AN **ACTIVE LEARNING** APPROACH TO RESEARCH AND PEDAGOGY

Journey of Research sections trace the evolution of ideas in the field and encourage interaction with the latest evidence-based research

JOURNEY OF RESEARCH *Invincible, Invulnerable, and Resilient*

Until the 1970s, psychologists and psychiatrists had primarily focused on understanding circumstances that threatened or disrupted the developmental process, using what is known as a *deficit model* or *risk perspective*. They wanted to understand what placed a child at risk for less-than-optimal development so they would be able to intervene in ways that would prevent problems or correct ones that already existed. A change in perspective emerged in the 1970s and 1980s when several researchers caught people's attention with stories of children who had overcome great adversity and gone on to become extraordinary individuals in the process.

In one of the best-known studies, Emmy Werner (1992) followed almost 700 children on the Hawaiian island of Kauai from birth until their 30s. Almost one third of the children were initially considered to be at high risk due to their life circumstances. These children had difficult births, lived in poverty,

had parents impaired by alcoholism or mental illness, or experienced parental divorce or discord, and many had multiple risk factors. But as Werner and Smith (1985) tracked these high-risk children over time, they found that one third had very good outcomes by the time they entered adulthood. With the advent of this type of resiliency research, the focus in the field began to shift from what could go wrong in development to what could go right. What helps a child recover or bounce back from adversity?

Protective factors identified in resiliency research include an active, outgoing personality that engages other people; good communication and problem-solving skills; a talent or ability that attracts other people; and faith in your own ability to make good things happen (Werner, 2005). These children also are emotionally stable and not easily upset. Often they make good use of whatever resources are available to them,

Chapter-opening "Test Your Knowledge" assessments challenge students' misconceptions

Marginal notes and highlighted text reinforce an understanding of the answers

5 Physical Development in Infancy and Toddlerhood

T/F Test Your Knowledge

Test your knowledge of child development by deciding whether each of the following statements is *true* or *false*, and then check your answers as you read the chapter.

1. T☐ F☐ Humans use only 10% of their brains.

2. T☐ F☐ Infants are born with almost all the brain cells they will ever have.

3. T☐ F☐ Newborn babies form synapses (the connections between nerve cells) in their brains at the rate of a hundred new connections each second.

4. T☐ F☐ Babies are unable to see when they are first born.

5. T☐ F☐ Infants are born with a preference for the foods common in their culture.

6. T☐ F☐ Within the first 2 months of life, infants do not experience pain.

7. T☐ F☐ Babies triple their birth weight by the time they are 1 year old.

8. T☐ F☐ It is important that infants crawl before they walk. If they go directly to walking, they are more likely to develop learning disabilities later in life.

9. T☐ F☐ Potty training most often becomes a battle of wills between a toddler and her parents.

10. T☐ F☐ Baby walkers help babies walk at an earlier age.

Correct answers: 1(F), 2(T), 3(T), 4(F), 5(T), 6(F), 7(T), 8(F), 9(F), 10(F)

T/F #7
Babies triple their birth weight by the time they are 1 year old. *True*

them, and this is in part because of the effect their bodily proportions have on us.

Growth from infancy to age 2 is very rapid. The average infant doubles her birth weight by about 5 months of age and triples it by her first birthday. During this same time, she will add about 10 inches or 50% to her length at birth. If the same rate of growth applied to the average 11- or 12-year-old, it would be terrifying, but after a child's second birthday, growth slows. Two-year-olds are approximately half the height they will be in adulthood, so to get an estimate of a child's adult height, you can double the child's height at age 2. However, a better indicator is to look at the height of family members. Assuming adequate nutrition, height is highly genetic, so it is very likely a child's eventual height will fall somewhere within the range of the height of her close relatives.

Figure 5.5 shows average growth rates for boys and girls. Despite the smooth curve of growth, real growth may occur in spurts. In fact, infant sleep patterns have been found to predict these growth spurts. If babies begin to sleep longer or take more naps, they may be about to have a jump in both height and weight (Lampl & Johnson, 2011).

Learning Questions

Additional chapter pedagogy includes **Learning Questions, Check Your Understanding questions, Chapter Summaries, marginal video links,** and more.

9.1 What occurs during Piaget's preoperational stage of cognitive development?

9.2 What are the basic processes described by Vygotsky's sociocultural theory?

9.3 How do attention and memory develop in early childhood?

9.4 Why is play important for cognitive development in early childhood?

9.5 How does language develop in early childhood?

9.6 How do children develop preacademic skills in reading, writing, and arithmetic?

9.7 What risk factors and supports exist for cognitive and language development in early childhood?

Chapter Summary

9.1 What occurs during Piaget's preoperational stage of cognitive development?

Children in the preoperational stage advance in their thinking when they begin to use symbols to manipulate information in their minds rather than with their hands, although symbols at this age are still very concrete. Limitations in their thinking include **transductive reasoning**, **egocentrism**, **animism**, and lack of **conservation**.

9.2 What are the basic processes described by Vygotsky's sociocultural theory?

Children learn through social interaction with more capable others that moves them just beyond their current level of understanding. The difference between what they can do independently and what they can do only with assistance is the **zone of**

INTERACTIVE RESOURCES THAT GIVE YOU AN EDGE

$SAGE edge™

edge.sagepub.com/levinechrono

SAGE edge for Instructors supports teaching by making it easy to integrate quality content and create a rich learning environment for students.

SAGE edge for Instructors features

- Test bank
- PowerPoint slides that include text, images, figures, and video links
- Original video, created specifically for the text
- Sample course syllabi for semester and quarter courses
- Exclusive! Access to full-text SAGE journal articles
- Multimedia content that spans different learning styles
- Lecture notes
- Course cartridge for easy LMS integration

SAGE edge for Students provides a personalized approach to coursework in an easy-to-use learning environment.

SAGE edge for Students features

- Original video, created specifically for the text
- Mobile-friendly eFlashcards and quizzes
- An online action plan with feedback on your course progress
- Chapter summaries with learning objectives
- Exclusive! Access to full-text SAGE journal articles

Child Development From Infancy to Adolescence is also available as an **Interactive eBook** which can be packaged with the text at no additional cost or purchased separately. The Interactive eBook offers

- Immediate access to original SAGE videos created specifically for the text
- Hyperlinks to additional web, audio, and video resources

PRAISE FOR CHILD DEVELOPMENT FROM INFANCY TO ADOLESCENCE: AN ACTIVE LEARNING APPROACH

▶ On the Active Learning Experience

"This book reads with more flow . . . and more connections to prior learning and more examples the students will relate to. There is more author-reader connection as the authors ask the reader to predict, try things out, and connect to their own experiences."

—Nancy Hughes, SUNY Plattsburgh

"The Active Learning sections are excellent . . . These provide support for students to understand complex, unfamiliar, and/or abstract concepts. The activities and questions scaffold students through the act of taking a child's perspective and/or being a researcher."

—Lisa Huffmann, Ball State University

"I think [the Test Your Knowledge and Active Learning] activities actively engage the students in the learning process and also help the retention of information."

—Martha Ravola, Alcorn State University

"The explanation of the Test Your Knowledge feature within the margins of the text will do much to engage students as they read."

—Margaret Annunziata, Davidson County Community College

▶ On Accessibility and Real Life Application

"I am very impressed with this chronologically organized edition of this text. Reading level and writing style and tone are accessible . . ."

—Christina Gotowka, Tunxis Community College

"This text is very easy to read and well organized to guide understanding and knowledge of the material."

—Joyce Bloomingburg, Freed-Hardeman University

"I think the students would do well using this text."

—April Grace, Madisonville Community College

"The authors have incorporated vignettes and exercises that push the students beyond the confines of the text, forcing them to think about and also internalize material."

—C. Timothy Dickel, Creighton University

▶ On Research and Diversity

"I very much like the Journey of Research [sections], which help students understand what motivated the research, why it's useful, and how it's done—that it's a process."

—Judith Bryant, University of South Florida

"The Journey of Research [sections] provide a good supplement to the developmental facts in the chapter. It is good for students to see where information comes from and how research is a window into development."

—Juliana Raskauskas, California State University, Sacramento

"Not only do I believe that this text really makes an effort to discuss both culture and diversity within the body of the text, but it also makes a point of providing both discussion and research that is relative to understanding how culture affects child development."

—Maria Pagano, New York City College of Technology, CUNY

THE **ACTIVE LEARNING** EXPERIENCE

This exciting chronological introduction to child development employs the lauded active learning approach of Levine and Munsch's successful topical text, creating an interactive learning experience that equips students with tools they can use long after the class ends.

Active Learning exercises in each chapter engage students in a personal and applied understanding of the material

Active Learning

Using Linguistic Constraints

You can use this activity to learn some made-up words and see how a young child might experience learning them. In each situation, decide how you would answer the question and name the linguistic constraint that guided your decision.

1. You know a bat is a long, thin object, and a ball is small and round. If I ask you to hand me the glumph, which object do you pick up?

    Which constraint did you use to make your decision?

    Polka Dot/Polka Dot Images/Thinkstock

2. The creature with the pink hair is a lorum. When you have more than one lorum, what do you call them?

    How did you know what more than one lorum is called?

    iStockphoto.com/rididiw

3. These are both floogles, but the green one is a flinger and the purple one is a flagger.

    What constraint helps you understand how these creatures are similar and how they are different?

    iStockphoto.com/yayayoyo

4. This glumbug is dingling.

    How do you know which of these new words is a noun and which is a verb?

    iStockphoto.com/DimaChe

5. If I tell you this is a boblabo, am I naming the creature's beak, its wings, or something else?

    What constraint allows you to determine what the word boblabo refers to?

    iStockphoto.com/totallyjamie

Active Learning

Head-to-Body Proportions

Take your right hand and reach over your head to touch your left ear. No problem, right? Now ask the parent or caregiver of an infant or toddler to help the child do the same thing. How far does the child's hand get over her head? Most likely the child's arm will not reach the opposite ear because her head is much larger in relationship to the rest of her body than the head of an adult is to his body.

As children mature, their arms and legs lengthen, and the rest of the body catches up in size to the head. The ability to reach overhead and touch your opposite ear has been used in some countries, such as Tanzania where there were inadequate birth records to document children's ages, as a rough test of a child's maturation and readiness to attend school (Beasley et al., 2000). ∎

Custom Active Learning videos demonstrate activities and concepts discussed in the text

Child Development
From Infancy
to Adolescence

SAGE was founded in 1965 by Sara Miller McCune to support the dissemination of usable knowledge by publishing innovative and high-quality research and teaching content. Today, we publish more than 750 journals, including those of more than 300 learned societies, more than 800 new books per year, and a growing range of library products including archives, data, case studies, reports, conference highlights, and video. SAGE remains majority-owned by our founder, and after Sara's lifetime will become owned by a charitable trust that secures our continued independence.

Los Angeles | London | Washington DC | New Delhi | Singapore | Boston

Child Development
From Infancy
to Adolescence

An Active Learning
Approach

Laura E. Levine / Joyce Munsch

Central Connecticut State University — California State University, Northridge

SAGE

Los Angeles | London | New Delhi
Singapore | Washington DC | Boston

Los Angeles | London | New Delhi
Singapore | Washington DC | Boston

FOR INFORMATION:

SAGE Publications, Inc.
2455 Teller Road
Thousand Oaks, California 91320
E-mail: order@sagepub.com

SAGE Publications Ltd.
1 Oliver's Yard
55 City Road
London EC1Y 1SP
United Kingdom

SAGE Publications India Pvt. Ltd.
B 1/I 1 Mohan Cooperative Industrial Area
Mathura Road, New Delhi 110 044
India

SAGE Publications Asia-Pacific Pte. Ltd.
3 Church Street
#10-04 Samsung Hub
Singapore 049483

Executive Editor: Reid Hester
Development Editor: Nathan Davidson
Digital Content Editor: Allison Hughes
Associate Digital Content Editor: Lucy Berbeo
Editorial Assistant: Morgan McCardell
Production Editor: Melanie Birdsall
Copy Editor: Deanna Noga
Typesetter: C&M Digitals (P) Ltd.
Proofreader: Susan Schon
Indexer: Molly Hall
Cover and Interior Designer: Scott Van Atta
Marketing Manager: Shari Countryman

A catalog record of this book is available from the Library of Congress.

ISBN: 978-1-4522-8881-9

Printed in Canada

This book is printed on acid-free paper.

15 16 17 18 19 10 9 8 7 6 5 4 3 2 1

Brief Contents

Detailed Contents

Zephyr Picture/Photolibrary/Getty Images

© Marmaduke St. John/Alamy

Chapter 2. Theory and Research in Development   26

Ian Boddy/Photo Researchers, Inc.

Chapter 4. Prenatal Development, Birth, and the Newborn 100

© Buddy Mays/Corbis

Emmanuel Rogue/Photo Researchers, Inc.

Mauro Fermariello/Science Source

Chapter 7. Social and Emotional Development in Infancy and Toddlerhood   214

PART IV: EARLY CHILDHOOD   251

Michael Stuparyk/Toronto
Star via Getty Images

Chapter 8. Physical Development in Early Childhood   252

Chapter 9. Cognitive Development in Early Childhood   286

Guido Mieth/Moment/Getty Images

Jupiterimages, Brand X Pictures/
Stockbyte/Getty Images

Chapter 10. Social and Emotional Development in Early Childhood   324

Picture Partners/Photo Researchers, Inc.

Bill O'Leary/The Washington Post/
Getty Images

Chapter 12. Cognitive Development in Middle Childhood   390

Stephen B. Morton for The Washington
Post via Getty Images

© Andrew Fox/Corbis

Chapter 16. Social and Emotional Development in Adolescence   540

Villerot/Science Source

Preface

This book is designed to create significant learning experiences for students who want to learn about children. *Child Development From Infancy to Adolescence: An Active Learning Approach* provides the field's most current evidence-based knowledge about the development of infants, children, and adolescents. Our pedagogical goal is to help students understand, retain, explore, and apply that knowledge. A central, organizing feature of this text is the learning activities embedded within each chapter. These activities take a variety of forms so that they stay interesting and fresh to the student and are integrated with the flow of information in the chapter rather than being stand-alone features that are easily skipped or ignored. We also provide opportunities throughout the book for students to learn about how our understanding of child development has evolved through the scientific process to reach our current state of knowledge.

This book can be used effectively by students who want to apply theory and research about child development to interactions with infants, children, and adolescents in many settings. The chronological approach allows students to integrate knowledge about the different facets of physical, cognitive, and social/emotional growth to bring about an understanding of the whole child at each age. The coverage and pedagogical features in this book have been conceived and carefully executed to help students discover the excitement of studying child development and to equip them with tools they can use long after they take this class.

Philosophical Approach

Challenging Misconceptions

One of the challenges in teaching a child development course is to help students give up some of the intuitive ideas or simplistic thinking that they have about the topic. Many students enter courses on child and adolescent development confident that they already know most of what they need to know about development and that this is "all just common sense," but experienced instructors know that some of the most important information in their courses is, in fact, counterintuitive. Unfortunately, students' original ideas are often quite difficult to change, and many of them complete courses in child development with their misconceptions intact. To counteract this tendency, we ask students to begin each chapter by testing their initial knowledge of the topics in that chapter. Unexpected or surprising answers to these questions draw the students into the chapter to find information related to their misconceptions. In addition, the activities throughout the book encourage students to seek out further information and to learn to evaluate that information rather than accepting what they hear without question.

Active Learning

Features intended to engage students are often included in textbooks as "add-ons," but our active learning philosophy is at the heart of all of the pedagogy provided throughout this book. Note that Active Learning activities do not appear in "boxes," which we believe students often skip or ignore. Rather they are an integral part of the text itself. The chapter narrative leads directly into the material in the Active Learning feature, and the feature smoothly transitions back into the narrative at its end. As educators, we know that students must *act* on the material presented in a course to make it their own. We all try to do this in a number of ways in our classrooms, but for the student, reading a textbook is a solitary and often passive process. To help guard against this passivity, our unique pedagogical features (described in the next section) are designed to capture students' interest and turn reading into an active process.

Focus on What Constitutes Evidence

We help students realize that although there is a place for "what I think" and for individual examples, the strength of a social science rests on marshaling convincing evidence within an agreed on framework. Basic concepts about research and the scientific method are presented within the text and in an activity-based appendix available as a downloadable file on the companion website, but these ideas are also reinforced and developed throughout the book.

Emphasis on Learning How to Learn

Long after they leave the classroom, students who interact with children and adolescents will need to find information to answer questions that arise. We want to encourage students' independent pursuit of knowledge about child development so we provide them with tools that will help them do that. They are introduced to the use of databases including PsycInfo and learn to evaluate Internet sources to identify legitimate, research-based sources of information.

Critical Thinking Skills

When students look for information on their own, they need to critically evaluate the content of what they find. In Chapter 1, we talk about how to be a good consumer of information on development and lead them through a critical evaluation of a website. In addition, the true/false questions that appear throughout each chapter continuously challenge students to reflect on what they believe about children and to evaluate the sources of those beliefs. The instructor teaching site and student study site provide access to peer-reviewed research articles that students can explore independently to add to their understanding of topics. This ability to critically evaluate ideas about children and their development will be beneficial to students who plan to go on for graduate study, those who will work directly with children and families in professional careers, and those who will use these ideas when caring for their own children.

Neuroscience

To reflect the burgeoning interest in the field of neuroscience and its implications for child development, we have included information on brain function where it is relevant throughout the book. This information is presented in clear language that makes it appropriate for the student of child development who may not have a strong background in biology.

Diversity and Culture

Because an understanding of diversity and culture is essential for anyone working in the field of child development, these topics are integrated into each chapter to give the broader picture of how each aspect of development is influenced by the many different circumstances that constitute children's lives around the world.

Psychopathology

Coverage of topics related to psychopathology or developmental differences gives students a better understanding of the continuum of human behavior. Rather than relegating these topics to a separate, stand-alone chapter or to feature boxes, we include them within the chapters where they give students a deeper understanding of how these differences relate to the full range of development of all children.

Pedagogical Features

Our philosophical approach is reflected in the pedagogical features that make this text a unique and powerful educational tool.

Active Learning

A variety of active learning activities in the text complement and enhance the ideas presented in each chapter. Activities might ask students: (a) to reflect on their own experiences while growing up (and perhaps compare those experiences to the experiences of classmates), (b) to immediately test their understanding of a concept, (c) to conduct an observation or interview related to text material, (d) to carry out a simple activity and reflect on what they've learned, or (e) to seek out information that goes beyond the text through the use of library resources or the Internet. Each of these activities is designed to consolidate student learning through personal experiences that illustrate the ideas presented in the book.

Test Your Knowledge

To challenge misconceptions that students often bring with them to a course in child development, each chapter begins with a true/false quiz that contains interesting and provocative questions related to the material in that chapter. The quizzes are designed to tap into commonly held beliefs or ideas that have a strong intuitive sense of what should be right. Students can immediately check whether their answers are correct. When they get a question wrong, they can satisfy their curiosity about the topic by finding that question in the margin of the relevant section in the chapter, where they also will find information related to the question highlighted in the text. It is our intention to pique student interest by challenging their assumptions. The initial question plants a seed that is reinforced when they again read about the topic in the context of the chapter.

Journey of Research

It is not unusual for students in child and adolescent development courses to expect that by the end of the semester, they will have simple answers to a number of very complex questions. Of course we can seldom provide these simple answers. Instead, we need to help students understand that the science of child development is an ongoing endeavor and that we continue to build and add to our understanding each day. Although it is important that students learn about our current best knowledge, this information is more meaningful when students understand it in the context of our evolving ideas about a given topic. To help students better understand this material, we keep the focus of the text on the current state of knowledge and use the Journey of Research feature to provide the historical contextual information on the topic. This helps students understand that what they learn today in their class may be information that changes—sometimes substantially—in the future as our body of knowledge grows. This is, after all, how the scientific process works.

Learning Objectives and Self-Testing Review

Each chapter begins with a set of learning objectives that help guide students as they read. These opening learning objectives are then linked to a chapter summary at the end of each chapter in which students can review what they have learned. Research has increasingly demonstrated that the best way for students to retain information they are learning and also to transfer that knowledge to new situations is by periodically testing their own knowledge. Other study approaches such as rereading, highlighting, and even summarizing have not been found to be as effective as self-testing. On the student study site that accompanies the text, we provide chapter quizzes as well as flash cards that students can use to test themselves. However, we believe it is important to provide this opportunity within the book as well. Therefore, we have written our review at the end of each major topic and at the end of the chapter in the form of questions to help students test themselves on what they have learned. Answering these questions will promote greater retention of what they are learning and increase the likelihood that they will be able to apply this knowledge in useful ways.

Understanding Research

Scientific research is the foundation for our understanding of development. In Chapter 2, we describe basic aspects of research that are important for students to understand so they can evaluate new information. The Appendix on Research Methodology on the companion website provides a guided activity that allows students to walk through the scientific process while checking their understanding of each step.

Graphics, Artwork, and Videos

Because many individuals learn best when there is a visual component to instruction, and because child development is a field that is rich in imagery, each chapter contains photos, graphics, and links to videos that illustrate important concepts in a memorable way. Many of the photos in the text include questions embedded in their captions that prompt the student to think further about the topic. Important concepts are further illustrated through the videos that accompany the text.

Ancillaries

SAGE edge offers a robust online environment featuring an impressive array of tools and resources for review, study, and further exploration, keeping both instructors and students on the cutting edge of teaching and learning. Go to **edge.sagepub.com/levine-chrono** to access the companion site.

SAGE edge for Instructors

SAGE edge for Instructors supports teaching by making it easy to integrate quality content and create a rich learning environment for students. This password-protected site gives instructors access to a full complement of resources to support and enhance their child development course. The following chapter-specific assets are available on the teaching site:

- **Test banks** provide a diverse range of questions as well as the opportunity to edit any question and/or insert personalized questions to effectively assess students' progress and understanding
- **Sample course syllabi** for semester and quarter courses provide suggested models for structuring a course

- Editable, chapter-specific **PowerPoint slides** offer complete flexibility for creating a multimedia presentation for the course
- **Video and multimedia content** includes new videos created by SAGE specifically for this book, featuring real-life demonstrations of some of the Active Learning exercises that appear throughout the text
- Additional **original videos** created in several childcare settings illustrate important concepts from the book
- EXCLUSIVE! Access to full-text **SAGE journal articles** that have been carefully selected to support and expand on the concepts presented in each chapter to encourage students to think critically
- **Lecture notes** summarize key concepts by chapter to assist in the preparation for lectures and class discussions
- A **course cartridge** provides easy LMS integration

SAGE edge for Students

SAGE edge for Students provides a personalized approach to help students reach their coursework goals in an easy-to-use learning environment. To maximize students' understanding of child development and promote critical thinking and active learning, we have provided the following chapter-specific student resources on the open-access portion of edge.sagepub.com/levinechrono:

- Mobile-friendly **eFlashcards** strengthen understanding of key terms and concepts
- Mobile-friendly practice **quizzes** allow for independent assessment by students of their mastery of course material
- A customized online **action plan** includes tips and feedback on progress through the course and materials, which allows students to individualize their learning experience
- **Learning objectives** reinforce the most important material
- **Video and multimedia content** includes new videos created by SAGE specifically for this book, featuring real-life demonstrations of some of the Active Learning exercises that appear throughout the text
- Additional **original videos** created in several childcare settings illustrate important concepts from the book
- EXCLUSIVE! Access to full-text **SAGE journal articles** that have been carefully selected to support and expand on the concepts presented in each chapter

Acknowledgments

Our team at SAGE put an enormous amount of work into this book. We send a special thank you to our editor, Reid Hester, for his unfailing support and encouragement. We are grateful to our developmental editors Cheri Dellelo and Elisa Adams, our copy editor Deanna Noga, and to Nathan Davidson, Lucy Berbeo, Lauren Habib, Melanie Birdsall, and Allison Hughes for their contributions. Thanks also go to Shari Countryman for directing the marketing aspect of the book's production.

We want to thank all the children, parents, and staff at the California State University at Northridge who participated in the filming of videos that accompany the text. We also are grateful to our students from whom we learn so much.

Thanks go to the following individuals who reviewed the manuscript:

Margaret H. Annunziata, Davidson County Community College

Joyce Bloomingburg, Freed-Hardeman University

Judith B. Bryant, University of South Florida

Melissa M. Burnham, University of Nevada, Reno

Dixie R. Crase, University of Memphis

Sharon DeLeon, Fullerton College

Gayle J. Dilling, Olympic College

Kari L. Dudley, PhD, University of New Hampshire

Charles Timothy (Tim) Dickel, EdD, Creighton University

Warren Fass, University of Pittsburgh at Bradford

Victoria Fu, Virginia Polytechnic Institute and State University (Virginia Tech)

Christina J. Gotowka, Professor Emerita, Tunxis Community College

April M. Grace, Madisonville Community College

Helen I. Green, MEd, PC, Cuyahoga Community College

Joel A. Hagaman, University of the Ozarks

Deborah Harris O'Brien, PhD, Trinity Washington University

Lisa Huffman, Cameron University

Nancy C. Hughes, SUNY Plattsburgh

Sonya Kitsko, Robert Morris University

Elizabeth Levin, Laurentian University

Micheline Malow, Manhattanville College

Rebecca Martin, South Dakota State University

Philliph Masila Mutisya, North Carolina Central University

Ms. Jana L. Moore McCurdy, College of Western Idaho

Matt Nordlund, Cleveland State University

Alexa Okrainec, Brandon University

Maria Pagano, New York City College of Technology, City University of New York

Lindsay Blau Portnoy, Hunter College, CUNY

Juliana Raskauskas, California State University, Sacramento

Martha D. Ravola, Alcorn State University

Pamela Schuetze, SUNY Buffalo State

Julia Tang, Mount St. Mary's College

Michelle Tichy, University of Northern Iowa

Margot Underwood, Joliet Junior College

Jennifer A. Vu, University of Delaware

Bridget A. Walsh, University of Nevada, Reno

Denise L. Winsor, University of Memphis

As always, we are grateful to our families and friends for their continuing support, as well as their ideas and stories that have contributed to the creation of this book.

About the Authors

Laura E. Levine received her PhD in developmental and clinical psychology from the University of Michigan. After working with children and families at the Children's Psychiatric Hospital and in private practice in Ann Arbor for 10 years, she moved to Connecticut and was a stay-at-home mother of her two children. She returned to academia in 1994 and has been teaching child psychology and life span human development for 20 years at Central Connecticut State University, where she is currently a professor in the Department of Psychological Science. She has received three university teaching awards, and her research on the social development of young children and on the relation between media use and attention difficulties has appeared in journals such as *Developmental Psychology*, the *Journal of Applied Developmental Psychology*, *Infant Mental Health Journal*, *Infant and Child Development*, *Computers and Education*, and *CyberPsychology, Behavior, and Social Networking*.

Dr. Levine has been very active in promoting excellence in college teaching. She was involved in the creation of the Center for Teaching Excellence at Central Connecticut State University and served on the board of the Connecticut Consortium to Enhance Learning and Teaching. She created numerous programs for faculty both at her university and at regional and national conferences. Her work on the scholarship of teaching and learning can be found in *New Directions for Teaching and Learning*, *College Teaching* and the *International Journal for the Scholarship of Teaching and Learning*.

Joyce Munsch received her PhD in human development and family studies from Cornell University. She was a faculty member in human development and family studies at Texas Tech University for 14 years, where she also served as associate dean for research in the College of Human Sciences for 2 years. In 2002, Dr. Munsch came to California State University at Northridge as the founding chair and professor in the Department of Child and Adolescent Development.

Dr. Munsch's research has focused on adolescent stress and coping and social network research. Her work has been published in the *Journal of School Psychology*, *Adolescence*, the *Journal of Early Adolescence*, the *Journal of Research on Adolescence*, and the *American Journal of Orthopsychiatry*. Throughout her career, Dr. Munsch has administered grants that support community-based programs. She was the codirector of the Early Head Start program at Texas Tech University and co–principal investigator for three Texas Youth Commission (Department of Juvenile Justice) grants. At Cal State Northridge, she administered the Jumpstart program for 10 years. Her commitment to community service learning was recognized in 2005 when she was awarded the CSUN Visionary Community Service Learning Award. At Texas Tech, she was the College of Human Sciences nominee for the Hemphill-Wells New Professor Excellence in Teaching Award, the Barnie E. Rushing Jr. Faculty Distinguished Research Award, the El Paso Energy Foundation Faculty Achievement Award, and the President's Excellence in Teaching Award, and she received the Kathryn Burleson Faculty Service Award and the College of Human Sciences Outstanding Researcher Award. Dr. Munsch has recently worked with the Los Angeles County Early Childhood Education Workforce Consortium. The Consortium is dedicated to preparing a well-qualified ECE workforce for the Los Angeles community. She also is one of three faculty members from the California State University system who review courses at the California Community Colleges for transfer to the CSUs.

Cameron Spencer/Thinkstock

© Sandro Di Carlo Darsa/PhotoAlto/Corbis

Issues, Theory, and Research in Child Development

Zephyr Picture/Photolibrary/Getty Images

1

Issues in Child Development

Take a moment to think about why you want to learn about children, adolescents, and their development. You may have a career goal that involves working with children or adolescents. Perhaps you want to better understand yourself or those you know by exploring how childhood has affected who you have become. You may enjoy the interactions you have with children and want to understand them better, or your interest may be more scientific, with a focus on understanding the research that explains the processes of development. Your particular goal will influence how you approach the information in this book.

In this book, we provide you with information and activities that will stimulate your thinking in all these ways. We want to share with you the excitement that we feel about the topic of child and adolescent development and to pique your curiosity so that you will want to learn even more about it.

By the time you have finished reading this book, you will have a solid foundation in a number of important topics related to development. It is our hope that this will motivate you to take additional courses about children and their development.

In this first chapter, we introduce some of the basic concepts of child and adolescent development. We first look at why people study children, and present some ways that people use knowledge about children to promote positive development. We then discuss some of the basic issues about how development occurs. We introduce you to the different contexts that influence children's lives and give you some ways to differentiate reliable information on child development from other material you may encounter. Because a variety of careers require a solid understanding of child and adolescent development, we also show you some ways you can learn more about careers that interest you.

Why Study Childhood?

Many people are interested in studying child development because the topic itself is fascinating and important. Others want information they will be able to use in their role as a parent or in a future career. These goals are not mutually exclusive. Many students have a natural curiosity about development and know that they will be able to use the information in the future as a professional who works with children or a policymaker who shapes social policy that affects children and families. We begin this chapter by looking at all of these alternatives.

Understanding the Process of Development

One reason why students are interested in studying child development is that experiences in childhood influence who we become as adults. Understanding that process helps us understand the role that infancy, childhood, and adolescence play in forming our abilities, beliefs, and attitudes.

Researchers who study children as they develop over long periods of time have provided ample evidence that early traits, behaviors, and experiences are related to many adult outcomes. For example, Lewis Terman began a study of gifted children that has lasted over 80 years (Leslie, 2000). Although Terman died many years ago, others are still mining his data to answer questions about life span development. One finding is that those children who were rated high in the quality Terman called conscientiousness or social dependability had many positive outcomes in adulthood, including a reduction of 30% in the likelihood they would die in any particular year (Friedman et al., 1995). How does earlier conscientiousness link with these later outcomes? The connection is partially explained by the fact that conscientious individuals were less likely to smoke and drink alcohol to excess, both of which are predictive of a shorter life span. Some have hypothesized that conscientious people have better marriages, while others think they may be better prepared to handle the emotional difficulties they encounter (Friedman et al., 1995). Ongoing research is continuing to explore the full complexity of these connections.

As another example of the continuity between early and later development, Walter Mischel and his colleagues have carried out studies demonstrating that self-control in 4-year-olds is predictive of their ability to delay gratification in adolescence and beyond (Shoda, Mischel, & Peake, 1990). In their original research, 4-year-olds were told they could immediately have something desirable like a marshmallow, or they could have two marshmallows if they waited until the researcher returned a while later. Children who were able to wait for longer periods of time were the ones who demonstrated greater self-control at age 18 (Eigsti et al., 2006). Even 30 years later, those who had waited to eat the marshmallow at age 4 had lower body mass index than those who could not wait, perhaps indicating a continuing ability to control food-related urges (Schlam, Wilson, Shoda, Mischel, & Ayduk, 2013).

The earliest stages of development are clearly important for later development and functioning. However, Charles Nelson (1999), neuroscientist and developmental psychologist, has argued that the first 3 years of life are no more important than later periods of development. He likens early development to building the foundation of a house. A solid foundation is essential, but the ultimate shape and function of the house depends on adding the walls, the roof, the pipes, and all the rest. Nelson's focus is on

Learning Questions

1.1 Who needs to have a good understanding of child development?

1.2 What are the domains of child development and some recurring issues for debate?

1.3 What are the contexts for child development?

1.4 How can you be a smart consumer of information about development?

1.1

Who needs to have a good understanding of child development?

VIDEO LINK 1.1
Marshmallow Test

Resisting temptation.
Longitudinal research has found that children who are not able to control themselves and resist temptation while they are young are likely to become teenagers who also cannot control their impulses. ■

the development of the brain, but his comments could apply to many other areas of child development. He states that the basic form of the brain is set down within the first years of life but it is continually affected by the experiences we have later in life. Another example is the research by Alan Sroufe and his colleagues who found that the nature of infants' secure relationship with their mother was an important predictor of their ability to have close romantic relationships with adults. However, the nature of their peer relationships through middle childhood also related to later relationships (Sroufe, Egeland, Carlson, & Collins, 2005). Experiences early in life have consequences for functioning later in life, but experiences all along the path to adulthood also contribute to an adult's psychological functioning.

Using Our Knowledge of Child Development

A second reason to study child development is to be able to use this information to improve the lives of children and adolescents. An understanding of how children think, feel, learn, and grow, as well as how they change and stay the same, is essential to the ability to foster positive development. This understanding can help parents and family members, professionals who work with children and families, and people who create and carry out social policies and programs that affect children and their families.

JOURNAL ARTICLE 1.1
Applying Developmental Science

Parents and Family Members

A solid understanding of child development can help all parents do their best in this important role. Many parents read books, search websites, and browse magazines designed to help them understand their children so they can become better parents. How useful any of these sources of information will be to an interested parent depends in large part on how solidly the information in them is grounded in scientific research. Parents' understanding of their children's needs and abilities at each stage of development helps them provide the appropriate amount and type of support and stimulation to enhance their children's growth and development.

For some parents, knowledge about child development is even more crucial. For example, teen parents are more likely than older parents to lack knowledge about what to expect from their child at different ages, so they may underestimate what children understand and can do and, as a result, may not provide the kind of stimulation that will help their child's mind grow. On the other hand, they may expect things that their children are not yet able to do and become impatient or punitive when their child does not live up to these unrealistic expectations (Culp, Culp, Blankemeyer, & Passmark, 1998). When teen parents are provided with information about child development, along with other types of support from a trained home visitor, their ability to empathize with their child increases and they understand more about how to discipline their child without resorting to physical punishment.

Programs to support parents. Incarcerated parents have been helped by programs such as The Family Nurturing Program. Such programs help parents maintain a relationship with their children while they are physically separated from them and also help the parents learn how to promote positive development in their children. ■

Another high-risk group that can benefit from parenting interventions is incarcerated parents. When one group of incarcerated parents took part in a program called The Family Nurturing Program, many showed the same kind of gains as those found among teenagers given home visits. They became more empathic and less punitive and developed more realistic expectations for their children (Palusci, Crum, Bliss, & Bavolek, 2008).

WEB LINK 1.1
Family Nurturing Program

Child Development Professionals

You may be interested in studying child development because you see yourself in a future career that involves working with children and families. In different ways and at different levels, people in all the helping professions are engaged in the identification and prevention of problems, in providing interventions when problems do occur, and in promoting positive development for all children and teens.

Community organizers, community psychologists, and outreach workers are a few of the professions that focus on preventing problems before they emerge. Child therapists and family therapists are two of the professionals who help families address existing problems. In child therapy, the therapist meets individually with the child, while family therapy involves the whole, or a significant part of, the family. Social workers, psychologists, child psychiatrists, and marriage and family therapists are other professionals who provide these and other types of interventions to families. Promoting the optimal development of children and adolescents is a primary goal of professionals who work in the field of education (especially classroom teachers, resource teachers, administrators, and counselors) and mental health professionals, youth service workers, and representatives of community organizations who run a variety of programs for children. A strong foundation in child development helps each of them find and use information about development in ways that support and encourage children and adolescents to reach their full potential.

We recognize that students today are interested in knowing where their education can eventually lead them and are hungry for information about future careers. If you are taking this course because you are considering a career related to child development, how much do you know about the career you are thinking about entering? You can assess your current knowledge about a career related to child development by completing **Active Learning: How Much Do You Know About Careers in Child Development?**

Careers in child development. Knowledge about child development is essential to people working in many different careers (including pediatricians, teachers, social workers, counselors, therapists, lawyers, and nurses). If you are interested in a career working with children, there are many opportunities available to you. ■

Active Learning

How Much Do You Know About Careers in Child Development?

If you are interested in a career that includes working with children, begin by completing the table below with what you currently know about the career you would like to enter when you finish your education. If you haven't settled on a career yet, simply choose one that holds some interest for you. Even if you feel you have very little information on a particular topic, take your best guess at every answer.

Next, use the *Occupational Outlook Handbook* to find current information on your career. At the Bureau of Labor Statistics (2014b) website at www.bls.gov, type "Occupational Outlook Handbook" into the search box or select it from the dropdown menu under "Publications." There also is likely a copy of the Bureau of Labor Statistics *Occupational Outlook Handbook* in your campus library. Select the career you are interested in from the alphabetic dropdown menu, or type the name of your career in the search box on the page. For each career, you will find information on the following:

- What people in this career do—duties and responsibilities.
- Work environment—where people in this career work and conditions affecting their employment.
- How to become one—the education and training required both for entry into the field and for advancement within this career. You will also find information about any certifications or licenses required to work in this profession and the skills and personal qualities required for success on the job.
- Pay—the median salaries earned in this career.
- Job outlook—information about the job prospects for this career. You'll learn how many people are currently employed in it and whether the demand for this profession is increasing or decreasing.

- Similar occupations—additional helpful information about careers related to the one you are researching. For instance, if you think you would like to be a child psychologist, here you can find that related careers include being a counselor, social worker, special education teacher, or recreation worker. If you click on any of these links, it will take you to the page in the *Occupational Outlook Handbook* that provides all the information about that alternative career.
- Contacts for more information—links to professional organizations that support and advocate for people working in that career. The organization webpages are rich sources of information about each career, and you should look at one or two of them before you finish exploring this page.

Although the *Handbook* lists hundreds of occupations, you won't find every conceivable job title. For instance, *child life specialist* and *early interventionist* are not yet in the *Handbook*, but you can find information about a related career to begin your search (child life specialists do work similar to what a counselor does, but they work with children and their families in the specialized setting of a hospital).

VIDEO LINK 1.2
Child Life Specialist

Name of the career you researched: _____

Does it appear in the *Occupational Outlook Handbook* (OOH)? _____Yes _____ No

(If no, name the related career you researched): _____

Topic	Your Current Knowledge	Information From the OOH
Educational level required for entry into this career (for example, high school diploma, associate's degree, bachelor's degree, master's degree, PhD, or other advanced degree)		
Educational level required for advancement in this career		
Important day-to-day work responsibilities (that is, what you will do each day in this career)		
Work setting (for example, office, school, hospital), and how much travel is required (if any)		
Median annual earnings		
Demand (for example, is the demand for this career expected to increase or decrease over the next 10 years, and by how much?)		

Another very useful website to examine if you are specifically interested in a career in the field of psychology is the American Psychological Association's site. You can find career information at http://www.apa.org/careers/resources/guides/careers.aspx ▪

Making social policy. Social policy that affects children and families is made at the highest levels of the federal government down to local school boards and neighborhood councils. Interested citizens also take part when they write letters to elected officials, sign petitions, work for causes they support, and vote. ■

Social policy Government or private policies for dealing with social issues.

Policymakers

Most often we think about applying our understanding of child development directly to the children with whom we work. However, the well-being of children and families is also affected by the laws and programs that make up social policy. Research on child development informs and guides the people who make these policies. For example, Walter Gilliam (2005), director of the Edward Zigler Center in Child Development and Social Policy at Yale University, found that preschool children in Connecticut were more than 3 times as likely to be expelled as children in Grades K–12. His research also showed that when a mental health consultant was available to help teachers develop ways to handle problem behaviors, far fewer young children were expelled (Bell, 2008). His research and advocacy led to legislative changes in five states that have increased the number of mental health consultants provided to preschools. Consider how many young children are being better served because of the research and advocacy of Dr. Gilliam.

Another example of social policy in action is the work done by Child Trends. Based on research it had conducted, this organization presented evidence to legislators about both the human and the monetary costs ($9.2 billion a year) of teen childbearing (Holcombe, Peterson, & Manlove, 2009). This type of presentation is far more convincing to those who must provide the funds for programs to prevent teen pregnancy than simple statements of need, unsupported by research evidence. **Active Learning: Social Policy Affecting Children and Adolescents** provides some additional information about the type of issues social policy organizations have focused on in recent years.

Active Learning

Social Policy Affecting Children and Adolescents

A number of organizations in the United States devote resources to informing legislators and private citizens about topics of importance to the country. Their goal is to help bring about changes in social policy based on solid research. You can visit their websites to retrieve reports that interest you.

The Annie E. Casey Foundation (2014) has a primary mission to "foster public policies, human-service reforms, and community supports that more effectively meet the needs of today's vulnerable children and families." From its home page at http://www .aecf.org, you can click on the tabs at the top of the page for "Kids," "Families," and "Communities" to see research that has been done on various topics, including child protection, foster care, youth and work, poverty, and working families. For instance, under the topic "Education," you will find research reports and policy briefs on the importance of early reading for later academic success and strategies for reducing the school dropout rate.

The mission of the *Future of Children* is "to translate the best social science research about children and youth into information that is useful to policymakers, practitioners, grant-makers, advocates, the media, and students of public policy." You will find the website at http://futureofchildren.org. This organization publishes two issues of its journal each year, each devoted to a single topic. Recent issues have included children with disabilities, work and family, immigrant children, the transition to adulthood, and preventing child maltreatment. Future of Children is dedicated to making scientifically based information available to the widest possible audience. From its home page, you can click on webcasts to see presentations on subjects such as fostering adolescents' transition to adulthood and helping fragile families.

The Society for Research in Child Development is a professional organization with close to 6,000 members in the United States and around the world. It periodically produces policy briefs on a variety of topics related to child development. Go to its home page at http://www.srcd.org and select "Social Policy Report" from the drop-down menu of publications, then select individual reports from that page.

There is a wealth of information at each site. Visit at least one site and identify a topic or two that interest you, review the information available, and make a mental note to revisit the site when you are looking for up-to-date information for one of your course papers. ▪

As citizens, we all have a responsibility to vote and to speak out for the well-being of children. The more we understand about their needs, the more effective we will be in advocating on their behalf and supporting the policies we believe will best serve them.

Check Your Understanding

1. What are some reasons for studying child development?
2. Who is likely to benefit from being knowledgeable about child development?
3. What is the relationship between social policy and research on child development?

Understanding How Development Happens

Now that we have described reasons for studying how children grow and develop, we describe some of the basic issues you will encounter as you study child development. We all have our own ideas about children. You brought some of your own with you when you entered this class. Stop for a few minutes and think of a couple of sentences or phrases that capture what you believe to be true about how child development occurs.

Do you believe that if you spare the rod you will spoil the child? Or that as the twig is bent, so grows the tree? Do you think that children are like little sponges? Or that they grow in leaps and bounds? Each of these bits of folk wisdom touches on an issue that has been debated within the field of child development. We briefly discuss several of those issues here, but we revisit them at various points throughout the book.

Domains of Development

When studying development, we often distinguish between three basic aspects or domains of development: physical, cognitive, and social-emotional. Physical development includes the biological changes that occur in the body, including changes in size and strength, as well as the integration of sensory and motor activities. Neurological, or brain, development has become a major area for research in physical development in recent years. Cognitive development includes changes in the way we think, understand, and reason about the world. It includes the accumulation of knowledge as well as the way we use that information for problem solving and decision making. Social-emotional development includes all the ways we learn to connect to other

1.2

What are the domains of child development and some recurring issues for debate?

Physical development Biological changes that occur in the body and brain, including changes in size and strength and integration of sensory and motor activities.

Cognitive development Changes in the way we think, understand, and reason about the world.

Social-emotional development Changes in the ways we connect to other individuals and express and understand emotions.

Domains of development. When we study development, we look at changes in the physical, cognitive, and social-emotional development of children and adolescents. ■

VIDEO LINK 1.3
Pretend Play

JOURNAL ARTICLE 1.2
Nature versus Nurture

Nature The influence of genetic inheritance on development.

Nurture The influence of learning and experiences in the environment on development.

individuals, understand our emotions and the emotions of others, interact effectively with others, and express and regulate our emotions.

Although it is useful to make distinctions between these domains, it is important to understand that they continually interact with each other. For instance, during puberty adolescents undergo dramatic physical changes over a short period of time, but these changes also affect social development. As adolescents grow to look more like adults and less like children, adults begin to treat them more like adults, giving them new responsibility and expecting greater maturity from them. These opportunities, in turn, contribute to the cognitive development of adolescents as they learn from their new experiences. In a similar way, when infants learn to walk and can get around on their own, their relationship with caregivers changes. The word *no* is heard much more frequently, and infants need more careful supervision because they now can get themselves into dangerous situations. And, of course, infants' enhanced ability to explore the environment gives them many new opportunities to learn about the world in ways that advance their cognitive development.

Nature and Nurture

Throughout history, the question of whether our behavior, thoughts, and feelings result from nature, our genetic inheritance, or from nurture, the influence of the environment, has shaped our understanding of why we act certain ways and how we can influence human behavior. The controversy was originally described as nature *versus* nurture. For example, let's say you are an aggressive (or shy, or outgoing) person. Researchers wanted to find out whether you became aggressive because you were "born that way," with genes from your parents determining the outcome, or whether you learned to be aggressive because of what you saw or experienced in your environment. People initially argued for one side or the other, but in more recent times it has become clear that the outcome is a mixture of both.

Researcher D. O. Hebb said that asking whether behavior is due to nature or to nurture is similar to asking whether the area of a rectangle is due to its length or its width (Meaney, 2004). Just as both length and width are necessary to determine area, genes and environment interact to determine behavioral development. More recent research has indicated that nature and nurture are inextricably intertwined in surprising and complex ways (Coll, Bearer, & Lerner, 2004). We have left behind the era of "nature *versus* nurture" and entered the era of "nature *through* nurture," in which many genes, particularly those related to traits and behaviors, are expressed only through a process of constant interaction with their environment (Meaney, 2010; Stiles, 2009). We discuss these ideas further in Chapter 3.

© Sandro Di Carlo Darsa/PhotoAlto/Corbis

Quantitative change and qualitative change. As children grow, there are quantitative changes that are evident in this photo (for example, they grow taller and weigh more), but there are also qualitative changes that are less easy to see (for example, they move from one cognitive stage to the next). ■

Continuous Versus Stage-Like Development

Is development a series of small steps that modify behavior bit by bit, or does it proceed in leaps and bounds? In Chapter 2 and throughout the rest of the book, you will learn about some theories in the field of child development that describe development as a series of stages children move through, similar to the "leaps" described above. Each stage has characteristics that distinguish it from the stages that come before and after. Other theories, however, describe processes that change development in small increments.

Another way to think about this issue is to differentiate between quantitative and qualitative change. Quantitative change is change in the amount or quantity of what you are measuring. For instance, as children grow, they get taller (that is, they add inches to their height), they learn more new words (that is, the size of their vocabulary grows), and they acquire more factual knowledge (that is, the amount of information in their knowledge base grows). However, some aspects of development are not just the accumulation of more inches or words. Instead, they are qualitative changes that alter the overall quality of a process or function, and the result is something altogether different. Walking is qualitatively different from crawling, and thinking about abstract concepts such as justice or fairness is qualitatively different from knowing something more concrete, such as the capitals of all 50 states. Stage theories typically describe qualitative changes in development, while incremental theories describe quantitative changes. Both types of change occur, and that is why we don't have just one theory that describes all aspects of development. Some theories are more appropriate for describing certain types of changes than others.

Stability Versus Change

How much do we change during the process of development? As we grow, develop, and mature, are we basically the same people we were at earlier ages, or do we reinvent ourselves along the way? We find evidence of both stability and change as we look at development. For instance, characteristics such as anxiety (Weems, 2008), shyness (Dennissen, Asendorpf, & van Aken, 2008; Schmidt & Tasker, 2000), and aggressiveness (Dennissen

Quantitative changes Changes in the amount or quantity of what you are measuring.

Qualitative changes Changes in the overall nature of what you are examining.

Stage theories Theories of development in which each stage in life is seen as qualitatively different from the ones that come before and after.

Incremental theories Theories in which development is a result of continuous quantitative changes.

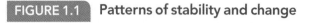

FIGURE 1.1   Patterns of stability and change

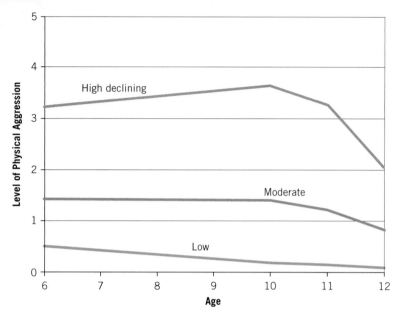

By looking at individual differences in patterns of change over time, the researchers who carried out this study were able to see that children who started the study with low or moderate levels of aggression showed little change in their level of aggressive behavior as they got older (those represented by the bottom two lines), while children who started at high levels of aggression changed over time (those represented by the top line).

SOURCE: Kokko, K., Tremblay, R. E., Lacourse, E., Nagin, D. S., & Vitaro, F. (2006). Trajectories of prosocial behavior and physical aggression in middle childhood: Links to adolescent school dropout and physical violence. *Journal of Research on Adolescence, 16*(3), 403–428. This is a modification of the graph found on p. 415.

et al., 2008; Kokko & Pulkkinen, 2005) tend to be relatively stable over time. However, the specific way in which these characteristics are expressed changes with a child's age. For example, young children hit, kick, or throw things when they are angry, but school-age children express their aggression through teasing, taunting, and name-calling (Kokko & Pulkkinen, 2005; Loeber & Hay, 1997), and adolescents attack each other through social means (for example, spreading rumors or excluding people from social activities).

Figure 1.1 shows the results of a study of aggressive behavior in children aged 6 to 12. Kokko, Tremblay, Lacourse, Nagin, and Vitaro (2006) identified three different patterns of stability or change in this behavior, shown by the three lines in the figure: (a) The "low" group starts at a low level and remains at a low level through the period of time studied; (b) the "moderate" group starts at a moderately high level at age 6 and stays close to that level over the period studied; (c) the "high-declining" group starts at a relatively high level but ends at a considerably lower level, although still significantly higher than the other two groups. As you look at Figure 1.1, do you wonder what factors contributed to change in a pathway or to its stability? That would be a logical thing to think about next because such information could help us develop interventions to change pathways that lead to problem behavior.

Individual Differences

Scientific research strives to identify general principles that describe average or typical patterns. We want to be able to make general statements about what usually happens. But you cannot spend much time observing children or adolescents without recognizing how different each one is from all the others. Our study of children needs to deal with both aspects of development—those aspects that are universal and shared by all or almost all individuals, and those in which we are different from each other. Throughout this book you will learn about general conclusions that are drawn from research. For example, adolescents who do well in school generally have high self-esteem and children who are raised by harsh, punitive parents are often aggressive.

Although these are true as general statements, there also are numerous exceptions that give us insights we would not have otherwise. For example, children who grow up in poverty with parents who cannot effectively care for them are at risk for a number of developmental and mental health problems, but a small group manages to thrive in the face of great difficulty. By looking at these children, we can identify factors that help protect a child from some developmental risks.

Individual differences. Characteristics of individual children, such as age, gender, or ethnic background, can affect the developmental process, so outcomes that apply to one child will not necessarily apply to another. This means we must always be mindful of individual differences when we reach our conclusions. ∎

The developmental pathways of any given individual are difficult to predict. *Different* pathways can result in the *same* outcome, a process known as equifinality (*equi* = equal, *finality* = ends). For example, depression may result from biological and genetic processes, but it also can result from early traumatic experiences. However, it is also true that the *same* pathway can lead to *different* outcomes, known as multifinality (Cicchetti & Toth, 2009). For example, children who are victims of abuse can have many different long-term outcomes that can include not only depression but also resiliency and healing. Individual characteristics of a child or an adolescent, including the child's gender, age, ethnic or racial background, and socioeconomic status are just some of the characteristics that may influence the specific outcome in any given situation.

Equifinality Different developmental pathways may result in the same outcome.

Multifinality The same pathways may lead to different developmental outcomes.

This understanding of individual differences has changed the way we view behavioral and emotional disorders. In the field of developmental psychopathology, psychological disorders are now seen as distortions of normal developmental pathways (Cicchetti & Toth, 2009; Sroufe, 2009). Accordingly, in this book we include these disorders in our discussions of typical development. For example, language disorders appear with the discussion of typical language development, and attention deficit disorder appears in the section in which we describe typical development of attention. Thinking about atypical development this way may help reduce the stigma associated with mental disorders, because it helps us see them as variations in development rather than as illnesses.

Developmental psychopathology An approach that sees mental and behavioral problems as distortions of normal developmental processes rather than as illnesses.

The Role of the Child in Development

Some of the most influential theories in child development describe ways in which the circumstances of children's lives shape their development. The clearest example of this type of theory is called learning theory or behaviorism. As you will see in Chapter 2, this approach explores the way the systematic use of rewards and punishment affects the likelihood that a child will—or won't—behave in certain ways. The theory of behaviorism was originally based on the idea that children are passive recipients of forces outside their control. You may agree with this point of view if you think children are like sponges who absorb whatever they are exposed to or like lumps of clay parents shape into the type of children they want.

However, other theories in child development have given children a much more active role in shaping their own development. For example, Jean Piaget, a Swiss psychologist, developed a theory of cognitive development proposing that children actively explore their environment and in the process create their own theories about how the world works. Another influential theorist, Lev Vygotsky, a Russian psychologist, proposed that learning is a collaborative process in which the child seeks to solve problems while more experienced people provide just enough help to allow the child to continue learning independently. Sandra Scarr later described a process of active niche picking in which people express their genetic tendencies by actively "seek[ing] out environments they find compatible and stimulating" (Scarr & McCartney, 1983, p. 427).

Richard Lerner (1982) succinctly captured the idea that children are affected by and also affect their environments when he said that children are both the products *and* the producers of their own development. Characteristics of individual children evoke different reactions from the people with whom the children interact, and these reactions provide feedback in a way that can change the children. For example, the way peers respond to socially skilled children is different from the way they respond to socially awkward ones. These reactions feed back to children and affect their level of self-esteem, which, in turn, will affect their future interactions with peers.

As you continue to read this book, think about the ways you conceptualize development. You should expect your ideas to undergo some significant changes as your understanding of this process grows.

Niche picking A process in which people express their genetic tendencies by finding environments that match and enhance those tendencies.

Check Your Understanding

1. What are the differences between physical, cognitive, and social-emotional development?
2. Why is the relationship between nature and nurture relevant to the study of child development?
3. Contrast quantitative and qualitative changes that occur in development.

1.3

What are the contexts for child development?

AUDIO LINK 1.1
Nurturing the Young Child

Contexts of Development

Children around the world are similar to one another in many ways, but the way development occurs varies widely depending on the context in which a child grows up. *Context* is a very broad term that includes all the settings in which development occurs. Children develop in multiple contexts that include family, schools, neighborhood, peer groups, and communities (Lerner, 1982). Throughout this book you will learn about these different contexts and the way they influence various aspects of children's development.

Family

Families are the primary context for development for most children. Families today take many different forms, but whether they are nuclear families, single-parent families, step- or adoptive families, they all serve one important function: They are responsible for the socialization of their children. They instill the norms, values, attitudes, and beliefs of their culture so that children grow up to be positive, contributing members of their society. We discuss the effects of different family forms on child development, and also examine the ways that families link children and adolescents to the other contexts that influence their development.

Within most cultural groups some families have more resources than others and some have less, and these differences affect children's development. Socioeconomic status (SES) is a combined measure of a family's income and parental education and occupation (Bradley & Corwyn, 2002). In general, a higher SES allows a family to have more resources that can support healthy child development. Beginning before the child is born, low SES parents have less access to good prenatal care, and their babies are more likely to be born prematurely or at low birth weight and to develop other long-term health

Socialization The process of instilling the norms, values, attitudes, and beliefs of a culture in its children.

Culture The system of behaviors, norms, beliefs, and traditions that form in order to promote the survival of a group that lives in a particular environmental niche.

Socioeconomic status A person's social standing based on a combined measure of income, education, and occupation.

problems. Children who spend time living in poverty are found on average to have lower academic performance than those who do not. This makes sense if you consider that parents with more resources are able to provide books, educational experiences, and other activities that a family with few resources cannot. In addition, poor nutrition and low access to health care affect the growing brain and body, influencing a child's ability to learn. Finally, families with few resources are more likely to experience highly stressful events, such as loss of income, relocation, divorce and separation, and violence (Bradley & Corwyn, 2002). Children's response to stress such as this, especially when it is repeated, puts severe strains on their ability to develop optimally. You will learn about the effects of socioeconomic status on children's development as you read about development at each age level throughout this book.

WEB LINK 1.2
Children of Poverty

School

In most countries, school is another important context for development. During the academic year, children spend 6 to 7 hours a day at school (Juster, Ono & Stafford, 2004). Within that context, children learn academic skills, such as reading, writing, and arithmetic, and older children and adolescents are prepared for higher education or entry into the workforce, but schools also play a role in socializing children to become good citizens. In recent years, schools have increasingly taken on other functions, providing nutritious meals for students, some health care, and social services (de Cos, 2001). School also is where most children and adolescents make friends, and sometimes become the victims of bullies. You can see from this description why we talk about schools as an important developmental context when we are talking about physical, cognitive, and social-emotional development.

Community

The characteristics of the community in which children live impact many aspects of development. It affects the range and quality of support services available to children and their families, including the educational opportunities and out-of-school activities that are available. Whether a neighborhood is safe or not affects the amount of time children might spend outside their homes and the kinds of things they do with this time.

Culture

The general findings from research on development are modified not only by individual differences, but also by group differences, such as those between different cultures. For example, a very strict parenting style would likely have a different effect on children raised in a culture that views strictness as a sign of love and care than in one that views the same behavior as a sign the parent doesn't like the child. Matsumoto and Juang (2004) point out that culture is a way of describing similarities within one group of people and differences between groups of people. It emerges from a particular group's *environmental niche*; for example, a desert society will have different rules and traditions than a society located on rich farmland. Even the technological landscape, such as availability of television or cell phones, shapes the environmental niche. Culture forms to promote the survival of the group in its niche.

Throughout the book we draw on cross-cultural studies to illustrate both research that finds similarities across cultures, which suggests there is a universal process at work, and research that illustrates important differences between cultures. Much of what you will read is based on research carried out in Western, developed countries, but increasingly the study of child development seeks to understand children within the context of their own cultures. One of the important changes in the field of child development in recent years has been a deeper, richer appreciation of this diversity.

Cultural differences. Does this photo fit your idea of how to raise a child? Culture affects what we expect parents to do. In Western society, young children generally do not take care of infants; however, in some African societies, older siblings are expected to contribute to the care of infants in their families. ■

We often assume the way we do things is the right way and that other ways are wrong. For example, Robert LeVine et al. (1994) showed U.S. mothers videos of mothers from the Gusii people in Kenya. The U.S. mothers were appalled that 5- and 6-year-old children were put in charge of their infant siblings and that mothers did not praise their children. On the other hand, when he showed tapes of the U.S. mothers to the Gusii mothers, they were appalled that mothers did not nurse their babies immediately when they cried and could not understand why they talked to their babies when the babies clearly could not understand them.

To understand a culture other than our own, we must understand its environmental context and its values. Infant mortality is a major problem for the Gusii, so the protection and health of their infants is the primary concern. Mothers in this culture soothe and calm babies to keep them in an equilibrium conducive to healthy development by nursing them often to prevent the stress of crying. Health is also an issue in the United States but can usually take a backseat to our emphasis on engaging and teaching infants. Stimulating the infant's cognitive development is a priority, so talking to babies, offering toys, and interacting are important. Neither of these approaches is right or wrong. Both are responsive to the realities of the environment, usually in a way to best promote the well-being of the children. When we look at parenting practices in other cultures, we need to guard against labeling those practices as deficient when in reality they are simply different from practices that are more familiar to us. For an example of how we may misinterpret the actions and intentions of people whose culture is different from our own, see **Active Learning: Cultural Competence and Grief.**

AUDIO LINK 1.2
Tiger Moms

Active Learning

Cultural Competence and Grief

Joanne Cacciatore (2009) recounts an experience she had with a family who had just suffered the unexpected death of an 18-month-old son. Although two sets of grandparents and the young child's parents were present, no one except one of the grandfathers would talk with a representative of the medical examiner's office. When the grandfather did talk with her, he stayed at least 4 feet away and did not make eye contact. He steadfastly insisted that no autopsy be performed on the child's body, even though the law required one in cases of sudden child deaths in his state. The family sat in the medical examiner's office for almost 2 hours in silence, with little or no show of emotion. When they finally were asked whether they wanted to have some time with the dead child to say their good-byes, they adamantly refused.

How would you interpret this family's behavior? What circumstances could account for it? How does it fit with your cultural beliefs regarding the way a family grieves for the death of a young child? Does their behavior seem typical, atypical, or pathological to you?

■ **Answer:** This case involved a Native American family and their behaviors were completely expected and normal for some families in their culture. In this culture it was the proper role of the grandfather to be the spokesman for the family. Native Americans may not make sustained eye contact when talking to others and may not display emotion even when they are dealing with personal grief. Because this culture values listening, it is not unusual for its members to remain silent even while sitting together. Autopsies are usually prohibited, as is postmortem contact with the deceased. In the cultural context of this family, their behavior was appropriate, respectful, and in keeping with their traditions and beliefs (Cacciatore, 2009). However, within any culture, there is a range of individual differences. Other Native American families who are more assimilated to the larger culture might not adhere to all these cultural traditions.

One way in which cultures vary is along a continuum from individualism to collectivism. U. S. culture is based on values of rugged individualism. Our heroes often are those who are self-made and managed to rise from deprived circumstances to become successful by their own efforts. In other cultures, the emphasis is more on an obligation to those around you: your family or your group, however you define it. Throughout this book we discuss children's experiences in relation to which of these types of culture forms the context for their lives.

Culture is expressed in overt behaviors such as how we greet people, but there are also much more subtle ways in which culture becomes a part of us, guiding not only our behaviors but also the ways in which we think or experience our feelings. In a relatively new field called cultural neuroscience, researchers are now examining how people who grow up in different cultures develop differences in the way their brains function (Kitayama & Park, 2010). Jenkins, Yang, Goh, Hong, and Park (2010) demonstrated how cultural differences can affect our perceptions. They studied the brain function of Chinese and U.S. adults while they showed them photos of objects in settings that made sense and objects in nonsensical settings, as shown in the photos on this page. Chinese culture values individuals within the context of all that surrounds them, whereas U.S. culture values individuals independent of the surrounding environment. Chinese participants focused their attention more strongly on the object when the background didn't make sense than when it did, whereas U.S. participants were less affected by the background. The Chinese participants were more affected by the context of the objects, while the U.S. subjects paid much less attention to the context.

Because culture is a powerful influence on our behavior, perceptions, and expectations, it is important that we strive to understand children's development within the context of their cultural background and experiences.

Collectivism The cultural value that emphasizes obligations to others within your group.

Individualism The cultural value that emphasizes the importance of the individual with emphasis on independence and reliance on one's own abilities.

Cultural neuroscience The study of the interaction of culture, the mind, and the development of the brain.

Check Your Understanding

1. What is the primary context for most children's development?
2. How does socioeconomic status affect a child's development?
3. What are the goals of cultural neuroscience?

Cultural differences in perception. The context in which these animals appear has different effects on viewers from a Chinese cultural background and on those from a U.S. cultural background. ■

1.4

How can you be a smart consumer of information about development?

Being a Smart Consumer of Information About Development

Information about children and child development is everywhere—in books, magazines, and television programs, at home, and online. How can you judge the quality of the information you see, both in this course and afterward? The solution is to become an informed consumer of information about development so we provide some suggestions for how you can do this.

Know Your Sources

Your campus library owns many journals in the field of child development, as well as many books and professional publications, and you can trust these to be reliable sources of information on child development. You can probably access many of them through your library's electronic databases. Among those of greatest interest to students in child and adolescent development are PsycINFO and ERIC (Education Resources Information Center). PsycINFO contains more than 3 million records that include peer-reviewed journals, books, and dissertations from the 17th century to the present (American Psychological Association [APA], 2014b). ERIC is sponsored by the U.S. Department of Education and has more than 1.3 million bibliographic records of journal articles and other education-related materials (Education Resources Information Center, n.d.). In these databases, you can find abstracts of articles (brief summaries of the research done and the conclusions drawn from it) and information that will allow you to locate many of the complete articles, whether on the shelves of your library or online.

Many journals use a peer review process to determine which articles they will publish. After researchers submit an article to a journal, the journal's editors send it out to a group of professionals knowledgeable about the topic of the research. These research peers, in turn, tell the editors whether they think the article should be published and often make suggestions to improve it before publication. This process ensures that the information you take from a peer-reviewed journal has passed professional scrutiny before it ever got into print.

However, when you turn to the Internet to find information and use a search engine such as Yahoo!, Google, or Bing, you need to provide your own scrutiny and use good judgment. Remember that anyone can post information on the web, and the authors of some web pages do not necessarily have any particular expertise. Their information may simply be wrong, or it may be opinion masquerading as fact. This is especially a risk when you are researching a controversial topic. Commercial sites provide some amount of legitimate information, but their real intent is to sell you a product (Piper, 2000).

Although the Wikipedia website is popular with college students, anyone can add to an existing post on the site. For these reasons, Wikipedia is *not* considered a reliable source of information for most purposes. If you do use a site like this, use it as a starting point only, and be sure to expand your search to include other professional sources of information. Many Wikipedia entries include a bibliography of professional books and articles that may help send you in the right direction to find scientific information on the topic you are researching.

Many libraries currently use Jim Kapoun's 1998 guidelines for evaluating web pages you want to use for research. You can use these guidelines to evaluate a web page that interests you by completing **Active Learning: Evaluating Information on the Web.**

Peer review A process in which professionals critique an article and make suggestions for improvement before a decision is made whether to publish it.

VIDEO LINK 1.4
Peer Review

Active Learning

WEB LINK 1.3
Evaluating Sources

Evaluating Information on the Web

Begin this activity by picking a topic related to child development that you would like to know more about. For example, what is the effect of violent video games on children's level of aggression, or how does parental divorce affect teens' romantic relationships? Find a website devoted to this topic through a search engine such as Google and evaluate it using the criteria below.

Name of the site you found: _____

URL: _____

1. Accuracy of Web Documents

- Who wrote the page and can you contact him or her?
- What is the purpose of the document and why was it produced?
- Is this person qualified to write this document?

2. Authority of Web Documents

- Who published the document and is it separate from the "Webmaster"?
- Check the domain of the document, [and ask] what institution publishes this document?
- Does the publisher list his or her qualifications?

3. Objectivity of Web Documents

- What goals/objectives does this page meet?
- How detailed is the information?
- What opinions (if any) are expressed by the author?

4. Currency of Web Documents

- When was it produced?
- When was it updated?
- How up-to-date are the links (if any)?

5. Coverage of Web Documents

- Are the links (if any) evaluated, and do they complement the documents' theme?
- Is it all images or a balance of text and images?
- Is the information presented/cited correctly?

SOURCE: Kapoun (1998, July/August). Reprinted by permission of the author.

What is your overall evaluation of the accuracy and helpfulness of this site?

Next, log on to PsycINFO through your campus library website and search for the same research topic. Be sure to enter specific search terms for the topic you've chosen, not a full sentence or phrase; for example, enter *video games* on one line and *aggression* on the next rather than entering *effect of video games on aggression* on one line. Chances are your search will return many, many published articles. If it doesn't, try changing one or more of your search terms. For instance, if you searched for *teenagers*, you could try searching for *adolescents*. Choose one or two of the articles you find that give you electronic access to the full text of the articles and look over the information.

What are advantages and disadvantages of using the Internet versus PsycINFO for finding information on child development? How much do you trust the information in each? What gives you confidence in the results you found? ■

Become a Critical Thinker

As you learn about child development, don't hesitate to look for answers to your own questions. No single book can contain all the information you need on any topic, so seek out divergent opinions on topics that intrigue you. Expose yourself to a wide range of ideas. You will probably find some that make sense to you and some that are harder to accept, but keep an open mind and don't stop asking questions and learning. Just be sure you turn to credible sources of information as you go through this process. As you learn more about research methods in Chapter 2, you will become better able to examine the evidence behind the ideas you find rather than just relying on what someone else has said.

A science is an organized body of knowledge that is accumulated over time; therefore, that body of knowledge changes and grows. New ideas come into existence, and old ideas fall out of favor because they are replaced with better information. For instance, autism was once attributed to (or perhaps we should say "was blamed on") mothers who were cold and rejecting toward their children, but today research on autism focuses on differences in the structure and functioning of the brain in autistic children as an underlying cause. The fact that an idea has been around for a long time—or that many people endorse it—does not necessarily mean it is true. Remember that for a very long time, everyone believed that Earth was flat. Likewise, just because an idea is new doesn't necessarily mean it is better than what we believed before. All new ideas that enter a science are subjected to review and critique by people in the field, and research findings need to be tested and replicated or produced again by others before we can gain confidence that they are accurate and reliable. The best suggestion is to be open to new ideas but to be cautious about jumping on a bandwagon until there is good evidence that the bandwagon is going in the right direction. If new ideas cannot be replicated, they are not a fact—they are a fluke!

VIDEO LINK 1.5
**Brain Development
and Autism**

Replicate To find the same results as in a previous research study.

Beware Generalizations

As you learn about child development, you will need to guard against taking a particular instance or example and generalizing it to other people. It is easy to assume others have had experiences the same as or similar to yours with the same or similar consequences. Your own experiences are meaningful and real. They all become part of what has made you the person you are today and help shape the person you will be tomorrow. That fact is never in question, but your experiences may not represent the average or typical experience of other people. Trying to generalize from one particular experience to general statements is always dangerous. Likewise, when we conduct research, we cannot necessarily generalize findings based on one population to another population that might have different characteristics.

The converse of this is also true. When you read about conclusions drawn from research, they may not describe what your personal experiences were, but this does not mean the research is invalid. Rather it reminds us that research describes the outcome for groups, not for every individual within a group. When we say men are more physically aggressive than women, for instance, it does not mean every man is more aggressive than any woman, only that on average there is a difference between the groups, and within the groups there is a good deal of individual variability.

Avoid Perceptual Bias

It will be easier for you to remember the facts you encounter in this book that fit well with your expectations, and to forget or ignore those that don't. This tendency to see and understand something based on the way you expected it to be is called a **perceptual bias**, and it can affect your learning. That is one reason we use common misconceptions to begin each chapter. Identifying them can help you pay more attention to those ideas that challenge the preconceptions you bring to your reading.

Perceptual bias The tendency to see and understand something based on the way you expected it to be.

Question "Common Sense"

Finally, students sometimes think that child development is just common sense. Unfortunately it isn't that simple. While some findings sound like common sense, others will be counterintuitive. Sometimes we fall back on folk wisdom, or ideas that are widely accepted but have not been scientifically tested, to describe our ideas about development. Folk wisdom may have a grain of truth in it, but it usually does not help us understand the reasons for what we see, and sometimes it is simply wrong. Do you believe sticks and stones may break your bones but names will never hurt you? That "wisdom" may not hold true for children who are victims of verbal bullying. At other times, folk wisdom is contradictory. Do you believe that opposites attract . . . or that birds of a feather flock together?

Active Learning: Testing Your Knowledge of Child Development provides a selection of questions appearing in the chapters that follow. Test your current knowledge about these topics.

Active Learning

Testing Your Knowledge of Child Development

1. T☐ F☐ Genes have been found to play a role in the development of almost all behaviors that have been studied.

2. T☐ F☐ Research has shown that exposing a fetus to extra stimulation (for example, playing music near the woman's stomach) can stimulate advanced cognitive development.

3. T☐ F☐ Humans use only 10% of their brain.

4. T☐ F☐ Children who are gifted or talented often pay a price for their giftedness because they are likely to be socially or emotionally maladjusted.

5. T☐ F☐ It is perfectly fine to use baby talk with infants.

6. T☐ F☐ Programs that build students' self-esteem not only improve their grades but also help reduce delinquency, drug use, and adolescent pregnancy.

7. T☐ F☐ Having a lot of conflict between parents and adolescents is normal in families with adolescents.

8. T☐ F☐ Adolescents are much less likely to be victims of violence while in school now than they were 20 years ago.

9. T☐ F☐   Children who grow up without siblings tend to be more self-centered, maladjusted, lonely, and neurotic than children who have siblings.

10. T☐ F☐   Adults who were abused as children are very likely to become abusive parents themselves.

Answers:

1. **True.** Behavioral genetics has shown that almost all behaviors studied have some genetic component. However, different traits and behaviors are more or less heritable (Chapter 3).

2. **False.** Although a fetus is able to hear and even respond to sounds prior to birth, there is no evidence that auditory stimulation beyond the level provided by the natural prenatal environment has any extra cognitive benefits (Chapter 4).

3. **False.** Neurologist Barry Gordon, who studies the brain, finds the notion that we use only 10% of our brain ridiculous. He says, "It turns out . . . that we use virtually every part of the brain, and that [most of] the brain is active almost all the time" (Boyd, 2008, para. 5) (Chapter 5).

4. **False.** Gifted children have generally been found to be socially and emotionally well-adjusted and to feel positive about their gifts and abilities (Chapter 12).

5. **True.** The way adults often talk to babies—in a high-pitched voice, with a great deal of exaggeration, and in a singsong rhythm—is actually well suited to the hearing capabilities and preferences of a baby. Babies pay attention to us when we talk this way, and doing it will not delay their language development (Chapter 6).

6. **False.** Self-esteem programs have not been effective at improving school performance or reducing adolescent problem behavior. It appears more likely that better achievement promotes high self-esteem rather than the other way around (Chapter 13).

7. **False.** A lot of parent-adolescent conflict does occur in *some* families, but conflict is not overwhelming or pervasive in most families (Chapter 16).

8. **True.** In 1992, the rate of violent victimization of teens was 53 students per 1,000, while in 2010 the same rate was 14 students per 1,000 (Chapter 16).

9. **False.** Research has generally failed to support the negative predictions made about only children. Rather it has found that only children show high achievement, good adjustment, strong character, and positive social relationships (Chapter 13).

10. **False.** This is one of the most serious misunderstandings about child abuse. About 30% of abused children perpetuate the cycle by repeating abuse in the next generation, but the majority does not. They successfully break the cycle when they reach adulthood (Chapter 10).

How did you do? Many of these questions represent common beliefs, so it wouldn't be surprising if you got a number of them wrong. We hope your results make you eager to learn more about these topics, but remember to pay extra attention to those ideas that contradict your preconceived ideas. The explanations you will find in the chapters are more extensive than the brief ones we provide here, so you will learn a great deal more about each. ■

Check Your Understanding

1. How does peer review help assure readers that scientific information is valid and reliable?
2. What does it mean to be a critical thinker?
3. What is perceptual bias?

Conclusion

We hope this chapter has made you eager to explore child development through the topics presented in this book. In this chapter we have introduced you to some of the basic concepts in the field of child development. The rest of the book elaborates on these concepts in many ways. Our understanding of the nature of child development has important consequences for our ability to foster children's positive growth. As you read this book, we want you to take an active role in your own learning process through the use of the activities we have provided that will help you examine your current beliefs about children and adolescents and move to a new level of understanding that you can build on long after this course is over.

Chapter Summary

The chapter summary at the end of each chapter is designed in a question/answer format so that you can use it to test yourself on what you have learned. While looking at each question, cover the answer and try to answer it yourself. Then see how the answer corresponds to your own understanding. Self-testing is a very effective way to study and learn.

1.1 Who needs to have a good understanding of child development?

Informed parents and family members are better able to understand their children's needs and abilities at each stage of development, which helps them respond empathically as well as provide the appropriate type of stimulation to support their children's growth and development. In addition to pediatricians and teachers, social workers, counselors, therapists, lawyers, nurses, and people in many other careers all draw on child development knowledge in their work. Lawmakers and program developers responsible for **social policy** must understand how policies will affect children and their families. Citizens who are knowledgeable about child development can advocate and/or vote for policies that promote positive child development.

1.2 What are the domains of child development and some recurring issues for debate?

Physical development consists of the biologically based changes that occur as children grow. **Cognitive development** consists of the changes that take place in children's thinking and learning. **Social-emotional development** consists of the changes that occur in children's understanding and expression of emotions as well as their ability to interact with other people. Issues in the study of development include debate about the relative contribution of **nature** and **nurture** to development, **incremental theories** or **quantitative changes** versus **stage theories** or **qualitative changes,** and stability versus change over time. In addition, different developmental pathways may result in the same outcome (**equifinality**), or the same developmental pathways may result in different outcomes (**multifinality**). Examining less adaptive processes and outcomes is the domain of **developmental psychopathology**. Another debate examines whether children play an active role in their own development or are passive recipients of external influences.

1.3 What are the contexts for child development?

The contexts for development include a child's family, as well as their schools, neighborhoods, communities, and culture. Family is the primary context for development for most children and family resources make a significant impact on the experiences a child will have. Characteristics of the school a child attends and the community in which the child lives affects every aspect of development. **Culture** includes the behaviors, norms, beliefs, and traditions that a particular group has developed as it has adapted to its environment. **Cultural neuroscience** has shown that culture affects the way our brains develop and even the way we perceive the world. Although we see cultural differences in how parents raise their children, one approach is not better than another because each culture prepares children to be successful in the context of their particular environment.

1.4 How can you be a smart consumer of information about development?

Be sure your information is based on scientific evidence that has been **replicated** in studies conducted by more than one researcher. Look for convergence from many different sources of information and think critically about them. Don't generalize from a single example, but also don't reject the results of research because your individual experiences don't agree with the research findings. Try to be objective so that you don't fall prey to **perceptual bias** that just confirms what you already expected. Finally, examine your preconceptions carefully to determine what is scientifically based fact and what is unproven folk wisdom.

Key Terms

Cognitive development   9

Collectivism   17

Cultural neuroscience   17

Culture   14

Developmental psychopathology   13

Equifinality   13

Incremental theories   11

Individualism   17

Multifinality   13

Nature   10

Niche picking   14

Nurture   10

Peer review   18

Perceptual bias   21

Physical development   9

Qualitative changes   11

Quantitative changes   11

Replicate   20

Social policy   8

Social-emotional development   9

Socialization   14

Socioeconomic status   14

Stage theories   11

Sharpen your skills with SAGE edge at edge.sagepub.com/levinechrono

SAGE edge for Students provides a personalized approach to help you accomplish your coursework goals in an easy-to-use learning environment.

Go to edge.sagepub.com/levinechrono for additional exercises and video resources. Select Chapter 1, Issues in Child Development, for chapter-specific activities. All of the Video Links listed in the margins of this chapter are accessible via this site.

2

Theory and Research in Development

T/F Test Your Knowledge

Test your knowledge of child development by deciding whether each of the following statements is *true* or *false*, and then check your answers as you read the chapter.

1. **T** ☐ **F** ☐ Well-designed research can tell us whether a theory is true or false.

2. **T** ☐ **F** ☐ The best way to establish and maintain a behavior is to reward people every time they perform the behavior you are interested in.

3. **T** ☐ **F** ☐ The best way to get rid of an undesirable behavior in a child is to punish the child for doing it.

4. **T** ☐ **F** ☐ There are times when it can be an advantage for a girl to go through puberty at an early age.

5. **T** ☐ **F** ☐ If a child is experiencing a lot of stress at home, the child will show behavior problems in the classroom.

6. **T** ☐ **F** ☐ A good theory should be universal, applying to all children in all situations.

7. **T** ☐ **F** ☐ The best way to do research on development is to conduct experiments.

8. **T** ☐ **F** ☐ When conducting research by doing an observation, it is important that the person who is doing the observation does not know the purpose of the research.

9. **T** ☐ **F** ☐ Standardized tests (such as the SATs or ACT) are not biased against American-born ethnic or racial minorities.

10. **T** ☐ **F** ☐ Even if research consistently finds that children whose mothers talk to them a great deal have high self-esteem, we should not conclude that frequent conversations with parents build self-esteem in children.

Correct answers: (1) F, (2) F, (3) F, (4) T, (5) F, (6) F, (7) F, (8) F, (9) T, (10) T

Theories of development are central to our understanding of children and adolescents. In this chapter we introduce you to some of the major theories in the field of child development that have influenced the direction that the study of children and adolescents has taken. These theories differ in the way they describe the developmental processes and what drives them. Some of the theories have their origins in the late 19th and early 20th centuries, but each has modern applications that we have included in this chapter. All theories must be testable, so we describe a variety of methods that are a part of the scientific method used to test these theories and to build our knowledge base. We begin with a discussion of why theories are an important basis for our understanding of development.

Learning Questions

2.1 What do child development theories tell us?

2.2 What are the hypotheses of the major child development theories?

2.3 How is research on child development conducted?

2.4 What are ethical considerations in research with children and adolescents?

Why Theories of Development Are Important

To make progress in our understanding of child development, it is not enough simply to observe children. Our observations become the basis for our thoughts about why and how children develop the way they do, but when we systematize and organize these thoughts, we develop a model that allows us to predict how children will behave. This model is called a developmental theory. Although we all have our own personal theories about various aspects of human behavior, the theories we use to build a scientific understanding about child and adolescent development must be public and testable. Theories in any science serve two important functions: They help us *organize* the knowledge that we already have, and they help us *make predictions* about new information that we then can investigate and test.

For example, a parent might react to an infant's excessive crying very differently depending on his understanding of what this crying means. If he subscribes to the theory of behaviorism, he might believe that picking up the crying baby will reward that behavior and make the baby cry more. However, if he subscribes to the theory of ethology, he might believe the crying is a behavior that signals that the baby needs comfort. If that need is met, it will help the baby develop a secure attachment that will eventually help the baby cry less (Bell & Ainsworth, 1972).

Now that we have stated opposing theoretical ideas, we can design research that will test those ideas. St. James-Roberts (2007) studied two types of parenting: *demand parenting*, in which babies were reliably picked up when they cried (based on an ethological approach), and *structured parenting*, in which standard bedtimes and routines were put in place and some crying was acceptable (based on a behavioral approach). Note that no one simply left babies to cry uncontrollably! Demand parenting resulted in babies crying less during the first 3 months of life but continuing to cry at night after that age. Structured parenting resulted in more crying during the first 3 months but reduced crying at night thereafter. The results support the idea that quickly responding to a crying infant meets the infant's needs (ethological theory), but also that it establishes a pattern that reinforces the crying itself (behavioral theory).

As this research suggests, most theories can never be proved beyond a shadow of any doubt, but the scientific process allows us to provide evidence that supports or opposes the truth of these ideas. For example, some say Darwin's theory of evolution is not a proven fact, and technically this is true. However, the enormous body of evidence that supports its ideas outweighs the evidence against it. Consequently, evolutionary theory

2.1

What do child development theories tell us?

Developmental theory A model of development based on observations that allows us to make predictions.

T/F #1
Well-designed research can tell us whether a theory is true or false.
False.

is widely accepted in scientific circles today. On the other hand, other theories have come and gone as evidence piled up that did not fit with the predictions that emerged from them. At one time, we thought inadequate early mothering was the cause of the severe mental illness known as schizophrenia (Ambert, 1997), but as research continued, it became clear that the more likely culprit in the development of schizophrenia is a combination of genetic endowment and environmental influence (Boksa, 2008). As our understanding advanced, the idea that mothers' behavior was the cause for this mental disorder disappeared.

In Chapter 1, you were introduced to some of the major issues in the field of child development. Next we discuss how theories address two of these issues: How and why change happens.

How Does Change Happen?

As you will remember from Chapter 1, development has to do with both stability and change over time, so each developmental theory must address how change happens and explain why some aspects of behavior remain the same. You learned that some theories describe development as a series of quantitative changes that happen little by little, smoothly over time, such as growing physically inch by inch, while other theories describe development as a series of large qualitative changes that occur at certain ages and alter the nature of the child or adolescent in significant ways. These qualitative theories are called stage theories, because each stage in life is seen as different from the ones that come before and after. One way to understand the difference between the two types of change is to consider the development of memory. Children can remember more and more as they get older (quantitative change), but they may suddenly increase their memory capacity when they develop a new way of encoding information into memory (qualitative change) (Siegler & Crowley, 1991).

Why Does Change Happen?

Developmental change may be driven by biological processes inside each person, by environmental events that affect each person, or by an interaction between the two. Development is also affected by the way we make sense out of our experiences. One of the important ways developmental theories differ from each other is the relative weight they attach to internal and external influences on development.

Check Your Understanding

1. What two functions do theories serve in science?
2. What is the relationship between theory and truth?
3. What are two ways in which theories of development differ from each other?

2.2

What are the hypotheses of the major child development theories?

Theories of Child and Adolescent Development

As we begin this description of developmental theories, it is important for you to understand that theoretical ideas do not appear in a vacuum. The influential theorists in our field all have developed their ideas in a particular culture and at a particular point in historical time, and their ideas about child development reflect these influences. However each of these theories has been tested over time, retaining those concepts and principles that continue to be useful and losing or changing those that don't. In different ways, each of these theories has helped shape the type of questions we ask, the type of research we conduct, and often the interpretation we place on our findings.

Psychoanalytic Theory

We begin our discussion of theories with psychoanalytic theory (*psyche* = the mind; *analysis* implies looking at the parts of the mind individually to see how they relate) because it was the first theory to describe stages of development through childhood. Although psychoanalytic theory has been very controversial throughout its existence, many of its concepts have become part of our assumptions about how the mind works. Sigmund Freud (1856–1939), the father of psychoanalysis, has been recognized as one of the 100 most influential people of the 20th century (Gay, 1999).

Freud believed we are aware of some of our thoughts, which are in our conscious mind, but unaware of other thoughts, which are in our unconscious mind. When we have thoughts, memories, and feelings that would be unacceptable to us, we repress them and hide them from ourselves (Freud, 1953). According to Freud, the key to healthy psychological functioning lies in discovering the unconscious thoughts or memories associated with psychological symptoms and bringing them back into the conscious mind. Techniques such as free association, in which a person allows thoughts to float freely without censorship, and dream analysis are two ways of gaining insight into the working of the unconscious mind (Freud, 1950). To experience the technique of free association, try **Active Learning: Free Association.**

Free Association

Free association starts with a stimulus, which could be a dream or a word. The person who is free associating tries to let her mind float freely and says the first thing that comes to her mind in response to that stimulus. For example, if someone is told to free associate to the word *blue*, her first association might be to say the word *green*. She then says what *green* brings to mind and ends up with a list like this: *blue, green, sea, ocean, fish, swim, water, drink, lemonade, lunch*. This example might come from a person in an 11 a.m. class who is hungry!

Now you try it. When you read the word at the end of this sentence, write down a series of 10 words that spontaneously come to mind: *child*

_____   _____   _____   _____   _____

_____   _____   _____   _____   _____

Freud would say that this type of free association gives a clue to the unconscious contents of your mind. Did the words you wrote reflect particular concerns, interests, or issues on your mind recently? If you were in psychoanalytic psychotherapy, the process would lead you ever deeper into your unknown thoughts and feelings. You might find it interesting to compare the last word on your list of free associations with that of other students in your class to see in how many different directions the word *child* can take you. ■

Freud theorized that personality is made up of three parts: the id, the ego, and the superego. According to Freud, we are all born with an id, which consists of our basic drives. The id operates on what Freud called the pleasure principle because it seeks immediate gratification for all its urges. Infants have no way to control their drives. They want *what* they want, *when* they want it.

VIDEO LINK 2.1
Sigmund Freud

Psychoanalytic theory Freud's theory in which the way we deal with biological urges moves the person through a series of stages that shape our personality.

Unconscious mind The part of the mind that contains thoughts and feelings about which we are unaware.

Free association The process used by psychoanalysis in which one thinks of anything that comes to mind in relation to a dream or another thought to reveal the contents of the unconscious mind.

Id According to psychoanalytic theory, the part of the personality that consists of the basic drives, such as sex and hunger.

Pleasure principle The idea that the id seeks immediate gratification for all of its urges.

Sigmund Freud. Sigmund Freud developed the theory of psychoanalysis in the early 1900s. Many of his ideas continue to influence the way we think about the impact of early experience on later development. ■

Ego The part of the personality that contends with the reality of the world and controls the basic drives.

Reality principle The psychoanalytic concept that the ego has the ability to deal with the real world and not just drives and fantasy.

Superego Freud's concept of the conscience or sense of right and wrong.

Psychosexual stages Freud's idea that at each stage sexual energy is invested in a different part of the body.

Oral stage Freud's first stage, in which infants' biological energy is centered on the mouth area.

Anal stage Freud's second stage, in which toddlers' sexual energy is focused on the anus.

Phallic stage Freud's third stage, in which children ages 3 to 6 overcome their attraction to the opposite-sex parent and begin to identify with the same-sex parent.

Latency stage Freud's fourth stage, involving children ages 6 to 12, when the sex drive goes underground.

As children grow older they develop an ego, which has the ability to negotiate between their basic drives and the demands of the real world. The child is still motivated by her basic drives, but she now is able to interact in the real world to get her needs met. Even though she is hungry, she might realize that if she waits until you are off the phone and asks politely, she may be more likely to get the cookie she wants. This way of dealing with wants and desires is known as the reality principle.

Finally, sometime between the ages of 5 and 7, the child begins to incorporate moral principles that work against the drive-motivated functioning of the id. These moral principles are maintained by the superego. Freud believed that children do not have any internal sense of guilt that guides their actions until they develop a superego. Whereas a younger child might simply take a cookie when hungry, an older child will be able to control herself and resist the temptation because she knows that taking a cookie when she isn't supposed to is wrong.

Sigmund Freud's Psychosexual Stages

In Freud's theory, our most basic drive is the sex drive. Freud outlined five stages in child and adolescent development, which he called psychosexual stages. At each of these stages, sexual energy is invested in a different part of the body, and gratification of the urges associated with those areas of the body is particularly pleasurable. Freud believed that the way in which gratification of urges is handled during each of these stages determines the nature of an adult's personality and character. We next describe these stages and Freud's ideas about the effects later in life if development during these stages does not go well.

The first stage is the oral stage which lasts from birth to about 18 months of age. The zone of pleasure is the mouth, which is what drives any 6-month-old baby to put a toy immediately in her mouth. Freud developed the idea that someone can get "stuck" or fixated in one of the first three psychosexual stages if her needs are not adequately met at that stage, or if she receives so much gratification that she is not willing to move on to another stage. That person will then exhibit characteristics of that stage later in life (Freud, 1953). For example, an individual who is fixated in the oral stage may want to continue to try to satisfy his oral urges by overeating or smoking. Many of us have some remnants of this stage as we chew on our fingers or pencils; however, a fixation is really a concern only when it interferes with adaptive functioning in some critical way.

The anal stage lasts from 18 months to 3 years. At this age the pleasure center moves to the anus, and issues of toilet training become central. Although many of us squirm to think of the anus as a pleasure center, we have only to listen to the "poopy talk" of young children to see the hilarity it brings about. The task of the child at this age is to learn to control his bodily urges to conform to society's expectations. A person who is fixated at this stage may become overcontrolled (referred to as *anal compulsive*) as an adult (Freud, 1959). Everything must be in its proper place to an extreme degree. Conversely, someone might become *anal expulsive*, creating "messes" wherever he goes.

The phallic stage lasts from 3 to 6 years of age. Sexual energy becomes focused on the genitals, and boys and girls develop what has been called "the family romance." Boys imagine marrying their mother when they grow up and girls imagine marrying their father. Children must learn to give up these desires and begin to identify with the parent of the same sex.

The latency stage occurs between 6 and 12 years of age. *Latent* means inactive, and Freud believed that during this time the sex drive goes underground (Freud, 1953). Children move from their fantasies during the phallic period of marrying their parent to a new realization that they must take the long road toward learning to become a grown-up. The sex drive provides energy for the learning that must take place, but the drive itself is not expressed overtly. Children transfer their interest from parents to peers (Freud, 1965). At this age children who had cross-sex friendships often relinquish them as each sex professes disgust for the other.

This separation of the sexes begins to change at age 12, when young adolescents enter the genital stage. At this point, sexual energy becomes focused on the genital area, and sexual interest occurs between peers.

Erik Erikson's Psychosocial Stages

Many followers of Freud further developed his theory, but one of the most influential was Erik Homburger Erikson (1902–1994). Erikson believed that issues of the ego are more important than those linked with the id. He believed that a major issue is the development of identity. He described a set of psychosocial stages (as opposed to Freud's psycho*sexual* stages), each rooted in the social experiences typical at each stage of development rather than in sexual urges (Erikson, 1963). At each age he believed a central conflict needs to be resolved based on the interaction between our biological development and

Freud's latency stage. Does this picture of girls interacting with girls and boys interacting with boys remind you of your own experience in elementary school? ■

our experiences in our environment. The way in which we resolve that conflict lays the groundwork for the next stages of our development.

For example, Erikson believed that it is extremely important for infants to establish trust in the world around them, so he called the developmental issue for infants *trust versus mistrust*. Infants are totally dependent on the adults who care for them. When caregivers are dependable and reliably meet the infant's needs, the infant learns to trust the world and feel safe and secure in it. However, when caregivers are inconsistent in providing care or are emotionally unavailable, the infant develops a sense of mistrust in the world. These early experiences can color the way the individual approaches social relationships later in life. In a similar way, each subsequent developmental stage presents a different developmental conflict. The way infants resolve the issue of trust versus mistrust sets the stage for the way they will go on to deal with issues of autonomy versus shame and doubt at the next stage. Erikson's eight stages are compared to Freud's psychosexual stages in Table 2.1.

Of course none of us have a completely positive or completely negative set of experiences; therefore, we can think of the two possible outcomes of each stage as two sides of a seesaw, with one side higher than the other but both actively in play. For example, we will all have some trust and some mistrust in our relationships; it is the balance of the two that lays the foundation for later development. The other important aspect of Erikson's theory is that he believed development does not stop in adolescence. He went beyond Freud's stages to add three stages of adulthood, becoming the first theorist to recognize that we continue to grow and develop throughout our lives.

Modern Applications of Psychoanalytic Theory

While some concepts in psychoanalytic theory have been supported by research, others have not. Psychoanalytic theory has been controversial, yet ideas that come from it are still very influential, particularly in the study of mental and emotional disorders (Fonagy, Target, & Gergely, 2006). Many psychotherapists continue to use therapy based on Freud's idea that inner conflicts from earlier life experiences, especially early trauma, form the basis for current psychological symptoms and bringing those inner conflicts into consciousness will be therapeutic.

Genital stage Freud's fifth and final stage in which people 12 and older develop adult sexuality.

Psychosocial stages Erikson's stages that are based on a central conflict to be resolved involving the social world and the development of identity.

VIDEO LINK 2.2
Erik Erikson

AUDIO LINK 2.1
Freud's Contributions

TABLE 2.1	A comparison of Freud's and Erikson's stages of development				
Ages	**Freud's psychosexual stages**			**Erikson's psychosocial stages**	
Infancy	Oral	Pleasure is focused on the mouth and "taking in"		Trust versus mistrust	Development of trust in maternal care and in one's own ability to cope versus hopelessness
Toddlerhood	Anal	Pleasure is focused on the anal region and control of one's own body and its products		Autonomy versus shame and doubt	Independence and self-control versus lack of confidence
Early childhood	Phallic	Pleasure is focused on the genital area; development of the "family romance"		Initiative versus guilt	Exuberant activity versus overcontrol
Middle childhood	Latency	Sexual energy goes underground as child focuses on peers and learning		Industry versus inferiority	Learning the tasks of one's society versus a sense of inadequacy
Adolescence	Genital	Sexual energy reaches adult level, with focus on intimate relationships		Identity versus role confusion	Integration of previous experiences to form an identity versus confusion about one's role in society
Early adulthood				Intimacy versus isolation	Ability to form close relationships versus fear of losing the self
Middle adulthood				Generativity versus stagnation	Guiding the next generation versus preoccupation with one's own needs
Later adulthood				Ego integrity versus despair	Achievement of a sense of meaning in life versus focus on fear of death

SOURCE: Compiled from Kahn (2002) and Erikson (1963).

© Ted Streshinsky/CORBIS

Erik Erikson. Erikson was a psychoanalyst who focused more on the role of social issues in development than Freud and who introduced stages of life that continued through adulthood. ■

Erikson's ideas about the effect of social experiences on development have influenced contemporary child care practices and our understanding of the way development occurs as a series of interrelated experiences. For instance, we urge new parents to be sensitive and responsive to their infants as a way to establish a sense of trust, as Erikson described. We better understand the challenge of adolescence when we see it as a struggle to establish a coherent sense of individual identity. We also use Erikson's theories in the treatment of children with emotional disturbances to provide a framework for understanding the central issues that children deal with at different ages.

Erikson's ideas also have remained influential because they are a good reflection of the way we think about development today, as we outlined these issues in Chapter 1. The role Erikson gives to the influence on development of culture, the environment, and social experiences fits well with our current interest in understanding the contexts in which development occurs. His portrayal of the child as an active participant in shaping his or her own development and the incorporation of both change (as reflected in different crises in each of the stages) and stability (as seen in the idea that later stages continue to be influenced by the resolution of earlier issues) also dovetails with our current thinking.

Behaviorism and Social Cognitive Theory

A very different school of thought about how children develop is offered by the learning theories. Whereas psychoanalytic theory focuses on internal processes of the mind, the learning theories focus on observable behavior. These theories are based on the link between a stimulus (an event in the external environment) and the individual's response. The two learning theories we describe are behaviorism, based on principles of classical and operant conditioning, and social cognitive theory, based on principles of modeling and imitation.

John B. Watson and Classical Conditioning

Unlike other psychologists in the early 1900s, John B. Watson (1878–1958) was not interested in studying the impact of internal factors such as genetic influences and the workings of the mind on human development (Buckley, 1989). Instead, he concentrated on what he could see: behavior, or what people *do*. The modern academic field of psychology was just emerging, and psychologists in America were trying hard to establish the field as an experimental science, with testable predictions based on observable phenomena rather than unseen concepts such as Freud's unconscious mind.

Watson studied the ways in which the environment influences human behavior. He described a process called classical conditioning, illustrated in Figure 2.1. In this process, a particular stimulus or event in the environment is paired with another stimulus over and over again. The first stimulus, known as the *unconditioned stimulus*, provokes a natural response, known as the *unconditioned response*. For example, Ivan Pavlov (1849–1936), a Russian physiologist who was studying reflexes and the processes of digestion, presented food to hungry dogs in his lab. In response, the dogs salivated, just as you would if you were hungry and walked by a bakery. The food is the unconditioned stimulus because it elicits a natural or unconditioned response, salivation. Then Pavlov preceded each presentation of the food with a distinctive noise, such as a bell ringing. At first the bell did not provoke salivation from the dogs, so initially it was considered a neutral stimulus. However, over time the dogs began to associate the sound of the bell with the food, so the animals had *learned* something about the bell, and it now became a *conditioned stimulus*. Finally, Pavlov presented only the bell and found that the dogs continued to salivate just as if the food had been presented. Salivation to a formerly neutral stimulus, such as the ringing of a bell, is known as a *conditioned response* (Pavlov, 1927).

In a well-known experiment with a 9-month-old infant known only as Little Albert, Watson applied the idea of classical conditioning by demonstrating that he could use it to create fear in a human infant (Watson & Rayner, 1920). Clearly this type of research would be considered unethical today and would not be conducted unless strict safeguards were implemented to assure the infant's safety and well-being. Watson found that Little Albert, like many infants, was frightened by a sudden loud sound so the noise was an unconditioned stimulus and would bring about fear as an unconditioned response. When Little Albert was first shown a white rat, he was curious and unafraid, so the rat was initially a neutral stimulus because it did not produce a fear response. However, Watson then made the loud clanging noise at the same time that he presented the white rat to the infant. He did this numerous times over a number of days, and Little Albert soon began to cry as soon as he saw the white rat. Eventually Watson stopped making the loud sound, and yet every time he showed Little Albert the white rat, which by now had become a conditioned stimulus, the infant continued to show fear, which now was a conditioned, or learned, response.

© Underwood & Underwood/Corbis

John B. Watson. John B. Watson is called the father of the theory of behaviorism, which focuses on what people do, rather than on what they think. ■

Behaviorism The theory developed by John B. Watson that focuses on environmental control of observable behavior.

Classical conditioning The process by which a stimulus (the unconditioned stimulus) that naturally evokes a certain response (the unconditioned response) is paired repeatedly with a neutral stimulus. Eventually the neutral stimulus becomes the conditioned stimulus and evokes the same response, now called the conditioned response.

VIDEO LINK 2.3
Little Albert

Classical conditioning

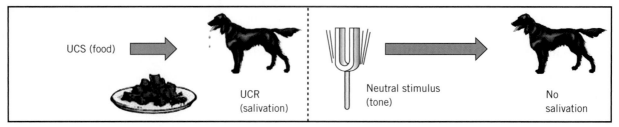

BEFORE CONDITIONING

An unconditioned stimulus (UCS) produces an unconditioned response (UCR).

A neutral stimulus produces no salivation response.

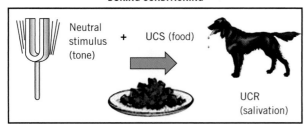

DURING CONDITIONING

The unconditioned stimulus is repeatedly presented just after the neutral stimulus. The unconditioned stimulus continues to produce an unconditioned response.

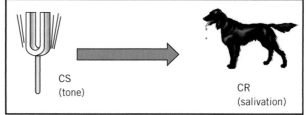

AFTER CONDITIONING

The neutral stimulus alone now produces a conditioned response (CR), thereby becoming a conditioned stimulus (CS).

This figure shows the steps in the process of classical conditioning.

Other people who subsequently carried out this type of classical conditioning with other infants were unable to replicate the results Watson described (Harris, 1979). However classical conditioning does have relevance to some common everyday experiences. A child who gets sick from eating asparagus may later find that just seeing asparagus makes him feel queasy. The sick feeling has become classically conditioned to the sight of that vegetable. To check whether you understand the steps of the classical conditioning process, try **Active Learning: Understanding the Process of Classical Conditioning**.

Active Learning

Understanding the Process of Classical Conditioning

Read the following paragraph and then answer the questions below.

Every time your roommate leaves the room he says "Goodbye!" and loudly slams the door, making you flinch. After this has happens a number of times, your roommate says to you "Gotta go now. Goodbye!" and you realize that you are flinching even before you hear the door slam. Can you identify all the elements in this classical conditioning paradigm listed below?

Unconditioned stimulus (the stimulus that naturally is tied to a response that you can't control):

_____

Unconditioned response (the response that is automatic):

_____

Conditioned stimulus (the stimulus that starts out neutral but is paired with the unconditioned stimulus):

_____

Conditioned response (the response you have learned):

_____

■ Answer: Originally, the unconditioned stimulus always produces the unconditioned response. In this case, the slamming door made you flinch so the *slam* is the *unconditioned stimulus* and the *flinch* is the *unconditioned response*. However, over time the slam has been paired with your roommate saying "Goodbye!" You didn't originally flinch when he said it, so "Goodbye" *was originally a neutral stimulus*. With repeated pairings with the slamming door, "Goodbye" has become a *conditioned stimulus* and your flinch has become a *conditioned response*, and you begin to flinch when your roommate says "Goodbye."

One of the dangers of this type of learning is that once the conditioned (or learned) response has been established, people understandably avoid the stimulus that produces the unpleasant unconditioned response, so they don't have the opportunity to find out that they really have nothing to fear. If you once got very sick after eating asparagus you avoid it in the future and never find out that it had nothing to do with your illness. Classically conditioned fears can be so powerful that they begin to limit what people who experience them are able to do. This type of unreasonable fear is called a phobia.

Phobia An irrational fear of something specific that is so severe that it interferes with day-to-day functioning.

Modern Applications of Classical Conditioning

People who experience phobias go to extremes to avoid the object of their fears. Modern psychologists have used classical conditioning to treat such phobias by exposing patients to their feared situations in a controlled way. This idea began long ago when Mary Cover Jones (1924) followed Watson's experiment with Little Albert with a study of a 2-year-old boy who seemed to have the exact phobias of rats, rabbits, and other objects that Watson had conditioned into Little Albert. Jones was able to undo these fears by *deconditioning* the child; she presented him with candy at the same time a rabbit was brought to him and encouraged imitation when he saw another child holding the rabbit.

Virtual reality. A virtual reality helmet such as this one allows a therapist to expose a client to a feared stimulus in a gradual and controlled way. This allows the client to overcome strong fears and phobias. ■

AP Photo/CHRISTOPHER A. RECORD

More recently, virtual reality has been used in the treatment of children with anxiety disorders to expose them to feared stimuli in a controlled way that they can tolerate. Although the amount of research on this approach has been limited, it has been shown to be helpful for children with school phobias and phobias of spiders (Bouchard, 2011).

B. F. Skinner and Operant Conditioning

B. F. Skinner (1904–1990) further developed the theory of behaviorism by introducing the idea of operant conditioning. While studying rat behavior at Harvard, Skinner noticed that the rats were affected not by what came *before* their behavior, as was true of classical conditioning, but by what came *after* (Vargas, 2005). He concluded that spontaneous behaviors are controlled by the environment's response to them. A reinforcement is anything that occurs after a behavior that increases the likelihood the behavior will continue or happen again. Reinforcement can be *positive* or *negative*. While it is easy to think of examples of positive reinforcement, understanding negative reinforcement is more difficult. Positive reinforcement occurs when you get something you like and want. Negative reinforcement occurs when something disagreeable is removed by a behavior. For instance, when a parent picks up a crying baby and the baby stops crying, stopping the unpleasant sound of the infant crying reinforces the parent's behavior and makes it more likely the parent will respond this way again when the baby cries. Do you wear your seat belt when you drive? You should simply because it helps keep you safe, but car manufacturers weren't sure that was enough of an incentive, so they installed an obnoxious buzzer that won't turn off until you buckle your belt. Eliminating that annoying sound is another example of negative reinforcement. The habit of buckling your seatbelt is reinforced when the sound goes away.

Skinner described several concepts related to operant conditioning that help us understand how the process works. The first is the process of shaping behavior. Reinforcement of a behavior cannot occur if that behavior doesn't occur. For example, you cannot reinforce positive peer interaction with a child who does not interact with his peers. However, Skinner developed the idea, based on his work with pigeons, that behavior could slowly be "shaped" through reinforcement of behaviors that progressively get more and more like the behaviors desired. To shape the behavior of a child who does not interact with peers, you could use a series of rewards that begin when the child is simply near another child. The next step might be that the child is reinforced only when he looks at the other child, and finally the reinforcement might be provided only when he speaks while looking at the child. Eventually, the reward would be contingent only on true interaction with a peer.

Operant conditioning is also affected by the schedules of reinforcement that are used. These schedules can be based on *time* or on *number of responses*. In a fixed interval schedule, a reinforcement is delivered after a fixed period of time. In a variable interval schedule, the reinforcement comes after different time periods. Likewise, in a fixed ratio schedule, the reinforcement occurs after the same number of behaviors each time. In a variable ratio schedule it occurs after differing numbers of behaviors (Skinner, 1953). Think about how each of these schedules affects the pattern of responses that we observe. When reinforcement depends on time, we typically see response frequency picking up at around the time of the anticipated reward, then dropping off sharply until near the time of the next reward. You might see this pattern in students who have regularly scheduled

Operant conditioning The process by which the likelihood of a response is increased or decreased due to the consequences that follow that response.

Reinforcement A response to a behavior that causes that behavior to happen more.

Negative reinforcement A response that makes a behavior more likely to happen again because it removes an unpleasant stimulus.

Schedules of reinforcement Schedules (ratio or interval) on which reinforcement can be delivered based on a fixed or variable number of responses or fixed or variable lengths of time.

VIDEO LINK 2.4
BF Skinner

Everett Collection/Newscom

B. F. Skinner. Skinner's theory is based on the process of operant conditioning. Rewards and punishments (or simply ignoring a misbehavior) are used to change the likelihood of that behavior continuing to occur. ■

quizzes. Their behavior (studying) may be low until around the time of the quiz, when it picks up substantially (cramming). By contrast, with "pop quizzes," we would expect to see a steadier level of studying so students are always ready for a quiz, whenever it occurs (Steiner & Smith, 1999). If your reinforcement depends on the number of responses and that number is fixed, you would maximize your reward by working at a constant high level of responding so you complete the required number of responses as quickly as possible. On a variable ratio schedule, you are never quite sure how many times you will need to respond before you receive your reward, so this schedule can result in very persistent behavior (such as seen in gambling situations) because you anticipate that every response might be the one that produces the reward you are chasing (Steiner & Smith, 1999). Reinforcing someone every time she performs a behavior may be less effective in establishing and maintaining that behavior than these other patterns of reinforcement. While continual reinforcement might help establish a behavior quickly, once the reinforcement stops, the behavior will quickly disappear. Behavior is better maintained on a variable schedule.

If reinforcement increases the likelihood of a response, punishment is intended to decrease it. Punishment consists of administering a negative consequence (such as a spanking) or taking away a positive reinforcement (such as "no dessert because you didn't eat your dinner") in response to an unwanted behavior. However, Skinner (1953) believed that a more effective way to control behavior is to ignore undesirable behavior rather than punish it, while reinforcing an alternative desirable behavior. This is a process that Skinner called extinction. A child may be looking for *any* response from a parent; therefore, even yelling or spanking may unintentionally reinforce the undesirable behavior because it gets the child the parental attention she wants. In this case, ignoring the child when she misbehaves, but giving her attention when she behaves well, should help extinguish the misbehavior.

Figure 2.2 summarizes the differences among positive reinforcement, negative reinforcement, and punishment.

Modern Applications of Operant Conditioning

Operant conditioning has been used as a classroom management strategy for many years. Students may be given tokens, stickers, or check marks on a classroom chart to reward good behavior. At some point these tokens can be redeemed for gifts, privileges, or special activities (Landrum & Kauffman, 2006). Operant conditioning techniques also have been used extensively with children in special populations. In research with autistic children, their use has been associated with improvement in IQ, language, and sociability (Lablanc, Richardson, & McIntosh, 2005; Simpson et al., 2005), as well as with the reduction of behavioral problems in children with multiple disabilities (O'Mea, 2013).

Albert Bandura and Social Cognitive Theory

Albert Bandura, who was originally trained as a behaviorist, became discontented with the ideas of behaviorism because it is difficult or impossible to identify either stimuli or reinforcements for the entire range of human behavior we see (Pajares & Schunk, 2002). Bandura proposed that, in addition to classical and operant conditioning, people can learn new behaviors simply by watching others and imitating them rather than by receiving direct reinforcement of their own behaviors from the environment (Bandura, 1986). He had returned to the view, rejected by both Watson and Skinner, that internal mental processes or cognition play an important role in human learning and human behavior. For this reason, he initially called his theory a *social learning theory* because the learning occurs from watching other people (social) and processing this information.

T/F #2
The best way to establish and maintain a behavior is to reward people every time they perform the behavior you are interested in. *False*

Punishment Administering a negative consequence or taking away a positive reinforcement to reduce the likelihood of an undesirable behavior occurring.

T/F #3
The best way to get rid of an undesirable behavior in a child is to punish the child for doing it. *False*

Extinction In operant conditioning, the process by which a behavior stops when it receives no response from the environment.

FIGURE 2.2   Illustration of positive reinforcement, punishment, and negative reinforcement

Positive Reinforcement		

Stimulus → Response → Positive Reinforcement You receive a pat on the back (reward) for working hard (response).	over time	Stimulus → Response (the connection becomes stronger)
Punishment		

Stimulus → Response → Punishment You are sent to your room (punishment) for misbehaving (response).	over time	Stimulus → Response (the connection becomes weaker)
Negative Reinforcement		

Stimulus → Response → Negative Reinforcement Your baby stops crying (negative reinforcement) when you pick him up (response).	over time	Stimulus → Response (the connection becomes stronger)

VIDEO LINK 2.5
Bobo Doll

Bandura's earliest work was designed to show how children learn by direct observation. In his classic experiment, one group of children observed an adult on television act aggressively to a Bobo doll (a large inflated figure of a clown that is weighted on the bottom), hitting it, kicking it, throwing it, and striking it with a toy hammer (Bandura, Ross, & Ross, 1963). These children and another group of children who had not seen the video were then brought individually into a room containing the Bobo doll and other toys. The children who had seen the adult attacking the Bobo doll were much more likely to hit, kick, or throw the doll or strike it with a hammer. In contrast, the children who hadn't seen the adult model attacking the Bobo doll were less likely to carry out these aggressive acts. Bandura concluded that observation of a model may provoke a more generalized response based on the children's cognitive understanding of what was happening. In this case, they may have specifically seen the adult hit the Bobo doll, but they also understood that the generalized idea was to be aggressive to the doll.

Bandura's later development of his theory placed greater emphasis on the cognitive, or thinking, aspects of behavior development and specifically on thinking about our own ability to have control in our lives. He renamed his theory social cognitive theory to emphasize that thought has social origins but is then processed through our own individual cognitive interpretations.

Albert Bandura. Albert Bandura's social cognitive theory contributed the idea that people learn new behaviors by watching and imitating them rather than being directly reinforced. ■

Social cognitive theory The theory that individuals learn by observing others and imitating their behavior.

Modern Applications of Social Cognitive Theory

Bandura's recent research based on social cognitive theory has focused on self-efficacy or "the core belief that one has the power to influence one's own functioning and life circumstances" (Bandura, Caprara, Barbaranelli, Pastorelli, & Regalia, 2001, p. 125). These beliefs play a crucial role in understanding motivation because they are powerful predictors of which goals we will pursue (Pajares, 2005). We tend to pursue tasks at which we believe we can succeed and to avoid ones at which we believe we will fail. The concept of self-efficacy has found wide applications in a variety of situations that involve people's personal decisions to make changes in their lives. Health self-efficacy, the belief that you can make decisions or change behaviors that affect your health and well-being,

Self-efficacy A belief in our ability to influence our own functioning and our life circumstances.

AUDIO LINK 2.2
"Fixed Mindset" of Intelligence

Bandura's experiment on modeling. What did this boy and girl learn by watching the adult in the film at the top? ■

© Farrell Grehan/CORBIS

Jean Piaget. Based on his detailed observation of children, Piaget described them as "little scientists" who actively explore their environment and learn from those experiences. ∎

Schema A cognitive framework that places concepts, objects, or experiences into categories or groups of associations.

Assimilation Fitting new experiences into existing mental schemas.

Accommodation Changing mental schemas so they fit new experiences.

Equilibration An attempt to resolve uncertainty to return to a comfortable cognitive state.

has been associated with positive lifestyle changes in adolescents who are HIV-positive, patients in cardiac rehabilitation, and adults suffering from osteoporosis (Jones, Renger, & Kang, 2007). Perhaps the most important application has occurred in the area of education because students with a sense of self-efficacy work harder and longer at academic tasks, tackle more difficult tasks, and have a greater sense of optimism that they will succeed (Pajares, 2002).

Theories of Cognitive Development

The following theories take the area of cognitive development, which focuses on the processes of the mind, including thinking and learning, as their major focus. We introduce these ideas in this chapter and then examine them further in Chapters 6, 9, 12, and 15, where we discuss cognitive development at each age.

Jean Piaget's Cognitive Developmental Theory

Jean Piaget (1896–1980) was a Swiss scientist whose theory greatly influenced the way we think about child development. Piaget studied children's thinking using what is called the *clinical method*. He encouraged children to talk freely and learned about their thoughts from a detailed analysis of what they said (Piaget, 1955).

Piaget believed we are constantly adapting to our environment by organizing the world in ways we can understand. The units that we use to organize our understanding are called schemas. They consist of a concept and all the associations to that concept that we have developed through our past experiences. For example, we all have a schema for gender, which contains all the expectations and associations we activate when we see women and men.

According to Piaget, adaptation consists of two processes: assimilation and accommodation. In assimilation, we take new information and put it into an existing schema, whether it really fits there or not. Take the example of a little boy who goes to the zoo and sees an elephant for the first time. He turns to his mother and says, "Look, it's a big doggy with two tails." This child does not have a schema that helps him make sense of an animal with both a trunk and a tail, so he tries to fit this new experience into one of his existing concepts. Will he always think the elephant is a strange dog? Of course not, and this is where the process of accommodation comes in. As his mother points out the unique features of an elephant, the child accommodates this new information by creating a new schema, one for elephants. In Piaget's theory, a process he called equilibration is the constant seesaw between assimilation and accommodation. As we have new experiences and learn new things about the world, we assimilate new information into existing schemas, but if the new information cannot be assimilated, it throws us into a state of disequilibrium. We then need to change our schemas to accommodate the information, so we can return to a steady state of equilibrium.

Like Freud and Erikson, Piaget believed children change in qualitative ways from one age period to the next. The stages he described were based on the way he believed children thought about and understood the world at each age level. Remember that Freud's stages are based on the progression of the sex drive and Erikson's on the social development of the self. Piaget believed children are not just less knowledgeable than adults; rather, they think in qualitatively different ways at each developmental stage. We describe these stages when we examine Piaget's theory in more depth in each of the chapters on cognitive development.

Modern Applications of Piaget's Theory

Criticism of Piaget's theory has focused largely on the methodology he used and his conclusions about when children enter each of the stages in his theory, but his greatest legacy may lie in his concept of constructivism (Newcombe, 2011). Piaget understood that we do not operate like video cameras, taking in what is around us passively and indiscriminately. Instead, he believed that we are active learners, always working to *construct* our understanding of the world. He saw children as being like "little scientists," always actively experimenting on the world to increase their understanding of it.

These ideas have had a great impact on educational practices, fostering a teaching style that promotes the child's active approach to constructing his own learning. Many teachers use Piaget's ideas as the basis for their teaching style (Hinde & Perry, 2007), and research in this area is ongoing. For example, Constance Kamii and her colleagues (Kamii, Rummelsburg, & Kari, 2005) gave low-socioeconomic status, low-achieving students in first grade math-related activities to explore (for example, pick-up sticks and group-based arithmetic games) instead of traditional math assignments (for example, "What is 2 + 2?"). At the end of the year, these students scored higher on tests of mental arithmetic and logical reasoning than did similar students who had received teacher-directed, pencil-and-paper instruction.

Lev Vygotsky's Sociocultural Theory

Lev Semyonovich Vygotsky (1896–1934), a Russian psychologist, had somewhat different ideas about cognitive development, emphasizing the importance of the social world and of culture in promoting cognitive growth (Vygotsky, 1978b). According to Vygotsky (1986), learning first takes place in the interaction between people; then the individual internalizes that learning and it becomes a part of his own independent thinking.

Vygotsky believed that looking at what the child is capable of learning in interaction with a skilled helper is a better indicator of his level of cognitive development than just testing what he already knows. He was more interested in what the child could become than in how the child currently functioned (Wertsch, 1985). Vygotsky (1978a) developed the concept of the zone of proximal development, which was defined as "the distance between the actual developmental level as determined by independent problem solving and the level of potential development as determined through problem solving under adult guidance or in collaboration with more capable peers" (p. 86).

Proximal refers to being near or close. A good teacher stays close to what children already know but then helps them take the next step. Of necessity the teacher must first determine what the children know in order to shape the next step. The process by which this learning happens is referred to as scaffolding. A scaffold is a structure put around a building to allow people to work on it. In Vygotsky's concept, adults help the "construction" of the child's understanding by providing guidance and support (the scaffolding). Just as the scaffold comes down when a building is completed, so too the adult can step back when the child fully understands. For example, if you have a jack-in-the-box and want to play with a 6-month-old baby, you will likely just turn the handle for him and watch his reaction. When the child is 2 years old, you might hold his hand on the handle so he can learn to turn it. When he is 4, you might just give him the toy and watch. Your input is no longer needed, and your "scaffolding" can come down.

Modern Applications of Vygotsky's Theory

Like Piaget's theory, Vygotsky's ideas have had a powerful influence in the field of education. One specific educational practice that developed out of Vygotsky's ideas is known as dynamic assessment. In this approach, instead of testing what a child knows or can do at one particular time, the instructor uses an interactive assessment process to identify the child's zone of proximal development and provides the help the child needs to progress to

Constructivism The idea that humans actively construct their understanding of the world rather than passively receiving knowledge.

VIDEO LINK 2.6
Zone of Proximal Development

Zone of proximal development According to Vygotsky, this is what a child cannot do on her own but can do with help from someone more skilled or knowledgeable.

Scaffolding The idea that more knowledgeable adults and children support a child's learning by providing help to move the child just beyond his current level of capability.

Dynamic assessment A testing procedure that uses a test-intervene-test procedure to assess the examinee's potential to change.

a higher level of achievement. The teacher asks a question to assess the child's understanding of a concept. When a child answers the question incorrectly, the instructor starts with the most indirect help, such as a hint that the child think about whether he or she has seen a problem like this before. If this help is not enough, the adult will increase the level of direction, potentially ending by giving and explaining the correct answer. Some children will only need the small hint, while others need a more direct approach (Poehner, 2007).

Information Processing

Whereas Piaget and Vygotsky provide more global concepts about cognition and its development, information processing theory breaks down the way we understand and use information into steps, such as acquiring information, storing it, and retrieving it (Robinson-Riegler & Robinson-Riegler, 2008). When this approach first appeared in literature, it proposed that we process information in a way that is similar to the way that computers process information. Since then we have realized that our brains are much more complicated than computers, so a newer way of thinking about the memory process has developed, known as the connectionist or neural network model. Using this model, you can think of memory as a neural network that consists of concept nodes interconnected by links, as shown in Figure 2.3. For example, when we see a white duck, different concept nodes may be activated. One node can represent a specific concept (*white*), one can represent a higher-order concept (*duck*), and one can represent a superordinate concept (*bird*) depending on how the neurons are activated (Robinson-Riegler & Robinson-Riegler, 2008). The concept nodes are analogous to nerve cells, or neurons, in the brain, and the links are connections between individual neurons. When information is stored in memory, it becomes a new node that is connected to other nodes in the network.

Connectionist/neural network model A model of memory in which the process is envisioned as a neural network that consists of concept nodes that are interconnected by links.

FIGURE 2.3   Neural network model of memory

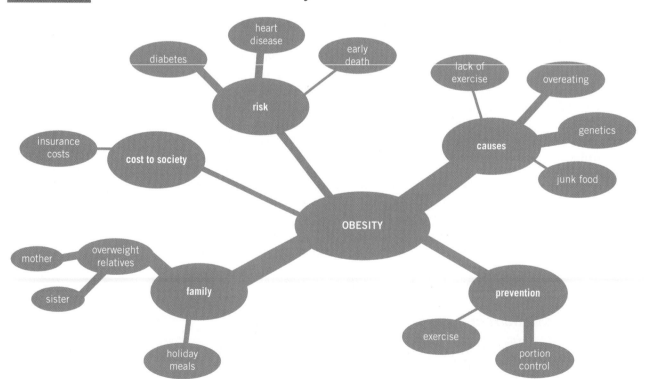

Neural networks are a newer way of thinking about information processing. Concepts are made up of information (or nodes) and the links that connect that information to represent a concept.

Although each node is connected in some way to other pieces of information in our memory, the strength of these connections can vary, and learning involves modifying the strength of the connections. When input comes into the system (for example, the sight of a bird in flight), certain nodes are activated. If the links between those nodes are strong enough, the output is a concept (in this case, *bird*). This way of thinking about information processing more closely reflects our current understanding that neurons operate through multiple simultaneous connections with other neurons throughout the brain.

Modern Applications of Information Processing

The fact that the information processing approach breaks cognitive processes down into their component steps has been used to design better teaching techniques. For example, the process of learning to read has been broken down into two important parts: the ability to name letters accurately and the ability to name letters quickly. A child must do both automatically in order to read fluently (Ritchey & Speece, 2006). Research has shown that the speed with which a child can name letters, even with mistakes, is more important for later reading efficiency than total accuracy of letter naming. With this information, teachers will have a better idea how to develop skills that will help children learn to read.

Other applications of principles from information processing theory to classroom practice include being sure you have the learner's attention before you start (for example, by changing the volume and tone of your voice), connecting new knowledge to other information that is already in the individual's memory (for example, by including a lot of examples), and requiring the learner to actively process new incoming information (for example, by using discussion groups and classroom activities to actively engage the students in using the new information) (Huitt, 2003). Completing the Active Learning activities and answering the true/false questions in this book are examples of ways you can use these principles to enhance your own learning.

Evolutionary Theories

Charles Darwin's theory of evolution is based on the idea that living things that adapt to their environment are more likely to pass on their genes to the next generation. His focus was largely on physical characteristics, but his basic idea that human behavior that has adaptive value will persist is central to the application of ethology and sociobiology to development.

Ethology

Konrad Lorenz (1903–1989) is considered the father of modern ethology, which is the study of the adaptive value of animal and human behavior in the natural environment (Tinbergen, 1963). As a zoologist studying animal behavior in Munich, Germany, Lorenz found that ducks and geese would *immediately* follow their mothers after they were born. This automatic behavior, called imprinting, is adaptive because the mother provides her offspring with food and protection from predators. Lorenz showed that this behavior was innate and not learned. When he removed the mother goose and substituted himself, the newly hatched geese responded to him in the same way they would have responded to the mother goose: by following him.

Some researchers attempted to apply the idea of imprinting to human behavior. They claimed that infants must have skin-to-skin contact with their mother within the first few hours after birth for *bonding*, or love, to develop. Like many direct applications of animal behavior to humans, this has turned out not to be the case. Although animal behavior can give us some ideas about human behavior, the direct application of one to the other is usually too simplistic, so we must exercise caution in applying these ideas. Although there is no evidence for this concept of bonding in human beings, ethological

VIDEO LINK 2.7
Lorenz and His Geese

Ethology The study of the adaptive value of animal and human behavior in the natural environment.

Imprinting In ethology, the automatic process by which animals attach to their mothers.

Konrad Lorenz and imprinting. Konrad Lorenz observed the behavior of geese (left) and demonstrated the presence of imprinting by removing the mother goose and substituting himself (right). ▪

principles contributed to our understanding of the slower, less automatic development of attachment between infant and mother during the first year of life. You will learn more about attachment in Chapter 7.

Sociobiology

Sociobiology The application of principles of evolution to the development of social behavior and culture.

In 1975, biologist Edward O. Wilson introduced the field of sociobiology, which examines the role principles of evolution have played in the development of social behavior and culture. One example of what sociobiologists study is the impact of kinship on relationships. According to sociobiology, people are more likely to protect, help, and give to relatives than to other people because they share some of their genes with biological family members, and therefore they have a stake in making sure family members survive to pass on the genes they share (Pollet, 2007).

Modern Applications of Evolutionary Theory

Ideas taken from evolutionary theory have influenced research on several important topics in the field of child development, including aggression, altruism, attachment, and social dominance hierarchies. Understanding the adaptive value of each of these behaviors gives us insight into the mechanisms that contribute to them. Evolutionary approaches such as ethology and sociobiology have contributed to a newer approach known as *evolutionary developmental psychology* which applies the principles and ideas of evolutionary theory specifically to questions of how and why children develop as they do (Blasi & Bjorklund, 2003; Causey, Gardiner, & Bjorklund, 2008). Children's behavior is seen as an adaptation to the environment in two ways: (1) What children do is adaptive because it is a preparation for adult life, and (2) what children do is adaptive at their own stage of development and in their specific life circumstances.

One example of research based on an evolutionary developmental approach has focused on the onset of puberty in girls. Age of onset is affected by many factors but is largely controlled by our genes. However, research has shown that girls enter puberty at earlier ages when their parents have a high level of conflict with little support or satisfaction in their marriage, when their father is absent or severely dysfunctional, or when they have an insecure relationship with their mother at age 15 months (Belsky, Houts, & Fearon, 2010; Saxbe & Repetti, 2009; Tither & Ellis, 2008). Evolutionary developmental psychologists point to the fact that a girl with a dysfunctional childhood may not be able to count on reaching adulthood successfully; therefore, the adaptation of an early puberty may ensure that she will be able to pass on her genes by enabling her to get pregnant earlier in life.

T/F #4
There are times when it can be an advantage for a girl to go through puberty at an early age. *True*

Ecological Theory

We tend to think of the study of ecology as focusing on plants and animals and their relationships to the environment, but in the 1970s, Urie Bronfenbrenner (1917–2005) applied the idea of how organisms interact with their environment to the field of developmental psychology to create a theory of human ecology. Using this framework, he defined development as the "interaction between the developing organism and the enduring environments or contexts in which it lives out its life" (Bronfenbrenner, 1975, p. 439). Bronfenbrenner believed we cannot understand the life course of an individual without understanding how that person interacts with all the different facets of his environment. He also believed this interaction is a dynamic process: All aspects of the environment affect the individual, and the individual affects all aspects of his environment.

Bronfenbrenner's Model

Bronfenbrenner (1977) proposed that individuals grow and develop within a nested set of influences that he divided into four systems: the microsystem, mesosystem, exosystem, and macrosystem, as shown in Figure 2.4. He subsequently added a dimension of time, called the chronosystem (Bronfenbrenner, 1986). These systems are embedded one within the other, each influencing the other in a back-and-forth fashion. The relationship between the systems also changes as the child grows and develops. Bronfenbrenner emphasized the importance of understanding the individual, not on her own or with one or two other people, but rather within all these contexts. His theory is, in part, a criticism of some of the techniques of experimental psychology, in which children are tested in the laboratory with an experimenter and perhaps a parent, and the results are then assumed to be true in the child's natural setting (Bronfenbrenner, 1977).

The microsystem includes the face-to-face interactions a person has in her immediate settings, such as home, school, or friendship groups. The interaction between a mother and a child forms a microsystem, as does the interaction between a child and a peer, or between a pair of siblings. The mesosystem brings together two settings that contain the child. For example, when parents meet and talk to a child's teacher, the home setting interacts with the school setting and this interaction influences the child's progress at school. The exosystem consists of settings the child never enters, that is, that are *external* to the child, but that affect the child's development nevertheless (Bronfenbrenner, 1986). For example, even if the child never goes to a parent's workplace, what happens in that setting can have an effect on the child. A job so demanding that it leaves parents exhausted at the end of the day affects the way parents will interact with children when they come home. The macrosystem consists of cultural norms that underlie the institutions and activities that make up someone's everyday life. For example, the macrosystem in the United States includes the ideology of democracy, as well as the value placed on individual achievement. The chronosystem consists of the events that take place at different times of a child's life, as well as the time in history in which the child lives. For example, parental divorce affects a 2-year-old child much differently than a teenager. Also, the current experience of divorce, when it has become more common, is different than it would have been in 1940 (Bronfenbrenner, 1986).

It will be easier for you to remember the various systems that make up ecological theory if you are able to recognize examples of each of them. **Active Learning: Examples of Ecological Systems** gives you a chance to do this.

Cornell University

Urie Bronfenbrenner. Urie Bronfenbrenner developed ecological theory to explain the importance of the context in which children develop. ■

JOURNAL ARTICLE 2.1
Ecological Systems Theory

Microsystem In ecological theory, the face-to-face interaction of the person in her immediate settings, such as home, school, or friendship groups.

Mesosystem The interaction among the various microsystems, such as a child's school and home.

Exosystem Settings that the child never enters but that affect the child's development nevertheless, such as the parents' place of work.

Macrosystem Cultural norms that guide the nature of the organizations and places that make up one's everyday life.

Chronosystem The dimension of time, including one's age and the time in history in which one lives.

FIGURE 2.4   Bronfenbrenner's ecological systems model

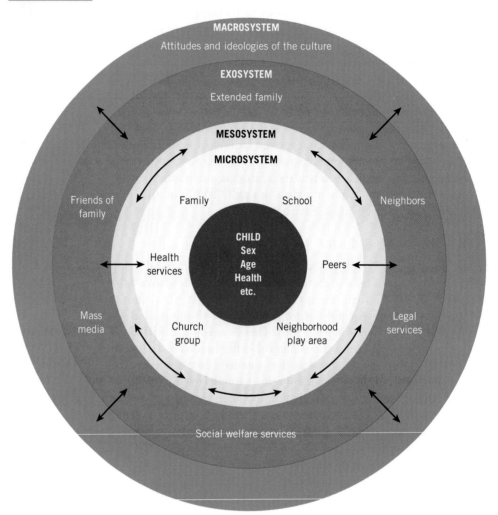

Think of the various systems in the ecological systems model as a set of nested environments, but with interactions both within a level and across levels. The chronosystem, not shown here, gives the context of time to all of these levels of influence.

SOURCE: Kopp & Krakow (1982). Reprinted and reproduced electronically with permission.

Active Learning

Examples of Ecological Systems

Match each description below with the correct level of the ecological system it represents. The levels are the microsystem, mesosystem, macrosystem, exosystem, and chronosystem.

Example	System Level
1. The number of mothers with children under the age of 5 who were employed outside the home doubled between 1970 and 1990.	
2. A child's parents go to school for a parent-teacher conference so they can find out how their child is doing.	
3. Native American parents raise their children to avoid interpersonal conflicts and to cooperate with others to work for the greater good.	
4. The child's preschool teacher shows the child how to stack two blocks on each other.	

5. New parents in Germany are entitled to 47 weeks of paid parental leave after the birth of their baby.

6. A parent gets a promotion and a big raise, but that also means working longer hours.

7. Parents invite a teen's group of friends to their house to watch some movies.

8. Fathers today take a more active role in parenting than fathers in the past did.

9. A teenager and his best friend make plans for how they will spend time together on the weekend.

10. A new mother spends some time with her friends, who tell her she is too worried about caring for her baby and should just relax and enjoy being a mother.

■ **Answers:** (1) chronosystem, (2) mesosystem, (3) macrosystem, (4) microsystem, (5) macrosystem, (6) exosystem, (7) mesosystem, (8) chronosystem, (9) microsystem, (10) exosystem

Modern Applications of Ecological Theory

Ecological theory has expanded the range and number of variables (characteristics that can be measured and that can have different values) that researchers include to more fully understand a child's development within multiple contexts. For example, Brophy-Herb, Lee, Nievar, and Stollak (2007) used ecological theory as a basis for understanding the development of social competence in preschoolers. Instead of looking at single variables like socioeconomic status or family stress as predictors of children's social competence, they examined an intersecting and nested array of variables they believed would have an influence on social competence. These variables included individual characteristics of the child (age, sex, and level of stress); family characteristics (married or divorced parents, level of stress, and socioeconomic status); teacher behavior; and classroom climate. One example from this study illustrates the complexity of the findings: Although children with more stress in their lives were rated as having lower social competence, the nature of the child's classroom modified this relationship. A child experiencing high stress was more likely to have lower social competence in a classroom in which many children had behavioral problems than a stressed child in a classroom where few other children had behavior problems.

Another legacy of human ecology is the application of theory to social policy. A human ecologist believes all levels of society affect human development. The logical extension of this belief is to become active in the creation of social policy, including legislation and programs at all levels of government. Bronfenbrenner himself was active in the creation of Head Start, a program designed to help disadvantaged children by providing interventions at several different levels. Head Start not only provides an excellent educational program for children but also helps their families' well-being by providing help with financial, social, educational, and psychological difficulties they might be experiencing. It also works hard to create links between the classroom setting and the child's home.

Variable A characteristic that can be measured and that can have different values.

T/F #5
If a child is experiencing a lot of stress at home, the child will show behavior problems in the classroom. *False*

Social policy in action. The development of the Head Start program was strongly influenced by Bronfenbrenner's ecological systems theory because it was designed to provide interventions at several of the levels described in the theory. ■

Dynamic Systems Theory

As the study of children has become increasingly sophisticated, researchers have realized that development is a complex process that includes

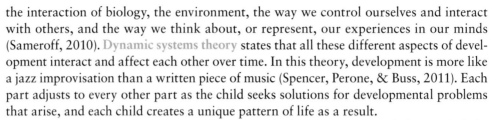

Dynamic systems theory The theory that all aspects of development interact and affect each other in a dynamic process over time.

JOURNAL ARTICLE 2.2
Dynamic Systems Theory

WEB LINK 2.1
Gene Mapping

Neuropsychology The study of the interaction of the brain and behavior.

Behavioral genomics The study of the interaction of genes and behavior.

the interaction of biology, the environment, the way we control ourselves and interact with others, and the way we think about, or represent, our experiences in our minds (Sameroff, 2010). Dynamic systems theory states that all these different aspects of development interact and affect each other over time. In this theory, development is more like a jazz improvisation than a written piece of music (Spencer, Perone, & Buss, 2011). Each part adjusts to every other part as the child seeks solutions for developmental problems that arise, and each child creates a unique pattern of life as a result.

To illustrate how this process works, we can look at how Esther Thelen applied the theory of dynamic systems to the development of motor skills. Whereas earlier theories linked motor development to body and brain maturation, her research provided evidence that biological maturation operates in interaction with environmental influences (Spencer et al., 2006). Thelen found that the nature of physical development was flexible, not absolute. For example, newborn babies have a stepping reflex in which they appear to be walking when held upright, even though they cannot support their own weight. This reflex typically disappears at about 2 to 3 months of age, and the disappearance was initially thought to be a product of brain maturation. However, Thelen found that babies who seem to have lost their initial stepping reflex will begin stepping again if placed up to their chests in water so their legs are not so heavy, which means the disappearance of this reflex is not driven solely by brain development (Thelen, 1989). Infants stop "stepping" reflexively when their legs become too heavy for them to lift. Thelen posited that the development of real walking is not just a matter of biological maturation but a coming together of many different experiences, bodily growth, and motivation. She showed that infants develop these abilities in different ways, depending on such characteristics as weight and activity level. They experiment with how to do things, and each action influences what the next action will be.

Neuropsychology and Behavioral Genomics

Neuropsychology, the study of the interaction of the brain and behavior, and behavioral genomics, the study of the interaction of genes and behavior, are on the cutting edge of research in the field of child development today because new technology has allowed researchers to investigate both the brain and genes in much more detail. We discuss these fields in some depth in Chapter 3 and in each of the physical development chapters, so we introduce them only briefly here.

Researchers can now use technology to see the structure and functioning of our brains and to identify specific genes to begin to understand their role in development. These findings have produced an avalanche of new research. The earliest approach to the study of both genes and the brain was very deterministic; the belief was that biology determines behavior. However, the more we learn about the functioning of both the brain and genes, the clearer it becomes that the effects go in both directions. Biology has an impact on behavior, but the environment also affects our biological functioning. The brain's development to some extent depends on an individual's experiences. The development of connections between nerve cells, the coating of the nervous system, and the neurochemistry of the brain are all shaped in part by what a person does. The expression of genes is also affected by environmental events.

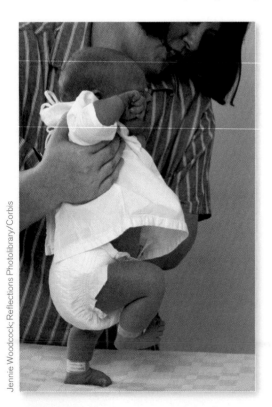

Jennie Woodcock; Reflections Photolibrary/Corbis

The stepping reflex. The stepping reflex is present in young infants. If you support their weight and allow their feet to touch a flat surface, they will raise and lower their legs as though they are walking. What causes babies to lose this reflex? ■

Before we leave this discussion of developmental theories, Table 2.2 provides a summary that will help you identify whether each theory deals with quantitative or qualitative change, and the relative emphasis each places on the role of biology or environment as the driving force in development.

TABLE 2.2 **Comparison of developmental theories**

Theory	Quantitative or qualitative change	Biology and/or environment	Contribution to the study of child development
Psychoanalytic theory	Qualitative: Freud has 5 stages Erikson has 8 stages	Biology drives development and is affected by environmental experiences.	Children's unconscious thoughts and motivations help to explain their behavior. Erikson's stages describe typical developmental issues from infancy through adolescence.
Behaviorism	Quantitative	Environment.	Reinforcement is used to change children's problem behaviors. Imitation plays a big role in children's learning.
Piaget's cognitive theory	Qualitative: Piaget has 4 stages	Biology drives development, and the environment shapes it.	Understanding children's active construction of knowledge shapes teaching approaches.
Vygotsky's cognitive theory	Quantitative	Environment, in the form of culture and social influence, drives development.	Scaffolding and the zone of proximal development form the basis for teaching approaches.
Information processing	Quantitative	Biology and environment interact.	Basic processes of cognitive development are central to understanding the process by which children learn.
Evolutionary theories	N/A	Biology underlies adaptation to the environment.	Children's behaviors are explained as a result of adaptation to the environment.
Ecological theory	Quantitative	A nesting of environmental influences are also affected by a child's characteristics.	Children interact with and are influenced by numerous levels of social influence.
Dynamic systems theory	Quantitative	Biological growth interacts with environmental experiences.	Children's behavior results from a complex interaction of biological, environmental, cognitive, and social-emotional factors.

Culture and Developmental Theory

Although some of the theories we have described take cultural differences into account, all were developed by European or American theorists. If we assume all societies must conform to Western values, we forget that different ideas and behaviors may be more adaptive for children growing up in different contexts and environments. To understand the diversity of development, we must take into account the indigenous theories of child development that guide the way children are raised in a variety of cultures.

T/F #6
A good theory should be universal, applying to all children in all situations. *False*

As an example of these cultural differences, many of the theories we've described in this chapter focus on the development of the individual. However, a focus on individual identity and individual needs and achievements is largely a Western value. Developmental theory in many non-Western cultures focuses instead on the role of the individual in the context of the social group. For example, Nsamenang and Lo-oh (2010) explain that in sub-Saharan Africa, the overarching theory of development "positions the child not in his or her sovereignty but as socially integrated in a human community" (p. 386). You will learn more about these cultural comparisons throughout the book.

As you learn about developmental theories, you might be tempted to say "I agree" or "I don't agree" with any particular theory, but your opinions should ultimately depend on reasoned, testable evidence that supports or refutes each one. In the next section, we examine how psychologists carry out research that advances our theoretical understanding of human development.

> **Check Your Understanding**
>
> 1. How do Freud's and Erikson's theories differ from each other?
> 2. Compare Piaget's and Vygotsky's theories of child development.
> 3. What do the two evolutionary theories of child development tell us?
> 4. Describe the five systems that influence development in Bronfenbrenner's theory.
> 5. What are neuropsychology and behavioral genomics?

2.3

How is research on child development conducted?

Research Methods

As we mentioned at the beginning of this chapter, theories must be subjected to rigorous testing before we are willing to accept them as reliable and valid. In this section we look at the methods researchers use to study children and adolescents to add to our understanding of growth and development. We provide a brief introduction to the major methods, but additional information about these topics appears in the Appendix: The Scientific Method, available as a downloadable file on the companion website. Because each research method has its own advantages and disadvantages, there isn't one best way to study development. Rather we look for the most appropriate method to investigate the particular topic we want to examine. After this overall description of research methods, we consider the special challenges that come along with conducting research with children and adolescents.

The Scientific Method

Child development is one of many disciplines that use the scientific method to add to their body of knowledge. The scientific method is a self-correcting process because the outcome of our inquiry, whether it supports our initial ideas or not, informs and guides our future efforts. We begin by asking a question (often based on our theories), next we identify the factors or elements that need to be examined to answer that question, and then we put our question to the test. Based on what we find, we can accept or reject the premise on which the original question was based (Salkind, 2004). Each of these steps is described in more detail in the remainder of this chapter.

Research often begins with our careful observation of a behavior we are interested in understanding. In trying to make sense of what we see, we draw on theories to formulate a testable prediction about the nature and causes of the behavior, called a hypothesis. A hypothesis is most often designed to relate two or more variables. However, before we can test our ideas, we need to figure out how we will measure the behavior we want to

Hypothesis A testable prediction about the nature and causes of behavior.

study. If, for example, we are interested in studying aggression, we need to decide which observable behaviors will fit the way we conceptualize "aggression." We can include physical aggression, such as hitting or biting, but we need to decide whether we also want to include verbal aggression, such as name calling, or relational aggression, such as excluding someone from a group activity. Deciding what we will include and what we will exclude is called operationalizing a concept.

Two essential characteristics of any measure used in scientific research are reliability and validity. A measure is reliable when it produces the same or similar results each time it is used. For example, if we use a measure of self-esteem, we would expect a given child or adolescent to score at about the same level if we administered the measure on several occasions. We also need to be sure that our measures accurately reflect the construct or characteristic in which we are interested. A measure is considered valid if it measures what it purports to measure. If researchers used a test of mathematical skill as a measure of general intelligence, you would probably question the validity of their measure because this one ability is too narrow to be considered a valid measure of general intelligence.

Another important decision involves choosing a sample of participants to take part in our research. We try to make our samples representative of the population we are interested in, because we want our research to do more than say something about the particular group of children or adolescents who take part in our research. We want to be able to generalize our results from a particular sample to a larger population, but we must be careful how we take this step. For example, if we conduct research in kindergartens in suburban schools, we need to be careful not to mistakenly assume that our findings would apply equally to children from social, economic, or ethnic backgrounds that are very different from those of the children we studied. We might not find the same results if we studied children from low-income families enrolled in a Head Start program, or children from higher-income families enrolled in an expensive private school.

Methods and Measures

Once researchers have developed their hypothesis, operationalized the concepts within it, and chosen their sample, they must decide how they will gather the data for their study. Many methods are used to gather scientific information, and each has advantages and disadvantages (see Table 2.3). There isn't a single "right" or "best" method. Some methods simply are more appropriate for answering certain types of questions than others.

We describe seven of the most common ways of studying children and adolescents: observations, self-report measures, standardized tests, physiological measures, archival records, case studies, and ethnography.

Observations

We can learn a great deal about anything we are interested in, including development, by making careful observations. Scientific observations differ from our casual, everyday observations of the world because they need to be both systematic and objective and must be carefully planned and executed if they are to be valid.

If researchers are testing their own hypotheses, there is a risk that they might see or pay more attention to observations that tend to support those hypotheses and overlook those that don't. This tendency is called observer bias. Having more than one observer code or score the observations helps assure us that the observations are objective rather than subjective. Another safeguard is to use observers who don't know the specific hypothesis being tested (that is, observers who are "blind" to the hypothesis) so that it cannot affect their perception of the events they are observing.

Observations in naturally occurring settings allow us to see children behaving as they normally do within the social relationships that shape their development every day of

Operationalizing a concept Defining a concept in a way that allows it to be measured.

Reliability The ability of a measure to produce consistent results.

Validity The ability of a research tool to accurately measure what it purports to measure.

Generalize To draw inferences from the findings of research on a specific sample about a larger group or population.

WEB LINK 2.2
Validity and Reliability

T/F #7
The best way to do research on development is to conduct experiments.
False

Observer bias The tendency for an observer to notice and report events that he is expecting to see.

T/F #8
When conducting research by doing an observation, it is important that the person who is doing the observation does not know the purpose of the research. *True*

TABLE 2.3   A comparison of research methods

Method	Advantages	Disadvantages
Observation	Is a rich source of information	Can be confused with interpretation
	Allows observation of behavior as it naturally occurs	Risks observer bias
	Can be conducted in a laboratory to gain control in the situation	Can produce large amounts of raw data that must be coded and analyzed
	Can lead to new hypotheses	Risks changing the behavior being observed
		Cannot identify the causes of behavior
Survey, questionnaire	Gathers information quickly and efficiently	Requires precisely worded questions
	Can gather information on many different topics	Requires questions that are not misleading or biased
		Risks respondents not answering honestly
		Risks respondents not being able to accurately recall or report on behavior
		Risks socially desirable rather than truthful answers
Interview (structured and clinical)	Can be a first-person or third-person account	Lacks a second observer to verify the information
	Can gather in-depth information	
Standardized test	Can assess many qualities or characteristics	Needs periodic updating
	Allows an individual to be compared to the average performance of a group	Must be scored and interpreted by trained examiner
Physiological measures	Can gather data that don't require language or an active response from participants	Requires equipment that is expensive and can be difficult to maintain
		Does not always allow for clear interpretation of data
Case study	Is a rich source of information and hypotheses	May yield information with limited generalizability
	Can utilize multiple methods	Is time-intensive
		Risks observer bias
Ethnography	Can provide a rich look at cultural groups	Risks changing the behavior of group members
		Is time intensive
		Risks observer bias
Experiments	Can identify the causes of behavior	Requires test groups to be comparable
		Cannot be used to study some topics

their lives, and we see them in situations that have real emotional significance for them (Dunn, 2005). However, moving observations into a laboratory gives researchers greater control over the situation and allows them to create a specific set of conditions in which to conduct their observations.

Making a detailed record of everything that happens in a stream of behavior can make researchers aware of aspects of behavior they haven't noticed before and can be a good source of new hypotheses for future research. However, recording everything that happens even in a fairly short period of time produces a tremendous amount of raw data

Jeffrey Greenberg/Science Source

Scientific observation.
Carefully conducted observations, either in natural settings or in a laboratory, can give us insight into behavior as it naturally occurs. ■

that need to be analyzed and reduced before useful information emerges, so researchers often use checklists to collect data. While observing the child, you simply mark the presence or absence of each item on the checklist or count how many times each behavior occurs. Checklists have been used to assess many aspects of development, including social skills, physical skills, language development, and problem behaviors. They provide a quick way to look at a child's development in relationship to general norms or to other children, and to keep track of children's progress as they grow and develop. For this reason, checklists are often used in educational, medical, and other settings that require quick, efficient assessment of a child's level of functioning.

Although observations are very useful sources of information about behavior, they have some limitations. First, although we want to capture behavior as it naturally occurs, the mere presence of an observer might change the way people behave. Fortunately children usually adapt to the presence of an observer without too much difficulty. Although they are initially curious and might ask questions about what the observer is doing, the lure of getting back to what they were doing, such as playing with their friends, is usually far stronger. Another limitation of observational research is that it doesn't tell us directly about the causes of behavior. If you observe a child who stays on the sidelines when other children are playing, there are many possible explanations for this behavior. From observation alone, it is impossible to tell whether this is the behavior of a child who simply is not very social, a temporary reaction to something that occurred earlier in the day, or an indication of an adjustment problem for the child. Based on these observations, the researcher might formulate a hypothesis to explain the child's behavior, but additional research would be needed to identify the cause.

Self-Report Measures

Another way to gather information relatively quickly and efficiently is to use self-report measures such as surveys, questionnaires, and interviews. However, the usefulness of the conclusion you can draw from self-report measures largely depends on the accuracy and validity of the responses received, so having questions that are precise, well written, and understandable is essential to the validity of the research. If the questions in a survey are unclear or difficult to answer, it wouldn't matter how much you wanted to give accurate information because a poorly designed questionnaire might not allow you to do so.

Checklist A prepared list of behaviors, characteristics, or judgments used by observers to assess a child's development.

Surveys A data collection technique that asks respondents to answer a common set of questions.

Questionnaires A written form of a survey.

Interviews A data collection technique in which an interviewer poses questions to a respondent.

Another possibility is that the person taking the survey is unwilling or unable to give complete or accurate responses. And sometimes respondents give the answer they think the researcher is looking for, or the answer they think makes them look good in the researcher's eyes, a problem that is called social desirability. You can see how social desirability becomes a challenge for researchers investigating a sensitive topic such as sexuality, drugs, or prejudice. The **Journey of Research: Children's Eyewitness Testimony** illustrates the powerful influence the wording of our questions can have on the results we obtain.

VIDEO LINK 2.8
Children as Eyewitnesses

JOURNEY OF RESEARCH *Children's Eyewitness Testimony*

A revealing illustration of the impact of how we ask a question on the answer we get comes from research on children's eyewitness testimony. Think for a minute about the subtle difference between asking someone "Did you see that?" and asking "Didn't you see that?" The first alternative suggests there can be one of two legitimate answers ("Yes, I saw that" or "No, I didn't see that"), but the second implies you may have missed something someone else saw. The pressure is to respond to the second question by saying "Of course I saw that." Although you may feel you would respond to such a question by simply saying what you did or didn't see regardless of how the question was phrased, a child is more likely to be swayed by the question itself.

In the 1990s, there were several high-profile cases of alleged child abuse. Under relentless and often suggestive questioning, children described horrific abuse at the hands of adults who were caring for them. Based on this testimony, a number of defendants initially received jail sentences, but in all these cases the charges were later dismissed or the plaintiffs were released from prison because of the improper way evidence had been gathered.

In the notorious McMartin Preschool case, seven teachers were accused of sexually abusing several hundred young children based on interviews such as this one:

Interviewer:	Can you remember the naked pictures?
Child:	(Shakes head "no")
Interviewer:	Can't remember that part?
Child:	(Shakes head "no")
Interviewer:	Why don't you think about that for a while, okay? Your memory might come back to you.

SOURCE: Interview Number 111, p. 29 as cited in Garven, Wood, Malpass, & Shaw (1998, p. 349).

It is clear from this example that the interviewer had a particular answer in mind and wanted the child to give that answer. The questioning is not at all unbiased. Even though young children are able to accurately recall events, when the questions they are asked are misleading, when they are subjected to repeated questioning, or if the interviewer makes overt suggestions about what has happened, we cannot trust their answers (Krähenbühl & Blades, 2006). Because children are limited in their ability to understand and interpret language, we need to be particularly careful about the wording of questions used in surveys, questionnaires, and interviews used with them. ■

Usually interviewers ask everyone in the sample group the same set of questions, but sometimes they might want to ask additional follow-up questions or ask the respondent to expand on the original answers or provide examples. In this case, researchers use a clinical interview as the research method. This method allows greater flexibility.

Because infants and children may be too young to respond to an interviewer's questions, we may need to rely on information provided by a second party, such as parents, child care providers, and teachers. The more time these people have spent with the child and the more familiar they are with the child's behavior, the more likely they will be able to provide high-quality information. For example, parent reports have been used to describe the antisocial and acting-out behavior of their adopted adolescents (Klahr, Rueter, McGue, Iacono, & Burt, 2011), and teacher reports have been used to rate the social-emotional competence of their students (Merrell, Cohn, & Tom, 2011).

Standardized Tests

You are probably familiar with standardized tests such as IQ tests and achievement tests. We standardize a test by administering it to large groups of children to establish norms. A norm is the average or typical performance of a child of a given age on the test. Once we have established the norms for a test, we can compare an individual child's performance to the appropriate age norms to determine whether that child is performing at, above, or below the level of the average child of the same age.

Standardized testing has been a controversial topic for many years. Much of the debate has centered on the validity of these tests, that is, whether they actually measure what they say they are measuring. A related controversy arose over the way test results are interpreted and used. Early wide-scale use of standardized intelligence tests during World War I and World War II found that native-born Americans scored better than immigrants, immigrants from Northern and Western Europe scored better than those from Southern and Eastern Europe, and Black Americans received the lowest scores of all (Glaser, 1993). Critics asked whether the differences in test scores really reflected inherent differences in mental abilities between these groups, or whether they were simply measuring knowledge of American mainstream culture and environment (Arbuthnot, 2011). This latter view became known as the *cultural test bias hypothesis* (Reynolds, 2000).

College entrance tests such as the SAT and the ACT have been subjected to the same types of criticisms charging they are biased or discriminate against certain groups of students. A number of psychometric reviews have come to the conclusion that "well-constructed, reliable, well-standardized psychological tests are not biased against native-born American racial or ethnic minorities" (Reynolds, 2000, p. 145) and that any content bias is usually quite small, but in response to concerns about possible bias, some colleges have stopped using SAT/ACT results or have made the tests optional (Hiss & Franks, 2014).

In addition to helping determine whether children's development is on track, standardized tests are also useful for assessing the effectiveness of programs and interventions. For example, the effectiveness of a summer enrichment program that paired talented young adolescents from limited-opportunity backgrounds with high school or college-aged students was assessed using standardized tests of mathematics and reading skills (Laird & Feldman, 2004).

Physiological Measures

Gathering valid and reliable data from infants and young children presents a special challenge to researchers (de Haan, 2007). Young children have limited language ability so they can't understand and follow complex instructions or provide complex verbal responses to questions, and their attention spans are notoriously short, so keeping them on task is another challenge. Fortunately, researchers now have an arsenal of devices that allow them to measure and interpret biological responses without needing to rely on verbal skills.

Electroencephalograms (EEGs, which measure electrical activity in the brain) and event-related potentials (ERPs, which measure the brain's electrical response to meaningful sensory stimuli) can measure neural activity during a number of brain states (Banaschewski & Brandeis, 2007). The photo here shows a type of cortical cap with

Standardized test A test that is administered and scored in a standard or consistent way to all examinees.

Norm The average or typical performance of an individual of a given age on a test.

T/F #8

Standardized tests (such as the SATs or ACT) are not biased against American-born ethnic or racial minorities. *True*

AUDIO LINK 2.3
IQ Tests

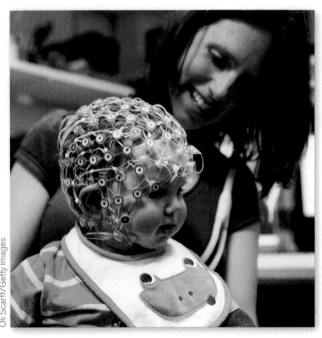

Oli Scarff/Getty Images

Cortical measurement. This infant's brain activity is being measured by means of a specially designed "electrode hat." This noninvasive method of studying the brain has given us new insights into its functioning. ■

▶
VIDEO LINK 2.9
fMRI and Dyslexia

Archival records Data collected at an earlier date that are used for research purposes.

electrodes embedded in it that records brain activity. To make the necessary measurements, researchers place the cap snugly on the child's head; the technique is noninvasive and is not painful for the child. Magnetic resonance imaging (MRI) gives us a picture of the structures of the brain; functional magnetic resonance imaging (fMRI) measures changes in the flow of blood in different parts of the brain and produces a computerized image of this activity.

Although these techniques require expensive and sophisticated equipment, they are helping us achieve a new understanding of processes we would not be able to study without them. For example, studies comparing cortical functions in adults and adolescents have found that these two groups process information differently; adolescents often use different brain regions than adults (Yurgelun-Todd, 2007). Research in which fMRIs are used to scan the brains of children diagnosed as autistic has found that the part of the brain controlling face recognition is underactive (Kalb, 2005). As you may know, children with autism often do not make eye contact with others and show little or no interest in social relationships. Because this is a relatively new technology, we must be sure that we understand and are correctly interpreting the results that we get from it.

Archival Records

Researchers don't always collect their own data. They may use archival records, or data that were collected by others. For instance, a researcher might use historical diaries, letters, or photographs to gain insight into what childhood was like in the past. Reports and statistics collected by the U.S. government provide a historical snapshot of many topics relevant for a developmental researcher, as do medical records and school records.

MRIs and fMRIs. The MRI image (left) shows pictures of successive sections through the brain from the back to the front. The fMRI image (right) shows where the blood is flowing through the brain when the person thinks about an activity and actually does that activity. ■

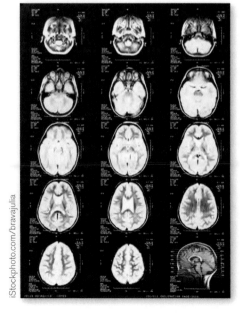

iStockphoto.com/bravajulia

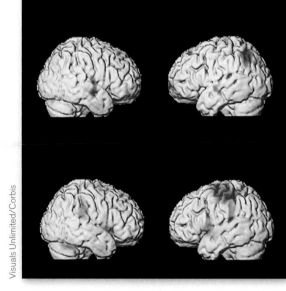

Visuals Unlimited/Corbis

Case Studies

A **case study** takes a comprehensive and intensive look at a single individual or a small group. The subjects of case studies are often exceptional in some way, which is what makes them interesting subjects for scientific study. In one well-known case study, a group of researchers worked to rehabilitate a young girl named Genie who had been raised in conditions of horrible deprivation. In the process, the researchers kept detailed case notes on her attempts at recovery.

Because of the close relationship that can develop over time between the researcher and the subject of a case study, the researcher must strive to remain objective when making observations and interpreting data. Despite this challenge, case studies offer us a rich and deep picture of development because they can bring together information from multiple sources using multiple methods, including interviews, observations, tests, and documents. Although the findings may have limited generalizability, case studies can be a rich source of new hypotheses that future researchers can explore with other more typical or representative groups of individuals.

Ethnography

Ethnography is a technique from the field of anthropology in which a researcher lives with a group of people as a participant observer, taking part in the group's everyday life while also observing and interviewing the people in the group. This technique is especially helpful when studying children in different cultures because it allows the researcher to see the whole context of the children's development. For example, Samantha Punch (2012) lived in an area of Bolivia to study children's development in a poor, rural community. Sudhir Venkatesh (2008) wanted to administer questionnaires to gang members in inner city Chicago and ended up living among them for almost 10 years. This resulted in a rich account of their lives in a book titled *Gang Leader for a Day: A Rogue Sociologist Takes to the Streets.*

Ethnographies allow a rich look at a cultural group from someone embedded in that group for an extended period of time. However, researchers must be aware that their presence may change the behavior of the group. Also, the researchers' own biases may

Case study An in-depth study of a single individual or small group of individuals, which uses multiple methods of study.

Ethnography A technique in which a researcher lives with a group of people as a participant observer, taking part in the group's everyday life while observing and interviewing people in the group.

MICHAEL NICHOLS/National Geographic Creative

Ethnography. This ethnographic researcher entered into the everyday life of this group of people to gain a rich picture of all aspects of their environment. ■

affect how they interpret what they see. Other drawbacks include risks to the researcher's safety and the amount of time needed to carry out an ethnographic study.

How Research Is Designed

To test a hypothesis, researchers use one of two ways to relate the variables within the hypothesis: experimental or correlational research designs. In this section you will learn the differences between these two approaches and the strengths and limitations of each.

Experimental Designs

As useful as other methods are, conducting experiments occupies a central place in our repertoire of research methods. One reason is that experiments allow us to do something other methods can't—they can *identify the causes* of behavior. With other methods, we can speculate about the causes, but we do not have enough control over the situation to make a firm determination. However, when a researcher designs an experiment, the goal is to control as many aspects of the experimental situation as possible to draw conclusions about the causes of the outcome.

Experiments can take different forms and can include one, two, or more groups of participants, but these are the essential features you will find in an experimental research design:

- The experimental group is the group that receives the special treatment of interest to the researcher.
- The control group does not receive the special treatment and provides a baseline against which the experimental group can be compared.
- The participants are randomly assigned to either the experimental or the control group. Because this assignment is made by chance, the two groups will likely start out being very similar to each other, without any systematic differences that could affect the outcome of the experiment. To get a random assignment to groups, you could simply flip a coin for each participant, with all "heads" going into one group and all "tails" into the other; or you could put all the names in a hat and pull them out one by one, alternately assigning them to one group or the other.
- The independent variable is the special treatment the researcher hypothesizes will make a difference between the experimental and control groups after the experiment. The assumption is that the independent variable is the cause of any change we observe following the experiment.
- The dependent variable is the outcome of interest to the researcher. We measure it at the end of the experiment to see whether manipulating the independent variable has produced the expected effect.

If we look at an example of experimental research, this terminology will have more meaning for you. Researchers wanted to know whether changing the way in which teachers read to preschoolers would affect the children's awareness and understanding of the printed word (Justice, McGinty, Piasta, Kaderavek, & Fan, 2010). Fifty-nine teachers and their classes were randomly assigned to the experimental group or the control group. The children in both groups were tested at the start of the study to be sure they did not differ on several measures of language milestones. Such a pretest comparison gives us confidence that the two groups are similar before we begin any experimental intervention.

The teachers in the control group were asked to keep reading to their students in the same way they had been doing. Remember, the control group provides the baseline for detecting any changes that result from the experimental manipulation during the

---

Experimental research design A research design in which an experimental group is administered a treatment and the outcome is compared with a control group that does not receive the treatment.

Experimental group The group in an experiment that gets the special treatment that is of interest to the researcher.

Control group The group in an experiment that does not get the special treatment and provides a baseline against which the experimental group can be compared.

Random assignment Assigning participants to the experimental and control groups by chance so that the groups will not systematically differ from each other.

Independent variable The variable in an experiment that the researcher manipulates.

Dependent variable The outcome of interest to the researcher that is measured at the end of an experiment.

research. The teachers in the experimental group read to their students following specific instructions for referring to the print in the book, for example, asking the children where the title of the book was or whether a particular letter was upper or lower case. Remember, the experimental group gets the treatment whose effect the researchers are interested in studying. The independent variable in this study was whether teachers used this special program while reading to their students or not, and the dependent variable was the children's print knowledge.

When print knowledge was tested again in the spring, the children in the experimental group demonstrated significantly greater understanding of the nature of print, an important prereading skill. Because the two groups of children were similar at the start of the experiment on the measure of interest to the researchers, and because the only relevant difference between them during the experiment was the way their teachers read to them, the researchers concluded that the intervention was the *cause* of the difference they observed at the end of the experiment. Figure 2.5 shows the steps in the experimental process and the way they relate to each other. **Active Learning: The Experimental Method** gives you an opportunity to review the terminology used in experiments and to check that you can recognize each element when you see it in the description of an experiment.

FIGURE 2.5   The experimental process

Step 1	Step 2	Step 3: Pretest	Step 4: Treatment	Step 5: Posttest	Step 6: Compare Results
A representative group of children is chosen to be in the study	Children are randomly assigned to groups	Pretest establishes groups are the same	Independent variable is administered to the experimental group	Dependent variable is measured	Supports hypothesis
Sample	Experimental Group	Score on test of language development	Training sessions on reading to children	Score on test of language development	Experimental group score > Control group score
	Control Group	Score on test of language development	No training sessions	Score on test of language development	

This figure shows you how an experiment (in this case an experiment to promote language development) is conducted, starting with a sample of the population of interest to the researcher and ending with results that can be interpreted.

Active Learning

The Experimental Method

You can test your understanding of the experimental method by identifying the components of an experiment in this example taken from a study by Beth Hennessey (2007) designed to measure the effects of a program to build social competence in a sample of school-age children.

A total of 154 fourth graders in eight classrooms participated in the study. In half the classrooms, teachers used the Open Circle Program, a social skills training program that "encourages students, teachers and administrators to learn and practice communication, self-control and social problem-solving skills" (Hennessey, 2007, p. 349). The classroom teachers were asked to rate their students' social competence in the fall before the program began and again in spring after the program ended. Based on the teachers' reports, Hennessey concluded that the students in the classrooms that used the Open Circle Program training showed greater improvement in their social skills and problem-solving behavior than students who didn't receive this training.

From the description of this experiment, identify the following:

Experimental group: _____

Control group: _____

Independent variable: _____

Dependent variable: _____

Experimental group: The group that received the Open Circle Program training

Control group: The group that did not receive the Open Circle Program training

Independent variable: Whether the group received the social skills training or not

Dependent variable: The measure of social competence and problem solving

■ Answers:

Although the experimental research method lets us control many aspects of a situation that might affect an outcome, some other variable or condition we haven't taken into account could still be responsible for the outcome. For this reason, experiments must be carefully planned and carefully executed. It also may have occurred to you by now that, as appealing as the experimental method might be, it cannot answer many of the questions that are of great interest to us as developmentalists. There are many situations we could never ethically create as experiments. For example, if we want to study the effects of divorce on children, we cannot randomly assign half our sample of families to divorce one another while the other half stays married.

Correlational Designs

In a correlational research design, a researcher examines the relationship between two or more variables, such as self-esteem and children's academic achievement. When we look at correlations, we are interested in two characteristics: the *strength* of the relationship and the *direction* of the relationship. Figure 2.6 will help you visualize these aspects of correlations as we describe them. We'll talk first about the direction of the relationship. Correlations can be *positive* or *negative*. In a positive correlation, the value of one variable increases as the value of the second variable increases. For example, lifetime earnings are positively correlated with the number of years in school. As years completed in school go up, so do lifetime earnings. In a negative correlation, as the value of one variable increases, the value of the second variable decreases. For example, the more often people brush their teeth, the lower their rate of tooth decay.

The second characteristic of correlations is the strength of the relationship between the two variables. This can range from a correlation of +1.0 (a perfect positive correlation) to a correlation of −1.0 (a perfect negative correlation). At either of these extremes, a change of one unit of measurement in one of the variables is accompanied by a change of one unit of measurement in the second variable, so if we knew someone's score on one variable, we could perfectly predict her score on the second variable. As a correlation moves from +1 or −1 toward 0, the relationship between the variables gets weaker and

Correlational research design Research that measures the strength and direction of the relationship between two or more variables that are not created by the experimenter.

FIGURE 2.6   **Examples of correlations**

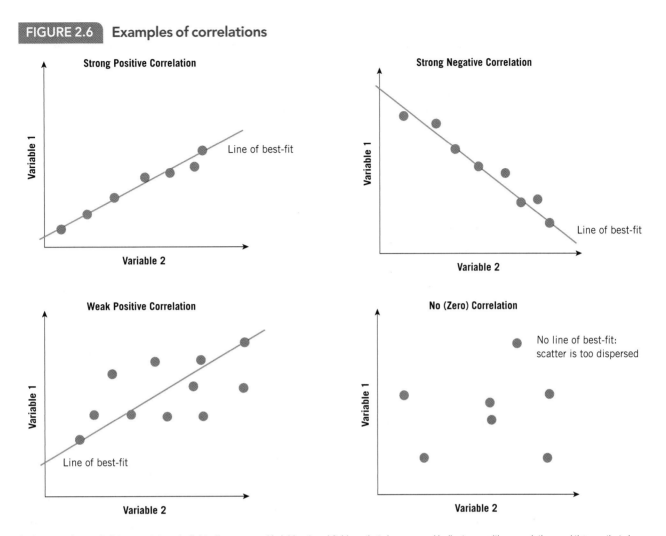

In these graphs, each dot represents an individual's scores on Variables 1 and 2. Lines that slope upward indicate a positive correlation, and the one that slopes downward indicates a negative correlation. The spread of the data points around the line shows how strong the correlation is. The closer the points are to falling on a straight line, the stronger the correlation.

weaker and the spread of the data points around the central line increases. An increase in the value of one of the variables is now associated with a *range* of values for the second variable. For instance, the correlation between people's shoe size and their IQ is probably close to zero because there is no reason to think these characteristics are related to each other in any systematic way. Many correlations in developmental research are in the moderate range of ±.15 to ±.40.

If you read an article claiming a fairly strong positive correlation between the amount of stress children report in their lives and the number of days they miss school because they are ill, it would be dangerous to conclude that high levels of stress *cause* illness. This *might* be the case, but just because two things are correlated, we cannot determine if one of them caused the other. We do not have enough information from this correlational study alone to draw that conclusion because both variables (stressful life conditions and poor health) might be affected by a third variable that was not included in the study. In this case, impoverished living conditions could be that third variable. Children who come from poorer families probably have more stress in their lives, but they may also

T/F #10
Even if research consistently finds that children whose mothers talk to them a great deal have high self-esteem, we should not conclude that frequent conversations with parents build self-esteem in children.
True

WEB LINK 2.3
Correlation, Not Causation

Longitudinal design A research design that follows one group of individuals over time and looks at the same or similar measures at each point of testing.

Cross-sectional design A research design that uses multiple groups of participants who represent the age span of interest to the researcher.

have less healthy lifestyles and less access to medical care when they need it. In this case, the family's financial status is responsible for both high levels of stress and illness.

Does this mean we can never answer the question whether stress or economic circumstances causes poor health in children? Not exactly. We could conduct a natural experiment in which we control the variable of financial status by including only children from the same economic background. Or we can use statistical techniques that allow us to take economic status out of our equation. Both approaches allow us to see whether stressful life circumstances are related to health outcomes *over and above* the effect of the family's economic situation.

Developmental Research Designs

Each of the methods we've described can test scientific hypotheses, but each can also be used within research designs that look at development. Three developmental research designs are longitudinal, cross-sectional, and cross-sequential.

A longitudinal design follows one group of individuals across time and looks at the same or similar measures at each point of testing. The biggest advantage of a longitudinal study is that it gives us the clearest picture of how the variables we are interested in change as a function of age. However, it takes a good deal of time and money to conduct multiple waves of data collection for a large group of individuals. Many researchers do not have the resources necessary to conduct this type of research. Also, because participants need to be tested or measured repeatedly over the course of the study, it is inevitable that some will drop out, compromising the representative nature of the original sample. For example, children from poorer families tend to change schools more frequently than children from more affluent families. If you are doing your research in a school, over time it is likely that more of the poorer students will move away during the course of the study, so by the time they reach the end of the study, those in your sample may be of a higher socioeconomic status than your original group.

Longitudinal studies also lock researchers into using one set of measures even if better alternatives come along. If they switch measures during the study and find changes in the level of the outcomes they are tracking, the researchers cannot be sure whether the changes are attributable to the fact that the participants are older or the new measure is actually measuring something slightly different than the original measure. Despite these concerns, however, longitudinal research provides a very powerful way to look at developmental change, and that is the reason this design is widely used.

A cross-sectional design studies multiple groups of participants who cover the age span of interest to the researcher. If you were interested in developmental changes between elementary and middle school, you could collect data from groups of participants who were 8 years old, 10 years old, and 12 years old. Then, by comparing the results from the groups, you could construct a picture of the changes that occur over that period of development. Because you collect all your data at the same time, you can do so in a relatively quick, cost-effective manner. Obviously participant dropout is not an issue because there is only a single data collection. Based on cross-sectional research, you will know that children of different ages show differences on the outcome you measured, but you won't know *why*. We presume age changes are responsible, but we need to be careful when making these assumptions.

One of the big challenges in cross-sectional research is that the different age groups in the study must be as similar as possible on any variable that might affect the study's outcome. Here is an extreme example. Imagine you are interested in how self-esteem changes during the transition from elementary to middle school. To examine these changes, you use a group of 8-year-old students who attend a public elementary school in a disadvantaged neighborhood, a group of 10-year-old students from a private school with a religious affiliation, and a group of 12-year-old students from a suburban public school. Even if you found differences in self-esteem between the groups, could you correctly interpret them as age-related changes associated with school transitions? Clearly you could not. Because the groups came from such widely different school settings (and, therefore, it is likely that they differ from each other in a variety of other ways), you could not make any valid interpretation of these data. Differences between groups in actual cross-sectional research are much more subtle than those in this example, but any difference that is not recognized and accounted for by the research can be a threat to the validity of the conclusions drawn from this type of research.

Another difficulty with cross-sectional research is that different age groups or cohorts have lived during different times in history. These differences create what is called a cohort effect. For example, people in their 70s are likely to be less skilled with computers than those in their 20s. This does not mean computer skills decline with age; rather it reflects the effects of the introduction of the home computer in the late 1970s, when those people now in their 70s were already older than 30 years of age. The skill advantage of younger people reflects their use of the computer from a much younger age.

Finally, the cross-sequential design brings together elements of cross-sectional research and longitudinal research. This design uses several groups of people of different ages who begin their participation in the study at the same time (just as cross-sectional research does) and follows them over a period of time that can vary from a few months to many years, just as longitudinal research does. What makes this method unique is the overlap of the groups' ages. For example, if we were looking at children's health over the age range from birth to 20 years, we could begin by assessing four different groups: infants, 5-year-olds, 10-year-olds, and 15-year-olds. After we repeat our assessment 5 years later (when the infants are 5 years old, the 5-year-olds are 10, and so on), we will have two different groups that were assessed at age 5, two assessed at 10, and two assessed at 15. Because we needed to follow the groups for only 5 years to cover our age span of interest, the risk of participants dropping out of the research study is lower than it would have been in a 20-year study, which reduces sample bias. We also have reduced the time, money, and labor needed to conduct the study compared to a 20-year-long study of children's health. Finally, if there were any cohort differences between the groups, those effects would become apparent when we compare the results of the overlapping groups who are the same age in different years.

Even though cross-sequential research offers advantages, the cohort groups still need to be as much alike as possible at the start of the study, and you still need to be able to track and reassess the groups at regular intervals, so sample attrition is still a potential problem. Test your understanding of these three different developmental research designs by trying **Active Learning: Developmental Research Designs.**

Cohort effect Differences between groups in a cross-sectional study that are attributable to the fact that the participants have had different life experiences.

Cross-sequential design A research design that uses multiple groups of participants and follows them over a period of time, with the beginning age of each group being the ending age of another group.

Active Learning

Developmental Research Designs

Look at the chart below and answer the following questions:

1. If only Group A was tested, what type of developmental research design would this be?

2. If only Testing Year 2015 was carried out, what type of developmental research design would this be?

3. If all the groups were tested in years 2015 and 2020, what type of developmental research design would this be?

Testing Year 2015	Testing Year 2020
Group A age 10	Group A age 15
Group B age 5	Group B age 10
Group C newborn	Group C age 5

followed and retested after 5 years.

3. Cross-sequential research design, because different age groups are compared and the groups also are

time.

2. Cross-sectional research design, because different age groups are tested and compared at the same

5 years.

1. Longitudinal research design, because the same group of participants is followed and retested after

■ Answers:

Interpreting the Results of a Study

After we conduct research, we must still interpret the results. The accuracy of our final understanding of what the study showed is greatly affected by the way we interpret the data, and two people may look at the same data and interpret them in different ways. In reaching our conclusions, we must be careful not to generalize beyond the characteristics of the sample that participated in the research. We also need to remember that conclusions drawn from research—even very carefully conducted research—are generalizations that apply to groups of individuals. As you learned in Chapter 1, there is a great deal of diversity among individuals within any group. Therefore, our conclusions will not apply to every single child, and the fact that some children do not fit the general pattern does not invalidate the general conclusion.

Research results are tested using various statistical methods to determine whether the outcomes may have happened by chance. However, even if the results are statistically significant (that is, they did not happen by chance), you still might wonder whether they make any difference in the real world. As an example, consider research on the relationship between birth order and intelligence (Kristensen, & Bjerkedal, 2007). An analysis of the IQ test scores of over 250,000 young men in the Norwegian military service found that the scores of first-borns in the sample were higher than the scores of second-borns at a statistically significant level of .05 (meaning that there are only 5 chances in 100 that this is an accidental difference). But before any first-born readers of this text begin celebrating their intellectual superiority over their siblings, note that the difference in test scores between the two groups was only 2.82 points. Although these results are statistically significant, it is not likely that a difference of fewer than 3 IQ points will have any practical significance in the lives of these men.

Our confidence that our conclusions are valid is strengthened if we are able to replicate or repeat our findings using other groups that are the same as or similar to the group we originally studied. We can extend the research to groups that differ from our original sample to determine whether we can generalize the conclusions to new populations. We also expect that other researchers will be able to replicate our results by conducting their own independent research and coming to the same or similar conclusions (Makel, Plucker, & Hegarty, 2012). When findings are published in research journals or presented at professional meetings, it gives other researchers the opportunity to critique the way the research was conducted and identify any possible flaws in the logic or problems with the methodology, analysis, or interpretation of the findings. Sometimes a statistical procedure called meta-analysis is used to combine the data from different studies and determine whether there is a consistent pattern of findings across studies. We discuss the results from meta-analyses on important topics throughout this book.

Meta-analysis A statistical procedure that combines data from different studies to determine whether there is a consistent pattern of findings across studies.

Check Your Understanding

1. What is the difference between reliability and validity?
2. What are the most common self-report measures used in research?
3. What are the essential features of the experimental research design?
4. How do longitudinal research, cross-sectional research, and cross-sequential research differ?
5. What are some of the challenges in interpreting research results?

Ethics in Research With Children and Adolescents

2.4

What are ethical considerations in research with children and adolescents?

Any research with human participants must ensure their safety and well-being. U.S. Department of Health and Human Services (2005a) regulations provide specific protections for research participants. They can only be exposed to minimal risks during their participation, and any potential risk must be weighed against the anticipated benefits from the research. They must be informed of the purpose of the research and its risks and benefits and must freely agree—without coercion—to participate; they have the right to withdraw from participation at any point. Finally, the privacy of participants must be protected, and the data collected must be treated as confidential.

Because of their particular vulnerability, children are given additional protections when they participate in research. The Society for Research in Child Development (SRCD, 2007) has developed specific guidelines that include the expectation that no physical or psychological harm will be done to children who participate in research and that the researcher will use the least stressful research procedures possible. The researcher also must seek consent from both the children and their parents. If children are not old enough to give consent because they do not necessarily understand the full significance of the research, they still must assent if they are old enough to do that. That means that the children freely choose to participate and are able to terminate participation at any point if they want to. If, during the course of the research, the researcher becomes aware of any threat to the child's well-being, it is the responsibility of the researcher to inform the parents and arrange for assistance for the child.

WEB LINK 2.4
Ethics and Children

Check Your Understanding

1. What does the U.S. Department of Health and Human Services require as ethical guidelines for research with children?
2. What additional considerations arise in the Society for Research in Child Development recommendations?

Conclusion

In this chapter you have been introduced to the basic theories that organize our information about child development and guide our ongoing research in the field. You will find more theories as you read through the rest of this book. You also were introduced to a variety of methods that are used as a part of the scientific process to test these theoretical ideas. As you continue to read about theories and methods throughout this text, remember that our body of knowledge is dynamic. It grows and changes as our understanding grows and changes. You will be able to apply your knowledge of theories and research methods not only to examples in this text, but also to information on child development that you encounter beyond this course.

Chapter Summary

2.1 What do child development theories tell us?

Theories of development give us models that allow us to predict how children will behave. Some theories propose that development occurs in stages, while others see development as a continuous process. Theories also differ in their emphasis on biological and environmental influences that bring about growth and development.

2.2 What are the hypotheses of the major child development theories?

a. **In the psychoanalytic perspective, how do Freud's and Erikson's theories compare?**

In Freud's theory, sexual energy shifts from one area of the body to another as the child develops, forming the basis for five psychosexual stages. Erik Erikson believed the social world and the development of identity were driving forces for development through psychosocial life stages.

b. **In the theory of behaviorism, what are classical and operant conditioning?**

In **classical conditioning** an unconditioned stimulus is paired with a neutral stimulus. After repeated pairings, the neutral stimulus elicits a conditioned response. In **operant conditioning** something that follows a behavior affects the likelihood of that behavior happening again. Reinforcement increases the behavior, while punishment decreases it.

c. **What is the basic learning process of social learning theory?**

Bandura's social learning theory emphasizes the importance of imitation as a learning process.

d. **How do Piaget and Vygotsky describe the learning process?**

Piaget's theory of cognitive development states that we organize the world into **schemas** and either **assimilate** new information that fits into them or **accommodate** it by changing our schemas. Vygotsky emphasized the role of social interaction and believed adults or more skilled peers build children's knowledge through **scaffolding**.

e. **What model for mental functioning does information processing use?**

The connectionist or **neural network model** describes mental processing as a neural network of concept nodes that are interconnected by links.

f. **How has Darwin's theory of evolution been applied to the study of child development?**

Ethology studies animals' and humans' behavior in relationship to their adaptation to the natural environment. **Sociobiology** proposes that human social behavior is affected by genes that evolved to promote adaptation.

g. **What are Bronfenbrenner's five systems of influence?**

Bronfenbrenner proposed that individuals grow and develop within a nested set of influences that he divided into five systems: **microsystem, mesosystem, exosystem, macrosystem**, and **chronosystem**.

h. **What are neuropsychology and behavioral genomics?**

Neuropsychology is the study of the brain and behavior. **Behavioral genomics** is the study of genes and behavior. Both brain development and the expression of genes are influenced and shaped by environment and experiences.

i. **What is dynamic systems theory?**

Dynamic systems theory examines the way all aspects of development—biological, cognitive, and socioemotional—influence one another.

2.3 How is research on child development conducted?

The **scientific method** begins with observations, which generate **hypotheses**. After we **operationalize** the concepts in our hypotheses, we select a **representative sample** for research. Any measures we use must be **reliable** and **valid**.

Research can draw on naturalistic observation, **checklists** of behaviors, or self-report measures that include **surveys**, **questionnaires**, and **interviews**. We also gather data via **standardized tests**, physiological measures, **archival records**, **case studies**, and **ethnography**.

Participants in experimental research are **randomly assigned** to an **experimental** or **control group**. The **independent variable** is the treatment given to the experimental group, after which we measure the **dependent variable** for both groups. If there is a difference, we can conclude the independent variable caused it. **Correlational research** is designed to examine the relationship between variables. Results are examined for the direction and the strength of the relationship but a correlation does not mean that one of the variables caused the other.

A **longitudinal design** follows and assesses a single group of participants over a period of time. **Cross-sectional designs** assess comparable groups of participants of different ages at the same time. In a **cross-sequential design**, several groups are followed for a period of time, with an overlap in the age at which one group begins the study and another group finishes it.

In interpreting study results, we must not **generalize** beyond the characteristics of our sample and we expect to find individual exceptions to the results.

2.4 What are ethical considerations in research with children and adolescents?

All research must protect the physical and psychological safety and well-being of participants and safeguard the confidentiality of results. Participation must be voluntary, and children (or their parents) have the right to withdraw at any point.

Key Terms

Accommodation 40

Anal stage 30

Archival records 56

Assimilation 40

Behavioral genomics 48

Behaviorism 33

Case study 57

Checklist 53

Chronosystem 45

Classical conditioning 33

Clinical interview 54

Cohort effect 63

Connectionist/neural network model 42

Constructivism 41

Control group 58

Correlational research design 60

Cross-sectional design 62

Cross-sequential design 63

Dependent variable 58

Developmental theory 27

Dynamic assessment 41

Dynamic systems theory 48

Ego 30

Equilibration 40

Ethnography 57

Ethology 43

Exosystem 45

Experimental group 58

Experimental research design 58

Extinction 37

Free association 29

Generalize 51

Genital stage 31

Hypothesis 50

Id 29

Imprinting 43

Independent variable 58

Interviews 53

Latency stage 30

Longitudinal design 62

Macrosystem 45

Mesosystem 45

Meta-analysis 65

Microsystem 45

Negative reinforcement 36

Neuropsychology 48

Norm 55

Observer bias 51

Operant conditioning 36

Operationalizing a concept 51

Oral stage 30

Phallic stage 30

Phobia 35

Pleasure principle 29

Psychoanalytic theory 29

Psychosexual stages 30

Sharpen your skills with SAGE edge at edge.sagepub.com/levinechrono

SAGE edge for Students provides a personalized approach to help you accomplish your coursework goals in an easy-to-use learning environment.

Go to edge.sagepub.com/levinechrono for additional exercises and video resources. Select Chapter 2, Theory and Research in Development, for chapter-specific activities. All of the Video Links listed in the margins of this chapter are accessible via this site.

Fuse/Thinkstock

© Sandro Di Carlo Darsa/PhotoAlto/Corbis

part

II

3 Nature Through Nurture

Genes and Environment

T/F Test Your Knowledge

Test your knowledge of child development by deciding whether each of the following statements is *true* or *false*, and then check your answers as you read the chapter.

1. T ☐ F ☐ Each human being has hundreds of thousands of genes that make him or her a unique individual.

2. T ☐ F ☐ When a child is conceived, it is the mother's genetic material that determines the gender of the child.

3. T ☐ F ☐ The tendency to have identical twins runs in families.

4. T ☐ F ☐ Two parents with brown eyes can still have a child with blue eyes.

5. T ☐ F ☐ Carrying one recessive gene for sickle-cell anemia can be beneficial for an individual.

6. T ☐ F ☐ Every gene in your body has one specific function.

7. T ☐ F ☐ Males are more likely to have a genetic disorder than females.

8. T ☐ F ☐ At age 17, Mike is already a heavy drinker. Because both of his parents have struggled with alcoholism for a long time, genes must have determined that Mike would also become an alcoholic.

9. T ☐ F ☐ Genes have been found to play a role in the development of almost all behaviors that have been studied.

10. T ☐ F ☐ The experiences you have in your life can change the structure of your genes.

The Study of Genetics and Behavior

In this chapter, we examine what we know about the effects of genes, the basic unit of inheritance made of DNA molecules, and the interaction of genes and environmental influence on children's development. We focus first at the molecular level to examine how genes work and what happens in genetically based disorders. We then describe behavioral genetics and examine research based on the study of twins and adopted children that is designed to discover whether and how certain behaviors are linked to our genetic inheritance. Finally, we discuss the intricate interaction of specific genes and environmental experiences, deepening our understanding of nature and nurture. We can no longer describe many aspects of development as a result of either genetic or environmental influence because we now know that genes and environment interact in complex ways. To see how far our scientific knowledge of the role of genes has come in the last 150 years, see **Journey of Research: The History of Research on Genetics.**

Learning Questions

3.1 What are the differences between molecular genetics, behavioral genetics, and behavioral genomics?

3.2 How do genes and chromosomes function?

3.3 How do genetic disorders develop, and what role do genetic testing and counseling play in identifying, preventing, and treating these disorders?

3.4 How do we study the relationship between our genetic inheritance and our traits and behavior?

3.5 How do genes and the environment interact?

3.1

What are the differences between molecular genetics, behavioral genetics, and behavioral genomics?

Gene A segment of DNA on a chromosome that creates proteins that are the basis for the body's development and functioning.

....

JOURNEY OF RESEARCH *The History of Research on Genetics*

The modern study of genetics began in 1866 when Gregor Mendel, a Central European scientist and monk, published a paper outlining a number of the principles that guide the transmission of genetic information from one generation to another. These principles, which Mendel discovered by studying the way characteristics of pea plants passed from one generation to the next, came to be known as *Mendelian inheritance.* However, Mendel did not know about genes, and it was not until 1900 that the significance of his work was recognized (Lane, 1994).

Also around 1900, the English psychologist and anthropologist Francis Galton concluded that just as pea plants could be bred to have certain characteristics, so could desirable traits be bred into human beings, while undesirable ones could be bred out. This process, which Galton called *eugenics*, would require promoting reproduction by "superior" human beings and inhibiting reproduction by "inferior" ones. The idea became so influential that, beginning in 1907,

30 states in the United States passed laws allowing for the forced sterilization of about 60,000 people considered "criminals, idiots, rapists, and imbeciles" (Watson, 2003, p. 27). (The terms *idiot* and *imbecile* in those days indicated levels of performance on IQ tests.) As the Nazis came to power in Germany in the 1930s, they enthusiastically adopted a policy that embraced eugenics. They began with sterilization but then moved to mass murder of all those deemed unfit to reproduce for a multitude of reasons. This came to include annihilation of entire ethnic groups in the service of creating a pure "Aryan race" (Watson, 2003).

As a result of eugenics and its excesses, genetics research came to be seen as suspect. It was not until the 1950s that the American biologist James Watson and his British colleague Francis Crick developed a basic understanding of genetic structure and function. Their findings allowed scientists to understand the exact process that underlies the genetic transmission first described by

VIDEO LINK 3.1
Eugenics

Genome All of a person's genes, including those that are active and those that are silent.

Genome-wide association A system that allows scientists to examine the whole human genome at once.

Mendel almost 100 years earlier. In 1990, with James Watson as its first director, the Human Genome Project undertook the ambitious goal of mapping all the human genes (National Human Genome Research Institute, 2010). In 2003, exactly 50 years after Watson and Crick's discovery, the map of the human genome was completed (Human Genome Project Information, 2008b). Research on the human genome took another step forward in 2005 when a new technique, called genome-wide association, was developed. With this technique, instead of studying particular genes believed to be responsible for a particular disorder or trait, researchers can now study the whole genome at once to identify the relevant genes (Hu, 2013). Developments in the study of the human genome are occurring rapidly, yet much work remains to make the connections between specific genes and most human traits and behaviors (Plomin, 2013). ■

Genes are linked to our most basic physical characteristics. However, in the study of children and adolescents we are most interested in the way they relate to behavior and its development. Scientists investigate genetic effects on behavior in three ways: (1) Molecular genetics is focused at the level of the cell, (2) behavioral genetics is focused at the level of behavior, and (3) behavioral genomics examines the connections between the behavioral and the cellular levels. We now describe each of these in more detail.

Molecular Genetics

In molecular genetics, scientists study processes at the molecular level, examining both the structure and the function of genes and the DNA molecules they contain. Molecular genetics thus focuses on identifying particular genes to understand how they work within the cell. A gene carries a chemical set of instructions that tells the cell how to produce specific proteins (Jorde, Carey, Bamshad, & White, 2006). For example, a particular gene contains the instructions to produce an enzyme, which is a type of protein, called phenylalanine hydroxylase (PAH) that breaks down a common amino acid in the human diet. Through the study of molecular genetics, scientists discovered that when this gene has a certain defect, it does not contain the correct information to produce PAH. A child who inherits a gene with this defective information from both parents will have a potentially deadly condition known as phenylketonuria or PKU (Scriver, 2007), which we discuss again later in the chapter.

Molecular genetics Research focused on the identification of particular genes to describe how these genes work within the cell.

Behavioral Genetics

Behavioral genetics begins with behavior rather than molecules and attempts to define the heritability of a characteristic (that is, how much or how little of a trait is based on genetics). Behavioral genetics studies natural situations, such as adoption and the occurrence of twins, to understand this connection between genes and behavior. Children who are adopted share genes with their birth parents, but they share their environment with their adoptive parents. If we look at large numbers of adopted children and find they are generally more similar to their birth parents than their adoptive parents on a trait such as fearfulness, we can conclude that genes play a large role in determining who is more fearful.

Behavioral genetics Research to determine the degree of genetic basis for a behavior, trait, or ability.

Heritability A measure of the extent to which genes determine a particular behavior or characteristic.

Behavioral Genomics

The new field of behavioral genomics has emerged to bridge molecular genetics, which focuses on activity at the level of the cell, and behavioral genetics, which focuses on activity at the level of human behavior (Plomin, DeFries, Craig, & McGuffin, 2003a). While behavioral genetics examines the heritability of a characteristic, behavioral genomics seeks to identify which specific genes are linked to specific behaviors. When scientists find a genetic association for a particular behavior using the approaches of behavioral genetics described above, they can use molecular genetics to attempt to identify the specific genes that may be active in producing that behavior.

Check Your Understanding

1. What is the basic unit of inheritance?
2. What is the focus of molecular genetics?
3. What do behavioral geneticists study?
4. What field of study bridges molecular and behavioral genetics?

How Do Genes Work?

When the Human Genome Project completed mapping all the genes that make a human being one of the biggest surprises was that the total came to only about 20,000 to 25,000 genes, not the 100,000 or more that researchers had expected to find (U.S. Department of Energy Genome Programs, 2012). If the number of genes alone governed how complex and sophisticated we are as a species, then it would appear we are only a little more complicated than mice or fruit flies. Even rice has between 46,000 and 55,600 genes (National Human Genome Research Institute, 2007). Something other than simply the number of genes must account for the large differences between species.

Genes are made up of nucleotides, which are organic molecules containing a chemical base, a phosphate group, and a sugar molecule. Only 2% of the 3 billion nucleotides in the human genome are needed to make up the 20,000 genes that create proteins (Plomin, 2013). The other 98% of the genome was long considered to be "junk" and to have no effect, but this idea is changing rapidly. With new technology, scientists are now able to use whole-genome sequencing to study all the nucleotides, not just those that make up active genes (Plomin, 2013). Some of these nucleotides play an important role in regulating the functioning of the 20,000 genes (Zhang et al., 2013).

Think of genes as simply a set of instructions, such as you might get when you purchase a new cell phone with many unfamiliar features. If you read and follow the instructions you will be able to perform all the functions built into the cell phone. However, if you don't, you may never use some of them. In the same way, genes may be either read or ignored, with consequences for the aspects of human structure and functioning to which they are related. Later in this chapter we will learn more about the ways in which genes are either expressed or their instructions remain silent.

Although most of the genes have been identified, we are still a long way from knowing exactly what each actually does (Human Genome Project Information, 2009; U.S. Department of Energy Genome Programs, 2008). Figure 3.1 shows the characteristics associated with the genes found by the Human Genome Project on one chromosome.

Our Genetic Beginnings

Every person's life begins when a father's sperm penetrates a mother's egg during fertilization. The fertilized egg that results is called a zygote. The egg and sperm cells each contain half our genetic material, organized into 23 chromosomes. When fertilization occurs, the chromosome strands from the sperm join those from the egg to form 23 matched pairs in which genes with the same function pair up. As you can see in Figure 3.2, in 22 of these pairs of chromosomes (called *autosomes*) the two chromosomes look very similar. The chromosomes in the 23rd pair can be the same or different, because the chromosome contributed by the father can be either an X chromosome or a Y chromosome. The mother can only contribute an X chromosome to the 23rd pair, so it is the information from the father that determines the sex of the child. A conception with

---

3.2

How do genes and chromosomes function?

T/F #1
Each human being has hundreds of thousands of genes that make him or her a unique individual. *False*

Nucleotides Organic molecules containing a chemical base, a phosphate group, and a sugar molecule.

WEB LINK 3.1
Human Genome Mapping

Fertilization The union of a father's sperm and a mother's egg to produce a zygote.

Zygote A fertilized egg.

Chromosomes The strands of genes that constitute the human genetic endowment.

T/F #2
When a child is conceived, it is the mother's genetic material that determines the gender of the child. *False*

FIGURE 3.1   Chromosome 12

Lupus erythematosus	Dentatorubro-pallidoluysian atrophy
Hypophosphatemic rickets, autosomal dominant	Emphysema
Coagulation factor VIII (von Willebrand factor)	Alzheimer disease, susceptibility to
Tumor necrosis factor receptor superfamily	Inflammatory bowel disease
Periodic fever, familial	Leukemia, acute lymphoblastic
Keutel syndrome	Hypertension, essential, susceptibility to
Periodic fever, familial (Hibemian fever)	Leukemia factor, myeloid
Episodic ataxia/myokymia syndrome	Spastic paraplegia, autosomal dominant
Pseudohypoaldosteronism, type I	Taste receptors
Hemolytic anemia	Glycogen storage disease, type 0
Diabetes-associated peptide (amylin)	Hypertension with brachydactyly
Lactate dehydrogenase-B deficiency	Alzheimer disease, familial
Colorectal cancer	Retinoblastoma-binding protein
Fibrosis of extraocular muscles, autosomal dominant	Ichthyosis bullosa of Siemens
Adrenoleukodystrophy	Telangiectasia, hereditary hemorrhagic
Palmoplantar keratoderma, Bothnia type	Leukemia: myeloid, lymphoid, or mixed-lineage
Melanoma	Allgrove syndrome
Rickets, vitamin D-resistant	Diabetes insipidus, nephrogenic, dominant and recessive
Anti-Mullerian hormone receptor, type II	Human papillomavirus type 18 integration site
Persistent Mullerian duct syndrome, type II	Epidermolytic hyperkeratosis
Activating transcription factor I	Keratoderma, palmoplantar, nonepidermolytic
Soft tissue clear cell sarcoma	Cyclic ichthyosis with epidermolytic hyperkeratosis
Myopathy, congenital	White sponge nevus
Meesmann corneal dystrophy	Pachyonychia congenita
Epidermolysis bullosa simplex	Fundus albipunctatus
Cataract, polymorphic and lamellar	Glioma
Sarcoma amplified sequence	Myxoid liposarcoma
Enuresis, nocturnal	Stickler syndrome, type I
Achondrogenesis-hypochondrogenesis, type II	SED congenita
Osteoarthrosis, precocious	Kniest dysplasia
Wagner syndrome, type II	Glycogen storage disease
SMED, Strudwick type	Rickets, pseudovitamin D deficiency
Scapuloperoneal syndrome	Interferon, immune, deficiency
Sanfilippo syndrome, type D	Cornea plana congenital, recessive
Lipoma	Growth retardation with deafness and mental retardation
Salivary adenoma	Spinal muscular atrophy, congenital nonprogressive
Uterine leiomyoma	Cardiomyopathy, hypertrophic
Myopia, high grade, autosomal dominant	Brachydactyly, type C
Darier disease	Noonan syndrome
Spinocerebellar ataxia	Cardiofaciocutaneous syndrome
Mevalonic aciduria	Tyrosinemia, type III
Hyperimmunoglobulinemia D and periodic fever	Lymphoma, B-cell non-Hodgkin, high-grade
Spinal muscular atrophy	Holt-Oram syndrome
Phenylketonuria	Alcohol intolerance, acute
Ulnar-mammary syndrome	Tumor rejection antigen
Diabetes mellitus	Human immunodeficiency virus-1 expression
Maturity-onset diabetes of the young	Amyloidosis, renal
Oral cancer	

The Human Genome Project found that chromosome 12 contains genes that are linked with the variety of body functions, diseases, and behaviors shown in this figure. This is just a partial list of all the gene functions found for this chromosome.

SOURCE: U.S. Department of Energy, Genome Programs (2003). http://genomics.energy.gov

FIGURE 3.2   Human chromosomes

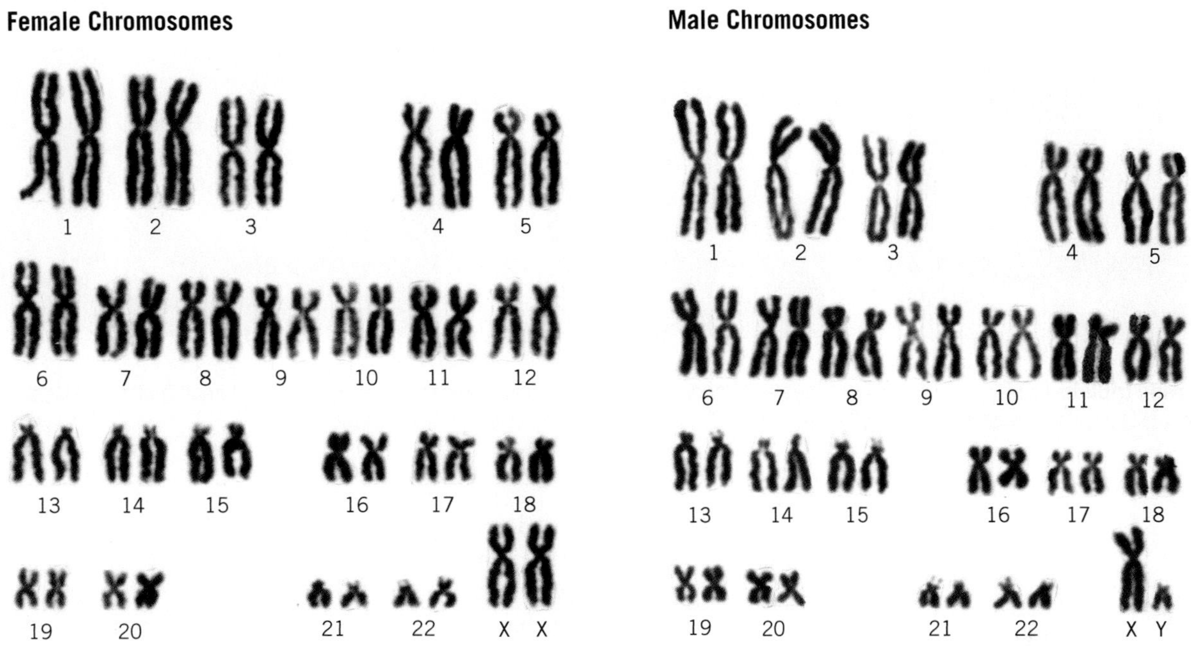

Female Chromosomes

Male Chromosomes

This image shows a full set of 23 pairs of chromosomes for a female and for a male. Note the difference between the 23rd chromosome pairs. XX is a genetic female, and XY is a genetic male.

an X chromosome from both parents is a female. One with an X chromosome from the mother and a Y chromosome from the father is a male.

Sometimes fertilization results in the conception of more than one child. About 3.3% of pregnancies result in the birth of twins (Martin, Hamilton, & Osterman, 2012). Other multiples, such as triplets or higher-order births such as quadruplets, are considerably more rare, accounting for only 124 out of every 100,000 births (Martin, Hamilton, Osterman, Curtin, & Mathews, 2013).

The occurrence of twins has been important in the study of behavioral genetics, as we will see later in this chapter. Twins are conceived in two ways. In the first way, a mother's ovary releases two eggs during a menstrual cycle and each is fertilized by a different sperm. The resulting twins are referred to as dizygotic (DZ), because they develop from two (di-) fertilized eggs (zygotes). They are only as genetically similar to each other as any other pair of siblings, meaning they have about half their genes in common (see Figure 3.3), and thus they don't have an identical appearance. In fact, DZ or *fraternal twins* don't even have to be the same sex. Because each egg is fertilized by a different sperm, one can be carrying an X chromosome while the other is carrying a Y chromosome.

The second way twins develop occurs when a single egg is fertilized by a single sperm to form a zygote. The zygote begins replicating and producing additional cells, but early in this process, for reasons we don't really understand, the ball of cells splits into two (Gilbert, 2000). Each ball of cells continues to develop prenatally to become one of two *identical twins*, referred to as monozygotic (MZ) because they are the product of a single (mono) fertilized egg (zygote). Because monozygotic twins both have the same set of genetic material (including the information on chromosome pair 23), they are always the same sex and look much alike. This type of twinning occurs by chance, so the tendency to have MZ (identical) twins does not run in families.

Dizygotic (DZ) twins Twins formed when a woman produces two ova or eggs, which are fertilized by two sperm; genetically DZ twins are as similar as any siblings.

Monozygotic (MZ) twins Twins formed when a woman produces one egg that is fertilized by one sperm and the resulting ball of cells splits to form two individuals with the same genes.

T/F #3
The tendency to have identical twins runs in families. *False*

Twins and triplets. Identical twins are always the same gender, but fraternal twins can be the same gender or different. Triplets can be identical or fraternal, or a set of identical twins with a fraternal sibling. ■

It has always been a puzzle why identical twins can have small differences in their basic appearance or develop different genetically based disorders. Scientists had previously assumed the environment was responsible. However, recently researchers have discovered that even identical twins have small differences in the arrangement of their genes, and these differences may result in observable and sometimes significant differences (Bruder et al., 2008). In addition, as we discuss later, we now know that environmental influences affect the expression of genes. Even identical twins have different experiences, which may program their genes to function in different ways.

FIGURE 3.3   Genetic similarities between monozygotic and dizygotic twins

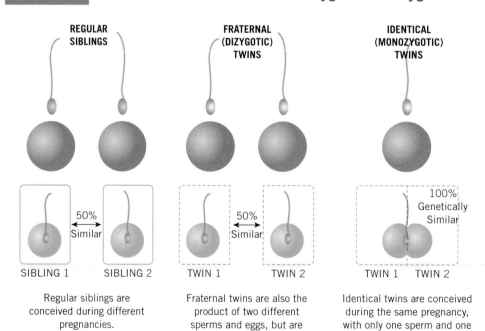

The difference in the degree of gene similarity of dizygotic and monozygotic twins as shown in this figure has been used by researchers to study the effects of genes on many human characteristics.

FIGURE 3.4   A human DNA molecule

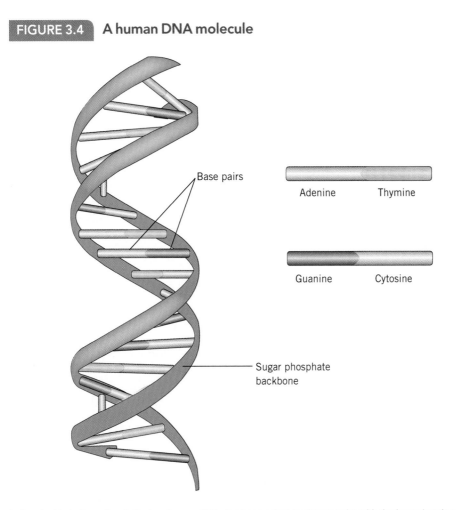

In the double helix molecule that makes up DNA, the base adenine always pairs with the base thymine, and the base guanine always pairs with the base cytosine. This "alphabet" of only four letters produces strings of bases that write the instructions for all the cells in our body.

SOURCE: U.S. National Library of Medicine (2011).

Chromosomes, Genes, DNA, and Bases (GATC)

Chromosomes are made up of genes, and genes are made up of DNA (*deoxyribonucleic acid*). DNA consists of two chains of nucleotides that twirl around each other in a *double helix* that looks much like a winding staircase with a banister, as illustrated in Figure 3.4. The chemical bases that make up the alphabet of genetic inheritance are guanine (G), adenine (A), thymine (T), and cytosine (C) (Alberts et al., 2002). One way to remember this is to think of the science fiction film called *Gattaca*, which is about a time in the future when all human beings are genetically manufactured (DeVito & Niccol, 1997). The name *Gattaca* will remind you of the four bases: G, A, T, and C. As you can see in Figure 3.4, each base is paired with another, adenine with thymine and cytosine with guanine, and this holds the double helix together.

A gene is made up of these bases as a sentence is made up of words. A sentence can contain all kinds of information and instructions. Likewise a gene contains information and instructions for the body to make a protein (Jorde et al., 2006). The trick to identifying a particular gene is to identify the combination of G, A, T, and C that gives the body directions to create a certain protein. To better understand this process, look at the following:

Gotothegrocerystorepickupmilkcomehome

One way to group these letters is:

Got oth egro

Ceryst orepick upm

ilk comeho me

We all know this is wrong and makes no sense. You would really divide this sequence of letters into three meaningful instructions:

Go to the grocery store.

Pick up milk.

Come home.

In a similar way scientists have taken sequences of bases such as ATCATCTTTGGTGTT and identified how to divide them into units that give clear instructions to produce proteins. This particular sequence is part of a gene called CFTR that is actually 250,000 base pairs long. The arrangement of many millions of combinations of these four bases governs how the basic proteins used by the body will be created, and these proteins are active in the development of both the form and function of our bodies.

All human beings share 99.5% of their genome; the remaining one-half of one percent is what contributes to our differences (Human Genome Research Institute, 2012). Changes that can occur in the structure of genes, called mutations, also differentiate among human beings. We can inherit mutations from our parents, but we each have approximately 175 new mutations that are unique to ourselves (Plomin, 2013). Most are inconsequential because they make no difference to our growth and development. In fact, evolution of the species depends on the occurrence of mutations that turn out to be adaptive and are therefore handed down from generation to generation (Wolters Kluwer Health, 2009). However, mutations have been linked to diseases such as cystic fibrosis and disorders such as autism and schizophrenia (Plomin, 2013). Some mutations consist of variations in a single nucleotide, referred to as a single nucleotide polymorphism, or SNP (Grigorenko & Dozier, 2013). Other mutations consist of large-scale changes in the order of nucleotides in a gene, called sequence variations: insertions of groups of nucleotides, deletions of groups of nucleotides, and variations in the number of copies of groups of nucleotides. These mutations can affect between one and thousands of nucleotides.

Let's return to our sentence analogy to illustrate the nature of these types of mutations. In each type of mutation described below, you can see that the initial instruction has been changed in some important way so the outcome will be quite different:

Single nucleotide polymorphism:

PICK UP MILK becomes PACK UP MILK

Change in the number of copies:

PICK UP MILK becomes PICK UPUPUPUPUPUP MILK

Mutations Changes that occur in the structure of a gene.

VIDEO LINK 3.2
Genetic Mutations

Insertion:

PICK UP MILK becomes PICK UP NO MILK

Deletion:

PICK UP MILK becomes PICK MILK

With this very basic understanding of how genes operate within the cell, we now discuss how genes are translated into our physical appearance and our behaviors.

Mendelian Inheritance: Dominant and Recessive Genes

You may have been told that you look very much like your father or exactly like your mother. How can this be, when you received an equal number of chromosomes from each parent?

When eggs and sperm cells are formed, the chromosomes in each "unzip" along the double helix so they each contain half the genetic material usually found in a cell. When egg and sperm combine at conception, chromosomes from each parent pair up and the genes from one parent are zipped up to similar genes from the other parent. Traditional Mendelian genetics tells us that each pair of genes is made up of some combination of dominant and recessive genes and the genes that are present are called the genotype. The information contained in the dominant genes is what is usually expressed in the person's body. What we see when we look at a person's bodily traits and characteristics is called the phenotype. The information from a recessive gene is usually not expressed in the phenotype unless the gene is paired with another recessive gene. To use a simple example, brown eye color is dominant over blue eye color. If your mother has brown eyes because she has two genes for brown eyes in her genotype, and your father has blue eyes because he *must* have two recessive genes for blue eyes, you will have brown eyes because you have received at least one dominant gene for brown eyes in your genotype. Your mother can pass along only the dominant brown-eye genes to her children (because that is the only genetic information she has for this trait), and your father can pass on only recessive genetic information for blue eyes (because that is all he has for this trait). The only possible genetic combination you can inherit is one dominant gene for brown eyes and one recessive gene for blue eyes. Therefore, brown eyes will be expressed as the phenotype of all the children in your family. However, you will still carry in your genotype the one recessive gene for blue eyes you received from your father. And if you have a child with someone who has brown eyes but who also carries one recessive gene for blue eyes, you will have a blue-eyed child if those two recessive genes are paired in the child. See Figure 3.5 to better understand how this might happen.

Although eye color is frequently used to illustrate the idea of dominant and recessive genes, you may have already realized that it isn't that simple. People also have green eyes, gray eyes, and hazel eyes. Although brown as an eye color is dominant over any of these alternatives, green, gray, and hazel eyes have their own dominance hierarchies. Also, the color of some people's eyes is bright and clear, and the color of other people's eyes is soft and washed out. You may even know someone who has one blue eye and one brown eye. But while the genetic process is more complicated than our example

Gene dominance. Do you look as similar to one of your parents as this girl does to her mother? Inheritance of dominant genes from one parent or the other can result in striking resemblances. ■

Dominant genes Genes that are usually expressed in the phenotype.

Recessive genes Genes that are generally not expressed in the phenotype unless paired with another recessive gene.

Genotype All the genes that make up a human being, or the specific genes at a particular location on a chromosome.

T/F #4
Two parents with brown eyes can still have a child with blue eyes. *True*

Phenotype A person's bodily traits and characteristics.

FIGURE 3.5   Genetic transmission of eye color (dominant and recessive genes)

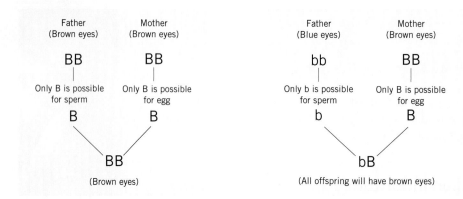

Both parents have only dominant genes for brown eyes, so that is the only genetic information they can pass to their children. All their children will have brown eyes.

The father only has recessive genes for blue eyes, so that is all he can pass along to his child. The mother only has dominant genes for brown eyes, so that is all she can pass along. Each child will have one gene for blue eyes and one gene for brown eyes, so all the children will have brown eyes.

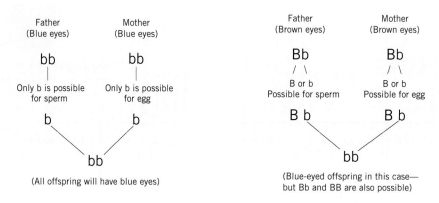

Both parents only have recessive genes for blue eyes. They both have blue eyes and can only pass genes for blue eyes to their children, so all their children will have blue eyes.

Each parent has both a dominant gene for brown eyes and a recessive gene for blue eyes (so both have brown eyes). However, if each passes along a recessive gene for blue eyes, the child will have blue eyes, but if either parent passes along a gene for brown eyes, the child will have brown eyes.

indicates, understanding the way dominant and recessive genes work is still central to understanding genetic inheritance.

Whether you have blue eyes or brown eyes is not crucial to your future development. Other types of gene pairings are, however, because some genetic disorders are caused by two recessive genes pairing up with each other. One such disease is *sickle-cell anemia*, found in 1 of every 500 African Americans. Sickle-cell anemia is a painful and destructive disease in which the shape of red blood cells is distorted. Normal red blood cells are smooth and round, but sickle cells look like the letter C (National Heart, Lung and Blood Institute [NHLBI], 2007). Normal red blood cells also have a large surface area, which enables them to transport oxygen throughout the body, but sickle cells are not able to do this effectively. They are hard and tend to clump together, restricting the flow of blood into smaller blood vessels, as shown in Figure 3.6. This failure to transport oxygen where it is needed results in pain and can eventually cause damage to the organs (NHLBI, 2007).

You may wonder why such maladaptive genes have not disappeared from the human gene pool, but there is a good evolutionary reason. It turns out that, although having two such recessive genes is harmful, having *one* may be protective in certain environments. The recessive gene for sickle-cell anemia, carried in the genotype of about 1 in 10 African Americans, appears to protect them from malaria (Wolters Kluwer Health, 2009). The first hint that this might be true came from the observation that the areas in Africa in which this gene is found in the population are almost identical to the areas in which malaria is a major problem. With its protective advantages, individuals with the recessive gene are more likely to survive to pass it on to the next generation (Ringelhann, Hathorn, Jilly, Grant, & Parniczky, 1976). However, if two people who carry the recessive gene have children, there is a 1-in-4 chance their children will inherit two recessive genes and suffer from sickle-cell anemia. For a better idea about how disorders can result from recessive genes, try to answer the questions in **Active Learning: Understanding the Inheritance of Tay-Sachs Disease.**

Transmission of eye color. This father must carry the recessive gene for blue eyes in his genotype. When his daughter received one recessive gene from her father and another recessive gene for blue eyes from her mother, she ended up with blue eyes. ■

T/F #5

Carrying one recessive gene for sickle-cell anemia can be beneficial for an individual. *True*

FIGURE 3.6 **Sickle-cell anemia**

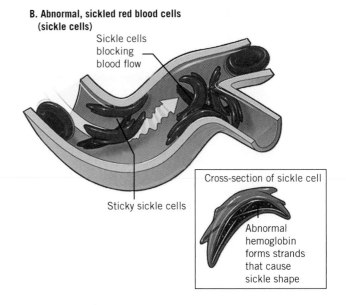

Normal red blood cells move freely through the blood vessels (A). Sickle-shaped red blood cells stick together and block the normal flow of blood, depriving the organs of needed oxygen (B).

SOURCE: National Heart, Lung and Blood Institute (2007).

Active Learning

Understanding the Inheritance of Tay-Sachs Disease

Tay-Sachs is a genetic disease that results in progressive neurological deterioration and death, usually by age 5. The highest incidence occurs among Ashkenazi Jews, whose ancestors came from Eastern Europe (Wolters Kluwer Health, 2009), and elevated levels are also found in French Canadians living in Quebec (Hechtman et al., 1990). A recessive gene is responsible for Tay-Sachs, and a simple blood test can locate it. Answer the questions below to enhance your understanding of how a recessive gene works:

1. A woman decides to be tested for the Tay-Sachs gene and finds she is a "carrier" of Tay-Sachs, meaning she has the gene for the disease. If she is a carrier, does she have to worry that she will develop Tay-Sachs herself? What, if anything, does she have to worry about?

2. Can you establish the likelihood that any child she has will inherit Tay-Sachs disease, or do you need other information to do this?

3. The woman's husband decides to be tested and finds he does *not* carry the Tay-Sachs gene. What is the likelihood this couple will have a child with the disease?

4. If the husband *is* a carrier, what is the likelihood that a child of theirs will have Tay-Sachs?

4. Look at the chart below (referred to as a Punnett square), which shows the possible pairings of a mother's and a father's genes, to see what the likelihood is of a child having Tay-Sachs disease when both parents are carriers:

Father	Mother	
	Tay-Sachs (ts) gene (recessive)	Normal (N) gene (dominant)
Tay-Sachs (ts) gene (recessive)	ts/ts*	ts/N
Normal (N) gene (dominant)	N/ts	N/N

* This is the only combination that will result in the child having Tay-Sachs because both parents are contributing a recessive gene for the disease. Therefore, each time this couple conceives a child, there will be a 1-in-4 (or 25%) chance the child will have the disease.

Answers:

1. The woman will not develop the disease herself. Because the gene is recessive, the dominant partner in this gene pair will determine the outcome for the person carrying it. In this case, she "carries" the gene but does not experience its effects.

2. We cannot know how likely it is that a child will inherit a recessive gene disorder unless we know the genotype of both the mother and the father. If the father also is a carrier, he could pass a recessive gene for the condition on to his children. A baby must inherit the recessive Tay-Sachs gene from both the mother and the father to develop the disease.

3. If the husband is not a carrier, there is no chance the child will have Tay-Sachs because the baby must have two Tay-Sachs genes, one from the mother and one from the father. Any children from this couple will inherit one dominant gene from the father that will protect them from having this condition.

As we've shown, a single gene pair can be responsible for deadly disorders. At least in animals, a single gene pair also can be linked with behaviors that appear quite complex. For example, in a small animal called a vole, one particular gene for producing the hormone vasopressin governs whether the animal is monogamous. While the prairie vole chooses a partner for life, the meadow vole, whose gene is slightly different, mates with whoever is available. Scientists discovered that the gene that produces the hormone vasopressin differs in these two types of voles. When they switched that gene between the two types, the monogamous prairie vole became a wanderer and the wandering meadow vole immediately began to direct his mating energies toward one female only and gave up his wandering ways (Lim et al., 2004). It is unlikely we will find a single gene that governs such complex behavior in human beings. However, research in Sweden found that men with a certain form of the vaso-

Pair-bonding. This type of vole mates for life. Researchers have found that a single gene can make the difference between a vole who is monogamous and one who isn't. ■

pressin gene are more likely than other men to have trouble with long-term, committed relationships (Walum et al., 2008). Clearly, human genes interact with cultural expectations to shape practices such as monogamy. However, it is interesting to begin uncovering in the animal world the role of some genes similar to those found in humans.

One Behavior, Many Genes; One Gene, Many Effects

Certain disorders, such as PKU and Tay-Sachs, are created by a single recessive gene pair. However, most human behaviors are unlikely to be the result of only one gene. Polygenic inheritance means many different genes may interact to promote any particular trait or behavior (McGuffin, Riley, & Plomin, 2001). In addition, they may interact with our environmental experiences in ways we describe later in this chapter. Therefore, the occurrence of any trait or ability is likely to be multifactorial; that is, it depends on many factors, including a number of genes interacting with one another and with various aspects of the environment. In addition, any one gene may influence a variety of outcomes. This is referred to as pleiotropic effects. For example, one gene might be implicated in aggression but might also be active in regulating heart rate (Rowe, 2003).

A specific type of pleiotropic effect occurs when some genes or combinations of genes seem to have a general effect on many related abilities. These have been labeled generalist genes (Kovas & Plomin, 2007). For example, genetic analyses have shown that the same genes that influence abilities in reading also influence abilities in language and math (Haworth et al., 2009). Researchers believe they will find a set of many genes, each having a small effect, that together exert a general effect on a range of cognitive abilities (Trzaskowski, Shakeshaft, & Plomin, 2013). For example, instead of looking for one gene that determines mathematical ability, scientists now look for groups of many genes, each contributing a small amount to mathematical and other learning abilities. The more of these genes that are active, the greater the person's learning ability (Kovas & Plomin, 2007). Therefore, although scientists have identified the functions of some individual genes, we must be careful not to oversimplify the findings that emerge as research continues.

Polygenic inheritance Numerous genes may interact to promote any particular trait or behavior.

Pleiotropic effects The many different influences any single gene may have.

T/F #6
Every gene in your body has one specific function. *False*

Generalist genes Genes that affect many related abilities.

1. What are chromosomes?
2. How do monozygotic twins and dizygotic twins occur?
3. What is polygenic inheritance?
4. What are pleiotropic effects?

3.3

How do genetic disorders develop, and what role do genetic testing and counseling play in identifying, preventing, and treating these disorders?

Genetic Disorders

We have discussed some of the outcomes in human functioning in which genes play a role. Now we focus on situations in which genes contribute to disorders that interfere with the healthy functioning of the human mind and body. We describe three types of genetic disorders: single-gene disorders, chromosomal disorders, and multifactorial inheritance disorders (Wolters Kluwer Health, 2009).

Single-Gene Disorders

Single gene disorders Genetic disorders caused by a single recessive gene or mutation.

Some genetically based disorders result from a single gene. In **Active Learning: Understanding the Inheritance of Tay-Sachs Disease**, you saw that Tay-Sachs is one of them. Others are phenylketonuria (PKU) and cystic fibrosis. Phenylketonuria is a condition in which the child cannot digest a common protein in the human diet. This condition can result in intellectual disability (de Groot, Hoeksma, Blau, Reijngoud, & van Spronsen, 2010). In cystic fibrosis the child's body produces a thick, sticky mucus that clogs the lungs, making the child vulnerable to pulmonary infections. It is also associated with nutritional deficiencies (Ratjen & Döring, 2003).

Single-gene disorders can occur in two ways: (1) An individual inherits a pair of recessive genes that carry the instructions for that disorder, or (2) mutations occur as cells divide so that some of the bases that give the instructions to create proteins are out of order or missing. In the case of cystic fibrosis, the genetic cause of the disorder is a missing sequence (or what we had called a "deletion" earlier in this chapter) in a specific gene called the CFTR gene. The normal sequence is ATCATCTTTGGTGTT, but some children inherit a version of this gene in which the three bases that are highlighted here are missing. As a result, a critical part of the protein the gene creates is also missing (Human Genome Project Information, 2003).

Many genetic disorders are based on recessive genes, but most of the time the recessive gene is paired with a dominant gene that does not carry this disorder so the information in the dominant gene protects the individual from developing the disorder. One student put this succinctly: "If one gene is screwed up, you have a backup." As long as the dominant gene is doing its job, the dysfunctional gene will likely not be noticed. However, in one situation a single recessive gene will be expressed because there is no second gene to create a pair. As you can see in the photo on this page, the Y chromosome is much smaller than the X chromosome and contains only 70 to 200 genes, the fewest of all the chromosomes. By comparison, the X chromosome contains 900 to 1400 genes

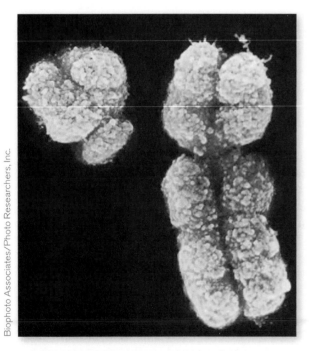

Biophoto Associates/Photo Researchers, Inc.

X and Y chromosomes. Do you see the potential problem when the X chromosome and the Y chromosome pair up? Large portions of the X chromosome (the one on the right) do not have a partner on the Y chromosome (the one on the left), and therefore any recessive gene on the X chromosome without a partner will appear in the male's phenotype. If the recessive gene is the source of a genetic problem, the man is vulnerable to it. ■

(U.S. National Library of Medicine, 2010a; 2010b). In addition, only some of the genes on the Y chromosome are active. Thus when an X chromosome pairs with a Y chromosome to create a boy, some of the X chromosome's active genes will not find a partner on the Y chromosome. These genes will be expressed whether they are normally recessive or dominant. The outcome is increased vulnerability in boys to the effects of recessive genes on the X chromosome that cause such problems as red-green color blindness, hemophilia, and Duchenne muscular dystrophy (Jorde et al., 2006).

Chromosomal Disorders

Genetic disorders can also occur at the level of the chromosome. Chromosomal disorders occur when one of the 23 pairs of chromosomes contains a number of chromosomes other than two. For example, Figure 3.7 shows the chromosomal configuration of an individual with Down syndrome. In the 21st position, there are three chromosomes rather than two. In another condition, Turner's syndrome, there is only a single chromosome in the 23rd position in a female. The second way a chromosomal disorder occurs is when there is a change in the structure of the chromosome caused by breakage (National Human Genome Research Institute, 2011a). When sections of chromosomes break apart, they may not come back together in their original form. Some sections may be backward or may even link to a different chromosome. Both these types of abnormality may occur by chance, but the second type also can be passed along to a child by a parent who has this type of chromosomal pattern. Table 3.1 describes a number of conditions caused by chromosomal abnormalities.

As with all disorders, there is a range of effects resulting from chromosomal disorders. For instance, children with Down syndrome have intellectual impairment, but some are profoundly impaired while others are better able to lead productive lives. It is impossible to tell at birth what level a child will reach. Therefore, it is important that these infants and their parents receive early intervention to help them achieve as much as they can.

Multifactorial Inheritance Disorders

Multifactorial inheritance disorders result from the interaction of many genes that also interact with environmental influences. Many disorders, including depression, alcoholism, schizophrenia, and autism, appear to have some genetic input. However, it is likely they result from the interaction of many genes that also interact with environmental influences. There are currently no genetic tests for these types of multifactorial problems (National Human Genome Research Institute, 2011b), but individuals can take preventative steps when they know from their family history that they are at higher risk of developing a disorder. For example, an individual with high levels of alcoholism in the family may choose to avoid alcohol. Someone whose family has a high level of depression may learn to identify those symptoms early to get appropriate treatment if needed.

Genetic Counseling and Testing

Our increasing ability to identify specific genes has led to the creation of commercial genetic tests that promise to help you assess your genetic risk of developing certain diseases or conditions. You can purchase a testing kit online, provide the company with a saliva sample or swab from the inside of your cheek, and receive in turn a report that outlines your individual genetic risks (often expressed as "high," "low," or "average" for a variety of possible disorders or characteristics), as well as some strategies that can help reduce the risk (Harvard Medical School, 2010).

T/F #7
Males are more likely to have a genetic disorder than females. *True*

AUDIO LINK 3.1
Genetics and Autism

Chromosomal disorders Disorders that result when too many or too few chromosomes are formed or when there is a change in the structure of the chromosome caused by breakage.

© Richard Bailey/Corbis

Down syndrome. This girl has facial features that are typically associated with Down syndrome, including small upturned eyes, small ears, and a flat facial profile. ■

Multifactorial inheritance disorders Disorders that result from the interaction of many genes in interaction with environmental influences.

FIGURE 3.7   Chromosomes for Down syndrome

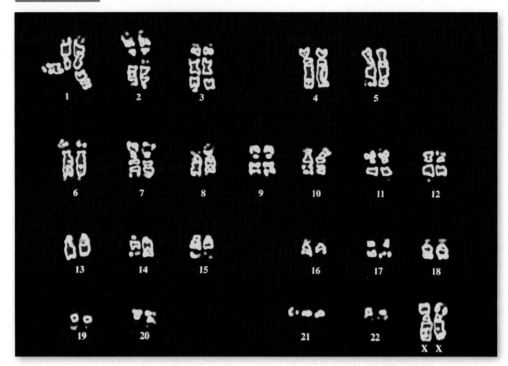

Compare these chromosomes from someone with Down syndrome with those in Figure 3.2. Did you notice the extra copy of the 21st chromosome? This is referred to as trisomy because there are 3 chromosomes instead of 2.

TABLE 3.1   Chromosomal abnormalities

Disorder	Chromosomal description	Symptom description	Treatments
Down syndrome	One extra chromosome 21	Intellectual disability; typical facial features; poor muscle tone; possible problems with heart, digestion, and hearing	Physical, occupational, speech, and educational therapy; medical intervention as needed
Klinefelter syndrome	An extra X chromosome in men (XXY in the 23rd position)	Infertility; small genitals; enlarged breasts; reduced facial, armpit, and pubic hair; possible autoimmune disorders	Testosterone therapy, medical intervention as needed
Turner syndrome	A missing X chromosome in women (XO in the 23rd position)	Short stature, webbing of the neck, lack of development of ovaries resulting in lack of sexual maturation at puberty	Estrogen replacement therapy, growth hormone administration is possible
Fragile X syndrome	One gene segment (CGG) on the X chromosome in the 23rd pair is repeated 200 times rather than 5 to 40 times	Intellectual disability and learning disabilities; distractibility and impulsivity; twice as likely in males, who have typical facial features and possible autism	Early intervention, special education, treatment for ADHD

SOURCE: Merck Manual Home Health Handbook (2013).

As simple and appealing as this process may appear to be, there is good reason to be cautious before deciding to spend money on it. First, the Food and Drug Administration (FDA) has questioned the value of such tests in making health decisions. The tests themselves are also relatively expensive, ranging from a couple of hundred dollars to several thousands of dollars, but most important, their results are based on incomplete information (Harvard Medical School, 2010). As you already know, genetic factors are only one part of the equation in assessing your risk of developing a genetically based condition. Your lifestyle and environmental factors also play an important role that commercial tests do not take into account.

Before making a final decision, you should be aware of the fact that you cannot be denied employment or health insurance based on genetic information (except in companies with fewer than 15 employees), but this protection does not extend to life, disability, or long-term care insurance (Harvard Medical School, 2010). For this reason you want to be sure that, if you purchase a test, your information will be securely stored and protected. There are also other low- or no-cost ways to assess your risk of developing a genetic disease. **Active Learning: Assessing Genetic Risk** gives you several sources you can use to do this.

Active Learning

Assessing Genetic Risk

You can begin assessing your own risk by collecting information about genetic conditions that have affected your blood relatives. These include cancer, diabetes, heart disease, high blood pressure, stroke, and alcoholism (National Society of Genetic Counselors, n.d.). Also record the age at which the condition appeared in each of your relatives. The likelihood of developing these conditions increases with age, so you will need to periodically update your information. Because health issues are a sensitive subject and some family members may be reluctant to share information, be careful about how you approach this topic with them.

A number of well-established risk calculators are available at no cost on the Internet. You can use a search engine to find the Framingham Risk Assessment Tool available through the National Institutes of Health to assess your risk of developing heart disease or suffering a heart attack, or you can use My Health Advisor from the American Diabetes Association to help you assess your risk of developing diabetes. If you do use an Internet assessment tool, however, be sure the source is a legitimate health authority and not just a company trying to sell you a product or service. ■

People become particularly concerned about genetics when they are about to start a family. In each pregnancy, any couple statistically has a 3% chance of having a child with a genetically based disorder (Centers for Disease Control and Prevention [CDC], 2008a). Based on these low odds, there is usually no reason for genetic counseling. However, in some cases individual risk is higher, and individuals may want to seek out a genetic counselor to help them assess the type and amount of risk. See Table 3.2 for additional information about couples who are at increased risk of conceiving a child with a genetic disorder or birth defect and who might consider having genetic counseling.

Genetic counseling and testing can occur before or during a pregnancy. Counselors ask about the couple's own medical histories and their families' history of diseases and genetic disorders and may recommend certain tests. Blood tests can identify the presence of single recessive genes that are more common in certain populations, such as those for Tay-Sachs disease (Ashkenazi Jews), sickle-cell anemia (African Americans

VIDEO LINK 3.3
Genetic Counseling

TABLE 3.2   Who should receive genetic counseling?

The March of Dimes organization (2014a) recommends that the following individuals consult with a genetic counselor:

- Those who have, or are concerned that they might have, an inherited disorder or birth defect.
- Women who are pregnant or planning to be after age 35.
- Couples who already have a child with intellectual disability, an inherited disorder, or a birth defect.
- Couples whose infant has a genetic disease diagnosed by routine newborn screening.
- Women who have had babies who died in infancy or three or more miscarriages.
- People concerned that their jobs, lifestyles, or medical history may pose a risk to outcome of pregnancy. Common causes of concern include exposure to radiation, medications, illegal drugs, chemicals, or infections.
- Couples who would like testing or more information about genetic conditions that occur frequently in their ethnic group.
- Couples who are first cousins or other close blood relatives.
- Pregnant women whose ultrasound examinations or blood testing indicate that their pregnancy may be at increased risk for certain complications or birth defects.

SOURCE: March of Dimes (2014a). Used with permission.

or Africans), and thalassemia, a blood disorder associated with reduced production of hemoglobin (Southeast Asians, Taiwanese, Chinese, Filipinos, Italians, Greeks, or Middle Easterners) (American Medical Association, 2008). As we saw in **Active Learning: Understanding the Inheritance of Tay-Sachs Disease,** couples should be concerned about these possible disorders only if both partners carry the recessive gene for the condition.

During pregnancy, several tests can identify some possible genetic abnormalities in the developing fetus. Tests of the mother's blood, such as the *alpha-fetoprotein test*, can uncover abnormalities in hormone levels that signal the possibility of spina bifida, which is a defect in the neural tube, the structure from which the brain and spinal cord develop, or Down syndrome (Larson, 2002). Amniocentesis and chorionic villus sampling can be carried out to identify chromosomal disorders as well as some single-gene disorders, such as sickle-cell anemia. However, these tests do not look for other genetic and nongenetic factors that can cause birth defects, and most women will not have these tests.

Amniocentesis A test to look for genetic abnormalities prenatally, in which a physician uses a long, thin needle to extract amniotic fluid, which is then tested.

Chorionic villus sampling (CVS) A test to look for genetic abnormalities prenatally, in which a small tube is inserted either through the vagina and cervix or through a needle inserted in the abdomen, and a sample of cells from the chorion is retrieved for testing.

As shown in Figure 3.8, in amniocentesis, a long, thin needle is inserted through the mother's abdomen and into the amniotic sac, which surrounds the fetus. Cells from the skin surface of the developing embryo are routinely shed into the amniotic fluid that surrounds the embryo. When fluid from the sac is withdrawn, it contains fetal cells that can be analyzed for genetic abnormalities. In chorionic villus sampling or CVS, cells are obtained from microscopic projections called villi found on the outside layer of the embryonic sac, called the chorion. These cells can be obtained either through the abdomen or through the vagina and cervix, and the sample is then analyzed (Jorde et al., 2006). Because all the structures that support the pregnancy (including the placenta, the amniotic sac, and the chorion) are the result of the conception, the cells they contain have the same genetic makeup as the embryo, and that is why they can be tested for genetic problems. CVS is performed at 10 to 11 weeks of gestation, while amniocentesis cannot be performed until 15 to 17 weeks. The risk of miscarriage resulting from the procedure itself is slightly higher for CVS than for amniocentesis, but the parents receive information about any possible genetic problems earlier in the pregnancy (Jorde et al., 2006).

Ethical Considerations in Genetic Testing

Questions about privacy and the use of genetic screening results raise many ethical questions for genetic research, particularly when children are the subjects (National Human Genome Research Institute, 2011b). For example, the American Academy of Pediatrics (AAP) raises several objections to the suggestion that more extensive prenatal genetic screening be offered to all pregnant women (Beaudet, 2013). One is the likelihood of false positive results (that is, results indicating a problem where none exists), which can cause parents much anxiety and could force them to make reproductive decisions with enormous impact on their families. A second issue is preserving the privacy of the results of such tests. There is great concern that employers, insurers, and others might gain access to these records and use them to discriminate against individuals with genetic disorders by denying them insurance or employment.

The Institute of Medicine has recommended that all prenatal genetic tests meet the following guidelines: "(1) identification of the genetic condition must provide a clear benefit to the child; (2) a system must be in place to confirm the diagnosis; and (3) treatment and follow-up must be available for affected newborns" (American Academy of Pediatrics [AAP] Committee on Bioethics, 2001). In addition, the American Academy of Pediatrics recommends that testing for conditions that develop in adulthood should not be carried out until a child is at an age to make his or her own informed decision about having the test, especially when earlier knowledge of the condition has not led to a better outcome through early interventions.

Parents and others considering genetic testing must be educated about the risks, including stigmatization, discrimination, and psychological harm, before making their decision (AAP Committee on Bioethics, 2001). There is much to be gained from genetic research and testing, but we should proceed carefully in order to avoid harm, especially to children.

Treatment of Genetic Disorders

Given the toll that genetic disorders take on individuals, we continue to search for ways to treat these conditions. One approach is to attempt to correct the genetic defects themselves, but this is difficult to do with the state of our current knowledge. A different approach is to alter the environment in ways to reduce or eliminate the damaging effect of the genetic disorders.

Although gene therapy, the treatment of genetic disorders through the implantation or disabling of specific genes, is still in its infancy for humans, scientists are working on several ways to use our new knowledge about genes to prevent and treat human disorders. We've all experienced the unpleasant effects when a virus infects our cells, but researchers are using viruses that have been genetically altered to "infect" cells with healthy genes to replace disordered ones (U.S. Department of Energy Genome Programs, 2012). They have also been able to localize and then disable certain problematic genes. For example, researchers at Leiden University Medical Center in the Netherlands were recently able to block the action of a gene implicated in the development of Duchenne muscular dystrophy (Grady, 2007) and a nationwide clinical trial is currently underway

FIGURE 3.8   Genetic testing

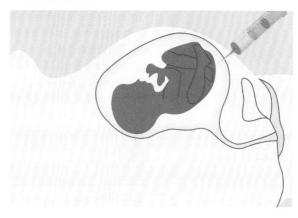

During amniocentesis (shown here), a physician uses a sonogram to show a picture of the fetus in the amniotic sac and then uses a long, thin needle to extract about 4 teaspoons of amniotic fluid. Fetal cells floating in the fluid can be tested for genetic problems. In chorionic villus sampling, a small tube, or catheter, is inserted either through the vagina and cervix or through a needle inserted in the abdomen, and a sample of cells from the chorion (which has the same genetic makeup as the fetus) is retrieved for testing.

SOURCE: ©VEM/Photo Researchers, Inc.

AUDIO LINK 3.2
Ethics and Genetic Testing

JOURNAL ARTICLE 3.1
Mental Disorder Stigmatization

Gene therapy Treatment of genetic disorders through implanting or disabling specific genes.

in the United States (UC Davis Health System, 2013). The idea that we may intervene at the level of genes is intriguing. At present gene therapy is being conducted only on an experimental basis (National Cancer Institute Fact Sheet, 2006), but it is one of the exciting avenues of research in the field of behavioral genetics.

The effects of gene-based disorders can sometimes be controlled through environmental interventions. For example, we have long known that the effects of the genetic disorder phenylketonuria (PKU) can be prevented by removing phenylalanine from the diet of those newborns found to carry the recessive gene (Plomin, DeFries, Craig, & McGuffin, 2003b). A child who has PKU cannot produce an enzyme essential in the digestion of phenylalanine, a common protein in foods such as beef, poultry, fish, eggs, milk, and wheat products (de Baulny, Abadie, Feillet, & de Parscau, 2007). When phenylalanine is only partially digested because of the missing enzyme, harmful substances are produced that can damage the child's brain and central nervous system, resulting in intellectual disability (de Groot et al., 2010). It is not the gene itself that causes the problem, but rather the interaction of the gene with the newborn's intake of food containing phenylalanine. By eliminating phenylalanine from the diet of an infant through the use of a special formula, the harmful effects are eliminated (Wappner, Cho, Kronmal, Schuett, & Seashore, 1999).

Because the brain is growing so rapidly during the early years, it is particularly vulnerable to these damaging toxic effects, but the National Institute of Child Health and Human Development (2006) recommends that people with PKU maintain a low-phenylalanine diet throughout their lives to prevent the appearance of symptoms. That diet primarily includes fruits, vegetables, and low-protein grain products. In the future, perhaps we will be able to provide early intervention for babies with other identifiable genes that cause behavioral disorders.

Check Your Understanding

1. When do single-gene disorders occur?
2. What causes chromosomal disorders such as Down syndrome?
3. What is amniocentesis?
4. What are some risks of genetic testing?

Behavioral Genetics

3.4

How do we study the relationship between our genetic inheritance and our traits and behavior?

WEB LINK 3.2
Behavioral Genetics

With some understanding of how genes function, we now look at the question of how behavior is related to the genes we inherit. The scientific study of behavioral genetics began before we had knowledge of which specific genes might affect specific behaviors, and, in spite of the fact that scientists have identified the genes that make up the human genome, we are still a long way from knowing what most of our genes actually do and how our behaviors relate to gene functioning. Although molecular genetics, which focuses on identifiable individual genes, has become a major area of research in recent years, the more traditional approach of behavioral genetics continues to provide important information.

Behavioral genetics begins with the study of a particular behavior. Historically researchers have used several approaches to try to separate the relative influence of genes and environment on individual differences in that behavior. You might think that simply noting how similar children are to their parents could tell us how much of a particular behavior is genetic, but genetic influences and environmental setting are often intertwined in complex ways. For example, imagine walking into the home of a new friend and discovering this friend is a very talented pianist. You then find out both parents in this family perform with a local choir and the youngest child is a gifted violinist. What would you conclude about the source of this musical talent? Did the children in this family inherit genes for their musical ability, or did they learn about music from the experiences their parents provided for them? In this situation, there is no way to know which has happened. It's likely both genes and environment have had an influence, but scientifically it is impossible to sort out which factor had what effect. The effect of genes on complex behaviors such as musical ability and alcoholism is not that straightforward. A variety of factors, including the effects of a person's environment, may also play an important role.

In theory we might solve this problem by taking children from musical families and placing them in families that are not musical to see what happens. If musical ability is produced by genes, these children will still develop this talent. If it is produced by environmental influences, they will not necessarily be musical after growing up in a nonmusical family. Obviously it is unethical to do anything like this with human beings, so psychologists have had to look for natural situations that might provide the same information. Three types of studies have been carried out that take advantage of such natural situations: (1) studies of adopted children, (2) comparisons of identical (monozygotic, or MZ) and fraternal (dizygotic, or DZ) twins, and (3) studies of identical twins adopted in infancy and reared by different families.

The goal of this type of research is to establish the level of heritability, a measure of the extent to which genes determine a particular behavior or characteristic. However, heritability levels are specific to the population and environment that is studied. If a study in Sweden finds a high level of heritability for the trait of shyness, the only way to know whether this same characteristic is highly related to genes in Mexicans is to study a sample of Mexicans (Benson, 2004). However, for disorders such as schizophrenia, autism, and attention deficit hyperactivity disorder, heritability rates have been high across many populations (Wray & Visscher, 2008).

Studies of Adopted Children

Children who are adopted have birth parents from whom they inherit their genes and adoptive parents who provide the environment in which they grow up. To look at the relative contribution of genes and environment on whatever developmental outcome they are studying, researchers must have information about both the adoptive and the biological parents. They then look at the concordance rate, the degree to which a trait or an ability of one individual is similar to that of another. One example of this type of research has been carried out to determine the heritability of alcoholism. Cadoret, Troughton, and O'Gorman (1987) found that adoptees who had one or more birth parents and/or grandparents who had alcoholism were 4.6 times as likely as others to develop alcoholism themselves. By comparison, if the adoptive parents were alcoholic, the risk of the child developing alcoholism was raised 2.7 times. This indicates that both genes and environment played a role, but in this instance the stronger influence appeared to be genetic.

Studies Comparing Identical and Fraternal Twins

Another approach to measuring the relative influence of genes and environment has capitalized on the fact that there are two types of twins. As you'll remember, identical or monozygotic twins are more likely to share all or almost all their genes in common, while fraternal or dizygotic twins share only about half of their genes in common, just as any two siblings would. However, twins usually grow up together in the same family, so their environment is very similar. Therefore, differences and similarities between twins are more likely to be a result of their genetics than their environment. After all, they are born to the same parents in the same family at the same point in time.

T/F #8
At age 17, Mike is already a heavy drinker. Because both of his parents have struggled with alcoholism for a long time, genes must have determined that Mike would also become an alcoholic.
False

Concordance rate The degree to which a trait or an ability of one individual is similar to that of another; used to examine similarities between twins and among adopted children and their biological and adoptive parents.

JOURNAL ARTICLE 3.2
Twin Studies

Scientists have tried to identify behaviors or personality traits linked with genetic inheritance by looking at the concordance rate between twins on those behaviors or traits. If identical twins are more similar to each other (that is, they have a higher concordance rate) on a trait such as shyness than are fraternal twins, the researchers conclude that genes play a role in determining whether someone is shy. Using this type of study to look at the causes of alcoholism, Pagan et al. (2006) followed twins from adolescence through early adulthood. They found the age of initiating use of alcohol was no more similar between identical twins than between fraternal twins, but identical twins were more similar to each other regarding the amount they drank and who became problem drinkers in late adolescence and early adulthood. This study provides additional evidence that genes play a role in the development of problem drinking.

Studies of Identical Twins Reared Apart

The third type of research combines twin and adoption research by looking at identical and fraternal twins who were adopted into separate families and studying how similar they are to each other (Bouchard, Lykken, McGue, & Segal, 1990). This research has reached the conclusion that identical twins reared apart are about as similar to each other on some aspects of their personality, interests, and social attitudes as identical twins reared together, and more similar than fraternal twins reared together (Lehman, 2005). This appears to provide strong evidence for the powerful influence of genes on many characteristics.

VIDEO LINK 3.4
Separated at Birth

Despite widespread media reports that identical twins reared apart were eerily similar—marrying spouses with the same name, wearing identical clothes, giving their dog the same name—there has been much criticism of the way this research was done. Joseph (2001) makes the case that many of these "separated" twins actually knew each other. For instance, they may have been adopted by relatives who lived in the same area, and this could account for many of their similarities. Some children were not adopted at birth but were raised together for a number of years before they were separated. Finally, Joseph argues that these twins should be compared to pairs of unrelated strangers who are the same age, sex, race, and ethnicity and who have a similar level of attractiveness, because each of these characteristics is also likely to make people similar to each other. Only if the identical twins were truly separated at birth and really didn't know each other while they were growing up—but still turned out to be significantly more similar to each other than the strangers—would there be evidence for a strong genetic influence. **Active Learning: Twins Separated at Birth** will give you some sense of the role coincidence might play in similarities found between identical twins reared apart.

Twins Separated at Birth

The research on twins separated at birth has reported some striking similarities among reunited twins (Lykken, McGue, Tellegen, & Bouchard, 1992). The Minnesota Study of Twins Reared Apart reports a pair of reunited twins who were habitual gigglers, another pair who used the same brand of toothpaste and shaving lotion, and even one pair who had both been married to women named Linda whom they later divorced only to marry women named Betty. The challenge with this type of report is to distinguish characteristics and behaviors that have genetic or environmental underpinnings from those that are merely coincidences.

Would you be surprised to find out you were sitting in class next to someone who had your birthday? You should be, because that is not a very likely occurrence. However, even if your class has only 23 students in it, there is a 50-50 chance there is at least one shared birthday among your classmates (Mathematical Association of America, 1998). The likelihood of a shared birthday increases as the size of the group increases, so in a large class, you are almost certain to find some "birthday buddies" among your classmates.

The point is that the odds of finding a similarity between people who don't know each other are sometimes surprisingly high. Your professor may give you the opportunity to complete the following activity during one of your classes, but you can do it on your own outside class. Take a few minutes to talk to someone you don't know. Introduce yourself and tell each other a little about yourselves. In your conversation include some discussion about where you grew up and went to school, the number of brothers or sisters you have, what you like to do with your time, some personal preferences (such as your favorite brand of clothes, favorite foods, or favorite recording artists), how you would describe yourself (for example, outgoing, friendly, kind, or thoughtful), and finally describe some of the things you are good at (for example, sports, academics, or arts). Keep track of any similarities you discover. At any point, did you begin to wonder whether you were twins separated at birth? Probably not, but in all likelihood some interesting—if not eerie—consequences emerged from your conversation. Did you remember to ask the person you were talking to when his or her birthday is? ■

Recent Research Approaches

Until recently, research based on behavioral genetics has focused on establishing heritability and has not examined the specific effect of the environment. Newer studies, however, have included a focus on particular aspects of the environment and their impact on human behavior by expanding the methods used in earlier twin and adoption studies. For example, Dick and Rose (2004) not only studied twins but also included one close friend of each twin in the study. All the children had neighborhood, school, and community in common, but only the twins also shared some genes and their family setting. This approach allowed the researchers to conclude that the age at which these children began to smoke and drink was more strongly related to neighborhood, school, and community characteristics than it was to genes or family upbringing. In other words, the twins were no more similar to each other in these behaviors than they were to their friends.

Although behavioral genetics has shown that almost all behaviors studied have some genetic input (Dick & Rose, 2004), different traits and behaviors are more or less heritable. It is useful to discover which traits and behaviors are *highly* likely to develop from genetic input because this will aid the search for the specific genes responsible. On the other hand, we also want to know which aspects of the environment are influential in the development of behavior, so we can promote environments associated with positive outcomes.

In the next section we further explore the interaction of specific genes and environment. It may surprise you to learn that some genes are activated *only* by environmental experiences. As we find out more about these interactions, we may be able to intervene early to change the environments that switch on genes that support destructive behavior.

T/F #9
Genes have been found to play a role in the development of almost all behaviors that have been studied. *True*

Check Your Understanding

1. Why do genetics researchers study adopted children?
2. What does a concordance rate measure?
3. What may explain many of the striking similarities reported between identical twins separated at birth?

3.5

How do genes and the environment interact?

JOURNAL ARTICLE 3.3
Gene-Environment Interactions

The Interaction of Genes and Environment

We have now seen how genes work within our bodies at the molecular level, and we have looked at the ways in which scientists seek to discover which behaviors, traits, and abilities are linked to our genetic inheritance. As scientists have learned more about specific genes and how they function, it has become clear that gene influence on behavior is affected by the environment and the experiences that the individual with those genes has, especially early in life.

How the Environment Shapes Gene Expression

Our understanding of genetic inheritance has become much more complex since the time of Mendel. We now know that genes can act differently in a variety of circumstances. One of the major findings in recent research on genes is that the environment can influence gene expression. Two ways in which this happens are through *canalization* and *epigenesis*.

Canalization

Canalization The degree to which the expression of a gene is influenced by the environment.

There is considerable variability in how strongly genes affect different traits or characteristics. Although some characteristics seem relatively impervious to environmental factors, others are much more easily influenced. The degree to which the expression of a gene is influenced by the environment is captured in the concept of canalization proposed by Conrad Hal Waddington (1942). Imagine yourself looking down from the top of a steep hill. You see that water and weather have carved gullies (or canals) into the hillside. Some are deep and narrow, and others shallow and wide. If you begin rolling balls down the hillside, some will travel down the deep, narrow pathways and end up in about the same place every time, but others will travel down the shallow, wide pathways and may end up on one side or the other of the gully by the time they reach the bottom of the hill.

In a similar way, we can think of some traits as being deeply canalized. Genes for deeply canalized traits have a self-righting tendency that produces the expected developmental outcome under all but the most extreme environmental conditions (Black, Hess, & Berenson-Howard, 2000; Gottlieb, 1991). For example, across a wide spectrum of environmental conditions, almost all infants reach the early motor milestones, like sitting up and walking. In contrast, a trait such as intelligence is much more variable in its outcome. This genetic pathway is *less* constrained or less deeply canalized, so it is *more* influenced by the landscape of the child's environment. Children raised in the relatively enriched environment of middle- and upper-income status are likely to express the levels of intelligence provided by their genetic inheritance. However, genetic inheritance plays a smaller role for children raised in low-income families. The relative deprivation they experience limits their ability to express genes for high intelligence and restricts them to a narrower range of outcomes (Turkheimer, Haley, Waldron, D'Onofrio, & Gottesman, 2003). The concept of canalization thus gives us insight into the complex interaction between our genetic endowment and the influence of the environment.

Epigenetics

Epigenetics A system by which genes are activated or silenced in response to events or circumstances in the individual's environment.

T/F #10
The experiences you have in your life can change the structure of your genes. *False*

What determines the way individual genes are influenced by environmental experiences? One answer comes from epigenetics, which is the study of the chemical reactions that activate and deactivate parts of the genetic material of an organism, as well as the factors that influence these chemical reactions (Zhang & Meaney, 2010). While the structure of the genes remains the same, the way each gene is expressed may be very different depending on these chemical tags, which determine where and when genes should be "turned on" or expressed and the action of these tags can be influenced by experiences an individual has in the environment.

Epigenetics has demonstrated how early life experiences can literally get "under the skin" by activating or silencing certain genes (Szyf & Bick, 2013). One example of how epigenetics works has been demonstrated by Michael Meaney, a researcher at McGill University, who studied rat mothers and their offspring. He and his colleagues found that rat babies reared by mothers who ignored them and did not touch them were more fearful and stressed by environmental events later in their lives, shown both by the babies' behavior and by the levels of stress hormones they produced. The researchers were able to link the behavior with a particular gene that is active in babies reared by nurturing mothers but which had been "turned off" in the neglected babies.

To be sure this genetic effect was due to the mother's behavior and not to her genes, the researchers switched babies between nurturing and non-nurturing mothers, and the results were the same. In those babies reared by non-nurturing mothers, it was again found that the gene was turned off by these early experiences even though their biological mothers were very nurturing (Diorio & Meaney, 2007). In an evolutionary sense, it appears that baby rats that do not experience adequate mothering "reprogram" their genes. The structure of the gene remains the same, but the way it functions is changed. The result of this reprogramming is that the babies respond more quickly to stress. The evolutionary advantage of their increased responsiveness is the ability to respond more quickly when facing danger rather than waiting for unresponsive mothers to protect them.

Although there are obviously large differences between rats and humans, biologically there also are some similarities. Research has shown that when human mothers are highly unresponsive to their infants, the babies respond to stressful situations with higher levels of stress hormones, just like the baby rats whose mothers ignored them (Gunnar & Cheatham, 2003; Gunnar & Quevedo, 2007). Increased levels of stress hormones have also been found in children who suffered severe neglect in orphanages during their first 8 months of life, even when they were subsequently adopted into well-functioning families (Gunnar & Cheatham, 2003). Research on this topic has also focused on the molecular level. Essex et al. (2013) found that teens whose parents reported high levels of stress when these teens were infants had different patterns of activation of genes by those chemical tags than those whose parents had not been stressed. The next step for scientists is to link these different patterns with the behaviors associated with early deprivation.

Another example of the impact of epigenetics is research on the development of high levels of aggression. Researchers have found that humans have one of two versions of a gene on the X chromosome that determines how much of an enzyme called MAO-A (monoamine oxidase-A) is produced in their bodies. There is some evidence that individuals with less MAO-A tend to be more aggressive. You might think this is evidence that some forms of aggression are genetically determined, and you would be partially right. However, in a longitudinal study in New Zealand, not all boys with the version of the gene that produces lower levels of MAO-A turned out to be aggressive. Only boys were studied because it is more complicated to study girls, who have *two* X chromosomes. Boys with this version of the gene who *also* experienced abuse during their childhood were much more likely to become aggressive adults. The environmental trigger of abuse early in life "turned on" the negative effects of the lower level of MAO-A (Caspi et al., 2002). Those boys with the other version of the gene were much less likely to become aggressive, whether they experienced child abuse or not.

See Table 3.3 for a visual representation of the relationship between genetic inheritance and environmental experiences in producing higher levels of aggression. This finding has been confirmed in several subsequent studies (Kim-Cohen et al., 2006; Reif et al., 2007), and similar results have been found for different genes relating to depression and posttraumatic stress disorder (Binder et al., 2008; Caspi et al., 2003).

VIDEO LINK 3.5
Epigenetics

TABLE 3.3   Interaction of genes and environment

		Version of gene that produces MAO-A	
		Gene version producing low levels of MAO-A	Gene version producing average levels of MAO-A
Experience of child abuse	Yes	Higher average levels of aggression	Typical levels of aggression
	No	Typical levels of aggression	Typical levels of aggression

This table shows the outcomes for boys who have different versions of the gene that produces MAO-A in relationship to their early life experiences. When they have the predisposing version of the gene *and* they experience child abuse, they are more likely to be highly aggressive as adults.

Aggression is also addressed in a study of adults adopted at birth. Cadoret, Yates, Troughton, Woodworth, and Steward (1995) found these adults were more likely to be aggressive if their biological parents had shown antisocial behavior problems *and* their experience with their adoptive parents had been difficult, for example if there was divorce or substance abuse in their adopted family. Again, a specific combination of genes and environmental experiences was necessary to produce the behavior. Based on studies such as these, it appears certain genes can make individuals more or less susceptible to environmental effects (Dick & Rose, 2004).

Can epigenetic changes be handed down to the next generation? When a woman has a baby, any epigenetic changes to the chemical tags that turn on or off certain of *her* genes are usually wiped clean. That is, infants start with a fresh slate and build their own epigenetic pattern as they grow and develop (Daxinger & Whitelaw, 2012). However, some epigenetic changes may actually be passed down to the developing fetus. For example, animal research has shown that prenatal exposure to certain chemicals can have epigenetic effects on the animal that appear in its great-grandchildren even if they were never exposed to the chemical (Skinner, Haque, Nilsson, Bhandari, McCarrey, 2013). Scientists are just beginning to research these effects and the ways they might influence human development.

Complexities in the Study of Gene-Environment Interaction

Another example of recent research designed to show the interaction of genes and environment has focused on the timing of the onset of puberty, especially for girls. Puberty is triggered by the action of certain genes, and its individual timing is in part inherited. If your mother entered puberty at an early age, you are also more likely to experience puberty early (Belsky et al., 2007; Ellis & Essex, 2007). However, a variety of environmental factors also appear to turn on the genes for puberty.

There is evidence that girls are more likely to enter puberty earlier when they experience a difficult early family life and when their fathers are absent (Ellis & Essex, 2007; Posner, 2006). This finding appears to indicate an environmental effect on the timing of puberty; however, it is possible that a purely genetic explanation may be adequate. One particular gene associated with aggression in men (the X-linked AR gene) also can be inherited by a daughter. However, as the principle of pleiotropism indicates, genes may have more than one outcome. In girls, this same gene is not associated with aggression but instead acts to trigger early puberty. Therefore, a father with this gene is more likely to be aggressive and have more interpersonal conflict, creating a more difficult family life in the process. His daughter may inherit this gene, but instead of influencing her to be more aggressive, it triggers early puberty. It is not the father's aggression that turned on the gene for puberty, but rather inheritance of the gene itself that both promotes

Bettmann/Corbis

Bettmann/Corbis

Like father, like son. Is it genes or environment that creates the similarity? Evel Knievel attempted to jump the Caesars Palace fountains in Las Vegas on his motorcycle in 1967. The attempt landed him in a coma for a month. His son Robbie took up the challenge and completed it successfully in 1989. ■

aggression in the father and turns on early puberty in the daughter (Posner, 2006). This is another example of the complexity that awaits us as we try to fully understand the interaction of genes and the environment.

How Genes Shape the Environment

So far we have described the way genes affect physical and biological processes and the way the environment influences the expression of genes to produce various developmental outcomes. In a third developmental mechanism, genes influence the nature of the environment in which they exist.

Sandra Scarr (1992) proposed that one way to think about how genes shape the environment is to see them as passive, active, or evocative. When genes are passive, they don't have to do much to be expressed, as when children are born into a family that provides them with both their genes and an environment that encourages the expression of those genes. For example, Robbie Knievel probably inherited genes for risk-taking from his famous father Evel Knievel, who was known for his daredevil stunts. However, it is also likely that his father encouraged and trained him in motorcycle jumping as he grew up. In the end, Robbie outdistanced his dad. He jumped 150 feet over the fountains at Caesars Palace in Las Vegas, a trick Evel had paid for with a month in the hospital (BBC News, 1998).

Passive gene-environment interaction A situation in which a child's family shares his own genetically determined abilities and interests.

Active gene-environment interaction A situation in which a child's genetic endowment becomes a driving force to seek out experiences that fit her genetic endowments.

Genes are active when they become a driving force for children to seek out experiences that fit their genetic endowments (Rowe, 2003). A child with genes that promote risk-taking may be drawn like a magnet to snowboarding, bungee jumping, or whatever is offered that provides a physical and risky challenge. On the other hand, a child with a genetic predisposition to be timid will seek out activities that are solitary and not overly stimulating or exciting. This type of gene effect is also called niche-picking or niche-building. You find the part of your environment (the niche) in which you feel most comfortable, and you actively make this choice (Feinberg, Reiss, Neiderhiser, & Hetherington, 2005).

VIDEO LINK 3.6
Sensation Seeking

Evocative gene-environment interaction A situation in which children's genetic endowment causes them to act in a way that draws out or "evokes" certain responses from those around them.

Finally, genes are evocative when they cause the children to act in a way that draws out or evokes certain responses from those around them. In research by Cadoret et al. (1995), the hostile behavior of an adopted child, which may have its origins in the genes inherited from the child's birth parents, evoked harsh discipline from the child's adoptive mother. This harsh discipline further promoted the hostility and aggression of the child.

On the other hand, an infant with an easy temperament may evoke more positive social interaction from others just because it is such a pleasure to interact with an infant who smiles and coos at everything you do. In this way, we can think of children as shaping the environment in which they live and have their experiences.

1. What does the concept of canalization describe?
2. What is epigenetics?
3. What are the differences between passive gene-environment interaction, active gene-environment interaction, and evocative gene-environment interaction?

Conclusion

All human beings begin with the combination of the genes of their two parents. However, we are then born into an environment that shapes the way those genes will be expressed. As we have seen, our genetic inheritance also shapes the environment we will experience. We are a long way from understanding all the complex interaction between our genetic inheritance and our environmental experiences. As we continue our study of child development, we examine the way development is shaped both by our genetic inheritance and by the environmental context of our lives.

Chapter Summary

3.1 **What are the differences between molecular genetics, behavioral genetics, and behavioral genomics?**

Scientists have examined behaviors of twins and adopted children to try to discover the extent to which genes produce specific behaviors. This approach, which focuses on behavior, is called **behavioral genetics**. More basic research, called **molecular genetics**, focuses on particular genes and the way they function within the cells. A third approach, known as behavioral genomics, attempts to link specific behaviors with specific genes.

3.2 **How do genes and chromosomes function?**

Chromosomes are made of chains of **genes**, which consist of chains of the nucleotide bases guanine, adenine, thymine, and cytosine. The order of these bases gives a cell the instructions for producing different proteins. The **genotype** consists of all the genes a person has, and the **phenotype** is the characteristics that result in part from the genes. Genes are generally paired up. **Dominant genes** are expressed in the phenotype regardless of the gene they are paired with, but **recessive genes** are expressed only

if they are paired with another recessive gene, or if they are carried on the X chromosome of a male child. Each trait or behavior can be produced by the interaction of many genes, a process called **polygenic inheritance**. In addition, any one gene may have many different influences, called **pleiotropic effects**. Disorders such as cystic fibrosis result when **mutations** occur in a gene.

3.3 **How do genetic disorders develop, and what role do genetic testing and counseling play in identifying, preventing, and treating these disorders?**

Single-gene disorders such as sickle-cell anemia and Tay-Sachs disease result when an individual inherits a pair of recessive genes that carry that disorder. Chromosomal disorders such as Down syndrome occur when a child receives the wrong number of chromosomes or when there is a change in the structure of the chromosome caused by breakage. **Multifactorial inheritance disorders,** such as depression and alcoholism, result from the interaction of many genes that also interact with environmental influences. Genetic counseling helps parents assess the risk that their child might have certain conditions. During pregnancy the *alpha-fetoprotein test*, **amniocentesis,** and **chorionic villus sampling** can assess genetic defects. Important ethical considerations are the possibility of false positive results for prenatal tests which will cause unnecessary worry for parents, and the need to maintain the confidentiality of test results to avoid discrimination in employment or availability of health insurance.

3.4 How do we study the relationship between our genetic inheritance and our traits and behavior?

Studies of **concordance rates** between adopted children and their birth parents and their adoptive parents, twin studies comparing the concordance rate between **monozygotic** and **dizygotic twins,** and studies of identical twins reared apart have examined the relative contributions of genes and environment on children's behavior.

3.5 How do genes and the environment interact?

Canalization is the degree to which genes are affected by environmental variations. **Epigenetics** is a system through which chemical tags activate or silence gene activity in response to events or circumstances in the individual's environment. Genes can also affect the nature of an individual's environment. In **passive gene-environment interaction,** children are born into a family that shares and promotes their own genetically determined abilities and interests. In **active gene-environment interaction,** children seek out experiences on their own that fit their genetic endowments. In **evocative gene-environment interaction,** children act in a way that draws out or evokes certain responses from those around them.

Key Terms

Active gene-environment interaction 97

Amniocentesis 88

Behavioral genetics 72

Canalization 94

Chorionic villus sampling (CVS) 88

Chromosomal disorders 85

Chromosomes 73

Concordance rate 91

Dizygotic (DZ) twins 75

Dominant genes 79

Epigenetics 94

Evocative gene-environment interaction 97

Fertilization 73

Gene 79

Gene therapy 89

Generalist genes 83

Genome 72

Genome-wide association 72

Genotype 79

Heritability 72

Molecular genetics 72

Monozygotic (MZ) twins 75

Multifactorial inheritance disorders 85

Mutations 78

Nucleotides 73

Passive gene-environment interaction 97

Phenotype 79

Pleiotropic effects 83

Polygenic inheritance 83

Recessive genes 79

Single gene disorders 84

Zygote 73

$SAGE edge™

Sharpen your skills with SAGE edge at edge.sagepub.com/levinechrono

SAGE edge for Students provides a personalized approach to help you accomplish your coursework goals in an easy-to-use learning environment.

Go to edge.sagepub.com/levinechrono for additional exercises and video resources. Select Chapter 3, Nature Through Nurture, for chapter-specific activities. All of the Video Links listed in the margins of this chapter are accessible via this site.

4

Prenatal Development, Birth, and the Newborn

T/F Test Your Knowledge

Test your knowledge of child development by deciding whether each of the following statements is *true* or *false,* and then check your answers as you read the chapter.

1. T☐ F☐ When a child is conceived, there is a 50-50 chance the child will be a male.

2. T☐ F☐ More than half of all conceptions never implant in the woman's uterus.

3. T☐ F☐ Research has shown that exposing a fetus to extra stimulation (for example, playing music near the pregnant woman's stomach) can stimulate advanced cognitive development.

4. T☐ F☐ Using techniques that are available today, it is possible for some parents to choose the sex of their baby with 100% accuracy.

5. T☐ F☐ The amount of alcohol that a woman consumes while she is pregnant doesn't matter because all amounts of alcohol are equally harmful to the infant.

6. T☐ F☐ Adolescents who were exposed to marijuana prenatally are no more likely to use marijuana than adolescents who were not exposed.

7. T☐ F☐ Infants who are born to women who are HIV-positive are almost certain to develop AIDS.

8. T☐ F☐ An infant born prematurely will have developmental problems and lag behind other children of the same age.

9. T☐ F☐ When a woman gives birth she instinctively knows what to do to care for her new baby.

10. T☐ F☐ Following the birth of a baby, couples today pretty much share household and child care responsibilities.

From the moment a sperm unites with an egg in the process of fertilization, the complicated process of development begins. As you learned in Chapter 3, that moment determines the genetic makeup of the new individual, but from that very moment the fertilized egg, or zygote, also begins interacting with the environment. What happens in the prenatal environment of a woman's womb over the next 9 months can have a tremendous effect on the course of development. As you'll see in this chapter, the process has some built-in safeguards that help ensure the newborn is healthy and fully ready to enter the world, but the system is not perfect, and the number of potential prenatal threats is substantial. Fortunately, we know a great deal today about ways to help a mother go through her pregnancy without complications and get the newborn off to the best possible start in life.

In this chapter we describe the process of prenatal development and birth. We then take a look at what happens following the birth of a new baby. We examine the amazing capabilities of the newborn as well as the way the parents handle the transition to becoming a family.

Learning Questions

4.1 What happens during the three stages of prenatal development?

4.2 What are some risks and health issues during pregnancy?

4.3 What do the mother and baby experience during birth?

4.4 How do newborns function, and what threatens their well-being?

4.5 How do people experience the transition to parenthood?

Prenatal Development

4.1

What happens during the three stages of prenatal development?

We begin by looking at the process of prenatal development, describing how over the period of 9 months a single fertilized cell develops into a fully formed and functional newborn. We also look at how assistive reproductive technology can help couples who are dealing with infertility.

The Three Stages of Prenatal Development

The prenatal journey begins when a follicle in a woman's ovary matures and releases an ovum or egg during her monthly menstrual cycle in the process called ovulation. The ovum begins to travel down the fallopian tube toward the uterus. This is where fertilization occurs, when the egg is penetrated by one of the approximately 300 million sperm cells released into the woman's reproductive system during an act of intercourse.

Usually only one child is conceived at a time, but sometimes there are more than one. In Chapter 3 you learned that there are two types of twins: monozygotic (MZ) or identical twins who are the result of a single fertilized egg that splits early in development, and dizygotic (DZ) or fraternal twins who are the result of two eggs being released in a single cycle, each of which is fertilized by a different sperm. About 70% of twins are dizygotic. The tendency to have DZ twins rather than a single child is genetically related, so some families are more likely to have them than others. Although fertility declines with age, women over 35 are more likely to have DZ twins (Fletcher, Zach, Pramanik, & Ford, 2009). The rate of twinning for women 35 to 40 is double the rate of women who are younger, and women who become pregnant after the age of 45 have a 1-in-3 chance of having a multiple birth (Bortolus et al., 1999). Some part of this increase is due to the greater likelihood in recent years that older mothers will have used fertility drugs or in vitro fertilization to get pregnant, but normal changes in the woman's reproductive system account for most of the increase. After 35, a woman's ovaries decline in their ability to release eggs, so the woman's body increases its production of a hormone

Ovum An unfertilized egg.

Ovulation The release of a mature egg from an ovary.

that can counter this decline (Beemsterboer et al., 2006). If the body creates too much of this hormone, multiple eggs are released. When more than two eggs are fertilized the result may be triplets or even more. These babies can be any combination of identical and fraternal because they may result from multiple eggs and any one of the fertilized eggs can divide to form an identical pair.

If the sperm that unites with the egg is carrying a Y chromosome in the 23rd position, the conception is a male, but if the sperm is carrying an X chromosome, the conception is a female. It may surprise you to learn that there is quite a substantial difference in the rate of conception for males and females. Between 107 and 170 males are conceived for every 100 females (Kalben, 2002). If you look back at Figure 3.2, the picture of chromosomes in Chapter 3, the reason for this gender disparity will be clear to you. Because the Y chromosome is much smaller than the X chromosome, sperm with a Y chromosome are lighter than those with an X chromosome, so they can swim faster and are more likely to reach the egg first.

However, males may be more vulnerable to the detrimental effects of toxins in the prenatal environment, so fewer male conceptions survive (Davis et al., 2007). This may help explain the decline in recent years in the proportion of male births in industrialized countries (Davis et al., 2007). By the time of birth, the ratio of males to females drops to 106 live male births for every 100 live female births (Cunningham et al., 2005; Kalben, 2002). Another way in which male fetuses are more vulnerable is that male fetuses grow more rapidly in the womb than female fetuses and this rate of growth may outpace the ability of the placenta to provide the nutrients needed to support development of the organ systems. It has been hypothesized that this prenatal deprivation may result in long-lasting changes in organs and metabolism that make males more vulnerable to maternal malnutrition or illness during the pregnancy, and thus create a lifelong vulnerability in males to conditions such as heart disease or high blood pressure throughout their lives (Barker et al., 1993; Eriksson, Kajantie, Osmond, Thornburg, & Barker, 2009).

Prenatal development is divided into three stages of very different lengths. We next describe what happens in each of these stages in detail.

The Germinal Stage (Conception to 2 Weeks)

The first stage of prenatal development is the germinal stage, and it begins when the sperm penetrates the egg. Once fertilization occurs and there is a zygote or fertilized egg, the outside thickens so no other sperm will be able to enter. The zygote continues the journey through the fallopian tube, and the process of cell division begins (see Figure 4.1). It takes about 15 hours for that single cell to become 2 cells, and then the process continues with 2 cells becoming 4, then 8, and so on until there is a ball of 32 cells at 4 to 5 days following conception. At this stage, the mass of cells is ready to implant in the lining of the uterus. During the woman's menstrual cycle, her hormones have prepared the lining for just this purpose. If the ball of cells fails to implant for any reason, it passes out of the woman's body without her even realizing there had been a conception. This is not at all uncommon. In fact, it is estimated that up to about 60% of conceptions fail to implant and do not survive (Moore & Persaud, 2003).

T/F #1

When a child is conceived, there is a 50-50 chance the child will be a male. *False*

AUDIO LINK 4.1
Mother's Diet and Baby's Gender

Germinal stage The prenatal stage that lasts from conception to 2 weeks postconception.

FIGURE 4.1 **The germinal stage**

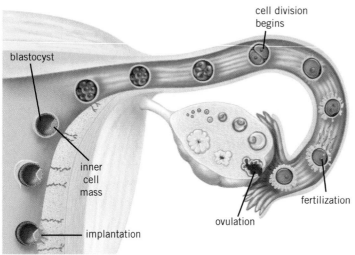

In the week following the fertilization of the ovum, the newly formed zygote travels down the fallopian tube, and the developing blastocyst implants in the lining of the uterus.

T/F #2

More than half of all conceptions never implant in the woman's uterus. *True*

As the cells continue to proliferate, the solid ball becomes a hollow ball called a blastocyst, which now has a solid group of cells at one end called the inner cell mass and an outer ring of cells called the trophoblast (see Figure 4.2). The inner cell mass will go on to become the embryo and part of the amnion that surrounds the embryo, and the outer ring will become the support system for the pregnancy, which includes the placenta and the chorion. We describe these structures and their functions when we discuss the next stage of prenatal development.

Cells in the trophoblast secrete an enzyme that digests some of the lining in the uterus so that the blastocyst can securely embed itself there. After implantation, fingerlike extensions from the outer layer of the trophoblast grow into the uterus, and a connection between the embryo and the woman is established (Galan & Hobbins, 2003). Now that an outside source of nourishment is available, the blastocyst can really begin to grow in size.

The Embryonic Stage (2 Weeks to 2 Months)

The embryonic stage begins at about 2 weeks postconception and lasts until 8 weeks. At this point, the conception is called an embryo. The embryo is surrounded by a support system that connects it to the mother. This support system includes two fetal membranes as well as the placenta and umbilical cord. You can think of the membranes as two sacs, one inside the other. The chorion is the outer one, and the connection that it establishes with the uterus gives rise to the placenta. The inner one, called the amnion, surrounds the developing embryo and is filled with amniotic fluid to cushion and protect the embryo, and later the developing fetus.

The placenta performs the essential functions of bringing oxygen and nutrients from the mother to the developing embryo and carrying away fetal waste products. As shown in Figure 4.3, this transfer between the mother and the embryo occurs *without* any intermingling of their blood (Cunningham et al., 2005). Maternal blood (which has a high concentration of oxygen and nutrients) flows into the placenta, where it fills up empty spaces. If you look carefully at Figure 4.3, you'll see that the fetal arteries occupy these spaces, where they spiral around within the spaces and then return to the fetus as a closed loop. They do *not* directly connect to the maternal arteries or veins. This is why a mother and her child can have different blood types. The two blood systems remain separate throughout the pregnancy.

Because the concentration of oxygen and nutrients in the fetal blood is low, these substances move from the mother's blood to the fetal blood and are carried back to the developing fetus. In a similar way, the waste products that are in high concentration in the fetal blood move into the spaces in the placenta, where the maternal blood picks them up to transport back to the mother for disposal through her organ systems. This transport system can prevent some substances from moving from the mother to the fetus because their molecules are too large to pass through the walls of the arteries, but many substances that are potentially damaging to the developing embryo unfortunately *can* move across the placenta and enter the fetal blood system.

During the embryonic stage, the inner cell mass differentiates into three layers, each of which goes on to become different organs and structures of the embryo. This differentiation is shown in Figure 4.4. The outermost layer, called the ectoderm (*ecto* means "outside" or "external"), becomes the skin, the sense organs, and the brain and spinal cord. The innermost layer, called the endoderm (*endo* means "within" or "inner"), goes on to become the respiratory system, the digestive system, the liver, and the pancreas. The layer between these two other layers, the mesoderm (*meso* means "middle"), becomes the muscles, bones, blood, heart, kidneys, and gonads (Gilbert, 2006).

FIGURE 4.2 | **Development of the blastocyst**

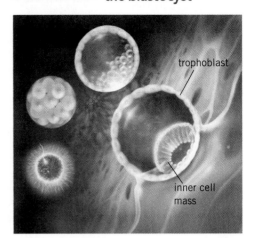

As the zygote continues to replicate and divide, a solid ball of cells forms. The cells fold over themselves and form a hollow ball of cells called the blastocyst, which contains the inner cell mass (which becomes the embryo) and an outer ring of cells called the trophoblast (which becomes the support system for the pregnancy).

Blastocyst A hollow ball of cells that consists of the inner cell mass, which becomes the embryo, and an outer ring of cells, which becomes the placenta and chorion.

Inner cell mass A solid clump of cells in the blastocyst, which later develops into the embryo.

Trophoblast The outer ring of cells in the blastocyst that later develops into the support system for the pregnancy.

Embryonic stage The prenatal stage that lasts from 2 weeks to 2 months postconception.

Embryo The developing organism from conception to the end of the second month of a pregnancy.

Chorion The outer fetal membrane that surrounds the fetus and gives rise to the placenta.

Amnion The inner fetal membrane that surrounds the fetus and is filled with amniotic fluid.

Placenta The organ that supports a pregnancy by bringing oxygen and nutrients to the embryo from the mother through the umbilical cord and carrying away fetal waste products.

FIGURE 4.3   Functions of the placenta

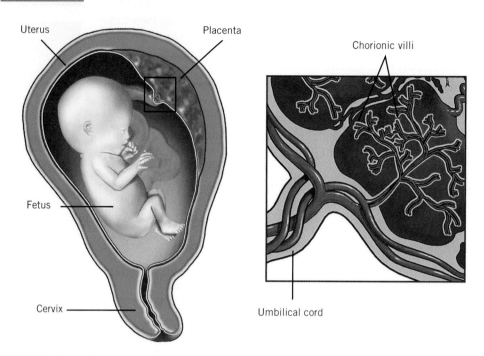

It is within the placenta that oxygen and nutrients in the maternal blood are picked up by the fetal blood, and waste products carried in the fetal blood are released into the maternal blood to be disposed of by the mother's body.

FIGURE 4.4   Differentiation of the inner cell mass

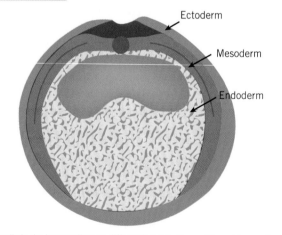

Ectoderm → skin, sense organs, brain, and spinal cord.

Mesoderm → muscles, blood, bones, and circulatory system.

Endoderm → respiratory system, digestive system, liver, and pancreas.

The cells in the inner cell mass differentiate into three different types of cells, each of which goes on to have a different function.

Ectoderm The outermost layer of the inner cell mass that later becomes the skin, sense organs, brain, and spinal cord.

Endoderm The innermost layer of the inner cell mass that later becomes the respiratory system, digestive system, liver, and pancreas.

Mesoderm The middle layer of the inner cell mass that later becomes the muscles, bones, blood, heart, kidney, and gonads.

Cephalocaudal development A principle whereby development proceeds from the head region down through the body.

Organogenesis The process in prenatal development by which all of the major organ systems of the body are laid down.

Throughout the prenatal period, development is from the head region down through the body. This is called cephalocaudal development (*cephalus* means "head," and *caudal* means "tail"). Throughout the pregnancy, but especially in the early months, the development of the upper half of the embryo (and later of the fetus) is more advanced than the lower half. At 9 weeks of age, the head represents about half the entire length of the fetus because the brain is developing so rapidly that it outpaces the rest of the body.

During the embryonic stage, all the major organ systems of the body are laid down in a process called organogenesis, meaning the *genesis* or beginning of the organs.

At 4 weeks, a primitive heart begins beating, and at about 5 to 6 weeks, spontaneous movement begins, although the mother cannot yet feel this movement. By 8 weeks, the end of this stage of prenatal development, all the major organs and structures of the body have been laid down and are in place and the brain and nervous system are developing rapidly. Because so much development occurs within a very short period of time, this is a critical period for development. Anything in the prenatal environment that disrupts the process at this point can cause damage that is both severe and irreversible. Unfortunately, at this point the woman may not even realize she is pregnant. If genetic abnormalities are present in the embryo, they may result in an early miscarriage that ends the pregnancy. It is estimated that 50% to 80% of miscarriages occurring in the first trimester of pregnancy are caused by chromosomal abnormalities and not by anything the woman has done (Simpson, 2007).

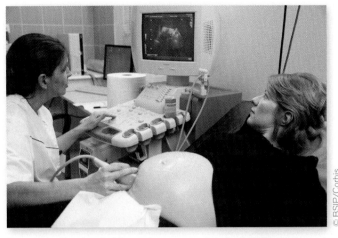

Prenatal testing. A technician performs a prenatal ultrasound for a pregnant woman. What information does this test provide for the patient? ■

The embryo now is just over 1 inch in length and weighs less than one thirtieth of an ounce, but it is already an amazingly complex organism. Although the organ systems are formed, they will need quite a bit more time before they are developed enough to do the work they are intended to do.

Many women have a prenatal ultrasound between 6 and 10 weeks of the pregnancy. During the test, high-frequency sound waves pass through the woman's uterus and bounce off the baby. The returning sounds create a video image that shows the embryo's size, shape, and position in the womb. The test is often repeated midpregnancy at about 20 weeks. At this point, the test can confirm that the baby is growing at the expected rate, and the physician can check for any physical abnormalities, confirm if there is more than one fetus, determine whether other aspects of the pregnancy appear to be normal, and visually determine the sex of the baby, if the parents want that information. Because this is a medical procedure, the American Congress of Obstetricians and Gynecologists (ACOG, 2013a) recommends that ultrasounds be performed only when there is a specific medical reason for them, so women with low-risk pregnancies may not have this test performed at all.

The Fetal Stage (2 Months to Birth)

The third stage of development, called the fetal stage, begins at the third month postconception and lasts until the baby is born. This stage is characterized by the continued growth of the fetus and a remarkable increase in size and weight. All the organ systems need to complete their development and become functional, so the newborn will be capable of surviving independently of the mother after birth.

One particularly significant event during this period is the transformation of the genitalia of the fetus into male or female genitalia. Until now, the development of males and females has followed the same pathway, but at 9 weeks, the testes of a male fetus begin to produce the male hormone *androgen*, and that hormone alters the development of the genitalia from this point on (McClure & Fitch, 2005). In the absence of androgen, the genitalia of a female fetus continues along its developmental pathway, and a female reproductive system is laid down.

Hormones produced prenatally not only shape the physical development of the fetus, but they also influence the development of the brain. The concentration of testosterone peaks at about 8 to 24 weeks postconception, and the changes it produces are permanent (Hines, 2006). By the 26th week of the pregnancy, anatomical differences in

Critical period A period of time during which development is occurring rapidly and the organism is especially sensitive to damage, which often is severe and irreversible.

Ultrasound A prenatal test that uses high-frequency sound waves to create an image of the developing embryo's size, shape, and position in the womb.

Fetal stage The prenatal stage that lasts from the beginning of the third month postconception until birth.

Fetus The developing organism from the end of the eighth week postconception until birth.

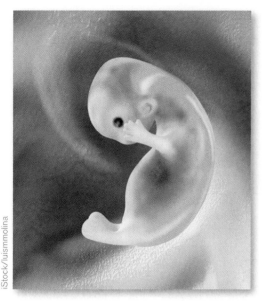

Embryonic development. At 6 weeks postconception, you can see that a primitive heart has formed in this embryo. You also can see how the cephalocaudal principle affects prenatal development. The head and arms are considerably more developed than the lower parts of the body. ■

Gestational age The length of time since the conception of a developing organism.

brain structure of male and female fetuses are apparent (Achiron, Lipitz, & Achiron, 2001). For instance, the two hemispheres of the male brain are more symmetrical than the hemispheres of the female brain, there is more gray matter and less white matter in the female brain, and the concentration of gray matter in the neocortex is higher in female brains (Good et al., 2001). However, there are many more similarities than differences between male and female brains, and many other factors, such as experiences later in life, also affect the formation of boys' and girls' brains.

At about 10 weeks, fetal breathing movements begin, although there is no air in the amniotic sac to breathe. Instead, fetuses breathe in and then expel amniotic fluid. Between week 12 and week 16, most women will begin to feel the movement of the fetus. At first it feels like a light fluttering and first-time mothers may mistake it for digestive functioning, but as time goes on, the movement becomes more and more marked. By a gestational age of 20 weeks, fetuses have been recorded moving more than 50 times in a single 50-minute session (DiPietro et al., 2004). Fetal movement declines from this point until the baby is born. At 32 weeks, the fetus spends between 90% and 95% of its time sleeping (Hopson, 1998), but it still develops quite a repertoire of activities prior to birth. We have learned a great deal in recent years about behavioral competencies that develop prenatally so the newborn is ready to begin interacting with the world.

Although the fetus is protected from extreme stimulation within its uterine environment, it is not isolated from the sensory world. In fact, it interacts with a complex intrauterine environment (Smotherman & Robinson, 1996), and by the time the baby is born, all the senses are functional to some extent (Hopkins & Johnson, 2005). The cutaneous senses, "skin senses" such as touch and pain, and the proprioceptive senses, the ones that detect motion or the position of the body, are the first to develop. Dr. Heidelise Als, a developmental psychologist at Harvard Medical School, has commented on the amount of tactile stimulation the fetus gives itself: "It touches a hand to the face, one hand to the other hand, clasps its foot, touches its foot to its legs, its hand to its umbilical cord" (Hopson, 1998, p. 45).

The cutaneous senses are followed by the chemical senses, such as smell and taste, and the vestibular senses, such as the sense of equilibrium and balance. The last to develop are the auditory and visual senses (Lecanuet, Graniere-Deferre, & DeCasper, 2005). The intrauterine environment provides at least some stimulation for all these senses. For instance, sounds are transmitted through the mother's abdomen to provide auditory stimulation (Smotherman & Robinson, 1996). Recent research has found that newborns respond differently to vowel sounds that were part of the native language they were exposed to in utero than to sounds they did not hear prenatally (Moon, Lagercrantz, & Kuhl, 2013). Amniotic fluid carries chemosensory molecules that stimulate the smell and taste receptors, and movement of the fetus stimulates the vestibular senses (Lecanuet et al., 2005). What we see throughout the prenatal period is a great deal of continuity as systems develop and later become functional. This prepares the newborn to begin interacting with—and responding to—the environment almost immediately after birth.

We now even have evidence that some simple forms of learning can occur before birth. These are all signs of an intact and functional central nervous system, but Lecanuet et al. (2005) caution that we should not presume prenatal differences in stimulation are related to later differences in cognitive functioning. The research on prenatal sensory capabilities has led to the development and marketing of a variety of gadgets that purport to stimulate neural growth or to facilitate learning, memory, thinking, and even social interaction prenatally. However, this shows a lack of understanding of the meaning of the research. Stimulation beyond what is normally provided to the developing fetus is *not* necessarily better and could, in fact, be harmful. The normal prenatal environment provides enough stimulation for optimal development.

Many other common beliefs about pregnancy have been handed down from generation to generation. Test yourself by answering the questions in **Active Learning: Old Wives' Tale or Scientific Fact?** to see which of these ideas have a scientific basis and which do not.

T/F #3
Research has shown that exposing a fetus to extra stimulation (for example, playing music near the pregnant woman's stomach) can stimulate advanced cognitive development.
False

Active Learning

Old Wives' Tale or Scientific Fact?

Throughout this book we ask you to test your commonsense or intuitive knowledge of development against what we know about it scientifically. There are probably more old wives' tales about pregnancy than about any other period in development. Which of the following statements about pregnancy are *true*, and which are *false*?

1. T ☐ F ☐ A fast fetal heart rate means the woman is having a girl.

2. T ☐ F ☐ When a woman is pregnant, she is eating for two.

3. T ☐ F ☐ A woman shouldn't dye her hair while she is pregnant.

4. T ☐ F ☐ A pregnant woman shouldn't jog.

5. T ☐ F ☐ Pregnancy will be the happiest time in a woman's life.

6. T ☐ F ☐ Women may have difficulty concentrating in the first 3 months of a pregnancy.

7. T ☐ F ☐ Pregnant women have a special glow.

8. T ☐ F ☐ A woman's hair will fall out after her pregnancy.

SOURCES: Felsenthal (2006); Gardephe & Ettlinger (1993); KidsHealth (2008); Warnick (2010); Vora (n.d.).

■ Answers:

1. **False.** Fetal heart rate changes with the amount of fetal activity but does not differ by gender.

2. **True.** But the second person the woman is "eating for" probably weighs 8 pounds or less. That means an additional 300 calories a day on average are all the extra calories she will need to consume.

3. **False.** There is no definitive link between hair coloring and fetal health, although some animal studies have found a link between dyes and cataracts (Bouchez, 2010). For that reason it is probably best not to use hair coloring during a pregnancy, especially in the early months, unless it is natural coloring such as henna.

4. **Probably true.** We say "probably true" because a woman who was an avid runner before becoming pregnant can probably safely continue the activity, but the ligaments and tendons in a woman's body become softer, her breasts enlarge, and her center of gravity shifts during her pregnancy, so there is increased risk for the pregnant casual runner. For these women, other physical activity, like swimming or walking, might be a better choice.

5. **False.** While pregnancy can be a very happy time of life for most women, between 10% and 16% of pregnant women suffer a major depressive disorder during their pregnancy and even more experience depression at a subclinical level (Marcus & Heringhausen, 2009). We should not mistakenly dismiss these symptoms as unimportant by simply attributing them to hormonal mood swings.

6. **True.** Fatigue, morning sickness, and preoccupation with the pregnancy itself can make a woman forgetful early in her pregnancy.

7. **True.** The woman's body produces a great volume of blood to support the pregnancy, which results in more blood flow in the vessels and an increase in oil gland secretions. This could be responsible for the "glow" we associate with pregnancy.

8. **True.** Hormones secreted during a pregnancy cause hair to grow faster and fall out less, but the hormonal changes that follow the birth of the baby can cause a significant amount of hair to fall out as the body readjusts.

Infertility

Infertility The inability to conceive within 1 year of frequent, unprotected sex.

Couples who engage in frequent, unprotected sex can expect to conceive a child within 1 year, so failure to conceive within that length of time may mean that infertility is a problem for the couple. About 12% of married U.S. women have difficulty either getting pregnant or carrying a pregnancy to term (RESOLVE: The National Fertility Association, 2014). One-third of the cases are attributable to female factors and one-third to male factors; in the remaining cases the cause is mutual or cannot be determined (RESOLVE, 2014). Infertility can be the result of physical problems in either partner, such as a blocked fallopian tube in the woman or a reduced sperm count due to illness in the man. Lifestyle factors, including heavy use of alcohol or tobacco, exposure to environmental toxins, and stress, also can play a role.

One of the most influential factors in infertility, however, is maternal age. Women in the United States are waiting longer to have children, and today 20% don't have their first child until they are 35 or older (CDC, 2013d). About one-third of these women will have a problem with fertility, compared to 12% in the general married population, but medical science today can offer infertile couples a wide range of interventions. Several are described in Table 4.1.

The term *assisted reproductive technology* (or ART) is usually reserved to describe procedures in which both the egg and the sperm are handled. It does not include procedures that involve only the sperm, such as artificial insemination, or in which the woman receives medication intended to stimulate egg production (CDC, 2014a). By this definition, about 1% of infants born in the United States are conceived using assisted reproductive technology.

WEB LINK 4.1
Older Parenthood in the United States

Check Your Understanding

1. What occurs in each of the three stages of prenatal development?
2. What is an ultrasound, and why is it used?
3. What are some of the ways that medical science can help infertile couples?

4.2

What are some risks and health issues during pregnancy?

Health and Risks in Pregnancy

In this section we describe some of the things that a woman can do to help ensure her health and the well-being of her baby during the pregnancy. In addition to getting early and continuing prenatal care and being careful about her diet, the woman needs to avoid

TABLE 4.1	Infertility treatment and interventions
Female fertility drugs	Drugs can stimulate the production and release of eggs from a woman's ovaries.
Artificial insemination	Sperm (from the woman's partner or from a donor) is placed in the womb at the time of ovulation. Can be used in conjunction with fertility drugs to increase the chance of success.
Gamete intrafallopian transfer	The egg and sperm are collected and placed directly in the woman's fallopian tubes so fertilization takes place in her body rather than in a laboratory.
In vitro fertilization	Eggs are surgically removed from a woman and mixed with a sample of sperm (from the woman's partner or a donor) to create one or more embryos, which are then placed in the uterus.
Intracytoplasmic sperm injection	If sperm count is low, the sperm are damaged, or they show poor motility, a single sperm cell that is viable can be injected directly into an egg to create an embryo.
Preimplantation genetic diagnosis	Embryos are created in a lab and genetically tested before they are implanted in the woman's womb. Originally developed to help families at risk of having children with gender-related genetic disorders, this technique can be used to select embryos by gender, though this use is highly controversial and is against the law in some European countries.

SOURCE: Kalb (2004); Turkington (2002).

T/F #4

Using techniques that are available today, it is possible for some parents to choose the sex of their baby with 100% accuracy. *True*

potentially harmful substances such as tobacco and alcohol. There are critical periods in early development when these substances are particularly damaging.

Maternal Health and Well-Being

The three stages of prenatal development describe what is happening to the developing infant during the 9 months of the pregnancy. However, from the point of view of the pregnant woman, those 9 months are divided in a different way, into 3-month periods called *trimesters*, each of which has its own characteristics.

During the first trimester, it may not be apparent to other people that the woman is pregnant, but changes in the level of her hormones can cause fatigue, breast tenderness, and *morning sickness*, a nausea that often subsides as the day progresses. During the second trimester, most women start to feel better and the pregnancy begins to become apparent as the fetus grows larger. The woman now is able to feel the fetus moving inside her. These first fetal movements are called the *quickening*. In the third trimester, the fetus continues to grow and the woman becomes more tired and uncomfortable (Chye, Teng, Hao, & Seng, 2008). At the end of this trimester, she will experience the fetus dropping lower within her as it begins to move into position to begin the birth process.

Seeing a physician on a regular basis, beginning early in the pregnancy, is one of the best things a woman can do to avoid problems later on. In fact, good self-care even before a woman becomes pregnant is a very wise idea. When a woman does not receive prenatal care, she is three times more likely to give birth to a baby of low birth weight and five times more likely to have her infant die (U.S. Department of Health and Human Services, 2006).

Most women see their doctor for the first time between 2 and 4 weeks after they have missed a period. Women in the United States typically see their doctors about every 4 weeks through their second trimester, and then every 2 weeks until they are a month away from their due date, when they move to weekly visits. Women who have chronic

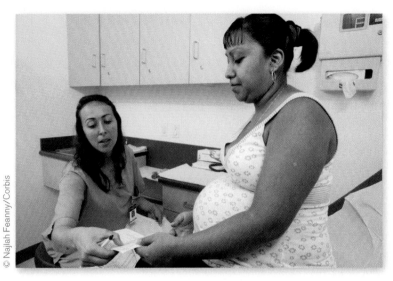

Prenatal care. Regular visits to a doctor throughout a woman's pregnancy are essential to good prenatal care. What do you think we could do in the United States to help ensure that more pregnant women get this type of care? ■

conditions, such as diabetes, asthma, or allergies, may need to see their health care provider more frequently or may be referred to a physician who specializes in high-risk pregnancies. They also may need to eliminate or change the dosage of any medication they are taking, but these changes should only be made in careful consultation with a physician.

Although the United States spends about twice as much per person on health care as any other country (Peter J. Peterson Foundation, 2013), U.S. maternal and infant health are *not* the best in the world (Central Intelligence Agency, 2014; Heisler, 2012). Each year nearly one million American women give birth without having received adequate medical attention during their pregnancy (Health Resources and Services Administration, n.d.). Black, Hispanic, and Native American women are more than twice as likely as White women to receive late or no prenatal care (Child Trends, 2014a).

In a 2014 comparison of worldwide maternal health data, the United States ranked 60th in the world, with a maternal death rate of 18.5 deaths per 100,000 live births. This is triple the rate in the United Kingdom and eight times the rate of Iceland, the country with the lowest maternal mortality rate (Almendrala, 2014). These figures represent an increase in the United States since 1990, when the rate was 12.4 deaths per 100,000 births. The United States was one of only eight countries in the world that experienced an increase in maternal mortality during this period. Many of the deaths result from complications of conditions such as heart disease, diabetes, obesity, or kidney problems that begin during the woman's pregnancy or are exacerbated by it. Adopting a healthy lifestyle before and during a pregnancy and getting early prenatal care go a long way toward ensuring a healthy delivery for both mother and infant (CDC, 2013g).

Miscarriage

Miscarriage The natural loss of a pregnancy before the fetus reaches a gestational age of 20 weeks.

Unfortunately it is not an uncommon occurrence for a pregnancy to result in miscarriage, which is the natural loss of a pregnancy before 20 weeks gestational age of the fetus (Branch & Scott, 2003). Most miscarriages occur during the early weeks of a pregnancy, before the woman even knows she is pregnant, but women who know they are pregnant and miscarry a wanted pregnancy experience a real sense of loss that should be acknowledged. Although genetic abnormalities are the most common cause of miscarriage, in about half the cases the cause is unknown. However, when medical professionals can identify a cause, it is easier for women to come to terms with the loss, and knowing the cause relieves some of the initial distress (Nikčević & Nicolaides, 2014).

Women utilize a number of different coping strategies to deal with the loss of a pregnancy (Van, 2012). Most talk with others about their loss. Talking with another woman who has herself experienced the loss of a pregnancy can be particularly helpful. Not only is there a feeling of shared understanding, but if the other woman has subsequently carried a pregnancy to term, it also provides reassurance and a sense of hope in the situation. Partners or others who feel they don't know what to say or do should be aware that "just being there" is an important and effective way to help the grieving process (Van, 2012, p. 82). Recurrent miscarriage affects only 1% to 3% of couples (Alijotas-Reig & Garrido-Gimenez, 2013), so most women who have a miscarriage can take comfort from the fact that they will be able to have children through a future pregnancy.

In some cases, a mother may choose to terminate a pregnancy by having an induced abortion. Worldwide about 20% of pregnancies end in abortion (Sedgh et al., 2012). In the United States, some of the major reasons women gave for having an abortion were financial difficulty, lack of support from a partner, and the need to care for other children (Biggs, Gould, & Foster, 2013). Abortion is a difficult choice to make, but research has shown that most women feel most anxious *before* the event. Although they may feel some grief and sadness afterward, the predominant feeling is relief (Weitz, Moore, Gordon, & Adler, 2008). The American Psychological Association's Task Force on Mental Health and Abortion concluded that adult women with an unplanned pregnancy who have an abortion during the first trimester have no worse psychological outcome than those who deliver the baby (APA, 2014a). Women who have multiple abortions are at higher risk for emotional difficulties, but there may be other related factors that predispose them to have several unwanted pregnancies. Negative reactions to abortion are more likely if the woman has little support for the procedure, has had previous mental health problems, and if the pregnancy was wanted (APA, 2014a).

WEB LINK 4.2
Abortion Debate

Maternal Diet

One of the best ways to ensure a healthy pregnancy is for a mother to have a healthy diet. Because the developing baby is so small relative to the size of the mother, an average of 300 extra calories a day is all that is needed to support prenatal growth (Katz, 2003), with fewer calories required early in the pregnancy and more nearer the time for delivery. The recommended weight gain for women who begin their pregnancy at a normal weight is 25 to 35 pounds (ACOG, 2013b). Women who are underweight at the beginning of their pregnancy can safely gain a bit more, and women who are overweight should gain less. The goal is a newborn who weighs between 7 and 8 pounds (Olds, London, & Ladewig, 2002). Infants who are born smaller than average for their gestational age are more vulnerable to infections, and those who are much larger than average increase the length of labor and risk difficulties in the delivery itself.

AUDIO LINK 4.2
Maternal Diet and Obesity

When a mother is malnourished because of a severely restricted diet, the negative consequences can be severe and long-lasting, affecting the future health of the infant, as well as cognitive skills, problem-solving abilities, developmental levels, and behavioral functioning (Boulet, Schieve, & Boyle, 2011; Kessinich, 2003; Morgane et al., 1993). Evidence that an infant is vulnerable to effects of the maternal diet in other ways comes from research conducted on primates. Coe and Lubach (2008) found that when a primate mother's diet was inadequate for a sustained portion of the pregnancy, infants who were later raised in an environment where food was abundant were more prone to obesity. What accounts for this surprising outcome? When infants are "starved" prenatally, it lowers their basal metabolic rate (the rate at which they use energy when they are resting) so their bodies are programmed to burn calories more slowly after they are born, placing them at greater risk of obesity and potentially of diabetes later in development.

Because pregnant women need to be sure their diet has an adequate amount of vitamins and minerals, doctors usually prescribe a multivitamin or prenatal vitamin. Folic acid, which is one of the B vitamins, plays an important role in preventing defects of the brain and spinal cord, so women who are planning on becoming pregnant should be sure their diet contains an adequate amount of this essential vitamin even before they become pregnant (Chye et al., 2008).

Healthy eating while pregnant. Healthy eating is always important, but particularly while you are pregnant. The mother's diet provides all the nutrients her developing child needs. Avoiding foods that can be harmful is equally essential. ■

Folate not only occurs naturally in foods such as fortified breakfast cereals, beans, leafy green vegetables, and orange juice, but it also is available as a food supplement. Doctors also may recommend iron or calcium supplements (Katz, 2003).

There also are some foods that should be avoided because of risks associated with them. For instance, luncheon meats and soft cheeses such as Brie and feta can contain bacteria, and certain fish including shark and swordfish may have high levels of mercury or industrial pollutants (Chye et al., 2008). Although there has been some concern about the relationship between caffeine consumption and preterm birth, a recent meta-analysis did not support this concern (Maslova, Bhattacharya, Lin & Michels, 2010). Moderate caffeine intake that is the equivalent of 1 or 2 cups of coffee per day is usually considered safe (Morgan, Koren & Bozzo, 2013). However, caffeine also can come from tea, soda, and chocolate, so consumption of these foods should be taken into account when figuring daily caffeine consumption. Bottled water and energy drinks also may contain caffeine even though their labels do not indicate the caffeine content of the product.

Teratogens

Teratogens Agents that can disrupt prenatal development and cause malformations or termination of the pregnancy.

A number of factors can have a negative impact on prenatal development. Agents that can cause malformations in an embryo or a fetus are broadly referred to as **teratogens**. They include diseases a mother has or contracts during her pregnancy (such as rubella, syphilis, or HIV/AIDS), things the mother ingests (such as alcohol, medication, or drugs), and toxins in the environment (such as mercury in the foods she eats or exposure to radiation or environmental pollution). Because there are so many potential teratogens, we can talk only briefly about some of the most common ones in this chapter.

Each teratogen has a specific effect on the developing embryo or fetus and can result in a *structural abnormality*, such as missing or malformed limbs, or a *functional deficit*, such as hearing loss or intellectual disability. Figure 4.5 shows the sensitive periods for the impact of various teratogens on development. The level of the impairment can range from mild to severe. The nature and magnitude of the effect depends on *when* in the prenatal period the fetus or embryo is exposed to the teratogen, the *amount* or dosage of the exposure, and the *length of time* the exposure continues. For example, an exposure that could end a pregnancy if it occurred early in the germinal stage might produce serious physical defects if it occurred during the embryonic stage but much less severe defects if it occurred late in the fetal stage.

The effect when a woman contracts rubella or German measles at different points in her pregnancy provides a good illustration of this point. The effect on an adult woman is rather mild, but the effects on her pregnancy can be devastating. Exposure in the first 11 weeks results in birth defects that include significant problems with vision, hearing, and heart function in 90% of cases, while exposure later in the pregnancy leaves 20% of infants with congenital defects (Reef & Redd, 2008). Fortunately rubella rarely occurs in the United States because children are routinely vaccinated for the disease, but it continues to be a threat to fetal development in other parts of the world, so most of the cases of maternal rubella in the United States occur among foreign-born residents who came to the United States from countries that do not have vaccination programs (CDC, 2013i).

Alcohol

Alcohol should never be a part of a pregnant woman's diet. When you drink an alcoholic beverage—whether it is beer, wine, or hard liquor—the alcohol in it enters your bloodstream and circulates through your system until your liver can break it down over the next couple of hours and pass it from your system. During that time, because the concentration of alcohol in a pregnant woman's bloodstream is higher than the concentration in the fetal blood, the alcohol crosses the placenta and enters the developing embryo or fetus where it can cause damage. The relatively small size of the embryo, together with

FIGURE 4.5   Sensitive periods in prenatal development

		Main Embryonic Period (in weeks)						Fetal Period (in weeks)			
1	2	3	4	5	6	7	8	9	16	32	38

Period of dividing zygote, implantation, and bilaminar embryo

Embryonic disc

Morula

Amnion

Blastocyst

Embryonic disc

Not susceptible to teratogenesis

Neural tube defects (NTDs)	Mental retardation	CNS
TA, ASD, and VSD	Heart	
Amelia/Meromelia	Upper limb	
Amelia/Meromelia	Lower limb	
Cleft lip	Upper lip	
Low-set malformed ears and deafness	Ears	
Microphthalmia, cataracts, glaucoma	Eyes	
Enamel hypoplasia and staining	Teeth	
Cleft palate	Palate	
Masculinization of female genitalia	External genitalia	

Legend:
- • Common site(s) of action of teratogens
- ▬ Less sensitive period
- ▬ Highly-sensitive period

TA—Truncus artoriosus; ASD—Atrial septal defect;
VSD—Ventricular septal defect

| Death of embryo and spontaneous abortion common | Major congenital anomalies | Functional defects and minor anomalies |

This figure shows parts of the body that are most vulnerable to the effects of teratogens at specific times throughout the pregnancy. It also shows types of problems that might develop, such as ASD or atrial septal defect, which affects the heart.

SOURCE: Moore & Persaud (2003).

---

the fact that vital organ systems may be in critical stages of development, helps explain why even a small amount of alcohol can be a problem. The effect of alcohol on a 120-pound woman is different from its effect on a 1- or 2-pound fetus.

The most clear-cut effect of alcohol on a pregnancy is seen in children born to women who have consumed large quantities of alcohol (usually defined as 7 to 14 drinks a week throughout their pregnancy) or had occasional bouts of binge drinking (defined as having 5 or more drinks at one time). Either pattern of drinking can result in fetal alcohol syndrome (FAS), which includes physical characteristics such as

Fetal alcohol syndrome (FAS) A condition in the child resulting from heavy or binge consumption of alcohol during a pregnancy; associated with abnormal facial features, small stature, and a small head, and functional problems such as problems with learning, memory, and attention span.

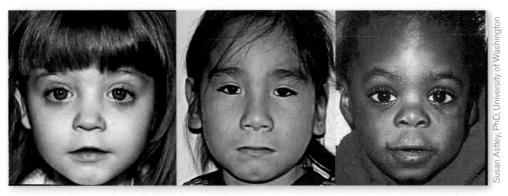

Susan Astley, PhD, University of Washington

VIDEO LINK 4.1
FAS

Facial characteristics of children with fetal alcohol syndrome. These photos show some of the facial features that are characteristic in children with fetal alcohol syndrome, including a smooth ridge between the nose and upper lip, a thin upper lip, wide-spaced eyes, underdeveloped ears, and a short nose with a flat bridge. ■

Fetal alcohol spectrum disorders (FASDs) A range of impairments in a child resulting from consumption of alcohol during a pregnancy; associated with any subset of characteristics of fetal alcohol syndrome at varying levels of severity and other more subtle or functional deficits.

abnormal facial features, small stature, and a small head and functional problems such as problems with learning, memory, and attention span (CDC, 2012d), as well as trouble controlling behavior and regulating emotions. FAS represents the extreme end of a continuum of problems known as fetal alcohol spectrum disorders (FASDs), which can include any subset of characteristics at varying levels of severity and other more subtle or functional deficits that include difficulty with abstract thinking, poor problem-solving skills, mood swings, or being defensive or stubborn (CDC, 2012d). According to the CDC (2012a), fetal alcohol syndrome is the leading preventable cause of intellectual disability and birth defects in the United States. The ongoing study of the way alcohol affects a pregnancy is described in **Journey of Research: Understanding the Effects of Alcohol on a Pregnancy.**

JOURNEY OF RESEARCH *Understanding the Effects of Alcohol on a Pregnancy*

As far back as ancient Greece and Rome, people suspected that alcohol could have a negative impact on pregnancies (Calhoun & Warren, 2006). However, concern did not appear in the medical literature until the 1700s, when a group of physicians in England described women alcoholics giving birth to children who were "weak, feeble, and distempered" (Calhoun & Warren, 2006, p. 169). In 1899, an English deputy medical examiner noted that alcoholic mothers had an increased risk of having a child who died at birth, but these early observations linking alcohol and birth defects were largely ignored by the medical community until a group of French researchers published a paper in the 1960s describing some commonly occurring problems noted in the offspring of a group of 100 women who drank heavily during their pregnancy (Calhoun & Warren, 2006). In the 1970s, British researchers identified the shared anomalies among children born to chronic alcoholic mothers, concluded that alcohol was the cause of these anomalies, and coined the term *fetal alcohol syndrome* (Calhoun & Warren, 2006). As interest in this topic took hold, research examined other factors that contributed to the problems seen in children born to alcoholic mothers. In addition to drinking, for example, these women may have smoked, been malnourished, received no prenatal care, or had untreated medical conditions.

As public concern continued to grow, the U.S. Food and Drug Administration issued a bulletin in 1977 that discouraged "binge" or "chronic, excessive" drinking during pregnancy (Bobo, Klepinger, & Dong, 2006, p. 1062). A decade later, the federal Alcoholic Beverage Labeling Act was passed requiring that alcoholic beverages carry a warning that they should not be consumed during pregnancy because of the risk of birth defects. Several health initiatives since then have tried to inform women of this danger. In 2005, the Surgeon General updated an advisory originally issued in 1981 that suggested pregnant women "*limit* [emphasis added] the amount of alcohol they drink," saying "*no amount* [emphasis added] of alcohol consumption can be considered safe during a pregnancy," and warning women that alcohol can damage the fetus at any stage in a pregnancy (U.S. Department of Health and Human Services [USDHHS], 2005b). How successful have our efforts been to educate women about the dangers of drinking while pregnant? According to the CDC (2012a), between 2006 and 2010, 7.6% of pregnant women reported using alcohol in the past 30 days and 1.4% reported at least one episode of binge drinking during that period. Although accurate numbers are difficult to obtain, the American Academy of Pediatrics estimates that there may be as many as 40,000 infants born each year in the United States with FASDs (AAP, n.d.).

Researchers continue to study the effects of prenatal alcohol exposure. In the past few years, several large studies conducted by European researchers have

challenged the idea that complete abstinence is required. In a study of over 5,000 women in New Zealand, Australia, Ireland, and the United Kingdom, no association was found between alcohol consumption before 15 weeks of gestation and the infant being small-for-gestational age, having a reduced birth weight, or a preterm birth (McCarthy et al., 2013). In another study with a sample of 1,628 women and children from the Danish National Birth Cohort, no statistically significant association was found between low to average moderate weekly alcohol consumption and measures of planning, organization, and self-control in the children when they were 5 years old (Skogerbø et al., 2013). Perhaps even more surprising, this study found there was only weak or no consistent association between maternal binge drinking and these outcome measures. A third study based on the same Danish National Birth Cohort found a small positive association between binge drinking and emotional/peer problems and hyperactivity/inattention/conduct problems, but no association with lower levels of alcohol consumption. Although these researchers controlled for many factors that could influence the outcomes, they warn that there may be other characteristics of the home environment that they did not consider that may be masking the potentially damaging effect of small amounts of alcohol.

In addition, it is difficult to diagnose some effects of alcohol on brain and cognitive development. In another recent study carried out in South Africa, researchers compared children with FASD to those who did not have any symptoms. Even mothers of children who did not have FASD had some history of drinking while pregnant, and the more drinking mothers in this sample had done, the more symptoms of FASD their children were likely to have (May et al., 2013). Drinking during the first trimester raised the likelihood of FASD 12 times, while drinking throughout pregnancy raised the risk 65 times.

None of these studies assert that heavy alcohol consumption during pregnancy is safe, and the Centers for Disease Control and Prevention (2014g) continues to caution women that there is no known safe amount of alcohol to drink while pregnant. Given the importance of this topic and the fact that many women do drink some alcohol while they are pregnant, research will continue to try to clarify the consequences of alcohol consumption for the woman and her child. ■

T/F #5
The amount of alcohol that a woman consumes while she is pregnant doesn't matter because all amounts of alcohol are equally harmful to the infant. *False*

Any effects of prenatal exposure to alcohol are permanent and irreversible. Although stopping drinking at any point in a pregnancy prevents further damage, it does *not* reverse any harm that has already been done. Although the estimated incidence of FAS differs depending on the population studied and the way the condition is identified and assessed, the CDC (2014g) puts it at 0.2 to 1.5 per 1,000 live births, with FASDs occurring at 3 times that rate. Although intervention programs can help improve the functioning of children born with FAS and FASDs, this is a completely preventable condition. Because so much development occurs in the weeks before a woman realizes she is pregnant and because nearly half of all pregnancies in the United States are unplanned (Finer & Zolna, 2012), abstaining from alcohol if you are sexually active is a good idea even before you become pregnant.

Tobacco

Another completely preventable source of developmental risk is maternal smoking, along with exposure to secondhand smoke during pregnancy (CDC, 2007b; Rogers, 2009). Cigarette smoke contains over 4,000 chemicals, including formaldehyde, arsenic, and lead, and the more a woman smokes, the greater her risk of having a baby with low birth weight (Rogers, 2009). As a woman smokes, the level of carbon monoxide in her blood increases, reducing the capacity of her blood to carry oxygen. Because the nicotine in the smoke constricts the blood vessels, this further limits the flow of oxygen and nutrients to the fetus through the placenta. Also, nicotine is an addictive substance that tends to suppress appetite, so pregnant smokers eat less. All these factors contribute to the growth retardation so strongly associated with babies born to smokers.

Smoking also has been associated with an increased risk of miscarriage, premature birth, and sudden infant death syndrome (Shea & Steiner, 2008). The effects are so pervasive that Jauniaux and Greenough (2007) have made the claim that in many countries smoking has replaced poverty as the most important risk factor for all these negative pregnancy-related outcomes. In their estimation, smoking while pregnant costs the United States $250 million in direct medical costs each year, and they predict that a reduction of just 1% in smoking prevalence would lower the incidence of babies born at low birth weight by 1,300 infants each year.

AUDIO LINK 4.3
Smoking in Pregnancy

Maternal smoking while pregnant also is a major contributor to later developmental problems for the child. The risk of developing asthma is significantly increased if a mother smokes while pregnant, even if she does not smoke after the baby is born (Neuman et al., 2012). A recent systematic review of studies published over the past 40 years found a positive association between maternal smoking and defects of the heart, musculoskeletal system, face, eye, and gastrointestinal system and malformation of the genitals (Hackshaw, Rodeck, & Boniface, 2011). Behavioral effects include attention deficit hyperactivity disorder (ADHD), conduct disorders, and learning disabilities (Rogers, 2009; Shea & Steiner, 2008; Slotkin, 2008).

While smoking has decreased among the general population over the last couple of decades, it has decreased at a slower rate among young women ages 19 to 29 than among other groups, and in 2010, 10.7% of pregnant women still reported smoking during the last 3 months of their pregnancy (CDC, 2014j). The good news is that when pregnant women stop smoking, even as late as the second trimester, the weight and body measurements of their infants are comparable to those of infants whose mothers were nonsmokers (ACOG, 2005).

Babies born to mothers who smoke during their pregnancy appear to undergo withdrawal symptoms similar to those seen in babies born to mothers addicted to illicit drugs (Law et al., 2003), and maternal smoking during pregnancy is a strong predictor of whether adolescents begin smoking and become addicted themselves, regardless of whether their parents smoked during their childhood (Abreu-Villac, Seidler, Tate, Cousins, & Slotkin, 2004). Even when women are persuaded to stop smoking while they are pregnant or breastfeeding, many resume shortly thereafter (Xu, Wen, Rissel, & Baur, 2013). Most people know that secondhand smoke is equally dangerous both before and after birth, but it is important to know that even "thirdhand smoke," the residue found in dust, carpets, and many other surfaces in a household where people smoke, may affect infants who spend more of their time playing with toys at floor level (Winickoff et al., 2009). It would be beneficial to both mother and infant if we could find ways to make a smoke-free environment a long-term lifestyle change rather than a brief adaptation to the pregnancy itself.

Prescription and Over-the-Counter Drugs

It is difficult to make general statements about the use of drugs (whether prescription or over-the-counter) because the potential effect on a pregnancy depends on the specific type of medication taken, when in the pregnancy it is taken, for how long, and at what dosage. If a woman wants to use over-the-counter medications to relieve the discomfort of colds, headaches or nausea, she should discuss this decision with her physician first so they can weigh the potential benefits from using the drugs against the possible risks for the fetus. Because most herbal remedies and food supplements have not been tested by the U.S. Food and Drug Administration for safety, it is best to avoid these completely during a pregnancy. To see how safe your own medications would be for a pregnant woman, try **Active Learning: Safety of Medications During Pregnancy.**

Active Learning

Safety of Medications During Pregnancy

Do you know whether the medications in your medicine cabinet right now are safe for use during pregnancy? Make a list of all your medications (both prescription and over-the-counter), vitamins, and herbal supplements, and check their safety.

You can use the *Physicians' Desk Reference* (*PDR*), which contains the information that comes in the insert with your prescriptions, including any warnings or contraindications for a drug's use. A separate volume of the *PDR* deals specifically with nonprescription drugs, dietary supplements, and herbal medicines. This information is available through the PDR Network website at www.PDR.net.

You also can search the Internet by typing the name of a specific drug and the word *pregnancy* to see whether there are any advisories against its use. Remember to check the credentials of the site you are using. Sites maintained by the Centers for Disease Control and Prevention, the National Institutes of Health, or the American Congress of Obstetricians and Gynecologists will give you information you can trust.

After you complete your search, take some time to think about what a pregnant woman would need to consider when weighing the benefits of these medications and supplements against the potential risk to her pregnancy and developing fetus. ■

Medications and pregnancy. A woman should be very careful about what medications she uses during her pregnancy. The labeling on the medication itself may provide a warning about use during pregnancy, but the Physicians' Desk Reference also contains information about safety. ■

Medication is most likely to be harmful in the early critical weeks of the pregnancy, but there are some medications that should never be used during a pregnancy. They include Accutane for acne (Honein, Paulozzi, & Erickson, 2001), Soriatane for psoriasis (Stiefel Laboratories, 2008), and thalidomide, which is used to treat multiple myeloma, complications of AIDS, and leprosy (Ito et al., 2010). Soriatane can be harmful if used up to 3 years before the woman becomes pregnant. All three of these medications can result in severe birth defects.

When a woman has a chronic condition such as asthma, diabetes, or high blood pressure, continuing her medication during pregnancy may be necessary. For example, women who are diabetic have an increased risk of miscarriage, stillbirths, and some birth defects if they do not effectively control their glucose level while pregnant (Cunningham et al., 2005). For women living with AIDS, the National Institutes of Health (2014) recommend that they continue a regimen of antiretroviral drugs during pregnancy because it lowers the risk of passing HIV to the unborn child. There also is a large body of research on the use of antidepressants during pregnancy, but the findings have been mixed, so women taking these drugs should discuss their situation with their doctor immediately if they become pregnant (Field, 2007; Mayo Clinic Staff, 2012a).

Illegal Drugs

Conducting research on the effect of illegal drugs on a human pregnancy is challenging because it is difficult to get accurate information from mothers who are using illegal substances about the amount or type of drugs they use, or the length of time they have

WEB LINK 4.3
Accutane

WEB LINK 4.4
Heroin Epidemic

used them. It is also hard to disentangle the effect of the drugs themselves from the effect of other factors that might negatively affect the pregnancy. A woman who is using illegal drugs may be less likely to see a doctor during her pregnancy, and she may be less likely to take good care of herself in other ways. Despite these difficulties, there has been a good deal of research on the effect of marijuana and cocaine on pregnancies in recent years.

Infants exposed to cocaine prenatally are significantly more likely to be born prematurely, to be born at a low birth weight, or to be small for their gestational age (Gouin, Murphy, Shah, & Knowledge Synthesis Group on Determinants of Low Birth Weight and Preterm Births, 2011). These newborns also show signs of withdrawal several weeks after they are born, and prenatal exposure can affect the way they interact with their parents after birth. Infants rely on crying to signal distress to their caregivers. However, infants prenatally exposed to cocaine are less clear in the signals they send (Field, 2007), so it is more difficult for their parents to adequately care for them.

At the height of the cocaine epidemic in the 1980s, many were concerned about how our society would be able to meet the needs of infants damaged prenatally by cocaine exposure. However, as longitudinal data has accumulated, we have seen that developmental impacts are less severe than originally anticipated (Bandstra, Morrow, Mansoor, & Accornero, 2010), although there are subtle effects. Exposed children are less able to regulate their own behavior at age 7 (Accornero et al., 2011) and have lower language ability through age 12 (Bandstra et al., 2011). Cocaine use is often connected with other risk factors, including prenatal exposure to other toxic substances and a poor-quality early environment (Frank, Augustyn, Knight, Pell, & Zuckerman, 2001), but there is now clear evidence that cocaine exposure itself has negative effects on several areas of a child's subsequent development.

Marijuana is the most commonly used illicit drug among U.S. women in their childbearing years. According to the National Survey on Drug Use and Health, in 2009, 16.7 million people in the United States aged 12 or older used marijuana at least once in the month prior to being surveyed (National Institute on Drug Abuse, 2010), and 4.6% of pregnant women report using marijuana during the first trimester of their pregnancy (Substance Abuse and Mental Health Services Administration [SAMHSA], 2009). The psychoactive ingredient in marijuana, cannabis, crosses the placental barrier to enter the bloodstream of the fetus (Huizink & Mulder, 2006). Most of the studies on the effect of marijuana have been done with mothers who are heavy users, and these have found a pattern of neurological and behavioral effects on infants who were prenatally exposed, including tremors and startle responses (Fried & Makin, 1987) and altered sleep patterns in infancy (Huizink & Mulder, 2006).

The findings from research on the effect of prenatal exposure to marijuana on cognitive development of young children have been mixed. Research with older children has more consistently found a negative effect on executive functioning (which includes the ability to organize and integrate information), cognitive flexibility in problem solving, sustained and focused attention, impulsivity, hyperactivity, and abstract reasoning (Huizink & Mulder, 2006). A possible explanation for this finding is that cannabis alters the neurology in the prefrontal cortex, the site in the brain responsible for higher cognitive functioning that develops later in childhood.

Studies that exposed animals to cannabis prenatally have found evidence that changes occur in the sensitivity of specific circuits in the reward system of the brain, potentially making cannabis even more reinforcing for adult animals with this prenatal history (Malanga & Kosofsky, 2003). A longitudinal study of human infants exposed prenatally found that even after controlling for a number of other risk factors (including family and peer substance use, current alcohol and tobacco use by the adolescent, and characteristics of the family environment), prenatal exposure to cannabis still predicted marijuana use at age 14 (Day, Goldschmidt, & Thomas, 2006).

VIDEO LINK 4.2
Newborn Withdrawal

T/F #6
Adolescents who were exposed to marijuana prenatally are no more likely to use marijuana than adolescents who were not exposed.

False

Women who stop using marijuana while pregnant are likely to resume use after they have their babies (Bailey, Hill, Hawkins, Catalano, & Abbott, 2008), creating an environment in which children with a possible neurological sensitivity to marijuana also have role models who use the drug. Although the effects of marijuana use may be subtle, "even subtle effects can have both short-term and long-term implications" for the child's development (Huizink & Mulder, 2006, p. 36), so women need to think carefully about these implications before using recreational drugs.

A recent study that compared the independent effects of alcohol, tobacco, cocaine and marijuana on the likelihood of a preterm delivery or restricted fetal growth concluded that the legal substances, alcohol and tobacco, were more harmful than the illegal ones (Janisse, Bailey, Ager, & Sokol, 2014). While cocaine use was associated with preterm delivery and marijuana was associated with restricted fetal growth, alcohol and cigarettes were associated with both negative outcomes. This research serves as a reminder that the legal/illegal distinction should not be equated with the harmfulness of a substance. Each of these substances is potentially harmful to fetal development in its own way.

Sexually Transmitted Diseases

Women should be screened for sexually transmitted infections (STIs) early in their pregnancy because untreated STIs can affect their pregnancy and possibly their unborn child. Fortunately bacterial infections such as chlamydia, gonorrhea, and syphilis can be cured with antibiotics during the pregnancy (CDC, 2008b). Although viral STIs such as genital herpes and HIV/AIDS cannot be cured, antiviral medication can reduce the symptoms and their effect on the developing fetus (CDC, 2009c).

JOURNAL ARTICLE 4.2
Managing HIV in Pregnancy

The virus that causes AIDS can cross the placental barrier and be transmitted from mother to baby during the pregnancy, but it also can be passed along when the baby is being delivered vaginally or through the mother's breast milk after the baby is born. This is why it is recommended that HIV-positive mothers continue taking their antiviral medication during their pregnancy, have their babies by cesarean section, and not breast-feed their infants. Taking antiviral medication while pregnant lowers the viral load in the woman's blood, and, if the baby also is treated with anti-HIV medication after birth, the risk of passing the infection to the infant drops to less than 2% (USDHHS, 2012b). Figure 4.6 on page 120 illustrates the dramatic decline in perinatally acquired pediatric AIDS in the United States as a result of these efforts.

Neonatal herpes is another maternal infection that can have devastating consequences for an infant. Infants born with the disease who do not respond to treatment are at risk for neurological damage, intellectual disability, or death (American Social Health Association [ASHA], 1999–2011). Fortunately the risk of prenatal herpes infection appears to be low. An estimated 25% to 30% of pregnant women have genital herpes, but the infection rate for their babies is 0.1% (that is, one tenth of one percent; ASHA, 1999–2011). Ninety percent of cases of herpes in infants are transmitted as the infant passes through the birth canal. Consequently, if a mother has active genital herpes at the time she goes into labor, the infant is usually delivered by cesarean section (CDC, 2008b). Neonatal herpes also can be transmitted after the baby is born, often through kissing by an adult with an active oral herpes infection (ASHA, 1999–2011).

T/F #7

Infants who are born to women who are HIV-positive are almost certain to develop AIDS. *False*

Maternal Stress

Whenever we are under stress, our body produces stress hormones, and one of those hormones, cortisol, can pass through the placenta. High levels of maternal stress hormones during a pregnancy have been associated with lower birth weight and a slower growth rate in the fetus, and with temperamental difficulties in infants (Wadhwa, 2005). As we have seen for other conditions, the exact effects of prenatal stress and maternal cortisol production on a pregnancy depend on the nature, timing, and duration of exposure.

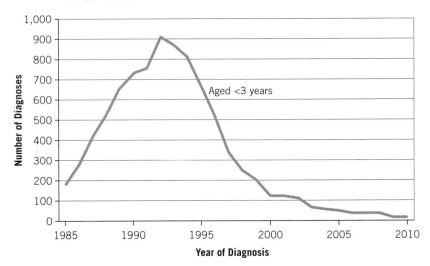

FIGURE 4.6 AIDS diagnoses among perinatally infected persons, 1985–2010

"Perinatal transmission" includes the transmission of the virus that causes AIDS from mother to child during pregnancy, labor and delivery, or breastfeeding. With the use of antiretroviral medications during pregnancy, the rate of transmission has decreased dramatically in recent years. Continued treatment of infected infants after birth further reduces the number who go on to develop AIDS.

SOURCE: National Center for HIV/AIDS, Viral Hepatitis, STD & TB Prevention (n.d.). *AIDS trends.* Retrieved from http://www.cdc.gov/hiv/pdf/statistics_surveillance_aidstrends.pdf

NOTE: All displayed data have been statistically adjusted to account for reporting delays, but not for incomplete reporting.

Several studies have shown that maternal stress early in the prenatal period has a greater impact on fetal growth, length of gestation, infant reactivity to stress, and cognitive development at 12 months of age (Davis & Sandman, 2010; Davis, Glynn, Waffarn, & Sandman, 2011; Wadhwa, 2005).

Maternal stress. Pregnancy brings with it some unique stresses, but excessive stress from any source can affect the fetus because stress hormones cross through the placenta. What are some things a pregnant woman could do to manage her level of stress? ∎

Environmental Pollutants

There are any number of toxic chemicals in our homes and workplaces that have the potential to be harmful to a pregnant woman (Sahin & Gungor, 2010; Wilson, 2014). Women need to carefully follow the usage warnings that appear on the labels of household cleaning products, insect repellants, pesticides, and solvents. Whenever possible, products that are toxic should be replaced by ones that are more environmentally friendly. Women who live in older homes can be exposed to lead in paints that were used before 1978 or from old lead pipes used in the plumbing, and living in an urban area or near heavily traveled roads can expose a woman to air pollutants. To avoid exposure to radiation pregnant women need to avoid exposure to X-rays. They also need to consider whether they are exposed to harmful substances in their workplace and talk with their employer and physician about ways to reduce or eliminate the exposure.

In conclusion, a number of factors can adversely affect prenatal development, but there is much a pregnant woman can do to help ensure the health and well-being of her baby. The goal of any pregnancy is to have a healthy baby, and fortunately this is exactly what happens in most cases. Although the risks are real and we need to guard against them whenever possible, there also is a great resiliency in the developing child. And, as we point out throughout this book, what happens to the child after birth has a huge impact on the eventual developmental outcome. Children who start life with birth defects or developmental deficits benefit greatly from growing up in a nurturing, supportive environment. Early intervention also can do a great deal to help these children develop to their fullest potential.

Check Your Understanding

1. What can the mother expect during each of the three trimesters of pregnancy?
2. What are the risks to the baby of maternal smoking and drinking during pregnancy?
3. What other factors can pose a risk to the developing embryo or fetus?

The Birth Experience

4.3

What do the mother and baby experience during birth?

After months of waiting, the parents-to-be are understandably excited—and likely a bit apprehensive—when labor finally begins. How long the process will take and the mother's subjective experience of the birth can be quite variable from one woman to the next.

Labor and Delivery

Earlier in the pregnancy the woman may have felt some *Braxton Hicks contractions*. These uterine contractions can begin as early as the 6th week of pregnancy but aren't noticeable until midpregnancy. They usually are infrequent, painless, and sporadic (Cunningham et al., 2005). However, as the woman gets closer to her due date, the contractions begin to soften and thin out the cervix, preparing it for true labor. We now look at each of the three stages of labor in detail.

First Stage: Early and Active Labor

For first-time mothers, the first stage of labor usually lasts between 10 and 20 hours, although it could be much briefer or go on for days. So much happens during this stage that it is divided into three phases. During the first phase called early labor, true contractions begin. At first they last about 30 to 60 seconds and come every 5 to 20 minutes. At this point, the contractions themselves are usually not very painful, and most women can safely remain at home, taking part in light activities or getting some rest, if possible. The contractions begin to thin out, or *efface*, and open up, or *dilate*, the cervix. As the cervix opens, a mucus plug is discharged from the vagina.

When the cervix has dilated to 4 centimeters, the second phase called active labor begins, and the contractions become longer, stronger, and more frequent (Cunningham et al., 2005). The cervix continues dilating, but now at a more rapid pace. When contractions last 1 minute and are coming about every 5 minutes, it is time for the woman to get ready to give birth, whether at a hospital, birthing center, or at home (ACOG, 2007). It is during this phase of active labor that women may feel they need some pain medication or will want to use the breathing and relaxation strategies they learned during childbirth classes. About half of American women use an *epidural* during their labor. An epidural

Early labor The first phase in the first stage of labor in which contractions are usually not painful but the cervix begins to thin out and dilate.

Active labor The second phase in the first stage of labor in which contractions become longer, stronger, and more frequent and the cervix dilates to 4 centimeters.

is a regional anesthesia that blocks the nerve impulses from the lower spine and decreases sensation in the lower half of the body to give some pain relief (American Pregnancy Association, 2007). On average, the second phase of labor lasts between 3 and 8 hours.

Once the cervix has dilated 7 centimeters, the woman enters the third phase called transition because it marks the movement into the second stage of labor (Cunningham et al., 2005). It is the shortest, but also the most difficult, phase of labor, lasting on average between 15 minutes and 3 hours. Contractions are now coming in very rapid succession and last up to 90 seconds each, with little or no pause between them. For about three-quarters of women, the amniotic sac ruptures (that is, the "water breaks") near the end of this phase.

Transition The third phase in the first stage of labor in which contractions come in rapid succession and last up to 90 seconds each, with little or no pause between them, and which ends when the cervix has dilated 10 centimeters.

Second Stage: Pushing

When the cervix has dilated 10 centimeters, the second stage of labor begins and uterine contractions begin to push the baby down through the birth canal. Many women feel a strong urge to push with each contraction. Between 30% and 35% of vaginal births in the United States involve an episiotomy, a surgical incision from the back of the vagina to the anus intended to allow the baby to exit the birth canal without creating more of a tear in the tissue, but the medical necessity of this procedure has recently been called into question (Hartmann et al., 2005).

Most babies enter the birth canal head first, with the back of their head toward the front of their mother's stomach and their chin tucked against their chest. Abnormal positioning of the fetus is called a malpresentation. Labor can be slower and more difficult if the baby's head is facing upward, a position called sunny-side-up; the baby's feet or bottom are positioned to come out first, called a breech presentation; or the baby is laying crosswise in the uterus, called a transverse position. The doctor may try to rotate the baby into a better position, but sometimes a malpresentation necessitates a surgical delivery (Center of Excellence for Medical Multimedia, n.d.). Once the baby's head emerges from the birth canal, one shoulder and then the other are delivered, and the rest of the baby's body quickly follows. If everything is going normally, the baby may be placed on the mother's stomach while the umbilical cord is clamped and cut.

Malpresentation An abnormal positioning of the fetus in the uterus.

Third Stage: Delivering the Placenta

Now the uterus begins to contract again to expel the placenta. This generally occurs without any pain or discomfort to the mother, and this stage lasts only 5 to 10 minutes (ACOG, 2007). The contraction of the uterus helps close off the blood vessels where the placenta has separated from the uterus, to prevent further bleeding. If an episiotomy has been performed, the doctor will close that incision at this time.

BSIP/UIG Via Getty Images

Just born. This baby is immediately put onto the mother's stomach so she can touch and hold her baby right away. ∎

Birthing Options

Today there is a wide range of birthing options available. Women can choose a birth setting, the type of professional assistance they receive, and a birthing technique. Deciding which is the best option depends on her personal preferences and her medical condition, but she also needs to consider both the risks and the benefits of each alternative to make the best decision. Pregnant women receive information about childbirth options from a variety of sources. In a nationally representative sample of over 1,500 mothers, 56% of first-time mothers reported taking a childbirth education class, most often at a hospital site. Two-thirds of the sample also said they had watched one or more television shows depicting birth. Information from friends and relatives and the Internet were other important sources of childbirth information (Declercq, Sakala, Corry, & Applebaum, 2006).

Births can occur in a hospital, at a birthing center (either a free-standing center or a center affiliated with a hospital), or at home. When a woman decides to give birth in a hospital, she has access to medical professionals and medical technology, including access

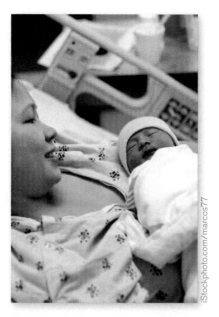 

Birthing options. Women have a choice about where and how they give birth. The birth can take place in a hospital, in a birthing center, or at home. The birth can be attended by a physician or midwife. What do you think are advantages or disadvantages of each of these alternatives? ■

to pain medications, but hospitals are sometimes seen as impersonal settings in which the woman gives up much control over the circumstances of the birth (Williams & Umberson, 1999). There also has been concern that medical interventions are overused when births occur in a hospital setting. For instance, labor can be induced through the use of medications or by rupturing the amniotic sac if the woman has passed her due date and the baby is becoming too large, but labor is sometimes induced as an elective procedure for the convenience of the family or a physician (Dublin, Lydon-Rochelle, Kaplan, Watts, & Critchlow, 2000). Approximately 22% of pregnant women in the United States undergo induction of labor (ACOG, 2009), a rate that has doubled since 1990 (Lydon-Rochelle et al., 2007). Although the associated risks are small, it can trigger contractions that are too frequent or that are abnormally long and strong and this can physically exhaust the woman and make her feel unprepared and out of control during her labor.

A birth center provides a home-like atmosphere and gives the woman greater autonomy in her experience of labor. For instance, she has freedom to move around and can get into different positions, such as squatting, that may help alleviate her discomfort and assist the birth process. Birth centers are staffed by certified nurse-midwives, not obstetricians (Bouchez, 2008). While a birth center will have standard medical equipment, the staff does not perform surgical procedures such as epidural or cesarean deliveries and does not induce labor or administer drugs. For that reason, a woman might choose a hospital birth center rather than a freestanding center. Pain relief, fetal monitoring, and surgery if it is needed are all close at hand with this alternative (Bouchez, 2008).

Home births are reserved for low-risk pregnancies. Although the number of home births has increased in recent years, in 2012 less than 1.5% of U.S. births occurred in a residence (MacDorman, Mathews, & Declercq, 2014). Some studies have found that home births are as safe as hospital births for healthy women having a normal pregnancy, but the American Congress of Obstetrics and Gynecology has criticized the quality of the research behind such claims (Bouchez, 2008).

Births can be attended by a physician or a midwife. In the United States, 90% of births are attended by a physician, most often a gynecologist or obstetrician (Boston Women's Health Book Collective, 2005) and about 8% are attended by midwives (Martin, Hamilton, Osterman, Curtin, & Mathews, 2013). Although the number of births attended by midwives has more than doubled since 1990, it still significantly lags behind the number in other parts of the world. Ninety-eight percent of U.S. births attended by midwives occur in a hospital or a birth center (Mendola, 1999). Although the World Health Organization (2011) recommends that skilled health professionals be involved in childbirth, around the world 34% of births (largely in developing countries) are not attended by a professional.

Doula A trained, knowledgeable companion who supports a woman during her labor and delivery.

VIDEO LINK 4.3
Doula

In addition to these healthcare professionals, doulas and birth coaches may support a woman during labor. Unlike a physician or midwife, a doula does not directly assist in the birth process but rather is a trained, knowledgeable companion who is present to support the woman through her labor and delivery. In one controlled study, women who were randomly assigned to receive continuous support from a doula during labor had lower rates of cesarean section deliveries and fewer forceps deliveries, needed less epidural anesthesia, and had shorter labors than women in the control group who were simply observed during their labor (Kennell, Klaus, McGrath, Robertson, & Hinkley, 1991). Because women find it comforting to have someone who can assure them that what they are experiencing is normal and to be expected, one possible explanation of these results is that the doula's presence reduces the amount of stress hormones the woman produces during her labor.

Having a labor coach can provide invaluable support for the woman. A personal labor coach usually is a husband, partner, relative, or close friend who has attended childbirth preparation classes with the woman and is committed to being supportive of her through the delivery process. A coach may do specific things that help the woman relax, such as tracking and reporting her progress through each contraction, providing some distraction to get her mind off the contractions, or doing physical things to make her more comfortable like providing a massage or helping her change her position.

During their labor, 69% of the women in one study reported using at least one non-pharmacological method of pain relief, including breathing techniques (49%); changing position or moving around (42%); mental strategies such as relaxation, visualization, or hypnosis (25%); or massage or acupressure (20%) (Declercq et al., 2006). However, in this sample, 76% of women reported receiving an epidural in which medication is injected into the spine, and 81% of those women rated it as a very effective means of pain relief.

One of the most dramatic changes in American childbirth in recent years is the number of children born by cesarean delivery (see Figure 4.7). In 2012, 32.8% of all births were by cesarean delivery (unchanged from 2011), compared to 22.9% in 2000 (Martin et al., 2013). Although rates increased across all age and ethnic groups, the rate is highest among older mothers (49.2% for women over the age of 40) and non-Hispanic Black women (35.5%) (Martin et al., 2013). Cesarean deliveries were once the result of medical necessity, but at least part of the recent increase has been attributed to nonmedical reasons that include maternal choice, more conservative practice guidelines that call for surgical intervention sooner, and physicians' fear of litigation. In 2006, cesarean deliveries were the most frequently performed surgical procedure in U.S. hospitals (Menacker & Hamilton, 2010). A panel of experts convened by the National Institutes of Health said that it was difficult to fully evaluate the benefits or risks of elective cesareans compared to planned vaginal delivery, but concluded that the wishes of the woman should be honored, barring any medical contraindications, as long as the known risks and benefits have been discussed with her (Viswanathan et al., 2006).

We used to believe that a woman should not attempt a vaginal birth once she had had a cesarean delivery, but that idea began to change in the 1980s when a panel convened by the National Institutes of Health questioned that assumption. Following their recommendations for when a vaginal birth after cesarean (VBAC) could be considered, the number of VBAC deliveries increased through the 1980s and 1990s but has declined since 1996 (Cunningham et al., 2010). Because it is difficult to compare the benefits of a VBAC delivery for the woman with the possible increased risk for the fetus, clinicians and medical facilities continue to resist promoting VBACs.

FIGURE 4.7   Cesarean delivery rates: United States, 1989–2011

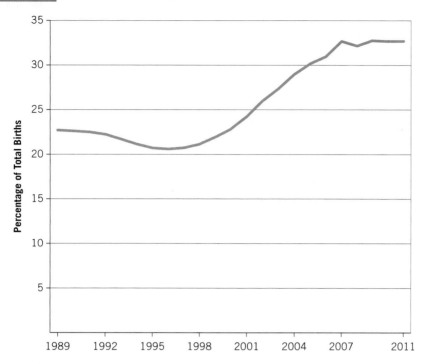

The number of births by cesarean delivery in the United States has increased dramatically in recent years for a variety of reasons, including an increased number of women who elect to have a surgical delivery.

SOURCE: Figure 1, p. 2 in American College of Obstetricians and Gynecologists (2014).

In non-Western cultures, the birth process may be quite different from what we have described above. For example, an Ifaluk woman, who lives in Micronesia on one of two tiny islands in the Pacific Ocean, gives birth in a birth house, accompanied by a midwife and her female relatives (Le, 2000). When the baby is ready to be born, the woman kneels on a mat and helps the baby out by herself. She must try not to show distress or pain, in accord with the Ifaluk value of remaining calm at all times. If there are complications, the other women will help. After the baby is born, the woman's mother helps by holding the baby and then bathes the baby in the ocean. This is a sharp contrast to the Western, hospital-based approach to childbirth.

The Birth Experience of the Baby

You probably have heard stories about labor and delivery from the perspective of the mother, but have you ever wondered how the baby experiences birth? It might seem pretty traumatic. The baby is pushed through the birth canal, with uterine contractions intermittently causing oxygen deprivation (Lagercrantz & Slotkin, 1986), and the newborn rapidly goes from a warm, quiet, and dark prenatal environment into a bright, noisy, and cold postnatal world. Fortunately babies are physiologically well prepared to handle the stress of being born. For one thing, the skull of a baby is composed of separate plates that can overlap and compress during the birth process, allowing the head to elongate so it can fit through the birth canal. For another, the compression of the baby's head and the oxygen deprivation that accompanies the contractions trigger the release of stress hormones that help clear the lungs after birth and promote normal breathing, and ensure a rich supply of blood to the heart and brain (Lagercrantz & Slotkin, 1986).

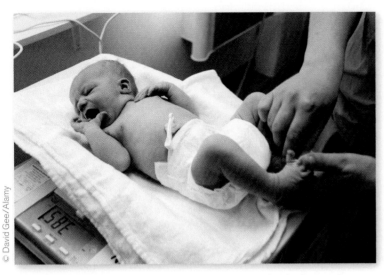

Apgar assessment. The condition of a newborn is assessed at 1 minute and 5 minutes after birth by the Apgar Scale to determine whether any medical intervention is needed. ▪

Apgar Scale An assessment of a newborn's overall condition at 1 minute and 5 minutes after birth that is based on the newborn's activity level, pulse, grimace, appearance, and respiration.

As soon as the baby's head is delivered, the doctor or midwife will use a rubber syringe to clear away any material in the mouth and air passages. Most babies begin breathing spontaneously at this point, but as many as 10% of newborns need some form of resuscitation to help them (Cunningham et al., 2005). After the baby emerges, the umbilical cord is clamped and cut when it has stopped pulsing and a few drops of an antibiotic such as tetracycline or erythromycin are placed in the baby's eyes to prevent infection that could be caused by any organisms that were present in the birth canal (Cunningham et al., 2005).

The baby's overall condition is assessed using the Apgar Scale at 1 minute and again at 5 minutes after birth. The newborn receives 0, 1, or 2 points each for its *Activity* level, *Pulse*, *Grimace* (reflex irritability), *Appearance*, and *Respiration*. A total score of 7 to 10 points is the normal range, and for newborns in this range, routine care will continue, with a reassessment of their status at 5 minutes. The baby will be kept warm and placed on the mother's stomach for some skin-to-skin contact or in her arms so mother and baby can meet for the first time. An Apgar score in the range of 4 to 6 indicates that some intervention is needed. This might be some additional suction to help the baby breathe, massage, or the administration of oxygen. A score of 3 or less means some immediate lifesaving intervention is needed (Bregman, 2005).

Check Your Understanding

1. What happens during each of the three stages of labor?
2. How do the roles of a doula and a midwife differ?
3. What does the baby typically experience during birth?

4.4

How do newborns function, and what threatens their well-being?

The Newborn

Babies enter the world equipped in many ways to begin their journey of development and to interact with the people who will love and care for them along the way. The journey is easier for some newborns than others, but in this section we examine the capabilities newborns possess from birth, and some of the challenges they face in the early months of life.

Newborn Capabilities

In the early days of the field of psychology, William James (1890/1990) described the world of the infant as "one great blooming, buzzing confusion" (p. 462), and the idea that newborns were unable to make sense of their world persisted for years. Today we know this statement seriously underestimates the capabilities of newborns to receive information about the world through all their senses in an organized way and to respond to that information. As we said earlier in this chapter, all the senses begin developing during the prenatal period and become functional before birth. Some are more advanced in their development than others when the infant is born, but there is no doubt the newborn can hear, see, taste, smell, and respond to touch.

Infant states. Infants continually move through a series of states that allow them to regulate the amount of stimulation that they receive. Can you see how this is an adaptive way for an infant to meet his or her needs for rest, stimulation, and physical care? ■

Infant States

Newborns have a set of infant states that represent different levels of consciousness that help regulate the level of stimulation they receive and keep the input at a level they can process. At one end of the continuum is crying and at the other is deep sleep. Let's start at the quiet end of this continuum.

Newborns spend most of their time asleep, and it is normal for them to sleep 16 to 18 hours each day (Hanrahan, 2006). About half this time is spent in REM (rapid eye movement) sleep, which is the light sleep in which dreams occur, and half is spent in regular sleep, which ranges from drowsiness in which the eyes open and close to a deep sleep in which the infant is quiet and doesn't move. Because infants' stomachs are so small, they will wake up to eat about every 3 or 4 hours throughout the day and the night. By 6 months of age, most babies will sleep through the night for 12 hours or more and continue to take daytime naps (Hanrahan, 2006).

When infants are awake, they can be in a state of *quiet alertness* in which their eyes are open and they are attentive to what is going on around them but are very still, or in a state of *active alertness* in which they are alert to what is going on in their environment but are moving around. Young infants are quiet and awake for only about 1 hour each day, and this state comes in episodes that last only 5 to 10 minutes at a time (Maurer & Maurer, 1988). The last state on the continuum is crying, which is the way infants signal that they need something, but infants may also cry for no discernible reason. The amount of time that infants cry increases to an average of 2.6 hours a day at 6 weeks of age, but decreases after this time (Hiscock, 2006). Sensitively responding to an infant's needs can help this state pass.

Even at this young age, there are individual differences in how regular infants are in their behavior. Some have regular and predictable schedules and are easy to calm when they are upset, but others are much more variable in their schedule and much more difficult to soothe. Some infants smoothly transition from one state to another, and others move rapidly or unexpectedly between states. Some signal what they need in a way that is clear and easy for parents to interpret so they can promptly respond, and others are

Infant states Different levels of consciousness used to regulate the amount of stimulation an infant receives; states range from crying to deep sleep.

much more difficult for new parents to "read." Over the early weeks, parents come to know the unique characteristics of their infants, and in most cases, parents and infant are able to get in sync with each other so things go relatively smoothly. That doesn't mean, however, that there won't be plenty of nights with too little sleep for the new parents and times when they worry about how well they and their infant are doing.

Risks to the Newborn's Health and Well-Being

A number of factors can place a newborn at risk, but being born prematurely or at a low birth weight are significant ones. A premature birth is one that occurs before a gestational age of 37 weeks. Babies born weighing less than 5 pounds, 4 ounces are considered low birth weight. Babies who are smaller in size than normal for their gestational age are considered small for gestational age. This is an indication that some circumstance restricted physical growth in the prenatal environment so that the infant developed more slowly than normal.

After increasing from the 1980s through 2006, the number of preterm or premature births in the United States declined slightly to 11.5% of live births in 2012 (March of Dimes, 2014a, 2014b). This decrease is significant because premature infants are at risk for a number of neurological and development problems. Beyond the human cost, prematurity carries a high financial cost as well. The direct health costs for the first year of a premature baby's life average $49,033, versus $4,551 for a baby whose birth is uncomplicated (March of Dimes, 2008).

We have made great strides in recent years in our ability to care for babies born prematurely. Medical technology helps ensure not only their survival but also their healthy development. The modern neonatal intensive care unit (NICU) has roots that reach back more than 100 years. Read **Journey of Research: From Child Hatchery to Modern NICU** to understand the progress that has been made.

Premature birth A birth that occurs before a gestational age of 37 weeks.

Low birth weight A full-term infant who weighs less than 5 pounds, 4 ounces.

Small for gestational age Babies who are smaller in size than normal for their gestational age.

....

JOURNEY OF RESEARCH *From Child Hatchery to Modern NICU*

One of the first attempts to improve the survival rates of premature infants was an incubator developed by obstetrician Étienne Stéphane Tarnier in the 1880s (Sammons & Lewis, 1985). It consisted of a wooden box with walls insulated with sawdust. The box was divided into two compartments. Half of the bottom compartment was left open to allow for circulation of air, and the other half held stone bottles filled with hot water to control the temperature. As the air circulated into the upper compartment, which contained the infant, it passed over a wet sponge to pick up moisture. A chimney in the top compartment allowed the air to pass over the infant and exit into the room (Neonatology on the Web, 2007). In addition to controlling heat and humidity and isolating sick infants from healthy ones (Sammons & Lewis, 1985), the "incubator is so simple that

any village carpenter can make it, and cheap enough to be within the means of all but the most destitute" (Neonatology on the Web, 2007, para. 3).

In 1896, Martin A. Couney supervised a display of incubators with six premature infants in them at the Berlin World's Fair, in an exhibit named "Kinderbrutanstalt" or "child hatchery." The exhibit was such a commercial success (yes, people were willing to pay admission to see these wonders) that Couney repeated it at other expositions around the world until the 1940s, when the public's interest waned (Snow, 1981). He did provide excellent care to the infants in his charge and claimed that 6,500 of the 8,000 infants in his care survived, including one as small as 1.5 pounds (Snow, 1981).

After World War II, the care of premature infants increasingly moved into the hands of medical specialists, and neonatology emerged as a recognized medical specialty dedicated to the care of newborns. Because physicians believed parents were the source of dangerous infections and that premature infants could easily be overstimulated, parents were routinely excluded from the nursery. This practice continued until the early 1970s (Davis, Mohay, & Edwards, 2003), but today parents are an important part of the team that cares for a premature infant. They are encouraged to participate in the care and feeding of their infant, to ask questions so they understand the complicated medical interventions that may be sustaining their infant, and to get close to their infant to begin building a bond.

Another important change in our care of premature infants is based on research showing that touch and stimulation at an appropriate level are beneficial, not harmful to the infant. Parents might even be encouraged to provide *kangaroo care*, in which the baby is placed in skin-to-skin contact with the parent's bare chest and draped with a blanket, or the infant may receive infant massage (Field, Diego, & Hernandez-Reif, 2007). Studies of the effect of systematic massage

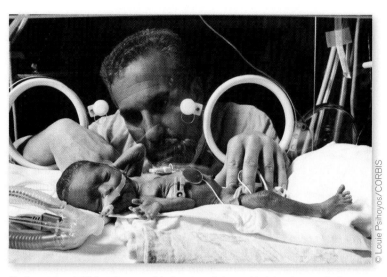

Modern neonatal intensive care. Modern hospitals provide intensive medical care for premature infants by carefully controlling their environment and continually monitoring their bodily functions. However, even in this intensive medical environment, human touch is an important part of their care. ■

on premature infants have shown that three 15-minute sessions daily for 10 days can result in a 47% greater weight gain than is experienced by infants who don't receive massage (Field et al., 2007). Take a look at the picture of a modern NICU on this page to see how far we have come from that first sawdust-filled box. ■

Although in many cases the underlying cause of premature births remains unknown (Edgren, 2002), we have identified several factors that increase the risk. A lack of prenatal care for women who lack health insurance plays a role in 20% of premature births (March of Dimes, 2013). The increase in the number of multiple births is another factor, because multiples are more likely to be born prematurely. Unhealthy maternal behaviors during pregnancy, such as smoking, drinking, or using drugs, also are responsible for some premature and low-birth-weight births (Browne, 2005). In some cases there is an abnormality in the woman's reproductive system, such as a placenta that prematurely separates from the uterus or a cervix that opens too soon.

Premature infants are not yet able to regulate their bodily functions in the same way full-term infants can, so the neonatal intensive care unit (NICU) has been specifically designed to monitor the functioning of the infants and to compensate for what they cannot yet do for themselves. For instance, premature infants do not have a layer of body fat that helps them regulate body temperature and fluid loss, so incubators provide constant levels of heat and moisture. They may not yet have a sucking reflex or gag reflex, so they need special feeding procedures. Their immature central nervous system means they can be easily overwhelmed by stimuli, so the light level is kept low, noise is minimized, and the infants are handled slowly and gently (VanderBerg, 2007). Staff in the NICU need to be particularly sensitive toward infants who cannot signal what they need (Smotherman & Robinson, 1996; VanderBerg, 2007).

Medical technology continues to advance the care of premature infants, and modern NICUs are very successful at saving even very small, fragile babies. The survival rate for premature babies born at very low birth weight of less than 1500 grams, or about 3.3 pounds, is approximately 90%, and for infants born at extremely low birth weight of less than 1000 grams, or about 2.2 pounds, the rate is still between 50% and 70% (Volpe, 2009). However, as birth weight goes down, the risk of complications goes up. This has created a dilemma for medical professionals who work with these tiny patients. Most NICUs provide intensive care to infants born at a gestational age of 25 weeks or more, but they may provide it to infants at a gestational age of 23 or 24 weeks only with the agreement of the parents (Tyson, Nehal, Langer, Green, & Higgins, 2008; see also Cunningham et al., 2005). The question is whether there is a point at which a premature infant is so small and the chance of survival so low that the humane thing to do is provide comfort care rather than trying to save the life of the infant. Comfort care provides for the basic needs of the infant but stops short of heroic measures that might cause additional pain and suffering without being likely to prolong the infant's life.

T/F #8
An infant born prematurely will have developmental problems and lag behind other children of the same age. *False*

Despite our best efforts, a number of premature infants do not survive, and prematurity accounts for more than 70% of neonatal deaths (Williamson et al., 2008). Premature infants who do survive demonstrate a wide range of developmental outcomes. Some go on to have few, if any, developmental problems and do not differ substantially from full-term infants, while others experience lifelong disabilities that can range from mild to very severe (Tyson et al., 2008). Many factors—prenatal conditions, birth circumstances, number and quality of medical services utilized by the family, access to intervention services, and many more—come together to affect the quality of the outcome.

When infants finally are large enough to leave the NICU, their parents need to turn their attention to helping their children reach their fullest potential. A consistent finding from numerous studies is that low-birth-weight and premature infants are at increased risk of cognitive impairment and academic failure as they grow up (Hill, Brooks-Gunn, & Waldfogel, 2003; Jepsen & Martin, 2006). They also can have sensory or motor impairments or be medically fragile. Those who are born the earliest are also those at greatest risk (Cunningham et al., 2005; Dombrowski, Noonan, & Martin, 2007), but even among very premature infants born at 24 to 26 weeks, 20% were "totally free of impairment at 5 years of age or more" (Cunningham et al., 2005, p. 857).

To have good developmental outcomes, premature infants and their parents need access to comprehensive services that start early in development and are delivered consistently over a period of time (Hill et al., 2003). Even under the best of circumstances, caring for a premature infant places extraordinary demands on a parent. That means parents need to stay motivated to use the services and follow through on the recommendations made by the professionals who work with their child. For this reason, the way the parents view their infants and the expectations they have for them are crucial.

If parents see their infant in a negative way and have low expectations for her, they may unconsciously treat the infant in ways that actually hinder development. This way of perceiving a premature infant is called a *prematurity stereotype*, and both mothers of premature infants and mothers of full-term infants may see premature infants in a stereotypically negative way. When parents watched videotapes of premature infants and full-term infants, they rated premature infants as less physically mature in appearance, less sociable, less cognitively competent, and less behaviorally mature (Stern, Karraker, McIntosh, Moritzen, & Olexa, 2006). Yet all the videotapes actually showed full-term infants. When the researchers labeled the infant in a video "premature," the mothers saw that infant's behavior less favorably simply because of the label and the preconceptions that came with it. For this reason it is important that we help parents of premature infants understand that their infants can have good developmental outcomes so they can see and appreciate the progress their children make.

Check Your Understanding

1. What is the newborn capable of doing at birth?
2. What are some risks to the newborn's health and wellbeing?
3. What promotes optimal development in premature infants?

The Transition to Parenthood

Becoming a parent affects all aspects of your life including your sense of identity, your relationships with your partner and others, and your career, so it is not surprising that it can be accompanied by a good deal of stress as well as many positive feelings. We describe families as systems of interrelated individuals. In a system, the addition of a new member affects the roles and functioning of all other individuals and, like any major life transition, adjusting to the new situation takes time. In this section, we look at the impact of the birth of a new baby on the mother and the father, but also at the impact on the couple.

Becoming a Mother

Pregnancy, childbirth, and child rearing are experiences that will touch on the full range of a woman's emotions. In a society that idealizes mothers as being totally self-sacrificing, all-giving nurturers, women who struggle with the normal array of mixed feelings may have an added burden of guilt that they are not living up to this ideal if they are not ecstatic following the birth of their baby. Women are happiest about having a baby when they have had a choice about whether to have a child; have support from a partner, family, and others; and have adequate resources to support the child (Lips, 2006).

It is a common misconception that after a baby is born, a new mother automatically follows her instincts and knows just what to do (Redshaw & Martin, 2011). In fact, many first-time mothers around the world must learn to be comfortable with breastfeeding, changing diapers, and soothing a crying baby. The way they themselves were mothered as a child provides an unconscious model for most women of what a mother should be like. New mothers also frequently turn to their own mothers, relatives, child care professionals, and books or websites on child care for support and advice (Walker, 2005). However, when a woman receives conflicting advice from different sources, it adds to her stress rather than relieving it. Mothers report that when this happens, they fall back on their own instincts or experiences, or they use the baby's cues to guide their decision (Walker, 2005).

New mothers are also helped by their biology. Nurturing behavior gets a boost from hormones such as oxytocin and prolactin, which are at elevated levels in expectant and new mothers (Bower, 2005; Brunton & Russell, 2008; Lim & Young, 2006). There also is evidence to suggest that hormonal changes in men may be linked with fathering behavior (Gettler, McDade, & Kuzawa, 2011). Storey, Walsh, Quinton, and Wynne-Edwards (2000) studied expectant couples who were living together and found that immediately before their baby's birth both men and women had higher-than-normal levels of prolactin and cortisol, and following the birth both also showed lowered levels of testosterone, the hormone often linked with aggressive behavior. For fathers, the pattern was strongest in men who had experienced symptoms of a sympathetic pregnancy, such as weight gain, nausea, and mood swings, during their partner's pregnancy.

The rapid hormonal changes that follow childbirth, along with other stresses new mothers experience, frequently result in mood swings, sadness, loss of appetite, trouble sleeping, and irritability that we associate with the "baby blues" (Cunningham et al., 2005). Often a little time, together with some rest and help with caring for the newborn, are enough to alleviate the symptoms. Postpartum depression is a more severe response that typically begins within the first 3 months of delivery and lasts more than 2 weeks (Cunningham et al., 2005). Symptoms include sadness, lack of energy, trouble concentrating, and feelings of guilt or worthlessness, and are severe enough to interfere with the woman's ability to function. Women who experience depression should consult their doctor, because effective treatments can help restore their well-being. The most common approaches to treating postpartum depression are antidepressant medications and counseling or therapy (Logsdon, Wisner, & Shanahan, 2007).

4.5

How do people experience the transition to parenthood?

T/F #9
When a woman gives birth she instinctively knows what to do to care for her new baby.
False

AUDIO LINK 4.4
Postpartum Depression

Postpartum depression A severe depression that typically begins within the first three months after childbirth that lasts for more than 2 weeks; symptoms are severe enough that they interfere with the woman's ability to function.

In some cultures, including many Asian, Middle Eastern, Latin, and indigenous cultures, the month or so following the birth of a baby is considered a crucial time for the new mother to recover. In this process, she has support from a female-oriented cultural network and cultural traditions that celebrate the birth as a new beginning for the woman and her family (Chang, 2011). In contrast, for women in Western society there is little recognition by society that their new role is valued, and they may have only limited social support (Munhall, 2007). They often receive some help from the baby's father and from their own mother or other relatives, but they may spend much of the day alone with the baby. Some new mothers feel pressure (or financial need) to quickly return to work and may be torn between this need and their desire to devote themselves completely to the care of their infant. Women in American society have many choices, but having many choices means that they can also second-guess their decisions, whatever they are.

Becoming a Father

Couvade A sympathetic pregnancy in which a man experiences a variety of symptoms associated with pregnancy or childbirth while his partner is pregnant.

Many changes also occur for a man when he learns that he is about to become a father. Most of these changes are psychological and emotional, but some men from different cultures around the world experience what anthropologists call couvade, from the French word *couver*, meaning "to hatch" (Brennan, Marshall-Lucette, Ayers, & Ahmed, 2007; Chernella, 1991). In *ritualistic couvade*, the man might feign contractions and labor pains at the same time the mother is in labor. In the modern world, a fairly common type of *psychosomatic couvade* occurs in which men experience a variety of physical symptoms associated with pregnancy, including weight gain, nausea, indigestion, backaches, mood swings, and food cravings. Between 11% and 65% of husbands of pregnant women report such symptoms (Bartlett, 2004; Masoni, Trimarchi, dePunzio, & Fioretti, 1994).

An expectant father expresses his emotional investment in the pregnancy by nurturing and caring for his partner. He supports her by helping her choose a healthy diet, encouraging her to get enough rest and an appropriate amount of exercise, and supporting her as she deals with the emotional and physical changes of pregnancy. Many men accompany their partners to doctor's appointments or childbirth classes and actively prepare for the birth process. Having good information about what is happening to his partner and learning ways that a man can provide tangible assistance can help him prepare for his transition into fatherhood (Boyce, Condon, Barton, & Corkindale, 2007).

For many men today, choosing to actively participate in the birth of their baby by being present during labor and in the delivery room is one of the ways they express their empathy for their partner. However, the actual experience may fall short of their expectations (Bartlett, 2004; Dolan & Coe, 2011; Reed, 2005). Men describe feeling marginalized by medical professionals both during the pregnancy and the birth itself

©iStockphoto.com/toos

A new father is born. The transition to becoming a new father can be a powerful experience for men. A father's role today involves much more than being the breadwinner for the family. Fathers also can be sensitive and nurturant caregivers for their newborn infants. ∎

(Dolan & Coe, 2011; Hanson, Hunter, Bormann, & Sobo, 2009). Despite these feelings, many men are overcome with a powerful and perhaps unexpected rush of emotions following the birth of their baby (Erlandsson & Lindgren, 2009; Reed, 2005). Those early moments and the opportunity to see and hold their newborn become rich rewards for the new father.

However, in many cultures women prefer to have their mothers present at the birth rather than their husbands (Abushaikah & Massah, 2012). In some cultures fathers and other men are strictly prohibited from taking part in the birth experience and early care of the baby, while in others they assume a major role in caring for young children. Ifaluk men are only allowed to see their newborn from a distance while the mother and baby stay in the birth house for the first 10 days. During this time, the father has two responsibilities: to provide the mother with fish to eat and to make a cradle for the baby. The Ifaluk mother hands over the responsibility of caring for the child to the father when the child is 2 years old, and he becomes the major caretaker for the next 2 to 3 years (Le, 2000). Clearly, the role of the father can differ enormously from one culture to another.

Becoming a Family

In their classic book *The Transition to Parenthood*, Jay Belsky and John Kelly (1994) say that while men and women become parents at the *same time*, they don't become parents in the *same way*. Researchers have identified a number of issues that surface for new parents, including fatigue and exhaustion (especially in the early weeks after the birth and especially for the mother), as well as anxiety, depression, and self-doubt about their parental competence. Women are more likely to worry about changes in their physical appearance, and men are more likely to worry about providing for their family financially (Belsky & Kelly, 1994; Halle et al., 2008). Both worry about the increase in household responsibilities and changed relationships with in-laws (who also have an adjustment to make as they become grandparents, aunts, and uncles). And of course, they both find sources of gratification, including the fact that they find the new baby irresistible and may become totally preoccupied with thoughts about the baby. If you have spent time with new parents, you have probably noticed that it is difficult to get them to talk about anything else.

Dividing the additional work that results from having a baby in the household often becomes a sore point for the couple. One reason is that men and women may use different yardsticks to measure their contribution to this workload. If men compare what they do around the house and their direct contribution to caring for the newborn—that is, changing diapers, feeding the infant, getting up during the night—against what their fathers did, their contribution is significant. Between 1965 and 2011, the amount of time men spent in child care almost tripled (Parker & Wang. 2013). However, in most cases, men's contribution still is only about half what their partners are doing (see Figure 4.8.). Between 1965 and 2011, the amount of time women spent in child care increased almost 50% (Parker & Wang, 2013). Using that yardstick to measure the parents' relative contribution to child care, new mothers can end up feeling unhappy and disgruntled. Despite the idealized notion of equally shared parenting, a traditional gender division of labor in parenting often continues to exist, with father assuming the role of a helper while mothers assume the role of primary caregiver (Fox, 2001; Gjerdingen & Center, 2005; Kotila, Schoppe-Sullivan, & Kamp Dush, 2013).

To better understand the type of help and support that can help parents transition into their new roles, use **Active Learning: Easing the Transition to Parenthood** to explore the range of services available to parents in different circumstances.

WEB LINK 4.5
**Postnatal Marital
Satisfaction**

JOURNAL ARTICLE 4.3
Postnatal Gender Dynamics

T/F #10

Following the birth of
a baby, couples today
pretty much share
household and child
care responsibilities.
False

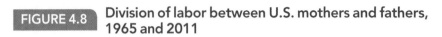

FIGURE 4.8 Division of labor between U.S. mothers and fathers, 1965 and 2011

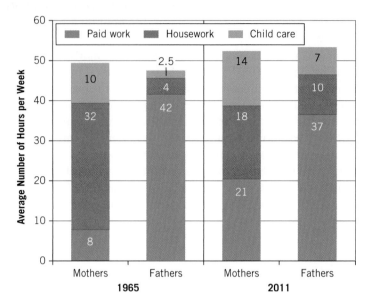

Although fathers have increased their involvement with their children significantly since 1965, they still spend much less time with them than mothers do.

SOURCE: Bianchi, Robinson, & Milkie (2006); Parker & Wang (2013).

NOTE: Based on adults ages 18–64 with their own child(ren) under age 18 living the household. Total figures (at the top of each bar) may not add to component parts due to rounding.

Active Learning

Easing the Transition to Parenthood

Research the services or supports available to new parents living in your community in each of these circumstances. In each case, note whether parents need to pay for the services and whether the provider is a professional (for example, a nurse or a parent educator) or a nonprofessional (for example, an experienced parent).

- An older married couple with a premature infant
- A single mother with a healthy, full-term infant
- An unmarried couple with a low-birth-weight infant

Searching online for early intervention programs and the name of your state or community should lead you to some useful information. ∎

In light of the stress associated with becoming a new parent, it is not surprising that a number of studies report a significant decrease in marital satisfaction following the birth of a baby (Hansen, 2012; Luhmann, Hofmann, Eid, & Lucas, 2012; Pinquart & Teubert, 2010; Twenge, Campbell, & Foster, 2003). However, this is not a universal finding. At least some couples report increased marital satisfaction and happiness following the birth of a child or a stable pattern of marital satisfaction across time (Anderson, Van Ryzin, & Doherty, 2010; Dush, Taylor, & Kroeger, 2008).

Recent research on parenthood and marital satisfaction has moved in the direction of identifying the circumstances that are associated with a smooth transition to parenthood versus a rocky one (Holmes, Sasaki, & Hazen, 2013). First, having realistic expectations for how parenthood will change your life helps new parents adjust to this transition (Holmes et al., 2013). For instance, if a new mother expects that both parents will equally share the extra work created by an infant and this expectation is not fulfilled, it can lead to dissatisfaction with the relationship. Other areas where reality can fall short of expectations include the impact of parenthood on career goals, energy level, money pressures, relationships with friends and family, and more. Second, personal goals usually need to change following the transition to parenthood. When there is a good fit between an individual's life goals and opportunities offered by parenthood, new parents are happier (Salmela-Aro, 2012). In one study, this shift occurred when there was a decline in achievement-related goals and an increase in family- and motherhood-related goals following the transition to parenthood. Third, paternal involvement in childcare is associated with more positive satisfaction trajectories for both parents (Agache, Leyendecker, Schäfermeier, & Schölmerich, 2014).

Keep in mind that a family is a system, and for most couples it is likely that any decline in satisfaction with their marriage is offset by other satisfactions from their new role as parents. For instance, becoming a parent adds a new dimension to our sense of personal identity (Lee, MacDermid, Dohring, & Kossek, 2005; Nomaguchi & Milkie, 2003; Reeves, 2006) and most parents feel very good about the job they are doing as a parent and the way their child is developing (Wenger & Fowers, 2008).

Check Your Understanding

1. What is the new mother's experience usually like?
2. How do men typically adjust to fatherhood?
3. How does the birth of a baby often affect the parents' relationship?

Conclusion

Prenatal development starts with a single fertilized cell and ends with a newborn ready to begin interacting with the environment and the people in it. Despite many risks, the vast majority of pregnancies end with the birth of a healthy, well-functioning baby, and in spite of the difficulties parents encounter along the way, most would, and do, choose to do it all over again. In the next chapters, we take a look at infants and toddlers. We learn about how they develop physically, cognitively, socially, and emotionally during this critical time of life, and the implications of this development for their future well-being.

Chapter Summary

4.1   What happens during the three stages of prenatal development?

During **ovulation**, a woman's ovary releases an egg or ovum. If the ovum is fertilized by a sperm, the resulting single cell multiplies until it becomes a hollow ball of cells called a **blastocyst**, which implants in the lining of the uterus. This is the **germinal stage**, from conception to 2 weeks postconception. In the **embryonic stage**, from 2 weeks to 2 months

postconception, the cells increase until they form an **inner cell mass** that becomes the **embryo**, and a ring of cells that becomes the support system, including the **placenta**. The three layers of the inner cell mass (the **endoderm**, **mesoderm**, and **ectoderm**) become different systems of the body. The developing embryo is vulnerable to **teratogens**, which can disrupt the developmental process. In the third stage, the **fetal stage**, from 2 months to birth, the fetus grows in size and weight, and all the organ systems become functional prior to birth.

4.2 What are some risks and health issues during pregnancy?

Seeing a physician for early and regular prenatal visits will help ensure that a pregnancy progresses normally, as will a healthy diet. A pregnant woman should avoid alcohol, which can result in **fetal alcohol spectrum disorders**, and stop smoking, which is associated with low birth weight, premature deliveries, and later developmental problems. The use of illegal drugs threatens a pregnancy directly. Prescription and over-the-counter drugs should be taken only in consultation with the woman's physician. Preexisting illnesses (such as a sexually transmitted infection) should be treated to protect the unborn baby, and pregnant women should reduce their stress level since stress hormones can cross the placenta.

4.3 What do the mother and baby experience during birth?

In the first stage of labor, contractions dilate and efface the cervix to 10 centimeters. In the second stage, the infant is born, and his or her condition is assessed using the **Apgar Scale**. In the third stage, the placenta is delivered. Couples who take childbirth preparation classes learn about labor and delivery and practice techniques that can help control the pain of childbirth, but many women in the United States also use medication (such as an epidural) to do this. The experience of childbirth varies greatly across cultures. During the birth process babies will have some oxygen deprivation and the skull will elongate as the head goes through the birth canal. These experiences release stress hormones that promote adaptation to the external world.

4.4 How do newborns function, and what threatens their well-being?

All the newborn's senses are functional by the time of a full-term birth. The infant has different **infant states**—sleep, quiet alertness, active alertness, and crying—that help keep sensory stimulation at a manageable level. Infants differ in how regular their schedules are and how easy they are to soothe. Rates of **infant mortality** in the United States are higher than in many other industrialized countries. Infants born **prematurely** or at **low birth weight** are at increased risk of physical and cognitive developmental problems, but early intervention can ensure that these infants reach their full potential.

4.5 How do people experience the transition to parenthood?

New parents often become enthralled with their new baby. However, exhaustion, anxiety, depression, and doubts about their competence may cause problems for them. Some new mothers suffer from the "baby blues," which are relatively mild and short-term, but others experience **postpartum depression**, which is more severe and long-lasting and requires intervention. Marital relations must go through a period of readjustment; some dissatisfaction is a common outcome. Having realistic expectations for how becoming a parent will affect other aspects of the parents' lives helps make this transition positive. Learning to care for their new baby promotes feelings of competence in most parents and a sense of satisfaction in the parenting role.

Key Terms

Active labor   121

Amnion   103

Apgar Scale   126

Blastocyst   103

Cephalocaudal development   104

Chorion   103

Couvade   132

Critical period   105

Doula   124

Early labor   121

Ectoderm   104

Embryo   103

Embryonic stage   103

Endoderm   104

Fetal alcohol spectrum disorders (FASDs)   114

Fetal alcohol syndrome (FAS)   113

Fetal stage   105

Fetus   105

Germinal stage   102

Gestational age   106

Infant states   127

Infertility   108

Inner cell mass   103

$SAGE edge™

Sharpen your skills with SAGE edge at edge.sagepub.com/levinechrono

SAGE edge for Students provides a personalized approach to help you accomplish your coursework goals in an easy-to-use learning environment.

Go to edge.sagepub.com/levinechrono for additional exercises and video resources. Select Chapter 4, Prenatal Development, Birth, and the Newborn, for chapter-specific activities. All of the Video Links listed in the margins of this chapter are accessible via this site.

iStockphoto.com/jfairone

iStockphoto.com/nyul

Infancy and Toddlerhood

part
III

5 Physical Development in Infancy and Toddlerhood

T/F Test Your Knowledge

Test your knowledge of child development by deciding whether each of the following statements is *true* or *false,* and then check your answers as you read the chapter.

1. **T ☐ F ☐** Humans use only 10% of their brains.

2. **T ☐ F ☐** Infants are born with almost all the brain cells they will ever have.

3. **T ☐ F ☐** Newborn babies form synapses (the connections between nerve cells) in their brains at the rate of a hundred new connections each second.

4. **T ☐ F ☐** Babies are unable to see when they are first born.

5. **T ☐ F ☐** Infants are born with a preference for the foods common in their culture.

6. **T ☐ F ☐** Within the first 2 months of life, infants do not experience pain.

7. **T ☐ F ☐** Babies triple their birth weight by the time they are 1 year old.

8. **T ☐ F ☐** It is important that infants crawl before they walk. If they go directly to walking, they are more likely to develop learning disabilities later in life.

9. **T ☐ F ☐** Potty training most often becomes a battle of wills between a toddler and her parents.

10. **T ☐ F ☐** Baby walkers help babies walk at an earlier age.

Correct answers: (1) F, (2) T, (3) T, (4) F, (5) F, (6) F, (7) T, (8) F, (9) F, (10) F

In this chapter, we open our study of infants and toddlers by examining some of the central issues regarding their physical development. We begin by looking at the infant brain and how it develops (including some information on disabilities associated with brain development). We then describe how infants' senses develop and how they predispose babies to form social relationships. We look at how infants' bodily proportions are different from those of adults and examine how infants and toddlers develop gross and fine motor skills during the first 2 years of life. We also explore issues of health and nutrition, including breastfeeding, sleep, illnesses, and infant mortality and child abuse. We conclude by examining the effects of stress on physical and emotional well-being.

Learning Questions

5.1 What are the structures of the brain and related developmental processes and disabilities?

5.2 How do the five senses develop in infancy and toddlerhood?

5.3 What reflexes and motor skills do infants and toddlers possess?

5.4 What are the major health and nutrition issues in infancy and toddlerhood?

Brain Development

Brain development begins prenatally, and by the time a baby is born, all the basic structures of the brain are in place. But, as we are about to see, infancy is a time when there is rapid growth and change in the young brain, just as there is rapid growth throughout the rest of the body.

We begin our discussion of brain development by addressing two common misconceptions. The first is the myth that humans use only 10% of their brains. As we describe the parts and the functions of the brain in the following sections, it should become clear to you that we use *all parts* of our brains. Neurologist Barry Gordon, who studies the brain, says, "It turns out . . . that we use virtually every part of the brain, and that [most of] the brain is active almost all the time" (Boyd, 2008, para. 5). The second misconception is that what we *think* has little to do with how our bodies function, and that our body's functioning has little to do with our thoughts. In fact, what affects the brain affects the body, and what affects the body affects the brain (Diamond, 2009). To begin to see the surprising ways in which the brain and the body interact, try **Active Learning: Brain and Body.**

5.1

What are the structures of the brain and related developmental processes and disabilities?

T/F #1
Humans use only 10% of their brains. *False*

Active Learning

Brain and Body

Sit comfortably in a chair. Cross your right leg over your left (at the knee or ankle). Circle your right foot to the right (in a clockwise direction). Now, using your right hand, draw a number 6 in the air. Were you able to keep your foot circling to the right? A few people can, but most people cannot. This is easy to do using your right foot and your *left* hand, so the difficulty arises from the fact that the left side of your brain controls the right side of your body and seems to be able to direct movement in only one direction at a time. You know your body is physically capable of doing both actions, but your brain may not let you do both at the same time. Children too are limited in their physical abilities, in part because of their brain development. Not only will you be learning about the impact of the brain on the body's activities in this chapter, but you will also learn about the impact the body has on the brain and the effect that experience has on the development of *both* body and brain. ■

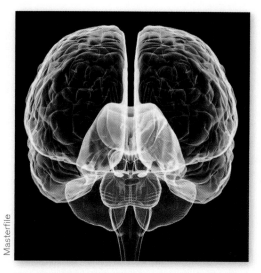

Masterfile

The two hemispheres of the human brain.
Although the two hemispheres of the brain may look similar, some brain functions are handled mainly by one side, other functions are handled mainly by the other side, and some are handled by both. The corpus callosum (shown in green in this picture) connects the two hemispheres so they can communicate with each other. ▪

Hemispheres The two halves of the brain.

Corpus callosum The band of fibers that connects the two hemispheres of the brain.

Structures of the Brain

The brain is an organ of the body made up of a number of different parts. We can examine it from two perspectives: from side to side and from back to front. As you can see in the photo shown here, the brain is divided down the middle into two halves, or hemispheres. Some parts of the brain are found on both sides, and some are located in only one hemisphere. For example, the motor cortex that controls the body's movements is similar on both sides, but only the right side of the brain controls the left side of the body, and vice versa. However, the language centers of the brain appear largely on the left side, at least for right-handed people. Lefties may have their language centers on either or both sides. The two sides of the brain communicate with each other through a band of fibers that connects them, called the corpus callosum.

Although the two sides have some distinct functions, there is no such thing as being totally "right-brained" or "left-brained." Both halves of our brains are involved in complex ways in almost everything we do. For example, although much of language is processed on the left side, specific aspects, such as humor and the emotional tone of what we say, are processed in the right hemisphere (Kinsbourne, 2009).

We get a different view of the brain when we look at it from the side. The parts, or lobes, of the brain have some distinct functions, which we describe below. However, as we saw with the two hemispheres, it is important to realize that most aspects of human functioning engage many parts of the brain in coordination with one another. For example, the occipital lobe is known to control vision, but the parietal, temporal, and frontal lobes also play a role in vision (Merck Manual, 2008).

Look at Figure 5.1 along with Table 5.1, to identify the parts of the brain in this image, working from the back of the head (on the right side) toward the front (on the left side). Starting at the lower back of the head, the *brain stem* (in blue) includes the spinal cord, which controls our basic functions such as breathing. Next, the *cerebellum* (in green) controls balance and movement. Above the cerebellum, the *cerebrum* or *cortex* controls the higher functions of thought and action. The cerebrum includes many different parts, including the *occipital lobe* (in yellow), which processes vision; the *temporal lobe* (in pink), which processes hearing; the *parietal lobe* (in orange), which processes sensory input and spatial awareness; and the *frontal lobe* (in red), which processes complex thoughts, movement, language, and self-control. The very front of the cerebrum is called the *prefrontal cortex*, and it controls judgment and the ability to plan. Within the cerebrum, but not visible in Figure 5.1, are the *amygdala* and the *hippocampus*, which are important in the experience and expression of emotions, memories, and sensations (Bear, Connors, & Paradiso, 2007).

Although this is a good description of some of the functions that we currently know are associated with different areas of the brain, brain research is one of the most active areas in the field of child development, so our understanding of brain functions will undoubtedly change as research continues. As we continue our discussion of the brain, think about how different aspects of physical development are linked back to the different parts of the brain and the functions they control. In future chapters you will learn more about the cognitive, language, and emotion centers of the brain and their functions.

FIGURE 5.1	Side view of the human brain

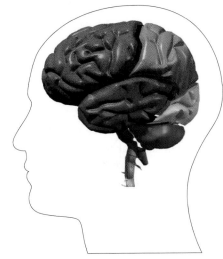

Use the color code in Table 5.1 to locate the different areas of the brain in this photo. Pay attention to the different functions controlled by each brain structure.

SOURCE: Based on *The Merck Manuals, Online Medical Library*. (2008). Neurologic Disorders: Function and Dysfunction of the Cerebral Lobes, Introduction (2010–2014).

TABLE 5.1   Brain structures and functions

Name of structure	Color in figure	Some functions of each structure
Brain stem	Blue	Includes the spinal cord, which controls basic functions such as breathing, heartbeat, and blood pressure
Cerebellum	Green	Controls balance and movement
Occipital lobe	Yellow	Processes visual information
Temporal lobe	Pink	Active in hearing, language, memory for facts, visual memory, and emotion
Parietal lobe	Orange	Processes sensory input and spatial awareness
Frontal lobe	Red	Processes complex thoughts, movement, language, working memory, and self-control

SOURCE: Based on *The Merck Manuals, Online Medical Library*. Neurologic Disorders: Function and Dysfunction of the Cerebral Lobes, Introduction (2010–2014).

Developmental Processes

The infant brain grows and develops through the interaction of biological forces and environmental influences. This process directs the way the cells of the brain connect with one another and the pattern of connections relates to many aspects of physical, cognitive, and social-emotional development.

Neurons and Synaptic Connections

The adult brain and nervous system is made of 100 billion nerve cells, called neurons (Pakkenberg & Gundersen, 1997). Each nerve cell sends nerve impulses via special chemicals called neurotransmitters to other nerve cells. As you can see in Figure 5.2, each cell sends neurotransmitters through extensions of the cell called axons and receives messages through receptors called dendrites. Axons are the part of the nerve cell that conducts impulses away from the cell body, and dendrites are the parts that receive impulses from other neurons. The place where the axon from one neuron meets the dendrite of another neuron is called the synapse. Just about everything we do depends on communication between nerve cells. Adults have approximately 1 quadrillion (!) of these synaptic connections.

Infants are born with almost all the neurons they will ever have; however the synapses or connections between them are largely formed after birth. As a result, babies have fewer inborn behavior patterns than other animals, and they are more open to learning from their environment. The experiences they have actually shape the development of synaptic connections and the formation of their brains (Rosenzweig, Breedlove, & Watson, 2005). The development of new synapses is referred to as synaptogenesis. After a baby is born, new synapses may be formed at the rate of more than *one million* connections *per second* (Greenough, Black, & Wallace, 1987). One reason infants' brains are more active than adults' is that they are so busy forming connections (Gopnik, Meltzoff, & Kuhl, 1999).

Neurons The cells that make up the nervous system of the body.

Neurotransmitters Chemicals that transmit nerve impulses across a synapse from one nerve cell to another.

Axon The part of a nerve cell that conducts impulses away from the cell body.

Dendrites The parts of a neuron that receive impulses from other neurons.

Synapse The place where the axon from one neuron meets the dendrite of another neuron.

Synaptogenesis The development of new synapses.

T/F #2

Infants are born with almost all the brain cells they will ever have. *True*

T/F #3

Newborn babies form synapses (the connections between nerve cells) in their brains at the rate of a hundred new connections each second. *False*

VIDEO LINK 5.1
Brain Overview

VIDEO LINK 5.2
**Infant Brain
Development**

FIGURE 5.2   **Neurons and synapses**

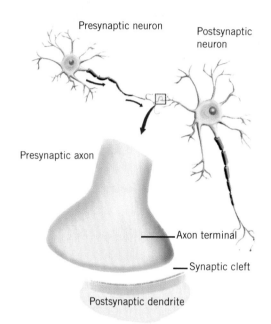

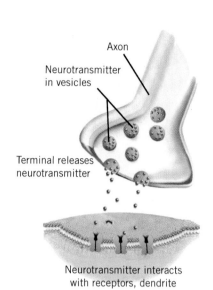

Two nerve cells (neurons) communicate with each other as the axon of one reaches the dendrite of the other at the synapse (shown at the left). At the synapse, chemicals called neurotransmitters are released from one cell and bring their "message" to the second cell (shown at the right).

SOURCE: Garrett, B. *Brain & Behavior: An Introduction to Biological Psychology.* © 2009 SAGE.

Plasticity of the Brain

Plasticity The ability of an immature brain to change in form and function.

The ability of the infant brain to change in form and function is referred to as plasticity. If you, as an adult, had half your brain (one hemisphere) removed, the result would be catastrophic. You would lose movement in the opposite side of your body, and you would lose the functions handled in that hemisphere. For example, people who have damage to the language centers in the left hemisphere may be unable to speak. However, until about age 4 or 5, children who have had one hemisphere removed to treat an otherwise untreatable condition, such as severe epilepsy, can recover almost full function (Eliot, 1999).

In one study of children who had an entire temporal lobe removed, there was no significant decline in the group's overall IQ following the surgery (Westerveld et al., 2000). Even when the surgery removed the left temporal lobe (the part of the brain associated with language), there was no loss of verbal intelligence and nonverbal intellectual functioning actually improved significantly. This occurs because the brain at this young age has enough plasticity that brain cells originally intended to serve one function (for example, controlling movement) can turn into cells that control another function instead (for example, language). In the study by Westerveld et al. (2000), the small group of children who did experience significant loss of function following the surgery tended to be the oldest in the group.

VIDEO LINK 5.3
Hemispherectomy

At various times within the first years of life, babies' brains produce so many new synaptic connections that the density of connections is greater than that found in the adult brain (Blakemore & Choudhury, 2006). However, in the normal process of brain development, many of these synaptic connections do not survive. In a process called pruning, synaptic connections that are used remain, and those that are not used deteriorate and

Pruning The deterioration and disappearance of synapses that are not used.

disappear. Just as pruning dead branches strengthens a tree, pruning unused synapses strengthens the brain. Rather than being a terrible loss, this process results in a brain that is much more efficient (Huttenlocher, 1999). As an example, newborn infants can distinguish between speech sounds found in all languages, but during their first year of life they are exposed only to the specific sounds in the language that they hear each day. By one year of age, they can no longer distinguish between sounds found in other languages they don't regularly hear. This fine-tuning of the ability to categorize sound is thought to be the result of pruning of synapses in the part of the brain that processes sound during early development (Blakemore & Choudhury, 2006).

The process of pruning follows a "use it or lose it" principle. Greenough et al. (1987) described two ways this happens: experience-expectant mechanisms and experience-dependent mechanisms. Experience-expectant brain development occurs because our brain encounters experiences that it *expects* to happen. For example, in the normal course of events our eyes will be exposed to light. When these expected events occur, the pathways in the brain that are used are retained. In experiments with kittens, Hubel and Wiesel (1965) showed that if this does not happen, the eye still develops normally, but the part of the brain that processes visual information does not function. Kittens with one eye closed for a period of time after birth were never able to develop vision in that eye, even when it was later open. This is why children who have an eye that has considerably less vision or doesn't coordinate with the other eye (a condition called amblyopia or "lazy eye") must have intervention early in their lives or they may lose effective vision in that eye.

Experience-dependent brain development is much more individual and depends on each person's particular experiences. In addition to unused synapses being pruned away, it appears that new synapses develop in response to stimulation. For example, Elbert, Pantev, Wienbruch, Rockstroh, and Taub (1995) studied the brains of violinists. If you pretend to play the violin, on which hand are the fingers more active? The fingers of your left hand move all around, pressing on the strings to produce different notes, while the fingers of your right hand usually stay in one position, holding the bow. Elbert et al. (1995) found that in violinists the area of the right side of the brain that controls the left hand had many more synaptic connections than the same area of the left side of the brain. It is unlikely that these people are born this way, making them more likely to become violinists. Instead, the constant use of the fingers of the left hand to move and press the appropriate strings on the violin further develops that part of the right side of the brain.

Myelination of Neurons in the Brain

So far we have discussed the development of synapses through the process of synaptogenesis, but for messages to be sent successfully, myelination, another process in the development of the nervous system, is necessary. For neurons to work efficiently, they need to be coated with a fatty substance known as myelin, as shown in Figure 5.3.

Picture an electrical cord between the wall socket and your lamp. How does the message travel from the light switch to turn on the lamp? Within the electrical cord is a metal wire that carries the electrical current. If bare wire were used with no insulation, not only would you get a shock when you touched it, but also your light would not work very well. Only some of the current, not all of it, would be likely to arrive at its destination. For that reason, an electrical cord is always insulated with some material that cannot carry an electric current. As a result the electrical message all goes to turn your light on. In a similar fashion, the neurons in the nervous system are insulated with myelin so the message sent by the neurotransmitters will be received most effectively.

When babies are born, just as the synaptic connections are not complete, so too the myelin sheath does not cover all the neurons in the nervous system. The process of producing synaptic connections, pruning away those that are not being used, and myelinating

Experience-expectant brain development Development that occurs when we encounter experiences that our brain *expects* as a normal event.

Experience-dependent brain development Development that occurs in response to specific learning experiences.

JOURNAL ARTICLE 5.1
Neural Plasticity

Myelination The process of laying down a fatty sheath of myelin on the neurons.

FIGURE 5.3   **The myelin sheath**

The myelin sheath is a fatty coating that wraps around the nerves to ensure that the chemical messages sent between neurons are delivered efficiently. In this figure, the axon is shown in blue with the myelin sheath wrapped around it. A cross section is shown here so you can see how the coating wraps around the axon.

the connections that are left begins in infancy and continues throughout childhood and adolescence (Paus et al., 1999). We have only recently developed imaging techniques that can trace the developmental pattern of myelination in the human brain as it proceeds from the lower centers at the base of the brain through the higher centers of the cortex (Deoni et al., 2011). As researchers learn more about the normal progression of myelination, they are also likely to find evidence of the abnormal processes that may underlie such disorders as autism and schizophrenia (Deoni et al., 2011).

We have already learned that synaptogenesis is affected by our experiences through the process of experience-dependent brain development. There is also evidence that myelination is affected by our experiences. Bengtsson et al. (2005) compared brain development in children who spent long hours practicing piano to that in children who did not play piano. Their evidence indicates that the extra stimulation certain neurons experience when children are practicing results in more myelination of those neurons, including those in the corpus callosum, which connects the two hemispheres of the brain. The corpus callosum assists your ability to coordinate movements of your two hands at the same time. In this study, children who played piano had increased brain efficiency, and this increased ability continued into adolescence.

Disabilities Related to Brain Development

When brain development does not occur as expected, or when there is damage to the brain at any point, a number of disabilities may result. We discuss cerebral palsy here because specific brain abnormalities are known to cause this disability. We also include autism in this section because brain development has been linked to the development of this disorder, although the exact mechanism remains to be discovered.

Cerebral Palsy

Cerebral palsy A chronic condition that appears early in development and primarily involves problems with body movement and muscle coordination.

Cerebral palsy is an umbrella term that describes a group of brain-based disorders that affect a person's ability to move and maintain balance and posture. People with cerebral palsy may experience difficulties with muscle tone, coordination, movement, and speech. These abnormalities arise early in development and are the result of brain injuries that can occur during fetal development or at any point up to about 3 years of age (Abdel-Hamid, 2011). About 70% of cases of cerebral palsy result from brain injury during prenatal development, most often with no known cause, and an additional 10% to 20% are due to brain injury during the birth process itself (United Cerebral Palsy, 2007). The remaining cases occur after the infant is born but early in development, when an infection or injury causes damage to the brain. Approximately 800,000 children and adults in the United States live with one or more symptoms of cerebral palsy (National Institute of Neurological Disorders and Stroke [NINDS], 2011), and the percentage of children afflicted by this condition has remained largely unchanged over the past 30 years (Abdel-Hamid, 2011).

Risk factors include premature birth, low birth weight, conception of two or more fetuses, maternal exposure to toxins or infections, and lack of oxygen during the birth process (Abdel-Hamid, 2011). While some children are profoundly affected and will need total care throughout their lives, others show only mild impairment and require little or no special assistance. Although this condition does not worsen with age, early intervention and therapy can be beneficial to the child because it can help prevent or delay the onset of secondary problems. The goal of intervention is to create an individual treatment plan that meets each child's unique needs. Medications can help control seizures and muscle spasms, surgery can lengthen muscles and tendons that are too short to function, and physical therapy can help the child build necessary skills. You also may have seen new technologies that let children with cerebral palsy use even limited head movements to operate a computer with a voice synthesizer that enables them to communicate.

Assistive technology for cerebral palsy. Computer technology that is available today can enable a young person with cerebral palsy to participate in classroom activities and communicate his thoughts and feelings, even though he has limited physical mobility. ■

An exciting new avenue of research is investigating the use of a drug that allows regrowth of the myelin coating on nerve cells in the brain (Fancy et al., 2011). When a lack of oxygen disrupts the nerve cells' ability to create myelin, those cells die, which can lead to cerebral palsy. Although far from being ready to use in humans, this research offers hope for a new pharmaceutical treatment of this type of brain injury.

Autism Spectrum Disorder

Autism spectrum disorder (ASD) includes a range of symptoms that can vary greatly in severity from one child to the next. ASD is characterized by pervasive impairment in social communication and interaction and by restricted or repetitive behaviors, interests, or activities (American Psychiatric Association, 2013). Severity is classified in the *Diagnostics and Statistics Manual-5* (*DSM-5*) of the American Psychiatric Association by how much support the individual needs to function effectively. Some children with autism have few words and respond only to very focused, direct approaches from other people, while those with less severe symptoms may speak normally, but are not successful at maintaining the normal back and forth of conversation (American Psychiatric Association, 2013). Research is ongoing about the ways in which brain structure and function underlie the symptoms of ASD. In young children with ASD, imaging has shown enlargements of certain parts of the brain, in particular the amygdala, which is active in emotional experience and expression. This research found that the larger the amygdala, the more difficulty the person has with social relationships (Sparks et al., 2002).

For children with ASD the brain may have too many synapses in certain areas. Instead of having efficient, strong connections among specific neurons, they have less efficient connections among many more neurons (Shih et al., 2011). You can see this illustrated in Figure 5.4. We do not yet know whether the brains of children with ASD produce an overabundance of synapses, or whether the normal number of synapses are not pruned away as they should be.

Although we typically don't label a child as autistic until he or she is 3 years or older, there is a growing body of evidence that symptoms of autism are apparent earlier in development (Kalb, 2005; National Institute of Mental Health [NIMH], 2009). In one

Autism spectrum disorder (ASD) A disorder characterized by pervasive impairment in social communication and interaction and by restricted or repetitive behaviors, interests, or activities. Severity is classified by how much support the individual needs to function effectively.

VIDEO LINK 5.4
ASD: Diagnostic Criteria

FIGURE 5.4 The atypical brain: Autism

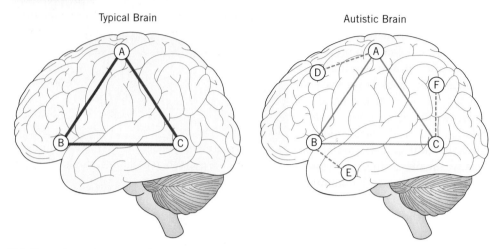

This figure shows the pattern of connectivity in a typical brain in comparison to those in the brain of a person with autism. The blue lines represent strong connections, while the orange lines represent weak connections. Note that the brain of an autistic person has more connections than is typical, but they are much weaker.

SOURCE: Akhgarnia (2011, May 26).

recent study researchers found that infants who were later diagnosed with ASD began to decrease their attention to other people's eyes beginning at two months of age (Jones & Klin, 2013). If other researchers confirm this new information, we might be able to begin intervention even earlier than we can now. Current methods can make valid and reliable diagnoses as early as 18 months (Chawarska, Klin, Paul, & Volkmar, 2007; Lord, Risi, DiLavore, Shulman, Thurm, & Pickles, 2006), and new tests for infants as young as 12 to 18 months are being developed. For instance, research has shown that the brains of typically developing infants respond differently when they see faces than when they see objects, but in infants with ASD, the brain does not seem to differentiate faces from objects (McCleery, Akshoomoff, Dobkins, & Carver, 2009). This may relate to the tendency of individuals with ASD to avoid looking at other people's faces.

The Centers for Disease Control and Prevention (2014c) recommend screening infants for developmental delays that might indicate the presence of an ASD at well-baby check-ups throughout the first 2.5 years of life. Table 5.2 shows some of the behaviors that health care providers may check for during the first 2 years.

TABLE 5.2 Infant screening for autism spectrum disorders

Some behaviors in infancy that are possible indications of autism include:

- child does not babble or coo by 12 months of age
- child does not gesture, such as point or wave, by 12 months of age
- child does not say single words by 16 months
- child does not say two-word phrases on his or her own (rather than just repeating what someone else says) by 24 months
- child has lost any language or social skills (at any age)
- child does not establish or maintain eye contact
- child does not make facial expressions or respond to your facial expressions
- child does not respond to his name by 12 months of age

SOURCE: WebMD (2013).

There is good reason to identify this condition as soon as we can because the optimal intervention consists of at least 2 years of intensive intervention during the preschool years (Filipek et al., 1999; NINDS, 2008). Although there is no cure, such early intensive behavioral intervention has brought about substantial improvement in IQ and adaptive behavior (skills needed for everyday life) for many autistic children. Intensive early intervention also has improved the ability to discriminate faces from objects and many other behaviors associated with ASD (Dawson et al., 2012). Results are less clear so far for language and social development (Reichow, 2012).

Because ASD has a strong genetic component, not all children will eventually benefit from early intervention, but we do not yet know who will benefit and who will not, so it is important that all children take part in treatment as soon as they are diagnosed. Because the plasticity of the infant brain allows for growth and change, there is hope of an improved outcome for children with ASD (Dawson, 2008).

Check Your Understanding

1. What are the roles of neurons and synapses?
2. What happens in the process of pruning?
3. What role does myelination play in brain development?

Sensation and Perception

Infants use the information that comes to them through their senses to learn about the world in which they live. In the next section, we describe how the development of the brain and the senses promotes learning and also predisposes babies to form the all-important attachments to their caregivers.

When we talk about sensations, we are referring to the information from the environment that is picked up by our sense organs. For instance, light from the environment stimulates the retina of the eye, sound waves stimulate the auditory nerves in the inner ear, and chemical compounds in the food we eat stimulate the taste receptors on our tongue. However, it is the brain that puts the sensory information that it receives together so that it can interpret what is happening in the world and attach meaning to that information. This is the process of perception. For example, light within a certain range of wavelengths is the color red and within another range of wavelengths is the color blue. But when the retina of your eye is stimulated with the wavelength for red, it is the process of perception that interprets the wavelengths as color. Before we discuss development of the five senses, we begin this section by describing a special way in which our senses link us to other human beings.

Mirror Neurons

Newborn babies are capable of imitating adults' simple facial expressions (Meltzoff & Moore, 1997). If you stick out your tongue at a baby, the baby may stick her tongue out at you. Until recently, scientists had little idea how infants were capable of manipulating parts of their body they can't even see, but in the 1990s, a team of Italian researchers was studying the brains of macaque monkeys when they discovered what are now called mirror neurons (Winerman, 2005). The researchers found that the same neurons fired whether the monkey put something in its own mouth or saw the researcher put something in the researcher's mouth. Although the exact neurons that perform these functions have not yet been found in humans, results from brain imaging studies indicate that for humans the same regions are activated for both experienced and observed motor movement and emotional expression. For newborns, this built-in system may activate an automatic

5.2

How do the five senses develop in infancy and toddlerhood?

Sensations The information from the environment that is picked up by our sense organs.

Perception The process of interpreting and attaching meaning to sensory information.

AUDIO LINK 5.1
Mirror Neurons

Mirror neurons Neurons that fire both when an individual acts and when the individual observes the same action performed by another.

© Jennie Woodcock; Reflections Photolibrary/CORBIS

Mirror neurons. Mirror neurons may give infants the ability to imitate simple actions that they see others do. This baby is copying her mother's facial expression. How would you feel if an infant responded to you by doing what you just did? ■

imitative response. Just as we automatically cringe when we see a baby cry in response to an injection, or open our mouths as we feed babies, or laugh when we hear others laugh, babies also imitate some of our actions automatically. This is a powerful way in which babies are brought into the social world. They learn from us, and we enjoy seeing ourselves reflected in our babies. By contrast, when autistic children were shown pictures of faces expressing a range of emotions and were asked to imitate those faces, there was less activity in the brain regions associated with mirror neurons than in children without autism. Further, the more severe the child's condition, the lower the level of neural activity (Dapretto et al., 2006). This imitative deficit may contribute to the social isolation we associate with autism.

You know that yawns are contagious because you see it happen in classrooms all the time. When we see someone else yawn, think about yawning, or even hear the word "yawn," 40% to 60% of us will yawn (Platek, Critton, Myers, & Gallup, 2003). In a study in which researchers measured and mapped brain activity using functional magnetic resonance imaging (fMRI), they found that when adults saw a video of someone yawning, a certain area of the brain associated with the mirror neuron system was activated (Haker, Kawohl, Herwig, & Rössler, 2013). This involuntary "matching" of our behavior to another person's behavior is one way we show that we are in sync with others during our social interactions. Helt, Eigsti, Snyder, and Fein (2010) examined how the tendency to mimic behavior changed as a function of a child's age and explored whether it differed between typically developing children and children with autism spectrum disorders. They found that if an experimenter yawned four times while reading a book to young children, 10% of 3-year-olds, 35% of 4-year-olds, and 40% of 5- and 6-year-olds would also yawn on at least one of those occasions. However, children with autism spectrum disorders were significantly less likely to yawn under the same conditions, regardless of their age. You can see for yourself how we mirror the behavior of others by completing **Active Learning: Contagious Yawning—Mirror Neurons at Work.**

Active Learning

Contagious Yawning—Mirror Neurons at Work

Ask to read a short story to a child between the ages of 2 and 7 years. Because older children may be reading themselves and don't still expect to be read to, tell the child you want to ask some questions after the story. Sit across from the child so she can easily see what you are doing, and yawn 4 different times during the story, watching to see whether the child mirrors your behavior by yawning herself.

Either try this with several children of different ages, or pool your findings with those of others in your class to see whether your results resemble the age-related findings of Helt and colleagues. Remember to ask a few simple questions about the story at the end and thank the child for listening.

Keep in mind that in the research by Helt et al. (2010) the majority of children at all ages do NOT yawn, so do not think that there is something wrong with the child you are observing if he or she does not yawn when you do. ■

Development of the Five Senses

Why do infants look us in the eye? How is it that they recognize their mother's voices? These and other abilities that foster infants' relationships with others result from the rapid development of the five senses in the early weeks and months of life.

Vision

Infants are able to see from the time they are born although their vision is much weaker than normal adult vision. Young infants' visual acuity, the ability to see things in sharp detail, is about 20/400, which means an infant can clearly see at 20 feet what an adult with normal vision can see at 400 feet (Balaban & Reisenauer, 2005). Until they are about 3 months old, infants focus on objects that are 8 to 10 inches in front of them (American Optometric Association, 2013). That is one reason we often put our faces close to infants when we are talking to them—they don't see us clearly until we get that close. Infants will not develop adult levels of visual acuity until sometime between 6 months and 3 years (Slater, Field, & Hernandez-Reif, 2007).

However, infants can see faces, and from birth they are attracted to the faces of people around them, especially their mothers (Farroni, Menon, & Johnson, 2006). In addition, they tend to concentrate on areas of high contrast—that is, where darkest dark meets lightest light. At first this may mean they scan the parent's hairline, but at 2 months of age, infants concentrate attention on the eyes, where the white of the eye surrounds a darker center (Ramsey-Rennels & Langlois, 2007).

Think about how you would feel when holding a baby who looks you directly in the eye. Many parents respond with a sense that "this baby *knows* me." Haith, Bergman, and Moore (1977) have argued that babies are responding to social stimuli, not just high contrast, because their research showed that babies focused more on their mothers' eyes when their mothers were talking than when they were silent. If high contrast were the only factor, the child would pay equal attention to the eyes whether the mother was talking or not. More recently, Farroni and her colleagues (2006) found that newborns look more at the face of a person who is gazing directly at them than at the face of someone who is looking away. However, regardless of whether this is a "trick of nature" or a true social response, the fact that babies tend to look us in the eye is surely an adaptive way they attract others to interact with them. In fact, research has shown that mothers are more likely to continue to interact warmly with their infants when they are looking their mothers in the eye (Haith et al., 1977).

Hearing

Hearing becomes functional while the fetus is still in the womb, and one sound fetuses hear loudly is their mother's voice. Subsequently, babies show a preference for their mother's voice within the first 3 days of life (DeCasper & Fifer, 1987). Although they don't know the meaning of the words, they even

T/F #4
Babies are unable to see when they are first born. *False*

Visual acuity The ability to see things in sharp detail.

VIDEO LINK 5.5
Infant Vision

© Tim Clayton/Corbis

Infants' vision. From a very early age, infants are able to focus on other people's eyes when they look at them. How does this help infant and parent to form an initial bond? ∎

remember the specific sounds the mother said if she repeats them regularly while she is pregnant. In a famous experiment, mothers were assigned a story such as The Cat in the Hat to read aloud twice a day to their unborn fetus during the last 6 weeks of their pregnancy (DeCasper & Spence, 1986). Within hours of their birth, the newborns were given a special pacifier. If the infants sucked on the pacifier in a certain way, they heard a recording of either their mother or another woman reading the assigned story, but if they sucked in a different way they heard a recording of a different story. The researchers concluded that babies showed memory for what they had heard prenatally because they were more likely to suck the pacifier in the way that produced the recording of the story they had heard prenatally.

What else do babies hear prenatally? To get a little bit of an idea, press your ear against another person's stomach (choose someone you know well!). What sounds do you hear? Babies hear all this and more: the mother's heartbeat and sounds of digestion, as well as talking and other outside sounds. In fact, many babies seem to need a certain level of noise in their first few months after birth in order to sleep. Many parents resort to leaving a vacuum cleaner running or putting the baby near a running clothes dryer to provide a level of background sound. Teddy bears with built-in "heart sounds" also can help soothe babies.

Smell

Babies know their mother's smell from very early in their lives. Within the first 6 days of life, they will turn toward their mother's smell more often than toward another mother's scent (MacFarlane, 1975), and research has shown that babies who are being breastfed recognize their mother's scent in the first weeks of life (Cernoch & Porter, 1985; Vaglio, 2009). This may be linked to a similarity between the smell of the amniotic fluid they experienced before birth and the smell of the mother's breast milk (Marlier, Schaal, & Soussignan, 1998). Babies are even soothed by the scent of clothes their mother has been wearing (Sullivan & Toubas, 1998).

Taste

Infants prefer sweet tastes and react negatively to salty, sour, and bitter tastes (Rosenstein & Oster, 2005). Mother's milk is sweet, so this draws the baby to the food and to the mother. This taste preference has been used to help infants who must undergo a painful procedure: baby boys sucking a sweet pacifier while undergoing circumcision cried less than those who used an unflavored pacifier (Blass & Hoffmeyer, 1991). Mother's milk, as well as amniotic fluid, takes on some of the flavor of the foods the mother eats (Fifer, Monk, & Grose-Fifer, 2004). Therefore, babies are introduced to the tastes of their local foods even before birth, and there is evidence that early experience with particular tastes becomes acceptance or preference for such tastes later in life (Mennella, Griffin, & Beauchamp, 2004).

Touch and Pain

Touch can be very soothing. In one study, babies who were held in skin-to-skin contact with their mothers cried less when given a slightly painful medical procedure (in this case, a heel stick to extract a small amount of blood) (Gray, Watt, & Blass, 2000). As we discussed in Chapter 4, Tiffany Field and her colleagues at the Touch Research

WEB LINK 5.1
Newborn Sense of Smell

AUDIO LINK 5.2
Baby's Palate

T/F #5
Infants are born with a preference for the foods common in their culture. *True*

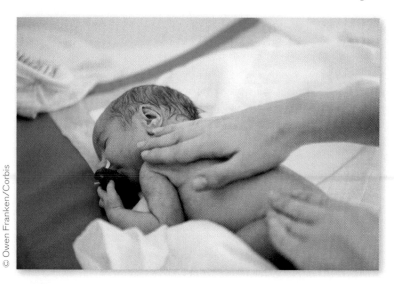
© Owen Franken/Corbis

Response to touch. Infants respond positively to gentle massage, and research has shown it can soothe babies and even improve growth. ■

Institute at the University of Miami have found that infant massage improves growth and effectively soothes babies of all ages, even premature babies (Dieter, Field, Hernandez-Reif, Emory, & Redzepi, 2003; Field et al., 2004). Many adults who have had a massage know how relaxing it can be. Massage with children can be helpful in improving conditions that range from anxiety (Field et al., 1992) to HIV (Diego, Hernandez-Reif, Field, Friedman, & Shaw, 2001). The research by Field and her colleagues appears to show that massage can not only make you feel better, but it can also raise the level of your body's ability to fight off the effects of disease.

You may be surprised to know that until about 35 years ago, many physicians and scientists believed infants were insensitive to pain. Read **Journey of Research: Do Infants Feel Pain?** to find out the history of these ideas.

JOURNEY OF RESEARCH *Do Infants Feel Pain?*

Strange as it may sound, until the 1980s, many physicians believed that infants did not feel pain. Because doctors also knew that anesthesia can have negative side effects, particularly for the smallest patients, they concluded it was best to use little or no anesthesia during painful medical procedures. The best-known case is that of an infant named Jeffrey Lawson who was born prematurely with a defect to his heart. He underwent open heart surgery with medicine designed to paralyze him during the surgery, but with no pain medication (Rodkey & Pillai Riddell, 2013).

Where did this idea come from? In a series of experiments on infant sensitivity to pain conducted in 1873, Alfred Genzmer pricked premature infants with pins, often causing blood to flow. (This would not meet current ethical standards for research!) Genzmer reported the infants showed no evidence of pain, even though their eyes grew wet (Rodkey & Pillai Riddell, 2013). In experiments conducted in the 1920s, infants between a few hours and 12 days of age were stuck with needles on their cheeks, thighs, and calves (Chamberlain, 1999). Almost all the infants cried, regardless of their age, but the oldest cried more in response to the mildest stimuli than the youngest did to the most painful stimuli. Based on this observation, the researchers concluded that the youngest infants in their study were relatively impervious to pain, while the older infants had become more sensitive. What they failed to take into account, however, was that mothers at that time were routinely given anesthesia during delivery. It is likely the maternal anesthesia was still in the systems of the youngest infants at the time they were tested, and these effects wore off gradually over the first few days of life.

Similar experiments were conducted in the 1930s by Myrtle McGraw, who reported on research in which infants from birth through 4 years of age were pricked with a pin. She reported that some infants did not respond to the pin pricks, but she also noted that others tried to pull away and cried. However, she concluded that these infant reactions were local reflexes that did not reach the higher levels of brain function, implying again that infants do not experience pain the way older children and adults do. Over the years, McGraw's *speculations* about brain function came to be cited as real *evidence* that brain immaturity was the reason infants were insensitive to pain.

In reading about this research, you may be wondering how these scientists could so badly misinterpret what they were seeing. Wasn't it obvious to them that sticking a pin in an infant was painful and made the infant cry? In the 1980s, research finally joined with parent advocacy to reach the conclusion that infants do experience pain. Owens and Todt (1984) found "that the increases in heart rate and crying in the context of a tissue damaging stimulus indicated that the infants experienced pain and that pain in infants can be reliably measured in clinical settings" (p. 77). The earlier research—and the misguided interpretation of its results—reminds us how careful we must be not to let our initial beliefs override the evidence that is right in front of us. When we observe an infant undergoing a

T/F #6
Within the first 2 months of life, infants do not experience pain.
False

medical procedure and crying, furrowing his brows, struggling and squirming, or breathing heavily while his heart races, we should accept the logical conclusion that the infant is in pain, not assume infants do not experience pain because others have said so. ■

Circumcision Surgical removal of the foreskin of the penis.

The most common surgical procedure for infants is circumcision, removal of the foreskin from the penis, usually performed within the first 10 days after birth (Taddio, 2001). About 77% of male infants in the United States are circumcised, which is a decrease from 83% in the 1960s (Morris, Bailis, & Wiswell, 2014). Non-Hispanic White males are most likely to be circumcised (91%), followed by non-Hispanic Black males (76%) and Mexican American males (44%) (Morris et al., 2014). For many families, it is part of a cultural tradition, but for others it is a personal choice. Because circumcision is a painful procedure, many parents weigh its pros and cons before deciding whether to circumcise their baby boys. However, the American Academy of Pediatrics has supported circumcision as a procedure whose benefits outweigh its risks. The health risks associated with neonatal circumcision are very small while the risks associated with not circumcising an infant include higher rates of urinary tract infections, HIV, and a number of other conditions for the male and increased rates of cervical cancer, chlamydia, and other conditions for any female sexual partner (Morris et al., 2014). Pain control is very important during circumcision and can include a variety of local anesthetics as well as stress reducers such as use of a pacifier dipped in sucrose (Taddio, 2001).

Cross-Modal Transfer of Perception

So far we have described how infants perceive the world through their individual senses. However, the senses also have to work together. For example, if you closed your eyes and touched an apple, when you opened them and someone showed you an apple and an orange, you would know you had just touched the apple by looking at it. In other words, your perception of "apple" crosses from the tactile mode to the visual mode because your senses work together in a process called cross-modal transfer of perception.

Cross-modal transfer of perception Perception with one sense (for example, seeing an apple) enables recognition of that object with another sense, such as touch.

Infants, even from birth, show some aspects of cross-modal transfer of perception, but their abilities are limited in a number of ways. They can visually recognize something they have only touched and not seen (like the apple in the example above), but they cannot recognize by touch something they have only seen but not touched (Sann & Streri, 2007). These abilities strengthen as infants grow older and have more experience seeing, touching, hearing, smelling, and tasting many things in their world.

Many toys designed for young children incorporate features that let them use their senses to explore the world. **Active Learning: How Toys Stimulate Babies' Senses** helps you identify some of these features for yourself in a popular infant's toy.

Lamaze International, Inc.

Active Learning

How Toys Stimulate Babies' Senses

Given what you now know about infant sensory preferences, think about how toys you have seen are designed to promote infant sensory development. For example, the toy shown here can be held by any of the handles, all of which have different textures. When a baby shakes it, it makes a soft chiming sound. The faces will attract babies' attention. Now use what you know to design your own baby toy. Describe how each feature of your toy can foster development of the baby's senses. ■

Sensory Preferences and Connection to Caregivers

To review, we have seen that infants prefer to look at faces, naturally "look you in the eye," recognize their mother's voice, and prefer her scent and the taste of her milk. In addition, infants are able to naturally imitate people from their first days of life. Clearly, from the minute we are born we are well equipped to enter a social world, and we are prepared to form relationships with those who take care of us. Although true attachment will not develop until later in the first year of life, as we discuss in Chapter 7, infants prefer the special people who care for them, and they have inborn mechanisms that draw these people into relationships with them.

Check Your Understanding

1. What are sensations, and how do they differ from perceptions?
2. How do each of the senses develop during infancy?
3. How do infant sensory preferences connect infants to their caregivers?

Infant Body Growth and Motor Development

5.3

What reflexes and motor skills do infants and toddlers possess?

Of course all babies are beautiful, but beyond that they share some physical characteristics that draw us to them. In this section, we discuss the proportions and growth of the normally developing infant's body. We then describe the ways in which babies develop their motor skills, from the earliest reflexes to the ability to walk and manipulate objects.

Infant Bodily Proportions

When infants are born, the comparative proportions of their heads and bodies are very different from those of older children and adults. A baby's head is very large in comparison to his small, helpless-looking body. If you do the activity described in **Active Learning: Head-to-Body Proportions** with an infant or toddler, you will see for yourself how short the child's arms are in comparison to the size of her head.

ACTIVE LEARNING
VIDEO 5.1
Head-to-Body Proportions

Active Learning

Head-to-Body Proportions

Take your right hand and reach over your head to touch your left ear. No problem, right? Now ask the parent or caregiver of an infant or toddler to help the child do the same thing. How far does the child's hand get over her head? Most likely the child's arm will not reach the opposite ear because her head is much larger in relationship to the rest of her body than the head of an adult is to his body.

As children mature, their arms and legs lengthen, and the rest of the body catches up in size to the head. The ability to reach overhead and touch your opposite ear has been used in some countries, such as Tanzania where there were inadequate birth records to document children's ages, as a rough test of a child's maturation and readiness to attend school (Beasley et al., 2000). ■

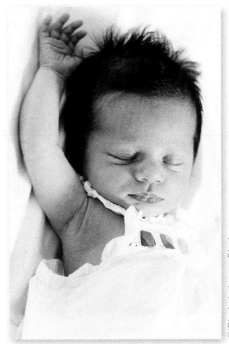

©iStockphoto.com/YsaL

In addition to their large head, infants also have large eyes, a small nose and mouth, and relatively fat cheeks. There may be an evolutionary reason for this appearance. It makes babies appear cute, and we are attracted to taking care of them (Vance, 2007). This attraction is even stronger for women who have larger amounts of reproductive hormones in their system (Sprengelmeyer et al., 2009). A secret few parents will reveal is that some aspects of baby care can be unpleasant because they include dealing with all kinds of bodily fluids, smells, and being up half the night, but as a new mother once wrote: "It's a good thing God made babies so cute, otherwise you would send them right back to the hospital!" Anyone who has seen the movie *E.T.* (Spielberg, 1982) knows that in spite of how frightening the extraterrestrial in the title looked, with his large head, large eyes, and helpless-looking body, we loved him and wanted to help him get home again. In the same way, we protect and nurture our babies in spite of the difficulties of caring for them, and this is in part because of the effect their bodily proportions have on us.

Growth from infancy to age 2 is very rapid. The average infant doubles her birth weight by about 5 months of age and triples it by her first birthday. During this same time, she will add about 10 inches or 50% to her length at birth. If the same rate of growth applied to the average 11- or 12-year-old, it would be terrifying, but after a child's second birthday, growth slows. Two-year-olds are approximately half the height they will be in adulthood, so to get an estimate of a child's adult height, you can double the child's height at age 2. However, a better indicator is to look at the height of family members. Assuming adequate nutrition, height is highly genetic, so it is very likely a child's eventual height will fall somewhere within the range of the height of her close relatives.

Figure 5.5 shows average growth rates for boys and girls. Despite the smooth curve of growth, real growth may occur in spurts. In fact, infant sleep patterns have been found to predict these growth spurts. If babies begin to sleep longer or take more naps, they may be about to have a jump in both height and weight (Lampl & Johnson, 2011).

Motor Development

In the following section we examine the development of motor skills. We begin with a description of babies' first movements: the reflexes. We then describe the role the myelination of the nervous system plays in determining the sequence in which motor milestones are achieved. Finally, we discuss other factors, such as physical activity, that influence the development of early motor skills.

Infant Reflexes

Newborns can't move around on their own, and they don't have much control over their limbs, but from the time they are born, they have a set of involuntary, patterned motor responses called **reflexes** that are controlled by the lower brain centers and that help them respond to some of the stimuli in the environment. These reflexes are hardwired into the newborn's nervous system, so they are automatic and don't need to be learned. Within the first few months of life, the higher centers of the brain develop and take over from the lower centers. As this happens, most of the infant reflexes disappear on a predictable timetable and are replaced by voluntary and intentional actions. Table 5.3 lists many of the infant reflexes and shows when they usually disappear. For instance, if you gently touch a newborn's cheek, she will reflexively turn in the direction of the touch to find a source of food. It doesn't take very long, however, for even a young infant to learn the signals indicating she is about to be fed. At that point, she will begin to turn in the direction of her caregiver as soon as she recognizes it is mealtime, but now with a voluntary action. Reflexes that have survival value persist beyond infancy.

It is not that reflexes and voluntary behavior are two distinct types of response. There is a continuum that represents different mixes of reflexive and voluntary behavior that we see as motor development proceeds (Anderson,

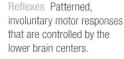

T/F #7
Babies triple their birth weight by the time they are 1 year old. *True*

Reflexes Patterned, involuntary motor responses that are controlled by the lower brain centers.

VIDEO LINK 5.6
Reflexes

Prenatal thumb sucking. Reflex activities may result in thumb sucking as early as 12 to 14 weeks of gestational age. ▪

Neil Bromhall

FIGURE 5.5 Average growth curves from birth to 24 months

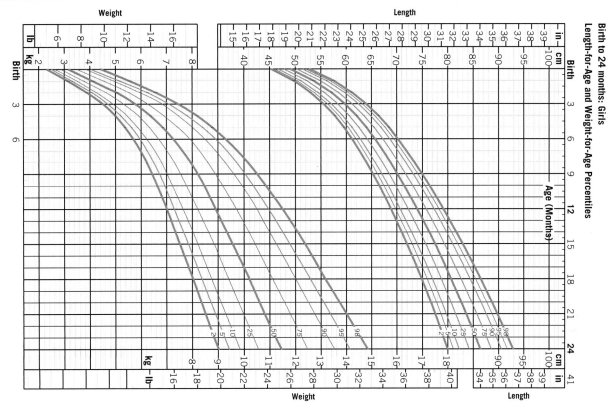

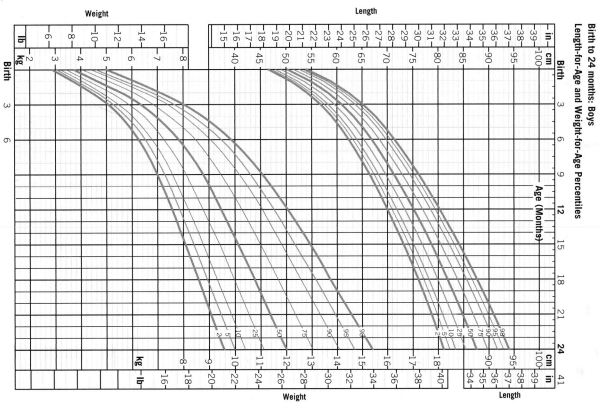

On these growth charts, the line marked "50" represents the growth of the average child. Half the children at any given age are above that average and half are below. The other lines represent the growth of children above or below the average. For example, children who fall on the line marked "90" are taller or heavier than 90% of the children of that age.

SOURCE: Centers for Disease Control and Prevention (2009a, 2009b).

TABLE 5.3   Newborn reflexes

Reflex	Description	When this reflex disappears
Sucking reflex	When something touches the roof of the baby's mouth, her lips close, and she will suck reflexively.	About 2 months
Crawling reflex	When the baby is placed on his tummy, his legs will make crawling motions even though he is not able to move forward.	About 2 months
Moro reflex (or startle reflex)	When a baby loses support and feels like she is falling or hears a loud sound, she will flail her arms and legs outward. Most babies will cry when startled and then pull their limbs back in.	About 3 months
Stepping reflex	If you support the baby's weight but let his feet touch the ground, he will lift and set his feet in a "walking" motion.	About 3 months
Tonic neck reflex	When a baby is placed on his back and his head is turned to the side, he will stretch out the arm and leg in the direction he is facing and pull inward the opposite arm and leg, often called a "fencer's pose."	About 4 months
Babinski reflex	When you stroke the side of a baby's foot, her big toe points up and the other toes will fan out.	About 4 months
Rooting reflex	If you gently stroke the baby's cheek, he will turn in the direction of the touch and begin to suck with his mouth.	About 4 months
Palmar grasp	When you touch the baby's palm with your index finger, she will clench your finger.	About 6 months
Gag reflex	The throat contracts to expel objects too large to be ingested. This reflexive gag helps prevent choking.	This reflex does not disappear.
Blinking reflex	Eyes blink when touched or exposed suddenly to bright light.	This reflex does not disappear.

SOURCE: National Institutes of Health (2009).

Roth, & Campos, 2005). However, if a reflex is missing or fails to disappear when it should, this can be an indication of a neurological problem and the infant should be assessed by a doctor.

Infants begin moving even before birth, exercising their developing muscles and giving feedback to the motor cortex of the brain that helps develop voluntary movements after birth (Eliot, 1999). Although the fetus cannot voluntarily control its movements, we can see prenatal ultrasound pictures of babies sucking their thumb. It appears that some kind of reflexive behavior may result in the fetus "finding" its thumb (Becher, 2006). Interestingly, the preference for one thumb or the other is predictive of whether the child later will be right-handed or left-handed (Hepper, Wells, & Lynch, 2005).

Development of Motor Skills

Two basic forms of motor skills are gross motor and fine motor. Gross motor skills call on the large muscle groups of the body (for example, the legs and arms). Fine motor skills enable us to make small movements, mostly of the hands and fingers, but also of the lips and tongue. The development of these skills is linked with the development of the brain and the entire nervous system.

The motor cortex is the strip at the top of the brain that goes from ear to ear and controls the conscious motor movements of the body (Bower, 2004). If you were to guess, which parts of the body do you think take up most of the area in the motor

Gross motor skills Skills that involve the large muscle groups of the body—for example, the legs and arms.

Fine motor skills Skills that involve small movements, mostly of the hands and fingers, but also of the lips and tongue.

FIGURE 5.6   **Homunculus**

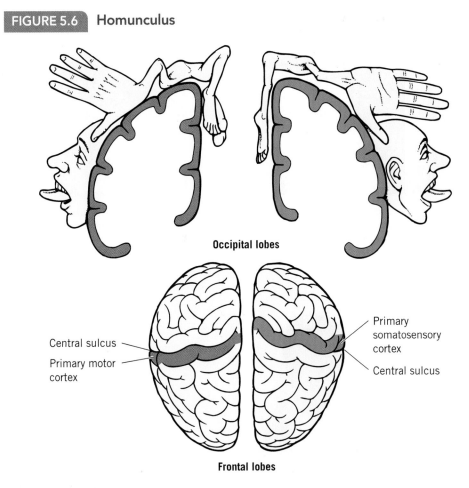

Occipital lobes

Central sulcus

Primary motor cortex

Primary somatosensory cortex

Central sulcus

Frontal lobes

The term *homunculus* means "little person." This drawing of a strange "little person" indicates where in the brain the different parts of the body are controlled and how much space is allocated to each part.

SOURCE: Reprinted with permission from Porter, R. (Ed.). (2008). *The Merck Manual of Diagnosis and Therapy, 18th Edition.* Whitehouse Station, NJ: Merck. © 2008 by Merck & Co., Inc. Available at http://www.merck.com/mmpe

cortex? If you guessed the legs, because they are large and have so much range of motion, you will be surprised to learn the majority of the motor cortex is used to control the mouth and hands, which contain many more muscles than the legs. Look at Figure 5.6 to see how the body is represented in the brain, both for motor activities and for sensory input. Neuroscientists in England recently found the motor cortex is so complex that it is activated not just when we actually act, for example when we kick something, but also when we read action words, such as *kick* (Bower, 2004).

Myelination of Motor Neurons

The brain connects through the spinal cord to all the neurons in the body. As we discussed, the nervous system works more efficiently when it has been coated with the fatty substance known as myelin. This is true not only for the neurons in the brain but also for the motor neurons in the body. The myelin sheath is set down in the nervous system in the body in two directions: from the head downward, referred to as the cephalocaudal direction, and from the torso out to the extremities of fingers and toes, referred to as the proximodistal direction.

The effects of the cephalocaudal direction of myelination are illustrated in the following photo series.

Proximodistal Development that proceeds from the central axis of the body toward the extremities.

The cephalocaudal direction of myelination results in infants gaining control of their bodies in the following sequence that corresponds to the motor milestones that most babies go through and that parents joyfully record in their baby books. ■

iStockphoto.com/Stefan_Redel

1. Head and neck: Parents of newborn infants must be careful to support the baby's head, but as myelination proceeds downward, babies become able to hold up their head independently.

iStockphoto.com/alexsl

2. Shoulders: A newborn placed on his stomach will remain in that position, but as myelination moves down the neck, the baby will be able to raise his head to see the world.

Laura Dwight/Corbis

3. Shoulders: As the shoulders come under control, the baby will reach the next milestone: rolling over (from stomach to back and from back to stomach).

iStockphoto.com/toos

4. Arms and chest: With control of this region, the baby will be able to use his arms to push up from his stomach to survey a larger area around him. However, his legs are still flat to the floor.

iStock/Igor Stepovik

5. Hips: When the hips and back come under the baby's control, she can now begin to sit up, at first with support and then independently.

iStockphoto.com/zulufoto

6. Thighs: With control of the legs, babies can pull their legs underneath them and begin to crawl. Often babies will initially crawl backward, in part because their control of their arms is greater than their control of their legs (Greene, 2004).

BananaStock/Thinkstock

7. Lower legs: With control traveling from the thighs to the lower part of the legs, babies begin to pull up on furniture to a standing position.

Ryan McVay/Photodisc/Thinkstock

8. Feet: Control of the feet is needed to walk independently. At first babies walk with feet wide apart and hands raised to help with balance. As they gain more control of their feet and toes and better balance, their gait becomes more like that of an adult.

The proximodistal direction of myelination, from the central axis of the body out to the extremities, results in the following steps in development:

1. **Torso:** Babies will roll over, using control of their chest and shoulders.

2. **Arms:** Control of the arms begins with the infants' ability to swipe at objects they see. They become able to use their arms to push up from the ground, which eventually develops into crawling.

3. **Hands:** When infants begin to purposefully grasp objects, they scoop objects with all their fingers up against their palms, in what is called the palmar grasp.

4. **Fingers:** As they gain control of their fingers, they can use thumb and forefinger to pick up things as small as Cheerios. This is called the pincer grasp. Only later can they control the rest of their fingers to use a tripod grasp, using thumb, forefinger, and middle finger to hold a pencil.

Variability in Motor Milestones

The sequence of motor milestones happens in the same way for most babies around the world. This fact indicates that motor development is strongly controlled by our genes, which dictate the expected sequence of development. Thus, we can describe motor development as strongly canalized, as noted in Chapter 3; that is, genes allow for only a few possibilities in response to the environment. However, there is some variation in the timing of motor milestones. For example, although most infants in the United States walk

Proximodistal development of motor skills. Look at how you hold your pen or pencil. Which fingers do you use, and how do you use them? Compare how your hand works to how these children are able to use their hands. Why do you think that preschoolers are often given "fat crayons" to use instead of pens? ■

by 12 to 14 months, some walk as early as 9 months and some not until 18 months. Development may be uneven, so an infant might forge ahead with cognitive development but take longer to develop motor skills. A pediatrician can discuss with parents whether a later onset of walking is of concern for their child or whether it is just a normal variation in development of motor skills.

In addition to individual differences, there are cultural differences in the age at which children begin to walk. These differences are linked to cultural practices and beliefs. For example, Super (1976) found that Kenyan parents practiced walking and sitting skills with their babies, and as a result their babies reached these particular milestones sooner than babies in the United States. In the United States, babies' stepping reflex typically disappears at about 3 months of age as babies become chunkier and cannot lift their legs as easily. Their muscle development does not keep pace with the weight they add to their legs (Thelen, Fisher, & Ridley-Johnson, 2002). In contrast, the Kenyan babies who exercised their legs did not lose their reflex before they developed real walking. Other activities they did not practice, such as rolling over, did not develop more quickly. Clearly, specific skills developed earlier because these babies practiced them, with the help of their parents.

To test this hypothesis, Zelazo, Zelazo, Cohen, and Zelazo (1993) had Canadian parents practice walking skills or sitting skills with their 6-week-old babies. They found that skill development was quite specific. Those trained in walking were able to walk at an earlier age, while those trained in sitting performed this action at an earlier age. Therefore, even though genes are responsible for the general development of these skills, the environment can affect their fine-tuning. Although this research supports the idea that these motor skills can be advanced by practice, remember that it is not necessary to practice them. Even when a culture's child-rearing practices do not include "practice walking," all infants learn to walk given the opportunity and encouragement.

Another example of the effects of experience on the development of motor skills is the Back to Sleep program instituted by the American Academy of Pediatrics. In 1992, this group began to recommend that infants be put to sleep on their backs to reduce the risk of sudden infant death syndrome (SIDS). Since that time, the incidence of SIDS has decreased by more than 50% (National Institute of Child Health and Human Development, 2010). However, there is some evidence that an unintended consequence of this policy is that infants are starting to crawl at later ages (Davis, Moon, Sachs, & Ottolini, 1998). When babies sleep on their stomachs they reflexively move their arms and legs, strengthening those muscles, but when they sleep on their backs they do not get this stimulation. As a result, pediatricians and others are now recommending that parents put their infants on their stomachs for some period of time every day while they play with the baby or at least keep a watchful eye to be sure the baby is safe. On the other hand, going directly from sitting to walking is not associated with later motor problems, and infants who sleep on their backs walk at the same age as other infants (Davis et al., 1998). We also have debunked the myth that children not having the experience of crawling later develop learning disabilities. Crawling is has nothing to do with cognitive skills such as reading (Kasbekar, 2013).

Dynamic Systems

We have seen that the development of motor skills results from input from genes, maturation, and the environment. However, researcher Esther Thelen, whose dynamic systems theory we described in Chapter 2, has shown that development of motor skills is even more complex. For example, newborns are unable to control the movements of their arms to reach for something, and it was assumed that the development of eye-hand control is the necessary factor for achieving this control. But Thelen and her colleagues were able to show that the infant's activity level is another major factor. Infants have to control the speed with which they move their arm to successfully grasp a desired object,

AUDIO LINK 5.3
SIDS

T/F #8

It is important that infants crawl before they walk. If they go directly to walking, they are more likely to develop learning disabilities later in life.

False

so those who are more active have to learn to slow down and control their reach, while those who are less active have to increase the velocity of their reach to be successful (Thelen et al., 1993). Infants need to find the best fit between their physical style and the demands of the task. In the human dynamic system, many factors, including physical, cognitive, and social factors, must come together to determine all behaviors.

Although research is showing the complexity of motor development, the real-world approach to fostering early motor skills remains simple. Parents can promote normal development of motor skills by providing a safe, babyproofed space that is large enough for infants and toddlers to explore and by enthusiastically encouraging the development of each motor milestone in its turn. Under these conditions, over the course of a normal waking day, when infants begin walking, they will take more than 9,000 steps, the equivalent of the length of 29 football fields (Adolph & Berger, 2006).

You can learn more about the development of motor skills in infants and toddlers by carrying out **Active Learning: Checklist of Motor Skill Development** with a child.

Active Learning

Checklist of Motor Skill Development

The following checklist of motor skills from the National Center for Education in Maternal and Child Health shows you what to expect an average or typical infant to do with regard to gross motor skill development. You can use it to observe an infant or toddler under 2 years of age to see how the child's ability corresponds to what is average or typical. There is a great deal of variability between individuals, however, so any individual infant may not do everything expected at a particular age but still be developing within the normal range.

ACTIVE LEARNING
VIDEO 5.2
Checklist of Motor Skill Development

Motor Skill	Mean	Age Range
Holds head erect and steady	1.6 months	0.7–4 months
Sits with support	2.3 months	1–5 months
Lifts head, shoulders, and forearms while lying down	3.5 months	2–4.5 months
Sits momentarily without support	5.3 months	4–8 months
Reaches with one hand	5.4 months	4–8 months
Rolls over from back to front	6.4 months	4–10 months
Crawls and pulls on objects to achieve upright position	8.1 months	5–12 months
Walks with handholds ("cruises")	8.8 months	6–12 months
Stands momentarily without support	11 months	9–16 months
Walks independently	11.7 months	9–16 months

SOURCE: American Academy of Pediatrics: Bright Futures (n.d.); Adapted from Bayley (1969).

Were you surprised by any of the actions the child you observed could or could not perform? How would you explain the upper limits of the child's abilities—lack of practice, level of brain maturation, development of motor coordination, or other reasons? If you were able to compare your observations with those of other people, did you find trends of physical development across ages, and did you find individual differences between children of the same age? ■

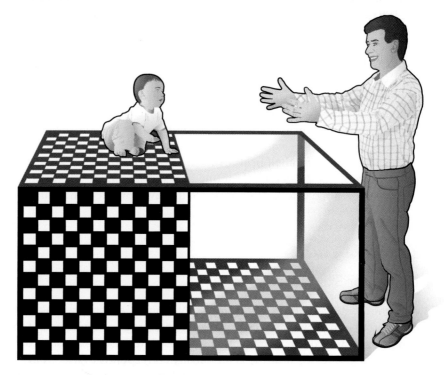

FIGURE 5.7   **The visual cliff**

As infants learn to crawl, they become fearful of crossing the apparent "cliff" in this apparatus designed by Eleanor Gibson to assess infants' depth perception.

Effects of Motor Skill Development

The timing of motor milestones interacts with other areas of infant development. In a classic work, Eleanor Gibson developed what she called the visual cliff, a Plexiglas-covered table that gives the illusion that one side drops off from table level to floor level as shown in Figure 5.7 (Gibson & Walk, 1960). Although babies can perceive depth from an early age, Gibson's research showed they do not develop a fear of sudden "drop-offs" until they have started to crawl. About 4 to 6 weeks after they have learned to crawl, they become fearful of what looks to them like a fall about to happen (Campos, Bertenthal, & Kermoian, 1992). The new ability to move around has other effects as well. Infants can now try to stay near their parents as attachment develops; but they also can explore more freely, which increases learning; and they can also get into more trouble, which requires more control from parents and others (Campos, Kermoian, & Zumbahlen, 1992).

Bladder and Bowel Control

WEB LINK 5.2
Potty Training

Like all motor skill development, the progress children make with regard to toilet training is dependent not only on their physical ability to control their bladder and bowel muscles, but also on their cognitive, social, and emotional development. This development takes place within a cultural context that reflects wide differences in the expectations for and even the definition of toilet training. In the United States, young toddlers often begin potty training between 18 and 24 months of age. Caucasian families generally begin training later (about 25 months) than non-Caucasian families (18–19 months) (Horn, Brenner, Rao, & Cheng, 2006). In contrast, in other countries, infants are trained to have some control over elimination during the first year of life. In Vietnam, infants usually do not wear diapers and parents are alert to signs their baby needs to pass urine or have a bowel movement. Vietnamese mothers report that when the infant passes urine the parent makes a whistling sound, and the infant soon becomes conditioned to urinate when hearing the sound. As a result of this type of training, infants are capable of remaining dry with parental support by a year of age (Duong, Jansson, & Hellström, 2013).

In the United States and other Western societies, infants do wear diapers and potty training takes place in a very different way. Rather than using parents' observations of when the child seems to need to urinate or defecate, a child-centered approach relies on signs that the child is ready for training to begin. They are:

- The child stays dry at least 2 hours at a time during the day or is dry after naps.
- Bowel movements become regular and predictable.
- The child can follow simple instructions.
- The child can walk to and from the bathroom and help undress.
- The child seems uncomfortable with soiled diapers and wants to be changed.
- The child asks to use the toilet or potty chair.
- The child asks to wear "big-kid" underwear. (American Academy of Pediatrics [AAP], 2009a)

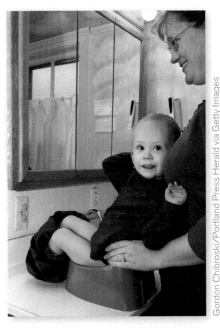

Potty training. Learning to use the potty should be a process that encourages a toddler's autonomy and never shames him or her for accidents. ■

In the process of potty training, parents need to decide what words they will use for body parts and for urine and feces. They may use a child-sized potty chair. The child may begin by telling the parent when she has a dirty or wet diaper. Parents can make regular use of the potty as a part of the child's routine. When the child achieves a level of dryness, training pants can be introduced (AAP, 2009a). However, the child should never be shamed for having accidents. For many parents potty training is a time for encouraging and rewarding the child's attempt to master this new skill. The more parents can treat this as a learning process and less as a battle of wills, the better off everyone will be. The goal for this approach is a child who can independently use the bathroom without parental help.

T/F #9

Potty training most often becomes a battle of wills between a toddler and her parents. *False*

Check Your Understanding

1. What reflexes does an infant possess?
2. What is the difference between gross motor skills and fine motor skills?
3. How do motor skills develop as the process of myelination proceeds?

Health and Nutrition

In this section, we discuss how to get babies off to a healthy start, as well as some of the risks to health that may affect infants.

5.4

What are the major health and nutrition issues in infancy and toddlerhood?

Breastfeeding

The American Academy of Pediatrics Section on Breastfeeding (2005) describes human breast milk as "uniquely superior for infant feeding" (p. 496) and recommends that babies be exclusively breastfed until 6 months of age, with other foods gradually added between 6 months and 1 year. In 2010, about 77% of new mothers in the United States began breastfeeding their babies, about 49% were still doing so when the babies were

iStock/jo unruh

Breastfeeding while at work. Places of employment can support the decision of their female employees to breast feed their infants by providing a space that the employees can use for nursing breaks or to pump breast milk that can be stored and used later by their infants while their mothers are away from them. ■

JOURNAL ARTICLE 5.2
Breastfeeding in Public

6 months old, and 27% continued to breastfeed at one year of age (CDC, 2013j). This is a significant improvement; rates in 2000 were 71% breastfeeding at birth, 35% at 6 months, and 16% at 12 months (CDC, 2013j). Women who are more likely to breastfeed are older, have more education, are married, and live in metropolitan areas (Li, Darling, Maurice, Barker, & Grummer-Strawn, 2005). Serious questions have been raised about how well hospitals, places of work, and other institutions support a woman's decision to breastfeed her infant (Gartner et al., 2005; Lindberg, 1996; Skafida, 2012). For example, the rate of breastfeeding might be improved if workplaces provided private settings for mothers to pump milk for their babies or if hospitals did not give new mothers free samples of formula provided by the companies that produce them.

Breastfeeding offers benefits to both the baby and the mother. Breast milk provides the baby with antibodies that come from the mother's body and help fight off infection. In both developed and developing countries, breastfeeding is associated with a decreased incidence and/or severity of infectious diseases such as diarrhea, respiratory infections, and ear infections (Gartner et al., 2005). There is some evidence that breastfeeding promotes earlier development of the infant's own immune system (Jackson & Nazar, 2006). Other benefits include lower rates of type 2 diabetes and lower rates of SIDS (CDC, Division of Nutrition and Physical Activity, 2007). There is even some indication that breastfeeding may help prevent childhood and adolescent obesity, although more evidence is needed to prove this conclusively (CDC, Division of Nutrition and Physical Activity, 2007; Dewey, 2003; von Kries et al., 1999). In some studies, breastfeeding has even been associated with slightly enhanced performance on tests of cognitive development and brain development (Gartner et al., 2005; Isaacs et al., 2010). However, this research must be interpreted with some caution. Because mothers who choose to breastfeed their infants tend to be older and have more education than those who don't, we need to be sure we have taken maternal differences into account before attributing the cognitive advantage only to the decision to breastfeed. These other maternal characteristics would have a positive influence on cognitive development on their own (Der, Batty, & Deary, 2006).

For the mother, production of breast milk is related to production of the chemical *oxytocin*, which helps her uterus return to shape. Although this chemical also delays the return of fertility, women are advised not to rely exclusively on breastfeeding to prevent another pregnancy. Lactation also appears to make mothers more relaxed and less reactive to stress, possibly by reducing blood pressure (Light et al., 2000; Tu, Lupien, & Walker, 2005). In the long term, it has been found that women who breastfeed have a reduced risk of some breast and ovarian cancers and type 2 diabetes (Gartner et al., 2005; Ip et al., 2007).

Breastfeeding also benefits the individual family and society as a whole. It has been calculated that increasing the rate of breastfeeding in the United States to the level recommended by the Surgeon General would save a minimum of $3.6 billion through lower health care costs and less loss of wages caused by caring for a sick child (Weimer, 2001). Additional benefits are that the family does not have to pay for formula, and society does not need to deal with the disposal of formula cans and bottles and the cost of transporting these products to market.

In certain rare circumstances breastfeeding is not recommended. You learned in Chapter 4 that HIV can be transmitted from an infected mother to her infant through breast milk, so HIV-positive mothers should not breastfeed. Most drugs prescribed by a physician are not likely to be harmful to the infant, but when a woman is undergoing chemotherapy or using antibiotics, antianxiety medications, or antidepressants, these substances enter her breast milk (American Academy of Pediatrics Committee on Drugs, 2001). For this reason, women should consult with their doctor concerning the safety of any medication they are taking. Because nursing women who smoke have nicotine in their breast milk, this is another good reason to give up smoking (Gartner et al., 2005).

Caring for Teeth

Babies are usually born toothless, although about 1 in every 2,000 to 3,000 newborns have what is called a natal tooth that has very little root structure and is usually removed before the baby leaves the hospital (Fotek, 2012). When a baby is born, 20 baby teeth are already almost entirely formed below the gums, and these teeth begin to emerge when an infant is between 6 and 9 months old (American Dental Association [ADA], 2005). Figure 5.8 illustrates the usual order in which teeth emerge during the first 2½ years. Generally, the central bottom teeth come in first, followed by other teeth near the center of the mouth, and then those to the side of the central teeth. Teething is often rather uncomfortable for babies and may cause fussiness. Sore gums can be soothed by a massage with a clean finger, or by a chilled teething ring to chew on. A physician may prescribe an anti-inflammatory medication if the pain is not controlled in those ways.

Even though baby teeth will eventually fall out and be replaced by permanent teeth, they should receive good care, since they are important both for eating and for learning

FIGURE 5.8 **Baby teeth**

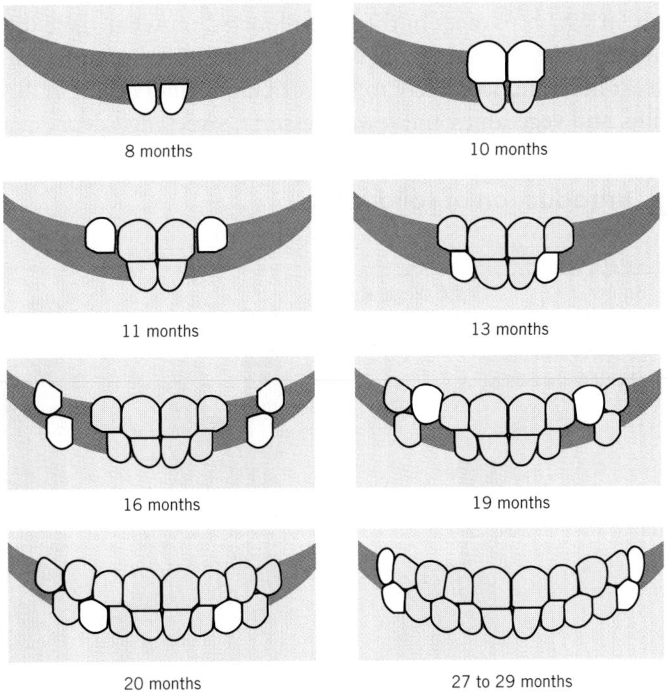

8 months	10 months
11 months	13 months
16 months	19 months
20 months	27 to 29 months

Baby teeth usually emerge in the order and at the ages shown.

to talk (ADA, 2005). Tooth decay in baby teeth can lead to infection that can damage the permanent teeth growing in the gums. The American Dental Association (2005) recommends that a caregiver begin brushing the child's very first tooth with a little water and infants should not sleep with a bottle in their mouth, because the milk or juice stays on the teeth for a long time, promoting tooth decay. Finally, limiting sweets is important for everyone's dental health, but it is especially important for infants.

Starting Solid Foods

As we've seen, the American Academy of Pediatrics recommends waiting to offer babies solid food until they are 6 months old. However, 40% of parents give their babies solids before even 4 months of age (Clayton, Li, Perrine, & Scanlon, 2013). In one study, mothers reported doing so because they thought the baby was old enough or because they thought solid foods would help the baby sleep through the night, although this appears to be a myth with no evidence to support it (Zero to Three, 2012). Many said their doctor had told them to start, indicating many pediatricians are not following the AAP guidelines.

Mothers who introduced solid food early were more likely to be young, single, and with a lower level of education. Mothers who were feeding the baby with formula rather than breastfeeding also tended to introduce solids earlier (Clayton et al., 2013). For some families the high cost of formula was a reason for introducing solid food (Quenqua, 2013). Babies who were more irritable also were more likely to receive solid food early (Wasser et al., 2011). Babies get all the nutrients they need in the right proportions from either breast milk or formula, so introducing solid foods too early often means the baby won't drink enough milk to get the balanced nutrition it offers. Figure 5.9 shows the types of foods infants are being fed at different ages during the first year of life.

Nutrition and Malnutrition

A national study in which parents in the U.S. reported on what their infants' and toddlers' ate found that most are eating a healthy diet. In 2008, infants were more likely to be receiving breast milk and less likely to be receiving formula than in 2002. They were eating more fruits and vegetables and fewer desserts, sweetened drinks, and salty foods

FIGURE 5.9   Introduction of solid foods

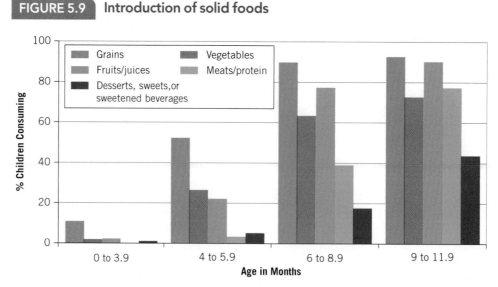

Are you surprised by any of the types of foods parents are feeding their infants during the first year of life?

SOURCE: Siega-Riz, Deming, Reidy, Fox, Condon, & Briefel (2010).

than 6 years earlier. However, many were still not receiving enough fiber, which comes from fruit, vegetables, legumes, and whole grains and were receiving too much salt and saturated fat. All these are risk factors for heart disease and high cholesterol later in life (Butte et al., 2010).

Obviously malnutrition is an even greater risk for infant development than a poor diet. An estimated 19 million children in developing countries suffer from severe malnutrition, and the younger the child is, the more vulnerable she is to the effects of malnutrition on growth (Management of Acute Malnutrition in Infants (MAMI) Project, 2009). Being malnourished is not just going hungry; it means not getting the nutrients needed for growth and development. This affects brain development as well as other aspects of physical health and growth. If the infant survives malnourishment, and many do not, the effects may last a lifetime even if the person later gets plenty of food. In a study in Barbados, adults who had been malnourished as infants were more likely to have ongoing attention deficit and conduct problems that began in childhood and continued through adulthood (Galler et al., 2012a; Galler et al., 2012b). It is essential that infants receive adequate nutrition; otherwise, the results of the early assault on their growth and development become irreversible.

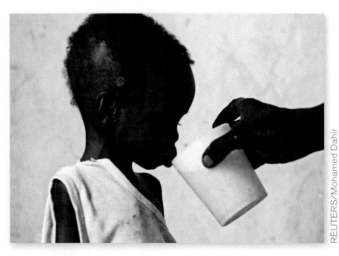

Malnutrition. A malnourished two-year-old is fed at a hospital in Sudan, in an area the UN calls "the hungriest place on earth." Early malnourishment affects brain development, as well as other aspects of physical health and growth, and its effects may last a lifetime. ■

WEB LINK 5.3
Malnutrition

Sleep

Newborns sleep a total of 16 to 18 hours per day (Hanrahan, 2006). By 6 months of age, most will sleep through the night for 12 hours or more and continue to take daytime naps (Hanrahan, 2006). Figure 5.10 shows how sleep patterns typically change over the first 2 years of life.

About one-third of babies do not sleep through the night until much later than 6 months. There is much controversy about how parents should deal with infants who awaken during the night. Some say they should be attended to whenever they cry, and many parents are comfortable doing so, but some parents may find themselves exhausted during the day because their baby continues to get up one or more times during the night. Exhaustion can lead to depression, which interferes with effective parenting, so addressing sleep issues for baby and parent is very important (Martin, Hiscock, Hardy, Davey, & Wake, 2007).

In one experimental study in Australia, parents who reported that their infants had sleep problems were assigned to either a sleep education program or a control group. In the sleep education program, parents were taught about normal infant sleep cycles and learned that infants older than 6 months of age can be taught to settle back to sleep on their own without a parent soothing them. Parents were taught to respond to infant crying at night at increasing intervals of time until the infant learned to go back to sleep without parental help. The families were also advised to gradually reduce the number of times infants were fed during the night. After two months, infants in the intervention group had greater reduction in sleep problems, and mothers in the intervention group who were depressed had a greater decrease in depression (Hiscock & Wake, 2002).

Some parents fear that allowing their baby to cry at night may be harmful, and there is some evidence that simply allowing the baby to "cry it out" alone

Infant sleeping. Infants will wake throughout the night and need care from a parent. During the first six months the number of wakings will normally decrease, and most babies will begin to sleep through the night. ■

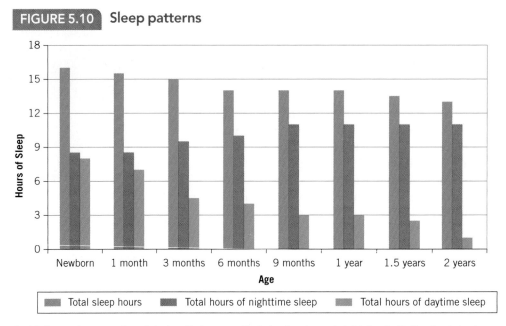

FIGURE 5.10 **Sleep patterns**

As this figure shows, newborn infants will sleep equally during the day and night. Gradually they begin to sleep more during the night, with naps during the day.

SOURCE: Hanrahan (2006).

WEB LINK 5.4
Sleep Patterns

for the whole night is stressful and should be avoided. However, in a follow-up study of those infants who received the more gradual approach described above, no detriment was found at age 6 in the child's emotional development, security of attachment to the parents, or any aspects of psychosocial functioning the researchers examined (Price, Wake, Ukoumunne, & Hiscock, 2012).

Illnesses and Injuries: Prevention and Care

So far we have discussed the basic issues of health, including nutrition and sleep. We now examine the more medical issues of vaccinations to prevent illness and some of the threats to infants' health such as illness, abuse, and stress.

Vaccinations

Vaccinations are an important way to prevent illness. Not vaccinating a child puts both the child and those around the child at greater risk of contracting preventable diseases. In 2010, there were more cases of whooping cough (pertussis) reported in California than in any year since 1947. When researchers examined the location of these outbreaks, they found children were more than twice as likely to get whooping cough if they lived in areas where large numbers of parents had refused to have their infants vaccinated for this disease (Atwell et al., 2013). Whooping cough causes severe and prolonged coughing in infants, along with apnea, or periods when the baby stops breathing. Half of infants who get this disease are hospitalized (CDC, 2013f). Any small risk that might result from a vaccination is far outweighed by the risk of getting any of the serious diseases that vaccines help prevent.

Common Illnesses and Injuries

As important as immunizations are, they cannot protect against common illnesses, and it is not unusual for infants to develop these illnesses. Because infants are not able to tell us what they are feeling, adults have an extra obligation to watch for and correctly interpret symptoms of illness when they occur in young children, and to learn when these require medical attention. Frequent well-baby checkups during the first year of an infant's life give a doctor the chance to monitor the infant's physical growth and weight gain and are excellent opportunities for parents to ask health-related questions. The American Academy of Pediatrics (2009b) recommends checkups every 3 to 6 months between ages 1 and 3, and on a yearly basis thereafter.

Fortunately, most common childhood illnesses are self-limiting (that is, they resolve without needing any medical intervention), but when a symptom is severe or long lasting, parents need to consult a physician. Any temperature of 105° or higher taken with an oral thermometer requires immediate medical attention because it can be life-threatening, but even a low-grade fever can be a medical concern for infants and young children because it could be a sign of a serious infection.

Ear infections are another common childhood illness. Three out of four children will have at least one ear infection before their third birthday, and this is the most common reason for taking a young child to a physician (U.S. National Library of Medicine, 2013). Ear infections occur when fluid builds up behind the eardrum and becomes a breeding ground for viruses or bacteria (Mayo Clinic Staff, 2008). Bacterial infections will respond to antibiotics, but in most cases this is not necessary. Warm compresses may give the child some relief from pain without overusing antibiotics. However, repeated ear infections become a concern because they can affect a child's hearing and interfere with the ability to learn language (Shapiro, Hurry, Masterson, Wydell, & Doctor, 2009). When infections become chronic and begin to pose this type of threat, doctors can perform surgery in which tubes are placed in the ears to keep the fluids from building up to restore hearing so language can develop normally (Kogan, Overpeck, Hoffman, & Casselbrant, 2000).

Falls account for over 50% of injuries to children under the age of 1, and they are the number-one reason for visits to the emergency room in this age group (CDC, 2013e). Infants should never be left unattended on a high surface because you never know when the baby will start rolling over. As infants become mobile, it is essential to take safety precautions to protect them from falls down stairs by installing a safety gate at the top of the stairway. Baby walkers are linked with many accidents because toddlers take off in them without control at 3 feet per second, faster than parents can catch them (AAP, 2008). Although walkers have been redesigned so they are too wide to go through most doorways (or down the stairs), the American Academy of Pediatrics still recommends that parents avoid them and use a stationary activity center instead. Many parents have the mistaken idea that baby walkers encourage the development of walking, but infants sitting in walkers are not really practicing the skills needed to walk, such as balance. The bottom line is that walkers are very dangerous and babies who use them do not walk any earlier than others.

Infant Mortality

In general, developed countries have far lower rates of infant mortality, deaths within the first year of life, than less developed countries. However, even developed countries vary in how effectively they prevent infant death. Figure 5.11 shows the infant mortality rates for a number of developed countries. Note where the United States ranks in this figure. Despite its wealth and the availability of (but not always access to) world-class medical facilities, in 2010 the United States had a higher infant mortality rate than 34 other industrialized countries (Organisation for Economic Co-operation and Development, 2012).

In the United States, an average of 6.1 babies of 1,000 live births die within the first year; the precise rates vary significantly by race. In 2009, the infant mortality rate for non-Hispanic Black women was 12.4 deaths per 1,000 live births, compared to 5.33 deaths for non-Hispanic Whites (MacDorman, 2013). The difference was largely attributable to the large number of premature births to non-Hispanic Black women (18.3%). As you know from Chapter 4, premature infants are at far greater risk of not surviving infancy.

WEB LINK 5.5
Global Immunization

AUDIO LINK 5.4
Vaccinations

T/F #10
Baby walkers help babies walk at an earlier age. *False*

Infant mortality The rate of infant death within the first year of life.

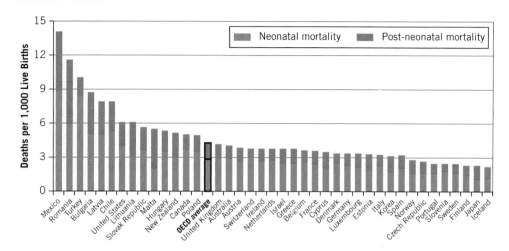

FIGURE 5.11   Infant mortality rates around the world, 2010

This figure shows the number of deaths of infants under one year of age (neonatal = the first 28 days of life, postneonatal = 28 days to one year). The United States has a higher rate than all but six countries.

SOURCE: OECD (2012).

However, there is some good news for the United States. Between 2005 and 2011, the infant mortality rate decreased by 12%, with the largest decreases among the highest-risk group, non-Hispanic Black infants (MacDorman, Hoyert, & Mathews, 2013). Although the biggest decreases occurred in southern states, the South still continues to have the highest levels of infant mortality, as shown in Figure 5.12.

The major causes of infant mortality, including birth defects, prematurity/low birth weight, Sudden Infant Death Syndrome, and maternal complications of pregnancy, declined in recent years, but there was no decrease in unintentional injuries (Borse et al., 2008; MacDorman, Hoyert, & Mathews, 2013). Suffocation most often occurs for infants while they are sleeping, so it is important to provide a firm surface free of loose bedding or soft objects, especially for very young infants. For toddlers, suffocation is most often a result of what they put in their mouths, including food that is not cut up well enough or other small objects (CDC, 2012g). It is important to babyproof the home to keep these types of objects out of young children's reach.

Sudden infant death syndrome (SIDS) The unexpected death of an apparently healthy infant.

Sudden Infant Death Syndrome (SIDS)

The unexpected death of an apparently healthy infant is a parent's worst nightmare. Sudden infant death syndrome (SIDS) is the leading cause of death for children between the ages of 1 month and 1 year. It rarely occurs before 1 month and peaks between 1 and 4 months (Task Force on Sudden Infant Death Syndrome, 2011).

We do not understand the cause of SIDS, but it is likely to be a combination of factors including a physical vulnerability in the infant (for example, some abnormality in the part of the brain that controls breathing, a brain chemical imbalance, a bacterial infection), a stressor in the environment (such as secondhand smoke, overheating due to too much clothing or an overly warm room), and a critical period of vulnerability in early development (Mayo Clinic Staff, 2014).

Blend Images - Mike Kemp/Brand X Pictures/Getty Images

Back to sleep. The "back to sleep" program (the recommendation that parents place an infant on his or her back to sleep) on a firm surface has greatly reduced the incidence of Sudden Infant Death Syndrome in the United States. ■

FIGURE 5.12   **Infant mortality rates by state**

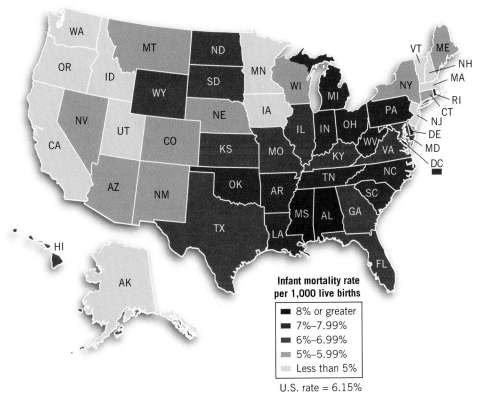

Infant mortality rate
per 1,000 live births

■ 8% or greater
■ 7%–7.99%
■ 6%–6.99%
■ 5%–5.99%
□ Less than 5%

U.S. rate = 6.15%

The rate of infant deaths varies by region of the country, with the highest rates in the South.

SOURCE: MacDorman, Hoyert, & Mathews (2013). Retrieved from http://www.cdc.gov/nchs/data/databriefs/db120.htm

Because the list of risk factors for SIDS is quite long and not all of them are under parents' control, it may seem there is little a concerned parent can do, but in fact a couple of preventive strategies are both simple and effective. Putting an infant down to sleep on his or her back has done a great deal to reduce the incidence of SIDS (AAP, 2005). Of course, once babies can roll over on their own and lift their heads voluntarily to avoid anything blocking their air supply, the position in which they are put to sleep is less important. Other simple but effective precautions are to use a firm mattress for the infant and forbid smoking in the home. Maternal smoking during pregnancy or after the baby is born significantly increases the risk of SIDS. While these precautions do not guarantee an infant will be safe, they are easy ways to lower an infant's risk.

Abusive Head Trauma and Shaken Baby Syndrome

Sometimes an adult who is frustrated with a baby may shake the baby hard. This causes the baby's brain to bounce against the skull, particularly if the baby's head hits something, even an object as soft as a pillow. The damage caused can include bruising, bleeding, or swelling in the brain that results in permanent brain damage or even death. In addition, because babies' heads are large in proportion to their bodies and their neck muscles are weak, they may suffer whiplash, much like what you might experience in a car accident. Symptoms of shaken baby syndrome may include:

- Convulsions (seizures)
- Decreased alertness

- Extreme irritability or other changes in behavior
- Lethargy, sleepiness, not smiling
- Loss of consciousness
- Loss of vision
- No breathing
- Pale or bluish skin
- Poor feeding, lack of appetite
- Vomiting (Kaneshiro & Zieve, 2011)

Within the first 3 months of life, episodes of prolonged crying for no apparent reason are common and normal for infants; however, these times can be very stressful for a new parent. The incidence of shaking by a caregiver is highest when the infant is between 2 and 3 months of age, when this crying is at its peak (Parks, Annest, Hill, & Karch, 2012). It is important for all caregivers to know that although they may feel anger at a baby, they should never act on that anger. Learning techniques for self-control is important to prevent abusive behavior. These may include simply putting the baby down, getting some help with childcare, and expressing emotions to a supportive person. If these feelings of frustration become common, counseling or parenting classes can be helpful. Child abuse hotlines are available for emergency situations.

Stress and Coping

A certain amount of stress is normal for everyone, including infants. For example, many infants experience stress when separated for even a short time from their mother or father. However, for some infants stress is more extreme and may become chronic. This type of stress might be the result of abuse, neglect, hunger, or lack of adequate care.

The stress response is our body's reaction to experiences we find threatening. Whenever you are exposed to stressful situations, your hypothalamus sends signals to your adrenal gland, which then produces high levels of cortisol, a hormone that prepares your body to deal with threats in the environment by increasing blood pressure and heart rate. Cortisol also shuts down other functions that are not essential at that moment, such as digestion and growth processes (Mayo Clinic Staff, 2013).

Under normal stress, cortisol rises to help deal with the threat and then decreases to let the body return to normal, but when infants experience overwhelming and ongoing stress, their brains become less capable of developing normal mechanisms for responding to stressful situations. The resulting persistent high levels of cortisol can cause brain cells to die or can reduce the connections between areas of the brain that are essential for learning and memory (National Scientific Council on the Developing Child, 2005/2014; Shonkoff & Phillips, 2000).

The neural circuits in the stress response system are particularly malleable during infancy, so prolonged exposure to stressful situations can make these systems overreactive or slow to shut down throughout the remainder of the individual's life. Behaviorally, infants who are under chronic stress may become children and adults who are overly anxious and fearful. Physically, they may produce large amounts of cortisol over a longer period of time. Stress-related production of cortisol is linked with lowered immune responses, so these infants may be more likely to become sick. Cognitive functions are also affected by elevated cortisol, so learning and memory do not develop as well as they would for an infant who experiences a relaxed, organized, and loving environment (National Scientific Council on the Developing Child, 2005/2014). As we've learned, infants' brains are plastic, or changeable, so the good news is that many of the effects of stress early in life can be reversed with sensitive caregiving. However, without intervention, the maladaptive stress response can become a long-term reaction to life experiences that may severely limit the child's growth and development.

Cortisol A hormone produced as part of the stress response that prepares the body to deal with threat and also shuts down nonessential functions.

1. What are some benefits of breastfeeding, for mothers and babies?
2. Why are vaccinations recommended?
3. What is the role of cortisol in the infant's response to stress?

Conclusion

In infants and toddlers, brain and body are developing faster than they will at any later time in life. Care that provides all the basic elements necessary for good health is essential. Physical development is linked to many aspects of emotional, social, and cognitive development, so healthy growth and development in infancy lays the groundwork for future growth in all these areas, as you will see in the chapters that follow.

Chapter Summary

5.1 What are the structures of the brain and related developmental processes and disabilities?

The brain is made up of **neurons** and is divided into two specialized **hemispheres**, connected by the **corpus callosum**. Although infants have billions of neurons, they have relatively few **synapses** that connect them. In early brain development, **synaptogenesis** forms connections between neurons, and **myelination** improves the efficiency of the neural impulses. Unused synapses are **pruned**, but when an individual encounters typical experiences, **experience-expectant brain development** occurs and those synaptic connections are retained. When an individual encounters unique experiences, **experience-dependent brain development** occurs and new synapses are formed.

Cerebral palsy results from damage to the brain before or shortly after birth and is characterized by problems with body movement and muscle coordination. **Autism spectrum disorders** may be caused by different patterns of brain development (such as failure to prune unnecessary synapses). Symptoms include impairment in social communication and interaction and restricted or repetitive behaviors, interests, or activities. Severity is classified by how much support the individual needs to function effectively.

5.2 How do the five senses develop in infancy?

Infants are born with a fully functional set of sense organs. **Sensations** registered by the sense organs are transmitted to the brain and integrated into a coherent picture of the external world in the process of **perception**. Infants also may automatically imitate simple behaviors they see because **mirror neurons** in the brain fire in the same way when they see a behavior as when they actually perform it.

Although an infant's **visual acuity** is initially poor, it develops to adult levels by 6 months to 3 years after birth. Hearing is well developed at birth, and infants have shown a preference for their mothers' voices. The sense of smell also is highly developed at birth, and infants prefer sweet to other tastes. Both smell and taste preferences are shaped by experiences prenatally. Infants are sensitive to touch. Soothing touch promotes development and well-being while pain produces stress.

5.3 What reflexes and motor skills do infants and toddlers possess?

Infants are born with a set of **reflexes**, most of which are soon replaced by voluntary movement as the nervous system matures. Children gain control over both **fine motor skills** and **gross motor skills**, and these skills develop following the **cephalocaudal** and **proximodistal** principles (moving from the head to toe, and from the center of the body to the extremities).

Motor development is shaped by a complex interaction of genes, maturation, and environmental experiences. Parenting practices can influence how quickly infants develop specific motor skills. **Dynamic systems theory** makes it clear that motor skill development is affected by cognitive and social factors as well as purely physical characteristics.

5.4 What are the major health and nutrition issues in infancy?

Health is promoted in infancy through breastfeeding when possible and development of regular sleeping patterns. Threats to health include colds, fevers, ear infections and injuries from falls. Major causes of infant mortality include SIDS, birth defects, prematurity/low birth weight, maternal complications of pregnancy, and unintentional injuries (mostly due to suffocation). Child abuse is also a major risk for infants, including abusive head trauma and shaken baby syndrome. Finally, all infants will experience some amount of stress from everyday events, but in case of overwhelming or ongoing stress the long-term production of **cortisol** will increase the likelihood of illness, cognitive deficit, and fearfulness.

Key Terms

Autism spectrum disorder (ASD)　147

Axon　143

Cerebral palsy　146

Circumcision　154

Corpus callosum　142

Cortisol　174

Cross-modal transfer of perception　154

Dendrites　143

Experience-dependent brain development　145

Experience-expectant brain development　145

Fine motor skills　158

Gross motor skills　158

Hemispheres　142

Infant mortality　171

Mirror neurons　149

Myelination　145

Neurons　143

Neurotransmitters　143

Perception　149

Plasticity　144

Proximodistal　159

Pruning　144

Reflexes　156

Sensations　149

Sudden infant death syndrome (SIDS)　172

Synapse　143

Synaptogenesis　143

Visual acuity　151

$SAGE edge™

Sharpen your skills with SAGE edge at edge.sagepub.com/levinechrono

SAGE edge for Students provides a personalized approach to help you accomplish your coursework goals in an easy-to-use learning environment.

Go to edge.sagepub.com/levinechrono for additional exercises and video resources. Select Chapter 5, Physical Development in Infancy and Toddlerhood, for chapter-specific activities. All of the Video Links listed in the margins of this chapter are accessible via this site.

Cognitive Development in Infancy and Toddlerhood

6 Cognitive Development in Infancy and Toddlerhood

T/F Test Your Knowledge

Test your knowledge of child development by deciding whether each of the following statements is *true* or *false*, and then check your answers as you read the chapter.

1. **T ☐ F ☐**   If a young child drops an object from her high chair over and over again, she is probably just asserting herself and testing her parents' patience.

2. **T ☐ F ☐**   Infants appear to have an intuitive understanding of how gravity works.

3. **T ☐ F ☐**   Few people have clear memories of what happened in their lives before the age of 3.

4. **T ☐ F ☐**   Being attracted to novelty as an infant is associated with intelligence in later childhood.

5. **T ☐ F ☐**   Infants are born with a preference for listening to their native language.

6. **T ☐ F ☐**   A sensitive parent should be able to tell the difference between a baby who is crying because he is hungry and one who is crying because he is in pain or is lonely.

7. **T ☐ F ☐**   It is perfectly fine to use baby talk with infants.

8. **T ☐ F ☐**   Teaching babies to use sign language will delay development of spoken language.

9. **T ☐ F ☐**   Intellectual disability is diagnosed when an individual has an IQ below 70.

10. **T ☐ F ☐**   Babies who watch videotapes designed to improve cognitive development (like Baby Einstein videos) have larger vocabularies than babies who don't watch these videos.

Correct answers: (1) F, (2) T, (3) T, (4) T, (5) T, (6) F, (7) T, (8) F, (9) F, (10) F

What do babies know about the world, and how do they understand and interpret their experiences in it? One of the challenges in answering these questions is that when we study cognitive development of infants, we cannot use the techniques we usually use with older children and adults. Infants cannot answer questions about what they are thinking, for instance, and it is difficult for us to remember and report on the way we thought when we were that young. Jean Piaget, whose theory was briefly described in Chapter 2, based his ideas about infant cognitive development on detailed observation of his own children when they were infants and toddlers. More recently, researchers have developed clever ways to test these and other theories through the use of technology that can monitor eye movements, brain function, and many other biological responses that give us clues into the nature of babies' thoughts.

In this chapter, we describe theory and research about cognition, including the first stage of Piaget's theory of cognitive development. We also introduce you to a newer theory of cognitive development, called the theory of core knowledge, which proposes different ideas about the nature of infant thought. We describe how basic infant cognitive processes develop, including attention, memory, and executive function, and which aspects of infant cognitive skills relate to later intelligence. Finally, much of cognitive development relies on language; therefore, we describe the ways in which infants develop their understanding and use of language, beginning even before they are born. We conclude the chapter with a discussion of some of the factors that put an infant's cognitive and language development at risk and some that enhance and support it.

Learning Questions

6.1 What occurs during Piaget's sensorimotor stage of cognitive development?

6.2 What is the premise of the theory of core knowledge?

6.3 How do infants learn?

6.4 What cognitive processes develop during infancy?

6.5 What aspects of infants' cognitive development are the best predictors of later intelligence?

6.6 How do infants develop language?

6.7 How can we ensure optimal cognitive and language development in infants?

Piaget's Theory of Cognitive Development

6.1

What occurs during Piaget's sensorimotor stage of cognitive development?

Jean Piaget (1896–1980) was a student of biology before he studied psychology and child development. By age 10, he had already published his first article in the field of biology, a study of an albino sparrow he had seen in a park (McKeachie & Sims, 2004). He continued his biological interests with research on mollusks, those hard-shelled sea creatures such as oysters, snails, and clams. He had published over 20 articles on the subject by the time he was 21, and he later completed his doctoral dissertation on the mollusks of the Valais region in Switzerland (Singer & Revenson, 1996).

If one of your friends were like the young Piaget, you might be concerned that his or her life was too narrowly focused on one thing, as was Piaget's godfather. He introduced the young man to the study of philosophy, and Piaget then became interested in the philosophical question of how we come to know and understand our world, an area of study referred to as *epistemology*. His approach to studying the development of the human mind was a synthesis of ideas drawn from biology and philosophy, along with an interest in finding evidence for theories based on careful observation. On the one hand, he looked at human beings as biological organisms who must adapt successfully to their environment, just as snails and clams do. On the other hand, he looked at the unique characteristics of the human mind, with its capacity for reflection and understanding,

Genetic-epistemology The study of the development of knowledge through biological adaptation and development of the mind.

and wondered how it all worked. As we will see, both approaches contributed to the theory of genetic-epistemology (*genetic* from biology, *epistemology* from philosophy) Piaget developed.

Basic Principles

Many developmental researchers credit Piaget with revolutionizing the study of children's cognitive development (Flavell, Miller, & Miller, 2002). Although his theory has received some criticism and undergone some revision over the years, it provides a set of basic principles to guide our understanding of cognitive development that is still found in most current theories. They include the following ideas:

- Intelligence is an active, constructive, and dynamic process.
- Mistakes children make in their thinking are usually meaningful because the mistakes give us insight into the nature of their thought processes at their current stage of development.
- As children develop, the structure of their thinking changes, and their new modes of thought are based on earlier structures. (Flavell et al., 2002)

Piaget believed that we are always actively trying to make sense of our experiences to adapt successfully to our environment and ensure our survival. By "making sense" he meant organizing our experiences into schemas, as we described in Chapter 2. **Active Learning: Organizing by Cognitive Schema** gives you a chance to explore the different ways to organize a single set of objects, depending on which schemas you use. Remember that a schema is a cognitive framework that places concepts, objects, or experiences into categories or groups of associations. Each person has a unique way of organizing experiences based on the schemas he or she has developed.

Ly Wylde Photography/Moment Select/Getty Images

Active Learning

Organizing by Cognitive Schema

Look at this photo of footwear. List as many ways to organize or categorize these shoes as you can.

You can do this in several different ways: (a) by type, (b) by color, or (c) by wearer. What other categories did you use? In Piaget's terms, each of these ways of organizing the shoes might indicate a schema you have for footwear. ■

Often, when we have a new experience, it immediately makes sense to us because we can fit it into a schema we already have. For example, a child may have a new kind of sandwich that she easily understands is a kind of food similar to foods she's had before. When we can fit new experiences easily into our pre-existing schemas, we engage in what Piaget called assimilation because we can *assimilate* or take the new experience into an existing schema. However, let's say this child has never seen crab served in its shell. If the child is served something that is this different from the foods she is familiar with, she may not connect it with her schema for food. Piaget would say she is thrown into a state of confusion, or disequilibrium, by the experience.

Disequilibrium A state of confusion in which your schemas do not fit your experiences.

People generally find the uncertainty of disequilibrium uncomfortable, so they try to make sense of what they are seeing in order to return to a comfortable cognitive state through a process Piaget referred to as equilibration. When we need to change our schemas to fit new experiences, we use accommodation because we are *accommodating* or changing the way we think about something in order to understand the new information. In this case, if a parent can convince the child to try eating the crab, she may discover it is a delicious food, and she accommodates her existing schema for food by including crab in it and equilibrium is restored.

The Sensorimotor Stage

As a result of his research and his conversations with children, Piaget believed children think in a different way than adults do; that is, not only are there quantitative differences in that children have less information or less skill in thinking than adults do, but more important there are qualitative differences as well, meaning children think in a particular way unique to their developmental level. Based on his detailed observations, Piaget identified four stages from infancy through adolescence, each representing a new quality of thought but each building on the cognitive abilities acquired during the previous stage. We introduce the stages here, but you will learn about the nature and qualities of each when we describe cognitive development at each age level throughout the book. The first stage, which corresponds to infancy, is called the *sensorimotor stage* and we describe it in detail in this chapter. The second stage is called the *preoperational stage* and corresponds to early childhood; the third is the stage of *concrete operations* in middle childhood, and the final stage is *formal operations*, which begins in early adolescence. Although Piaget set out ages for each stage, you should think of them as approximations; some children reach the stages sooner or later than others. What Piaget felt was most important is that the stages can occur only in the order he described. Children cannot jump from sensorimotor thinking to formal operations and then back to concrete operations. The path of development moves in only one direction.

As its name implies, the **sensorimotor stage** is the time during which Piaget believed infants organize their world by means of their senses. He felt they do little internal mental processing of the world; rather they understand it based on the direct action they take on it. For example, a rattle is not a toy with its own existence, but a "shake-able" because the infant can shake it. The infant understands it according to what he or she does to it. It is only at the end of the sensorimotor period that infants are capable of internal mental representation, in which they will view the rattle as an object that exists in its own right.

Although Piaget described six substages of the sensorimotor period, he believed that "the facts remain so complicated and their sequence can be so rapid that it would be dangerous to separate these stages too much" (Piaget, 1952, p. 331). Therefore, we summarize these substages briefly in Table 6.1, but we believe it is more useful to examine four general trends in development within the sensorimotor period: (1) development from reflexes to goal-directed activity, (2) from the body to the outside world, (3) development of object permanence, and (4) from motor action to mental representation.

As we learned in Chapter 5, all infants are born with reflexes, which are automatic, patterned behaviors that have some survival value. These behaviors are not learned but are built into the nervous system. However, Piaget said that learning begins even in the first month of life as infants begin to adapt these reflexes to the environment. For example, the sucking reflex is usually evoked when the lips are touched. However, the infant soon begins to suck before his lips are touched, perhaps when he is placed in his mother's arms where he anticipates being fed. In this way, even automatic behaviors begin to accommodate to the environment (Piaget, 1962).

Between 1 and 4 months, infants begin to use reflexes in different ways. When the reflex results in a pleasurable experience, the infant intentionally repeats it over and

Sensorimotor stage
Piaget's first stage in which infants understand the world through the information they take in through their senses and through their actions on their environment.

| TABLE 6.1 | Six substages of the sensorimotor period |

Substage	Age	Characteristics	Examples
1. Use of reflexes	0–1 month	Automatic reflexes	Infant makes sucking motion with mouth when stroked on the cheek.
2. Primary circular reactions	1–4 months	Adaptation of reflexes to the environment	Infant adjusts sucking to accommodate a new pacifier.
3. Secondary circular reactions	4–8 months	Repetition of actions that make interesting events last	Infant swings arm and happens to hit bell; repeats this action many times.
4. Coordination of reactions and application to new situations	8–12 months	Action schemas applied to new objects	Infant taps bell and it rings; tries tapping a new object in the same way.
5. Tertiary circular reactions	12–18 months	Intentional discovery of new means to explore	Toddler rings bell and discovers hitting bell with a stick also makes it ring.
6. Invention of new means of exploration through mental combinations	18–24 months	Use of mental activity to guide exploration	Toddler sees cracker on table and pulls chair over to climb up and get it.

SOURCE: Adapted in part from Piaget (1952).

over again. For example, when the infant somehow gets his thumb in his mouth, it begins what Piaget called a circular reaction. The action produces a good feeling, which prompts the infant to continue the action, and the good feeling continues to stimulate the action, in a circular fashion. When the baby's thumb falls out of his mouth, he has to rediscover the action that will place it back where it feels good (Piaget, 1962). The different circular reactions the infant is developing are examples of motor schemas. Infants organize their understanding of the world into motor schemas through their action on it. We all know that if you give an 8-month-old any object, the first thing she will do is put it in her mouth. She is using this sucking or mouthing schema as her way of organizing the world: Is this object a "suckable"? How does it taste? How does it feel in my mouth?

Between 8 and 12 months, infants combine the motor schemas they have already developed to begin solving problems. No longer do they just repeat actions over and over for the pleasure of it. Now they have a goal in mind and use motor schemas such as grasping, hitting, and mouthing in combinations to reach that goal. At the next stage, usually between the ages of 12 and 18 months, infants develop new behaviors that allow them to achieve their goals. Although they still repeat actions over and over, now they do it with planned variations designed to "see what happens when I do *this*!" For example, any parent knows the stage babies go through when they continually drop things on purpose. If you watch carefully, you'll see that each time the child does this, the action is likely to be a little different as he experiments with "What happens when I drop it this way? What happens when I drop it and Mommy is there? What happens when I drop it and she's not there?" This can be very frustrating for parents, but Piaget saw it as an example of the active experimentation children engage in at all ages.

When babies are very young, their major interest is meeting their bodily needs for food, sleep, and comfort. As they grow, their attention is increasingly focused on the world around them. Their vision and coordination improve, and they begin to apply circular reactions to objects outside their own bodies. For example, if a baby kicks her legs

Circular reaction An infant's repetition of a reflexive action that results in a pleasurable experience.

Motor schema Infants' organization of knowledge through action on the world.

T/F #1

If a young child drops an object from her high chair over and over again, she is probably just asserting herself and testing her parents' patience. *False*

and sees the mobile hanging over her crib move in response, she repeats the kicking over and over until she tires of the excitement over the response she can create in the world (Rovee-Collier, 1999).

Piaget believed newborns do not understand that objects (or people for that matter) exist outside their own action on them; that is, infants lack object permanence. An infant grasping a toy experiences "grasping a toy," not "I, a separate entity, am grasping this toy, which also has an existence of its own" (Fast, 1985). While the child is grasping the toy, it is part of his experience, but when he is not, the toy doesn't exist for him. As the infant develops new means of exploration, he learns that he can grasp the toy and also chew on it and also look at it. When he applies *several* motor schemas to an object, the motor schemas become detached from the object itself. The toy is no longer just "something I grasp," but "a thing separate from my actions on it." Finally, by the end of the sensorimotor stage, the child understands that objects exist independently and act according to their own rules (Fast, 1985). **Active Learning: Testing Object Permanence** will walk you through the procedures Piaget used to assess object permanence in infants.

© BSIP SA/Alamy

Motor schema. This baby is using the motor schema of sucking to explore objects. As long as this activity is pleasurable, the baby will continue to repeat it in a pattern called a circular reaction. ■

Active Learning

Testing Object Permanence

Piaget (1954) devised a series of experiments to test infants' understanding of object permanence. You can carry out this test if you have access to a child between 6 months and age 2. If others in your class test children of different ages within this age range, you can compare results to see how object permanence changes during this period of time. You will need to have an interesting toy or object that is safe for an infant to have (that is, nothing the child can choke on or that is otherwise unsafe to put in the mouth) and two cloths to cover the object. There are three steps to the series of experiments Piaget carried out:

1. Show the child the toy and be sure he is interested in it and is watching you. Then hide the toy under one of the cloths, which are set side by side between you and the child. Observe and record whether the child searches for the toy.

2. If the child searches and finds the toy, begin Step 2 by hiding it again under the same cloth. Then, while the baby is still watching, move the toy from under the first cloth to under the second cloth. Observe and record where the baby searches.

3. If the child finds the toy the second time, repeat Step 2 but try to move the toy from the first cloth to the second without letting the child see what you are doing. Observe and record where the child searches.

Follow-up: Does the child show through his behaviors that he understands objects continue to exist even if he can't see them?

In Piaget's experiments, young infants would not search at all when an object was hidden; it was as if they believed the toy simply disappeared. At an older age they

Object permanence The understanding that objects continue to exist when no one is interacting with them.

ACTIVE LEARNING
VIDEO 6.1
Testing Object Permanence

The development of object permanence. How does the concept of object permanence explain why this baby loses interest in the toy dog when it is hidden? ■

VIDEO LINK 6.1
A-not-B Error

A-not-B error In a test of object permanence, an infant searches for an object hidden under cloth A, but continues to look under cloth A when it is moved under cloth B.

would search under the first cloth, but if the toy was moved under a second cloth, they would continue to search in the first location or give up even if they clearly saw the experimenter move the object under the second cloth. This is known as the A-not-B error because the infant continues to look in the first location, *A*, and does not switch to the second location, *B*, where the object is now hidden. A third stage occurs when the baby searches after seeing the object moved from *A* to *B*, but not after *not* seeing the switch. Finally, when the infant has true object permanence, she will continue to search regardless of the movement of the object. There is no question in the baby's mind that the toy still exists even though she can no longer see it, and she will search until she recovers it. ■

In recent years, the validity of Piaget's ideas about the development of object permanence has been questioned. Read about this ongoing controversy in **Journey of Research: The Debate About Object Permanence.**

· ·

JOURNEY OF RESEARCH *The Debate About Object Permanence*

One of the challenges for any stage theory is that once we place an ability at a certain stage, people can begin asking "But could it happen earlier?" Much of the controversy about object permanence has centered around whether this is a cognitive ability that develops over time (as Piaget suggested) or one that arises much earlier in development, or perhaps even is innate.

Research on object permanence done from a Piagetian perspective has found a developmental progression as his theory would predict. Infants younger than 7 months do not search for a hidden object. As they get older they will retrieve an object that is partially hidden, and finally by 8 to 10 months of age, they can retrieve an object that is totally hidden (Moore & Meltzoff, 2008). However, Piaget believed this still did

not indicate complete object permanence. He found that when infants between 7 and 12 months of age see someone hide an object in one location (position A) and then move that object to a second hiding place (position B), they continue to look for the object in position A. It is not until 1 year of age that infants reliably know to search in position B and master the A-not-B task.

Contrary to this idea of a developmental progression, Baillargeon (2008) proposed that infants are *born* with "persistence"— that is, an understanding that objects persist through time and space. In other words, they are born with object permanence. This idea is part of the *theory of core knowledge*, which we discuss a little later in this chapter. Piaget's critics have pointed out that the way he tested for object permanence—retrieving an object from under a cover—requires much more than understanding that the object continues to exist. Infants also must be able to remember where the object was, plan for its retrieval, and have the motor skills to reach out and grasp the object (Baillargeon, Li, Ng, & Yuan, 2009).

How can we look for evidence of object permanence without relying on these other abilities? When modern researchers have used more sophisticated techniques that reduce the difficulty of the task, they report evidence of object permanence (or persistence) much earlier than previous research. For example, researchers are now able to use computer software to track where a baby is looking. Based on the idea that infants will look longer at events that surprise them, researchers have found that babies look longer at events that violate an expectation of object permanence. Baillargeon, Spelke, and Wasserman (1985) showed 4-month-old babies a toy. A screen was then placed in front of the toy and tipped slowly backward. In the real world, the screen would hit the toy and stop tipping. Some babies saw exactly that (the expected outcome). However, some babies saw the screen continue to tip all the way back, as if it were going right through the toy (an unexpected outcome). Babies in the unexpected-outcome condition looked significantly longer than those in the expected outcome condition. Therefore, it appeared the babies knew the object should still be there even though they couldn't see it.

This line of research has continued to be controversial. Sirois and Jackson (2012) have questioned whether longer looking time is really a measure of surprise. Instead they examined changes in the dilation of infants' pupils during the same task as the one developed by Baillargeon et al. (1985). Pupils dilate based on how much light is present, but dilation also changes due to interest, arousal, and the amount of information being processed, referred to as cognitive load. In their research with 10-month-old infants, Sirois and Jackson found no change in pupil size when it appeared to the infant that the screen was going right through the box. Their interpretation of the results reported by other researchers was that longer looking time reflected the infant's interest in other factors, such as the movement of the screen, not surprise indicating object permanence. Using this interpretation, they concluded there was no evidence for object permanence in these infants.

Other researchers have explained Piaget's results as a lack of memory rather than a lack of object permanence; that is, they would argue that infants know an object still exists, but they forget about it. Bremner et al. (2005) showed that 4-month-olds would track an object that moved behind a screen to the point where it emerged again, but only if the time behind the screen was very short. It appears that a longer disappearance overtaxes a young infant's memory ability.

Clearly Piaget's work provided a rich source of hypotheses for research on cognitive development, but this ongoing debate about object permanence is also a good illustration of the way we have used new techniques to try to answer longstanding questions in our field. It reminds us that the conclusions we draw from new research still depend on the way we interpret the results we find. ▪

As we have seen, Piaget believed infants understand the world through motor schemas, such as grasping, sucking, and shaking. Motor schemas are quite different from the kinds of schemas based on concepts and inner thought you used earlier in **Active Learning: Organizing by Cognitive Schema**. Piaget theorized that ultimately motor schemas would become the basis for internal, cognitive representations of the world. He believed children's first thoughts are mental representations of the actions they have been performing. In other words, the motor schemas are internalized, and the infant can *think* of them instead of actually *doing* them. Piaget (1963) provides the following example of the planning that can now occur. His daughter Jacqueline, at the age of 1 year and 7 months, tried to put a chain necklace into a matchbox. Over and over she tried to put one end of the chain in, then the next part, and then the next. However, each time the first part would fall out as she was trying to put the rest in, and she remained unsuccessful. Piaget reported that at an older age his other daughter Lucienne used her new abilities to think ahead rather than just act. With the same objective of putting the necklace into the matchbox, she rolled the necklace into a ball and successfully placed it into the box. Instead of the trial-and-error approach of her sister at a younger age, Lucienne was able to think about an effective way to accomplish this goal and then do it.

Piaget did not have the means to test young infants that have since led modern researchers to conclude that infants understand some concepts earlier than he thought. A basic tenet of Piaget's ideas is that infants create knowledge through an interaction of brain development and their own action within the environment, and that this requires time to develop. In the next theory we present, called the theory of core knowledge, researchers propose that infants are born with some of the basic knowledge Piaget believed they had to learn.

Check Your Understanding

1. In Piaget's theory of cognitive development, what is the difference between assimilation and accommodation?
2. What occurs during Piaget's sensorimotor stage of cognitive development?
3. What is object permanence?

6.2

What is the premise of the theory of core knowledge?

Theory of core knowledge The theory that basic areas of knowledge are innate and built into the human brain.

Theory of Core Knowledge

The theory of core knowledge is based on the idea that humans are born with innate cognitive systems that provide basic, or core knowledge for understanding the world (Spelke & Kinzler, 2007). These basic systems are not developed from experience; rather they represent knowledge that appears to be built into the human brain. This theory is a direct challenge to Piaget's ideas that children construct even very basic knowledge about the nature of objects and people through experience. Would you be surprised by any of the following?

1. A ball that was buried in the sand in one location is pulled out of the sand in a different location (Newcombe, Sluzenski, & Huttenlocher, 2005).

2. You see one doll in a case. Someone then hides the case, and you see that person add one other doll. When the case is later opened, there are three dolls in it; in other words, 1 + 1 = 3 (Wynn, 1992).

3. You see a block pushed to the end of a small platform and then beyond the edge so that most of it is not supported, and yet it does not fall, as shown in Figure 6.1 (Baillargeon, Needham, & DeVos, 1992).

Violation of expectation A research methodology based on the finding that babies look longer at unexpected or surprising events.

These are just a few of the classic scenarios that have been presented to babies within their first year of life to assess their understanding of the nature of objects and the way they function. As we described earlier, looking longer at an event is interpreted as an indication that a baby is surprised by an event that is a violation of expectation. Research from the core knowledge perspective has found that there appear to be some innate cognitive systems for understanding some aspects of the world. Babies look longer at the events described above even before their first birthday. This is seen as evidence that the infant's understanding of some aspects of the world do not have to be learned as Piaget implied; nor is it the "blooming, buzzing confusion" described long ago by William James (1890/1990, p. 462). From the three experiments described above, it appears that (1) infants understand that objects remain in the same place unless moved, an indication that they have a form of object permanence; (2) they have a basic concept of number, at least up to three; and (3) they have a basic understanding of the effects

T/F #2

Infants appear to have an intuitive understanding of how gravity works. *True* of gravity. Many other competencies have been explored, and many have been found so early in life that researchers claim they are innate abilities.

Although researchers who subscribe to the theory of core knowledge claim infants are born with certain basic knowledge, they differ about the content of that knowledge. Spelke and Kinzler (2007) present evidence for four areas of core knowledge:

1. Knowledge that an object moves as a cohesive unit, it does not contact another object unless they are close to each other, and it moves on a continuous path.

2. Knowledge that agents (people) act purposefully toward a goal. Infants also know that objects are not acting with a goal "in mind" in the same way that people are.

3. Knowledge (within limits) of number, as experienced in all modalities—for example, *hearing* a number of tones or *seeing* a number of objects. This understanding is not exact and gets less precise as the number gets larger. The knowledge of number also includes a basic understanding of addition and subtraction.

4. Knowledge of spatial relationships, including how to use the shape of the environment to find out where they are when disoriented.

Spelke (2000) argues that later learning is largely based on these earliest core understandings of the world.

Researchers are actively studying the question of whether certain aspects of knowledge are innate or whether infants must construct their knowledge through experience in the world. For example, although Spelke and Kinzler (2007) argued that infants know from birth that people but not objects act with intention, other researchers have provided some evidence that these abilities are learned very early but are not innate. Woodward (2009) found that infants are more likely to understand other people's intentions in reaching for objects after they themselves have learned to intentionally reach for an object. She argues that they learn from their own actions about how to interpret the actions of other people.

The ongoing research in this area is a wonderful example of the scientific process, as evidence and counter-evidence refine our understanding of the beginning stages of cognitive development. The findings will help us see how children and even adults develop more sophisticated understandings based on these early concepts. They may also provide insight into some of the difficulties children may have when they move from their primitive core knowledge to a higher level of understanding of the same concept (Spelke, 2000).

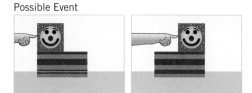

FIGURE 6.1   Do infants understand gravity?

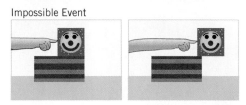

Even babies are surprised when they see an object seemingly defying gravity, as in the last frame above.

SOURCE: Baillargeon (1994).

Check Your Understanding

1. What are four areas of core knowledge that have been identified?
2. What is violation of expectation and what does it tell us about how infants understand the world?
3. How does the theory of core knowledge differ from Piaget's theory of cognitive development?

Learning

You studied some basic principles of learning when you read about the theories of behaviorism and social cognitive theory in Chapter 2. Research has shown that even very

6.3

How do infants learn?

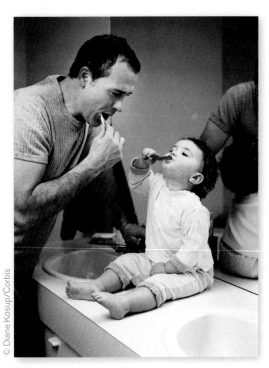

© Diane Kosup/Corbis

Learning by doing. Imitation is an effective way for infants to learn. What does this suggest for parents of babies and young children? ∎

VIDEO LINK 6.2
Imitation

young infants learn through the basic mechanisms of behaviorism—classical and operant conditioning—and through imitation, as described by social cognitive theory.

Learning through classical conditioning, the association of one stimulus with another, has been shown in young infants based on a reflexive response all of us have: blinking when a puff of air is directed at our eyes. In a study of 4- to 5-month-old babies, the puff of air (the unconditioned stimulus) was preceded by a tone the infants could hear (the neutral stimulus). When this was done repeatedly over two sessions, infants began to blink when they heard the tone (now the conditioned stimulus) before the puff of air was introduced (Ivkovich, Collins, Eckerman, Krasnegor, & Stanton, 1999). This behavior demonstrates that the infants had learned to associate the tone with the puff of air. In the same way, an infant might associate the sounds of her mother's footsteps with the satisfaction of being fed and stop crying when she hears her mother coming.

Infants also learn through the process of operant conditioning, the reinforcement of spontaneously produced behavior. One procedure designed to assess memory in infants began by teaching them to kick using operant conditioning. Infants were placed in a crib with a mobile swinging above, and for 3 minutes researchers counted the number of times each infant naturally kicked her legs. They then tied a ribbon from her leg to the mobile so that when she kicked, the mobile moved around, creating a pleasing visual display. With this display as reinforcement, infants learned to kick much more often (Gerhardstein, Dickerson, Miller, & Hipp, 2012).

Imitation is another very basic way in which infants learn, as described by social cognitive theory. The tendency to imitate begins with newborns, who often copy simple adult actions like sticking out their tongue. By 14 months, infants will imitate adults' novel actions designed to reach a certain goal. When an adult gets an infant's attention and shows how he can turn on a light box by bending over and touching it with his head, the infant tends to imitate that action despite the fact that she can achieve the same goal by simply touching the lightbox with her hands (Király, Csibra, & Gergely, 2013; Meltzoff, 1999). Clearly infants are learning both the actual task at hand (turning on the lightbox) and the social message that there is much to learn by watching others and imitating what they do.

Check Your Understanding

1. What are some of the ways infants learn?
2. How do we know whether infants can be classically conditioned?
3. Describe an experiment demonstrating the effect of operant conditioning on infants.

6.4

What cognitive processes develop during infancy?

Cognitive Processes

The ways in which we take in and process information have been described by the theory of information processing. In this section, we first describe what research has shown about two of the most basic cognitive processes, attention and memory, as they develop in the first 2 years of life. Other specific cognitive abilities also are beginning to develop during this period as well, including infants' ability to categorize and to understand numbers. Finally, we describe the higher mental function called executive function that helps young children inhibit their immediate responses to achieve a desired goal. Although we find the roots of these processes in infancy, each continues to mature and develop throughout childhood and adolescence, so we return to these topics in future chapters.

Attention in Infancy

When someone is told to "Pay attention!" it means that person should focus her mental processes on one thing (maybe a teacher's words) and not on another (maybe her friends' conversation). Tuning in to certain things while tuning out others is called selective attention, and maintaining focus over time is called sustained attention (Fan et al., 2009; Parasuraman, 1998). Telling a baby to pay attention is often futile because the infant does not yet have the capacity to control his attention very well.

What attracts infants' attention? We know infants will look longer at something they haven't seen before. This preference for novelty makes it highly likely infants will learn as much as they can about the world by focusing their attention on what is new. The other side of this attraction to novelty is that infants lose interest and respond less to what they have seen before, a process known as habituation. For example, if you entered a room that had a noisy air conditioner, you would probably be very aware of the sound at first. After a while, however, you would habituate to the sound, and you would no longer pay any attention to it. In the laboratory, habituation has been used to assess many aspects of cognition that infants cannot tell us about in words. In the habituation procedure, a researcher shows an object to an infant over and over again and records how long the infant looks each time the object is presented. In addition, the infant's heart rate is monitored because attention is also indicated by a decrease in the heart rate. Normally, the infant will lose interest over time and will decrease the amount of time spent looking. The rate of habituation measures how quickly the infant decreases the time spent looking with repeated showings.

As infants get older, their ability to process information becomes more efficient so they habituate to familiar stimuli more quickly (Colombo & Mitchell, 2009). Although the rate at which babies habituate is somewhat predictive of later cognitive abilities, Colombo and Mitchell (2009) conclude that rate of habituation itself does not indicate intelligence; rather, habituation is a basic ability that is essential for the development of higher level learning.

Although sustained attention decreases as infants become familiar with an object and this happens more quickly as infants get older, sustained attention *increases* in older infants when they are shown more complex stimuli, such as a Sesame Street video, and this change continues through preschool (Courage, Reynolds, & Richards, 2006). Think about completing a three-piece jigsaw puzzle over and over again. Clearly you would quickly lose interest. However, if you were given a complex puzzle to solve, your interest might grow with each new aspect of the puzzle you noticed. This difference has also been observed in infant attention.

Memory in Infancy

After we have paid attention to something, we must move it into memory if we want to use that information in the future. How do we know whether infants can remember? In her classic work on infant memory, Carolyn Rovee-Collier (1999) developed the procedure described earlier based on operant conditioning to find out how long infants can remember. She had infants lie in a crib under a mobile with attractive toys hanging on it. She then tied a ribbon from the baby's ankle to the mobile so that when the baby kicked, it would make the mobile shake in a pleasing way. Each baby learned to kick to move the mobile. The babies were then brought back into this situation, some after a day, some

Selective attention The process of tuning in to certain things while tuning out others.

Sustained attention The process of maintaining focus over time.

Habituation The reduction in the response to a stimulus that is repeated.

VIDEO LINK 6.3
Infant Memory

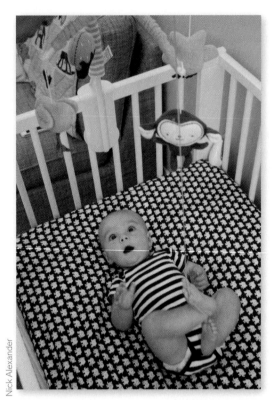

Nick Alexander

Do they remember? Rovee-Collier's research has shown that infants can learn to kick to make a mobile move in an interesting way. When they are in the same situation even days or weeks later, they will remember how to do this. ■

after several days, and some after a week or longer. If the baby remembered the mobile, she would kick right away. If not, she would learn all over again how to make the mobile move. Using this and another paradigm appropriate for somewhat older babies, Rovee-Collier found that 3-month-olds could remember what they needed to do for 1 week and 18-month-olds could remember for 13 weeks.

However, one limitation of infant memory is that infants are much more likely to remember something when they are in the same circumstances in which they first encountered it (Hayne, 2004). You may have had the experience of seeing your professor or a classmate in the supermarket or the gym and not recognizing that person in such a different context. Infants appear to have this difficulty to a much greater degree than older children and adults. However, just as your memory may return when the person reminds you how you know them, infants can recover memory with just a little reminder. In this case, when the experimenter shook the mobile briefly 3-month-old infants remembered what to do after a month, four times as long as they could remember without the reminder (Bearce & Rovee-Collier, 2006).

Memory gradually increases between ages 1 and 2. Bauer and Leventon (2013) taught 13-, 16-, and 20-month-olds to imitate specific actions. The 16- and 20-month-olds could remember these actions for 1 month, but not for 3 months unless they were given reminders. The 13-month-olds could not remember them for even 1 month unless they were given reminders. Gradually toddlers increase their ability to retain and retrieve information.

Before learning about what is called infantile amnesia, try **Active Learning: Infantile Amnesia** so you can use your own experience to help you understand the information that follows.

Active Learning

Infantile Amnesia

Infantile amnesia Adults' inability to remember experiences that happened to them before they were about 3 years of age.

T/F #3
Few people have clear memories of what happened in their lives before the age of 3.
True

Find a quiet place to try this activity. Close your eyes for a minute and try to think of the earliest memory you can call to mind. Give yourself some time to relax and let your mind wander. When people try to recall early memories, they sometimes recall an event like a trip to the hospital to treat an injury (Peterson, 2002), but you also may recall an event that was fun and exciting, like a birthday party, your first trip to a beach, or a pony ride. Whatever memory you find, go back and try to bring up another early memory. After you have identified two or three early experiences, figure out how old you were at the time each event occurred. What is your earliest childhood memory? ■

Most people cannot recall events before age 3 because of what we call infantile amnesia. The existence of infantile amnesia does not mean infants cannot remember things that happened to them early in life, because we have already seen that they can. Rather it seems that later in life it becomes difficult to recall what happened in that earlier time.

Various explanations have been proposed for the occurrence of infantile amnesia; one involves physical changes occurring in the brain. As we saw in Chapter 5, the brain is far from complete when an infant is born. Two areas that are necessary for memory processes are the hippocampus and the prefrontal cortex. Important parts of these two areas only become functional between 20 and 24 months of age (Bauer, 2007). We will see that memory ability improves as these areas of the brain continue to develop throughout childhood and adolescence. A related idea is that the production of new neurons in the hippocampus during infancy causes reorganization of this area of the brain that interferes with the formation of stable memories (Akers et al., 2014; Josselyn & Frankland, 2012).

Other explanations have relied on psychological or cognitive explanations. Courage and Howe (2004) have argued that before infants have a clear sense of self (which we discuss in Chapter 7), their memories are not organized into a coherent story of their own lives, in other words into an autobiographical memory. It is much harder to remember random events than those that tie together in a meaningful way. Rovee-Collier (1999) has argued that memory requires the ability to use the same memory processes that were used when the first experience happened. Infants remember nonverbally (because they have not yet developed language), so when older children and adults try to use their usual verbal memory methods, they are not able to recall the earlier events that were processed without words.

One interesting study illustrated how verbal and nonverbal processes affect our memory. Toddlers were shown a demonstration of how a Magic Shrinking Machine could turn large toys into smaller ones (Simcock & Hayne, 2002). The toddlers were then allowed to turn the crank themselves to make this happen. Most of the toddlers who were originally tested this way did not have enough language to describe what had happened. When they were brought back either 6 months or 1 year later, they had developed adequate vocabulary to describe the event, but they could not do so, even when shown the device and toys again. However, when they were allowed to use the Magic Shrinking Machine, they remembered just what to do and how it worked. Their nonverbal memory remained, but since the events had never been coded into verbal memory, they were unable to remember them with words to tell others. It appears that we can remember things from infancy nonverbally through our emotions and actions, but it is very difficult to translate those memories into language. It has been argued that only when we can talk about events do we remember them in conscious thought (Fogel, 2002). In fact, when mothers talk with young children about their past experiences, their children are more likely to retain memories from early life when they enter adolescence (Jack, MacDonald, Reese, & Hayne, 2009).

Categorization

To understand what we see in the world, we learn to group things together into categories. We would experience the world quite differently if every dog we saw were unrelated in our minds to any other dog. Instead, we categorize all these animals into a category called *dog* that we define through general characteristics such as four paws, a tail, barking, and so on. There is now surprising evidence that even 4-month-old infants can put things into certain simple categories. In one study, 4-month-olds were shown a series of pictures of two cats. Researchers were able to track exactly where the infants were looking. Many of the infants looked back and forth between the two cats, probably comparing them to each other. After seeing this series, they were then shown pairs in which a dog and a cat appeared. As we've learned, infants' attention is drawn to novelty. If the infants have put all the cats into one category, then dogs would be in a different category and therefore novel. The researchers found, in fact, that infants looked more at the dogs than the cats, indicating that they had developed two different categories, one for cats and one for dogs. This was particularly true if there was a pet cat in the infant's home and if the infant had looked back and forth between the pairs of cats in the first series shown. In other words, both real-life experience and focusing attention on similarities and differences in a laboratory setting contributed to the development of categories even

Categorization in infancy. Four-month-old infants saw a series of pictures showing two cats, like the picture on the left. They were then shown a picture of a dog and a cat like the one on the right. Their preference for looking at the dog indicates they knew the difference between the category of cat and dog. ■

at this very early age (Kovack-Lesh, Oakes, & McMurray, 2012). By the second year of life, toddlers appear to understand much more complex categories, such as animate versus inanimate (Rostad, Yott, & Poulin-Dubois, 2012).

Development of the Number Concept

JOURNAL ARTICLE 6.1
Number Concept

Do infants have to develop language to understand the concept of numbers? There is increasing evidence that they do not. In fact, a very basic understanding of number is one of the capabilities the theory of core knowledge posits as an innate capability. In laboratory settings, an infant is shown one object, which is then hidden behind a screen. The infant next sees a researcher put one more object behind the screen. However, when the screen is removed, lo and behold there are three objects, like a magic trick. In fact, babies too see this as magical and nonsensical because they look longer at this outcome than if there are just two objects present when the screen is removed. It appears they are puzzled by the outcome. Therefore, they have a basic understanding that $1 + 1 = 2$ and $1 + 1$ does not equal 3. This same result was found for $5 + 5$ and $10 - 5$. Infants looked longer when the screen was removed and saw that $5 + 5$ resulted in 5 objects and $10 - 5$ resulted in 10 objects (McCrink & Wynn, 2004).

Executive Function

Executive function The aspect of brain organization that coordinates attention and memory and controls behavioral responses for the purpose of attaining a certain goal.

Inhibition The ability to stop more automatic behaviors in order to stay on task and ignore distractions.

If you put a cookie near a 1-year-old, point at it, and tell her "No, no, don't eat that cookie," how long will it take for her to grab the cookie and devour it? In all likelihood there will be little hesitation; she will simply take the cookie and eat it. She does not yet have the ability to control her impulses, which is part of the skill called executive function. Executive function is that aspect of brain organization that coordinates attention and memory and controls behavioral responses for the purpose of attaining a certain goal (Blair, Zelazo, & Greenberg, 2005). It includes inhibition, the ability to stop our automatic responses in order to stay on task and do what is needed to carry out a task correctly (A. Diamond, 2006). These abilities begin to develop during the first 2 years of life and are essential for learning.

What factors promote the development of inhibition? If you have visited the toddler room at a childcare center you have likely heard caregivers respond to children who impulsively grab an object from another child or hit the child by telling them "Use your words!" The growing ability to use language is one central factor that promotes children's ability to control themselves. In addition, parents help when they support their toddler's attempts to master age-appropriate tasks (Matte-Gagné & Bernier, 2011). Brain development is also a factor. The prefrontal cortex is the seat of self-control and is far from fully developed during infancy. Development will continue through adolescence.

Photograph by Stephen Ausmus, U.S. Department of Agriculture, Agricultural Research Service.

Testing infant intelligence. This examiner is administering the Bayley Scales of Infant Development to this young child. These scales assess the physical, social, and emotional development of the infant, without needing to rely on language. ∎

Check Your Understanding

1. What are selective attention and sustained attention?
2. What is infantile amnesia?
3. Describe a typical infant's understanding of numbers.
4. What is executive function?

Infant Intelligence

So far we have discussed some of the cognitive processes found in all infants. However, many parents are proud of how "smart" their baby is, while some worry about their baby's abilities. In other words, there are individual differences in how effectively infants develop and use these various cognitive processes. Long before children enter school, their intellectual abilities are taking shape. Being able to assess these abilities can serve two purposes: (1) to determine whether infant abilities are predictive of later intelligence, and (2) to offer services to infants whose development is not optimal *before* they reach school.

Assessing intelligence in infants is difficult because we rely heavily on language for tests of older children, but infants cannot understand test instructions or provide verbal responses. For this reason, most tests of infants' development assess physical, motor, sensory, and/or early language development. Although such tests can identify intellectual impairment and developmental delays based on a neurological impairment, infants' scores on these tests have not been found to predict intelligence as measured at older ages (Roze et al., 2010; Thompson, Fagan, & Fulker, 1991).

While tests such as these continue to be used in both clinical and research applications, they are used more as an assessment of general developmental issues rather than intelligence. A newer approach to assessing intelligence in young children draws on information processing approaches. They include measures of cognitive ability we have already described: infant attention, attraction to novelty, and habituation to a repeated stimulus. Responses to novelty and habituation appear to be particularly important predictive factors of later intelligence (Bornstein et al., 2006; Fagan, Holland, & Wheeler, 2007; Kavšek, 2004). These information-processing abilities have been related to later global intelligence and to specific cognitive abilities. For instance, attention, processing speed, and memory in infancy have been found to predict general intelligence at age 11 (Rose, Feldman, Jankowski, & Van Rossem, 2012). A preference for novelty has been associated with both general intelligence and several specific cognitive abilities (Fagan, Holland, & Wheeler, 2007; Rose, Feldman, & Wallace, 1992). Infants' ability to regulate themselves (for example, to settle back to sleep after a brief disruption) is also an important predictor of intelligence measured at age 6 (Canals, Hernández-Martínez, Esparó, & Fernández-Ballart, 2011).

6.5

What aspects of infants' cognitive development are the best predictors of later intelligence?

AUDIO LINK 6.2
What Do Babies Think?

T/F #4

Being attracted to novelty as an infant is associated with intelligence in later childhood. *True*

This newer research, which measures information-processing abilities and executive control functions, is providing evidence that the efficiency and effectiveness of certain cognitive processes in infancy do predict intelligence in children and adults. Cognitive processes such as attraction to novelty help infants learn from their environment. An infant who is attracted to novel elements in the environment is more likely to learn from his experience, and this ability continues to support new learning as the infant moves into childhood and adolescence. Although the basics of attention, self-regulation, and number concept set the stage for future learning, they are not a guarantee that learning will occur. Cognitive growth needs support from teachers, parents, and others throughout a child's development.

Check Your Understanding

1. Why are researchers interested in assessing infant intelligence?
2. What aspects of infant development predict later intelligence?

Language in Infancy

6.6

How do infants develop language?

From their very first cries, human beings communicate with the world around them. Infants communicate through sounds (crying and cooing) and through body language (pointing and making other gestures). However, sometime between 8 and 18 months of age, a major developmental milestone occurs when infants begin to use words to speak.

We can define language as a system of symbols we use to communicate; its development is one of the most significant cognitive achievements. Words are symbolic representations; that is, when a child says "table," we understand that the word represents the object. Although we use language to communicate with others, we may also talk to ourselves and use words in our thinking. The words we use can influence the way we think about and understand our experiences.

Language A system of symbols we use to communicate with others or to think.

After defining some basic aspects of language, we describe some of the theories proposed to explain the amazing process by which we understand and produce language. We examine the brain's role in processing and producing language. Once we have established this background, we show the ways in which language development proceeds during infancy.

Aspects of Language

Researchers have studied four basic aspects of language: phonology, syntax, semantics, and pragmatics. Phonology is the study of the sounds of a language. (To remember this term, think of the sounds that come from your tele*phone*, or the word cac*ophon*y, meaning a lot of loud, annoying sounds.) Syntax is the grammar of a language—that is, how we put words in order and how we change words in a rule-based fashion to create meanings. For example, *play* becomes *played* when we talk about the past. Semantics refers to the meanings of words. Pragmatics is the way we use language in a social context. For example, you probably speak in different ways to your professor, to your friends, and certainly to a 2-year-old. In each case, you are using language in a different way so you can communicate effectively with your listener. When children develop the ability to communicate with language, they are developing all four of these areas (Gleason, 2005). They must understand and form the sounds of the language they are learning. They must learn what words mean and how to put them together so they make sense, and they must learn when and how to use language to accommodate their listeners and to accomplish their goals. We consider all these aspects as we describe language development.

Phonology The study of the sounds of a language.

Syntax The grammar of a language.

Semantics The study of the meanings of words.

Pragmatics The rules guiding the way we use language in social situations.

Morpheme The smallest unit in a language that has meaning.

Two basic units are central to the study of language and its development: morphemes and phonemes. A morpheme is the smallest unit that has meaning in a language. For example, the word *cats* has two morphemes: *cat* and *s*. *Cat* refers to the animal, and *s* means more than one. A phoneme is the smallest distinct sound in a particular language. For example, *go* has two phonemes: *g* and *o*, and *check* has three: *ch*, *e*, and *ck* (National Reading Panel, 2000). Different languages have distinct types of phonemes. For instance, in Japanese, the length of a vowel can indicate different words. The word *toko* means "bed," while *toko* with a long final *o* means "travel" (Sato, Sogabe, & Mazuka, 2010). In English, no matter how long we draw out the *a* in *cat*, it still means "cat."

Theories of Language Development

There are many different ideas about how children learn to talk and understand language, and many controversies persist to this day. We are still learning about how this process can occur so quickly in the first years of life.

Behaviorism and Social Cognitive Learning Theory

If you took a survey of people on the street and asked them how children learn language, many would probably answer, "By imitation." Of course imitation must play an important role. After all, children learn the language they hear, not some other language. The idea that language is learned through imitation is connected with Bandura's theory of social cognitive learning (Chapter 2). Imitation is the central learning principle of this theory.

According to B. F. Skinner (1957/1991), language is also shaped through operant conditioning and the use of reinforcement. When we respond to a baby's babbling with a smile or some vocalization of our own, babies babble even more. If we respond to a request for a cookie with the desired cookie, it becomes more likely the child will use that word again the next time he wants a cookie. If we remember that reinforcement is anything that makes a behavior continue, then it is clear we reinforce the development of a child's language in many ways. Consistent with these ideas, research has shown that the more mothers respond to their babies' vocalizations, the sooner the babies develop language (Tamis-LeMonda, Bornstein, & Baumwell, 2001).

Nativism

In contrast to operant conditioning and social cognitive theory, both of which focus on our interactions with the environment, Noam Chomsky (1968) proposed that the human brain is innately wired to learn language, a theory known as nativism that is often linked with the theory of core knowledge described earlier. Chomsky believes children could not learn something as complex as human language as quickly as they do unless there is already a grammatical structure for language hardwired in their brains before they ever hear human language. He calls this structure universal grammar and suggests that hearing spoken language activates it, achieving more than just imitation.

Chomsky believes the language we usually hear is not enough on its own to explain the construction of all the rules of language children quickly learn. For instance, nativists point to the fact that children will say things they have never heard, such as "The cats eated the mouses" rather than "The cats ate the mice." We *hope* children have never heard adults say "eated" or "mouses," and therefore they could not be just imitating language they have heard. However, you can easily see that, although the first sentence is grammatically incorrect, in some respects it *could be* correct. In English we do add *-ed* for the past tense and *-s* for plurals. However, we have exceptions to those rules, called irregular verbs and nouns. When children make this type of grammatical error they are showing that they have learned a pattern, but they are applying it to words that don't follow that pattern. This process of acting as if irregular words follow the regular rules is called overregularization. Children are creating these words from their own understanding of grammar.

Chomsky believes the basic principles of grammar are innate. Clearly, we do not all speak the same language and the rules for grammar are not the same in all languages, so how can there be a universal grammar? Chomsky believes basic language principles are hardwired in the brain, similar to the basic principles that underlie the basic operation

VIDEO LINK 6.4
Noam Chomsky

Nativism A theory of language development that human brains are innately wired to learn language and that hearing spoken language triggers the activation of a universal grammar.

Universal grammar A hypothesized set of grammatical rules and constraints proposed by Noam Chomsky, thought to underlie all languages and to be hardwired in the human brain.

Overregularization A type of grammatical error in which children apply a language rule to words that don't follow it (for example, adding an s to make the plural of an irregular noun such as *foot*).

Phoneme The smallest distinct sound in a particular language.

of your computer. Just as your computer can run many different types of software, the language structures in your brain can process the specific characteristics of whichever language or languages you are hearing around you.

Interactionism

A third approach incorporates aspects of both behaviorism and nativism. According to interactionism, both children's biological readiness to learn language and their experiences with language in their environment come together to bring about language development. Just as we learned in Chapter 3 that nature is expressed through nurture, interactionist theorists argue that both readiness and experience are equally necessary for the child to develop language and must work together.

In addition, interactionism suggests language is created socially, in the interaction between infant and adult. For example, adults naturally simplify their speech to young children, not because they think "I need to teach this child how to speak" but because the child then understands and responds to what the adult is saying. The adult is sensitive to the effectiveness of his communication so that when the child does not understand, he simplifies his language until the child does understand (Bohannon & Bonvillian, 2005). Research on mother-infant speech has found that mothers in a variety of cultures make many of the same modifications in their speech to infants, perhaps because these changes produce a good fit between the mother's speech and the infant's perceptual and cognitive capabilities (Fernald & Morikawa, 1993). In addition, adults often repeat what children say but recast it into more advanced grammar. For example, a child might say, "More cookie," and the adult might respond, "Oh, do you want more cookies?" In the process, he is modeling a slightly higher level of language proficiency, which the child can then imitate. The child in this example might then say, "Want more cookies."

Cognitive Processing Theory: Statistical Learning

Are social interaction and biological readiness enough to explain how children learn language? A newer view is that learning language is a process of "data crunching," in which children take in and statistically process the language they hear (Hoff & Naigles, 2002, p. 422). Proponents of this cognitive processing theory argue that infants are processing language even during the first year of life, before they can speak (Naigles et al., 2009). Therefore, their understanding of language is learned, not innate as Chomsky's theory asserts. Although the learning may be *motivated* by social interaction, cognitive theory says the actual process of learning words and their meanings may rely more on the computational ability of the human brain.

One basic question cognitive processing theory has addressed is how infants learn to differentiate words out of the stream of sounds they hear. Although we can see the spaces between words on a written page, these "spaces" are often not evident when we speak. For example, if you heard someone say, "Theelephantisdrinkingwater," how would you figure out that *elephant* is a separate word and *antis* is not? One answer is that infants' brains are constantly figuring out statistically how likely it is that certain sounds will follow each other. This likelihood is referred to as the transitional probability (Karuza et al., 2013). For example, when we hear *ele*, it is most often followed by *phant* or *vator*, so there is a high transitional probability between these syllables. However, the entire word *elephant* can be followed in a sentence by many different sounds, and any particular one has a low transitional probability. Researchers have used made-up words embedded in random syllables to see whether adults, children, and infants can differentiate the "words" from the rest of the utterance (Lew-Williams & Saffran, 2012; Saffran, Johnson, Aslin, & Newport, 1999). Take a look at the "sentence" below and see whether you can figure out what the "word" is:

Bupadapatubitutibubupadadutabapidabupada

Did you discover *bupada?* When people of all ages hear lengthy readings such as this, they are able to pick out the "words" even though they have no real meaning. When researchers applied this idea to the processing of discriminating words in a real but unfamiliar language (Italian), they found 8-month-olds were able to use conditional probabilities to differentiate between nonwords and words they had heard in a stream of conversation (Pelucchi, Hay, & Saffran, 2009). Infants were also likely to figure out the meaning of the words (Hay, Pelucchi, Estes, & Saffran, 2011; Lany & Saffran, 2010). Now, if you heard someone say *bupada* in addition to hearing the string of sounds shown above, you would be much more likely to pick *bupada* out as a word, and researchers have found that infants too are helped to discriminate words when they hear them separately as well as in sentences (Lew-Williams, Pelucchi, & Saffran, 2011).

Language and the Brain

The brain's left hemisphere contains two areas that are central to language: Broca's area and Wernicke's area. As shown in Figure 6.2, Broca's area, which is active in the production of speech, is located near the motor center of the brain that produces movement of the tongue and lips (Gleason, 2005). A person with damage to this area will have difficulty speaking and as a consequence will use the fewest words needed to get his message across. For example, when a man with damage in Broca's area was asked about his upcoming weekend plans, he answered, "Boston. College. Football. Saturday" (Gleason, 2005, p. 17).

You can also see in Figure 6.2 that Wernicke's area, which helps us understand and create the meaning in speech, is located near the auditory center of the brain. Someone with damage to this area of the brain has no trouble producing words, but has difficulty

Broca's area The part of the brain active in the physical production of speech.

Wernicke's area The part of the brain that helps us understand the meaning in speech.

FIGURE 6.2   **Language centers of the brain**

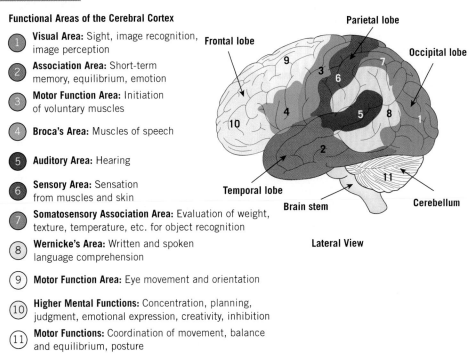

Functional Areas of the Cerebral Cortex

1. **Visual Area:** Sight, image recognition, image perception
2. **Association Area:** Short-term memory, equilibrium, emotion
3. **Motor Function Area:** Initiation of voluntary muscles
4. **Broca's Area:** Muscles of speech
5. **Auditory Area:** Hearing
6. **Sensory Area:** Sensation from muscles and skin
7. **Somatosensory Association Area:** Evaluation of weight, texture, temperature, etc. for object recognition
8. **Wernicke's Area:** Written and spoken language comprehension
9. **Motor Function Area:** Eye movement and orientation
10. **Higher Mental Functions:** Concentration, planning, judgment, emotional expression, creativity, inhibition
11. **Motor Functions:** Coordination of movement, balance and equilibrium, posture

Broca's area (shown here in green), which controls speech production, is next to the motor cortex that controls movement. Wernicke's area (shown in light green), which controls language comprehension, is next to the auditory area that controls hearing.

making sense. For example, one patient with damage to Wernicke's area responded as follows to the question "What brings you to the hospital?"

> Boy I'm sweating, I'm awful nervous, you know, once in a while I get caught up, I can't mention the tarripoi, a month ago, quite a little, I've done a lot well, I impose a lot, while, on the other hand, you know what I mean, I have to run around, look it over, trebbin and all that sort of stuff. (Gardner, 1976, p. 68)

This patient speaks without any problem but is not making any sense and makes up words, such as *trebbin*.

The brain is not a simple organ, and we continue to learn about its complexity. For instance, although language is primarily handled by the left hemisphere of the brain, some aspects of language, such as recognition of the emotion in someone's words, are controlled by the right hemisphere (Gleason, 2005).

The capabilities of these two regions do not develop at the same time. Infants *understand* words before they can *say* them. Another way we describe this is to say comprehension of language precedes production of language. When you tell a 1-year-old to put a toy in a box, she will most likely *understand* you and might follow your directions, yet she is not likely to be able to *say* anything close to "put the toy in the box." This difference between receptive and expressive language continues throughout life (Celce-Murcia & Olshtain, 2001). Even college students can understand a sophisticated or technical lecture in class, while their own speech and writing are likely to be less complex.

Stages of Language Development

In this section we describe the development of language. We purposely de-emphasize the ages at which these developments occur because children differ enormously in the rate at which they develop language. One major question that remains controversial is whether there is a specific age beyond which children are not capable of developing language. To see how our thinking has changed on this issue, see **Journey of Research: Is There a Critical Period for Language Learning?**

Receptive language The ability to understand words or sentences.

Expressive language The written or spoken language we use to convey our thoughts, emotions, or needs.

WEB LINK 6.1
Early Speech

....

JOURNEY OF RESEARCH *Is There a Critical Period for Language Learning?*

If there is a limited window of opportunity for children to learn language, then infants and children who are deprived of environmental stimulation and early facilitation of language learning may have basic difficulty with language that lasts their whole lives. Evidence for the existence of such a critical period comes from studies of children who were severely deprived during the early years of life. One famous case is that of a girl called Genie.

Throughout her childhood, Genie spent most of her time strapped to a chair in a back bedroom of her family home, where she had little social contact or interaction with others. In 1970, the girl's situation came to the attention of welfare authorities in Los Angeles, and at age 13 Genie was removed from her home. At that point her overall development was severely delayed, and she had

little functional language. Genie provided a unique opportunity for scientists to examine the idea that there is a critical period for language development. At 13, she was already past the age when children normally develop language. Developmentalists used a variety of methods to promote her language development and carefully documented her progress (Rymer, 1993). Although Genie learned words, researchers concluded that she could never develop the use of grammar (Curtiss, 1977).

This conclusion has been reported over and over again as evidence for a critical period for language learning. However, Peter Jones (1995) reexamined data from Curtiss's earlier study of Genie and came to a different conclusion. Look at several things Genie was able to say in 1974 and 1975:

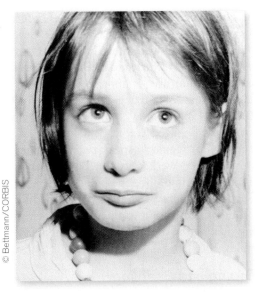

A critical period for language learning? Genie was raised in almost complete isolation. When she was rescued from her abusive home, she had no functional language. She later became the subject of an intensive case study that looked at whether she could develop language long after the time when this typically occurs. ■

"I want think about Mama riding bus."

"Teacher said Genie have temper tantrum outside."

"I do not have a toy green basket."

While these sentences may not be perfect, they show quite complex levels of grammatical construction. Jones (1995) concluded that Genie was able to develop language, and in particular grammar, even at her advanced age.

On the other hand, a woman called Chelsea was incorrectly diagnosed as intellectually disabled until she was 31 years old, when it was discovered that she was deaf. She lived with her family and received no education and no language input. When she was given hearing aids she was able to learn words, but she was never able to develop normal grammar. Here are some sentences she produced:

"banana the eat"

"Peter sandwich bread turkey"
(Herschensohn, 2007, p. 91)

The importance of the window of opportunity for language learning is illustrated by research on orphans who lived the first months of their lives in poorly equipped and poorly staffed orphanages in Romania where they suffered extreme deprivation. Those who were placed with foster families before the age of 2 had few problems with language development, while those adopted at an older age had marked language delays (Windsor et al., 2011) but not disorders likely to last throughout their lives. In a similar way, children who are born deaf but who receive cochlear implants have better language outcomes if the implantation occurs when they are younger (Nicholas & Geers, 2007). Early implantation appears to better preserve or restore the auditory system that supports language development in infants (National Institute on Deafness and Other Communication Disorders, 2013).

In the area of brain research, evidence has also shifted from the idea that language can be learned only early in life to the idea that it can be learned later as well, but it is more difficult at older ages. Researchers originally speculated that brain development was responsible for a critical period for language learning. Specifically, the hypothesis was that certain parts of the brain worked most efficiently until a certain age, and then the restructuring of the neural connections forced the brain to use entirely different areas for learning language. However, recent research using brain imaging techniques has shown that individuals continue to learn language, including a second language, with the same parts of the brain as in first language learning (Stowe & Sabourin, 2005).

Clearly, language is learned most efficiently in early life, but we have moved away from the idea of a critical period beyond which language cannot develop. Instead we think about a sensitive period when it is easiest to develop language. ■

VIDEO LINK 6.5
Critical Periods

Prenatal Foundations for Language Learning

Language learning begins before birth. During the last trimester of prenatal development, changes in fetal heart rate and motor activity when the mother is speaking show that the fetus can hear her voice, and this affects the infant's preferences for language after birth in a number of ways (Karmiloff & Karmiloff-Smith, 2001). In one study, pregnant women read passages from a specific book, such as Dr. Seuss's *The Cat in the Hat*, twice a day when they thought their fetus was awake (DeCasper & Spence, 1986). After the babies were born, those who had heard the story were more likely to try to elicit the sound of their mother reading *The Cat in the Hat* (rather than a new poem they had never heard before) by sucking a pacifier in a certain way. It appears that infants become familiar with and prefer "the rhythms and sounds of language" they have heard prenatally (Karmiloff & Karmiloff-Smith, 2001, p. 43) and show a preference for the particular language their mother speaks, whether it is English, Arabic, or Chinese.

In addition, newborns who had heard their mothers regularly speak two languages showed a preference for both (Byers-Heinlein, Burns, & Werker, 2010). This prenatal awareness of language sets the stage for language learning once the baby is born. In one study, it was even shown that when they cry, babies only 3 to 5 days old sound like the language they have been hearing. French babies cried from low pitch to high, while German babies cried from high pitch to low, mimicking the sounds of the language they hear (Mampe, Friederici, Christophe, & Wermke, 2009).

Infants' Preverbal Communication: Cooing and Babbling

Babies cry as soon as they are born. At first this is a reflexive behavior, not an intentional communication. The process of communication begins when babies begin to learn that crying can act as a signal that brings relief from whatever is bothering them because it motivates adults to do what it takes to make it stop.

Although babies cry for many reasons, there does not appear to be clear evidence that they have different cries for hunger, pain, or loneliness. Research shows only that parents differentiate the intensity and severity of crying, not the specific reason for the cry (Gustafson, Wood, & Green, 2000). Knowing this should relieve parents who have been told they should recognize *why* their baby is crying but realize they cannot.

Between 2 and 4 months after birth, babies begin to make more pleasant sounds (Menn & Stoel-Gammon, 2005). The first ones are soft vowel sounds, a bit like doves cooing. At this stage babies also begin to laugh, which is a great reward for parents, and to join in a prelanguage "conversation" (Tamis-LeMonda, Cristofaro, Rodriguez, & Bornstein, 2006). The baby coos, the parent talks back, the baby looks and laughs, the parent smiles and talks. In this way, babies begin to learn how to have a conversation even before they can speak.

Babies typically begin to make one-syllable sounds, such as ba and da, when they are 4 to 6 months old, and they begin to combine those sounds repetitively (baba, gaga) when they are 6 to 8 months old (Sachs, 2005). Among the most common consonant sounds are /b/, /d/, and /m/. At this point, parents get very excited, thinking the baby means "daddy" when he says "dada" or "mommy" when he says "mama." Although it does not appear that these first vocalizations are meaningful, babies may start to learn they have meaning because of the way their parents respond to them (Menn & Stoel-Gammon, 2005). In many languages around the world, even those with no common origins, the words for father—dada (English), abba (Hebrew), and baba (Mandarin Chinese)—and mother—mama (English), ahm (Arabic), and manah (Greek)—start with the earliest sounds babies make.

Saying *Bababa* changes to saying something like *daDAW ee derBEH* as babbling begins to sound more and more like the language the baby is hearing and not like other languages (maybe the second phrase sounds like *the doggie under the bed*). Although babies initially are able to make all the sounds in all languages, at this point a baby growing up with English will not produce the type of /r/ sounds used in French or Spanish because the baby is not hearing those sounds in the language environment. Now the feedback from hearing speech plays more of a role in language development than it did earlier. Deaf babies will babble early on, but at the age when hearing babies increase the variety of their sounds,

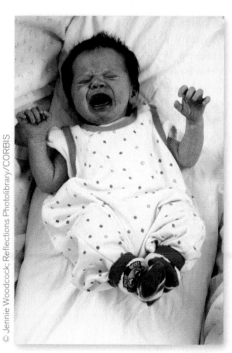

Why is this baby crying? Babies' cries do not communicate specific information, except intensity of pain or discomfort. However it does signal that the baby needs something and caregivers respond to give the baby some relief. ■

© Jennie Woodcock; Reflections Photolibrary/CORBIS

deaf babies do not because they are not receiving this language input from their environment (Menn & Stoel-Gammon, 2005). On the other hand, deaf babies who are learning sign language appear to go through the same stages of language learning as hearing babies, in this case "babbling" with hand gestures instead of sounds.

Preverbal Perception of Language

We've already seen that infants respond to language even before they are born. It is also true that they are learning a great deal about language before they can say even one word. Babies younger than 6 months of age can distinguish the sounds made in all languages, but by 10 months, they have lost some of that ability (Best & McRoberts, 2003). For example, Hindi has two distinct phonemes that sound like "da" to English speakers. One is made the same way as in English, but the other is made with the tongue on the roof of the mouth. Babies in an English language environment can discriminate these two sounds until about 10 months of age, when they lose the ability to differentiate between sounds they are not hearing in their native language (Conboy & Kuhl, 2011). Asian infants can tell the difference between the English language sounds "ra" and "la," but Asian adults have a more difficult time because this distinction is not found in the language they speak (Sheldon & Strange, 1982).

The process by which infants narrow their perception to the specific language they are hearing appears to be linked to their later language production. Infants who are better at discriminating sounds in their native language at 7 months have better language development during the second year of life, while infants who are better at discriminating sounds in a nonnative language at 7 months have more delayed language development (Kuhl, Conboy, Padden, Nelson, & Pruitt, 2005). It appears that part of learning a language depends on identifying the specific sounds that make up that language. Infants who develop this ability later also develop language at a later age.

How Adults Foster Early Language Development

Before we continue our description of the stages of language development, let's take a focused look at the role adults play in fostering young children's language development. In many cultures, adults begin to shape infants' developing language ability by talking to them even when it is clear the babies do not understand. Adults act as if they do understand and carry on conversations, taking turns with the baby, whatever the baby's response. Karmiloff and Karmiloff-Smith (2001) provide the following illustration:

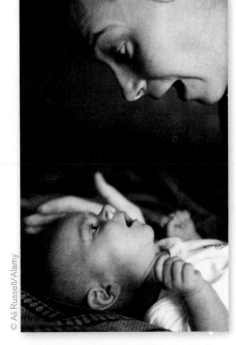

Mother: Oh, so you're HUNgry, are you?

(Baby kicks.)

Mother: YES, you ARE hungry. WELL, we'll have to give you some MILK then, won't we?

(Baby coos.)

Mother: Ah, so Mommy was RIGHT. It's MILK you want. Shall we change your diaper first?

(Baby kicks.)

Mother: RIGHT! A clean diaper. THAT's what you want. GOOD girl. (p. 48)

This type of exchange provides the baby with early experience of the back-and-forth of dialogue that will be important in later speech, but we must be careful about concluding that what adults do is the *most* important factor for children's developing speech. Research with some cultures, such as the Gusii people of Kenya, shows that parents in these cultures speak to their babies much less often than American parents,

Laying the foundation for speech. This mother is laying the foundation for her infant's later speech. What is the infant learning about language from this interaction? ■

but their infants still develop language. In fact, when LeVine and his colleagues (1994) instructed Gusii mothers to talk and play with their babies while they were videotaped, they complied but said "it was of course silly to talk to a baby" (p. 210). However, Gusii children become as proficient with their language as American children are with English despite these different early experiences with language. There are many roads to language competence, and we must be careful not to apply one standard to all people.

Think about the way you talk to babies or hear others do so. You are unlikely to approach a baby and say in a low, monotone voice, "Hello, baby, how are you today? I hope you are having a fine day." You would be much more likely to say, "Hel-LO, BAAAA-BEEEE. How are YOU today?" The special way we talk to infants and young children in a high-pitched voice with a great deal of exaggeration and a singsong rhythm was once referred to as motherese. However, since we have found that in most cultures, all adults, and children, too, change the way they speak to infants and young children, this type of speech is now known as child-directed speech (Weisleder & Fernald, 2013). Although adults in some cultures do not usually talk to their babies, child-directed speech has been found in cultures around the world (Bryant & Barrett, 2007). Some people believe child-directed speech is harmful to infants, teaching them the wrong way to speak, but the evidence is that what we naturally do in this way actually fosters language development (Rowe, 2008; Weisleder & Fernald, 2013).

In one study, if 4-month-old babies turned their head in one direction they would hear regular adult speech and if they turned in the other direction they would hear child-directed speech. Most infants turned more often in the direction that started the child-directed speech (Fernald, 1985). This finding supports the idea that the reason we speak in this silly way is that infants pay more attention to us when we do; it creates a good fit with the infant's sensory and cognitive capabilities and helps hold the infant's attention (Fernald & Morikawa, 1993). In addition, the musical quality of child-directed speech appears to promote early perception of the phonemes in a language (Lebedeva & Kuhl, 2010). An interesting variation is found among the Kaluli of Papua New Guinea. Although the Kaluli tend not to talk *to* their babies in this way, they hold up the babies to face people and use a similar type of speech to speak *for* the baby (Feld & Shieffelin, 1998). Whether we are talking *with* our baby or talking *for* our baby, either approach shows the infant that speech is a type of interaction between people.

In the first months after birth, infants are focused mostly on their own bodies and on interaction with the people in their world. At about 6 months they begin to develop more interest in the objects and events around them. At this point, caregivers begin to talk about what the infant sees as both infant and caregiver gaze at objects and events. When babies look or point at what they see, adults tend to label what it is for them (Goldfield & Snow, 2005). In fact, one researcher has referred to pointing as "the royal road," if not the only road, to language development (Butterworth, 2003, p. 9).

Pointing is just one of the gestures children use to communicate. Infants use many gestures before they can speak and continue to use them along with speech (Volterra, Caselli, Capirci, & Pizzuto, 2005). Parents have begun to take advantage of this fact by introducing forms of sign language. Nonverbal signs are representations that have meaning, just like words. Using signs can reduce frustration for both parent and child when the child can sign what he wants instead of crying. Some people fear

Child-directed speech Speech tailored to fit the sensory and cognitive capabilities of infants and children so it holds their attention; includes speaking in a higher pitch with exaggerated intonation and a singsong rhythm and using a simplified vocabulary.

T/F #7

It is perfectly fine to use baby talk with infants. *True*

© age fotostock Spain, S.L./Alamy

What is this toddler saying? Toddlers use pointing as a way of communicating before they have words. Parents often respond by describing whatever the toddler is interested in. ■

Sign language for babies. Babies can gesture long before they can use words. They can learn to use signs taken from American Sign Language to communicate what they want and need, and this does not delay their development of spoken language. ∎

© Christina Kennedy/Alamy

babies will rely on these signs and it will delay the development of spoken language while others believe it may accelerate language, but a recent study found no difference in infants' language development whether mothers signed with their babies or did not (Kirk, Howlett, Pine, & Fletcher, 2013). Although most parents gesture as they talk to their infants, the amount and type of gesturing differs from parent to parent. Rowe and Goldin-Meadow (2009) found that parents in families of higher socioeconomic status (SES) use gestures with their infants to communicate a broader range of meaning than parents from families of lower SES. In turn, children from the higher-SES families used more gestures to communicate meaning by 14 months of age, a difference that contributed to differences in the size of their vocabulary when they were 4-1/2 and about to begin kindergarten.

Gesturing may enhance language learning in several ways. First, when a child points to an object and a parent translates that gesture into a word by naming the object, the word enters the child's vocabulary sooner than it otherwise might (Rowe & Goldin-Meadow, 2009). Using gestures without naming also enhances vocabulary development. Iverson and Goldin-Meadow (2005) found that when children use a gesture, such as flapping their hands to signify a bird, the actual word *bird* tends to show up about 3 months later. The representation of the idea through gesturing may help the child learn the word meaning and eventually say and use the word.

There also are cultural differences in the use of gestures. For example, Italians tend to use many more gestures than Americans (Iverson, Capirci, Volterra, & Goldin-Meadow, 2008). However, Iverson et al. (2008) found that gesturing seemed to serve the same purpose in both populations. For both Italians and Americans, the child's use of gestures together with speech was predictive of the development of two-word utterances.

Development of Words and Growth of Vocabulary

Through their interactions with caregivers, infants begin to associate words with familiar objects and people. Remember that comprehension of language precedes the production of language. While infants begin to *understand* words at about 9 months, they do not begin to *say* words, on average, until about 13 months (Tamis-LeMonda et al., 2006). The sounds they play with while babbling may be the sounds they use for the first words they say (Menn & Stoel-Gammon, 2005). These first words may be made up by the baby and may not correspond to an adult word. For example, one baby referred to any motorized

T/F #8
Teaching babies to use sign language will delay development of spoken language. *False*

vehicle as a *gogo*, and *baba* meant water. When the family drove through a car wash, the baby created a new word combination of these two made-up words to describe his experience. He called it a *baba-gogo*.

At 1 year, babies typically have only a few words, but by 2 years of age they generally have between 200 and 500 words (Fernald, Pinto, Swingley, Weinberg, & McRoberts, 2001). Although they initially learn new words slowly, over the second year of life they begin to learn them more quickly (Ganger & Brent, 2004). For some babies, the learning of new words explodes in what has been called a vocabulary burst, but for others the learning is more gradual.

How do toddlers manage to master their native language so quickly? First, during their second year, children begin to understand that words are symbols standing for objects in the world (Preissler & Carey, 2004). This realization provides a strong incentive for them to acquire and use language. Second, children use several assumptions and principles that seem to facilitate the expansion of their vocabulary. These assumptions are called constraints because they limit or constrain the alternatives the child considers when learning a new word, which makes the process of acquiring vocabulary easier. One of these constraints is the whole-object bias. When a child sees a giraffe for the first time and someone points to the animal and says "giraffe," the child assumes the word describes the entire animal—not its strange, long neck; not its skinny legs; and not its brown spots. Children make this assumption even when the new object obviously has two parts, and even if one of the parts is more prominent than the other (Hollich, Golinkoff, & Hirsh-Pasek, 2007).

Another constraint is the mutual exclusivity constraint. Children assume there is one and only one name for an object. If they hear a novel word, they assume it describes an object they do not already know the name for, because the object wouldn't have two different names (Hansen & Markman, 2009). The taxonomic constraint leads children to assume that two objects with features in common can have a name in common, but that each object also can have its own individual name (Markman, 1990). For example, both dogs and cats have four legs and a tail and are covered with fur so they are both *animals*, but they each have some unique characteristics that distinguish between them so they also can have their own individual names.

As children apply these principles to their acquisition of new words, they can quickly learn new words, often based on a single exposure, in a process called fast mapping. The constraints allow the child to form an initial hypothesis, which they can test in future situations that provide a basis for rapid acquisition of words (Pan, 2005). The first time a child sees a bus but says "truck," someone will probably point out how a bus and a truck are different. As the child continues to see buses, the use of that particular word will be quickly refined.

Around the world children typically add nouns to their vocabulary before they add verbs. Nouns are thought to be easier to learn because they refer to objects in the child's world and the child has realized things should have names (Waxman et al., 2013). However, different languages express verbs in a variety of ways; for example, an English-speaker would likely always say "the girl *is* young," but speakers of many other languages would leave the verb out, knowing it is implied by the meaning of the rest of the sentence. Because verbs are handled in different ways, the ease with which children learn them varies depending on the language they are learning (Waxman et al., 2013). Just as infants can use fast mapping to learn new words, they can use specific types of fast mapping called syntactic bootstrapping to use syntax to learn the meaning of new words (Gleitman, 1990) and semantic bootstrapping to use conceptual categories (action words or object names) to create grammatical categories (verbs or nouns) (Johnson & de Villiers, 2009; Pinker, 1984). To pull yourself up by your bootstraps is an expression that means to solve a problem using your own resources. In this case, children use knowledge they have in one domain of language to help them learn another domain (Karmiloff & Karmiloff-Smith, 2001).

For instance, there are differences in the forms words take that help you determine whether they are nouns or verbs. If you were introduced to two new words—*klumfs* and *pribiked*—which would you think was a noun and which a verb? You know we add *-s* to

---

Vocabulary burst The rapid growth of a child's vocabulary that often occurs in the second year.

Constraints Assumptions that language learners make that limit the alternative meanings that they attribute to new words.

Whole object bias An assumption made by language learners that a word describes an entire object rather than just some portion of it.

Mutual exclusivity constraint An assumption made by language learners that there is one (and only one) name for an object.

Taxonomic constraint An assumption language learners make that two objects that have features in common can have a name in common, but that each object also can have its own individual name.

Fast mapping A process by which children apply constraints and their knowledge of grammar to learn new words very quickly, often after a single exposure.

Syntactic bootstrapping The use of syntax to learn the meaning of new words (semantics).

Semantic bootstrapping The use of conceptual categories to create grammatical categories.

nouns to form a plural in English; therefore that is a strong clue that *klumfs* is a noun. Likewise, a verb can have a past tense, so the *-ed* at the end of *pribiked* is a strong clue that this is a verb. Second, where a word appears in a sentence (its syntax) provides clues to word meaning. In English the noun usually precedes the verb, so if someone told you "the thrulm progisted the car," you could assume *thrulm* is a noun and *progisted* is a verb. If someone told you "you have a very *glickle* smile," you might guess that *glickle* is an adjective that modifies or describes your smile.

One-year-olds also use verbs they know to learn new nouns. In one study 15- and 19-month-olds were shown a picture of a small animal and a colorful abstract object. They then heard a conversation in which one person says "The *dax* is crying." When the 19-month-olds were shown the two original pictures again and were asked "Where is the *dax*?" they were likely to look at the animal rather than the abstract object. They were more likely to do so than if they heard someone say "The *dax* is right here." By 19 months of age, children understand that only living things can cry, therefore the use of the verb helped them learn that the word *dax*, a made-up word, refers to the animal and not to an abstract design (Ferguson, Graf, & Waxman, 2014). To see for yourself how constraints can help guide a young child's word learning, try **Active Learning: Using Linguistic Constraints**.

Active Learning

Using Linguistic Constraints

You can use this activity to learn some made-up words and see how a young child might experience learning them. In each situation, decide how you would answer the question and name the linguistic constraint that guided your decision.

1. You know a bat is a long, thin object, and a ball is small and round. If I ask you to hand me the glumph, which object do you pick up?

Which constraint did you use to make your decision?

Polka Dot/Polka Dot Images/Thinkstock

2. The creature with the pink hair is a lorum. When you have more than one lorum, what do you call them?

iStockphoto.com/ddraw

How did you know what more than one lorum is called?

3. These are both floogles, but the green one is a flinger and the purple one is a flagger.

iStockphoto.com/yayayoyo

What constraint helps you understand how these creatures are similar and how they are different?

4. This glumbug is dingling.

How do you know which of these new words is a noun and which is a verb?

iStockphoto.com/DimaChe

5. If I tell you this is a boblabo, am I naming the creature's beak, its wings, or something else?

What constraint allows you to determine what the word boblabo refers to?

iStockphoto.com/totallyjamie

Two-Word Phrases

After children have acquired a number of words in their vocabulary, they enter a stage of language development in which there is enormous growth in understanding of word meanings and in use of more sophisticated grammatical construction. At around a year and a half, children begin to combine words in phrases such as *Mommy up* or *All gone kitty*. This is the beginning of their use of grammar, and it demonstrates that children create their own grammar rather than simply making mistakes in using adult grammar (Karmiloff & Karmiloff-Smith, 2001). At this stage, children around the world use language in the same way, by including only the most basic information in what they say. For example, they may say, "Eat apple," but they cannot say, "I'm eating an apple" or "You ate the apple." For some children, one word, such as *allgone* or *more*, becomes a "pivot" word to which other words are attached, as in *allgone apple* or *allgone mommy*. As infants reach their second birthdays, they have established a strong foundation for further language learning. The story of how children learn language continues when we explore early childhood cognitive development in Chapter 9.

Check Your Understanding

1. What do behaviorism, nativism, interactionism, and cognitive processing theory tell us about infants' acquisition of language?
2. What evidence is there for a sensitive period for language learning?
3. How do adults contribute to an infant's acquisition of language?
4. What are some strategies toddlers use to acquire vocabulary so quickly?

6.7

How can we ensure optimal cognitive and language development in infants?

Threats to and Supports for Cognitive and Language Development

So far in this chapter, we have looked at typical development of cognition and language in infants and toddlers. The good news is that in most cases parents and caregivers are well equipped to provide infants with the stimulation they need to support their cognitive development. However, there are a number of genetic and environmental reasons that infants may not develop in a typical way. In this section we start by describing two different types of threats to optimal cognitive and language development: intellectual disability and poverty. We also examine some ways we can reduce their negative effects on development. We conclude with a discussion of early intervention programs designed for families who need extra help to provide the best possible context for their infants to grow and develop.

Developmental Risks

The level of intellectual development any child attains depends on that child's genetic potential, together with environmental influences of many kinds. We also should remember that a child's cognitive development does not happen in isolation; it is related to the other aspects of development, including emotional, social, and physical development. For example, good health is a basic requirement for the brain development that underlies cognitive growth, and a warm, nurturing environment provides the kind of security that allows babies to explore freely and learn from their experiences.

Intellectual Disability

Parents understandably take great joy from seeing their infants reach various cognitive and language developmental milestones, but they worry if their child does not reach these milestones when anticipated. A considerable range of ages is appropriate for each of these achievements, so parents shouldn't be overly concerned when there are minor delays, but if an infant's cognitive abilities are not developing as well as expected, the infant should be evaluated by the appropriate professional.

A number of conditions can contribute to a delay. In most cases, early intervention can set the infant back on the optimal developmental path. For instance, a hearing impairment could significantly delay language development, but many types of hearing impairment can be easily treated. However, about 1% to 3% of infants have an intellectual disability (NIH, 2013), a reduced mental capacity that will affect the child throughout life. An intellectual disability can be caused by a genetic condition such as Down syndrome or fragile-X syndrome, infections, extreme malnutrition, prenatal exposure to toxins such as drugs and alcohol, head injuries, or child neglect and abuse (Guralnick, 2005; NIH, 2013). Although there are many causes for intellectual disability, no specific cause can be identified for 75% of people with this diagnosis (NIH, 2013).

At one time we used a score of less than 70 on a standardized test of intelligence as the sole indicator of an intellectual disability. Today we recognize that intellectual disability includes difficulties in three areas of functioning—conceptual, social, and practical—and we are more interested in gauging how the disability affects the individual's everyday life than in relying on a single number for a diagnosis. Therefore, the child's ability to think clearly, to socialize effectively, and to manage everyday activities and responsibilities are all examined before a diagnosis of intellectual disability is made.

Sometimes diagnosis is fairly easy because the child is born with physical signs of the disability, such as those that accompany Down syndrome. In this case, the diagnosis can be confirmed through chromosomal analysis. The Food and Drug Administration has approved a new test that looks at an entire genome at one time and can detect both large and small chromosomal abnormalities responsible for some intellectual disabilities (FDA, 2014). However, diagnosis begins for all babies with an assessment of their developmental level in comparison to that of other infants their age. Even if a specific diagnosis such as Down syndrome is made genetically, there is still a great range in the cognitive abilities each child can achieve.

Poverty

A child's experiences in the environment are an important influence on cognitive development, and this effect begins early in development. Research has shown that children whose families have few material resources show lower levels of cognitive development as early as 18 to 24 months of age (Ryan, Fauth, & Brooks-Gunn, 2006). Even at 6 months of age, babies growing up in poverty were less attentive to objects in the environment than those in higher-income families (Clearfield & Jedd, 2013).

Factors that have been found to mediate between SES and cognitive development are disorganization and family enrichment, a combination of parental stimulation and

T/F #9
Intellectual disability is diagnosed when an individual has an IQ below 70. *False*

Intellectual disability A type of intellectual impairment that includes a low score on a standardized test of intelligence (usually 70 to 75 or lower), deficits in cognitive functioning, and impaired adaptive functioning.

WEB LINK 6.2
Poverty and Cognitive Development

responsiveness. As you can imagine, trying to raise a baby without adequate financial resources can be very stressful for parents. As they struggle to make ends meet, their lives can become chaotic. In one study of infants in poor families, the degree of disorganization in the household was related to the infant's development of receptive and productive language (Vernon-Feagans, Garrett-Peters, Willoughby, & Mills-Koonce, 2012).

The amount of stimulation provided by parents and their responsiveness to the infant, a characteristic called *home enrichment*, is important. In a large-scale longitudinal study, children were followed from 6 months of age until they were in third grade (National Institute of Child Health and Human Development Early Child Care Research Network, 2005). Families often move in and out of poverty so comparisons were made between those families that were never poor, those that were chronically poor, those that were poor only during the child's first 3 years, and those that were poor only between preschool and third grade. As you might expect, home enrichment was highest in the group of families that had never been poor and lowest in those who had always been poor. Further, enrichment declined over time for both the chronically poor families and the families who became poor. Researchers also found the quality of parenting was lower in poor families, but this was more the case for families experiencing chronic poverty than for those who experienced shorter periods of poverty. Lower-quality parenting and less enrichment were both related to poorer language and cognitive development in the children.

Promoting Cognitive and Language Development in Infants

Based on what we know about conditions that threaten optimal cognitive development, it should be clear what conditions support it. The Home Observation for Measuring the Environment (HOME) Inventory is a scale for assessing the amount and quality of stimulation and support provided to children in their family environment (Caldwell & Bradley, 2003). In a supportive environment:

1. Parents are responsive to infant needs and communications, both verbal and nonverbal.

2. Parents show acceptance of and warmth toward their infant, with appropriate discipline that is not harsh.

3. The infant's home is organized rather than chaotic and there is a flexible but regular pattern to the infant's day.

4. Age-appropriate learning materials, such as toys and books, are available.

5. Parents actively promote learning in a natural and relaxed way.

6. A stimulating variety of activities is provided.

From this description, it is clear that infants can develop their cognitive skills when caregivers talk to them and respond to their efforts to communicate, read to them, play with them by creating simple games such as peek-a-boo and singing songs with actions, and watch them carefully to see what interests them while providing activities that encourage the development of new skills. In this type of environment, infants will feel secure enough to explore the world and be motivated to understand what they experience.

Media Use in Infancy

Research using the HOME Inventory suggests some simple ways to promote cognitive development, including talking, singing, and playing with infants, but there is no magic way to turn them into geniuses, despite the claims of products with names like *Little*

Einstein. Likewise, playing Mozart for babies may encourage their interest in music, but there is no evidence for the claim that it will actually increase their IQ (Pietschnig, Voracek, & Formann, 2010). Although most media designed for infants purports to be educational, there is no evidence that TV or DVDs of any kind are helpful for their cognitive development (Kirkorian, Wartella, & Anderson, 2008). By now you should understand why: Watching videos is a passive activity, but the research evidence shows over and over again that infants and toddlers learn much more effectively from real-life interaction (Anderson & Pempek, 2005; DeLoache et al., 2010; Krcmar, Grela, & Lin, 2007). For this reason, the American Academy of Pediatrics Committee on Public Education (2001, reaffirmed in 2011) recommends that pediatricians "discourage television-viewing for children younger than 2 years and encourage more interactive activities that will promote proper brain development . . .." (p. 424).

While 34% of children under 2 do not watch any screen-based programming, 66% do watch TV sometimes and 43% watch TV, including recorded programming, every day for an average of almost an hour a day (Rideout, 2013; Rideout & Hamel, 2006). It may surprise you that babies age 8 to 16 months who watched videotapes designed specifically to improve cognitive development, such as the Baby Einstein videos, developed a *smaller* vocabulary than those who did not (Zimmerman, Christakis, & Meltzoff, 2007). One reason is that both the amount and the quality of interactions between parents and child decrease when the videos are playing (Pempek, Demers, Hanson, Kirkorian, & Anderson, 2011; Tanimura, Okuma, & Kyoshima, 2007). In a study by Robb, Richert, and Wartella (2009), 1-year-olds who watched an educational video called Baby Wordsworth, designed to promote language development, did not have better language development. What did predict vocabulary use and understanding was how much adults read to the infants. In another study by this research group, parent engagement with the baby and the video determined how much the baby learned from watching the video. The more engaged the parent was, the more the baby learned (Fender, Richert, Robb, & Wartella, 2010).

In addition to programming specifically directed at infants and toddlers, children under age 3 are exposed on average to 5.5 hours a day of background TV (Lapierre, Piotrowski, & Linebarger, 2012). More than one-third of families with young children have the TV on all or most of the time, even if no one is watching it (Rideout, 2013). Although toddlers usually will not continue to watch shows they don't understand, TV is designed to grab a viewer's attention, with techniques that work on young children as well as on adults. Think about being in a room or a restaurant where a TV is on that you are not even watching. Do you find your eyes drawn to the TV over and over again, distracting you from your conversation or other activities? The same appears to be true for infants and toddlers, to the detriment of their ability to develop their play (Anderson & Hanson, 2013; Setliff & Courage, 2011). Infants and toddlers will look at background TV over 25 times during a 30-minute show, disrupting the play and social interactions (Schmidt, Pempek, Kirkorian, Lund, & Anderson, 2008) that are crucial for optimal cognitive development in the early years. The more adult-focused background TV they are exposed to at age one, the lower children's cognitive functioning at age 4 (Barr, Lauricella, Zack, & Calvert, 2010). Clearly, background TV can be detrimental to young children's cognitive development.

A new topic relevant to cognitive development has emerged in the rapidly changing world of electronic media. A big change in the lives of many infants and toddlers has been the introduction of handheld electronic devices such as smartphones and tablets. Today even toddlers in their strollers are focusing their attention on iPads and other mobile devices. The number of children

WEB LINK 6.3
Baby Einstein Controversy

WEB LINK 6.4
Infants and Media

T/F #10
Babies who watch videotapes designed to improve cognitive development (like Baby Einstein videos) have larger vocabularies than babies who don't watch these videos.
False

Media use in infancy. Despite marketing claims to the contrary, there is no evidence that exposure to media is helpful for infants' cognitive development. Why do you think products such as music CDs for babies remain popular with parents? ∎

© StockShot/Alamy

Hand-held electronics for babies. Even babies are using screen-based electronic media. What do you think will be the consequences of such early exposure to electronic communication? ∎

AUDIO LINK 6.3
Infant Screen Time

under 2 who have used these devices jumped from 10% in 2011 to 38% in 2013 (Rideout, 2013). What does it mean for cognitive development when a 23-month-old can assemble a six-piece puzzle on a screen but has no idea what a real puzzle is? Victoria Rideout, author of survey research on this topic, has said these handheld devices "are gamechangers because they're so easy to use . . . a young child who can touch a picture can open an app, or swipe a screen" (Lewin, 2013, p. A17). Researchers are only beginning to examine the effects of this new use of media by infants and toddlers.

Many parents are quick to offer media to infants to keep them busy, and those with fussier babies are more likely to use media as a way to quiet the baby (Radesky, Silverstein, Zuckerman, & Christakis, 2014). However, the American Academy of Pediatrics (2011b) reminds parents that "Unstructured playtime is more valuable for the developing brain than any electronic media exposure. . . . Even for infants as young as 4 months of age, solo play allows a child to think creatively, problem-solve, and accomplish tasks with minimal parent interaction" (p. 1043). In other words, even infants do not have to be entertained all the time, either by parents or by media.

Early Intervention for Language and Cognitive Development

For many aspects of cognitive and language development, it is essential that infants get off to a good start because later development builds on these earliest experiences. Therefore babies who show signs of difficulty with cognitive and language development are good candidates for early intervention from professionals trained to help them and their families. Legislation known as IDEA (Individuals with Disabilities Education Act) requires that early intervention programs be made available for infants between birth and age 3. Each family works with professionals to develop an Individual Family Services Plan designed to provide individualized special services to the infant. Professionals who assess and treat babies and toddlers include speech and language therapists, psychologists, social workers, physicians, and other health professionals.

Home visiting can be an effective intervention with families of young children who are at developmental risk. In 2010, the U.S. Congress passed the Maternal, Infant and Early Childhood Home Visiting (MIECHV) program, which provides funding to states for home-visiting programs shown through research to make a difference for children from birth to age 5. Forty-eight states currently provide such programs (DiLauro & Schreiber, 2012). Effective intervention programs not only teach infants language and cognitive skills but also support their overall well-being, including health and emotional and social development. Effective intervention programs help families access necessary services, interact in a loving manner with their baby, and promote cognitive and language growth through activities such as reading to the child.

Research has found some positive effects on cognitive and language development when high-risk parents receive visits during pregnancy and after the baby is born. In one longitudinal study, high-risk pregnant mothers who were young, unmarried, and low income were visited by nurses on a regular basis. When the children reached age 12, they scored higher on tests of math and English than children from a comparable group of families that did not receive home visits (Kitzman et al., 2010). In another study, an extensive home-visiting program for infants from 6 months to 36 months of age resulted in improved language development (Lowell, Carter, Godoy, Paulicin, & Briggs-Gowan, 2011).

Check Your Understanding

1. What are the benefits of diagnosing intellectual disability early in life?
2. How does poverty affect early cognitive development?
3. How can parents promote optimal cognitive and language development?
4. What are the effects on infants' cognitive and language development of watching educational TV programs and videos?

Conclusion

The first 2 years of life are an exciting time of discovery and exploration. You have seen some of the ways in which infants' cognitive abilities grow and also some of the threats to optimal development. A solid foundation with loving caregivers who provide security, structure, and stimulation is essential for infants to develop the basic skills that will allow them to move on to the next level of cognitive development, as language sets the stage for further achievements.

Home visiting. This professional is helping the infant's parent develop effective parenting skills by showing how to engage the baby with toys appropriate to the baby's developmental level. ■

Chapter Summary

6.1 **What occurs during Piaget's sensorimotor stage of cognitive development?**

During the sensorimotor stage infants go through 6 substages that describe their development from primitive reflexive response through **circular reactions** to intentional exploration of the world. **Object permanence** develops when infants understand that objects continue to exist even when they can't see them.

6.2 **What is the premise of the theory of core knowledge?**

The **theory of core knowledge** posits that humans are born with innate areas of knowledge built into the brain. There are some differing ideas about what that knowledge is, but it may include basic understanding of how objects and agents move, the nature of number, and spatial relationships.

6.3 **How do infants learn?**

There is evidence that even very young infants learn through classical and operant conditioning and through imitation.

6.4 **What cognitive processes develop during infancy?**

Selective attention means tuning in to certain things while tuning out others, while **sustained attention** is maintaining focus over time. Infants pay more attention to something that is novel and will spend more time paying attention to complex rather than simple stimuli. Infant memory is nonverbal, so older children and adults have difficulty recalling experiences that happened before the age of 3, referred to as **infantile amnesia**. Infants appear to have a basic understanding of numbers. Even 4-month-olds seem to understand basic categories such as *cat* and *dog*, while older toddlers can understand broader categories such as animate and inanimate. **Executive function** is that aspect of brain organization that coordinates attention and memory and controls behavioral responses for the purpose of attaining a certain goal. Infants are just beginning to develop the ability to inhibit certain behaviors to achieve a desired goal.

6.5 **What aspects of infants' cognitive development are the best predictors of later intelligence?**

Preference for novelty, speed of habituation, and self-regulation ability all appear to be important predictive factors for later intelligence.

6.6 **How do infants develop language?**

Language includes **phonology** (the sounds that make up the language), **syntax** (the grammar of the language), **semantics** (the meanings of words), and pragmatics (the way we use language in social situations to communicate). Behaviorism emphasizes the role of reinforcement in the environment as a way to motivate and shape children's language development, but social cognitive learning theory emphasizes the role of imitation. **Nativism** emphasizes the role of biology by explaining language development as a result of our brain's inborn capacity to learn language. **Interactionism** brings these ideas together by stating that children's biological readiness to learn language must work together with their experiences to bring about language development. **Cognitive processing theory** suggests that infants' brains are capable of statistically analyzing the speech they hear to figure out language. Two areas of the brain are central for language development and use: **Broca's area** controls the production of speech, and **Wernicke's area** supports understanding language. Before they can use words, infants communicate by crying, cooing, babbling, and gesturing. Infants and toddlers begin verbalizing by using one word at a time and then create primitive sentences when they put two words together.

6.7 How can we ensure optimal cognitive and language development in infants?

Cognitive and language development are impaired in infants with intellectual disability, an overall reduced mental capacity that will affect the child throughout life. Poverty is an environmental threat to optimal cognitive development as early as 6 months of age. Parents promote cognitive development by providing a warm and accepting environment, responding to their infants' cues, providing age-appropriate stimulation, and maintaining an organized home. Despite claims that educational media can improve infants' cognitive growth, the best way for infants to learn is from interacting with the people around them.

Key Terms

A-not-B error   184

Broca's area   197

Child-directed speech   202

Circular reaction   182

Cognitive processing theory   196

Constraints   204

Disequilibrium   180

Executive function   192

Expressive language   198

Fast mapping   204

Genetic-epistemology   180

Habituation   189

Infantile amnesia   190

Inhibition   192

Intellectual disability   207

Interactionism   196

Language   194

Morpheme   194

Motor schema   182

Mutual exclusivity constraint   204

Nativism   195

Object permanence   183

Overregularization   195

Phoneme   195

Phonology   194

Pragmatics   194

Recast   196

Receptive language   198

Selective attention   189

Semantic bootstrapping   204

Semantics   194

Sensorimotor stage   181

Sustained attention   189

Syntactic bootstrapping   204

Syntax   194

Taxonomic constraint   204

Theory of core knowledge   186

Transitional probability   196

Universal grammar   195

Violation of expectation   186

Vocabulary burst   204

Wernicke's area   197

Whole object bias   204

$SAGE edge™

Sharpen your skills with SAGE edge at edge.sagepub.com/levinechrono

SAGE edge for Students provides a personalized approach to help you accomplish your coursework goals in an easy-to-use learning environment.

Go to edge.sagepub.com/levinechrono for additional exercises and video resources. Select Chapter 6, Cognitive Development in Infancy and Toddlerhood, for chapter-specific activities. All of the Video Links listed in the margins of this chapter are accessible via this site.

7

Social and Emotional Development in Infancy and Toddlerhood

T/F Test Your Knowledge

Test your knowledge of child development by deciding whether each of the following statements is *true* or *false,* and then check your answers as you read the chapter.

1. **T □ F □** Emotions are universal, so people all over the world understand each other's emotional expressions.

2. **T □ F □** When a young boy in the United States is hurt, he may express what he is feeling as anger, not sadness.

3. **T □ F □** Infants are too young to have empathy for the feelings of others.

4. **T □ F □** When babies cry because a parent has left, it is evidence that they are too attached to their parents.

5. **T □ F □** Mothers must have immediate contact with their babies after they are born if a secure attachment is to be formed.

6. **T □ F □** If a child has developed an insecure attachment to a parent, that child can still become securely attached later in her life.

7. **T □ F □** Infants are too young to be affected by parental divorce.

8. **T □ F □** Most adopted children are adopted as infants.

9. **T □ F □** Most mothers of infants and toddlers who work outside the home do so out of necessity.

10. **T □ F □** Infants are not capable of forming relationships with other children before the age of 2.

Correct answers: (1) F, (2) T, (3) F, (4) F, (5) F, (6) T, (7) F, (8) F, (9) T, (10) F

Infants enter the world with a basic repertoire of emotions that lets them communicate what they are feeling. They are also born with a characteristic way of responding to their experiences that we call temperament. At first the infant does not feel separate from his caregiver, but early in development he begins to distinguish the *self* from *the other*. From their earliest days of life, infants are primed to form social relationships with those who care for them. We saw in Chapter 5 that newborns quickly begin to look at faces, recognize their mother's voice, and prefer her scent, the beginnings of a relationship that will last a lifetime. In this chapter, we learn more about how infants' social world develops. We examine the attachments infants develop to the important caregivers in their lives and the important role families, culture, and peers play in their social and emotional development.

Learning Questions

7.1 What are emotion and temperament?

7.2 How do infants and toddlers develop a sense of self?

7.3 How does attachment develop?

7.4 What other life experiences shape infants' development?

Emotions: Universality and Difference

Are you usually a pleasant and positive person, or do you struggle with feelings of sadness? Are you easily frightened, or are you unflappable? Are you calm and easygoing, or are you readily provoked to anger? In this section, we discuss both the biological underpinnings and the environmental influences that shape our expression, experience, and interpretation of emotions. We also talk about how temperament influences the way infants react to experiences and how they begin to learn how to control and regulate their emotional response to events.

What Is Emotion?

When you are sitting in a scary movie, you may experience a rapid heartbeat and a sense of tension, you may grip the arm of your friend next to you, and you may actually jump when the hidden menace leaps out at you. This experience of fear includes your body's physiological reaction, your interpretation of the situation, communication with another person, and your own actions, which are all parts of what we call emotion. We all experience a range of emotions, from happy to sad, angry to afraid, and embarrassed to disgusted.

One way to understand the role of emotions in communication is to look at situations in which emotions are absent. See **Active Learning: Why We Use Emoticons** to recognize problems that arise when our electronic communication lacks emotional expression and the ways people have tried to solve these difficulties. You will also learn about some cultural differences in the expression of emotions.

7.1

What are emotion and temperament?

Emotion The body's physiological reaction to a situation, the cognitive interpretation of the situation, communication to another person, and actions.

Active Learning

Why We Use Emoticons

Have you ever had an online conversation with someone only to realize later that you misunderstood what she really meant to say? If someone writes, "I want to see you," how do you interpret that? Is this person saying she longs to see you, or is she preparing to scold you? In 1982, Scott Fahlman, a professor of computer science at Carnegie

Mellon University, sent the first emoticon, designed to add emotions to online communication. He wrote, "I propose the following character sequence for joke markers: :-)" (Lovering, 2007, p. E2). These markers were meant to distinguish sarcastic or silly comments from serious ones, because people were badly misunderstanding each other, going as far as to interpret jokes as real safety warnings (Fahlman, n.d.). Using emoticons, you would read "I want to see you :-)" very differently from "I want to see you >:-(". Emotions are necessary to make sure our meaning is communicated clearly.

You may not know that other cultures have their own emoticons, which you might not recognize. Western-style emoticons typically are written so that you need to tip your head to the left to see them. East Asian emoticons appear right-side up. Emoticons also reflect cultural differences in the way individuals understand other people's emotions. For example, when trying to interpret photographs of faces expressing different emotions, Westerners tend to scan the whole face, while East Asians focus on the eyes (Jack, Blais, Scheepers, Schyns, & Caldara, 2009). This difference is apparent when we compare emoticons used in these two cultures:

East/West Differences in Emoticons		
Emotion	West	East
Happy	:-)	(^_^)
Sad	:-(	(;_;) or (T_T)
Surprised	:-o	(0.0)

Can you identify the emotions expressed by these emoticons used in East Asia?

(a) ☆⌒(>。≪)   (b) (–︿–)   (c) (>^_^)> (;_;) <(^_^<)   (d) ポッ(´｡•ω•｡`)(´｡•ω•｡`)ポッ

Answer: (a) Getting hurt/experiencing pain; (b) complaint/discontent; (c) offering a hug to a person who is crying; (d) love.

Because emotions have a physiological component, we might expect them to be rooted in our biology and thus to be similar among human beings of all cultural backgrounds. In fact, there is remarkable similarity around the world in the display and understanding of facial expressions that indicate basic emotions: happiness, sadness, fear, anger, interest, and disgust (Izard, 2007; Oatley, Keltner, & Jenkins, 2006). In addition, there is some evidence for the universality of more complex emotions, such as pride (Tracy & Robins, 2008). The argument has been made that basic emotions are automatic and unlearned because all infants demonstrate these basic emotions, and particular neural systems in the brain are at least partially dedicated to the expression of each of these emotions (Izard, 2007). Prevalence of these emotions has also been found to change over the course of the first year, with positive affect such as happiness increasing, fear decreasing, and frustration (anger) increasing (Rothbart, Derryberry, & Hershey, 2000).

Although some aspects of emotional expression appear to be universal, there is also considerable evidence that the way we display our own emotions and understand those shown by others is mediated in part by our culture, language, gender, temperament, and personality (Izard, 2007; Kayyal & Russell, 2013; Matsumoto, 1992, 2006; Matsumoto & Assar, 1992; Russell, 1994). Although our basic emotions appear to be biologically determined, we quickly develop ways of thinking about emotions, called

T/F #1
Emotions are universal, so people all over the world understand each other's emotional expressions. *False*

Universal emotions. These girls from Myanmar in Southeast Asia (left) and from the Himba tribe in Namibia, Africa (right) would likely recognize each other's smiles as expressing the same emotion. ■

emotion schemas, that affect the way we experience and show emotions (Izard, 2007). You'll remember that a schema is a cognitive framework that organizes the world into categories and associations. When we experience sadness, we draw on a wealth of associations and memories to understand what we are feeling. We label the experience, connect it to our memory of other experiences when we felt sad, and judge whether our expression of sadness is allowable or appropriate, especially in front of other people.

For example, the idea that "big boys don't cry" is a powerful control on the expression of sadness for many boys and may make it difficult for them to get help or even to understand their own sad feelings. A boy in the United States who is hit by a baseball may automatically begin to cry, but if his schema for crying includes "big boys don't cry," he decides "I cannot let myself cry," and his facial expression may then reflect anger at himself for experiencing this forbidden emotion. Sadness is then often expressed as anger, which is more acceptable for boys in the American culture. Matsumoto, Consolacion, and Yamada (2002) reported that people in individualistic cultures, such as the United States, show their feelings more openly than do people from collectivist cultures, such as Japan. Knowing this, a Japanese person interprets someone's small smile as indicating great happiness, while an American interprets a broad grin as moderate happiness.

Emotion schemas All the associations and interpretations that an individual connects to a certain emotion.

T/F #2
When a young boy in the United States is hurt, he may express what he is feeling as anger, not sadness.
True

Social Referencing

When we experience emotions, they produce various physiological effects on our body, but what does it mean to you when your heart races or you find yourself shaking and trembling? One way we begin to understand how to label our emotions is to look at the way others are reacting when we are uncertain about how we should react, a process called social referencing. Social referencing first develops between 9 and 12 months of age (Hennighausen & Lyons-Ruth, 2005). You may have seen a toddler fall and immediately look around for his parent. If his father gasps and runs over with fear on his face, the child is likely to begin crying. However, if his dad smiles and says, "You're OK" (if the child really isn't hurt), the toddler is likely to pick himself up and return to play. The child is learning to interpret his feeling of mild upset as either something that is very frightening or a slight bump that he can manage and overcome. Of course, any child who is truly hurt will cry and needs comfort.

Social referencing Using the reaction of others to determine how to react in ambiguous situations.

Empathy

In addition to checking with other people for clues about their emotional expression, infants and toddlers have a natural tendency to share other people's feelings, which is the essence of empathy. As we saw in Chapter 5, from their first days of life, infants imitate the actions of others. The same is true for emotions. If a baby hears another baby crying, he is quite likely to start crying himself (Geangu, Benga, Stahl, & Striano, 2010). Have you experienced something similar yourself? When you see someone crying on television or a movie, do you ever find your own eyes getting wet? Experiencing the feelings of others is a form of empathy and is the basis for much human interaction. When we experience another's distress, we are more likely to try to show sympathy by helping or comforting that person. See how toddlers express empathy by completing **Active Learning: Empathy and Sympathy.**

Active Learning

Empathy and Sympathy

You can carry out the following experiment designed by Carolyn Zahn-Waxler and her colleagues to look at empathy and sympathy in toddlers (for more information, see Robinson, Zahn-Waxler, & Emde, 1994). When you are with a child you know, pretend to hurt yourself. You can pretend to pinch your finger in a drawer, stub your toe, or experience some other noticeable but minor hurt. Practice beforehand so you can react in a realistic way.

How does the child respond? Young children may ignore you, laugh, look hurt, or cry themselves, or show sympathy by asking whether you are OK or need a Band-Aid. Think about what each type of behavior means regarding the child's ability to take another's point of view as well as empathizing with another's pain. As children get older, they move from showing personal distress when they empathize with you (for example, crying themselves) to being more oriented to your feelings and helping you feel better.

After you note the child's reaction, be sure to reassure the child that you now are feeling much better and do not hurt anymore. Also thank the child if he or she tried to help you. ■

Temperament

Although most of us will be frightened when we see a horror film, some people will be so terrified that they will never go to see another film like that again, while others will be scared but also excited by it and will take every opportunity to see more. Temperament is the general way in which we respond to experiences in the world, whether seeing horror films, doing a class presentation, or being cut off in traffic. Although different experiences evoke different emotional responses, the concept of temperament implies that individuals have a general emotional style that guides their tendency to respond in certain ways to a variety of events in their environment. Some people are usually timid, fearful, and anxious; some are fearless and outgoing; and others are often aggressive and angry.

Some of these differences reflect characteristic ways we have learned to respond to our experiences, but parents report that their children were different from each other from the moment they were born; one

Empathy. Even young children can experience empathy and will attempt to soothe another person, as this girl is doing for her friend. ■

child was quiet while the other was boisterous, or one was demanding while the other was content. There is some evidence that they are right, that we are born with a certain temperament based to some degree on our genetic inheritance (Goldsmith, Lemery, Aksan, & Buss, 2000; Rothbart, 2007).

Among the several different approaches to describing and measuring temperament (Strelau, 1998), one of the most influential was developed by Alexander Thomas and Stella Chess (Chess & Thomas, 1999; Thomas & Chess, 1977). Based on semistructured interviews with parents, Thomas and Chess identified nine characteristics that contribute to the infant's temperament. These are activity level, adaptability, approach or withdrawal, attention span and persistence, distractibility, intensity of reaction, quality of mood, rhythmicity (or regularity), and threshold of responsiveness. Any individual infant can score high, low, or average on each of these characteristics, and combining this information produces three temperament profiles: an easy temperament, a difficult temperament, and a slow-to-warm temperament. Table 7.1 shows where infants with each of these temperament profiles fall on each of these dimensions.

Infants with an easy temperament have a generally positive mood, adapt fairly easily to change, and are regular and predictable in their patterns of eating, sleeping, and elimination (Chess & Thomas, 1999). In contrast, infants with a difficult temperament have a more negative mood, are easily frustrated and slow to adapt to change, and have irregular patterns of eating, sleeping, and elimination. Infants with difficult temperaments also tend to react more intensely to situations than those with easy temperaments. For these children, it is even more important that parents try to keep their environments regular and predictable and introduce changes gradually. The third temperament described by Chess and Thomas (1999) is the slow-to-warm temperament. The reaction of these infants to new experiences is milder than the reaction of a difficult child, whether they are exposed to something they like or something they dislike. However, if they are given some time and are not pressured by adults, with repeated exposure to the new experience they gradually come around on their own. Slow-to-warm infants also are less irregular in their eating, sleeping, and elimination patterns than difficult infants but less regular than easy infants.

VIDEO LINK 7.1
Temperament

JOURNAL ARTICLE 7.1
Temperament and Obesity

Easy temperament A child's general responsiveness marked by positive mood, easy adaptation to change, and regularity and predictability in patterns of eating, sleeping, and elimination.

Difficult temperament A child's general responsiveness marked by a more negative mood, intense responses, slow adaptation to change, and irregular patterns of eating, sleeping, and elimination.

Slow-to-warm temperament A general responsiveness marked by a slow adaptation to new experiences and moderate irregularity in eating, sleeping, and elimination.

TABLE 7.1   Temperament profiles

Dimension of temperament	Easy	Slow to warm	Difficult
Activity Level	Varies	Low to moderate	Varies
Adaptability	Very adaptable	Slowly adaptable	Slowly adaptable
Approach/Withdrawal	Positive approach	Initial withdrawal	Withdrawal
Attention Span and Persistence	High or low	High or low	High or low
Distractibility	Varies	Varies	Varies
Intensity of Reaction	Low or mild	Mild	Intense
Quality of Mood	Positive	Slightly negative	Negative
Rhythmicity	Very regular	Varies	Irregular
Threshold of Responsiveness	High or low	High or low	High or low

This table shows where infants who are classified by Thomas and Chess as *easy, slow-to-warm, or difficult* fall on each of the nine dimensions of temperament they describe. Note that about 35% of infants show a mixture of traits that do not fit any of the profiles.

SOURCE: Adapted from Chess, Thomas, & Birch (1965).

In their early studies of children's temperament, Thomas and Chess (1977) found that easy infants made up about 40% of their sample, difficult infants made up 10%, and slow-to-warm infants made up about 15%. The remainder could not be classified because they displayed the 9 characteristics in a different configuration or were not consistent in the type of behaviors they showed from one occasion to another. According to Chess and Thomas (1999), what is most important in shaping the consequences of having one type of temperament versus another is the goodness of fit between the child's characteristics and the demands of the environment. For instance, if an infant doesn't like a lot of noise and crowds of people, a sensitive parent tries to avoid these situations or plans to take the infant into these situations only when she is well rested, fed, and comfortable (Sturm, 2004).

The question whether the temperament with which we are born remains the basis for our emotional responses for the rest of our lives is a complicated one. Research shows a tendency for many children to maintain the same temperament over time (Carranza, Gonzalez-Salinas, & Ato, 2013; Casalin, Luyten, Vliegen, & Neurs, 2012; Neppl et al., 2010; Rothbart et al., 2000). However, there also are many children who change. Although they do not tend to go from one extreme to another, smaller changes do occur (Goldsmith et al., 2000; Carranza et al., 2013). Think about your own temperament. If you are shy now, were you also shy as a child? If you are outgoing now, have you been told you were very friendly as a child? Were you shy until a certain age and then you changed to become more outgoing? In recent years, Mary Rothbart and her colleagues have added to the work by Chess and Thomas with rigorous analyses of parent questionnaires about children's temperament (Rothbart, Ahadi, Hershey, & Fisher, 2001). They have examined two basic aspects of temperament: (1) involuntary reactivity to external events, including emotional, motor, and attentional reactivity; and (2) ability to self-regulate reactions. To learn more about Rothbart's approach and apply it to your own understanding of your temperament, interview your parents as suggested in **Active Learning: Temperament.**

Goodness of fit How well a child's temperamental characteristics match the demands of the child's environment.

AUDIO LINK 7.1
Temperament into Adulthood

Temperament. Children's temperament ranges from shy and retiring to outgoing and adventurous, and where a child falls on this continuum influences how that child interprets new experiences. Where would you place yourself? Have you always been that way? ■

Active Learning

Temperament

Mary Rothbart and her colleagues developed some different ideas about the dimensions of temperament than those of Chess and Thomas. In their research, they found three basic dimensions: (1) extraversion, (2) negative emotion, and (3) self-control (Rothbart et al., 2001). Use these dimensions to interview your parents about what you were like as a young child. Ask your parents how similar you were to the following characteristics from the Children's Behavior Questionnaire for each dimension (Rothbart et al., 2001):

> Extraversion: "Usually rushes into an activity without thinking about it"; "Gets so worked up before an exciting event that s(he) has trouble sitting still."

> Negative emotion: "Has temper tantrums when s(he) doesn't get what s(he) wants"; "Has a hard time settling down for a nap."

> Self-control: "Can lower his/her voice when asked to do so"; "When picking up toys or other jobs, usually keeps at the task until it's done." (p. 1406)

Did you respond quickly to experiences, like grabbing an object you wanted right away, or did you move slowly into new situations? Were you able to calm yourself down when upset or angry? Do you feel that your parents' descriptions of you as a child still describe you now in any way? If you feel your temperament has undergone some significant change, can you identify anything that initiated that change (for instance, becoming more outgoing after you had to move to a new school and make new friends)? These indicators of temperament seem to stay the same for most people, but they can change if experiences provide the impetus for those changes. ■

Emotional Self-Regulation in Infants and Toddlers

When children (and adults) can control the expression of their emotions, they are more likely to be able to use emotions in a positive way. One example of an adult who is not in control of his emotions is a person who experiences road rage. This person may chase after someone who has cut him off in traffic, putting himself and others at risk. In children, we see a similar inability to control rage in the form of a temper tantrum.

Regulating emotions. A driver in the throes of road rage looks a great deal like a young child having a temper tantrum. In both cases, the individual has failed to regulate and control their negative emotions. ■

Infants have little self-control and have difficulty regulating their emotional reactions. As adults, we recognize and accept this. For example, when they begin to cry, they may cry harder and harder, stressing their body's resources. They rely on parents to help control and modulate these feelings. A special relationship forms with the parent as the parent learns to comfort the child effectively. However, even young infants make some effort to exercise self-control. Early in development they begin to develop ways to soothe themselves through behaviors such as thumb sucking, holding a favorite "blankie," or avoiding a feared or frustrating object by looking away (Eisenberg, Hofer, & Vaughan, 2007). They may also signal in a subtle way when they are being overstimulated. If you are playing with an infant who suddenly yawns, stretches, and turns away, the infant is letting you know he is feeling overwhelmed and you need to reduce the amount of stimulation he is trying to process. Being sensitive to the infant's signals—whether of hunger, tiredness, or discomfort—helps the infant learn to regulate his own emotions because he comes to know he doesn't need to get frantic to get a response from his caregivers.

As children become toddlers, the important adults in their lives continue to be powerful models of ways to regulate and control emotions and behaviors. If parents react to their own frustrations with negative outbursts, toddlers learn that such behavior is acceptable. When parents are angry or become frustrated but stop for a minute to regain their composure, this models exercising self-control rather than behaving impulsively for their children.

Another way parents help infants develop self-control is providing an environment with predictable routines. Parents don't need to be rigid about this, but regular times for meals, sleep, and play help keep an infant from becoming overly hungry, tired, or bored. You know from your own experience that it is more difficult to exercise self-control when you are feeling very tired or hungry, and the same is true for infants.

Parents and other caregivers can also help redirect their child's behavior. For instance, if a toddler bites someone in frustration, parents can give him an alternative behavior to express his feelings. People who work with young children know that biting at this age is not unusual, and you frequently hear them saying "Use your words" to remind children they can express their frustration in other more acceptable ways. As children develop conversational skills, their struggles over possessions decline in frequency (Hay, 2006).

AUDIO LINK 7.2
Self-Regulation

Check Your Understanding

1. What is emotion?
2. What is temperament?
3. What categories of temperament have been identified in infants?
4. How do infants learn to control their emotions?

7.2

How do infants and toddlers develop a sense of self?

The Self in Infants and Toddlers

What conception of self is present when we are born? Psychoanalyst Margaret Mahler argued that infants are not born with a sense that they have a self that is separate from those who take care of them (Mahler, Pine, & Bergman, 1975). Babies must develop this sense, and they appear to do it in two stages. The first understanding of self is based on the infant's growing ability to make things happen: "*I make this mobile move*" or "*I make my mommy smile*." The baby's *intention* to make things happen reflects her awareness that she is the agent of change. Rochat (2001) has proposed that this first understanding then leads to a new concept of "me" when the child can begin to think *about* herself. Self-awareness means the child is the object of her own perceptions and thoughts (Gallup, Anderson, & Shillito, 2002). This second type of awareness begins to develop in the second year of life.

We describe four ways in which this new sense of self is expressed: mirror self-recognition, use of the pronouns *I* and *you*, visual perspective taking, and possessiveness. All four develop at about the same time, somewhere near the child's second birthday (Rochat, 2001; Stipek, Gralinski, & Kopp, 1990).

Mirror Self-Recognition

The classic experiment establishing whether a toddler has physical self-awareness is the mirror self-recognition task. In this task, the toddler's parent pretends to wipe the toddler's nose but secretly puts rouge or lipstick on the tissue and marks the child's nose with it. The child is then placed in front of a mirror. If she realizes the image in the mirror is really herself and not another child, she will touch her own nose when she sees the funny red mark on it. At 1 year of age children will not do this. Instead they react as if their mirror image were another child with whom they can interact. Sometime between 18 and 24 months, children in Western societies understand that the mirror image is a reflection of themselves, and they begin touching their own nose (Broesch, Callaghan, Henrich, Murphy, & Rochat, 2011; Gallup et al., 2002).

That's me! Before their second birthday, toddlers begin to recognize their own image in the mirror. Before this, they may have been fascinated by the baby in the mirror, but now they know who that baby is—they are looking at themselves. ∎

VIDEO LINK 7.2
Rouge Test

Use of Pronouns

You may hear toddlers say something like "Daddy, pick you up, pick you up!" when what they mean is "Daddy, pick me up!" Using *I* and *you* appropriately is not something we can learn by imitation. The child only hears Daddy say, "I'll pick you up," so he imitates what he hears. Only when he understands that *I* is different from *you* does he become able to use the pronouns correctly and say "Pick me up!" Toddlers develop this ability several months before or after their second birthday. Before this time, many resort to the strategy of referring to themselves by name—for example, "Ethan do it!" (Bates, 1990). Infants begin to use personal pronouns like *my* and *mine* between the ages of 15 and 18 months (Saylor, Ganea, & Vazquez, 2011). Those as young as 12 months of age can correctly retrieve an object an experimenter has played with when asked to give the experimenter *my ball* (Saylor et al., 2011).

Visual Perspective-Taking

If you ask a toddler to show you her drawing, she may hold it up so she can see it but you cannot. She assumes that because she can see it, you must be able to see it as well. The child must develop an understanding that you and she are separate people with different points of view to develop what is called visual perspective-taking. This ability develops in toddlers between 18 and 24 months of age (Moll & Tomasello, 2006). Ricard, Girouard, and Gouin Décairie (1999) found it was linked with the ability to use *I* and *you* correctly as described above.

Visual perspective-taking The understanding that other people can see an object from a point of view that is different from one's own.

Possessiveness

Two-year-olds are entering what Erik Erikson (1963) referred to as the stage of *autonomy versus shame and doubt*. Being "autonomous" means you are independent and have some control over what happens to you. Toddlers assert their autonomy, or separation of self from others, through two of their favorite commands: "No!" and "Mine!"

As they develop a clearer sense of themselves as separate from those around them, toddlers are motivated to defend their own way of doing things and what they think belongs to them. In one study, Levine (1983) found that 2-year-old boys who recognized themselves in a mirror and were able to understand and use *I* and *you* accurately were more likely than those with a less clear self-concept to claim toys when interacting with

Brooks Kraft/Corbis

It's mine! Possessiveness is another component of toddlers' growing sense of self. Once they know that they are a separate individual, they also understand that there are things that belong to them. ■

an unfamiliar peer. Caregivers who deal with toddlers should see this toy-claiming not as selfishness but as a first expression of the child's understanding that "I have a self that is different from yours." Hay (2006) found that toddlers who used possessives when interacting with a peer were more aggressive initially, but 6 months later they were more likely to share with a peer.

Toddlers who have a clearer sense of self are better able to play successfully with peers (Hay, 2006; Levine, 1983). Girls who have a clearer sense of self will try to create a sense of similarity when interacting with an unfamiliar peer by playing with the same type of toy (Levine & Conway, 2010). At this point, toddlers begin to imitate each other (Asendorpf & Baudonniere, 1993), and they can work together with a peer to solve a problem. For example, in one study two toddlers were shown a clear box containing toys. The only way to retrieve the toys was for one child to press a lever while the other took the toys out of the box. One child could not physically do it alone. Toddlers who had shown a clearer sense of self-other differentiation were better able to coordinate with their partner to retrieve the toys successfully (Brownell & Carriger, 1990).

Check Your Understanding

1. What is mirror self-recognition?
2. What is the significance of a toddler's use of personal pronouns?
3. What is visual perspective taking?
4. How does possessiveness demonstrate the toddler's growing sense of self?

7.3

How does attachment develop?

Attachment An emotional bond to a particular person.

Attachment

Love is one of the most important and formative of emotions. The first love we develop is for those who care for us, usually our parents. The love in this relationship consists of an emotional bond, known as attachment, which is central to the well-being of infants and children as they grow. In this section, we look at how attachment develops, how it differs from person to person, and what its consequences are. Before continuing, try **Active Learning: Experiencing a Sense of Secure Attachment.**

Active Learning

Experiencing a Sense of Secure Attachment

In a quiet place, close your eyes and relax for a brief time. Keeping your eyes closed, try to remember a time in your life when you felt cared for, secure, and loved. If you are able to bring forth a memory, stay with it for a few minutes. Experience that feeling. Who are you with in this memory? What is happening? Now slowly open your eyes and return to the present. Reflect on your experience. How did you feel? Was there one person in particular who helped you feel that way? This activity is designed to elicit feelings connected with the experience of emotional attachment. These are feeling-memories that we may call on in times of stress. This exercise is not necessarily an easy one to do, so do not be alarmed if you were not able to call forth a memory. ■

Secure attachment A strong, positive emotional bond with a person who provides comfort and a sense of security.

Secure attachment is a strong, positive emotional bond with a particular person who provided comfort and a sense of security. If you are attached to someone, you are more likely to turn to that person when you are distressed. You are usually happy to see that person and may be unhappy about separations. This is a person with whom you can feel free to be yourself in the fullest sense. Although we talk quite a bit about the development of attachment in infants, attachment remains central to our well-being throughout our lives.

Journey of Research: The History of the Study of Attachment gives you more information about how our thinking about the roots of attachment has changed over the years.

JOURNEY OF RESEARCH *The History of the Study of Attachment*

In the early to mid-1900s, both psychoanalytic and behavioral theorists developed ideas about how the bond between child and parent is formed. Both theories of attachment were based on the idea of drive reduction—that is, that human behavior is motivated by the need to satisfy basic needs, such as hunger. When we feel hungry, we are driven to seek out food, and our drive is reduced when we eat. In both theories, the development of a child's attachment to his mother is based on the mother's ability to satisfy such drives. Specifically, as the mother provides food to satisfy the infant's hunger drive, the infant learns to associate his sense of satisfaction, or drive reduction, with her presence and as a result develops an attachment to her.

In the 1950s, new ideas about the nature of attachment appeared. In 1958, Harry Harlow published an article titled "The Nature of Love," in which he reported the results of his research with macaque monkeys. To test his ideas about how attachment forms, Harlow separated infant monkeys from their mothers at birth and raised them with two surrogate mothers. One "mother" was a wire mesh tube, and the other was a wooden tube covered in sponge rubber with terrycloth wrapped around it so it would be comfortable to touch. Half the monkeys were fed from a bottle protruding from the wire mother, and half were fed from the cloth mother.

Harlow found that infant monkeys spent the majority of their time clinging to the cloth mother regardless of which surrogate mother provided milk. When the infant monkeys were frightened by a loud, moving toy, they were more likely to run to the cloth mother for security. When they were placed in a new, unknown setting, they again preferred to cling to the cloth mother

Nina Leen/Time & Life Pictures/Getty Images

Harlow's monkeys. In his research, Harry Harlow (1958) found that monkeys preferred a soft cloth "mother," even if it did not provide food, over a wire "mother" that provided food through a bottle. How did this finding challenge the ideas of both psychoanalytic and behavioral theories of attachment? ■

Drive reduction The idea that human behavior is determined by the motivation to satisfy or reduce the discomfort caused by biological needs or drives.

VIDEO LINK 7.3
Harlow's Monkeys

and eventually were able to explore the room, using it as a safe base to return to when they became frightened. When the cloth mother was absent, the babies were distressed and unable to explore the environment or play. Harlow came to believe that the primary function of nursing a baby might actually be to provide contact comfort with the mother, and that this contact comfort created the mother-infant attachment, not feeding as the behaviorists and psychoanalysts believed.

At about the same time, John Bowlby, a child psychiatrist trained in psychoanalysis, was exploring his observation that separations from parents had an enormous impact on the psychological well-being of children seen in a psychiatric clinic (Ainsworth & Bowlby, 1989). Bowlby believed Harlow's research with monkeys confirmed his suspicions that a psychoanalytic explanation for attachment was not adequate.

Bowlby also was intrigued by a new theory based on the observation of natural behavior of animals. Remember from Chapter 2 that Konrad Lorenz's theory of ethology proposed that genes produce certain behaviors, and that if these behaviors help the animals adapt successfully to their environment, the genes that produce them will be handed down from one generation to the next. In 1958, Bowlby set forth his new theory of attachment based on ethology. He argued that attachment is a biologically based, active behavior related to the infant's need for protection in order to survive. Bowlby believed infant behaviors such as crying, smiling, sucking, clinging, and following are adaptive behaviors that promote the survival of the child by helping develop attachment between mother and child.

In what ways is attachment adaptive? First, because infants are dependent on an adult caregiver to provide all the things that keep them alive, it makes sense biologically that they would have built-in behaviors designed to keep that adult near. A baby who feels threatened, whether by a scary noise or uncomfortable hunger pains, will act to keep the parent, or caregiver, close. Crying, smiling, and following all serve this purpose. Second, when infants feel secure, they are able to explore their environment, checking back from time to time with a parent as a form of "emotional refueling," like a car that runs out of gas and needs to be filled up to continue on its travels (Mahler, Bergman, & Pine, 2000, p. 69). The child uses the parent as a secure base for exploration, and because exploration is essential for human learning, these behaviors are adaptive.

In 1950, Mary Ainsworth joined Bowlby's research team (Ainsworth & Bowlby, 1989). Ainsworth was interested in assessing and classifying different types of emotional security. When she moved from England to Uganda in 1954, she began her research by observing mothers and their infants. These and subsequent observations led to the classification of four categories of attachment: secure attachment, anxious avoidant attachment, anxious ambivalent/resistant attachment, and disorganized/disoriented attachment (described in the text below). The basic theory outlined by Bowlby and Ainsworth remains the underlying model for most of the work on attachment being done today. ■

Secure base for exploration The use of a parent to provide the security that an infant can rely on as she explores the environment.

WEB LINK 7.1
Bowlby's Stages

Preattachment The stage of development of attachment from birth to 6 weeks, in which infant sensory preferences bring infants into close connection with parents.

Attachment in the making The stage from 6 weeks to 6–8 months in which infants develop stranger anxiety, differentiating those they know from those they don't.

Clear-cut attachment The stage from 6–8 months to 18 months–2 years, when an infant develops separation anxiety when a person he is attached to leaves him.

Goal-corrected partnership The stage of development of attachment from 18 months on, when toddlers create reciprocal relationships with their mothers.

The Development of Attachment: Bowlby's Stages

As John Bowlby (1969) brought new ideas from Harlow's research and from ethological theory into his research on attachment, he described the following four stages in the early development of attachment:

1. Preattachment (birth to 6 weeks)

2. Attachment in the making (6 weeks to 6–8 months)

3. Clear-cut attachment (6–8 months to 18 months–2 years)

4. Goal-corrected partnership (also referred to as the formation of reciprocal relationships; 18 months on) (Ainsworth, Blehar, Waters, & Wall, 1978)

Preattachment (Birth to 6 Weeks)

From their earliest days, infants act in ways that attract others to care for them. It is very difficult to sit and do nothing when we hear a baby crying, especially if that baby is our own. Both new mothers and new fathers experience hormonal changes following childbirth that may increase their responsiveness to their baby's distress, such as more rapid heartbeats and other physiological responses that promote caregiving to their new babies (Berg & Wynne-Edwards, 2001; Feldman, Weller, Zagoory-Sharon, & Levine, 2007; Fleming, Corter, Stallings, & Sneider, 2002; Weisman, Zagoory-Sharon, & Feldman, 2014).

As we discussed in Chapter 5, the sensory preferences of infants, such as smell and vision, predispose them to social interactions with the world in general, and with their mothers in particular. Infants can immediately imitate some facial expressions, they prefer to look at faces rather than inanimate objects, they respond to voices, and most love to be touched and held. Their cry communicates their needs to those around them and draws others to care for them. Even at birth infants look at other people's eyes and begin to follow the direction in which someone is looking with their own gaze (Farroni, Massaccesi, Pividori, & Johnson, 2004).

Joint attention. As this infant follows his mother's gaze and they share the experience of looking at this tree, the infant monitors his mother to be sure they are involved in the same thing. ■

Within the first year, their attraction to eyes helps them engage in a process called joint attention (Flavell, 1999; Gredebäck, Fikke, & Melinder, 2010). In joint attention, the infant looks at the same object someone else is looking at but also looks at the person; that is, he monitors the other person's attention to make sure they are both involved with the same thing (Akhtar, 2005). When infants engage in joint attention, they begin to explore the world together with their caregivers.

Joint attention A process in which an individual looks at the same object that someone else is looking at, but also looks at the person to make sure that they are both involved with the same thing.

Attachment in the Making (6 Weeks to 6–8 Months)

Babies begin to smile at about 6 weeks of age. At first these smiles seem almost random, but by about 2 months, babies clearly have developed a social smile directed specifically at people (Ellsworth, Muir, & Hains, 1993). Very quickly, smiling becomes reserved for people the baby recognizes. A 3-month-old baby may look seriously at a stranger but begin to grin when he sees his mother. These early signs of recognition and responsiveness begin to lay the foundation for a special relationship with the familiar and important people in the baby's social world.

In many infants, this early discrimination between familiar and unfamiliar intensifies. If you have ever gone to babysit for a 6-month-old infant who has never met you before, you know what stranger anxiety means. Sometimes all the baby has to do is see a stranger and she begins wailing. In other cases, the baby may interact and smile as long as she is in her mother's arms, but if the stranger tries to hold her, the crying begins.

Stranger anxiety Fearfulness that infants develop at about 6 months of age toward people they do not know.

Clear-Cut Attachment (6–8 Months to 18 Months–2 Years)

In the stage of clear-cut attachment, infants begin to move about on their own and become able to actively maintain contact with their caregiver. Infants now clearly discriminate between their attachment figures and strangers. During this stage, babies seek out their parents when they are stressed or afraid, but separation from parents, in and of itself, becomes frightening, and infants begin to protest when their parents leave. This distress is referred to as separation anxiety. An infant crying at the departure of someone who helps the infant feel secure does not indicate an excessive attachment to that person. It is quite a normal reaction. In addition, the parent becomes a secure base for exploration. When a parent is around and the infant can get to the parent, he is comfortable to explore, but if the parent is absent, exploration may stop. Although you can control your emotions better than an infant, you may remember a time when you were separated from the people you love and felt anxiety about being on your own without them. Did you call or text your parents or friends back home more frequently? In this situation, you can see that we continue to need the "emotional refueling" we see in infants.

Separation anxiety Distress felt when separated from a parent.

T/F #4
When babies cry because a parent has left, it is evidence that they are too attached to their parents. *False*

Goal-Corrected Partnership (18 Months On)

As the baby becomes a toddler, she becomes increasingly aware that her mother has goals and motives different from her own. At this point, she realizes she must create a partnership with her mother through their interaction. This partnership is based on

Attachment and a secure base for exploration. Securely attached children will play away from the parent, as long as they can go back from time to time for some "emotional refueling." ■

Internal working model
A mental representation of particular attachment relationships a child has experienced that shapes expectations for future relationships.

▶

VIDEO LINK 7.4
Strange Situation

Strange Situation Mary Ainsworth's experimental procedure designed to assess security of attachment in infants.

the idea of two separate individuals interacting, each with an equal part in keeping the interaction going (Bowlby, 1969).

Toddlers now are able to form symbolic representations of the particular attachment relationships they have been experiencing (Bowlby, 1969). This concept, referred to as an internal working model of attachment, has helped psychologists understand how early attachment patterns contribute to the close relationships that children—and even adults—develop later in life. Based on our past experiences, an inner script develops, so in this sense our future interactions are shaped by our past interactions. For example, a child who has been abused may expect aggression from others, and this expectation will shape how the child behaves when meeting new people. Abused children may respond to new people by provoking them to anger, possibly recreating the abuse situation they have experienced. In a similar way—but with a very different outcome—children who have been warmly cared for come to expect that others will treat them positively, so they themselves act in a warm and engaging way. Their own positive interactions then elicit positive responses from others.

Although research supports the idea that internal working models are fairly stable over time, they can be modified (Pietromonaco & Barrett, 2000). It takes time and patience to overcome the expectations a child with a negative working model of attachment has developed for new relationships, but it can be done.

Security of Attachment

As you read in **Journey of Research: The History of the Study of Attachment,** Mary Ainsworth worked with John Bowlby and further developed his ethological theory. Ainsworth was interested in looking at individual differences in the types of attachment that infants and mothers formed together, based on the degree of security the infant felt in that relationship. She developed an experimental procedure to classify types of attachment known as the Strange Situation. The Strange Situation places an infant and mother in a series of situations that become increasingly stressful for the infant. Except for the first episode, each lasts 3 minutes unless the baby is crying, in which case the time period is cut short.

1. An observer brings mother and baby into a comfortable room equipped with a one-way mirror and immediately leaves.

2. Baby plays while mother responds naturally.

3. Stranger enters, and at the end of 3 minutes the mother leaves.

4. Baby is in the room with the stranger, who may interact with the baby.

5. Mother returns, stranger leaves, and at the end of 3 minutes the mother again leaves.

6. Baby is alone for 3 minutes.

7. Stranger enters and may interact with the baby.

8. Mother returns (Ainsworth & Bell, 1970).

Based on her observations of infants' reactions during the Strange Situation, Ainsworth described four types of attachment: secure attachment, anxious avoidant attachment, anxious ambivalent/resistant attachment, and disorganized/disoriented attachment, which we describe below.

Ainsworth found two behaviors in her observations that best identified the type of attachment relationship infants had with their mother. The first was the child's ability to be comfortable and explore a new setting while the mother was in the room, with the mother acting as a secure base for exploration. The second was the child's response to the mother's return to the room, known as *reunion behavior*—that is, the child's ability, when stressed by the mother's departure, to use the mother on her return to calm down and return to playing. Interestingly, distress at separation by itself was *not* a reliable indicator of type of attachment. Table 7.2 describes the typical infant and mother behaviors for each type of attachment.

Infants with secure attachment rely on their parent to respond to their needs and turn to their parent when they are stressed. The baby's reliance on a trustworthy parent allows her to explore the environment, knowing mother is there to help if needed. In contrast, infants with insecure attachment have learned that their parent is not as available to them and have adapted in one of two ways. In anxious avoidant attachment, the mother has been unresponsive to her infant, and the infant has learned not to rely on her help and support. This infant is not distressed when his mother leaves the room, is just as comfortable with the stranger as with his mother, and, when his mother returns to the room, does not rush to greet her. In anxious ambivalent/resistant attachment, the mother may interact positively with her infant, but she does not respond to the infant's cues. For example, she may ignore the baby when he is trying to get her attention but interacts when the baby is more interested in sleeping than interacting. In anxious ambivalent/resistant attachment, the infant is reluctant to move away from his mother to explore the room, is very distressed when his mother leaves the room, and will not let the stranger comfort him. However when mother returns, the infant's behavior is described as "ambivalent" because he seems to want to approach his mother but also appears angry and resists the mother's attempt to pick him up (Bosma & Gerlsma, 2003).

Although the first three types of attachment differ in the level of security or trust in the relationships, all are organized and coherent ways of responding to a particular situation. The fourth category, disorganized/disoriented attachment, describes infants whose behavior is unpredictable and odd and shows no coherent way of dealing with attachment issues (Hennighausen & Lyons-Ruth, 2010). This category is often linked with parental abuse or neglect and is connected with unmanageable fear. Think about how this pattern would develop. The very person to whom the baby would normally turn when afraid is the same person causing the fear. The babies don't know what to do or where to turn. They cannot organize their behavior because they do not have a predictable environment. They never know what to expect or what is expected of them.

Attachment as a Relationship

Attachment is based on the relationship between two people, each of whom has an impact on the nature of the relationship. The interaction of a particular child and a particular parent creates a unique relationship different from that between any other two people.

The Role of the Mother

Sometimes the literature on attachment makes it sound like an insecure attachment is the fault of the infant's mother because she wasn't sensitive enough or responsive enough. However, the quality of an infant's attachment is the product of a number of different factors working together. Parents don't have to be perfect to have a securely attached

Anxious avoidant attachment An attachment classification in which the infant is not distressed when his mother leaves, is as comfortable with the stranger as with his mother, and does not rush to greet his mother when she returns.

Anxious ambivalent/ resistant attachment An attachment classification in which the infant is reluctant to move away from his mother to explore and is very distressed when she leaves, but when she returns, he approaches her but also angrily resists her attempt to pick him up.

Disorganized/disoriented attachment An attachment classification in which behavior is unpredictable and odd and shows no coherent way of dealing with attachment issues; often linked with parental abuse or neglect.

TABLE 7.2	**Types of attachment**			
Type of attachment	**Security/ organization**	**Safe base for exploration**	**Reunion with caregiver**	**Early mothering**
Secure	Secure/ organized	Explores freely with caregiver present	Seeks out caregiver and is easily soothed by caregiver	Is responsive to infant's needs
Anxious avoidant	Insecure/ organized	Explores with or without caregiver's presence	Does not seek out caregiver	Is emotionally unavailable, dislikes neediness
Anxious ambivalent/ resistant	Insecure/ organized	Stays close to caregiver, doesn't explore freely	Both seeks and rejects contact with caregiver	May be attentive, but not in response to baby's cues or needs
Disorganized/ disoriented	Insecure/ disorganized	May "freeze," explores in a disorganized fashion	May go to caregiver while looking away, shows a dazed expression or fear	Shows intrusiveness, maltreatment, and/or emotional unavailability, confuses or frightens the child

This table shows Ainsworth's four types of attachment with their associated behaviors in the Strange Situation and aspects of mothering that have been related to each type.

SOURCES: Ainsworth (1979); Shamir-Essakow, Ungerer, & Rapee (2005); Sroufe (2005); Sroufe, Egeland, Carlson, & Collins (2005).

infant. There is enough resiliency in both infants and parents that most often the outcome is a positive one.

What could affect the mother's ability to be a sensitive, responsive caregiver to her baby? The factors are remarkably similar to those that help someone through any stressful situation. Remember from Chapter 4 that the transition to becoming a new parent can be a stressful one. Having social, emotional, and material support is important to new mothers because it helps them maintain a positive relationship with their babies. Mothers are more likely to respond positively to their babies when they have the following:

- A positive relationship with their partner
- Adequate economic resources
- Good psychological health (for example, maternal depression has been linked to insecure attachment)
- A history of good care in their own childhood
- An infant who is easy to care for (Cox, Paley, Payne, & Burchinal, 1999; Crockenberg & Leerkes, 2003; Figueiredo, Costa, Pacheco, & Pais, 2009; Martins & Gaffan, 2000)

In 1979, two medical doctors, John Kennell and Marshall H. Klaus, vigorously promoted the importance of early attachment. They presented research they believed demonstrated that newborn human infants must experience close physical, skin-to-skin contact with their mothers within a few hours after birth for the mothers to be able to form a bond with them. This research transformed the way that hospitals treated new mothers and their infants. Rather than being separated, newborns and their mothers were given an opportunity to interact immediately following birth. However, subsequent research failed to support the long-term effect of early contact on attachment

T/F #5

Mothers must have immediate contact with their babies after they are born if a secure attachment is to be formed. *False* for full-term infants (Eyer, 1992; Myers, 1984). When the newborn is healthy, immediate skin-to-skin contact is wonderful for mother and baby but does not determine their emotional attachment to each other. However, the situation is somewhat different for premature infants. When normal attachment processes are disrupted because of the medical care required by premature infants, taking infants out of the incubator to allow mothers to have skin-to-skin contact with their baby does help promote attachment and also improves the baby's development through age 10 (Feldman, Rosenthal, & Eidelman, 2014).

The Role of the Father

Fathers have often been neglected in the research on infant attachment, but it has become clear that infants are capable of forming more than one relationship and that the unique relationship they develop with their fathers plays an important role in their lives (Braungart-Rieker, Courtney, & Garwood, 1999). Some research has shown that fathers are more likely to react sensitively to their sons than to their daughters, and that baby boys are more likely than baby girls to be securely attached to their fathers (Schoppe-Sullivan et al., 2006). However, both boy and girl infants form attachments to both parents during their first year, and the attachment to the father is likely to be as secure as that to the mother (Schneider Rosen & Burke, 1999).

The Role of the Infant

Infants, too, play a role in the type of attachment relationship formed with the parent. Infant temperament is particularly important if the infant is irritable, cries easily and with intensity, and is difficult to soothe. In one study, maternal sensitivity predicted whether the attachment was secure or not, but it was the infant's temperament that predicted the *type* of insecurity an insecurely attached infant exhibited (Susman-Stillman, Kalkose, Egeland, & Waldman, 1996). For instance, at 3 months of age, infants who had lower levels of sociability were more likely to have an avoidant attachment at 6 months of age, and infant irritability predicted anxious ambivalent/resistant attachment.

In addition to temperament, other infant characteristics such as premature birth and neurological problems can affect the way attachment is first formed (Brisch et al., 2005). One factor is a condition called *infantile colic*, in which babies cry inconsolably for long periods of time for no apparent reason. Mothers of colicky infants may interpret the babies' inability to be comforted as a personal rejection, leading them to question their efficacy as a parent (Landgren & Hallström, 2011; Pauli-Pott, Becker, Mertesacker, & Beckmann, 2000). At the very least, infantile colic is exhausting, both emotionally and physically, for all members of the family (Landgren & Hallström, 2011).

All Together Now

Rather than looking only at the parent or only at the baby, researchers are increasingly focusing on the ongoing relationship in which the characteristics and behaviors of the parent and the baby shape each other over time. For example, in one study, when infants in the first 6 months of life had a high level of intense and frequent crying, mothers were less likely to be highly sensitive to their infants by the time they were 6 months old. This combination of factors, in turn, led the infant to have an insecure attachment at 1 year of age (Sroufe, 2005). In other words, the baby's behavior affected the mother's ability to respond sensitively, and this interaction influenced the quality of the attachment

©iStockphoto.com/Zurijeta

Not "bonding," but...Although their research was flawed, the ideas of Kennell and Klaus (1979) about early bonding helped change hospital practices. This mother reflects the joy of being handed her newborn. ■

WEB LINK 7.2
Father's Attachment

relationship. To further complicate the picture, Crockenberg and Leerkes (2003) found that mothers were likely to be less sensitive to these infants only when they were at risk because of poverty, inadequate social support, or a history of parental rejection. Mothers who were *not* at risk were often *more* engaged with their fussy babies.

A way to check your own understanding of the various factors that influence attachment is to see whether you can apply it. Try **Active Learning: Educating Parents.**

Active Learning

Educating Parents

Imagine you are a parent educator. Given what you now know about the formation of attachment, plan a class for new parents to explain what attachment is and how they can promote secure attachment in their baby. To get started, think about how you would define attachment for these new parents. What would you tell them about where attachment comes from and how stable it is? What are the best things parents can do to help ensure their infant will develop a secure attachment? What can parents do for themselves to become effective and loving parents? ∎

The Biology of Attachment

Researchers are uncovering many links between behavior and biology. In the study of attachment, they have looked for neurochemical explanations of the development of adaptive and maladaptive behaviors. Researchers have studied adopted children reared in conditions of severe neglect in orphanages in Romania and Russia (Fries, Ziegler, Kurian, Jacoris, & Pollak, 2005). Many of these children continued to have problems forming secure attachment relationships with their adoptive parents even though their situations had dramatically improved and they now had parents who wanted and loved them very much.

Fries et al. (2005) found that 3 years after they had been adopted, these children had different biochemical responses to social interaction than other children. Children raised by their parents from birth experienced a rise in the neurochemical oxytocin after interacting with their parents. This neurochemical may be linked with a positive feeling that arises in connection with warm social interactions (Carter, 2005). However, previously neglected children did not demonstrate a similar rise in oxytocin following interaction with their adoptive parents. Many also produced very low levels of vasopressin, a neurochemical linked with the ability to recognize individuals as familiar. Children reared in deprived situations sometimes will run to any available adult when distressed rather than to their parents. It is not yet clear whether these chemical responses are set for life or whether they can change with experience.

Attachment and Culture

Remember that Bowlby (1969) thought attachment behaviors were adaptive behaviors that helped ensure the survival of infants. This suggests that we should see attachment in cultures all over the world, and quite a few cross-cultural studies have tested this premise. Many have focused on one of two questions: (1) Is the proportion of secure versus insecure attachments in infants similar from one culture to another? (2) What does a "securely attached" infant look like to mothers in different cultures?

In regard to the first question, cross-cultural research has found that the proportion of infants classified by the Strange Situation as having a secure attachment does not differ very much from one country to another (Posada & Jacobs, 2001; Svanberg, 1998;

van IJzendoorn & Sagi-Schwartz, 2008). Secure infants typically account for about two-thirds of the subjects in a study. What is more likely to differ across cultures is the proportion of infants in the different categories of insecure attachment.

In American and Northern European cultures, the most common insecure category is avoidant attachment, but in Israel, Korea, and Japan it is anxious/ambivalent attachment (Jin, Jacobvitz, Hazen, & Jung, 2012; Svanberg, 1998). Table 7.3 shows a comparison of secure, avoidant, and resistant attachment types in the United States, Japan, Korea, and a larger international sample of infants. Disorganized/disoriented attachment, which is not included on this table, was found in 15% of infants in Korea as well as in North American and Europe (Jin et al., 2012; Lyons-Ruth & Jacobvitz, 2008). In Japan, research on attachment has been complicated by the Japanese concept of *amae*, an emotional interdependence between a caregiver and child encouraged by the Japanese culture but not identical to the Western concept of attachment (Rothbaum, Kakinuma, Nagaoka, & Azuma, 2007). This has led Nakagawa, Lamb, and Miyaki (1992) to question whether a measure such as the Strange Situation, which has been used primarily with middle-class Western samples, is valid as a cross-cultural measure.

That leads us to our second question. Rather than asking where children in different cultures fall in Ainsworth's classification scheme, we can ask what parents in different cultures think a securely attached infant looks like. In the United States, mothers are more likely to associate secure attachment in their infants with autonomy and self-determination. In other words, a child is seen as secure if she can move away from her mother and play independently. Mothers in Japan are more likely to see their children as secure if they show behaviors that put them into harmony with others: accommodating to other people, behaving well, and cooperating (Rothbaum et al., 2007). In addition, Japanese mothers are more likely to see their children's unreasonable demands for attention (such as crying every hour through the night while all their needs have already been met) as a need for closeness or interdependence, whereas American mothers tend to see this behavior as testing the limits and asserting one's self.

Likewise, although sensitive mothering is related to secure attachment in most cultures, the definition of sensitivity may vary. For example, Carlson and Harwood (2003) found Puerto Rican mothers more likely than mothers in Boston to be physically controlling of their infants. In the United States, this type of physical control has been seen as insensitive, but for Puerto Rican babies, this type of physical control is a positive value in their culture because it leads to respectful behavior, which is highly valued.

This research reminds us of how difficult it is to search for universal developmental processes when they can take so many forms as we move from one culture to another.

TABLE 7.3	Distributions of infant–mother attachment classification in diverse cultures		
	Avoidant A	Secure B	Resistant C
Sapporo, Japan	0 (0%)	41 (68%)	19 (32%)
Baltimore, USA	22 (21%)	70 (67%)	13 (12%)
Global Sample	23 (21%)	1,294 (65%)	273 (14%)
Taegu, Korea	1 (1%)	66 (78%)	18 (21%)

Although there are similar percentages of securely attached infants in many cultures, the type of anxious or insecure attachment differs between countries.

SOURCE: Jin, Jacobvitz, Hazen, & Jung (2012).

We always need to guard against assuming that the way things work in one culture will describe how they work somewhere else.

Continuity and Discontinuity in Attachment

In this section we examine the long-term effects of attachment in infancy, and we also look at other factors that limit or change the impacts of early attachment on later development.

Long-Term Outcomes of Infant Attachment

Research has shown long-term effects of security of attachment in infancy, as Bowlby's concept of internal working models would predict. Securely attached infants have more internal resources with which to cope with difficult events. In their early years, their relationship with their parents serves to soothe and modulate their reactions to frightening or other arousing events. This soothing is then internalized so that at an older age the child or adolescent is able to soothe himself when needed. Table 7.4 gives you some examples of what is going on in the minds of children with different types of internal working models.

One reason security of attachment in infancy can predict later outcomes is that there is a good deal of continuity in attachment styles over time. Several factors contribute to this continuity. Most families do not change drastically over time, so characteristics of parenting remain stable and the patterns of attachment and adaptation developed in infancy continue to be reinforced by later experiences. Also, as we have already described, children usually continue to behave in ways that cause their later relationships to replicate their earlier ones.

TABLE 7.4   Internal working models

Type	Internal working model
Secure	• I can trust and rely on others. • I am lovable, capable, significant, and worthwhile. • My world is safe.
Anxious avoidant	• Other people are unavailable and rejecting. • I have to protect myself. • If I deny my needs, I will not be rejected. • If I do what is expected of me, I will not be rejected. • If I take care of others and deny my own needs, I will be loved.
Anxious ambivalent/ resistant	• Others are unpredictable, sometimes loving and protective, sometimes hostile and rejecting. • I don't know what to expect—I am anxious and angry. • I cannot explore—I may miss an opportunity for love and affection. • If I can read others and get them to respond, I will get my needs met.
Disorganized/ disoriented	• My caregiver, at times, seems overwhelmed by me and, at other times, seems very angry with me. • Others are abusive—neglectfully, physically, emotionally, and/or sexually. • I am unable to get my needs met. I don't know how to protect myself.

Think about how having each type of internal working model of attachment would affect a child's approach to and interaction with new people.

SOURCE: Public Health Agency of Canada (2003).

However, what happens when a child's life circumstances *do* change? For instance, what happens when a mother who had developed a secure attachment with her baby becomes preoccupied with a bad marital relationship or becomes depressed? Ample evidence shows that new life circumstances can change a secure attachment to an insecure one and vice versa (Weinfield, Whaley, & Egeland, 2004). Moss and colleagues studied attachment in children at age 3-1/2 and assessed their attachment again 2 years later (Moss, Cyr, Bureau, Tarabulsy, & Dubois-Comtois, 2005). The majority maintained the same attachment style, but children whose attachment style changed from secure to insecure and/or disorganized/disoriented were more likely to have experienced events such as parental hospitalization or death, decreased quality of mother-child interaction, and decreased marital satisfaction of their parents.

A child's attachment also can change for the better if the parents take part in interventions designed for parents of infants with insecure attachments. These programs can and do change parenting patterns and allow for changes in attachment over time (for example, see Bernard et al., 2012). Therefore, it is clear that infants' earliest attachment experiences do not doom those who begin with insecure attachment and are not a guarantee for those who begin with secure attachment. Even though insecurely attached infants are at increased risk of psychological problems compared to securely attached infants, a variety of factors, including a positive relationship with some other caring adult or the child's own characteristics, can help promote positive development.

The Effects of Later Experiences

Even if attachment style remains consistent as children grow and develop, many other life circumstances may affect and moderate the effects of early attachment experiences. As Alan Sroufe and his colleagues have found, later experiences interact with early attachment relationships to help influence adult functioning. In 1974 and 1975, they recruited 257 low-income pregnant women for a longitudinal study of their children from birth through age 26 (Sroufe, Carlson, & Shulman, 1993). In early research reports, Sroufe and his colleagues reported straightforward effects of secure attachment in infancy on later development. Securely attached infants became children who were more competent in their interactions with peers, were more self-reliant, and had better self-control (Sroufe et al., 1993).

However, as the children got older, the picture became much more complicated. For example, while the researchers did not find a *direct* link between early attachment and the ability to have intimate, romantic relationships in early adulthood, there was an indirect link, mediated through subsequent experiences in the person's life. Although secure attachment in infancy prepares the child for later positive peer relationships, the child's history with peer relationships independently predicted some aspects of adult relationships more clearly than early attachment history, and the combination of early attachment and later experiences with peers was even more predictive of some aspects of later romantic relationships. Each stage provides the foundation for the next, but experiences at each successive stage also change the nature and direction of a child's development (Van Ryzen, Carlson, & Sroufe, 2012).

Attachment Disorders

Only a rare few children have such difficulties in all their attachment relationships that they require intervention (Balbernie, 2010). The *DSM-5* (APA, 2013) recognizes two such conditions, reactive attachment disorder and disinhibited social engagement disorder. Both are based on caregiving experiences in infancy such as abuse and neglect that interfere with the formation of secure relationships.

A child with reactive attachment disorder (RAD) does not seem able to form any attachment. The child is withdrawn with caregivers and shows disturbance in both

T/F #6
If a child has developed an insecure attachment to a parent, that child can still become securely attached later in her life. *True*

JOURNAL ARTICLE 7.2
Reactive Attachment Disorder

Reactive attachment disorder (RAD) A disorder marked by an inability to form attachments to caregivers.

Disinhibited social engagement disorder An attachment disorder in which children approach strangers indiscriminately, not differentiating between attachment figures and other people.

social and emotional functioning (APA, 2013). A child with disinhibited social engagement disorder is indiscriminate in whom he goes to. He does not seem to have any special relationship with his caregiver, and his reaction is the same whether he is interacting with a stranger or someone he knows well (APA, 2013). It has been argued that this type of behavior is actually adaptive for children who have been abandoned or mistreated, because children who have no effective parenting may do best when they approach a broad range of adults for help (Balbernie, 2010). The problem is that these children do not change their behavior even when adopted into caring families, and this can cause problems if the adoptive parents do not understand the cause.

Much research has focused on children raised in the deplorable conditions found in orphanages in Romania. In the 1980s, the country's leader, Nicolae Ceausescu, wanted to increase the population and therefore abolished access to contraception and abortion and forced women to continue having children beyond the ability of their families to care for them. As a result, over 100,000 children were sent to Romanian orphanages that were not prepared to care for their physical, mental, or emotional needs (Kaler & Freeman, 1994). One study reported that an individual child would be cared for by as many as 17 different caregivers in a single week (Zeanah et al., 2005). After reading about how an infant forms a secure attachment with a caregiver, you can see why children in these orphanages could not form attachments. They never had the consistent, sensitive, or responsive caregiving necessary for this bond to form.

One group of researchers developed a foster care program that could accommodate some of the institutionalized children (Smyke et al., 2012). They compared the incidence of reactive attachment disorder in those who remained in the institutions to those in foster care and to a control group who had never been institutionalized. Institutionalized infants and toddlers between the ages of 6 and 30 months had more signs of RAD than the control group. However, for those who were then moved into foster care, the incidence of RAD declined to the same level as the noninstitutionalized control group. The researchers also assessed the children for indications of disinhibited social engagement disorder and found that these behaviors also declined, but remained higher than the level of the control group. It appears that moving infants to a more secure environment improves attachment, but there may be limits, at least in the early years of a child's life. Families that adopt children with attachment disorders need to recognize that much hard work will be needed to try to reverse the negative effect of the child's earlier experiences.

Although the eventual outcome for many Romanian orphans who were adopted was positive, it is much better to try to prevent and/or treat attachment disorders in high-risk populations, such as children living in poverty or in abusive families, than to try to fix the problem after it occurs. Bakermans-Kranenburg, van IJzendoorn, and Juffer (2003) found that the most effective therapies focused on developing the mother's sensitivity to her baby. As maternal sensitivity increased, so did infant-mother attachment. Although only a few programs to date have targeted the sensitivity of both mothers and fathers, those that did found an even greater effect than those that intervened only with the mother.

Romanian orphans. The terrible conditions in Romanian orphanages created lasting problems, even for children who were eventually adopted. The inability of these children to form emotional attachments was one of the most serious ones. ■

> **Check Your Understanding**
>
> 1. What are Bowlby's stages of attachment?
> 2. Describe the Strange Situation.
> 3. How does early attachment have an effect on later relationships?
> 4. What are reactive attachment disorder (RAD) and disinhibited social engagement disorder?

Contexts of Development

The primary context for infants' social-emotional development is the family, but other influences such as nonfamily care, culture, media, and peer relationships all play a role in their lives. In this part of the chapter, we examine some of the life experiences that shape the development of infants and toddlers.

Family Relationships

"Few would dispute that the family is the basic social unit in the organization of human society and a primary context for the development and socialization of society's children" (McLoyd, Hill, & Dodge, 2005, p. 3), yet the definition of family may differ widely from one cultural setting to another. For instance, in southern India, a woman marries all of her husband's brothers, and her children are each assigned to one of the brothers, not necessarily the biological father (Coontz, 2000). In Micronesia, an Ifaluk family consists of two sets of parents: biological and adoptive. Anyone can ask a pregnant woman for permission to adopt her baby. The baby will live with its mother until age 3 when it will move in with the adoptive family, with both families being involved with the child's upbringing (DeLoache & Gottlieb, 2000).

Families differ in many ways within the United States as well. The U.S. Census Bureau (2008a) defines a family as any two individuals living together who are related by birth, marriage, or adoption. Many people think of a family as being a husband and wife living with their biological and/or adopted children, or what is called a nuclear family, but a family can have a number of different structures. There are single-parent families, multigenerational families, families with two same-sex partners, and families formed by adoption, divorce, or remarriage. Coontz (2000) has concluded that the major difference between current and earlier levels of diversity in family form is not "the *existence* of diversity but by its increasing *legitimation*" (p. 28). Diverse forms of family life have been increasingly recognized as acceptable ways to raise children.

Divorce

You may have heard the statistic that half of all marriages in the United States end in divorce. How children understand and react to their parents' divorce will depend in large part on their age. For that reason, we talk about this topic in several chapters, each time focusing on age-specific information. Most of the research on family transitions has studied school-age children and adolescents. Only limited research on the effects of divorce and separation has been conducted with infants (Clarke-Stewart, Vandell, McCartney, Owen, & Booth, 2000; Tornello et al., 2013), despite the fact that a considerable number of very young children are exposed to these events. Nearly 20% of first marriages end in separation or divorce within the first 5 years (Tornello et al., 2013) so, if there are children in the marriage, the chances are high that they will be infants or toddlers.

Infants and toddlers do not understand what is happening when parents separate. Instead they resonate to their parents' distressed feelings and to disruptions in their normal routines and this can result in a number of behavioral problems. These can include

7.4

What other life experiences shape infants' development?

Nuclear family A family consisting of a husband, a wife, and their biological and/or adopted children.

T/F #7

Infants are too young to be affected by parental divorce. *False*

anger and aggression, separation anxiety, eating or sleep problems, or loss of recent developmental achievements such as toilet training or language development (Cohen & the American Academy of Pediatrics Committee on Psychosocial Aspects of Child and Family Health, 2002; Kalter, 1990).

Given the central role attachment plays in infant development, it is not surprising that the limited research conducted has focused on the impact of marital transitions on attachment security. It is not uncommon for children whose parents are separated or divorced to spend some amount of time with the nonresident parent, but overnight separations from the primary caregiver can be stressful for an infant (George, Solomon, & McIntosh, 2011). We ordinarily think that maintaining contact with both parents following a divorce is a good thing for a child, but based on what we know about attachment theory, we could argue that infants who are still in the process of forming an attachment relationship should not spend a lot of time away from their primary caregiver because it can contribute to attachment insecurity. On the other hand, infants can form qualitatively different attachments to multiple caregivers, so frequent overnight visits with the nonresident parent give the young child the chance to do this and in this way such visits may be beneficial to the child.

To test these ideas, Tornello et al. (2013) looked at infants and toddlers from low-income, primarily racial/ethnic minority families. In this sample of fragile families, they report that 6.9% of infants under the age of 1 year and 5.3% of toddlers ages 1 to 3 spent an average of one overnight per week with their nonresident parents. This research found that frequent overnight visits (at least one night a week) with nonresident fathers were associated with attachment insecurity among infants but the association was not clear for toddlers. This suggests that an attachment relationship is more vulnerable when it is in the early stages of formation, as attachment theory would predict (McIntosh, Smyth, Kelaher, Wells, & Long, 2010). The percentage of infants classified as insecurely attached was 43% for the frequent overnight group, 25% for infants who had only day contact with their fathers, and 16% for infants who had fewer than one overnight visit per week. However, more frequent overnights were not related to adjustment problems at older ages.

None of this means nonresident fathers should not have contact with their infants. Rather the recommendation is that the visitation of the nonresident parent should be "frequent, short, on a very regular and stable basis" and should take place in surroundings familiar to the infant (Ram, Finzi, & Cohen, 2002, p. 46). As the infant gets older, they can better tolerate separation from their primary caregivers, and overnight visits will cause less distress.

Is the effect on attachment security of a parental divorce in infancy specific to the parental relationship, or does it generalize to all future relationships, as the idea of an internal working model would suggest? There is evidence that people who have secure attachment relationships with parents also tend to have secure attachment relationships with romantic partners (Sibley & Overall, 2008), but the different experiences we have across types of relationships could result in qualitatively different working models. In a test of these ideas, people who were younger when their parents divorced were more likely to have an insecure attachment to their parents than people whose parents had divorced when they were older, with the highest level of insecurity for those who experienced parental divorce during the first few years of life (Fraley & Heffernan, 2013). The effects of parental divorce were much stronger for the future relationship with parents than it was for romantic relationships, suggesting that we can form different working models for different relationships in our lives.

Three out of 4 people who divorce will remarry (Coleman, Ganong, & Warzinik, 2007), and when there are children are involved, stepfamilies form. In fact, 1 out of every 3 American children will live in a stepfamily at some point during their childhood or adolescence (Braithwaite, Schrodt, & DiVerniero, 2009). Parents who remarry should remember that young children need consistency and stability in their relationships and

Stepfamilies Families in which there are two adults and at least one child from a previous relationship of one of the adults; there also may be biological children of the couple.

environments. With some effort, this consistency can be maintained even while parents' relationships are undergoing change. Recall that infants can form multiple attachment relationships, and the addition of new attachment figures does not necessarily harm the quality of existing attachments.

Grandparents Raising Grandchildren

According to the 2010 U.S. Census, almost 7.8 million children under the age of 18 are raised by their grandparents or other relatives and those under the age of 6 are more likely to live with a grandparent than older children. About 20% of these grandparents raising grandchildren live below the poverty line (American Association of Retired Persons, 2014).

Even when grandparents are not the main caregivers for their grandchildren, their role has been expanding to fill gaps in single-parent and divorced families or families in which both parents work outside the home (Bengtson, 2001; Dunn, Fergusson, & Maughan, 2006). When parents are still in their children's lives and are close to their own parents, then grandparent-grandchildren relationships are likely to be close as well, with help going both ways. The children help the grandparents, and the grandparents care for their grandchildren (Dunn et al., 2006).

Grandparents become their grandchildren's main caretakers for many reasons: death of the parents, illness, incarceration, drug addiction, or other difficulties that prevent parents from filling their parental role (Dunifon, 2013). Sometimes grandparents are formally named as the major caretakers by child welfare agencies, but more often the arrangements are informal. In these cases, the agencies that help families find resources may not know about the arrangements so they are not able to help the grandparents in this way (Raphel, 2008). Without formal legal rights, grandparents can be hindered in taking care of their grandchildren's needs. For instance, they cannot give permission for medical care and may have difficulty enrolling the child in school (AARP, 2014).

Although grandparent-headed families are marginalized, some programs are specifically designed to help them. For example, in Hartford, Connecticut, a program called the Community Renewal Team provides help to 24 families in which grandparents are raising their grandchildren (AARP, 2014). Housing is provided with rent on a sliding scale, along with free after-school child care on a campus separated from the dangerous neighborhood that surrounds it. A variety of services are offered both to the grandparents and to the children. Not only does this program benefit the families participating in it, but it also saves taxpayers the money that otherwise would be spent placing the children in foster care.

Adoptive Families

In 2008, approximately 136,000 children were adopted in the United States (Child Welfare Information Gateway, 2011). Infants under 2 account for only 6% of adoptions; another 9% are toddlers and preschoolers (Vandivere, Malm, & Radel, 2009). This compares to the 60% of adoptees who are between the ages of 5 and 12.

Professionals who study and work with adoptive families point to the value of developing the "family story" for adopted children. Parents can begin to tell children the story of their adoption, in simple terms and in a loving context, even before they can really understand it. This sets the stage to fill in details as the child grows and is able to understand more. When the details are difficult, the parents walk a fine line between "honoring the birthparent and acknowledging hardships and limitations" (Rampage, Eovaldi, Ma, Weigel-Foy, 2003, p. 217). About 14% of adoptions are intercountry adoptions. Respecting the child's cultural origins becomes especially important in these families.

Most adoptions today are **open adoptions**, in which the child and the birth and adoptive families have access to each other, although the amount of information shared and the frequency of contact between the adopted child and the biological parents or other

AUDIO LINK 7.3
Grandparents Raising Grandchildren

T/F #8
Most adopted children are adopted as infants.
False

Open adoptions Adoptions in which the children and their biological and adoptive families have access to each other.

Multicultural adoption. About 14% of U.S. adoptions involve children who come from another country. Whenever an adoptive child's cultural background is different from the adoptive parents, it is important that the parents try to honor the child's cultural heritage. ∎

Foster care The temporary placement of children in a family that is not their own because of unhealthy situations within their birth family.

WEB LINK 7.3
International Adoptions

WEB LINK 7.4
Foster Care

relatives are very variable (Siegel, 2012). In one study, adoptive parents were interviewed about their attitudes about their open adoption of an infant at the time of the adoption and 20 years later (Siegel, 2013). None regretted having an open adoption, and nearly half wished it was even more open.

Foster Care

In some circumstances children must be removed from their homes for their own well-being. They may have experienced abuse or neglect, or their parent may be unable to care for them because of mental or physical illness, incarceration, substance abuse, or even death (American Academy of Child and Adolescent Psychiatry [AACAP], 2005). When there are no alternative caregivers within the family, these children are likely to be placed in the foster care system with a foster family that receives financial support from the state. Everyone involved in this placement knows this is a temporary situation. The child may return home, move to another foster home or institution, or eventually be legally released for adoption. Currently there are slightly less than 400,000 children in foster care in the United States (Adoption and Foster Care Analysis and Reporting System, 2013).

The temporary nature of a foster care placement brings particular challenges for infants and toddlers who need consistent care to promote development. Experiencing child abuse or neglect and then a change in caregivers when the child is removed from the home contributes to higher levels of disorganized attachment among infants and toddlers in the child welfare system (Dozier, Zeanah, & Bernard, 2013). Toddlers are more likely to reject their temporary caregivers, which can, in turn, elicit rejection from even well-meaning caregivers. The more changes in caregiving the child experiences, the more likely the child is to develop difficulties with self-control and inhibition (Lewis, Dozier, Ackerman, & Sepulveda-Kozakowski, 2007). Foster parents vary in how committed they are to a particular child. Children who experience a lack of commitment from caregivers are more likely to see themselves negatively and have problem behaviors (Dozier et al., 2013).

Foster parents must not only be able to fully commit to an infant or toddler in their care, but also be ready to support the child's return to the birth parents. The participation of foster parents in supervised visits with the birth parents is important to help the infant make a smooth transition between homes. Ideally the foster parent would remain involved with the infant as a "foster aunt, godmother" to prevent the abrupt changes that are so detrimental in the child's first years (Dozier et al., 2013, p. 169).

Infant Development in Contexts Beyond the Family

Infants spend most of their time within the family context, but they are not completely isolated from other influences. Many infants and toddlers spend at least part of their day in the care of other people while their parents work. The larger world also plays a role through the influence of children's cultural surroundings. An infant's exposure to media should be limited because face-to-face interactions with a live person are much more important for development, but we can't ignore the impact of this context on early development. The peer context in infancy and toddlerhood is different from what it will become later in development, but in this section we look at the early roots of peer relations as they are laid down in the first couple of years.

Nonparental Child Care

Reading all this information about mother-infant attachment may make you wonder whether mothers are the only ones who can or should take care of infants and young children. One argument made against the use of nonmaternal child care is that the quality of the child's attachment to the mother might suffer. Although some parents are concerned that attachment to a child care provider will undermine the child's attachment to them, infants are capable of forming more than one secure attachment.

The issue of early child care has been a controversial topic. Today the United States is one of only a few Western countries that do not provide universal, publicly funded child care for their citizens. One reason is a continuing belief that women should be at home taking care of their young children, but the reality is that over half of married mothers with children under the age of 6 are in the workforce (Cohany & Sok, 2007). Despite what some people think, most women work today out of necessity. Although many have jobs they enjoy and that give them a sense of identity and feelings of accomplishment, their paychecks are necessary because their partners' salaries are too low to adequately support a family, their partners are unemployed, or the woman is the head of the household.

For these women, child care may consist of care by relatives, a nanny or babysitter, a day care home, or a day care center. Figure 7.1 shows the historical rates of maternal employment. As you can see, the likelihood of a woman's being in the workforce increases as her children get older. The availability of child care is one important factor influencing whether a woman is employed outside the home. Figure 7.2 shows the types of child care used by mothers of young children. Each type has its strengths and weaknesses.

Figure 7.2 shows that about two-thirds of infants and toddlers are cared for by their parents or another relative, but what do we know about other care arrangements? In 1991, the National Institute of Child Health and Human Development (NICHD) began

T/F #9
Most mothers of infants and toddlers who work outside the home do so out of necessity. *True*

© Ariel Skelley/Corbis

Daycare. Research has found that high-quality child care does not interfere with a young child's secure attachment to his or her parents. Children can form secure attachments to more than one person. This is fortunate because most women who work outside the home do so out of necessity. ∎

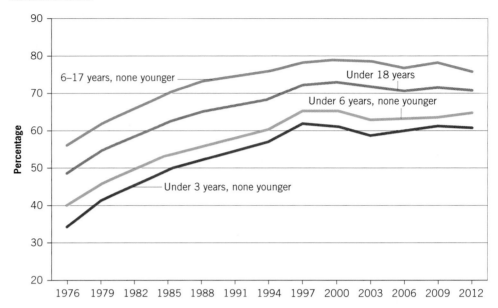

FIGURE 7.1 U.S. women in the workforce

The number of mothers employed outside the home has steadily increased over the last 3 decades, until quite recently, but mothers with the youngest children have the lowest rates of labor force participation.

SOURCE: Bureau of Labor Statistics, Current Population Survey. Graph by the Women's Bureau, U.S. Department of Labor (1976–2012). http://www.dol.gov/wb/stats/facts_over_time.htm

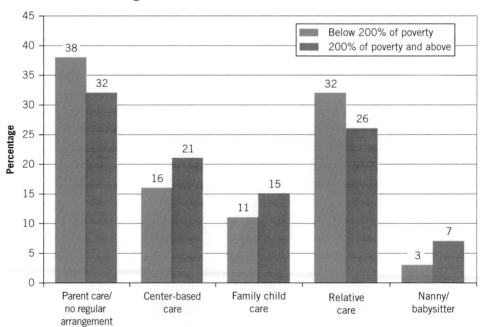

FIGURE 7.2 Child care arrangements used by U.S. mothers of children from age 0 to 3, 2013

Mothers of infants and toddlers need to rely on a variety of child care arrangements to care for their children while they are at work.

SOURCE: As appears in *Better for Babies: A Study in State Infant and Toddler Child Care Policies,* Stephanie Schmit and Hannah Matthews (2013, August). Data based on *Children in Low-Income Families Are Less Likely to Be in Center-Based Care,* Jeffrey Capizzano and Gina Adams, Urban Institute (2003).

a large longitudinal research project at 10 locations across the United States designed to examine the effects of early nonmaternal child care on child development. It found that insecure attachment to the mother was first and foremost linked to insensitive mothering rather than to whether the child was in nonmaternal care. However, three factors magnified the negative effect of insensitive mothering: (1) The quality of the nonmaternal care also was poor, (2) the infant spent more than 10 hours a week in care, or (3) the infant had experienced more than one child care arrangement within his or her first 15 months (Belsky, 2005; NICHD Early Child Care Research Network, 1997). Interestingly, in a different study, infants with difficult temperaments were *more* likely to have secure attachment with their mother when they spent *more* of their time in out-of-home care (McKim, Cramer, Stuart, & O'Connor, 1999). Perhaps when mothers got a break from these difficult infants, they were able to provide the care they did give with more enthusiasm.

Clearly the quality of child care can have an impact on attachment and emotional development overall, but what is high-quality care? In 2013, Child Care Aware of America surveyed state program requirements and how well programs complied with these requirements. The benchmarks used to rate the states are found in Table 7.5 on the next page.

WEB LINK 7.5
Child Care

Although there are high-quality child care settings that meet these standards, many others have been found inadequate for providing for even the basic needs of children, especially children from low-income families (Forry et al., 2012; Shonkoff & Phillips, 2000). Child Care Aware of America graded each state on their benchmarks and found that no state earned an A or B, 10 states earned a C, 21 earned a D, and the remaining 20 states failed (Child Care Aware of America, 2013b).

The National Association for the Education of Young Children recommends that there be one caregiver to every four infants between the ages of 6- to 18-months. However, each state sets its own standards for how many children may be cared for in a group and how many caregivers must be there. State regulations for adult:child ratios range from 1:3 to 1:6 for infants 6 to 9 months old and between 1:3 and 1:9 for 18-month-olds (Child Care Aware of America, 2013a). If you have ever cared for just one infant, you know what a difficult job it can be. The goal for high-quality care is to keep this ratio as low as possible.

Early childhood educators earn less than parking lot attendants, cooks, and cashiers and child care teachers earn about one-third of the salary of a public school kindergarten teacher, although both have a similar level of education (Porter, 2012). Consequently in many child care centers, staff turnover is a great problem. The average annual turnover rate for teaching staff in child care settings is 30% (Porter, 2012), which gives child care one of the highest rates of turnover of any profession. When child care workers receive a living wage and health care benefits, they stay longer at their jobs (Shonkoff & Phillips, 2000). This is important because consistency of care allows a caregiver to get to know the infant and the infant to become attached to the caregiver. High rates of staff turnover also have a negative impact on children's social, emotional, and language development (Korjenevitch & Dunifon, 2010).

The reality is that many parents of infants and toddlers need to work outside the home, and the availability of high-quality care of their children is essential. For this reason, we need to continue to build a well-qualified workforce in early care and education that can provide the consistent, stimulating, and warm environment in which young children can thrive.

How Parents Transmit Culture to Infants

How do children learn about the culture into which they are born? Certainly some cultural expectations are explicitly taught to children, but much cultural information is conveyed in more subtle ways. One way in which cultures vary is along the continuum from individualism to collectivism. U.S. values are based on rugged

TABLE 7.5	Benchmarks used to assess state requirements for child care programs and oversight of compliance.

Program benchmarks:

1. A comprehensive background check is required, including using fingerprints to check state and FBI records, checking the child abuse registry and checking the sex offender registry.

2. Child care center directors are required to have a bachelor's degree or higher in early childhood education or a related field.

3. Lead teachers are required to have a Child Development Associate (CDA) credential, college courses in early childhood education or an associate degree in early childhood education or a related field.

4. Child care center staff are required to have an orientation and initial training in child development, child guidance, child abuse prevention, emergency preparation, licensing regulations, learning activities, health and safety, safe sleep, shaken baby prevention, CPR, and first aid.

5. Child care center staff are required to have 24 hours or more of annual training in child development, child guidance, child abuse prevention, emergency preparation, licensing regulations, learning activities, health and safety, safe sleep, shaken baby prevention, CPR, and first aid.

6. Child care centers are required to plan learning activities that address language/literacy, dramatic play, active play, cognitive development, self-help skills, creative activities, limited screen time, social development, emotional development and culturally sensitive activities.

7. Child care centers are required to follow recommended health practices in 10 specific areas: hand washing/diapering/toileting, nutritious meals and snacks, immunizations, exclusion of ill children, universal health precautions, administration of medications, toxic/hazardous substances, sanitation, weekend/evening care, and incident reporting.

8. Child care centers are required to follow recommended safety practices in 10 specific areas: SIDS prevention, discipline/guidance, fire drills, outdoor playground surfaces, emergency plans, electrical hazards, water hazards, supervision, transportation supervision, and firearms (prohibited or access controlled). Corporal punishment is prohibited.

9. Child care centers are required to encourage parent involvement, including regular communication with parents, total parental access to the center and to all written policies.

10. Staff:child ratio requirements comply with NAEYC* accreditation standards for seven age groups.

11. Group size requirements comply with NAEYC accreditation standards in seven age groups.

Oversight benchmarks:

1. Child care centers are inspected at least four times per year, including visits by licensing, health, and fire personnel.

2. Inspection and complaint reports are available to parents on the Internet.

3. Programs to licensing staff ratio does not exceed 50:1.

4. Licensing staff have a bachelor's degree in early childhood education or a related field.

SOURCE: Child Care Aware of America (2013). http://www.naccrra.org/sites/default/files/default_site_pages/2013/wcdb_benchmarks_040813.pdf.

NOTE: *NAEYC is the National Association for the Education of Young Children.

individualism. Our heroes often are those who are self-made and managed to rise from deprived circumstances to become successful, and people are admired for being independent and autonomous. In other cultures, the emphasis is more on an obligation to those around you: your family or your group, however you define it. These values are communicated from parent to child even before the child can speak. For example, in many collectivistic cultures around the world, the value of connection to others is communicated in infancy because babies are constantly kept close to the

Cultural differences in feeding. Babies in individualistic cultures are often encouraged to try to feed themselves, but babies in collectivist cultures are more likely to be fed in a way that emphasizes that eating is an opportunity to enjoy family closeness. Do you see how these different cultural values are reflected in these pictures? ■

mother's body, sleeping with her while she anticipates the baby's needs. Contrast this with individualistic cultures in which babies are expected to sleep through the night in their own bed and are praised for soothing themselves when they cry (Greenfield, Keller, Fuligni, & Maynard, 2003).

Robin Harwood was interested in how the individualistic values of U.S. society and the more collectivist values of Puerto Rican society might be taught even to infants through the way their mothers interacted with them. Harwood and her colleagues set out to see whether the feeding practices of mothers in the two cultures reflected different value systems (Miller & Harwood, 2002). Think about the scene you expect to see when a mother feeds her 1-year-old baby. If you were born in the United States, most likely you have an image of the baby sitting in a high chair. The mother spoon-feeds the baby but often lets the baby take the spoon to begin learning to feed herself, usually with messy and somewhat hilarious results, as shown in the leftmost photo on this page. She may also put some "finger food," like dry cereal, on the tray for the baby to take on her own. Contrast this picture with that of the typical Puerto Rican mother and baby. This mother feeds the baby to make sure the baby eats well, with the feeding remaining under her control and not the baby's, as shown in the photo at the right.

What subtle message is each mother giving her baby from the earliest days of life? The American mother is saying, "Be independent. Learn to do things on your own separately from me. We will watch and praise you." The Puerto Rican mother is saying, "Be close to family. Listen to and cooperate with your parents. Enjoy your food in the context of family love and expectations for proper behavior." Thus, cultural values are translated directly into parenting techniques. Babies are learning the values of their culture even with their first bites of food.

Although we have emphasized the comparison between individualism and collectivism in different cultures in this particular example, it is clear that all people have both individual and social needs and all cultures acknowledge both aspects of life. However, they may do so in different ways. For example, in Western cultures parents encourage their children to interact socially because the children choose to do so. In

Latino cultures, parents expect children to interact socially as an expression of the obligation to promote the well-being of the group as a whole (Raeff, Greenfield, & Quiroz, 2000).

Development of Peer Relationships

From infancy onward, there is something qualitatively different and special about children's interactions with other children their own age. When a child interacts with adults and even older children, the older people are largely in charge of the interactions, both because they are more powerful and because they can keep the interaction going in spite of the young child's less-developed social abilities. Peer interactions are different because children must work out how to maintain the relationship themselves, at their own level of social and cognitive functioning. Another reason the relationship between peers is special is that peers are often more fun and exciting (Dunn, 2004). Mom and Dad will tire of "chase me" games long before two toddlers do. Preschoolers may share a deep interest in dinosaurs that the adults in their lives encourage but do not necessarily share.

What is the youngest age at which children are able to interact in a meaningful way with peers? While most people are very aware that preschoolers are able to play with other children, they often believe infants and toddlers are not yet capable of real peer relationships. However, there is some evidence that even before age 2, infants can form relationships with other children. Babies are often very interested when they see other babies, smiling at them and trying to touch them (Hay, Caplan, & Nash, 2009). Near the end of their first year of life, infants want to be near other young children, seek them out, and engage in a number of behaviors such as offering their toys that are meant to draw them into a social interaction (Williams, Ontai, & Mastergeorge, 2010). By their second year, infants bring reciprocity into their peer interactions as they imitate what other children are doing.

As young children develop language, they add this new ability to their interactions. Language allows them to begin to coordinate their activities in a more cooperative way, planning what they will do together or solving problems as they arise (Eckerman & Didow, 1996; Howes & Matheson, 1992). Language also indicates that children are developing the ability to use symbols, and this ability leads to pretend play. Now, instead of using just their bodies to imitate each other's behavior ("I see you jump and it looks like fun, so I jump"), they can begin to arrange a tea party, with pretend tea and cookies, or other make-believe games.

In a variety of ways, adult caregivers help infants and toddlers develop early social skills in a cultural context by scaffolding their social behaviors (Williams, Mastergeorge, & Ontai, 2010). This scaffolding can take a direct, adult-centered form, such as moving an infant away from another infant or telling the child what the social rule is, and it also can be more child-centered. A child-centered approach follows the lead of the child so, for instance, a caregiver might help an infant who is looking at peers to approach a peer group and join it or might express to the infant what another

T/F #10

Infants are not capable of forming relationships with other children before the age of 2.

False

© Rebecca Drobis,/Blend Images/Corbis

Early social relationships. By the time they are toddlers, children are able to engage in meaningful social interactions with each other. They begin to enjoy following each other's behavior while they are playing. ∎

child is feeling (for example, "Curtis was playing with that toy and now he seems angry that you tried to take it away from him").

All relationships have their conflicts, and relationships with peers are no exception. Adults who work with toddlers know "Mine!" and "No!" are two of their favorite words. Especially when these words are linked with hitting or biting, adults are not likely to see them in a positive light. However, as we noted at the beginning of this chapter, being able to use these words reflects some positive aspects of toddlers' development. Claiming toys indicates a developing sense of self as an individual (Levine, 1983; Rochat, 2011). In addition, conflicts are not just about possessing objects. They also reflect a new social awareness. Research has shown that toddler conflicts are reciprocal in nature (Hay, Hurst, Waters, & Chadwick, 2011; Hay & Ross, 1982)—that is, "If you take my toy, the next time I see you, I will take yours." This becomes part of the way that children learn how to make friends. If you want someone to play with you, you will not succeed if you take his toy.

The nature of children's attachment relationships with their parents is another important influence on their ability to develop close relationships with peers. Toddlers and preschoolers who have secure attachments to their parents receive more positive responses from peers (Fagot, 1997). In one large study, children who had secure attachments to their mothers at age 3 were more likely to have high-quality friendships in third grade (McElwain, Booth-LaForce, Lansford, Wu, & Dyer, 2008), while insecurely attached children became increasingly withdrawn from their peers (Booth-LaForce & Oxford, 2008). It appears that children who have secure attachments to their parents have a higher sense of self-worth, and this translates into more confident interactions with peers (Booth-LaForce et al., 2006). However, relationships with peers also play an independent role in children's development, and the quality of relationships they develop will further affect many aspects of their lives.

Check Your Understanding

1. How can divorcing or separated parents minimize negative effects on infants and toddlers?
2. What is an open adoption?
3. How do parents transmit culture to infants?
4. What do we know about the effect of media exposure on infants and toddlers?
5. How do infants and toddlers develop peer relationships?

Conclusion

By the end of infancy, infants have started to develop a sense of self and are learning to express and control their emotions as guided by caring adults. They have established important relationships that will shape and influence many aspects of their lives as they develop. Most have established a secure attachment to their primary caregivers and are prepared for the world of peers and play they will encounter as they move into early childhood.

Chapter Summary

7.1 What are emotion and temperament?

The experience of an emotion includes your body's physiological reaction to a situation, your interpretation of the situation, communication of the feeling to another person, and your own actions in response to the feeling. Although basic emotions appear to be universal, the way we express them can differ from one culture to another. One of the ways we learn how to react in an ambiguous situation is through **social referencing**. **Temperament** is the general way in which we respond to experiences in the world, such as being timid or fearless. Infant temperaments have been characterized as **easy**, **difficult**, or **slow-to-warm**.

7.2 How do infants and toddlers develop a sense of self?

Infants have little self-awareness, but within the first 2 years of life, they develop the ability to recognize themselves in a mirror, to use the pronouns *I* and *you* correctly, and to understand that other people see the world differently than they do, called **visual perspective taking**. They also become possessive of their toys.

How does attachment develop?

7.3 **Attachment** is a strong, positive emotional bond with a particular person who provides a sense of security. It is adaptive because it provides children a safe place from which they can explore the environment and learn. According to John Bowlby, attachment develops in four stages: **preattachment** (birth to 6 weeks), **attachment in the making** (6 weeks to 6–8 months), **clear-cut attachment** (6–8 months to 18 months–2 years), and **goal-corrected partnership** (or formation of reciprocal relationships; 18 months on). **Stranger anxiety** typically appears during the stage of attachment in the making and **separation anxiety** appears

during the stage of clear-cut attachment. As the result of the attachment process, we develop an **internal working model** of relationships that we carry with us into new relationships. Based on response to Mary Ainsworth's **Strange Situation**, the infant's attachment can be classified as **secure**, **anxious avoidant**, **anxious ambivalent/resistant**, or **disorganized/disoriented**. Although the percentage of infants with secure attachment does not differ much among cultures around the world, what constitutes sensitive parenting and security in infancy does. Individuals can change their type of attachment as a result of their later life experiences. Children are capable of forming a secure attachment to more than one person at a time. High-quality child care does not harm children's attachment to their parents, but poor-quality child care can interact with poor mothering to create less secure attachment. A **reactive attachment disorder** occurs in children deprived of a consistent caregiver or abused early in their lives. They withdraw from emotional connections to people. In **disinhibited social engagement disorder** children attach indiscriminately to anyone.

7.4 What other life experiences shape infants' development?

Families may take many forms, including divorced parents, grandparents raising their grandchildren, adoption, and foster care. Each of these may pose risks and opportunities for infant development. Many infants spend much of their day in the care of adults other than their parents and will be affected by the quality of that care. Media use has not been shown to benefit the cognitive development of infants and toddlers. Even before they are 2 years old, infants are interested in other children and try to engage them socially. Infants who already have a secure attachment with their caregivers receive more positive responses from peers.

Key Terms

Sharpen your skills with SAGE edge at edge.sagepub.com/levinechrono

SAGE edge for Students provides a personalized approach to help you accomplish your coursework goals in an easy-to-use learning environment.

Go to edge.sagepub.com/levinechrono for additional exercises and video resources. Select Chapter 7, Social and Emotional Development in Infancy and Toddlerhood, for chapter-specific activities. All of the Video Links listed in the margins of this chapter are accessible via this site.

Mauro Fermariello/Science Source

Tony Anderson/Digital Vision/Getty Images

Tyrone Turner

part
IV

8 Physical Development in Early Childhood

T/F Test Your Knowledge

Test your knowledge of child development by deciding whether each of the following statements is *true* or *false,* and then check your answers as you read the chapter.

1. T ☐ F ☐ By the time they are 5 years old, children show an anti-fat bias.

2. T ☐ F ☐ Parents should be concerned when their young child is curious about sexual issues.

3. T ☐ F ☐ Left-handed children are at a greater risk of dying at a younger age or suffering from an autoimmune disease.

4. T ☐ F ☐ There has been an alarming increase in the incidence of autism spectrum disorder in recent years.

5. T ☐ F ☐ Overweight preschoolers usually will grow out of their weight problem as they get older.

6. T ☐ F ☐ Many preschoolers do not get the recommended amount of physical activity each day.

7. T ☐ F ☐ Because children are still growing, they are more resistant to the effects of environmental toxins than adults are.

8. T ☐ F ☐ The incidence of childhood cancer has increased in recent years.

9. T ☐ F ☐ Spouses in custody disputes frequently file false reports of child abuse against each other.

10. T ☐ F ☐ In the United States, one child dies from child abuse or neglect every 4 days.

Correct answers: (1) T, (2) F, (3) F, (4) F, (5) F, (6) T, (7) F, (8) F, (9) F, (10) F

In this chapter, we look at physical changes to body growth and proportions as young children look less like babies and more like adults. We examine how gross motor and fine motor skills develop, enabling young children to do many things for themselves. We also look at the way the brain and central nervous system change in early childhood. We identify important contributors to healthy development including diet, exercise, and sleep, as well as common illnesses that most young children experience at one time or another, and chronic illnesses that can make their first appearance in early childhood. Finally, we examine threats to young children's physical well-being, including environmental toxins, accidents and injuries, and child maltreatment.

Body Growth and Changes

As children move out of infancy and into early childhood, their rate of growth slows and their bodily proportions change and become more similar to those of an adult. Monitoring the rate of physical growth helps to assure us that physical development is on track. Young children develop fine and gross motor skills that enable them to dress themselves, draw and begin writing, and engage in physical play. There is great variability in the timing of motor skill development, but for some children significant delays may result from a developmental coordination disorder. Young children are also becoming more aware of their own body in many ways.

Measuring Growth

Physical growth during infancy is very rapid, but as children move out of infancy and into early childhood, we see a significant decrease in the rate of their physical growth. The one exception between infancy and adolescence is a slight growth "bump" that occurs around age 5 for girls and age 6 for boys. Between the ages of 2 to 5 years, the average child grows about 2-1/2 inches and gains 4 to 5 pounds each year (Shield & Mullen, 2012). Birth length typically doubles by the fourth year (Huelke, 1998). You can get a fairly accurate estimate of average body height in inches for a given age between 2 and 14 years by multiplying the age of the child by 2.5 and adding 30 (Weech, 1954). Using this formula, we can estimate that the average 7-year-old will be 47-1/2 inches tall (7 years × 2.5 = 17.5 + 30 = 47.5 inches). This is a very close approximation to the average height of a 7-year-old given by the Centers for Disease Control and Prevention (CDC) growth charts.

Growth charts show us growth patterns in percentiles. A *percentile* is simply a measure of the percent of the population represented by a certain number. If you are in the 90th percentile in height, you are taller than 90% of people your age. If you are in the 15th percentile in weight, only 15% of the population weighs less than you do. Parents like to have this information, but they should not use it in isolation. While being at either extreme might be a reason for concern and an indication of some type of problem, other factors also influence a child's development and are important for our interpretation of a percentile ranking. For instance, heredity contributes heavily to physical characteristics and some ethnic or racial groups are generally larger (or smaller) than is average in the U.S. population, so these factors need to be taken into account. A pediatrician can help a parent interpret growth chart percentiles to determine whether there is reason for concern and

Learning Questions

8.1 What physical changes occur as children move from infancy into early childhood?

8.2 How do young children see and think about their changing bodies?

8.3 How are typical and atypical brain development similar, and how are they different?

8.4 What role do nutrition and good health habits play in early development?

8.5 What types of health threats can children in early childhood face?

8.6 How is child maltreatment a threat to young children?

8.1

What physical changes occur as children move from infancy into early childhood?

VIDEO LINK 8.1
Growth Hormones

Body mass index (BMI) A
measure of body fat
calculated as a ratio of
weight to height.

rather than looking at a single measure, will usually watch the child's ranking over time to see whether it is changing. A significant change in percentile ranking could be a sign of a potential problem. For example, if a child is in the 50th percentile for weight at one visit to the doctor but drops to the 20th percentile at the next visit, this is worrisome.

Another important measure of physical growth is the body mass index (BMI), which considers weight relative to height. It is often used as a screening tool to determine whether a child is at a healthy weight. Figure 8.1 shows a BMI chart for boys between

FIGURE 8.1   Using the body mass index (BMI)

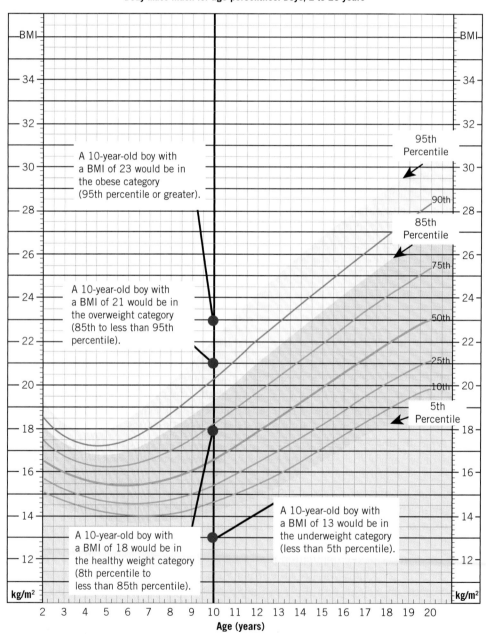

Body mass index-for-age percentiles: Boys, 2 to 20 years

A BMI chart such as this one for boys can help us determine whether a child's ratio of weight to height places him at a healthy weight or one considered underweight, overweight, or obese. This chart shows how some sample BMI numbers would be interpreted for a 10-year-old boy. Note there are different charts for girls and for people over 20.

SOURCE: Centers for Disease Control and Prevention (2011a).

2 and 20 years of age (CDC, 2011a). Children are considered underweight if their BMI falls below the 5th percentile and overweight if it is in the 85th to less than the 95th percentile. A BMI equal to or greater than the 95th percentile is considered obese. This means a healthy weight includes every BMI between the 5th and the 85th percentile.

Overweight Being at or above the 85th percentile and lower than the 95th of the body mass index (BMI) compared to children of the same age and sex.

Obese Being at or above the 95th percentile of the body mass index (BMI) for children of the same age and sex.

Changing Bodily Proportions

In addition to height and weight, the proportions of the child's body change pretty dramatically during early childhood, as the trunk and limbs catch up with the earlier growth of the head. You learned earlier that development proceeds from the head region down through the body by the cephalocaudal principle of growth. This makes the heads of infants disproportionally large compared to their bodies. As the bones in the arms and particularly in the legs grow at a more rapid rate during early childhood, the toddler's body begins to stretch out, and bodily proportions become more similar to those of an adult. Figure 8.2 shows how the size of the head relative to the body changes between birth and 6-1/2 years of age.

Because parts of the body that are undergoing rapid development are the ones most vulnerable to negative environmental conditions, research has found that nutritional deficiency, infections, and other stressful environmental conditions during early childhood have a relatively greater impact on the leg bones while leaving the head largely unaffected and the trunk only moderately affected. As a result, children who have suffered some physical adversity that affected their growth in early childhood are not only at risk of having shorter legs, but also at increased risk of being overweight or suffering from diabetes, coronary heart disease, and even some types of cancer later in their lives (Bogin & Varela-Silva, 2010).

During this period of development, the proportion of body fat and muscle in the body also is changing. The layer of subcutaneous fat in a 5-year-old is only about one-half the thickness of the layer of fat in a 9-month-old infant (Huelke, 1998), so young children lose some of that chubbiness that we associate with infants. Both boys and girls lose fat and gain muscle during early childhood, but in slightly different proportions. By the time they are 5 years old, girls have slightly more fat than males, and males have slightly more muscle (Sakai, Demura, & Fujii, 2012).

Motor Skill Development

As the bodies of young children undergo these changes, the amount and type of physical activity they can engage in also changes. As their upper body continues to develop, they can throw and catch balls. As they become more streamlined and less top-heavy, their balance improves and they no longer "toddle." They now can walk with a gait and stride that allow them to run, jump, and hop. All these actions are examples of gross motor skills that rely on the larger muscles of the body. Physical development also follows the proximodistal principle, so young children gain motor control from the center of the body out toward the extremities. Fine motor skills require control of the small muscles of the body. Developing control over the small muscles of the hands and fingers enables the 3-year-old to hold a crayon using her fingers rather than her fist, to build a tower of blocks, and to use scissors to cut paper. Four-year-olds begin to feed and dress themselves, ride a tricycle, and color inside the lines (American Academy of Pediatrics, 2009a).

Table 8.1 summarizes many of the motor milestones we see during early childhood. You can learn more about the development of children's motor skills by carrying out **Active Learning: Checklist of Motor Skill Development** with a child.

FIGURE 8.2 **Changing bodily proportions**

Birth   6½ years   15½ years

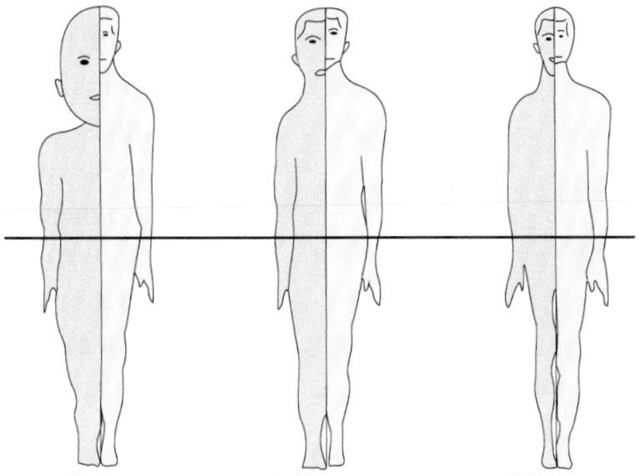

As children move through early childhood, their body proportions begin to look more like the proportions of an adult. Their heads, which were disproportionately large in infancy, become relatively smaller as their trunk and lower extremities grow more rapidly than their head region during this period.

SOURCE: Burdi, Huelke, Snyder, & Lowrey (1969).

| TABLE 8.1 | Development of fine and gross motor skills in early childhood |

Age	Fine skills	Gross skills
3 years	Picks up blocks	Stands on one foot
	Places shapes in holes	Walks backwards and sideways
	Turns the pages of a book	Jumps down from a step
	Paints at an easel	Kicks a large ball with force
4 years	Holds a pencil in an adult way	Pedals a tricycle
	Copies a square accurately	Hops in place and with forward movement
	Brings thumbs into opposition	Bounces a large ball
	Colors inside lines	Runs smoothly
5 years	Uses a knife and fork competently	Can touch toes when upright
	Threads a needle and sews	Jumps for height up to 30 cm
	Copies a triangle accurately	Dances rhythmically to music
	Does jigsaws with joining pieces	Walks downstairs with alternating feet
6 years	Ties own shoe laces	Skips with alternate feet
	Writes first and last names	Catches a ball with consistency
	Holds a pencil with finger tips	Kicks a football up to 6 meters
	Builds a straight tower of cubes	Throws a ball using wrists and fingers

Children between the ages of 3 and 6 develop a wide range of fine motor and gross motor skills. As you review the developmental milestones in this table, think about the ways in which they enable the young child to more effectively interact with his or her environment while at the same time making him or her more independent.

SOURCE: Bailey (2005).

Active Learning

Checklist of Motor Skill Development

Use the checklist in Table 8.1 to assess a young child's motor skills. Choose either the gross skills list or the fine skills list. Begin testing a little below your child's age level and continue until the child is unable to perform several actions. Always respond positively to the child's attempts and don't let the child become frustrated by asking him to perform actions that are much too difficult for him. You can demonstrate the motor skills and ask the child to perform them after you.

Were you surprised by any of the actions your child could or could not perform? How would you explain the upper limits of the child's abilities—lack of practice, level of brain maturation, development of motor coordination, or other reasons? If possible, compare your observations with those of other students in your class. Did you find trends of physical development across ages, and did you find individual differences between children of the same age? ■

WEB LINK 8.1
Developmental
Coordination Disorder

Developmental coordination disorder (DCD) A condition in which delays in reaching motor milestones interfere with daily living and/or academic performance.

Motor Disability: Developmental Coordination Disorder

The Diagnostic and Statistical Manual of Mental Disorders (DSM-5) (APA, 2013) recognizes a condition called developmental coordination disorder (DCD) in which delays in reaching motor milestones interfere with daily living and/or academic performance. It is usually first noticed when a young child has a significant delay in reaching normal milestones like sitting up, walking, jumping, or standing on one foot, or has problems with fine motor skills such as writing, using scissors, or tying shoelaces. Over time, these difficulties can interfere with a child's social development because they lead him or her to resist playing with other children; they can also affect academic performance once children begin school.

Although these problems appear in the early years of life, the diagnosis is generally not made until age 5, because there is such a wide range at which children normally develop different motor skills. About 6% of school-aged children may have this condition, and it is more common in boys (APA, 2013). Possible causes include biological factors such as prenatal malnutrition (Davidson, 2003) and abnormalities in the neurotransmitter or receptor systems in the central nervous system (Barnhart, Davenport, Epps, & Nordquist, 2003). The condition can be improved with physical education and daily exercise that help the brain and body work together, and in some cases occupational therapy or physical therapy is necessary to help children master daily self-help activities (Barnhart et al., 2003; Tokolahi, 2014).

Developmental coordination disorder. This boy is using assistive technology programmed to respond to what he does with this "mission control panel" in order to direct a cartoon robot on a computer screen. How do you think this technology helps him physically, cognitively, and emotionally? ∎

Body Awareness, Body Image, and Sexuality

As young children gain more control over their bodies by walking, running, and hopping, and as they increase their ability to pick up and manipulate objects, they are also developing their sense of body awareness. Feedback from receptors in our joints, muscles, and ligaments travels to the part of the brain that controls movements to give us a sense of where the different parts of our body are in space without our needing to look at them. This sense is called proprioception. We usually are not aware of the information our brain is receiving unless we consciously think about it. Were you thinking about where your feet were before you read that last sentence? Probably not. But you will need this information if you decide to stand up right now and walk across the room to get a snack.

Young children must learn how to use this feedback to move effectively through their environment and control their motor activity. Until they do, their movement may appear clumsy or awkward, or they may have difficulty judging how much force or strength they need to accomplish a task. Children develop body awareness naturally as a part of their normal activity, but parents and caregivers can enhance this development with some of the simple games young children love to play. Simon Says ("Simon says do this. . . . do this. . . . do this") or the hokey-pokey allow children to consciously move specific parts of their body and gain a sense of where they are in relationship to the rest of their body. Many people have enjoyed asking a young child, "Where is your nose? Where are your ears?" and children delight in showing they know the answer. Body awareness also can be facilitated by structured activities, such as introducing children to simple forms of yoga (Wenig, 2014). Yoga can help children develop strength, flexibility, coordination, and body awareness while engaging in a relaxing and noncompetitive physical activity.

You can observe the development of body awareness in young children for yourself if you complete the activity described in **Active Learning: Developing Body Awareness.**

8.2

How do young children see and think about their changing bodies?

Body awareness Conscious knowledge of one's own body parts and movements.

Proprioception The sense of knowing where the parts of your body are located in space.

ACTIVE LEARNING
VIDEO 8.1
Developing Body Awareness

VIDEO LINK 8.2
Body Image

Body image How a person subjectively sees and feels about his or her physical characteristics.

T/F #1

By the time they are 5 years old, children show an anti-fat bias.
True

Active Learning

Developing Body Awareness

Offer to play the game Simon Says. A young child may not understand that he or she shouldn't do a behavior unless "Simon says" to do it, so just give the directions for the child to follow. Begin by having the child do the movements with you. As you say "Simple Simon says touch your nose" or "Simple Simon says touch your knees," do the action with the child watching you. Then just give the directions and allow the child to do the actions on his or her own without a model. Finally, ask the child to keep following the directions but with eyes closed. Because body awareness is a sense of where your body is in space even when you can't see it, this last task is much harder for a young child. Note how many errors the child makes in the three conditions. Does he or she have more difficulty touching different parts of the body with eyes closed? If you have a chance to try this activity with children of different ages, do you see differences in their ability to do the tasks as they get older? As always, if the game becomes difficult or frustrating for the child, thank him or her for playing with you and end the game. ▪

Related to body awareness is our body image, or the way we see and feel about our physical body. Poor body image has been associated with a number of developmental problems that include depression, anxiety, and eating disorders, and a positive body image can promote confidence and self-esteem. Most of the research on body image has been done with older children because the way they see themselves becomes increasingly important as they move toward adolescence, but we now realize that early childhood is the time that body image begins to emerge as children internalize the models they see in their culture. Play is one way children internalize these standards. Think of the most popular doll little girls in Western cultures play with. Did Barbie come to mind? She should, because 99% of 3- to 10-year-olds in the United States own at least one Barbie doll (Dittmar, Halliwell, & Ive, 2006).

As early as 5 or 6 years of age, children in the United States have begun to take in the societal stereotypes Western culture offers for an ideal physique. Dissatisfaction with body image has been reported in children as young as 6 or 7 years of age (Birbeck & Drummond, 2005; Tiggmann, 2001). By age 5, children are already showing an anti-fat bias (Smolak, 2004). Girls especially see thinness as desirable, and being fat as "nasty" or mean (Birbeck & Drummond, 2005, p. 592). The picture is a bit more complicated among boys because they associate being larger with being more powerful and physically competent but also with being a bully, so boys want to be tall but not necessarily big.

The fact that we see the beginning of a thinness ideal and body dissatisfaction at these young ages suggests this may be an opportune time to initiate programs designed to prevent body image problems (Smolak, 2004) rather than waiting until adolescence when cultural ideals have become much more entrenched. We can take a number of positive steps to promote a positive body image in young children. Parents should avoid letting their children hear them talk about their own weight concerns, plans for dieting, or dissatisfaction with their own size and shape. Instead they should focus more on health and less on weight, be sure their children get nutritious meals and snacks, and provide lots of opportunity for physical activity (Academy of Nutrition and Dietetics, 2012). We return to these topics of health and nutrition later in this chapter.

Another facet of physical development that sometimes is difficult for us to accept as adults is the fact that children are sexual beings from the earliest days of their lives. They are naturally curious about their bodies and learn at an early age that touching it can feel good. For young children, self-stimulation is a type of soothing behavior rather than something used for sexual pleasure.

Adults are often caught off guard when they discover pre-schoolers "playing doctor" or imitating adult behavior like kissing. Children of this age also may try to see adults when they are undressed or going to the bathroom. These behaviors are all expression of a child's natural curiosity about the human body and how it works. It is best not to overreact to these situations. Instead we can address young children's curiosity by talking with them in an age-appropriate way about the parts of the body or bodily functions and by answering their questions in a simple but honest manner. For instance, it is a good idea to teach young children the correct names for body parts and give them a simple, basic description of the difference between male and female anatomy. However, we need to be careful not to overwhelm them with too much information. Being open and willing to talk with children while they are young about these topics lays the groundwork for the type of positive and frank communication parents will want to have with their children as they get older and need more information about their sexuality.

Even when they understand this, parents and caregivers can be shocked and react strongly when they come upon sexual play between children. Experts say there is no reason for undue concern as long as certain conditions surround the event: it occurs between children who know each other, play together frequently, and are about the same age and size, the play appears to have been spontaneous and unplanned, and none of the children seem distressed or upset by it, and they stop when they are told to and can be re-directed to another activity (National Child Traumatic Stress Network, 2009; National Sexual Violence Resource Center, 2013). The adult can use this opportunity to remind the children about respecting each other's privacy.

This is another example of the way parents socialize their children. They help their children learn there are times when being naked is acceptable (for example, when it is time to take a bath) and other times when it is not (for example, at nursery school). Table 8.2 describes some common behaviors related to sexuality that we see in young children and makes suggestions for encouraging healthy development.

Although curiosity about sex and occasional masturbation are normal behaviors in young children, there is a point at which they become indicators of a problem that may require the help of a professional. Some of these indicators are having a precocious knowledge about sexual activity, using coercion or force on other children to get them to take part in sexual play, and being preoccupied with sexual behaviors (including masturbation) and engaging in them frequently after being told by an adult to stop (Gil & Shaw, 2014).

These behaviors can indicate the child has been a victim of sexual abuse, but there also can be more innocent explanations. For instance, a child who has a urinary infection might frequently rub the genitals in an attempt to ease the pain. Children who are overly stressed may use masturbation as a way of trying to relieve that tension. Knowing when a child's behavior has crossed a line and become problematic is difficult, so any concerns should be discussed with a qualified professional who can evaluate the behavior and identify its causes. If the child has been victimized, therapeutic services are available to treat even very young children to help them cope with these experiences.

©iStockphoto.com/waldru

Building healthy body awareness. Simple forms of yoga can help children develop not only strength and flexibility but also body awareness that aids their physical development. ∎

T/F #2
Parents should be concerned when their young child is curious about sexual issues.
False

VIDEO LINK 8.3
Talking About Sex

TABLE 8.2	Healthy sexual development in young children	
Healthy sexuality development and behaviors		
Stage of development	**Common behaviors**	**Ways to encourage healthy development**
Infancy (Ages 0–2)	• Curiosity about the body, including genitals • Touching of the genitals, including masturbation, in public and in private • No inhibitions around nudity	• Teach correct names of body parts, such as penis and vagina • Explain basic information about the differences between male and female anatomy • Help children begin to understand how to interact respectfully with peers • Provide very simple answers to questions about the body and bodily functions
Early Childhood (Ages 2–5)	• Occasional masturbation either publicly or privately, usually occurs as a soothing behavior rather than for sexual pleasure • Consensual and playful exploration with children of the same age (for example, "playing house" or "playing doctor") • Questions about sexuality or reproduction, such as, "Where do babies come from?" • Curiosity regarding adult bodies (wanting to go into the bathroom with parents, touching women's breasts) • Continued lack of inhibition around nudity (taking off diaper or clothes in public) • Use of slang terms for body parts and functions	• Provide basic information about reproduction (babies grow in the uterus of a woman) • Encourage a basic understanding of privacy and when behaviors are appropriate and inappropriate • Explain the difference between wanted and unwanted touch (a hug that is welcome and positive versus one that is unwelcome and uncomfortable) • Talk about boundaries, including letting children know their body belongs to them and they can say no to unwanted touch

Young children are naturally curious about their bodies and are beginning to explore their sexuality. Adults need to know what behaviors are typical of young children of different ages to support their development.

SOURCE: Adapted from National Sexual Violence Resource Center (2013).

Check Your Understanding

1. How do we measure a child's growth?
2. How are bodily proportions changing during early childhood?
3. What are fine and gross motor skills?
4. What is a developmental coordination disorder (DCD)?
5. What is the difference between body awareness and body image?
6. When does a child's curiosity about sex become a concern?

8.3

How are typical and atypical brain development similar, and how are they different?

Brain Development

The brain continues to change both its structure and its functions during the period of early childhood. The two hemispheres become more specialized, affecting the development of handedness. One significant neurological problem we introduced in Chapter 5 is autism spectrum disorder. We return to this topic here because children are most likely to be diagnosed with this disorder during the period of early childhood.

Typical Brain Development

During the prenatal period and during infancy, a child's brain adds synaptic connections between neurons at an astonishing rate. By the time children enter early childhood, synaptogenesis in areas of the brain responsible for vision, hearing, and language have already greatly diminished, but production in the prefrontal cortex is just reaching its peak (see Figure 8.3) and this process is not completed until late adolescence or early adulthood (Shonkoff & Phillips, 2000).

The volume of the entire brain increases 25% between early childhood and adolescence (Courchesne et al., 2000), reflecting changes in both the gray matter (the nerve cell bodies) and the white matter (the myelinated nerve fibers). The amount of gray matter increases from about 18 months until 6 to 9 years of age, at which point it decreases (Courchesne et al., 2000). The white matter of the brain, which is essential for the development of the neural pathways that connect individual parts of the brain, undergoes its most prominent increase in the first 3 to 4 years of life (Moon et al., 2011). The corpus callosum, the thick band of nerve fibers that connects the two hemispheres of the brain, also myelinates rapidly during early childhood, allowing the two hemispheres to communicate and better coordinate activities that use both sides of the body at the same time.

You'll remember that although the two hemispheres of the brain share many functions, they also each have some specialized functions. The left hemisphere controls the right side of the body and the right hemisphere controls the left. The localization of a function in one hemisphere of the brain or the other is called lateralization. One of the most important specialized functions is language, which is lateralized in the left hemisphere of the brain for about 70% to 90% of humans. For the remainder of the population, language is either lateralized in the right hemisphere or is not strongly lateralized (Alic, 2006).

Lateralization is also associated with whether you are right-handed, like 90% of people, or left-handed (Fagard, 2006), and the differentiation of brain functions between the two hemispheres is much stronger for righties than it is for lefties (Price, 2009). Humans are the only species that shows such a strong bias in handedness, although the reason is still being debated. It most likely results from a complex interaction of genetic factors and environmental or cultural ones (Fagard, 2006). Parents sometimes wonder whether they should be concerned if their child shows a preference for using the left hand. After all, much of our environment is organized in a way that is better suited for right-handed rather than left-handed individuals. Beyond practical considerations, there really isn't much basis for concern. There are no consistent findings regarding a relationship between hand preference and general intelligence among children in the normal range of intelligence (Leconte & Fagard, 2006). Among the myths surrounding handedness are the belief that left-handed individuals are more creative (they aren't), that they die at younger ages (they don't), or they suffer from more autoimmune diseases (they don't) (McManus, 2002). In fact, left-handers

AUDIO LINK 8.1
Play and Brain Development

Lateralization The localization of a function in one hemisphere of the brain or the other.

T/F #3

Left-handed children are at a greater risk of dying at a younger age or suffering from an autoimmune disease.
False

FIGURE 8.3   **Synaptogenesis in early childhood**

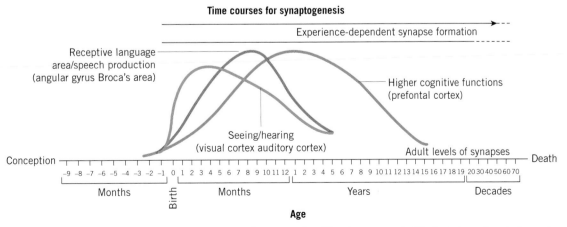

The rate of synaptogenesis, or creation of new synapses between cells, differs from one part of the brain to another during early childhood. While the rate in the visual and auditory cortex and the angular gyrus has greatly slowed by age 2, development in the prefrontal cortex is just reaching its peak in early childhood, and synaptogenesis will continue there into adolescence.

SOURCE: Shonkoff & Phillips (2000).

Being left-handed in a right-handed world. A child who shows a preference for left-handedness by early childhood should never be forced to use his or her right hand. It is possible to adapt to a primarily right-handed world (but thank goodness for left-handed scissors). ■

are among some of our most accomplished individuals, including four of our most recent presidents: Barack Obama, Bill Clinton, George H. W. Bush, and Ronald Reagan.

Atypical Brain Development: Autism Spectrum Disorder

In Chapter 5, we introduced you to aspects of autism spectrum disorder that are recognized in infants and toddlers, but most children are not diagnosed with this disorder until early childhood. Accurately estimating the prevalence of autism spectrum disorder (ASD) is not easy, but in June 2014, the CDC (2014d) released statistics indicating yet another increase in the United States (see Table 8.3). By this most recent estimate, 1 in 68 children have been identified with an ASD, an estimated prevalence that is 30% higher than in 2008 and a staggering 120% higher than the estimate in 2002. Researchers in Asia, Europe, and North America have reported similar prevalence rates of about 1% of the population, although in some cases they are considerably higher, as high as 2.6% in a recent study conducted by Kim et al. (2011) in South Korea. What could account for this dramatic increase? To answer this question, we must first understand the causes of ASD. To see the history of how our understanding of the causes of ASD has changed, read **Journey of Research: Searching for the Cause of Autism Spectrum Disorder.**

TABLE 8.3   Prevalence of autism spectrum disorder

Identified Prevalence of Autism Spectrum Disorder ADDM Network 2000–2010 Combining Data From All Sites				
Surveillance year	Birth year	Number of ADDM sites reporting	Prevalence per 1,000 children (range)	This is about 1 in X children...
2000	1992	6	6.7 (4.5–9.9)	1 in 150
2002	1994	14	6.6 (3.3–10.6)	1 in 150
2004	1996	8	8.0 (4.6–9.8)	1 in 125
2006	1998	11	9.0 (4.2–12.1)	1 in 110
2008	2000	14	11.3 (4.8–21.2)	1 in 88
2010	2002	11	14.7 (14.3–15.1)	1 in 68

The prevalence of autism spectrum disorder in the United States continues to increase. The most recent estimate from the Centers for Disease Control and Prevention in June 2014 is that 1 in every 68 American children has this disorder, a 120% increase since 2002.

SOURCE: Centers for Disease Control and Prevention (2014d).

JOURNEY OF RESEARCH *Searching for the Cause of Autism Spectrum Disorder*

In an early description of autism spectrum disorder, the psychiatrist Leo Kanner (1949) identified the cause as parental coldness, marked by a mechanical attention to the child's needs that lacked any genuine warmth or enjoyment. From this perspective, the infant's aloofness and withdrawal were seen as an adaptive response to an almost intolerable situation. As a result of Kanner's description, the psychological literature from the 1940s through the early 1970s was filled with references to "refrigerator mothers" (Frith, 2003). Today inadequate parenting has been eliminated as a possible cause of ASD as more contemporary research has focused on possible biological causes.

Strong evidence for a possible genetic cause comes from the observations that ASD runs in families (Bailey, LeCouteur, Gottesman, & Bolton, 1995), that boys are 5 times more likely than girls to be diagnosed (1 in 54 boys and 1 in 252 girls) (CDC, 2013a), and that siblings of children who are autistic are 20 to 50 times more likely to be diagnosed than the general population (Salmons, 2010). Other lines of research mentioned in Chapter 5 have identified structural differences in the brains of children with ASD, such as a massive overgrowth of brain synapses and a lack of synaptic pruning (Carper & Courchesne, 2005), a process important for efficient brain function. In one study, 90% of autistic boys between 2 and 5 years of age had a brain volume larger than average (Courchesne et al., 2000). As early as ages 2 and 3, boys with ASD had more white matter in the cerebellum and more gray matter in the cortex than average. Still other research has found functional differences in the brains of autistic children, such as reduced activity in the dorsal medial-frontal cortex, the portion of the brain that mediates emotional and social responsiveness (Mundy, 2003). These differences may contribute to the difficulty children with ASD have in understanding what other people are thinking.

Another line of research has examined possible environmental causes (or triggers) of autism spectrum disorder. You may have heard of research that looked at the role of mercury used as a preservative in the measles-mumps-rubella (MMR) vaccine given to infants. In 1998, the British medical journal *Lancet* published a study that appeared to find a link between ASD and this vaccine (Wakefield et al., 1998). In response to that report and similar research (California Department of Developmental Services, 1999), public concern about the safety of the vaccine grew. In 2004, however, 10 of the 12 original authors of the *Lancet* article issued a retraction of their research that said, in part, that the data were insufficient to establish a causal link between the MMR vaccine and ASD (Murch et al., 2004).

The current scientific consensus is that the clinical evidence does not support the idea that immunizations are a cause for autism spectrum disorder (CDC, 2012b; National Research Council, 2011). This conclusion found support from research conducted in Montreal, Canada. When the mercury compound was removed from the vaccine, there was no corresponding decrease in the incidence of ASD. In fact, the incidence of ASD in the group of children who had not received the vaccine was slightly higher (Fombonne, Zakarian, Bennett, Meng, & McLean-Heywood, 2005). The far stronger research evidence for a genetic and/or neurological component makes it unlikely that some event after birth, such as an immunization, is the cause (Taylor, 2006). Because understanding the cause of autism spectrum disorder is of such great importance, research on this topic is sure to continue. The Centers for Disease Control and Prevention (2013b) is currently working with the National Vaccine Advisory Committee to coordinate future research on this issue. ∎

VIDEO LINK 8.4
Neurological Explanations for ASD

It is possible that something in the environment aside from mercury in vaccinations is responsible for the increase in the incidence of ASD, and research on possible environmental causes continues. However, Gernsbacher and colleagues have suggested that a better explanation is that the increased prevalence rate reflects changes in the way we diagnose autism spectrum disorder. When autism spectrum disorder first appeared in the *Diagnostic and Statistical Manual of Mental Disorders* (*DSM*) in 1980, the diagnosis included six criteria that all had to be present. However, in 1994, the updated *DSM-IV* had 16 criteria, only half of which needed to be present. The description of the criteria also was broadened. For instance, "gross deficits in language" became "difficulty sustaining a conversation" (Gernsbacher, Dawson, & Goldsmith, 2005, p. 56), a much lower hurdle. It is not possible at this point to anticipate the effect the most recent change in the diagnostic criteria for ASD in the *DSM-5* will have on the number of cases diagnosed in the future. The broader definition of ASD, some true increase in the risk of a child's developing an ASD, and greater community awareness of the disorder that brings more children in for assessment probably all contribute to the increase in the reported number of children with this diagnosis.

T/F #4
There has been an alarming increase in the incidence of autism spectrum disorder in recent years. *False*

Of course any increase in the true incidence of ASD would be a cause for concern, but the identification of a greater number of children with an autism spectrum disorder is not, in and of itself, necessarily a bad thing. Some children now identified as autistic represent a group that might otherwise have been overlooked and not have received early and comprehensive intervention services. Although we typically don't diagnose ASD until a child is 3 years or older, there is good reason to identify the condition as soon as we can because the optimal intervention consists of at least 2 years of intensive early behavioral intervention during the preschool years (Filipek et al., 1999; National Institute of Neurological Disorders and Stroke [NINDS], 2008). Although there is no cure, early treatment can bring about substantial improvement for many children with ASD (Reichow, 2012). For instance, highly structured programs that include intensive skill-oriented training can help young children develop social and language skills they lack (NINDS, 2008).

Under the Individuals with Disabilities Education Act (IDEA), all states have specialists trained specifically to work with young children diagnosed with ASD (National Institute of Mental Health [NIMH], 2009). In 2010, almost 50,000 children between the ages of 3 and 5 received these services (CDC, 2013b). Children are typically assessed by a team of specialists, which can include a psychologist or psychiatrist, a neurologist, a speech therapist, and/or other professionals who work with children with ASD (NIMH, 2009). Based on their evaluation, the child's strengths and weaknesses can be identified and an effective treatment plan will be designed to target the symptoms. Together with the family, the team develops an Individualized Family Service Plan (IFSP) that describes the services to be provided to the family, not just the child, and this plan is reviewed at least once every 6 months.

Check Your Understanding

1. How does the rate of synaptogenesis change in early childhood?
2. What is lateralization of the brain?
3. What do we know about the causes of autism spectrum disorder?

Health and Nutrition

8.4

What role do nutrition and good health habits play in early development?

Early childhood is an important time in life to establish good health habits. Young children need good nutrition to support their physical activity and growth. Poor nutrition and obesity at this point in development have serious implications for the child's future well-being. As young children spend more time outside the home, they are exposed to many common illnesses, and some serious lifelong health problems can emerge at this age. After describing some of these problems, we look at ways to protect young children from illness, accidents, and injuries.

Healthy Eating

You may remember learning about the food pyramid in elementary or high school. Recently, the U.S. Department of Agriculture (2012) replaced the pyramid with a new image, "My Plate," that shows the proportion of fruits, vegetables, grains, protein, and dairy that make up a healthy meal. As Figure 8.4 shows, fruits and vegetables fill half the plate. The U.S.D.A. also recommends cutting back on solid fats and added sugars and salt, and making sure at least half the grains we consume are whole grains.

Children who get off to a good start with a diet that contains a variety of healthy foods benefit not only in childhood but throughout adolescence and into adulthood. Remember that when we talk about "diet," we are *not* talking about "dieting." We are interested in the amount, quality, and diversity of the food a child or an adolescent eats, not the restriction of calories with the goal of losing weight.

While good nutrition is important at any age, early childhood is a particularly critical time for two reasons. First, food preferences set early in life establish a pattern that persists into adulthood (Sternstein, 2007). A child who eats a lot of fat, sugar, and salt comes to prefer these tastes and may have lifelong difficulty restricting their intake. The second reason is that obesity has its roots in this stage. In a review of the literature, every longitudinal study found an increased risk of overweight children becoming overweight adults (Singh, Mulder, Twisk, van Mechelen, & Chinapaw, 2008). An overweight child is twice as likely to become an overweight adult as a normal weight child. A child who has a BMI above the 85th percentile at least once at 24, 36, or 54 months of age is 5 times more likely to be overweight at age 12 than a child with a normal BMI at these young ages (Sternstein, 2007).

In 2013, the Centers for Disease Control and Prevention said that 1 in 8 preschoolers were obese (12%). The rates are even higher for Black children (19%) and Hispanic children (16%). However, some positive changes appear to be on the horizon. When the CDC recently updated its statistics, obesity rates among 2- to 5-year-old children decreased from 13.9% to 8.4% between 2003–2004 and 2011–2012. This represents a 43% decline in less than a decade. Declines were *not* found among other age groups studied. Only time can tell whether the trend will continue as these very young children get older, but there is hope for the future if healthy patterns are being established at this early age. Reasons for

| FIGURE 8.4 | Choose My Plate |

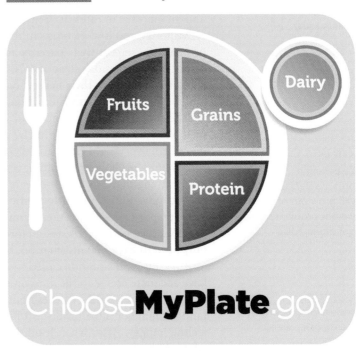

The new "Choose My Plate" logo from the U.S. Department of Agriculture helps you see the proportions of different types of food that make up a healthy meal.

SOURCE: U.S. Department of Agriculture, ChooseMyPlate.gov.

WEB LINK 8.2
Junk Food in Schools

Fighting childhood obesity. After her mother received nutritional education, this young girl replaced television watching with outdoor exercise and became a slimmer and much more active child. ∎

© Mark Richards/Corbis

WEB LINK 8.3
Healthy Eating

T/F #5
Overweight preschoolers usually will grow out of their weight problem as they get older. *False*

Food insecurity A situation in which food is often scarce or unavailable, causing people to overeat when they do have access to food.

AUDIO LINK 8.2
Picky Eaters

the decline are hard to identify, but lower consumption of sugary beverages, more nutritious meals and snacks at child care centers, more emphasis on physical activity, and an increase in rates of breastfeeding may all be making a contribution.

Minority and low-income children continue to be at a disproportionately high risk of being obese, but their parents are often in denial about their children's weight. In a study by Rich and colleagues (2005), all the children were at or above the 95th percentile in weight for their height, but 81% of their parents said their child was healthy and 50% were not concerned about their child's weight. Parents often explained their lack of concern by saying the child would simply grow out of it, was tall or big-boned, or looked just fine. Unfortunately, as we know from the longitudinal research we just described, overweight children do not typically grow out of the problem. Results such as these remind us how important it is to understand parents' perspectives on a situation if we are going to try to design interventions to change their behavior, because even when parents have nutritional information, there is no guarantee they will actually apply it when preparing meals for their families if they do not see their family as having a problem (Weatherspoon, Venkatesh, Horodynski, Stommel, & Brophy-Herb, 2013). They not only need to have the information, but they also need to be motivated to use it.

A paradoxical situation called food insecurity can exist in families that do not always have adequate access to the amount of nutritious food required to meet their basic needs (Franklin et al., 2012). In these families, hunger and obesity can exist side by side. A family might consume lower-cost foods that are relatively high in calories to keep from feeling hungry. Also, when food is not consistently available, adults and children may adopt the strategy of overeating when it *is*. This pattern of feast and famine can result in weight gain over time. It is estimated that one in seven U.S. households experience food insecurity, with low-income, ethnic minority, and female-headed households being at greatest risk (Franklin et al., 2012). Children who experience food insecurity also have other negative outcomes, including higher rates of illness, lower academic achievement, and more aggression, withdrawal, and emotional distress (Ashiabi & O'Neal, 2008).

Although we want our children to eat a wide variety of healthy foods, parents often report their 2- to 5-year-olds are picky eaters (Serrano & Powell, 2013). In the Feeding Infants and Toddlers Study (FITS), the number of parents who considered their children picky eaters increased from 19% in infancy to 50% in toddlerhood (Weatherspoon et al., 2013). One reason may be that children have more taste buds in certain areas of the tongue than adults do, and there is some evidence they taste both sweetness and bitterness more strongly (Mennella, Pepino, & Reed, 2005; Segovia, Hutchinson, Laing, & Jinks, 2002). Some young children decide they will only eat one or two favorite foods, or they decide to eat only foods of a certain color or texture. As long as the choices are healthy and the child continues to have enough energy and appears healthy, parents can probably go along with this for at least a while, but should continue to offer different foods for the child to try (Serrano & Powell, 2013). A young child's taste for new foods develops slowly, so parents need to be patient about introducing them. A child may have to try a new food at least 10 times before developing a taste for it (Sternstein, 2007).

Young children have small stomachs, so they need to have snacks between meals. Children in the United States get about 30% of their daily calories from snacks (Sternstein, 2007), but too often these are high in sugar and fat and low in nutrients. Figure 8.5 shows the Healthy Eating Food Plan for Preschoolers from the U.S. Department of Agriculture, with healthy snack alternatives that appeal to a young child. The figure gives you a good idea of what the size of a portion should be, as well as the variety of foods a preschooler might eat in a day.

What we know about a typical preschooler's diet can point the way to changes that improve it (Sternstein, 2007). For instance, most young children eat few dark green vegetables. Fried potatoes make up most of their vegetable consumption. Thirty percent to 50% drink a sweetened beverage every day. While fruit juice can be a healthy food,

FIGURE 8.5 Healthy eating food plan for preschoolers

Healthy Eating for Preschoolers — Daily Food Plan

Use this Plan as a general guide.

- These food plans are based on average needs. Do not be concerned if your child does not eat the exact amounts suggested. Your child may need more or less than average. For example, food needs increase during growth spurts.

- Children's appetites vary from day to day. Some days they may eat less than these amounts; other days they may want more. Offer these amounts and let your child decide how much to eat.

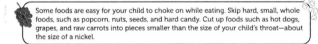

Food group	2 year olds	3 year olds	4 and 5 year olds	What counts as:
Fruits	1 cup	1 - 1½ cups	1 - 1½ cups	**½ cup of fruit?** ½ cup mashed, sliced, or chopped fruit ½ cup 100% fruit juice ½ medium banana 4-5 large strawberries
Vegetables	1 cup	1½ cups	1½ - 2 cups	**½ cup of veggies?** ½ cup mashed, sliced, or chopped vegetables 1 cup raw leafy greens ½ cup vegetable juice 1 small ear of corn
Grains Make half your grains whole	3 ounces	4 - 5 ounces	4 - 5 ounces	**1 ounce of grains?** 1 slice bread 1 cup ready-to-eat cereal flakes ½ cup cooked rice or pasta 1 tortilla (6" across)
Protein Foods	2 ounces	3 - 4 ounces	3 - 5 ounces	**1 ounce of protein foods?** 1 ounce cooked meat, poultry, or seafood 1 egg 1 Tablespoon peanut butter ¼ cup cooked beans or peas (kidney, pinto, lentils)
Dairy Choose low-fat or fat-free	2 cups	2 cups	2½ cups	**½ cup of dairy?** ½ cup milk 4 ounces yogurt ¾ ounce cheese 1 string cheese

Some foods are easy for your child to choke on while eating. Skip hard, small, whole foods, such as popcorn, nuts, seeds, and hard candy. Cut up foods such as hot dogs, grapes, and raw carrots into pieces smaller than the size of your child's throat—about the size of a nickel.

There are many ways to divide the Daily Food Plan into meals and snacks. View the "Meal and Snack Patterns and Ideas" to see how these amounts might look on your preschooler's plate at www.choosemyplate.gov/preschoolers.html.

This plan, developed by the U.S. Department of Agriculture, shows the variety of foods and portion sizes that would meet the dietary needs of a typical preschooler. New foods should be introduced slowly into a young child's daily diet to give the child time to develop a taste for them.

SOURCE: U.S. Department of Agriculture, ChooseMyPlate.gov.

it should be limited to 4 to 6 ounces a day for children under the age of 6. Infants need enough fat in their diet to support the myelination process, but after age 2, they can safely begin transitioning to lower-fat milk.

In addition to the foods that are included in a healthy diet, there are some foods that should be avoided because they pose a risk for young children. Unpasteurized milk, fresh juice made at home from unwashed fruits, and juice bought from a roadside stand can contain harmful bacteria. Honey can contain the botulinum organism, and raw eggs can contain salmonella. Adults should be particularly careful about giving young children firm, round foods such as popcorn, whole grapes, and hot dogs, because these are approximately the size of a child's airway and can lodge in the throat and cause choking (American Academy of Pediatrics, 2006).

Parents need to be good role models of healthy eating behavior. Although there isn't much we can do about our genetic propensity to gain weight, we can control our calorie intake and activity level. Meal time should be an opportunity for the family to be together to enjoy each other's company. This is a daily opportunity to create habits that benefit the young child by establishing a healthy pattern for a lifetime.

© Mitch Diamond/Alamy

Losing baby teeth. Do you remember feeling as excited about losing your baby teeth as this boy appears to be? Notice that his two bottom teeth are new ones coming in and are larger than the others. ■

WEB LINK 8.4
Food Allergies

Oral Health

Obviously healthy eating is related to having healthy teeth, so good dental practices should be developed in early childhood. As children enter early childhood, their permanent teeth begin to push up through the gums, loosening their baby teeth. It is a very exciting development for children when, at about age 6, they lose their first baby tooth. Over the next few years, baby teeth will fall out in about the same order that they emerged in infancy.

Parents can begin gently brushing an infant's teeth as soon as they emerge, but by the time children are 2 to 3 years old and can understand that they should spit and not swallow the toothpaste, they can begin learning to take care of their own teeth. Developing good oral health habits is important because tooth decay is a type of infection that is largely preventable. Despite this fact, about 25% of children begin kindergarten with at least one cavity (American Dental Association, 2014). Many cities add fluoride to their water supplies to strengthen tooth enamel and make it more resistant to the acids that cause tooth decay, but if a family's water supply does not already contain fluoride, parents can get a prescription from their dentist for drops or chewable tablets that will accomplish the same purpose.

Food Allergies

Between 4% and 8% of children suffer from one or more food allergies (Branum & Lukacs, 2009; Gupta et al., 2011), with the incidence peaking among 3- to 5-year-olds (Gupta et al., 2011). The 8% estimate means almost 6 million children in the United States have a food allergy (Gupta et al., 2011), at an estimated cost of $20.6 billion annually (Gupta et al., 2013). That represents an annual cost of $4,184 per family, often for special food or parents' time lost from employment. Because most of these expenses are not reimbursed by medical insurance, they can affect a family's quality of life.

Although any food could cause an allergic reaction, 90% of childhood allergies are caused by just 6 common foods: milk, eggs, peanuts, tree nuts (such as walnuts or cashews), soy, and wheat (American Academy of Pediatrics, 2013). Think for a moment about how common each of these foods is in a typical American diet, and you'll realize how challenging it can be to live with a child with an allergy to any of these foods. To make the situation even more challenging, in a recent national sample of over 38,000 children, 30.4% of those who had allergies were allergic to more than one food (Gupta et al., 2011).

It is fortunate that most allergic reactions to food are not serious or life threatening (Sicherer, Mahr, & The American Academy of Pediatrics Section on Allergy and Immunology, 2010), but they can be. In one study, 38.7% of the children with allergies had a history of severe reactions (Gupta et al., 2011). Parents can exercise great care and control over their child's diet at home, but the challenge increases as young children spend more time outside the home. If the child is going to attend preschool, parents need to discuss the school's policies and procedures regarding management of allergies (Sicherer et al., 2010). Although *anaphylaxis*, a severe reaction to an allergen that affects many systems in the body, is rare, preschool children may experience this severe reaction more often than older children. Parents should provide the school with details about the child's allergy, emergency instructions and contact information, and a self-injectable epinephrine pen if one has been prescribed by the child's physician. To help prevent allergy-related problems, many preschoolers have "no-share" food policies and guidelines regarding food that can be brought into the classroom.

A very promising new therapy is on the horizon for children with peanut allergies. Researchers at Addenbrooke's Hospital in Cambridge (UK) have recently conducted the first large-scale test of an immunotherapy that gave children tiny amounts of peanut protein in the form of peanut flour that were gradually increased over a period of 4 to 6 months. By the end of the second phase of the study, between 84% and 91% of the children could safely eat at least 5 peanuts a day, and between 54% and 62% could eat almost twice that many (Anagnostou et al., 2014). This is enough not only to allow children to eat some peanuts, but also to protect them from the level they would find in snacks or meals inadvertently contaminated with peanuts or peanut products. If successful, the therapy can improve the children's quality of life because it gives them the chance to take part in typical childhood activities like going to birthday parties and eating in restaurants without the fear of an unexpected allergic reaction to the food.

Physical Activity

We all have the idea that young children have boundless energy, and we know they are developing the motor skills that let them run, jump, skip, and ride scooters and bikes. Why shouldn't we assume they are getting plenty of physical activity? As intuitive as this sounds, there is evidence that many children do not get the amount of vigorous physical activity recommended by the National Association for Sport and Physical Education (2009). The Association recommends that preschoolers get at least 60 minutes of structured physical activity and 60 minutes or more of unstructured physical activity each day. Children should not be sedentary for more than 60 minutes at a time unless they are sleeping.

That seems like a reasonable expectation, but a meta-analysis that systematically reviewed 39 studies of preschool programs for children between the ages of 2 and 6 found that only slightly more than half the children reached the minimum of 60 minutes of vigorous physical activity a day (Tucker, 2008). Not surprisingly, researchers have found that children spend more time in vigorous physical activity when they are outdoors, boys engage in more activity than girls, and the amount of physical activity can vary considerably from one preschool to another (Pate, Pfeiffer, Trost, Ziegler, & Dowda, 2004; Tucker, 2008).

It is not likely that children will be much more physically active at home than at school (Frömel, Stelzer, Groffik, & Ernest, 2008), but parents can give young children opportunities to use their new gross motor skills by getting them outside whenever possible or

T/F #6

Many preschoolers do not get the recommended amount of physical activity each day. *True*

©iStockphoto.com/STEFANOLUNARDI

The joy of physical activity. Based on the recommendations of the National Association for Sport and Physical Education, how much daily physical activity should these young schoolchildren get? ■

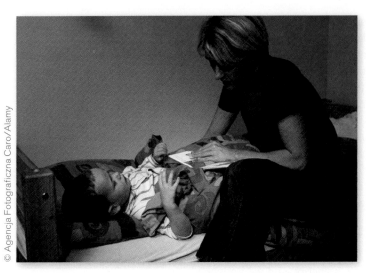

Bedtime. Going to sleep is easiest with a routine that helps the child wind down. What is this mother doing that will help her child drift off to sleep? ▪

JOURNAL ARTICLE 8.1
Sleep Disturbance

creating some space inside where they can move freely. Young children don't need a lot of structured activities. They just need the opportunity to run, jump, and climb. Walking the dog with their parents, riding a tricycle or bike, and playing catch or throwing a Frisbee are all fine activities. When the weather doesn't cooperate, caregivers can play hide-and-seek or follow the leader in the house. Parents also encourage physical activity in their children when they are physically active themselves and limit the amount of time children spend watching television.

Sleep

Young children need enough rest to support their physical and cognitive growth, although the amount changes as they move through early childhood. Research has found that the ratio of nighttime sleep to the total amount of sleep a 1-year-old gets is related to his or her level of executive functioning at 4 years of age (Bernier, Beauchamp, Bouvette-Turcot, Carlson, & Carrier, 2013). The proposed explanation has to do with the structural changes in the young brain we described earlier in this chapter, including the increase in neuronal connections and in the white matter and gray matter in the frontal lobes, so good sleep habits in young children play a role in brain development.

Between the ages of 3 and 5, preschoolers need about 11 to 13 hours of sleep each night. Most will have given up their afternoon naps by the time they are 5. Many preschoolers have some nighttime fears or occasional nightmares. This is also the developmental period when sleepwalking and night terrors peak (National Sleep Foundation, 2013). During a night terror, the child cries intensely and shows extreme fear while remaining asleep, unlike a nightmare which will wake a child up. A cool, quiet, dark sleep environment with no distraction such as a TV in the bedroom and a relaxing bedtime routine will help ensure that children get the rest they need.

As children begin school, they still require 10 to 11 hours of sleep, but now there are more demands on their waking hours so settling down and falling asleep can be more difficult. Watching TV or using a computer right before bedtime can disrupt a child's (or adult's) sleep, so children should avoid such stimulating activities right before bedtime. A regular bedtime routine and sleep schedule continues to be helpful in maintaining a healthy sleep pattern.

Check Your Understanding

1. Why is good nutrition particularly critical in early childhood?
2. What are the effects of food insecurity on healthy eating habits?
3. What are the most common allergens affecting young children?
4. How much physical activity is healthy for toddlers and preschoolers?
5. How do children's sleep needs change during early childhood?

8.5

What types of health threats can children in early childhood face?

Illnesses and Threats to Health

A good diet, an appropriate amount of physical activity, and good sleep habits all contribute to the physical development and well-being of children in early childhood. In this section, we turn our attention to threats to that well-being, including common illnesses, chronic illnesses, and accidents. Where we can, we also describe ways to avoid or prevent the harm these things can cause.

Common Illnesses

The immune systems of young children are still developing, so they are not as resistant to common germs as older children and adults. That is why physicians recommend that young children receive a series of immunizations on a specific schedule, to provide protection against 14 common diseases including measles, mumps, whooping cough, polio, and rubella (or German measles) (CDC, 2012e). Some of these diseases have been greatly reduced or even eliminated in recent years, but if parents don't continue to immunize their young children, they will regain a foothold in the population. Recently whooping cough, which had been virtually eradicated, made a resurgence in an area of California where rates of vaccinations were low (Atwell et al., 2013), so we must continue immunization programs to maintain the progress we have made.

Although some parents have concerns about the safety of vaccines, all formulas are subjected to clinical trials before they go into general use, and the Centers for Disease Control continually monitors vaccines for their effectiveness and safety. Parents need to understand that preventable diseases have very serious health consequences for children who are not protected by a vaccine. For instance, mumps is usually a relatively mild disease that causes fever, headaches, and swelling of the salivary glands in the cheeks and jaw, but it can lead to meningitis, encephalitis, deafness, or even death (CDC, 2012e).

While immunizations offer good protection against a number of contagious diseases, they do not protect against common illnesses such as diarrhea, sore throats, or colds. It is not unusual for young children to get these illnesses, but parents need to learn when they require medical attention.

Diarrhea is fairly common in young children and can be caused by a mild infection or as a reaction to a new food or medication. In developed countries such as the United States, it is not usually seen as a critical symptom. If the child is kept well hydrated to replace lost fluids, the illness will run its course in a couple of days. However, in countries with inadequate sanitation and few medical resources, diarrhea is one of the most common causes of childhood death (World Health Organization, 2012). Even in the United States over 350 children die annually from diarrhea-related disorders (Esposito et al., 2011; Mehal et al., 2012), so severe diarrhea should not be ignored, especially if the child has a fever. If the child shows signs of dehydration, the diarrhea lasts for more than 24 hours, or there are signs of blood or pus in the stools, the child should be seen by a health care provider.

Over-the-counter antidiarrheal medications are not recommended for young children (Iannelli, 2006). Instead it is best to feed a child small, frequent meals of easily digestible foods like bananas, rice, applesauce, and toast (sometimes called the BRAT diet) to help the symptoms subside. Children should not be given foods that contain large amounts of sugar (such as soda pop, sports drinks, or ginger ale) or fat (such as ice cream or milk). Water can be supplemented with an oral rehydration solution because it contains the right amount of salt, sugar, potassium, and other minerals to replace the body fluids being lost. While this won't treat the diarrhea itself, it will help prevent dehydration, which is the most serious threat.

Fever is an indication that the body is trying to fight off an infection. If a mild fever is making a child uncomfortable, the parent can give the child a lukewarm bath and dress him in light clothing. However any temperature of 104° or higher taken with an oral thermometer requires immediate medical attention, as does a fever accompanied by a severe headache or sore throat, ear pain, repeated vomiting or diarrhea, or a seizure (Bacher, 2013). While a fever can be a symptom of something as simple as a cold, it also can be associated with a wide range of more serious health threats such as appendicitis, strep throat, and pneumonia. A doctor will need to know what other symptoms are present to identify the possible cause of the fever. For children 2 years of age and up, a dose of acetaminophen can help to bring a temperature down (Bacher, 2013), but children under 18 years should never be given aspirin to try to bring down a fever because of a possible link between aspirin and Reye's syndrome, a rare but dangerous condition that includes swelling of the liver and the brain (Mayo Clinic Staff, 2011).

Mild sore throats also are common in children and will usually run their course in a few days. They can be caused by viral or bacterial infections. They also can be the result of a postnasal drip, which causes mucus to collect in the throat, or mouth breathing, which dries out the throat. If a sore throat lasts longer than a week or is accompanied by a fever or red and swollen tonsils, the child may have strep throat and should be seen by a physician who may prescribe antibiotics (Mayo Clinic Staff, 2012b). The child should complete the entire course of antibiotics by using all the medication as prescribed. If she doesn't, the infection can spread to other parts of the body and cause kidney problems or even rheumatic fever, a disease that affects the heart (Shelov & Altmann, 2009).

Few signs of childhood illness get a parent's attention as quickly as vomiting. Nausea can result from simple causes, such as gastroenteritis (an infection of the gut that will usually run its course in a few days), eating too quickly, or eating a food that doesn't agree with you, but it also can be a symptom of more serious illnesses such as appendicitis or poisoning. In either of these latter cases, parents need to quickly get emergency treatment for their child. When vomiting occurs repeatedly over a period of several hours, the child is at risk of dehydration, so all the precautions against dehydration that we have already discussed should be taken. As with diarrhea, liquids given in small doses keep the child from becoming dehydrated and easily digestible foods are best tolerated by an upset stomach.

Once a child catches a cold or the flu, there isn't much that will treat or speed up the progress of the illness. Parents can be sure their children stay well hydrated and get plenty of rest, and use a humidifier or a saline nose spray to make them more comfortable, but contrary to what many parents believe, over-the-counter cough and cold medicines should *not* be given to young children. Because these medications do not treat the cause of the cold or make it go away sooner but do have a number of potentially serious side effects, the U.S. Food and Drug Administration (2013) strongly recommends not giving them to children under the age of 2 and is currently assessing their appropriateness for children between 2 and 11 years of age.

Finally, ear infections are the most common reason children see a doctor. Bacterial infections will respond to antibiotics, but in most cases medication is not necessary. Warm compresses may give the child some relief from the pain without overusing antibiotics. As you learned in Chapter 5, repeated ear infections can impair a child's hearing and interfere with the ability to learn language so they may require medical intervention to prevent reoccurrence.

When children first enter preschool or day care, they have contact with many new people over the course of a day and are exposed to new illnesses. Children under the age of 2 who are in out-of-home care do have more upper respiratory tract infections, gastrointestinal tract infections, and ear infections than children cared for at home, but a 2001 study by the National Institute of Child Health and Human Development Early Child Care Research Network found that by 3 years of age these differences subsided and there was no effect on children's language

Preventing the spread of illnesses. This child is learning that washing hands frequently is important to staying healthy because it helps prevent the spread of colds and the flu. ■

David Buffington Blend Images./Newscom

competence or school readiness. Although their mothers reported slightly higher rates of behavioral problems, preschool teachers did not see a difference between those who had experienced more illness and those who had not, so out-of-home care does not seem to pose any substantially increased developmental risk.

The rate of illnesses for children in groups can be reduced with several simple procedures. Of course children who are ill should be kept at home and away from other children. Thoroughly washing hands and covering mouth and nose when you sneeze are other simple but important prevention strategies. As we have already discussed, immunizations protect children from contagious diseases such as diphtheria, measles, polio, whooping cough, and influenza.

Chronic Illnesses

The types of common illnesses we just described are called self-limiting or acute because they usually run their course in a fairly short amount of time, often without any treatment. By contrast, chronic illnesses are long-lasting, do not resolve themselves spontaneously, and in most cases cannot be completely cured (Compas, Jaser, Dunn, & Rodriguez, 2012). Some chronic illnesses are present at birth, including certain heart problems, spina bifida (a condition in which the spinal column doesn't close completely), sickle-cell anemia, and hemophilia. Other chronic illnesses can appear at any time in life. These include asthma (the most common chronic illness), arthritis, diabetes, and cancer. Chronic illnesses can be the result of infection such as HIV/AIDS, genetics, environmental exposure, or an interaction of genetics and environmental factors.

Estimates of the number of children living with chronic conditions will vary depending on the definition used, but by one estimate, 25% of children in the United States live with at least one of these conditions (VanCleave, Gortmaker, & Perrin, 2010). The recent increase in the number of children living with chronic illness is attributable, at least in part, to the fact that many diseases that once were fatal are now treatable (Halfon & Newacheck, 2010). The child is now *living with* rather than *dying from* the illness. Many chronic illnesses run in families. How much do you know about your own health history? You are routinely asked for this information when you see a new physician. **Active Learning: Creating a Personal Health History** will help you compile it.

Active Learning

Creating a Personal Health History

You might want to use this activity as an opportunity to track down information from your childhood that you may not have or to ask questions about your family's health history that you have not discussed with your parents before. The Surgeon General of the United States maintains a webpage at https://familyhistory.hhs.gov/fhh-web/home.action where you can compile a detailed family health history, but you can also create one informally by finding answers to these general questions:

- What childhood illnesses did you have (for example, mumps, rubella or German measles, chicken pox, rheumatic fever, or strep throat)? At what age did you have each, and how severe was it?
- Are your immunizations for diseases such as tetanus, polio, rubella, and diphtheria up to date? Find out when you received each and remember they need to be updated from time to time.
- What are the names and dates of any surgical procedures you have had?
- What are the dates and reasons for any hospitalizations?

- What allergies (if any) do you have?
- What medications do you take (both prescription and over the counter), and how much and how often?
- What major illnesses have affected your parents, grandparents, and siblings, such as arthritis, diabetes, hypertension (high blood pressure), heart disease, kidney problems, seizure disorders, major depression, alcoholism, or other substance abuse problems? ■

Environmental Toxins and Threats

T/F #7
Because children are still growing, they are more resistant to the effects of environmental toxins than adults are. *False*

Because children are still growing and because they eat and drink more in proportion to their body size than adults, they are even more vulnerable than adults to environmental toxins (U.S. Environmental Protection Agency, 2012). A large number of environmental hazards have been identified, including asbestos, dioxin, household chemicals, lead, mercury, molds, pesticides, radon, and secondhand smoke. As an estimate of the impact of the environment on health, in her 2000 presidential address to the Ambulatory Pediatric Association, Dr. Ellen Crain made the claim that "the environment may account for 25% to 40% of the global burden of disease" (p. 871).

Adults are often surprised by what young children will put into their mouths, including medicines, cleaning products, and even kitty litter. This behavior can place children at considerable danger of ingesting something harmful. Almost 60% of the 2 million victims of poison exposure each year are under the age of 6 (Children's Hospital of Philadelphia, 1996–2014). All potentially harmful substances should be kept safely out of the reach of young children and in their original containers, which will contain information about how to deal with accidental poisoning. Parents and caregivers should keep a poison control center number where they can easily find it if they need it or call 911 if their child collapses or stops breathing. The national poison control number is 1–800–222–1222.

Pesticides

Children are frequently exposed to pesticides in their homes, at school, and on the playground. Pesticides are found in rodent and insect control products, household chemicals and cleaning products, lawn and garden products, and pet products. They are even present in the food we eat and in household dust, which young children can ingest unintentionally (Egeghy et al., 2007). Some families choose to eat organic foods in an attempt to lower this risk. In 2010, U.S. consumers spent $26.7 billion on organic foods, but a recent review of studies found limited evidence they are superior in nutrition or safety to nonorganic foods, although organic produce may reduce exposure to pesticide residue (Smith-Spangler et al., 2012). Adults can further reduce the risk of children's exposure to pesticides by looking for safe alternatives to toxic products. If a family does use pesticides, they should purchase products in child-resistant packaging and store the products where children cannot get to them. Consumers should always follow the warnings on the containers about how to use the product safely (U.S. Environmental Protection Agency, 2012).

Lead

WEB LINK 8.5
Lead Poisoning

Children also can be exposed to lead in their environment, though the risk has been greatly reduced by the elimination of lead as an ingredient in household paint and motor fuel (Federal Interagency Forum on Child and Family Statistics, 2009). However, the risk that remains is not evenly distributed among the population. Because lead was an additive in paint until the 1980s, many older houses still have surfaces covered in lead-based paint. Before lead was outlawed as an additive to motor fuels in 1995, millions of metric tons of lead poured into the environment so lead continues to be found in the soil near roadways. This places children who live in older housing and in traffic-congested areas at the greatest risk of exposure to lead in the environment (Godwin, 2009). In recent years, an additional source of lead exposure has been certain candies produced in Mexico and the paint used on imported toys, primarily ones manufactured in China (Godwin, 2009). These sources are of particular concern because the products are marketed specifically for children.

The differential risk of exposure to lead is illustrated by the fact that from 2003 to 2006, blood lead levels at or above 5 micrograms per deciliter were found in 12% of Black children versus 2% of White and Mexican American children (Federal Interagency Forum on Child and Family Statistics, 2009). While childhood deaths from lead poisoning are extremely rare today, blood lead levels in even the moderate range are associated with lower IQ scores and shortened attention spans, and chronic lead poisoning in early childhood is associated with violent and criminal behaviors later in life (Godwin, 2009; Jusko et al., 2008; Surkan et al., 2007; Zhang, Baker, Tufts, Raymond, Salihu, & Elliott, 2013).

Parents can help reduce children's exposure to lead by testing the paint in their homes with kits available in home improvement stores. If lead is detected, only a licensed contractor should remove it, since removal will produce a large amount of contaminated dust. Lead poisoning does not produce any easily recognizable symptoms, but if parents have reason to think their child has been exposed to lead, they can have them tested for the presence of lead in their blood. Simple steps to reduce lead exposure include wet-mopping floors and window sills, asking people to remove their shoes when they come indoors, and having children frequently wash their face and hands.

Environmental Effects on Chronic Diseases

We also see the impact of environmental factors on several of the chronic illnesses that affect a significant number of children each year. The most common chronic illness among children in the United States and the one that places more limits on children's activity than any other disease (Mayo Clinic Staff, 2010) is asthma. Asthma is an inflammation of the bronchial airways that results in chest tightness, coughing and wheezing, and shortness of breath. Most children who have asthma developed their first symptoms before they were 5 years old (National Institutes of Health, 2012a), with boys being more vulnerable than girls, although this gender difference disappears in older age groups. The incidence of children currently living with asthma has increased substantially in recent years to a level of 10% of all children (see Figure 8.6) (National Center for Environmental Health, 2011). The greatest increase occurred among African American children. Between 2001 and 2009 there was almost a 50% increase of asthma cases in this group (National Center for Environmental Health, 2011). The increase in the incidence of asthma and related respiratory problems has paralleled the increase in the use of fossil fuels, and today the incidence is highest among poor children who live in urban environments filled with coal-burning furnaces and diesel-fueled vehicles (Crain, 2000).

While we don't know the exact cause of asthma, many researchers think the interaction of a genetic vulnerability and exposure to an environmental trigger, most often early in life, produces the symptoms (National Institutes of Health, 2012b). Possible triggers that have been identified to date include allergies, cigarette smoke, and air pollutants. More than half of all cases are triggered by allergies. A mother's smoking during pregnancy has been associated with an increased risk of asthma in her child, possibly as a result of stunted prenatal growth of the lungs (Jaakola & Gissler, 2007), and even exposure to secondhand smoke in the

Asthma The most common chronic illness in childhood, in which a child's airways constrict, making it difficult to breathe.

Chris Lowe/Newscom

Treatment of asthma. Asthma is affecting increasing numbers of children. Treatment with an inhaler helps this girl to breathe more easily when she has symptoms. Why are more children in cities struggling with this problem? ■

FIGURE 8.6   Percentage of children ages 0 to 17 with asthma, 1997–2011

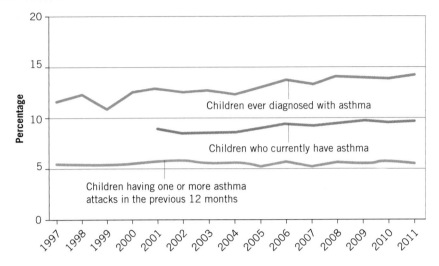

The number of children in the United States who have been diagnosed with asthma has climbed steadily in recent years. Most children who have asthma experience their first symptoms before they are 5 years old.

SOURCE: Federal Interagency Forum on Child and Family Statistics (2013a).

environment is a risk. Air pollutants such as ozone, particulates, nitrogen dioxide, and sulfur dioxide are other triggers for an asthma attack.

The hygiene hypothesis has been proposed as a possible explanation for the increase in asthma and allergies. According to this hypothesis, as our environment has become cleaner, it has lowered our exposure to germs. As a consequence, our immune system is now less able to differentiate between harmful substances and less harmful irritants so it overreacts to harmless irritants like pollen. Support for this idea came from a research finding that children from Amish farm families had lower rates of asthma, hay fever, and allergies than are found in most population studies (Holbreich, Genuneit, Weber, Braun-Fahrlander, & vonMutious, 2012; Holbreich, Genuneit, Weber, Braun-Fahrlander, Waser, & von Mutius, 2012). The researchers argue that exposure while young to farm animals and the variety of allergens found on a farm, together with growing up in a larger family, provides the protective effect.

This hypothesis does not have unequivocal support. Some countries that expose children to a variety of microbes still have high rates of asthma so exposure does not seem to provide the protection predicted by the hygiene hypothesis, and the overall rate of asthma is declining in some Western countries even though there is no evidence they are less clean than in the past (Brooks, Pearce, & Douwes, 2013). The role that early exposure to allergens plays in the development of asthma and allergies remains under investigation.

Cancer is the number-one cause of death by disease during childhood. About 15,000 children between birth and 19 receive this diagnosis each year. Young children are particularly vulnerable to several types of leukemia and cancers of the brain and central nervous system. According to the Centers of Disease Control (2013c), the highest incidence of these two cancers occurs in children between 1 and 4. The causes of childhood cancer are still poorly understood, but there is evidence that exposure to toxins, such as radiation and pesticides, may contribute to some types (U.S. Environmental Protection Agency, 2013). The statistics on childhood cancers contain both good news and bad news. As you can see from Figure 8.7, the good news is that the number of fatalities has decreased over the last 30 years, but the bad news is that the incidence of childhood cancers has continued to climb during that same period (U.S. Environmental Protection

Hygiene hypothesis The idea that living in a germ-free environment is causing our immune system to become more reactive to allergens.

T/F #8
The incidence of childhood cancer has increased in recent years. *True*

Agency, 2013). Research will need to determine whether this is an actual increase in the incidence of the disease or simply a reflection of better detection and reporting.

Accidents

Between 1981 and 2000, the rate of deaths due to injuries among children from birth through 19 fell by nearly 43% (Child Trends, 2012b). We can easily think of societal changes that have contributed to this overall decline. Laws now require that children be restrained while riding in motor vehicles, school and community programs promote bicycle safety (including the wearing of helmets and safety gear), organized sports for children focus more on the safety of participants, and toys are screened for health and safety hazards. But injuries continue to be the leading cause of death for children 19 years and younger (Gilchrist, Ballesteros, & Parker, 2012), so there is still room for improvement. Nearly 9,000 children in the United States die from unintentional injuries each year (Child Trends, 2012b), and as you can see from Figure 8.8, many more are hospitalized or require medical treatment.

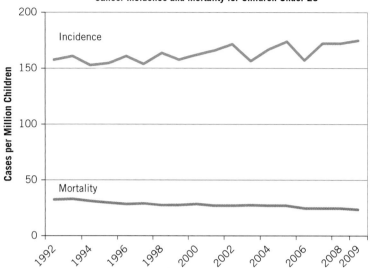

FIGURE 8.7 **Incidence and mortality rates of childhood cancer in the United States**

The number of cases of diagnosed cancer in children has gone up over time, but fortunately with better treatment, the death rate has gone down.

SOURCE: U.S. Environmental Protection Agency (2013).

Figure 8.9 shows the annual number of childhood deaths in the United States from different causes. It also shows the increase or decrease in deaths from each cause from 2000 to 2009. While we have made progress in reducing some risks to children, others have increased, but we can do a great deal to reduce each of these risks.

FIGURE 8.8 **Childhood death and injury from accidents**

Each year in the United States, over 9,000 children under the age of 19 die from accidents. However, many more are hospitalized or require medical treatment for their injuries.

SOURCE: Centers for Disease Control and Prevention (2012h).

FIGURE 8.9   Changes in the cause of childhood death from accidental injury, 2000–2009

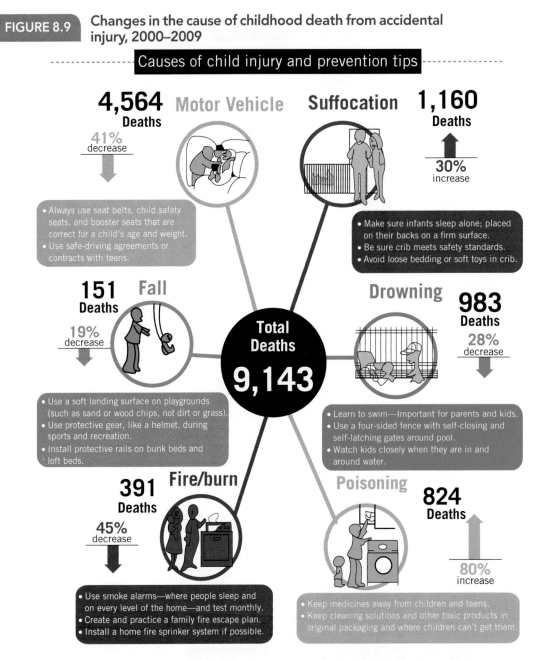

Causes of child injury and prevention tips

4,564 Deaths Motor Vehicle
41% decrease
• Always use seat belts, child safety seats, and booster seats that are correct for a child's age and weight.
• Use safe-driving agreements or contracts with teens.

Suffocation **1,160** Deaths
30% increase
• Make sure infants sleep alone; placed on their backs on a firm surface.
• Be sure crib meets safety standards.
• Avoid loose bedding or soft toys in crib.

151 Deaths Fall
19% decrease
• Use a soft landing surface on playgrounds (such as sand or wood chips, not dirt or grass).
• Use protective gear, like a helmet, during sports and recreation.
• Install protective rails on bunk beds and loft beds.

Total Deaths **9,143**

Drowning **983** Deaths
28% decrease
• Learn to swim—Important for parents and kids.
• Use a four-sided fence with self-closing and self-latching gates around pool.
• Watch kids closely when they are in and around water.

391 Deaths Fire/burn
45% decrease
• Use smoke alarms—where people sleep and on every level of the home—and test monthly.
• Create and practice a family fire escape plan.
• Install a home fire sprinker system if possible.

Poisoning **824** Deaths
80% increase
• Keep medicines away from children and teens.
• Keep cleaning solutions and other toxic products in original packaging and where children can't get them.

Motor vehicle accidents continue to be the leading cause of death for children under the age of 15. Although deaths from motor vehicle accidents, falls, burns, and drownings decreased between 2000 and 2009, deaths from suffocation and accidental poisoning increased. There are things that we can do to prevent all of these accidental causes of death.

Percentages show changes in death rates from 2000 to 2009. Deaths are from 2009. Total deaths include 1,070 from other causes.

SOURCE: Centers for Disease Control and Prevention (2012h).

Although deaths from unintentional injury have been declining for all children, children 4 years of age and younger were the group at greatest risk in all these years. It is easy to see why young children are at particular risk. First, they are naturally curious and have a strong desire to imitate what they see others do. Although their physical capability increases throughout this developmental period, their muscles, bones, and ability to balance and control their bodies are all still developing. They also do not yet have good decision-making skills that help protect older children from harm. Preschoolers are proud of their growing independence, but this independence can translate into resistance to being put into a car seat or a newfound ability to get themselves out of it while their parents are driving. Motor vehicle and transportation accidents are the leading cause of death for children between ages 1 and 4, accounting for 31% of deaths (Borse et al., 2008).

The curiosity of young children may lead them to experiment with matches or lighters as they imitate what they see grownups doing. Parents can try to protect their children from danger by putting things they shouldn't play with on top of a piece of furniture, but preschoolers can be skilled climbers who see this as an interesting challenge. The developing motor skills that serve them well in so many ways also allow them to open drawers, cabinets, and jars that contain things they shouldn't have, so parents need to remain very vigilant to protect young children from harm.

Check Your Understanding

1. Why should young children be vaccinated against common childhood illnesses?
2. Why are over-the-counter cough and cold medicines not recommended for young children?
3. How can children be protected from environmental toxins like lead and pesticides?
4. Why are young children so prone to accidents?

Child Maltreatment

8.6

How is child maltreatment a threat to young children?

Stop for a moment and count slowly to 10. In the time it took you to count to 10, it is likely that another report of suspected child maltreatment was made. In 2012, more than 3.4 million reports of suspected abuse or neglect involving 6.3 million children were made to child protection agencies in the United States (U.S. Department of Health and Human Services [USDHHS], 2013).

Maltreatment is the broad, overarching term that covers both abuse and neglect. It includes any act by a parent or caregiver that results in harm or potential harm to a child. Abuse more specifically includes deliberate and intentional words and actions that cause harm or potential harm to a child, whether the abuse is physical, sexual, or psychological. Neglect is the failure to provide for the basic physical, emotional, medical, or educational needs of a child or failure to protect the child from harm or potential harm (CDC, 2014e). In the sections that follow, we describe how the Child Protective Services system deals with reports of suspected maltreatment, who are its victims and perpetrators, and what can be done to help families and victims.

Maltreatment Any act committed by a parent or caregiver that results in harm or potential harm to a child.

Abuse Deliberate and intentional words and actions that cause harm or potential harm to a child; can involve physical, sexual, or psychological abuse.

Neglect Failure to provide for the basic physical, emotional, medical, or educational needs of a child or to protect the child from harm or potential harm.

Child Protective Services (CPS)

Before we describe the current child protective services system, you can read about the history of efforts to protect children from abuse or neglect in **Journey of Research: Child Protective Legislation.**

JOURNEY OF RESEARCH *Child Protective Legislation*

Throughout much of human history, children were considered the property of their parents and parents were free to do whatever they wanted to them. As long as children were seen as property, society chose not to interfere with decisions made by individual families about how they treated their children. Today we think of children as individuals who need to be nurtured and protected, but the view of children in the 1800s was that they needed hard work and strict discipline if they were to be kept on the straight and narrow path and to grow up to be honest, moral people (Bagnell, 2001).

A pivotal event in the history of child protection in the United States occurred in 1873, when a church worker became aware of a 9-year-old girl named Mary Ellen who was being horribly mistreated by her family (Miller-Perrin & Perrin, 1999). However, when the church worker tried to have Mary Ellen removed from her home, she found that there was no legal precedence for such an action, and the authorities refused to act. Being persistent, the church worker next turned to the American Society for the Prevention of Cruelty to Animals (ASPCA) for help, arguing that as a member of the animal kingdom, Mary Ellen deserved at least the same protection that would be offered to a mule that was being mistreated. With the help of the ASPCA, Mary Ellen was removed from her abusive home and placed in foster care (Miller-Perrin & Perrin, 1999). The following year, in 1874, the Society for Prevention of Cruelty to Children was formed with the mission of protecting children from abuse and maltreatment (Miller-Perrin & Perrin, 1999). However, the case of Mary Ellen did not lead directly to broadly based efforts to protect children.

That had to wait for almost another 100 years. In the 1960s, Dr. Henry Kempe, a pediatrician in Denver, Colorado, found evidence in the X-rays of some children he treated of broken bones and fractures in different stages of healing, indicating that whatever had caused them had happened repeatedly over a period of time. Dr. Kempe and some of his colleagues published the groundbreaking article "The Battered Child Syndrome" in 1962 and began a campaign to raise awareness not only among doctors but also among the general public of a situation that had remained hidden behind the closed doors of private homes before this (Leventhal, 2003).

Even with the growing recognition that child abuse existed and might be widespread, it took more than another decade before the United States passed comprehensive legislation intended to protect children from abuse. In 1974, Public Law 93–247, the Child Abuse Prevention and Treatment Act—CAPTA, was enacted by Congress. This legislation established a mechanism for reporting cases of suspected abuse or neglect to child protection agencies and for tracking the disposition of those cases. The act has been amended several times, most recently in 2003, but it remains the foundation for our efforts to identify and protect children who are being mistreated and to provide support to families so that children can safely remain in their homes with their parents. ■

WEB LINK 8.6
Child Protective Services

In broad overview, this is how the Child Protective Services (CPS) system handles the reports it receives: The Child Abuse Prevention and Treatment Act established a toll-free hotline in each state to receive reports of suspected maltreatment. Calls made to the hotline are evaluated to determine whether the reported incidence is covered by the laws regarding child abuse or neglect. If it is, the report is referred to a local CPS agency for investigation of the allegations (USDHHS, 2013). Based on the investigation, the agency makes a determination that the allegations are *substantiated* (an official decision that a child has been mistreated), *indicated* (there is enough evidence to support the allegation that a child has been maltreated but not enough to support a formal substantiation), or *unsubstantiated* (there is not enough evidence to support the allegation). Children can be removed from the family if they are considered in imminent danger, or services can be provided to the family to prevent further maltreatment if the child is not at imminent risk. The balance between protecting the child and preserving the family as a unit is a central concern of child welfare agencies (Roberts, 2002), so agencies are reluctant to remove children unless they are clearly in danger. In 2012, families with approximately 3.2 million children who were considered at risk of abuse and neglect received prevention services that allowed the children to stay in their homes. Services provided to families can include parent education, child day care, and assistance with finding employment for the parents or housing for the family.

In the 1970s, when the original child protective legislation was written, the goal was to uncover every possible case of abuse that was occurring. That is one reason why the law was written to allow any concerned citizen to report suspicions to a state hotline. Although there was initially some concern that making a false report would become a way for disgruntled neighbors or vindictive ex-spouses to harass a parent, only two tenths of 1% of all reports are intentionally false (USDHHS, 2013), and people who knowingly file false reports can be prosecuted.

Although anyone can report suspected maltreatment, three fifths of reports in 2012 came from professionals who work with children and families. These individuals are considered mandatory reporters who are required by law to report their suspicions to authorities (Child Welfare Information Gateway, 2014). Included among mandatory reporters are health care providers, teachers, child care providers, social workers, police officers, and clergy. Failure by a professional to report a suspicion of maltreatment carries a legal penalty, which can be a fine or even imprisonment, but all states also provide immunity from civil liability and criminal penalties for mandatory reporters because their reports are considered to have been made in good faith (Crosson-Tower, 2003). The identity of the reporter is not disclosed to the family.

One consequence of the original decision to cast a wide net is that the system has often been nearly overwhelmed by the number of reports it receives. It takes an enormous amount of resources to screen and investigate the almost 3-1/2 million reports received annually by CPS, but in 2012, only one fifth of the reports were substantiated following an investigation (USDHHS, 2013). In the remaining four fifths of referrals, children were found to be nonvictims of maltreatment. We could change the legislation to make reporting abuse and neglect more difficult and that would reduce the number of cases the system must investigate, but then more cases might go undetected. So far we have not been willing to make this trade-off, so we continue to have a broad-based approach designed to discover as many families as possible in which abuse is occurring.

There is no doubt that preventing child maltreatment is expensive. A recent estimate of the total lifetime economic burden resulting from one year's new cases of fatal and nonfatal child maltreatment was $124 billion (Fang, Brown, Florence, & Mercy, 2012), but the authors of this study note that a "promising array of prevention and response programs have great potential to reduce the economic burden" (p. 163) and conclude that the benefits of effective prevention programs outweigh their costs.

Incidence of Maltreatment

Although cases of child abuse are the ones that often grab our attention, the incidence of neglect is much higher than the incidence of abuse. In 2012, 78.3% of the victims were neglected, 18.3% were physically abused, 9.3% were sexually abused, and 8.5% were psychologically maltreated (USDHHS, 2013). An additional 10.6% of victims experienced such other types of maltreatment as abandonment or parental drug addiction. Cases can be substantiated on more than one allegation, which is why the total is greater than 100% (USDHHS, 2013). In this same year, there were 1,593 child fatalities from maltreatment (USDHHS, 2013). That means that on average 4 children each day die as the result of abuse or neglect in the United States.

When we try to estimate the magnitude of child maltreatment, we should keep in mind that reported cases are only a portion of all the cases that actually occur. Based on a nationally representative sample of over 4,500 children and adolescents, David Finkelhor and his colleagues estimated that 1 in every 10 children had been a victim of maltreatment during the year preceding their study (Finkelhor, Turner, Ormrod, & Hamby, 2009).

Victims and Perpetrators

Although children of any age might be abused or neglected, younger children are at particular risk. Children age 3 and younger accounted for 26.8% of the victims in 2012 (USDHHS, 2013), and children 3- to 5-years-old accounted for another 19.9%. Nearly

T/F #9
Spouses in custody disputes frequently file false reports of child abuse against each other. *False*

Mandatory reporters Individuals who work with children who are required by law to report suspicions of child maltreatment to authorities.

T/F #10
In the United States, one child dies from child abuse or neglect every 4 days. *False*

three quarters of the children who die as a result of maltreatment are under 3 years of age (USDHHS, 2013). Think of all the reasons why young children are at an increased risk. They are small and defenseless. They spend all or most of their time in the care of adults, and caring for a young child can be frustrating for a parent or caregiver. Because young children spend most of their time in the home, no one outside the family may be aware that maltreatment is occurring. For all these reasons we need to be especially concerned about the abuse and neglect of young children.

There are some child characteristics in addition to age that are associated with an increased risk of maltreatment. Children who have a physical, behavioral, or mental disability are at an increased risk (USDHHS, 2011). More victims are White (44.0%) than African American (21.8%) or Hispanic (21.0%) (USDHHS, 2013), although this does not necessarily represent an additional risk, because the White population is larger than either of the other minority groups (Sedlak et al., 2010). The risk of being a victim does not differ substantially between boys and girls for most types of maltreatment (Finkelhor, Ormrod, Turner, & Hamby, 2005; USDHHS, 2013), although girls are 4 times more likely to be victims of sexual abuse than boys. However, boys are at greater risk of suffering a fatality than girls; in 2012, 57.6% of fatality victims were male.

In 80.3% of maltreatment cases, the perpetrator was a parent (or parents). In those cases, mothers were the sole perpetrator in 36.2% of the cases, fathers in another 18.7%, both parents in 19.4%, and a parent and another adult in the remaining cases. Although child abuse and neglect can occur at any socioeconomic level, low-income families are at greater risk of being reported (Laskey et al., 2012). The higher reporting rate may reflect an actual difference in incidence because a number of circumstances associated with poverty contribute to the risk of maltreatment. Poorer families are exposed to more life stressors, for instance, and increased stress makes it more likely that parents can lose control and strike out at their children. Fewer financial resources can result in living conditions associated with neglect. When the economy takes a downturn, reports of both abuse and neglect typically increase (Freisthler, Merritt, & LaScala, 2006). Parents who have substance abuse problems are both more likely to be living in marginal conditions and more likely to be abusing or neglecting the children in their households. It also is much more likely that low-income families will be in contact with agencies such as welfare agencies, probation services, and public health clinics that are staffed by mandatory reporters of suspected abuse or neglect. Families in better financial circumstances are unlikely to have contact with these agencies. Another possibility is that racial and socioeconomic bias makes it more likely that people will report a poorer family than a family with greater economic resources to the authorities (Laskey et al., 2012).

The consequences of physical abuse are not entirely clear (Fergusson, Boden, & Horwood, 2008). Although some research has found increased rates of suicidal thoughts, depression, antisocial behavior, and substance abuse, other studies have not found differences in these outcomes between physically abused children and matched control samples of children who were not abused. In a study of 16,000 adults who had experienced physical abuse while growing up, the researchers found that physical abuse occurs more often to boys than to girls, but health-related outcomes in adulthood seemed to be worse for girls (Thompson, Kingree, & Desai, 2004).

Few studies have examined the long-term impact of neglect on children's development. This is a very difficult topic to research because neglect coexists with a number of other circumstances that also place a child at risk. A recent study of young children with a substantiated report of neglect found that 17% had been born to a teenage mother and 40% had high blood-lead levels; almost two thirds of the mothers had received inadequate prenatal care, 45% had been homeless, and almost two-thirds lived in poverty. Neglected children experienced even higher levels of these risk factors than children who had suffered physical abuse. While victims of neglect had poorer academic achievement outcomes, there was no similar significant association between abuse and academic outcomes (Fantuzzo, Perlman, & Dobbins, 2011).

JOURNAL ARTICLE 8.2
Child Neglect

The research conducted by Fergusson and his colleagues (2008) was particularly important because it controlled for a number of other life experiences known to be associated with the same negative mental health and psychosocial outcomes we associate with child abuse. For instance, we know that children who grow up in unstable families, who are not securely attached to their caregivers, who live in poverty, or who live in difficult and dangerous environments are more prone to these types of mental health problems. When Fergusson et al. (2008) controlled for these factors within their sample, the relationship between childhood physical abuse and later mental health problems became statistically nonsignificant. This type of analysis helps us understand that abuse most often occurs within a context of other negative influences that contribute to the negative outcomes we see in children.

Check Your Understanding

1. What is child maltreatment?
2. Who are mandatory reporters?
3. What are the advantages and disadvantages of casting a wide net in efforts to uncover child maltreatment?
4. What are the long-term consequences of abuse and neglect in childhood?

Conclusion

During early childhood, children build the skills that they will need as they prepare to move beyond their family into a broader world that includes new people and new experiences. Healthy physical development, including a good diet and adequate amounts of sleep and physical activity, build a strong foundation for facing those new challenges. Adults can do a great deal to protect young children from threats to their well-being while supporting and encouraging healthy development.

Chapter Summary

8.1 **What physical changes occur as children move from infancy into early childhood?**

The rate of physical growth in infancy slows as children move into early childhood. We assess their rate of growth by looking at the percentile they are in for their height, weight, and ratio of weight to height or **body mass index**. Children's body proportions change as growth in their trunk and legs catch up with their head in size and they lose fat and gain muscle. These physical changes are reflected in children's new gross and fine motor skills, which help them do more tasks for themselves. Young children become much more aware of many aspects of their body and how it functions.

8.2 **How do young children see and think about their changing bodies?**

Body image and **body awareness** develop during early childhood. Body dissatisfaction may also begin this early. Young children are normally curious about their bodies and sexuality, so parents should talk with them at a level appropriate for their level of understanding.

8.3 **How are typical and atypical brain development similar, and how are they different?**

The rate of synaptogenesis slows down in some parts of the brain, while the production of new synapses in the part that handles higher cognitive functions peaks. Myelination of the corpus callosum improves motor coordination between the two sides of the body, while lateralization of the brain contributes to specialization of functions in the two hemispheres. A diagnosis of **autism spectrum disorder** is often made in early childhood, and differences in the brains of autistic children are the most likely cause of the disorder. **Developmental coordination disorder** is a brain condition that specifically affects motor development.

8.4 **What role do nutrition and good health habits play in early development?**

Good nutrition is essential, but young children may become picky eaters. Obesity may be decreasing in this age group, which is encouraging because **obese** preschoolers are likely to remain obese as they get older. When people experience **food insecurity**, it predisposes them to later obesity. Between 4% and 8% of young children suffer from allergies. Young children need get enough sleep and physical activity to stay healthy.

8.5 **What types of health threats can children in early childhood face?**

Children may experience common, short-term illnesses or long-term, chronic illnesses. Environmental toxins may contribute to the development of some chronic illnesses such as asthma or cancer. The **hygiene hypothesis** proposes that the increased cleanliness of children's environments has contributed to the increase in allergies and asthma, but this hypothesis has not received unequivocal support. Rates of injury and death from accidents in childhood have been decreasing but young children are particularly vulnerable to these risks.

8.6 **How is child maltreatment a threat to young children?**

Maltreatment includes both **abuse** and **neglect.** Young children are at greater risk than older children of being a victim of maltreatment. Child abuse and neglect most often occur in the context of many other types of dysfunction within a family, so it has been very difficult to determine the specific long term effects. The Child Protective Services system investigates reports of suspected maltreatment and makes a determination whether a child can remain at home. **Mandatory reporters** are required to report suspected maltreatment, but private citizens also can report in most states. The child protection system must balance the need to protect children from harm against the desire to preserve the family unit.

Key Terms

Abuse   279

Asthma   275

Body awareness   257

Body image   258

Body mass index (BMI)   254

Developmental coordination disorder (DCD)   256

Food insecurity   266

Hygiene hypothesis   276

Lateralization   261

Maltreatment   279

Mandatory reporters   281

Neglect   279

Obese   255

Overweight   255

Proprioception   257

Sharpen your skills with SAGE edge at edge.sagepub.com/levinechrono

SAGE edge for Students provides a personalized approach to help you accomplish your coursework goals in an easy-to-use learning environment.

   Go to edge.sagepub.com/levinechrono for additional exercises and video resources. Select Chapter 8, Physical Development in Early Childhood, for chapter-specific activities. All of the Video Links listed in the margins of this chapter are accessible via this site.

9 Cognitive Development in Early Childhood

T/F Test Your Knowledge

Test your knowledge of child development by deciding whether each of the following statements is *true* or *false,* and then check your answers as you read the chapter.

1. **T ☐ F ☐** We describe preschoolers as egocentric because they are selfish.

2. **T ☐ F ☐** We can improve a preschooler's memory by teaching the child to use memory strategies.

3. **T ☐ F ☐** It is important for children to play because they have fun when they are playing, but the real learning happens in the classroom.

4. **T ☐ F ☐** It is beneficial for young children to talk out loud to themselves while working on projects.

5. **T ☐ F ☐** If a young child says "I goed outside," it helps develop his language skills if the parent

corrects him by saying "No, you mean to say, 'I *went* outside.'"

6. **T ☐ F ☐** Using flash cards and workbooks is the best way to ensure that a child develops early literacy skills.

7. **T ☐ F ☐** When young children use spelling they have "invented" (rather than conventional spelling), it slows down their ability to learn how to spell correctly.

8. **T ☐ F ☐** Many children who grow up in poverty go on to become adults who contribute positively to society.

9. **T ☐ F ☐** Participating in a high-quality preschool program can increase a child's chance of graduating from high school or attending college.

10. **T ☐ F ☐** The fast pace used on the television program *Sesame Street* does not affect the attention span of children who watch it.

Correct answers: (1) F, (2) F, (3) F, (4) T, (5) F, (6) F, (7) F, (8) T, (9) T, (10) T

The period of early childhood is marked by great steps forward in cognitive development. At age 2, toddlers are just developing language, and their ability to think logically and in complex ways is very limited. Between 2 and 7, children develop a level of thinking that prepares them to attend school and learn in new ways. In this chapter, we describe Piaget's stage of preoperational development and explore Vygotsky's sociocultural theory and its application in early childhood. We then examine development of the basic mental processes of attention, memory, and executive function. Young children are also applying their cognitive skills to social problems, and we describe the development and limitations of young children's social cognition. We then continue the description of language development that began in infancy. In addition, we discuss the development of preacademic skills, including reading, writing, and arithmetic, and the important role of play in young children's learning. Finally, we look at how young children's cognitive and academic abilities are supported both at home and in preschool settings and what factors may put them at risk.

Learning Questions

9.1 What occurs during Piaget's preoperational stage of cognitive development?

9.2 What are the basic processes described by Vygotsky's sociocultural theory?

9.3 How do attention, memory, executive function, and social cognition develop in early childhood?

9.4 Why is play important for cognitive development in early childhood?

9.5 How does language develop in early childhood?

9.6 How do children develop preacademic skills in reading, writing, and arithmetic?

9.7 What risk factors and supports exist for cognitive and language development in early childhood?

Piaget's Theory of Cognitive Development: The Preoperational Stage (2–7 Years)

Piaget defined his second stage of development largely by what it lacks: operations. For Piaget, operations are mental actions that follow systematic, logical rules. When children are *pre*operational, they do not think in a logical way (perhaps this is why we do not have them start formal schooling until late in this stage). However, Piaget also described a new development that will help set the stage for more sophisticated thinking: the ability to use symbols.

Use of Symbols

According to Piaget, the major accomplishment of the preoperational stage is the ability to represent actions mentally rather than physically. Toddlers can think about and refer to objects that are not in their immediate vicinity because they can represent them in their minds. They can *tell* you about an apple they ate yesterday, unlike the infant who must *show* you an actual apple. A symbol is anything that represents something else that is not present, but symbols at this age are still very concrete. Abstract symbols, such as a balance scale representing the concept of justice, are still outside the comprehension of the preoperational child. Three ways in which children demonstrate their ability to use symbols are through play, language, and drawings.

Young children use objects or themselves and other people in play to symbolically represent something that is not there. While they are actually holding a block, in their mind they are imagining it is a telephone, and they can pretend to talk to someone at the other end of the line who is also a figment of their imagination. Some children create an

9.1

What occurs during Piaget's preoperational stage of cognitive development?

Operations Mental actions that follow systematic, logical rules.

Preoperational stage Piaget's second stage of development, in which children ages 2 to 7 do not yet have logical thought, and instead think magically and egocentrically.

VIDEO LINK 9.1
Symbolic Development

© Urban Zone/Alamy

Fantasy play. By using a tube of rolled up paper as a telescope, this girl shows she can use symbols in fantasy play, indicating that she is in Piaget's preoperational stage. ◼

entire person, an imaginary companion, who is so real to them that he or she must have a seat and be served at the dinner table.

For Piaget, the development of language is important because it shows that children can use symbols. Whenever we use a word, it represents something that is not there. Look at this word: **APPLE**. You will notice that it is not round, and if you were to lick the page in your textbook, you will find that it isn't sweet. It isn't even red, but you knew the real-world object it stood for when you first read it. In a similar way, if we say "table," we no longer have to have the table in front of us.

Finally, children demonstrate the use of symbols whenever they make a drawing of something, even if no one else can recognize it. Young children demonstrate that they understand the representative nature of pictures because they do not try to eat a picture of an apple but instead understand that the picture only represents a real apple (Preissler & Bloom, 2007).

While the use of symbols is a major step forward and liberates children from the immediate physical world, Piaget also placed considerable emphasis on the limitations of children's thought at this age. In their attempt to understand the world, they put together events that merely happen close in time as though one explains the other, even if they aren't logically related to each other. They also may try to explain events by giving inanimate objects human thoughts and feelings. They see and understand experiences only from their own perspective and tend to focus on one aspect of the physical appearance of objects while ignoring others. Piaget names and describes each of these limitations in his description of preoperational thinking.

Intuitive Thought

Intuitive thought According to Piaget, the beginning forms of logic developing during the preoperational stage.

Beginning around age 3 or so, many children enter the "why" stage (Piaget, 1955, 1973). They have some understanding of what they are seeing and experiencing, and now they ask "why?" about anything and everything as they try to figure out the world around them. Piaget believed young children are beginning to put together logical explanations but are still influenced more by what they perceive than by logical reasoning. He called this initial reasoning intuitive thought.

Transductive Reasoning

Transductive reasoning Thought that connects one particular observation to another by creating causal links where none exist.

Adults and older children usually think logically, using deductive and inductive reasoning to figure out problems. *Deductive reasoning* starts with a general premise (for example, "All apples have cores") and moves to specific conclusions ("This is an apple; therefore it must have a core"). Deductive reasoning is the basis of hypothesis testing, which we described in Chapter 2 as necessary for scientific research. *Inductive reasoning* starts with individual examples ("I see many apples, and they all have cores") and ends with general principles ("Therefore all apples have cores"). This reasoning is similar to the way we collect observations to develop theories.

Piaget found in his interviews with children that their logic was not consistently either deductive or inductive. Instead, they moved freely from one particular observation to another, creating causal links where none existed. He called this transductive reasoning. One example he gives is his daughter Lucienne's statement: "I haven't had my nap, therefore it isn't afternoon," as if taking her nap caused it to be afternoon (Piaget, 1962,

p. 232). Preoperational children may base their conclusions on a set of unrelated facts, or they may assume things cause each other that just happen to occur at about the same time. For example, an angry child might accuse an innocent bystander of doing him harm by reasoning, "You were there when I fell, so it's your fault that I hurt myself."

Egocentrism

Piaget believed that young children find it difficult to see the world from another person's point of view, especially if that point of view differs from their own. Piaget called this difficulty egocentrism (*ego* means "I" or "self"; therefore the child's world centers around his own point of view). Notice it is *not* the same as selfishness or egotism (thinking you are the greatest), although young children may have plenty of each of those characteristics as well. It really means the child's mind is insufficiently developed to allow her to understand that someone else's perspective could be different from her own. The result may be an apparently "selfish" child who grabs toys from others, but the reason is that she only knows how much *she* wants the toy and cannot yet understand that someone else wants it just as much. Adults should set appropriate limits on children's behavior at this age, but they should also help the child become aware of the thoughts and feelings of others to gradually overcome behavior that otherwise appears to be willfully selfish.

We see this cognitive limitation in the youngest preoperational children even regarding what they think someone else sees. For example, if someone on the phone asks a child how old she is, the child may hold up two fingers to indicate 2 years old, thinking that if she can see her fingers, then the person at the other end of the line can, too. Piaget and Inhelder (1956) used the "three mountains task," illustrated in Figure 9.1, as a way to assess egocentrism. First the child was shown a large model of three mountains on a table. Piaget lived in Switzerland and mountains were very familiar to the children he tested. Then, while standing on one side of the table, the child was shown pictures of what the mountains looked like from all four sides of the table. Finally the child was asked what a doll would see from each side of the table. Regardless of where the doll was, 4-year-old children reported that the doll saw the same view they themselves saw. In other words, children in the preoperational stage did not differentiate between their own point of view and that of another person. Egocentrism is expressed in other ways

T/F #1
We describe preschoolers as egocentric because they are selfish. *False*

Egocentrism The inability to see or understand things from someone else's perspective.

FIGURE 9.1   **Piaget's three mountains task**

In Piaget's three mountains task, a child who is egocentric believes that the teddy bear always sees the same view that she herself sees.

SOURCE: Adapted from Papalia, Olds, & Feldman (1998); Piaget & Inhelder (1956).

you may recognize. For example, if you ask a 3-year-old what to get Mommy for her birthday, he may reply "A toy truck!" If that is what he likes, he believes she must like it as well. Egocentrism makes it difficult for children to understand that other people see, feel, think, and understand things differently than they do.

Animism

Animism Giving human characteristics, such as thought and intention, to inanimate or natural things.

Another form of thinking seen in a preoperational child is animism, in which they give human characteristics, such as thought and intention, to inanimate or natural things. Piaget (1962) gave the following examples: A child saw a swirl of dead leaves and asked, "Do they like dancing?" and another child stated when she missed a train, "Doesn't the train know we aren't in it?" (pp. 251–252). Notice that animism is not the same as pretending. A child who knows she is pretending when she has her doll play a game with her is not displaying animism. However, if she truly believes the doll can be angry about losing a game, this would be an example of animism.

Conservation

Conservation The understanding that a basic quantity of something (amount, volume, mass) remains the same regardless of changes in appearance.

Centration Focusing on only one aspect of a situation.

Decenter The ability to think about more than one aspect of a situation at a time.

Another important cognitive skill preoperational children have not yet acquired is conservation, the understanding that the basic quantity of something (its amount, volume, or mass) remains the same even if its appearance changes. If you were to take a lump of clay and flatten it into a pancake, make it into a ball, or roll it into a tube, you would realize you still had the same amount of clay because you did not add or remove anything. However, preoperational children are fooled by the change in appearance and might think the new shape has more or less clay than the original.

Piaget believed one reason preschool children are fooled in this way is that they can focus on only one aspect of a problem at a time, a cognitive limitation he called centration. For instance, when preoperational children see water in several glasses, they notice only the height of the water and decide the glass with the highest level has more water in it regardless of the width of the different glasses. In Piaget's terms, they "center" on one aspect (the height of the glass) and ignore the other (the width). When children are in the next stage of development, concrete operations, they begin to decenter and are able to think about more than one aspect of a situation at a time. Now children might see that the level of the water is higher in one glass but the glass is narrow, while the level in the other is lower but the glass is wider. Once children understand that they need to consider both the level of the water and the width of the container, they will be able to come to the correct solution more easily. See **Active Learning: Conservation** for tests you can carry out with preschool and school-age children to understand more about the development of conservation.

ACTIVE LEARNING
VIDEO 9.1
Conservation

Active Learning

Conservation

To see the development of conservation, have a preschool child (age 3–5) and/or a school-age child (age 6–10) carry out the following tasks. Be sure to test the children separately so neither knows what the other has answered.

1. **Conservation of volume** (see Figure 9.2a). Equipment: two identical transparent containers and a third transparent container of a different shape. Fill the two identical containers with the same amount of water. Show these to the child

and ask, "Do these containers have the same amount of water, or does one have more than the other?" Be sure to adjust the amount of water until the child agrees the containers have the same amount. Then tell the child to watch while you pour the water from one of the identical containers into the third container. Ask the child, "Now do these two containers have the same amount of water, or does one have more than the other?" If the child answers that one has more, ask which one. However each child responds, be sure to ask *why* he or she came to that conclusion.

2. **Conservation of mass** (see Figure 9.2b). Equipment: play dough or clay. Make two identical balls of clay. Show them to the child and ask, "Do these two pieces of clay have the same amount of clay [play dough], or does one have more than the other?" Be sure to adjust the amount of clay until the child agrees the two pieces have the same amount. Then take one ball and, with the child watching, roll it into a long tube. Ask the child, "Now, do these two pieces of clay have the same amount of clay, or does one have more than the other?" However each child responds, be sure to ask *why* he or she came to that conclusion.

3. **Conservation of number** (see Figure 9.2c). Equipment: eight identical items, such as pennies or cookies. Make two rows of four items parallel to each other. Ask the child, "Does this row have the same number of pennies [or cookies] as this other row?" If the child does not agree they are the same, show the child by counting that each has four, and then ask again. Once the child has agreed that the rows are the same, move the pennies or cookies in one row so they are much farther apart than those in the other row. Then ask the child, "Now, are there the same number of pennies [or cookies] in these two rows, or does one have more than the other?" Again, be sure to ask the child to explain his or her answer.

The child's explanation for his or her answer is the most important part of this experiment, because it will tell you how the child reasoned about the changes you made. If the child is fooled by the change in the appearance of the liquid, the clay, or the row of objects, he or she is still in the preoperational stage and cannot yet conserve volume, mass, or number. If the child is not fooled, he or she has developed the ability to conserve and is in concrete operations. Some children may show conservation for some of the tests but not for all. These children are in a transitional state, moving from preoperational to concrete operational thinking. ■

To summarize what Piaget tells us about the preoperational stage, it is marked by an advance to symbolic thinking, but children's thinking at this stage is tied to what they

FIGURE 9.2a   **Conservation of volume**

These illustrations show you the types of transformations that occur when you are testing a child's ability to use decentration to solve conservation problems.

Piaget's Conservation Tasks

Part I

Part II

FIGURE 9.2b   **Conservation of mass**

Part I

Part II

FIGURE 9.2c   **Conservation of number**

Part I

Part II

©iStockphoto.com/peterspiro

see rather than what they reason out with the use of logic. Their perception is still tied to their own point of view, although they gradually begin to realize that others may see and understand the world differently than they do. Many of the limitations found in preoperational children are overcome in the next stage, called concrete operations. We describe these changes in Chapter 12 when we learn about cognitive development during middle childhood.

Check Your Understanding

1. Why did Piaget call his second stage of cognitive development "preoperational"?
2. In Piaget's theory, what is transductive reasoning?
3. What did Piaget mean when he described young children as egocentric?
4. What is animism?
5. How is centration related to young children's inability to understand conservation of volume, mass, and number?

9.2

What are the basic processes described by Vygotsky's sociocultural theory?

Vygotsky's Sociocultural Theory of Cognitive Development

Lev Vygotsky (1896–1934) lived in Russia during the time of the communist revolution, when the tsarist government was brought down and a new government based on Marxist principles was established. These principles, including a focus on the process of development, collective activities, and the importance of understanding development within its cultural and historical context (Fu, 1997; Gielen & Jeshmaridian, 1999), played an important role in shaping Vygotsky's thinking about human behavior and the study of the human mind.

Although Vygotsky had supported much of the ideology of the communist government, his work was banned during his lifetime in favor of the "reflexology" of Pavlov, which denied the importance of the mind and its inner processes (Trevarthen, 1991). Vygotsky's work did not become available in the West until 1962, when his book *Thought and Language* was published in English. Since then, his ideas have become very influential in the study and application of cognitive theory. Piaget lived to be 84 and made contributions to the field of child development over a long period of time. By contrast, Vygotsky's life was cut short when he died at age 37 (McKeachie & Sims, 2004). All his significant contributions to the field came from only 10 years of work, but they have had a profound effect, particularly in the field of education.

Before we describe Vygotsky's theory of cognitive development in more detail, let's review how his theories are similar to and different from Piaget's theory. Vygotsky's theory of cognitive development begins with the social world, and in that way it is very different from Piaget's theory. In contrast to Piaget, who saw the child as an active but largely independent learner, Vygotsky saw all learning and ideas as beginning in the social world of interactions between children and those with whom they have contact. As a result, Vygotsky believed learning is culturally based, because all people are situated within their own culture. The tools, language, and actions of a particular culture are transmitted to children and serve to shape their cognitive abilities (Gauvain & Parke, 2010).

Lev Vygotsky. Vygotsky's sociocultural theory describes cognitive development as a result of children's social interactions within their particular culture. ∎

You will remember one example of this principle from the research on *cultural neuro-science* described in Chapter 1 demonstrating that culture shapes whether we focus on one central object or the whole context of a scene we are viewing (Jenkins et al., 2010).

Central to Vygotsky's theory is the idea that children learn through the process of social collaboration with someone who is more knowledgeable than they are. As developmentalists, when we hear this description, we usually think of interactions between adults and children, but we should not assume the more knowledgeable person is necessarily an older one. Children learn a great deal from their peers, and there certainly are some areas of expertise where a younger person teaches an older one. Vygotsky described three ways in which ideas are transmitted from a more experienced person to a less experienced one: the zone of proximal development, scaffolding, and private speech. We describe the first two in detail here. The concept of private speech is discussed later in this chapter in the context of language development.

The Zone of Proximal Development (ZPD)

Vygotsky began his work as a psychologist by working with children who had physical and mental impairments. At first, he simply tested their mental abilities. However, he soon developed the idea that children should be tested twice: the first time performing on their own, and the second time performing with a little help from an adult. This technique assesses both the child's actual level of achievement and the child's readiness to learn. The difference between what the child can do independently and what the child can do with the help and guidance of a more skilled adult or peer is what Vygotsky (1978b) called the zone of proximal development, or ZPD. It is within this zone that learning occurs.

If we present learners with information that is very far above their current level, it is not likely to be beneficial. On the other hand, if we simply give them information they already have, it does not advance their knowledge or understanding. Children get the greatest benefit from interactions that focus on information just slightly beyond what they are capable of doing on their own. One of the challenges of being an effective teacher is determining where the ZPD is and staying within it. It is, of course, a moving target. As soon as we have been effective as a teacher, our learner's ZPD shifts upward, and we need to adjust our teaching to match this new ZPD.

Scaffolding

Vygotsky saw adults and older children forming a cognitive structure around a child that they could use to move the child to fuller understanding. This process is what he called scaffolding. Scaffolding is a sensitive process of providing the support that helps the child achieve what is just out of reach. When the child has achieved understanding, the scaffolding is no longer needed and the child can now carry out the task independently.

To better understand scaffolding, think about teaching a child to tie her shoes. With an infant, you would simply

© Roy McMahon/CORBIS

Scaffolding. Teaching a child to become progressively more independent in tying his or her own shoelaces is a good example of the scaffolding technique. ∎

do it for her. With a 2-year-old, you might hold her hands and do it with her. With a preschooler, you might teach the "bunny ears" approach, in which the child forms two loops and circles one around the other, maybe with a song or rhyme that goes with the process. By age 6 or 7, you can teach the child how to wrap one string around and through the other. The amount and type of help you provide at each of these steps is the scaffold that supports the child's learning. Finally, no scaffolding is necessary when the child can perform this task alone.

You will find several applications of Vygotsky's theory throughout this chapter as you learn more about the development of executive function, language development, fantasy play, and learning to read.

Check Your Understanding

1. Why did Vygotsky believe social collaboration is central to children's learning?
2. What is the zone of proximal development?
3. How does scaffolding function in Vygotsky's view of cognitive development?

9.3

How do attention, memory, executive function, and social cognition develop in early childhood?

Cognitive Processes

In this section, we look at some of the cognitive processes that undergo significant change during early childhood. Although attention, memory, executive function, and social cognition all improve substantially from infancy, young children still have many limitations in each of these areas. For instance, their memory is still quite suggestible, so they may develop false memories of things that did not happen to them. We look at both the advances and the limitations that remain in this period of early childhood.

Attention in Early Childhood

The process of learning usually begins when we pay attention to what we will be learning. As children grow, they are increasingly capable of directing and sustaining their attention (López, Menez, & Hernández-Guzmán, 2005). However, as anyone who has worked in a preschool can tell you, some children can sit in circle time and pay attention, and others have great trouble doing so. Individual differences in the ability to focus and sustain attention have consequences for later development. In a longitudinal study, parents rated their 4-year-old child's attention span ("Plays with a single toy for long periods of time," "Child goes from toy to toy quickly") and the child's persistence ("Child persists at a task until successful," "Child gives up easily when difficulties are encountered"). Children who had more ability to maintain focused attention and who persisted even when faced with difficulties had higher math and reading achievement at age 21 and a greater chance of college completion by age 25 (McClelland, Acock, Piccinin, Rhea, & Stallings, 2013).

Although individual differences in attention may in part be genetic (Posner, Rothbart, & Sheese, 2007), they are also influenced by the child's experiences. For example, attention in preschool children has been linked to differences in parenting that are related to families' economic circumstances. Low-income mothers are likely to experience more parenting stress and tend to provide less stimulation and support to their children. These differences in parenting are related to more impulsivity and less sustained attention in 5-year-olds, and these characteristics, in turn, are related to lower cognitive, academic, and social competence (Dilworth-Bart, Khurshid, & Vandell, 2007).

Helen Neville and her colleagues (2013) also found that low-income preschoolers had less effective *selective attention* than did children from families with more resources; that is, they were less able to ignore distracting stimuli. Neville developed a training program for these children focused on games that allowed them to practice attention skills. Her program also trained parents to promote their child's attention skills. After 8 weeks she found positive changes in the way these children's brains functioned and also in their language skills, nonverbal IQ, and social skills, as well as a reduction in problem behaviors. Parents benefited from the program, too, showing reduced stress and a better ability to maintain conversations with their children. It is clear that focused and sustained attention is an important building block for future academic success.

Memory in Early Childhood

Certainly young children's memory is improving, but there are still limitations in their ability to encode information into memory, how much information they can retain, and how suggestible their memory is.

Encoding Processes

Memory is a process of taking in information and encoding, or organizing, it so that you can later retrieve and use it. When you read this book, you will want to remember the information and ideas presented in it. When you study you use encoding processes, such as repetition or association to known material, to help ensure you will remember the information. Children younger than 5 or 6 usually do not use a deliberate strategy to try to remember something, and even when we try to teach them, they are unable to use memory strategies. By 5 to 6 years of age, they still do not use these strategies spontaneously, but they can use them when they are taught to do so. Children tend not to use memory strategies spontaneously until middle childhood, but the age of acquisition and use of these strategies varies enormously between individual children (Schneider, Kron, Hünnerkopf, & Krajewski, 2004). When 6-year-olds were asked how they memorized a group of pictures they had been shown, their answers reflected individual differences in their use of encoding strategies. While one child used an active encoding strategy: "I looked carefully and I repeated: red, blue, brown," another had no strategy: "I looked at them, and I remembered them . . . I just looked at them" (Visu-Petra, Cheie, & Benga, 2008, p. 101).

One of the memory strategies young children do use is scripts to help them remember what to do in a familiar situation (Nelson, 2014). Just as a script tells the actors what to say and do in a dramatic play, a script as we are using it here is a memory of what to say and do in particular situations. Children as young as 3 might have a script for going out to lunch at a fast-food restaurant or going to the grocery store (and may act out that scenario in play with friends).

How can adults foster memory development in young children? It is important to talk with children about their activities. If a parent asks the child what he did at preschool that day and has a conversation about it, the child will be more likely to form memories. Another wonderful way to promote memory is through music. You can probably remember the words to a song you have not heard for years when the first few notes are played. Music helps form powerful memories, which is one reason we teach children using songs. Can you say the alphabet without singing it?

Working Memory

Another aspect of memory that undergoes developmental change is the capacity of working memory. Working memory is the amount of information we can actively hold in our conscious mind at one time. The working memory of young children has a very limited capacity. The average 5-year-old can hold one or two pieces of information in mind at a time (Alloway, 2010). This means that "Put your book in your cubby, and come sit at the table" may be all the information he or she can handle in working memory at once. A three- or four-item sequence is likely to exceed that capacity. However, we see the

T/F #2

We can improve a preschooler's memory by teaching the child to use memory strategies. *False*

Encoding processes The transformation processes through which new information is stored in long-term memory.

Scripts Memory for the way a common occurrence in one's life, such as grocery shopping, takes place.

Working memory The amount of information we can actively hold in our conscious mind at one time.

capacity of verbal working memory and visual-spatial working memory steadily increase from age 4 to age 11 (Alloway, Gathercole, & Pickering, 2006; Gathercole, Pickering, Ambridge, & Wearing, 2004).

False Memories

JOURNAL ARTICLE 9.1
False Memories

We all create the story of our lives from our autobiographical memories. However, have you ever been told that a memory you thought happened to you actually happened to your sister or friend? How reliable are our memories?

Research has shown it can be fairly easy to influence young children to think they experienced something that never happened. In one study, children were told to imagine taking a hot-air balloon ride and to think in detail about what it was like (Ceci, Bruck, & Loftus, 1998). They were then asked whether this had really happened to them. They were given similar instructions to remember in detail other events, some of which had really happened to them and some of which had not. The researchers repeated this process for 11 weeks, and gradually children began to agree that they had in fact gone on a hot-air balloon ride. In the 12th week, another researcher interviewed each child, telling the child that the previous researcher had said some things that were not true. When the child was asked which things had really happened, many still remembered having taken the fictional balloon ride. Younger preschoolers were more likely to make these mistakes than older preschoolers. As we mentioned in Chapter 2, the suggestibility of young children's memories makes it especially important that interviewers taking eyewitness testimony from children are trained not to inadvertently create false memories for the child.

Executive Function

As we learned in Chapter 6, executive function is a higher-order ability of the brain to organize our attention, memory, and behavior in order to reach a goal. It enables us to inhibit some behaviors, switch from task to task, and remain focused on what we are doing. Young children have limited ability to do these things, and we see this limitation in how they follow rules. At 3 years of age they are capable of following two rules, such as "If you get a red card put it in this pile, but if you get a blue card, put it in this pile," but if you ask these children to do more they will not be able to remember and carry out the task (Center on the Developing Child at Harvard, 2011). By age 4 most children can change rules, for example, first sorting cards into a pile for flowers and a pile for cars and then taking all the cards and sorting them into one pile for red pictures and one for blue pictures (Zelazo, 2004–2014).

By age 5, executive function has developed to allow more complex tasks. For example, many children can play Simon Says, inhibiting an action when the leader doesn't say "Simon says." However, there are large individual differences in this ability, so some young children will not be able to carry out the task. **Active Learning: Executive Function** gives you an opportunity to do a simple assessment of several aspects of executive function in young children, including attention, working memory, and inhibitory control.

Active Learning

Executive Function

ACTIVE LEARNING
VIDEO 9.2
Executive Function

Behavioral regulation is a manifestation of executive function skills that are crucial to children's ability to function well in a classroom setting (Ponitz, McClelland, Matthews, & Morrison, 2009). They include being able to pay attention, follow directions, and inhibit or regulate behavior. You can make a simple assessment of these skills by playing Head-Shoulders-Knees-Toes with preschool children.

Tell the child you are going to play a game in which he or she should follow your directions when you say "touch your head" or "touch your toes." Give the child several opportunities to do this while mixing up the order of your directions, something like this: Touch your head, touch your toes, touch your toes, touch your head, touch your head, touch your toes. After you have established that the child can follow your directions, tell the child "Okay, now let's be silly. When I tell you to touch your head, you should touch your toes. When I tell you to touch your toes, you should touch your head." Again give the child a set of directions, observing how easy or difficult it is for the child to inhibit the original response and shift to the contrary response.

Repeat the activity, using the instructions to "touch your shoulders" and "touch your knees."

If you observe children from about age 3 to age 6, you will see how much these executive functions develop in a relatively short period of time. Three-year-olds will find it difficult to behave contrary to what they are hearing, but 6-year-olds will find it easy and fun. ■

Executive function provides the basis for learning preacademic skills. Preschool children who show greater ability to pay attention, inhibit irrelevant behavior, and actively remember are able to learn basic language, literacy, and arithmetic skills more quickly than others (Center on the Developing Child at Harvard, 2011). Children develop these skills through play with peers as well as through sensitive scaffolding by adults (Lengua, Honorado, & Bush, 2007). They do best when both their home and preschool provide organized and predictable environments.

When young children experience chaotic or threatening environments, their executive function may suffer. If you think about a time when you were highly stressed, you may remember finding it difficult to think clearly about what you should do. Recall from Chapter 8 that when children experience high levels of stress for long periods while their brains are developing, the effect on the brain may last longer than the stress itself. For example, children who have experienced abuse and neglect early in life generally have lower executive function ability (National Scientific Council on the Developing Child, 2005). The good news is that intervention in the preschool years can improve these abilities. In one program called Tools of the Mind, children were encouraged to tell themselves out loud what they were supposed to do, to carry out extended dramatic play, and they were given aids to memory and attention. Children in this program were later found to have greater executive function, which correlated with greater academic skills, than a comparable group of children who did not take part in the program (Diamond, Barnett, Thomas, & Munro, 2007).

Social Cognition: Theory of Mind

When we study social cognition, we are looking at the ways we use cognitive processes to understand our social world. One important aspect of social cognition that develops in childhood is called theory of mind, which refers to "young children's developing abilities to understand self and others as agents who act on the basis of their mental states (i.e., beliefs, desires, emotions, intentions)" (Astington & Filippova, 2005, p. 211). For example, if you ask a child why she took her friend's toy away, she may answer, "Because I *wanted* it!" She explains her behavior in terms of her *own* mental state of wanting the toy. It takes children longer to understand that the other child is now crying because he, too, wanted it.

We see the beginning of the development of a theory of mind in young children as they leave infancy and enter early childhood. Within the first 2 years of life, young children begin to use their understanding of some basic aspects of other people's minds in their interactions with them. For example, they seem to understand that they should give a

Social cognition The ways we use cognitive processes to understand our social world.

Theory of mind The ability to understand self and others as agents who act on the basis of their mental states.

particular type of food to someone who has reacted with a smile to that food and not to someone who has reacted with disgust, even if they themselves prefer the rejected food (Repacholi & Gopnik, 1997). This growing understanding also helps the child's early language learning. Children have a primitive understanding of what an adult is thinking when the adult says "doll" while *looking* at an object. The child understands that the adult is labeling *that* object rather than something else (Baldwin & Moses, 2001). Young children also begin to develop language to describe internal states, and they seem to progress from an understanding of wants and desires ("she wants that cookie") to an understanding of beliefs ("he thinks the cookie is over there") (Tardif & Wellman, 2000).

Over time, as we understand more and more about the motives, emotions, and thoughts of others, we all become pretty accomplished "mind readers." See **Active Learning: Mind Reading and Mindblindness** to experience what it might be like if you did not have a theory of mind.

Active Learning

Mind Reading and Mindblindness

Simon Baron-Cohen (1995) presents the following scenario in his book *Mindblindness*: "John walked into the bedroom, walked around, and walked out" (p. 1). Think about how you might try to explain this behavior. What could possibly be going on to make this happen?

Write down your ideas about what John might be doing. Next, underline each word in your explanation that reflects something about his possible mental state—for example, *wanted, heard, wanted to know, looked for, was confused*. After you do this, try to write an explanation for John's behavior that does *not* include anything about his mental state. It is hard for us to do. Here is one attempt by Baron-Cohen (1995): "Maybe John does this every day, at this time: he just walks into the bedroom, walks around, and walks out again" (p. 2). Not very satisfactory, is it? Most of us automatically put ideas about others' thoughts into our explanations for their behavior.

It is hard for us even to imagine what it would be like if we did not have theories about what goes on in other people's minds. Baron-Cohen uses the term mindblindness to describe the inability to understand and theorize about other people's thoughts. Mindblindness is characteristic of many people who have autism spectrum disorders. ∎

Mindblindness The inability to understand and theorize about other people's thoughts.

Children actively construct their ideas about what happens in their own and other people's minds, and they become better at doing this as they get older (Peterson, Wellman, & Slaughter, 2012). Between ages 2 and 4, a child develops some ability to understand that other people can believe something the child knows is untrue, called a false belief. A classic experiment designed to test whether children understand that what goes on in someone else's mind might be different from what is going on in their own is called the false belief paradigm. In these experiments, a child views a scene something like this: A doll named Louise is shown that a piece of candy is hidden in a certain drawer in a toy kitchen. Louise then leaves, and the experimenter takes the candy and moves it into the refrigerator. When Louise returns, she wants the candy. The child is asked where she thinks Louise will look for it. A child who doesn't understand that others can have false beliefs will say that Louise will look in the refrigerator. The child knows where the candy is, and, if she doesn't yet have a theory of mind, it seems to her that Louise must know that, too.

False belief The understanding that someone else may believe something that a child knows to be untrue.

False belief paradigm An experimental task used to assess a child's understanding that others may believe something the child knows to be untrue.

Children who do understand that others may have false beliefs understand that Louise will look first in the drawer where she last saw the candy. By age 4, most children can respond based on an understanding of false beliefs, and recent research has indicated that younger children can carry out similar tasks successfully when verbal responses are not required. For example, 2-year-olds watched while an adult saw a puppet place a ball in a particular box. Then a phone rang and the adult turned away, while the puppet moved the ball to a different location. When the adult went to retrieve the ball, these toddlers looked toward the box that the adult would have falsely believed still contained the ball (Southgate, Senju, & Csibra, 2007). Similar results have been found for even younger infants (Scott & Baillargeon, 2009). You can determine for yourself whether a young child has developed an understanding of false beliefs he or she can express verbally by following the instructions in **Active Learning: False Beliefs**.

Active Learning

False Beliefs

Try the following simple experiment with a child between 3 and 4 and another child who is older.

1. Before you see each child, take a box a child would recognize as containing crayons. Remove the crayons and put something else inside: short drinking straws, for example.

2. When you sit down with the child, ask her what she thinks is in the box. She should answer "crayons." Then show her what is really inside. Close the box.

3. Ask her the following: "If [name of a friend] came into the room right now, what would she think is inside this box?"

If the child replies "crayons" (or whatever she said the first time), then she has demonstrated a good understanding that a friend may think something different from what she herself does. If she replies that her friend would know it is not crayons but is instead whatever you have put in the box, then she does not understand that her friend could have a false belief. Instead, she thinks her friend knows everything that she herself knows, despite the fact that her friend never saw that you had replaced the crayons with some other objects (adapted from Flavell, 1999). Whether the child understands that her friend can have a false belief is an indication of where she is in the process of developing a theory of mind. ■

ACTIVE LEARNING
VIDEO 9.3
False Beliefs

The ability to understand what others are thinking is a skill that is affected by children's experiences. When parents discuss emotions with their children, the children are more likely to develop a theory of mind at a younger age (Lewis & Carpendale, 2002). Children also are more likely to understand false beliefs if their parents' discipline techniques include asking the child to think about how another person felt when the child is disciplined for hurting that person (Ruffman, Perner, & Parkin, 1999).

Researchers also have looked at the impact of cultural differences on the development of theory of mind (Ahn & Miller, 2012; Shahaeian, Peterson, Slaughter, & Wellman, 2011). Although children in many different cultures develop theory of mind at about the same age, the way in which it develops differs. In collectivist cultures such as Iran and China, children are encouraged to obtain knowledge but not to express opinions that challenge their elders' points of view and disrupt family harmony. Consequently their first understanding of theory of mind is that others can know things that they do not or vice versa. Children in individualist cultures such as Australia and the United States are more often encouraged to express their own opinions and they learn that others can have different opinions before they understand that they can have different knowledge (Shahaeian et al., 2011).

9.4

Why is play important for cognitive development in early childhood?

T/F #3

It is important for children to play because they have fun when they are playing, but the real learning happens in the classroom. *False*

Discovery learning An approach to teaching that emphasizes allowing children to discover for themselves new information and understanding.

Play and Cognitive Development

Play has increasingly been seen as an activity that simply takes time away from the "important work" of childhood: academic learning (Pellegrini, 2005). For example, several years ago the U.S. government wanted to narrow the focus of the Head Start preschool program for disadvantaged children to one outcome: literacy. While literacy is certainly a core skill all children should have, this restricted goal ignores preschoolers' developmental need to learn through exploration and play (Zigler & Bishop-Josef, 2006). As Joan Almon (2003) of the Alliance for Childhood said, "The child's love of learning is intimately linked with a zest for play" (p. 18). Children not only have fun while they play, but it also is one important way that they learn about the world.

Educators in early childhood programs have felt a continuing pressure to focus on academic achievement, preparing children to do well on standardized tests, and to make a choice between play-based, child-centered programs and academic, teacher-directed programs. However, Kyle Snow (n.d.), Director of the National Association for the Education of Young Children's Center for Applied Research, has proposed that we think of preschool environments as shown in Figure 9.3. Rather than thinking about play *versus* learning, we can think about ways to incorporate learning into play so we have play *and* learning.

Discovery learning is one approach that combines play and instruction, with the focus on allowing children to discover for themselves new information and understanding. The advantage of including discovery learning in preschool is illustrated by research in which children were shown a novel toy with four different interesting results. For example, one tube squeaked, a second one had a hidden mirror, and so on. For one group of 4-year-olds, the experimenter acted as though she discovered the first tube could squeak by accident and seemed surprised and delighted by what she discovered. With the second group, she acted more like a traditional teacher and told the children to watch her as she showed them how to make the first tube squeak. Both groups were then allowed to play with the toy on their own (Bonawitz et al., 2011). All the children could repeat what they saw the researcher do, but the first group played with the new toy longer and discovered more of its features than the group that had received instruction on how to use the toy. The researchers concluded that direct instruction made the children less curious and less likely to discover new information on their own. Of course we also want learning to be efficient, and direct instruction does accomplish that so that is why a balanced approach may be best.

What is play? See **Active Learning: What Is Play?** to try to define its characteristics for yourself.

FIGURE 9.3 The interaction of play and direct instruction

Child active

Teacher passive / Teacher active

Discovery
Free play

Scaffolding
Guided play

Maturation
Rest

Direct instruction
Rule-based games

Child passive

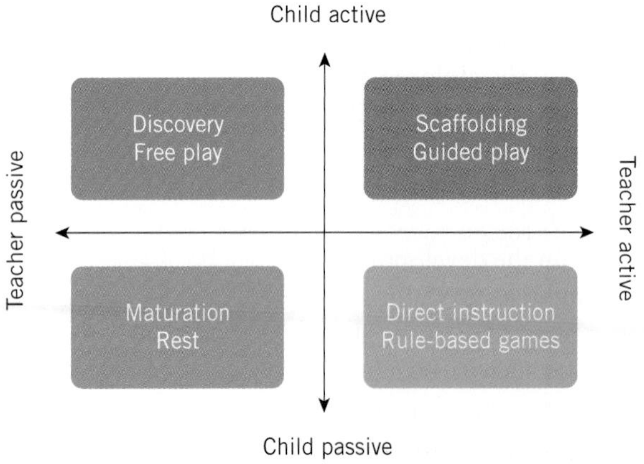

Rather than thinking of the preschool environment as being either play-centered or teacher-directed, we can look at the way those two approaches can be combined. If you were choosing a preschool for your young child, which balance would you prefer? Why?

SOURCE: Snow (n.d.).

Active Learning

WEB LINK 9.1
Play

What Is Play?

Read the following descriptions of play situations with 4-year-olds in two different cultures.

Scenario 1. In the following translated dialogue, a 4-year-old boy (Dagiwa) and girl (Hoyali) in Papua New Guinea are pretending to be doctors taking care of patients, which are represented first by the visiting anthropologist's feet and then by a tree stump:

Dagiwa:	(addresses foot-patient) "Are you also sick?"
Hoyali:	"Hold this one" (takes foot in hands and places it down on ground). "I am letting it stay here."
Dagiwa:	"Has this one also been sick, eh?"
Hoyali:	"Yes, this one has been sick."
Dagiwa:	(pretends to give the foot-patient an injection) "The injection is finished."

(Dagiwa leaves Hoyali and focuses his attention on a small banana tree stump . . . which is treated as if it is a new patient. Hoyali moves to join him.)

Dagiwa:	"Is this one ill?"
Hoyali:	"I am giving it an injection." (adapted from Goldman & Smith, 1998, pp. 226–227)

Scenario 2. In this second example, a group of 4-year-olds is interacting in a day care center in the United States.

Elisha and Max are in their make-believe library in their day care center pretending to read a book about building castles. Elisha counts the blocks as she hands them to Max, who repeats the numbers as he places each block in the structure. Max is growing impatient, however, and says that he will be the castle's "big green dragon." Elisha responds, "OK, I will be the princess with a purple dress, but let's finish making the castle." Juan joins them and wants to play. Max agrees and offers Juan a role as the prince. But Juan wants to be the green dragon. Much negotiating takes place. Finally, Juan agrees to assume this role, but he insists on wearing a gold crown (Bellin & Singer, 2006, p. 101).

Based on these scenarios, reflect on these questions and keep your answers in mind as you read the rest of this section on play and cognitive development:

1. How would you define play based on these two examples? What characteristics make this play rather than some other kind of activity?

2. What cognitive, language, social, and emotional abilities must children have to be able to play in these ways?

3. Finally, how does this play help children develop physically, cognitively, linguistically, socially, and emotionally? What are the children learning in each of these domains? ■

What definition of "play" did you come up with? Perhaps the chief characteristic of play is that it is fun. Children are actively and fully engaged in the "private reality" that makes up their play (Segal, 2004, p. 38). Other characteristics that have been proposed include the following:

1. Play is done for its own sake, not for any outside goal or purpose.

2. Even when it is an imitation of adult work, play is marked as being different through signals such as exaggeration of activities, role reversals, or laughing.

3. Play is voluntary and spontaneous (Burghardt, 2004, p. 294).

Some have argued that play is a universal human behavior, though it is not unique to humans, as anyone with a puppy knows. Even children who must work at an early age find ways to play while they are working (Drewes, 2005). For example, fantasy play was found among both poor and middle-class Brazilian children regardless of their ethnic group and location within the country (Gosso, Morais, & Otta, 2007). In 2013, the United Nations Committee on the Rights of the Child affirmed its long-time commitment to the importance of play for children's development around the world. As a part of this reaffirmation, the Committee said, "Play and recreation are essential to the health and well-being of children and promote the development of creativity, imagination, self-confidence, self-efficacy, as well as physical, social, cognitive and emotional strength and skills. They contribute to all aspects of learning . . ." (p. 4).

Development of Play

Piaget (1962) described a developmental sequence of play based on a child's cognitive maturity. He hypothesized that the nature of children's play would change as the level of their thinking changed. Based on this sequence, he proposed three levels:

Practice play Performing a certain behavior repetitively for the mere pleasure of it.

1. **Practice play:** performing a certain behavior repetitively for the mere pleasure of it—for example, jumping back and forth over a puddle for no purpose other than the enjoyment of doing so. An infant in the sensorimotor stage of development is capable of practice play such as dropping a ball over and over just to see it happen.

Symbolic/sociodramatic play Using symbolic representations and imagination for play.

2. **Symbolic/sociodramatic play:** using symbolic representations and imagination for play—for example, pretending to drink tea. Toddlers begin to use symbols in play at the end of the sensorimotor period, and preschoolers in the preoperational stage of cognition develop sociodramatic play to a much greater extent.

Games with rules Making up rules for a game or playing games with preestablished rules.

3. **Games with rules:** making up rules for a game or playing games with preestablished rules, such as baseball or soccer. This type of play is developed most clearly in the next stage, the stage of concrete operations. Piaget argued that younger children try to fit reality to their own purposes through fantasy, while older children begin to fit themselves into the larger reality of the social world around them by following rules.

Constructive play Building or making something for the purposes of play.

Since Piaget proposed these stages, researchers have further developed his ideas about the cognitive levels necessary for different types of play. Sara Smilansky (1968) added a stage after practice play, which she labeled constructive play, consisting of building or making something for the purposes of play. While practice play begins in infancy when, for example, babies shake a rattle over and over, both symbolic/sociodramatic and constructive play develop during early childhood as children develop the cognitive abilities necessary to pretend, plan, and carry out different scenarios. Young children are not very good at games with rules, as anyone who has ever tried to play Candyland or Chutes and Ladders with a preschooler soon finds out. They are interested in winning but don't understand the nature of rules and that they apply equally to all players.

Symbolic/ Sociodramatic Play

Symbolic/sociodramatic play, also referred to as fantasy play, appears as children move from infancy to early childhood in widely diverse cultures around the world, but the content reflects the culture in which it is embedded. For example, in one study, American children based their play on toys and the ideas they represented, so a toy rocket might trigger fantasy about a trip into outer space. In contrast, Chinese children tended not to use objects but rather based their pretend play on social interactions, such as pretending to address a guest or interacting with a shopkeeper (Haight, Wang, Fung, Williams, & Mintz, 1999).

While the content of fantasy play differs, the development of the ability to use symbols and understand social roles, both of which are used in fantasy play, may have a more universal pattern. Watson and Fischer (1977, 1980) proposed that fantasy play using symbols goes through several stages in accordance with the child's level of cognitive development. They saw a sequence of steps, based on the toddler's development from a focus only on himself to greater ability to take the role of another as follows:

I win! Young children have difficulty understanding and following the rules of a game. Trying to play a game like Monopoly or Candyland with a young child often ends the way the child wants, regardless of the rules. ■

1. The child performs the action—for example, pretending to sleep (18 months).

2. The child acts on the other—for example, combing the doll's hair (18 months–2 years).

3. The child has the other perform an action—for example, the doll washes its face (2 years).

Preschoolers then build on these skills as they learn to perform social roles:

1. The child performs or has a doll perform several different actions linked to a social role, such as doctor (3 years).

2. The child performs a social role with another person performing a complementary role—for example, doctor and patient (4 years).

3. The child performs more than one role—for example, she is the doctor and then the mother of the patient (6 years).

Both social and cognitive abilities contribute to a child's ability to play. Play becomes more sophisticated and complicated as children can coordinate activities with others socially while at the same time developing the ability to use symbols and understand rules. We discuss the social side of play in Chapter 10.

Fantasy play seems to promote what Vygotsky called private speech more than other activities do. **Private speech** involves talking to oneself, often out loud, to guide one's own actions. In one study, researchers observed children's play with their mothers. They found the children often incorporated what their mothers had said during play when they talked to themselves during their own private fantasy play (Haight & Miller, 1992). If you have been with preschoolers, you have most likely seen the way they

🎙️ AUDIO LINK 9.1
Changes in Play

Private speech Talking to oneself, often out loud, to guide one's own actions.

talk to themselves as they make-believe, giving voice to different characters and having whole conversations all by themselves. In one study, almost all the mothers who were interviewed reported that their 3- to 5-year-olds used private speech during their fantasy play, and the preschoolers were more likely to engage in private speech while they were playing than when they were problem solving (Winsler, Feder, Way, & Manfra, 2006)

The way that fantasy play can facilitate cognitive development is shown by its use as an intervention strategy to help young children learn preacademic skills. Together with colleagues, Dorothy Singer developed a program called *My Magic Story Car* in which parents and caregivers of low-income children are taught to use fantasy play to help their children develop the skills necessary for school (Bellin & Singer, 2006). For example, in the Trip to Mars game, the parent or caregiver helps children teach Martian children about life on Earth by creating a book explaining it in their own words. The children then fly to Mars and pretend to teach the Martian children how to use the book. Clearly, children should and do respond with more enthusiasm to this way of learning literacy than by using worksheets to learn letters. Research has shown this program to be successful in improving young children's school readiness.

> ### Check Your Understanding
>
> 1. Why is play important for developing cognitive skills?
> 2. How did Piaget categorize types of play?
> 3. What is constructive play?
> 4. What are some benefits for children of fantasy play?

9.5

How does language develop in early childhood?

Language Development in Early Childhood

As we saw in Chapter 6, toddlers up to age 2 have learned to use single words and are beginning to combine them into two-word sentences. This early language ability forms the basis for the rapid developments in language that occur during early childhood.

Development of Syntax

Telegraphic speech A stage in language development in which children only use the words necessary to get their point across and omit small words that are not necessary (for example, *Go bye-bye*).

When children put three or more words together, they are beginning to develop the syntax or grammar of their language. They use the simplest combination of words in the right order to convey the meaning they intend. Long before instant messaging and texting, people used to send telegrams. Because they had to pay by the word, they did not say, "I am going to arrive at 11:00 p.m. at the train station"; instead they said, "Arriving station 11 p.m.," leaving out all unnecessary words. When young children begin to put words together, they act as if they have to pay for each word, and they use only the ones necessary to get their point across. This is called telegraphic speech.

Word order used in telegraphic speech reflects the language children are hearing. For example, word order in English is very likely to be a subject, then a verb, and then the object of the verb: *The dog* (subject) *chased* (verb) *the cat* (object). English-speaking children find it difficult to produce and understand passive sentences in which this order is changed: *The cat was chased by the dog*. However, children who speak Sesotho, a language found in southern Africa, hear passive sentences frequently and can produce these forms as soon as they learn to speak (Demuth, 1990). You can try **Active Learning: The Impact of Word Order** to see whether the language development of a child you know has advanced to the point where the child understands passive sentences.

Active Learning

The Impact of Word Order

First take two pieces of paper and draw a picture on each. On one piece of paper, draw a dog facing right and running. On the second piece of paper, draw a cat facing right and running. Ask a child between 3 and 6 years of age to arrange the pictures to show *The dog is chasing the cat*. Then ask the child to arrange the picture to show *The dog is chased by the cat*. Does the child understand that in the second sentence, which is in the passive form, the cat is actually chasing the dog? If not, this shows that the child still understands language only through the grammatical structure of subject-verb-object. Some 4-year-old English-speaking children can understand passive sentences, but many children in elementary school still have trouble with this form (Vasilyeva, Huttenlocher, & Waterfall, 2006). Compare your results with those of others in the class who tested children of different ages. ▪

ACTIVE LEARNING
VIDEO 9.4
Impact of Word Order

Overregularization

Not only are young children beginning to use sentences with more complex word structure, but they also are beginning to use more complex forms of the words themselves. Whereas younger children use only the basic forms of words, such as *I go store*, preschoolers begin to add morphemes. In Chapter 6, we defined a morpheme as the smallest unit that has meaning in a language. A morpheme may be a word like *house, car,* or *alligator*, or it may be any part of a word that has meaning, such as *-ed*, which indicates past tense, or *-s*, which indicates a plural. As the preschooler learns to use morphemes appropriately, she no longer says "I walk home" but rather "I walked home" when she means the past tense.

When children first learn to use added morphemes, they often use them on words for which they don't work. We called these mistakes overregularization in Chapter 6 because children are using the regular forms on words that follow an irregular pattern. For example, the past tense of *I ride* is not *I rided* but rather *I rode*. Young children seem to learn a rule or pattern, such as "add 'ed' to make past tense" but then apply this rule to words that are irregular in form. Interestingly, they may use both the correct and the incorrect version, even in the same sentence: *I goed to the store and then went home.*

Follow the directions in **Active Learning: Collecting a Language Sample** to look at the nature of a young child's language development.

VIDEO LINK 9.2
Overregularization

Active Learning

Collecting a Language Sample

Take a 10- to 15-minute language sample of a child between 2 and 4 years of age by watching while the child is playing with another child or talking with an adult. Try to write down exactly what she says. How many words does the child put together: one, two, three, or more? If the child is using single words, how does she make herself understood (for example, by using gestures)? If she puts two or more words together, are they in the same order we find in adult grammar? Are words left out as in telegraphic speech (for example, *I go store*)? Do the words have appropriate endings (for example, *kicked, playing, desks*)? Does the child overregularize and put endings on irregularly formed words (for example, *wented, sitted*)? Compare your findings with those of others in your class who observed children older or younger than the child you observed. ▪

ACTIVE LEARNING
VIDEO 9.5
Collecting a Language Sample

Egocentric Versus Private Speech

Although their use of language is rapidly increasing, preschoolers still have some limitations to their ability to communicate with others. Piaget (1973) described the inability of young children to take the role of other people in their conversations as egocentric speech. For example, a child may say something like "I went to that place and saw someone going round and round." He does not realize that you have no idea what "that place" is or how someone can go "round and round" because he doesn't understand that you don't know everything that he knows. For Piaget, the explanation for egocentric speech is that children are not born social beings; they must learn to be social and to understand other people's points of view. Children's speech reflects this imperfect understanding. Eventually children begin to learn that when others don't understand them they must adjust what they say to accommodate what the other person does or does not know. When they begin to do this, their communication becomes much more effective. Schematically, Piaget described the development of speech as follows:

Presocial speech ⟶ Egocentric speech ⟶ Socialized speech

Vygotsky (1962) had a very different idea about what egocentric speech was. For Vygotsky, children are born social beings so they always intend to communicate, but at some point their speech divides into two types: speech directed at other people and speech directed at themselves. As we noted earlier in the chapter, Vygotsky referred to self-directed speech as private speech. Speech directed at other people continues to be communicative, but private speech becomes increasingly silent. Younger children talk to themselves out loud, for example, "I'm using the red crayon." Somewhat older children more often whisper or mutter to themselves when carrying out a task. Some children may even move their mouths silently. Vygotsky said that this speech becomes internalized eventually as silent speech ("saying it in my head") and then as thought. Schematically, Vygotsky described the development of speech as follows:

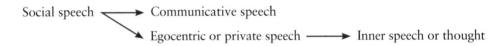

The research has tended to support Vygotsky's point of view. Although children do, at times, engage in egocentric speech that does not take into account the needs of the listener, more often this speech is for the purpose of self-direction, as Vygotsky describes (Berk & Winsler, 1995). Vygotsky stated that children hear what others say to them and then they say it in some form to themselves. Scaffolding is what the *adult* does to help children learn, but private speech is what the *child* does to change external interactions into internal thoughts. For example, an adult might scaffold a child's attempts to put together a jigsaw puzzle by saying, "First try to find the pieces with one flat side to put on the outside edge of the puzzle." You may then hear the child saying to himself, "Flat pieces, find flat pieces." The child is talking to himself to guide his own actions. Vygotsky and others have shown that the more difficult the task, the more children talk to themselves in this way (Duncan & Cheyne, 2002; Fernyhough & Fradley, 2005). Research has shown that young children who use private speech to guide themselves through difficult tasks are able to carry out these tasks more successfully than those who do not talk to themselves as they work (Berk, Mann, & Ogan, 2006).

Private speech does not end in early childhood. When confronted with a difficult task, 10% of 17-year-olds were found to talk openly to themselves and another 20% talked covertly by mumbling or whispering (Winsler & Naglieri, 2003). Try **Active Learning: Private Speech** to see when even adults may still engage in private speech.

Active Learning

Private Speech

If you ever find yourself talking out loud when you are alone (that is, using private speech), think about what you are most likely to say to yourself. The chances are you talk about tasks you need to do, giving yourself direction or organizing yourself, as in "Oh . . . the psych assignment!" or "Almost forgot that!" As adults, we usually do not vocalize this way, but when we are alone or attempting to do something difficult, we may.

Get a friend to help you with this activity and find a quiet place to do it. Your friend will need a desk or table to work on so he can write and a page from a book or a sheet of newspaper that he will be able to write on. Tell him you are looking at how accurately people can scan written material to find target letters and that he should "cross out the Ts, circle the Os, and square the Ls" (meaning he should draw a box around the letter L) on the page you give him. Repeat these instructions a couple of times to be sure he understands (you can say it like a little rhyme) and ask him to repeat it to you a time or two to further confirm his understanding, but do not let him write it down. Tell him that you will later count how many letters he was able to mark up correctly in 3 minutes.

After you are sure your friend understands the instructions, tell him that you will sit out of the way so you don't distract him and will tell him when to start and when to stop. After 2 minutes, give him a 1-minute warning (to create a little more pressure). While he is working, listen carefully to hear whether he resorts to using private speech to help him perform the task. Kronk (1994) found that 37 of 47 participants talked to themselves while working on a difficult cognitive task she gave them, and 46 of 47 talked to themselves if others were working on the same task and talking to themselves. ■

How Parents Promote Language Development in Young Children

One thing parents tend *not* to do with young children is to correct their grammar explicitly. The following story helps show what effect it might have if you were to spend much time correcting young children's grammar. In the 1970s, before the age of the computer, when people still wrote letters to each other, a young man carried on a correspondence with his girlfriend who was at a different college far away. Both these young people were highly intellectual, as you will see. They wrote each other love letters, and the recipient then *corrected the grammar* in the letter and returned it to the sender. You probably reacted quite negatively to this scenario, but why? Clearly, dealing with the grammar instead of the content of a love letter took all the meaning—in this case, the romance—out of the exchange. In the same way, when a child is trying to tell us something, we respond to the content, not the form of what he is saying. When the child says, "Me go store," we answer, "Oh, are you going to the store?" We do not answer, "You should say, 'I am going to the store.'" If we did, the child would be totally confused. Karmiloff and Karmiloff-Smith (2001) provide the following example of what happened when a mother tried to correct her child's grammar:

Child:	Daddy goed to work.
Mother:	Yes, that's right. Daddy went to work.
Child:	Daddy goed to work in car.
Mother:	Yes, Daddy *went* in his car.
Child:	Daddy goed his car very fast.

| Mother: | Ah ha, Daddy *went* to work in his car. Say *went* to work, not *goed*. Daddy *went* to work. |
| Child: | Daddy wented to work. (p. 102) |

T/F #5

If a young child says "I goed outside," it helps develop his language skills if the parent corrects him by saying "No, you mean to say, 'I went outside.'" *False*

As this example shows, sometimes even when we directly try to correct grammar, it doesn't work. Parents best promote children's language development when they talk to them frequently, model correct language usage, and elaborate on what the child says. For instance, if the child says "Daddy goed to work," the child learns best when the parent responds by modeling the correct grammar and then elaborates, promoting further speech by the child: "Yes, Daddy went to work, but he'll be home in a while. Do you want to talk to Daddy on your (toy) phone?"

Socioeconomic Status and Language Development

JOURNAL ARTICLE 9.2
SES and Language

Family socioeconomic status plays a large role in children's development of language, with consequences for later development including level of readiness to enter school. In a classic study of children's language environment, Betty Hart and Todd Risley (1995) followed 42 families over a 2-1/2-year period, observing and recording their everyday conversation. The sample consisted of families who were receiving welfare, working-class families, and families in which the parent or parents held professional jobs. The difference in the amount of language to which the children were exposed was striking. On average, parents on welfare used 600 words an hour with their toddlers, working-class parents 1,300, and parents with professional jobs 2,100. Although parents in professional families did not initiate verbal interactions with their children any more frequently than other parents, they were more likely to respond to what their children said. They also used more affirmative or encouraging statements and fewer prohibitions, such as "Stop that" or "Don't." By the time the children were 3 years old, those in professional families had been exposed to 8 million more words on average than children in welfare families. The effect these different experiences had on the growth of the children's vocabularies is shown in Figure 9.4.

The effect of a family's socioeconomic status (SES) on children's language development continues as the children get older. Vasilyeva, Waterfall, and Huttenlocher (2008) looked at the type of early sentences used by children whose parents had different levels of education. One group had high school diplomas as their highest level of education, the second group had college degrees, and the third group had professional degrees (for example, a master's degree, a doctorate, or a professional degree in medicine or law). The researchers found no differences across groups in the children's use of *simple* sentences. The children did not differ in the age at which they started producing simple sentences or in the proportion of simple sentences they used. However, differences emerged later in the acquisition and

FIGURE 9.4 **Differences in toddlers' vocabulary**

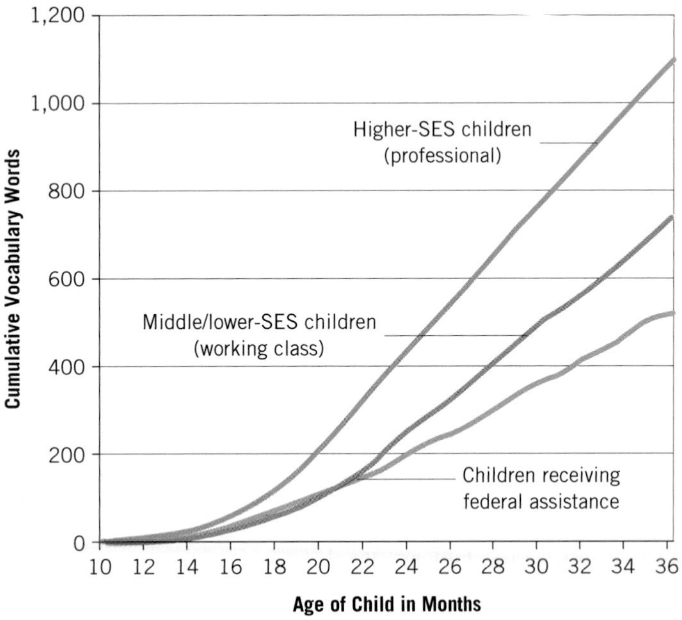

The more words toddlers hear in their everyday life, the more they produce when they learn to speak. Children in families in which the parents are professionals hear significantly more words than children in working-class families or families on welfare, and this is reflected in the size of their vocabularies.

SOURCE: Hart, B., & Risley, T. R. (1995). *Meaningful differences in the everyday experience of young American children.* Copyright © 1995 by Paul H. Brookes Publishing Co., Inc. Reprinted by permission of the publisher.

FIGURE 9.5 Differences in the complexity of toddlers' sentences

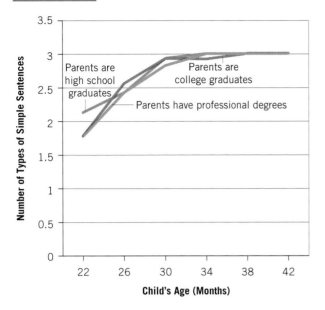
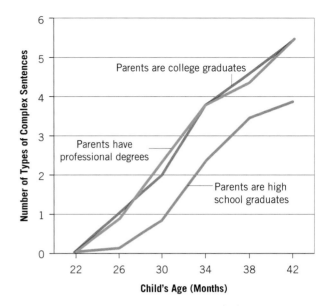

There is little difference in the use of simple sentences among children from families with different levels of education (left). However, there are differences in how many types of complex sentences these children produce (right).

SOURCE: Vasilyeva, M., Waterfall, H., & Huttenlocher, J. (2008). Emergence of syntax: Commonalities and differences across children. *Developmental Science, 11*(1), pp. 90–91. © 2008 Wiley-Blackwell. Reprinted with permission.

use of *complex* sentences. Children from families with higher levels of education began producing complex sentences earlier and used them more frequently. Figure 9.5 shows the different paths of development for these two types of sentences. The authors say that children from different educational backgrounds move further apart as they grow older, and other research has shown that the disparity continues beyond the preschool years.

Check Your Understanding

1. Give an example of telegraphic speech.
2. Why do young children use overregularization in their speech?
3. Compare egocentric speech and private speech.
4. How can parents help develop their children's language development?

Preacademic Skills: Reading, Writing, and Arithmetic

9.6

How do children develop preacademic skills in reading, writing, and arithmetic?

Until now, our discussion of language development has focused on spoken language. In this section we introduce another very important aspect of language: the ability to understand and use written language. In addition, we look at how children begin to learn number skills that underlie the ability to do arithmetic.

Learning to Read

School is the context in which most children learn to read, write, and do arithmetic, but the groundwork for these achievements is laid throughout the preschool years. We

Emergent literacy The set of skills that develop before children begin formal reading instruction, which provide the foundation for later academic skills.

use the term emergent literacy to describe the set of skills that develop before children begin formal reading instruction which provide the foundation for later academic skills. Picking up a book, holding it right-side-up, turning the pages, "reading" a story by talking about the pictures, or picking up a pencil and scribbling on a paper are all examples of these early skills.

Research on reading typically has looked at how a child acquires specific skills such as phonetics (or decoding sounds from letters) within the school context, but children also learn about reading, writing, and print material through informal processes, such as parents reading to children before they start school (Lonigan, Purpura, Wilson, Walker, & Clancy-Menchetti, 2013). As in the development of spoken language, the heart of emergent literacy is the interaction between an adult and the child, in this case as the adult reads to the child or tells a story. From these shared experiences the child develops an awareness of print, learns to recognize and name letters, and becomes aware of the sounds associated with different letters. In 2014, the American Academy of Pediatrics put out a new policy statement recommending that physicians promote parents reading to their young children to promote language skills and create an interest in reading (O'Keefe, 2014). Reading to young children serves other purposes than actually teaching them to read. Regular reading to children in the first 3 years of life has been linked to a higher level of both language development and cognitive development (Rodriguez et al., 2009; Rodriguez & Tamis-LeMonda, 2011). In 2009, half of U.S. children between 1 and 5 years of age were read to every day by members of their family (U.S. Census Bureau, 2011b). This was true for 59% of children in families above the poverty level but only 45% of those below that level. It is important to help all parents, but especially poorer parents, better understand the importance of this early experience.

WEB LINK 9.2
Dialogic Reading Works

Dialogic reading A technique used to facilitate early literacy, which involves an adult and a child looking at a book together while the adult asks questions and encourages a dialogue, followed by switching roles so the child asks questions of the adult.

Using Dialogic Reading

Many adults love to read to children to expose them to books and new ideas that come from them, but the child shouldn't just be a passive listener. The child must be an active participant in the process. A technique known as dialogic reading is particularly effective in developing early literacy skills (Zevenbergen & Whitehurst, 2008). As the adult and child look at a picture book together, they actively talk about it. The adult engages the child in the process by asking questions and encouraging a dialogue about what is going on in the story. What is essential to this process, however, is that the partners then switch roles and the child becomes the storyteller and the adult the active listener and questioner (Ghoting & Martin-Díaz, 2006; Institute of Education Sciences, 2007). Dialogic reading provides the essential dimension of active involvement and practice, practice, practice that is required to develop a complex skill like reading.

Vygotsky's zone of proximal development helps explain why dialogic reading is such an effective technique. As you know, Vygotsky believed children learn best when adults (or more skilled peers)

Reading aloud. Few simple activities affect children's language and cognitive development more than being read to every day. Why do you suppose only about half of all U.S. children have this experience? ∎

expose them to ideas that are just a bit beyond where they are in their own development. When an adult is successful at keeping the dialogue and questioning during dialogic reading within the child's zone of proximal development, the interactions build on the child's existing skills and move the child to the next level of understanding. Techniques such as word-and-picture flash cards and word books that emphasize drill and basic skills acquisition are popular with some parents (Neuman, Kaefer, Pinkham, & Strouse, 2014). However, these techniques separate acquiring specific literacy skills from the rich context of reading and do not provide the same sort of sensitive feedback and interaction that dialogic reading can provide. Techniques such as flash cards have helped low-achieving children and children with cognitive disabilities (Browder, Wakeman, Spooner, Ahlgrim-Delzell, & Algozzine, 2006; Foorman, Francis, Fletcher, Schatschneider, & Mehta, 1998), but most children can benefit from informal reading-related activities (Gerard, 2004).

The basic technique in dialogic reading is the PEER strategy. During the interaction with the child, the adults *prompt* the child to talk about the story, *evaluate* the child's response, *expand* upon it by rephrasing or adding information, and, to reinforce them for the child, *repeat* the expanded utterances (Zevenbergen & Whitehurst, 2008). If you are looking at a book with a picture of several animals, you might *prompt* the child to respond by saying, "Do you see a kitty here?" If the child says, "Here's a kitty," you can say, "Yes [*the evaluation*], and she is sitting next to a doggie [*the expansion*]." And to complete the sequence, ask the child to *repeat* what you said. The goal is to ask questions that encourage the child to think about what she is seeing and to build her language skills in answer to your questions. Follow the directions in **Active Learning: Using Dialogic Reading** to see how you can use this approach when reading with a child.

T/F #6
Using flash cards and workbooks is the best way to ensure that a child develops early literacy skills. *False*

Active Learning

Using Dialogic Reading

Dialogic reading is a skill and requires practice. Use this as an opportunity to read to a young child, preferably 3 or 4 years old. If you choose a book you are familiar with (perhaps a favorite from your own childhood), you will know the story well enough that you can focus your attention on providing prompts for the child. You might want to create a little "cheat sheet" for yourself of the following prompts before you begin, because when you are first using dialogic reading, you will probably find yourself stumped from time to time about what kind of prompt to use next.

- *Completion prompts* leave a blank at the end of a sentence that the child can fill in: "When the girl went to the store, she bought a _____."

- *Recall prompts* ask the child for information about what has already been read: "Where did the little girl want to go?" or "Why was Emma feeling sad?"

- *Open-ended prompts* ask the child to describe what is happening in a picture.

- *W-prompts* are the w-questions that reporters use when gathering information for a story—who, what, when, where, why, and how (not a w word, but still important for gathering information): "*What* is Keisha going to do next?" or "*Why* is Larry excited?"

- *Distancing prompts* take the child out of the storybook to make her think about the real world: "This dog looks a lot like the dog we saw at Aunt Cindy's house last week. Do you remember that dog? What did you like about him?" (Whitehurst, 1992; Zevenbergen & Whitehurst, 2008)

ACTIVE LEARNING
VIDEO 9.6
Using Dialogic Reading

If you practice this technique, creating these opportunities for learning will become quite natural to you. Finding that *zone of proximal development* and pitching your comments and questions to a child at just the right level to advance his or her understanding is what many parents, and *all* good teachers, do all the time. ■

By the age of 3 or 4, children usually can "read" familiar books by retelling stories using the pictures as cues (Johnson & Sulzby, 1999). As children gain experience with books, they begin to understand the relationship between the words on the page and the content of the story. They learn that it is the words, not the pictures, that tell the story, and they learn the conventions of written language (for example, in English the text is read from the top of the page to the bottom and from left to right) (Gunn, Simmons, & Kameenui, 1995).

Learning to Write

Even very young children love to take a crayon or marker and "write" a letter or story. The earliest writing skills (similar to early reading skills) are basic: Children understand that writing moves from left to right (in English-speaking countries) and from the top of the page down, and that it is meant to convey information. As their fine motor skills improve, they can begin to write recognizable letters. Remember from Chapter 6 that children develop their fine motor skills as motor control moves down their arms to their fingers. Figure 9.6 is an example of how writing skills develop in young children. Children love being able to write their own names and often master this skill even before they enter school.

Children will sound out familiar words and often begin to invent their own spelling of words based on how the words sound. The results may initially be incomprehensible—for example, a child might write *train* as *chran*—but this first writing is the basis for further learning about spelling and writing. Contrary to what some adults think, using invented spelling does not slow down or prevent a young child from learning conventional spelling and it does allow children to be more creative in their writing by letting them use more words in what they write (Brasacchio, Kuhn, & Martin, 2001). It can even help with the task of learning to read (Sénéchal, Ouellette, Pagan, & Lever, 2012).

T/F #7

When young children use spelling they have "invented" (rather than conventional spelling), it slows down their ability to learn how to spell correctly. *False*

Early writing

This is how I write my name:	This is how I write my name:	This is how I write my name:
September 2007	December 2007	February 2008

This writing sample from a prekindergarten child shows how much progress is made in just a few short months. Children take great pride in learning how to write their names.

SOURCE: Karen Cox © 2010, www.prekinders.com. Reprinted with permission.

Learning Arithmetic

As young children are learning to recognize and understand letters and words, they are also beginning to recognize and understand numbers. How do we know when a child understands numbers? The answers three children gave to the question "Which is bigger: seven or nine?" help illustrate the development of the concept of number:

> Brie responds quickly, saying "Nine." When asked how she figured it out, she says, "Well, you go, 'seven' (pause) 'eight', 'nine' (putting up two fingers while saying the last two numbers). That means nine has two more than seven. So it's bigger."
>
> Leah says, hesitantly, "Nine?" When asked how she figured it out, she says, "Because nine's a big number."
>
> Caitlin looks genuinely perplexed, as if the question was not a sensible thing to ask, and says, "I don't know." (Griffin, 2004, p. 173)

Clearly Brie understands what numbers represent while Caitlin does not. Leah is beginning to get the idea. How did Brie learn this concept?

Theorists have hypothesized that human beings have two ways of understanding numbers. The first way is an intuitive sense of quantity that is unlearned and emerges early in infancy. As we saw in Chapter 6, even young infants are surprised when shown one object, then another is added behind a screen and when the screen is removed there are three objects, in other words, 1 + 1 = 3. Children are using this sense of number when they tell you a basket with 10 apples has more than a basket with five apples even though they have not counted the apples. This sense is called the approximate number system (ANS). The ANS does not require language or numerical representation (Bonny & Lourenco, 2013). The second way is a more precise one that relies on the ability to count and perform basic arithmetic. It requires children to learn the words and symbols for numbers and then to map quantities onto the symbols that represent them. In other words, the child must learn that when they see three objects this corresponds to the symbol 3 and the word *three*.

Preschool children appear to develop and use the ANS and the symbolic system of numbers separately. They can estimate that 10 apples is more than 5 apples. They are also learning to count to ten. However, it is not until age 6, on average, that they put this all together to realize that counting is a way to figure out which group has more apples (Kolkman, Kroesbergen, & Leseman, 2013).

There are many different elements young children must bring together when they learn about numbers. They must learn the basic concept that many things are more than one or a few things. They must learn the names of numbers and the order in which they appear. They must learn the symbols for numbers, and finally they must apply all this information to create a one-to-one correspondence between numbers and the objects being counted. This process may be a slow and winding path to the ultimate outcome of the number concept.

Developing an understanding of numbers. Our understanding of numbers begins in early infancy with an intuitive sense of quantity that becomes more precise and sophisticated during early childhood. ■

Approximate number system (ANS) An intuitive sense of quantity that appears to be innate.

VIDEO LINK 9.3
Approximate Number System

Check Your Understanding

1. What is emergent literacy?
2. Describe the process of dialogic reading.
3. What effect does invented spelling have on children's ability to learn to write?
4. In what two ways do young children understand numbers?

9.7

What risk factors and supports exist for cognitive and language development in early childhood?

Risk Factors and Supports for Cognitive and Language Development in Early Childhood

What factors promote children's cognitive and language development, and what factors create risks that may interfere with children's ability to achieve their highest potential? In this section we look at one of the major threats to optimal cognitive development: poverty. We then look at ways that early education can support optimal cognitive development.

The Effects of Poverty

Poverty exists around the world and is a threat to healthy growth and development of all children who grow up without adequate resources. In the United States in 2011, almost half of children under age 6 (17.5 million) lived in poverty or in low-income families (Addy, Englehardt, & Skinner, 2013). Even with the challenges of growing up in poverty, most of these children grow up to contribute positively to society. However, we must recognize that poverty is a major risk factor that may stop a child from reaching his or her full potential (Shonkoff & Phillips, 2000). Childhood poverty has been associated with difficulties for children in all areas of development, but the deficits in cognitive functioning and academic achievement have been most clearly documented (McLoyd, 2000; Nikulina, Widom, & Czaja, 2010).

Research has found that children whose families have few resources show lower levels of cognitive development as early as 18 to 24 months of age (Ryan et al., 2006). By the time they entered kindergarten, they were already significantly behind their middle-class peers in preacademic skills that would lead to basic skills in reading and arithmetic and in measured IQ (McLoyd, 2000). When children begin school at a low level, it becomes increasingly difficult to catch up, and school can become a source of frustration.

If you think about all the problems associated with poverty, you can come up with a very long list that includes the following examples:

- Poor health due to unavailability of health care, unsafe living conditions, and poor diet
- Lack of resources in the neighborhood, including structured after-school activities
- High rates of depression and posttraumatic stress disorder in both parents and children
- Anxiety linked to caring for a family in a dangerous neighborhood where loved ones may be lost to violence or individuals may witness frightening events
- High levels of stress that contribute to marital discord and instability
- Safety concerns that limit children's ability to explore their environment
- Poor schools with inadequate facilities
- Racism or other discrimination
- Segregation leading to a lack of opportunities and social exclusion (McLoyd, 2000; Ryan et al., 2006)

These factors interact with each other in complex ways to decrease academic performance in children. For instance, parents who are struggling with the stresses of poverty are less likely to provide educational stimulation and guidance in the home. They also have lower expectations for their children's achievement. Teachers also are more likely to have low expectations for the achievement of students from impoverished families

T/F #8

Many children who grow up in poverty go on to become adults who contribute positively to society.

True

Affluence and poverty. Compare these two scenes and think about what each setting provides for the children in it and what the consequences might be for the children's academic achievement. ∎

(Benner & Mistry, 2007; McLoyd, 2000). Families in poverty move their homes much more frequently than other families, most often due to unplanned events such as evictions or foreclosures. Moving three or more times is linked with more attention and behavioral problems in children, both of which set the child up for academic difficulties (Ziol-Guest & McKenna, 2014).

Supporting Academic Readiness

Early childhood education helps prepare all children for the transition into elementary school, but this experience is particularly important for young children growing up in disadvantaged circumstances. We know a good deal about what constitutes high-quality early care and education, but we must be willing as a society to invest the necessary resources to ensure the availability of these opportunities to all children.

Early Childhood Education

In his 2013 State of the Union address, President Barack Obama recognized the crucial role early childhood education plays in the children's development. He said:

> In states that make it a priority to educate our youngest children . . . studies show students grow up more likely to read and do math at grade level, graduate high school, hold a job, and form more stable families of their own. We know this works. So let's do what works and make sure none of our children start the race of life already behind.

In 2011, 78% of 4-year-olds in the United States attended preschool. If that sounds like a lot to you, you may be surprised to learn that in Denmark, France, Iceland, Spain, and Norway 85% of 4-year-olds attend preschool programs, and in those countries, early education begins earlier than is typical in the United States. In a

Early childhood education. President Barack Obama uses a magnifying glass to play a game with pre-kindergarten children while visiting their classroom. The President's agenda has promoted the idea of high-quality preschool for all. ∎

number of Western European countries, 90% of 3-year-olds attend preschool, while only 50% of American 3-year-olds do (Organisation for Economic Co-operation and Development, 2013). Even more disheartening, only 33% of American 4-year-olds attended what would be considered a high-quality program that adequately prepares children for school (U.S. Department of Education, n.d.-b).

There is much evidence that attending preschool has positive benefits later on in life. However, these benefits accrue only when preschool education is of high quality. How can we know when a preschool program is of high quality? The National Institute for Early Education Research identifies these essential indicators:

AUDIO LINK 9.2
High-Quality Day Care

- Aspects of Structure

  - Adult-child ratios do not exceed 20 children in a group, with 2 teaching staff (the ratio for toddlers is 1:6 and for infants 1:4).
  - Teachers and staff are qualified and compensated accordingly.
  - All staff are supervised and evaluated and have opportunities for professional growth.

- Aspects of Process

  - There are positive relationships between teachers and children.
  - The room is well-equipped, with sufficient materials and toys.
  - Communication occurs throughout the day, with mutual listening, talking/responding, and encouragement to use reasoning and problem solving.
  - Opportunities for art, music/movement, science, math, block play, sand, water, and dramatic play are provided daily.
  - There are materials and activities to promote understanding and acceptance of diversity.
  - Parents are encouraged to be involved in all aspects of the program. (Espinosa, 2002)

A program with these characteristics is likely to be costly, so low-income parents are often unable to give their children the advantage of attending a high-quality preschool. In the United States, the Head Start program was designed to help parents below a certain income level provide their children with this type of program and get the resources and knowledge they need to support their children's cognitive growth.

Head Start and Early Head Start

The Head Start program was developed in the 1960s to narrow the gap between children from different socioeconomic backgrounds so economically disadvantaged children could enter school on par with their more economically advantaged peers. Most people think of Head Start as solely a preschool program, but it is much more than that.

Poverty affects families, not just children, so Head Start was designed to help the whole family and the whole child. To this end, a caseworker partners with each family to find resources for whatever the family decides are its most pressing needs, including the need for education, employment, health care, or mental health counseling. Children are given two nutritious meals each school day, even if they are in the classroom only in the morning, and dental care and vision screening are provided. Finally, parental involvement is central to children's progress in Head Start and beyond. Because many parents whose children are participating also grew up in poverty, school may not have been a positive experience for them. Head Start helps parents learn new skills and attitudes that promote their active role in their children's educational experiences both at home and at school. When parents are active in the program, their children's preacademic skills, including literacy skills and vocabulary, are more likely to improve (Head Start Family and Child Experiences Survey [FACES], 2007; Hindman & Morrison, 2011). Many also have argued that Head Start must continue to be a program that addresses the whole child, not just cognitive skills because we know cognitive skills do not develop in a vacuum; they are intricately related to physical health, emotional well-being, and family support.

Although there are differences between families in how involved they are with Head Start and with their young children's learning, generally families who take part in this program are more involved in activities such as reading books, playing games, and talking, both during their time with the Head Start program and through the first years of elementary school (Gelber, Isen, & National

Off to a good start. Head Start children, such as this boy, who come from low-income families receive a good beginning to their education through the help of teachers in the federal Head Start program. ■

Bureau of Economic Research, 2011). When parents were involved, their children's literacy skills and vocabulary were improved (Hindman & Morrison, 2011).

In 1994, Head Start was expanded to create the Early Head Start (EHS) program to serve parents and younger children. EHS is focused on pregnant women and children under 3, and its services vary according to the needs of the community. It may include child care provided at a center or in a home, and weekly home visits to promote the parents' ability to support their children's development (Head Start, 2014).

Research has been conducted on the short-term and long-term effectiveness of Head Start. Short-term research has shown some significant cognitive gains by the end of the program that prepare students for the transition into kindergarten. Unfortunately, longer-term follow up studies have found that these gains typically disappear at some point before the end of third grade (Karoly et al., 1998; Puma et al., 2012). Needless to say, these results are disappointing for a program with such ambitious goals, but we need to remember that Head Start is designed as an intervention for disadvantaged children who often are growing up in very difficult circumstances. Even high-quality preschool will not be able to compensate entirely for the effects of growing up in poverty.

To some extent, these findings also reflect variability in the quality of the programs offered. In Tulsa, Oklahoma, quality of teaching is emphasized and lead teachers must have a college degree and an early childhood education certification, and teaching is rewarded with salaries similar to those earned by public school teachers. In this situation, early cognitive effects of Head Start experience were considerably larger than the average (Gormley, Phillips, & Gayer, 2008; Pianta, Barnett, Burchinal, & Thornburg, 2009). In an effort to ensure that Head Start will offer consistently high-quality programs across its sites, there is a federal mandate that by September 2013 at least 50% of Head Start teachers nationwide would have a bachelor's degree in early childhood education or a closely related major. It is too soon to know how this change will impact the outcomes for Head Start participants.

Other research has looked beyond outcomes in early elementary school and has assessed more than cognitive skills. Across this research, low-income children who attended high-quality preschool programs had a number of positive developmental outcomes, including fewer grade retentions and special education placements than nonparticipants. They were more likely to graduate high school and attend college, earned more as adults, and were less likely to be imprisoned (Garces, Thomas, &

T/F #9

Participating in a high-quality preschool program can increase a child's chance of graduating from high school or attending college. *True*

Currie, 2002; HighScope Educational Research Foundation, 2014; Reynolds, Temple, Robertson, & Mann, 2001; Schweinhart, 2013). The positive long-term effects appear to be strongest for children who came from the most disadvantaged backgrounds (Garces et al., 2002).

If the cognitive gains from attending an early intervention program such as Head Start dissipate over the first couple of years, what accounts for positive long-term outcomes? One possible answer comes from Fuhs and Day (2011), who followed a group of 132 mostly African American and Hispanic preschoolers and found significant improvement in executive functioning over the preschool year. Stop to remind yourself what executive functioning entails. It includes the ability to inhibit behavior when you need to, to think flexibly and shift your attention from one task to another, to regulate your emotional responses, to monitor and assess your own performance, and to plan and organize the tasks you must accomplish. Do you see how developing this set of skills would help you succeed in school and avoid some problem behaviors? In addition, on average Head Start children also show increases in cooperative behavior in the classroom (FACES, 2007).

Based on such research, the argument has been made that the money spent on Head Start (approximately $9,000 per child in 2008) reaps financial benefits that clearly outweigh the initial expense (Ludwig & Phillips, 2008). When you consider the costs incurred when children require special education services, do not complete high school, or enter the criminal justice system, you can begin to see how the initial expenditures are justified. Ludwig and Phillips (2008) estimate that the benefits of reducing special education placements and grade retention alone can offset 40% to 60% of original program costs. Head Start is intended to be an investment that helps children throughout their lives, and long-term research has found some ways it has done that. James Heckman (2011), Nobel prize-winning economist, summarized his research on the effects of early intervention as follows:

> The logic is quite clear from an economic standpoint. We can invest early to close disparities and prevent achievement gaps, or we can pay to remediate disparities when they are harder and more expensive to close. Either way we are going to pay. And, we'll have to do both for a while. But, there is an important difference between the two approaches. Investing early allows us to shape the future; investing later chains us to fixing the missed opportunities of the past." (p. 47)

Motivated by arguments such as these, an extra $2.1 billion was added to Head Start and Early Head Start funds through the American Recovery and Reinvestment Act.

Educational TV: Sesame Street

As you recall from Chapter 6, infants do not learn well from TV, but this situation is somewhat different in early childhood. There is evidence that educational TV (but not entertainment TV) can improve cognitive functioning and academic performance in preschool children. Research on the educational TV show *Sesame Street* has found positive effects on preacademic skills when children watched beginning even at age 2 (Wright, Huston, Scantlin, & Kotler, 2001). Although there are many educational programs on television, *Sesame Street* has included a research component since the very beginning of its programming and, as a result, has more data on its effectiveness than any other program. See **Journey of Research: Educational TV and *Sesame Street*** for additional information about the history and effectiveness of *Sesame Street*.

JOURNEY OF RESEARCH *Educational TV and* Sesame Street

Following World War II, the number of television sets in U.S. homes quickly climbed to about 8 million by the late 1950s (Levine & Waite, 2002). Educational programs for children at that time often filmed a teacher leading activities typical of a preschool or kindergarten classroom. The teachers were not trained actors, and surveys at the time showed that children greatly preferred commercial TV (Lemish, 2007).

In the 1960s, research by Joan Ganz Cooney for the Carnegie Corporation found that preschoolers were watching a great deal of television every day (Friedman, 2006), and the vast majority of homes had a television regardless of their income level. Cooney and her colleagues promoted the idea that a different kind of TV show could engage and teach young children, especially those being raised in poverty, to help get them ready for school. She created the Children's Television Workshop (CTW, now called the Sesame Workshop) to achieve this goal. Bringing together top educators, psychologists, and television producers, the group used the latest research to determine how children would best learn from this relatively new medium (Lemish, 2007). From the observation that children are greatly attracted to commercials, CTW developed a show that used the same techniques found in commercials, such as short segments, bright colors, and music, but with educational rather than commercial goals in mind. With the addition of Jim Henson's Muppets, this show became *Sesame Street*, which first aired in 1969 (Friedman, 2006; Williams-Rautiolla, 2008).

Today, the U.S. version of *Sesame Street* is watched by about 8 million people each week, but *Sesame Street* has gone far beyond the borders of the United States. Twenty versions of the show appear in more than 150 countries around the world (Sesame Street Workshop, 2014). In each version, *Sesame Street* staff members from the United States work together with local producers, artists, and actors to create a program appropriate for that culture.

Die Burger/AFP/Newscom

Sesame Street around the world. In November 2009, Sesame Street celebrated its 40th anniversary. It now appears in 120 countries around the world. In each country, the cast of Muppets is adapted to the local culture. In 2002, Sesame Street in South Africa introduced Kami, a Muppet who is living with HIV. ■

Sesame Street sets very specific goals based on research-supported knowledge about children's development. For example, it has been shown that children learn more from TV when they interact with an adult about what they've seen, so *Sesame Street* has designed segments that will encourage parents to watch with their children so they can discuss and reinforce what the show teaches (Wright et al., 2001). Many celebrities, actors, and musicians have done guest segments on *Sesame Street*, including Amy Poehler, Maya Angelou, Hillary Clinton, Garth Brooks, LL Cool J, and the band One Direction, and the program often features parodies of programs adults watch, such as Upside Downton Abbey and True Mud. Three- and 4-year-old children are not going to understand these jokes, but their parents will.

Because *Sesame Street* is designed to teach preacademic skills that prepare

WEB LINK 9.3
Sesame Street and Social Issues

children for reading, writing, and arithmetic, each show is "sponsored" by a particular letter and number, but the show teaches much more than preacademic skills. "Social, moral and affective" teaching goals have guided the programming throughout its history (Mielke, 2001, p. 84). For example, diversity has always been a central value, with characters from all backgrounds represented in the cast. *Sesame Street* also has not shied away from big issues that impact children's lives. In South Africa, on *Takalani Sesame*, the show introduced a Muppet character, Kami, who was HIV positive and showed both the prejudice Kami experienced and the love and fun the character could have with others (Hawthorne, 2002).

There is much research evidence that watching *Sesame Street* does make a difference for young children. Viewers were better prepared to learn to read and do arithmetic, and this readiness seemed to be truly a result of watching the show and not of other variables, such as how educated their parents were or how much they read to their children. The advantage held even through high school, when students who had watched the program at age 5 had higher grades in English, math, and science (Huston, Anderson, Wright, Linebarger, & Schmitt, 2001; Schmidt & Anderson, 2007). You might

wonder how watching one TV series could have such a long-term effect. Longitudinal research has shown that watching *Sesame Street* is related not only to developing preacademic skills but also to gaining a greater sense of competence, being less aggressive, and demonstrating more motivation for academic achievement (Huston et al., 2001). Teens who are less aggressive can take part in school more effectively, feel good about what they are accomplishing there, and maintain their motivation to achieve.

Criticisms of *Sesame Street* have focused on the fast pace of the program, which some have claimed may contribute to shortening the attention span of the children who watch it. However, Anderson, Levin, and Lorch (1977) found no immediate effects of pacing in *Sesame Street* on impulsivity or task persistence, and they argue that viewers' increase in academic competence is evidence that attention is not harmed.

Sesame Street remains a major force in children's educational television. To keep pace with rapidly changing media, it has added a website with podcasts, computer games, and other activities and ideas for parents and caregivers to help children develop all types of abilities that will help when they enter school. ∎

T/F #10
The fast pace used on the television program *Sesame Street* does not affect the attention span of children who watch it. *True*

Starting School

When should children start school? Is it important that they start school-based learning as early as possible, or should they wait until they are mature enough to profit from education? This debate has been ongoing for many years. Most U.S. children start school by entering kindergarten when they are about 5 years old, but each state or school district sets its own dates for school entry. In Connecticut, children enter kindergarten if they will be 5 by January 1st of that school year, while in Nebraska and Hawaii they must be 5 by July 31st before the school year begins (Education Commission of the States, 2014), so some children will be 4 years 8 months when they enter school while others will be 6 years 1 month. As you can imagine, a year and five months difference in age can make a big difference in a child's maturity or school readiness.

In addition, some parents believe either that their child is not ready to enter at the designated age, or that the child will have an advantage if he or she is older when beginning school, so they intentionally hold the child out for a year (called *redshirting* after a similar practice in college athletics). This practice makes the age range of those entering kindergarten even larger. Are children better off starting at younger or older ages? The research indicates that younger children may have some disadvantages in the earliest years of school, but those differences disappear by later elementary school (Stipek, 2002). Some have argued that instead of holding children back, schools should accommodate teaching to the needs of their students (Stipek, 2002). For example, not all children will be ready to learn to read in kindergarten, so the curriculum should be flexible enough to

VIDEO LINK 9.4
Redshirting

allow teachers to teach basic prereading skills to younger children to foster their readiness as they enter first grade. Accommodating the needs of the younger children should help ensure that they will catch up as they progress through school.

1. What problems associated with poverty can hinder cognitive and language development in early childhood?
2. List some of the National Institute for Early Education Research's indicators of a high-quality preschool program.
3. What are some short- and long-term benefits associated with attending a Head Start program?
4. What qualities make for sound educational television programming for young children?
5. What might be an advantage of holding a child out of kindergarten for a year so he starts school at age 6?

Conclusion

Young children's natural curiosity is a wonderful basis for their cognitive growth during the period of early childhood. Young children are constantly asking "Why?" as they try to figure out the world around them. Sensitive scaffolding of information and skills by adults can help promote children's new knowledge and more sophisticated ways of thinking. Children also learn best through the fun of play, which can maintain their zest for learning. Although there are many limitations on their cognitive abilities, young children who are active and involved in their world are preparing the learning abilities that will help them thrive as they enter school.

Chapter Summary

9.1 What occurs during Piaget's preoperational stage of cognitive development?

Children in the preoperational stage advance in their thinking when they begin to use symbols to manipulate information in their minds rather than with their hands, although symbols at this age are still very concrete. Limitations in their thinking include **transductive reasoning**, **egocentrism**, **animism**, and lack of **conservation**.

9.2 What are the basic processes described by Vygotsky's sociocultural theory?

Children learn through social interaction with more capable others that moves them just beyond their current level of understanding. The difference between what they can do independently and what they can do only with assistance is the zone of proximal development (ZPD). Through scaffolding an adult helps move the child through the ZPD to full independent achievement.

9.3 How do attention, memory, executive function, and social cognition develop in early childhood?

Young children have limited sustained and selective attention abilities. Young children have difficulty using **encoding processes** so their memory is quite limited, but they can use **scripts** to help their recall. **Working memory** allows them to recall only one or two things at a time. Memory is highly suggestible and this can lead to false memories. As preschool children develop executive function, they show greater ability to pay attention, inhibit irrelevant behavior, and actively remember. However, they still have a limited ability to understand that others don't know what they know, an aspect of **theory of mind**.

9.4 Why is play important for cognitive development in early childhood?

Play provides a setting in which children are free to explore and interact in an environment of fun that keeps them motivated to learn. Piaget and his followers described four cognitive levels of play: functional, symbolic/sociodramatic, constructive, and games with rules.

9.5 How does language develop in early childhood?

Young children put together very short sentences, called **telegraphic speech**, and make grammar mistakes through overregularization, but by the end of this period, their language is quite complex. Vygotsky believed children talk out loud to themselves in **private speech** as a way of directing their own thoughts and actions. Substantial evidence supports Vygotsky's ideas. Parents tend to model the correct way to say something rather than directly correcting their children's grammar. By the time they reach kindergarten, young children growing up in poverty hear and produce fewer words and less complex sentences than children in higher income families.

9.6 How do children develop preacademic skills in reading, writing, and arithmetic?

Emergent literacy is development of the set of skills that provide the foundation for reading. **Dialogic reading** is one good approach to helping young children learn about reading. Children are encouraged to write even before they know all the rules for correct spelling. They develop their number concept both from the **approximate number system**, which they seem to understand very early in infancy, and from the precise number system used by adults.

9.7 What risk factors and supports exist for cognitive and language development in early childhood?

Young children growing up in poverty tend to have lower levels of cognitive skills. High-quality preschool has been shown to increase young children's cognitive abilities in the near term and several life outcomes in the long term. Head Start is a federally funded program that helps children and families in poverty improve children's cognitive development through education and intervention. Carefully designed and researched educational programs on television such as *Sesame Street* have also been shown to improve cognitive development in young children. Children may start kindergarten at a range of ages, and younger children struggle more academically in the early grades; however, these differences disappear in later elementary school if kindergarten teachers teach them basic skills.

Key Terms

Animism 290

Approximate number system (ANS) 313

Centration 290

Conservation 290

Constructive play 302

Decenter 290

Dialogic reading 310

Discovery learning 300

Egocentric speech 306

Egocentrism 289

Emergent literacy 310

Encoding processes 295

False belief 298

False belief paradigm 298

Games with rules 302

Intuitive thought 288

Mindblindness 298

Operations 287

Practice play 302

Preoperational stage 287

Private speech 303

Scripts 295

Social cognition 297

Symbolic/sociodramatic play 302

Telegraphic speech 304

Theory of mind 297

Transductive reasoning 288

Working memory 295

$SAGE edge™

Sharpen your skills with SAGE edge at edge.sagepub.com/levinechrono

SAGE edge for Students provides a personalized approach to help you accomplish your coursework goals in an easy-to-use learning environment.

Go to edge.sagepub.com/levinechrono for additional exercises and video resources. Select Chapter 9, Cognitive Development in Early Childhood, for chapter-specific activities. All of the Video Links listed in the margins of this chapter are accessible via this site.

Jupiterimages, Brand X Pictures/Stockbyte/Getty Images

10 Social and Emotional Development in Early Childhood

T/F Test Your Knowledge

Test your knowledge of child development by deciding whether each of the following statements is *true* or *false,* and then check your answers as you read the chapter.

1. T☐ F☐ Preschoolers are too young to experience complex feelings like guilt and shame.

2. T☐ F☐ When a child is struggling to do something like move a heavy object, an adult should always help him do it.

3. T☐ F☐ Today most parents do not reinforce gender-specific stereotypes and instead treat their sons and daughters in very similar ways.

4. T☐ F☐ Spanking is an effective way to teach children how to control their behavior.

5. T☐ F☐ Children who are raised by permissive parents are most likely to grow up to be self-reli-ant, confident, and explorative.

6. T☐ F☐ Good parenting looks the same regardless of where we find it.

7. T☐ F☐ If a child chooses to play alone when there are other children to play with, there is no reason for concern.

8. T☐ F☐ Preschoolers are not likely to maintain a friendship for more than a few weeks.

9. T☐ F☐ Families are unlikely to move out of poverty once their income is at that level.

10. T☐ F☐ Adults who were abused as chil-dren are very likely to become abusive parents themselves.

Correct answers: (1) F, (2) F, (3) F, (4) F, (5) F, (6) F, (7) T, (8) F, (9) F, (10) F

Young children are developing new emotions and new abilities to express and control their emotions. As they begin to understand their own feelings better, they develop a better understanding of the thoughts and feelings of other people. Their self-concept is based on simple concrete characteristics, but their self-esteem is extraordinarily high. Part of their developing sense of self includes what they understand about their own gender.

Young children also are learning what is right and wrong, but at this age their definition is largely determined by what others tell them rather than their own independent judgments. Families play a major role in helping children understand social rules. The parenting strategies they use and the parenting style they adopt are major influences in shaping their children's personalities. Parents also are each child's first social partners, and they form the base from which young children enter the world of peers and play.

Finally, young children may live in circumstances that have long-term consequences for all areas of development. Poverty, homelessness, and trauma are all situations that compromise a young child's ability to grow and flourish so we look at these situations and their consequences.

Learning Questions

10.1 How do emotions change during early childhood?

10.2 How does the sense of self develop in early childhood?

10.3 How do different theories describe the development of gender identity?

10.4 What roles do environmental influences, cognitive development, and emotional development play in the development of morality?

10.5 How are children socialized by their family so they behave in an appropriate way for their culture?

10.6 What are play and peer relationships like during early childhood?

10.7 What risks and resources are relevant to emotional development in early childhood?

Emotional Development in Early Childhood

10.1

How do emotions change during early childhood?

You learned about how infants begin to experience and regulate emotional states in Chapter 7. In early childhood, emotions become somewhat more complex. Preschoolers now have a stronger sense of self, and this leads them to become aware of emotions related to the self, such as pride and guilt. They begin to represent their emotions through words and images, and this helps in the process of regulating their emotional responses. Tantrums decrease as children learn to use words to express their feelings.

Self-Conscious Emotions

Infants within the first year of life demonstrate the basic emotions: happiness, sadness, fear, anger, interest, and disgust (Izard, 2007), but as they get older, they develop the ability to recognize these emotions in others. Before age 3, most children recognize happiness when they see it in others, and by 4 or 5 they can identify the other basic emotions (Tracy, Robins, & Lagattuta, 2005).

It takes a bit longer for complex emotions to develop. Very young children do not have emotions that depend on an awareness of self, or what are called self-conscious emotions. Emotions such as pride, shame, and guilt all require children to think about how an event affects their evaluation of themselves (Tracy et al., 2005). Children begin to experience pride by age 3, and by age 4 or 5 they can identify pride in other people from their nonverbal signals.

While it is pretty easy to recognize differences between the basic emotions, the differences between the complex emotions are more subtle and require more explanation. By

Self-conscious emotions Emotions that depend on awareness of oneself, such as pride, guilt, and shame.

WEB LINK 10.1
Guilt

T/F #1

Preschoolers are too young to experience complex feelings like guilt and shame. *False*

Guilt Feelings children have when they think about the negative aspects of something they have done, particularly moral failures.

Shame A feeling that occurs as a result of personal failure or when children attribute their bad behavior to an aspect of themselves that they believe they cannot change.

one definition, guilt occurs when children think about the negative aspects of something they have done, whereas shame occurs when they attribute their bad behavior to an aspect of themselves they believe they cannot change (Tracy & Robins, 2006). Shame has also been linked with personal failures, such as poor performance at school or in sports, whereas guilt is linked to moral issues, such as hurting others. Many researchers claim that children do not develop the complex abilities necessary to fully understand shame and guilt until well into middle childhood, but they first emerge in early childhood. Shame emerges at a younger age, but children begin to show guilt as they better understand the rules for their behavior and the mental states of others (Bafunno & Camodeca, 2013).

Berti, Garattoni, and Venturini (2000) found that 5-year-old Italian children were just as likely as older children to understand that guilt is caused by something a person has done wrong and that it can be dealt with by trying to repair the damage done. However, the 5-year-olds also tended to believe they had to feel guilty only if someone else was there to see what happened. If no one was there, they would feel happy. Older children's sense of guilt was not affected by whether someone else was there. You can see whether you are clear on the distinction between shame and guilt by answering the questions in **Active Learning: Shame and Guilt.**

Active Learning

Shame and Guilt

Read the following scenario imagining that you are a child. Decide which answer would indicate guilt and which would indicate shame:

> You see a cookie that your mother has told you not to take but you eat it anyway.

Would you think, "I am a bad kid"? Or would you think "I did something bad"? Which of these reactions indicates shame and which indicates guilt? If you were 5 years old, in what circumstances would you be most likely to feel guilty?

■ Answers: Ferguson, Stegge, Miller, and Olsen (1999) suggest that thinking you are a "bad kid" is indicative of shame, and feeling "you did something wrong" is indicative of guilt. If you were a 5-year-old, you might not feel guilty unless someone saw you take and eat the cookie.

Representation and Regulation of Emotions

As children move into early childhood, they begin to represent events in their lives through language and images. Conversations with parents about events they have experienced now help shape the way in which children understand and cope with their emotions. Parents who use more words to label and describe emotions have children who are more comfortable talking about their feelings. For example, for children with asthma, emotional well-being was related to their mothers' use of emotion words and explanations in conversations with them about their disease (Sales & Fivush, 2005).

When children are able to talk about their feelings, they become better able to regulate and control their expression of those feelings. Rather than exploding into a temper tantrum, young children become able to say, "I am mad that I can't have a cookie!" Children who can regulate their emotions and behaviors are more socially and academically competent, more agreeable and sympathetic, and more resilient (Izard, 2007; McCabe & Brooks-Gunn, 2007; Mischel & Ayduk, 2004). Emotional regulation is also linked to lower levels of problematic behaviors, such as impulsivity, delinquency,

VIDEO LINK 10.1
Emotion Regulation

aggression, and several behavioral disorders seen in older children, including conduct disorder and oppositional defiant disorder, which are discussed in Chapter 13 (McCabe & Brooks-Gunn, 2007).

These findings are consistent with the ideas expressed by Daniel Goleman (1995) in his book *Emotional Intelligence*. Goleman believes the ability to deal with emotions is as important to our success as our cognitive abilities. The ability to understand and control one's emotions, to understand the emotions of others, and to use this understanding in human interactions are all aspects of emotional intelligence that help us navigate human interactions successfully.

> **Emotional intelligence** The ability to understand and control one's emotions, to understand the emotions of others, and to use this understanding in human interactions.

Check Your Understanding

1. What are self-conscious emotions?
2. Compare guilt and shame in young children.
3. What is emotional intelligence?

The Self in Preschoolers

When we talk about the self, we make an important distinction between self-concept, which is the way that we think about or describe ourselves, and self-esteem, which is the way we feel about the characteristics in our self-description. Young children include a wide range of characteristics in their self-descriptions and, as we will see, they feel almost uniformly positive about them.

> **10.2**
>
> **How does the sense of self develop in early childhood?**
>
> **Self-concept** How we think about or describe ourselves.
>
> **Self-esteem** How we feel about characteristics we associate with ourselves.

Self-Concept in Early Childhood

For Erik Erikson, toddlers are in the stage of *autonomy versus shame and doubt*. They are trying to become autonomous in relation to their parents; that is, the child is becoming a separate self. For preschoolers, the self becomes tied to what they can do. Erikson (1963) describes the central issue of this stage as *initiative versus guilt*. Preschoolers try to initiate activity; that is, they want to do things, to create, and to make things happen. However, young children may fail at these attempts to do things by themselves, and that can lead to guilty feelings that they have done something wrong. Adults should be patient with and allow them to see what they can do on their own.

The young child's definition of self as being "what I do" is reflected in Susan Harter's (1999) illustration of a preschooler's self-description:

> I'm 3 years old and I live in a big house with my mother and father. . . . I have blue eyes and a kitty that is orange. . . . I know all of my ABC's, listen: A, B, C, D, E, F, G, H, J, L, K, O, M, P, Q, X, Z. I can run real fast. . . . I can count up to 100. . . . I can climb to the top of the jungle gym, I'm not scared! I'm never scared! I'm always happy. . . . I'm really strong. I can lift this chair, watch me! (p. 37)

T/F #2
When a child is struggling to do something like move a heavy object, an adult should always help him do it. *False*

Can you list the characteristics that make up this description? It includes physical description (blue eyes), possessions (a kitty), abilities (knowing ABCs, climbing, lifting a chair), feelings (never scared), and some basic information—the child's age and where he lives. We will see in later chapters how self-descriptions change as children get older.

At this age, children begin to develop a coherent set of memories about their lives, referred to as an autobiographical memory. Memory for the events in one's life plays an important role in the development of a self-concept (Prebble, Addis, & Tippett, 2013). The content of our autobiographical memories reflects cultural differences. In individualistic cultures these memories tend to focus more on events that have significance for

VIDEO LINK 10.2
Self-Concept

> **Autobiographical memory** A coherent set of memories about one's life.

the individual, such as getting a desired toy, while in collectivist cultures they highlight the interconnectedness of the individual to others, such as family vacations (Ross & Wang, 2010; Wang, 2008).

Research has shown that the way parents talk with their children about what happens in their lives also has an effect on the way children remember their lives. When parents guide their children in complex discussions about events, children are better able to remember details about their lives and may even understand them in more complex ways (Haden, 2003).

Self-Esteem in Early Childhood

Young children tend to have very high self-esteem. If you look back at the self-description of the 3-year-old above, you may be struck by the fact that the child had an unrealistically high opinion of his abilities. This 3-year-old claimed he knew *all* his ABCs (although he clearly did not), could run *fast* and climb to the *top* of the jungle gym, and was *never* scared. Another example of this unrealistic self-appraisal comes from a little girl who was asked whether she knew how to swim. "Yes" was her reply, but when she was asked to swim over to the adult, she let go of the side of the pool and sank like a stone.

To understand why young children have such a positive evaluation of themselves, you need to consider the standard of comparison they use when making self-evaluations. When a 3-year-old compares what she can do now to what she could do just a year earlier, it is a very impressive improvement. Also preschoolers are not yet able to compare themselves to others because cognitively they cannot keep two things—their own behavior and the behavior of another person—in mind at the same time. Without being able to compare their own performance to the performance of another person, almost everything they do can be the "best" in their eyes (Harter, 1999).

Self-Control and Delay of Gratification

Effortful control The ability to consciously control one's behavior.

As you learned in Chapter 9, executive function is the brain's ability to choose goals, initiate appropriate responses, inhibit inappropriate ones, monitor success, and correct errors, if they occur (Zhou et al., 2007). The development of executive function has been linked with effortful control, the ability to consciously control our own behavior. In a well-known study, 4-year-old children were told they could eat one marshmallow right away or wait and get two marshmallows later (Eigsti et al., 2006). When tempted in this way, children who actively tried to inhibit their immediate impulse to grab that marshmallow and eat it—by doing things such as sitting on their hands, looking away from the marshmallow, or whistling a tune—were better able to wait than those who concentrated on the marshmallow. **Active Learning: How Do Children Resist Temptation?** will show you how you can try this experiment with a child.

Active Learning

How Do Children Resist Temptation?

Walter Mischel and his colleagues found that children who exert active self-control at 4 years of age are better able to concentrate and tolerate frustration when they become teenagers (Eigsti et al., 2006). Infants have little ability to delay gratification, but by age 4 many children can use intentional tactics to help themselves do so. Try the following task with a preschool child:

Equipment needed:

2 marshmallows (or other attractive reward)

A table and chair for the child

Procedure:

1. You can do this activity with a boy or a girl between 3 and 5 years of age. In a room with no distractions (for example, no toys or books), seat the child at a table with one marshmallow (or other treat) on a plate.

2. Tell the child you have to leave the room for a little while. Ask whether the child would prefer to have one marshmallow or two marshmallows. Explain that if the child can wait until you come back, he will receive two marshmallows. However, if he feels unable to wait, the child can eat the one marshmallow but will not receive the second marshmallow. Be sure the child understands the instructions.

3. Leave the room and secretly observe the child for up to 10 minutes, or return if the child eats the marshmallow or appears greatly distressed. Ideally you will have a one-way mirror, or if not, find another way to be sure the child cannot see you watching. Observe whether and how the child tries to stop himself from taking the marshmallow. Does he sit on his hands, look around the room, sing to distract himself, and so on? These are all observable ways he may try to exercise effortful control.

4. If the child waited and did not eat the marshmallow, give him two when you return to the room. If he ate the one on the plate, he does not receive the second marshmallow.

5. Be sure to tell the child how helpful he was and thank him regardless of whether he got one marshmallow or two.

6. Compare your results with those of others in your class. Were children who had more tactics to try to control themselves more successful in waiting until the time was up to receive the marshmallows? Were there differences depending on the ages of the children; for example, were 4-year-olds able to wait longer than 3-year-olds? ▪

Children use effortful control to help them delay immediate gratification in favor of waiting for a later, larger reward. A similar situation you may find familiar is a party with lots of wonderful food to tempt you. To avoid overeating, you might move away from where the food is being served and engage in conversation so you aren't thinking about all that temptation. Young children who waited for the second marshmallow were more likely to distract themselves from the marshmallow by looking at or thinking about other things. In addition, when preschoolers were taught to "reframe" the temptation by thinking of the marshmallow as a cloud or a cotton ball rather than a treat, they are better able to wait for the larger reward (Mischel et al., 2011).

As they get older, children become better able to delay gratification and wait until later to get something desirable. McCabe and Brooks-Gunn (2007) looked at this topic by using **delay of gratification** tasks in a preschool classroom rather than in a research laboratory. First, they asked children to wait to eat an M&M candy until the researcher blew a whistle, and then they placed the children in groups of four and repeated the procedure. They also asked the children, first individually and then as part of a group, not to peek as the researcher wrapped a present for them. Not surprisingly, they found that older children were better able to regulate their behavior and delay gratification than

Delay of gratification The ability to wait until later to get something desirable.

younger children, whether they were tested individually or as part of a group. Although girls waited longer than boys before peeking in the gift wrap task, there was no gender difference in the likelihood that children would peek at some point. Finally, the researchers found no consistency across the different situations they tested. This highlights that children's ability to delay gratification is the result not only of their characteristics but also of the context of a particular situation. Ask yourself honestly what situation would be tempting enough that you too would peek even when you know you shouldn't.

Self-control at a young age has been associated with a number of positive outcomes in school-age children (Zhou et al., 2007), but lack of control and high negative emotionality in children as young as 3 to 5 have been found to predict later delinquency and even adult criminal convictions (Henry, Caspi, Moffitt, Harrington, & Silva, 1999). In longitudinal studies of more than 500 children who were given the marshmallow test at age 4, those better able to resist temptation had the following later outcomes: lower body mass index, higher SAT scores and academic achievement, better ability to cope with stress, and a higher sense of self-worth and self-esteem. In research with a more diverse population, outcomes included less aggression and bullying (Mischel et al., 2011; Schlam et al., 2013).

When a child has difficulty delaying gratification, there are opportunities for interventions that can change the course of development before a persistent pattern sets in (Zhou et al., 2007). These interventions include helping the child develop coping skills and helping parents learn behavioral management skills that support and assist their child's coping efforts.

JOURNAL ARTICLE 10.1
Delay of Gratification

Check Your Understanding

1. How do autobiographical memories form?
2. What is effortful control?
3. Describe a delay-of-gratification experiment.
4. What do we know about the later advantages of developing self-control while a preschooler?

10.3

How do different theories describe the development of gender identity?

Development of Gender Identity

"It's a boy!" "It's a girl!" One of the first and most central aspects of our sense of self is our gender. Our gender determines much about what our experiences in life will be. Every society prescribes certain roles and expectations for the behavior of men and women, girls and boys. Whether you are a boy or a girl biologically is determined by genes, hormones, and physical body parts. However, the concept of gender includes all the roles and stereotypes that our society connects with being a boy or a girl. Take a minute to think about what you connect with the concept of "boy" and the concept of "girl." Numerous theories have contributed ideas about how children develop their concept of gender and their own gender identity. We describe three of these approaches: behavioral and social learning theory, cognitive developmental theory, and gender schema theory, as well as the research that has been guided by them.

Behavioral and Social Learning Theories

T/F #3
Today most parents do not reinforce gender-specific stereotypes and instead treat their sons and daughters in very similar ways. *False*

As we learned in Chapter 2, a central concept of the theory of behaviorism is reinforcement, those environmental responses that cause a behavior to continue or be repeated. For behaviorists, gender identity results from direct and indirect reinforcement of gender roles and activities. Adults may claim they do not discriminate between boys and girls and think all the observed differences between the sexes have biological origins, but considerable research shows that parents do, in fact, reinforce sex-typed play activities and household chores for their children (Berenbaum, Martin, Hanish, Briggs, & Fabes, 2008).

While both boys and girls receive positive reinforcement for gender-appropriate behavior, boys receive more active discouragement for behaviors and activities that are defined as feminine than girls do for their masculine activities, at least in part because feminine boys are expected to stay that way through adulthood, while masculine girls are expected to outgrow these characteristics (Sandnabba & Ahlberg, 1999). Fathers are more likely than mothers to respond negatively to cross-gender activities (Bussey & Bandura, 1999). In one study, young children believed their parents would disapprove of cross-gender play, especially for boys, even if the parents claimed they did not have gender stereotypes (Freeman, 2007). Children may be picking up on parents' unconscious attitudes about gender roles.

What is gender-appropriate behavior? How do you think this boy's peers or parents would react if they saw him playing with dolls? What would their response communicate to him? ■

The central concept of social learning theory is the role of imitation, and children are exposed every day to numerous examples of gender roles and activities they can imitate. Even when their parents do not demonstrate strongly differentiated gender roles, children still see these roles portrayed in the world around them and in the media. As just one example, in a study of superhero cartoons, male superheroes outnumbered females 2 to 1, and the male superheroes were rated more likely to show anger while the female superheroes were more concerned about their appearance (Baker & Raney, 2007).

Cognitive Developmental Theory

Lawrence Kohlberg (1966) was the first theorist to examine the development of gender identity through the lens of cognitive theory. He believed children's understanding of gender goes through stages based on their level of cognitive development. When they are younger, they do not understand that gender is a characteristic that is stable and permanent. He found that young children thought gender could change over time ("I'm a boy, but I can be a mommy when I grow up"), or with changes in appearance such as hairstyle or clothing.

The first stage Kohlberg hypothesized, called gender identity, begins at about age 2. In this stage children can identify gender—"I am a girl, and you are a boy"—but their concept of gender relies on external appearance. They may believe that if a girl were to wear a tie, she might become a boy. As toddlers learn these gender labels, there is some evidence that they begin to take part in more gender-stereotyped play (Zosuls et al., 2009). The second stage, called gender stability, begins at age 3 when children understand that their gender will remain stable over time—that is, a girl will become an adult woman, and a boy will become an adult man. However, they are still not clear that a girl playing with trucks does not become a boy. Finally, in the third stage, called gender constancy, 5-year-old children have a more sophisticated level of understanding that despite superficial changes, a girl remains a girl and a boy remains a boy (Halim & Ruble, 2010). For example, at this age a child understands that a girl who plays with trucks is still a girl and a boy with long hair is still a boy.

Ruble et al. (2007) found support for these ideas, including the fact that children who had achieved gender constancy were less likely to be rigid in their adherence to gendered characteristics. They asked children questions such as "Is it wrong for boys to wear nail polish?" and "Would it be OK for a boy to wear nail polish if he didn't

AUDIO LINK 10.1
The Princess Obsession

Gender identity Stage when children can identify gender but their concept of gender relies on external appearance.

Gender stability Stage when children understand that their gender will remain stable over time, but aren't sure that gender won't change if they do activities usually performed by the other gender.

Gender constancy The understanding that despite superficial changes, one's gender remains constant.

get into trouble and nobody laughed?" to determine how rigidly the children held gender role standards. It appears that before children have gender constancy, when there is still some question in their minds about whether they can turn into the other sex, they are more likely to have rigid standards. Therefore, preschool children often adhere more tightly to gender stereotypes than school-age children. Once the children are clear that they will forever be a boy or a girl, they are more flexible about activities and external appearance like clothing, hairstyles, and nail polish. A boy may or may not want to wear nail polish, but he knows that he will still be a boy if he does. A girl knows she can play with trucks and still be a girl. **Active Learning: Kohlberg's Cognitive Developmental Theory of Gender Development** is designed to show you how to test these concepts with a young child.

Active Learning

Kohlberg's Cognitive Developmental Theory of Gender Development

ACTIVE LEARNING
VIDEO 10.2
Gender Development

To identify the level of gender concept a child has reached according to Kohlberg's developmental theory, interview a child between the ages of 2 and 6 and ask the following questions:

1. Gender identity: Are you a girl or a boy? Whatever the child answers, ask the opposite; for example, if the child says she is a girl, ask whether she is a boy.

2. Gender stability: "When you were a baby, were you a boy, or a girl, or sometimes a boy and sometimes a girl?"

3. Gender stability: "When you grow up, will you be a man, a woman, or sometimes a man and sometimes a woman?"

4. Gender constancy: If you went into the other room and put on clothes like these [name other-sex clothes], would you then really be a boy or really be a girl? Follow-up question (if correct): Why did you say you would really be a [same sex]? Is it because you didn't want to be a [other sex] or because you can't change from a [same sex] to a [other sex]?

5. Gender constancy: When you grow up, if you do the work that [other sex] do, will you really be a man or really be a woman?

6. Gender constancy: "If a boy wore nail polish, would he become a girl? . . . If a girl had really short hair, would she become a boy? If a boy played with baby dolls, would he become a girl? . . . If a girl played with trucks, would she become a boy?

7. Gender constancy: "If you really wanted to be a [other sex: boy/girl], could you be?" (Arthur, Bigler, & Ruble, 2009, p. 444).

You can also ask the child the names of male and female friends and substitute their names above, instead of asking the child directly about himself or herself.

If the child can answer only Question 1 correctly, she is in the gender identity stage. If she can answer only the first three questions correctly, she is in the gender stability stage. If she can answer at least the first five correctly, she has full gender constancy. Children who answer some but not all questions correctly within a stage are still working on the understanding in that stage. If possible, compare your results with those of classmates who interviewed children who were younger or older than the child you interviewed. ■

Sandra Bem believed that much of what Kohlberg found about the stages of gender understanding was based on children's ignorance of the real physical differences between the sexes. In raising her own child, she made sure he did know the difference. She tells the following story to illustrate the idea that when children understand the physical differences between the sexes, they are not as affected by superficial differences.

Because Bem was trying to raise her son not to be gender-stereotyped, she accepted his request to go to school with barrettes in his hair. One of his buddies told him, "You're a girl, because only girls wear barrettes." Her son decided to show him in no uncertain terms that he was a boy, not a girl, so he pulled down his pants, but his friend replied, "Everybody has a penis; only girls wear barrettes!" (Bem, 1989, p. 662). Without the knowledge of physical differences between the sexes, his friend had to rely on superficial characteristics like barrettes to determine his friend's gender.

Meet Chris. Imagine you were just introduced to this child named Chris. What would your initial reaction be? What are the first questions you would ask this child? Does this child's appearance make you feel uncomfortable in any way, and if so, what is the source of your discomfort? By the way, this is a picture of a 6-year-old boy. ∎

Gender Schema Theory

In Chapter 2, we describe a schema as a way that we organize our understanding of the world. Gender is one important schema that guides the way we see the world. Most people find it easier to navigate the world and social relationships in it when they can categorize others as "male" or "female." For example, when people were asked to evaluate the images other people chose to represent themselves online, most respondents preferred avatars that had clear indicators of being male or female rather than ones that were androgynous and difficult to categorize in terms of gender (Nowak & Rauh, 2008). Uncertainty about a person's gender made them uncomfortable. Look at this photo of Chris. What questions does this photo bring to your mind?

A gender schema contains more than simply whether someone is a male or a female. It also contains all the things an individual connects with each gender, such as expected behaviors, abilities, and occupations. Sandra Bem believed that gender development does not follow stages based on cognitive development, as Kohlberg said. Instead, she believed we learn gender concepts from our particular society. Children's self-concepts are formed in part by what they believe is assigned to their gender. In many Western cultures, a boy is likely to have "strong" but not "nurturing" in his self-description. Parents will proudly exclaim how strong their little boy is or "what an arm" he has when he throws a ball. Little girls are more likely to hear their parents talk with excitement about how their little girl is so loving to her dolls, a real "little mommy." As children learn what is expected for their gender, they try to fill those expectations (Hyde, 2014).

WEB LINK 10.2
Pink

Check Your Understanding

1. What do behavioral and social learning theories tell us about gender development in early childhood?
2. Describe the stages in Kohlberg's cognitive development theory of gender development.
3. What are gender schemas?

Moral Development

Earlier in this chapter, we said that your self-concept included all the ways you think about and describe yourself. Would you describe yourself as honest or trustworthy? As caring and compassionate? As respectful and patient toward others? All of these are characteristics of your self-concept that are rooted in moral development.

10.4

What roles do environmental influences, cognitive development, and emotional development play in the development of morality?

Young children are just beginning to learn how to discriminate between right and wrong; in other words, they are developing a sense of morality. At this age, what is moral or right is primarily determined by the people around the child. For that reason, children feel less ownership of their actions (Hardy & Carlo, 2011). They do what is right because they will be rewarded if they do or punished if they don't, but we want children to develop an internal sense of morality so they will choose to do what is right because of their own thoughts and feelings, not because of the external consequences. Children who have a warm, supportive relationship with parents who help them understand how their behavior affects themselves and others are more likely to internalize the parents' moral values (Hoffman, 2000). These children are learning to think about right and wrong not just in terms of what is good for them but rather in terms of what is good for everyone.

In this section, we describe how different theories have connected moral development with the influences in the environment, such as role models, and with emotional and cognitive development. In addition, because understanding morality is not the same as behaving in a moral fashion, we examine not only the development of moral thought but also the development of moral behavior.

The Role of the Environment

The theory of behaviorism offers an environmental explanation for how children first learn right from wrong. According to this theory, when a child does something good, like helping a friend, he may receive praise from an adult or a positive reaction from the friend. This reinforcement makes it more likely the child will behave this way again. However, when the child does something bad, like taking a toy away from a friend, he is likely to be scolded by an adult and receive a negative reaction from his friend. He will associate negative events with this behavior, and that should make it less likely the behavior will occur again in the future.

Social learning theory adds another mechanism for moral development. Children will imitate what they see others do, especially if the other person's behavior receives reinforcement. Without being directly reinforced for their own behavior, they learn what is good behavior and what is bad from what they see. For example, young children imitate both the aggressive behavior and helping behavior they see when they watch television shows. When high-quality prosocial television programs and DVDs were substituted for more aggression-laden programming for a sample of 3- to 5-year-old children, social competence scores increased and angry/aggressive/oppositional behavior decreased. The effects were particularly strong for boys from low-income families (Christakis et al., 2013).

However, the biggest question in the development of morality is how children move from responding to external consequences, such as rewards and punishments, to internalizing a moral sense of right and wrong so they do what is right even if no one is around. Some of the theories about how this happens emphasize the role of emotional development in the process, while others emphasize the role of cognitive development.

The Role of Emotional Development

Emotions enter into the development of morality in two ways. First, we don't want to do what we

AUDIO LINK 10.2
Morality

Time out. Consequences such as time out and a scolding should make it less likely that this little girl will repeat negative behaviors. ■

Comstock/Stockbyte/Getty Images

think is wrong because we will feel guilty about it, and that is an uncomfortable emotion. As we have seen, guilt is an emotion that develops during early childhood. Second, we want to do what is right because we will feel good about doing it and possibly even proud of ourselves. These emotions are the result of our conscience, an autonomous inner guiding system that is based on our understanding of moral rules (Kochanska & Aksan, 2006).

Kochanska and Aksan (2006) have shown a link between conscience and moral behavior. They found that responsiveness of the mother to her infant leads to the toddler's eager willingness to comply with the parent's guidance and rules. In preschoolers these rules become internalized to form the basis of the child's internal conscience. In turn, children who develop an effective internal conscience are much less likely to engage in disruptive and negative behavior (Kochanska, Barry, Aksan, & Boldt, 2008; Hardy & Carlo, 2011).

The central role of a different aspect of emotions in moral development is shown in the following simple example: A young child bumps her head as she emerges from a play structure. The teacher says, "Oooh, ouch! That must hurt. Should we put some ice on it?" This example illustrates the two basic aspects of emotional response that underlie prosocial behavior: empathy and sympathy. The teacher is experiencing *empathy* when he says, "Oooh, ouch!" It is almost as if he too were experiencing the hurt. As we learned in Chapter 7, even newborns seem to experience this type of emotional sharing. When they hear other babies crying, they are likely to start crying themselves (Geangu et al., 2010). However, unlike a newborn, the teacher is able to manage his own emotional response to react with concern for the child. This response is called *sympathy* (Eisenberg, Spinrad, & Sadovsky, 2006). If you feel empathy for other people, it is likely to lead to sympathy for their plight. You also are more likely to want to do something to help them and less likely to want to hurt them. In a recent study of older children, the likelihood of sharing with a peer was affected in some children by their ability to be sympathetic, and for others by their feelings of guilt (Ongley & Malti, 2014).

Just as empathy and sympathy can lead to prosocial behaviors that help and support other people, anger can lead to antisocial behaviors that hurt other people physically or emotionally. We judge these behaviors to be moral in the case of prosocial behaviors, or as a violation of moral standards in the case of antisocial ones. The use of aggression by children at different ages is related to the level of their moral understanding. We are less concerned by a preschooler who pushes a friend away to get to a toy than we are by a teenager who uses the Internet to destroy another teen's reputation, in part because we don't expect the preschooler to understand how her behavior is hurtful to the other child.

The Role of Cognitive Development

Cognitive theories link the development of moral thought to the development of thought in general. It has been argued that young children learn the basic rules of right and wrong by first grade. This moral knowledge is based on their understanding of what is considered right or wrong in the context of their culture. For example, do unto others as you would have them do to you, or honesty is the best policy, are moral principles endorsed by many cultures. Moral judgment is the way we reason about moral issues and reach conclusions. For example, two children may know it is wrong to take a cookie without asking. They have the same moral knowledge. However the reason why they don't take a cookie differs based on their stage of cognitive development. A young child doesn't take the cookie because she knows she will be punished if she does. A child at a higher level of moral judgment understands that taking the cookie is wrong because it breaks trust with a parent.

To test some of his ideas about moral development, Piaget (1965) posed moral dilemmas to children of different ages to see how they would respond. He described their resulting judgments as falling into three stages: premoral reasoning, heteronomous morality,

Conscience An autonomous inner guiding system that is based on our understanding of moral rules.

JOURNAL ARTICLE 10.2
Sharing

Prosocial behavior Actions that help and support other people.

Antisocial behavior Actions that hurt other people, physically or emotionally.

Moral knowledge Understanding of right and wrong.

Moral judgment The way people reason about moral issues.

Premoral reasoning The inability to consider issues on the basis of their morality.

Heteronomous morality Moral judgments based on the dictates of authority.

Autonomous morality When children are aware of the rules and realize that they must adhere to them to maintain their interaction with others rather than because an adult has told them what to do.

Immanent justice The belief that unrelated events are automatic punishment for misdeeds.

and autonomous morality. Piaget believed that before the age of 4, young children were premoral; that is, they were unable to consider issues on the basis of their morality. He described the moral thought of children from ages 4 through 7 as heteronomous, which means "subject to external controls and impositions" (Merriam-Webster, 2010). In this stage, young children base their judgments on adult authority. They do not really understand why moral rules should be followed, so their behavior often is not consistent from one situation to another (Lapsley, 2006).

Another aspect of this second level of moral thought is immanent justice, or the belief that unrelated events are automatic punishment for misdeeds. Piaget (1965) argued that young children believe in "the existence of automatic punishments which emanate from things themselves" (p. 251). For example, in one moral dilemma he tells a story about a boy who stole apples and ran away but then fell through a rotten bridge. He asks the child whether the boy would have fallen if he had not stolen the apples. A child in the heteronomous stage will say that the boy would not have fallen into the water if he had not stolen the apples. Falling into the water was a punishment for what he did. One difficulty with this kind of thinking is that children who have experienced a negative event, such as being hospitalized for an illness, may believe it is a punishment for something they did. In fact, many adults still show this kind of thinking when they ask "What did I do to deserve this?" if something terrible happens to them. It is as if they think they are being punished for something they did earlier that really has no connection with the bad event that happened.

By age 7 or 8, children have generally moved on to the stage known as autonomous morality, in which they are aware of the rules and realize they must adhere to them to maintain their interaction with others. In Piaget's (1965) words, they come to understand that "everyone must play the same" (p. 44). The issue of fairness to all becomes central as children become less egocentric and more aware of others' points of view. Piaget believed children's play with peers contributes to moral development because in play everything must be negotiated, not handed down from adults, so children must figure out together how to play fairly and treat each other decently if they want to continue playing.

Check Your Understanding

1. How do the reactions of other people affect a young child's sense of which actions are right and which are wrong?
2. What is conscience?
3. Which emotions might lead a child to prosocial behaviors? Antisocial behaviors?
4. Compare moral knowledge and moral judgment.
5. Describe Piaget's stages of premoral, heteronomous, and autonomous morality.

10.5

How are children socialized by their family so they behave in an appropriate way for their culture?

Family Relationships

It is the goal of parents to raise their children in a way that makes them positive and productive members of their society. In this section, we describe some of the techniques and strategies that parents use to help shape their children's behavior.

Socialization

Parents are the first teachers and first models of what social relationships are like. In a process called socialization, parents, peers, and other important figures in the child's world help the child learn how to interact in appropriate ways according to the rules and norms of their society (Damon, 2006). Of course, what is considered appropriate varies from one culture to another. The main goal of socialization is to promote the child's acceptance and internalization of the attitudes, beliefs, and values held by their society. We next look at how parents promote their children's ability to understand society's expectations for their behavior, to act on this understanding, and to use those values to guide their own behavior.

> **Internalization** The process by which individuals adopt the attitudes, beliefs, and values held by their society.

Parenting Strategies and Techniques

Parents use many different techniques to teach their children appropriate behavior, depending on their own personality characteristics, their understanding of the nature of child development, and the characteristics and behavior of the child. Adults use a number of types of discipline to channel their children's behavior in positive ways and/or to stop negative behavior.

Inductive discipline sets clear limits for children, gives consequences for negative behavior, and provides explanations to the child about why the behavior was wrong and what he might do to fix the situation (Hoeve et al., 2009). Self-oriented induction asks the child to think about the consequences of his behavior for himself—for example, "Put the cookie back [setting limits], or you will ruin your appetite for dinner [explaining why]," while other-oriented induction focuses the child on thinking about the consequences for someone else—for example, "Look how sad Joey looks when you said that mean thing to him. Can you help him feel better?" (Gibbs, 2014).

In many situations, parents influence their children's behavior simply because children recognize and respect their parents' authority (Gibbs, 2014). When using the command strategy, parents simply state what should be done. They do not make any overt threats of punishment, but the child responds to the parents' legitimate authority to make this request—for example, "It is time to turn off your computer and get ready for bed."

According to social learning theory, behavior changes through the processes of modeling and imitation, and we are more likely to want to imitate models we like or admire. In the technique of relationship maintenance, parents try to create a positive relationship with their child so they will have a greater influence on the child's behavior or be a more attractive model for the child to imitate. When parents display affection toward a child, praise the child for things she has done well in the past, or show that they understand how the child feels, it helps motivate the child to comply with what the parents want the child to do (Grusec, Goodnow & Kuczynski, 2000).

In contrast to these types of positive discipline, power assertion relies on "adult-oriented, coercive, restrictive, and firm discipline techniques and emphasizes the negative aspects of control such as harsh punishment" (Hoeve et al., 2009, p. 750). Power assertion can use physical or nonphysical threats of punishment. Another approach is love withdrawal, in which parents withhold their love until the child conforms to the parents' expectations for his behavior—for example, "I'm not speaking to you until you apologize." While some power assertion or love withdrawal may be necessary to get the child's attention, the more positive approaches of inductive discipline, command strategy, and relationship maintenance will help the child internalize ideas about what is good and bad behavior (Choe, Olson, & Sameroff, 2013; Hoffman, 2000; Kristjánsson, 2004).

What are the outcomes of each of these strategies? The use of inductive discipline has been related to reduced behavior problems, such as aggression (Choe et al., 2013), and greater empathy which results in more prosocial behavior in children, meaning they are more likely to share and to show sympathy and other positive social behaviors (Krevans & Gibbs, 1996).

Although inductive discipline is beneficial to children in Western cultures, the same may not be true in all cultures. You can see how a discipline strategy that gives children the opportunity to make choices within certain limits and tells them how they can rectify a situation if they've done something wrong fits well with cultural values that emphasize

> **Inductive discipline** A parenting technique that involves setting clear limits for children and explaining the consequences for negative behavior, why the behavior was wrong, and what the child might do to fix the situation.
>
> **Self-oriented induction** A parenting technique in which the child is asked to think about the consequences that the child might experience as a result of his behavior.
>
> **Other-oriented induction** A parenting technique in which the child is asked to think about the consequences of the child's behavior for someone else.
>
> **Command strategy** A parenting technique in which the parent does not make any overt threats of punishment, but the child responds to the legitimate authority that the parent has to make a request of the child.
>
> **Relationship maintenance** A parenting technique in which the parents try to create a positive relationship with their child so that the parents will have a greater influence on the child's behavior.
>
> **Power assertion** A disciplinary technique that emphasizes control of the child's behavior through physical and nonphysical punishment.
>
> **Love withdrawal** A parenting technique in which parents withhold their love until a child conforms to the parents' expectations for his behavior.

VIDEO LINK 10.3
French Parenting

T/F #4

Spanking is an effective way to teach children how to control their behavior. *False*

VIDEO LINK 10.4
Spanking

choice, independence, and self-motivation. The same might not be as effective for children in a culture that emphasizes interdependence, behavior that is proper in the eyes of others, and a family hierarchical structure. For instance, in Japan if children misbehave, rather than reprimanding them the mother is likely to apologize for the children's behavior to anyone who saw what happened (Miyake & Yamazaki, 1995). The mother's apology preserves social harmony with others while preserving her close emotional bond with her child.

There is quite a bit of evidence that power assertion in the form of spanking often has negative effects. Statistics on the use of spanking vary dramatically from one study to the next, but in a 2013 Harris Interactive poll, two-thirds of parents in the United States said they have spanked their children. This is down from 80% in 1995, and younger parents were less likely to have spanked their children than older parents. This change is positive because research has shown no evidence that spanking is a positive socialization practice. In fact, children who are spanked tend to be more aggressive than those who are not, and this seems to be true across all ethnicities studied (Gershoff, 2013).

There are several reasons why spanking is not a good strategy to use to try to change a child's behavior. First, while spanking can be an effective way to immediately stop a behavior, it does not help children understand how to control themselves in the long run. Second, because parents may be out of control themselves when they spank their children, they model exactly the opposite of what they want their children to learn. And third, physical punishment can cross a line and become abusive, and abuse is clearly linked with negative outcomes for children, as we discuss later in this chapter (Kazdin & Benjet, 2003; Lansford et al., 2004).

Another reason spanking is ineffective in the long term is that when children become angry and resentful, their emotional distress gets in the way of hearing their parent's message about correct behavior. They are less likely to internalize the values the parent is trying to instill in them and won't be able to use these values in the future. Finally, research among young children with behavior problems found spanking was no more effective than time-out in bringing about children's compliance with their mother's commands (Gershoff, 2013).

You might wonder whether some parents are more strict and punitive because their children are more difficult to control. In that case, the parents' punitive behavior would be a response to the child's behavior rather than the cause of later problems. This is a very reasonable question to ask, but parents' use of spanking is more likely to precede and escalate children's aggressive behavior rather than the other way around (Gershoff, 2013; MacKenzie, Nicklas, Waldfogel, & Brooks-Gunn, 2013). It appears that the most important factor for whether parents are likely to use power assertion was whether they themselves were raised that way (Hoeve et al., 2009).

Parents are not always consistent in the way they discipline their children. They are more likely to resort to power assertion when they are under stress, especially when they are in a bad mood; when they believe the child's bad behavior was deliberate rather than accidental; or when the child has done something hurtful to others rather than committing some minor infraction of the rules (Critchley & Sanson, 2006).

The American Academy of Pediatrics, along with a number of other organizations of professionals who work with children, urges parents to abandon spanking in favor of other, more effective styles of discipline. The characteristics of more effective practices in response to children's misbehavior include:

- clarity on the part of the parent and child about what the problem behavior is and what consequence the child can expect when it occurs
- a strong and immediate initial consequence when the targeted behavior first occurs
- an appropriate and consistent consequence each time a targeted problematic behavior occurs

- instruction and correction delivered calmly and with empathy
- a reason for a consequence for a specific behavior, which helps children beyond toddler age to learn the appropriate behavior and improves their overall compliance with requests from adults. (American Academy of Pediatrics, 1998, reaffirmed in 2012)

Parenting Styles

Now that we have looked at specific parenting techniques, we examine different parenting styles based in part on these techniques. Diana Baumrind (2013) took dimensions that had recurred in research on parenting and combined them to describe four different parenting styles. The first dimension is parental acceptance/responsiveness, and the second is parental demandingness/control. Parents who are high on acceptance/responsiveness show a good deal of warmth and affection in their relationship with their child and provide a lot of praise and encouragement. In contrast, parents who are low on this dimension can be cool and even rejecting (sometimes ignoring the child completely), and they are more likely to criticize or punish the child than to praise him.

Parents who are high on the demandingness/control dimension promote and expect appropriately mature behavior from their children and will step in to control children's misbehavior (Baumrind, Larzelere, & Owens, 2010). In contrast, parents low on this dimension impose much less structure and fewer limits on their children. If we combine these two dimensions, we get the four distinct parenting styles shown in Table 10.1.

Authoritative parents combine high levels of control with a good deal of warmth and encouragement. Although they do make demands on their children, their expectations are reasonable and appropriate for the child's age and are directed at specific behavior they want the child to change (Baumrind, 2013). A hallmark of this style is that authoritative parents are willing to provide rationales for their rules and expectations and are open to listening to their children's point of view (Heath, 2005). Sometimes they are even persuaded by their children to be flexible about the rules because the situation warrants it. Overall these parents treat their children with respect and respond to their child's unique characteristics.

Authoritarian parents are high on control and often have a large number of rules that they expect their children to obey. These parents highly value unquestioning compliance from their children. They feel no obligation to explain the reasons for their rules and are generally unyielding about the rules themselves. They are not sensitive to the feelings of their children and are, therefore, considered low on the dimension of acceptance/responsiveness. The most negative aspect of this kind of parenting is discipline that is arbitrary, harsh, and demeaning (Baumrind et al., 2010).

Permissive parents provide a great deal of warmth and acceptance to their children, but this acceptance is coupled with few, if any, rules or restrictions. Children are free to express their ideas and opinions (often having an equal say with parents in decision

Acceptance/responsiveness A dimension of parenting that measures the amount of warmth and affection in the parent-child relationship.

Demandingness/control A dimension of parenting that measures the amount of restrictiveness and structure that parents place on their children.

Authoritative parents Parents who combine high levels of control with a good deal of warmth and encouragement, together with reasonable expectations and explanation of the parents' rules.

Authoritarian parents Parents who combine high levels of control and low levels of warmth, and who expect compliance from the child.

Permissive parents Parents who provide a great deal of warmth and acceptance but have few, if any, rules or restrictions.

WEB LINK 10.3
Parenting Styles

TABLE 10.1   Baumrind's parenting styles

		Acceptance/responsiveness	
		High	Low
Demandingness/control	High	Authoritative	Authoritarian
	Low	Permissive	Disengaged

The combination of two basic dimensions of parenting (acceptance/responsiveness and demandingness/control) creates four different parenting styles.

Disengaged parents Parents who do not set limits or rules for their children and are not emotionally connected to them.

making in the family), and parents usually do little monitoring or restricting of the child's activities.

Disengaged parents provide neither control nor warmth to their children (Baumrind, 2013). They do not demand good behavior or set rules or limits, and they also are not emotionally connected to their children. Some parents in this category are so consumed with problems in their own lives that they appear to have nothing left to give to their relationship with their children.

These brief descriptions provide a good sense of the different parenting styles, but parents do not always fit neat, clear-cut textbook descriptions. Even the most authoritarian parent might relent and show some flexibility occasionally, and even the most permissive parent might have to draw the line at some point to stop a child's behavior. However, parenting styles are fairly regular and consistent patterns that play themselves out in a variety of situations. It would not be surprising if, as you read these descriptions, some parents you know came to mind for at least a couple of them.

A great deal of research has been done on the consequences of each of these different parenting styles. We describe next what the research has shown, but bear in mind that most of it has been done on White middle-class children from Western cultures. The characteristics of individualistic cultures that differ from those of collectivist cultures might influence parenting styles and their outcomes.

Baumrind's research has continued for over 45 years. In both the original and the current longitudinal research, children raised by authoritative parents have been found to be "the most self-reliant, self-controlled, explorative, and content" (Baumrind, 1971, p. 1; see also Baumrind et al., 2010). The high achievement orientation Baumrind (1967) found in preschool children raised by authoritative parents continues to be reflected in older children and adolescents in their academic achievement (Aunola, Stattin, & Nurmi, 2000; Gray & Steinberg, 1999).

Baumrind and her colleagues found that when preschool children experience authoritative parenting, they are more likely to become highly competent and well-adjusted adolescents (Baumrind et al., 2010). They are more socially skilled, show greater psychosocial maturity, and exhibit fewer internalizing (or self-directed) behaviors such as anxiety and fewer externalizing (or other-directed) behaviors, such as aggression. They are more likely to be seen as outgoing; as leaders (Baumrind, 1991a); as more cooperative with peers, siblings, and adults (Denham, Renwick, & Holt, 1991); and as more empathetic and altruistic (Aunola et al., 2000). They also have been found to have higher self-esteem (McClun & Merrell, 1998), to be more self-reliant (Steinberg, Mounts, Lamborn, & Dornbusch, 1991) and to have a lower likelihood of using drugs, alcohol, and tobacco (Adamczyk-Robinette, Fletcher, & Wright, 2002; Baumrind, 1991a; Fletcher & Jefferies, 1999; Gray & Steinberg, 1999).

In comparison, children raised by authoritarian parents are likely to be defiant, resentful, and withdrawn (Baumrind, 2012). Two of the most destructive aspects of authoritarian parenting are parental hostility and indirect and intrusive control (Baumrind et al., 2010). Baumrind described the situation as one in which children feel trapped and angry but are afraid to protest because of possible negative consequences. They are not encouraged to think for themselves or make their own decisions. Authoritarian parents often rely on physical punishment (Baumrind, 2012), so they model aggressive behaviors for their children. This may help explain why authoritarian parents are more likely to have children who become bullies (Baldry & Farrington, 2000). A child who has, in effect, been bullied by authoritarian parents may then vent the resulting anger and frustration he or she feels on other weaker victims.

Children of authoritarian parents have lower self-esteem (Martinez & Garcia, 2008; Rudy & Grusec, 2006) and less ability to play positively with peers (Gagnon et al., 2014). Use of punitive discipline by authoritarian parents is associated with both externalizing and internalizing behavior problems (Fletcher, Walls, Cook, Madison, & Bridges,

Internalizing (or self-directed) behaviors Behaviors in which a child's emotions are turned inward and become hurtful to themselves.

Externalizing (or other-directed) behaviors Behaviors, such as aggressive or destructive behavior, in which the child "acts out" on the environment.

2008). The picture that emerges suggests that across a range of developmental outcomes, authoritarian parenting has negative repercussions for child development.

Children raised by permissive parents were described as "the least self-reliant, explorative, and self-controlled" (Baumrind, 1971, p. 2). Permissive parents are at the other extreme on the dimension of control, although they combine permissiveness with a good deal of warmth and affection. Parents may choose this style with the best intentions, but the child outcomes are not particularly positive. Adolescents who had experienced permissive parenting as preschoolers were less autonomous, perhaps as a result of having a less solid grounding in appropriate expectations and controls in their early years (Baumrind et al., 2010). Nijhof and Engels (2007) describe children of permissive parents as "self-centered, impulsive and aggressive" (p. 711), as having poor social skills, and as feeling unworthy of the love of another person.

Children with disengaged parents have the worst outcomes. Young children raised by parents who are less warm and less involved have been found to be more angry and defiant (Miller, Cowan, Cowan, Hetherington, & Clingempeel, 1993). In middle childhood, they have lower levels of academic achievement (Murray, 2012) and as adolescents, they score more poorly than peers on measures of psychosocial development (self-reliance, work orientation, social competence), school achievement (grade point average, school orientation), internalized distress (psychological and somatic symptoms), and problem behavior (drug use, delinquency; Lamborn, Mounts, Steinberg, & Dornbusch, 1991).

In looking at the pattern of findings from these studies, you would likely conclude that certain parenting styles have more positive outcomes for children than other styles, but the outcomes associated with different parenting style are not universal. Other factors, including the age and temperament of the child and the cultural context in which the parenting occurs, interact with parenting styles to produce the outcomes so the same parenting style might have different outcomes in different settings (Davidov, Grusec, & Wolfe, 2012; Lansford et al., 2005). Some recent research highlights these cultural differences. Research in Europe has not found negative effects of permissive parenting, and for some outcomes, children with permissive parents did better than children with authoritative parents (Calafat, García, Juan, Becoña, & Fernández-Hermida, 2014; Garcia & Gracia, 2009). Authoritarian parenting in collectivist cultures such as Egypt, Iran, India, and Pakistan teaches children to inhibit the expression of their own wants and needs in accordance with their culture's expectations and is not associated with lower self-esteem in the children (Rudy & Grusec, 2006). It has been suggested by Lansford and Deater-Deckard (2012) that when physical discipline is the cultural norm, children understand and accept it and consequently it is not as likely to lead to the aggressiveness seen in children living in cultures where physical discipline is associated with parental rejection. These findings remind us to be careful to take cultural norms into consideration whenever we discuss parenting approaches. Good parenting does not look the same in all cultures.

You are likely to have some reaction when you see the photo in **Active Learning: Parents' Reaction to Misbehavior.** This activity will help you better understand how parents with different parenting styles would deal with this situation. How would *you* react?

T/F #5
Children who are raised by permissive parents are most likely to grow up to be self-reliant, confident, and explorative. *False*

T/F #6
Good parenting looks the same regardless of where we find it. *False*

Active Learning

Parents' Reaction to Misbehavior

Imagine a parent comes into the living room to find this scene. Now think about each parenting style Diana Baumrind identified. Describe what you think an authoritative parent would say and do. Next do

iStockphoto.com/BanksPhotos

the same for an authoritarian parent, a permissive parent, and a disengaged parent. Now imagine you are one of the children in the photo and think about what you would learn from the response of each type of parent. In the long run, which type of response is likely to be most effective in making you want to behave differently in the future? Why? ▪

JOURNAL ARTICLE 10.3
Fathering

Much of the research on parenting has looked at mothers' parenting styles (Winsler, Madigan, & Aquilino, 2005), but once researchers began to look at fathers' parenting styles as well, the issue of how much agreement there was between mothers and fathers arose. Several consistent differences have been found. Mothers are more likely than fathers to use an authoritative style, and fathers are more likely than mothers to use an authoritarian style (Russell, Hart, Robinson, & Olsen, 2003; Winsler et al., 2005).

Within the same family, the congruence between parents' styles is only modest. In one study, there was fairly high agreement between parents who were permissive, moderate agreement between parents where one was authoritarian, and no agreement where one parent was authoritative (Winsler et al., 2005). What can explain these differences? Being a permissive parent is often an intentional choice by parents who want to create a specific type of child-rearing environment, so these parents may discuss and reach agreement on a shared philosophy of child rearing. In other families, one parent may adopt a style that balances the style of the other parent. If one parent is authoritarian, it may be more important that the second parent be authoritative or even permissive. However, if one parent is authoritative, it may matter less which style the second parent adopts.

Fortunately, children can adapt to the fact that their parents have different styles, and, of course, children sometimes try to use these differences to their own advantage. When children want something from their parents, they often have a pretty good idea of which parent to approach and just how to frame that request to increase the chance that they will get what they want. The one potential problem with this strategy arises when the lack of agreement between parents becomes a source of conflict within the family.

Interventions for a Better Family Life

As we are learning, children tend to thrive when they grow up in families in which they have positive relationships with their caregivers in an organized living situation with clear expectations and opportunities to learn (Shonkoff & Phillips, 2000). Ecological systems theory tells us that children and their families are affected by influences at many different levels, from broad cultural expectations to government policies, to the neighborhoods in which they live, and to their own individual, even internal, experiences in life. When a family is struggling, intervention may occur at any of these levels, support can be provided at different points in the development of the family, and programs can be designed to prevent as well as to fix problems that have already occurred. We next look at a few examples to illustrate these approaches.

At the level of government, some of the central policies that influence families include those concerned with economic security, child care and education, health care, and reproductive rights (Hartman, 2003). For example, the Family and Medical Leave Act (FMLA) of 1993 allows many workers up to 12 weeks of unpaid leave, with the guarantee of return to the same or a comparable job when they need to care for a newborn, adopt, take a child into foster care, or care for a family member with a serious health problem (U.S. Department of Labor, 2010).

While this is an improvement from when there was no job protection for parents who have children, it does not cover all workers. The provisions of the FMLA only apply to people who work in companies with at least 50 employees and the worker must have been employed for at least 1,250 hours for one year before the leave is taken. This also is much less protection than governments in other countries offer. In France, parents can take off 16 to 26 weeks at 100% of their current salary (Stebbins, 2001), and they may take up to 2 years of unpaid leave. In Sweden, parents can share more than 12 months of paid leave to care for a new baby (Duvander & Andersson, 2006).

Intervention for families can also come at the level of the community. One example is the Safe Start Promising Approaches program sponsored by the U.S. Department of Justice. This ongoing program was originally set up in 11 communities to help children 6 and younger and their families who had been exposed to violence. As a wraparound program, it included services from the justice system, health and mental health care providers, and other human services (Arteaga & Lamb, 2008). In communities that implemented this program successfully, new screening protocols used by police, teachers, and others working with children were able to identify more children who had been exposed to violence. The program resulted in less exposure to violence and fewer psychological symptoms for the children, and less stress for parents and a better understanding of the effects of violence on their children (Hyde, Lamb, Arteaga, & Chavis, 2008).

Family therapy. A family therapist counsels the whole family, not just the child who has been identified with a problem. ◼

Wraparound program A comprehensive set of services offered to families to strengthen them or reunite them.

Interventions at the level of the individual family may consist of family therapy for those with identified difficulties. Often a child presents with a problem, but the therapist, who might be a psychiatrist, psychologist, social worker, or marriage and family therapy counselor, may meet with the whole family or with various combinations of family members, such as father and daughter or parents and one son (Fox, 2006). Like any psychotherapy, family therapy begins with a family history, a discussion of the nature of the problem, and an evaluation of the family's strengths and possible barriers to treatment (Eyberg, Nelson, & Boggs, 2008). Interventions can include teaching parenting skills, helping parents understand their children's behavior, and helping parents with their own emotional problems. Therapists also may help families reflect on their interactions or coach the families while they interact.

Another type of family-based program targets families whose children are at high risk of developing psychological and behavioral problems and attempts to intervene *before* those problems emerge. For example, a program for preschool children with behavioral problems such as aggression and impulsivity provided an 8-week intervention the summer before the children began school. The goal of the program was to help the children develop skills that would help them make a successful transition into kindergarten. In the classroom, trained educators used a behavior modification program to teach the children to follow instructions, complete tasks, comply with teacher instructions, and interact in a positive and cooperative way with peers. During this time, the children's parents received training on how to use the same behavioral management strategies with their children at home to reduce the problem behaviors (Graziano, Slavec, Hart, Garcia, & Pelham, 2014).

Shonkoff and Phillips (2000) conclude that interventions with families work best when they consist of "empowering parents as the true experts with respect to their own child's and family's needs and . . . building a strong, mutually respectful, working partnership in which parents and professionals relate comfortably in a collaborative effort to achieve family-driven objectives" (p. 366).

Check Your Understanding

1. What is the relationship between socialization and internalization of norms?
2. Compare the parenting strategies of inductive discipline, command strategies, relationship maintenance techniques, power assertion, and love withdrawal.

3. How do the parenting styles called authoritative, authoritarian, permissive, and disengaged differ?
4. Give examples of some interventions that help support better lives for families.

10.6

What are play and peer relationships like during early childhood?

Peer Relationships and the Role of Play

A strong family life forms the basis for young children's new interactions in the world of their peers. We saw in Chapter 7 that even infants are interested in peers and begin to interact through imitation of each other. However, with the development of language, preschool children take peer interactions to a higher level. Play is the hallmark of preschool peer interaction.

In make-believe play, children take on different identities as they create a whole world of their own. As adults, we must appreciate the social skill this takes. One researcher has likened it to the level of coordination that must be achieved by a jazz quartet (Dunn, 2004). Children must learn to control their own impulses and understand others' intentions. At this stage, imitation is no longer enough to maintain an interaction. Instead the children develop complementary roles: "You be the mommy, and I'll be the baby." Judy Dunn (2004) believes that taking part in shared make-believe in which children can express and explore their feelings, including their fears, dreams, and disappointments, becomes the basis for the development of the trust and closeness essential to relationships among older children.

Parents from many different cultures engage in fantasy play with their young children (Haight, Black, Ostler, & Sheridan, 2006), and this play is associated with the development of social skills in children's interactions with peers. For example, when Lindsey and Mize (2000) studied play between parents and their 3- to 6-year-old children, they found that children who engaged with their parents in more pretend play that was mutually responsive (that is, parent and child each responded effectively to each other's cues) had higher social competence with peers in their preschools.

Play disruption An inability to play because the child's emotions are preventing the kind of free expression linked with the fun of play.

When children have the opportunity to play but are unable to do so, it can be an indication of a variety of behavioral problems. In the *DSM-5* (APA, 2013), one characteristic of autism spectrum disorder consists of "Deficits in developing, maintaining, and understanding relationships. . . . These difficulties are particularly evident in young children, in whom there is often a lack of shared social play and imagination (e.g., age-appropriate flexible pretend play) and, later, insistence on playing by very fixed rules" (p. 54). Other children who are highly stressed and anxious may have the cognitive and social abilities to play but experience play disruption, an inability to play because their emotions are preventing the kind of free expression linked with the fun of play (Scarlett, Naudeau, Salonius-Pasternak, & Ponte, 2005). Play is such a central aspect of children's lives that difficulties with play often indicate larger problems in the child's life.

Emotional Development

In the psychoanalytic tradition of Sigmund Freud, play is seen as the expression of the child's inner emotional conflicts (Scarlett et al., 2005). Children play out in fantasy what is bothering

Design Pics/Ron Nickel/Ron Nickel/Design Pics/Newscom

Early social interactions. Toddlers' first interactions are often imitations of each other. Can you see how the imitative play of these children as they follow each other on this play equipment might lead to turn taking and eventually cooperative interaction as they develop more social skills? ∎

them in real life. For example, children may become the "mean mother" with their dolls to express their frustration with parental discipline they have experienced. This fantasy gives children some sense of control that helps them deal with real situations in which they feel helpless, as all children do at some times when dealing with the powerful adults in their lives. It also allows them to express in play certain emotions that might be unacceptable in real life, such as anger at a baby sibling (Haight et al., 2006).

Play therapy developed as a way to help children work through difficult feelings with the help of an adult who is trained to understand play as a type of communication. Many children, especially young children, are unable to sit and talk with a therapist about their feelings as adults do. Instead they present their thoughts and emotions in symbolic form through their

Emotional development. This 6-year-old girl is participating in a play therapy session. Games help her express her inner world in a secure space. ■

play. As their thoughts and feelings become clear in their play, the therapist helps the children manage them in more adaptive ways.

One example was provided by Jones and Landreth (2002) in a study on play therapy for children with chronic, insulin-dependent diabetes who experience frightening symptoms, such as diabetic coma, along with many mystifying and painful interventions from doctors and nurses. In one case, a child was experiencing stomachaches every day. Over five sessions of play therapy, he acted out battle scenes, which initially used play soldiers but eventually came to include doctors and nurses as the "bad guys" who would never go away, because "they just keep coming back!" (Jones & Landreth, 2002, p. 127). After expressing his feelings in this symbolic way, the child was able to talk about the "anxiousness" in his stomach. When the therapist clarified that "feeling worried or nervous" could be experienced as a stomachache, the boy was able to move on to a less conflicted and less compulsive type of play, and his stomachaches did not return.

In a meta-analysis of studies on the efficacy of play therapy, Bratton, Ray, and Rhine (2005) found this type of treatment was generally very helpful to children and resulted in changes in their maladaptive behavior. It was especially effective when parents were active in the treatment and could begin to understand what their child was communicating to them through play. When parents can see more clearly how things appear from their child's point of view, they are better able to help the child resolve conflicts rather than acting them out in negative ways, such as fighting with other children or experiencing stomachaches.

Play therapy A way to help children work through difficult feelings with the help of an adult who is trained to understand play as a type of communication.

VIDEO LINK 10.5
Play Therapy

Social Development

Play with other children is intrinsically social, so it is no surprise that it has been linked with the development of social skills and the formation of friendships. In the 1930s, Mildred Parten (1932) described the following levels of play, still used by researchers and those who work with children (for example, Dyer & Moneta, 2006, and Freeman & Somerindyke, 2001). The levels are based on the social skills a child is capable of using with peers.

1. **Unoccupied behavior:** looking around at whatever occurs, but engaging in no activity
2. **Onlooker behavior:** watching others play

Unoccupied behavior Looking around at whatever occurs, but engaging in no activity.

Onlooker behavior Watching other children play.

Solitary independent play Engaging actively with toys that are different from those being used by other children.

Parallel play Playing next to a peer with the same type of materials, but not interacting with the other child.

Associative play Sharing toys and interacting with peers, but without a common goal.

Cooperative play Play with peers that has a common goal.

3. **Solitary independent play:** engaging actively with toys that are different from those being used by other children

4. **Parallel play:** playing next to but not in interaction with others, often using the same type of materials—for example, blocks or dolls

5. **Associative play:** playing with other children, sharing toys, and interacting, but with no overall organization of the group to achieve a common goal

6. **Cooperative play:** playing as part of a group that has a common goal such as erecting a building, creating a make-believe scene such as "house" with assigned roles, or playing sports

Many studies have provided support for Parten's idea that children become more interactive and more cooperative with age, and that the tendency to take part in more socially interactive play reflects better social adjustment (Coplan & Arbeau, 2009; Fantuzzo, Bulotsky-Sheare, Fusco, & McWayne, 2005). However, the exact levels of play Parten proposed have been called into question. For example, children take part in solitary and parallel play at about the same age, so these may not reflect distinct levels of social maturity. Contrary to what Parten proposed, research has not consistently shown that parallel play is a higher level of social interaction than solitary play. Parallel play is prevalent throughout the preschool years and may be more related to the nature of the school curriculum than to the children's social skills. In one study, children were more likely to engage in parallel play if the school provided many activities that promoted an individual task orientation rather than less structured or more cooperative activities (Provost & LaFreniere, 1991).

Whereas unoccupied and onlooker activities have been linked to immaturity and lack of social skills, solitary independent play, such as when a child plays alone but imaginatively with dolls or creates block buildings, has been linked with positive development, autonomy, and maturity (Luckey & Fabes, 2005). The meaning of solitary play is in part determined by the reason behind it. Some children may prefer to play alone because they can be in control of what happens and can create what they have in mind without interference. Others prefer play with objects rather than with people, and this type of social disinterest has not clearly been linked to any long-term problems for these children (Coplan & Armer, 2007). However, children may play alone because they have been rejected by others, are too shy to approach them, or lack the social skills to initiate contact with them, and these causes are more likely to be connected with later difficulties. For example, children who are shy and anxious in new social situations are more likely to have difficulties such as academic problems and low self-esteem, particularly if their shyness is combined with lower verbal skills, overprotective parents, and/or the lack of a high-quality friendship (Coplan & Armer, 2007).

To test yourself on your understanding of Parten's stages of play, see **Active Learning: Parten's Stages of Social Play.**

T/F #7
If a child chooses to play alone when there are other children to play with, there is no reason for concern.
True

Active Learning

Parten's Stages of Social Play

Next to each level of Parten's play scale write the number of the description that best matches it.

Unoccupied behavior _____	1. Francisco and Martha decide to play house and agree that Devorah will be the baby.
Onlooker behavior _____	2. Keisha sucks her thumb while gazing randomly around the room.
Solitary independent play _____	3. Jon and Claudia each work on a puzzle, occasionally looking at each other's work.
Parallel play _____	4. Ted builds a tower with blocks.
Associative play _____	5. Carol is new in class. She watches the children play with great interest.
Cooperative play _____	6. Sadie and Sabine play in the sandbox, talking with each other and exchanging the tools and cups they need for their individual sand castles.

■ Answers: Unoccupied behavior—2; Onlooker behavior—5; Solitary independent play—4; Parallel play—3; Associative play—6; Cooperative play—1

Play and social development are inextricably linked, so researchers have difficulty determining what comes first, play or social competence. While play undoubtedly contributes to social development, children whose social development is more advanced probably also make better playmates. Some research has shown that preschool children who were more likely to engage in fantasy play were also more likely to demonstrate theory of mind, or the ability to understand what others are thinking. Research has shown that children who spend more time in fantasy play have a better understanding of the emotions of self and others (Lindsey & Colwell, 2003). However, in a review of this research, Lillard et al. (2013) conclude that there is limited evidence for a direct relationship between play and theory of mind. The evidence indicated that a third factor, such as parenting techniques, might underlie the development of both skills.

By the age of 3, children begin to show preferences for specific playmates, and friendships develop. Friendship has been defined as a mutual relationship, meaning both people must agree they have a friendship, that is marked by companionship, closeness, and affection (Dunn, 2004). Although preschoolers are notoriously fickle, many form friendships that last months or even years (Dunn, 2004). Preschool children who are friends are more comfortable with each other, have more fun when they play together, and can resolve conflicts and show sympathy and support for each other. Their interactions are more complex than those found among preschoolers who are not friends (Dunn, 2004).

However, friendships at this age are not based on sophisticated qualities that will enter into relationships at an older age, such as how trustworthy the friend is. Preschoolers are more attracted to another child who enjoys the same kinds of play activities they do. Rubin, Lynch, Coplan, Rose-Krasnor, and Booth (1994) studied the role of play in the formation of friendship. They brought groups of four previously unacquainted 7-year-olds together to play and then asked the children which child they liked to play with most. The children were drawn to those who shared their same play style. A child who took part in fantasy play preferred to play with another child who also played this way, while a child who liked to build things (constructive play) preferred playing with another who also liked this activity.

We have made the argument that play is related to emotional expression and social skills. Clearly, the opportunity to play should be available for the benefit of all children.

Friendship A mutual relationship marked by companionship, closeness, and affection.

T/F #8
Preschoolers are not likely to maintain a friendship for more than a few weeks. *False*

Check Your Understanding

1. Describe the process of play therapy.
2. What are Parten's levels of play?
3. How is play related to development of theory of mind?
4. What characterizes friendships between preschoolers?

10.7

What risks and resources are relevant to emotional development in early childhood?

WEB LINK 10.4
Poverty

T/F #9

Families are unlikely to move out of poverty once their income is at that level. *False*

Risks, Resources, and Resilience

Many young children grow up in situations that put their social and emotional development at risk. In this section, we discuss several important ones: poverty, homelessness, and trauma. Knowing about these threats to children's well-being helps us develop the tools to intervene early in their lives.

Poverty

As Figure 10.1 shows, 25% of children under the age of 6 in the United States lived in poverty in 2011, while 49% lived in low-income families with income less than 2 times the federal poverty line. The poverty line is the minimum income considered necessary for adequate support of basic needs (Addy et al., 2013). This rate has been on an upward trend since 2006 and reflects the economic reality that has afflicted many families in the United States. Children are even more likely to live in poverty if they are raised in a single-parent household. While 35% of those with married parents are in poverty or near-poverty, 75% with single parents live at this level of income (Addy et al., 2013). Minority children are also more likely to grow up in a low-income family; about 35% of White children, 67% of Hispanic children, and 70% of Black children live in poverty or near-poverty (Addy et al., 2013). The negative effects of growing up in poverty may be magnified for children who also are marginalized as the result of discrimination (Yoshikawa, Aber, & Beardslee, 2012).

Of course poverty is not a static condition. Families move in and out of poverty as their circumstances change. In any particular year, individuals living in poverty have a one in three chance of moving out of poverty. Most people experience periods of poverty

FIGURE 10.1   **Percentage of young children raised in poverty**

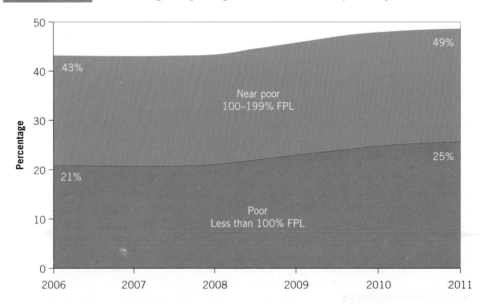

The percentage of young children raised in families whose income is at or below the federal poverty line (FPL in the figure) and at or below twice that level has risen significantly in recent years.

SOURCE: Addy, Engelhardt, & Skinner (2013).

that last 1–4 years. However, the more extreme the poverty and the longer its duration, the worse the child's outcome. Chronically poor children have worse outcomes than those who have only brief periods of economic disadvantage, and those with even brief experiences of poverty do more poorly than those who have never been poor (Allhusen et al., 2005).

Poverty reduces both material and nonmaterial investments, such as the amount of time that parents can devote to supporting their children's development (Aber, Morris, & Raver, 2012). It also creates enormous ongoing stress in parents, which can affect their physical and mental health. Depression is more common in low-income families, and depressed parents are much less able to care for their children in a way that supports their optimal growth. Poverty decreases the resources available to help mothers with depression, resulting in worse outcomes for the children (Petterson & Albers, 2001). Low-income parents also are less likely to provide a cognitively stimulating environment, with the toys and books that promote academic achievement, and are less likely to talk with their children than parents who are better off (Hart & Risley, 1995; Leffel & Suskind, 2013; McLoyd, 1998). The result is a lower level of verbal proficiency in the children, which has an important impact on later academic achievement.

The many risk factors associated with poverty, such as dangerous neighborhoods, high levels of noise, crowding, and substandard housing, are also linked to behavioral problems in poor children (Aber et al., 2012). An additional risk factor is the fact that parents who are dealing with the issues associated with poverty are more likely to be highly punitive and less warm toward their children, and this pattern of parenting is linked with behavioral problems (Bradley, Corwyn, McAdoo, & Garcia Coll, 2001). There is more evidence for a link with children's externalizing problems, such as aggression, than with their internalizing problems, such as depression, but both results are elevated in poor children and increase the longer the child lives in poverty (Allhusen et al., 2005).

When income relative to family needs increases in low-income families, child outcomes improve. A large study carried out by the National Institute of Child Health and Human Development followed children from birth to age 3 (Dearing, McCartney, & Taylor, 2001). Although increases in income for middle- and upper-income families did not affect children's abilities at age 3, increases in income for low-income families had a large effect. Children's language abilities, readiness for school, and social behaviors all improved, even reaching the same level as that for children in families that were not deprived. It was also true that poor families that became poorer had children with even worse outcomes. These same results were found when these children were retested at age 9. In a separate study, antisocial behavior was found to decrease in 4- to 7-year-olds when their families moved out of poverty and to increase the longer the families remained in poverty (MacMillan, McMorris, & Kruttschnitt, 2004).

There are some nonfinancial factors that are linked with better outcomes for children growing up in low-income families. Having parents who are not only very loving but also very strict seems to help children succeed in difficult circumstances (McLoyd, 1998). Attendance at an early education program, such as Head Start, also helps. However, direct financial aid to low-income families may be the most direct and effective way to improve the lot of children in those families. Several programs that directly reduce poverty by providing child allowance or tax credits for poor families have yielded significant increases in academic achievement and reductions in behavioral problems for children in those families as income increases (Dahl & Lockner, 2008; Duncan, Huston, & Weisner, 2007; Gennetian & Miller, 2000).

VIDEO LINK 10.6
Trauma

Homelessness. One outcome of poverty can be homelessness. The mother cuddling her daughter in this photo searched for work for 6 months and then was unable to pay her rent, so the family lost their house and ended up in a homeless shelter. ■

Homelessness

According to the National Center on Family Homelessness, one in every 45 children in the United States (or 1.6 million children) was homeless between 2006 and 2010 (Bassuk, Murphy, Coupe, Kenney, & Beach, 2011). Forty percent of those children were under 6. Homeless families share many stresses and risks with families living in poverty. Their children often go hungry, lack access to medical care, and miss many educational opportunities.

Homeless families try to cope by moving in with relatives, doubling up with other families or friends, staying in motel rooms, or sleeping in cars or public spaces. Children may be separated from their parents and from siblings if they are sent to live with friends or relatives. Emergency shelters may be available to the family, but they often are crowded, noisy, and at times unsafe, so most families consider them a last resort. If families need to move repeatedly, it forces children to change schools often. An estimated 40% of homeless children attend two different schools in a year, and 28% attend three or more (Bassuk et al., 2011). Families who become homeless often have other serious problems such as parental substance abuse, domestic violence, or mental illness, but they have limited access to services that meet those needs.

Homelessness has no easy solutions. Economic recovery would help many families, as would more affordable housing options. Meanwhile, services that address problems associated with homelessness—including medical services, substance recovery services, job training, and child care for working families—are needed to improve the lives of homeless children.

Trauma and Its Effects

Recent years have seen a rapidly growing interest in trauma and understanding how it affects physical and mental well-being (Aldwin, 2012). According to the National Child Traumatic Stress Network (n.d.), a traumatic event is one a child either witnesses or participates in that is perceived as extremely threatening. In some studies over two thirds of children reported experiencing a potentially traumatic event, and 25% report such experiences before the age of four, but these numbers vary in different populations and different studies (American Psychological Association Presidential Task Force on Posttraumatic Stress Disorder and Trauma in Children and Adolescents, 2008; Grasso, Ford, & Briggs-Gowan, 2013). The percentage is higher among children with psychological disorders.

The type of experiences that can fall under the umbrella term *trauma* include, but are not limited to, exposure to domestic violence, physical or sexual abuse, neglect, loss of a parent, natural disasters, school violence, medical trauma, terrorism, and refugee and war zone trauma. However, children react very differently to these experiences. A child's reaction can be affected by the exact nature of the experience, whether the child was in any way prepared for it, how the child perceives the threat, how long it lasts, the severity of the incident, the child's age or gender, and whether the child has a personal history of other traumatic experiences, as well as by the child's personality characteristics, coping abilities, and pretrauma psychological health (Skuse, Bruce, Dowdney, & Mrazek, 2011). Following a traumatic event, children may be left with the feeling that their world is neither secure nor predictable (Aldwin, 2012). They do not feel safe. Almost all will suffer some immediate reactions, which might include the development of new fears, separation anxiety, sleep disturbances or nightmares, loss of interest in normal activities, lack of concentration, anger, sadness, or somatic complaints (such as stomachaches or headaches) (American Psychological Association Presidential Task Force, 2008).

Although children's play often helps them work out emotional problems, following a traumatic event they may engage in a rigid reenactment of the event that does not seem to give them any relief (Hamblen & Barnett, 2009). Some will continue to reexperience the trauma through intrusive thoughts, distressing dreams, flashbacks, or extreme reactions to situations that resemble the event (Aldwin, 2012), all of which are characteristics of posttraumatic stress disorder (PTSD).

Preschoolers are particularly reactive to events that occur in their immediate family. Domestic violence, foster placement, parental separation, and divorce all threaten their secure attachment to their caregivers (Graham-Bermann et al., 2008). Like younger children, preschoolers may experience separation anxiety when a parent leaves the household because they reason that since one parent has left, the other could also abandon them. Intrusive thoughts, nightmares, and feelings of hopelessness may become more common (Graham-Bermann et al., 2008). Finally, children may become aggressive toward peers as a result of anger at what has happened at home or in imitation of parents' aggression toward each other (Cohen, Chaput, & Cashon, 2002).

Active Learning: Intrusive Thoughts gives you a bit of the experience of what having an intrusive thought might feel like.

Dealing with the aftermath of a disaster. Children can experience posttraumatic stress disorder following a traumatic event. As shown in this child's drawing of the events of September 11, 2001, art therapy can help children relive the experience in a way that allows them to deal with their emotions and control some of their anxiety. ∎

Active Learning

Intrusive Thoughts

Sit quietly for several minutes with your eyes closed and think about anything you want, except do *not* think about the green rabbit on this page.

Were you able to keep this rabbit out of your mind? People with PTSD often try very hard not to think about the traumatic events they have experienced. In fact, some actually develop amnesia for those events. However, for many, the more they try to keep the memories and thoughts out of their minds, the more these thoughts and emotions intrude in a way that is out of their control. Consider a messy closet, with toys and clothes falling out. When you examine items and put them back in a more orderly way, you can keep the closet closed and open it only when you choose to take something out. In a similar way, examining and understanding your thoughts, emotions, and memories allows you to put them in the past so you can fully engage in your current life (adapted from Vickers, 2005). ∎

Many behaviors preschool children show as a result of the experience of trauma can be disruptive when they are with other children. Preschoolers and children in kindergarten have a very high rate of expulsion and suspension from school—13 times the national average for older children (Giliam & Shahar, 2006)—and some who are expelled may be suffering from the aftereffects of trauma. A new program model called Head Start Trauma Smart is specifically designed to identify and help children whose difficulties are related to experiences of trauma. It is based on a program called ARC, which stands for attachment, self-regulation, and competency. Identified children meet individually with therapists trained in this approach. In addition, all adults who work with the children, from parents and teachers to bus drivers, are taught about the ways trauma affects both brain and behavior development. They learn to help children talk about their feelings rather than getting out of control.

Posttraumatic stress disorder (PTSD) Reexperiencing a traumatic event through intrusive thoughts, distressing dreams, flashbacks, or extreme reactions in situations similar to the original trauma.

Coping with trauma. A new program called Head Start Trauma Smart helps children deal with traumatic experiences. In this photo the child is learning to identify and discuss how he is feeling. ■

WEB LINK 10.5
Programs for Emotional Development

T/F #10
Adults who were abused as children are very likely to become abusive parents themselves. *False*

If children need help calming down, they can use "breathing stars" made from file folders to help them concentrate on just breathing to relax, or they can go to "calming corners" where there are sensory items that may help soothe them. Once the child is more relaxed, the adult can help the child find a better solution to the problem. The main point is to help the child take control of his or her own feelings and behavior (Bornstein, 2014; Smith, 2013). As adults learn to see these children as *troubled* rather than *as trouble*, they become more capable of making a warm connection with them, which is essential to helping the children manage their feelings and form relationships. Of course all children, not just those subjected to trauma, benefit from an educational environment in which adults are sensitive to their emotional needs and one which helps them build coping skills that they can draw on throughout their lives.

What can we take from this research on child outcomes? First, children have a great deal of resilience, and with appropriate help they can recover from early traumatic experiences. Second, children growing up in difficult circumstances often face multiple threats to their healthy development. The fact that inadequate parenting, domestic violence, poverty, and abuse occur together is not surprising, but their combination multiplies the stress a child must cope with, so many children are not dealing with a singular problem. Children who face fewer developmental challenges are more likely to overcome them and have a more positive prognosis for their future.

One good illustration of this ability to recover from early trauma comes from research with survivors of child abuse. You may have heard that abused children grow up to become abusive parents. The situation is not as simple as that. When we look at the histories of parents who have abused their children, it is true that many were victims of abuse themselves, but most estimates are that about 30% of children with a history of abuse perpetuate the cycle with their own children. This means 70% (or over two thirds) manage to break the cycle and do not repeat the pattern with their own children (Kim, 2009). It is encouraging to know that many adults who have experienced the pain of abuse can overcome these experiences to become positive, effective parents themselves. In Chapter 1, you learned about the concept of multifinality, or the idea that a range of outcomes can result from the same starting point. When thinking about the effect of trauma, it is important to remember that a child's resiliency, together with appropriate intervention and support, and improved life circumstances can all work together to bring about positive developmental outcomes for many traumatized children. We all have a role to play in preventing traumatic experiences for as many children as possible, and then aiding in their recovery when that becomes necessary.

Check Your Understanding

1. What are the developmental consequences of poverty and near-poverty during early childhood?
2. Why does homelessness affect young children's academic achievement?
3. What are some of the effects on young children of witnessing or experiencing a traumatic event?
4. How are children able to overcome the negative effect of early traumatic experiences?

Conclusion

As young children move into a world of peers and play, they gain a clearer idea of their own thoughts and feelings and understand that others have thoughts and feelings that may be quite different from their own. Family remains central for these young children as they learn right from wrong and how to interact with the wider social world. Although we often think of early childhood as a carefree time, many young children undergo traumatic experiences. Intervention at this early age supports positive social and emotional growth so children can move forward into their school years with confidence. Young children often show considerable resiliency in the face of adversity, and can go on to recover from early traumatic experiences.

Chapter Summary

10.1 How do emotions change during early childhood?

Emotions that rely on self-awareness, including pride, shame, and guilt, do not develop until the preschool years or beyond. Preschool children begin to represent their emotions through language and images.

10.2 How does the sense of self develop in early childhood?

Erikson's psychosocial stages of development are based on the development of identity. Toddlers deal with the developmental conflict of *autonomy versus shame and doubt*, and preschoolers with *initiative versus guilt*. Preschoolers think about themselves in very concrete ways. They develop an **autobiographical** memory as adults talk with them about their experiences. They have very high self-esteem because they do not yet compare themselves to others. Some young children exhibit self-regulation through **effortful control**, which predicts positive outcomes later in life.

10.3 How do different theories describe the development of gender identity?

Behavioral theories emphasize reinforcement and imitation of gender-appropriate behaviors. Kohlberg's cognitive developmental theory ties gender identity development to Piaget's stages of cognitive development. Gender schema theory emphasizes the development of ideas associated with each gender based on societal expectations and experiences.

10.4 What roles do environmental influences, cognitive development, and emotional development play in the development of morality?

Children learn right and wrong through reinforcements they receive from the environment and learn socially accepted behavior through imitation. Empathy and guilt influence them to behave in moral ways. Piaget describes the development of moral judgment in early childhood from the first stage called **premoral** to a higher stage called **heteronomous morality**, marked by belief in **immanent justice**. By age 7 or 8, children move to the stage of **autonomous morality**, in which they are aware of the rules and realize they must adhere to them to maintain their interaction with others.

10.5 How are children socialized by their family so they behave in an appropriate way for their culture?

Parents use a variety of types of discipline to socialize their children: **inductive discipline, command strategies, relationship maintenance techniques, power assertion**, and **love withdrawal**. In Western cultures, inductive discipline is associated with greater empathy, but the effectiveness of any strategy depends on the values of the culture. Power assertion has been associated with bullying, fighting, and delinquency. Based on the amount of parental **acceptance/responsiveness** and **demandingness/control**, we can describe four styles of parenting: **authoritative, authoritarian, permissive**, and **disengaged**. Authoritative parenting is associated with a number of positive child characteristics in most Western cultures but what constitutes effective parenting can differ from one culture to another. Intervention to promote better family life may include family therapy. Effective programs empower parents to advocate for their children and build a working relationship with professionals.

10.6 What are play and peer relationships like during early childhood?

Play is related to emotional and social development. Parten described levels of play based on children's developing ability to coordinate activity with a peer: **unoccupied behavior, onlooker behavior, solitary independent play, parallel play, associative play**, and **cooperative play**. By age 3 children can form **friendships** based on shared enjoyment of the same activities.

10.7 What risks and resources are relevant to emotional development in early childhood?

The longer a child lives in poverty, the worse the outcomes are likely to be. Homelessness has many of the same negative effects as living in poverty. Children also can experience many negative effects from experiencing traumatic events, including posttraumatic stress disorder. However, children have the ability to recover from early traumatic events.

Key Terms

Acceptance/responsiveness   339

Antisocial behavior   335

Associative play   346

Authoritarian parents   339

Authoritative parents   339

Autobiographical memory   327

Autonomous morality   336

Command strategy   337

Conscience   335

Cooperative play   346

Delay of gratification   329

Demandingness/control   339

Disengaged parents   340

Effortful control   328

Emotional intelligence   327

Externalizing (or other-directed) behaviors   340

Friendship   347

Gender constancy   331

Gender identity   331

Gender stability   331

Guilt   326

Heteronomous morality   335

Immanent justice   336

Inductive discipline   337

Internalization   337

Internalizing (or self-directed) behaviors   340

Love withdrawal   337

Moral judgment   335

Moral knowledge   335

Onlooker behavior   345

Other-oriented induction   337

Parallel play   346

Permissive parents   339

Play disruption   344

Play therapy   345

Posttraumatic stress disorder (PTSD)   351

Power assertion   337

Premoral reasoning   335

Prosocial behavior   335

Relationship maintenance   337

Self-concept   327

Self-conscious emotions   325

Self-esteem   327

Self-oriented induction   337

Shame   326

Solitary independent play   346

Unoccupied behavior   345

Wraparound program   343

$SAGE edge™

Sharpen your skills with SAGE edge at edge.sagepub.com/levinechrono

SAGE edge for Students provides a personalized approach to help you accomplish your coursework goals in an easy-to-use learning environment.

Go to edge.sagepub.com/levinechrono for additional exercises and video resources. Select Chapter 10, Social and Emotional Development in Early Childhood, for chapter-specific activities. All of the Video Links listed in the margins of this chapter are accessible via this site.

©iStockphoto.com/dcdebs

©iStockphoto.com/dcdebs

11 Physical Development in Middle Childhood

T/F Test Your Knowledge

Test your knowledge of child development by deciding whether each of the following statements is *true* or *false*, and then check your answers as you read the chapter.

1. **T☐ F☐** Growth during middle childhood is slow and steady.

2. **T☐ F☐** It is normal for the first changes associated with puberty to occur in girls as young as 5 years of age.

3. **T☐ F☐** Children who are sexually abused are more likely to be victimized by someone they know than by a stranger.

4. **T☐ F☐** The primary cause of attention deficit/hyperactivity disorder is poor parenting.

5. **T☐ F☐** The diets of most American children do a good job of meeting their nutritional needs.

6. **T☐ F☐** The rate of childhood obesity in middle childhood has finally leveled off in the United States.

7. **T☐ F☐** Pulling a loose baby tooth will allow the permanent tooth to emerge more quickly.

8. **T☐ F☐** Parents of children who participate in organized sports worry a great deal about their child being injured while playing.

9. **T☐ F☐** Children who participate in organized sports develop skills they use to keep them physically active throughout their lifetime.

10. **T☐ F☐** When children diagnosed with ADHD play outdoors, their symptoms are reduced.

Correct answers: (1) F, (2) T, (3) T, (4) F, (5) T, (6) T, (7) F, (8) F, (9) F, (10) T

Physical development during middle childhood is substantially different from what it was at younger ages. Growth is not as rapid as it was in infancy and early childhood, nor as dramatic as it will be in adolescence, but many important changes do occur. Think for a moment about the difference between what a 7-year-old child can do on the playground and what an 11-year-old can do. Compare what you looked like in first grade to what you looked like in sixth. That is some indication of the amount of physical change we describe in this chapter.

In many ways, middle childhood is a time for consolidation of the changes that occurred earlier that prepare the body for the changes to come in adolescence. Brain development in the cerebral cortex continues and, just as important, so does synaptic pruning. As children in middle childhood continue to develop their gross motor skills, organized activities play a larger role in many of their lives. As their fine motor skills develop, their handwriting improves and their drawing becomes more detailed and complex. Good health practices like eating well and getting enough sleep and exercise all help keep the child on track for developing a healthy body and lifestyle. In this chapter, we also talk about new research that highlights how children's experiences in the natural world contribute to their physical development in positive ways.

Learning Questions

11.1 How is physical growth different in middle childhood than in early childhood?

11.2 How does the brain change in middle childhood?

11.3 Describe healthy practices for children in middle childhood and ways they deal with chronic illnesses, such as asthma and diabetes.

11.4 What kinds of physical activities are best for children in middle childhood and what are the risks of participating in them?

11.5 Why is contact with the natural world important for children?

Body Growth and Changes

Physical growth continues in middle childhood but at a slower pace than in early childhood. Children add on average a little over 2 inches in height each year and gain about 6.5 pounds (American Academy of Pediatrics, 2004). Although growth charts usually show a smooth and continuous function, growth typically occurs in spurts of about 24 hours, followed by days or weeks of no growth (Adolph & Berger, 2006). The pattern only *appears* smooth because we average the data from a number of children to create the growth curve so the individual daily growth spurts cancel each other out. Many children also will experience growth spurts during one season of the year in which they grow as much as 3 times as fast as during their slow season of growth (American Academy of Pediatrics, 2004). The rate of growth picks up again as children near the end of middle childhood and get ready for the transition into adolescence with the changes that prepare the body for sexual reproduction known as **puberty** (American Academy of Pediatrics, 2004).

For girls, the peak period of growth is about 1 year after puberty begins, and for boys, who begin puberty about 2 years later than girls, it is about 2 years after puberty begins (American Academy of Pediatrics, 2004). Boys generally are taller than girls during middle childhood, but as children approach puberty, girls will start to become taller than boys as they hit their growth peak and begin transitioning into adolescence. Other factors that affect the amount and rate of physical growth include nutrition, level of physical activity, and overall health and well-being.

As we described in Chapter 8, physicians use growth chart percentiles and trajectories of growth to determine if a child's rate of growth is in the normal range. These growth charts track where an individual child falls relative to others of the same age

11.1

How is physical growth different in middle childhood than in early childhood?

T/F #1
Growth during middle childhood is slow and steady. *False*

Puberty The physical changes that make adolescents capable of sexual reproduction.

VIDEO LINK 11.1
Physical Development

Physical change in middle childhood. Even though physical growth during middle childhood is slower than it was in early childhood—or than it will be in adolescence—quite a bit of change still occurs. See how much physical change occurs by comparing the girl who is at the beginning of middle childhood with the one who is approaching early adolescence. ∎

regarding their height or weight. For children whose growth rate is significantly less than the average, hormonal treatments can increase the rate of growth (Lee & Menon, 2006), but these treatments are usually reserved for treating specific conditions such as Prader-Willi syndrome, juvenile arthritis, or Turner's syndrome. While they are usually considered both safe and effective, growth hormone treatments cost about $30,000 a year. Because clinical studies of children of short stature have *not* found they are at any greater risk of psychosocial disorders than children of normal stature (Lee & Menon, 2006), parents need to carefully consider whether the treatments are necessary and advisable. There is some concern in the medical community that use of hormone therapy for children without a specific medical condition creates a slippery slope because it is difficult to define how short is *too* short. Doctors will not provide treatment for children of normal stature who want—or have parents who want the child—to be taller. To be effective, treatment must be given before the growth plates at the end of the long bones of the body harden and stop growing.

Between 25% and 40% of children between the ages 3 and 5 experience *growing pains*, which are sharp, throbbing pains in their legs, usually coming in the late afternoon or evening (American Academy of Pediatrics, 2007). These pains can recur between ages 8 and 12. Although their cause is not clear, it appears that "growing pains" may be a misnomer because the pain is not actually caused by growth. It is more likely the result of fatigue from excessive physical activity (de Permentier, 2012). A gentle massage, warm bath, or gentle stretching is usually all that is needed to provide relief.

Changing Bodily Proportions

You'll remember that growth proceeds in a cephalocaudal direction, from the head downward through the body. By the time children move into middle childhood, their legs are growing more rapidly than their trunk or upper body, so their bodies continue to move closer to the proportions of an adult as the relative sizes of the head, trunk, and lower extremities finally come into balance (Cain, 2005). Although the amount of body fat they have stays relatively stable, the change in body proportions makes them look slimmer (American Academy of Pediatrics, 2004). Girls tend to have less muscle mass than boys of the same age. **Active Learning: Your Growth in Childhood** guides you through a review of your own growth patterns.

Apple Tree House/Iconica/Getty Images

How tall am I? School age children enjoy keeping track of their growth, which can be rapid at times. ∎

Active Learning

Your Growth in Childhood

Families often keep track of their children's growth. See whether your family kept a baby book detailing your growth in your early years. If your parents later marked your growth on a wall, look at the rate of change over time. Were there some periods of more rapid growth in your childhood? If possible, compare these changes to those of your siblings or of your friends or classmates. At what points were girls taller than boys? If your family has saved your yearly school pictures, compare what you looked like in second grade to what you looked like in sixth or seventh grade. What physical changes do you see in your pictures over this developmental period?

Fine and Gross Motor Skills

Both fine and gross motor skills show considerable development over the school years. Table 11.1 summarizes some of the changes typical between the ages of 5 and 10 years. Although most children develop these skills on a similar timetable, we always need to remember there will be individual differences based on genetics, the range of experiences the child has had, and environmental supports for these various activities.

The development of fine motor skills is reflected in improvements in handwriting, both printing and cursive, and in the detail and complexity children now incorporate into their drawings. Many children also now enjoy activities that rely on fine motor skills and good eye-hand coordination, such as beading, sewing, building models, and playing complex video games.

As children have become increasingly skilled at keyboarding, there has been a debate within the educational community about whether children still need to learn cursive writing. Some advocates make the philosophical arguments that cursive is a skill all educated people should possess and that handwritten letters are more gracious and personal, but there also is brain research to support the idea that

Developing motor skills. By fifth or sixth grade, most children have motor skills nearly as refined as an adult's, as this young rhythmic gymnast demonstrates. At this age they also are quite flexible compared to children of other ages. ■

TABLE 11.1	Fine and gross motor skills	

Age	Fine motor/visual perception	Gross motor skills
5–6 years	• Picks up and replaces minute objects • Has good control when writing and drawing with pencils and paint brushes • Prefers to use dominant hand • Copies a square and triangle • Copies 'V,' 'T,' 'H,' 'O,' 'X,' 'L,' 'A,' 'C,' 'U,' 'Y' • Writes a few letters spontaneously • Draws a person with 6 or more body parts and facial features • Cuts out a simple picture • Draws a house with door, windows, roof, and chimney • Starts to color neatly within outlines • Counts fingers on one hand with index finger of the other hand • Prints first name	• Walks easily on a narrow line • Skips on alternate feet • Stands on one foot (right or left) for 8 to 10 seconds • Hops 2 to 3 meters forward on each foot • Catches a beanbag without trapping against the body • Throws a beanbag onto a target 5 out of 10 times • Rides a two-wheeled bike without stabilizers
6–7 years	• Prints all numbers 1 to 9 without a model to copy (some may be reversed) • Prints first and last name • Discriminates left from right • Has good control over pencil, with change in direction • Threads small beads onto a cord confidently • Uses scissors to cut more complex shapes	• Catches a tennis ball two-handed, away from the body • Aims and throws accurately • Stands on either leg for 15–20 seconds • Walks along a narrow line on tiptoes • Jumps repeatedly with feet together
7–10 years	• Prints all numbers and letters (without reversing any) • Becomes competent in cursive handwriting • Manipulates and places pegs competently in a peg board with either hand • Manipulates scissors competently	• Stands and balances on either leg for 30 seconds and beyond • Walks along a narrow line heel to toe • Hops repeatedly on either leg with controlled landing

Motor skills continue to develop throughout middle childhood as children gain control, flexibility, balance, and coordination.

SOURCE: Adapted from Lammas & Poland (2014). Reprinted with permission from the authors.

cursive writing affects brain functioning in a way that keyboarding does not. Think about the difference between shaping a complex series of curves, loops, and slants as you form words versus what is involved when you copy the same sentence by striking keys on a keyboard. Writing in cursive activates different circuits in the brain than keyboarding (Klemm, 2013) and the use of the fine motor skills and eye-hand coordination required by cursive writing promotes reading, writing, and cognitive skills (James & Engelhardt, 2012). One advocate for cursive writing, William Klemm (2013), a professor of neuroscience at Texas A&M University, has said it benefits brain development like learning to play a musical instrument does, but while not everyone can afford to take music lessons, everyone can use paper and pencil to write.

When children begin school, their gross motor skills are still relatively undeveloped, but by fifth or sixth grade, most have made great strides and their motor skills are almost as coordinated as those of an adult. They are increasingly able to control and coordinate parts of their body as they run, skip, jump, and throw. Their flexibility, balance, reflexes, and strength all improve. Because the ligaments in their limbs are not yet firmly attached to the bones, children in middle childhood are quite flexible compared to children of other ages (Cain, 2005). For all these reasons, many enjoy participating in physical activities that depend on gross motor skills, including group and individual sports.

Prepubescence

Prepubescence refers to the years immediately before puberty when hormonal changes begin. We include this topic in this chapter because the earliest events in the pubertal sequence occur in middle childhood, sooner than many people realize. The pubertal changes and range of ages at which they typically occur are shown in Figure 11.1. At some point between ages 5 and 9, the adrenal gland increases its production of androgens in both boys and girls. These hormones will later be linked to the growth of facial hair and increased muscle mass in boys and to the growth of pubic and armpit hair in both boys and girls. A few years later, estrogen produced by the girl's ovaries will trigger changes in the growth of her uterus, vagina, and breasts and will cause fat to accumulate in the distribution pattern typical of females. Estrogen is also necessary to support the girl's menstrual cycles, which can begin as early as age 10.

Although the sequence of milestones in sexual development is nearly universal, the timing can vary considerably from one child to another. Many factors, including diet and health, body type, heredity, and racial background, affect the timing of puberty, but the first thing you may notice in Figure 11.1 is that girls begin and end the process at earlier ages than boys. In girls, fat cells release a protein called *leptin* that tells the brain that the fat stores in the body are adequate to sustain puberty. As a result, girls who are heavier than average are likely to go through puberty at a younger age than girls who are average in weight or thinner (Lee et al., 2007).

Heredity also plays a role, because daughters go through puberty at about the same age their mothers did (Ersoy, Balkan, Gunay, & Egemen, 2005). This means that early-maturing girls are likely to have mothers who also matured at an early age. Finally, there are some consistent racial differences. On average African American girls mature earlier than White girls (Herman-Giddens, 2006). For instance, the average age of appearance of breast buds in prepubescent girls is 8.8 years for African American girls, 9.3 years for Hispanic girls, and 9.7 years for White non-Hispanic and Asian girls (Herman-Giddens, 2013).

In a small percentage of girls, the earliest physical changes in the pubertal sequence, such as the beginning of breast buds and appearance of pubic hair, have been reported as early as 6 or 7 years of age (Nield, Cakan, & Kamat, 2007). This occurrence, known as precocious puberty, has received increasing attention (Parent et al., 2003). Rare medical

---

T/F #2
It is normal for the first changes associated with puberty to occur in girls as young as 5 years of age. *True*

Prepubescence The period before puberty when hormonal changes begin.

Precocious puberty A condition in which pubertal changes begin at an extraordinarily early age (as young as 6 or 7 years of age).

conditions, such as hormonal disorders or brain tumors, can be responsible for these early changes, but in some cases the girls are simply the earliest-maturing girls in their peer group (Kaplowitz, 2006).

For boys, the earliest sign of puberty is an enlargement of the testes and a thinning and reddening of the scrotum (American Academy of Pediatrics, 2004), which can occur as early as 9 years of age, although for most boys these events occur closer to an average age of 11. Look again at Figure 11.1 to see the set of pubertal changes that typically begin at about this age for boys.

The approach of puberty provides an opportunity for parents to talk with children about the changes their bodies will go through. Children maturing on about the same timetable as most of their peers have support from their peer group. They see what others are experiencing and how they are coping with their bodily changes. Early maturers, however, are the pioneers in this regard and don't have the same type of peer support. In fact, their peers may be intimidated by them. For this reason, parents need to be particularly careful to provide both information and support for early-maturing children.

AUDIO LINK 11.1
Precocious Puberty

FIGURE 11.1   **The pubertal sequence**

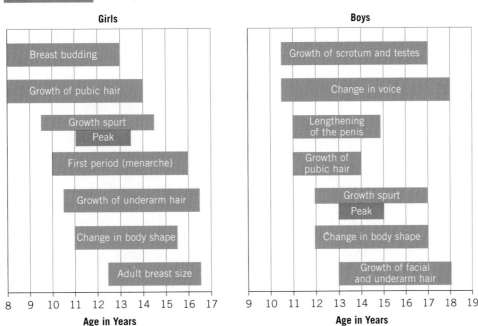

During puberty, sexual development occurs in a set sequence of changes, the timing and speed of which vary from person to person. This chart shows a typical sequence and normal range of development for the milestones of sexual development.

SOURCE: Porter (2013). From the *Merck Manual Home Health Handbook,* edited by Robert Porter. Copyright 2013 by Merck Sharp & Dohme Corp., a subsidiary of Merck & Co, Inc, Whitehouse Station, NJ. Available at http://www.merck-manuals.com/home.

Sexual Abuse and Its Consequences

Child sexual abuse Any interaction between a child and an adult (or another child) in which the child is used for the sexual stimulation of the perpetrator or an observer.

Child sexual abuse has been defined as "any interaction between a child and an adult (or another child) in which the child is used for the sexual stimulation of the perpetrator or an observer" (Child Welfare Information Gateway, 2013). Although children of any age can be victims of sexual abuse, the greatest risk of victimization occurs between the ages of 8 and 12 years. Other factors that place a child at risk of being sexually abused include living in a single-parent household, not living with a biological parent, living in a household marked by discord or violence, and having a physical or cognitive disability (Finkelhor, 2009; March & Schub, 2013; Pinto & Schub, 2013). Although sexual abuse occurs in families from all ethnic and racial backgrounds and at all socioeconomic levels, children who live in poorer families or are members of racial or ethnic minorities are at higher risk (March & Schub, 2013; Pinto & Schub, 2013). It also occurs in countries around the world in many different cultures, with rates that average below 10% for boys and between 10% and 20% for girls. However, rates vary from country to country and research has found rates as high as 50% to 60% in South Africa (Pereda, Guilera, Forns, & Gómez-Benito, 2009).

Although many people think that sexual abuse is perpetrated by strangers, most children who are sexually abused are victimized by someone they know (Cromer & Goldsmith, 2010; Finkelhor et al., 2005). Abusers often use tactics known as *grooming* to lure children into increasingly sexualized contact. They might give the child gifts or do special activities with them. They also may threaten the child to keep him or her from telling others what is happening. This gradual seduction of the child lowers the chance of the child's telling someone about the abuse. Boys who are sexually abused are even less likely than girls to disclose what has happened to them (Ullman & Filipas, 2005). A retrospective study conducted in Australia found that men were significantly less likely to disclose the abuse around the time it occurred (26% of men versus 64% of women did so), and it took significantly longer for them to tell anyone about what happened (O'Leary & Barber, 2008). In fact, some of the study participants took over 20 years to discuss their abuse with someone, even if they were experiencing a great deal of distress.

Sexual abuse has been associated with a number of negative outcomes for the physical health of the survivor, including gastrointestinal and gynecologic symptoms, cardiopulmonary symptoms, and obesity (Irish, Kobayashi, & Delahanty, 2010). It also has been associated with higher rates of depression, anxiety disorders, antisocial behavior, substance abuse, and attempted suicide (Finkelhor & Hashima, 2001; Irish et al., 2010; Putnam, 2003). Children who have been sexually abused at younger ages may show age-inappropriate sexual knowledge or engage in sexualized behaviors (Hornor, 2010; Irish et al., 2010; Putnam, 2003). Because children normally do show certain types of sexually oriented behavior, it is important to know which behaviors are typical and which constitute inappropriate sexuality.

Survivors of more severe sexual abuse are more likely to engage in high-risk sexual behaviors as they get older (Hornor, 2010). In general, the outcomes are poorer for sexual abuse survivors who suffered more severe abuse (for example, the abuse began at a younger age, or it included penetration or attempted penetration) or who found little or no support following disclosure (Hornor, 2010; Lacelle, Hébert, Lavoie, Vitaro, & Tremblay, 2012).

Because so many adults go years without revealing they were abused (Lyon & Ahern, 2011), we had come to believe it would be difficult to get children to speak about it. It turns out, however, that children are neither in denial about the reality of their abuse, nor in need of specific suggestions about what happened in order to talk about what happened to them. Lamb et al. (2003) found that 83% of 4- to 8-year-old children willingly answered open-ended questions about their abuse, and 66% were willing to name the perpetrator when questioned by specially trained police. Disclosure that abuse is occurring is a critical first step in stopping it so that the process of helping the child recover can begin. Adults need to be sensitive to signs of possible abuse, help children disclose if they are being victimized, and support them as they deal with the aftermath. With support from caring adults, many can go on to live healthy and successful lives (Draucker et al., 2011; Hornor, 2010).

T/F #3
Children who are sexually abused are more likely to be victimized by someone they know than by a stranger. *True*

VIDEO LINK 11.2
Sexual Abuse

Check Your Understanding

1. What new capabilities result from children's improved fine and gross motor skills in middle childhood?
2. At what age do girls begin puberty? Boys?
3. What might cause precocious puberty?
4. What are possible negative outcomes of sexual abuse that occur in middle childhood?

Brain Development

The changes that occur in the brain during middle childhood prepare the brain for the more complex learning and thinking that we see in middle childhood and later in adolescence. Brain-based disorders that become evident when children are in the school environment include specific learning disorder and attention deficit/hyperactivity disorder.

Typical Brain Development

During middle childhood, changes occur in both the structure and the functioning of the brain that support the cognitive development we discuss in Chapter 12. Overall, the brain reaches 95% of its peak size by age 6, and peak volume at age 10-1/2 for girls and 14-1/2 for boys (Giedd & Rapoport, 2010). The myelin, or white matter in the brain, continues to increase, and parts of the brain become more interconnected as more fibers are added. These changes are important for the formation of long-term memories and our ability to connect new information to things we have previously learned.

Specific brain structures that experience growth during middle childhood include the frontal lobe, the parietal lobe, and the corpus callosum. The frontal lobe is responsible for executive functioning, including planning, reasoning, and impulse control (Cain, 2005). Younger children begin to develop executive functions, but these abilities improve significantly during middle childhood. Changes in the frontal lobe also improve working memory, or the amount of information we can retain in our conscious mind at one time (Semrud-Clikeman, 2014). The parietal lobe, which processes sensory information and supports language and memory, undergoes major development during middle childhood. This plays a role in the development of language and reading. The third brain structure that undergoes significant change is the corpus callosum, the thick band of fibers that connects the two hemispheres of the brain (Cain, 2005). This change improves communication between the two hemispheres, increases the lateralization of function that began in early childhood, and improves coordination between different parts of the brain.

Changes also occur in the chemistry of the neuronal pathways that support both long-term and short-term memory functioning (Semrud-Clikeman, 2014). These chemical changes continue for hours or even days after we learn something, consolidating the learning and making the information available in our long-term memory (Gazzaniga, Ivry, & Mangun, 2013). The improved connectivity and coordination between different areas of the brain all contribute to the improvement of motor skills, visual-spatial skills, and coordination (American Psychological Association Division of Educational Psychology, 2014c). During middle childhood, activity is focused largely in the posterior regions of the brain, where the areas that process auditory, visual, and tactile information come together and where long-term memories are stored (Semrud-Clikeman, 2014).

Research using electroencephalographs (EEGs) to measure brain activity has identified another important change in brain functioning. Alpha waves are the brain pattern

11.2

How does the brain change in middle childhood?

AUDIO LINK 11.2
Football and Concussions

we associate with alert attention, while theta waves are the pattern associated with sleep. In early childhood, we have more theta waves than alpha waves, but the ratio changes as we enter middle childhood. Between 5 and 7 years of age, the amount of each type of wave is about equal, but by age 7, alpha waves, the ones associated with engaged attention, become predominant (Cain, 2005).

Hormonal changes in middle childhood known as adrenarche also affect brain development. These changes begin when the adrenal gland begins producing the androgen dehydroepiandrosterone (or DHEA). It is hypothesized that DHEA promotes synaptogenesis in the cortex and prolongs the development of the prefrontal cortex (Campbell, 2011). The changes associated with adrenarche have been described as "a signature feature of middle childhood" and as important as the hormonal changes of puberty (Angier, 2011, para. 4).

All these changes come together to advance the way children in middle childhood think and learn, and this, in turn, supports the work they do in the school environment. The process does not play out in exactly the same way for all children, however, and some deviations from these patterns are associated with problems in learning and communication that affect a number of school-aged children.

Brain-Related Disabilities

In Chapter 8, we described some of the differences found in the brains of children who are autistic. Along a similar line of research, psychologists and neurologists have discovered a number of differences in the brains of children diagnosed with a specific learning disorder or attention deficit/hyperactivity disorder (ADHD). Some of these are differences in the actual structure of the brain, and some are variations in the way the brain functions as different parts become activated when the child engages in specific types of activities. We discuss specific learning disorder and ADHD in this chapter because these conditions are most often identified when children enter school and begin to learn how to read and write and are expected to sit still and pay attention to their teacher. Our focus here is on what we know about the physical causes of these conditions and, in the case of ADHD, what we know about medical treatments that can improve the condition. In Chapter 12, you will learn more about how these conditions affect a child's cognitive development.

The *DSM-5* has eliminated the term "learning disability" and grouped together the different subtypes of learning disabilities under one diagnostic term: specific learning disorder. There are different subtypes based on impairment in reading, in written expression, and in mathematics, and these are now described as *specifiers* rather than separate disorders (APA, 2013). A specific learning disorder manifests as difficulties in acquiring academic skills resulting in achievement that is substantially below the expected level for the child's age. It is severe enough that it interferes with academic or daily living activities that require that skill. It is presumed to have a biological origin and cannot be attributed to pervasive intellectual disability or to other developmental, neurological, sensory, or motor disorders (APA, 2013).

We have known for years that specific learning disorders are neurological disorders that affect the brain's ability to process information, but it is only recently that sophisticated imaging tools have allowed us to identify some of the brain differences that cause these problems. We now can use MRIs to record the structure of the brain and functional MRIs to measure brain activity in response to neural activity. We look more closely at the research on dyslexia, the most widely studied specific learning disorder, to illustrate the variety of possible causes currently being investigated.

Dyslexia refers to a "pattern of learning difficulties characterized by problems with accurate or fluent word recognition, poor decoding, and poor spelling abilities" (APA, 2013, p. 67). Brain chemistry may play a role. Recent research conducted at Yale

Adrenarche The increase in adrenal androgen production that occurs early in the pubertal sequence and affects brain development.

Specific learning disorder Difficulty with learning and academic performance based on impairment in reading, written expression, and/or mathematics.

VIDEO LINK 11.3
Dyslexia

Dyslexia An alternative term for a specific learning disorder that is characterized by problems with accurate or fluent word recognition, poor decoding, and poor spelling abilities.

University with children between 6 and 10 found that those whose brains had higher levels of two key chemicals (glutamate and choline) scored lower on tests for reading and language (Pugh et al., 2014). Functional differences may also exist in the brains of children with learning disorders. For instance, we usually use the left hemisphere of the brain when we read, but individuals with dyslexia show more activity in the right hemisphere (Breier, Simos, & Fletcher, 2002). The right hemisphere is ordinarily used to process new or novel information, so this suggests that dyslexics find reading to be more of a novel task than a familiar one (Semrud-Clikeman, 2014). Finally, there is evidence for structural differences. For instance, the connection between Broca's area of the brain, which controls speech production, and Wernicke's area, which controls our understanding of written or spoken language, is smaller in kindergartners who have poorer awareness of the sound of letters (Saygin et al., 2013; see also Boets et al., 2013). Keep in mind that learning disorders are a group of conditions, not a single condition, and we may eventually find different specific causes for each of the specific subtypes.

The possibility that genetics play a role in specific learning disorder comes from studies suggesting they run in families. Children who have dyslexia have parents or other close relatives who are 4 to 8 times more likely to also have them compared to children who do not have the disorder (APA, 2013). Research also has found a moderate genetic influence for mathematical and reading ability, with monozygotic twins being more similar in ability than dizygotic twins (Kovas et al., 2007). Other possible causes include damaging effects in the prenatal environment or injury during the birth process, or a serious illness or injury shortly after birth. It is also possible that extremely poor nutrition or exposure to environmental toxins can play a role (National Institute of Child Health and Human Development, 2012).

Attention deficit/hyperactivity disorder (ADHD) is another neurodevelopmental disorder described in the *DSM-5*. It is "a persistent pattern of inattention and/or hyperactivity-impulsivity that interferes with functioning or development" (APA, 2013, p. 59). There are three patterns of symptoms: predominantly hyperactive-impulsive presentation, predominantly inattentive presentation, and a combined presentation. A child with a hyperactive-impulsive presentation always seems to be in motion, fidgets, has trouble staying on task, and does everything quickly and without much apparent thought. This is more than a child with high energy. The child cannot control the impulsive behavior that interferes with the ability to function effectively on a day-to-day basis. A child with an inattentive presentation is easily distracted, has trouble getting organized, has trouble following directions, continually loses things, and often shifts from one task to another without completing either of them (CDC, 2014b). A child with a combined presentation shows symptoms of both inattention and hyperactivity-impulsivity.

Research on the causes of ADHD also is ongoing. Both twin studies and adoption studies support the likely role of genetics, with some specific genes playing a part in the development of behaviors associated with ADHD. Differences in brain structure and function also have been identified (Frank-Briggs, 2011; Steinhausen, 2009). For example, the brain volume of hyperactive children has been found to be 5% smaller than that of children who are not hyperactive. There are also differences in the neurotransmitters that help with focusing attention and controlling impulses, and there is reduced communication between the posterior part of the brain that retrieves previously learned information and the front part of the brain that uses and applies the information to a current situation (Semrud-Clikeman, 2014). However, numerous environmental factors also have been investigated (ADHD Educational Institute, 2014). These include prenatal factors such as maternal use of alcohol and/or tobacco or other environmental toxins, and adverse family living conditions as the child grows up. Genetic and neurobiological factors can interact with environmental factors in complex ways to produce differences in the specific symptoms of ADHD, their severity, and course of development.

Attention deficit/ hyperactivity disorder (ADHD) A persistent pattern of inattention and/ or hyperactivity-impulsivity that begins in childhood and interferes with functioning or development.

VIDEO LINK 11.4
ADHD

No medical interventions are available to treat learning disabilities, but a variety of medications are used to treat ADHD, most often stimulants such as Ritalin. The clinical guidelines for the diagnosis and treatment of ADHD from the American Academy of Pediatrics (2011a) recommend the use of an approved medication, together with behavioral therapy. The therapy helps parents provide structure in their child's environment and positive reinforcement for good behavior, in addition to helping children gain a more positive self-image. Although the exact way medication helps regulate behavior is not clear, it appears to alter the neural activity in the frontal-striatal area of the brain, which ordinarily inhibits behavior (Barkley, 2006).

Because this therapeutic approach has been effective in increasing attention, improving impulse control, reducing task-irrelevant behavior, and reducing disruptive behavior, it is widely used in school-age populations (Barkley, 2006). Although there is less research on the use of medication to treat ADHD symptoms in teens and adults than in children, the existing studies support the continued effectiveness of these medications beyond childhood (Barkley, 2006; Vaughan, March, & Kratochvil, 2012). Some critics have charged that we rely too heavily on medication and that ADHD is being overdiagnosed, but other professionals attribute the increase in the number of children with this diagnosis to better identification of those who otherwise would have gone unrecognized and, therefore, untreated.

Some families use complementary and alternative therapies such as dietary modification or nutritional supplements as part of their child's treatment. Little or no scientific evidence exists to support the effectiveness of such approaches (Ballard, Hall, & Kaufmann, 2010; Barkley, 2006; Karpouzis & Bonello, 2012). Eliminating sugar has produced no behavioral improvement in ADHD symptoms, and eliminating food additives has had only small effects. Dietary interventions are not even mentioned in the American Academy of Pediatrics (2011a) practice guideline for treating ADHD. We have, however, dispelled the idea that poor parenting causes ADHD (Kutscher, 2008). The challenging behavior exhibited by children with ADHD can no doubt disrupt effective parenting, so parents need to learn how to deal effectively with the child's behavior. However in this case, the parents' behavior is more likely a response to the child's characteristics, not a cause of them.

AUDIO LINK 11.3
Treating ADHD

T/F #4
The primary cause of attention deficit/hyperactivity disorder is poor parenting. *False*

Check Your Understanding

1. What changes take place in the brain during middle childhood?
2. What differences in the brain may account for specific learning disorder in some children?
3. What treatments have been found effective for ADHD? Which have shown few or no results?

11.3

Describe healthy practices for children in middle childhood and ways they deal with chronic illnesses, such as asthma and diabetes.

Health and Well-Being in Middle Childhood

Overall, middle childhood is a relatively healthy time for most children. They can suffer any of the short-term illnesses described in the chapter on early childhood, but they will probably be ill less often than younger children because their immune system has become stronger and they have built up some resistance from previous bouts of illness. Some, of course, will continue to suffer chronic health problems such as asthma, heart conditions, and cancer that originated earlier in development, and some new cases of any of these chronic conditions may appear in middle childhood for the first time. Good health practices, a nutritious diet, and adequate amounts of sleep and physical activity all play an important role in maintaining a child's health. There also is a great deal that we can do to help protect children from injuries during middle childhood.

Healthy Living in Middle Childhood

Health is not just the absence of illness. Well-being depends on the ways in which children maintain their good health. In this section, we discuss the importance of healthy eating, dental and oral health, and sleep to a child's overall health. We also discuss the effects of being obese or overweight and carrying heavy backpacks on children's developing bodies.

Healthy Eating

Healthy eating continues to be important as children enter middle childhood, but as they get older, they have more autonomy over what they eat because more of their food is consumed away from home. The good news is that the diets of most American children do a good job of meeting their nutritional needs (Clark & Fox, 2009), although, of course, there also is room for improvement.

A recent report based on the National Health and Nutrition Examination Survey looked at the diets of American school-aged children and concluded that most children have an adequate amount of protein and carbohydrates in their diets, although there was concern about excessive calories from solid fats and added sugars, excessive amounts of sodium and saturated fat, and inadequate amounts of nutrient-dense, high-fiber foods like whole fruits, dark green and deep yellow vegetables, legumes, and whole grains (Volkarsky, 2010). More than 92% of the children in the survey had adequate amounts of 8 of the 13 essential vitamins and minerals in their daily diets, but 10% had inadequate amounts of vitamins A, C, and E and magnesium and phosphorus. The root of some of these nutritional problems lies with the kind of foods often favored by school-aged children. Hamburgers, cheeseburgers, and pizza contribute substantial amounts of fat and sodium to the diet, and whole milk and ice cream contribute saturated fat. Children need to continue to be educated about healthy food choices, especially as they get older and make more of these choices for themselves.

We often assume that fast foods are a primary culprit contributing to the poor quality of the diet of school children. On a typical day, one third of American children and over 40% of American adolescents consume food or beverages from a fast-food restaurant (Poti, Duffey, & Popkin, 2014). A number of studies have found that the foods consumed away from home at fast-food and full-service restaurants are high in calories, total fat, saturated fat, sugar, and sodium (see, for example, Bowman, Gortmaker, Ebbeling, Pereira, & Ludwig, 2004; Powell & Nguyen, 2013; Sebastian, Wilkinson Enns, & Goldman, 2009). These meals also tend to be low on nutritious foods such as milk, fruits, and vegetables (other than potatoes). For these reasons, it has been easy to conclude that eating fast food is a major contributor to the high rates of obesity in the United States, but that connection may not be as strong as many people assume. Recent research has found that it is the quality of the *remainder* of the child's diet that is more strongly associated with weight status and dietary outcomes (Poti et al., 2014). This reminds us that fast food is only one part of the picture. That does not mean we should ignore it. Reducing the amount of fast food consumed is a good step in the direction of improving the overall quality of children's diets, but we have much more work to do. The same study found that 2- to 5-year-olds were less likely to be consumers of fast food than were 6- to 11-year-olds who, in turn, had lower rates than the adolescents in the study. The picture

© David Page/Alamy

A high-calorie diet. Fast foods may be convenient and popular, but they usually are low in nutritional value. What would make a better lunch for this young boy? ■

is one of deteriorating nutritional quality as children get older. Educating children during middle childhood about wise food choices can help ensure that the quality of their diet improves rather than deteriorates as they move through the elementary school years.

Many American school children eat one or more meals a day at school. The Food and Nutrition Service of the U.S. Department of Agriculture operates the program responsible for providing food to schools, including the School Breakfast Program and the National School Lunch Program, as well as snacks for children in after-school educational and enrichment programs. In 2012 and 2013, about 13.2 million children participated in the School Breakfast Program on a typical day, and 85% received a free or reduced-price breakfast (Food Research and Action Center, 2010). You probably have heard someone say that breakfast is the most important meal of the day. There is a good deal of research support for the importance of a good breakfast—one based on high-fiber, nutrient-rich whole grains, fruits, and dairy products. If you think skipping a meal isn't a bad idea if we are concerned about children's weight, you would be wrong. Children who eat breakfast generally do consume more calories in a day than children who don't, but a review of 47 studies found that they also were *less* likely to be overweight (Rampersaud, Pereira, Girard, Adams, & Metzl, 2005). The foods that children eat at breakfast tend to be more nutrient-dense than the foods they eat at either lunch or dinner (Volkarsky, 2010), so these calories make a positive contribution to the overall quality of a child's diet.

Whether a child eats breakfast also is related to cognitive performance in the classroom because eating breakfast improves attention and memory (Hoyland, Dye, & Lawton, 2009; Rampersaud et al., 2005), with the effect being greater for children who otherwise have poorer diets (Hoyland et al., 2009; Kristjansson et al., 2007). However the reason why school breakfast programs are associated with better academic performance is not what you might expect. Children who eat their breakfast at school have better attendance than those who don't, so when we try to interpret the impact of a school breakfast program on students' cognitive performance, at least part of that effect may be attributable to their better school attendance rather than to the nutritional value of the meal itself (Hoyland et al., 2009; Kristjansson et al., 2007).

On a typical day, 30.7 million U.S. children participate in the school lunch program, with about 70% receiving free or reduced-price lunches. Children who participate are more likely than those who don't to consume low-fat milk, fruits, and vegetables and less likely to consume less healthy items like dessert and snacks (Condon, Crepinsek, & Fox, 2009). As part of a continuing effort to improve the nutritional quality of the foods served at schools, the 2010 Healthy Hunger-Free Kids Act implemented comprehensive reforms that included offering some cook-from-scratch options, using students as taste testers before adding new items to the menu, and promoting fruit and vegetable consumption by featuring a "fruit or vegetable of the month" program. When the reforms were first announced, critics doubted children would embrace the healthier menu, but a study of 10 school districts in California found that nearly 90% of the students said that they liked the taste of the food at least sometimes (The California Endowment, 2013). Beginning with the start of the 2014 school year, the Smart Snacks in School program extended these nutritional standards to foods sold on school campuses in vending machines, at school stores, and in à la carte food lines as part of the continuing effort to improve the quality of food eaten in the school environment.

VIDEO LINK 11.5
Lunchroom Undercover

Tim Boyle/Getty Images

A better diet. If they are exposed to healthy choices at a young age, children can develop good eating habits for a lifetime. ∎

While these changes have been well accepted by many students and applauded by parents, the study notes some real challenges that remain. For one thing, many elementary schools give children only 20 minutes for lunch, hardly enough time to wait in line to get their food and enjoy a nutritious meal, and many school kitchens do not have the space or equipment to prepare many of its foods from scratch. Try **Active Learning: School Lunches** to find out about the choices that children make from the foods currently offered by their schools.

Active Learning

School Lunches

Talk to a couple of elementary school-aged children who regularly get their lunch from their school cafeteria. It doesn't matter whether they purchase their lunch or get it through the school lunch program. Ask them what they like and don't like about the lunches, whether they usually get low-fat milk or 100% fruit juice with their meals, and whether they usually eat any fruit or vegetables. Some schools even offer salad bars, although these are more common in high schools than in middle schools or elementary schools. Ask the children you talk to what they would do to improve the foods they are served. You can decide whether their suggestions would make the meals more nutritious or not. For instance, they might say they would prefer white bread to the whole wheat bread their cafeteria uses, but this would not be a more nutritious change. ■

▶

ACTIVE LEARNING
VIDEO 11.1
School Lunches

Obesity and Overweight

Being overweight or obese has serious negative consequences for children, so both conditions are concerns. We know overweight children are likely to become overweight adolescents who in turn become overweight adults (Malina, Bouchard, & Oded, 2004), and we know children who are overweight or obese have an increased risk of developing a number of life-threatening health conditions throughout their lives (Long, Mareno, Shabo, & Wilson, 2012).

Being overweight has been linked to the dramatic increase in type 2 diabetes among children in recent years. Children who are overweight also have an increased risk of having asthma compared to children of normal weight, and that risk is even greater for children who are moderately or extremely obese (Black, Smith, Porter, Jacobsen, & Koebnick, 2012; see also Brüske, Flexeder, & Heinrich, 2014). Children who are more overweight also make more visits to the doctor and to emergency rooms and use more medication. Although the full clinical effects of childhood obesity may not become apparent for years, in the long term they include elevated blood pressure, increased levels of cholesterol, and even some cancers (Malina et al., 2004). The cost of these problems to society—in addition to the tremendous personal cost to the individual—is staggering (Koplan, Liverman, & Kraak, 2005). However, the social and emotional consequences of obesity also are very real.

One study by Long, Mareno, Shabo, and Wilson (2012) used data from the National Health and Nutrition Examination Survey (NHANES) to look at rates of being overweight or obese in children ages 6 to 11 over a decade to get a picture of how these numbers change with the age of the child and how they have changed in recent years. Figure 11.2 shows the results from this research. You can see that the youngest children (6–7 years of age) had the lowest rates of overweight and obesity, but the risk increased for each subsequent age group. In the older age groups (8–11 years of age), the rates were highest among Mexican American males and non-Hispanic Black females (not shown in the figure).

FIGURE 11.2   Obesity and overweight in children 6 to 11 years of age

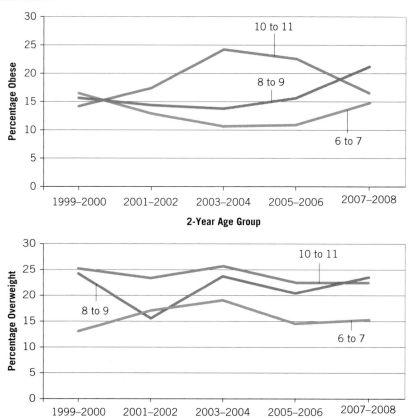

This figure shows the percentage of children who were obese (OB) or overweight (OW) according to the National Health and Nutrition Examination Survey over the 10-year period from 1999 to 2008. Note how the risk of being classified as either overweight or obese increases with the age of the child.

SOURCE: Long, Mareno, Shabo, & Wilson (2012). Reprinted with permission.

After years of national attention to the problem of childhood obesity, we may finally be turning a corner and making some progress. As you learned in Chapter 8, recent statistics have found a decrease in the rate of obesity among 2- to 5-year-old children (Ogden, Carroll, Kit, & Flegal, 2014). Although there was no comparable decrease in other age groups in this study, we can hope that as these young children move from early childhood into middle childhood, they will sustain this progress. Another part of the good news is that the percentage of children in middle childhood who were obese has not increased in the last few years (Ogden et al., 2014).

Controlling childhood obesity will require a multifaceted approach that includes a healthy diet, exercise, counseling, and commitment by the family (U.S. Preventive Services Task Force, 2010). One thing families can do to help control their children's weight is to limit the amount of television they watch. A good deal of research has linked television viewing with obesity (for example, Crespo et al., 2001). It has both a direct and an indirect effect on body weight (Boulos, Vikre, Oppenheimer, Chang, & Kanarek, 2012). Viewing affects weight directly because the more time we spend watching television, the less time we have for physical activities, the more advertisements promoting high-calorie but low-nutrition foods we see (Ferguson, Muñoz, & Medrano, 2012), and the more mindless eating we do (Boulos et al., 2012). However, television also promotes obesity in indirect ways. Beyond the advertisements during television programs

T/F #6

The rate of childhood obesity in middle childhood has finally leveled off in the United States. *True*

WEB LINK 11.2
Childhood Obesity

themselves, product placement of food within shows produces less obvious promotion of particular brands of food, and through television programming, we have come to see losing great amounts of weight as entertainment and a competition rather than as a lifelong challenge (Boulos et al., 2012). Because watching more television appears to cause greater problems with weight as children grow and develop, limiting their viewing while they are still in their formative years should be helpful and healthful under any circumstances.

Teeth and Oral Health

Of course healthy teeth are essential for healthy eating. Children normally have 20 baby teeth that they begin losing at around 6 years of age (Sterling & Best-Boss, 2013). The first to be lost are in the middle of mouth. Even though a wiggly tooth can be a bit uncomfortable and may make it difficult to eat, parents and children should let the teeth come out on their own without pulling and twisting them. The root of the tooth will dissolve naturally when the tooth is ready, and the permanent tooth is usually right under the gum and will begin pushing its way out or erupting (Schulman, 2001). Pulling the baby tooth prematurely will not speed up this process. Instead the gum can bleed, it will probably be painful, and the child will run the risk of developing an infection at the site.

T/F #7
Pulling a loose baby tooth will allow the permanent tooth to emerge more quickly.
False

As permanent teeth appear, the child's smile will have a mixture of small baby teeth and larger permanent teeth, but by 12 or 13 years of age, all the baby teeth should be replaced by adult teeth that will match in size. Teeth further back in the mouth will continue to erupt until almost the end of adolescence.

Regular visits to the dentist and daily oral care, including brushing and flossing, help ensure the child's teeth will remain strong and healthy. A dentist might recommend that a sealant be applied to the chewing surfaces of the back teeth to help prevent caries (or cavities). Without proper care, a child can develop cavities or an infection of the gums. When children suffer pain from oral health problems, it affects their appetite and consequently their nutrition and can interfere with their ability to concentrate at school or ability to get a good night's sleep (Holt & Barzel, 2013). Because low-income children are more likely to suffer from oral health problems, and because dental care can be expensive and often is not covered by insurance, school-based programs can be an effective way to get preventive services to these children.

Sleep

Getting an adequate amount of sleep supports a child's physical and psychological well-being, but evidence suggests children are getting less sleep than they did in the past (Astill, Van der Heijden, Van IJzendoorn, & Van Someren, 2012) and may not be getting an optimal amount. Children in middle childhood require 9 to 10 hours of sleep a night, but in one recent study of over 4,000 Australian children and adolescents, 17% of participants did not meet the recommendation of the U.S. Centers for Disease Control and Prevention for the amount of sleep a child needs (Olds, Maher, Blunden, & Matricciani, 2010). The percentage of children falling short of this goal increased with age. Most other studies of sleep duration have likewise found that as children get older, they get less sleep (Biggs, Lushington, Martin, van den Heuvel, & Kennedy, 2013; Olds et al., 2010), primarily because their bedtime gets later (Biggs et al., 2013).

JOURNAL ARTICLE 11.1
Sleep

Other differences consistently found in research are that girls sleep more than boys (Astill et al., 2012; Biggs et al., 2013; Olds et al., 2010), and children from lower SES families and non-Caucasian families report sleeping less (Biggs et al., 2013). In one study, non-Caucasian children from lower SES families had the shortest sleep duration of any group in the sample (Biggs et al., 2013). In international studies of sleep patterns, children from Asian countries sleep the least, perhaps because they report spending more time on homework than children from other countries (Biggs et al., 2013).

Fortunately most children do not have sleep problems (Simola, Liukkonen, Pitkäranta, Pirinen, & Aronen, 2012). However, the school-aged child may have some trouble winding down at the end of day. Having a television in the bedroom and watching more than 2 hours of television a day is one of the circumstances that has been associated with getting less sleep (Garmy, Nyberg, & Jakobsson, 2012), but fortunately this is something a family can control. Families also can continue to maintain regular bedtime routines, as they did when the child was younger, to help them settle down for the evening. Some parents may not appreciate the value of a fixed bedtime and a regular sleep schedule, so they may need to be educated about the importance of sleep to a child's health and well-being (Biggs et al., 2013; Olds et al., 2010).

In addition to sleep duration (that is, the number of hours of sleep you get a night), sleep quality matters. Do you fall asleep quickly, stay asleep through the night, and feel rested when you wake up? Younger children do well on these measures (Astill et al., 2012), but as they get older, sleep problems occur with more frequency. In a study conducted in Sweden, the youngest children in the sample (6 or 7 years old) did not have trouble falling asleep or waking up and did not report feeling tired at school, but the percentage of participants reporting each of these problems increased with age (Garmy et al., 2012). Another age-related difference was that younger children slept about the same amount of time every day, both on school days and on weekends. As children get older, however, there is more "catch-up sleeping" on weekends as they try to make up for sleep lost during the week (Garmy et al., 2012; Olds et al., 2010).

Both lack of sleep and poor sleep quality have been associated with a number of negative consequences for children, including somatic complaints, poorer school performance, mood disorders, motor skills problems (Olds et al., 2010), and behavior problems (Astill et al., 2012). In one study, a persistent pattern of sleep problems over a 4-year period from preschool to school age was associated with a 16-fold increase in the risk of psychosocial symptoms, especially aggression, problems with social interactions, and anxious/depressed mood (Simola et al., 2012).

In adults, sleep problems are related to problems with attention and memory, but, surprisingly, when researchers did a meta-analysis of many studies on sleep in children, they did not find that less sleep was related to problems with attention and memory (Astill et al., 2012). However, insufficient sleep has been connected with being overweight (Olds et al., 2010). When you are sleep deprived, your body produces *more* of the hormone that tells you when it is time to eat and *less* of the hormone that tells you when to stop eating. Sleep deprivation also slows your metabolism.

Most children are able to stay dry through the night by the time they are 5 years old, but 15% to 20% of 5-year-olds experience nocturnal enuresis, an involuntary emptying of the bladder during sleep beyond the age at which children usually gain bladder control (Caldwell, Nankivell, & Sureshkumar, 2013). Although the percentage of children who wet their beds at night declines with age, 1.5% of children at 9-1/2 years of age still have accidents two or more times a week (Jacques, 2013; Prynn, 2012). There are a number of causes. Some children sleep so deeply that they do not respond to the urge to get up and urinate when their bladders are full, and others produce an unusually large amount of urine or have relatively small bladders. Bedwetting can affect a child's emotional well-being because it keeps them from taking part in activities that other children enjoy, like sleepovers, and sets the child apart as different. If parents are harsh and judgmental toward a child with this problem, it compounds the emotional burden. A child who wets the bed at night should never be humiliated or punished for this behavior, which he or she cannot control.

Research evidence on the effectiveness of treatment of nocturnal enuresis is quite limited, but pediatricians recommend a number of remedies (Franco, von Gontard, & De Gennaro, 2013). Simple strategies include ones like setting up a simple reward system (for example, a star on a chart for each night the child remains dry), waking the child

Nocturnal enuresis An involuntary emptying of the bladder during sleep beyond the age at which children usually gain bladder control.

during the night to void, or restricting liquid consumption in the evening. If these strategies don't work, there are underpants wired to sound an alarm or vibrate when the child begins to pass urine and medications that decrease urine production at night or reduce bladder contractions and increase bladder capacity (Prynn, 2012). Almost all children gain bladder control at night as they get older, but the help we can give them lets them reach that goal more easily and sooner.

Backpacks

By one estimate, over 40 million American children routinely carry backpacks to school (Moore, White, & Moore, 2007), and many of those backpacks are heavier than the weight recommended by professional organizations such as the American Physical Therapy Association, the American Chiropractic Association, and the American Academy of Pediatrics (Bryant & Bryant, 2014; Moore et al., 2007). The recommended maximum weight is 10% to 15% of the child's body weight (KidsHealth, 2013). Girls and younger children are at greater risk of pain or injury because the backpacks they carry are more likely to exceed the recommended weight for their smaller size (KidsHealth, 2013; Moore et al., 2007). Girls, on average, carry backpacks heavier than those carried by boys of the same age (Moore et al., 2007).

In 2011, the U.S. Consumer Product Safety Commission estimated that 9,701 serious injuries resulted from carrying backpacks and book bags (Bryant & Bryant, 2014), and many more children report back or shoulder pain severe enough to interfere with their participation in school or leisure activities. The problem is made worse when children carry their backpacks on one shoulder or wear them too high on their back. A backpack worn correctly evenly distributes its weight across the body.

At risk of injury? Many young children carry more weight in their school backpacks than is ideal for their size. How can parents address this problem to reduce the risk of injury? ■

Parents can reduce the likelihood of injuries by purchasing backpacks that are lighter, have wide padded shoulder straps, a padded back, and a waist belt to evenly distribute the weight across the body, and by making sure their child knows the correct way to pick it up, put it on, and wear it (KidsHealth, 2013). Parents also can remind their children that they shouldn't be carrying a lot of unnecessary things in their backpacks. Schools play a role too by educating children about backpack safety. Having periodic backpack weigh-ins makes students aware of how much they are carrying. Some schools have begun replacing print textbooks with digital ones, and the California Department of Education has set weight limitations on the textbooks that can be adopted for use in its schools (California Department of Education, 2013). These precautions should limit children's experience of back, neck, or shoulder pain from the backpacks they carry each day.

Chronic Illnesses

Healthy lifestyle choices are particularly important for children who suffer from chronic illnesses. One of the important developmental changes that occurs in middle childhood for children with a chronic illness is that they typically assume more responsibility for self-care and the management of their disease (Brown, Gallagher, Fowler, & Wales, 2010). Once they enter school and begin spending a good portion of their day away from the immediate oversight of parents, children need to learn how to recognize the signs that their condition may need attention and know the appropriate action to take.

For instance, they need to recognize that an asthma attack is about to begin or that their blood sugar is falling dangerously low. At this point, parents become coordinators for the people who have contact with their child throughout the day (Brown et al., 2010). In a school setting, this includes classroom teachers, school nurses, and school administrators. This shift can be challenging for parents who have been vigilant for years in managing a potentially life-threatening condition for their child. Next we look specifically at two chronic illnesses that affect a great number of school-aged children: Asthma and diabetes.

Asthma

As we noted in Chapter 8, asthma is a common chronic illness among children. Although the majority of the cases are diagnosed before the age of 5, children between 5 and 17 have the highest prevalence rates as new cases continue to be diagnosed throughout the elementary school years (American Lung Association, 2012). Because some individuals eventually outgrow their symptoms, the prevalence rate then declines in older age groups.

According to the CDC (2010b), in an average classroom of 30 children, 3 are likely to have asthma. By one recent estimate, 14.4 million school days a year are missed because of it (Meng, Babey, & Wolstein, 2012). School absence obviously has a negative impact on the academic performance of the child who is missing class time, but it also has an indirect effect on other children in the school if state funding is based on average daily attendance. More student absences translate into less money for the school. Because children from low-income families are more likely to have asthma and to miss more school, schools in low-income neighborhoods are disproportionately penalized financially by these absences. Children who attend schools in low-income neighborhoods are at another disadvantage because older buildings that are poorly maintained or that are located in congested urban neighborhoods harbor more irritants that can trigger an asthma attack (Meng et al., 2012).

The Centers for Disease Control and Prevention has several initiatives designed to make schools healthier environments for children with asthma. An effective school-based program of asthma management requires a partnership between the school, the family, and health-care providers (Wheeler, Buckley, Gerald, Merkle, & Morrison, 2009). It identifies students who have been diagnosed, keeps a written action plan from the child's physician on file at the school so staff can deal with asthma episodes, makes trained staff available to administer medication or implement emergency protocols, and communicates with the family and physician when a child's symptoms are not being well controlled (Wheeler et al., 2009). Schools also can play a role in identifying children who may have asthma but who have not yet been diagnosed and are not receiving appropriate treatment for the condition.

Diabetes

Diabetes A metabolic disorder in which the body does not produce insulin, or cannot use the insulin produced by the body.

Diabetes is a group of diseases in which the body cannot make efficient use of sugars and carbohydrates in the diet because it either doesn't produce insulin or can't use the insulin that it does produce. The result is high blood glucose levels. When blood glucose is too high, it can result in serious damage over time to the heart and blood vessels, kidneys, nerves, and the retina. However, if the treatment for diabetes causes blood sugar to drop too low, an immediate and potentially life-threatening condition called *hypoglycemia* can occur. Hypoglycemia causes irritability, shakiness or confusion, rapid heartbeat, and in extreme cases loss of consciousness or coma (National Diabetes Education Program [NDEP], 2006). Fortunately, with good management and control, the person with diabetes can lead a full, normal life.

There are two types of diabetes. Type 1 diabetes is an autoimmune disease in which the body's immune system destroys the cells in the pancreas that produce insulin (NDEP, 2006), possibly as a result of a virus (Suomen Akatemia, 2013). This form typically occurs during childhood or adolescence and is the leading cause of diabetes in children. In type 2 diabetes, the body becomes resistant to the insulin produced by the pancreas. This type usually occurs in adults who are over the age of 40 and overweight and is rare among children under the age of 10 (NDEP, 2006; Scott, 2013).

Before 1990, fewer than 4% of children with diabetes had type 2 diabetes (Scott, 2013), but this number has been increasing as more children have become overweight and physically inactive. Today about 3,600 new cases of type 2 diabetes are diagnosed in the United States each year among youth under the age of 19 (CDC, 2011c). Although the numbers are increasing for all children, some ethnic groups are at particularly high risk. Type 2 diabetes accounts for 14.9% of new cases of diabetes among non-Hispanic Whites, but this number climbs to 46.1% of new cases for Hispanic children, 57.8% for African American children, and is even higher for Asian/Pacific Islanders (69.7%) and Native Americans (86.2%) (Scott, 2013).

Type 1 diabetes is managed with insulin therapy. This therapy requires that blood glucose levels be monitored so an appropriate amount of insulin can be calculated and injected at each meal to match diet and activity patterns (Kelo, Martikainen, & Eriksson, 2011). Children with type 1 diabetes can also use an insulin pump that is worn on the body to provide insulin continuously. Although children may be self-conscious about wearing a pump, those who

Treating diabetes in a child. Children with diabetes can live full, normal lives but at this age they require help from adults with monitoring and treating their condition. ∎

do have good long-term control of their diabetes (Johnson, Cooper, Jones, & Davis, 2013). Both types of treatment are too complex for younger children to manage without consistent help from adults (Kelo et al., 2011), but school-aged children can begin to take responsibility for their self-care.

Management of type 2 diabetes depends on balancing healthy eating and portion control with the required level of physical activity and medication, if any. Children need to restrict their intake of refined sugars and carbohydrates. This can be difficult because foods high in carbohydrates and refined sugars are very popular in this age group. Some children with type 2 diabetes also need to take oral medications, and some may even require insulin. The goal is to keep blood sugar levels within a safe range, neither too high nor too low.

In the school setting, diabetes is recognized as a disability, and it is illegal for a school to discriminate against a child because of it. The child's condition must be accommodated just as other special needs are (American Association of Diabetes Educators, 2014). Parents, school staff, medical professionals, and peers can all act as part of a support team for the child dealing with diabetes (Kelo et al., 2011).

The symptoms of type 2 diabetes can come on slowly and may be misdiagnosed. They include fatigue, excessive thirst, weight loss, blurred vision, and slow healing of sores (NDEP, 2006). Although no available test detects diabetes in a child before symptoms develop (Wilson, 2013), we know the factors that place a child at increased risk. They include having a family history of diabetes and being a member of a high-risk population group, female, overweight, or physically inactive. Although we can't change a child's family history, ethnicity, or gender, some steps can prevent or greatly reduce the risk of type 2 diabetes. The most important are losing weight and increasing physical activity. Because stress can alter blood sugar levels, stress management can also be a help.

VIDEO LINK 11.6
Diabetes

1. List some effects of insufficient and poor-quality sleep for children in middle childhood.
2. How does eating breakfast benefit children in middle childhood?
3. Identify recent trends in obesity and overweight among children in middle childhood.
4. How can schools assist children who have asthma and their families?
5. What is the difference between type 1 diabetes and type 2 diabetes?

11.4

What kinds of physical activities are best for children in middle childhood and what are the risks of participating in them?

Physical Activity

As children enter middle childhood, they become faster, stronger, and better coordinated, and as a consequence, their gross motor skills develop rapidly during this period. We see these changes reflected in the amount and types of physical activity they engage in. The Centers for Disease Control and Prevention (2011b) recommend that children get 60 minutes of physical activity each day. This activity can include a mix of aerobic activity, muscle-strengthening activity, and bone-strengthening activity. To be effective, aerobic activity should be vigorous enough to make you breathe heavily and make your heart beat much faster than normal. Examples of aerobic activity that school-aged children would enjoy include brisk walking, running, swimming, biking, skateboarding, and dancing. Children at this age do not need to take part in weight training to strengthen their muscles. Instead activities such as playing on a jungle gym or playing a game of tug-of-war, climbing trees, and taking part in gymnastics accomplish the goal. Bone-strengthening activity can be as simple as a game of hop-scotch or jumping rope, skipping, or playing sports like basketball, volleyball, or tennis. These activities probably sound like ones you think children enjoy and spend time doing, but most American children fall short of the goal of 60 minutes of physical activity a day (Bryan, Sims, Hester, & Dunaway, 2013).

The Role of Schools in Promoting Physical Activity

In middle childhood, children spend most of their day in a school classroom, and most of the activity that takes place during a school day is sedentary. However, opportunities for physical activity exist during recess and as part of structured physical education classes. Unfortunately, in recent years, many schools have reduced or eliminated either or both from the school day (Bocarro, Kanters, Casper, & Forrester, 2008; Chin & Ludwig, 2013). According to Healthy People 2020 (2013), the 10-year agenda of the Federal government to improve America's health, in 2006 only 3.8% of public and private elementary schools required daily physical education for all their students. The numbers for recess are a little better, with 57% of school districts requiring daily recess and 33% recommending it (Beighle, 2012).

What do we know about how children use their time during physical education classes and recess, and do they use it in a way that increases their daily level of physical activity?

It's not work; it's fun. Exercise can be fun, as this boy knows. Why do most U.S. children get less physical activity per day than they should? ■

Physical Education Classes

Physical education classes seem to be a logical way to ensure that all children participate in some physical activity during the day because all children attend school, but only 5 states (Illinois, Iowa, Massachusetts, New Mexico, and Vermont) require physical education for all grades from kindergarten through twelfth grade (Bryan et al., 2013). Figure 11.3 shows the impact that recent budget cuts to education have had on schools' ability to offer physical education classes to students. The typical total duration of physical education classes in elementary school over the course of a week is about 90 minutes (Kahan, 2008), which means that even if every minute of physical education classes were spent in physical activity, it would still fall far short of the recommended 60 minutes a day.

Although younger children have a generally positive attitude toward physical education, attitudes become more negative as children get older (Bocarro et al., 2008). Because not all children enjoy physical education class and a number of them want to get out of it, educators have tried to offer fun and engaging alternatives. In recent years, the focus of physical education has broadened to include more than sports and athletics. It now plays a public health role by including topics such as nutrition, physical fitness, and wellness (Bryan et al., 2013). While these topics are an important part of the picture, they do take time away from actual physical activity. The Let's Move campaign initiated by First Lady Michelle Obama in 2010 calls for physical education programs to devote at least 50% of their class time to vigorous activity.

One of the goals of physical education is to develop an interest in activities students can pursue on their own and throughout their lifetime. The idea is that rather than being deeply invested in one or two physical activities, physical education programs should offer a wide range of activities students can choose to continue participating in as they get older (Bocarro et al., 2008). This concept is known as leisure repertoire theory.

Supporting physical education. First Lady Michelle Obama (shown here with young soccer players) initiated the Let's Move campaign to ensure that physical education programs continue to devote at least 50% of their time to vigorous activity. ■

JIM WATSON/AFP/Getty Images

WEB LINK 11.3
Physical Education

Leisure repertoire theory The theory that says if children develop a wide repertoire of activities while young, they will be more likely to continue to participate in physical activity as they get older.

Recess

While more schools offer recess than offer physical education classes, 29% of schools do not have regularly scheduled recess for students in the elementary grades (Story, Kaphingst, & French, 2006). Even when students do have recess, they usually have a lot of discretion in deciding what they want to do with this time. Rather than being physically active, some choose to use this time to catch up with school work or to play video games in the classroom. Others engage in sedentary activities like talking with their friends.

Although recess makes up a relatively small part of the school day (typically lasting only 20 to 30 minutes), it can account for a substantial part of the physical activity some children get. Boys can obtain as much as 40% of their daily physical activity during recess, and girls 31% (Beighle, 2012). Although the amount of time they spend in physical activity during recess varies from one study to another, boys spend between 16% and 68% of their recess being physically active, and girls between 15% and 52% (Beighle,

FIGURE 11.3   The impact of budget cuts on physical education

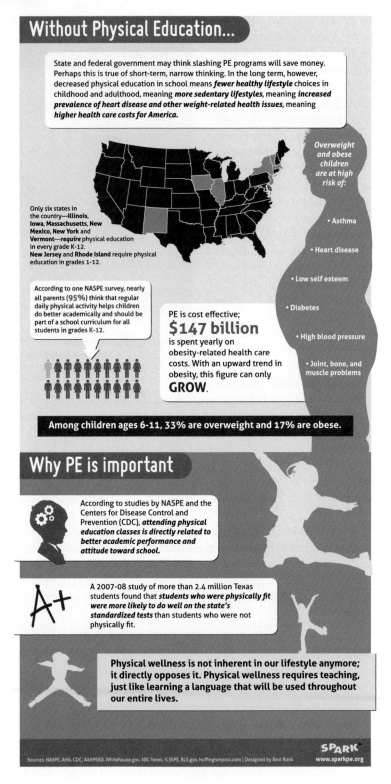

In the face of budget cuts, a number of schools have cut physical education classes as a cost-saving strategy. However, given the number of ways in which physical education benefits school children, this decision may be very short-sighted.

SOURCE: SPARK (2009–2014).

2012). It has been a pretty consistent finding that boys get more physical activity than girls (Chin & Ludwig, 2013; Ridgers, Saint-Maurice, Welk, Siahpush, & Huberty, 2011), but there have not been consistent differences by socioeconomic status (Chin & Ludwig, 2013) or ethnicity (Chin & Ludwig, 2013; Ridgers et al., 2011).

Schools can promote getting a greater amount of moderate or vigorous physical activity during recess with some simple strategies. Providing children with inexpensive equipment such as flying disks, plastic hoops, jump ropes, beanbags and balls; training playground supervisors to show children new games and activities; and painting lines for simple games like hopscotch or marking off court areas all lead to increased physical activity (Beighle, 2012; Kahan, 2008; see also Chin & Ludwig, 2013).

In a recent policy statement from the American Academy of Pediatrics, recess was described as a "crucial and necessary component of a child's development" that offers cognitive, social, emotional, and physical benefits (Murray & Ramstetter, 2013, p. 183). The statement goes on to note that recess benefits the whole child. Children are more attentive and productive in the classroom following a break from rigorous cognitive tasks. They learn valuable social skills because play during recess gives them an opportunity to communicate, negotiate, cooperate, and problem solve with peers. They also develop self-control in the context of this play. And, of course, they also receive the benefits we have already described of any physical activity that occurs during this time outside the classroom. The national Parent Teacher Association (PTA) was so concerned about the trend toward eliminating playtime that it began a program called Rescuing Recess to convince the 40% of public schools that have eliminated or are planning to eliminate recess to rethink their priorities (PTA, 2006).

Simple games. Providing opportunities for exercise need not be expensive for schools and communities. Simple sidewalk games encourage movement and participation. ■

Intramural and Extracurricular Activity

A third opportunity for physical activity in the school environment takes place in the context of intramural and extracurricular activities. About half of American schools offer intramural sports and sports clubs that allow students to compete against other students at their school (Story et al., 2006). By comparison, 82% of middle school and 94% of high schools offer interscholastic sports teams that compete with other schools (Bocarro et al., 2008). You can use **Active Learning: After-School Physical Activity** to compare how children's activities in their after-school hours have changed over the years.

WEB LINK 11.4
Learning Self-Control

Active Learning

After-School Physical Activity

The way children use their time after school—and consequently how physically active they are—has changed in recent years. Taking music lessons and going to academic enrichment programs or religious instruction are all worthwhile activities, but they do not require a child to be physically active. Watching television, playing video games, and reading help pass the time, but they don't get your heart rate up.

Take a few minutes to think about how you would spend a typical afternoon when you were in elementary school from about third to fifth grade. Did you spend your time at school, in your neighborhood, in your own yard, or in the house? What kind of activities did you engage in? How much physical activity was part of your regular routine? Would you describe it as sedentary, moderately physically active, or vigorously physically active? Ask a child who is 8 to 10 years old a similar set of questions using language that they will be able to understand. Also talk with someone who is at least 10 years older than you about the same topics. If you can talk to someone else even older than that, take that opportunity also.

Does a pattern emerge? Do children seem to be spending more time in or near their homes, and have their activity choices become more sedentary? ■

While interscholastic sports offer a wonderful opportunity for a child who is a skilled athlete to compete and hone his or her athletic skills, intramural programs encourage the larger group of students who are not as skilled or motivated to participate in competitive sports to get some physical activity while having fun. For after-school activities to be successful, schools need to listen to what students say they want from the programs. Schools can make intramural programs appealing to students by providing a safe and attractive physical space they can use and by emphasizing the mastery of skills, fun, and the achievement of personal best rather than competition. Elementary schools are often neighborhood schools that are within walking distance of a child's home, but middle schools are often farther away, so transportation can become an issue for older children who want to participate in extracurricular activities. Only 22% of schools provide transportation home after sports, which can disproportionately affect low-income children's ability to take part in these activities (Story et al., 2006).

The Role of the Family in Promoting Physical Activity

At home, parents can encourage physical activity by being good role models for their children and being active themselves. They can make physical activity part of their family's daily routine. They also can be sure their children have access to places where they can be physically active and provide some age-appropriate equipment. It does not need to be expensive or elaborate; balls, jump ropes, hula hoops, and flying discs are all inexpensive items that encourage physical activity. The other important thing for parents to do is to monitor the amount of screen time their children have and to set limits on it.

The kind of physical activity children participate in outside school depends on their age. Younger children in the early elementary years spend more time in free play, while older children in the higher elementary grades are more likely to take part in organized activities. Play contributes directly to physical development by giving children the chance to use both gross motor and fine motor skills. Play is a natural tool that helps build healthy bodies while also contributing to brain development (Milteer & Ginsburg, 2012), but not all children have the same opportunity for these experiences.

One type of physical activity play is rough-and-tumble play in which children look like they are fighting or wrestling, but their goal is just to have fun, not to hurt or win. This type of play increases during the early school years and continues, although at a greatly reduced level, through early adolescence. Clearly these activities promote physical strength and endurance, but they may also affect brain development. The greatest amount of neuronal growth in rats was found when they were most engaged in rough-and-tumble play and exploration (Haight & Black, 2001). Rough-and-tumble play also correlates with social competence,

Rough-and-tumble play Play that looks like fighting or wrestling, where the goal is not to hurt or win, but to have fun.

Physical play. Play can promote physical development in children. This type of rough-and-tumble play builds strength, coordination, and self-control as children learn to have fun without hurting each other. ■

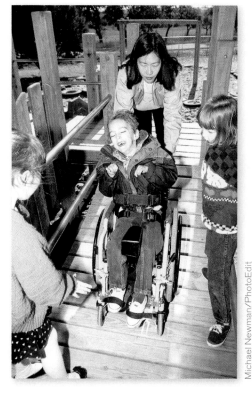

A universal playground. This playground has been specifically designed to be accessible to all children and adults—both those with disabilities and those without. The young boy in the second photo has a chance to play that he would not have had on a typical playground with all its steps and uneven surfaces. ■

possibly based on the same kinds of brain changes that have been found in monkeys and rats who take part in these activities (Pellis & Pellis, 2007). This type of play also helps develop self-control because children learn not to go too far and hurt someone (Pellegrini, 2002).

Accessible Playgrounds

Amy Jaffe Barzach's life changed after she saw a little girl in a wheelchair watching other children play on a playscape, unable to join in. Barzach believed play should be every child's right, and she set out to make it so. She developed a program called Boundless Playgrounds that creates universal playgrounds accessible to all children regardless of physical and mental limitations. Barzach quickly realized that typical playscapes also limit the interaction parents with disabilities can have when playing with their children. In a Boundless Playground built on an army base, soldiers who were missing limbs or were in wheelchairs were able to join in the fun with their children, creating a priceless opportunity to cement the bonds that may have been threatened when a parent who has been gone for a long time returns to his or her family but is very changed.

AUDIO LINK 11.4
Accessible Playgrounds

Play-Related Injuries

Although playgrounds are the setting for hours of healthy, vigorous play during middle childhood, they also are a leading source of injuries. Each year over 200,000 children age 14 and younger are treated for playground-related injuries (CDC, 2012f). Because falls are a major source of injury, playground equipment should be installed on a soft fall surface such as shredded rubber or fine sand, the height of equipment should be moderate, and guardrails should always be in place. Children should not be wearing loose clothing or scarves that can get caught in play equipment. Finally, it is essential that adults actively monitor the children's play (SafeKids, 2007). The U.S. Consumer Product Safety Commission (2010) provides detailed guidelines to create the safest possible playground experience for children.

Young athletes. Venus and Serena Williams began playing tennis as children and reached the very top levels of play as adults. The value of beginning intensive athletic training at an early age is widely debated. What is your opinion? Is it a rewarding experience that leads to fitness and skill, or does it lead to injury and burnout? ■

Organized Sports

Approximately 38 million children and teens in the United States take part in organized sports every year. That number includes about three quarters of all families with school-age children (Mickalide & Hansen, 2012). The kind of experience children have in sports can vary widely. They can participate in highly structured, adult-supervised, competitive activities, or they can play in informal activities organized by the children themselves that only loosely follow a set of rules. They can join team sports like football, basketball, or hockey, or pursue individual sports like track, swimming, or gymnastics. All types can help them achieve similar health benefits.

Between the ages of 6 and 9, posture and balance have improved to the point that children can participate in entry-level soccer, baseball, tennis, and gymnastics, and by ages 10 to 12, most are ready for sports that depend on more complex skills such as football, basketball, hockey, and volleyball (DiFiori et al., 2014). But chronological age alone is not a good indicator of a child's readiness to participate in a particular sport. Other factors, such as the skill set of an individual child and the child's motivation to participate, also need to figure into the decision.

When we hear stories about highly skilled adult athletes, they often mention that the individual began training in the sport at a very young age, but there is real debate within athletics about the value of early and intensive specialized training in a specific sport. This type of experience increases the potential for overuse injuries and eventual burnout. Some experts believe more generalized participation earlier in childhood, with a transfer of skills from one sport to another, and more specialized training later in adolescence is a better alternative (DiFiori et al., 2014).

Sports-Related Injuries

Given the potential health benefits of children's participation in sports, how likely is it that a child might be injured as a result of playing? The issue of safety is not trivial. One third of all children who play team sports suffer injuries serious enough to keep them off the field at least for a while, and some of these injuries have consequences that will last the rest of their lives (Mickalide & Hansen, 2012). Parents may not be fully aware of the level of risk their children are exposed to. In a recent national survey, many parents of children age 5 to 14 who play an organized team sport or participate in gymnastics said they did not worry that much about their child being injured as a consequence of participation (Hart Research Associates, 2011) (see Figure 11.4). Perhaps this finding is not surprising. If parents believed the risk of injury were high, they would be unlikely to allow their child to participate at all. Parents of children who spend more hours per week participating in a sport, who are younger, or who are minorities perceive a higher risk than other parents. And more than two thirds of parents correctly see football as the sport that carries the greatest risk of sustaining an injury.

Unfortunately, about one third of child athletes believe they should play even while injured, and almost half of coaches are pressured by the parents of injured children to let the players back into the game (Mickalide & Hansen, 2012). Although many people believe it is mainly in the intensity of actual games that children are injured, most injuries occur during practice; therefore, it is just as important for children to take the preventive steps of warming up, wearing protective gear, and drinking plenty of fluids during practice as it is for a game (SafeKids USA, 2011). There appears to be a significant gap between how important parents say it is for them or the child's coach to know the

T/F #8

Parents of children who participate in organized sports worry a great deal about their child being injured while playing. *False*

WEB LINK 11.5
Sports-Related Injuries

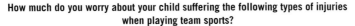

FIGURE 11.4   **Parental concern about sports injuries**

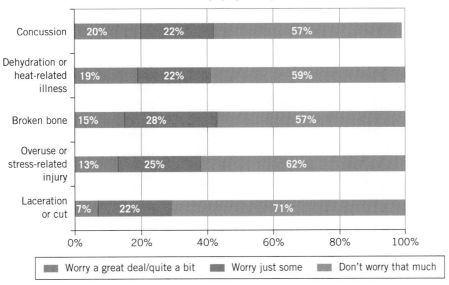

According to one survey, many parents of children who participate in organized sports activities do not appear very concerned about the likelihood of an injury. However, substantial numbers of children do sustain injury, and many require medical treatment.

SOURCE: Hart Research Associates (2011).

signs of specific types of injuries and how confident they are that they or the coach actually have this knowledge (Hart Research Associates, 2011) (see Figure 11.5).

About three-quarters of parents whose children play sports know that half of all sports injuries are preventable, but many seem willing to accept that risk for their children (Hart Research Associates, 2011). In a nationally representative sample of parents, 86% agreed with the statement that injuries are "just part of the game" (p. 5), with fathers less likely than mothers to think that injuries could be avoided.

There are actually several important ways to help prevent injuries when children are playing sports. Competitors should be fairly equally matched in size and weight. Adults should be sure players have a reasonable level of skills to participate safely and are matched by skill level, where appropriate. Parents and caregivers also must make sure children have the right safety equipment for their sports, and that it is the right size, fits well, and is not damaged or degraded in any way that reduces its effectiveness.

Children need to warm up before practice or a game to prepare their bodies for the activity. Preparation helps reduce the risk of injury during the game itself, and practice helps children develop the skills they need to play well in addition to improving their physical condition so they play safely. Practice also helps children learn how to coordinate their play with that of teammates. Many parents report that their children do wear properly fitted equipment, drink fluids regularly, and warm up before playing (Hart Research Associates, 2011), but these are self-reports so we must be cautious about their accuracy. Another safety issue is to provide child athletes with protection from the sun while they are outside.

The Role of Coaches

Connecting children to positive role models is often listed as one of the benefits of participating in organized sports, but the way adults see what they are doing in this role and the way the children see it can be quite different. Coaches' expectations for performance

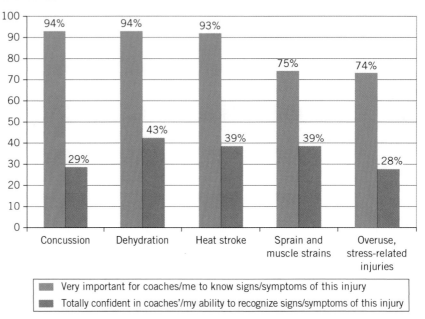

FIGURE 11.5   The knowledge gap about sports injuries

Very important for coaches/me to know signs/symptoms of this injury

Totally confident in coaches'/my ability to recognize signs/symptoms of this injury

Although most parents say it is important for them or their child's coach to know the signs and symptoms of specific types of sports injuries (especially the more serious ones such as concussion, dehydration, or heat stroke), relatively few are confident they or the coach actually have this knowledge.

SOURCE: Hart Research Associates (2011).

may exceed the children's capabilities (American Academy of Pediatrics, 2001), which can result in frustration, stress, and a lowered sense of self-esteem for the participants. Parents' unrealistic expectations can have the same effect. In one study of families in competitive hockey, mothers, fathers, and sons were asked to describe how much pressure parents exerted on their children and how much support they provided (Kanters, Bocarro, & Casper, 2008). Across all the questions, the boys consistently reported feeling more pressure and perceiving less support than their parents reported. When there is a lack of agreement between the experience of the children and the perception of the parents, it can become another factor that contributes to eventual burnout in the sport.

Most adults who volunteer their time to coach organized youth activities have the children's best interests at heart, but many lack experience working with children and may not have a good understanding of child development. An adult coach might push a young player, thinking it will help the child develop skills or inspire a sense of accomplishment, but the child is just looking for a way to have fun and spend some time with friends. When children participating in sports programs were asked what they *liked* about their coaches, they said their coach was nice, was fair, and "teaches us good things" (for boys) or "helps us play better" (for girls). However, when asked what they *liked least*, they said the coach "gets mad and yells at us," "works us too hard," "does not let me play enough" (for boys), or "doesn't teach us much" (for girls) (Humphrey, 2003, p. 58). Coaches may not understand how young players see their well-intended efforts to motivate them.

We may think of organized sports as a way to keep children physically active and set a pattern of lifelong physical activity, but 70% drop out by the age of 13 (Engle, 2004). About one quarter of those who stop say it was no longer fun for them, while another 16% say they stopped because they or their parents were concerned about the possibility of injuries (Mickalide & Hansen, 2012). Perhaps we could improve the retention rate if

T/F #9

Children who participate in organized sports develop skills they use to keep them physically active throughout their lifetime. *False*

we listened more to what children are telling us about their experiences. Emphasizing skills, teamwork, and fun rather than winning may a good way to put some of the spontaneity and joy back into organized sports for children.

Check Your Understanding

1. How much physical activity should children in middle childhood get every day?
2. What is the role of play in middle childhood?
3. How can parents help prevent sports injuries in their children?
4. Why might coaches and children have very different expectations of children's participation in organized sports?

Children and the Natural World

> Those who contemplate the beauty of the earth find reserves of strength that will endure as long as life lasts.
>
> —Rachel Carson, *Silent Spring*

Children today are less likely than children in previous generations to go outside to play with their friends because of parents' concerns for safety, the amount of time children spend using media, and their participation in adult-organized activities. One consequence of this trend is that children today are more cut off from the natural world. In this section, we examine the role that experiencing nature plays in children's healthy development. This entails giving children regular opportunities to experience the land, water, and living things in green environments, such as parks, forests, and gardens.

A recent book, titled *Last Child in the Woods: Saving Our Children From Nature-Deficit Disorder* by Richard Louv (2008), focused attention on the consequences of separating children from the natural world. Louv proposed a campaign he calls "Leave No Child Inside" (Charles, Louv, Bodner, Guns, & Stahl, 2009). Subsequently, President Obama began the America's Great Outdoors Initiative, designed to bring people of all ages back to the natural world. After listening to more than 100,000 people and conducting 21 sessions with children and teens, the initiative's leaders proposed four goals for youth:

1. Make the outdoors relevant to today's young people: Make it inviting, exciting, and fun.

2. Ensure that all young people have access to outdoor places that are safe, clean, and close to home.

3. Empower and enable youth to work and volunteer in the outdoors.

4. Build on a base of environmental and outdoor education, both formal and informal (America's Great Outdoors, 2011).

According to survey research by the Outdoor Foundation (2012), all this attention may be having the desired positive effect. The steep decline in outdoor participation that took place between 2006 and 2010 did not continue in 2011. That year, 63% of 6- to 12-year-old children took part in outdoor recreation at least once during the year, and many of them spent a great deal of time outdoors.

11.5

Why is contact with the natural world important for children?

© Stock Connection Blue/Alamy

The great outdoors. How does this family hike connect children to the natural world? ■

JOURNAL ARTICLE 11.2
Children and Nature

Researchers have begun to focus their attention on the effects of engagement with and isolation from the natural world on children, looking at a broad range of types of contact from play in green spaces to therapy using horseback riding. As you might imagine, when children are outdoors in green spaces they engage in more physical activity, which has been related to reduced levels of obesity (Bell, Wilson, & Liu, 2008; Cleland et al., 2008; McCurdy, Winterbottom, Mehta, & Roberts, 2010). A study carried out in eight European cities found that the higher level of obesity among low-income children is linked to their lowered access to green spaces in which to play (Evans, Jones-Rounds, Belojevic, & Vermeylen, 2012). Activity level is only one contributor to obesity; diet is the other. The natural world has been brought to thousands of children through school gardens, and there is some evidence that activity in these gardens increases their likelihood of choosing and enjoying healthy vegetables (Parmer, Salisbury-Glennon, Shannon, & Struempler, 2009).

Several studies have shown that time spent in nature can renew and revive the ability to focus attention (Berman, Jonides, & Kaplan, 2008; Kaplan, 1995). It also may allow for unstructured reflection, which often results in effective problem-solving. Several studies by Frances Kuo and Andrea Taylor have shown that exposure to natural outdoor environments can even reduce the attention-deficit symptoms of ADHD and is related to increased self-discipline in inner-city girls (Kuo & Taylor, 2004; Taylor & Kuo, 2009; Taylor, Kuo, & Sullivan, 2002).

T/F #10

When children diagnosed with ADHD play outdoors, their symptoms are reduced.
True

As you know if you have spent time at a beach or taken a walk through the woods, the natural environment can be relaxing. Even in rural areas, children who experience more life stress have lower levels of distress and higher self-worth when they have more access to natural environments in and around their homes. Although this access can be related to income, the relationship between natural environment and stress relief was found to be independent of the effect of income (Wells & Evans, 2003). The evidence from this emerging area of research suggests that public policy can work to ensure that everyone, regardless of income, has access to green space and the natural environment.

Finally, experience with nature, as well as parents' attitudes toward it, promotes children's positive attitudes toward the natural world, including their enjoyment of it and their wish to protect it (Cheng & Monroe, 2012). As we've seen, there is growing research on the link between children's well-being and access to and engagement with natural environments. The reasons behind this relationship still need to be explored. It is also not yet clear whether a nearby park, a natural view out a window, or indoor plants are sufficient to bring about these outcomes. There is a long way to go to understand the effects of nature on children's development, but it is important that we explore these effects now that children have less and less exposure to the natural world.

Check Your Understanding

1. Why are children spending less time with nature today than in the past?
2. What are the America's Great Outdoors Initiative goals for children?
3. What are some advantages for children of experiencing nature?

Conclusion

The rate of physical growth slows during middle childhood, but both fine and gross motor skills have improved and consolidated. The brain has nearly reached full adult size, and various regions are now interconnected in ways that support learning and memory. To sustain growth during this period of development, children need a healthy diet, an adequate amount of exercise, and enough sleep. Most children are doing well in these areas, although there is room for improvement in all three. During middle childhood, children are gaining greater control over health-related decisions in their lives, and we need to educate them about how to make good ones as their bodies prepare for the dramatic growth that will begin as they enter early adolescence and puberty. Finally, all children benefit from activities in the natural world and there are new initiatives to promote physical activity in these settings.

Chapter Summary

11.1 **How is physical growth different in middle childhood than in early childhood?**

Physical growth is slower in middle childhood, but children typically add 2 inches in height and gain 6.5 pounds each year during this time. Growth of the legs gives the child bodily proportions that are more adult-like. Improved fine motor control is reflected in children's ability to write and draw. Gross motor abilities are evident in their increased strength, balance, flexibility, and control. Girls typically begin **prepubescence** as early as ages 5 to 9 years and boys a couple of years later.

11.2 **How does the brain change in middle childhood?**

The brain reaches 95% of its peak size by age 6. As myelin in the brain increases, the two hemispheres become more interconnected, improving coordination between the brain's parts. These changes support long-term memory and the growth of executive function. Differences in brain chemistry, function, or structure can result in a **specific learning disorder** or in **attention deficit/hyperactivity disorder (ADHD)**. Medication is widely used along with behavioral therapy to treat ADHD.

11.3 **Describe healthy practices for children in middle childhood and ways they deal with chronic illnesses, such as asthma and diabetes.**

Most children have a reasonably good diet during middle childhood, but most ingest too much fat, refined sugars, and sodium and too few whole grains, fruits, and vegetables. School breakfast and lunch programs provide nutritious food for many children, and the quality of the food offered by the programs is improving. Overweight and obesity continue to be a problem although there are some promising signs that the situation is improving for younger children.

In middle childhood, baby teeth are replaced by permanent adult teeth and these must be cared for to prevent cavities and infections. Children need enough sleep to keep them healthy, but they get less as they get older. To prevent injuries, school children should not be carrying backpacks that weigh more than 10% to 15% of their body weight. Children in middle childhood can assume more responsibility for managing their chronic illnesses. Schools can do a great deal to become asthma-friendly environments. Although there is no way to prevent the development of type 1 diabetes, the risk of developing type 2 diabetes can be reduced through weight control and physical activity, which also help protect against physical damage from the illness.

11.4 **What kinds of physical activities are best for children in middle childhood and what are the risks of participating in them?**

Neither physical education classes nor recess provide enough daily activity for children to get the recommended amount of physical activity. While competitive extramural sports are good for children who are skilled athletes, other children benefit from intramural programs that emphasize skill building and fun. Playgrounds can be designed to be accessible to children and adults with physical disabilities. Adults can do a lot to protect children from injury while they are playing organized sports. Coaches and parents should follow all recommendations for children's safe participation and have reasonable expectations for their performance.

11.5 **Why is contact with the natural world important for children?**

There are national efforts underway to increase the amount of contact children have with the natural world. This contact has physical, cognitive, and psychological benefits. It may also encourage healthy eating if children grow some of their own food. Experiencing nature has been found to reduce distractibility in children with ADHD and helps children value and protect the natural world.

Key Terms

Adrenarche   364

Attention deficit/hyperactivity
   disorder (ADHD)   365

Child sexual abuse   361

Diabetes   374

Dyslexia   364

Leisure repertoire theory   377

Nocturnal enuresis   372

Precocious puberty   361

Prepubescence   359

Puberty   357

Rough-and-tumble play   380

Specific learning disorder   364

Sharpen your skills with SAGE edge at edge.sagepub.com/levinechrono

SAGE edge for Students provides a personalized approach to help you accomplish your coursework goals in an easy-to-use learning environment.

   Go to edge.sagepub.com/levinechrono for additional exercises and video resources. Select Chapter 11, Physical Development in Middle Childhood, for chapter-specific activities. All of the Video Links listed in the margins of this chapter are accessible via this site.

12 Cognitive Development in Middle Childhood

T/F Test Your Knowledge

Test your knowledge of child development by deciding whether each of the following statements is *true* or *false,* and then check your answers as you read the chapter.

1. T☐ F☐ It is more difficult to fool a school age child than a younger child into thinking he remembers something he never actually saw.

2. T☐ F☐ One third of U.S. fourth graders are not reading at even a basic level.

3. T☐ F☐ When a young child learns two languages at the same time, the extra effort it takes to learn the second language slows down the child's general cognitive development.

4. T☐ F☐ Well-constructed and reliable standardized intelligence tests are not biased against native-born racial and ethnic minorities.

5. T☐ F☐ Intelligence as measured by IQ tests is determined by genetics for some groups of people and by environment for other groups.

6. T☐ F☐ IQ tests are the best predictors we have of how well a child is going to do in school.

7. T☐ F☐ Children with a learning disorder have normal intelligence.

8. T☐ F☐ Children who are gifted or talented often pay a price for their giftedness because they are likely to be socially or emotionally maladjusted.

9. T☐ F☐ Placing high-, average-, and low-performing students together in groups to collaborate on a project is equally beneficial to all the children in the group.

10. T☐ F☐ Generally speaking, boys are not doing as well in school as they have in the past.

A shift in cognitive abilities occurs between early and middle childhood, sometimes referred to as the *5- to 7-year shift* because marked changes occur between these two ages (Sameroff & Haith, 1996). This is the age when children can begin to learn the skills they need to be successful adults in their society. In rural and less developed settings, children are now given more responsibilities, including care of younger siblings, taking care of animals, and doing household chores. They are seen as having reached the age of reason when they can use common sense and think logically. For those in modern societies, this means the beginning of school.

In this chapter we examine Piaget's stage of concrete operations and some of the abilities he described that underlie children's new capacity for logical thought. We then describe changes in children's attention, memory, and executive function during this developmental period. Language continues to develop in middle childhood as children become more aware of the nature of language and the way it is used. We examine the critical language-based development of reading and writing, as well as some of the difficulties children may have with these skills. Some children are developing two or more languages, and we describe the effects of bilingualism on cognitive development, as well as the way schools accommodate those learning English as a second language during this age period.

In the last sections of this chapter we look at the issues of intelligence, how it is defined and measured, and its relationship to school achievement. We look at the effect of different levels of ability on achievement and conclude by examining the role of schools and teachers in fostering every child's highest level of achievement.

Learning Questions

12.1 What occurs during Piaget's stage of concrete operations?

12.2 How do attention, memory, and executive function develop in middle childhood?

12.3 Describe the progression of language development, including literacy, in middle childhood.

12.4 How does intelligence affect academic achievement in middle childhood?

12.5 How do we define intellectual disability, specific learning disorder, and giftedness?

12.6 What aspects of the school environment affect children's academic achievement?

Piaget's Stage of Concrete Operations (7–12 Years)

Piaget was one of the first theorists to describe the effects of the 5- to 7-year shift, which he described as the beginning of his third stage of cognitive development, the stage of concrete operations. In the preoperational stage, children could not think logically about mental operations. Children in the stage of concrete operations now can think logically rather than magically, but their abilities are still limited because their thinking is concrete rather than abstract. For example, how would you explain the saying "Don't put all your eggs in one basket"? As an abstract thinker, you might say, "Don't count on only one plan. Have some backup plans." Now compare what a concrete thinker might say: "When you go to the store, take two baskets and put half your eggs in one and half in the other." Concrete thought focuses very much on the here and now. This is probably why we don't start teaching children subjects that require abstract thinking, such as political science or philosophy, until adolescence.

Piaget described three cognitive advances in concrete operational thinking: reversibility, classification, and seriation. Once children develop these cognitive skills, they are able to solve conservation problems, something they could not do during the preoperational stage in early childhood.

12.1

What occurs during Piaget's stage of concrete operations?

Concrete operations The third stage in Piaget's theory in which children between 6 and 12 years of age develop logical thinking but still cannot think abstractly.

VIDEO LINK 12.1
Reversibility

Reversibility

Reversibility is the ability to reverse mental operations. This ability allows a child to overcome the pull toward perceptual bias when making judgments about conservation tasks. For example, if the contents of a short, wide glass are poured into a tall, thin glass, the water level will be higher in the second glass. This may cause the preoperational child to think the second glass contains more water. However, a child who understands reversibility realizes that if you reverse the procedure and pour the water back into the short glass, the amount will still be the same. Reversibility is necessary for a child to understand that if $1 + 1 = 2$, then necessarily $2 - 1 = 1$, a basic foundation for understanding arithmetic. In the concrete operational stage, children are now paying attention to *how* something changes, not just its beginning and ending states. Children in the preoperational stage look only at the first level of the water and the second level in the two containers and not at the action that occurs as you pour from one glass to another one that has a different shape and therefore they reach the wrong conclusion and think the volume of the water has changed.

Classification

Piaget saw the ability to classify objects into hierarchical conceptual categories as central to concrete operations; for example, a terrier fits in the larger category of dogs and dogs fit in the larger category of animals. The game of *20 Questions*, in which a child must ask a series of questions that can be answered "yes" or "no" to figure out what the other person is thinking about, provides a good opportunity to see the difference in classification skills between preoperational and concrete operational stages. When playing *20 Questions*, a child in the concrete operational stage is likely to first ask something like "Is it alive?" This is a highly efficient question because it eliminates a very large number of potential items. Children in the concrete operational stage will continue to work their way down from larger to smaller categories (for example, "Is it an animal?" or "Is it a plant?"), but children in the preoperational stage may start with very specific questions like "Is it a cat?" or "Is it my chair?" These children do not yet understand how to organize smaller items or groups into larger categories.

Piaget tested children's ability to use classification by showing them 18 brown wooden beads and 2 white wooden beads and asking, "Are there more brown beads or more wooden beads?" A child who has developed classification ability will correctly answer that there are more wooden beads because he or she understands that both the white beads and the brown beads belong to the category of wooden beads. Children in the preoperational stage don't understand this hierarchy and are fooled by their perception so they will answer that there are more brown beads.

Classification. Are there more dogs or black dogs in this photo? Children in the stage of concrete operations understand that both tan dogs and black dogs belong to the category of "dogs" so they are not fooled by this question. ■

Seriation

Another skill gained in concrete operations is seriation, the ability to put objects in order by height, weight, or some other quality. A younger child may be able to take two or three sticks of different lengths and put them in order from shortest to tallest, but a child in concrete operations can correctly arrange an entire set of sticks according to their length relative to each other. However, one question is what it means if a young child can put a few items into a series, but not a larger number of items. Piaget's critics claim that children develop this ability before the stage of concrete operations. Younger children are capable of seriating but are unable to do so when their abilities are overwhelmed by the complexity of the task.

Evaluation of Piaget's Stage of Concrete Operations

A major criticism of Piaget's work is that children are found to be capable of carrying out some of his operations, such as seriation and classification, at earlier ages than he indicated if the tasks are simplified. As described above, a young child can put two or three sticks in order according to height but gets confused when there are many more. Similarly, a young child may classify many types of dogs as being in the category of dog but is unable to categorize correctly with more complicated questions. Although Piaget saw the acquisition of these skills as a unified, relatively quick process, the findings indicate that learning them is more likely to be a gradual than a sudden process.

Check Your Understanding

1. What characterizes Piaget's stage of concrete operations?
2. What is reversibility?
3. What can children with classification skills do?
4. What is seriation?

Cognitive Processes

Cognitive psychology and the theory of information processing have described the gradual processes by which children achieve the larger competencies described by Piaget and others. In this section, we describe the further development of attention, memory, and executive function during middle childhood.

12.2

How do attention, memory, and executive function develop in middle childhood?

Attention in Middle Childhood

The ability to sustain attention and avoid distractions increases greatly when children move into middle childhood. This ability has been linked to achievement in both math and reading (Anobile, Stievano, & Burr, 2013; Franceschini, Gori, Ruffino, Pedrolli, & Facoetti, 2012).

One aspect of cognitive functioning that affects attention at this age is processing speed, or the speed at which we can take in information (Demetriou, Christou, Spanoudis, & Platsidou, 2002; Kail & Ferrer, 2007). Processing speed has generally been found to increase throughout childhood and adolescence, possibly because of an increase in the efficiency of communication between neurons within the brain (Kail, 2000).

A second, related cognitive function is automaticity, the process by which skills become so well practiced that we can do them without much conscious thought, freeing up processing capacity for other tasks. Think of a time when you were learning a complex skill, like driving a car with standard transmission, and you needed to focus all your attention on what you were supposed to do and when you were supposed to do it. As you became more skilled these actions became more automatic and you did not need to think consciously about each step (A. Diamond, 2006). We see this process at work in the way children learn to count or recognize words. At first, these cognitive tasks take a good deal of effort on the child's part, but over time they become so automatic that they no longer take as much processing capacity. Children move from focusing their attention on the laborious process of sounding out letters to reading words and entire sentences for comprehension.

Processing speed The efficiency with which one can perform cognitive tasks.

Automaticity The process by which skills become so well practiced that you can do them without much conscious thought.

Short-term memory Brief, temporary storage of information in memory.

Memory in Middle Childhood

Short-term memory refers to brief, temporary storage of information, such as recall of a string of numbers shortly after it is given to you. This information quickly disappears unless it is actively moved into long-term memory. Short-term memory has limits both in how long we remember something and in how much information we can remember at one time. Working memory is a combination of short-term memory and attentional control (Tulsky et al., 2013). It allows you to briefly store information while you are manipulating it, such as when you are told a string of numbers and then asked to say them backwards.

To see one of the ways working memory has been assessed in children, try **Active Learning: Working Memory.**

Active Learning

Working Memory

To see how working memory has been assessed in children (Gaillard, Barrouillet, Jarrold, & Camos, 2011), get a piece of paper large enough to cover a page in this book and cut a hole about 1/2 inch high and 2 inches wide about halfway down the paper. Line up the left edge of the opening so you can see the START button below in the window. Slide the paper down so you can see the first letter in the line below. Read the letter out loud and then quickly move down to the next row and add 1 to each number appearing in that row, saying each result out loud. Continue with each letter and series of numbers, covering the letters after you have read them out loud. When you reach STOP at the end of the series, try to recall the letters you read in the order they were presented.

Gaillard et al. (2011) report that third graders remembered on average two letters, while sixth graders remembered between three and four. How effective were you at keeping the letters in mind briefly while you carried out the addition? If you found this task difficult, the reason is that the brain has difficulty processing information (adding numbers), while maintaining memory for a new stimulus (the letters) at the same time. When attention is diverted from the letters to perform the addition, the memory trace decays (Gaillard et al., 2011). ∎

	START	
	G	
7	2	5
	R	
3	6	7
	M	
1	4	5
	V	
3	8	2
	C	
9	1	6
	STOP	

One factor underlying the growth in working memory is the general increase in information processing speed we discussed earlier. A second factor is that children develop a number of encoding strategies that help them store and retrieve information, and these strategies improve in complexity and efficiency as children get older (Ghetti & Angellini, 2008). By age 7, children begin to use active strategies to maintain memory (Camos & Barrouillet, 2011), and spontaneous use grows throughout middle childhood (Schneider, 2002).

Encoding is important because it prepares information for memory storage. The more carefully information is encoded and stored away, the greater the likelihood that you will later be able to find and retrieve it when you need it. We look here at two of the encoding strategies children use as their techniques become increasingly sophisticated: grouping and elaboration.

If you can group pieces of information together while you learn them, you are more likely to be able to retrieve and use the information later. To remember a list that contains the words *horse, rose, hammer, bus, pig, cow, tulip, saw, airplane, wrenches, lily,* and *train,* you can group items into conceptual categories. Horses, pigs, and cows are animals; hammers, saws, and wrenches are tools; roses, tulips, and lilies are flowers; and buses, airplanes, and trains are modes of transportation. Another way to encode the words is by the settings in which you find these items: a farm for the animals, a workshop for the tools, a garden for the flowers, and an airport for the vehicles.

Another memory strategy you can use for organizing information you need to remember is called elaboration. The idea here is to create extra connections that can tie bits of information together, through the use of images or sentences. For instance, if you need to remember to buy lemons on the way home, you could picture yourself walking to the parking lot wearing lemons on your feet instead of shoes. As you walk to the parking lot after your classes, this odd picture should easily come to mind. If you were taking a course on anatomy and needed to remember that arteries are thick and elastic and carry blood that is rich in oxygen from the heart, you could make up a sentence such as "Art(ery) was thick around his middle so he had to wear trousers with an elastic waistband" (McPherson, 2001).

VIDEO LINK 12.2
Encoding Strategies

Elaboration A memory strategy that involves creating extra connections, like images or sentences, which can tie information together.

Knowledge Base

As children learn more about the world, they build their knowledge base. This has implications for memory because it becomes easier to store away and recall information when you can make many connections between new information and previously learned information. Several research studies have found that children who are already experts in a subject are able to remember more information related to the subject of their expertise than children who are not experts and increasing children's knowledge base on a particular subject results in better memory for new, related information (Blasi, Bjorklund, & Soto, 2003; Schneider, Bjorklund, & Maier-Bruckner, 1996).

You have seen this effect in action if you know a child who has become fascinated with dinosaurs or baseball statistics, or who knows everything imaginable about Harry Potter. These experts quickly digest any new information they encounter about their favorite subject and can remember and use it immediately with little effort. Likewise, your professor for this course can integrate new information about child development into his or her knowledge base more quickly and with less effort than you are likely to be able to do. By the end of the course, however, your expanding knowledge base will allow you to understand and remember any new information about child development more effectively than you could have before you studied this topic.

False Memories

There are several different types of false memories. One type is memory of an event that never happened that we described in

Building a knowledge base. This boy has built a large knowledge base about coins of the world. If he were given new coins to add to his collection, he would be able to remember these coins much more quickly than someone who does not have this background information. ■

Chapter 9 in which young children in an experiment became convinced they had taken a hot air balloon ride even though they never had. Another type of false memory, called false recognition, is more common in older children. Older children may create this type of memory when they remember the gist of what they experience rather than the specific details (Brainerd & Reyna, 2004). **Active Learning: Creating False Memories** will give you a chance to develop a false memory.

Active Learning

Creating False Memories

Cover the list of words in the right column on this page. Read the list on the left-hand side of the page, then cover that list and look at the list on the right side. Circle the words on the second list that you saw on the first list.

desk	blackboard
pen	pencil
blackboard	eraser
eraser	orange
PowerPoint	teacher
teacher	desk
student	grandfather

STOP: Don't read any further until you've tried this activity. Then look at the discussion written upside down below.

■ Did you mistakenly identify "pencil" as one of the words that you saw? If you did, you had a false memory, based on the fact that you knew that all the words you initially saw were related to the concept of school. Therefore, you mistakenly "remembered" "pencil" as one of the words you saw in the first list.

T/F #1
It is more difficult to fool a school age child than a younger child into thinking he remembers something he never actually saw.
False

Fuzzy trace theory The theory that there are two memory systems: a systematic, controlled memory for exact details and an automatic, intuitive memory for the gist, or meaning, of events.

Although you might think younger children are more likely to come up with false memories than older children or adults, in the case of false recognition the opposite is often true. Holliday, Brainerd, and Reyna (2011) showed 7- and 11-year-old children lists of words related to each other conceptually, such as *bed* and *dream* that related to the concept of *sleep*. The older children were more likely to mistakenly identify a new related word as one they had previously seen. They understand the category into which the words fall and remember in a general way that "these words all have to do with sleep" rather than remembering the specific words presented. Because younger children do not place the individual words into conceptual categories, they are more likely to remember individual words.

Brainerd, Reyna, and their colleagues describe this as the fuzzy trace theory. They believe there are two ways in which we remember. One is the intuitive, automatic way they describe as the fuzzy trace memory, while the other is a deliberate, strategic way, such as the use of strategies we described earlier (Brainerd & Reyna, 2004). Although children and adults of all ages use both types of memory, young children are more likely than older children or teens to have very specific, verbatim memories. Older children are more likely to have extracted the meaning of an event and then remembered the gist of it rather than each specific detail.

Executive Function

As we have learned, executive function is the aspect of brain organization that coordinates attention and memory and controls behavioral responses to help us attain our goals (Blair et al., 2005). Although its exact definition and components are subject to much debate, there is evidence that this form of top-down cognitive control is characterized by three abilities: cognitive flexibility, inhibitory control, and working memory (Weintraub et al., 2013). As you also have learned, executive function is linked to the development of the prefrontal cortex of the brain, which continues through adolescence.

Executive function is related to achievement in school and may even predict school success more accurately than IQ (Blair & Razza, 2007). A number of factors influence its development, including the socioeconomic status of a child's family. Children from poor families are at greater risk of difficulties with executive function (Raver, Blair, & Willoughby, 2013), which have been linked to ADHD and other disorders that include impulse and attention problems (Weintraub et al., 2013). Interventions can improve the executive functioning of children at greatest risk (Rueda, Posner, & Rothbart, 2005).

While executive function is related to academic achievement, it also has implications for performance of everyday tasks. Dawson and Guare (2013) provide the list of tasks shown in Table 12.1 that require executive function, showing the approximate age at which each task can reasonably be expected.

We have already examined one aspect of executive function: working memory. Now we look at the other two: cognitive flexibility and inhibitory control.

Cognitive Flexibility

Cognitive flexibility is the ability to switch focus as needed to complete a task. The National Institutes of Health has recently developed a set of tests to assess executive function across the life span. The task chosen to assess cognitive flexibility is the Dimensional Change Card Sort, in which children are asked to sort cards by one criterion (such as shape) and then switch to another (such as color) (Zelazo et al., 2013). See Figure 12.1 on page 399 for an illustration of this type of test. Cognitive flexibility improves through middle childhood.

Cognitive flexibility The ability to switch focus as needed to complete a task.

Inhibitory Control

Toddlers often grab toys from each other, but by age 6 most children are able to control their impulse to grab at something they want. Their developing inhibitory control also includes the ability to stop more automatic cognitive responses to do what is necessary to carry out a task correctly (A. Diamond, 2006). This type of ability is measured by the well-known Stroop Test. In a very simplified form, this test requires that you say the color in which each of the following words is written: blue, **green**, purple, red. You should have read this as "green, purple, red, blue." Did you have some difficulty saying the color of the words rather than reading the word itself? Reading is very automatic, so it takes effort to inhibit your tendency to read the words rather than look at the color. In a classic study, Comalli, Wapner, and Werner (1962) found that the time taken to read these colors correctly declined rapidly between 7 and 17 years of age, showing the increasing efficiency of inhibitory control through middle childhood and adolescence.

Inhibitory control The ability to stop more automatic cognitive responses to do what is needed to carry out a task correctly.

JOURNAL ARTICLE 12.1
Stroop Effect

> ### Check Your Understanding
>
> 1. What are processing speed and automaticity?
> 2. Compare short-term and working memory.
> 3. How do children encode information?
> 4. What is fuzzy trace memory?
> 5. What are three aspects of executive function?

TABLE 12.1   Developmental list of executive function skills

Preschool

- Run simple errands (e.g., "Get your shoes from the bedroom").
- Tidy bedroom or playroom with assistance.
- Perform simple chores and self-help tasks with reminders (e.g., clear dishes from table, brush teeth, get dressed).
- Inhibit behaviors: don't touch a hot stove; don't run into the street; don't grab a toy from another child; don't hit, bite, push, etc.

Kindergarten–Grade 2

- Run errands (two to three step directions).
- Tidy bedroom or playroom.
- Perform simple chores, self-help tasks; may need reminders (e.g., make bed).
- Bring papers to and from school.
- Complete homework assignments (20-minute maximum).
- Decide how to spend money (allowance).
- Inhibit behaviors: follow safety rules, don't swear, raise hand before speaking in class, keep hands to self.

Grades 3–5

- Run errands (may involve time delay or greater distance, such as going to a nearby store or remembering to do something after school).
- Tidy bedroom or playroom (may include vacuuming, dusting, etc.).
- Perform chores that take 15–30 minutes (e.g., clean up after dinner, rake leaves).
- Bring books, papers, assignments to and from school.
- Keep track of belongings when away from home.
- Complete homework assignments (1 hour maximum).
- Plan simple school project such as book reports (select book, read book, write report).
- Keep track of changing daily schedule (i.e., different activities after school).
- Save money for desired objects, plan how to earn money.
- Inhibit/self-regulate: behave when teacher is out of the classroom; refrain from rude comments, temper tantrums, bad manners.

Grades 6–8

- Help out with chores around the home, including both daily responsibilities and occasional tasks (e.g., emptying dishwasher, raking leaves, shoveling snow); tasks may take 60–90 minutes to complete. Baby-sit younger siblings or for pay.
- Use system for organizing schoolwork, including assignment book, notebooks, etc. Follow complex school schedule involving changing teachers and changing schedules.
- Plan and carry out long-term projects, including tasks to be accomplished and reasonable timeline to follow; may require planning multiple large projects simultaneously.
- Plan time, including after school activities, homework, family responsibilities; estimate how long it takes to complete individual tasks and adjust schedule to fit.
- Inhibit rule breaking in the absence of visible authority.

High School

- Manage schoolwork effectively on a day-to-day basis, including completing and handing in assignments on time, studying for tests, creating and following timelines for long-term projects, and making adjustments in effort and quality of work in response to feedback from teachers and others (e.g., grades on tests, papers).
- Establish and refine a long-term goal and make plans for meeting that goal.
- Make good use of leisure time, including obtaining employment or pursuing recreational activities during the summer.
- Inhibit reckless and dangerous behaviors (e.g., use of illegal substances, sexual acting out, shoplifting, or vandalism).

SOURCE: Dawson & Guare (2013).

FIGURE 12.1 The Dimensional Change Card Sort task measures cognitive flexibility

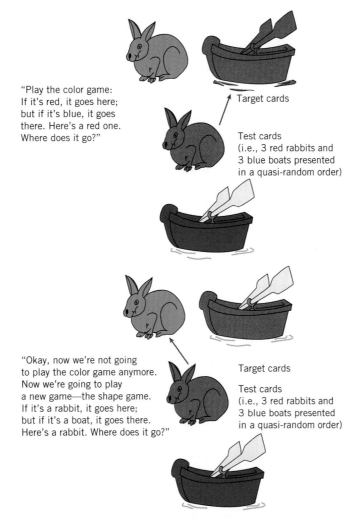

"Play the color game: If it's red, it goes here; but if it's blue, it goes there. Here's a red one. Where does it go?"

Target cards

Test cards (i.e., 3 red rabbits and 3 blue boats presented in a quasi-random order)

"Okay, now we're not going to play the color game anymore. Now we're going to play a new game—the shape game. If it's a rabbit, it goes here; but if it's a boat, it goes there. Here's a rabbit. Where does it go?"

Target cards

Test cards (i.e., 3 red rabbits and 3 blue boats presented in a quasi-random order)

In the task above, children are shown the blue rabbit and the red boat and told to match a series of pictures by color first (red rabbit goes with the red boat) and then subsequently on shape (red rabbit goes with blue rabbit). If the child can switch successfully from the first task to the second, he is then told to match by color if there is a black border around the object or by shape if there is not.

SOURCE: Zelazo (2006).

Language Development in Middle Childhood

Describe the progression of language development, including literacy, in middle childhood.

Language becomes increasingly sophisticated in school-age children. They learn that words are not the same as what they represent, a new understanding that allows them to comprehend both verbal humor and sarcasm. Children are now fully engaged in applying their language skills to learning to read and write. We discuss these processes as well as the problems that occur for some children who have difficulty learning these important skills. Finally, some children must also deal with learning a new language, and we discuss the ways in which the education system helps these students.

Metalinguistic Ability

The understanding that words are not the same as what they stand for is the basis for metalinguistic ability, which enables children to begin to think about language and how to use it (Pan, 2005). Try **Active Learning: Metalinguistic Awareness** to see how children

Metalinguistic ability The ability to think about and talk about language.

in middle childhood start to appreciate words as words (for example, "I like the sound of the word *brussels sprouts*, even though I don't like to eat them.").

ACTIVE LEARNING
VIDEO 12.1
Metalinguistic Awareness

Active Learning

Metalinguistic Awareness

To see whether children at various ages understand that a word is not the same as what it refers to, ask the child, "What are your favorite things?" and then ask, "What are your favorite words?" For each response to each question, ask why it is her favorite. Compare your child's responses with those of classmates who interviewed children at different ages. Preschoolers are not likely to differentiate words from the things they refer to; they are likely to say their favorite word is *lollipop* because they like the candy itself. Children in middle childhood are more likely to know the word is not the same as what it represents. They may say they like the word *lollipop*, but their reason is that they like the sounds the word makes (Pan, 2005). ■

Their new metalinguistic abilities allow children to use language in new ways. For example, humor takes on a new dimension, as in this example:

Knock, knock.

Who's there?

Lettuce.

Lettuce who?

Lettuce in, we're hungry!

As we can see from this example, many jokes require a fairly sophisticated understanding of language and of the fact that words can sound alike but indicate very different things.

School-age children also develop the ability to use words to mean something beyond their literal meaning. For example, they can use metaphors such as *School is a ball!* or *Time is money*. They also begin to use irony or sarcasm, in which the speaker means the opposite of what he is really saying. For example, Filippova and Astington (2010) asked school-age children to respond to a scenario in which Billy helps his mom empty the dishwasher and breaks a plate. His mom says, "You sure ARE a GREAT helper!" Although 5-year-olds did not understand that the mother was not really complimenting Billy, 7- and 9-year-olds understood the sarcasm.

Reading in School-Age Children

Children begin to acquire the skills of conventional literacy as they move from kindergarten to first grade. **Journey of Research: What's the Best Way to Learn to Read?** describes the approaches and debates that have surrounded this question over the years.

Phonics (or basic skills) approach An approach to teaching reading that starts with basic elements like letters and phonemes and teaches children that phonemes can be combined into words before moving on to reading as a whole.

Whole language instruction A way to teach reading that emphasizes understanding the meaning of words from the context in which they appear.

. . . .

JOURNEY OF RESEARCH   *What's the Best Way to Learn to Read?*

There has been quite a debate over the years about which is the best way to teach children how to read. Two widely used approaches are the phonics or basic skills approach, which focuses on letter-sound relationships, and whole language instruction, which focuses on using reading materials that are inherently interesting to the child (Education Week, 2004).

Children traditionally learned to read using what today is called authentic literature, such as the Bible or literary classics. However, in the 1930s, U.S. schools began using books specifically designed to teach children how to read, called basal readers. They contained a limited vocabulary that was built gradually (a first-grade reader used only 300 words) and a great deal of repetition (Moran, 2000), so students would easily learn to recognize all the words. New words were added slowly and repeated frequently after they were introduced. Perhaps you are familiar with another children's book that uses this same look-say approach. Theodor Seuss Geisel (better known as Dr. Seuss) was asked by his publisher to create a children's primer that used only 225 "new reader" vocabulary words. The result was the publication in 1957 of one of the most popular children's books ever, *The Cat in the Hat* (Dr. Seuss Enterprises, 2002–2004).

However, basal readers fell out of favor in the 1970s as phonics became the dominant approach to teaching reading (Carbo, 1996). The phonics approach is a *bottom-up approach* because it starts with basic elements like letters and phonemes and moves up to words before advancing to reading (Armbruster, Lehr, & Osborn, 2001). Children learn that words are composed of separate sounds or phonemes that can be combined into words; for example, they learn the sounds associated with the letters *c* and *a* and *t* before they combine those sounds into the word *cat*. They learn to sound words out by breaking them down into their phonemes (Texas Education Agency, 2004). It is equally important that children be able to break down a word like *chat* into its phonemes *ch – a – t* (recall that phonemes are not the same as letters). Phonics emphasizes building these skills through exercises and practice. The phonics approach has been shown to be effective with at-risk students when they are first learning to read (Moustafa, 2001), and phonological skills are considered by some to be the best predictor of children's success in learning to read (Bingham & Pennington, 2007).

In the 1990s, however, the whole language approach gained favor over phonics in the educational community (Pearson, 2004). Whole language is a *top-down approach* that emphasizes understanding the meaning of words from the context in which they appear (Armbruster et al., 2001). Advocates draw a parallel between this way of learning to read and the way children naturally learn spoken language (Armbruster et al., 2001). In a language-rich environment, children first learn individual words to represent objects, actions, or desires and then learn to put the individual words together into meaningful sentences. In this view, the purpose of reading is to extract meaning from the text rather than to decode individual letters, phonemes, and syllables (Ryder, Tunmer, & Greaney, 2008).

The whole language approach returned to an emphasis on authentic literature that had an inherent interest for children rather than on books built around teaching a set of reading skills. However, this change did not always sit well with teachers, who knew students benefit from instruction and that it was not enough to immerse them in literature and expect them to figure out the principles of reading on their own. Not only did reading suffer, but so did the students' mastery of subject content because many had difficulty reading textbooks (Pearson, 2004). By the end of the 1990s, the effectiveness of the whole language approach was being questioned, as much by politicians emphasizing accountability in schools as by educators critical of the negative effect this approach had on students' performance in subjects other than reading.

In 2001, the National Institute of Child Health and Human Development, together

Learning to read. This teacher is conducting a phonics lesson. A recent study by the U.S. Department of Education concluded that phonics instruction contributes significantly to children's mastery of reading. ∎

John Prieto/The Denver Post via Getty Images

Balanced reading approach An approach to teaching reading that combines elements of the whole language approach (which emphasizes comprehension and meaning) with elements of the phonics approach (which emphasizes decoding of words).

AUDIO LINK 12.1
Common Core Reading

T/F #2
One third of U.S. fourth graders are not reading at even a basic level.
True

Knowledge telling A style of writing (typical of younger children) in which the writer proceeds with little or no evidence of planning or organization of ideas, with the goal of telling as much as he knows about a topic.

Knowledge transforming A style of writing in which the goal is to convey a deeper understanding of a subject by taking information and transforming it into ideas that can be shared with a reader.

with the U.S. Department of Education, convened a panel of reading experts who were charged with surveying the scientific literature on reading. The panel conducted a meta-analysis of 38 studies and found "solid support for the conclusion that systematic phonics instruction makes a more significant contribution to children's growth in reading than do alternative programs providing unsystematic or no phonics instruction" (National Reading Panel, 2000, Section 2, p. 45). The report almost immediately came under criticism (see Camilli, Vargas, & Yurecko, 2003; Garan, 2001; Shanahan, 2004; Yatvin, 2002).

Where do we stand today? Although there still is controversy about which approach is best, support is growing for a balanced reading approach that combines elements of the whole language and the phonics approaches (Pearson, 2004). Children not only need to be able to decode words, but they also need to comprehend the meaning of what they read. However, the balance between these two skills might change from one situation to another. For instance, the emphasis on phonics might be greater early in the process of learning to read and shift gradually to a whole language approach as the need to read for comprehension becomes greater. ∎

Whichever approach—or combination of approaches—schools adopt to teach reading, there is reason for optimism that reading ability is getting better, but there still is a great deal of room for improvement. Results from the 2013 National Assessment of Educational Progress showed some modest gains from earlier assessments for fourth-grade students (National Center for Education Statistics [NCES], 2013b). In this sample, 33% of fourth-grade public school students were reading below what is considered a *basic* level (partial mastery of prerequisite knowledge and skills), 68% were reading at or above the basic level, 35% at or above a level considered *proficient* (solid academic performance), and 8% at an *advanced* level (superior performance).

Writing Skills

In the early elementary grades, children begin to learn and apply conventional spelling rules (such as adding the suffix -*ed* to a word to form the past tense) and to learn more about the typical patterns of occurrence of certain letters in their written language (Kemp & Bryant, 2003). The eventual goal is for the process of spelling to become automatic (Rittle-Johnson & Siegler, 1999) so remembering how to spell a word is very quick and very accurate.

However, writing is more than correctly shaping letters on a piece of paper or stringing words together. We use writing to communicate our ideas, so writing also must include composition skills. Children in the early elementary grades may write about a topic by simply tying together a series of statements that describe the facts but there is an important difference between this knowledge telling and the knowledge transforming that adolescents and adults do (Alamargot & Chanquoy, 2001). When you rely on knowledge telling, you proceed with little or no evidence of planning or organization of ideas with the goal of telling as much as you know about the topic on which you are writing. In knowledge transforming, however, the goal is to transform information into *ideas* that you can share with your reader so the reader understands and learns from them. It attempts to convey a deep understanding of the subject. As children move through middle childhood, their ability to do this increases.

Communication Disorders

Children vary widely in the age at which they reach language milestones. However when children begin school, teachers and other school staff may recognize language-related problems that have gone unnoticed or need continued attention. The *DSM-5* (APA,

2013) identifies several communication disorders that affect children's ability to listen, speak, and use language in their social communications and in school:

- **Language disorder** causes both the child's understanding of language (receptive) and the ability to use language (expressive) to be substantially below his performance on a standardized measure of nonverbal intelligence. The child has a limited vocabulary and has difficulty using tense correctly, recalling words, or producing sentences of the length and complexity expected of a child of that age. In addition, the child has difficulty understanding words or sentences.
- **Speech-sound disorder** causes difficulty producing sounds or using sounds correctly for the child's age (for example, the child substitutes one sound for another). The child's speech is difficult to understand as a result and this interferes with social and academic skills.
- **Childhood-onset fluency disorder or stuttering** is a disorder in which the child has difficulty with fluency and time patterning of speech. The child may repeat sounds or syllables, repeat whole words, pause within a word, or pause in speech.
- **Social or pragmatic communication disorder** results in difficulty with both verbal and nonverbal communication. The child does not use communication appropriately in different situations. For example, the child does not greet others, does not change the way she communicates to a young child or to an adult, has trouble taking conversational turns or explaining misunderstandings, and cannot understand humor or metaphors that rely on multiple meanings of the same word.

Any child (or adult, for that matter) might show any of these language problems from time to time, but we wouldn't consider this a disorder unless the problems are persistent, the child's language is substantially below that expected for a child of the same age, and the problem interferes with other aspects of the child's life, such as her ability to communicate with others or her performance in school. Because some studies have found that language disorders are associated with difficulties in parent-child interaction and in social-emotional development, it is important that we identify and treat them as early as possible so we don't let secondary problems develop (Desmarais, Sylvestre, Meyer, Bairati, & Rouleau, 2008).

Bilingualism and Bilingual Education

Learning to speak a language is a complex cognitive task, so learning to speak two different languages is even more cognitively complex. For this reason, parents sometimes wonder whether being bilingual is so demanding that it will hurt a child's overall cognitive development. Fortunately this does not appear to be the case and there is evidence that in some ways bilingualism may actually enhance cognitive abilities. Many people around the world speak more than one language, and a growing body of research on bilingualism indicates that parents do *not* need to worry about having their children learn two languages at the same time at an early age (Bialystok & Viswanathan, 2009; Kovács & Mehler, 2009; Sorace, 2006). Although there is evidence that bilingual children have smaller vocabularies in each language than monolingual children (Bialystok & Craik, 2010; Bialystok, Craik, Green, & Gollan, 2009), they reach language milestones at approximately the same age (Petitto et al., 2001), and learning a second language at a young age makes it more likely the child will speak it without a detectable accent and will be proficient in using the language (Huang, 2014).

Bilingual children and adults may also have advantages in some areas of cognitive function, particularly executive function (Barac & Bialystok, 2012; Bialystok, 2011). Bialystok and Viswanathan (2009) reported that bilingual 8-year-old children demonstrated more skill than monolingual children on tasks that required the ability to inhibit

Language disorder A disorder in which a child's understanding and use of language is significantly below his nonverbal intelligence.

Speech-sound disorder Difficulty producing or using sounds at an age-appropriate level.

Childhood-onset fluency disorder or stuttering Difficulty with fluency and time patterning of speech.

Social or pragmatic communication disorder Difficulty with appropriate use of both verbal and nonverbal communication.

VIDEO LINK 12.3
Stuttering

T/F #3
When a young child learns two languages at the same time, the extra effort it takes to learn the second language slows down the child's general cognitive development.
False

Bilingual classrooms. Many children in U.S. classrooms speak more than one language. The American educational system has adapted to this diversity through a variety of programs designed to teach English as a second language (ESL). ■

a response when necessary and the ability to be cognitively flexible and to shift focus from one task to another. These abilities begin to develop much earlier in bilingual children. Differences in executive function even appear in preverbal infants who are from bilingual homes. After infants from monolingual and bilingual homes had learned to anticipate an event based on a verbal clue, when the clue changed the infants from bilingual homes were able to more easily shift to a new response (Kovács & Mehler, 2009).

Research also has found that bilingual children have an advantage in solving problems that require ignoring irrelevant or misleading information, have greater mental flexibility and greater creativity, are better at scientific problem solving, and have better concept formation (Andreou & Karapetsas, 2004; Bialystok, 2001). In other words, they have metalinguistic skills that allow them to understand and think about language in a more advanced way, including an understanding of the relative nature of language (for instance, they understand that the same object can be called by different names in different languages). However, on other measures there are no differences between monolingual children and bilingual children, and in some cases monolingual children have the advantage (Bialystok, 2007).

Thus far, we have focused on children who have already achieved competence in two languages. However, in the United States there are over 4.6 million children for whom English is not the first language, or the language spoken in their home or neighborhood. The vast majority of children with limited English proficiency speak Spanish as their first language, followed by Vietnamese, Chinese, Hmong, and Arabic (U.S. Department of Education, 2013). When these children get to school, they are generally expected to understand and speak English. There has been much debate about what is the best way to handle this situation and help ensure that these bilingual learners will be successful in school. At some times in history our educational system has accommodated bilingualism, at times there has been opposition to it, and at still other times it has been largely ignored (Menken & Solorza, 2014). The original assumption was that non-English speakers would want to be assimilated into the great American melting pot and would try to learn English as quickly as they could, so the educational system wouldn't need to do anything special to help them. However, this turned out not always to be the case. For instance, in the 18th and 19th centuries, immigrants often lived in their own communities and ran their own schools in which instruction was given in their native language (Public Broadcasting Service [PBS], 2001).

Over time, virtually all bilingual education in public schools was eliminated (PBS, 2001), but the tide turned again in the 1960s against a backdrop of desegregation in public schools and the civil rights movement (Crawford, 1995). By the mid-1960s, immigrant populations were increasingly demanding instruction in their native language and the incorporation of their culture into the curriculum. In the years that followed, the need for language services for children who were not native English speakers continued to grow. By the 1980s, 40% of the U.S. population consisted of minority-language speakers (PBS, 2001). Today an estimated 5 million children with limited English proficiency are enrolled in U.S. schools, and they are the fastest-growing segment of the school-age population (Uro & Barrio, 2013).

Programs designed to teach English to children who are not native speakers have taken a variety of forms in the United States. Some of the most common are the following:

- **Immersion programs** in which the students are taught academic subjects in English, with teachers tailoring the language they use to the current language level of their students.
- **English as a second language (ESL) pull-out programs** in which students spend part of the day in a separate classroom designed specifically to teach English and there is no accommodation for their native language in their regular classrooms.
- **Transitional bilingual education programs** in which the students receive some instruction in their native language while they also receive concentrated instruction in learning English. The goal of transitional programs is to prepare the students to *transition* to regular classes in English as soon as possible, so they do not fall behind their peers in content areas such as math, science, and social studies.
- **Developmental bilingual programs** that build on students' skills in their native language while they learn English as a second language. Students initially receive instructions in the core subjects in their native language but receive instruction in art, physical education, and music in English. As soon as they have sufficient skills, English is used for their instruction in the core subjects as well. Students typically remain in these programs longer than in traditional transition programs, but they continue learning English throughout their time in the program.
- Less frequently used than other alternatives is a **two-way immersion program** in which children who are native speakers of English and children who are non-native speakers work together in a classroom where *both* majority and minority languages are used. This type of program requires highly trained and skilled teachers who can support the development of both languages in their students in a language-integrated classroom (U.S. Department of Education, 2013).

It has been challenging to determine which approach might be considered best or most effective. Many programs are not pure forms of the approaches we have just described, so it becomes difficult to compare and evaluate programs that are actually hybrids of several approaches (Guglielmi, 2008). The intended goal of such programs has shifted from time to time as well, so the assessment of program effectiveness must change with the goal. For instance, if the goal is to assimilate recent immigrants into the English language and U.S. culture, an immersion approach fits well. On the other hand, if the goal is to promote multiculturalism, a dual language approach may be best (Ginn, 2008).

A committee of the National Research Council (1997) has recommended that rather than trying to find a one-size-fits-all solution, research needs to identify a range of educational approaches that can be tailored to the characteristics of the children in a specific community, while taking into account local needs and the resources available to support the language program.

Immersion programs Programs in which English language learners are taught academic subjects in English.

English as a second language (ESL) pull-out programs Programs in which students are taught English in a separate classroom.

Transitional bilingual education programs Programs in which English language learners receive some instruction in their native language while they also receive concentrated instruction in learning English.

Developmental bilingual programs Programs in which English language learners receive instruction in core subjects in their native language until they have the language skills to be instructed in English.

Two-way immersion program Programs in which children who are native speakers of English and children who are not work together in a classroom where both English and the children's other native language are used.

WEB LINK 12.1
Bilingual Education

Check Your Understanding

1. What do metalinguistic abilities allow children in middle childhood to do?
2. Compare knowledge telling and knowledge transforming.
3. What types of communication disorders are identified in middle childhood?
4. Describe the various types of bilingual education programs.

Intelligence

In this section, we talk about some of the important issues in the school context that affect student achievement. Student success can be determined by many different factors, from the intelligence and self-control of the individual to socioeconomic status and teacher expectations. We begin with a discussion of the role of intelligence. We examine

12.4

How does intelligence affect academic achievement in middle childhood?

whether intelligence is one ability or many different abilities and what effects intelligence may have on school achievement. As a part of this discussion, we describe how intelligence has been defined and measured over the years, and some of the controversies that have surrounded the use of intelligence tests.

How Do We Define Intelligence?

Intelligence Those qualities that help us adapt successfully so that we achieve our goals in life.

What is intelligence? A simple but useful definition suggested by Robert Sternberg (2002a) is that intelligence includes those qualities that help us adapt successfully to our environment so we achieve our goals in life, not just in school. That seems simple and straightforward, but keep in mind that when 24 prominent experts in the field were asked to define intelligence, they could not agree on a definition (Sternberg & Detterman, 1986).

One challenge when trying to define intelligence is deciding whether it is one ability or many. The idea of a single general intelligence, which has been called *g*, has a history that goes back to the very early days of intelligence testing (Gould, 1996). Some researchers accept the idea of a general intelligence factor but believe different abilities lie within it. For example, the Wechsler Intelligence Scale for Children (WISC), a widely used intelligence test, gives three scores: a total IQ, a verbal IQ, and a performance IQ. General intelligence has also been subdivided into fluid intelligence and crystallized intelligence. Fluid intelligence allows us to solve novel problems for which we have little training and is measured by how effectively we solve the problems and by how quickly. Crystallized intelligence, on the other hand, is a measure of the knowledge we already have that we can draw on to solve problems (Cattell, 1963). Research on brain function has supported the idea that these two separate types of intelligence exist. Performance on tasks requiring fluid intelligence has been linked with activity in the prefrontal cortex in the brain, while tasks requiring crystallized intelligence rely on specific frontal and posterior temporal and parietal areas of the brain (Nisbett et al., 2012).

Fluid intelligence Intelligence that allows us to quickly and effectively solve novel problems for which we have little training.

Crystallized intelligence What we already know and can draw on to solve problems.

However, some researchers believe there is no generalized intelligence that underlies all mental abilities. In the 1950s, J. P. Guilford proposed a theory of intelligence that encompassed 120 distinct abilities (Cianciolo & Sternberg, 2004). Researchers such as Howard Gardner and Robert Sternberg have described intelligence as a much smaller collection of separate and independent abilities, which we describe in more detail below. Thinking of intelligence as a collection of abilities suggests that someone could be strong in one area and weak in another because each type of intellectual ability operates somewhat independently.

To understand more about how intelligence has been conceptualized and measured in the field of education, read **Journey of Research: The History of Intelligence Tests.**

. . . .

JOURNEY OF RESEARCH *The History of Intelligence Tests*

The modern history of intelligence testing began in the early 1900s when Alfred Binet was asked by the French Minister of Public Instruction to develop a test for identifying students with mental difficulties who would need alternative teaching strategies to succeed in school (Wasserman, 2012). Before this time, students judged mentally deficient were simply kicked out of school. For example, Thomas Edison's teacher thought he was "addled," so he was not allowed to continue in the classroom and was taught at home (Detterman & Thompson, 1997, p. 1082).

Binet made modest claims for the test he developed. It was designed to reflect a child's level of performance on tasks similar to those required in school (van der Veer,

2007). An individual child's mental achievements were compared with those of other children of the same age who were performing well in school, and the comparison determined the child's mental age. In other words, a child of any age who performed on the test in a way typical for a 7-year-old had a mental age of 7.

Lewis Terman, a psychologist at Stanford University, standardized Binet's test on a sample of U.S. children and adapted it for use in schools in the United States. However, Terman began scoring the test not as a mental age, but as a single number representing the child's general level of intelligence, called the intelligence quotient or IQ. At that time the IQ score was calculated by dividing a child's mental age by her chronological age and then multiplying by 100. For example, if a 10-year-old scored at the 10-year-old level, her IQ score would be 10 (her mental age) divided by 10 (her chronological age) multiplied by 100, or IQ = 100. However, if another 10-year-old scored at the 12-year-old level, her IQ would be 12/10 × 100 = 120 (Wasserman, 2012).

Eventually researchers became concerned about using mental age as the basis for the IQ score so David Wechsler developed IQ tests for adults and children that were based on a deviation IQ (Wasserman, 2012), or how much the individual deviates from what is average for a person of the same age. To find a deviation IQ, researchers first administer an intelligence test to a very large sample of individuals of all ages to establish the norms for the test, or the expected scores for that population. For each specific age, the expected mean score is arbitrarily set to 100, with a standard deviation from the average score of 15 points. This ensures that most people will score between 85 points and 115 points on the test. As you move farther away from the average (that is, the greater the deviation from average), fewer and fewer people will score at those more extreme levels. When individuals take the WISC, their score is compared only to scores for others of the same age, and the IQ score indicates where they fall relative to the average performance for their age group. See Table 12.2 for sample questions that give an idea of what is included in the WISC.

It is crucial that the tests we use are both reliable (they produce the same or similar results each time they are used) and valid (they accurately measure what they claim to measure). In the 1960s, IQ tests were criticized as invalid because many in the educational community believed they systematically underestimated the true knowledge, skills, or aptitudes of certain children (Reynolds, 2000). Their argument was based on research that consistently found children from ethnic and racial minorities on average scored lower than other children (Hurn, 2002). This cultural test bias hypothesis claimed that items in the test were really measuring the experiences people have rather than any inherent characteristic or ability of the individual and that they are biased toward experiences of non-minority children. For example, if you were asked a question about snow, but you lived in a hot

Mental age The age level at which a child is performing on a test of mental ability.

Intelligence quotient (IQ) Originally a measure of intelligence calculated based on the ratio of a child's mental age to chronological age, largely replaced now by the deviation IQ.

Deviation IQ A measure of intelligence that is based on the individual's deviation from the norms for a given test.

Cultural test bias hypothesis The belief that standardized intelligence tests systematically underestimate the intelligence of minority groups because of bias built into the test.

AUDIO LINK 12.2
Cultural Test Bias

TABLE 12.2	Wechsler Intelligence Scale for Children (WISC)
Arithmetic	If 5 oranges cost 7 dollars, how much do 10 cost?
Vocabulary	What does "inconsistent" mean?
Block design	Use colored blocks to re-create a pattern.
Picture concepts	When shown a group of pictures, pick those that go together in some way.
Digit span	Remember increasingly long lists of numbers.
Digit span backward	Remember increasingly long lists of numbers and say them backward.

These are examples of subtests within the WISC and questions similar to those found on the actual test.

desert climate and had never had the chance to travel outside your area, you would feel the question was unfair to you compared to other children who had different life experience or had the chance to travel to different places. You might think that testing your intelligence by asking you this word is unfair. As a result of this controversy, psychologists attempted to develop intelligence tests that were culture-free, or at least culture-fair.

We have talked about whether an individual's abilities can be attributed to the person's inborn abilities or are a reflection of the person's experiences as an example of the nature/nurture debate. The controversy surfaced again in 1994 when Herrnstein and Murray published their book *The Bell Curve: Intelligence and Class Structure in American Life* in which they presented what they considered to be evidence of (in the words of critic Stephen Jay Gould, 1996, p. 34) "permanent and heritable differences" in IQ among individuals and, more specifically, among different racial groups.

The book stirred up so much controversy that the American Psychological Association set up a task force to respond to its claims (Neisser et al., 1996). This task force concluded that racial differences on IQ scores do exist, but the size of these differences was "well within the range of effect sizes that can be produced by environmental factors" (Neisser et al., 1996, p. 94) and that "there is certainly no . . . support for a genetic interpretation" (p. 97). In short, differences are more likely to be related to environmental issues than to inborn, genetic issues that are somehow connected with race. After a great deal of research and debate on this topic, today we can say that well-constructed and reliable standardized tests are not biased against native-born racial and ethnic minorities (Reynolds, 2000). Any differences found between different groups are not necessarily genetic because groups also have very different life experiences that can affect test performance.

When researchers looked separately at children in families of low socioeconomic status (SES) and those in families of middle to high SES in the United States, they found that most of the variability in IQ for low SES children is due to environmental influences, while IQ scores are largely determined by genes in higher SES groups (Turkheimer et al., 2003). Although differences in genetic potential among individuals or groups of individuals are likely, intelligence is one of those characteristics we described in Chapter 3 as not very deeply canalized. Whatever the genetic starting point, the environment has a substantial impact on the eventual outcome or end point for this characteristic. Where any individual ends up is determined by the quality of the environment and her experience in it, as well as other characteristics of the individual, such as her level of motivation or how hard she is willing to work to attain her goals. Although genes may roughly set an upper and lower limit, experiences, especially educational experiences, influence how much of that potential is fulfilled. When children grow up in poverty, their educational opportunities are limited. Just as a malnourished child may never express the genes that have the potential to make him 6 feet tall, a child with inadequate educational resources may not express the genes that would have increased his learning potential.

Despite the concerns raised about intelligence tests and their use over the years, we should keep in mind that Binet's original intent was to develop an assessment that would predict how a child was likely to do in school. Today's tests continue to do that well. They are valid and reliable predictors of school success (Ackerman, 2005). However, as we will see, they are not the only, or even the best, predictors of academic achievement. ■

IQ Scores and Academic Achievement

Although we have said scores on IQ tests do predict academic achievement, the prediction is far from perfect. In fact, other factors, such as self-control, may be better indicators. In a study by Duckworth and Seligman (2005), 164 children were given IQ tests at the beginning of the eighth grade, as well as a very simple test of self-control.

T/F #5
Intelligence as measured by IQ tests is determined by genetics for some groups of people and by environment for other groups. *True*

T/F #4
Well-constructed and reliable standardized intelligence tests are not biased against native-born racial and ethnic minorities. *True*

T/F #6
IQ tests are the best predictors we have of how well a child is going to do in school. *False*

They were given a dollar bill in an envelope and told they could either keep it or return it to the researchers and, if they returned it, they would receive $2 at the end of the week. For these children, evidence of self-control was twice as predictive of grades in school as their IQ scores. As you know, you sometimes need to exercise self-control and forego short-term pleasure to achieve long-term goals like academic success. The standardized tests used to assess intelligence don't typically measure factors like self-control.

Standardized Testing and Alternative Testing Methods

Most tests of intelligence are standardized tests. They are always administered and scored in the same way, and they are interpreted by comparing an individual's score to previously established age norms. There are a number of advantages to using standardized tests. Their norms and their degree of validity and reliability have been established by their developers. We have already discussed the concern that the tests may be biased against certain groups of students, but another concern is that test results can be influenced by a number of factors that are irrelevant to the test, for example, how the child is feeling that day, the child's motivation to do well on the test or not, and poor testing conditions such as a noisy testing room.

In response to the criticisms of standardized testing and with a desire to develop appropriate and specific educational plans for children, alternate forms of testing have been developed. One of those alternatives is dynamic assessment, based on Vygotsky's ideas about the zone of proximal development. Dynamic assessment attempts to measure the child's potential for change when the examiner intervenes and assists the child. This "potential to change" or modifiability can be measured by the number of hints a child needs to solve a problem he has previously failed and a second assessment of the child's ability after the assistance has been removed (Swanson, 2006–2014). The goal of dynamic assessment is to eliminate irrelevant factors that influence a child's performance, such as confusion on the child's part about what he or she is supposed to do. It is intended to supplement rather than replace standardized testing by providing additional information about the child's potential for change (Flanagan, Mascolo, & Hardy-Braz, 2006–2014).

A second alternative to standardized testing is authentic assessment, which places more emphasis on the process used to respond to the assessment than on the product (or answer) itself (Powers, 2006–2014). The content of an authentic assessment consists of complex problems that resemble real-life skills (Powers, 2006–2014). This approach has been advocated for student populations that are difficult to assess using standardized methods, including students with disabilities, very young children, and gifted students (VanTassel-Baska, 2014).

While the examiner in a standardized test is expected to administer the test in the exact same way to all individuals without interfering with the testing procedure in any way, the examiner for dynamic assessments or authentic assessments is an active participant who must have specialized training in the administration of this type of test. The test is given to only one child at a time. For these reasons, these tests are not widely used.

Authentic assessment A testing procedure that focuses on the process used in solving complex, real-life problems rather than the product that results from the process.

Alternate Views of Intelligence

Many critics of intelligence testing have argued that the kinds of abilities tested by most IQ tests are not the only ones related to success in modern society, and that no one type of intelligence underlies all others (that is, there is no g factor). Two of the most influential alternate contemporary theories have their origins in information processing theory. They are the theory of multiple intelligences and triarchic theory.

VIDEO LINK 12.4
Multiple Intelligences

Gardner's Theory of Multiple Intelligences

Howard Gardner proposed a theory of multiple intelligences, making the case that there are many different ways to express intelligence. He originally named seven types of intelligence but now includes two more, for a total of nine. However, he states, "there is not, and there never can be, a single irrefutable and universally accepted list of human intelligences" (Gardner, 1993, p. 60), so presumably his list may change and/or continue to grow.

To support the idea of separate intelligences, Gardner looked for evidence that each specific type resides largely in a different part of the brain that has a distinct way of processing information (Torff & Gardner, 1999). For example, a brain injury can impair one type while leaving others virtually unaffected. This means that following an injury to a specific part of the brain, a musician might lose the ability to speak but retain the ability to play music. Gardner argues that this supports the idea that the two intelligences (linguistic and musical) are relatively autonomous. As another example, we often see significant disparities of ability within a single individual. Gardner specifically points to special populations, such as savants or prodigies. Savants have low overall levels of attainment but exceptional ability in a very specific domain, like knowledge of the calendar or the ability to memorize the phone book. Likewise prodigies may be rather unremarkable in most areas but extremely gifted in one specific area such as playing a musical instrument or learning foreign languages.

Some critics disagree that there is strong evidence for nine different types of intelligence because there always is some degree of correlation between them (Klein, 1997). If they were truly independent as Gardner proposes, ability in one area would not correlate with ability in the others. Although certain functions are linked with certain parts of the brain, critics also point to the fact that few human activities rely on a single type of ability. A game of chess, for example, requires logical thought to plan your moves, spatial skills to help you visualize the board, and interpersonal skills to intuit the strategies your opponent is likely to use (Torff, 1996). Although these may be separate abilities, they need to work together in the process of completing the game.

Further, although Gardner (1999) has claimed that "accumulating neurological evidence is amazingly supportive of the general thrust of MI [multiple intelligences] theory" (p. 88), the neurological evidence we have to date shows that processing pathways in the brain are shared, not functionally isolated from each other (Waterhouse, 2006). In a critical review of the research on multiple intelligences, Waterhouse (2006) concludes that "to date there have been no published studies that offer evidence of the validity of the MI" (p. 208). A similar conclusion has been expressed by Allix (2000) and even by Gardner and Connell (2000). Proponents of the theory of multiple intelligences say it takes time for a new approach such as this to develop the methods needed to assess and validate it.

Despite critiques, Gardner's ideas about multiple intelligences have been widely accepted and implemented in education (Gardner & Traub, 2010; Waterhouse, 2006). One explanation for their being applied without the rigorous scientific examination we ordinarily expect is the fact that they simply make sense to many people. Waterhouse (2006) suggests that the theory of multiple intelligences seems more democratic than standard psychometric testing. Traditional intelligence tests appear to give a single estimate of a child's ability, whereas multiple intelligences offer the hope that every child will find some strength and distinctive talent.

Table 12.3 provides a brief definition of each of the nine types of intelligence on Gardner's list, together with examples of careers that could be based on each of these strengths. After looking at this table, try **Active Learning: Applying Multiple Intelligences** to see how you would apply Gardner's ideas in an educational setting.

| TABLE 12.3 | Gardner's multiple intelligences theory |

Type of intelligence	Description	Possible careers
Linguistic	The ability to use language	Public speakers and writers
Musical	The ability to make music	Composers and musicians
Logical-mathematical	The ability to reason about abstract concepts	Mathematicians and scientists
Spatial	The ability to see the world and then mentally manipulate or recreate what is seen	Engineers and artists
Bodily-kinesthetic	The ability to use your body effectively	Dancers and athletes
Interpersonal	Skill in interacting with other people	Sales representatives and politicians
Intrapersonal	The ability to understand your own emotions and thoughts and express them	Actors and poets
Naturalist	The ability to distinguish and categorize natural phenomena	Weather forecasters and park rangers
Existential	The ability to think about the ultimate questions of life and death	Philosophers and religious leaders

These are brief descriptions of the nine types of intelligence described by Howard Gardner and some possible careers associated with each type.

SOURCES: Gardner (1993); Gardner & Moran (2006).

Active Learning

Applying Multiple Intelligences

Imagine you are trying to teach a classroom of second graders about arithmetic. You know that within this class there are children with each type of intelligence Gardner has described. Decide how you would teach each one so he or she will best understand. For example, a child with high musical intelligence might learn best from a song about addition. Of course, in the real world, teachers cannot teach everything in nine different ways, but they can vary the ways they teach so all children will have a chance to learn using their own mental strengths. ■

Sternberg's Triarchic Theory of Intelligence

Robert Sternberg believes intelligence is related not only to success in school but also to success in life. He has said that "one's ability to achieve success depends on capitalizing on one's strengths and correcting or compensating for one's weaknesses through a balance of analytical, creative and practical abilities in order to adapt to, shape and select environments" (Sternberg, 2002a, p. 448). According to Sternberg's triarchic theory, living a successful life requires using these three types of intelligence—analytical, creative, and practical—to interact in the best possible way with one's particular environment.

Sternberg describes analytical intelligence as the one closest to g and the one prized highly in most schools. Creative intelligence is the ability to generate ideas and deal successfully with novelty. This type of intelligence is tested when children are asked to find as many possible solutions to a problem as they can rather than the one "correct"

WEB LINK 12.2
Triarchic Theory

Triarchic theory Sternberg's idea that intelligence represents a balance of analytical, creative, and practical abilities.

Analytical intelligence The type of intelligence that is the one closest to g or general intelligence and the one prized highly in most schools.

Creative intelligence The ability to generate ideas and to deal successfully with novelty (sometimes referred to as divergent thinking).

TABLE 12.4	Prompts used to teach and test memorization versus Sternberg's three types of intelligence	
Types of intelligence	**Prompts for teaching and testing**
Memory (the type of intelligence often emphasized in school)	Recall, recognize, match, verify, repeat
Analytical (Sternberg)	Analyze, evaluate, explain, compare and contrast, judge
Creative (Sternberg)	Create, explore, imagine, suppose, synthesize
Practical (Sternberg)	Put into practice, use, implement, apply

Schools have traditionally placed an emphasis on memorization, but Sternberg emphasizes intellectual skills beyond memorization. This table shows the kinds of questions used for teaching and assessment of each type of intelligence in his theory.

SOURCE: Sternberg (2002b).

Divergent thinking The ability to find as many possible solutions to a problem as possible rather than the one "correct" solution.

Practical intelligence The ability to solve everyday problems by changing yourself or your behavior to fit the environment better, changing the environment, or moving to a different environment in which you can be more successful.

Adaptive functioning A person's ability to function independently.

solution; it is sometimes referred to as divergent thinking. Practical intelligence allows you to solve everyday problems by changing yourself or your behavior to better fit the environment, changing the environment, or moving to a different environment in which you can be more successful. Although Sternberg's research has provided some support for the existence of these different types of intelligence, he admits the evidence is limited (Sternberg, 2003b; Sternberg, Castejón, Prieto, Hautamäki, & Grigorenko, 2001). Yet he has shown that learning is enhanced when teachers promote all these types of intelligence rather than emphasizing memory alone (Sternberg, 2002b). Table 12.4 illustrates the way teaching and assessment are different for each type.

Cognitive Deficits and Intellectual Gifts

12.5

How do we define intellectual disability, specific learning disorder, and giftedness?

Children's intellectual abilities vary in many ways. Some children fall at the lower range of general ability and are described as having an intellectual disability, while others fall at the upper range and are described as gifted and talented. Within the average range are some children with a specific learning disorder that limits their learning in particular ways. In this section, we describe these three variations that affect children's academic progress. Look at Figure 12.2 to see what the normal distribution of intelligence scores looks like.

Intellectual Disability

At the extreme low end are children who have an intellectual disability (APA, 2013). A score below 70 to 75 on a standard intelligence test is usually one of the criteria, in addition to overall deficits in cognitive functioning. The second important criterion is the child's ability to function independently, called adaptive functioning (APA, 2013). Limitations in adaptive behavior can hamper conceptual skills (such as reading and writing), social skills (such as handling interpersonal relationships), and practical skills (such as eating, dressing, and taking care of personal hygiene) (American Association of Intellectual and Developmental Disabilities [AAIDD],

FIGURE 12.2

Normal curve (distribution of IQ scores)

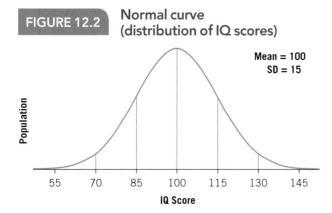

Mean = 100
SD = 15

IQ tests are designed so that the scores of most people fall near the midpoint (an IQ score of 100). As you move farther away from the center, there are fewer and fewer people at extremely high or extremely low scores.

SOURCE: Hart Research Associates (2011).

2013). A professional will use information from a variety of sources including interviews, observations, and informal assessments to compare the child's current level of functioning to that of other children of the same age (Biasini, Grupe, Huffman, & Bray, 1999). The third criterion for this diagnosis is that the condition begins before the age of 18.

By this comprehensive definition, about 1% of the population is considered to have intellectual disabilities (APA, 2013). A great deal can be done to help these children reach their full developmental potential through intervention programs and special education. Children who are intellectually disabled are able to learn new skills, but they do so more slowly than children with average or above-average abilities (Johnson & Walker, 2006).

We discussed a number of causes of intellectual disability in earlier chapters, including genetic causes such as Down syndrome and Fragile X syndrome, and environmental causes such as fetal alcohol syndrome, extreme malnutrition, and exposure to toxins such as lead or mercury, but professionals are able to identify a specific reason in only 25% of cases (U.S. National Library of Medicine, 2011). The more severe the intellectual disability, the more likely the child will also have other disabilities, such as impaired vision, hearing loss, cerebral palsy, or a seizure disorder (Centers for Disease Control and Prevention, 2005).

At one time children with intellectual disabilities were simply excluded from school, but the federal Individuals with Disabilities Education Act (IDEA) that you learned about in Chapter 8 now ensures they receive free and appropriate public education. Services are provided not only for children with intellectual disabilities, but also for those with "hearing impairments (including deafness), speech or language impairments, visual impairments (including blindness), serious emotional disturbance . . . , orthopedic impairments, autism, traumatic brain injury, other health impairments, or specific learning disabilities" and who need special education as a result (U.S. Department of Education, n.d.-a, para. 1).

Specific Learning Disorder

While intellectual disability affects general cognitive and adaptive functioning, many children have more specific difficulties with learning that are not linked to general intelligence (National Center for Learning Disabilities [NCLD], 2010). Between 5% and 15% of school-age children have difficulty with learning that is linked to a specific learning disorder (APA, 2013). In Chapter 11, we described some of the findings relating specific learning disorder to differences in brain development. In this section, we look at some of the cognitive deficits connected with these disorders as well as some of their effects. We again focus on problems with reading called dyslexia. Children with dyslexia have particular difficulty distinguishing or separating the sounds in spoken words, which creates problems when they are learning to spell and read written words (Council for Exceptional Children, 2009; Snowling & Hulme, 2011). Knowledge of letter-sound correspondence and phoneme awareness are the best predictors of a child's ability to learn to read (Duff & Clarke, 2011; Snowling & Hulme, 2011). Consequently, training children on these two abilities is central in successful attempts to intervene.

However, because the condition can vary in its nature and severity, it may be necessary to target specific reading skills or combine approaches, especially for students with the most severe disabilities (Snowling & Hulme, 2011). Evidence is accumulating that systematic training in phonics can improve a child's reading skills, although the size of the effect may not be large (Browder et al., 2006; Duff & Clarke, 2011), and even when reading accuracy improves, there may continue to be long-term problems with reading fluency and spelling (Snowling & Hulme, 2011). Early identification, before children begin to steadfastly avoid reading, and training embedded in a comprehensive literacy curriculum can benefit many children with reading difficulties.

T/F #7
Children with a learning disorder have normal intelligence. *True*

Children with a specific learning disorder face more than academic challenges in the classroom, so parents and teachers need to be sensitive to these other sources of stress in the child's life. The day-to-day expectations in a classroom are difficult for these children and can have a negative effect on their self-esteem (Alexander-Passe, 2006; NCLD, 2010). They may also lack the interpersonal and social skills that make it easy for others to make and keep friends, leading to feelings of loneliness (NCLD, 2010). Because children who are different can become a target for bullies, teachers and other school staff need to be particularly vigilant to protect them from harm to their self-esteem and physical and psychological well-being.

Although specific learning disorder cannot be cured, their effects on development can be reduced significantly with the proper educational support services. With help, children can work with their strengths and learn strategies to help them effectively deal with their disability. That is why the provision of special educational services is so important. Having a specific learning disorder does not mean children cannot achieve a great deal in their lives. You may know that actress Whoopi Goldberg, singer Solange Knowles, financier Charles Schwab, Olympic athlete Michael Phelps, and director Steven Spielberg each have a learning disorder (LD OnLine, 2008a, 2008b).

Giftedness

Gifted (or talented) children Children and youth who exhibit high performance capability in intellectual, creative, and/or artistic areas; possess an unusual leadership capacity; or excel in specific academic fields.

The other end of the continuum of cognitive ability represents children who are functioning at a very high level and have an extraordinary amount of potential for their development. These children are identified as gifted or talented. It has been difficult to arrive at a single, generally accepted definition of giftedness. We continue to rely primarily on measures of intellectual ability as the defining characteristic, even though giftedness includes a wide range of human abilities, talents, and accomplishments (McClain & Pfeiffer, 2012). Recent attempts to reconceptualize giftedness rely on a talent development model rather than seeing it as a "real" and permanent quality in the individual (Pfeiffer, 2012). In this view, giftedness is the ability to transform intellectual ability and talent into outstanding performance and innovation. It needs to be supported, encouraged, and nurtured for this to happen.

However, in contrast to the general agreement about the need to provide services to children with intellectual challenges, considerable debate and disagreement exist about the nature, amount, and type of services the educational system should provide to gifted children. When there has been some perceived threat to our country's status or well-being, such as the release of international statistics indicating that American children are lagging behind other nations in their academic achievement, there are calls for programs to support the development of our brightest children. When there is no such perceived threat, however, our traditional commitment to egalitarianism in our schools and fears of creating an elite class of students work against establishing and maintaining programs for gifted and talented students (Reis, 2004). This fear may be heightened by a chronic underrepresentation of Black and Latino students in gifted programs (Reis & Renzulli, 2010). When education budgets are tight, programs for the gifted are seen as a luxury (Reis, 2004). In general, the public's opinion seems to support special programs for gifted and talented youngsters as long as they do not reduce opportunities for average or below-average learners.

Because most classroom teachers report that they have never had training to tailor their teaching to accommodate

Gifted and talented programs. Programs for gifted and talented students may provide added educational enrichment. This girl rides on a hoverboard powered by a leaf blower as a way to learn about Newton's laws of motion. ■

Kelly Hunt

gifted students and few do so, a more effective way to teach gifted students may be to group them together for instruction geared to their level of ability (Reis & Renzulli, 2010). Special programs for gifted and talented students can take a variety of forms.

The enrichment approach covers the same curriculum as a typical class but in greater depth, breadth, or complexity. Enrichment teachers usually have a good deal of flexibility in structuring the students' exploration of the topics they cover. Many enrichment programs take place after school, on Saturdays, or during the summer and supplement the instruction the child receives in the regular classroom (Brody, 2005).

An accelerated program covers the standard curriculum, but more quickly than is typical as the student shows mastery of the material. A student who is advanced in a particular subject (for example, mathematics) might take that subject with a class at a higher grade level but remain in his or her regular grade for other subjects, or the student may be allowed to skip an entire grade to accelerate his or her progress in all subjects. Some people resist accelerated approaches because they fear children who complete their secondary schooling early will not yet be emotionally or socially ready to move on to a university to complete their education. However, the majority of studies that have looked at gifted children enrolled in accelerated programs have failed to find negative social or emotional outcomes (Lehman & Erdwins, 2004). Gifted students report feeling positively about themselves, do not feel socially isolated from their peers, and do not mind being identified as gifted (Boazman & Sayler, 2011; Sayler & Brookshire, 2004). On the other hand, they often report being bored, uninterested, and frustrated prior to being accelerated and were more satisfied emotionally and academically afterward (Vialle, Ashton, Carlon, & Rankin, 2001).

Outside the school environment, parents of gifted or talented children can do a great deal to foster and encourage their children's talents. James Alvino (1995) of the National Research Center on the Gifted and Talented at the University of Connecticut suggests that parents provide a rich learning environment for their children that allows for a lot of exploration but also help their children find a balance between their schoolwork and fun activities so they can manage their stress effectively. Adults should not have such high expectations that they lose sight of the fact that gifted children are, after all, still children.

Schools and Academic Achievement

Many aspects of the school environment affect children's academic achievement. We discuss the classroom environment, including the role of teachers, ability grouping and grade retention. Finally, we look at how boys and girls are doing in school.

Classroom Environment

Outside their family home, children spend the largest portion of their time in a school classroom. The most important structural feature in that environment is the teacher. The Center for Public Education (2005) has reviewed the literature on the effect of teacher quality on student achievement and reached these conclusions:

- Teacher quality is a more important influence on student performance than race, class, or the particular school the student is attending.
- The size of the teacher effect is substantial, especially for disadvantaged students. For example, the achievement gain for African American students with an effective teacher was 3 times as large as the gain for White students.
- The effect of having high-quality teachers accumulates over the years.
- Content knowledge, experience, training and certification, and general cognitive skills are all important characteristics of effective teachers.

Enrichment approach An educational approach for gifted children in which the curriculum is covered but in greater depth, breadth, or complexity than is done in a typical classroom.

Accelerated program A type of program that allows gifted students to move through the standard curriculum more quickly than is typical.

T/F #8
Children who are gifted or talented often pay a price for their giftedness because they are likely to be socially or emotionally maladjusted. *False*

WEB LINK 12.3
Gifted Students

12.6

What aspects of the school environment affect children's academic achievement?

Class size. Optimal learning occurs when well-trained, enthusiastic teachers can pay close attention to individual students. Small class size gives them the opportunity to interact in this way with their students. ■

Another classroom characteristic that impacts student learning is class size. Surveys in naturally occurring school settings support the idea that smaller classes, particularly in the early grades, can benefit students, sometimes substantially, and that these benefits continue into the upper grades (Biddle & Berliner, 2002). The differences favoring small classes also emerge from studies that assigned matched groups of children to large or small classes. The gains are similar for boys and girls, but the benefits are strongest for minority students, children from low-income families, and children attending inner-city schools (Biddle & Berliner, 2002; see also Whitehurst & Chingos, 2011), and again for children in early elementary school (Whitehurst & Chingos, 2011).

Although we can conclude that smaller classes are beneficial to certain children, it is more important to understand *why* this happens. Biddle and Berliner (2002) argue that the most important factors influencing learning for children in the early grades are whether they can understand and manage what is expected from them in a classroom and figure out whether they are going to be able to handle the challenge of education. Smaller classrooms in the early grades allow teachers to spend more time helping individual students establish effective work habits and positive attitudes toward school. Less time is spent on classroom management, which frees up more time for academic instruction.

However, smaller teacher-to-student ratios by themselves do not ensure better instruction, and reducing class size is an expensive undertaking. For instance, in a school with 300 pupils, reducing class size from 25 to 20 students will require hiring 3 new teachers and equipping 3 additional classrooms (Barnett, Schulman, & Shore, 2004). Some have questioned whether those resources might be better spent on directly improving teacher preparation and qualifications. When teachers have high-quality interactions based on warm and supportive relationships with their students and actively engage them in classroom activities, it positively affects student achievement (Guo, Connor, Tompkins, & Morrison, 2011). Again, while this is more likely to happen in a smaller classroom, simply having a smaller class does not guarantee it.

Expectancy Effects

Expectancy effects The effect that the expectations of others can have on one's self-perception and behavior.

We all can find ourselves living up—or down—to the expectations other people have for us. The same is true for children in the classroom, but when these expectancy effects influence the amount of effort that children expend on their schoolwork, there is good reason for concern. In 1968, Robert Rosenthal and Lenore Jacobson reported the results of an experiment in which they intentionally manipulated teachers' expectation for the academic performance of some of their students. The researchers told teachers in six grades that they were able to identify students who would be intellectual "bloomers" over the coming year and that teachers should expect to see significant intellectual growth in these children. The "bloomers" were, in fact, randomly selected from class lists. At the end of the school year, total IQ scores of the "bloomers" were significantly higher than those of the other students who acted as controls for this experiment in some of the grades tested (Snow, 1995). The explanation Rosenthal and Jacobson (1968) offered was that changing the expectations the teachers held for these students changed their behavior in a way that facilitated the children's intellectual growth. Perhaps the teachers spent more time with these children, believing it was being well used with children who would benefit from it. Perhaps they were more supportive and encouraging toward children who were about to "bloom" or gave them different learning opportunities than they gave the other children.

This research not only gained a lot of attention both within the fields of education and psychology and in the general public, but it also generated a lot of debate. It offered a very optimistic message and suggested an apparently simple way to improve academic performance—believe in the child and communicate that belief to him or her. Although some attempts to replicate the original findings have been successful, others have not. While believing in a child's ability to succeed is important, those beliefs will be successful only if they are paired with the help and support the child needs to be successful.

The mechanism that underlies teacher expectancy effects is called a self-fulfilling prophecy. Your expectations cause you to predict (that is, to make a prophecy about) what will happen in the future. Those same expectations or beliefs may lead you to behave in ways that, in turn, help ensure that you find exactly what you had expected to find (Madon, Guyll, Willard, & Scherr, 2011). For instance, if you have low expectations for a child's performance, you may spend little time working with or encouraging the child, or you might be overly critical of what the child does. These behaviors deny the child an opportunity to learn and may even make the child dislike school and withdraw from classroom activities. The child also may incorporate the way you see him into his own self-concept. He comes to see himself as a failure and gives up trying, so consequently he does poorly—just as you had expected—and your initial prophecy is fulfilled.

In a review of research carried out over the last 35 years, Jussim and Harber (2005) concluded that there was evidence for the effects of self-fulfilling prophecy but the effects were quite small, accounting for only 5% to 10% of the variance observed in students' grades (see also Tenenbaum & Ruck, 2007). However, they did find that "powerful self-fulfilling prophecies may selectively occur among students from stigmatized social groups" (Jussim & Harber, 2005, p. 131). This issue has become more important in school settings because the number of minority students in attendance has increased. According to the U.S. Census Bureau (2011a), 43% of elementary and high school students in 2009 were ethnic or racial minorities. Even teachers with egalitarian values have different expectations based on their students' ethnicity. A number of studies have found the highest expectations for Asian American students, and more positive expectations for European American students than for either Latino or African American students (McKown & Weinstein, 2008; Tenenbaum & Ruck, 2007). Early teacher expectations have a greater impact on children from poorer families, making them more vulnerable to negative expectations. Children whose first-grade teachers underestimated their abilities did more poorly later than their early test scores would have predicted, and the effect was stronger for the children from low-income families (Sorhagen, 2013).

However, teachers are not the only source of influence on student achievement. Parents also play a significant role, especially for Latino students because family is so central to Latino values. Alfaro, Umaña-Taylor, & Bámaca (2006) found that although academic support from teachers was important to Latino boys and girls, support from fathers was particularly important for boys and support from mothers was particularly important for girls. Latino parents also hold educational aspirations for their children similar to those of Anglo parents, although Latino parents sometimes feel schools do not welcome their involvement in their children's education (Quiocho & Daoud, 2006). There is good reason to make both teachers and parents aware of the potential effect of their expectations on their students' performance, and to use positive expectations to foster positive performance.

JOURNAL ARTICLE 12.2
Expectancy Effects

Self-fulfilling prophecy The process by which expectations or beliefs lead to behaviors that help ensure that you fulfill the initial prophecy or expectation.

High expectations. Extraordinary educators such as Erin Gruwell (left) and Joe Clark (right) have been represented in movies, but you may know others whose high expectations challenged you to excel. ■

There have been some very powerful movie portrayals of real teachers who have transformed the lives of their students through their high expectations. Have you seen any of these movies?

- In *Stand and Deliver* (Menéndez, 1988), a math teacher, Jaime Escalante, challenges a group of predominantly Hispanic students from the Los Angeles barrio to master calculus. The teacher and students work after school, on weekends, and during vacation to overcome cultural deprivation and to rise above the low expectations that everyone else seems to have for these students. By the end of the movie, 18 of the students successfully pass the Advanced Placement test in calculus.
- In *Freedom Writers* (LaGravenese, 2007), Erin Gruwell helps a group of gang-bangers in a racially divided high school find their voice. Through the reading assignments that she gives them and the daily journals that the students keep, they find hope for the future and for their personal educational aspirations.
- In *Lean on Me* (Schiffer & Avildsen, 1989), principal Joe Clark uses "tough love" to get the attention of the students in his school. He fights against city officials who don't agree with his tactics (such as chaining the doors shut to keep trouble-makers out), against teachers he considers incompetent, and against parents who don't understand what he is doing to save his school from being closed down. In the process, his high expectations for the students turn the school around and help make it a safe environment in which children can learn.

All of these educators have been publicly acknowledged for their inspirational work with students, but there are many such teachers who work with students and make a difference in their lives each day. **Active Learning: Teacher-Heroes in Movies and Real Life** guides you to think about such teachers in your own life.

Active Learning

Teacher-Heroes in Movies and Real Life

Think about the most inspirational teacher you have ever had. What did that person do that was different from what other teachers did that made this person special to you? Was it something she did, something she said, or the way she seemed to feel about you that made a difference? If you have seen any of the inspirational movies about teachers mentioned above, did you see any parallels between your experience and the teachers portrayed in the movies? What downside, if any, is there to these movies creating such high expectations in the mind of the public for what a really great teacher can do for students? ■

Ability Grouping

The positive and negative effects of expectations are one reason ability grouping in schools, also called streaming, tracking, or clustering (Trautwein, Ludtke, Marsh, Koller, & Baumert, 2006), has become another controversial issue in education. The rationale behind this educational approach is that ability groups allow individual students to be taught at the level most appropriate for their current level of understanding. It is intended to allow high-performing students to advance more rapidly (thus avoiding boredom and frustration as they wait for slower students to master the material) and to allow low-performing students to get the material at a slower pace that better matches their ability level. Critics, however, see this stratification as harmful to the low-performing students, because it can damage their self-esteem and create negative attitudes toward school and schoolwork (Ireson, Hallam, & Plewis, 2001). Other critics have charged that children in lower-ability tracks experience poorer quality teaching and a less supportive educational environment, which, in turn, contributes to their lower levels of academic achievement (Lucas, 1999; Nomi, 2010).

Ability tracking at the elementary school level has largely been abandoned in the United States in favor of collaborative learning. Collaborative learning allows students at different ability levels to work together on a common goal, such as a project or an assignment. Students in collaborative learning groups show higher achievement, better self-esteem, and greater social competency than those in other instructional approaches (Curry, De Amicis, & Gilligan, 2011). They also report liking what they are studying more and are more likely to develop friendships with students from different ethnic backgrounds (Curry et al., 2011).

One explanation for collaborative learning's benefits is that when tasks are complex, they make greater demands on cognitive processing, and under these circumstances, dividing the cognitive load among multiple people is helpful (Kirschner, Paas, & Kirschner, 2009). For this reason, collaboration would not be particularly productive for a simpler task that is within the cognitive processing abilities of any single individual. Of course, working in a group rather than as an individual requires some additional effort to maintain communication and to integrate individual information into a final group solution, but these efforts are justified for complex tasks.

While ability grouping creates homogeneous groups of students at similar ability levels, collaborative learning creates heterogeneous groups of students with varying ability levels. Proponents of collaborative learning maintain that all students in the group can benefit from this arrangement. You may have heard that the best way to learn something yourself is to teach it to someone else. Likewise, proponents of collaborative learning expect that high-achieving students will benefit from the opportunity to explain concepts to the lower-achieving group

Ability grouping An educational approach that places students of similar ability in learning groups so they can be taught at a level that is most appropriate for their level of understanding.

VIDEO LINK 12.5
Ability Grouping

Collaborative learning An educational strategy that allows groups of students who are at different ability levels to work together on a common goal, such as a project or an assignment.

Collaborative learning. These groups of students of different abilities are charged with completing a project together. Achievement and self-esteem can improve in this approach, and friendships often result. ■

members. The low-achieving members of the group benefit by getting assistance, encouragement, and stimulation from the more advanced group members (Marsh et al., 2008). Do you see the Vygotskian principle of scaffolding here when children are learning from their interactions with more skilled peers?

However, in general, collaborative learning seems to be more advantageous for low-performing students than for high-achieving ones (Nomi, 2010). High-ability students tend to achieve at the same level whether their collaborative group was homogeneous or heterogeneous (Saleh, Lazonder, & De Jong, 2005). Perhaps it shouldn't surprise us to find that high-ability students can do well under a variety of conditions. However, they benefit from their participation in a heterogeneous group in other ways, including the development of social and leadership skills and enhanced self-esteem (Neber, Finsterwald, & Urban, 2001).

Grade Retention

When children have not mastered the material for a grade level, they may be retained in that grade for another year so they can repeat it. Sometimes, however, children who have not mastered grade-level material are promoted to the next grade. The primary motivation for this type of social promotion is to keep the child in a class with same-age peers so he or she is not perceived as a failure and does not become alienated from school (Lorence & Dworkin, 2006).

One finding that consistently emerges from research on grade retention is that some children are at greater risk than others of being retained. African American and Latino students are more likely to be retained than Anglo students (Cannon, Lipscomb, & Public Policy Institute of California, 2011; Frey, 2005; Jacobs & Lefgren, 2004), boys are retained at higher rates than girls (Cannon et al., 2011; Frey, 2005; Karwelt, 1999), and children from low-income families are more likely to be retained than children from more affluent families (Cannon et al., 2011; Southern Regional Education Board, 2001). English-language learners are also at an increased risk (Cannon et al., 2011).

Research that looked at whether—or when—retention is beneficial to the child has produced mixed findings. Some in the educational community believe retention may have short-term benefits (Cannon et al., 2011), but concerns about the long-term consequences remain. Findings from several recent longitudinal studies in which retained students were compared to a comparison group who were promoted showed no significant benefits of retention, and the retained students were more aggressive during adolescence and more likely to drop out of high school (Jimerson & Ferguson, 2007). Meta-analysis of studies on grade retention has found small to moderate effects that favor promoted students over those who were retained, and longitudinal research has failed to find an overall positive effect of retention (Silberglitt, Jimerson, Burns, & Appleton, 2006).

To understand these findings we should think about the purpose of retention. Students are retained because they have not mastered the material at a certain grade level. If that hasn't happened on a first attempt, should we think that simply exposing the student to the same information a second time will make the difference? Contrary to what we might expect, 50% of students who repeat a grade do no better on their second attempt and 25% actually do worse (Kenneady & Intercultural Development Research Association, 2004). What works better is to provide students with extra help and assistance when they need to repeat a grade (Lorence & Dworkin, 2006). If you have ever had to retake one of your college courses, you know that if you simply do again what you did the first time, you will likely get the same results. However, if you change what you do or how you do it, you are more likely to have a better outcome. Although this makes sense, it means schools must be willing to spend the extra money to provide additional help to students who are repeating a grade.

T/F #9
Placing high-, average-, and low-performing students together in groups to collaborate on a project is equally beneficial to all the children in the group.
False

Social promotion Promoting a child who has not mastered grade-level material to keep the child in a class with same-age peers.

Boys and Girls in School

Some statistics seem to indicate that it is becoming more difficult for boys than for girls to be successful in school. For instance, a report prepared by the U.S. Department of Education (National Center for Education Statistics, 2004b) showed the following:

- Boys are more likely to repeat a grade than girls.
- Boys are more likely to be diagnosed with a learning disorder, emotional disturbance, or speech impediment than girls.
- Girls consistently outperform boys in reading and writing.

However, when the issue of boys' school performance was carefully reexamined, the picture appeared more complicated. Sara Mead (2006) reanalyzed some of the statistics on school performance and came to the conclusion that boys from middle-class or upper-middle-class families are, in fact, performing *better* in school than they have in the past, but the same is not true for minority boys or boys from disadvantaged families (see also Froschl & Sprung, 2008). The problem with boys may be specific to these particular groups of boys. If we are concerned about differential performance in school, it is not enough to look only at differences between boys and girls. We also need to look at differences *within* groups of boys and *within* groups of girls because there is great diversity within those groups.

T/F #10
Generally speaking, boys are not doing as well in school as they have in the past. *False*

Although girls generally outperform boys in many areas of school, they lag in participation in the STEM fields of science, technology, engineering, and math. We discuss this gap more thoroughly in Chapter 15 when we focus on adolescents, but we point out here that it is not too early to begin to intervene with girls on these issues at much younger ages. Most elementary school teachers are women, and many grew up with stereotypical ideas about gender and math, resulting in high levels of math anxiety. Girls, but not boys, who studied for one year in a classroom with one of these math-anxious teachers ended the year with more stereotyped ideas about math abilities and poorer math performance (Beilock, Gunderson, Ramirez, & Levine, 2010). Teachers can unintentionally communicate their own gender-based anxiety to their students.

Much is being done to break down stereotypes and encourage girls to enter careers in the STEM fields. Even the Barbie doll, the standard-bearer for female stereotypes, has begun to take an active role in promoting nonstereotypical roles for girls. Whereas in the past she was programmed to say, "Math class is tough!" in 2010 Computer Engineer Barbie was introduced. Commenting on the new Barbie, Rebecca Zook (2010) states that the "false dichotomy—that you have to choose between being feminine and 'looking the part' of a mathematician or scientist—might be part of what turns girls off from math and science in the first place" (para. 6).

Over 400 intervention projects have been sponsored by the National Science Foundation and the American Association of University Women (AAUW) Educational Foundation and have generally been successful in improving girls' participation and success in these fields (Darke, Clewell, & Sevo, 2002). One recommendation for improving these interventions is to incorporate more gender-equity projects directly into the

Girls and science. Young girls can be as interested in science as boys. To sustain this interest, many programs have been developed to encourage girls to enter the fields of math and science, but they are most effective when they begin with girls at young ages. ∎

©iStockphoto.com/dcdebs

school curriculum rather than having them occur outside the regular school day (AAUW Educational Foundation, 2004).

As a result of concern about whether boys and girls have different needs in the classroom, in 2006, then-U.S. Secretary of Education Margaret Spellings announced new regulations that allowed for the development of single-gender classrooms or schools within the public school system (U.S. Department of Education, 2006). However, critics of this move say there are many more similarities between the genders than differences (Paulson & Teicher, 2006). They fear this new interpretation of Title IX will roll back gains made since this landmark legislation barred sex discrimination in schools (AAUW, 2009). Most studies that have compared single-gender and mixed-gender educational settings have shown no benefit resulting from separating girls and boys (Nisbett et al., 2012). We are still searching for educational solutions that are fair to all: boys and girls, rich and poor, minority and nonminority students.

AUDIO LINK 12.3
Single-Sex Classes

Check Your Understanding

1. Compare fluid and crystallized intelligence.
2. Compare Gardner's and Sternberg's theories of intelligence.
3. How are children with intellectual disability identified?
4. What kinds of programs are available to encourage gifted children?
5. What are the effects of grade retention?

Conclusion

Middle childhood is the period of time when children begin to learn the skills they need to be successful adults in their society. As they enter their school years, their cognitive abilities, including logical thought, attention, memory, and mental organization, are growing to enable them to study and learn. Language use continues to develop and allows more sophisticated ways of thinking and interacting. Language also forms the basis for learning the skills of reading and writing required for success in school. Children's ability to perform well in school is related to intelligence, but self-control and the ability to pay attention also are central to being able to learn. Children may also excel at some types of cognitive abilities and not others. All children, regardless of their intellectual abilities or disabilities, socioeconomic status, gender, ethnicity, and race, deserve the care and education needed to raise them to their highest level of achievement.

Chapter Summary

12.1 What occurs during Piaget's stage of concrete operations?

The thinking of school-age children becomes much more logical, but it is not yet abstract. They understand **reversibility,** which allows them to solve conservation problems. They can also **categorize** objects into larger groups and **seriate** objects in order by a characteristic such as length or height.

12.2 How do attention, memory, and executive function develop in middle childhood?

Both maturation and the environment contribute to increases in children's ability to pay attention. **Processing speed**, or the speed and accuracy with which we can handle information, increases, and **automaticity** makes us able to do certain familiar tasks without having to pay much attention to them.

False memories can occur in young children because they can be very suggestible, but older children also develop false memories because they remember the gist, or meaning, of an event rather than the specifics of the experience. **Executive function** is that aspect of brain organization that coordinates attention and memory and controls behavioral responses for the purpose of attaining a certain goal. Three important aspects of executive function that are developing during middle childhood are **cognitive flexibility**, **inhibitory control**, and **working memory**.

12.3 Describe the progression of language development, including literacy, in middle childhood.

Metalinguistic ability develops as children begin to understand that a word is different from what it represents. Most children learn to read using a **balanced approach** that combines elements of **whole language instruction** and the **phonics** or **basic skills approach**. Bilingual children do not generally experience any cognitive disadvantage associated with their use of two languages, and they may show more advanced executive function. Difficulties with speech and language can be diagnosed as **language disorders**, **speech-sound disorder**, **childhood-onset fluency disorder** or **stuttering**, and **social** or **pragmatic communication disorder**.

12.4 How does intelligence affect academic achievement in middle childhood?

Debate has centered on whether there is one general underlying factor for intelligence, *g*, or whether intelligence is a set of relatively independent abilities or skills. Genes are thought to set the potential for a range of intelligence outcomes, while the environment determines where within that range the individual falls. Although IQ tests are effective at predicting a child's potential academic achievement, other factors (such as the ability to delay gratification) may predict achievement as well as or even better. Gardner's **theory of multiple intelligences** proposes at least nine types of intelligence, whereas Sternberg's **triarchic theory** proposes three—analytical, creative, and practical abilities.

12.5 How do we define intellectual disability, specific learning disorder, and giftedness?

Intellectual disability is indicated by a combination of IQ below 70–75, cognitive deficits, and limitations in **adaptive functioning** needed for everyday life. Specific learning disorder includes difficulties with reading, writing, and mathematics. One definition of **giftedness** is the ability to transform intellectual ability and talent into outstanding performance and innovation.

12.6 What aspects of the school environment affect children's academic achievement?

Factors in the ongoing debate about how to promote learning in school include the role of teacher training, class size, teacher **expectancy effects** that become **self-fulfilling prophecy** about student achievement, **ability grouping** versus **collaborative learning**, and grade retention versus **social promotion**. Although on average boys are not achieving as well as girls in school, this appears to be more of a problem for boys from disadvantaged families. Schools need to continue to encourage girls to participate in STEM courses to sustain their interest in careers in these fields.

Key Terms

Ability grouping 419

Accelerated program 415

Adaptive functioning 412

Analytical intelligence 411

Authentic assessment 409

Automaticity 393

Balanced reading approach 402

Childhood-onset fluency disorder/ stuttering 403

Classification 392

Cognitive flexibility 397

Collaborative learning 419

Concrete operations 391

Creative intelligence 411

Crystallized intelligence 406

Cultural test bias hypothesis 407

Developmental bilingual programs 405

Deviation IQ 407

Divergent thinking 412

Elaboration 395

English as a second language (ESL) pull-out programs 405

Enrichment approach 415

Expectancy effects 416

Fluid intelligence 406

Fuzzy trace theory 396

$SAGE edge™

Sharpen your skills with SAGE edge at edge.sagepub.com/levinechrono

SAGE edge for Students provides a personalized approach to help you accomplish your coursework goals in an easy-to-use learning environment.

Go to edge.sagepub.com/levinechrono for additional exercises and video resources. Select Chapter 12, Cognitive Development in Middle Childhood, for chapter-specific activities. All of the Video Links listed in the margins of this chapter are accessible via this site.

13 Social and Emotional Development in Middle Childhood

T/F Test Your Knowledge

Test your knowledge of child development by deciding whether each of the following statements is *true* or *false*, and then check your answers as you read the chapter.

1. **T** ☐ **F** ☐ Programs that build students' self-esteem not only improve their grades but also help reduce delinquency, drug use, and adolescent pregnancy.

2. **T** ☐ **F** ☐ School phobias usually are the result of children's worrying they won't do well in school.

3. **T** ☐ **F** ☐ Throughout childhood and adolescence, girls are more likely to suffer from depression than boys.

4. **T** ☐ **F** ☐ "Tough-love" programs (for example, wilderness camps and boot camps) for children with conduct problems have been very successful at rehabilitating these young people.

5. **T** ☐ **F** ☐ Children growing up in the same family usually are not very similar to each other.

6. **T** ☐ **F** ☐ Children who grow up without siblings tend to be more self-centered, maladjusted, lonely, and neurotic than children who have siblings.

7. **T** ☐ **F** ☐ The majority of women who are single but living with the father of their baby when their baby is born will marry the baby's father shortly after the baby's birth.

8. **T** ☐ **F** ☐ On average, there are only small differences between children of divorce and children from intact families.

9. **T** ☐ **F** ☐ School-wide programs that have attempted to reduce bullying in school have been highly successful.

10. **T** ☐ **F** ☐ Children who are able to rise above great adversity like poverty or child abuse have unusual abilities that have allowed them to succeed.

Correct answers: (1) F, (2) F, (3) F, (4) F, (5) T, (6) F, (7) F, (8) T, (9) F, (10) F

As children move into middle childhood, they begin to see themselves in more complex ways. Changes in gender identity and ethnic identity occur, and self-esteem becomes more realistic than it was in early childhood. Children are better able to express and control their emotions, but in this chapter we also describe several disorders rooted in emotional development, including depression, anxiety, and behavioral disorders. When children enter school, their social world becomes much larger. Although parents and siblings remain important, peers begin to play a larger role in children's lives. Friendships begin to develop at a deeper level, and whether a child is accepted by peers has consequences for his or her future emotional development. Before we end the chapter, we discuss children who manage to thrive in the face of great adversity and describe the characteristics of these resilient children.

The Self and Identity in School-Age Children

When people talk about the self, they often use the terms *self-concept* and *self-esteem* interchangeably, but in Chapter 10 you learned that they are not the same thing. When you are asked to describe yourself, your description is your self-concept. The way you feel about those characteristics, whether you like them or not, contributes to your self-esteem. To clarify that distinction, you can complete **Active Learning: The Difference Between Self-Concept and Self-Esteem.**

Learning Questions

13.1 How does the sense of self develop in middle childhood?

13.2 How does typical emotional development proceed during middle childhood and what problems do children have when they cannot manage or control their emotions?

13.3 What do we know about family relationships during middle childhood?

13.4 What affects the quality of a child's peer relationships?

13.5 How does media affect children's social relationships?

13.6 What makes some children resilient in the face of adversity?

13.1

How does the sense of self develop in middle childhood?

Active Learning

The Difference Between Self-Concept and Self-Esteem

In the column below labeled "Self-Concept," make a list of 8 to 10 characteristics that describe you. They can include physical characteristics (such as your height, weight, or body build), your skills and abilities, or your personality characteristics. After you complete your list, go back and circle a number for each characteristic to indicate how much you like or dislike this characteristic in yourself.

Self-Concept	Self-Evaluation										
	Like	10	9	8	7	6	5	4	3	2	1	Dislike
	Like	10	9	8	7	6	5	4	3	2	1	Dislike
	Like	10	9	8	7	6	5	4	3	2	1	Dislike
	Like	10	9	8	7	6	5	4	3	2	1	Dislike
	Like	10	9	8	7	6	5	4	3	2	1	Dislike
	Like	10	9	8	7	6	5	4	3	2	1	Dislike
	Like	10	9	8	7	6	5	4	3	2	1	Dislike
	Like	10	9	8	7	6	5	4	3	2	1	Dislike
	Like	10	9	8	7	6	5	4	3	2	1	Dislike
	Like	10	9	8	7	6	5	4	3	2	1	Dislike

The overall pattern of responses you gave for how you feel about the characteristics in your self-concept begins to tap into your self-evaluation or self-esteem. Most people have quite a few things that they like about themselves, but also some things that they dislike. Almost no one will have uniformly high esteem on every characteristic. Someone else with the same list of characteristics could end up with a different level of self-esteem because they feel differently about having those same characteristics as part of their self-concept. For instance, you may describe yourself as a very tall person, but you could love or hate that about yourself. Or you may see yourself as a very trusting person, but you could like the fact that you always think the best of everyone or hate the fact that you are so trusting that people frequently take advantage of you. Remember that self-evaluations occur in a cultural context. Is there anything you like on your list of characteristics that might *not* be seen as positively in another culture? ■

Self-Concept in Middle Childhood

As children enter middle childhood, they are able to think about themselves in more complex ways. While younger children describe themselves in very concrete terms ("I have red hair. I live in a big house and have a kitty"), children in middle childhood now include psychological terms, emotions, and attitudes in their self-descriptions ("I am a good friend. I like new things"). While children in early childhood tend to see themselves in an all-or-nothing way ("I'm never scared! I'm always happy"), children between 8 and 11 are refining their self-concepts to include shades of gray; for example, "I get sad *if* there is no one to do things with" (Harter, 2006b, p. 527). They can also experience more than one feeling at a time; for example, "I was happy that I got a present but mad that it wasn't what I wanted" (Harter, 2006b, p. 527).

Erik Erikson (1963) described middle childhood as a conflict of industry versus inferiority, when children need to set aside childhood fantasies and begin the work needed to learn the "industry" of their society. In most modern societies, this means going to school to prepare for adult life. When children enter school they get a great deal of feedback telling them how they are doing, and this helps shape their self-esteem. They begin to compare themselves to others, and they don't always come out on top. In carrying out this social comparison, they can think, "I am better than Joe at arithmetic but not as good as Arina at reading." This reflects a new ability to coordinate two or more concepts at the same time, their own performance and someone else's performance, as well as different types of performance, such as arithmetic and reading (Harter, 2006b). This is, of course, exactly what Piaget would say children of this age can do cognitively.

Industry versus inferiority The time in middle childhood during which Erikson says that children begin to learn what it takes to become an adult in their society.

Social comparison Comparing one's own performance or characteristics to those of other people.

Self-Concept and Culture

From previous discussions of individualistic and collectivist cultures, you will remember that some cultures place a high value on the role of the individual and individual achievement. Others conceptualize the self as part of a group, and in those cultures the group's goals take priority over individual accomplishments. In the United States, an individualistic culture, we tend to see people as separate, autonomous individuals who choose their own paths in life. Read these two self-descriptions from 6-year-old children:

> I am a wonderful and very smart person. A funny and hilarious person. A kind and caring person. A good-grade person who is going to go to [a prestigious university]. A helpful and cooperative girl.

> I'm a human being. I'm a child. I like to play cards. I'm my mom and dad's child, my grandma and grandpa's grandson. I'm a hard-working good child. (Wang, 2006, p. 182)

Cultural values. Children are socialized into the values of their cultures, and these values become part of how they see themselves. Children in individualistic cultures (such as the United States) often take great pride in individual achievement and success, while children in collectivistic cultures (such as China) are more likely to see themselves as embedded in a rich network of social relationships that take precedence over individual needs or accomplishments. ■

You can probably guess which description came from an American child and which from a Chinese child. Euro American children typically include more inner traits ("I'm smart") and abilities ("I am the fastest runner") in their descriptions, while Chinese children include more situational descriptions ("I play with my friend after school") and overt behaviors ("I like to tell stories"). Euro American children also are more likely to include positive evaluations like "beautiful" or "smart," while Chinese children described themselves in neutral terms like "work hard." Euro American children place more emphasis on the personal aspects of their lives, and Chinese children emphasize the social aspects of theirs (Wang, 2006). In all societies, individuals define themselves in terms of both individual characteristics and their relationships to others, but the *ratio* of personal-to-social references differs between the groups, with Euro American children using more personal references and Chinese children use more social references (Raeff, 2004).

Self-Esteem During Childhood

As children move from early childhood into middle childhood, their confidence in their own abilities often declines (Eccles, 1999; Harter, 2006a). Several factors contribute to this change. First, as children increasingly compare themselves to their peers, their self-evaluations become more realistic and drop from the inflated levels of early childhood. Second, the constant feedback children in elementary school receive from their teachers helps them develop a more accurate appraisal of their ability. When younger children receive feedback on their success or failure at a particular task, that information has little effect on their expectations for future success (Davis-Kean, Jager, & Collins, 2009). In contrast, older children take in this information and use it to change their predictions for their future behavior. This means that over time children's conceptions of self become more realistic.

Feedback and self-concept. How will her teacher's response to her efforts affect this girl's concept of herself? In middle childhood feedback from teachers and others leads children to develop a more realistic self-concept. ■

Third, children during middle childhood often participate in a variety of organized activities in which they are evaluated. They may be taking music lessons or gymnastics classes, playing sports, or participating in competitive activities such as the chess club or the debate team at school. In all these situations, they can clearly see when someone else can do more or less than they can.

When we talk about how we feel about our own general self-worth, we are talking about what is called global self-esteem. But if you are like most people, and as you saw when you did the **Active Learning** exercise above, there usually are some characteristics that we like about ourselves and some that we don't particularly like. Susan Harter (2012) has developed a model of self-esteem that identifies five separate dimensions that are relevant to the way children feel about themselves. They are:

1. Scholastic competence, or feeling you are doing well at school

2. Social competence, or feeling you are popular or well liked

3. Behavioral conduct, or feeling you act the way you are supposed to act

4. Athletic competence, or feeling you are good at sports

5. Physical appearance, or liking the way you look

Taken together, these dimensions form a profile across the developmental domains. Research has found that as children get older, they are better able to integrate these five dimensions into one overall assessment of global self-esteem (Harter, 2012).

High self-esteem has been associated with a number of positive developmental outcomes, and low self-esteem with a number of negative ones. For instance, students who have higher self-esteem tend to do better in school than students with lower self-esteem (Baumeister, Campbell, Krueger, & Vohs, 2003). Based on this observed relationship, school systems developed a number of programs designed to boost students' self-esteem, with the goal of eventually improving their academic performance. Collectively these efforts are referred to as the self-esteem movement. To learn how successful or unsuccessful these programs have been, read **Journey of Research: The Self-Esteem Movement.**

Global self-esteem The feelings you have about your own general self-worth.

Self-esteem movement School-based programs designed to boost students' self-esteem, with the goal of eventually improving their academic performance.

· ·

JOURNEY OF RESEARCH *The Self-Esteem Movement*

The self-esteem movement had its roots in the efforts of California state assemblyman John Vasconcellos, who created the California Task Force to Promote Self-Esteem and Personal and Social Responsibility in 1986 (Mecca, Smelser, & Vasconcellos, 1989). The foreword to an edited volume produced by the members of the Task Force said the data and testimony from public hearings they held led to "a consensus that a primary factor affecting how well or how poorly an individual functions in society is self-esteem" (p. vii). Social problems as wide-ranging as alcohol and drug abuse, crime, and even child abuse were linked to low self-esteem.

As a result of this conclusion, a number of school-based self-esteem programs designed to boost students' self-esteem were created. However, over the years critics charged that these were largely "feel good" programs that had little or no impact on actual school performance. While such programs emphasized the uniqueness and value of the individual, the praise they offered was not tied to achievement or accomplishments (and was specifically *not* tied to academic performance). Despite spending millions of dollars on these programs, research failed to find any significant positive outcomes that could be tied back to them (Baumeister et al., 2003; Twenge, 2006).

Roy F. Baumeister and his colleagues (2003) pointed out that these programs may have failed because we got it backward. Self-esteem and positive outcomes may be correlated, but remember that we can't determine the direction of an effect from a correlation. Children who are good students often feel good about themselves (that is, they have high self-esteem), but the question is whether feeling good about yourself makes you a good student. Imagine for a moment what would happen if you felt *great* about yourself but were required to take a test on matrix algebra when you had never studied matrix algebra. Although in theory the direction of the effect can move in either direction, most evidence supports the idea that high self-esteem is primarily an *outcome* that results from performing well rather than being the *cause* of good performance (Baumeister et al., 2003; Dweck, 1999). High self-esteem also has not been found to "prevent children from smoking, drinking, taking drugs, or engaging in early sex" (Baumeister et al., 2003, p. 1), which were other goals of the self-esteem movement. ∎

T/F #1
Programs that build students' self-esteem not only improve their grades but also help reduce delinquency, drug use, and adolescent pregnancy.
False

The failure of self-esteem enhancement programs to produce the hoped-for outcomes does not mean we shouldn't promote high self-esteem among children. We want children to feel good about themselves. Rather, it means we need to help children base their esteem on actual achievement rather than on empty praise (Dweck, 1999).

If the self-esteem movement simply failed to deliver the expected results, that would have been disappointing but not necessarily harmful. However, some critics have charged that these programs have contributed to an increase in narcissism (Twenge, 2006). Whether self-esteem programs actually help make people narcissistic has not yet been resolved, but the findings are clear that simply boosting self-esteem will not be a solution to the myriad problems children may experience.

Media, Self-Concept, and Self-Esteem

We have known for a long time that parents and peers are important sources of self-esteem, but more recently we have begun paying attention to media as another source. As social comparison becomes an increasingly important element in building children's self-concept and self-esteem, images they see on television and in movies, in advertising, and online present another standard against which they can compare themselves. Unfortunately the unrealistic images they find offered there can lead them to feel dissatisfied with their body (Martins & Harrison, 2012; Murnen, Smolak, Mills, & Good, 2003; Wonderlich, Ackard, & Henderson, 2005). Women and girls are almost universally portrayed as unrealistically thin, and being repeatedly exposed to this thin ideal can be damaging to girls' self-esteem. Girls as young as 6 or 7 years of age express their desire to be thinner (Dohnt & Tiggemann, 2006), and the situation is not much better for boys (Murnen et al., 2003) because the images of super heroes and super athletes are no more realistic for them than the images of women that girls see. For boys, these images can lead to body dissatisfaction tied to a desire to be bigger, stronger, and more muscular.

Women are frequently portrayed in movies, video games, ads, and television shows as dependent upon men and secondary to them, while male characters are independent and in charge of the situation. Minority characters are frequently portrayed as criminals, sex objects, and people of lower status (Martins & Harrison, 2012). In one study of 7- to 12-year-olds, television viewing was negatively related to self-esteem in White and Black girls and Black boys, but not in White boys (Martins & Harrison, 2012). One explanation for this finding is that exposure to the negative portrayal of women in general and Black men in particular lowers the self-esteem of these groups, while the positive portrayal of White men boosts the self-esteem of White boys.

In another study, children between the ages of 6 and 12 were shown images from media that stereotypically portrayed men and women. Girls who rejected these images and said that they did not want to look like them had higher body esteem than girls who endorsed

VIDEO LINK 13.1
Thin Ideal

Thin ideal The idea promoted by media images that it is best for girls and women to be thin.

AUDIO LINK 13.1
Disney and Race

the images (Murnen et al., 2003). These media images did not have the same impact on the body esteem of boys, perhaps because boys of this age do not necessarily expect to be heavily muscular, whereas girls of any age can strive to be thin like the media images.

The typical U.S. child between ages 8 and 18 spends an average of 7 hours a day with entertainment media (Rideout, Foehr, & Roberts, 2010). Simply the amount of time spent with entertainment media would make it a powerful influence on a child's self-concept, but another reason media exposure is such a strong influence is that the more time spent with media, the less time the child has to engage in other positive, productive activities that contribute to self-esteem (Martins & Harrison, 2012). Encouraging children to take part in activities they enjoy and are good at, such as sports, cultural or artistic activities, or hobbies, helps those in middle childhood build a positive self-concept based on diverse aspects of the self, not just on physical appearance.

Gender Identity

By the time children enter middle childhood, their gender identity is well developed (Charlesworth, Wood, & Viggiani, 2011). They also understand what their culture defines as masculine roles, attitudes, and behaviors and what it defines as feminine ones. Although young children tend to be rigid and inflexible about gender roles, some of that rigidity lessens as they get older (Carver, Yunger, & Perry, 2003). Children who are content with their gender role report a higher sense of global self-worth. Those who are not content report greater distress in their relationships with peers, and peers see these children as being depressed, anxious, and self-deprecating (Carver et al., 2003).

Androgyny represents a mixture of traits that are traditionally considered masculine with traits that are traditionally considered feminine. While boys' identification with traditional male role models increases during middle childhood, girls tend to be more androgynous (Charlesworth et al., 2011). For example, when boys spend time with other boys, they devote most of that time to sex-stereotyped masculine activities. By comparison, when girls are with their peers, they spend similar amounts of time in masculine and feminine activities (McHale, Kim, Whiteman, & Crouter, 2004). This probably reflects the fact that society is more accepting of girls taking on some qualities traditionally described as masculine (such as being more independent or assertive) than it is of males taking on qualities described as feminine (such as being more nurturing or expressive). As girls in middle childhood face increasing pressure to conform more to gender stereotypes, they may abandon masculine activities and behaviors in favor of more traditionally feminine ones. Because masculine behaviors and traits such as assertiveness or risk-taking are the ones more highly valued by society, pressure to conform to traditional feminine activities can in this way lower a girl's self-esteem (Carver et al., 2003).

WEB LINK 13.1
Gender Identity

Androgyny The idea that both sexes can have characteristics that are traditionally considered masculine and traditionally considered feminine.

© Tim Clayton/TIM CLAYTON/Corbis

Gender identity. Unlike boys who spend most of their time in masculine activities, girls in middle childhood spend about the same amount of time in activities considered to be feminine and masculine. There is generally more acceptance for a girl like this one playing baseball than for a boy studying ballet. ∎

Ethnic Identity

Developing a gender identity is a basic task all children must deal with, but many also need to develop a sense of

Ethnic identity. Children begin to understand and identify with their ethnic group, but their understanding is more concrete than it will be when they enter adolescence. ■

their ethnic identity that consists of all "the attitudes toward and feelings of belonging to an ethnic group" (Marks, Szalacha, Lamarre, Boyd, & Coll, 2007, p. 501). By the time they enter middle childhood, children have the cognitive capacity to begin to form coherent ethnic identities (Byrd, 2012).

Relatively little research has examined the development of ethnic identity in children before the age of 10 (Byrd, 2012; French, Seidman, Allen, & Aber, 2006). Children are able to label the ethnic group they belong to by age 6 to 8; understand that differences are based on biological features, as well as social features such as speech patterns and lifestyle by age 7 to 8; and develop ethnic constancy, or the understanding that race or ethnicity remains the same across time and in different settings, between age 8 to 10 (Byrd, 2012).

The way children respond to the question "What does it mean to be [ethnicity]?" differs by ethnic and racial group (Rogers et al., 2012, p. 101). Immigrant children are more likely to refer to their language, heredity, or birthplace, whereas White and Black children are more likely to refer to physical characteristics such as skin color or relative social position. Although different characteristics related to ethnicity are salient for different children, at this age, the concept of group membership is based on concrete and physical characteristics. The development of an ethnic identity continues during adolescence, so we return to this subject in Chapter 16.

Ethnic identity A person's attitudes toward the ethnic group to which they feel they belong.

Ethnic constancy The understanding that race or ethnicity remains the same across time and in different settings.

AUDIO LINK 13.2
Ethnic Identity

Check Your Understanding

1. Compare self-concept and self-esteem.
2. How does media exposure affect children's self-esteem?
3. Describe children's understanding of ethnic identity in middle childhood.

Emotional Development and Emotional Problems

13.2

How does typical emotional development proceed during middle childhood and what problems do children have when they cannot manage or control their emotions?

Children's ability to successfully manage their emotions plays a critical role in their ability to form and maintain social relationships. In this section we describe the typical patterns of development of emotions such as fear, sadness, and anger during middle childhood and then describe the difficulties some children experience when they are unable to regulate their emotional responses.

Emotional Development in Middle Childhood

Learning to express emotions in ways that are expected and sanctioned by your culture is crucial to healthy social and emotional development (Chaplin & Aldao, 2013) and by middle childhood, most children understand and behave in ways that reflect those expectations. There are some consistent gender differences in emotional development in middle childhood, although many of them are only small to moderate. They include the fact that in the United States and many European countries, girls are expected to be more emotionally expressive than boys. They typically show higher levels of happiness, but also of sadness, fear, anxiety, shame, guilt, empathy, and sympathy (Brody & Hall, 2008; Chaplin & Aldao, 2013). Boys show more anger and aggression, although all of these gender differences are quite small (Chaplin & Aldao, 2013). Aggressive behavior is more accepted by society for boys than it is for girls, and finds expression through the rough-and-tumble play in which boys in middle childhood frequently engage (Rose & Rudolph, 2006).

As children move through middle childhood, they become better at regulating their expression of all emotions (Chaplin & Aldao, 2013). Difficulties with managing emotions include externalizing behaviors, in which children "act out" on the environment, and internalizing behaviors, in which they experience painful emotions and may do things that are hurtful to themselves. When we discuss difficulties with fear, anxiety, sadness, and depression, we are generally describing internalizing behaviors, while anger and aggression are most often associated with externalizing behavior.

Fear and Anxiety

The difference between fear and anxiety is not always clear, but we generally think of fear as a response to a real event, whereas anxiety is the anticipation of events that may or may not occur. While younger children are primarily afraid of things in the physical world, these fears are replaced in middle childhood by social anxieties and anxiety about school performance (Beesdo, Knappe, & Pine, 2009; Southam-Gerow & Chorpita, 2007). There is a tendency for girls to be more fearful and shy than boys (Cummings, Caporino, & Kendall, 2014).

Some level of fear and anxiety during development is normal, but excessive amounts of either become problematic. When anxiety is so great that it interferes with everyday activities and creates a great deal of distress, it is considered an anxiety disorder (APA, 2013), one of most commonly diagnosed mental health problems in children, affecting between 15% and 20% of them (Beesdo et al., 2009). The most common form of anxiety disorder is separation anxiety disorder, which is a developmentally inappropriate and excessive amount of anxiety when the child is separated from a primary attachment figure (APA, 2013). While mild distress and clinging behavior is normal in children 3 or 4 years old, we do not typically see this behavior in older children. Another common form of anxiety disorder is an obsessive-compulsive disorder (OCD). An obsession is an intrusive thought that pops up in a person's mind time and time again and creates anxiety. You learned about intrusive thoughts in Chapter 10. Compulsions are behaviors people feel they must repeat to reduce or control the anxiety, such as washing your hands over and over again even though you know they are clean. A person may know that what he is doing is unreasonable, but engaging in the compulsive behavior provides some temporary relief from the obsessive thoughts so it is repeated (APA, 2013). Longitudinal studies of children with anxiety disorders have found that these conditions in childhood predict the development of emotional disorders in adolescence, so they should not be ignored with the assumption they will simply disappear with age (Beesdo et al., 2009; Bittner et al., 2007).

Anxiety A vague fear about events that may or may not occur.

Anxiety disorder A level of anxiety that is severe, lasts a long time, and interferes with normal functioning.

Separation anxiety disorder An anxiety disorder marked by a developmentally inappropriate and excessive amount of anxiety when the child is separated from a primary attachment figure.

Obsessive-compulsive disorder (OCD) A disorder marked by obsessions or intrusive thoughts and repeated behaviors that people feel compelled to do to control the obsessive thoughts.

Separation anxiety disorder. Young children normally are distressed when they are separated from their caregivers. However, when a child reaches school age and the fear of separation is still overwhelming, it becomes a concern that may require professional help. ∎

When a fear involving something specific has no rational basis and is so severe that it interferes with day-to-day functioning, it is called a phobia. Common phobias include fear of spiders, snakes, heights, flying, water, and public speaking. About 5% of children experience school phobia (Chitiyo & Wheeler, 2006; Tyrrell, 2005). Children who suffer from school phobias tend to be good students, so it is not likely they are avoiding school because they are afraid they will not do well. Rather it is likely they are suffering from separation or social anxiety. Typical treatment consists of gradually returning the child to the classroom while equipping him with strategies to help manage emotional distress (Chitiyo & Wheeler, 2006). Intervening as early as possible contributes to the success of this approach (Tyrrell, 2005), because the longer the child avoids school, the scarier it will seem.

Sadness and Depression

Sadness is a normal reaction to experiences such as loss and disappointment, but clinical depression refers to sadness that is long-lasting and severe enough to affect the individual physically, emotionally, cognitively, and socially. The person may have trouble sleeping or eating, feel worthless, be unable to concentrate, and stay socially isolated from others (Hammen & Rudolph, 2003).

Depression in preadolescent children is relatively rare, affecting less than 2% to 3% of children ages 6 to 11 (Hammen & Rudolph, 2003; Kazdin & Marciano, 1998); however, it can be diagnosed in children as young as 3 (Luby, 2010). It may surprise you to learn that some studies have found that in middle childhood, boys are at a *greater* risk of suffering from depression than girls (Hammen & Rudolph, 2003; Hankin et al., 1998). As you can see in Figure 13.1, the rate of diagnosed clinical depression is slightly higher in males than in females until early adolescence. It is likely that clinical depression is the result of a complex interaction of biological, genetic, psychosocial, and family factors.

Anger and Aggression

Problems with aggression and impulsivity have been described as "the most persistent and common forms of childhood maladjustment" (Olson, Bates, Sandy, & Lanthier, 2000, p. 119). Fortunately, most children learn to control their anger as they get older, but a relatively small group shows high levels of aggression that persist (Campbell, Spieker, Burchinal, Poe, & NICHD Early Child Care Research Network, 2006; Côté, Vaillancourt, LeBlanc, Nagin, & Tremblay, 2006). Aggressive behavior that persists until children enter school is associated with academic problems, relationship problems, peer rejection, and even later criminal behavior (Olson et al., 2000). Aggression also is a primary symptom in oppositional defiant disorder (ODD), disruptive mood dysregulation disorder (DMDD), and conduct disorder, so we next look at these disorders in more detail.

Oppositional Defiant Disorder

Being oppositional or defiant from time to time is one way children assert a need to be autonomous. However, when confrontation, defiance, and argumentativeness become part of an ongoing pattern of behavior, the child may have a behavioral disorder known as oppositional defiant disorder or **ODD**. Oppositional defiant disorder includes three

VIDEO LINK 13.2
School Anxiety

T/F #2
School phobias usually are the result of children's worrying they won't do well in school.
False

WEB LINK 13.2
Childhood Depression

Clinical depression
A condition marked by long-lasting and severe feelings of worthlessness and hopelessness, a lack of pleasure, sleep and appetite disturbances, and possibly suicidal thoughts.

T/F #3
Throughout childhood and adolescence, girls are more likely to suffer from depression than boys. *False*

Oppositional defiant disorder A pattern of behavior marked by defiant, disobedient, and hostile behavior toward authority figures.

FIGURE 13.1 **Gender differences in clinical depression**

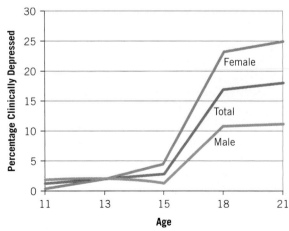

The percentage of clinical cases of depression changes by age and gender. Note the crossover that occurs at age 13.

SOURCE: Hankin, Abramson, Moffitt et al. (1998). © American Psychological Association.

VIDEO LINK 13.3
Oppositional Defiant Disorder

Coercive family environment A pattern of family interaction in which parents and children mutually train each other so that the child becomes increasingly aggressive and the parents become less effective in controlling the child's behavior.

Disruptive Mood Dysregulation Disorder Severe and frequent temper tantrums that are out of proportion with the situation.

Conduct disorder A persistent pattern of behavior marked by violation of the basic rights of others or major age-appropriate social norms or rules.

types of symptoms: angry/irritable mood, argumentative/defiant behavior, and vindictiveness (APA, 2013). Because the symptoms include fairly common behaviors such as temper tantrums, argumentativeness with adults, refusal to comply with adult requests, and aggressiveness toward peers, knowing when these behaviors have moved beyond the normal range to become disordered behavior is a challenge.

It has been difficult to determine the exact cause of oppositional defiant disorder, but both the child's temperament and factors within the family environment play a role. Gerald Patterson and his colleagues have described a common pattern of interaction in families with defiant children that they call a coercive family environment (Granic & Patterson, 2006). It starts when the child behaves in some way that irritates the parent, for instance jumping on the furniture, and the parent asks the child to stop. Instead of complying with this request, the child engages in some other coercive behavior like whining or throwing a temper tantrum that annoys the parent even more. The child's behavior is so annoying the parent finally gives up, perhaps with a statement like "You never listen to anything you are told to do."

This capitulation by the parent reinforces the child's behavior because, in the child's mind, he has won this battle when the parent stops trying to make him do something he doesn't want to do. Likewise, when the parent gives up and the child stops crying or whining, the peace and quiet reinforces the parent's ineffective parenting. This sets up a pattern of confrontation, followed by opposition, followed by defeat for the parent and success for the child, and the pattern repeats itself. Interventions that help parents provide structure in the home environment and establish daily routines can have some success in breaking the cycle, particularly if they are initiated before the child starts school (Egger, 2009; Shaw, Owens, & Giovannelli, 2001).

Disruptive Mood Dysregulation Disorder

Disruptive Mood Dysregulation Disorder (DMDD) is first diagnosed in children between 6 and 10 years of age when they have "severe recurrent temper outbursts . . . that are grossly out of proportion in intensity or duration to the situation . . ." that occur three or more times per week (APA, 2013, p. 156). Children with DMDD are irritable and angry most of the time and in many different situations. DMDD is a new diagnosis in the *DSM-5* and is considered more severe than oppositional defiant disorder.

Conduct Disorder

An even more serious diagnosis is conduct disorder, which the *DSM-5* describes as a "repetitive and persistent pattern of behavior in which the basic rights of others or major age-appropriate social norms or rules are violated" (APA, 2013, p. 469). The behaviors used to diagnose this condition include aggressiveness toward people and animals, property destruction, deceptiveness or theft, and serious rule violations, including frequently running away from home or being truant from school (McMahon & Kotler, 2006).

Rates of conduct disorder vary from less than 1% to 10% of the U.S. population (APA, 2013). The condition is 10 times more likely to affect boys than girls when onset occurs during childhood (Moffitt & Caspi, 2001). Early onset is associated with "inadequate parenting, neurocognitive problems, and temperament and behavior problems" (Moffitt & Caspi, 2001, p. 355), such as aggressiveness and irritability.

Conduct disorders are among the most difficult conditions to treat, but multisystemic treatment (MST) has shown some

Mauro Fermariello/Science Source

Conduct disorder. A conduct disorder involves aggression, a serious violation of another person's rights, or a major violation of societal rules. Age-inappropriate behavior such as drinking at this young age could be part of a pattern of behavior that indicates a potentially serious problem. ■

promise (Curtis, Ronan, & Borduin, 2004). Based on Bronfenbrenner's ecological systems theory described in Chapter 2, this approach examines many levels of influence that may contribute to the disorder, including family, peers, school, and community. The therapist and family work together to build on strengths within the family and the community to overcome problems. In a meta-analysis of 11 studies, MST made substantial improvements in family relationships and was able to decrease children's aggression toward peers, involvement with other conduct-disordered youth, and overall criminality (Curtis et al., 2004).

Treatments such as MST that include the family seem to work better than those that remove the child from the family, often in programs based on confrontation or "tough love." Because the child needs eventually to be able to function in his or her home, school, and community, treatment that keeps the family together as a unit makes achieving that goal more likely. If a child does acquire some positive skills as part of an out-of-home treatment program but returns to an environment that does not support those behavioral changes, the skills are not likely to persist.

Check Your Understanding

1. What are some gender differences in how boys and girls express emotions?
2. What is the difference between fear and anxiety?
3. What is clinical depression?
4. What are oppositional defiant disorder (ODD), disruptive mood dysregulation disorder (DMDD), and conduct disorder?

T/F #4
"Tough-love" programs (for example, wilderness camps and boot camps) for children with conduct problems have been very successful at rehabilitating these young people. *False*

Family Relationships

In this chapter, we have examined children's individual development of the sense of self and emotions. We now move on to an examination of children's social world. We first look at children's relationships with parents and siblings and then discuss their growing ability to interact with peers and develop friendships.

13.3

What do we know about family relationships during middle childhood?

Parenting in Context

In Chapter 10, we described the four parenting styles identified by Diana Baumrind: authoritative, authoritarian, permissive, and disengaged. At that time we noted that an authoritative style has been associated with a number of positive developmental outcomes for children, but we cannot ignore the cultural context in which parenting occurs. Parenting reflects the attitudes and values of a society, as well of its beliefs about how development occurs.

An authoritative style reflects some important values of individualistic cultures by showing respect for the child as an independent being in the context of a warm, affectionate relationship. The more authoritarian style adopted by many African American parents emphasizes important values in that culture, such as respect for authority and an obligation to family (Jambunathan, Burts, & Pierce, 2000). Research with Latino families has not identified a consistent parenting style (Jambunathan et al., 2000), but one study found that Baumrind's parenting types did not characterize Latino parenting very well. Most of these parents were high on control and high on warmth, just like authoritative parents, but they were low on autonomy-granting, a pattern called *protective parenting* (Domenech Rodriguez, Donovick, & Crowley, 2009). Although Asian mothers are usually permissive with young children, they emphasize a strong sense of family obligation as the children get older and rely on shame or guilt if children fail to live up to parental expectations (Jambunathan et al., 2000). Although Chinese parents

Familismo. Latino families share cultural values that include family loyalty, respect for social roles, and a strong moral sense. Each cultural group has its own traditions that emphasize the values that are important to it. ∎

are more controlling, their children typically do well in school. When children reach school age, mothers provide the drive for their efforts to succeed in school, but they do so in the context of the warm, supportive, and physically close relationship that was established when the child was much younger. Another important concept in Chinese culture is *guan*, which literally means "to govern" but can also mean "to care for" or even "to love" (Yi, 2013). The close monitoring and correcting of a child's behavior is seen by both parent and child as a fulfillment of parental responsibilities to the child and in the child's best interest.

Parenting style is based in part on parents' responses and adaptations to their individual children. For that reason even children growing up in the same family may have different experiences with parents. Before we take up the topic of siblings, use **Active Learning: Exploring Your Parents' Style** to connect your own experiences with your parents to the ideas presented here.

JOURNAL ARTICLE 13.1
Intercultural Parenting

Active Learning

Exploring Your Parents' Style

Review the four different parenting styles in Chapter 10, if you need to, before beginning this activity. Based on what you have learned about parenting styles, reflect on how you were raised by thinking about these questions:

- What style of parenting did each of your parents use? Did they use the same or different styles?
- If you have siblings, were there any differences in the styles your parents used with your siblings? Can you think of reasons they may have treated siblings differently?
- How did your parents' parenting style affect you?
- Did their parenting style change as you grew older? If so, *how* did it change?
- What would you do differently with your own children? What would you do the same way? Why? ∎

Relationships With Siblings

The longest-lasting relationships you will have in your life are likely to be with your siblings, on average lasting longer than parent-child relationships or marital relationships. About 80% of children in the United States have at least one sibling. How many siblings you have is not as important as who they are. Sister-sister relationships are different from brother-brother or sister-brother relationships, and siblings who are quite a few years apart in age have a different type of relationship than siblings who are born close together. Finally, in addition to birth siblings, many people have qualitatively different relationships with stepsiblings, half-siblings, and adoptive siblings.

Siblings occupy a special place in a child's social world. Some of the functions they fill overlap with those of parents and others overlap with those of peers, but the combination of roles they fill is unique. One unique characteristic is that sibling relationships can be marked *both* by warmth and by conflict (Buist & Vermande, 2014; Deater-Howe, Rinaldi, Jennings, & Petrakos, 2002). The sibling relationship can contain levels of jealousy and rivalry not usually seen in more discretionary relationships, like those between peers, but to varying degrees it also contains a sense of obligation. There is an expectation that siblings will be there to provide support and resources to each other in times of need (Cicirelli, 1994).

She's my sister! There is much more to sibling relationships than sibling rivalry. Most relationships are warm and supportive, and siblings learn a great deal from each other. ■

Sibling relationships often reflect the quality of the relationship between parents and their children. For example, McHale, Whiteman, Kim, & Crouter (2007) found that a warmer relationship with parents was related to more positive sibling relationships. However, siblings can sometimes compensate for difficulties in relationships with the parents. Warm sibling relationships can help children deal with stress in their lives, even when their relationship with their mother is not warm (Gass, Jenkins, & Dunn, 2007). Although siblings fill many positive roles for each other, they also can become "partners in crime," influencing each other to engage in more negative behavior (Richmond, Stocker, & Rienks, 2005, p. 556; see also Stormshak, Comeau, & Shepard, 2004).

Shared and Nonshared Environments

The assumption underlying much of the research done on siblings is that siblings grow up in the same family so they share the same environment, and the only difference between them is their genetics, but increasingly we have realized that each child growing up in the same family actually has many different experiences in that environment. This has led us to an interest in understanding the impact of the nonshared environment (Plomin, 2011).

VIDEO LINK 13.4
Sibling Relationships

Nonshared environment The different experiences that siblings in the same family have in that environment.

How important is the effect of nonshared influences? It is so great that one group of researchers has concluded that "one of the most notable findings in contemporary behavior genetics is that children growing up in the same family are not very similar" (Hetherington, Reiss, & Plomin, 1994, p. vii). In fact, once we take the effects of genetics into account, siblings are no more similar to each other than almost any two other children chosen at random (Turkheimer & Waldron, 2000). It is almost as though they were reared in completely different environments.

T/F #5
Children growing up in the same family are not very similar to each other. *True*

Previously, we had assumed that things like the quality of the parents' marital relationship, the neighborhood the children grew up in, and the family's socioeconomic status equally affected all children in a family, but factors such as these affect each child differently because each is born at a different point in the family's history. Let's assume you are the oldest child in the family. If you were a firstborn child, your family might still have been struggling to establish itself financially at the time of your birth, and money might have been tight during your early childhood. By the time your siblings were born, your family might have been better off financially, so their childhood was spent in more affluent circumstances than yours. Likewise your parents' relationship could have gotten either stronger or become more troubled between the time of your birth and the birth of your siblings. Your family may have moved to a better—or worse—neighborhood during this interval.

Any of these changes means you experienced a family environment in your childhood that was not necessarily the same as your siblings experienced later. And as children get older, they have increasing opportunities to select their own experiences outside the family. If you chose to play soccer, join the band, and hang out with the cool kids, did all your siblings make the same choices, or did they pick different activities, have different interests, and choose different friends than you did? **Active Learning: Examining**

Nonshared Environments allows you to continue thinking about ways in which you and your siblings grew up in separate worlds even though you grew up in the same family.

Active Learning

Examining Nonshared Environments

For this activity, choose one of your siblings as your focus. You might want to choose the sibling you feel is most different from you, but you don't need to do this. We apologize to only children for not being able to include them in this activity. For each item, write a brief description (just words or phrases) of your experiences and the experiences of your sibling as you see them. Then think about how these differences may have affected the two of you.

Event/Experience	You	Your Focus Sibling
Family interactions—The amount of each given by your parents:		
• Affection		
• Control/strictness		
• Responsibility		
Academic success		
Social relationships		
• Number of close friends		
• Quality of friendships (supportive, conflictual)		
• Peer group you spent time with (jocks, brains, populars, druggies, nerds)		
Participation in activities (list them)		
• At school		
• In the community		
• Lessons		
• Work (If "yes," at what age?)		
Major family life events (residential moves, major changes in finances, serious illness/injury of family members, parental separation or divorce). For each event, indicate your age and your sibling's age at the time.		

Based on this comparison, what did you conclude about the nature of the environment you and your sibling shared? In what ways did you have environments that were *not* shared and that may have contributed to differences between you and your sibling? ■

Birth Order

There have been several broad descriptions of differences between siblings by birth order, based on the idea that children have different experiences and play different roles in the family depending on whether they were born first, in the middle, or last. Personality research describes firstborn children as leaders and high achievers who behave responsibly, middle children as more socially skilled and popular, and youngest as the spoiled, rebellious, and artistic ones (Eckstein et al., 2010). However, the evidence for these differences is mixed, at best. One of the problems with this research is that birth order is confounded with family size, which is further confounded with other family

AUDIO LINK 13.3
Birth Order

characteristics such as ethnicity, education, and wealth (Hartshorne, 2009). The best we can say is that any effects of birth order on personal characteristics are extremely small.

Differential Parental Treatment

Parents are often quick to say that they treat all the children in their family the same way, but they may in fact adopt different parenting styles with different children within the same family. This really isn't surprising given that children within the same family differ by age and gender, as well as a number of personality and temperament characteristics (Plomin, Asbury, & Dunn, 2001). However, siblings who are treated less favorably—or who *perceive* they are treated less favorably—show lower levels of adjustment and more conflicted sibling relationships (Jensen & Whiteman, 2014; Jensen, Whiteman, Fingerman, & Birditt, 2013; Siennick, 2013) and can even be at an increased risk of engaging in delinquent activities (Jensen & Whiteman, 2014; Scholte, Engles, de Kemp, Harakeh, & Overbeek, 2007).

Of course in one situation, differential treatment between siblings is almost inevitable, and that is the case of stepsiblings (Baham, Weimer, Braver, & Fabricius, 2008). Each parent in the family likely has a qualitatively different relationship with his or her biological children and his or her stepchildren; plus, each stepsibling has a nonresident biological parent who comes into the mix. Under these complex circumstances, it is not surprising if rivalries or conflicts develop.

The impact of differential parental treatment of siblings is lessened if a child who receives less attention or is treated more harshly sees the differential treatment as legitimate or justified. For instance, when one of the siblings in a family has a developmental disability or other condition that necessitates special treatment by the parents, the healthy sibling usually recognizes and accepts the differences in parental treatment (Schuntermann, 2007).

Only Children

American families have gotten smaller in recent years for a number of reasons. In 2010, there were over 15 million one-child households in the United States (U.S. Census Bureau, 2012a), although of course many of these children might eventually have siblings. There are a number of negative ideas about what only children are like (Mancillas, 2006). Many people assume that if only children have their parents' exclusive attention, they will be selfish or totally dependent on others when they grow up. They believe the lack of social interactions with siblings will lead to a lack of communication or social skills.

The good news for only children is that research has generally failed to support these negative predictions. Rather, it has found that only children show high achievement, good adjustment, strong character, and positive social relationships (Falbo, 2012; Mancillas, 2006). In many comparisons, only children share the positive advantages firstborn children enjoy or are indistinguishable from children in small families. That also suggests they are *not* unique. Rather, they look like other children who have had the same advantage of parent-child relationships that support positive development and high achievement.

T/F #6
Children who grow up without siblings tend to be more self-centered, maladjusted, lonely, and neurotic than children who have siblings. *False*

Children's Living Arrangements

Children grow up in a variety of family structures. Figure 13.2 shows the percentage of children in the United States who live in each of several different family forms and how the percentage living in each household type has changed since 1970. Family-based households declined from 81% in 1970 to 66% in 2012 because more adults are living alone. Perhaps the most noticeable change is the decline in married couples living with their own children. They had been 40% of households in 1970, but accounted for less

FIGURE 13.2   Family household living arrangements

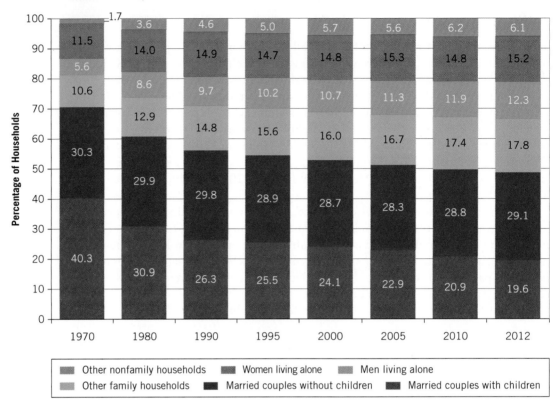

Family household type in the United States has changed substantially since 1970, with the number of married couples living with their own children declining from 40% in 1970 to slightly less than 20% in 2012. Over this same period of time, the number of households headed by an unmarried parent increased from 11% to 18%.

SOURCE: Vespa, Lewis, & Krelder (2013).

than 20% of households in 2012 (Vespa, Lewis, & Krelder, 2013). Each of these living arrangements has different consequences for children's growth and well-being, so we discuss them separately below.

Single Parenting

Single-parent households are formed in various ways. In some cases, the woman is unmarried when she has children, and in others she is divorced or widowed. In 2012, 40.7% of all births in the United States were to unmarried women (Martin, Hamilton, Osterman, Curtin, & Mathews, 2013). This percentage differs by racial and ethnic groups: 71.6% of Black or African American women, 66.9% of American Indian or Alaska native women, 53.5% of Hispanic women, 35.9% of non-Hispanic White women, and 17% of Asian or Pacific Island women were unmarried at the time of their child's birth (Martin et al., 2013). This does not, of course, mean the parent is the only adult in the household. In slightly more than half the births to unmarried women, the woman is cohabiting with a partner (Child Trends, 2012a). Although many unmarried women in this situation plan eventually to marry the father of their child, one large-scale study found that 1 year after the birth only 10% of the mothers had actually married the father, and only 20% of the fathers maintained regular contact with the child (McLanahan & Carlson, 2004).

Whether a single-parent household is created when a single woman gives birth or by divorce or the death of a parent has different consequences for children. Generally

T/F #7
The majority of women who are single but living with the father of their baby when their baby is born will marry the baby's father shortly after the baby's birth. *False*

children whose parent has died tend to do better in education and emotional adjustment in the long run than children whose parents are divorced. Society has established ways to support those who have lost a loved one, but it does not have comparable ways of supporting those who have undergone a divorce. For example, widows receive Social Security survivor's benefits (Tillman, 2007), but divorced mothers may or may not receive child support. On an emotional level, children are more likely to be able to hold on to positive thoughts about a parent who has died, while children of divorce are more likely to struggle with their feelings about both their parents.

If you were asked to describe the typical single parent, would you picture a mother or a father? Is this parent a teenager? Was this parent ever married? Is this parent employed, or does the family live in poverty or on public assistance? According to recent statistics from the U.S. Census, a single parent is more likely to be a mother than a father (84% female versus 16% male), to have been married at one point in time (only 34.2% of single mothers and 20.0% of single fathers were never married), to be employed (79.5% of mothers and 90% of fathers are employed either full or part time) (Grall, 2011), and not to live in poverty (although 41% of single mothers and 24% of single fathers do) (U.S. Census Bureau, 2012b). Also, only 8% of births to unmarried mothers occur to women under the age of 18 (Edin & Kefalas, 2005). How accurate were your ideas of what the typical single parent is like?

Divorce

In Chapter 7, you learned about the number of families who have experienced a divorce. In this chapter, we continue to look at the impact a parental divorce has on children. The earliest research tended to treat divorce as a single event. Children from divorced and intact families were compared, and there appeared to be many negative outcomes for children from divorced families. However, current thinking defines divorce as a process that unfolds over time rather than as a single event (Amato, 2010; Dowling & Elliott, 2012). After a divorce there will likely be a number of additional changes that affect the children in the family, including residential moves, changes in financial resources, new caretakers, custody changes, parental dating relationships, cohabitation, stepparents, new siblings, and more that may be disruptive and distressing for the children. All these factors play a role in how well children fare following a divorce.

Many studies have found that academic achievement suffers, with the biggest impact on school completion. Children from single-parent families formed by divorce are twice as likely as those with two parents to leave school before high school graduation (Martin, Emery, & Peris, 2004), they are less than half as likely to attend college (Elliott, 2009), and are less likely to complete college if they do begin (Biblarz & Gottainer, 2000).

Research also has examined both types of behavior problems, externalizing and internalizing behaviors. Children from divorced and single-parent families, especially boys, have generally been found to be more "disobedient, aggressive, demanding and lacking in self-control" (Martin et al., 2004, p. 284; see also Ehrenberg, Regev, Lazinski, Behrman, & Zimmerman, 2014) both in early childhood and later in life. To a lesser extent, parental divorce is also associated with internalizing behavior problems such as anxiety and depression (Ehrenberg et al., 2014; Franic, Middeldorp, Dolan, Ligthart, & Boomsma, 2010; Kim, 2011).

About 20% to 25% of children of divorce experience high levels of behavior problems, compared to 10% of children from intact families (Greene, Anderson, Hetherington, Forgatch, & DeGarmo, 2003). However, the average differences between children of divorce and children from intact families are small, and most children from divorced families score within the normal range of functioning on many measures (Amato & Anthony, 2014; American Psychological Association, 2004; Ehrenberg et al., 2014).

WEB LINK 13.3
Single Parenting

T/F #8
On average, there are only small differences between children of divorce and children from intact families.
True

Family conflict. What would it feel like to be this boy, listening to his parents fight? ■

JOURNAL ARTICLE 13.2
Divorce

Several factors associated with parental divorce are related to worse outcomes for children. One of the most important is ongoing high levels of conflict between the parents. If a parent resorts to criticizing the other parent, it is particularly damaging to the child's self-esteem and emotional well-being (Baker & Ben-Ami, 2011). When the parent says, "Your other parent doesn't love you," the child may hear, "You are not worth loving." However, when parents can handle their disagreements in a positive way (for example, they resolve conflict through problem solving and remain emotionally supportive of each other), children are more likely to experience positive emotional development (McCoy, Cummings, & Davies, 2009). In cases where high levels of family conflict and dysfunction are resolved by a divorce, children's functioning often improves (Booth & Amato, 2001; Strohschein, 2005; Yu, Pettit, Lansford, Dodge, & Bates, 2010).

It is not surprising that parent-child relationships often change as the result of a divorce. Parents who are highly stressed often provide less positive support for the child, use less effective communication, and provide less monitoring and control over the child's behavior (Greene, Sullivan, & Anderson, 2008; Martinez & Forgatch, 2002; Pett, Wampold, Turner, & Vaughan-Cole, 1999). Sometimes during or following a divorce, the children become more concerned with their parent's emotional needs than their own because they become a parental confidant or mediator between their parents (Jurkovic, Thirkield, & Morrell, 2001; Martin et al., 2004). At other times, they assume responsibility for actually managing the household by taking care of siblings, shopping, or cleaning for the family (Jurkovic et al., 2001). These children may appear to others to be doing well, and this added responsibility can contribute to the development of competence and maturity in older children, but it can be an overwhelming burden to younger ones (Jurkovic et al., 2001). When conflict between parents continues for years and the children are brought into it in many ways, divorce creates continuing anxiety in children.

Most psychologists today would agree that rather than asking whether divorce affects children, we should try to understand how and under what circumstances (Amato, 2010) and identify ways we can help children cope with this experience. When parents are able to disengage from each other while maintaining warm and consistent parenting for their children, children's cognitive and social development is less likely to be negatively affected in the long term (American Psychological Association, 2004; Ehrenberg et al., 2014). Parents can encourage their children to talk about how they are feeling, reassure them that both parents still love them and that the divorce is not their fault, and help them stay in contact with both parents. Keeping up with child support payments also helps reduce financial hardship, one of the greatest sources of stress during the divorce process (American Academy of Matrimonial Lawyers, 2009; Nemours Foundation, 1995–2012).

Most of the research that has been done on nonresident fathers has looked at the amount of face-to-face contact the father has with his children following a divorce or his provision of financial support to the family, while much less has looked at the quality of the relationship maintained despite the physical separation (Dunn, Cheng, O'Connor, & Bridges, 2004). One explanation for the variability in outcomes for children of divorce is that simple measures of paternal contact may not be adequate to assess the impact of nonresident fathers on their children's development. Instead we need to look at the quality of that relationship over time (Amato & Gilbreth, 1999).

The amount of contact children have with nonresident fathers varies greatly. In one longitudinal study, following a divorce two thirds of fathers were consistently either highly involved with their children or had little contact, another 23% had a pattern of declining contact, and a smaller group of 8% increased contact over time (Cheadle, Amato, & King, 2010). Although some children lose all contact with their fathers after a few years (Dunn et al., 2004), we should not presume that because a father does not reside in the same household as his children he is not part of their lives. In a study of older children in which about half the sample resided with their father and the other half lived apart, the children were asked to describe the perceived quality of their relationship with their father on a number of dimensions (Munsch, Woodward, & Darling, 1995). When children who lived with their father and children who lived apart but still had contact with him were asked to describe the quality of their relationship with their father, there were surprisingly few differences between their perceptions. Because maintaining contact with a child you no longer reside with takes effort, noncustodial fathers need to hear the message that they can be—and often are—important people in the lives of their children, an idea that continues to be supported by research (Dunn et al., 2004; Mandel & Sharlin, 2006).

There has been considerably less research on noncustodial mothers, but people often make negative assumptions about why a mother would not have custody of her children (Bemiller, 2010). They assume she is selfish, incompetent, or unfit, but it is more likely she has voluntarily relinquished custody to the children's father because she is unable to financially support the children, has physical or emotional problems, or the child has asked to reside with someone else (Bemiller, 2010). In fact there are several ways in which children's relationship with a noncustodial mother could be considered more positive than the relationship with noncustodial fathers. Noncustodial mothers are seen as maintaining greater emotional involvement in the lives of their children, even when they live apart, and as being more sensitive to their child's needs, more effective at providing support and comfort, and more knowledgeable about the child's day-to-day activities (Gunnoe & Hetherington, 2004). There also is some evidence that the relationship with a noncustodial mother plays a bigger role in the child's postdivorce adjustment (Gunnoe & Hetherington, 2004).

Stepfamilies

Three out of four divorced people remarry, so many children who have experienced a parental divorce later face the challenge of entering a stepfamily. It is not uncommon for children to dislike or show challenging behavior to a new stepparent (Ganong, Coleman, & Jamison, 2011). They may feel they are being disloyal to their biological parent if they like their new stepparent, may continue to harbor the fantasy that their parents will get back together, or may simply resent the attention their parent now pays to the new partner (Hetherington & Kelly, 2002). Strained relationships between stepparent and stepchild undoubtedly contribute to the fact that 60% to 67% of remarried couples experience a second divorce (Divorce Statistics, 2012). However, if the stepparent can ride out this period of adjustment, which lasts for 5 to 7 years on average, a better relationship can ultimately develop (Amato, 2005). On a positive note, if a parent's second marriage is better than the first, it provides the child with a new model of what a loving relationship can be (Kalter, 1990).

For many years stepfamilies were studied using a deficit comparison model that compared them to intact families and found them lacking or deficient. However, more recent research comparing children in stepfamilies to other groups of children has not shown any conclusive differences (Clarke-Stewart & Brentano, 2006; Pasley & Moorefield, 2004). Academic performance is somewhat lower for children from divorced families,

VIDEO LINK 13.5
Stepfamilies

AUDIO LINK 13.4
Gay Parents

and remarriage of a parent does not increase academic performance of the children over the level they achieved before the remarriage (Tillman, 2007). Overall adjustment and well-being of children in stepfamilies is slightly lower on average than that of children in well-functioning biological families, but individual differences are very large, which means many children in stepfamilies are thriving (Clarke-Stewart & Brentano, 2006; Dunn, 2002). The most important factors that relate to children's well-being in stepfamilies are the number of transitions and stresses a child has been exposed to and the quality of the parent-child relationship (Amato, 2005; Dunn, 2002). Parents and others need to be open to listening to children's thoughts and feelings about their complicated family lives.

Gay parents. Children growing up with loving parents who are gay appear to thrive as much as those whose parents are heterosexual. ∎

Gay and Lesbian Parents

According to the 2010 U.S Census, there are nearly 650,000 same-sex couples living in the United States, and an estimated 19% of same-sex couple households include children under the age of 18 (Gates, 2013). The majority of children in households with gay or lesbian parents were born when one of the parents was in a heterosexual marriage. However, increasingly, gay and lesbian couples are having children through pregnancy or adoption (Elliott & Umberson, 2004).

In 2005, the American Psychological Association released a comprehensive review of the research literature on gay and lesbian parenting and its effects on children. The authors of the report conclude:

> [T]here is no evidence to suggest that lesbian women or gay men are unfit to be parents or that psychosocial development among children of lesbian women or gay men is compromised relative to that among offspring of heterosexual parents. Not a single study has found children of lesbian or gay parents to be disadvantaged in any significant respect relative to children of heterosexual parents. Indeed, the evidence to date suggests that home environments provided by lesbian and gay parents are as likely as those provided by heterosexual parents to support and enable children's psychosocial growth. (p. 15)

Although this report came from the premiere professional organization in the field of psychology, almost immediately critics found problems with the conclusions based primarily on the methodology or the samples used for the studies (Marks, 2012; Regnerus, 2012). Most studies have relied on convenience samples, which are samples that are not necessarily representative of the population but rather are ones convenient and accessible to the researcher.

A more recent longitudinal study utilizing a large, random sample of adults ages 18 through 39 who grew up in diverse family forms came to a different conclusion that children do best when raised in continually married mother/father relationships. About one quarter of a large number of comparisons made in this study were "suboptimal" (p. 764) for adult children of LGBT parents (Regnerus, 2012). However, this study had its own methodological issues that may have biased the results and the conclusions drawn from it. First, many of the children raised in gay and lesbian families experienced a number of other stressful family events (for example, a contentious divorce or custody fight between heterosexual parents prior to formation of the LGBT family), and second, these adult children grew up in nontraditional families at a historical time when these family forms were less common, and probably less accepted, than they are in today's society (Regnerus, 2012).

The fact that most children currently residing with lesbian or gay parents have lived in other family structures as they grew up makes it extremely difficult to determine which of the observed effects are attributable only to the child's time in a lesbian or gay family. Paul Amato (2012) has joined the debate by saying that "if differences exist between children with gay/lesbian and heterosexual parents, they are likely to be small or moderate in magnitude" (p. 772). This may be the best conclusion we can draw about research on children in gay and lesbian families at this time.

Children in Foster Care

Children may be in foster care for a variety of reasons. Parents may not be able to care for their children, or children may be removed from their parental home because it is not a safe environment. One of the ways in which foster care is different from the other living arrangements we have discussed is that it is never intended to be a permanent situation for the child. The child not only goes into care with all the stress that brought him there in the first place but also must deal with the anxiety of living with a family he does not know, the need to change schools and lose contact with friends, and questions about when or whether he will have to move again, either to return to his own family, to be placed with another foster family, or to be adopted.

When 20 children in foster care were asked to provide advice to other children entering foster care and their foster families, these children indicated they knew that there was not one type of foster family, so new foster children had to be prepared for the fact that their new living situation might be quite different from other places they had lived (Mitchell, Kuczynski, Tubbs, & Ross, 2010). They also said that it would take time to adapt to the new foster families but that it gets easier as time passes. At least some of the children recognized that a new placement could mean new opportunities for the foster child. To handle the emotions that come along with this transition, the children recommended that newly fostered children try to stay calm, remain respectful, and have a positive attitude. It also helps if the child is able to keep some items that have sentimental value to them. We examine effects of foster care on adolescents in Chapter 16.

Check Your Understanding

1. Briefly compare parenting styles in families from different cultural backgrounds.
2. How do shared and nonshared environments affect sibling relationships?
3. How are only children similar to and different from children with siblings?
4. What are some ways that the negative effects of divorce on children can be reduced?
5. Why is it difficult to determine the effect of growing up in a LGBT family on children?

Peer Relationships

13.4

What affects the quality of a child's peer relationships?

Peers become increasingly important during middle childhood. Children's relationships both with friends and with the larger peer group will affect their well-being. In this section we look at the nature and impact of friendships and peer status and acceptance. We also look at a negative aspect of peer interactions: bullying.

VIDEO LINK 13.6
Friendships

Social status The level of peer acceptance or peer rejection of an individual in the peer group.

Sociometry A research technique used to assess a child's social status within the peer group.

Popular children Children who receive a lot of nominations as "like most" and few as "like least" on a sociometric measure.

Rejected children Children who receive a lot of nominations as "like least" and few as "like most" on a sociometric measure.

Average children Children who receive a number of nominations for "like most" and "like least" that is close to the median in the peer group on a sociometric measure.

Neglected children Children who receive relatively few nominations either as "like most" or as "like least" on a sociometric measure.

Controversial children Children who receive both a large number of nominations for "like most" and a large number of nominations for "like least" from peers on a sociometric measure.

Popular-prosocial children Children who are popular among peers because they are low on aggression and have a number of desirable characteristics.

Popular-antisocial children Children who are popular with peers by combining prosocial behavior with aggression as a way to manipulate people.

Friendships and Social Status

Children between the ages of 6 and 12 begin to value having a best friend, and this friendship is more likely to be marked by a commitment to each other based on trust. Friends spend time together, like to do the same kinds of things, and increasingly offer each other emotional support. However, friendships will vary in the amount of loyalty and commitment, self-disclosure, and conflict they contain. Another important aspect of peer relationships is social status, or the general acceptance or rejection of an individual within the peer group. Researchers have used a technique called sociometry to study peer acceptance. In this technique, researchers ask children to nominate the children they like most or like least (Poulin & Dishion, 2008). The choices of all the children are then combined to determine the overall level of social acceptance or rejection of each of the children in the peer group.

Figure 13.3 shows how we can combine peer acceptance and peer rejection to describe different social statuses of individual children. Children who receive a lot of nominations from the peer group for "like most" and few for "like least" are classified as popular children. Those who receive a lot of nominations for "like least" and few for "like most" are classified as rejected. Children who receive a number of nominations close to the median for the group are classified as average, and those who receive relatively few nominations in either category are classified as neglected. Finally, some children receive both a large number of nominations for "like most" from some peers and a large number of nominations for "like least" from other peers. They are classified as controversial children (Coie, Dodge, & Coppotelli, 1982).

More recently, researchers have recognized that there are two different ways a child can become popular within the peer group. Both groups of popular children are seen as attractive and having many friends, but popular-prosocial children are low on aggression and have highly desirable characteristics, such as helpfulness or athletic ability, while popular-antisocial children combine prosocial behavior with aggression as a way of manipulating people. This second group has been described by their peers as stuck

FIGURE 13.3   Determining sociometric status

Peer Acceptance

HIGH

	Peer Rejection HIGH ... LOW	
Controversial		Popular
	Average	
Rejected		Neglected

LOW

Popular children = High on peer acceptance, low on peer rejection
Rejected children = High on peer rejection, low on peer acceptance
Controversial children = High on peer acceptance, high on peer rejection
Neglected children = Low on peer acceptance, low on peer rejection
Average children = Average level of peer acceptance and peer rejection

After asking peers who they like the best (peer acceptance) and who they like the least (peer rejection), this information can be combined to produce the 5 sociometric status groups used in sociometric research.

SOURCE: Coie, Dodge, & Coppotelli (1982). © 1982 American Psychological Association.

up, bullies, and not caring about school, but at the same time they are seen as influential leaders and are admired for this characteristic (de Bruyn & Cillessen, 2006; Rodkin, Farmer, Pearl, & Van Acker, 2000).

In a similar way, we now distinguish between two groups of rejected children: rejected-aggressive children and rejected-withdrawn children. Some children are rejected by the peer group because they are aggressive, annoying, or socially unskilled (Sandstrom & Zakriski, 2004). For instance, they may try to enter a game other children are already playing by disrupting it and annoying potential playmates or they may have a tendency to interpret the innocent behaviors of others as hostile rather than benign. For instance, if someone walks past you in the cafeteria and some milk from his or her tray gets splashed on you, is it simply an accident or did that person want to humiliate and embarrass you? A tendency to interpret this behavior as aggressive is called a hostile attribution bias. An attribution is the explanation or cause we give for behavior. Children who have a hostile attribution bias respond negatively even to neutral events and are seen as more aggressive by their peers (Crick, Grotpeter, & Bigbee, 2002). The second group of rejected children are rejected because they are socially withdrawn and anxious (Juvonen, 2013; Zakriski & Coie, 1996). When children who are very shy, nervous, or depressed withdraw from contact with peers, they are not very appealing playmates for other children.

Research on popularity and peer rejection has been focused largely on the personal characteristics of the individual child; however, there is evidence that the context of peer relationships also influences who will be popular and who will be rejected. The characteristics that are seen as desirable can vary from one peer group to another. For example, although rejected children tend to be either aggressive or withdrawn, withdrawn children were more likely to be rejected in groups that are more aggressive, and aggressive children are more likely to be rejected in groups that are more withdrawn (Mikami, Lerner, & Lun, 2010). Children, like adults, also tend to accept and form friendships with others they perceive to be similar to themselves. Therefore, African American children are more likely to be rejected when the majority of their classmates are White, and White children are more likely to be rejected when their classmates are African American (Mikami et al., 2010).

Some children who are not popular with the larger group of their peers may still have friendships that buffer the negative effects of rejection or neglect by the peer group. Having one good friend can be enough to save a child from loneliness and to buffer the child from the physiological effects of stress experienced by rejected children who do not have a close friend (Peters, Riksen-Walraven, Cillessen, & de Weerth, 2011). On the other hand, some children who are widely accepted by the group as a whole do not have a close friend and describe themselves as lonely (Dunn, 2004). Children who are

Rejected-aggressive children Children who are rejected by peers because they are aggressive, annoying, or socially unskilled.

You gotta have friends! Popular children are liked by many of their peers, while rejected and neglected children are not. However, individual friendships are as important as social status for children's well-being. ∎

Rejected-withdrawn children Children who are rejected by peers because they are socially withdrawn and anxious.

Hostile attribution bias The tendency to interpret the innocent behaviors of others as hostile rather than benign.

unpopular also tend to have friendships that are less stable and supportive than those of their more accepted peers, and they are less able to resolve conflicts in their peer relationships (Dunn, 2004; Lansford et al., 2006).

How stable is peer status? The popular and rejected statuses are the most stable categories (Cillessen, Bukowski, & Haselager, 2000). We can easily understand why popular children might remain in this category over time. They regularly receive positive feedback from their peers, which should make it likely they will continue to engage in those behaviors that contribute to their popularity. However, rejected children also tend to maintain their status across various groups of peers and over time (Peets, Hodges, Kikas, & Salmivalli, 2007). That is more difficult to understand, because we would think negative feedback from peers might lead to a change in their behavior. However, aggression is a fairly stable characteristic across childhood, so rejected-aggressive children continue to show the behaviors that have alienated their peers. Those who are rejected-withdrawn may not have many opportunities to engage with peers and to develop their social skills, but some do and those are the children who move out of the rejected status over time (Haselager, Cillessen, Van Lieshout, Riksen-Walraven, & Hartup, 2002). In a similar way, the status of neglected children may change when they move into a different peer group (Zettergren, 2005). The reason is that neglected children tend to be socially unskilled, so with a little more time to mature and develop these skills, a number of these children become more accepted within the peer group.

Both peer rejection and lack of friends are related to difficulties in adulthood, while peer acceptance and having a good friend are related to better outcomes. In one study, preadolescents who had friends were more likely to have a high sense of self-worth when they became adults. Preadolescents rejected by their peer group were more likely to have trouble with the law later in life, probably because rejected children are more likely to seek out and form friendships with deviant peers who in turn are more likely to be engaged in criminal behavior (Juvonen, 2013).

Finally, the effects of peer rejection may be mediated by the child's sensitivity to rejection. A child who doesn't notice rejection or doesn't care very much about it is less likely to be negatively affected than a child who has a high level of rejection sensitivity. **Active Learning: Rejection Sensitivity** gives you an opportunity to better understand how this affects a child's peer relationships.

Rejection sensitivity The extent to which a child is affected by peer rejection.

Active Learning

Rejection Sensitivity

Begin by reading the following scenario:

> "Do you want to go to the movies with me on Saturday?" Ruben asked Carla on the playground. "Sorry," she told him, "I'm busy on Saturday." Ruben angrily stormed off the playground, knocking over a trash can as he passed the gate. Then Tony approached her. "Do you want to go skating with me on Saturday?" he asked. "No, I can't. I'm busy on Saturday," Carla said. "How about on Sunday?" Tony asked. "OK," she said. (Downey, Lebolt, Rincón, & Freitas, 1998, p. 1074)

1. Which boy demonstrates rejection sensitivity?

2. What is Ruben likely thinking about why Carla says she's busy? What is Tony thinking?

3. What do you think might explain the two boys' different reactions, including past experiences and current peer relationships?

4. How will the boys' reactions affect their future interactions with Carla?

5. Think about a time when you wanted to get together with someone and he or she said no. How did you interpret this response? What did you do? How did this affect your relationship with this person? ■

In the example in **Active Learning: Rejection Sensitivity**, Ruben sees Carla's response as an indication that she doesn't want to be with him, while Tony does not jump to that conclusion. If Ruben is generally rejected by his peers, his interpretation of Carla's response may be correct—maybe she really doesn't want to be with him, but children who experience more peer rejection over time come to expect rejection and may see it even when it is not there (London, Downey, Bonica, & Paltin, 2007). This is another example of hostile attribution bias, which can create a vicious cycle that perpetuates a child's rejection by potential friends. Rejection-sensitive children who are able to control the expression of their emotions have better long-term outcomes in adulthood (Ayduk et al., 2000).

Gender and Play

Gender segregation A preference for playing with other children of the same gender.

Gender segregation, the tendency of children to play and become friends with other children of the same gender, begins in preschool and becomes even stronger in middle childhood, especially for boys (Martin & Fabes, 2001; Munroe & Romney, 2006). Gender segregation during play is most likely to happen when there are many children to choose from, for instance in school. At home and in neighborhoods, choices may be more limited, so more mixed gender play occurs (Thorne, 1994). Often a boy and girl who play happily together at home actually hide this fact from their peers to avoid being teased at school.

One of the reasons boys and girls play separately may be that they have different styles of play. Many girls do not like the rough kind of play preferred by many boys. Although both boys and girls are cooperative with friends, boys' friendships are more likely to also include competition and dominance, while girls' friendships are more likely to include self-disclosure and agreement (Zarbatany, McDougall, & Hymel, 2000). Another possible reason is that boys do not respond to girls' style of communication during play, which is more likely to be in the form of suggestions rather than commands. When girls realize they can't influence boys as play partners, they turn to partners who *will* respond: other girls (Ayres & Leve, 2006). Beginning at about age 5, many girls prefer to interact in pairs or small groups, while boys are more likely to interact in large groups and involve themselves in organized games or projects (Markovits, Benenson, & Dolenszky, 2001). This difference in group size means that boys and girls are also engaging in different types of interactions. Large groups require cooperation, competition, conflict, and coordination, while small groups allow for intimate connection, with attention to the individual needs and feelings of the participants (Ayres & Leve, 2006; Maccoby, 2002).

To examine the question whether gender or play preference determines who boys and girls choose to play with, try **Active Learning: Gender Play Preferences**.

Active Learning

Gender Play Preferences

Interview a child between the ages of 4 and 8 using the following procedure, based on the *Playmate and Play Style Preferences Structured Interview* developed by Alexander and Hines (1994):

1. Prepare materials: Take four blank cards or pieces of paper. On two cards draw a plain stick figure. On the third card draw a "female" stick figure (for example, with a skirt and long hair) and on the fourth card draw a "male" stick figure (for

ACTIVE LEARNING
VIDEO 13.1
Gender Play Preferences

example, with a cap and bow tie). Then take a few more cards, and on separate cards draw a few gender-stereotyped toys, such as a baby doll and a toy truck, and a few gender-neutral toys, such as a slide and a puzzle. You could also glue pictures of toys from magazines or catalogs, if you prefer.

2. After reassuring the child that there are no right or wrong answers to the questions, show the child the two plain stick figures, one paired with a male gender-typed toy and the other with a female gender-typed toy. Explain that each figure is a child and the toy shows what that child likes to play with. Then ask the child to pick which figure he or she would want to play with. Do this with several toy pairs. Then use the gender-identified stick figures with gender-neutral toys like a kite or coloring book and ask which figure he or she would choose to play with. Finally, pair the gendered figures with opposite sex-typed toys and ask the child to choose the playmate he or she would prefer.

Did the child prefer to play with a figure who was using toys stereotyped for his or her own gender? Did the child prefer to play with a child of his or her own gender? When forced to choose, did he or she select a child of the same gender or the child who played with the gender-stereotyped toy? Alexander and Hines (1994) found that boys consistently chose an activity regardless of whether a boy or a girl was playing with it, perhaps rejecting boys who play outside the accepted range of activities. Younger girls (4–5 years old) chose to play with girls, regardless of the supposed toy preference of the figure, but older girls (6–8 years old) chose the activity over the gender of the figure. ■

Differences in play styles between boys and girls have also been found for non-Western cultures. A study conducted in four non-Western cultures found that boys played farther from home than girls and engaged in more physical play (Munroe & Romney, 2006). In many cultures, boys' play is more likely to be exploratory than girls' play, perhaps because adults put more limitations on where girls can go on their own. Among fourth-grade children in Bulgaria, Taiwan, and the United States, boys spent more time in free play and with computer games, while girls did more adult-chosen activities, chores, extracurricular activities, and reading (Newman et al., 2007).

Bullying

Although peers usually are positive influences and an important source of support and companionship during childhood, a darker side of peer relationships includes bullying, harassment, intimidation, and violence. Bullying has attracted increasing interest since the 1990s, when several highly publicized cases led to tragic consequences. In some cases, the bullying resulted in the suicide of the victim, and in others, the victims struck back violently through school shootings.

Bullying Repeated exposure to negative actions on the part of one or more other students; includes physical bullying, verbal bullying, and emotional bullying.

Bullying occurs when a victim is "exposed repeatedly and over time to negative actions on the part of one or more other students" (Olweus, 2003, p. 12). A wide range of behaviors are considered bullying, including physical bullying such as hitting, pinching, or punching; verbal bullying such as name-calling or teasing; and emotional bullying such as threatening or intimidating someone. Bullies appear to select as their targets other children who are not accepted by their same-gender classmates so they will not have others who stand by them (Veenstra, Lindenberg, Munniksma, & Dijkstra, 2010). In particular, bullies are likely to select children described as "anxious-solitary," whose vulnerabilities and fears are apparent to others rather than children who are simply unsociable (Ladd, Kochenderfer-Ladd, Eggum, Kochel, & McConnell, 2011).

Bullying has been studied in a number of different countries and large differences in self-reported rates of victimization have been found, from 9% of students in Norway and Sweden, to 21.9% of students in Japan, to 42% of students in Italy. The number of children who self-identify as bullies also varies from 7% in Scandinavia, to 28% of Italian primary school students, to 52% of Japanese elementary school students (Borntrager, Davis, Bernstein, & Gorman, 2009). Even taking into account these disparities, it appears that in many settings and across a number of cultures, the threat of being victimized by a bully is a significant concern for many school-age children.

Regardless of the form bullying takes, bullies share some common characteristics. They are more likely to be depressed (Harris, 2004), to have relatively poor self-concepts (MacNeil & Newell, 2004), to lack self-control, and to have lower levels of social competence than their peers (Demaray & Malecki, 2003). Another very important characteristic is that bullies often have a hostile attribution bias which causes them to see hostile intent in ordinary social interactions (Camodeca & Goossens, 2005). Bullies are more likely to misinterpret an accidental bump or an offhand comment as an intentional affront and then feels justified in attacking peers in retribution for the imagined offense.

Bullies. Bullying can take different forms, including physical, verbal, and psychological abuse. Intimidating or threatening someone is a type of psychological bullying, even if the bully never carries out any threats to physically harm the person. What form of bullying do you think occurs most frequently? ■

Bullies often also engage in deviant behaviors, such as smoking, drinking, carrying a weapon, stealing, or damaging property (Hay, Meldrum, & Mann, 2010; Nansel et al., 2001). They tend to have lower academic achievement, school adjustment, and bonding to the school environment (Demaray & Malecki, 2003; Harris, 2004; Sassu, Elinoff, Bray, & Kehle, 2004). Family characteristics include an insecure attachment to parents (Eliot & Cornell, 2009), a lack of parental supervision, punitive discipline, and family violence that models aggression as a way to resolve disputes (MacNeil & Newell, 2004). Parents of bullies may be uninvolved in their children's lives, and the child may feel unloved and uncared for (Demaray & Malecki, 2003).

Being a victim of bullying has serious emotional, psychological, and physical consequences for a child. Victims report feeling anxious and depressed and often have a poor self-concept (Sassu et al., 2004). Because victims often feel as though they have no friends, this sense of loneliness and powerlessness can contribute to thoughts of suicide or even a suicide attempt (Sassu et al., 2004). Being the victim of bullying also affects children's ability to be successful in school because victimization is associated with absenteeism, a lack of participation in extracurricular events (Harris, 2004), and a decline in academic performance (MacNeil & Newell, 2004). However, a victim's response also can take the form of violence against others.

AUDIO LINK 13.5
Consequences of Bullying

More than half of children who say they have been bullied say they have not told a teacher (Fekkes, Pijpers, & Verloove-Vanhorick, 2005; Holfeld & Grabe, 2012; Li, 2007). Many thought administrators or teachers were not interested in stopping bullying, and many adults have seemed unaware or unconcerned about the problem (Sassu et al., 2004). However, when adults within a school are perceived as being more supportive, children are more likely to say they would seek help if they were victims of a bully (Eliot, Cornell, Gregory, & Fan, 2010). Victimization can make people distrustful of others, and this contributes to the child's unwillingness to report what is happening. And, finally, some victims claim that being bullied simply didn't bother them (Harris, 2004).

Bullying is more than the interaction between a bully and a victim. To fully understand what happens—and why it happens—we need to look at the social context in which it occurs. Dan Olweus (2003) has provided such a description with the *bullying circle* (see Figure 13.4). As you can see, in addition to victim and bully, there are passive or possible

FIGURE 13.4   The bullying circle

The bullying circle shows that bullying involves more than just a bully and a victim. A number of others are involved to a greater or lesser extent.

A. Students Who Bully
These students want to bully, start the bullying, and play a leader role.

B. Followers or Henchmen
These students are positive toward the bullying and take an active part, but don't usually initiate it and do not play a lead role.

C. Supporters or Passive Bullies
These students actively and openly support the bullying, for example, through laughter or calling attention to the situation, but they don't join in.

D. Passive Supporters or Possible Bullies
These students like the bullying but do not show outward signs of support.

E. Disengaged Onlookers
These students do not get involved and do not take a stand, nor do they participate actively in either direction. (They might think or say: "It's none of my business," or "Let's watch and see what happens.")

F. Possible Defenders
These students dislike the bullying and think they should help the student who is being bullied but do nothing.

G. Defenders
They dislike the bullying and help or try to help the student who is being bullied.

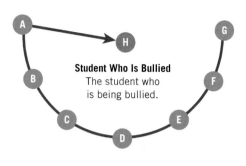

Student Who Is Bullied
The student who is being bullied.

SOURCE: Olweus, 2003. © 2001 by Guilford Publications, Inc. Reproduced with permission of Guilford Publications, Inc., via the Copyright Clearance Center.

WEB LINK 13.4
Stop Bullying

T/F #9
School-wide programs that have attempted to reduce bullying in school have been highly successful. *False*

supporters of what is happening and defenders or possible defenders of the victim, as well as curious onlookers. One goal of anti-bullying programs is to empower students so they can become someone who effectively acts as a defender in the face of bullying.

Public concern about bullying is increasing, and many individual states now have anti-bullying legislation (see Figure 13.5), but we still lack national legislation that treats bullying as a problem shared by all parts of the country. A number of different types of programs have been developed and implemented in U.S. schools, including (a) traditional programs such as the Olweus Bullying Prevention Program, which seeks to reduce the opportunities for bullying to occur while removing the rewards for it when it does happen (Olweus, 2003); (b) programs that increase social competence while reducing antisocial behavior such as aggression; (c) programs that teach students how to respond to conflict; and (d) restorative justice programs that try to restore a relationship between the victim and the bully through techniques such as reconciliation or peer mediation (Ferguson, San Miguel, Kilburn, & Sanchez, 2007).

Anti-bullying programs have had some limited success in reducing the problem. A review of anti-bullying programs (Ttofi & Farrington, 2011) found that on average they decreased bullying by 20% to 23% and victimization by 17% to 20%. This review also identified factors that contributed to the effectiveness of programs. More effective programs were longer and more intensive, involved the parents, and included more playground supervision. Perhaps surprisingly, this study found that peer-based interventions such as peer mediation, peer mentors, and bystander intervention programs actually increased victimization. The overall atmosphere of a school may also either promote or discourage bullying. Schools that offer both clear rules that are enforced and support to students have the lowest levels of bullying (Gregory et al., 2010).

Check Your Understanding

1. Compare popular-prosocial children and popular-antisocial children.
2. Compare rejected-aggressive children and rejected-withdrawn children.
3. How does gender segregation affect play in middle childhood?
4. How does the Olweus Bullying Prevention Program try to reduce bullying?

FIGURE 13.5 States with anti-bullying legislation

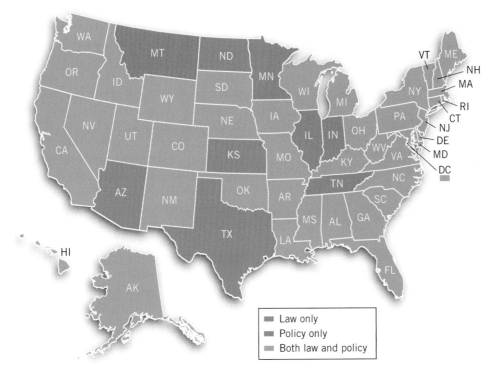

Does your state have laws that direct schools to develop policies to prevent and/or punish bullying? These are the states that had laws in place as of December 2010.

SOURCE: stopbullying.gov

Media Use

How does media affect children's social relationships?

The way children spend their leisure time affects their social relationships. A great deal of attention has been devoted specifically to understanding the effect that time with media violence has on peer relationships. In this section, we briefly review that research and then look at how parents can help mitigate those negative effects.

Media and Social Development

The study of media's impact on aggression began with Albert Bandura's study described in Chapter 2, in which children watched a film in which an adult attacked a Bobo doll. Since that time, a clear and consistent picture has emerged, namely that watching violence or playing violent video games promotes aggression in young viewers (Comstock & Scharrer, 2003; Gentile, 2003; Gentile, Linder, & Walsh, 2003; Kirsh, 2012). In one longitudinal study, Gentile, Coyne, and Walsh (2011) found that third- through fifth-grade children who were exposed to more violent media early in the school year showed higher levels of physical, verbal, and relational aggression 5 months later, at least in part because they had more hostile attribution bias. Likewise, Christakis and Zimmerman (2007) found that viewing violent television at ages 2 to 5 was linked with greater aggression at ages 7 to 10.

Violent video games increase aggressive tendencies even more than TV because players are acting out the violence rather than just watching it (Polman, de Castro, & van Aken, 2008). In a review of studies on violent video games, Anderson et al.

Violent video games. Research has found that playing violent video games brings out aggressive tendencies in children who are already aggressive and also in those who are not. ■

(2010) concluded that they increase the player's actual aggression, raise arousal levels, increase aggressive thoughts and feelings, and decrease prosocial behavior. The more blood there is in the game, the more intense these effects appear to be (Barlett, Harris, & Bruey, 2008). When the player identifies with and acts out the role of the "shooter," these effects are even stronger (Konijn, Bijvank, & Bushman, 2007). Although there is some evidence that children who are already more hostile and aggressive are more likely than others to be further affected by playing violent video games, it appears that even children who do not fit this profile become more violent. In one study, the least hostile children who played video games got into more fights than the most hostile children who did not.

In all cases, when parents limited the amount of time and controlled the content of the video games their children played, children had lower levels of aggression (Gentile & Anderson, 2003).

Helping Children Use Media Wisely

Good advice to parents regarding TV viewing can be very simple: Think about whether you want your child to act like the characters she sees on TV (Franklin, Rifkin, & Pascual, 2001) and let that guide your selection of programs. There are three ways in which parents can interact with children around TV: (1) by providing active mediation and guidance, which means talking with the child about what she is watching; (2) by setting limitations on what the child watches; and (3) by actually viewing programs with the child (Nathanson, 1999). Nathanson found that children were less likely to absorb messages of violence and aggression or to perform them when parents discussed these messages with their children.

Although limiting viewing had a positive effect, evidence also suggested that too much limitation might make the programs "forbidden fruit" and, therefore, even more appealing to children. Viewers between 8 and 22 years reported being *more* attracted to programs that were given restrictive ratings (Bushman, 2006; Bushman & Cantor, 2003). However, many families report that they have no rules for their children regarding TV viewing, and over 70% of children have TV and/or other media in their bedrooms, where no direct parental supervision occurs (Rideout et al., 2010).

Parents need to find a comfortable medium between being overly restrictive and having no restrictions at all. When parents watched shows containing violence with children without commenting on the show's content, children's aggression increased, possibly because it appeared to them that the parents tacitly approved of the messages they were seeing. We might speculate that giving children unfettered access to TV in the bedroom may also give the clear message of parental acceptance of all TV content (Barkin et al., 2006).

Check Your Understanding

1. How does use of violent media affect children in middle childhood?
2. How can parents help children use media more wisely?
3. What makes a particular type of viewing seem like "forbidden fruit"?

Stress, Coping, and Resilience

Stress is an inevitable part of growing up. It comes in many forms, from day-to-day hassles that are resolved in minutes to long-term stressors that persist over months or even years, to catastrophic events that change everything in our world in a matter of minutes. As we have noted in earlier chapters, the field of child development has increasingly recognized that facing adversity while growing up can produce stress responses that undermine the developing brain, cardiovascular system, immune system, and metabolic control system (Center on the Developing Child at Harvard University, 2010), but fortunately for most children, the stress they experience is within a range they can manage. Characteristics of the child, such as having an easygoing temperament or good problem-solving skills, or of the child's environment, such as a secure attachment figure or a strong network to provide social support, help in the process of coping. In this section, we focus specifically on what we have learned by looking at children who manage to thrive despite having extraordinary stress in their lives.

A number of experiences challenge the growth and development of children, from physical threats such as child abuse or chronic health conditions to emotional disorders to societal challenges such as poverty and discrimination. You may think it would be amazing if children who experience great adversity could not only survive these challenges but also thrive and grow up to be what Emmy Werner (2005) has described as "competent, confident, and caring adults" (p. 98), but this is exactly what her research has shown they can do. The ability to bounce back from adversity or thrive despite negative life circumstances is called resilience. **Journey of Research: Invincible, Invulnerable, and Resilient** describes how our understanding of children's ability to cope with developmental challenges has changed over the years.

13.6

What makes some children resilient in the face of adversity?

Resilience The ability to bounce back from adversity or to thrive despite negative life circumstances.

JOURNEY OF RESEARCH *Invincible, Invulnerable, and Resilient*

Until the 1970s, psychologists and psychiatrists had primarily focused on understanding circumstances that threatened or disrupted the developmental process, using what is known as a *deficit model* or *risk perspective*. They wanted to understand what placed a child at risk for less-than-optimal development so they would be able to intervene in ways that would prevent problems or correct ones that already existed. A change in perspective emerged in the 1970s and 1980s when several researchers caught people's attention with stories of children who had overcome great adversity and gone on to become extraordinary individuals in the process.

In one of the best-known studies, Emmy Werner (1992) followed almost 700 children on the Hawaiian island of Kauai from birth until their 30s. Almost one third of the children were initially considered to be at high risk due to their life circumstances. These children had difficult births, lived in poverty,

had parents impaired by alcoholism or mental illness, or experienced parental divorce or discord, and many had multiple risk factors. But as Werner and Smith (1985) tracked these high-risk children over time, they found that one third had very good outcomes by the time they entered adulthood. With the advent of this type of resiliency research, the focus in the field began to shift from what could go wrong in development to what could go right. What helps a child recover or bounce back from adversity?

Protective factors identified in resiliency research include an active, outgoing personality that engages other people; good communication and problem-solving skills; a talent or ability that attracts other people; and faith in your own ability to make good things happen (Werner, 2005). These children also are emotionally stable and not easily upset. Often they make good use of whatever resources are available to them, and form warm, emotional bonds with alternative caregivers when their own parents are unavailable to provide support.

Another important protective factor that emerged from longitudinal research is the ability to take advantage of major life transitions as opportunities to redirect your life (Werner, 2005). Entering a supportive marriage, returning to school, and joining military service are all opportunities for a second chance, and resilient individuals seize those opportunities. Werner (2005) summarized the process by saying the resilient children in her study "had relied on sources of support within the family and community that *increased* their competence and efficacy, *decreased* the number of stressful life events they subsequently encountered, and *opened* up new opportunity for them" (author's emphasis, p. 99).

The next shift in perspective came with the advent of the *positive youth development* perspective. This approach is discussed in Chapter 15, where we look at the impact of participation in positive community-based activities as a way to build strengths in children and adolescents. These protective factors work in *any* circumstance for *any* child, whether there is risk or not, to maximize the child's positive potential for growth. Sesma, Mannes, and Scales (2005) sum up this approach by saying, "The concept of thriving encompasses not only the relative absence of pathology, but also more explicit indicators of healthy and even optimal development" (p. 288). ■

WEB LINK 13.5
Resiliency

T/F #10
Children who are able to rise above great adversity like poverty or child abuse have unusual abilities that have allowed them to succeed. *False*

When research on resiliency first entered the literature, its portrayal of resilient children suggested they were remarkable—even heroic—in some way. Words like *invulnerable* and *invincible* were used to describe them, as though nothing could harm them (Masten, 2001). But as research on these children has matured, the picture that emerges is quite different from that of a superhero overcoming impossible odds. Anne Masten (2001), a researcher who has worked for many years with colleagues studying resiliency, concluded that resiliency is the product of what she calls "ordinary magic" (p. 227). She says, "The greatest surprise of resilience research is the ordinariness of the phenomena. Resilience appears to be a common phenomenon that results in most cases from the operation of basic human adaptational systems" (Masten, 2001, p. 227). Those systems include "connection to competent and caring adults in the family and community, cognitive and self-regulation skills, positive views of self, and motivation to be effective in the environment" (Masten, 2001, p. 234).

We have discussed each of these characteristics at some point in this book. Recall what you have learned about the role of attachment, effective parenting, self-esteem, self-regulation, and a drive to master the environment on the course of development. These are aspects of development we get right most of the time, and aspects that try to reassert themselves when things go wrong. Thinking about the "power of the ordinary" leads us to the conclusion that "resilience does not come from rare and special qualities, but from the everyday magic of ordinary, normative human resources in the minds, brains, and bodies of children, in their families and relationships, and in their communities" (Masten, 2001, p. 235). However, these adaptational systems need to be nurtured so they are available to children when they are needed. **Active Learning: Resilience** gives you a chance to think about where and when you have seen this "ordinary magic" happen in your own experiences.

Active Learning

Resilience

Children may experience many types of traumatic events or life circumstances, such as poverty, a natural disaster, child abuse, or a difficult parental divorce. Think about someone you know who appears to be doing well despite difficult life experiences that could have put that person at risk for emotional disturbance, criminal behavior, or other negative outcomes. If there have been potentially traumatic events or circumstances in your life, you can reflect on your own experiences.

Then think about what factors in that person's life may have contributed to his or her apparent resilience. For example, one boy was part of a tough, inner-city gang and headed for trouble. Instead he ended up going to college. He attributes his change in direction and resilience to the guidance of his stepfather, who got him into football where he found a different way to succeed, a positive group of peers, and a reason to do well in school. The factors you see for the individual you describe may come from the outside, such as loving support from one individual; they may come from the child, such as a lively intelligence or social skills; or, most likely, they may come from a combination of the two. ■

One of the greatest challenges to our understanding of the concept of resiliency is the great variability that we see in child outcomes. For example, as we described in Chapter 7, many Romanian orphans adopted by well-functioning families showed an incredible degree of recovery when their life circumstances changed (Masten, 2001), but some continued to show serious pathologies despite their improved living conditions. Most children who experience abuse while growing up do not perpetuate that pattern with their own children, but some do (Jaffee et al., 2013). Children of mothers who are clinically depressed have a high incidence of psychiatric disorders themselves, but a sizeable proportion are able to function adequately in their own lives (Goldstein & Brooks, 2005). Although children growing up in poverty are likely to have psychological and academic difficulties that could limit their achievements, the list of those able to overcome their early experiences includes people who have been successful in all fields of endeavor and several presidents of the United States.

What resiliency research shows us is that recovery is possible, even if it is not inevitable. As of now, we have not identified all the mechanisms that can protect children and the course of development is so complex that it is unlikely we will ever be able to devise a formula for resiliency that can correct every possible negative trajectory. What is important, however, is that work continues within the field to identify and understand the complex interactions between the individual and his or her environment that help children reach their full and unique potential whatever their life circumstances happen to be.

Check Your Understanding

1. What is resilience?
2. List some protective factors that help children cope with adversity.
3. What are some personal characteristics of resilient children?

Conclusion

During middle childhood, children's concept of self becomes more complex and self-evaluation becomes more realistic as they engage in social comparison with their peers. Children are better able to express and control their emotions, but those who have difficulty with this may develop emotional disorders, such as anxiety or oppositional defiant disorder. Families are still central to the well-being of children at this age whether the parents are married, single, divorced, or remarried. Peers become an increasingly important part of children's lives and both friendships and acceptance by the peer group are important influences on their development. Although stress is an inevitable part of growing up, with support from family or friends, many children show great resilience even if they go through very difficult circumstances. As children leave middle childhood, they prepare for the exciting and dramatic changes that occur physically, cognitively, and socially during adolescence.

Chapter Summary

13.1 How does the sense of self develop in middle childhood?

The self is composed of both the self-concept or how you see yourself, and self-esteem or how you feel about yourself. As school-age children get feedback on their performance and begin to make **social comparisons** of themselves with others, their self-evaluation becomes more realistic and self-esteem usually declines. Programs designed to build self-esteem have not been effective because self-esteem comes from accomplishments, not the other way around. Erikson describes school-age children as dealing with the conflict of **industry versus inferiority**. Media usage can be damaging to the self-esteem of children because of the unrealistic models it offers. Both gender and ethnic identity continue to develop in children at this age.

13.2 How does typical emotional development proceed during middle childhood and what problems do children have when they cannot manage or control their emotions?

By middle childhood, most children have learned how to manage their emotions in accordance with the expectations of their culture. Girls are slightly more emotionally expressive than boys, but anger and aggression are more accepted for boys than girls. Sometimes children's emotions become unmanageable and develop into internalizing disorders such as **anxiety disorders**, phobias, **clinical depression**, mood disorders, or externalizing disorders such as **oppositional defiant disorder, disruptive mood dysregulation disorder**, or a **conduct disorder**.

13.3 What do we know about family relationships during middle childhood?

Cross-cultural research has found that parents adapt their parenting style to reflect their cultural values. Siblings' relationships are affected by the gender configuration and age spacing of the children. Siblings are not as similar as we might think because of the significant impact of their **nonshared environment**. Children who have no siblings are as likely as those with siblings to be well-adjusted and happy. Single parent households are more likely to fall below the poverty line, but on average, children from divorced families are not very different from children in two-parent families. When remarriage occurs, most children eventually form positive relationships with stepparents. Noncustodial parents can be important in children's lives if they remain in contact. Children in foster care face special challenges because their living situation is not meant to be permanent.

13.4 What affects the quality of a child's peer relationships?

Children can be **popular, rejected, neglected, controversial,** or **average**. Those without friends or who are rejected by peers can have adjustment problems, but even a single good friend is enough to keep a child from being lonely. Girls and boys have different styles of play so we often see **gender segregation** at this age. **Bullying** creates psychological stress that can have long-term consequences.

13.5 How does media affect children's social relationships?

Children who watch media violence or participate in it through video games are more aggressive. Parents should monitor what their children watch and set limits around it. However, being too restrictive can make these programs "forbidden fruit" and more attractive to children.

13.6 What makes some children resilient in the face of adversity?

Resilient children thrive despite adversity because of "ordinary magic": a warm connection to a caring adult, self-control, good self-esteem, and a drive to master the environment. These children are able to take advantage of major life transitions as opportunities to change the direction of their lives.

Key Terms

Androgyny   432

Anxiety   434

Anxiety disorder   434

Average children   448

Bullying   452

Clinical depression   435

Coercive family environment   436

Conduct disorder   436

Controversial children   448

$SAGE edge™

Sharpen your skills with SAGE edge at edge.sagepub.com/levinechrono

SAGE edge for Students provides a personalized approach to help you accomplish your coursework goals in an easy-to-use learning environment.

Go to edge.sagepub.com/levinechrono for additional exercises and video resources. Select Chapter 13, Social and Emotional Development in Middle Childhood, for chapter-specific activities. All of the Video Links listed in the margins of this chapter are accessible via this site.

REUTERS/Larry Downing

iStock/Goodluz

©iStockphoto.com/fstop123

part VI

Adolescence

14 Physical Development in Adolescence

T/F Test Your Knowledge

Test your knowledge of child development by deciding whether each of the following statements is *true* or *false,* and then check your answers as you read the chapter.

1. **T ☐ F ☐** Adolescent girls who go through puberty earlier than their peers are happier and healthier than girls who go through puberty later.

2. **T ☐ F ☐** In the United States, 90% of adolescents between the ages of 15 and 19 have had sex at least once.

3. **T ☐ F ☐** The number of U.S. adults who today identify themselves as gay, lesbian, or bisexual is close to 20%.

4. **T ☐ F ☐** Many gay, lesbian, bisexual, or transgender adolescents say their school is one of the most accepting parts of their community.

5. **T ☐ F ☐** In recent years the adolescent pregnancy rate has reached a historic low.

6. **T ☐ F ☐** Adolescents as young as 14 years of age can obtain treatment for sexually transmitted infections in all 50 states without parental consent.

7. **T ☐ F ☐** The most effective way to prevent eating disorders is to give adolescents information about how harmful these behaviors can be to their bodies.

8. **T ☐ F ☐** Asian and Black adolescents have the lowest rate of smoking.

9. **T ☐ F ☐** In sports that both males and females play, girls are more likely to suffer a concussion than boys.

10. **T ☐ F ☐** When you are trying to deal with a stressful situation, you should try to ignore your emotional response and instead focus on solving the problem.

Correct answers: (1) F, (2) F, (3) F, (4) T, (5) T, (6) T, (7) F, (8) F, (9) T, 10 (F)

In this chapter, we examine the development of brain and body that will result in adult functioning by the end of adolescence. After examining the processes that contribute to the maturation of the brain, we look at the effects of puberty on the body. As adolescents go through puberty and move toward sexual maturity, their interest in sex develops, including clarification of their sexual orientation. If they become sexually active, they are exposed to certain risks, including becoming pregnant and contracting a sexually transmitted disease. We describe some of the other health-related risks of adolescence, including injury, disordered eating, and substance use. Despite these potential problems, most adolescents manage to cope well with the variety of stresses they experience as they navigate adolescence and move in a positive way toward young adulthood.

Learning Questions

14.1 What characterizes brain development in adolescence?

14.2 How do children's bodies change through adolescence?

14.3 How does sexual maturation affect adolescent development?

14.4 How are adolescents' health and well-being affected by their health practices?

14.5 How do adolescents deal with stress in their lives?

Brain Development in Adolescence

14.1

What characterizes brain development in adolescence?

The adolescent brain is still far from adult maturity. However, the changes over the course of adolescence are less about adding anything new and more about reorganizing the existing structures and functions to allow for greater efficiency and a higher level of cognition and behavior. As described by Jay Giedd (2008), "If we consider a literary/linguistic metaphor, maturation would not be the addition of new letters but of combining earlier formed letters into words, and then words into sentences, and then sentences into paragraphs" (p. 340).

Typical Development

In adolescence, certain aspects of brain structure and function become more streamlined. For example, there is another proliferation or overproduction of synapses in the brain in early adolescence at the very start of puberty, just as there was in infancy. This overproduction results in inefficiency of thought as demonstrated when young adolescents were shown a picture of a face (for example, a sad face) and heard a word that might or might not match that expression ("happy" or "sad"). It took young adolescents longer to decide whether the image and word matched than it did either younger or older participants in the study (McGivern, Andersen, Byrd, Mutter, & Reilly, 2002). The decrease in early adolescent performance was attributed to the proliferation of synapses at this age, and the increased efficiency at the task later in adolescence was attributed to the synaptic pruning that had occurred. The normal pruning process is complete in some areas of the brain by age 12, but in others, especially the prefrontal cortex which controls judgment and impulse control, the process is not complete until well into adolescence or early adulthood (Blakemore & Choudhury, 2006; Giedd, 2004; Gogtay et al., 2004). The changes that occur in the brain with this wave of pruning allow teens and young adults to develop the most sophisticated levels of thought (Petanjek et al., 2011).

Because the connections between the centers for reasoning and the centers for emotions (such as the amygdala) are still developing during adolescence, emotional responses are less tempered by reasoning than will be the case in adults (Society for Neuroscience, 2007). The tendency of adolescents to act on their emotions without thinking through

VIDEO LINK 14.1
Adolescent Brain

a situation may be related to the immaturity of this system in their brain. In **Active Learning: Teenage Brain Development** you will see how this information has even played a role in judgments made by the legal system.

Active Learning

Teenage Brain Development

Imagine you are the judge deciding the punishment in the following case: At age 17, Christopher Simmons brutally murdered an elderly woman, Mrs. Shirley Crook, as he robbed her house. Simmons was convicted of this crime. It is now your job to assign punishment: life in prison or the death penalty. What factors would you take into account in making your decision? Would the defendant's age be one of them? Give your decision and the reasons for it, and then see below to find out what the Supreme Court decided and why.

■ Answer: In fact, Christopher Simmons was initially sentenced to death by a lower court. The case eventually went to the Supreme Court, which overturned the penalty in favor of life in prison. During the Supreme Court considerations, the American Society for Adolescent Psychiatry entered into evidence an argument that adolescents may have impaired impulse control and judgment because of the immaturity of their brain development. In particular, the prefrontal cortex, which controls these functions, is not fully developed (Lehmann, 2004). In the final decision, Justice Anthony Kennedy stated, "The adolescent's brain works differently from ours. Parents know it" (Anderson, 2005, para. 25). Whether cognitive immaturity should be considered when determining a legal punishment is still a very controversial issue. Do you agree that adolescent brain development should be a factor in determining the harshness of punishment for crimes committed by teens? Why or why not?

The production and pruning of synaptic connections makes adolescence a time of opportunity for learning that shapes the brain, but the number of changes that occur also means the brain may be especially vulnerable to the effect of neurotoxins such as alcohol and other drugs during this period (Squeglia, Jacobus, & Tapert, 2009). Any cognitive deficits that result have potential consequences for future academic, occupational, and social functioning as the adolescent moves into young adulthood.

Brain Disorders: Schizophrenia

Schizophrenia A serious mental disorder in which individuals have difficulty discriminating external reality from their own internal states.

Some disorders of the brain do not appear until adolescence. Schizophrenia is a very rare but serious mental disorder that affects between 0.3% and 0.7% of the population (American Psychiatric Association [APA], 2013). It is related to both structural and functional differences in many regions of the brain (Ren et al., 2013). Diagnosis requires two or more of the following symptoms: delusions (unrealistic, fixed beliefs such as that the CIA is trying to get you), hallucinations (most commonly, hearing voices that are not there), disorganized speech, very disorganized or catatonic behavior (lack of reaction to the environment), or negative symptoms (for example, reduced expression of emotion and reduction in self-motivated behavior) which must be present for at least one month. Symptoms often first appear in late adolescence, but the onset can be much later into the mid-30s (APA, 2013). In the very rare cases when children and younger teens develop this disorder, it is referred to as *early-onset schizophrenia* (McDonell & McClellan, 2007). However, although schizophrenia may not be diagnosed until adolescence, in many cases the disorder is preceded either by a gradual deterioration in social and cognitive functioning or by ongoing difficulties in these areas (Quee et al., 2014). After the symptoms of schizophrenia develop, functioning in these areas continues to decline, resulting in difficulty with social, academic, and occupational functioning (McClellan & Stock, 2013; Tandon et al., 2013).

Although we do not understand all the causes of schizophrenia, it is clear that genes play a large role, as shown by research with twins. If one identical twin is schizophrenic, there is a 40% to 60% chance the other will be as well, while a fraternal twin has only a 5% to 15% chance of sharing this condition with a twin (McClellan & Stock, 2013). Prenatal disruption of brain development by factors such as the mother's experience of starvation or influenza increases the possibility the child will develop schizophrenia (Brown & Susser, 2008; Limosin, Rouillon, Payan, Cohen, & Strub, 2003), as do early head injuries for those with a genetic vulnerability (AbdelMalik, Husted, Chow, & Bassett, 2003). There also is a growing body of evidence that adolescent marijuana use can increase the risk of schizophrenia for some teens who are more vulnerable to the disorder because of a genetic predisposition, a dysfunctional environment, or other factors that are not yet entirely clear. For this reason, parents, teachers, and health care providers should be aware of the possibility and look for a decline in school performance and odd behavior in teens who are using marijuana (Evins, Green, Kane, & Murray, 2012).

Schizophrenia is a chronic disorder with little likelihood of a cure. Treatment includes medication, together with work with the adolescent's family to promote understanding of the disorder, and training for the individual in social skills, life skills, and problem-solving skills, together with specialized education programs (McClellan & Stock, 2013; Volkmar & Tsatsanis, 2002).

AUDIO LINK 14.1
Predicting Psychosis

Check Your Understanding

1. What is responsible for the inefficiency of thought demonstrated by many adolescents?
2. What is schizophrenia?
3. What role might genes play in the occurrence of schizophrenia?

Body Growth and Changes in Adolescence

Physical change occurs rapidly during adolescence. Adolescents experience the adolescent growth spurt, and the size and shape of their bodies take on the characteristic appearance of adult males and females. The timing of changes has implications for the young person both physically and socially.

14.2

How do children's bodies change through adolescence?

Physical Changes of Puberty

The adolescent growth spurt is one outward sign of a number of changes occurring as children move through puberty. The pubertal process moves the young person toward sexual maturity. As children approach adolescence, growth hormones work together with sex hormones (particularly estrogen for females and testosterone for males) to produce the rapid increase in height in both girls and boys known as the adolescent growth spurt. Girls, on average, begin their growth spurt at about 9 to 10 years of age and boys begin their growth spurt on average 2 years later than girls (Rogol, Roemmich, & Clark, 2002; Malina et al., 2004) and grow even faster. The pubertal growth spurt ends by about age 15 for girls, following the onset of menarche, and at age 16 or 17 for boys. Figure 14.1 shows how rapidly growth occurs.

Puberty is also a time of significant weight gain, with adolescents gaining 50% of their adult weight during this period of time (Rogol et al., 2002). Both boys and girls add both muscle and fat, but the amount of each and distribution in the body results in the typical gender difference in appearance of adult males and females. Boys add muscle

Adolescent growth spurt The period of rapid increase in height and weight that occurs in early adolescence.

FIGURE 14.1   Growth curves in adolescence

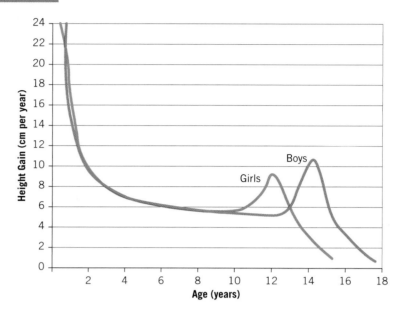

These curves show the rate of growth experienced by girls and boys during adolescence. Note the period of rapid growth that represents the adolescent growth spurt.

SOURCE: © Elsevier Ltd 2005. Standring: Gray's Anatomy 39e. http://www.graysanatomyonline.com

tissue at a faster rate than girls. Girls accumulate fat at a faster rate than boys and the fat migrates from the middle of their bodies to the upper and lower portions, giving them a curvier appearance (Rogol et al., 2002). By the end of puberty, boys have one and a half times as much muscle as girls (Archibald, Graber, & Brooks-Gunn, 2003).

We can estimate a person's *skeletal age* by examining the active growth centers at the ends of bones known as the epiphyses (eh-PIF-i-sees), as shown in Figure 14.2. Bones continue to grow until their soft spongy ends harden off, usually during adolescence; then growth is complete. Because girls reach this stage at a younger age than boys, on average they are shorter in stature than boys (Laycock & Meeran, 2013). One of the consequences of very early puberty is an early growth spurt and too-early bone maturation, resulting in short stature for these girls (Kaplowitz et al., 2013). Similar results have been found for males, with earlier pubertal timing associated with shorter adult status.

The production of androgens in both boys and girls that began in prepubescence is now linked to the growth of facial hair (in boys) and pubic and armpit hair (in both boys and girls) (Salkind, 2005). Estrogen produced by the girl's ovaries will trigger changes in the growth of her uterus, vagina, and breasts. Estrogen is also necessary to support the girl's menstrual cycles. Androgens (especially testosterone) produced by the boy's testes are responsible for the increase in muscle mass.

Although we know a fair amount about the hormonal changes that occur during puberty, we have not had a good understanding about what initiates the process until recently, when scientists discovered a gene called the KiSS-1 gene that appears to be the trigger (Plant, 2006). When the gene turns on, as it is genetically programmed to do, it stimulates the production of the kisspeptin protein molecule, which, in turn, leads to the release of gonadotropins that stimulate the testes in males and the ovaries in females.

During puberty, primary and secondary sex characteristics develop. **Primary sex characteristics** are the body structures necessary for reproduction—the vagina, ovaries, and uterus of the female, and the testes and penis of the male. For females, their maturation during puberty culminates in menarche, the first menstrual flow or period,

Primary sex characteristics The body structures necessary for reproduction—the vagina, ovaries, and uterus of the female, and the testes and penis of the male.

Menarche A girl's first menstrual period.

FIGURE 14.2   Epiphysis of the bones

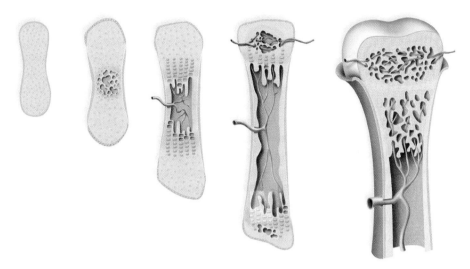

Growth centers are found at ends of bones. The ends remain soft until children reach their adult size, when the ends will harden and growth will stop. This image shows how the bone develops from cartilage (in blue) to hard bone with the soft tissue at the ends.

and the beginning of ovulation. For males, it culminates in spermarche, or the ability to produce viable sperm. Physical characteristics that are associated with gender that do not directly affect the sex organs are the secondary sex characteristics. Breast development in females, deepening of the voice in males, and growth of pubic and underarm hair in both genders are examples. These are important outward signs to others that a child is becoming physically mature. The way peers and adults interact with a young person often is affected by these changes. As young people look less like children and more like adults, they tend to be treated more like adults.

Spermarche The beginning of production of viable sperm.

Secondary sex characteristics Physical characteristics that are associated with gender that do not directly affect the sex organs, such as breast development in females or deepening of the voice in males.

The Timing of Puberty

Although the *sequence* of events that occur during puberty is fixed, the timing is variable. The age at which girls experience menarche has declined in industrialized countries since the mid-1800s (Laycock & Meeran, 2013), falling from about 16 years to about 12 years and leveling off over the last 20 to 30 years in the United States (Chumlea et al., 2003). Only recently have researchers looked at the timing of puberty in boys. In a study reported in 2012, pediatricians found male pubertal development was 6 months to 2 years earlier than reported in earlier studies. The earliest maturation occurred in African American boys, Hispanic boys were next, and the latest pubertal development occurred in White non-Hispanic boys (Herman-Giddens et al., 2012).

As we discussed in Chapter 11, the timing of puberty is influenced by multiple factors, including health, diet, body type, heredity, and ethnic background. Girls from families with more social and economic resources reach menarche 3 months to 3 years before girls from disadvantaged families (Parent et al., 2003), perhaps because of better diet and better overall health in more well-to-do families. A critical level of body fat is necessary for girls to maintain regular menstrual periods. That is why women who are anorexic, or who exercise so strenuously that their reserves of body fat drop to extremely low levels (for example, athletes and dancers), may have irregular periods or stop menstruating altogether. Population studies have consistently shown that a body weight of 47.5 kg (or 105 pounds) is associated with the menarche.

VIDEO LINK 14.2
Protein, Puberty, and Pollutants

Although the relationship is not as well established for boys as it is for girls, there is some evidence that body mass index also is related to the timing of puberty for boys (Burt Solorzano & McCartney, 2010; Kaplowitz, 2008). However, the evidence that does exist points to the opposite result for boys. Being overweight may delay the onset of puberty, although the reason for this delay is unclear at this time.

Because the physical changes of puberty have such a profound effect on how the young person is seen by others, undergoing these changes relatively earlier—or considerably later—than age-mates can have a significant impact on development. Research on pubertal timing goes back to the 1950s, but studies conducted since then have reached a consistent set of conclusions (Weichold, Silbereisen, & Schmitt-Rodermund, 2003). Although off-time pubertal maturation has been linked with depression in early adolescence for both boys and girls (Natsuaki, Biehl, & Ge, 2009), early maturation appears to have a number of advantages for adolescent boys, and late maturation a number of disadvantages. Early maturation can put the girls at some risk, but maturing at the same time as peers has some advantages.

Early maturing boys tend to have positive self-images and feel good about themselves in a number of ways, including being more self-confident and seeing themselves as independent. Late-maturing boys, on the other hand, have more negative self-concepts and are more likely to feel inadequate and rejected. Consequently, they may suffer from depression (Kaltiala-Heino, Kosunen, & Rimpela, 2003) or even engage in alcohol or substance use as a way of compensating for their low social status (Weichold et al., 2003). Because boys who mature earlier are taller and heavier than their peers in early adolescence, they are likely to be the athletes in the group, and this gives them a lot of status in the peer group (Eccles, 1999). However, early maturing boys tend to spend their time with older peers because their physical development is a better match with that of older adolescents, and this can expose them to behaviors they are not yet ready to handle (Goldstein, 2011; Mendle, Turkheimer, & Emery, 2007). For instance, they are more likely to begin using drugs and/or alcohol (Faden, Ruffin, Newes-Adeyi, & Chen, 2010; Westling, Andrews, Hampson, & Peterson, 2008). These risks are even greater for adolescents growing up in disadvantaged neighborhoods or with parents who are harsh or inconsistent in their discipline (Ge, Brody, Conger, Simons, & Murry, 2002).

Because early puberty has been associated with problematic behaviors during adolescence, it has been easy to think that the relative psychological immaturity of the early maturers or their association with older peers is responsible for those behaviors. We seldom look at child characteristics that existed before the onset of puberty that might increase the chance of the young person engaging in these risky behaviors. However there now is evidence from longitudinal research that boys who experience early puberty also had greater behavioral difficulties and poorer psychosocial adjustment earlier in their childhood. Early maturing girls tend to have problems only in psychosocial adjustment (Mensah et al., 2013). This research suggests that genetic and environmental factors may predate and influence the timing of puberty, as well as contribute to a greater risk of adjustment problems later in adolescence.

When a girl physically matures earlier than the other girls her age, it tends to set her apart and isolates her from them. In fact, it might even inspire a bit of jealousy or envy (Reynolds & Juvonen, 2011). Attention from boys (especially older boys) and the perceived popularity of early maturing girls can make them targets of peer rumors and gossip (Reynolds & Juvonen, 2011). Early maturing girls also tend to experience more anxiety in social situations because of their increased self-consciousness (Blumenthal et al., 2011). And because girls physically mature on average about 2 years before boys do, most boys the same age might even be a bit intimidated by a girl who is becoming a woman in front of their eyes (Reynolds & Juvonen, 2011).

Similar to what we saw with early maturing boys, this social isolation from age-mates might drive the girl to spend time with older adolescents (Weichold et al., 2003). A physically mature but chronologically young adolescent girl might be particularly

T/F #1
Adolescent girls who go through puberty earlier than their peers are happier and healthier than girls who go through puberty later. *False*

susceptible to peer pressure to drink, smoke, or be sexually active because she does not yet have the cognitive maturity to know whether, when, and how to say no—and to stick to it (Weichold et al., 2003).

Girls who mature at the same time as their age-mates have an advantage. They fit in comfortably with girls their own age and also with most of the boys and find support from a peer group dealing with the same issues and concerns they have. Later developers do not gain weight when their earlier developing peers do so they remain relatively thin, which fits well with the cultural stereotype of what an attractive young woman should look like. Consequently, these girls tend to have positive body images (Mendle et al., 2007).

The good news is that by the end of high school, almost all adolescents have undergone the physical changes of puberty, and a distinction between early and late maturers no longer has much meaning (Natsuaki et al., 2009). Unless the differences in timing of physical maturation have been responsible for other risky behaviors that become problematic in and of themselves (Copeland et al., 2010; van Jaarsveld, Fidler, Simon, & Wardle, 2007), adolescents are again on a pretty level playing field in this regard.

Celebrating Puberty: Adolescent Rites of Passage

Many cultures acknowledge the significant social transition that accompanies the physical changes of adolescence with rituals called rites of passage. Rites of passage are designed to provide the individual with an experience that marks his or her movement from childhood to adulthood, while simultaneously announcing this change to the community.

Rites of passage Rituals that publicly mark a change in status from child to adult.

Several rites of passage that are traditional in the United States may already be familiar to you. In the Jewish tradition, boys at age 13 and girls at age 12 celebrate the Bar Mitzvah or Bat Mitzvah (which means "son, or daughter, of the commandment" in Hebrew). In this ceremony, the boy or girl may lead a religious service to show all he or she has learned from religious education. This is followed by a party celebrating the child's acceptance as an adult member of the community, with the responsibility to carry out the religious commandments. A rite of passage that has come to the United States from Latin America is called the quinceañera. In this tradition, girls are given a special party to mark their 15th birthday (Alomar & Zwolinski, 2002). The girl dresses in an elaborate dress, possibly white, and is attended by a number of her friends. The high point of the event is a Catholic Mass of thanksgiving. Traditionally the quinceañera announces that the girl is of marriageable age; in other words, she is no longer a child but has become a young woman.

JOURNAL ARTICLE 14.1
Rites of Passage

In other parts of the world, rites of passage take a variety of forms that may not be familiar to you. In Bali it is believed that teeth are symbols of bad impulses, such as

Rites of passage. Milestones to adulthood include the Bar Mitzvah for the young Jewish boy on the left and the quinceañera being celebrated by the Hispanic girl on the right. ■

greed and jealousy, so in a rite of passage they are filed down to make the person more beautiful, both physically and spiritually (Bali Travel Guidebook, 2002). Young people are considered to be adults after taking part in this ceremony. In some cultures, the rites of passage are explicitly linked to the sexual maturation of adolescence. For example, the Navajo Kinaaldá ceremony is held the summer after a girl has her first menstrual period (Markstrom & Iborra, 2003). In southern Africa, traditional Zulu and Xhosa boys are supposed to perform an act of bravery, following which they are taken to a seclusion lodge where a circumcision ceremony takes place. They must show their manhood by not reacting to the pain, and after the ceremony they are painted with white chalk to show their purity. They are instructed by an elder on their adult responsibilities, including sexual responsibility. When the wounds have healed, the young men wash off the white chalk, and a great ceremony marks the end of their childhood and the beginning of their manhood (Mandela, 1994).

Reflect on the importance of any ritual that may have marked your movement from childhood to adulthood as you were growing up by answering the questions posed in **Active Learning: Rites of Passage.**

Active Learning

Rites of Passage

Have you experienced anything you might consider a ritual that marked your movement to adulthood? In your religion there may be rituals that happen in adolescence to mark a new level of responsibility and understanding. Although the United States has few formal rituals, you can probably think of important events that translate into the idea that "I am an adult now." A common and meaningful one is receiving a driver's license. In our mobile society, being able to get from place to place on your own is central to adulthood. What other events can you think of that are linked to public acknowledgement of a new maturity? Could you create a new rite of passage that would be meaningful to you and would symbolize the movement from childhood to adolescence in your community? ■

Teens and Sexuality

Although interest in sexuality can develop before adolescence, the surge of hormones during puberty gives a new force to sexual feelings (Diamond & Savin-Williams, 2009). Although researchers—and teens—often define "sex" and "sexuality" as genital intercourse, there are many other ways to express sexuality, so when we look at teen sexuality we are including a wide range of behaviors, from masturbation to kissing to oral sex. Teen sexuality is a normal and healthy part of development.

Teens learn about sex from friends, parents, and the media. Those who view more sexual content in the media are more likely to initiate sexual activity (Collins et al., 2004), and those who believe their peers are sexually active are more likely to engage in sexual activity themselves (O'Donnell, Myint, O'Donnell, & Stueve, 2003). Although some adolescents think that "everyone is doing it," in the United States, only 42% to 43% of all teenagers between the ages of 15 and 19 report they have had sexual intercourse at least once (Abma, Martinez, & Copen, 2010). U.S. teens today are waiting longer to become sexually active than in the recent past (Guttmacher Institute, 2012). The most common reasons sexually inexperienced teens gave for not having sex were that it was against their religion or morals, they did not want to become pregnant, and they hadn't yet found the right person.

14.3

How does sexual maturation affect adolescent development?

WEB LINK 14.1
Coercive Sex

T/F #2

In the United States, 90% of adolescents between the ages of 15 and 19 have had sex at least once. *False*

The reasons why adolescent boys and girls become sexually active differ between the genders. While teenage girls see sex as an expression of intimacy and commitment to a specific partner, boys are often motivated more by pleasure, curiosity, or a desire to feel loved. However, as teens get older, the differences between the motivations of young men and young women become smaller. Older teen boys become more likely to look for an intimate relationship than before, while older teen girls rely less on having a relationship as the context for having sex (Diamond & Savin-Williams, 2009).

Development of Sexual Preference

An important part of sexual development is sexual orientation, or preference for a same- or opposite-sex partner. As children enter adolescence, most find themselves attracted to members of the opposite sex, but some find themselves attracted to members of the same sex.

Estimating the prevalence of gay, lesbian, bisexual, and transgendered sexual orientation has been complicated by the fact that these preferences are often kept secret, and that individuals settle on a sexual orientation at different points in childhood, adolescence, or adulthood, so any estimate becomes a moving target. To try to overcome some of these methodological challenges, Gary Gates (2011) recently synthesized estimates from nine large-scale studies conducted in the United States, the United Kingdom, Australia, and Norway. The individual surveys varied considerably in the percentages they reported (see Figure 14.3), likely reflecting methodological differences in the surveys

Sexual orientation/ preference Sexual attraction to the same- or opposite-sex partners.

FIGURE 14.3   **Estimates of the percentage of individuals who identify themselves as gay, lesbian, or bisexual**

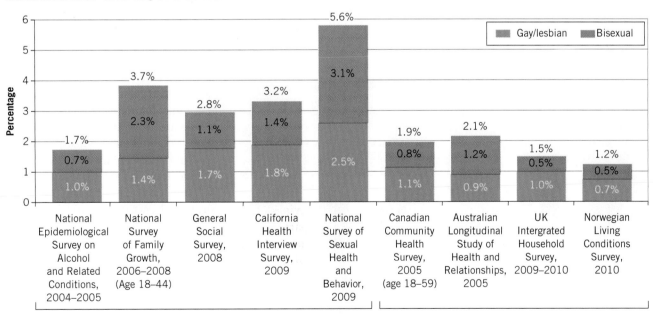

As you can see from this figure, the estimate of the percentage of individuals in different populations who are gay, lesbian, or bisexual varies considerably from one study to another, but any of these estimates are considerably lower than what many people think is the size of the LGB population.

SOURCE: Figure 1, p. 3 in "How many people are lesbian, gay, bisexual, and transgender" by Gary J. Gates, April 2011. Reprinted by permission of the author, Gary J. Gates, Williams Distinguished Scholar, The Williams Institute.

T/F #3

The number of U.S. adults who today identify themselves as gay, lesbian, or bisexual is close to 20%. *False*

themselves. Based on his analysis of the five surveys conducted in the United States, Gates concluded that 3.5% of the adults in the United States self-identify as gay, lesbian, or bisexual. Slightly more identify as bisexual than as lesbian or gay, and women are substantially more likely than men to describe themselves as bisexual. The estimated percentage of the population who report any lifetime same-sex sexual behavior rises to about 8.2%, while 11% acknowledge some attraction to an individual of the same sex.

Gays and lesbians often recall beginning to feel they were somehow different from their same-sex peers at some point during childhood (Carver, Egan, & Perry, 2004; Savin-Williams & Diamond, 1999). They may have engaged in cross-sex-typed behaviors (for example, girls playing masculine competitive sports, boys playing with feminine dolls) or have had cross-sex-typed interests. At around age 10, when many children have their first romantic attraction, these children find themselves being drawn to someone of the same sex, and this experience triggers a period of sexual questioning, often before they even enter puberty (Carver et al., 2004).

As teens work to come to terms with their sexual orientation, they may take the next step of exploring a same-sex relationship before finally adopting a gay, lesbian, or bisexual identity in late adolescence. However, this type of sexual exploration is not uncommon in adolescence and does not occur exclusively among young people who are homosexual. In one study, most youth who had taken part exclusively in same-sex behavior still identified themselves as heterosexual (Mustanski et al., 2014). However, for gay and lesbian youth, sexual experience often confirms their identity. In one study, half the gay and bisexual men surveyed said they had fully accepted their sexual identities and had a homosexual romance or homosexual experiences during high school or college (Dube & Savin-Williams, 1999).

Once young people have settled on a sexual orientation, they next need to integrate their sexual orientation into their identity. An important part of that process is disclosing this information to others (Savin-Williams & Ream, 2003). Young people today seem to be taking this step at younger ages than they did in the past. The first disclosure is still likely to be to a friend or a sibling, but with regard to parents, it is much more likely that young people will disclose to their mother, who is often more accepting, before disclosing to their father (Savin-Williams & Ream, 2003). Although there is relatively little information on how this disclosure affects the parent-child relationship in the long run, what information there is indicates that after an initial period of adjustment, most parent-child relationships rebound, and some even improve (Savin-Williams & Ream, 2003). Not surprisingly, acceptance and support from family members and friends is associated with better adjustment and mental health outcomes for the individual following disclosure of his or her sexual orientation (D'Augelli, 2003).

A recently published survey of over 10,000 self-identified lesbian, gay, bisexual, and transgender (LGBT) youth between 13 and 17 described some of the

Sexual orientation. When teens have support from their peers, regardless of their sexual preference, the process of developing a gender identity in adolescence becomes easier. ∎

difficulties they experience (The Human Rights Campaign, 2012). Although more than half said their immediate family knew of their sexual orientation and 25% said their extended family knew, acceptance by family members was still a major concern for these young people. About two thirds of teens whose families knew of their sexual orientation reported that their family members were accepting, but one third said they were not. Although 4 of 10 LGBT youth said that the community they live in is not accepting of their sexual orientation, most said they had "come out" about their sexual orientation at school and that friends, classmates, and teachers did not have a problem with their LGBT identity. In fact, many LGBT adolescents rated school as one of the most accepting parts of their community. They also reported participating in school-related and after-school activities at the same rate as their non-LGBT peers.

Despite the amount and type of acceptance they report, LGBT youth do experience isolation in some aspects of their lives. While about half say they have an adult in their family to whom they could turn if they felt worried or sad, this is fewer than the 79% of non-LGBT youth who said they had this type of support. It is not surprising that the experience of being an LGBT adolescent has an impact on well-being. They report a greater likelihood of being the victim of verbal harassment and physical assault than non-LGBT adolescents. Eighteen percent report being the victim of verbal harassment, and 5% report being the victim of physical assault, compared to 10% of non-LGBT adolescents who report being the victim of verbal harassment and 3% who have been victims of physical assault. That means LGBT adolescents experience these attacks at almost twice the rate of non-LGBT adolescents. Not surprisingly, these young people report lower levels of happiness, and a higher incidence of alcohol and drug use than non-LGBT adolescents.

The authors of the report note, however, that despite the concerns LGBT adolescents have, they show a great deal of optimism and hope for the future. Three quarters of the survey respondents said they know things will get better for them in the future, and 83% said they believe they will be happy. On the other hand, while half said they think the climate for LGBT individuals is getting better in their community, many feel they will need to leave in order to realize their hopes and dreams for their own future.

Before we leave this topic, we want to point out that the topic of sexual orientation is a very complex one. Being gay, lesbian, bisexual, or transgender are qualitatively different experiences. We will likely need more complex and better differentiated conceptualizations of sexual identity development to adequately cover the range of human experiences. And it is a mistake to assume sexual questioning happens at only one point in time and then is resolved (L. M. Diamond, 2006). It is more likely individuals return to and re-examine their sexual identity from time to time. When the process starts, when it ends, and how long it takes will differ from one person to another.

Gay and lesbian teens are often asked to explain their sexual orientation to others. To see what that experience might be like, try **Active Learning: The Heterosexual Questionnaire.**

T/F #4

Many gay, lesbian, bisexual, or transgender adolescents say their school is one of the most accepting parts of their community. *True*

VIDEO LINK 14.3
Being Gay

Active Learning

The Heterosexual Questionnaire

When gay, lesbian, and bisexual young people come out, they are often asked questions that are nearly impossible to answer. Advocates for Youth (Rochlin, 1977/2008) developed the following activity to help create greater understanding of their experiences. Regardless of your sexual orientation, try to answer the Heterosexual Questionnaire from the point of view of a heterosexual. Then reflect on the questions we have added at the end of the questionnaire.

The Heterosexual Questionnaire

Please answer the following questions as honestly as possible.

1. What do you think caused your heterosexuality?

2. When and how did you first decide you were heterosexual?

3. Is it possible that your heterosexuality is just a phase you may grow out of?

4. Is it possible that your heterosexuality stems from a fear of others of the same sex?

5. If you have never slept with a member of your own sex, is it possible that you might be gay if you tried it?

6. If heterosexuality is normal, why are so many mental patients heterosexual?

7. Why do you heterosexual people try to seduce others into your lifestyle?

8. Why do you flaunt your heterosexuality? Can't you just be who you are and keep it quiet?

9. The great majority of child molesters are heterosexual. Do you consider it safe to expose your children to heterosexual teachers?

10. With all the societal support that marriage receives, the divorce rate is spiraling. Why are there so few stable relationships among heterosexual people?

11. Why are heterosexual people so promiscuous?

12. Would you want your children to be heterosexual, knowing the problems they would face, such as heartbreak, disease, and divorce?

Reflection Questions

1. Did you find the questions hard to answer? Were some harder than others? Which ones were especially difficult? What, specifically, was so difficult about these questions?

2. How did the questions make you feel?

3. What does it say about our society that gay, lesbian, and bisexual youth are asked similar questions?

4. What can you do in the future if you hear someone asking a homosexual youth such questions? ∎

VIDEO LINK 14.4
Transgendered

Finally, remember that the process of exploring sexual orientation takes place in a cultural context and at a particular point in historical time. Acceptance of homosexuality varies greatly from one culture to another, but at least in some segments of society today, it appears to be growing. However, this generally positive picture is darkened by the significant fact that rates of suicide attempts continue to be higher among gay youth. In one recent study, lesbian, gay, and bisexual youth were 5 times more likely than heterosexual youth to have attempted suicide in the preceding 12 months, and this risk was even greater for adolescents in unsupportive environments (Hatzenbuehler, 2011). However, in a national study, homosexuality was found to be a risk factor for suicide among ninth graders, but not among eleventh graders (Fried, Williams, Cabral, & Hacker, 2013).

Our thoughts about the causes of homosexuality have changed substantially over the years. The evolution of our understanding is described in **Journey of Research: Explanations for Homosexuality.**

JOURNEY OF RESEARCH *Explanations for Homosexuality*

Homosexuality as a sexual orientation is as old as human history, but attempts to understand and explain it in a scientific manner are far more recent. In the late 1800s, Karl Heinrich Ulrichs proposed a scientific theory of homosexuality that claimed a biological basis for it (Kennedy, 1997), but this view was quickly overshadowed by a psychoanalytic explanation that then dominated the field for many years (Bieber et al., 1962).

The psychoanalytic explanation is based on a family dynamic that includes a dominant or seductive mother and a weak, hostile, or distant father, but the research that tested this idea was often based on the accounts of people who were already seeking help from a therapist, relied on small samples or single-subject designs, or did not have a comparison group. The fact that these studies were conducted by clinicians who already subscribed to the notion that a neurotic family was a root cause of homosexuality further compromised the scientific value of this work. Finally, it is hard to say whether the distancing of a father from a child who is exhibiting some cross-gender traits could be a response to the child's gender orientation rather than the cause of it (Isay, 1996).

The idea that homosexuality was pathological persisted until 1973, when the *Diagnostic and Statistical Manual of Mental Disorders* of the American Psychiatric Association (APA) officially excluded homosexuality as a disorder (Spitzer, 1981). Of course, there continues to be debate within our society about whether homosexuality is "normal" or "natural" and about whether people make a voluntary decision to adopt a heterosexual orientation.

Social learning theory provides a contemporary explanation for children's acquisition of their gender identity based on the processes of social reinforcement and observational learning (Bussey & Bandura, 1999). Although these ideas provide a helpful framework for understanding a heterosexual orientation, they are less satisfactory as an explanation for a homosexual or bisexual identity. Children in our culture are rarely positively reinforced by parents or peers for cross-gender behavior and are not as likely to observe homosexual role models as heterosexual ones. Even children raised by homosexual parents and exposed to homosexual role models daily are as likely to be heterosexual as children raised by heterosexual parents (Patterson, 2006).

Research continues to explore a potential biological basis for sexual orientation. Research on twins has found that genes play a role, but are not the entire story (Långström, Rahman, Carlström, & Lichtenstein, 2010). Other research has looked to neuroanatomy and neuroendocrinology as explanatory mechanisms. For instance, having an older brother increases the odds of homosexuality in later-born males. It has been proposed that the development of a male fetus may produce an immune reaction in the mother that results in antibodies that act on the sexual differentiation of the brain of males in subsequent pregnancies (Blanchard, 2008).

This research still has many unanswered questions, and in all likelihood the best possible explanation will include a complex set of interacting biological, social, and cognitive factors. ■

Risks of Sexual Maturation

When adolescents become sexually active, their decision carries with it a number of potential risks. After adolescents go through puberty, males can produce viable sperm, females can become pregnant, and both sexes are at risk of contracting a sexually transmitted infection. We look at the consequences of these possibilities on adolescent development and describe ways in which adolescents can protect themselves from these risks.

T/F #5
In recent years the
adolescent pregnancy
rate has reached a
historic low. *True*

WEB LINK 14.2
Teen Pregnancy

Adolescent Pregnancies

In 2012, the teen birthrate in the United States reached a historic low of 29.4 births per thousand teens age 15–19 (Martin et al., 2013). This rate has fallen almost 62% since 1991 (see Figure 14.4). The rates for Black and Hispanic teens are higher than the rates for non-Hispanic Whites (43.9 and 46.3 births respectively per 1000 women 15 to 19 years of age versus 20.5 births per 1000). Preliminary data for 2013 indicate that the decline in the teen birthrate is continuing to a new historic low of 26.6 per thousand teenage girls and the lowest number of births to teens ever reported for the United States.

Almost the entire decline in pregnancies among older teens (18 and 19 years of age) can be attributed to an increased use of contraceptives during this time period. Among younger teens, about one quarter of the decline was due to reduced levels of sexual activity, and the remainder to increased reliance on contraception (Guttmacher Institute, 2012). The condom is the most popular form of contraception (96% have ever used it), followed by withdrawal (57%) and the pill (56%). Injectable hormonal contraceptives were used by 20% and contraceptive patches by 10% of sexually active teens. Fourteen percent sought emergency contraception, or the "morning after" pill, while 15% relied on the calendar rhythm method, abstaining during times of higher fertility. About 5% used a newly developed vaginal contraceptive ring (National Center for Health Statistics, 2011).

As you can see from Figure 14.5, the adolescent pregnancy rate in the United States remains considerably higher than in other Western industrialized nations: 6 times the rate in the Netherlands, almost 4 times the rate in Germany, and almost 3 times the rate in France (Alford & Hauser, 2009; see also Hamilton & Ventura, 2012). What accounts for this difference between countries? U.S. teens and European teens have similar levels of sexual activity, but European teens are more likely to use contraception than their U.S. counterparts and to use more effective methods (Guttmacher Institute, 2012). Schalet (2007) has attributed the lower rates of adolescent pregnancy, births,

FIGURE 14.4   **Declining teen birthrate**

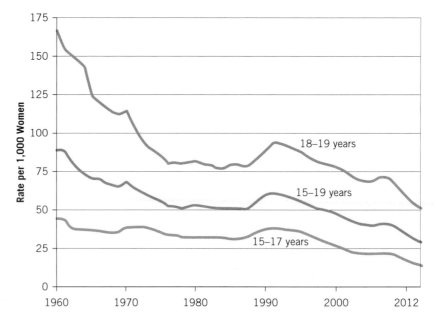

The teen birthrate declined to historically low levels in 2012.

SOURCE: Martin et al. (2013).

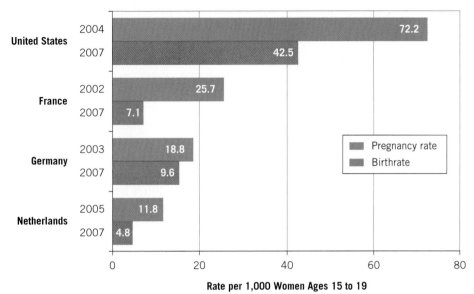

FIGURE 14.5 International comparison of teen pregnancy rate and teen birthrate

Both the adolescent pregnancy rate and the adolescent birthrate in the United States continue to be much higher than in other industrialized countries. What accounts for this large difference?

SOURCE: Used with permission of Advocates for Youth, Washington, DC. www.advocatesforyouth.org

abortions, and sexually transmitted infections among adolescents in the Netherlands to the fact that poverty is more widespread and more intense in the United States and that adolescents in the Netherlands have easier access to comprehensive sex education and reproductive health services than many in the United States. She illustrates the difference in attitude toward adolescent sexuality between the two countries with this quote from a government-funded youth initiative in the Netherlands:

> Parents, educators, and other professionals rarely tell young people to stay away from sex, or to say no to sex. Dutch policy is aimed at assisting young people to behave responsibly in this respect. The Dutch approach means spending less time and effort trying to prevent young people from becoming sexually active, and more time and effort in educating and empowering young people to behave responsibly when they do become sexually active. (Schalet, 2007, p. 4)

Why is it so important to prevent teen pregnancy? The impact of having a child during the teen years is felt by the mother, her child, and society. Research has found that only half of young women who give birth during high school go on to graduate, compared with 90% of those who do not give birth. Failure to graduate leads to lower incomes and higher rates of poverty. The children of teen mothers also suffer more health problems and are more likely to be put in jail during their teen years. They are more likely to be unemployed, and daughters of teen mothers are more likely to give birth themselves during their teen years. The cost to society of these problems plus increased foster care placement for teen mothers' children is estimated at almost $11 billion a year (CDC, 2013k). As a result, in 2010, the federal government initiated the President's Teen Pregnancy Prevention Initiative designed to reduce teen pregnancy, particularly among African American and Latino teens, by engaging communities in teen pregnancy prevention programs that research has shown to be effective.

Teen pregnancy. This teen mother is unusual because she is attending college. Only half of teens who give birth while still in high school will finish high school. ∎

In the United States, a variety of approaches to reducing teen pregnancy have been tried, including school-based clinic services, mentoring and role modeling programs, self-esteem initiatives, and opportunity development programs. Child Trends, a nonprofit and nonpartisan research center, assessed a wide range of interventions and found that the most successful ones included sex education and HIV education, early childhood programs that lift children's abilities and aspirations, and programs that engage teens in school-based and outside activities (Manlove et al., 2002). Allen, Seitz, and Apfel (2007) have suggested that the only effective approach will target the whole person instead of trying to deal with adolescents as a "bundle of sexual urges to be controlled" (p. 197). They suggest that we need to find ways to build competencies that protect the adolescent not only from risky sexual activity but also from a range of other risky behaviors.

Sexually Transmitted Infections and Diseases

Teens who are sexually active also risk contracting a sexually transmitted infection (STI) or a sexually transmitted disease (STD). Although these terms are sometimes used interchangeably, a sexually transmitted infection is an infection caused by a microorganism passed from one individual to another through intimate contact, but this infection is not considered a sexually transmitted disease until symptoms develop (American Sexual Health Association, 2014). Although STIs always come before an STD, all STIs do not turn into STDs. The CDC (2007a) estimates there are about 19 million *new* cases of sexually transmitted diseases each year, and almost half occur in young people between the ages of 15 and 24 (see Figure 14.6). Of course, many more cases go undiagnosed and are never reported.

An analysis of a representative sample of adolescent females between 14 and 19 found that among those who were sexually active, 37.7% tested positive for at least one of five common STDs, with the highest prevalence for the human papillomavirus (HPV) at 29.5% (Forhan et al., 2009). Prevalence of all the STDs was similar for non-Hispanic White and Mexican American adolescents but more than twice as high for Black participants. Even 26% of adolescents who had only recently become sexually active and 20% of those who had only a single sexual partner were part of these statistics.

Many STIs do not produce any symptoms that make the individual aware he or she should seek medical treatment, and some may not require treatment. For instance, 90% of new cases of HPV infection clear without treatment within 2 years (Forhan et al., 2009; National Cancer Institute, 2010). However, these infections can go on to produce cancerous cells. An estimated 12,000 women are diagnosed with cervical cancer annually and 4,000 die from it (National Cancer Institute, 2010). In June 2006, the Food and Drug Administration approved a vaccine that can prevent the types of HPV most likely to lead to cervical cancer. Since the vaccine was introduced in 2006, the prevalence of those types of HPV declined 56% among females between 14 and 19 (Markowitz et al., 2013). Despite the evidence of its effectiveness, the vaccination is only recommended, not required, for girls 11 or 12 years old, and voluntary vaccination rates remain relatively low. In 2010, 49% of females between 13 and 17 had received at least one dose of the vaccine, and 32% had received the three doses required for full protection (Markowitz et al.,

Sexually transmitted infection (STI) An infection caused by a microorganism that is transmitted by direct sexual contact.

Sexually transmitted disease (STD) A pathology that can result from a sexually transmitted infection.

| FIGURE 14.6 | Sexually transmitted infections among young Americans |

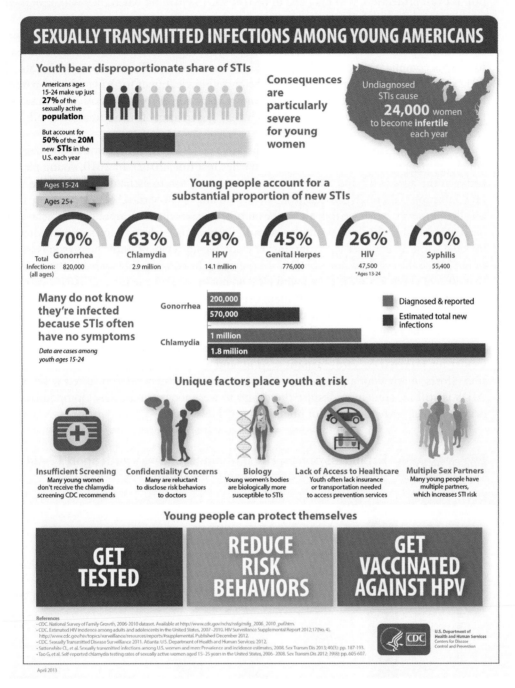

Adolescents and young adults are at greater risk of contracting a number of sexually transmitted diseases than the general population, as shown by these figures from the Centers for Disease Control and Prevention.

SOURCE: Centers for Disease Control and Prevention (2013h).

2013). If that rate were increased to 80% (a target other countries have met), it would prevent 50,000 girls who are alive today from developing cervical cancer during their lifetime (CDC, 2013c). The most frequent reasons given by parents for not having their daughters vaccinated were parents' belief that their daughters did not need the vaccine, were not sexually active, or the parents felt they did not have enough information to make an informed decision (Wong et al., 2011). However, 13% of teens become sexually active before age 15 (Guttmacher Institute, 2012). Because early vaccination is important for full protection, parents need to be realistic in deciding when they will have their adolescents vaccinated.

Other commonly occurring STIs include bacterial infections like chlamydia, gonorrhea, and syphilis. Each can be treated and cured, but if left untreated they can lead to serious complications, including death in the case of syphilis (Guttmacher Institute, 2012). Although adolescents 14 and older can obtain treatment for STIs without parental consent in all 50 states, they may not know where to get the care they need, may not be able to afford it, or may be afraid that if they get treatment, their treatment will not remain confidential (Forhan et al., 2009).

It is a different story with viral infections, such as HIV/AIDS, hepatitis B, and herpes, which are treatable but *not* curable (Guttmacher Institute, 2012). In 2010, young people between the ages of 13 and 24 years of age accounted for an estimated 26% of the new HIV infections, although this age group makes up only 17% of the U.S. population (CDC, 2014h). However, when we talk about the number of cases of AIDS among adolescents, we need to remember this infection takes about 10 years to develop. Even if an individual is infected while an adolescent, symptoms may not become evident until the person is in his or her 20s so the eventual rate of HIV infections may be considerably higher. Estimates are that 60% of young people infected with HIV do not know they are infected (CDC, 2014h).

Young men who have sex with men, especially minority young men, are at greatest risk. Figure 14.7 shows how the rate of new infections differs by the race/ethnicity and sex of the young person. Other risk factors are early sexual initiation, having an older sex partner, a history of sexual abuse, and infection with another STI (National Center for HIV/AIDS, Viral Hepatitis, STD, and TB Prevention, 2011). Despite education efforts, many young people are not concerned about becoming infected with HIV. AIDS is still an epidemic, despite the progress we have made in developing antiviral drugs that help extend the life of infected individuals.

T/F #6

Adolescents as young as 14 years of age can obtain treatment for sexually transmitted infections in all 50 states without parental consent. *True*

FIGURE 14.7   **Estimates of new HIV infections among youth aged 13–24 years, by race/ethnicity and sex, United States, 2010**

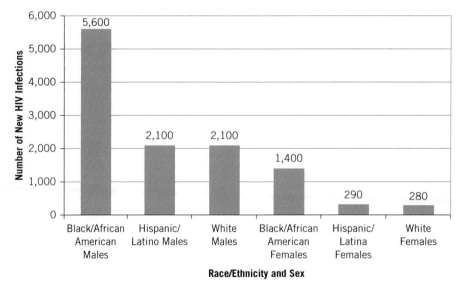

Young men are at considerably greater risk of being newly infected with HIV than young women, and this risk is substantially greater for young Black men, who accounted for 57% of all new HIV infections in 2010. A low perception of risk, low rates of HIV testing, and low rates of condom use are all contributing factors to this high infection rate.

SOURCE: Centers for Disease Control and Prevention (2012c).

Sex Trafficking and Prostitution

Of great concern worldwide is the problem of sex trafficking or the removal of children from their families for the purposes of commercial sexual exploitation or prostitution. For example, by one estimate there are 200,000 girls from Nepal who are currently working in brothels in India (Crawford & Kaufman, 2008), but this is not a problem only of less-developed countries. "U.S. children are being sold for sex not only on the streets, by pimps, but via craigslist and at truck stops across the country" (Kotrla, 2010, p. 182). Also, although most attention is paid to girls, young boys are also at risk but are often overlooked. Many boys are reluctant to admit what is happening to them and there are fewer services to help them (Chin, 2014).

Although it is difficult to measure the occurrence of sex trafficking, current estimates are that more than 100,000 children are being trafficked within the United States (Kotrla, 2010). A 2013 report issued by the Institute of Medicine and the National Research Council concluded that despite the serious long-term consequences of sex exploitation and sex trafficking for the youth victimized by it, as well as for the larger community, "efforts to prevent, identify, and respond to these crimes are largely under supported, inefficient, uncoordinated, and unevaluated" (p. 1). These shortcomings were attributed, at least in part, to the fact that the crimes happen at the margins of society and the general public does not know how to recognize the problem or what to do in response to it. Among the most vulnerable to this type of abuse are those children who have run away from home or who have been forced to leave. These are instances of severe and long-lasting abuse that have devastating consequences for the children who are victimized.

Whereas teens who were engaged in prostitution have been stigmatized as criminals, there now is a shift toward seeing them as victims (Reid & Piquero, 2014). Many of these young teens are escaping abuse, including sexual abuse, at home. For example, one young woman who began prostitution at age 11 reported, "[My grandmother] was also engaged in a lot of activities such as selling drugs, doing drugs, renting out the rooms of her house and stuff like that. So staying was basically out of the question because she had so many men in the house and I had been sexually molested and raped a lot of times, so I didn't want to stay there anymore and put up with that" (Cobbina & Oselin, 2011, p. 319). For some, prostitution gave them some sense of control over what was happening to them anyway, as one young woman explained, "[b]ecause from my childhood, I had been molested. And then as time went on, I was still getting molested, so I got tired. And I said well, if a man going to take it from me, why not sell myself?" (Cobbina & Oselin, 2011, p. 319). For other girls prostitution is a norm in their neighborhoods and they just expect to take part in it. In addition, they are attracted to the money and what they perceive as the glamour involved.

Young people who enter prostitution while they are teens tend to stay in it for many more years than those who begin at an older age. As a result they encounter many more of the risk factors involved, including violence, family problems, criminal convictions, and drug addictions that are an attempt to cope with the difficulties of this lifestyle (Cobbina & Oselin, 2011). They often suffer from health problems and post-traumatic stress disorder (Heilemann & Santhiveeran, 2011). Whether prostitution appears to be a choice or is a result of sex trafficking, both girls and boys need help to find a better way to live their lives.

Sex trafficking The forcible removal of children from their families for the purposes of prostitution or pornography.

VIDEO LINK 14.5
Sex Trafficking

Check Your Understanding

1. What are primary and secondary sex characteristics?
2. What is a rite of passage?
3. What challenges do LGBT adolescents face?
4. What is the difference between a sexually transmitted infection and a sexually transmitted disease?
5. How prevalent is sex trafficking of children in the United States?

14.4

How are adolescents' health and well-being affected by their health practices?

Health and Nutrition During Adolescence

Adolescents need nutritious food, appropriate amounts of physical activity, and adequate amounts of sleep to support their physical development. As young people gain greater autonomy and control over each of these aspects of their lives they have to make choices that affect their health at this point in their development, as well as in the future.

Sleep

As children move into adolescence, their sleep patterns begin to change. Only about 9% of adolescents report getting the optimal amount of sleep each night (9 or more hours), while almost two thirds report getting fewer than 8 hours (see Figure 14.8 on page 485; Garber et al., 2013). Whereas young children often get up quite early in the morning, teens often stay up late and then sleep late when they can. It is not clear how much of this shift is due to biological changes connected with puberty and how much is due to social expectations, but these differences are reported in many countries around the world (Randler & Frech, 2009). Even when school starts early, teens are more likely to stay up late, and as a consequence, many do not get enough sleep. Inadequate sleep has negative consequences including lower academic performance and higher levels of depression and anxiety (Short, Gradisar, Lack, & Wright, 2013). It also contributes to an increased rate of car accidents. Teens may be affected by both their lack of sleep and the poor quality of it.

You might suggest that teens just go to bed earlier, but it is often not that simple. Although teens can improve the quality of their sleep by avoiding video games and other screen-based activities near bedtime, their internal biological clock is directing later bedtimes for many, making it difficult for them to fall asleep earlier and leading to poorer sleep quality when they do finally get to sleep (Hasler & Clark, 2013). Many communities are discussing what time school should start for adolescents. In one school district, when high school was changed to start one hour later, teens got more sleep each night and the rate of teen car crashes declined 16.5% (Danner & Phillips, 2008). In another school, a mere 25-minute delay in the start of school significantly lowered daytime sleepiness, depressed mood, and caffeine consumption (Boergers, Gable, & Owens, 2014).

A sleepless night. Many adolescents get less sleep than they need. What effects does lack of sleep have? How do you do on exams or while driving a car when you are sleep-deprived? ∎

Healthy Eating and Eating Disorders

As adolescents spend more time away from their parents, they make more of their own choices about what to eat. Like younger children, however, many teens consume too much sugar, fat, and sodium and eat too few fruits, vegetables, and dairy products (Child Trends, 2013b). A report from the U.S. Department of Agriculture (2010) found that three of the top five food energy sources for teenagers included (1) soda/energy/sports drinks, (2) pizza, and (3) grain-based desserts such as cakes, pies, and cookies.

© Ben Welsh/Corbis

Parents may not be providing all the teenager's food, but it still is important that they continue to encourage healthy eating. Parental encouragement is associated with greater consumption of fruits and vegetables and lower consumption of fast foods (Bauer, Laska, Fulkerson, & Neumark-Sztainer, 2011). Some parents do become increasingly concerned about their teenage daughter's weight and encourage dieting, but the outcome is not always what they hoped. Under such pressure, teenage girls are more likely to increase binge eating and unhealthy ways of controlling eating, resulting in a higher likelihood of being overweight and depressed (Bauer et al., 2011).

Anorexia Nervosa

Although there are a number of eating disorders, the dramatic nature of anorexia nervosa and bulimia keeps them in the forefront of our attention. Anorexia nervosa is a condition in which individuals become obsessed with their weight and intentionally restrict their intake of food to a point that it may become life threatening. Anorexics lose 15% or more of their body weight, yet they still see themselves as grossly overweight and remain fearful of gaining weight. This condition takes a terrible toll on the young person's overall health. As the level of body fat falls, young women fail to begin menstruating, or their menstrual periods become erratic or cease altogether. Visible changes include thinning hair, brittle nails, a yellowing of the skin, and the growth of a fine downy hair on the face, arms, and back. Many anorexics experience more serious hidden changes, including gastrointestinal and cardiovascular problems and osteoporosis. Because anorexia can be life threatening, hospitalization may be required, but the prognosis is not encouraging. Hospitalization often occurs late in the process after a great deal of physical damage has already been done. Although some programs have had success with helping the anorexic regain weight, relapses following treatment are common, and mortality is higher than for other psychiatric disorders (Arcelus, Mitchell, Wales, & Nielsen, 2011).

Who is susceptible to this condition? Anorexics have been described as highly controlled individuals who set extremely high, and perhaps unrealistic, goals for themselves (Watkins, 2011). Psychological factors such as depression and low body esteem also are predictive of later eating disorders in both boys and girls (Berger, Weitkamp, & Strauss, 2009; Gardner, Stark, Friedman, & Jackson, 2000). Another possibility is that a dysfunctional family dynamic contributes to this disorder. An adolescent who sees his or her parents as demanding, overprotective, or overcontrolling can reassert some autonomy by controlling what and when he or she eats. Likewise, if the adolescent wants parental attention, this behavior is one way to get it.

Bulimia

Bulimia is an eating disorder characterized by eating binges in which enormous amounts of food are consumed, followed by self-induced vomiting or the excessive use of laxatives to get rid of the food. Individuals suffering from bulimia differ from those suffering from anorexia in several ways. First, the goal of an anorexic is weight loss, but the goal of most bulimics is to prevent weight gain. Second, anorexics try to have complete control

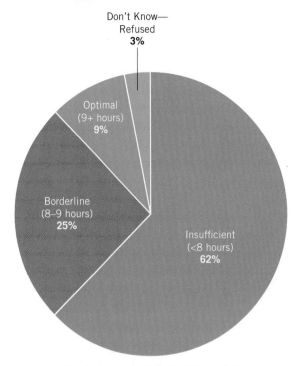

FIGURE 14.8 **Adolescent sleep habits**

Only about 9% of adolescents in Grades 9 through 12 report getting what is considered an optimal amount of sleep each night. By contrast, 62% report getting fewer than 8 hours each night. What do you think accounts for this sleep deficit for most young people? What suggestions would you make to improve the situation?

SOURCE: Garber et al. (2013).

NOTE. Percentages do not add up to 100% due to rounding.

Anorexia nervosa A condition in which individuals become obsessed with their weight and intentionally restrict food intake to a point that it may become life threatening.

WEB LINK 14.3
Eating Disorders

Bulimia An eating disorder characterized by eating binges, followed by purging (for example, self-induced vomiting or the excessive use of laxatives) to get rid of the food.

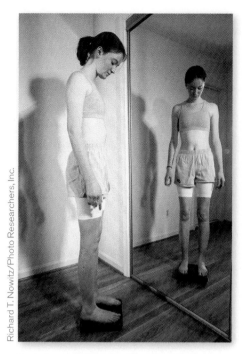

Body image. Eating disorders are often accompanied by inaccurate self-images and can lead to devastating consequences for a young person's health. Effective prevention programs have focused on changing maladaptive attitudes and behaviors. ■

Richard T. Nowitz/Photo Researchers, Inc.

over their behavior, but the eating behavior of bulimics is impulsive and out of control, and they often feel guilt and shame after an episode of binging. Third, the causes of bulimia are less well understood than the causes of anorexia. One reason is that many cases of bulimia go undetected because bulimics maintain their weight rather than losing a great deal of weight as an anorexic does.

There is no single known cause of bulimia, although the purging and other actions taken to control weight gain may make the person feel in control and thus help ease feelings of stress and anxiety (U.S. Department of Health and Human Services [USDHHS], 2012a). A combination of treatments that include individual and family therapy, nutrition counseling, peer support groups, and even medication seems to work best (Mitchell, Peterson, Myers, & Wonderlich, 2001; USDHHS, 2012a). The fact that bulimics often experience shame, guilt, or embarrassment about their condition can actually aid in their eventual recovery.

It is difficult to estimate the prevalence of eating disorders because much of the behavior associated with them is kept secret, but the lifetime rate for anorexia nervosa is estimated at 0.9% for women and 0.3% for men. The lifetime rate for bulimia is 0.5% for women and 0.1% for men (Hudson, Hiripi, Pope, & Kessler, 2007). Participation in activities where weight is a continuing issue (such as gymnastics or dance for females and wrestling for males) can put both girls and boys at risk.

There are no simple explanations for eating disorders. Both anorexia and bulimia can begin with normal dieting and concerns about weight that reflect the emphasis placed on thinness in our culture. Ongoing research has found some evidence for specific genes that may relate to certain types of eating disorders (Bergen et al., 2003). Girls who mature earlier than their peers are at risk because their early physical maturation is associated with being heavier (Berger et al., 2009; Tyrka, Graber, & Brooks-Gunn, 2000). Finally, psychological factors such as depression and low body esteem also are predictive of eating disorders in both boys and girls (Gardner et al., 2000; Keel & Forney, 2013).

In Chapter 13, we learned how watching television contributes to obesity in children. This is ironic because, at the same time, the media also promote thinness as the ideal for everyone, but especially for girls and women. Messages from the media are implicated in the rise in body dissatisfaction and eating disorders we see among girls and increasingly among boys (Grabe, Ward, & Hyde, 2008). Images in movies, in the press, online, and on TV promote what we described in Chapter 13 as the thin ideal. The relationship between thin ideal messages and eating disorders in teenage girls has been well documented (Harrison, 2000; Keel & Forney, 2013). The impact of television on bulimic symptoms was demonstrated on the island of Fiji. Before television was introduced, 3% of girls had symptoms of this disorder. Three years after TV was introduced, 15% of girls used vomiting to control weight. Although other variables may have changed along with the appearance of TV on the island, it does appear that the introduction of the Western thin ideal affected Fiji women's traditional norm of a more rounded body (Walcott, Pratt, & Patel, 2003).

In a review of programs designed to prevent eating disorders, Stice and Shaw (2004) found that the most effective ones target high-risk groups of adolescents rather than the general population of adolescents. They also found that older adolescents benefited more than younger ones, perhaps because the risk of developing an eating disorder increases after age 15. Contrary to what you might expect, programs that focus on providing information to adolescents about the harmful effects of disordered eating were ineffective at producing a change in behavior. Rather, those that focused on changing

T/F #7

The most effective way to prevent eating disorders is to give adolescents information about how harmful these behaviors can be to their bodies. *False* maladaptive attitudes (such as seeing a thin body as the ideal body type or feeling very dissatisfied with your own body) and maladaptive behaviors (such as fasting or overeating) were the most effective.

Obesity

Although obesity rates for adolescents have increased in recent years, this trend finally appears to be leveling off (Frederick, Snellman, & Putnam, 2014; National Center for Health Statistics, 2011). However, it is still true that one in six adolescents is overweight (Schwarz & Peterson, 2010), and being overweight carries with it both immediate health risks such as high cholesterol and high blood pressure and also potential future problems that include heart disease, stroke, diabetes, certain types of cancer, and osteoarthritis. Teens who are obese also are at higher risk of developing an eating disorder in an attempt to control their weight (Sim, Lebow, & Billings, 2013). Not all adolescents are equally at risk of being overweight or obese. Teens from low-income families are 1.6 times as likely to be obese as those from more affluent families (Lee, Harris, & Lee, 2013). Among adolescents between the ages of 12 and 19, non-Hispanic Black girls and Mexican American boys have the highest rates of obesity, and non-Hispanic White boys and girls have the lowest rate (Schwarz & Peterson, 2010).

The health gap between teens growing up in families in different socioeconomic circumstances appears to be widening rather than narrowing. Until 2002, rate of obesity was similar for all adolescents, but since then a decline has occurred among teens from higher socioeconomic backgrounds while the rate has continued to increase among teens from lower SES backgrounds (Frederick et al., 2014; Lee, Andrew, Gebremariam, Lumeng, & Lee, 2014). There are differences in both the caloric intake between the two groups of adolescents and their levels of physical activity. Low-income teens are likely to have less access to high-quality healthy food in their neighborhoods and in their schools, but they are also less likely to get adequate exercise through physical education in their schools or neighborhoods (Lee et al., 2013). While physical activity has increased since 2002 (Frederick et al., 2014), children in families of college-educated parents have participated in this increase but those of less educated parents have not. The neighborhoods in which poorer children and teens are growing up may lack safe places for recreation, but even when physical activities are available through high school sports and clubs, higher SES adolescents are more likely to participate than their lower SES peers (Frederick et al., 2014).

Smoking, Alcohol, and Illicit Drugs

Some of the choices adolescents make that have serious implications for health are about the use of alcohol, cigarettes, and drugs. According to *America's Children: Key National Indicators of Well-Being*, prepared by the Federal Interagency Forum on Child and Family Statistics (2013a):

- 2% of eighth graders, 5% of tenth graders, and 9% of twelfth graders reported smoking daily in the previous 30 days.
- 5% of eighth graders, 16% of tenth graders, and 24% of twelfth graders reported having five or more alcoholic beverages in a row during the last 2 weeks.
- 8% of eighth graders, 19% of tenth graders, and 25% of twelfth graders reported using illicit drugs in the previous 30 days.

Smoking

The decision to smoke has very serious long-term consequences for health. Nearly 80% of adult smokers begin as adolescents and every year over 443,000 deaths result from smoking (Federal Interagency Forum on Child and Family Statistics, 2013a). The

T/F #8
Asian and Black adolescents have the lowest rate of smoking.
True

JOURNAL ARTICLE 14.2
Smoking in Movies

good news is that cigarette use has significantly decreased and now is at historic lows. Although rates of smoking are similar for males and females, Native Americans and Alaska Natives have the highest prevalence, followed by Whites and Hispanics, with the lowest prevalence among Asians and Blacks (USDHHS, 2012c).

Because it is so difficult to stop smoking once the habit has been established, efforts designed to prevent young people from starting to smoke seem the wisest course. Some prevention efforts, such as the "truth® campaign" created by the American Legacy Foundation, have been quite successful. This campaign accounted for 22% of the decline in youth smoking over a 3-year period (Farrelly, Davis, Haviland, Messeri, & Healton, 2005). However, any prevention effort must compete with advertising that continues to portray smoking as pleasurable, product placement in movies that pairs cigarettes with attractive young performers, and the continuing perception by teens that smoking is "cool" and a sign of adulthood. For example, the more young teens watch movies in which there is a lot of smoking, the more likely they are to begin smoking themselves (Jackson, Brown, & L'Engle, 2007). Even controlling for parent and peer smoking, those who watched shows with the most smoking were 2.6 times more likely to start smoking than those who watched shows that had the lowest level of smoking (Wills, Sargent, Stoolmiller, Gibbons, & Gerrard, 2008). One solution would be for the movie industry to reduce the amount of smoking portrayed or to provide warning labels to indicate that smoking is shown in the movie, like the warnings that a movie contains sex, violence, or adult language.

In fact, the film industry has responded to these concerns. Some of the major companies have instituted specific policies to reduce tobacco use on screen. In 2010, the most popular movies contained less than half as much smoking as in 2005 (Glantz et al., 2011). However, smoking still occurred in 30% of movies rated G, PG, or PG-13. Therefore, another approach is to use media education to teach children and teens about why movies contain so much smoking. *Blowing Smoke* is the name of one project designed to teach sixth and eighth graders about smoking in movies (Bergsma & Ingram, 2001). The researchers found that most children and young teens initially believed smoking in movies was a random event with no particular purpose. *Blowing Smoke* taught them that smoking in films constitutes a form of advertising, sometimes even including brand names. By helping them understand the motivation behind smoking in movies and helping them think critically about it, we can change their desire to emulate admired movie stars (Bergsma & Ingram, 2001). Try **Active Learning: Cigarettes in the Movies** to see how much smoking there is in the movies and TV programs you watch and how you might talk with children about what you see.

Active Learning

Cigarettes in the Movies

In the next week, notice how many characters in movies and TV shows you watch smoke cigarettes. Do you see the same amount of smoking in real life as you see in these programs? Can you explain why the directors of the show would choose to have each character smoke? What, if anything, does it convey about the character? Can you think of any reasons, besides artistic ones, for having a character smoke?

At the following website you can find information and research about how teens are affected by seeing smoking in the media and how the tobacco companies have influenced the placement of tobacco products in films and TV shows: http://www.scenesmoking .org. You will also find ratings of current movies based on their presentation of tobacco use. ■

Several new tobacco products are designed to be attractive to teens. Electronic cigarettes, hookahs, and small cigars that may be flavored all find a market with adolescents. Between 2011 and 2012, the number of teens who had used e-cigarettes doubled from just under 5% to 10%, over 5% had used a hookah, and 6% had tried candy-flavored cigars (CDC, 2014l). The Food and Drug Administration does not have the authority to regulate the sale or use of electronic cigarettes, so children are not prohibited from using them (Glatter, 2014), however 38 states currently outlaw sales to minors. Although e-cigarettes may help current smokers quit, concern regarding adolescent use has centered on the question of whether e-cigarettes will become a gateway to the use of regular tobacco products by adolescents. A survey of 40,000 middle

Alternate forms of nicotine use. Electronic cigarettes, or e-cigarettes, have quickly become popular with teens, but we do not currently know that they are any safer than regular cigarettes. The U.S. Food and Drug Administration does not regulate the sale or use of electronic cigarettes, although this might change in the future. ∎

school and high school students found that use of e-cigarettes were associated with a greater likelihood of using conventional cigarettes. The study concluded that e-cigarettes do not discourage, and may even encourage, cigarette smoking (Dutra & Glantz, 2014). Although e-cigarettes do not contain the tar and other dangerous chemicals contained in tobacco smoke, they do contain nicotine, the highly addictive substance in tobacco.

Alcohol

The 2013 *Monitoring the Future* report asked adolescents whether they had ever used alcohol, had used it in the previous year, or had used it in the last 30 days. All measures were at historic lows (Johnston, O'Malley, Miech, Bachman, & Schulenberg, 2014). When young people do drink, however, they often engage in binge drinking, defined as drinking 5 or more drinks within a 2-hour period for men, or 4 or more drinks for women (National Institute of Alcohol Abuse and Alcoholism, 2004). According to the Office of Juvenile Justice and Delinquency Prevention (2005), about 90% of alcohol consumption by young people is binge drinking, and the highest proportion of binge drinkers (51%) are teens in the 18- to 20-year-old group (Naimi et al., 2003). Surveys consistently show that males report higher levels of both heavy drinking and daily drinking than females; however, the gender gap in binge drinking appears to be decreasing. White students report the highest levels of binge drinking and Black students the lowest (Johnston, O'Malley, Bachman, & Schulenberg, 2007).

Binge drinking places a young person at risk in a number of ways, including an increased chance of motor vehicle accidents, injuries, and fighting. Early onset of heavy drinking is particularly problematic because young adolescents are still immature in their decision-making skills and may not fully appreciate the consequences of their decision to start drinking. Those who do start at a young age have a longer period of exposure to alcohol than adolescents who wait to start drinking, so their alcohol consumption has a greater cumulative toll. A new threat is the marketing of "alcopops," sweet, fruity alcoholic drinks that are particularly appealing to underage drinkers and have been specifically marketed to teenage girls (Alcohol Justice, 2011). Many of these products come in 24-ounce cans and contain as much as 12% alcohol, making a single can the equivalent of more than 4-1/2 standard drinks. That is why these products are sometimes called a "binge in a can" (Alcohol Justice, 2011, p. 6).

Drug Use

Although the use of many types of illegal drugs by adolescents has declined in the past 20 years, marijuana use continues to increase. In 2013, 7% of eighth graders, 18% of tenth graders, and 22.7% of twelfth graders reported that they had used marijuana in the past month, and 6.5% of twelfth graders reported that they use marijuana every day (Johnston et al., 2014). In 2013, more high school seniors used marijuana than smoked cigarettes (Johnston et al., 2014). Adolescents increasingly perceive marijuana use as harmless, which does not bode well for future levels of use (Johnston et al., 2014). Marijuana use has been legalized for medical use with a doctor's prescription in 20 states and Washington, DC (Office of National Drug Control Policy, 2014), and recreational use has been legalized in Colorado and Washington, although it is still illegal for those under 21 to purchase and use it. A number of other states are considering legalization.

Patterns and percentages of use of illicit drugs other than marijuana are shown in Figure 14.9. Overall, there has been a decline in use of these drugs and upwards of 80% of high school students say they disapprove of their use (Johnston et al., 2014). Adolescent males and non-college bound students are somewhat more likely to use drugs than females and those who plan to continue their education (Johnston et al., 2014). African American teens generally have the lowest rates of drug use compared to White and Hispanic teens (Johnston et al., 2014).

Illicit drug usage is associated with a wide range of negative health outcomes; the specific effects depend on the particular substance used, its frequency, and dosage. Cocaine has been linked to heart attack and stroke, marijuana to both physical and cognitive impairment (such as lung damage and memory loss), and hallucinogens to problems in

WEB LINK 14.4
Marijuana

FIGURE 14.9   Teen drug use

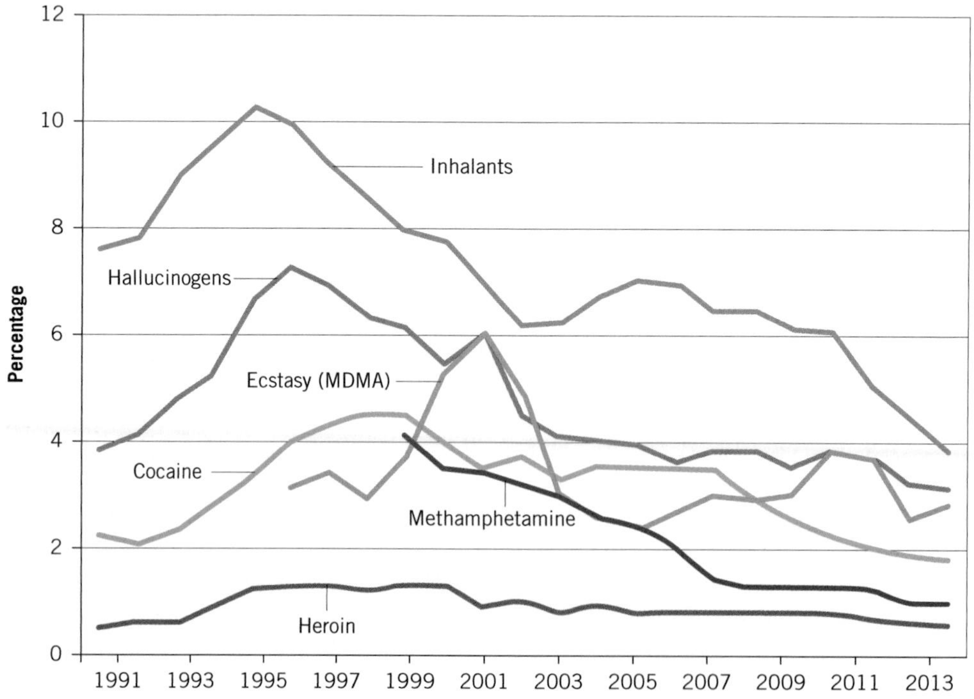

Since the early 1990s, there has been a general decline in the use of illicit drugs by adolescents.

SOURCE: National Institute on Drug Abuse (2014).

learning and retaining information (Federal Interagency Forum on Child and Family Statistics, 2009).

Nonmedical use of prescription and over-the-counter drugs also continues to be a problem for adolescents. In 2013, 15% of high school seniors reported that they had used these drugs during the previous year. The most abused drugs are Adderall, which is used to treat ADHD; Vicodin, which is used to treat pain; and cough medicines (Johnston et al., 2014).

Of course the use of any substance that affects physical or cognitive functioning can have collateral damage for your health. If your reaction time is slowed, you put yourself and others at risk when you get behind the wheel and drive. If your decision making is impaired, you put yourself and others at risk when you engage in unprotected sex or take foolish dares.

When teens use any of these substances to excess or develop significant life problems as a result of their use, they may be diagnosed with a substance use disorder (SUD). SUD is marked by (1) impaired control of the use of the substance so the teen craves it and uses more than intended; (2) social impairment including problems with peers, at home, or in school; (3) risky use of the substance when teens know it is causing problems in their lives; and (4) tolerance build-up so individuals need more and more of the substance and experience withdrawal symptoms when they try to stop (APA, 2013).

Substance use disorder (SUD) Use of drugs that is marked by impaired control, social impairment, risky use, and tolerance build-up and withdrawal symptoms.

Risks of Injury and Accidental Death

Although adolescence is a healthy time for most young people, it also is a time when the risk of accidents and injuries increases substantially. Adolescents do not always make the wisest decisions and are prone to take risks that compromise their well-being.

Accidents

Compared to younger children and adults, adolescents are at particularly high risk of injury or even death from accidental causes. Their willingness to take chances undoubtedly plays a role. Here are some of the specific risks to which adolescents expose themselves:

- 7.7% say they never or rarely wear seat belts when someone else is driving
- 87.5% who ride bicycles say they rarely or never wear helmets
- 24.1% report having ridden at least once in the last 30 days with a driver who had been drinking
- 8.2% say that in the previous 30 days they had driven a car or other vehicle after drinking alcohol
- 32.8% say they had texted or e-mailed while driving in the previous 30 days (CDC, 2012i; Palo Alto Medical Foundation, 2014)

In the United States more adolescents die from motor vehicle accidents than from all other causes combined (Child Trends, 2014b) (see Figure 14.10). Inexperience behind the wheel, a high tolerance for risk taking, and some poor driving habits (including distracted and drunk driving) all contribute to these frightening statistics. Males are more likely than females to suffer a fatal injury, and older adolescents (ages 15–19) are 5 times more likely to suffer a fatal injury than younger ones (ages 10–14) (Sleet, Ballesteros, & Borse, 2010). For every death due to injury from any cause, approximately 12 injuries require hospitalization and 641 require a trip to an emergency room.

In memoriam. Auto accidents—like the one whose three teenage victims are remembered here—are the leading cause of death among U.S. adolescents. What contributes to the high rate of auto accidents among young drivers? ■

Kathryn Osler/The Denver Post via Getty Images

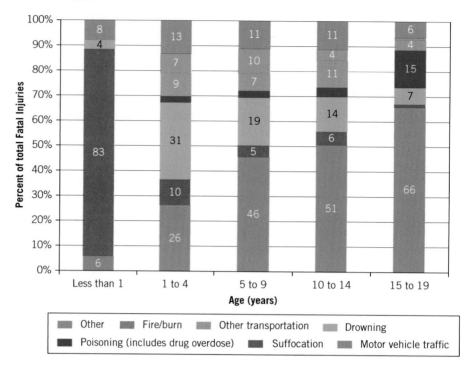

FIGURE 14.10 Adolescent deaths from unintentional injury

More U.S. young people between the ages of 15 and 19 die from motor vehicle accidents than from all other causes of death combined.

SOURCE: Child Trends (2014b); National Center for Injury Protection and Control (2014).

Concussion Traumatic brain injuries that change the way your brain functions and may result in headache, memory loss, and confusion.

Sports Injuries

In 2012, about 1.35 million children under the age of 19 were injured seriously enough while playing sports that they required treatment in an emergency room (Ferguson, Green, & Hansen, 2013). The risk of sports-related injuries increases as children get older, and at all ages it is greater for boys than girls (Wier, Miller, & Steiner, 2009). The exception, as Figure 14.11 shows, is that girls are 8 times more likely than boys to suffer a sprain or tear to the anterior cruciate ligament (ACL), the ligament in the knee that attaches the upper leg bone to the lower one. One possible explanation is that the notch in the knee that contains this ligament is narrower in women than in men, so it is easier for it to get pinched and torn when the knee twists or bends. About two thirds of catastrophic injuries to young women resulted from cheerleading and almost 20% of these injuries were to the neck and head (Mueller & Cantu, 2011).

Concussion

Recently awareness has risen of the long-term effects of one particular type of sports injury: concussion. Concussions are traumatic brain injuries that change the way

Sports injuries. Boys of all ages are at greater risk of sports injuries than girls, though girls are more likely to suffer injury to the ACL, a ligament in the knee. What can parents do to reduce these risks? ∎

Steve Satushek/Photolibrary/Getty Images

| FIGURE 14.11 | Sports-related injuries |

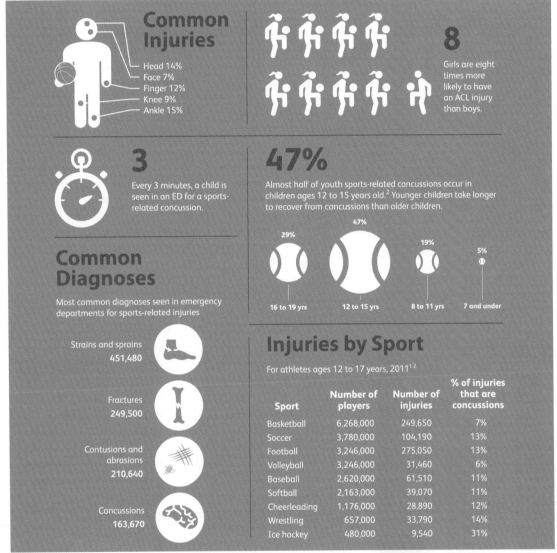

1.35 Million

Number of children seen in emergency departments with sports-related injuries in 2012

Common Injuries

Head 14%
Face 7%
Finger 12%
Knee 9%
Ankle 15%

8

Girls are eight times more likely to have an ACL injury than boys.

3

Every 3 minutes, a child is seen in an ED for a sports-related concussion.

47%

Almost half of youth sports-related concussions occur in children ages 12 to 15 years old.[2] Younger children take longer to recover from concussions than older children.

| 29% | 47% | 19% | 5% |
| 16 to 19 yrs | 12 to 15 yrs | 8 to 11 yrs | 7 and under |

Common Diagnoses

Most common diagnoses seen in emergency departments for sports-related injuries

Strains and sprains
451,480

Fractures
249,500

Contusions and abrasions
210,640

Concussions
163,670

Injuries by Sport

For athletes ages 12 to 17 years, 2011[1,2]

Sport	Number of players	Number of injuries	% of injuries that are concussions
Basketball	6,268,000	249,650	7%
Soccer	3,780,000	104,190	13%
Football	3,246,000	275,050	13%
Volleyball	3,246,000	31,460	6%
Baseball	2,620,000	61,510	11%
Softball	2,163,000	39,070	11%
Cheerleading	1,176,000	28,890	12%
Wrestling	657,000	33,790	14%
Ice hockey	480,000	9,540	31%

To learn more about youth sports safety, visit www.safekids.org

SAFE KiDS WORLDWIDE™

Founding Sponsor
Johnson&Johnson

One in five children who go to an emergency room for treatment is there because of a sport-related injury. What do you think places children in the 12- to 15-year-old age group at the greatest risk of suffering a concussion?

SOURCE: Ferguson, Green, & Hansen (2013).

NOTES: 1. National Sporting Goods Association. 2011 vs 2001 Youth Sports Participation, NSGA. Available at: http://www.nsga.org/files/public/2011vs2001_Youth_Participation_website.pdf. Accessed April 12, 2013. 2. Ferguson RW. Safe Kids Worldwide Analysis of CPSC NEISS data, 2013.

WEB LINK 14.5
Adolescent Concussions

T/F #9

In sports that both males and females play, girls are more likely to suffer a concussion than boys. *True*

your brain functions and may result in headache, memory loss, and confusion (Mayo Clinic Staff, 1998–2014). A sharp blow to the head makes the brain shake inside the skull, causing the injury. More than 160,000 children are seen in emergency rooms for sports-related concussions each year (Ferguson et al., 2013). Almost half of those concussions occur in children ages 12 to 15 (see Figure 14.12). In sports that both boys and girls play, such as soccer, lacrosse, and basketball, girls are proportionately more likely to suffer a concussion than boys (Ferguson et al., 2013). The reason for this gender difference is not clear. A biomechanical difference may make females more vulnerable, or it could be something to do with the way the game itself is played. Did you know that women lacrosse players are not required to wear helmets, while male players are (Ferguson et al., 2013)?

It is not always easy to tell whether someone has had a concussion because victims do not always lose consciousness. Other symptoms can include dizziness or "seeing stars," headache, vomiting, pressure in the head, problems with balance, blurry vision, and fatigue (Ferguson et al., 2013; Mickalide & Hansen, 2012). If concussion is suspected, the child or adolescent should be seen by a qualified heath care professional experienced in evaluating concussions to determine whether the child can return to normal daily activities (CDC, n.d.). Under no conditions should the player return to the sport or recreational activity on the same day the injury occurred. Following a concussion, a child's or teen's brain needs time to heal.

Repetitive impact on the head is most likely to occur while playing football. In one study, 95 high school football players were fitted with helmets that recorded head impact. In a single season, linemen averaged 868 impacts and receivers 372 (Broglio et al., 2011). Adults can help reduce the risk by making sure head contact is limited during play and players are taught correct tackling procedures (Ferguson et al., 2013). Adolescents also need to be told it is okay to speak up if they have been injured, and they are not letting their coach, their parents, or their teammates down if they need to sit out until they can be evaluated and cleared to re-enter the game. A new law due to take effect in California in 2015 limits practices that include tackling to two 90-minute sessions per week and forces schools to have players sit out for at least a week if they have a concussion (Jones, 2014).

Increasing evidence suggests that concussion can have long-term effects on cognitive function, motor skills, and mental health issues such as depression. Despite all this evidence, almost half of coaches still believe children can "see stars" from head impact without any negative effects (Mickalide & Hansen, 2012). When asked, the majority agree they need more training in prevention of sports injuries, but many are unable to get it due to the expense, lack of time, or unavailability of local training programs (Mickalide & Hansen, 2012). As of 2013, 48 states and the District of Columbia had enacted legislation intended to educate coaches, parents, and children about concussions and how to prevent them, although state laws vary in their rigor and implementation (Ferguson et al., 2013).

FIGURE 14.12   Who is at risk of concussion?

Almost half of youth sports-related concussions occur in children ages 12 to 15 years old.

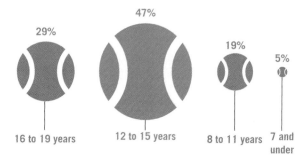

In sports that both boys and girls play, girls report a higher proportion of concussions among all injuries.

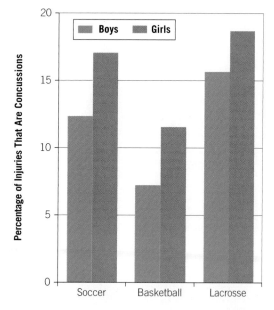

What do you think contributes to younger adolescents' and girls' having a higher risk of suffering a concussion while playing sports? When looking at the second figure, remember that more boys than girls play competitive sports, so boys suffer a greater number of total concussions, but for any individual child, the risk is greater for females than for males.

SOURCE: Ferguson et al. (2013).

1. Why do many adolescents get insufficient sleep?
2. Compare anorexia nervosa and bulimia.
3. Why is smoking so often portrayed in the media?
4. What constitutes binge drinking for men and for women?
5. What are the symptoms of concussion?

Stress and Coping in Adolescence

14.5

How do adolescents deal with stress in their lives?

Stress is a normal—and inevitable—part of life, and adolescence is a time when change, and therefore stress, is abundant. As we have said earlier in this book, when stress is very extreme or prolonged, it can affect the body in ways that have lifelong consequences for physical and mental well-being. However, most adolescents also have the cognitive ability and social resources that they need to cope effectively with stress.

What Is Stress?

In the broadest sense, stress is anything that places excessive demands on our ability to cope. When you experience stress, your body responds by releasing hormones that affect you physiologically. That is why your heart races, you breathe more rapidly, and you begin to sweat (American Psychological Association [APA], 2010). All these physiological reactions evolved as a part of the fight-or-flight response that was meant to protect us from real, physical threats in the environment. When we are dealing with short-term sources of stress, this response works the way it should—it energizes us just when we need it so we can deal with a real and immediate threat. The trouble occurs when our stress becomes long-term or chronic and the body tries to maintain this elevated level of readiness. Then the protective response can begin to take a toll on us physically in the form of physical symptoms like fatigue, headaches, and stomach upsets, or emotional consequences such as anxiety and depression (APA, 2010).

Which experiences we consider to be stressful can be subjective. For instance, some people find speaking before a group to be energizing and even fun, but others are nearly paralyzed with fright at the prospect of having to take the stage. The types of things we experience as stressful also change as a function of age (Humphrey, 2004). For adolescents, social experiences are important, so situations where they might suffer peer rejection can be stressful, and all adolescents need to cope with the changes their bodies go through during puberty. Whatever the source of the stress, however, adolescents also are developing coping resources that help them keep their level of stress manageable.

Normative Stress Versus Non-Normative Stress and Toxic Stress

Most of the stress we experience is normative stress. This type of stress is caused by experiences that happen to everyone (or almost everyone), that we can anticipate and prepare for, and that do not overwhelm our ability to cope. Starting college, going through puberty, learning to drive, and going out with someone you like are all examples of normative stress events. We can deal with them with a positive stress response in which the physiological reaction is mild in intensity and relatively brief (Shonkoff et al., 2012). Such experiences give us a chance to build coping skills and develop confidence in our ability to deal with challenges.

In contrast, non-normative stress is the result of a relatively rare occurrence that creates a great deal of stress and often overwhelms the individual, at least for a time. The death of a parent, a serious illness or hospitalization, and a natural disaster are all

Normative stress Stress that is predictable and that most people go through, and which requires a moderate and relatively brief response.

Non-normative stress Stress that results from a relatively rare occurrence that often overwhelms the individual.

Stress. Adolescence can be a stressful time as teens deal with academic demands, peer relationships, and some conflicts with parents. Chronic stress can affect a teen's mental and physical health. What can teens do to reduce their level of stress? ■

examples of non-normative stress events. Although this type of stress is intense, it often can be tolerated if the adolescent has a supportive relationship with an adult who can facilitate adaptive coping (Shonkoff et al., 2012). However, a more dangerous type of stress response to non-normative stressors is toxic stress. It can be brought on by experiences such as being a victim of child abuse, living with a parent who is a substance abuser, or experiencing ongoing discrimination. Toxic stress results in strong, frequent, and prolonged activation of the body's stress response system without any protective buffering from a supportive adult relationship. The unending exposure eventually impairs learning, behavior, and physical and mental well-being (Shonkoff et al., 2012).

Toxic stress Stress that results in strong, frequent, and prolonged activation of the body's stress response system without any protective buffering from a supportive adult relationship.

Coping Conscious efforts made to master, tolerate, or reduce stress.

Problem-focused strategies Coping strategies that focus on changing or improving a stressful situation.

T/F #10
When you are trying to deal with a stressful situation, you should try to ignore your emotional response and instead focus on solving the problem.
False

Emotion-focused strategies Coping strategies that are designed to reduce or manage emotional distress.

Coping

When faced with stressful situations, we do what we can to reduce that stress and return ourselves to a more balanced physiological status. Coping has been defined as the conscious efforts we make to regulate our emotions, our thoughts, and our behavior when challenged by stressful situations (Compas, Connor-Smith, Saltzman, Thomsen, & Wadsworth, 2001). Various ways of categorizing coping strategies have been proposed (Zimmer-Gembeck & Skinner, 2008). One way is to divide them into problem-focused and emotion-focused strategies.

Problem-focused strategies are designed to alter the situation in such a way that it reduces your stress, while emotion-focused strategies are designed to reduce or manage the emotional distress you are feeling. Table 14.1 provides examples of each of these strategies. For instance, you could try to improve a stressful situation by finding information you can use to change the situation, learning some new skills, using problem-solving strategies, or mobilizing social support for assistance. While trying to solve the problem is helpful in some situations, problem-focused strategies like these are most effective when the situation is one you can realistically change or control. Sometimes situations are beyond your control, and there aren't effective ways to change them. In these situations, you can reduce some of the stress by using emotion-focused strategies like sharing your feelings with trusted friends, changing your perception of the situation, using distraction, or trying to withdraw from the situation (Zimmer-Gembeck & Skinner, 2008). In most situations, people use a combination of strategies.

As adolescents get older they are better able to understand what is happening to them and to identify which strategies are most likely to work in any given situation. A recent study of older children and teens found, however, that a large number still rely on behaviors that may make them feel better (APA, 2010) but don't improve the situation that is causing them stress. They report using sedentary behaviors that include listening to music, playing video games, and watching television. Although these strategies may help them manage feelings of distress, they do not change the situation for the better, and when used extensively they can put the young person at risk for other problems such as obesity.

TABLE 14.1	Coping strategies
Problem-Focused Coping Strategies (efforts to change the source of the stress or your relationship to it)	
Strategy	**Example**
Active coping—taking action to remove the source of the stress or soften its effect	I put more time and effort into overcoming this problem.
Planning—thinking about the best way to handle the situation	I think about what I can do, step by step, to make the situation better.
Seeking instrumental social support—seeking advice, assistance, or information from others	I talk to others who have the same problem to get some advice from them.
Restraint coping—waiting for the right opportunity to take action	I make myself be patient until it is the right time to act.
Emotion-Focused Coping Strategies (attempts to manage or regulate the emotions caused by the situation)	
Strategy	**Example**
Expressing or venting your feelings—to release your feelings	When I get upset, I just let it all out because it makes me feel better.
Seeking emotional support—seeking moral support, sympathy, or understanding	I talk to my best friend because she is always there for me when I need her.
Acceptance of the situation	I just learn how to live with those things I can't change.
Positive reframing or reappraisal	I realize that what has happened to me is really all for the best in the long run.

This table contains examples of strategies that children and adolescents might use to cope with stress.

SOURCE: Adapted from Carver, Scheier, & Weintraub (1989; developed for use with adolescents).

AUDIO LINK 14.2
PTSD

Parents and people who work with adolescents want to help them deal with stress in their lives, and there are a number of things they can do. First, they need to simply watch the young person for signs of stress. Routine patterns of eating, sleeping, and leisure activities may be disrupted, or adolescents might begin having trouble at school because they can't concentrate or pay attention. They may become more aggressive or more withdrawn or have vague physical complaints about headaches or upset stomachs. Any of these changes should prompt a concerned adult to ask the adolescent how she is feeling and whether something is bothering her because disclosure is the first essential step for getting social support in a time of stress.

We can help adolescents think about problem-solving strategies that might work for them, or we can help them reappraise the stressful situation if it has been blown out of proportion. If stress is chronic, other behavior management strategies can be helpful, including relaxation techniques, meditation, and biofeedback (Humphrey, 2004). Other things that help all of us—children, adolescents, and adults—cope with stress include getting enough rest, eating a healthy diet, and getting some exercise. **Active Learning: Finding Resources to Cope With Stress** gives you the opportunity to explore some of the resources available on your campus if you are dealing with a good deal of stress.

Active Learning

Finding Resources to Cope With Stress

You may be well aware of the fact that being a college student can be stressful. Other people also recognize this, which is why most colleges and universities offer a wide range of services to their students to help them cope (and these services are usually free of charge).

Go to your college's home page and search for terms like *student workshops* or *counseling services* to see what your campus offers. On one campus, searching for the term *counseling services* found this information on the webpage for University Counseling Services:

- Counseling services—individual counseling, couples counseling, group counseling, psychiatric consultation, and urgent care
- Group therapy—Relationship Support, Gay/Lesbian/Bisexual Support, Men's Support, Making Peace with Your Body (body image, eating disorders), Saying Goodbye to Shy, First-Year College Experience
- Personal improvement workshops—Choice or Chance: Career Development, Improving Your Sleep, Relaxation Enhancement, Building Self-Esteem, Overcoming Procrastination

If you are aware that you are experiencing a high level of stress, you may want to look into the services your college offers to prevent future health problems. ■

Check Your Understanding

1. What are some physical and emotional consequences of stress?
2. What is the difference between normative stress, non-normative stress, and toxic stress?
3. Give examples of problem-focused and emotion-focused strategies for dealing with stress.

Conclusion

A great deal of physical change and development happens during adolescence as young people move through puberty and toward sexual maturity. As a part of this process, they develop their sexual preference and make important decisions about their sexual behavior. In the process, teens may expose themselves to a number of risks associated with those decisions. Many struggle to get the amount of sleep, nutritious food, and physical activity they need to support their growth. Their well-being also can be threatened by injuries and accidents, as well as by the use of alcohol, tobacco and drugs, and by stress. Despite these challenges, most adolescents make good choices and enjoy one of the healthiest times of their lives.

Chapter Summary

14.1 What characterizes brain development in adolescence?

Brain development continues in the prefrontal cortex during adolescence. A round of overproduction of synapses is followed by a round of pruning, as the brain becomes more streamlined and efficient. The serious brain disorder of **schizophrenia** can develop at this time.

14.2 How do children's bodies change through adolescence?

Adolescents experience an **adolescent growth spurt**. When they go through puberty, they become capable of reproducing. Girls experience **menarche**, and boys experience **spermarche**. Both **primary sex characteristics** and **secondary sex characteristics** develop. Maturing early has some advantages for boys and disadvantages for girls, but both early maturing boys and early maturing girls may be drawn into risky behavior if they associate with older peers. During adolescence, many young people develop their **sexual preference**. Adolescents who are gay, lesbian, bisexual, or transgender face additional challenges as they develop their sexual identities but many remain optimistic about their futures.

14.3 How does sexual maturation affect adolescent development?

Although the rate of adolescent pregnancies is at a historic low, the United States still has one of the highest rates of adolescent pregnancies in the industrialized world. In addition, unprotected sex can result in **sexually transmitted infections (STIs)** and **sexually transmitted diseases (STDs)** for both males and females. Rates of these diseases are highest in adolescence and early adulthood. Worldwide and in the United States, **sex trafficking** and prostitution have devastating consequences for some adolescents.

14.4 How are adolescents' health and well-being affected by their health practices?

Most adolescents do not get enough sleep. Many also have too much sugar, salt, and fats in their diets.

Some experience eating disorders, such as **anorexia nervosa** or **bulimia**, while others battle **obesity**. The thin ideal portrayed in the media can give adolescents unhealthy ideas about body weight and can contribute to disordered eating. The prevalence of smoking and drinking during adolescence has decreased, but adolescents who do drink often take part in binge drinking. Because it is so difficult to break the smoking habit, efforts have been directed at preventing adolescents from starting, including educating them about why smoking is portrayed in the media. Many adolescents use marijuana and many see it as harmless. The use of other illicit drugs can have a range of negative consequences. Many adolescents also are exposed to the risk of accidental injury or death; traffic accidents are the leading cause of accidental death. **Concussions** are a particularly serious type of sports injury associated with long-term effects on cognitive function, motor skills, and mental health.

14.5 How do adolescents deal with stress in their lives?

Stress is a normal part of life at any age, but the number of changes that occur during adolescence can make this time particularly stressful for young people. Most stress is **normative stress** and is resolved fairly quickly so the body can return to its normal level of functioning, but **non-normative** and **toxic stress** can lead to a number of long-term problems. Adolescents can use **problem-focused strategies** or **emotion-focused strategies** to cope with the stress, but they often rely on sedentary behaviors that make them feel better but do not help eliminate the stress.

Key Terms

$SAGE edge™

Sharpen your skills with SAGE edge at edge.sagepub.com/levinechrono

SAGE edge for Students provides a personalized approach to help you accomplish your coursework goals in an easy-to-use learning environment.

Go to edge.sagepub.com/levinechrono for additional exercises and video resources. Select Chapter 14, Physical Development in Adolescence, for chapter-specific activities. All of the Video Links listed in the margins of this chapter are accessible via this site.

15 Cognitive Development in Adolescence

T/F Test Your Knowledge

Test your knowledge of child development by deciding whether each of the following statements is *true* or *false,* and then check your answers as you read the chapter.

1. T☐ F☐ When teens are given statistical evidence to support an argument and personal opinions to support the same argument, they think logically and are more likely to base their own opinion on the statistical evidence.

2. T☐ F☐ Adolescents are able to study while listening to a favorite TV show because by this age their attentional processes are so well developed that they can split their attention between multiple activities.

3. T☐ F☐ The smarter you are, the more likely it is that you will also be creative.

4. T☐ F☐ Your moral values and beliefs are the best predictor of what you will actually do when faced with a moral dilemma.

5. T☐ F☐ Students who do a lot of texting do not differ from students who do not in their ability to spell or use Standard English.

6. T☐ F☐ Good writing skills are not as important in today's tech-savvy business world.

7. T☐ F☐ Throughout the elementary school years and into high school, girls do more poorly in math than boys.

8. T☐ F☐ In the past 40 years we have cut the high school dropout rate by more than half.

9. T☐ F☐ Nearly half the 14 million jobs that will be created in the United States by 2018 will go to people with an associate's degree or occupational certificate.

10. T☐ F☐ Many teens these days are overscheduled, spending most of their time after school in multiple organized activities like sports and music lessons.

Correct answers: (1) F, (2) F, (3) F, (4) F, (5) T, (6) F, (7) F, (8) T, (9) T, (10) F

Adolescence is a time of growth and consolidation in cognitive development. We begin this chapter by looking at the fourth stage in Piaget's theory of cognitive development, the stage of formal operations. In middle childhood, children developed logical thinking, but their thinking was limited to concrete reality. In adolescence, thinking expands to include ideas that are hypothetical and abstract. We also look at development in the basic cognitive processes and in social cognition. Changes in the way adolescents think about and understand the world affect their moral development, so we look too at moral reasoning and the way it relates to moral behavior. The second half of the chapter is devoted to an examination of the contexts in which cognitive development in adolescence occurs. We take a detailed look at schools as one of these contexts and examine the experience vulnerable adolescents have in the school environment. We also look at the way high schools prepare adolescents to transition into the workforce or college. The other contexts for education we examine include the family, the peer group, and the community.

Learning Questions

15.1 What changes occur as adolescents enter Piaget's stage of formal operations?

15.2 How do basic cognitive processes change during adolescence?

15.3 How does moral reasoning develop during adolescence?

15.4 How is teen language different from language in children and adults?

15.5 What threats to academic achievement do high school students face and what factors support their success?

Piaget's Stage of Formal Operations (12 Years and Older)

Thinking undergoes an important qualitative change as children enter adolescence. In middle childhood, children were able to think logically about concrete events but were not yet able to think about abstract or hypothetical concepts. Piaget's stage of formal operations is marked by the development of abstract thinking. Being able to think abstractly means teenagers no longer take literally a statement such as "Don't count your chickens before they hatch." They understand this does not refer to actual chickens. More important, in the formal operational stage, teens can think about broad abstract concepts such as democracy rather than just concrete concepts, such as counting votes in an election. A younger child can think about *doctors* and *nurses*, but someone in formal operations can think about the *field of medicine* (LeHalle, 2006).

Piaget (1999) said that by the age of about 12 children begin to reason logically about hypothetical possibilities rather than only about the concrete world. He called this new ability hypothetico-deductive reasoning. It has also been referred to as scientific thinking because it is the type of thinking scientists use when they set out to test a hypothesis. Remember we examined the scientific process in Chapter 2. In adolescence, hypothetico-deductive reasoning allows individuals to generate new possibilities and form hypotheses that they can test to answer questions. To test their hypotheses, they must use deductive reasoning, a form of logic in which a general principle leads to a logical conclusion. Piaget believed that someone with formal operations is able to follow a logical process even if it does not fit reality. For example:

1. Brown cows give chocolate milk.

2. This is a brown cow.

3. Therefore, it gives chocolate milk.

15.1

What changes occur as adolescents enter Piaget's stage of formal operations?

Formal operations Piaget's fourth stage in which people 12 and older think both logically and abstractly.

Hypothetico-deductive reasoning The ability to form hypotheses about how the world works and to reason logically about these hypotheses.

Scientific thinking The type of thinking scientists use when they set out to test a hypothesis.

Obviously this is a false premise leading to a false conclusion, but the logical process behind it is sound. A concrete thinker would not be able to separate herself from reality to reach the logical conclusion and would instead proclaim that no cows give chocolate milk. Piaget believed formal operations allow adolescents to step back from the concrete reality to reason in this more abstract, purely logical way.

One consequence of this ability to think hypothetically is that teens may become idealistic because they now can imagine what *could be* rather than simply what *is*. Idealism can motivate them to engage in activities in which they are committed to a larger goal. However, it can also cause them to question adult authority, for example, by confronting rules. They realize that even though there is a rule, it doesn't mean it always has to be that way. Other alternatives are just as reasonable and logical, and they may want to fight for these alternatives.

Formal operational thought also includes the ability to generate many possible solutions to a problem and test them before making a decision in order to discover which one is correct. To do this, you must understand that to measure the effects of any specific variable, you must hold all the other variables constant. To see one way in which Piaget tested this ability, see **Active Learning: Formal Operations**.

ACTIVE LEARNING
VIDEO 15.1
Formal Operations

Active Learning

Formal Operations

Piaget tested children of various ages on what he called the "pendulum problem." He provided each child with a pendulum, consisting of an object hanging from a string, and asked the child to figure out what determines how fast the string swings back and forth.

To carry out this activity yourself, find a length of string and attach an object to the end of it. Suspend the object so it can swing freely. Have available lighter and heavier objects and longer and shorter strings. Make a list of what you think might cause the string to swing quickly or slowly. Then write down the step-by-step process by which you would try to figure out which of the possibilities is the answer. If you have access to children of different ages, you can also do this with them, having each one generate her own list of possible causes and asking how she would test them.

Some possible answers to what determines how fast the string goes back and forth that you or the child might come up with are the weight at the end of the string, the length of the string, the strength of the initial push, and the height from which the weight is dropped.

To test these possibilities Piaget found that young children would simply try different combinations in an almost random fashion. For example, they might put a heavier weight on a longer string and then put a lighter weight on a shorter string, and in the process of trying different combinations they might stumble on the right answer. However, the hypothetico-deductive reasoning that appears in the stage of formal operations allows teens to approach this problem in a scientific way. They will think of possible answers to the problem and then test these specific hypotheses in a systematic way by controlling all the variables but the tested one. To learn the effect of the weight at the end of the string, they will vary the weight while keeping the length of the string, the strength of the initial push, and the height from which the weight is dropped the same. If varying the weight does not make a difference, they will test the strength of the initial push, and so on through all the possibilities. Did you (or a child you tested) carry out systematic experiments to determine the answer?

Have you figured out the answer to the pendulum problem? You can see the answer below.

■ **Answer: It is the length of the string that determines how fast it goes back and forth.**

When teens develop the ability to carry out the scientific process, they are able to take an idea or hypothesis and look at evidence to decide whether there is scientific support for it or not. This means they must understand what evidence is. Klaczynski (2001) had younger and older teens read the following:

> Ken and Toni are teachers who are arguing over whether students enjoy the new computer-based teaching method used in some math classes. Ken's argument is, "Each of the 3 years that we've had the computer class, about 60 students have taken it. They have written essays on why they liked or didn't like the class. Over 85% of the students say they have liked it. That's more than 130 of 150 students." Toni's argument is, "Stephanie and John (the two best students in the school, both high-honors students) have complained about how much they hate the computer-based class and how much more they like regular math classes. They say a computer can't replace a good teacher" (p. 859).

Then the researchers asked the teens to rate how likely they would be to take the computer-based course and how likely they would be to take the lecture course. The teens also rated how intelligent they thought each argument was.

Scientifically, which do you think is the better argument? Which course would you take based on what you know? Clearly, if the question is whether you are going to like the class, the statistical evidence is stronger than the testimony of two students, even if they are the highest-performing students in the school. In this research, 18% of 12-year-olds chose the statistical evidence and 42% of 16-year-olds chose this option. Still, the majority at both ages chose the intuitive evidence based on two people's opinions over the statistical evidence based on 150 students.

This type of choice may reflect the development of two systems of thought, one based on experience and the other on analysis (Kuhn, 2009). Effortless, intuitive thinking based on experience causes many people to make judgments without reflecting on all the possibilities. For example, Jonas plays violent video games but believes that he himself is not an aggressive person. On this basis he disagrees with research on large samples of teenagers showing that those who play these games are more likely than others to be aggressive. This is an example of putting personal experience above scientific thinking. To make a good argument against the research findings, Jonas would need to marshal other evidence based on more than his personal experience. For example, there might be a study in which boys who were aggressive before playing violent video games became more aggressive after playing, but other boys did not. Argument and counterargument, based on evidence, is the essence of the scientific process and develops only with formal operational thinking.

Piaget believed that not everyone reaches the stage of formal operations and that many people remain concrete thinkers all their lives. In one study in England, 14-year-old students tested on the pendulum task in 1976 were compared with 14-year-olds tested in 2007 (Shayer & Ginsburg, 2009). At both times, the majority of 14-year-olds did not reach the level of formal operations on this task, but the percentage who did declined over this time period from 23% to 10% for boys and from 25% to 13% for girls. Formal operational thinking continues to develop through adolescence, so it may be that these students will develop this level of thought later in their development. However, they may not ever develop formal operational thinking. There is some evidence that achieving this level of thought is not the product of maturation but rather is dependent on whether an individual's education trains him or her to develop it (Artman, Cahan, & Avni-Babad, 2006).

Adolescent Egocentrism

As you recall, Piaget described young children in the preoperational stage as egocentric because they are unable to see things from the perspective of people other than

T/F #1
When teens are given statistical evidence to support an argument and personal opinions to support the same argument, they think logically and are more likely to base their own opinion on the statistical evidence.
False

The imaginary audience. This girl likely assumes that others are looking as closely at her appearance as she is. Is her "audience" real or imaginary? ■

Imaginary audience The egocentric belief that one is the center of other people's attention much of the time.

JOURNAL ARTICLE 15.1
Adolescent Egocentrism

themselves. David Elkind proposed that there is a resurgence of egocentrism in early adolescence that is different from that of the preoperational child. According to Elkind, adolescent egocentrism is expressed through what he has called the imaginary audience and the personal fable (Alberts, Elkind, & Ginsberg, 2007).

When Elkind refers to an imaginary audience, he means that young teens believe they are the center of other people's attention in the same way they are the center of their own. Teens may refuse to go to school because their hair looks bad, or they may become self-conscious about the way their body looks. In the young teen's mind, everyone at school will also be very aware of such perceived flaws. Although teens can in fact be very cruel to one another, the chances are that most are more concerned about how they themselves look than about how other people look.

Although the "audience" can be seen as harsh and judgmental, it can also be positive. One teen said "Sometimes when I see a good-looking girl/boy, I think that they are looking at me in a very admiring way" (Alberts et al., 2007, p. 75). Or a teen may be dancing at a party and think everyone is looking at her because of how cool she looks. She is sure all the other people around her are spending a great deal of energy noticing and thinking about her. In these ways the teen, like the preschooler, has difficulty seeing the world from someone else's point of view and realizing she is not the center of the other person's world. Elkind developed the Imaginary Audience Scale to measure this aspect of adolescent egocentrism (Elkind & Bowen, 1979). The following is an example from that scale:

> **Instructions:** Please read the following stories carefully and assume that the events actually happened to you. Place a check next to the answer that best describes what you would do or feel in the real situation.
>
> You are sitting in class and have discovered that your jeans have a small but noticeable split along the side seam. Your teacher has offered extra credit toward his/her course grade to anyone who can write the correct answer to a question on the blackboard. Would you get up in front of the class and go to the blackboard, or would you remain seated?
>
> _____ Go to the blackboard as though nothing had happened.
>
> _____ Go to the blackboard and try to hide the split.
>
> _____ Remain seated. (Elkind & Bowen, 1979)

The first answer reflects a willingness to be exposed to the imaginary audience. The second reflects more discomfort, and the third reflects the most discomfort. Elkind and Bowen (1979) found that the highest scores on this scale, indicating acute awareness of an imaginary audience, were found in eighth grade, a time when adolescents are particularly sensitive about their appearance.

A personal fable is a belief held by teenagers that their experiences are unique and different from those of all other people. For example, a girl whose boyfriend has broken up with her may think, "My mother could never understand what I am going through. She could never have felt a love like I felt." Unfortunately, the personal fable can also be the basis of risky behaviors (Alberts et al., 2007). For instance, a teen may understand the effect of alcohol on reaction time but still believe he is such a good driver that "I can drive drunk and nothing will happen to me." Or a teen might understand the risks of unprotected sex but still feel that "I won't get pregnant—that only happens to other people."

Recently, Martin and Sokol (2011) proposed that the imaginary audience and personal fable represent more than the egocentric focus on the self that we associate with adolescence. We can also see them as adaptations that help the adolescent deal with some of the important developmental tasks of this stage of life. Adolescents are encountering many new interpersonal situations and are understandably concerned about how they will be perceived in them. The imaginary audience gives them the chance to imagine what might happen and anticipate some ways to handle it. The personal fable, with its focus on the uniqueness of the individual, helps prepare the young person for the individuation (or separation) from family that typically comes as the adolescent moves into young adulthood.

> **Personal fable** The belief (often held by teenagers) that you are in some way unique and different from all other people.

Is Formal Operations the Final Stage?

Piaget's studies led him to the conclusion that the stage of formal operations was the final, highest stage of mental development and, as we have already noted, not everyone reaches it. However, some theorists believe cognitive development can continue to another stage called postformal operations. Although this more advanced stage is beyond the scope of this chapter on adolescence, we briefly introduce it to show that adolescent thinking may not be the highest level of thought.

In the stage of postformal operations, the individual comes to understand that knowledge is not absolute; that is, there is not always one and only one right answer. Through this process, an individual can consider multiple perspectives and reconcile seemingly contradictory information (Labouvie-Vief, 2006). For example, people who agree with the following statements are indicating that they think at the postformal operational level: "I see that a given dilemma always has several good solutions," "There are many 'right' ways to define any life experience; I must make a final decision on how I define the problems of life," and "I am aware that I can decide which reality to experience at a particular time; but I know that reality is really multi-level and more complicated" (Cartwright, Galupo, Tyree, & Jennings, 2009, p. 185). Clearly the complexity of thought in this stage goes beyond the logical, abstract processes proposed by Piaget in the stage of formal operations.

> **Postformal operations** The cognitive ability to consider multiple perspectives and bring together seemingly contradictory information.

Check Your Understanding

1. What characterizes Piaget's stage of formal operations?
2. What is the role of the imaginary audience?
3. What is a personal fable?
4. How do postformal operations differ from formal operations?

Cognitive Processes

> **15.2**
>
> How do basic cognitive processes change during adolescence?

The cognitive processes we have examined as they develop earlier in life, including attention, memory, metacognition, executive function, and social cognition, all continue to develop from early to late adolescence.

The limits of attention. Teens believe that they can do homework while doing many other things at the same time. How effective do you think these boys' study time is with their attention so divided? ■

Attention in Adolescence

When you sit down to read this book or do other academic work, do you have music on, answer text messages, and/or have a TV running in the background? If so, you are like many students who have become so confident in their ability to control their attention that they believe they can attend to several things at the same time. However, research does not support this belief. In fact, our brain can carry out only one thinking activity at a time. When we are multitasking, we really are switching back and forth between tasks. In doing so, we often lose track of our original task and miss whatever is occurring while we make these switches.

One area of great concern is that teens often believe they can use electronic media successfully while driving, switching their attention from the road to their device and back again, but research does not support this belief. Recent studies have shown that teens who talk on cell phones while driving have delayed reaction times to events on the road, weave between lanes, and are much more likely to have an accident. Teens who text message while driving increase their chances of being in an accident even more (Drews, Yazdani, Godfrey, Cooper, & Strayer, 2009). In fact, reaction time for people who either talk or text on a cell phone while driving is slower than the reaction times of drunk drivers (Strayer, Drews, & Crouch, 2006), yet 49% of young adults report they have texted while driving (Tison, Chaudhary, & Cosgrove, 2011). Teens are not the only ones texting and driving. Adults are also setting a model for this type of dangerous behavior when they use technology while driving. In most states, texting while driving is now against the law (Governors' Highway Safety Association, 2014).

Use of electronic media can also interfere with schoolwork for teens. In one experimental study, adolescents were assigned to one of two groups. One group did homework with soap operas on TV in the background, and the other group did homework without background TV. Those with the TV on took longer to do their work because they were distracted by the programs, and even though the two groups spent the same amount of time actually looking at their homework, the students with TV remembered and understood less when they were tested on it (Pool, Koolstra, & van der Voort, 2003). Pool et al. (2003) argue that the distraction of TV interfered with the students' ability to integrate all the information from the homework. Consequently, they ended up with a much more superficial understanding of the material and remembered less.

This finding has been confirmed in neurological research. It appears that when we try to do two things at once, we do not use the part of the brain designed for deep processing of information. Instead we use a different part designed for more superficial, rapid processing (Foerde, Knowlton, & Poldrack, 2006). Finally, research on study habits has shown that the students who perform worst on exams are those who study with many distractions: music, television, e-mail, and/or conversations with friends (Gurung, 2005). See the effects of multitasking for yourself by trying **Active Learning: Studying and Distractions.**

AUDIO LINK 15.1
Multitasking

T/F #2
Adolescents are able to study while listening to a favorite TV show because by this age their attentional processes are so well developed that they can split their attention between multiple activities. *False*

Active Learning

Studying and Distractions

1. Set a goal of reading 10 pages of this textbook when you are likely to have distractions. Note the time that you start reading. Every time you are interrupted, note how long the interruption lasts and write down what the interruption was. Be sure to include when you interrupt yourself by texting someone, getting a snack, making a phone call, looking up at the TV, and so forth. Write down the time you finish reading the 10 pages. Subtract your starting time from your ending time and then subtract the total time of all the interruptions.

2. Now find a time and place to read 10 more pages of this textbook where you are reasonably certain not to be interrupted and will not to be tempted to interrupt yourself. Write down the time you start reading and the time you finish the 10 pages. Subtract to find out how long it took you.

3. Compare the results of studying both ways. Was one way more efficient than the other?

Bowman, Levine, Waite, and Gendron (2010) found that students who were interrupted with instant messages while reading a textbook online took much longer to do the same amount of reading than students who were not interrupted. If you are used to studying with the television, computer, and cell phone on, look at your results and decide for yourself whether the interruptions made you slower. You may want to consider putting off your other activities until you have finished studying. The end result is likely to be more efficient studying and more free time for you. ∎

Memory in Adolescence

In Chapter 11, we saw that memory ability improved considerably during middle childhood. Developmental changes continue to occur through adolescence in the way the brain manages working memory. In Chapter 14, we learned that the prefrontal cortex continues to develop, and this area of the brain is central to working memory in adults. However, when working on a memory task, younger teens are more likely to use both the prefrontal cortex and the hippocampus. By age 18, teens use only the prefrontal cortex, as adults do (Finn, Sheridan, Kam, Hinshaw, & D'Esposito, 2010). We can only speculate about the effects of using two areas of the brain instead of the more efficient use of just the prefrontal cortex. This difference may help younger teens be more open to storing information in more different types of situations, thus expanding their accumulation of new knowledge, while at the same time making them less efficient at storing specific information on which they are focusing (Finn et al., 2010).

Much evidence suggests that teens who drink heavily develop subtle differences in cognitive abilities, including a lower ability to use working memory efficiently. However, it also appears that teens who have poorer working memory are more likely to begin drinking heavily (Squeglia et al., 2012). Young teens with lower working-memory ability are also more likely to act without thinking and lack the ability to delay gratification. These teens are more likely to have early and progressively greater alcohol use through adolescence (Khurana et al., 2013).

Metacognition

As children move toward adolescence, they become increasingly able to think about and regulate their own thoughts and cognitive activities. This process is called metacognition

AUDIO LINK 15.2
Binge Drinking

Metacognition The ability to think about and monitor one's own thoughts and cognitive activities.

Metamemory The understanding of memory, how it works, and how to use it effectively.

(Vrugt & Oort, 2008). Metamemory specifically refers to the understanding of memory, how it works, and how to use it effectively.

To understand metacognition, think about what happens when you are studying for an exam in one of your courses. You might start by assessing how much you already know about a subject. That helps you determine how much time it will take you to prepare. You don't want to make a mistake at this step by underestimating how much work you need to do. Next you can consider which strategies you will use to prepare for your exam. You would most likely choose a different approach when studying for an English Literature exam than for a Chemistry final. You continue to evaluate your level of understanding as your studying progresses, to gauge how much more you need to do or to reevaluate the strategies you are using. After you get your grade, you can evaluate the effectiveness of the strategies you used, so the next time you can prepare more effectively or more efficiently.

Each decision you make when directing your own learning is an indication of your level of understanding of how cognition and memory work (Winn, 2004). As adolescents get older they get better at evaluating their own learning accurately (Weil et al., 2013). Studies with students from middle schools (Gaskins & Pressley, 2007) and college (Cano & Cardelle-Elawar, 2004) have shown that students' performance can be improved when they better understand how their cognitive processes work.

Executive Function

Executive function, the ability to organize and control our thinking and behavior to achieve a goal, continues to develop during adolescence. It is well known that teenagers are prone to engage in risky behavior, and the immaturity of executive function may be one reason. As with working memory, brain development underlies some of the further development of executive function. Further myelination and synaptic pruning, concepts you learned about in Chapter 5, occur in the prefrontal cortex, the area most responsible for executive function (Blakemore & Choudhury, 2006).

In a longitudinal study of teenagers, Boelema et al. (2013) examined three elements of executive function:

1. Control of attention, including *focused attention, sustained attention,* and *inhibition*

2. Information processing, including *speed of processing*

3. Cognitive flexibility, including the *ability to shift attention* to complete a task, and *working memory* (Boelema et al., 2013).

They examined Dutch adolescents by testing them at age 11 and then again at age 19 to determine the normative pattern of achievement of these aspects of executive function. They found that each aspect had its own timetable, but all improved over the teen years. Cognitive flexibility showed the most growth during this time, followed by speed of processing, and the smallest change was found in attention variables including inhibition. With the exception of cognitive flexibility, girls generally started at a higher level than boys, but boys went a long way toward catching up as they reached the end of their teen years. For most areas, teens from low-income families started at a lower level than their peers from higher-income families, but they seemed to catch up in the area of sustained attention. For inhibition, which is the ability to control our own behavior, there was even a larger difference between the high- and low-income groups by the end of adolescence.

Another central aspect of executive function is the ability to plan. Planning includes thinking through a task ahead of time and then evaluating the outcomes as you proceed through the task, changing what you are doing as necessary. This has often been assessed

FIGURE 15.1 **The Tower of Hanoi**

How many moves would it take you to get all of these disks to the right-hand pole without ever putting a larger disk on top of a smaller one?

with the use of the game The Tower of Hanoi, shown in Figure 15.1, in which the goal is to move all the disks to the right-hand rod by moving one disk at a time and never putting a larger disk on top of a smaller disk. Simpler versions of this task have fewer disks to move. Planning ability continues to develop through adolescence (Best, Miller, & Jones, 2009). When working on the Tower of Hanoi task, adolescents spend a longer time than younger children thinking about the problem before they begin moving pieces and are quicker to solve the problem using fewer moves (Asato, Sweeney, & Luna, 2006).

If adolescents are improving their ability to control their thoughts and behaviors to achieve a goal, why is it also true that they have a greater tendency to respond impulsively in many situations? Once again the answer is linked to brain maturation. Dopamine is a neurotransmitter, one of those chemicals that takes messages throughout the brain and nervous system. It helps carry messages of reward to the brain, and it appears that adolescence is a peak period for dopamine's availability and effective functioning (Luna, Paulsen, Padmanabhan, & Geier, 2013). This peak occurs around the same time that teens are most likely to seek immediate rewards, perhaps through risky behaviors (Wahlstrom, White, & Luciana, 2010). It appears that in teens the reward system is heightened while the control system in the brain is still developing.

Some have argued that a certain amount of risk taking in adolescents is important for the development of autonomy and learning about the larger world. Risk taking may have positive effects when it allows the teen to try new and exciting experiences, such as a trip to a foreign country. However, the obvious downside is the temptation to engage in activities that endanger the teen's safety such as experimenting with drugs or driving too fast.

Risky behavior is even more likely to occur when a teen is with peers than when alone. In a simulated driving experience, teens and adults had to make decisions about whether to stop at a light as it turned yellow (Chein, Albert, O'Brien, Uckert, & Steinberg, 2011). They were told that the faster they completed the course they were driving on, the more money they would receive, but they clearly risked having a crash if they ran the yellow light and this would slow them down even more than stopping. While having their brain function monitored through an fMRI, the participants completed this course once while alone and a second time while being observed by two friends who were in a different room. Adolescents, but not adults, took more risks in their decision making and had more crashes when their peers were observing them. fMRI results indicated a heightened response of the reward system in the brain when teens believed their peers could see what they did. This same result has been found even if the peer is a stranger (Weigard, Chein, Albert, Smith, & Steinberg, 2014).

VIDEO LINK 15.1
Peer Influence and Adolescent Behavior

T/F #3

The smarter you are, the more likely it is that you will also be creative. *False*

Convergent thinking Finding one correct solution for a problem.

Creativity

Creativity is central to the ability to move beyond what we know to the realm of possibility. While people of any age can be creative, some of the cognitive changes during adolescence are abilities particularly important for creativity. Being cognitively flexible, being able to think through a task and anticipate the outcome, and thinking hypothetically and abstractly are all essential elements of the creative process. Certain changes in the brain allow for more flexible and creative thinking (Kleibeuker et al., 2013).

Where does creativity fit into our understanding of intelligence? Is it an independent characteristic, or is it closely related to intelligence so that people who are high (or low) on one are also high (or low) on the other? A substantial amount of research has examined the relationship between creativity and intelligence, and a number of studies have found that the correlation is positive but moderately low (Kim, 2005; Wallach & Kogan, 1965). Although a certain amount of intelligence is necessary to be creative, high intelligence is not sufficient by itself.

What do we mean when we talk about creativity? In the 1950s J. P. Guilford proposed that creativity is based on an ability to see multiple solutions to a problem—that is, the ability to use divergent thinking. In contrast, many academic situations require that we come up with one correct solution, which is the result of convergent thinking. Robert Sternberg (2003a) has defined creative thinking as "thinking that is novel and that produces ideas that are of value" (pp. 325–326), and in this sense, we need both divergent thinking to produce new ideas and convergent thinking to narrow the alternative ideas down to the one that is most practical or likely to succeed.

According to Guilford (1950), being able to think divergently requires fluency, which is the ability to find multiple solutions relatively quickly; flexibility, which is the ability to consider multiple alternatives or shift your mind-set; and originality, which is the ability to come up with solutions that are unique. Most of the tests used to measure creativity are based on these ideas. See how **Active Learning: Creativity Tests** serves to stimulate your own creative thinking.

Active Learning

Creativity Tests

The following items are similar to items used on various tests of creativity. Give yourself a specific amount of time (perhaps 1 or 2 minutes) and provide as many alternate answers to each challenge as you can. You might want to do this activity with a small group of friends so you can observe whether there are substantial differences in the way different individuals perform.

Word fluency	Write as many words beginning with a given letter as you can in a specified amount of time.
Alternate uses	Give as many possible uses for a given item that you can (for example, a brick, a bicycle tire).
Consequences	Give as many consequences as you can for a hypothetical situation (for example, what if we could live underwater? What if animals could talk?).
Making objects	Draw as many objects as you can using only a specific set of shapes (for example, one circle and two squares).
Decorations	Use as many different designs as possible to outline a common object.

Scoring of this type of test is often quite complex, so this activity is simply an opportunity to stimulate your creativity, not to rate the results. How quickly were you able to generate multiple answers that were highly original? ■

As we discussed in Chapter 12, Robert Sternberg believes there are three types of intelligence—analytical, practical, and creative. Although Sternberg believes schools should foster all three, he also believes classroom teachers undervalue creativity because they presume it is the same thing as general intelligence or they just don't know how to teach it. He maintains that "to a large extent, creativity is not just a matter of thinking in a certain way, but rather it is an attitude toward life" and that "creative people are creative, in large part, because they have *decided* [author's emphasis] to be creative" (Sternberg, 2003a, p. 333). Table 15.1 presents 12 decisions that Sternberg says underlie the decision to be a creative thinker. Can you think of ways that a classroom teacher could help adolescents develop these creative attitudes and mind-sets?

We need to encourage teens to be creative, to experiment and try new things, and to think about situations in fresh ways without being bound to old practices and ideas. We must allow them to try and fail without becoming discouraged. As adults, we can also provide a stimulating environment that exposes them to new experiences, and we can urge them to find a passion and follow it.

TABLE 15.1   How to foster creative thinking

Redefine the problem	Don't necessarily accept things just because other people do. Allow yourself to see things differently.
Analyze your own ideas	Critique your own ideas and decide whether they are valuable and worth pursuing or not.
Sell your ideas	Just generating creative ideas is not enough. Because they challenge accepted ways of thinking, they must be "sold" to others.
Remember that knowledge is a double-edged sword	You cannot be creative without being knowledgeable, but existing knowledge also can hamper or hinder creative thinking.
Surmount obstacles	You need to be ready to "defy the crowd" and overcome these obstacles.
Take sensible risks	Rather than providing a safe and conventional answer, be willing to fail by trying new things.
Be willing to grow	Don't become so invested in your own original creative ideas that you are afraid to branch out or explore new ones.
Believe in yourself	Maintain a sense of self-efficacy even when no one else seems to believe in you.
Tolerate ambiguity	Be willing to tolerate some level of uncertainty while you are waiting to see whether your ideas will pan out or not.
Find what you love and do it	You are likely to be most creative when doing things you really care about.
Allow time	Realize that it takes time for incubation, reflection, and selection to develop a creative idea.
Allow mistakes	Recognize that mistakes will happen, but use them as an opportunity to learn.

These are suggestions Robert J. Sternberg makes that he believes teachers can use in their classrooms to encourage creative thinking.

SOURCE: Adapted from Sternberg (2003a, pp. 333–335).

Social Cognition in Adolescence

Social cognition and theory of mind, the ability to understand another person's thoughts, feelings, and beliefs, become more complex during adolescence in several ways. Anyone who has played poker knows that understanding what goes on in someone else's mind gets increasingly complicated. A good poker player not only has to figure out what the other players are thinking ("I have a good hand") but also has to keep in mind that the other players are trying to figure out what she is thinking. If she wants to bluff the others, she must make them think she has different cards than she really does. In other words, she is thinking about their thinking about her thinking. This is called recursive thinking and is an ability that is still developing through adolescence (Corballis, 2006). Figure 15.2 illustrates the way recursive thinking works.

Another way in which theory of mind becomes more complex is through its interaction with executive function, one aspect of which is the ability to inhibit, or stop, a behavior. Dumontheil, Apperly, and Blakemore (2010) gave a computer-based task to children, adolescents, and adults. All were shown a set of shelves with different objects on them, similar to what is shown in Figure 15.3. Although they could see balls of three sizes, a character called the Director could see only the two larger ones. In this task, the Director tells the person to move the small ball to the left. The person must inhibit an egocentric response, which is to move the small white ball, the one he or she can see but the Director cannot. Instead the person must move the green ball, which is the smallest one the Director can see. Dumontheil et al. (2010) found that older teens made fewer errors than younger teens, but more errors than adults. This result provides evidence that the ability to read another person's mind, even at the level of knowing what they actually see, is still developing through adolescence.

Social cognition and theory of mind have also been related to certain social outcomes in adolescence. For example, adolescents who had shown less ability to understand others' states of mind during childhood were more likely to become victims of bullies or to become both victim and bully (Shakoor et al., 2012). Therefore, it has been suggested that an important approach to preventing bullying is training in theory of mind. Goldstein and Winner (2012) attempted to promote theory of mind in teens through a 10-month intensive acting program while students in a control group took part in a

Recursive thinking The ability to think about other people thinking about your thinking.

FIGURE 15.2   **Recursive thinking**

Pictures like this have been used to test whether participants can describe the recursive thinking process. For instance, in the first picture, the boy is thinking about the girl and her father. In the second picture, the boy is thinking that he is thinking about himself. In the third picture, the boy is thinking about a girl thinking about what her father is thinking about her mother.

SOURCE: Oppenheimer (1986).

FIGURE 15.3 **Testing theory of mind**

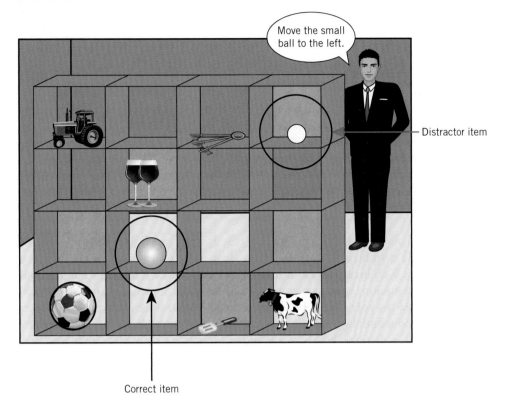

Correct item

In the picture shown here, which ball would you move if you were asked to move the small ball? Remember that the person asking you to move the small ball cannot see everything you can see. You might be fooled by the distractor item (in this case, the small white ball) because you can see it but the other person cannot.

SOURCE: Dumontheil, Apperly, & Blakemore (2010).

fine arts program. Acting, of course, requires that the individual step into the shoes of another person to portray that person's thoughts and feelings. The students who were trained in acting had a greater gain in theory of mind over this period of time than the control group did. Changes can and do still occur in this basic ability that underlies much of our ability to understand and successfully interact with others in our lives.

Check Your Understanding

1. How do memory and attention change during adolescence?
2. What are metacognition and metamemory?
3. Compare divergent and convergent thinking.
4. What is recursive thinking?

Moral Judgment

As adolescents develop the cognitive ability to think logically and hypothetically, they can think about the consequences of different decisions and this, in turn, affects the way they think about moral issues. As we learned in Chapter 10, Piaget believed moral judgments were based on a child's level of cognitive development. Lawrence Kohlberg developed and expanded upon Piaget's ideas.

15.3

How does moral reasoning develop during adolescence?

VIDEO LINK 15.2
Adolescent Morality

Kohlberg's Cognitive Developmental Theory

Kohlberg developed a series of moral dilemmas to assess moral judgment in children of different ages. Based on their responses, Kohlberg named and described stages of moral development. His most famous dilemma is a brief story titled "Heinz and the Drug":

> In Europe, a woman was near death from a rare form of cancer. There was one drug that the doctors thought might save her, a form of radium that a druggist in the same town had recently discovered. The druggist was charging $2,000, ten times what the drug cost him to make. The sick woman's husband, Heinz, went to everyone he knew to borrow the money, but he could only get together about half of what [the drug] cost. He told the druggist that his wife was dying, and asked him to sell it cheaper or let him pay later. But the druggist said, "No." So, Heinz got desperate and broke into the man's store to steal the drug for his wife. Should the husband have done that? Why? (Kohlberg, 2005, p. 214)

Children and adolescents of different ages read this dilemma, and some immediately say Heinz should definitely break in to get the drug while others say it would be wrong to do so. In fact, Kohlberg was less interested in what someone thought Heinz should do than in understanding how they came to their decision. Someone who says he would break in because his wife would be angry at him if he did not is at quite a different level of moral thought than someone who says he would break in because human life is sacred. Likewise, someone who says he would not break in because he might get caught and sent to jail is at a different level than someone who says he would not break in because it is important to respect each other's property.

Based on these different types of reasoning, Kohlberg described three levels of moral judgment: preconventional, conventional, and postconventional. He divided each level into two stages and these are described in Table 15.2. We describe here the broad outlines of the three major levels.

TABLE 15.2   **Kohlberg's stages of moral development**

Levels	Stages	Description (the basis for moral judgment)
I. Preconventional	1. Heteronomous morality	Obey the word of authorities and fear punishment
	2. Individualism, instrumental purpose, and exchange	Be fair; take everyone's self-interest into account
II. Conventional	3. Mutual interpersonal expectations and conformity	Act so as to be seen as "good" by those around you, in accordance with their expectations, including caring, loyalty, and gratitude
	4. Social system and conscience	Consider the good of society as a whole, maintaining order for the good of all
III. Postconventional	5. Social contract and individual rights	Understand that the rules of society may differ for different groups and that some values, such as life and liberty, are universal
	6. Universal ethical principles	Follow self-chosen principles of equal rights even when they conflict with society's rules

SOURCE: Adapted from Kohlberg (1987, pp. 285–286).

The first level, preconventional moral judgment, is most characteristic of young children. It is marked by self-interest and motivation based on rewards and punishments. In some circumstances, we all continue to think in these terms. For example, if you are driving faster than the speed limit and you hit the brakes when you see a police car, you are not thinking about the underlying reasons for the speed limit (such as safety or conserving gasoline). You are trying to get somewhere as fast as you can without getting caught breaking the law, and you hit your brakes because you don't want to get an expensive speeding ticket.

In the second level, conventional moral judgment moves beyond self-interest to take into account the good of those around you. In the first substage, a person bases moral decisions on the moral expectations of important people in his life. Here "trust, loyalty, respect, and gratitude" are central values (Kohlberg, 1987, p. 284). In the second substage, a person makes decisions based more on the expectations of society as a whole. Laws are to be followed because society would break down if everyone disobeyed them. In this stage, a person might respond to the Heinz dilemma by saying Heinz should not break in because if everyone did things like this, our society would be chaotic.

In the third level, postconventional moral judgment moves beyond society as a defining factor of what is moral or right. A person in this stage believes in the human rights of all people, so his or her moral judgments are based on universal principles that apply to all. Often these principles will correspond with society's rules, but when they don't, the person still chooses to follow the principles. For example, members of the organization Greenpeace broke the law in May 2014, when they tried to block a Russian oil tanker from offloading its cargo of oil from the Arctic. All were arrested but they felt that their moral principles were more important than the rules of their society. One protestor said, "This tanker is the first sign of a reckless new push to exploit the Arctic, a place of incredible beauty which is melting before our eyes" (Vidal, 2014, para. 7). Read about another situation in which an individual chose to break the law on behalf of what he believed was a higher moral purpose in **Journey of Research: Kohlberg's Life History and His Theory.**

Preconventional moral judgment Moral judgment that is marked by self-interest and motivation based on rewards and punishments.

Conventional moral judgment Moral judgment that moves beyond self-interest to take into account the good of those around you.

Postconventional moral judgment Moral judgment that moves beyond society as a defining factor of what is moral or right and is based on universal principles that apply to all.

....

JOURNEY OF RESEARCH *Kohlberg's Life History and His Theory*

Many times individuals' life experiences influence the theories they develop and the research they carry out. Lawrence Kohlberg's research is clearly connected to his life history. Kohlberg served with the U.S. Merchant Marines after World War II. Later, he volunteered to help sail ships that would move Jewish refugees out of Europe to the British-controlled territory of Palestine. In doing so, he was breaking British law, which made it illegal for these refugees to enter Palestine. Kohlberg was captured and held in Cyprus until he was liberated by the Jewish fighting force known as the Haganah. His research in later years focused on how people make decisions about what is right and wrong. As we described above, the highest level in Kohlberg's theory is one in which a person develops universal moral principles that may or may not conform to what a particular country or group of people believes is right. Can you see how his life experiences shaped his theoretical ideas? ■

SOURCE: Adapted from Levine (2002).

Like any stage theory, Kohlberg's seems to suggest that individuals will progress through the levels in a steady and systematic way, but research has shown that this is often not the case. Although these stages are usually described in terms of children's development, Kohlberg believed that even adults can remain in the first stage of moral judgment, and many individuals, regardless of their age, do not move beyond the stage of conventional moral judgment.

Some recent research has highlighted the complex nature of our moral reasoning (Nucci & Turiel, 2009). In one set of studies, children and adolescents between 8 and 17 were given a scenario in which the protagonist had been working to save up the money she needed for something she really wanted to do with her friends but was still $10 short. While she is riding on an empty bus, another passenger gets on and drops a $10 bill when getting out the change for the fare. The participant is asked whether the protagonist should tell the other passenger she has dropped the money or stay silent and pick it up and keep it. In a second scenario, participants were asked to decide whether it is acceptable to hit a child who is hitting or hurting another child as a way of stopping the incident.

The responses of the 8-year-old participants looked very similar to those of the 17-year-old participants, but the responses of the 14-year-olds looked very different. Relatively few 8- and 17-year-olds said the protagonist had the right to keep the money dropped on the bus, compared to the number of 14-year-olds who said this. Likewise, more 8- and 17-year olds than 14-year-olds said people had an obligation to intervene if someone else was being hurt.

What is most interesting is the reasoning behind these decisions. The youngest and oldest participants saw these moral dilemmas in a pretty straightforward light, but the 14-year-olds saw them as much more ambiguous, and thus their decision about whether a behavior was right or wrong was more variable. For instance, an 8-year-old said to give the lost $10 back "because it is someone else's $10 bill, she shouldn't keep it because it is not hers" and a 17-year old said, "You don't have the right to steal the money, and this is stealing because you know who dropped that money. It's not like breaking into someone's house, but it's still stealing" (Nucci & Turiel, 2009, pp. 154–155). In both cases the participants were clear on what made the behavior wrong.

In contrast, a 14-year-old said, "He's got every right to keep the ten dollars, like I said, because it's in nowhere land. And it's his, he found it. It's not in the kid's house or anything" (Nucci & Turiel, 2009, p. 154). For this 14-year-old, the decision to keep the money is seen as a personal prerogative because it is not clear it will necessarily harm the person who lost the money. If the money is "in nowhere land," it is there for anyone's taking. The explanation for these group differences offered by Nucci and Turiel (2009) is that the increasing cognitive abilities during adolescence allow the younger adolescents to consider more of the situational factors when making their decision and this makes the situation more complex and ambiguous for them.

Gender Differences in Moral Thought

When Kohlberg did his original research, he studied only boys. When he did include girls, they tended to perform at a lower level of moral reasoning than the boys. Carol Gilligan believed this occurred because Kohlberg's theory was gender-biased and reflected a masculine view of morality. Gilligan argued that women do not have a lower level of morality than men but rather have a different type. Her idea was that women base their moral judgments more on what she called the *principle of care* while men base their judgments on impersonal, abstract justice, which she believed was the basis for Kohlberg's stages. The perspective that women used to reason about Kohlberg's moral dilemmas necessarily placed them at a lower level on his stages of moral reasoning. Although Gilligan did much of her research using real-life moral dilemmas, she also set up hypothetical dilemmas, such as the following fable she presented to children:

The Porcupine and the Moles

> It was growing cold and a Porcupine was looking for a home. He found a most desirable cave, but saw it was occupied by a family of Moles. "Would you mind if I shared your home for the winter?" the Porcupine asked the Moles. The generous Moles consented, and the Porcupine moved in. But the cave was small, and every time the Moles moved around they were scratched by the Porcupine's sharp quills. The Moles endured this discomfort as long as they could. Then at last they gathered courage to approach their visitor. "Pray leave," they said, "and let us have our cave to ourselves once again." "Oh no!" said the Porcupine. "This place suits me very well."

After telling this fable, Gilligan would then ask, "What should the moles do? Why?" (Gilligan, 1987, p. 14).

Gilligan believed girls and women would be more likely to respond in terms of everyone's needs: "Cover the porcupine with a blanket [so that the moles will not be stuck and the porcupine will have shelter]" or "Dig a bigger hole!" (p. 7). Boys would be more likely to respond in terms of absolute right and wrong: "The porcupine has to go definitely. It's the moles' house" (p. 7).

Although several studies have reported such gender differences, the majority have found that both boys and girls think about morality from both the justice and the care perspectives (Jaffee & Hyde, 2000; Walker, 2006). Neither boys nor girls are consistent in the perspective they bring to resolving moral dilemmas, and the nature of the dilemma itself is the determining factor in which perspective they adopt (Walker & Frimer, 2009). In fact, Kohlberg's original findings that men were more moral than women also have not been borne out. In more recent research, the only gender differences found in Kohlberg's stages of moral reasoning have tended to favor girls, although these differences vary from country to country (Gibbs, Basinger, Grime, & Snarey, 2007). The major conclusion we can draw at the present time is that there is no clear gender difference in moral reasoning.

Cultural Differences in Moral Thought

Kohlberg believed the same stages of moral development he found in the United States would be found in cultures around the world. A review of studies carried out in 75 different countries found evidence for the universality of the move from preconventional to conventional morality (Gibbs et al., 2007). However, the universality of the move from conventional to postconventional moral reasoning has been much more controversial. Some have argued that the postconventional stage is reflective of Western and urban values. Which values represent the highest level of moral reasoning may differ from one culture to another, depending on the particular values of the culture. For example, in one study that compared Korean and British children, the researchers found that a concept Koreans refer to as *chung* could not be scored according to Kohlberg's method. *Chung* is a central value in Korean society that translates as an emotional bond between people in which "the boundary between individuals was dimmed and a sense of one-ness, sameness, affection, comfort, acceptance and so forth emerged" (Baek, 2002, p. 387). One example of how *chung* affects moral judgment comes from a 16-year-old Korean child's response when asked whether Heinz should steal the drug for his wife even if he didn't love her:

> Even though he doesn't love her, he should steal the drug. It is said that husband and wife live together based on *chung* rather than love. They (Heinz and his wife) might also have *chung* between them since they have been together for a long time. (Baek, 2002, p. 384)

JOURNAL ARTICLE 15.2
Culture and Morality

Although there are some cultural similarities, cross-cultural differences at the higher levels of moral thought may be the reflection of a Western bias in the way we assess moral reasoning rather than by any true differences in the level of moral reasoning in different cultures.

Moral Thought and Moral Action

Would you describe yourself as an honest person? Do you help others whenever you can? People often believe their behavior mirrors their values. In other words, they adopt a trait approach to understanding morality (Doris, 2002). They see themselves as a moral person and believe they act based on that morality. However, a substantial amount of research has shown there is only a moderately strong link between moral judgment and moral behavior (Hardy & Carlo, 2011), suggesting that morality is more state-like than trait-like because any number of situational factors affect how likely it is that we behave in accordance with our moral values or beliefs.

When you are given a hypothetical moral dilemma, you are largely free of situational constraints that might influence your actual behavior, but real life is filled with them. For example, divinity students were told they were going to give a practice sermon. Some were told to talk about the Good Samaritan who helped others in a time of need, while others were given unrelated topics. Then some students were told they were going to be late for their sermon, and some were not. On the way to deliver the sermon, each divinity student saw a man who appeared to be in pain and needed help. What do you think determined whether a student stopped to give help? The students' actual behavior was determined less by whether they had just been thinking about compassion and the Good Samaritan than by whether they were going to be late to give their sermon or not (Darley & Batson, 1973). These results clearly show how the constraints of the real world affect our moral behavior, even when we know what is the right thing to do.

T/F #4
Your moral values and beliefs are the best predictor of what you will actually do when faced with a moral dilemma. *False*

Check Your Understanding

1. Describe the three levels of moral judgment in Kohlberg's cognitive developmental theory.
2. According to Gilligan, how does the nature of boys' and girls' moral judgment differ?
3. What evidence is there that Kohlberg's stages of moral judgment are or are not universal?
4. Describe the relationship between moral thought and moral action.

15.4

How is teen language different from language in children and adults?

WEB LINK 15.1
Slang

The Language of Teenagers

We now move from the topics of moral reasoning and moral behavior to a very different aspect of cognitive development: language. In one sense adolescent speech becomes more adult-like in that sentences are longer and grammar is more complex. However, adolescents are also more likely to use slang or made-up words, especially when talking among themselves. They may do this for fun, to bond with a particular group, or simply to identify with being an adolescent. Teens often change the meaning of a word to its opposite: *That's sick* comes to mean *it's really good* (Karmiloff & Karmiloff-Smith, 2001). Shortcuts may be developed. The very polite *Hello, how do you do?* becomes *'sup?* Adolescent slang sometimes catches on with the wider society and becomes part of the way everyone talks (Ely, 2005).

We were going to include a list of teen slang words here but realized that slang changes so fast that they would likely be outdated by the time this book was published. Instead, if you are not far beyond adolescence yourself, think about which words you use with your friends but not with older people, like your parents. Do you have any idea about the origin of those words? Were you using different words when you were in high school or middle school? Is the slang you use particular to the area of the country in which you live or to a particular group to which you belong? Different regions of the country and different subgroups within the country develop their own particular slang. For example, teens from Nebraska are less likely than teens from California to use slang pertaining to surfing.

In recent years, teens' written language has been influenced by electronic communication, such as texting. Teens report sending a median of 60 texts a day, with older teens between ages 14 and 17 sending 100 texts a day, which far outdistances any other form of daily communication they use (Pew Internet & American Life Project, 2012). Since communicators try to make interactions as efficient as possible, they have developed shorthand methods, such as substituting the well-known *LOL* for *laugh out loud* and *u* for *you*. Try **Active Learning: Textisms** to see which ones you know.

Active Learning

Textisms

Which of the following textisms can you translate?

1. TYVM	6. NP
2. W/E	7. WBU
3. OATUS	8. ROFL
4. IIRC	9. OTOH
5. IMHO	10. SFSG

■ **Answers:** 1. Thank you very much, 2. Whatever, 3. On a totally unrelated subject, 4. If I recall correctly, 5. In my humble opinion, 6. No problem, 7. What about you?, 8. Rolling on the floor laughing, 9. On the other hand, 10. So far so good.

Although some have expressed concern that the continual use of texting abbreviations will negatively affect a young person's ability to spell or write Standard English, this does not appear to be the case (Varnhagen et al., 2010). When a group of college students who were regular users of "text speak" were compared to other college students who were not, there was no significant difference between the groups on tests of their literacy level or ability to correctly spell words they abbreviate when texting (Drouin & Davis, 2009). However, both frequent texters and those who did not frequently text *thought* that texting would hurt their ability to use Standard English. These shortcuts do occasionally sneak into students' written school papers, so it is important for students to learn when it is appropriate to use them and when it is not.

T/F #5
Students who do a lot of texting do not differ from students who do not in their ability to spell or use Standard English. *True*

While teens who communicate with others online do no more writing than other teens, the situation is different regarding blogging. About 28% of teens maintain a personal blog (Rideout et al., 2010), and blogging appears to promote more writing among teens. Of those who have a blog, 47% write outside of school assignments for their own personal reasons, while only 33% of teens without blogs do so. In addition, 65% of bloggers believe writing is important for their later success, while only 53% of nonbloggers have this belief (National Writing Project, 2014).

©iStockphoto.com/diane39

Teen communication. Many adolescents use their cell phones to text their friends. Although texting uses a lot of abbreviations and special terminology, it fortunately doesn't seem to interfere with adolescents' ability to use Standard English. ■

T/F #6
Good writing skills
are not as important
in today's tech-savvy
business world. *False*

VIDEO LINK 15.3
Texting

15.5

What threats
to academic
achievement do high
school students
face and what
factors support
their success?

Teens may not be negatively affected by texting, but their overall level of writing skills remains relatively low. As shown in Figure 15.4, in 2011, only 27% of students at grades 8 and 12 were able to write at or above the proficient level on the National Assessment of Educational Progress (NAEP), with girls scoring higher than boys and those in suburban areas scoring higher than those in urban and rural areas (National Center for Education Statistics, 2012).

University and business leaders alike are concerned about the number of high school graduates who do not have good writing skills. A survey conducted in 2004 by the National Commission on Writing gathered information from the human resource directors of 120 major U.S. companies. Half the respondents said they take writing into consideration when hiring an employee (especially salaried employees) and that an applicant who submits a poorly written application might not be considered for any position. They also reported that two thirds of salaried employees have some responsibility for writing as part of their job and that communicating clearly plays a role in promotion and retention. One respondent to the survey succinctly said, "You can't move up without writing skills" (p. 3). The National Commission on Writing concluded that employees' writing deficiencies cost U.S. businesses as much as $3.3 billion a year. Although teens may have their own ways of talking and writing, when they enter the business world they need to have a good set of language and writing skills if they expect to be successful.

Check Your Understanding

1. How is teenagers' speech different from that of adults?
2. How is texting affecting teens' literacy skills?
3. Why are good writing skills still important for teenagers?

Adolescent Cognitive Development in Context

So far in this chapter, we have discussed the development of basic cognitive skills, such as attention and memory, as well as academic skills such as writing. However, cognitive development takes place within certain contexts, and in this section we discuss the roles played by schools, parents, peers, and community in promoting or inhibiting cognitive development for adolescents.

The Role of Schools

School is the context in which formal instruction promoting cognitive development occurs in adolescence. A major transition in the lives of young adolescents is the move from elementary school to middle school. This typically occurs when the child is 11 or 12 (grades 6–8). It is usually considered the most stressful school transition students experience (Grills-Taquechel, Norton, & Ollendick, 2010; Martinez, Aricak, Graves, Peters-Myszak, & Nellis, 2011).

At the same time that they are dealing with the bodily changes associated with puberty, young teens must also move from a school in which they spend most of their day with one teacher and one group of peers to a middle school in which they must negotiate interactions with many different teachers and a much larger peer group (Eccles, 2004; Ryan, Shim, & Makara, 2013). Suddenly they are no longer the oldest in their school but the youngest, and the influence of older teens may or may not be beneficial. Their contacts with a larger number of peers often result in shifts in their friendships. The workload and academic expectations usually increase significantly, and teens are expected to be more independent in managing their work.

Some of the exciting changes of middle school include more choice in classes, more school-based activities such as student government, and more after-school activities including sports and the arts. Although young teens can thrive during the time of this transition, for some it is a time of decreased academic motivation and lower achievement. Similar issues arise when teens transition to high school.

FIGURE 15.4 **Reading achievement in adolescents**

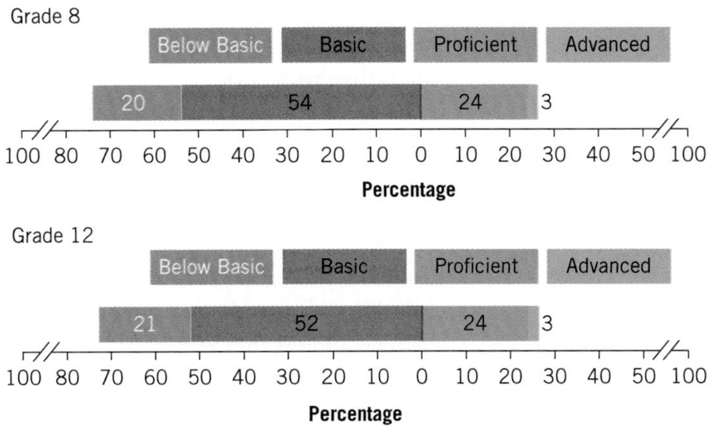

The assessment by the NAEP in 2011 shows that 73% of adolescents are not proficient in reading. Performance at the basic level indicates only partial mastery of knowledge and skills needed for proficient work at each grade.

SOURCE: U.S. Department of Education, Institute of Education Sciences, National Center for Education Statistics, National Assessment of Educational Progress (NAEP), 2011 Writing Assessment

Vulnerable Populations

In this section, we describe some of the students who are more at risk of poor academic performance during middle and high school for a variety of reasons.

Minority and Low-Income Students

Young adolescents from low-income or ethnic minority families, especially boys, are particularly at risk during the transition from elementary to secondary education (Moilanen, Shaw, & Maxwell, 2010; Serbin, Stack, & Kingdon, 2013). These students have generally developed fewer of the academic and social skills needed for success before they enter middle school, and they often have less support from family and others in their environment. However, when low-income and ethnic minority boys have developed these skills and have the support they need, their performance does not necessarily suffer as they enter middle school (Serbin et al., 2013). School programs can also help. In one high school, Latino males entering ninth grade were paired with seniors who provided support and meaningful connections in the school environment. The graduation rate of this group rose to 81%, while students in a control group had a graduation rate of only 63% (Johnson, Simon, & Mun, 2014).

Low-Performing Students

In most high schools, students are separated based on their abilities and high-achieving teens generally have a very different experience from low-performing students. School accelerates their learning, while those in the lower tracks often find their learning slowing down (Hallinan & Kubitschek, 1999). In Chapter 12, we described a number of problems associated with ability tracking in elementary grades. Many of those problems apply as well to the tracking that occurs in high schools. Students in the lower tracks often have teachers with fewer qualifications and may get a watered-down curriculum. They are more likely to see school as less valuable to them and are less active in the school (Eccles & Roeser, 2009). Peers in these classes are also more likely to be disconnected from school, which can lead to discipline problems. The most experienced teachers are likely to make sure they are not assigned to these classes but rather to advanced classes which are more gratifying for them to teach (Eccles & Roeser, 2009). Placement in the lower tracks can have an influence on the rest of teenagers' lives, because it is an important factor that affects whether they eventually attend college.

Adolescents With Specific Learning Disorder

Problems that arise in the elementary school years can persist and become worse as children with specific learning disorder move into adolescence. Research that looked at the way adolescents with dyslexia coped found some important and interesting gender differences (Alexander-Passe, 2006). Girls were more likely to try to find ways to make themselves feel better about the situation. For instance, they were more likely than boys to try to avoid the tasks at hand or to distract themselves from their problems by socializing with friends rather than studying. In contrast, boys were more likely than girls to attack the situation directly in an attempt to deal with it. They showed persistence and hard work and tried to analyze their past attempts to figure out what went wrong and could be corrected in the future. In this study, being dyslexic had a greater effect on the academic and general self-esteem of girls than it had on the self-esteem of boys, and girls reported higher levels of depression. Similar patterns of gender differences in coping have been found in other research (Greenglass, 2002).

You will remember from Chapter 14 that problem-focused coping can be an effective strategy when stress is caused by a situation that you can realistically change. Research conducted in Australia has shown that coping interventions can help adolescents with specific learning disorder develop a stronger sense of control over their situation and increase their use of coping strategies such as working hard and engaging in active problem solving (Firth, Frydenberg, & Greaves, 2008). A particularly encouraging note comes from a study that followed a group of students with learning disorders from age 10 into young adulthood (Seo, Abbott, & Hawkins, 2008). Across a number of outcomes, including postsecondary school attainment, rates of employment, amount of earned income, and receipt of public assistance, there were no significant differences between students with learning disorders and their peers except that the former were more likely to be receiving public aid at age 21 (but not at age 24).

While not all research on students with specific learning disorder has found such positive adult outcomes (for example, Zadok-Levitan & Bronz, 2004), when young people are proactive in dealing with their condition, set goals for themselves, are self-aware and emotionally stable, and have good social support, they can be highly successful (Goldberg, Higgins, Raskind, & Herman, 2003; Seo et al., 2008). Many colleges offer support services, such as untimed tests or note-taking services, for students with identified disabilities. You may want to explore the services available on your campus for these students.

Girls and the STEM Disciplines

When we talk about poor academic achievement, we don't usually think of girls as a vulnerable population. On average, girls do well in school, often outperforming their male classmates, but the one area in which they continue to lag regarding interest and involvement is the STEM disciplines—science, technology, engineering, and math. Women earn 60% of all bachelor's degrees but only 20% of degrees in the STEM fields (St. Rose, 2010), with the smallest numbers (18%) in Engineering and Computer Science (National Science Foundation, 2013).

The academic choices girls make that set them on a career pathway leading away from STEM careers begin early and persist and strengthen as they move into adolescence. High school girls are more likely than boys to say their goal in life is to help people, but they don't see the STEM fields as a way to do so (Hill, Corbett, & St. Rose, 2010). In general, girls tend to see science as a solitary profession and link it with violence and "blowing things up" (Miller, Slawinski Blessing, & Schwartz, 2006), and they connect both these things with being male. With few women professionals in these STEM fields, girls also lack models and mentors to encourage them to pursue careers in the sciences (Blackwell, 2010; Else-Quest, Hyde, & Linn, 2010). As one young woman interested in engineering stated, "It's intimidating being a girl who wants to go into the engineering field when it is definitely a male-dominated career" (Britsch, Callahan, & Peterson, 2010, p. 13).

For many years we attributed the shortage of women in these fields to lower ability and less interest in science and math, but we now have a very large body of research showing that girls do just as well as boys and take just as many science and math classes in high school as boys, although the particular courses vary. For instance, girls are more likely than boys to take biology, while boys are more likely than girls to take physics and engineering (Hill et al., 2010; National Science Foundation, 2012; Planty, Provasnik, & Daniel, 2007). Mathematical ability as measured by standardized tests is not significantly different in elementary school (Kenney-Benson, Pomerantz, Ryan, & Patrick, 2006; Lachance & Mazzocco, 2006), and girls frequently earn better grades in math classes than boys in elementary school and in high school (Kenney-Benson et al., 2006), although they do perform slightly more poorly than boys on "high stakes math tests," including the SAT, the ACT, and advanced placement exams (Hill et al., 2010, p. 5). Later, we discuss a concept called stereotype threat that may help explain why this is the case.

The one area of ability in which there are small but significant cognitive differences that favor boys is in spatial relationships, and it has been argued that this difference is wired into the brains of boys and girls before birth. Traditionally, boys have performed better on several aspects of spatial relationships including mental rotation. The type of test used to assess this ability is shown in Figure 15.5 (Voyer, Voyer, & Bryden, 1995). However, we know our brains continue to develop in response to our experiences. Terlecki, Newcombe, and Little (2008) demonstrated that training girls on spatial skills using computer games such as Tetris, that are based on shapes, could produce large improvements in their abilities in this area, and Tzuriel and Egozi (2010) found that specific training on spatial skills erased gender differences in mental rotation in

AUDIO LINK 15.4
STEM

T/F #7
Throughout the elementary school years and into high school, girls do more poorly in math than boys. *False*

FIGURE 15.5 **Mental rotation tasks**

Look at this object: Two of these four drawings show the same object. Can you find the two? Put a big X across them.

    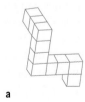

a   b   c   d

Answer: a and c

Items such as the one above are one of the few types of tests that consistently show higher performance for boys than girls.

SOURCE: Shepard & Metzler (1988). © 1988 American Psychological Association.

David Grossman/Science Source

Girls and math. By middle school most girls mistakenly believe they are not as good at math as boys are. Why do they arrive at this misconception? ■

first graders. Boys may have some initial genetic advantage in this area, or it may be that young boys gravitate toward activities that train those areas of the brain, such as playing with blocks. In either case, training can improve girls' performance significantly.

Despite our understanding that ability level does not clearly differentiate boys from girls, the idea that boys are better than girls at math persists (Else-Quest et al., 2010). Girls buy into the misconception that girls are not as good at math as boys starting long before adolescence. In one study, second-grade girls thought they were better at math than boys, but by fourth-grade they believed boys were better at it (Muzzatti & Agnoli, 2007). One consequence is that girls whose math ability is equal to that of boys perceive themselves as less skilled and are less likely to choose a career they believe requires that skill (Correll, 2004; Hill et al., 2010).

Where do these mistaken ideas come from? In large part, they come from the girls' social environment, including what happens in their school classrooms. There is evidence that within the school environment, girls are treated differently than boys, especially in science and math classes, in ways that subtly devalue their ideas and contributions. For example, when girls achieve at the same level as boys in math, teachers tend to attribute their success to hard work, while they attribute boys' success to ability (Espinoza, da Luz Fontes, & Arms-Chavez, 2014). Despite a great deal of attention given to these issues in 1995 when Myra and David Sadker wrote their book *Failing at Fairness: How Our Schools Cheat Girls*, a follow-up book called *Still Failing at Fairness* published in 2009 by Sadker and Zittleman reported that unequal treatment of boys and girls in the classroom remains.

Ideas about gender and math are also reinforced by the media. In one study, college women were shown either neutral commercials or commercials that promoted the stereotype that women are worse at math and science than men. When they were then asked to choose a career area, women who saw the stereotyped commercials were more likely to choose careers that did *not* involve math and science than those who saw the neutral commercial (Davies, Spencer, Quinn, & Gerhardstein, 2002). One successful intervention designed to displace these incorrect ideas taught girls that the brain is like a muscle that will grow when it is exercised rather than something that is fixed and unchangeable. When girls received this intervention, the gender gap on standardized tests in math disappeared (Good, Aronson, & Inzlicht, 2003). This new understanding of how the brain works counteracted the stereotype that girls are just not good at these subjects. Peers can also support a girl's interest in science and math. Girls who have friends who do well in school are more likely to take advanced math classes themselves (Crosnoe, Riegle-Crumb, Field, Frank, & Muller, 2008).

Stereotype threat The anxiety that results when individuals feel they are behaving in ways that confirm negative stereotyped expectations of a group with which they identify.

The math anxiety that many girls experience is linked to the idea of stereotype threat. This notion suggests that when girls take a difficult math test, like the SAT, ACT, or an advanced placement exam, they become anxious because they begin to think they are proving the negative stereotype about girls and math to be correct. Anxiety and high math performance do not go well together because anxiety decreases the working

FIGURE 15.6 | **Stereotype threat**

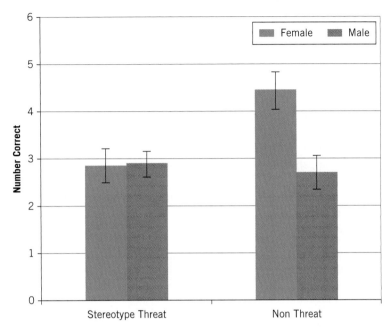

When given a difficult test in math, Anglo American women who were told that there were no gender differences for this test did better than men and better than women who heard instructions emphasizing that they were taking a test of mathematics ability.

SOURCE: Good, Aronson, & Harder (2008).

memory needed to carry out mathematical tasks (Schmader, 2010), and consequently, girls' performance goes down. However, when girls are specifically told that a test has not shown any gender differences in the past, their performance remains equal to, or even better than, that of boys as shown in Figure 15.6 (Good, Aronson, & Harder, 2008). The effects of stereotype threat are found even for performance on the spatial ability tests we described above. When young women in college were reminded of being female, they did much worse than young men on this test. However, when they were reminded that they went to a select private college they did significantly better than the women who had been reminded about their sex (McGlone & Aronson, 2006). There is some question whether stereotype threat operates the same way for women from all ethnicities. In the study by Good et al. (2008) the effects of manipulating stereotype threat were found only for Anglo American students, but not for Asian American, Hispanic American, and African American students.

Girls are often unaware of the stereotypes they believe. Unconscious stereotypes have been assessed by implicit association tests (Greenwald, Poehlman, Uhlmann, & Banaji, 2009) which measure the strength of the automatic associations you make between concepts. You can try a brief version of this test by doing **Active Learning: Implicit Associations Test.** In a study of 34 countries, implicit associations between science and gender predicted sex differences in science and math achievement in eighth-grade students (Nosek et al., 2009). In another study, girls as young as 9 were already showing implicit gender-based stereotypes about math ability. Middle school girls showed stronger implicit association between gender and math ability than boys did and the strength of this association was related to the adolescent's intentions or preference to take math classes and to their actual achievement in math (Steffens, Jelenec, & Noack, 2010).

VIDEO LINK 15.4
Stereotype Threat

Active Learning

Implicit Associations Test

Make cards with the following category words on them:

math, arts, female, male

Now make cards with the following words:

math, poetry, algebra, art, geometry, dance, calculus, literature, equations, novel,
female, woman, girl, she, lady, male, man, boy, he, sir

1. Put the category cards with the words *math* and *male* together on your left and
   the cards with *arts* and *female* together on your right. Put the rest of the cards in
   a pile in front of you.

2. For each card in front of you, think quickly about which of the two piles the card
   would best fit in and place the card on the left-hand pile or on the right-hand pile.
   Time yourself as you sort these cards to the left or the right as you think they
   belong.

3. Now take back all the cards into a pile. Put the category cards with the words *math*
   and *female* on your left and the cards with *arts* and *male* on your right.

4. Again, time yourself as you sort the rest of the cards either left or right as you
   think they belong.

Did it take longer to do one of these sorts than the other? If you implicitly associate
female with arts and male with math, it is easier and therefore quicker to sort each card
in your pile into these combined categories than into the pairs associating the categories of math with female and arts with male.

You can find an online version of this test at https://implicit.harvard.edu/implicit. ∎

SOURCE: Adapted from Greenwald & Nosek (2001).

Risk and Success in High School and College

We have described a number of groups who are at risk during their high school years.
We now examine the outcomes for those at risk and those who thrive. A teen's life trajectory is strongly influenced by whether the teen drops out of high school, completes high
school but doesn't go on to college, or continues on and completes college.

High School Dropouts

In 2012, about 7% of high school students dropped out of school without receiving a
diploma or equivalency certificate. This is a decline from a 17% dropout rate in the 1970s,
and we can see in Figure 15.7 that the percentage of students who drop out has declined
for all racial and ethnic groups studied. Another bit of good news here is that one study
found 63% of students who drop out of high school go on to eventually pass their GED
(General Educational Development test) within 8 years of their original anticipated graduation date (National Center for Educational Statistics, 2004a). However, even with these
improvements, the statistics mean that 1.1 million students did not graduate with their
class (Rumberger, 2013). It is in everyone's interest to find ways to keep these students in
school so they successfully complete their education sooner rather than later. Also, it is

T/F #8
In the past 40 years
we have cut the high
school dropout rate by
more than half. *True*

WEB LINK 15.2
Dropout Rates

important to note that these statistics do not include people who are incarcerated. As one in ten black males age 18–24 is in prison, this changes the numbers significantly for that group (Heckman & LaFontaine, 2010).

Researchers have examined school records to determine whether there were developmental pathways that distinguished high school graduates from dropouts (Hickman, Bartholomew, Mathwig, & Heinrich, 2008). The differences they discovered are what we might expect. Students who eventually dropped out of high school performed more poorly on standardized tests and received lower course grades than graduates, had higher levels of grade retention and absenteeism, and had more problem behaviors. More surprising was the origin of these differences. They began in kindergarten and persisted throughout elementary school, with the gap between future dropouts and their peers who would graduate on time widening as the students moved into middle school and continued into high school. These findings suggest that programs of early intervention, such as Head Start, do *not* start too early because the origins of eventual school dropout arise very early in a child's school career.

Although the dropout rate has been declining, there still is reason to be concerned about it and to look for ways to reduce it further. Young people who do not complete high school are ill-equipped for employment in today's marketplace. They are more likely to be unemployed than high school graduates, and when they are employed, they earn less and hold jobs with less occupational status (Child Trends, 2013a).

Declining dropout rates. The high school dropout rate has dramatically declined for all racial and ethnic groups, but more than 1 million students still do not graduate with their class. What can we do to reduce that number still further? ■

FIGURE 15.7   Dropout rates

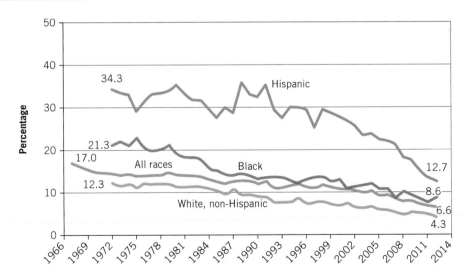

The dropout rate has been steadily declining over the past 50 years. This is especially important because employment is much more dependent on higher education than it was in the past. The dropout rate for Hispanics is inflated because it includes a large number of immigrants in this age group who never attended school in the United States.

SOURCE: Child Trends' calculations of U.S. Census Bureau, School Enrollment—Social Characteristics of Students: Detailed Tables. http://www.census.gov/hhes/school/data/cps/index.html

NOTES. * The status dropout rate measures the percentage of young adults aged 16 to 24 who were not enrolled in school and had not received a high school diploma or obtained a GED. This measure excludes people in the military and those who are incarcerated, but includes immigrants who never attended U.S. schools.

** Due to changes in the race categories, estimates from 2003 are not strictly comparable to estimates from 2002 and before. After 2001, the Black race category includes Hispanics.

Vocational training. During vocational training for metalworking, a trainer and an apprentice complete a welding exercise. Why are there so few apprenticeship programs like this in the United States despite their success in Europe? ■

Forgotten half High school students who graduate from high school but do not continue their education by going to college and are not well prepared for the transition to work.

AUDIO LINK 15.5
Non-College Options

T/F #9

Nearly half the 14 million jobs that will be created in the United States by 2018 will go to people with an associate's degree or occupational certificate. *True*

Non-College-Bound Adolescents

In 1988, the American Youth Policy Forum drew attention to another group of students they called the forgotten half who may be at risk in a different way. These are high school students who *do* graduate from high school but who do not continue their education by going to college. Because slightly more than two thirds of high school students go to college today, this group may now have become the "forgotten third," but it still represents a substantial portion of high school students (NCES, 2013a). The American Youth Policy Forum (2014) stated that these high school students were being shortchanged by the school system because they were not adequately prepared for the transition from school to work (see also America's Promise Alliance, 2009).

While higher education is still a pathway to prosperity for many young people, the fact that only 4 in 10 young adults obtain either an associate's degree or a bachelor's degree before they reach their mid-20s means college cannot be the *only* pathway. One reason so many students drop out of school is that they cannot see the connection between what they are studying and opportunities in the workplace (Symonds, Schwartz, & Ferguson, 2011).

Most European countries place a much greater emphasis on vocational education than the United States does. European students who do not plan to go to college enter apprenticeship programs that provide "a multi-year sequence of work-based and school-based learning opportunities providing formal certification of participants' competence" (Hamilton & Hamilton, 1997, p. 1) at the end of their training. Employers in Europe make this investment in training young people because they know it will make a highly qualified workforce available to them. Figure 15.8 shows the percentage of adolescents in various European countries who participate in these programs. There are few programs like this for students in the United States.

The School-to-Work Opportunities Act of 1994 created school programs that supported non-college bound students in the United States in their transition from school into productive careers (Hamilton & Hamilton, 1999) by providing information about careers and a range of work-related experiences. This approach allowed students, regardless of their eventual level of education, to make better informed decisions as they move through the educational system. A review of research on these programs found that although school-to-work programs did not raise grades, they did reduce drop-out rates and increased college enrollment. The programs helped students think about their future plans and develop skills useful in the workplace. However, this program's funding expired in 2001 and was not renewed. Although the American Recovery and Reinvestment Act of 2009 provides some funding that might include school-to-work programs, it does not mandate the creation of these types of programs (American's Future Workforce, 2013).

A report from the Harvard Graduate School of Education, titled *Pathways to Prosperity*, estimates that nearly half the 14 million jobs that will be created by 2018 will go to people with an associate's degree or occupational certificate (Symonds et al., 2011). The report concluded that a high school diploma is essential and college is desirable but "[t]he lessons from Europe strongly suggest that well-developed, high-quality vocational education programs provide excellent pathways for many young people to enter the adult work force" (p. 38).

FIGURE 15.8 Vocational education in European secondary schools

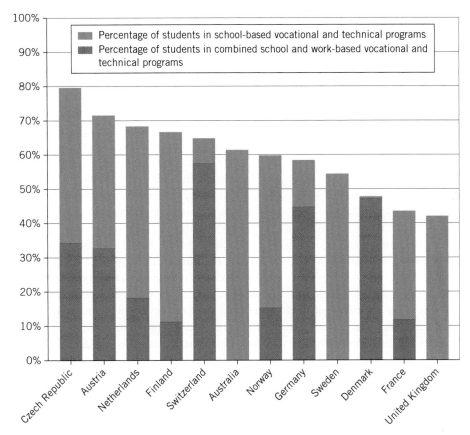

In many European countries, more than half of secondary school students are enrolled in vocational educational and training programs in which they develop work skills that are directly relevant to their future careers.

SOURCE: Organisation Economic Co-operation and Development (OECD). (2008). Education at a Glance 2008, OECD Indicators, Table C1.1, OECD, Paris. As appears in *Pathways to Prosperity: Meeting the Challenge of Preparing Young Americans for the 21st Century.* Harvard Graduate School of Education, February 2011, p. 18.

An evaluation of the effectiveness of various types of school-to-work transition programs found that cooperative education programs that combine classroom education and work experience, school enterprise programs that provide goods or services within the school environment, and internship/apprenticeship programs were positively related to employment for men (Neumark & Rothstein, 2005). The benefits for women were less clear, but internship/apprenticeship programs did have a positive effect on earnings.

College-Bound Students

Not all high school students are struggling. In fact many are thriving. According to the Federal Interagency Forum on Child and Family Statistics (2013b), in 2009, three quarters of high school graduates had successfully completed Algebra II, over a third had taken a mathematics course in analysis/precalculus, and over two thirds had taken at least one course each in biology and chemistry. During the 2009–2010 school year, over 1.8 million high school students took at least one advanced placement course (Aud, KewalRamani, & Frohlich, 2011). Students who receive a score on an advanced placement exam that exceeds a required minimum can use the course to fulfill a degree requirement in their college coursework. Slightly more females (56%) than males take advanced placement tests, although more males than females (61% versus 54%) receive a score above the required minimum.

A jumpstart to college. More high school students are taking Advanced Placement classes that will give them college credits before they leave high school. ■

About two thirds of high school graduates enroll in college in the fall immediately following their high school graduation (NCES, 2013a). From the high school graduating class of 2013, 68.4% of women and 63.5% of men were attending college in the fall. The enrollment rate by race/ethnicity was: Asian: 79.1%, White: 67.1%, Black: 59.3%, Latino: 59.9% (Bureau of Labor Statistics, 2014a).

Ideally, everyone who is intellectually capable should have the opportunity to attend college. However, some groups of students receive better preparation than others. Fewer than half those who take the SAT are prepared to succeed in college, a number that has not changed since 2009 (The College Board, 2013). Not being at this level of readiness can slow—or even derail—a student's college career. Fifty-four percent of students who achieved a benchmark level of achievement on the SAT completed college in 4 years, while only 27% of those who didn't meet this level graduated in 4 years. It is apparent that SAT scores are linked to family income, as shown in Table 15.3. Although these tests are good predictors of academic performance in college, high school grades have been found to be even better, especially for minority and first-generation students (Hiss & Franks, 2014) so many colleges are dropping the SAT and ACT as major admissions requirements.

TABLE 15.3   SAT scores for college-bound seniors by family income, 2013

Family income	Reading	Math	Writing	Total
$0–$20,000	435	462	429	1326
$20,000–$40,000	465	482	455	1402
$40,000–$60,000	487	500	474	1461
$60,000–$80,000	500	511	486	1497
$80,000–$100,000	512	524	499	1535
$100,000–$120,000	522	536	511	1569
$120,000–$140,000	526	540	515	1581
$140,000–$160,000	533	548	523	1604
$160,000–$200,000	539	555	531	1625
More than $200,000	565	586	563	1714

This table makes it very clear that family income correlates with SAT scores. What do you think might account for this correlation?

SOURCE: Calculated by FairTest from College Board, College-Bound Seniors 2013: Total Group Profile Report and College-Bound Seniors, 2006: Total Group Profile Report. Reprinted with permission from FairTest from http://www .fairtest.org/college-admissions-tests-show-testdriven-schooling.

Like the transition from elementary school to middle school or the transition from middle school to high school, the transition from high school to college can be stressful, and for many of the same reasons. College students usually have a great deal more autonomy than high school students, and many are living away from home for the first time. Despite their course work in high school, students may not have the academic preparation they need to be successful (Venezia & Jaeger, 2013). The skills and attitudes required to be successful in college are "habits of the mind" that include "critical thinking, an inquisitive nature, a willingness to accept critical feedback, an openness to possible failure, and the ability to cope with frustrating and ambiguous learning tasks" (Venezia & Jaeger, 2013, p. 120). Although older adolescents are capable of these things, as college students, they may find it difficult to meet all these expectations.

There are various ways of measuring college completion, but one of the most common is the 6-year-completion rate. This is the percentage of first-time undergraduate students at 4-year institutions who complete all their requirements for a bachelor's degree within 6 years. In 2011, the completion rate for 4-year institutions was 59% (NCES, 2013a). There was variability among different types of institutions: private nonprofit institutions had the highest completions rates (65%), and private for-profit institutions the lowest (42%). Not surprisingly, the most selective institutions had the highest completion rate (88%). The overall rate was higher for females than for males (61% versus 56%). At 2-year institutions the completion rate for an associate's degree within 3 years was 31%.

Completion rates are important because students who drop out of college often end up with significant education-related debt but none of the benefits they hoped for from a degree. Most college campuses devote considerable resources to their student support services. Efforts prior to college admission that help ensure students are well prepared for the demands of college, together with having given thought to the fit between their needs and the characteristics of the campus they have chosen, can help boost the likelihood that incoming students will be successful in college.

The Role of Family

The important people in our lives, including our friends and family, provide another crucial context for cognitive development during adolescence. Parents provide the structure and routine that supports achievement, are important role models for their children, and instill values and set expectations related to academic success (Roche & Ghazarian, 2012; Wang & Sheikh-Kahlil, 2014).

Effective parenting can occur in any type of family, but some family structures create added stress for parents and their children. These stresses, in turn, can interfere with children's focus on academics and parents' ability to support their child's efforts in school. As we described in Chapter 13, adolescents growing up in single-parent families formed by divorce are twice as likely as those with two parents to leave school before high school graduation (Martin et al., 2004). They are less than half as likely to attend college (Elliott, 2009) and less likely to complete college if they do begin (Biblarz & Gottainer, 2000).

Parenting style also relates to children's achievement in school. In Chapter 10, we learned about four types of parenting style as described by Diana Baumrind (2013)— authoritative, authoritarian, permissive, and disengaged—each of which has a different balance of control and warmth. Adolescents raised by authoritative parents, who not only are loving but also give structure and set limits, have higher achievement orientation than children raised with other parenting styles; that is, they are more motivated to learn and do well in school and less likely to drop out during high school (Aunola, Stattin, & Nurmi, 2000; Blondal & Adalbjarnardottir, 2014; Pong, Johnston, & Chen, 2010; Spera, 2005).

WEB LINK 15.3
Parental Involvement

Checking up. Parents who show an interest in their teenagers' school work promote better academic performance in their children. The poster behind this mother and daughter seems to indicate important values shared within the family. ∎

A good deal of cross-cultural research has found that cultural background affects how adolescents see their parents' behaviors and the impact those behaviors have on them. In collectivist cultures, greater amounts of control and the expectation that children will unquestionably obey their parents fits well with cultural values and expectations (Rudy & Grusec, 2006). Consequently, these parental behaviors may not have the same negative impact that they often have on adolescents in Western cultures.

Parents' views of their children's ability also are an important influence on the way children assess their own abilities (Tiedemann, 2000). In a way, parental beliefs can become a type of self-fulfilling prophecy for their children's behavior. To illustrate this point we return to our earlier discussion of girls' beliefs about their ability to do well in math and science. If parents see girls as less capable in math, their daughters, in turn, may begin to see themselves in that way and come to believe they are less capable. This may lead them to exert less effort or express more dislike for math, and the parents' prophecy is fulfilled when their daughters then perform more poorly. For instance, when parents offer uninvited help with their daughters' math homework, the girls are more likely to perceive their math abilities negatively (Bhanot & Jovanovic, 2005). Uninvited help unintentionally conveys the message that parents do not see girls as capable of doing this homework on their own. Parents, just like teachers (Espinoza et al., 2014), tend to attribute their daughters' success to the girls' hard work and their sons' success to both talent and effort (Jacobs, Davis-Kean, Bleeker, Eccles, & Malanchuk, 2005). Although boys and girls may be equally successful, they get different messages about *why* they are successful. Which type of career would you want to pursue, one that you could achieve in only if you worked really hard, or one that you were naturally good at?

The Role of Peers

Most adolescents spend a good deal of time in the company of other teens, and these peers can exert a considerable amount of influence on their academic achievement. This influence is both direct (for example, peers can accept or reject the high achiever) and indirect (for example, peers model academic behaviors and attitudes). Peers who devalue academic achievement can draw adolescents away from their schoolwork, but high-achieving peers exert a positive influence on an adolescent's own academic achievement (Hamm, Schmid, Farmer, & Locke, 2011; Lynch, Lerner, & Leventhal, 2013).

Teachers can intervene to change and support peer norms and expectations for academic success. The SEALS (Supporting Early Adolescent Learning and Social Success) professional development program has been designed to help sixth-grade teachers use the transition to middle school as a time to orient students toward positive engagement with academics by supporting "peer cultures of effort and achievement" (Hamm, Farmer, Lambert, & Gravelle, 2014, p. 216). In an intervention study, schools with the SEALS program were compared to a control group of schools without the program. As a result of what they learned in this training program, teachers became more attuned to the different peer groups that existed in their classes and were better able to manage the social dynamics, including bullying, that can interfere with learning. They were better able to use peers to promote positive classroom behavior. Students' attraction to peers who devalued school decreased, setting the stage for higher achievement through middle school and high school. Basically, young teens who participated learned that they could work hard in school and not give up acceptance and high esteem from their peers.

We have discussed contributions that parents and peers make to teens' motivation to succeed in school. **Active Learning: Academic Motivation** provides you with questions for thinking about the influences you (or a teen you know) experienced that helped shape your approach to school.

Peer influence. Peers exert a powerful influence both in and outside the classroom. How did your peers affect your high school experience? ■

Active Learning

Academic Motivation

Teens' motivation to do well in school is affected by both family and friends. You can carry out this activity in two ways. You can ask yourself these questions regarding how you felt during high school, or you can interview a teenager using these questions as a basis for further conversation about academic motivation:

- Did you talk about school much with members of your family?
- Did you think your family influenced the way you felt about school or how hard you tried?
- Was it important to you to try to do well in school to please your parents/guardians?
- How many of the friends you spent time with did well in school?
- How much did spending time with friends keep you from doing your schoolwork?
- Did you think your friends would make fun of you for doing well in school?

When considering your answers, think about whether family and friends have had different influences on your academic motivation or whether they influenced you in similar ways. Many times teens are influenced by parents to achieve and then choose friends who also are high achievers. However, it can also happen that teens are friends with others who reject school, and that influence may play a larger role than their parents on their motivation to do well in school. ■

SOURCE: Adapted from Urdan, Solek, & Schoenfelder (2007); Wong & Taylor (1996).

The Role of the Community: Positive Youth Development

The characteristics of the community in which the adolescent lives also influence cognitive development and academic achievement. Probably the most direct way we see this influence is through the quality of the neighborhood schools the adolescent attends, but communities offer numerous other opportunities and experiences beyond school that also contribute to cognitive development.

WEB LINK 15.4
Volunteering

Positive youth development An approach to finding ways to help all young people reach their full potential.

Developmental assets Common sense, positive experiences, and qualities that help young people become caring, responsible adults.

WEB LINK 15.5
Search Institute

A new way of thinking about development has emerged that adds a great deal to our understanding of the role activities play in the lives of young people. This approach is often called the positive youth development approach, because its primary focus is on finding ways to help young people reach their full potential (U.S. Department of Health and Human Services [USDHHS], 2007). It does more than help young people avoid the pitfalls associated with too much unsupervised time (Eccles & Templeton, 2002; National Research Council and Institute of Medicine, 2004; Roeser & Peck, 2003); it strives to identify the people, contexts, circumstances, and activities that help youth develop to their maximum potential. When organizations and communities give adolescents the chance to exercise leadership, build their skills, and engage in positive and productive activities, youth have the building blocks they need to grow into "healthy, happy, self-sufficient adults" (USDHHS, 2007, para. 1).

The Search Institute in Minneapolis has identified a set of 40 developmental assets that serve as these building blocks. It defines a developmental asset as "common sense, positive experiences, and qualities that help influence choices young people make and help them become caring, responsible adults" (Search Institute, 2012, para. 1). Constructive use of time is one of the sets of assets and can include creative activities such as lessons or practice in music, theater, or other arts, youth programs in the community, membership in a religious institution, and time spent at home rather than just hanging out with friends with nothing special to do.

Survey research conducted by the Search Institute found that only 21% of the youth surveyed said they participated in creative activities at least at the level the Search Institute considers adequate to support youth development, though 57% participated in youth programs, 58% participated in a religious community, and 51% did not spend more than 2 days a week outside their home just hanging out with friends. These results would indicate that for many young people, there still is room for higher levels of participation in the community that can support positive development, and there is particularly room for more adolescents to find creative outlets through the arts.

Different types of activities contribute to different aspects of cognitive development or contribute in different ways. For instance, earlier in the chapter we described a program in which older children and teens who received acting training over the course of a year showed gains in social cognition (Goldstein & Winner, 2012). Larson and Brown (2007) found that teens learn valuable lessons from involvement in theater programs. They learn more about understanding and managing emotions and they find new ways to deal with frustration and to celebrate success together as a result of these experiences.

Participation in service-oriented activities in the community also can directly contribute to academic success (Furco, 2013; Kraft & Wheeler, 2003; Schmidt, Shumow, & Kackar, 2007). This type of activity has an impact on a wide variety of academic outcomes, including "subject matter learning, standardized test performance, school attendance, earned grades, motivation for learning, and engagement in school" (Furco, 2013, p. 11). In addition, Roeser and Peck (2003) found that vulnerable youth who were highly active in both

Positive youth development. The positive youth development approach says that community activities such as this one help young people reach their full potential. What do teens gain when they participate in activities such as this clean-up of a park? ■

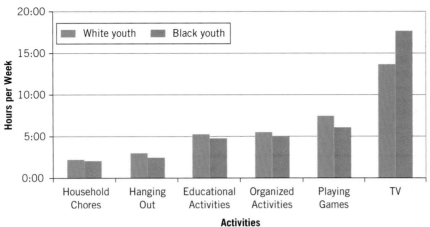

FIGURE 15.9 Weekly hours that White and Black youth (ages 5–18) spend in organized and nonorganized activities

Looking at this chart, do you think that American youth are overscheduled with organized activities or not?

SOURCE: Mahoney, Harris, & Eccles (2006). © 2006 Society for Research in Child Development.

school and community sports activities were twice as likely to graduate from high school and go on to college as students who did not have this level of engagement. On the other hand, vulnerable youth who spent time working in paid employment and simply watching television or hanging out with friends were less likely to go on to postsecondary education (Peck, Roeser, Zarrett, & Eccles, 2008).

Some worry that many adolescents are stressed out by doing too much, but relatively few young people appear to be overscheduled with organized activities. Figure 15.9 gives an overview of the amount of time spent in various activities. It is not surprising that adolescents tend to engage in more activities than younger children. In one national survey, 92.4% of U.S. teens took part in at least one activity, 27.1% in one to three, 31.4% in four to six, and 33.9% in seven or more activities in the previous year (Substance Abuse and Mental Health Services Administration, Office of Applied Studies, 2007). However, Mahoney, Harris, and Eccles (2006) found that only 3% to 6% of youth ages 5 to 18 report spending more than 20 hours a week in organized activities. These authors conclude that only 1 in 10 children could be described as overscheduled. That might still be too many, but overscheduling doesn't seem to be a typical pattern.

Perhaps more important, when older children and adolescents ages 9 through 19 were asked to describe why they participated in activities such as sports, after-school programs, clubs, and religious youth groups, the reasons they gave included enjoyment and excitement, encouragement and support from parents and friends, opportunities to challenge themselves and build skills, and anticipated social interactions with others. Mahoney et al. (2006) point out that in most cases adolescents have their own internal motivations for seeking out and participating in these experiences. In addition to the positive effect participation has on school-related outcomes, these activities are related to lower levels of substance abuse and better overall psychological adjustment (Mahoney et al., 2006).

T/F #10
Many teens these days are overscheduled, spending most of their time after school in multiple organized activities like sports and music lessons.
False

Check Your Understanding

1. What can schools do to promote or inhibit cognitive development in adolescents?
2. What factors contribute to the risk of underperformance in school for minority, low-income, and low-performing students?
3. What are some reasons why girls tend to stay away from the STEM fields?
4. What might a European-style apprenticeship program accomplish for U.S. students who do not plan to go on to college?
5. Compare the roles of family and peers in adolescents' academic success.

Conclusion

The cognitive changes that occur during adolescence allow the young person to think logically not just about concrete things but also about abstract and hypothetical concepts. Growth in basic cognitive processes affects the adolescent's social relationships and moral judgment and prepares the adolescent to cope with the increasing challenges of the school environment. Although some adolescents struggle with these challenges, most handle them quite well, and these educational experiences prepare them for their transition into young adulthood as they enter higher education and the workforce.

Chapter Summary

15.1 What changes occur as adolescents enter Piaget's stage of formal operations?

In the stage of formal operations, adolescents develop the ability to think about abstract concepts and use **hypothetico-deductive reasoning.** However, a type of egocentric thinking reappears in the form of the **imaginary audience** and the **personal fable.** The belief in the personal fable can be associated with risk-taking during adolescence. Some theorists believe there is a stage of **postformal operations** beyond Piaget's fourth stage.

15.2 How do basic cognitive processes change during adolescence?

Although teens think they can multitask successfully, research indicates they process information more superficially when they do this. The parts of the brain used for working memory continue to change over the teen years. Both **metacognition** and **metamemory** improve, and executive function continues to develop which improves adolescents' ability to plan. Teachers can support creativity in the classroom by requiring both divergent and **convergent thinking.** Adolescents' changing abilities are reflected in their social cognition, including the ability to engage in **recursive thinking,** and in further development in theory of mind.

15.3 How does moral reasoning develop during adolescence?

Kohlberg has described three levels of moral judgment: **preconventional, conventional,** and **postconventional moral judgment.** Many people (including most adolescents) reason at the conventional level, but some adolescents are cognitively capable of reasoning at the postconventional level. Most research supports the idea that there are no gender differences in levels of moral judgment. Men and women alike base their judgments on both justice and care, depending upon context. Research finds only a moderately strong link between moral reasoning and moral behavior.

15.4 How is teen language different from language in children and adults?

Adolescents' speech is more complex in grammar and subject matter than children's speech and differs from adult speech in its use of slang, especially in texting. Good writing skills remain important for success in the world of business.

15.5 What threats to academic achievement do high school students face and what factors support their success?

The transitions from elementary school to middle school and from high school to college are challenging because what we expect from the young person changes each time. Most adolescents are able to handle these transitions well, but minority, low-income, and low-performing students are particularly vulnerable to school failure or underachievement. Although girls generally do well in all subjects in school, including math, they still are not as likely as boys to have careers in the STEM disciplines. The idea that girls are not good at math or science persists in the form of a **stereotype threat,** which can have a negative effect on girls' performance in high-stakes testing situations. Girls with specific learning disorder are more likely to try to distract themselves and make themselves feel better about their difficulties, while boys are more likely to try to attack the situation and try to fix it. The high school dropout rate in the

United States has fallen by half in recent years, but low-income and Latino students continue to be more likely to drop out of high school than other groups of students. Many who drop out eventually earn a GED. The **forgotten half** who graduate from high school but do not go to college may not be well prepared to enter the workforce. The European model of apprenticeships provides alternate pathways to success for these young people but is rare in the United States. Slightly over two thirds of high school graduates enroll in college immediately following their graduation. College completion rates range from 88% in 6 years for very selective schools to 31% in 3 years for 2-year institutions. The family, peers, and the larger community play an important role in supporting adolescents' educational attainment.

Key Terms

Conventional moral judgment   517

Convergent thinking   512

Developmental assets   536

Forgotten half   530

Formal operations   503

Hypothetico-deductive reasoning   503

Imaginary audience   506

Metacognition   509

Metamemory   510

Personal fable   507

Positive youth development   536

Postconventional moral judgment   517

Postformal operations   507

Preconventional moral judgment   517

Recursive thinking   514

Scientific thinking   503

Stereotype threat   526

$SAGE edge™

Sharpen your skills with SAGE edge at edge.sagepub.com/levinechrono

SAGE edge for Students provides a personalized approach to help you accomplish your coursework goals in an easy-to-use learning environment.

Go to edge.sagepub.com/levinechrono for additional exercises and video resources. Select Chapter 15, Cognitive Development in Adolescence, for chapter-specific activities. All of the Video Links listed in the margins of this chapter are accessible via this site.

16 Social and Emotional Development in Adolescence

T/F Test Your Knowledge

Test your knowledge of child development by deciding whether each of the following statements is *true* or *false,* and then check your answers as you read the chapter.

1. **T□ F□** By comparison to other ethnic and racial groups, Asian American adolescents have the lowest self-esteem.

2. **T□ F□** The rate of violent crime committed by young people continues to climb from year to year.

3. **T□ F□** Rates of depression among adolescents have not changed in the last 30 years.

4. **T□ F□** Asking a teen whether he is thinking about committing suicide will make it more likely he will do it.

5. **T□ F□** Teens who are strongly attached to their friends are likely to also be strongly attached to their parents.

6. **T□ F□** A great deal of parent-adolescent conflict is normal in families with adolescents.

7. **T□ F□** Teens in the foster care system are extremely unlikely to attend college.

8. **T□ F□** Most adolescents say they feel a good deal of peer pressure to do things they know they shouldn't do.

9. **T□ F□** Adolescents today are much less likely to be victims of violence while in school than they were 20 years ago.

10. **T□ F□** Teens spend more time watching TV content than using any other kind of media.

Correct answers: (1) T, (2) F, (3) F, (4) F, (5) T, (6) F, (7) T, (8) F, (9) T, (10) T

Is adolescence a period of enormous "storm and stress," as suggested by G. Stanley Hall back in 1904 and as many people believe, or a time for exploration and self-discovery? In some ways, it can be both. In this chapter, we describe the development of identity that becomes a central focus in adolescence. We discuss how teens develop emotional self-regulation as well as what happens when they have difficulty with this task. We also look at the many changes in the context of adolescents' lives. Parents and siblings remain important, but increasingly teens are moving into the world of peers as they become more autonomous. Friendships and peer groups all become central to the life of the teen and romantic relationships begin. Beyond their attachments to family and peers, teens have important relationships with other adults such as teachers, coaches, and mentors who can make a difference in their lives. Teens take part in many structured and unstructured activities, and in the process they connect with some of these adults. They also use many forms of media extensively and this can have both positive and negative effects on their development. We begin this chapter by examining the various aspects of identity development during adolescence.

Learning Questions

16.1 How does identity develop in adolescence?

16.2 How do emotions develop in adolescence?

16.3 How do adolescents' relationships with their parents change?

16.4 What types of peer relationships do adolescents have?

16.5 What role do nonparental adults play in adolescents' lives?

16.6 What do adolescents do when they are not in school?

16.7 What is emerging adulthood and how does it differ from adolescence?

The Self in Adolescence

Erik Erikson described the developmental crisis of adolescence as identity versus role confusion. According to Erikson (1963, 1968), adolescents must figure out and get comfortable with who they are and who they want to become as they move into young adulthood.

It is not surprising that the physical, cognitive, and social changes of adolescence are reflected in changes in the self-concept. In particular, the cognitive changes that occur during the stage of formal operations are reflected in the way the adolescent can now think about the self. Self-descriptions become more abstract (Harter, 1999) and contain more psychological attributes (Martins & Calheiros, 2012). Adolescents also can incorporate contradictory traits in their self-descriptions. They now understand that they can show different characteristics in different situations and that these differences are all part of a unitary whole. For example, an adolescent might say, "I am usually a pretty friendly, outgoing person, but I really clam up when I am around adults." Adolescents have the cognitive ability to pull these divergent pieces of the self together into a coherent whole.

An important part of this process of identity development is "trying on" different identities, and that helps explain some of the behaviors we associate with adolescence. Teenagers experiment with new activities or associate with new friends, and sometimes they even take on new identities (Cross & Fletcher, 2009). An adolescent who has held conventional views and attitudes may flirt briefly with the Goth culture or begin spending time with the skaters or the stoners at school. Most of the time, adolescents settle on a positive identity, one that is approved by society. Being a *preppie*, a *jock*, or a *nerd* might be some examples. But sometimes the identity that the adolescent adopts is one that parents or other adults would not approve of, or what Erikson (1963) called a negative identity. Being a *druggie* or *burnout* provides a ready-made identity with a clearly defined set of attitudes, values, and behaviors that go with it, and these may clearly state to parents, "I am not you."

16.1

How does identity develop in adolescence?

Identity versus role confusion Erik Erikson's stage during adolescence when teens are dealing with consolidating their identity.

Negative identity An identity that is in direct opposition to that which parents or other adults would support.

Teen identities. As part of the process of identity development, adolescents may "try on" different identities like "skater," "jock," or "brain." ■

Marcia's Identity Statuses

James Marcia extended Erikson's work on identity development by describing the process by which adolescents work toward achieving an identity. According to Marcia (1966; see also Kroger, Martinussen, & Marcia, 2010), identity achievement requires adolescents to engage in a period of active *exploration* of the alternatives available to them, followed by a personal investment in the choices they make, a process Marcia calls *commitment*. By combining these two processes, Marcia named and described four identity statuses (see Table 16.1).

If you talk with some adolescents about their future, it becomes clear they haven't spent much time thinking about it and, what is more, they don't seem overly concerned about it. Adolescents experiencing identity diffusion feel both a lack of crisis (or the perceived need to explore alternatives) and a lack of commitment to a future identity.

Some adolescents make a firm commitment to an identity even before they have engaged in an active process of exploration and this is described as identity foreclosure. How can you feel you already know who you will become in the future without having actively looked for an identity? You may have grown up in a family in which everyone expected you to become a doctor, a teacher, or a police officer, and these expectations became an unquestioned part of the way you saw yourself. In this case, you have foreclosed (or cut off) other possibilities. In many parts of the world, identity foreclosure is the norm because choices are limited. In these cultures, adolescents simply become whatever their parents are.

Adolescents in the status of identity moratorium are actively exploring alternatives that can shape their future identity so, in Marcia's terms, they are in a state of crisis. However, they are not yet ready to commit to a specific choice. For example, you may remain undeclared in your major in college as you try out different subjects or even take time off from school to explore and define your interests before making a commitment to one.

Finally, adolescents who have actively explored the alternatives and who are now ready to commit to one are in the status of identity achievement.

There are a few general points that are important to note about Marcia's theory. First, keep in mind that Marcia's process of exploring and committing can apply to any aspect of identity development, as we see later in this chapter regarding ethnic identity (Bergh & Erling, 2005). People can also move between the statuses, although certain patterns are more likely than others. The trend in adolescence is from the low-commitment statuses of diffusion or moratorium toward a status that has a higher level of commitment (either

Identity diffusion A lack of interest in developing an identity.

Identity foreclosure Commitment to an identity before exploring possible options.

Identity moratorium A time of exploration in search of identity, with no commitment made yet.

Identity achievement The choice of an identity following exploration of the possibilities.

foreclosure or achievement) (Meeus, 2011; Meeus, van de Schoot, Keijsers, & Branje, 2012; Meeus, van de Schoot, Keijsers, Schwartz, & Branje, 2010), but even adolescents who have an achieved identity status can have new experiences that shake up their commitment to an identity and push them back into a state of moratorium. Having a close relationship with someone who has different attitudes or values than you have, traveling to a part of the world you have never seen before and experiencing a new culture, or coming to college and being exposed to new ideas—any of these experiences can unsettle a previously solid commitment to an identity.

Although movement between statuses is possible, the process of identity formation is *not* as dynamic as we might expect it to be. Researchers have found that stability within a status category over the course of a longitudinal study can be as high as 59% (which means almost 6 in 10 participants did not change their status over the course of the study) (Meeus et al., 2010). Where movement does occur, it is likely to be in the direction of identity achievement. Finally, people are likely to change at least some aspects of their identity *after* adolescence. Significant life events such as the birth of a child, a divorce, or a change in health can motivate you to reevaluate your identity.

Look back at Table 16.1. Where would you place yourself now? Where were you a year ago? Where do you think you'll be a year from now?

TABLE 16.1	**Marcia's identity statuses**		
		Crisis (exploration)	
		Low	High
Commitment	Low	Identity Diffusion	Moratorium
	High	Foreclosure	Identity Achievement

According to Marcia, identity development during adolescence reflects two processes: exploration of the alternatives available and commitment to an identity. Where an individual stands on these two processes determines the adolescent's identity status.

Self-Esteem During Adolescence

The transition into early adolescence is notoriously hard on a teen's self-esteem. Physical, social, and environmental factors come together in a way that is challenging for many (Finkenauer, Engels, Meeus, & Oosterwegel, 2002; Huang, 2010). As young adolescents go through the rapid physical changes of puberty, they can feel clumsy and awkward and often become self-conscious about their appearance. As we discussed in Chapter 15, the increasing demands of the school environment between elementary to middle school can be challenging. The cognitive changes of adolescence also affect self-esteem. Adolescents' ability to think hypothetically allows them to think not only about their real selves (the characteristics they currently have), but also about their ideal selves (the characteristics they aspire to have in the future). The impact this comparison has on self-esteem depends on both the discrepancy between the two selves and the importance of the domain for the individual (Harter, 2006b). You'll remember from Chapter 13 that Harter described five domains that contribute to self-esteem: scholastic competence, social competence, behavioral conduct, athletic competence, and appearance. For instance, there might be a relatively small discrepancy between your current weight and your ideal weight, but if the domain of physical appearance is very important to you, even a small discrepancy can have a large impact on your self-esteem. This domain is so important to most adolescents that Susan Harter (1999) found that self-rated physical attractiveness accounted for 70% of the variance or difference in self-esteem in adolescents.

The negative impact of the physical, social, and cognitive changes that accompany the transition into adolescence is relatively short-lived for most adolescents. Also, the impact may not be as great as we have thought them to be (Huang, 2010; Twenge & Campbell, 2001). Following the decline that typically occurs in early adolescence, self-esteem recovers and then stays stable throughout the remainder of middle adolescence and into early adulthood (Erol & Orth, 2011; Impett, Sorsoli, Schooler, Henson, & Tolman, 2008).

Gender differences in self-esteem appear fairly early in adolescence and persist until well into adulthood. However, even though girls' self-esteem is lower than that of boys,

Ideal self The characteristics one aspires to in the future.

WEB LINK 16.1
Adolescent Self-Esteem

it is not the same thing as saying it is low. A review of hundreds of studies of self-esteem that included thousands of participants found that although boys score higher on measures of global self-esteem than girls, the difference between them is actually quite small (Kling, Hyde, Showers, & Buswell, 1999).

Research that has looked at differences in self-esteem by race or ethnicity has found that African American adolescents on average score higher than White students, who are very similar to Hispanics. Asian American students had the lowest self-esteem (Bachman, O'Malley, Freedman-Doan, Trzesniewski, & Donnellan, 2011). However, the researchers note that differences *within* any of these groups are greater than the differences between them, so "on the whole the subgroups are more alike than different" (p. 462). In interpreting these results, we should remember that although Asian American teens often perform very well, children and adolescents in collectivist cultures are socialized to be modest so this may affect how they answer questions about self-esteem. In individualistic cultures, the expression of high self-esteem may be valued, but in collectivist cultures it may not. With this in mind, we look next at the development of an ethnic identity during adolescence.

Ethnic Identity

For many teens, a part of their identity is related to their ethnic background. Phinney (1989) proposed a theory that describes the process teens go through as they explore this aspect of their identity. The first stage is *unexamined ethnic identity*. The adolescent either has not thought about her ethnic identity and has no clear understanding of the issues (as in Marcia's status of identity diffusion) or has accepted without question the values and attitudes that others hold about her ethnic group (as in Marcia's status of foreclosure). In this stage, the adolescent often prefers the majority culture over her own ethnic culture (Marks et al., 2007).

The second stage is an *ethnic identity search* in which the adolescent actively tries to understand his culture and to explore the meaning of his ethnicity. He may read about

T/F #1

By comparison to other ethnic and racial groups, Asian American adolescents have the lowest self-esteem.

True

Finding an ethnic identity. Sharing family traditions—whether it is celebrating Kwanzaa, enjoying a birthday party with a piñata, or having a large Italian family dinner—helps children and adolescents form a sense of their ethnic identity. What family traditions did your family share while you were growing up? ■

TABLE 16.2	Phinney's stages of ethnic identity development

Stage	Comment
Unexamined ethnic identity	"My past is just there; I have no reason to worry about it. I'm American now." (diffusion)
	"I don't go looking for my culture. I just go by what my parents say and do, and what they tell me to do, the way they are." (foreclosure)
Ethnic identity search	"There are a lot of non-Japanese around me and it gets pretty confusing to try and decide who I am."
	"I think people should know what Black people had to go through to get to where we are now."
Achieved ethnic identity	"People put me down because I'm Mexican, but I don't care anymore. I can accept myself more."
	"I used to want to be White, because I wanted long flowing hair. And I wanted to be real light. I used to think being light was prettier, but now I think there are pretty dark-skinned girls and pretty light-skinned girls. I don't want to be White now. I'm happy being Black."

These comments from adolescents illustrate how they think about their ethnic identity at each of Phinney's stages of ethnic identity development.

SOURCE: Phinney (1989).

his culture, talk to others who share his cultural heritage, visit ethnic museums, or take part in cultural events (Marks et al., 2007). He may even actively reject the majority culture during this process. The result of this exploration is the final stage, *achieved ethnic identity*, in which the adolescent has "a clear, secure understanding and acceptance of one's own ethnicity" (Phinney, 1989, p. 38). Table 16.2 illustrates the adolescent's thinking at each of these stages. As you can imagine, this process is even more complex for the 5% or more of the school-age population that is multiracial (Brunsma, 2005).

Progress through these stages has been associated with a number of positive outcomes for the adolescent, including higher scores on measures of self-esteem, mastery, psychological adjustment, social and peer interactions, and family relations (Crocetti, Rubini, & Meeus, 2008; Seaton, Scottham, & Sellers, 2006; Umaña-Taylor, Gonzales-Backen, & Guimond, 2009). A strong sense of ethnic identity also can have a positive and protective role in reducing depression (Mandara, Gaylord-Harden, Richards, & Ragsdale, 2009) and promoting school performance. Wong, Eccles, and Sameroff (2003) found that a strong positive connection to their ethnic group reduced the impact of discrimination on academic self-concept and school achievement among African American adolescents and was associated with resistance to problem behaviors such as skipping classes, lying to parents about their whereabouts, bringing alcohol or drugs to school, and cheating on exams.

The formation of your ethnic identity is affected by society's attitudes toward the group with which you identify. Although many believe that racism is no longer an issue in the United States, those who experience it have a very different perception. In a variety of studies, between 49% and 90% of African American adolescents report having had experiences of racial discrimination in the form of harassment, poor treatment in public settings, or others' assumptions of lower ability or more violent behavior (Cooper, McLoyd, Wood, & Hardaway, 2008).

Racism has been defined as a pervasive system of advantage and disadvantage based on race. It is based on the belief that one race is superior to another. It consists of stereotypes (which are fixed beliefs about a particular racial group), prejudices (which are negative attitudes about that group), and discrimination (which is negative behavior directed at that group) (Cooper et al., 2008). Racism can be overt, meaning it is openly accepted and acted

JOURNAL ARTICLE 16.1
Adolescent Ethnic Identity

Racism A pervasive system of advantage and disadvantage based on race.

Stereotypes Conclusions made about someone based solely on the group with which he or she is identified.

Prejudices Negative attitudes toward individuals based on their race, ethnicity, religion, or other factors.

Discrimination Negative behavior directed at people on the basis of their race, ethnicity, religion, or other factors.

on, or it can be covert or hidden. When it is covert, the individual may not even be aware he or she carries racist attitudes but nevertheless is affected by them.

We also find racism in the way institutions are created and operate. For example, a large study carried out in Baltimore found that African American youth applied for jobs more often than their White peers but had lower rates of employment, even when they had the same socioeconomic status and academic achievement (Entwisle, Alexander, & Olson, 2000). The result of institutional racism is to provide fewer opportunities for African American youth, which then has an impact on later achievement and economic well-being.

Young people's perception that they are being treated unfairly because of their race is linked with a number of negative outcomes: lower levels of self-esteem; higher levels of depression, anxiety, and behavioral problems; and increased substance use (Pachter & Garcia Coll, 2009). Substance abuse or violence may become a way to avoid or fight against feelings of a lack of control over their lives (Cooper et al., 2008).

However, other teens who experience discrimination develop an attitude that "no one is going to stand in the way of my success" and take enormous pride in their ability to overcome adversity. Several factors allow them to take this approach. First, parental warmth and support and positive social support from others in their lives help minority teens maintain their self-esteem in the face of negative events. Second, through a process called racial socialization, minority parents teach their children about discrimination they may experience and prepare them with ideas and tactics that can help them deal with it. In addition, parents promote positive racial identification by instilling pride in their children's ethnic and racial heritage. Both parental support and racial socialization improve the outcomes for adolescents who have experienced racial discrimination (Brody et al., 2006; Cooper et al., 2008; Sellers, Copeland-Linder, Martin, & Lewis, 2006).

Racial socialization Efforts by minority parents to teach their children about discrimination, prepare them to deal with these experiences, and teach them to take pride in their heritage.

Check Your Understanding

1. How did Erikson describe the developmental crisis of adolescence?
2. What are the four identity statuses Marcia described?
3. How do adolescents develop their ethnic identity?
4. How can parents help adolescents deal with racism?

Emotions

Adolescence has often been thought of as a time of emotional storm and stress, and evidence suggests teens do experience more extreme emotions and more changeable moods than people of other ages. As they mature, however, adolescents become better able to regulate their emotions (Silvers et al., 2012). In this section, we concentrate on the role of empathy for others' feelings in both prosocial and antisocial or delinquent behavior. We then look at depression and suicide, both of which become more prevalent in adolescence.

Picture Partners/Photo Researchers, Inc.

Empathy. Adolescents with a secure attachment to their parents are more emotionally aware and sympathetic toward others. What do you think accounts for the relationship between attachment and emotional empathy? ■

16.2

How do emotions develop in adolescence?

Empathy and Prosocial and Antisocial Behavior

The ability to have empathy for other people underlies prosocial behavior, or voluntary actions that benefit someone else (Eisenberg, Morris, McDaniel, & Spinrad, 2009). Adolescents who report secure attachment with their parents and with their peers were found to be more emotionally aware, more sympathetic, more prosocial in their behavior, and more positive in their affect (Laible, 2007). Adolescents who are unable to empathize with others are more likely to be sexually abusive, delinquent, and antisocial, or to be bullies among their peers.

Children who were bullies in middle childhood are more likely to become delinquents in adolescence (Farrington, Loeber, Stallings, & Ttofi, 2011). Delinquency is defined as participation in criminal activity by minors. Both bullies and juvenile delinquents are more likely to lack empathy and guilt and to show little concern for other people (Kimonis et al., 2014). Teens who engage in criminal activity but who are capable of showing empathy toward others are more likely to be helped by intervention programs, because it is difficult to change youth who cannot understand and share the feelings of another.

Some good news about juvenile delinquency is that teen arrest rates for violent crimes by males have declined significantly in the last 15 years, as you can see in Figure 16.1. The rates for females have remained low and unchanged. No clear reasons have been found for this decline, but it is important that we go beyond sensationalistic newspaper headlines to see that, in this respect, young people seem to be doing better over time. In 2008, 75% of juvenile arrests were for assaults, vandalism, drug- and alcohol-related offenses, and broken curfews, and about 20% were for property crimes such as burglary or theft. Violent crime such as murder, rape, and aggravated assault represented fewer than 5% of arrests (National Center for Children in Poverty, 2014). We can be hopeful that continuing to intervene with positive youth development programs will reduce these numbers even more.

Depression and Suicide

As we mentioned in Chapter 13, depression can occur in younger children; however, the incidence increases markedly with puberty (APA, 2013). Adolescents are known for their moodiness, but depression is much more serious than a mood that passes. It is important to differentiate normal moodiness from depression because depression in adolescence is linked with both physical and mental health problems in adulthood (Maughan, Collishaw, & Stringaris, 2013). Teens with depression have low mood or irritability most of the time over at least a 2-week period, with loss of pleasure in activities

VIDEO LINK 16.1
Delinquency

Delinquency Youth involvement with criminal activity.

T/F #2

The rate of violent crime committed by young people continues to climb from year to year. *False*

FIGURE 16.1 **Violent crime arrest rates in young people 10–24 years old**

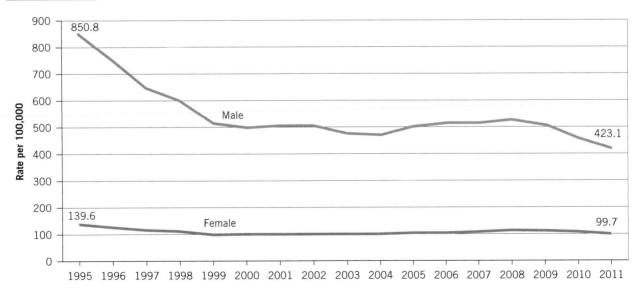

Despite all the publicity about violence in young people, the rate of arrests for violent crime committed by males has gone down significantly since 1995.

SOURCE: Centers for Disease Control and Prevention (2013l).

| TABLE 16.3 | Percentage of high school students who felt sad or hopeless*†, by sex, race/ethnicity, and grade—United States, Youth Risk Behavior Survey, 2013. | | |

Race/ethnicity	Female %	Male %	Total %
White¶	35.7	19.1	27.3
Black¶	35.8	18.8	27.5
Hispanic	47.8	25.4	36.8
Grade			
9	40.8	18.2	29.4
10	38.8	20.3	29.4
11	39.9	23.1	31.7
12	36.2	21.8	29.1
Total	**39.1**	**20.8**	**29.9**

SOURCE: Adapted from Youth Risk Behavior Surveillance—United States (2013).

* Almost every day for 2 or more weeks in a row so that they stopped doing some usual activities.

† During the 12 months before the survey.

¶ Non-Hispanic.

T/F #3
Rates of depression among adolescents have not changed in the last 30 years. *True*

and possibly weight change, sleep disturbance, feelings of worthlessness or guilt, and thoughts of suicide (APA, 2013). In a national survey in 2013, 30% of high school students reported feeling depressed for a 2-week period in the previous year, with higher levels for girls than boys in all racial categories (CDC, 2014m). Although these numbers may seem high, a review of studies conducted over a 30-year period found no increase in the prevalence of adolescent depression across that time (Costello & Angold, 2011).

As shown in Table 16.3, teen girls are almost twice as likely as teen boys to experience depression. Because of the sharp increase in depression in females at midpuberty, researchers have looked for biological causes such as hormonal changes, but there is little support for this hormonal hypothesis. However, girls' reactions to the physical changes associated with puberty (such as an increase in weight) are linked with lower body satisfaction and more depression (Vogt Yuan, 2007). Another possible explanation for higher levels of depression in girls is that they are more likely than boys to experience multiple stress events during adolescence, including daily hassles and interpersonal problems (Shih, Eberhard, Hammen, & Brennan, 2006). Finally, girls and boys are socialized differently. Boys are allowed to express their frustration and anger by acting out, while girls are socialized to internalize these feelings in a way that may take a psychological toll in the form of depression. Much of the research on depression in adolescents from ethnic minorities has found mixed results, but several recent large-scale studies have found no difference in depression among different ethnic groups, and in all groups girls have higher levels of depression than boys (Latzman et al., 2011; Twenge & Nolen-Hoeksema, 2002).

Although chronic or severe depression is a serious emotional condition, it is treatable. However, less than 40% of teens with depression receive treatment (SAMHSA, 2009), often because symptoms are mistaken for normal adolescent moodiness. Forms of therapy such as cognitive-behavior therapy and interpersonal psychotherapy for adolescents can help depressed adolescents change the way they think about and deal with their problems and improve their coping and social skills (Desrochers & Houck, 2013; Weersing & Brent, 2010). Although antidepressant medications are frequently used with success in the treatment of depression in adults, they may not work as well for adolescents and may even carry additional risks (Maughan et al., 2013; Wolfe & Mash, 2006), such as suicidal thoughts and behaviors (CDC, 2014m). These risks are most often outweighed by the benefits from taking the medication (Maughan et al., 2013), but families of teens who are taking antidepressants should make sure that their child will talk with them openly about any suicidal ideas.

Depression can lead to suicide, which is the third leading cause of death in adolescents. In addition to those who die from self-inflicted harm, many more make the attempt to kill themselves. When high school students were surveyed about suicidal thoughts in the previous year, 16% said they had seriously considered it, 13% reported having a plan, and 8% had tried to kill themselves (CDC, 2014m). Although more girls than boys attempt suicide, boys are more likely to actually die from a suicide attempt. Eighty-one percent of suicide deaths among 10- to 24-year-olds are male. There are also cultural differences. Native American and Alaskan Native teens had the highest rate of suicide, while Hispanic teens were more likely than others to make a suicide attempt (CDC, 2014m). Teens, especially girls, who have a friend who commits suicide are more likely to think about it and act on those thoughts themselves (Abrutyn & Mueller, 2014). Suicide is also more common among teens who cope with negative emotions by suppressing them rather than finding a way to express how they feel (Kaplow, Gipson, Horwitz, Burch, & King, 2014).

Many people think asking someone about suicidal thoughts will put ideas into that person's head, so they avoid the talking about the subject with teens. The fact is that asking about suicide will *not* make it more likely that someone will think about it or do it (SAMHSA, 2012). However, all thoughts about suicide should be taken seriously. If a depressed teen indicates he has a plan in place for killing himself, it is essential to get emergency care, remove objects he might use to harm himself, and not leave him alone.

When a young person does commit suicide, friends and other peers often need help with dealing with their reactions. Schools should have a plan in place that includes the provision of counseling to those requesting it. It is also important not to glamorize suicide, because this makes subsequent suicides by other students more likely. A toolkit for schools provided by the American Foundation for Suicide Prevention (2011) has a suggested statement that can be used by schools to help students understand what has happened. It says: "[Suicide] is usually caused by a mental disorder such as depression, which can prevent a person from thinking clearly about his or her problems and how to solve them. Sometimes these disorders are not identified or noticed; in other cases a person with a disorder will show obvious symptoms or signs. One thing is certain: there are treatments that can help. Suicide should never, ever be an option" (p. 15).

WEB LINK 16.2
Teen Suicide

T/F #4

Asking a teen whether he is thinking about committing suicide will make it more likely he will do it. *False*

Check Your Understanding

1. What role does empathy play in adolescent behavior?
2. How has the incidence of violent crimes committed by teens changed in recent years?
3. Compare the incidence of adolescent depression and suicide between boys and girls.

Family Relationships

Time spent with family remains important for adolescents. As they test their newly developing autonomy and independence, they continue to need the support of a solid home behind them. In this section, we describe how teens express this new drive for autonomy in their family relationships, and how disruption in the family system can negatively affect them as they strive to become independent individuals.

16.3

How do adolescents' relationships with their parents change?

Positive conflict. Not only are parent-teen conflicts less frequent than many people believe, but they can also be opportunities to work problems out together and maintain warm ties as the teen becomes more independent. ■

© Ariel Skelley/Corbis

Changes in Relationships During Adolescence

With so many changes occurring during adolescence, it is not surprising these events are reflected in adolescents' changing relationships with their parents. Rather than a massive change in the relationship, however, what occurs is better described as a renegotiation of that relationship (Collins & Laursen, 2004).

Most people would not question the importance of attachment relationships for preschoolers and school-age children, but the attachment relationship that began in childhood continues to be important to the well-being of adolescents as well. Adolescents spend less time with their parents and do not require their parents' physical presence to feel secure, but a sense that their parents are emotionally close and committed to them and their well-being continues to form a secure base that allows them to explore a widening world of social relationships and experiences (Gorrese & Ruggieri, 2012; Shearer, Crouter, & McHale, 2005; Smetana, Metzger, & Campione-Barr, 2004).

At one time, we thought parent and peer relationships were in competition, and that as the importance of one went up, the importance of the other would necessarily decrease. However, we now know that adolescents can maintain positive, high quality relationships with both their parents and their peers, just as the idea of internal working models for relationships described in Chapter 7 would suggest. Adolescents who report a secure relationship with their parents also tend to report a secure attachment with their close friends (Gorrese & Ruggieri, 2012).

Increasing Autonomy

Although most teens maintain their attachment to their parents, the nature of their relationship necessarily changes as they grow older. For instance, adolescents are less willing than children to accept the unilateral authority of their parents, so decision making evolves into a shared process in most families (Hill, Bromell, Tyson, & Flint, 2007). If parents tried to exercise the same type of behavioral control they used in childhood, their efforts could backfire and result in adolescent misconduct and rebelliousness. However, if parents relinquish some control and replace it with monitoring and tracking of their adolescent's activities, the teen is more likely to accept it as legitimate and comply with parents' expectations (Darling, Cumsille, & Martínez, 2008).

Some consistent differences appear between adolescents' relationships with their mothers and with their fathers. Adolescents report spending less time with their father and feeling closer to their mother (Shearer et al., 2005; Steinberg & Silk, 2002). Father-daughter relationships are typically the most distant parent-adolescent relationship (Shearer et al., 2005). Although mother-daughter relationships are the closest, they also are marked by more conflict, particularly around the time of puberty (Steinberg & Silk, 2002). In fact, mothers of both sons and daughters are more likely to experience conflict with their adolescents than fathers do, perhaps because they spend more time in contact with their children (Shearer et al., 2005).

Parent-Adolescent Conflict

Although many believe adolescents' relationships with their parents are marked by significant amounts of conflict, there is little research support for this idea. It is not unusual to find some level of conflict in most U.S. families (Smetana, 2011), but there is a good

T/F #5

Teens who are strongly attached to their friends are likely to also be strongly attached to their parents. *True*

WEB LINK 16.3
Parenting Styles and Teenagers

deal of variability from one family to another. The idea that adolescence is a time of conflict and alienation probably describes no more than 20% of families (Johnston, Walters, & Olesen, 2005).

The *frequency* of conflict is highest in early adolescence and declines as adolescents move into middle and late adolescence, but the *intensity* of conflict, when it does occur, tends to increase during middle adolescence (Laursen, Coy, & Collins, 1998; De Goede, Branje, & Meeus, 2009; Van Doorn, Branje, & Meeus, 2011). In **Active Learning: Sources of Parent-Adolescent Conflict** you can explore the kinds of issues that cause conflict in families.

T/F #6
A great deal of parent-adolescent conflict is normal in families with adolescents. *False*

Active Learning

Sources of Parent-Adolescent Conflict

In 1994, Brian K. Barber asked 1,828 White, Black, and Hispanic families of adolescents to rank-order the frequency of conflict in their family about each of the topics below. Go through the list and estimate how often you think *other families* with adolescents have conflict about each of these topics. Use 1 for most frequently and 10 for least frequently. Then go through the list again and mark how often you had conflict with your parents about each of these topics, using the same scale. When you are done, check your rankings against Barber's results below.

Topics of Conflict	1 = Most Frequent 10 = Least Frequent	
	In Most Families	In My Family
The way the adolescent dresses		
The adolescent's boyfriend/girlfriend		
The adolescent's friends		
How late the adolescent stays out at night		
How much the adolescent helps around the house		
The adolescent's sexual behavior		
The adolescent's drinking, smoking, or drug use		
Money		
School		
The adolescent's relationships with other family members		

■ Answers: This is the rank-ordering of actual conflict from Barber's (1994) sample: (1) helping around the house (*most frequent*), (2) family relationships, (3) school, (4) the way the adolescent dresses, (5) money, (6) how late the adolescent stays out, (7) the adolescent's friends, (8) the adolescent's boyfriend/girlfriend, (9) substance use, (10) sexual behavior (*least frequent*) (p. 379).

Many people believe conflict between adolescents and their parents typically focuses on explosive issues like adolescent sexuality or substance use, but it is much more likely to be about ordinary, everyday events like homework, curfews, loud music, and messy rooms (Eisenberg et al., 2008; Smetana, 2011). It would not be surprising if you

It's all a matter of how you see it. One thing that contributes to conflict between adolescents and their parents is the different ways that they define issues. To this teen, a messy room is a matter of personal choice and is nobody's business but her own, but to her parents, it may be seen as a violation of social conventions. ∎

identified these mundane issues as the most frequent sources of conflict in your family, even if you thought *other families* were fighting about the big things.

It seems the issues that create conflict between adolescents and their parents have not changed much over the last few decades. A 2008 study found that the four most frequent sources of conflict between parents and teens were cleaning chores, getting along with family, respect/manners, and school issues, and the least frequent were friends and dating, and smoking or alcohol (Eisenberg et al., 2008). These findings are very similar to what Barber reported 14 years earlier.

Despite the way it might feel when it is happening, conflict within families is *not* necessarily bad during adolescence (Smetana, 2011). In individualistic societies, some level of conflict is an inevitable part of the individuation and identity development that normally occur during adolescence (Adams & Laursen, 2001). The challenge for parents is to find the right balance between granting teens the autonomy they want and maintaining the connectedness or attachment they need. The right balance in early adolescence isn't the same as it will be in middle or late adolescence, so parents must be responsive to the developmental changes in their child. Conflict that takes place in the context of a warm, supportive family environment can be a positive thing that fosters personal growth (Smetana, 2011).

The amount and type of conflict tolerated will differ from one cultural context to another. As in Western families, conflicts in Indian families are most likely to be about minor things, like homework and household chores (Kapadia, 2008). However, Indian culture emphasizes honoring parents and maintaining harmony within the family. Consequently, adolescents are more likely to compromise to meet their parents' expectations and demands rather than believe they should decide for themselves what is best for them. We find similar patterns in other collectivist cultures, such as Mexico and Korea (Phinney, Kim-Jo, Osorio, & Vilhjalmsdottir, 2005).

Parents may be relieved to know that although conflict does cause some disruption in the parent-adolescent relationship, its effects are usually temporary. Most families successfully weather their children's transition through adolescence without any serious harm to the quality of their relationship (Shearer et al., 2005). In fact, parents report that their relationship with their adolescent children becomes closer during the process and there are more positive changes than negative ones (Shearer et al., 2005). Families are able to handle moderate levels of conflict because patterns of positive interactions were laid down throughout childhood (McGue, Elkins, Walden, & Iacono, 2005). The relationship becomes more egalitarian in adolescence, but the love, support, and responsiveness that were central to the earlier parent-child relationship remain strong (Van Doorn et al., 2011).

Family Time

Although the time spent with family decreases in adolescence, family activities remain important. Most teens report enjoying meals with their families and eat more healthfully when they do (Neumark-Sztainer, 2008). The positive sharing that may go on at meals contributes to lower level of risk taking and emotional problems teens in these families have (Larson, 2008). However, these effects depend on the quality of the interactions that occur. Almost half of U.S. families report having a television on during meals (Hersey & Jordan, 2007), which appears to disrupt the family's interactions. Use of other media, such as cell phones and videogames, can also interfere with the closeness family meals can foster. **Active Learning: Family Mealtime** will guide you in thinking about your own family's experiences with mealtimes.

Active Learning

Family Mealtime

Think about your own family when you were a teenager. How often did your family eat together? Did the frequency of eating together change from childhood to adolescence for you, and if it did, how did it change? When you ate together, remember what types of things were discussed and what the atmosphere was. What kinds of things interfered with your family eating together: job responsibilities, sports, or other extracurricular activities? Was the TV on in the room on a regular basis? Were there rules about use of individual media, such as cellphones, at the table? If so, what impact did this have on family interaction? Now consider your own experience in light of the general findings that connect family dinners with positive outcomes. How does your experience fit or not fit with this research? What does this activity tell you about your own experience; also what does it tell you about how the research might be refined so that it could capture other pertinent issues? ■

Yellow Dog Productions/The Image Bank/Getty Images

Family dinnertime. Families exchange more than food when they sit down to meals together. Family members have a chance to share the events of the day and spend time together. ■

Relationships With Divorced Parents

Although adolescence is a time for becoming more independent of parents, this task is easier when parents are in a position to give both support and control to help their teens become independent young adults. When parents are themselves embroiled in the emotional conflicts of a divorce, parenting becomes much more difficult. Adolescents may respond with problem behaviors to express their disappointment with their parents. Teen pregnancy is twice as high in divorced families as in married families (Martin et al., 2004). Depression, delinquent behavior, and substance abuse are also more likely to occur for these teens (Cohen, Chaput, & Cashon, 2002). The effects of divorce vary widely, however, and can be positive if the level of conflict decreases when parents separate (Hetherington, 2006).

A review of the literature on the effect of parental divorce or separation on adolescents found results similar to what we discussed in Chapter 13 regarding younger children: Academic performance often declines and levels of deviant or problematic behavior increase, as do anger and depression. At the same time, self-esteem decreases. Adolescents who have experienced parental divorce or separation express more negative attitudes toward marriage, but they also increase their dating and social involvement, perhaps as an attempt to find a supportive relationship outside the family. This same review also mentioned that too much disclosure of sensitive topics by the parents can make the young person feel caught between the parents and forced to mediate between them. However, maintaining a good parent-adolescent relationship and keeping the number of family transitions as low as possible helps buffer these negative effects (Hartman, Magalhães, & Mandich, 2011).

Adoption and Foster Care in Adolescence

Teens who grow up in adoptive homes or in foster care face special issues of family life, identity, and future plans.

Adoption

We have seen that young teens often have conflicts with their parents that center on everyday issues of family life. Families formed by adoption face some additional issues, as illustrated by the conversation below between a mother and a tall, red-haired boy who was adopted at birth by his much shorter, dark-haired parents:

Mother: Jack, you need to do your homework *now.*

Jack: *You* can't make me do my homework. I'm going to go find my *real* mother!

Mother: Your *real* mother is yelling at you right now!

This mother could have gotten defensive, based on her fear of abandonment (Rampage et al., 2003): "Go ahead, find your *real* mother," implying, "You were never really mine." Instead, she is comfortable being his real mother and knows he needs her to acknowledge their firm connection. He can express his need for independence with the security of knowing that he cannot really push her away; their bond is real and strong.

Jack is probably also wondering about his identity and wants to know more about where he came from. He clearly does not resemble his parents, and he is reminded of this fact every time he sees his own reflection. Differences between parent and child are also obvious with interracial adoption. In 2007, about 40% of adopted children were of a different race than their parents (Vandivere et al., 2009). As adolescents wrestle with developing their own identity, adoptees need to know as much as the adoptive parents know about their birth parents (Rampage et al., 2003). As they get older, they have greater control over their contact with birth relatives. It was satisfaction with the amount of contact adoptees have—rather than a specific amount or type of contact—that was associated with better outcomes as adoptees move into adulthood (Grotevant, McRoy, Wrobel, & Ayers-Lopez, 2013).

Foster Care

Adolescents living in foster care have undergone difficult circumstances in their family of origin, and some may continue to have problems in their foster families. A study conducted in Sweden found that youth who left long-term foster care after age 17 were 6 to 11 times more likely to be at risk for suicide attempts, substance abuse, serious crimi-

Foster families. Foster children may experience many different family situations as any one placement is likely to be temporary. Some, like this family, take in many children. What challenges and advantages do you think such a situation may provide? ■

John Ewing/Portland Press Herald via Getty Images

nality, and public welfare dependency than the majority population of peers (Berlin, Vinnerljung, & Hjern, 2011). However, the researchers determined that half the risk for these psychosocial problems could be attributed to the poor school performance of the foster youth. We can understand how entry into the foster care system can have a negative effect on the educational process. When a young person comes into foster care or moves from one foster care family to another he often has to change schools and records can be lost, days missed, and new situations may be uncomfortable for the children. These disruptions are reflected in the fact that only 50% of American children who have been in foster care either graduate high school or pass the General Educational Development (GED) test and fewer than 2% go to college (Bruskas, 2008).

    To help foster youth successfully transition out of care, Congress passed the Fostering Connections to Success and Increasing Adoptions Act in 2008 that allows states to provide support for foster children beyond age 18. Congress recognized that families in the United States today often help their children move into adulthood with both financial and emotional support, so this new act continues the role of government in providing care until foster adolescents reach age 21 if they are in school, in employment training, or employed at least 80 hours per month (Courtney, 2009). Research on the effectiveness of the programs that result from this new act will eventually give us an idea of what works best to transition adolescents from the foster care system into a successful adulthood.

T/F #7
Teens in the foster care system are extremely unlikely to attend college. True

---

Check Your Understanding

1. What role does autonomy play in adolescents' conflicts with their families?
2. What special issues do adolescents face when their parents divorce?
3. Why is forging an identity a particular challenge for adolescents who have been adopted?
4. What supports are available for adolescents aging out of foster care?

Peer Relationships

Peer relationships become an increasingly important context for development during adolescence. These take a variety of forms, from individual friendships to association with large groups of adolescents who share reputations and interests. In this section, we also discuss romantic relationships.

Friendships

Almost all adolescents can report having at least one close friend. Adolescent friendships tend to become more stable with age (Brown & Klute, 2006) as adolescents learn how to negotiate, to compromise, and to be more sensitive to the needs of others, and adolescents who perceive their friendships as higher quality have better emotional adjustment (Demir & Urberg, 2004).

Adolescent girls generally have smaller, more exclusive friendship networks than boys. They consider intimacy, loyalty, and commitment important qualities in those relationships, whereas boys are more likely to base their friendships on qualities such as status or achievement and have more open friendship networks (Vaquero & Kao, 2008). Girls say that within their friendships they can share their problems and be understood and cared for, while boys are more likely to feel that sharing problems is "weird" and a waste of time (Rose et al., 2012). However, because girls do more intimate sharing and disclosing in their relationships, they are understandably more concerned about possible betrayal by a friend, and this risk becomes one of the potential emotional costs of maintaining intimate relationships with friends.

Some other characteristics of adolescent friendships are that both equality and reciprocity are expected, that adolescents are likely to select as friends people they see as similar to themselves, and that close friendships are usually same-gender friendships (with a strong preference for friends from the same ethnic or racial background) (Brown & Klute, 2006; Hafen, Laursen, Burk, Kerr, & Stattin, 2011). Of course peer groups include more members of the opposite sex as the adolescent becomes older and begins dating (Hebert, Fales, Nangle, Papadakis, & Grover, 2013). Beyond similarity in demographic characteristics such as age, gender, and ethnicity, friends are similar in attitudes, values, and activity preferences (including delinquent and antisocial behavior) (Hafen et al., 2011; Solomon & Knafo, 2007).

Although friends have a number of characteristics in common at the beginning of their friendships, they become even more similar over time as they influence one another. Friendships are more likely to be maintained when this happens (Hafen et al., 2011). This process is often pleasant and positive, but it also means that teens can play a role in initiating friends into risky or problem behaviors, including sexual behavior (Baumgartner, Valkenburg, & Peter, 2011; Rew, Carver, & Li, 2011), smoking (Kobus, 2003), substance use (Dishion & Owen, 2002), and delinquency (Hafen et al., 2011). Peers do this by establishing the norms for the peer group, but also through their direct modeling of these

MoMo Productions/Stone/Getty Images

Friendships. How do friendships among adolescent girls differ from those among adolescent boys? ■

behaviors. You can use **Active Learning: Friends—Similar or Different?** to explore the similarities between you and your own friends during adolescence.

Active Learning

Friends—Similar or Different?

Think about your two best friends during your freshman or sophomore year of high school, and decide whether they were *similar to* or *different from* you on each of these characteristics.

	Friend #1		Friend #2	
Attitude toward school achievement	Similar	Different	Similar	Different
Level of participation in school activities	Similar	Different	Similar	Different
Hobbies or interests (for example, music, drama, video games, collections)	Similar	Different	Similar	Different
Religious values or beliefs	Similar	Different	Similar	Different
Attitude toward smoking	Similar	Different	Similar	Different
Attitude toward drinking	Similar	Different	Similar	Different
Crowd you were identified with	Similar	Different	Similar	Different
Degree of shyness or extroversion	Similar	Different	Similar	Different
Other characteristics that were important to you:				
1.	Similar	Different	Similar	Different
2.	Similar	Different	Similar	Different
3.	Similar	Different	Similar	Different

In what ways was the similarity between you and your friends beneficial to you? Were any differences beneficial? Did any differences cause stress or tension in your relationship? Can you think of any way in which you or your friend changed over time as the result of your friendship? ■

Cliques and Crowds

Peers influence each other even when they are not immediate friends. Small groups of friends who spend time together and develop close friendships are called cliques. Teens are also influenced by crowds, which are larger groups in which membership is based on an individual's abilities, interests, or activities (Brown & Klute, 2006).

Cliques are most common during early adolescence, and membership is often fairly fluid. In one study of adolescent cliques, fewer than 10% were stable over the 3 years they were followed (Engles, Knibbe, Drop, & deHaan, 1997). Within a clique, members can hold different roles. A leader often emerges, some are core members, and others are "wannabes" who hang around the periphery of the clique. Some adolescents are members of more than one clique at a time and link the cliques together

Cliques Small groups of friends who spend time together and develop close relationships.

Crowds Large, reputation-based groups that are based on a shared stereotype but whose members do not necessarily spend time together.

Brand X Pictures/Thinkstock

Punks and populars and jocks, oh my! Teenage crowds are groups of teens who share a similar taste in fashion, music, and activities. Although the members of a particular crowd may not know each other or spend time together, their peers see them as a part of an identifiable crowd. It isn't difficult to guess which crowd this group represents. ■

VIDEO LINK 16.3
Cliques and Crowds

ACTIVE LEARNING
VIDEO 16.1
Recognizing a Crowd

(Brown & Klute, 2006). And, of course, some adolescents are not a member of any clique. They may have friendships with individual peers who are not friends with each other, or they may be socially isolated. Young adolescents who were not part of any clique at age 11 to 13 experienced loneliness that made them more prone to depression by age 14 (Witvliet et al., 2010).

Although cliques can be an important source of social support, they also can use techniques like ridicule or the threat of being ostracized to control their members. Clique membership has been linked to increased externalizing behavior in boys as groups of friends influence and reward each other's negative behaviors (Witvliet et al., 2010).

Brown and Klute (2006) describe crowds as large, reputation-based groups that share a common identity among peers but whose members do not necessarily spend time together. One advantage of being identified as part of a crowd is that it gives you a ready-made identity among your peers. Crowd labels can be based on various characteristics that the members have in common, including residence (for example, the northenders), ethnicity or socioeconomic background (the Asians, the snobs), or abilities or interests (the jocks, the gangbangers). Think for a minute about the crowds you would recognize at your high school. The number of different crowds and how easily recognizable they are differs from one school setting to another.

Even though a teen probably does not know all the people in a particular crowd, they more often form friendships with others in the same crowd rather than with peers in different crowds because they do have some characteristics in common with their crowd members (Bagwell & Schmidt, 2011), and similarity is an important characteristic of most friendships.

As adolescents get older and develop a stronger sense of their own identity, crowds (just like cliques) become less important to them. **Active Learning: Recognizing a Crowd When You See One** gives you a chance to reflect on the crowd structure at your high school.

Active Learning

Recognizing a Crowd When You See One

Although most people report that they did not belong to just one clique or crowd in high school, most people are perceived as if they do. Name some of the different crowds that existed in your high school. What determined who belonged in which group? How were these groups similar to and different from each other in how they dressed, what music they listened to, how they spent their time, their attitudes toward school, and other things you can think of? How did the crowds relate to each other? Did they do some things together or have some values in common?

If you have classmates who came from a different type of school than you attended, it might be interesting for you to compare notes. The number and types of crowds in a given school vary by the size of school; its ethnic and socioeconomic composition; rural, urban, or suburban location; and a variety of other characteristics. Some of the crowds you were familiar with at your high school might not even exist in other high schools. ■

Peer Pressure

Peer pressure can be direct (for instance, when peers use direct rewards or punishment for compliance) or subtle (for instance, through modeling or by the establishment of group norms). Reports from adolescents support the idea that peer pressure, when it does occur, is more likely to be subtle rather than direct. For instance, Brown (1993) describes how adolescents responded to a question about peer pressure to drink at a party where alcohol is available. They said, in effect, that it is there if you want it but "nobody gives you a hard time if you don't. Like, no one comes up and shoves a beer in your hand and says, 'Here, drink it!'" (Brown, 1993, p. 190). However, they also said that if everyone else is drinking, they felt a "little weird just sipping a soda" (p. 190).

Peer pressure. Peer pressure can be direct, or it can be subtle. The group norms that develop within a clique are one way that pressure is exerted on friends to adopt similar attitudes and behaviors. ■

Burger/Phanie/Photo Researchers, Inc.

The way this type of pressure operates was illustrated in a study on teen smoking in the United States. Ali and Dwyer (2009) found that increases in the percentage of classmates and close friends who smoked were associated with small (3%–5%) but significant increases in the likelihood a teen would smoke. In China, too, smoking by teens was related more to peer than to parental smoking (Ma et al., 2008). In both urban and rural China, cigarettes are routinely offered as a gesture of goodwill, so Chinese youth risk being impolite by not accepting. This shows that peer pressure can be experienced in many different ways, including some that are rather subtle.

Despite the concerns of parents or other adults that peers are a constant source of pressure for adolescents to behave in negative ways (for example, to be sexually active, to use drugs, to engage in delinquent behavior), they are just as likely to influence each other away from these types of behaviors (Brown, Bakken, Ameringer, & Mahon, 2008). And although peers can devalue academic achievement and draw adolescents away from their schoolwork, having high-achieving peers in fact exerts a positive influence on an adolescent's own academic achievement (Robnett & Leaper, 2013; Véronneau & Dishion, 2011).

The type of influence peers have largely depends on whom the adolescents have selected as their peers. The risk of antisocial behavior increases substantially when an adolescent is a part of an antisocial peer group, because of both direct peer pressure to engage in antisocial behavior and more subtle forms of pressure like modeling or endorsement of it. As we saw with friendships, selection and influence work together. For instance, it is more likely that young adolescents who are aggressive or prone to deviance will gravitate toward other adolescents with similar inclinations (selection), and over time the norms within that group will reinforce antisocial behavior by group members (influence).

Susceptibility to peer pressure decreases as adolescents get older (Sumter, Bokhorst, Steinberg, & Westenberg, 2009) and, although peers exert pressure on adolescents, so do the important adults in their lives. Our understanding of the relative influence that parents and peers have on adolescents has changed over time, and these changes are described in **Journey of Research: The Influence of Parents and Peers.**

Peer pressure Influence exerted by peers to get others to comply with their wishes or expectations.

T/F #8

Most adolescents say they feel a good deal of peer pressure to do things they know they shouldn't do. *False*

VIDEO LINK 16.4
Peer Pressure

JOURNEY OF RESEARCH *The Influence of Parents and Peers*

Adolescents have qualitatively different relationships with their parents and their peers. For a long time, the field has debated the relative influence of these two relationships on adolescents. Must adolescents break away from parents and follow their peers before they can successfully become adults?

Historically it was assumed that parents were the primary influence on adolescent development and decision making. The goal of adolescents was to grow up and become adults, just like their parents. However, as a separate teen culture evolved following World War II, the perception that came to dominate our thinking was that adults and peers were in two separate worlds, with little or no meeting ground in the middle. Adolescents were enticed away from their parents' world as they succumbed to the lure of peers. In 1970, Urie Bronfenbrenner reflected this sentiment when he said that "where the peer group is to a large extent autonomous—as it often is in the United States—it can exert influence in opposition to values held by adult society" (p. 189). Kandel and Lesser (1972) popularized what became known as the *hydraulic model*, based on the assumption that there was a fixed amount of influence available, so increases in peer influence would necessarily mean that there would be compensating decreases in the influence of parents. The portrayal of adolescents as torn between two opposing forces continued to influence our thinking for decades.

In 1998, Judith Harris challenged many of these assumptions with the publication of her controversial book *The Nurture Assumption: Why Children Turn Out the Way They Do*. Although she never claims parents have no effect on their children, Harris puts forth very strong arguments that their influence has been significantly overestimated, and that peers are the primary force in the process of socialization. In a 1995 article in *Psychological Review*, she says, "What GS [group socialization] theory implies is that children would develop into the same sort of adults if we left them in their homes, their

Teens in the 1950s. In the 1950s, the goal of many teenagers was to be as much like an adult as they possibly could be. ▪

George Marks/Retrofile/Getty Images

schools, their neighborhoods, and their cultural or subcultural groups, but switched all the parents around" (p. 461). At the conclusion of this article, she says, "[T]he home environment has no lasting effects on psychological characteristics. The shared environment that leaves permanent marks on children's personalities is the environment they share with their peers" (pp. 482–483).

Harris's ideas represent an extreme position on the relative influence of parents and peers, and they have supporters and critics (see, for example, Vandell, 2000). Most contemporary research has walked the middle ground, finding that parents exert more influence than peers in some areas of adolescent development, while peers exert more influence in others. Peers usually have greater influence in areas related to peer culture (hairstyles, music preference, leisure activities), but parents continue to have the greater influence in more enduring aspects of adolescent development (educational and career plans, religiosity, and personal values) (Brown, 2004; Wang, Peterson, & Morphey, 2007). And parents and peers jointly influence adolescents in still other areas. ▪

Bullying and School Violence

Although the incidence of bullying typically peaks in the middle school years and then decreases through adolescence (Carney & Merrell, 2001; Nansel et al., 2001), recently a form of bullying has appeared that is more likely to involve adolescents than younger children. It is called cyberbullying. Cyberbullying is the use of e-mail, text messages, digital images, blogs, chat rooms, and webpages (including social network sites) to harm others. The harm can consist of posts intended to embarrass someone or hurt another's feelings, the spread of false or malicious information, or the use of someone else's user name to spread rumors or lies.

Eighty-eight percent of teens report having seen someone be cruel to someone else on a social network site at least "once in a while," and some report that it occurs much more frequently (Lenhart et al., 2011). Between 11% and 25% of students report having been a victim of cyberbullying (Kowalski & Limber, 2007; Li, 2007; Wang, Iannotti, & Nansel, 2009).

Cyberbullying differs from other forms of bullying in ways that make it particularly damaging (Kowalski & Limber, 2007). First, electronic messages can be sent instantaneously to a large number of people, making the impact even greater than in face-to-face bullying. Second, although you can try to avoid a bully at school or in the neighborhood, you can't hide from cyberbullying, which can happen at any time and in any place. Finally, the anonymity of the Internet means cyberbullies can say things they might not say in person. In fact, more than half of students who report having been a victim of cyberbullying say they do not know who the bully was (Kowalski & Limber, 2007).

School violence is another threat to the well-being of adolescents that has captured headlines in recent years, but, as Figure 16.2 shows, schools are safe for most adolescents and have become safer in recent years as the overall rates of school violence have fallen (Robers, Zhang, & Truman, 2012). In 1992, the rate of violent victimization of teens was 53 students per 1,000, while in 2010 the same rate was 14 students per 1,000. That being said, we can't ignore the fact that some schools do have serious problems with violence in its many different forms. In 2010, there were 358,600 victims of violent crimes

Cyberbullying The use of electronic technologies, including e-mail, text messages, digital images, webpages (including social network sites), blogs, or chat rooms, to socially harm others.

AUDIO LINK 16.1
Cyberbullying

T/F #9

Adolescents today are much less likely to be victims of violence while in school than they were 20 years ago.
True

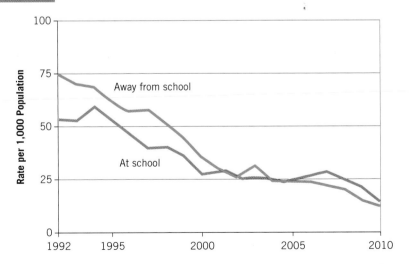

FIGURE 16.2 **Violent victimization of children in and outside of school**

Victimization rates for children age 12 to 18 have declined substantially in recent years according to the U.S. Department of Justice.

SOURCE: U.S. Department of Justice, Bureau of Justice Statistics, National Crime Victimization Survey (NCVS), 1992–2010.

at school (Robers et al., 2012), and in a nationwide survey of high school students, 7.7% said that during the previous 12 months they had been threatened or injured with a weapon on school property, and 11.1% said they had been involved in a physical fight (CDC, 2010c).

Efforts to reduce school violence have included services designed to help individual children at risk of perpetrating violence, as well as school-wide interventions designed to change the school climate in a more positive direction and broad-based community interventions designed to reduce violence in the community in which an individual school is located. In **Active Learning: School Violence From a Student's Perspective** you can compare your own experience of school violence with those of classmates.

WEB LINK 16.4
School Violence

Active Learning

School Violence From a Student's Perspective

Think about your own experience with violence in your elementary, middle, and high school. Talk with several friends and/or classmates who came from different high schools and compare your experiences. This activity will be most informative if the members of each group have had experiences in different types of schools. Violence on average is greater in middle school and high school than in elementary school and in urban schools than in suburban or rural schools. Males are more likely than females to be both perpetrators and victims. Fewer than half of public schools report a violent crime each year, and only 10% report a serious violent crime (National Youth Violence Prevention Resource Center, 2008), but in your discussion, remember to think about a full range of violent behavior, including threats of violence, assaults, and bullying in addition to other more clearly criminal acts. Also discuss what, if any, efforts were made by your schools to reduce school violence or to improve the school climate. ■

Romantic Relationships in Adolescence

Romantic relationships first emerge in adolescence, although the desire to have a boyfriend or girlfriend may begin before that. In one study of sixth, seventh, and eighth graders, there was no difference on a measure of how much the students wanted to have a boyfriend or girlfriend across the grades (Darling, Dowdy, VanHorn, & Caldwell, 1999), but the number who report being in a romantic relationship increases across adolescence, from 36% of 13-year-olds to 70% of 17-year-olds (Carver, Joyner, & Udry, 2003).

Adolescent romantic relationships are related to many of the developmental tasks of adolescence. They play an important role in the development of identity (including sexual identity), influence the process of individuation from the family of origin, change the nature of peer relationships, and lay the groundwork for future intimate relationships.

Although romance seems to occupy a prominent place in the thoughts of many adolescents, relatively little research has been done on the topic (Furman & Collins, 2009; Karney, Beckett, Collins, & Shaw, 2007). This is especially true when we compare the body of research on romantic relationships in adolescence to the body of research on adolescent sexual behavior described in Chapter 14. One of the reasons is that we do not have a commonly accepted definition of what a romantic relationship is (Furman & Collins, 2009; Karney et al., 2007). Many studies simply allow the participants to decide for themselves whether they are in (or have had) a romantic relationship (Karney et al., 2007). However, the problem with this approach is illustrated in one national longitudinal study in which participants were asked to name up to three people with whom they had had a romantic relationship. The researchers found that a large percentage of the named relationships were not reciprocated (in other words, the person with whom the adolescent reported having a romantic relationship did *not* include that adolescent on *his* or *her* list of romantic partners) (Karney et al., 2007).

Another challenge in doing research on romantic relationships is that the nature of these relationships changes a great deal over a relatively short amount of time. What a young adolescent wants from a romantic relationship and what makes that relationship satisfying or not is quite different from what an older adolescent wants. Younger adolescents place more importance on superficial characteristics such as physical appearance or having fun together, but older

Romantic relationships. Couples in adolescent romantic relationships are often similar in age, race, and attractiveness, among other factors. Why do you suppose they are also similar in their level of risk-taking behavior? ■

adolescents value qualities such as commitment and intimacy as they search for someone who could become a life partner (Montgomery, 2005). Also, various aspects of relationships have a different impact on adolescents depending on their age. While intimacy and exclusivity can be problematic in an early adolescent relationship, these same qualities are part of a strong romantic relationship in late adolescence (Karney et al., 2007).

Where do adolescents get their ideas about what a romantic relationship is like? They learn from observing the nature of their parents' relationships and the endless discussion of the topic with peers. The other important source of information is the media. Research by Ward and Friedman (2006) found that "sexy" primetime and talk shows influence teens to see romance in a stereotypical way, with men as sexual predators and women as sex objects. This was especially likely if the teen used the TV as a companion rather than watching it just for fun, suggesting that those who were more isolated were more influenced by what they saw on TV. In a different, longitudinal study, girls who watched reality shows centered on romance later talked more with peers about sexuality, and boys who watched these shows thought there was an unrealistically high level of sexual activity among teens in the real world (Vandenbosch & Eggermont, 2011). In a slightly older sample, college undergraduates who saw more romance media were more likely to have unrealistic ideas about relationships, including the belief that "I will feel an instant sense of oneness and indivisibility with my romantic soul mate" and "People who have a close relationship can sense each other's needs as if they could read each other's minds" (Holmes, 2007).

JOURNAL ARTICLE 16.2
Adolescent Romantic Relationships

There is a good deal of similarity in the quality of an individual's peer relationships and romantic relationships. Adolescents with high-quality peer relationships are more likely to enjoy a high quality relationship with their romantic partner, and likewise those with maladaptive peer relationships are more likely to have problematic romantic relationships (Karney et al., 2007; Kiesner, Kerr, & Stattin, 2004). Like peers, romantic partners are often similar to the adolescent on a number of characteristics, including age, race, ethnicity, attractiveness, academic interest, level of risk-taking behavior, and plans for attending college (Furman & Collins, 2009; Karney et al., 2007). Boys are more likely to prefer partners who are within a year of their own age, but girls often prefer partners who are slightly older.

The quality of early family relationships is also related to the quality of romantic relationships in adolescence (Karney et al., 2007; Laursen, Furman, & Mooney, 2006). Attachment theory, described in Chapter 7, proposes that the quality of our early relationships forms the basis for an internal working model of close relationships that we carry forward with us into future relationships (Shaver & Mikulincer, 2014). Internal working models continue to influence our significant relationships in late adolescence as we develop committed romantic relationships. In a romantic relationship, we use our partner as a safe haven in times of stress and as a secure base for exploring the environment, and we show evidence of separation distress when away from our partner for a significant period of time (Furman & Collins, 2009; Shaver & Mikulincer, 2014). These are all characteristics of a secure attachment we carry forward from early parent-child relationships. However, in a romantic relationship, each partner becomes an attachment figure for his or her partner. You can see how adolescent and adult attachment styles continue from Ainsworth's types of attachment described for infants in **Active Learning: Romantic Attachment Styles.**

Active Learning

Romantic Attachment Styles

Below are the descriptions used in Hazan and Shaver's (1987) research to describe romantic relationships. You should be able to recognize which of these descriptions fits the descriptions of three of the different infant attachment categories developed by Ainsworth and described in Chapter 7. Review that information, if you need to, then read each description and match it to the correct infant attachment category. Ainsworth's categories are *secure*, *anxious avoidant*, and *anxious ambivalent/resistant*.

Romantic Relationship Descriptions	Attachment Category
I find that others are reluctant to get as close as I would like. I often worry that my partner doesn't really love me or won't want to stay with me. I want to merge completely with another person, and this desire sometimes scares people away.	
I find it relatively easy to get close to others and am comfortable depending on them and having them depend on me. I don't often worry about being abandoned or about someone getting too close to me.	
I am somewhat uncomfortable being close to others; I find it difficult to trust them completely, difficult to allow myself to depend on them. I am nervous when anyone gets too close, and often, love partners want me to be more intimate than I feel comfortable being.	

Answers: Box 1—anxious ambivalent/resistant; Box 2—secure; Box 3—anxious avoidant.

Hazan and Shaver (1987) found that the percentage of adults in their sample who fell into each of these categories was very similar to the percentages found in infant attachment research conducted in the United States. The respondents' perception of the quality of their relationship with their parents (and the parents' relationship with each other) was the best predictor of their romantic attachment style. Hazan and Shaver are careful to say that relationships are complex and that personality variables such as attachment style are not enough, on their own, to explain romantic attachment, but their results point to continuity in the quality of personal relationships. ■

We also see this continuity from experience with parents to romantic relationships among adolescents who have been victims of abuse while growing up (Karney et al., 2007). Physical or sexual abuse during childhood places an adolescent at increased risk of either experiencing or perpetrating violence within an intimate relationship during adolescence. Survivors of more severe sexual abuse are more likely to engage in high-risk sexual behaviors as they get older (Hornor, 2010). This replication of violence in intimate relationships is not inevitable, but adolescents who are at risk in this way may benefit from intervention programs designed to help them develop healthy and happy relationships.

The prevalence of dating violence among teens is difficult to assess because many teens do not report it, and studies often define dating violence in different ways, but according to the Centers for Disease Control and Prevention (2014k), 22% of women and 15% of men recalled experiencing some form of partner violence when they were between the ages of 11 and 17. More than 9% of high school students report being physically hurt by someone they considered a boyfriend or girlfriend in the previous 12 months (CDC, 2014k). The incidence of psychological abuse is even higher, with 30% of heterosexual youth and 22% of homosexual youth between the ages of 12 and 21 reporting they had experienced psychological abuse from an intimate partner in the previous 18 months (National Institute of Justice, 2011). The earlier teens initiate sexual relationships and the more partners they have, the more likely they are to experience intimate partner victimization (Halpern, Spriggs, Martin, & Kupper, 2009).

Adolescents who have experienced dating violence are more likely to suffer depression and anxiety, to engage in unhealthy behaviors such as smoking and drinking, and to think about suicide (CDC, 2014k). They are also more likely to be revictimized in early adulthood (Halpern et al., 2009). On the other hand, adolescents who had high quality relationships and fewer partners had happier relationships in early adulthood. They were better able to resolve conflict and provide and receive support in their adult relationships (Madsen & Collins, 2011).

In conclusion, adolescents' experiences with romantic relationships should not be dismissed as unimportant (Meier & Allen, 2009). What teens learn in their early relationships can have an impact on their ability to form positive and long-lasting relationships in adulthood.

AUDIO LINK 16.2
Dating Violence

Check Your Understanding

1. How are girls' and boys' friendships different in adolescence?
2. Compare crowds and cliques.
3. Why is cyberbullying a particularly hurtful type of bullying?
4. How do friendships and family relationships influence the course of adolescents' romantic relationships?

Beyond Parents and Peers: Important Nonparental Adults

16.5

What role do nonparental adults play in adolescents' lives?

Research on adolescents' social relationships has largely focused on relationships with parents and peers. However, if we simply ask adolescents to name the people who are important to them, they spontaneously include a wide range of relatives and nonrelated adults that go beyond parents and peers (Chang, Greenberger, Chen, Heckhausen, & Farruggia, 2010; Farruggia, Bullen, & Davidson, 2013; Rishel et al., 2007).

These nonparental adults are about equally likely to be relatives or nonrelatives (Chang et al., 2010; Dubois & Silverthorn, 2005; Farruggia et al., 2013). When both parents and adolescents were asked to report on the strength of the adolescent's relationship with a number of people considered important in the adolescent's life, parents tended to underestimate the influence of extended family members but to overestimate the influence of unrelated adults who knew the adolescent in a formal or professional capacity, such as coaches, teachers, or clergy. Although people in these formal roles are devoted to working with young people, their time is often spread across many individuals, so their impact on any single adolescent may be diluted and the role they play is more limited than the role that a relative might play. An adolescent may seek out the help of a teacher for a school-related problem but wouldn't be as likely to go to that person for help with a personal issue or general concerns (Beam, Chen, & Greenberger, 2002).

Girls are more likely than boys to report having a very important adult in their lives and experiencing greater enjoyment and psychological intimacy in the relationship (Rishel et al., 2007). Although it is most likely the adult will be the same gender as the adolescent, boys have more cross-gender relationships than girls.

Functions Filled by Nonparental Adults

Adolescents' relationships with nonparental adults fill a number of functional roles. They are important sources of social support when the adolescent is trying to cope with a stressful experience (Munsch & Blyth, 1993), as well as a support for educational achievement (Farruggia et al., 2013), personal development, and efforts to try new things (Chen, Greenberger, Farruggia, Bush, & Dong, 2003). Nonparental adults are seen as role models, companions, teachers, guides, and confidants (Chen et al., 2003; Munsch & Blyth, 1993), and occasionally they are sources of more tangible support, such as financial assistance (Rhodes, Ebert, & Fischer, 1992).

Do nonparental adults in an adolescent's life simply provide more of the same functions parents provide, or are these relationships qualitatively different from those with parents? Nancy Darling and her colleagues have maintained that unrelated adults provide a unique context for development because they represent an adult point of view but are less judgmental than parents (Darling, Hamilton, & Shaver, 2003). Beam et al. (2002) found that a teen's relationship with a nonparental adult was not based on compensating for problems the teen was having with a parent. It appears these relationships do not substitute for parent-teen relationships but rather become a unique source of support.

VIDEO LINK 16.5
Role Models

Impact of Nonparental Adults

A relationship with a nonparental adult is associated with a number of positive outcomes for an adolescent, whether that relationship develops from a formal program or develops naturally. A **natural mentor** is a nonparental adult who provides support and guidance to a young person. Having a natural mentor has been associated with achieving higher levels of educational attainment for at-risk African American students (Hurd, Sánchez, Zimmerman, & Caldwell, 2012), lower levels of anxiety and depression among adolescent mothers (Hurd & Zimmerman, 2010), lower levels of reported use of marijuana and nonviolent delinquency, and higher levels of attachment to school (Zimmerman, Bingenheimer, & Notaro, 2002). This relationship may be so influential because it has both a direct and an indirect effect. The natural mentor directly reduces the risk of problem behavior by monitoring and sanctioning the behavior of the adolescent and also has an indirect effect because his or her support helps the adolescent resist peer pressure to engage in negative behaviors.

We often think about the importance of nonparental adult mentors for teens who have few other sources of support, but teens who already have many resources are more likely

Natural mentor A nonparental adult who provides support and guidance to a young person.

to have a mentor than those without such resources. When those with few resources do develop a mentoring relationship with an adult, they are more likely to reap more benefits than other teens, particularly if that mentor is a teacher (Erickson, McDonald, & Elder, 2009). **Active Learning: Relationships With Nonparental Adults** gives you an opportunity to think about the people who have filled the role of natural mentor in your life and the impact they have had on your development.

Mentoring. Mentors help many teens attain higher levels of education achievement and reduce the risk of negative behaviors. Would you make a good mentor for a teen? ■

Active Learning

Relationships With Nonparental Adults

Think about the relationships, other than with your parents and friends, that were important to you while you were a teenager. Was someone particularly influential, perhaps someone you would call a natural mentor? Did different people fill this role when you were in early, middle, and late adolescence, or did a single relationship continue throughout adolescence? What did the person or persons do that made this relationship an important one for you? Were these the same types of benefits you got from your parents and/or friends, or were they unique functions you did not find in other relationships? ■

There also are more than 3 million children and teens in the United States who are in formal mentoring relationships (MENTOR, 2012). In this case, a **mentor** is a constructed relationship in which a nonparental adult provides a range of functions to a young person. These relationships are established through programs in schools or organizations such as Boys and Girls Clubs or Big Brothers Big Sisters programs. The characteristics of a successful mentoring relationship sound very similar to those that make for the most positive parent-child relationship: closeness and warmth, consistency, and structure. Do you see the similarity to the description of authoritative parenting in Chapter 10? Mentoring relationships that are focused on and sensitive to the child's developmental needs and interests and that include a commitment of at least a year are most likely to result in positive outcomes (Grossman, Chan, Schwartz, & Rhodes, 2012; Rhodes & DuBois, 2006). When mentors also interact with the child's parents or peers, the positive effects increase. However, when relationships fall short on these factors, they are often linked with a *decrease* in well-being for the child or teen, so it is important for mentors to fully understand the nature of their commitment.

As appealing as mentor programs sound, the research has shown only small effects in many cases (Rhodes & DuBois, 2006). In a review of the effectiveness of 55 formal mentoring programs, in 10% of the programs the youth were worse off after participation, in one third there was no impact either positive or negative, and in the remainder there was a benefit for the youth, although it was usually small (DuBois, 2007). Mentoring is most effective when it includes intensive and ongoing training and support for mentors, interaction with the teen's parents, and clear guidelines for the duration of the relationship and how often the mentor and protégé will meet (DuBois, Holloway, Valentine, & Cooper, 2002).

Mentor A constructed relationship in which a nonparental adult provides a range of functions to a young person.

1. What role do nonparental adults play in an adolescent's life?
2. In what ways are relationships with mentors similar to and different from relationships with parents?
3. What characteristics help a formal mentoring program be successful?

16.6

What do adolescents do when they are not in school?

The Daily Lives of Adolescents

Adolescents spend time each day at school, with family and friends and perhaps working at a paid job, but the majority also have some discretionary time. In this section we describe the daily lives of adolescents in several different cultures.

Adolescent activities vary from one culture to another and reflect specific cultural values, as Table 16.4 shows. In Taiwan, academics outside school make up a relatively large portion of the day, and many activities for Taiwanese children are chosen and/ or directed by adults (Newman et al., 2007). In comparison, American teens are more likely to choose their own activities, and the one they choose more than teens in most other cultures is sports.

In general, American youth do less homework and have more free time. Larson (2004) describes three ways in which they use this free time: (1) playing or "hanging out" with others in unstructured activities; (2) engaging in structured activities, such as sports, drama or musical productions, or interest-based clubs; and (3) using media, such as television, video games, and computers. Try **Active Learning: The Daily Life of a Teen** to see how an adolescent you know uses his or her time and how much of that is discretionary leisure time.

TABLE 16.4   Average daily time use of adolescents

Activity	Nonindustrial, unschooled populations	Postindustrial, schooled populations		
		United States	Europe	East Asia
Household labor	5–9 hours	20–40 minutes	20–40 minutes	10–20 minutes
Paid labor	0.5–8 hours	40–60 minutes	10–20 minutes	0–10 minutes
Schoolwork	–	3.0–4.5 hours	4.0–5.5 hours	5.5–7.5 hours
Total work time	6–9 hours	4–6 hours	4.5–6.5 hours	6–8 hours
TV viewing	Insufficient data	1.5–2.5 hours	1.5–2.5 hours	1.5–2.5 hours
Talking	Insufficient data	2–3 hours	Insufficient data	45–60 minutes
Sports	Insufficient data	30–60 minutes	20–80 minutes	0–20 minutes
Structured voluntary activities	Insufficient data	10–20 minutes	10–20 minutes	0–10 minutes
Total free time	4–7 hours	6.5–8 hours	5.5–7.5 hours	4.0–5.5 hours

SOURCE: Larson (2004). © 2004 The Association for Psychological Science.

NOTE. The estimates in the table are averaged across a 7-day week. Time spent in maintenance activities like eating, personal care, and sleeping is not included. The data for nonindustrial, unschooled populations come primarily from rural peasant populations in developing countries (Larson, 2004, p. 146).

Active Learning

The Daily Life of a Teen

Ask a teenager to keep a journal reporting what she is doing every hour for 2 days (one school day and one weekend day). You might want to give her two sheets of paper divided into the hours of the day so she can note when she wakes up and goes to sleep (so you'll know how much time she was awake) and with one block of space for each hour. If this is not possible, think back to a typical day when you were in high school and describe for each hour what you were likely to be doing.

In either case, for each hour, decide whether you would classify the activity as school, paid work, or leisure time. Divide the number of leisure hours by the total number of waking hours to find the percentage that was leisure time.

For example, the teen below has a total of 18 hours in her day. She has 7 hours of leisure time, including sports, hanging out, dinner, and TV time. Therefore, seven eighteenths or .39 (almost 40%) of her day was spent in leisure activity.

8 a.m.	9 a.m.	10 a.m.	11 a.m.	12 p.m.	1 p.m.	2 p.m.	3 p.m.	4 p.m.
school	school	school	school	school	school	hanging out with friends	sports	sports

5 p.m.	6 p.m.	7 p.m.	8 p.m.	9 p.m.	10 p.m.	11 p.m.	12 a.m.	1 a.m.
homework	dinner with family	homework	TV with family	TV	homework	TV/Facebook/ phone	homework	sleep

Next try to categorize each leisure hour as one of the following: media use, structured activities like sports or school clubs, "hanging out" with friends, or interacting with family. Calculate the percentage of time spent on each type of activity by totaling the number of hours you decided are spent in leisure activities and dividing the number of hours in each type of leisure activity by the total number of hours. For example, if you decide the teen spent 6 hours in leisure activities and 2 of those hours were spent "hanging out," divide 2 hours (time spent hanging out) by 6 hours (the total leisure time) to get 33% or one third of the teen's leisure time. The teen shown in the chart above spent 3 hours watching TV; that is .43 or slightly more than 40% of her leisure time.

U.S. teens have been found to spend 40% to 50% of their day in leisure activities, compared with 25% to 35% for East Asians and 35% to 45% for Europeans (Larson, 2004). The particular type of activity that occurs during these leisure hours has an effect on teens' development, as we see later in this chapter. ∎

Unstructured Time

Parents of teens are especially concerned about risky or negative behaviors that can result from unsupervised time spent with peers. During such time, the likelihood of criminal behavior, teen sexuality, and drug and alcohol use increases (Mahoney, Stattin, & Lord, 2004). Especially when teens have delinquent friends, the more free time they have to hang out with them, the more likely they are to take part in criminal behavior (Svensson & Oberwittler, 2010).

However, even those who argue for the value of structured activities acknowledge that children and teens need some unstructured time. Just as younger children need free time to play, adolescents need time to just "hang out" with peers. This allows them to develop an identity separate from their parents and to learn how to manage themselves with

© Adrian Sherratt/Alamy

Hanging out at the mall. Children and teens need some unstructured time to spend in activities that they choose. Although too much unsupervised time is associated with problem behaviors, some time to "hang out" and enjoy being with friends is a positive thing for young people. ■

their peers, and that often includes some experimentation with somewhat risky behaviors. The trick is to provide teens with an appropriate balance of freedom along with structured time so they develop a sense of self-direction while minimizing risk (Osgood, Anderson, & Shaffer, 2005). As teens get older, parents increasingly allow them to spend time away from home in unstructured time with peers (Osgood et al., 2005).

Structured Time

In Chapter 15, we looked at whether children and adolescents were overscheduled with structured activities and found that for the majority this is not the case. Adolescents usually decide for themselves the number and types of activities they participate in and benefit in a number of ways from their participation. However, for structured activities to promote healthy development, they must be carefully planned. Programs should be scheduled when the teens would normally be hanging out with friends without adult supervision, usually directly after the school day (between 3 p.m. and 6 p.m.) when most problematic teen behavior would otherwise occur (Osgood et al., 2005).

Many teens take part in paid employment of some kind, whether informal work for neighbors or friends or more formal employment. Unless the work is tied to the development of school-related skills, evidence that employment promotes positive development for teenagers is mixed. Some research shows that teens who work have higher earnings 4 years after high school but are less likely to succeed in higher education (Casey, Ripke, & Huston, 2005). Other research found that teens who worked more than 20 hours per week were more likely to decrease their engagement with school and to exhibit problem behaviors (Monahan, Lee, & Steinberg, 2011). Teens who worked fewer than 20 hours did not differ academically or socially from those who did not work.

For teens from low-income families, working may be necessary to help their family. Their added income also may help them pay for extra educational expenses, such as field trips, that add to their academic interest and achievement (Lee & Staff, 2007). For teens from urban, low-income families, work in adult-type jobs after age 16 was related to a lower high school dropout rate, but the opposite effect was found for teens under age 16. However, younger teens who took jobs such as mowing lawns and babysitting were *less* likely to drop out than those the same age who had more adult-type jobs (Entwisle, Alexander, & Olson, 2005).

Media Use

Media consumption increases dramatically as children move into early adolescence, to an average of almost 9 hours a day, or 12 hours a day if we take multitasking into account (Rideout et al., 2010). There are large racial and ethnic differences in the use of electronic media. In research on 8- to 18-year-olds, Blacks and

Adolescent employment. Most teens work to have extra money. What are the benefits and the drawbacks of teen employment? ■

Hispanic children and teens spent 50% more time per day (12.5 hours) than Whites did (8 hours) using media (Rideout et al., 2010). This compares to 1 hour and 50 minutes of physical activity per day for younger teens and 1 hour and 34 minutes for older teens, and under 40 minutes of reading print media (Rideout et al., 2010). The use of print media peaks at age 10 and decreases as children move through adolescence, declining from 46 to 33 minutes of reading per day, while the use of music/audio increases steadily. A survey by the National Endowment for the Arts (2007) showed that in all age groups and at all levels of education, the ability to read well fell significantly between 1992 and 2003 as increasing amounts of time were spent on electronic media. This is hardly surprising given that reading itself promotes proficiency. The more we read, the better we become at reading.

Television viewing peaks in early adolescence and decreases as adolescents get older. In almost half of homes the television is always on and rules set by parents for media use tend to monitor content, not amount of time (Rideout et al., 2010). In those families that do have rules about media use, children use media an average of almost 3 fewer hours per day. A reduction of just 1 hour per day is the equivalent of 365 hours in 1 year, or more than 2 full weeks, so it is not an inconsequential amount of time to shift to other activities. Although TV is still the most frequently used medium (Nielsen, 2014), media use is constantly changing as new technologies develop. Although the statistics give a clear impression of extensive media use by children and teens, averages hide the fact that significant numbers of children use media only infrequently. For example, 21% of those surveyed by the Kaiser Family Foundation reported watching no TV on an average day (Rideout et al., 2010). We should not lose sight of the variability within any group of adolescents.

T/F #10
Teens spend more time watching TV content than using any other kind of media. *True*

Communication

Teens are avid users of electronic media for communication and the forms of communication are increasing exponentially. Subrahmanyam and Greenfield's (2008) most current description of electronic media used by youth is found in Table 16.5 but you can add at the bottom of the list any newer technologies you are using that were developed after this list was made.

In 2011, teens between ages 13 and 17 sent an average of 3,364 text messages per month, the highest rate for any age group (Nielsen, 2011). They talked on the phone less than other age groups (515 minutes per month), but almost 80% used social networks

TABLE 16.5   Forms of electronic communication

Communication form	Electronic hardware that supports it	Functions enabled
E-mail	Computers, cell phones, personal digital assistants (PDAs)	Write, store, send, and receive asynchronous messages electronically; can include attachments of Word documents, pictures, audio, and other multimedia files
Instant messaging	Computers, cell phones, PDAs	Allows for the synchronous exchange of private messages with another user; messages primarily are in text but can include attachments of Word documents, pictures, audio, and other multimedia files
Text messaging	Cell phones, PDAs	Short text messages sent using cell phones and wireless handheld devices
Chat rooms	Computers	Synchronous conversations with more than one user that primarily involve text; can be either public or private
Bulletin boards	Computers	Online public spaces, typically centered on a topic (such as health, illnesses, religion), where people can post and read messages; many require registration, but only screen names are visible (such as www.collegeconfidential.com)
Blogs	Computers	Websites where entries are typically displayed in reverse chronological order (such as www.livejournal.com); entries can be either public or private only for users authorized by the blog owner/author
Social networking utilities	Computers	Online utilities that allow users to create profiles (public or private) and form a network of friends; allow users to interact with their friends via public and private means (such as messages, instant messaging); also allow for the posting of user-generated content such as photos and videos (such as Facebook)
Video sharing	Computers, cell phones, cameras with wireless	Allows users to upload, view, and share video clips (such as YouTube)
Photo sharing	Computers, cell phones, cameras with wireless	Allows users to upload, view, and share photos (such as Instagram); users can allow either public or private access
Massively multiplayer online games (MMOGs)	Computers	Online games that can be played by large numbers of players simultaneously; the most popular type are the massively multiplayer online role-playing games (MMORPGs) such as World of Warcraft
Virtual worlds	Computers	Online simulated 3-D environments inhabited by players who interact with each other via avatars (such as Teen Second Life)
You can add other types of electronic technologies not included in the table here:		

This table summarizes common forms of electronic communication used by large numbers of children and adolescents. Newer technologies will continue to be added to this list as they develop.

SOURCE: Subrahmanyam & Greenfield (2008), p. 121. From *The Future of Children,* a collaboration of the Woodrow Wilson School of Public and International Affairs at Princeton University and the Brookings Institution.

or blogs (Nielsen, 2011). One gender difference that has been found is that girls are more likely than boys to use social and other media to maintain existing friendships, while boys are more likely to use them for flirting and for making new friends (Lenhart & Madden, 2007). Overall, teens report an enhanced sense of well-being as a result of maintaining friendships in this way (Valkenburg & Peter, 2007). Over half of teens in the United States use social media more than once a day, and 22% log on to a social media site such as Facebook more than 10 times a day. Social media not only make it easy to stay in touch with friends and family, but also promote community involvement, creativity and growth of ideas, connections with new people from diverse backgrounds, and identity development (O'Keeffe, Clarke-Pearson, & Council on Communications and Media, 2011). Students and schools have been using social media for group projects and to reinforce in-class learning. Social networking sites are also used to develop groups of people with common interests who may help each other. One study found that teens with cancer often used their websites to make contact with others who have cancer and to share information about their disease (Suzuki & Beale, 2006). Teens have also been found to use online peer advice bulletin boards to share information about general and sexual health and development. In this anonymous setting, they often feel freer to ask questions they may be too embarrassed to ask their parents or even their friends (Suzuki & Calzo, 2004).

There are also risks for teens using social media, such as the cyberbullying we discussed earlier. Teens can also put themselves at risk by their own online behavior. About 20% of teens report that they have exchanged nude or seminude pictures or videos of themselves, an activity known as **sexting**. Although the teen may think of this as harmless flirtation, the practice is illegal and can lead to child pornography charges or school suspension (O'Keeffe et al., 2011). In addition, the individual loses control of the image so it can be widely distributed without their permission or even their knowledge.

Sexting Sending nude or seminude pictures of oneself online.

Another risk of online communication is the presence of online predators. A study of online predators determined that most are adult men who create relationships with teenagers by developing trust over a long period of time (Wolak, Finkelhor, Mitchell, & Ybarra, 2008). Teens who eventually meet with the adult in person often believe they are having a romantic, sexual relationship with someone who cares for them. Most of the crimes that result from these contacts are statutory rapes rather than forced rapes, meaning the adult has sex with someone who is legally too young to be able to give consent. Clearly teens need to be better educated about the potential dangers of relationships with adults that are created through electronic communications, but it is often difficult for parents to know how to monitor the safety of their teen's interactions online, especially when teens are more familiar with the online landscape than they are.

Media and Self-Concept

Although media can have positive effects on self-concept, it also can limit the options adolescents see for their lives. Movies, TV shows, and other entertainments show the same types of characters with the same types of goals over and over again. As teens watch hours of these programs, do they define themselves according to these few possibilities as well?

Harrison (2006) argued that a positive self-concept relies to some extent on **self-complexity**—that is, the number of different ways in which an individual defines herself. For example, an individual with high self-complexity sees herself as someone who is an attractive person, a fairly good athlete, an excellent student, and a good friend. Someone with low self-complexity might tie her identity to her appearance and little else. In research with a largely nonminority sample of teens, Harrison found that the more television teens watched, the less complex their self-image was (see Figure 16.3). These limitations can cause trouble for teens when they experience stressful situations. For example, a boy whose identity is limited to being "a loving boyfriend" may become distraught when his girlfriend breaks up with him. Another boy with a more complex identity who is also very proud of his achievements in academics may be able to turn to this aspect of himself when faced with a breakup with his girlfriend.

Self-complexity The number of different ways in which an individual defines himself or herself.

The impact of the media on the self-concept of minority youngsters has received less attention. Television and movies, whose goal is to attract the most viewers, have tended

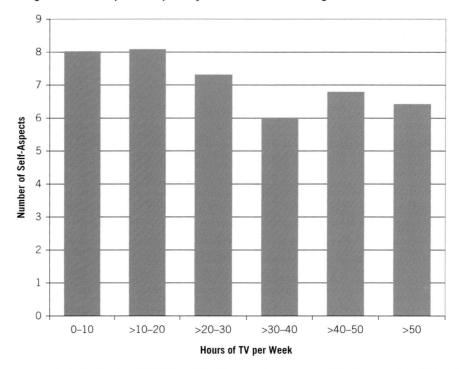

FIGURE 16.3 TV viewing and self-complexity

Average number of unique self-aspects by 10-hour television viewing increments for adolescents

Research conducted by Harrison (2006) found that the more hours per week that teens watched television, the less complex their self-images. This may reflect the stereotypical portrayal of characters and plots in many television shows.

SOURCE: Harrison (2006). © 2006 International Communication Association.

to portray White, non-Latino characters more often than minorities. When minorities are presented in the media, they are often shown in a negative light. For example, African American characters are often characterized by criminality, lack of intelligence, laziness, or inappropriate behavior (Tyree, 2011; Ward, 2004). Latino characters are 4 times as likely as others to be represented as domestic workers. They, too, are associated with crime and stereotypes, such as having a "hot temper" (Rivadeneyra, Ward, & Gordon, 2007). These portrayals are likely to affect minority youth, who are greater consumers of media than nonminorities (Rivadeneyra et al., 2007; Ward, 2004).

Research has confirmed this relationship, but the relationship is complex. The more media Latino teens viewed, the lower their social and body self-esteem was, but this relationship was strongest for women and for those who more closely identified with Latino culture (Rivadeneyra, Ward, & Gordon, 2007). For African American teens, only two types of programming, sports and music videos, were related to lower self-esteem. In addition, those who identified with Black characters on TV tended to have higher self-esteem, while those who identified with White characters had lower self-esteem. Finally, these relationships held only for those who reported themselves to be less religious. It appears that teens' background, the kind of programming they watch, and their reactions all play a role in the way viewing is related to self-concept for African American adolescents (Ward, 2004).

The portrayal of homosexual characters in the media is moving through the same stages of acceptance that minority characters have moved through in the past (Raley & Lucas, 2006). A recent report from the Gay and Lesbian Alliance Against Defamation (GLAAD) found that 4.4% of the characters scheduled to appear in prime-time network drama and comedies during the 2012–2013 season were gay, lesbian, bisexual, or trans-gendered (Moore, 2012). This represents an increase from 2.9% in the 2011–2012 television season.

A number of years ago, Clark (1969) proposed a way to assess the representation of minorities on television. Portrayals move from nonrepresentation (the group is excluded) to ridicule (the group is portrayed but primarily as objects of derisive humor), to regulation (the group is portrayed in limited but socially acceptable roles), to respect (the group is shown in both positive and negative roles). In an analysis of the portrayal of homosexual characters in television programming in 2006, Raley and Lucas concluded that TV shows had moved through Clark's first stage, were in the second (with much of the ridicule written for the gay characters themselves to say), and were moving into the third and even the fourth stage of portrayal. As the GLAAD report indicates, the number of portrayals continues to increase, and progress toward the fourth stage of portrayal continues. This is particularly important to adolescent viewers who may be dealing with gender identity issues but who lack real life role models and turn to the media for information about how to conduct themselves.

Media Literacy

Media literacy is the ability to understand the underlying purposes and messages of the media you use. Teaching media literacy to teens can help them become more savvy consumers of media so they can sort out what the producers are trying to do and decide for themselves whether they will accept it. Although even a single lesson can be effective, training that includes actual production of media helps teens learn how the messages are created and sent through media (Banerjee & Greene, 2007). In Chapter 14, you learned about efforts to help young teens understand that smoking in movies is really a form of advertising. Smoking-related media education has been successful at increasing reflective thinking about tobacco use and reducing susceptibility to smoking (Brown & Bobkowski, 2011; Pinkleton, Austin, Cohen, Miller, & Fitzgerald, 2007; Primack, Gold, Land, & Fine, 2006).

Another successful media education program targeted the influence of media on teen sexuality. Teens presented five lessons to their peers on topics such as "Using sex to sell." Compared to a control group, teens who took part in the program were more likely to report that "sexual depictions in the media are inaccurate and glamorized" (Pinkleton, Austin, Chen, & Cohen, 2012, p. 469). Some additional resources concerning media literacy include websites from The American Academy of Pediatrics' Safety Net and The Center for Media Literacy.

Media literacy The skills to understand the underlying purposes and messages of media.

> ### Check Your Understanding
> 1. How do U.S. teens spend most of their free time?
> 2. What role does "hanging out" in unstructured time play in teens' lives?
> 3. How are adolescents influenced by the media they watch?
> 4. What is media literacy?

Emerging adulthood A transition time between adolescence and adulthood, from 18–25 years of age.

Emerging Adulthood

16.7

What is emerging adulthood and how does it differ from adolescence?

If you are a college student between 17 and 22, do you think of yourself as an adolescent or an adult? On what basis did you make that decision? You can probably see that you have some things in common with adolescents, especially if you are not supporting yourself financially, and some things in common with adults, especially if you live away from your family. In 2000, Jeffrey Arnett proposed a new stage of development that links adolescence and adulthood. He called this period from age 18 through 25 **emerging adulthood**. Some of the traditional markers that a young person had moved into adulthood were marriage, childrearing, and career. Fifty years ago these all generally occurred when people were in their early 20s. However, today they occur at later ages, leaving the late teens and early 20s as a time when many young people still feel in-between adolescence and adulthood. They are focused more on a continued exploration of identity, establishing independence, and experimentation with possibilities for their lives (Lisha et al., 2014).

Although a thorough description of this stage is outside the scope of this book, keep in mind that the transition from adolescence to adulthood does not necessarily occur at a specific age. The definition of adulthood is subjective, and achieving it is an ongoing process.

> **Check Your Understanding**
>
> 1. What is Arnett's concept of emerging adulthood?
> 2. What are the traditional markers of arrival at adulthood?

Conclusion

Adolescence is a time for exploration of identity. As teens become more autonomous from their parents, they experiment with different aspects of who they are and who they will become. Families form the foundation for this development, but peers become central to teens' lives in potentially positive or negative ways. Teens also begin to find romantic partners. They explore activities both inside and outside school, and these may lead to supportive relationships with adults other than parents. As teens take on more responsibility for themselves, most find some form of paid employment, which may influence their future interests and careers. Finally, most teens are heavy users of media, which can also shape their self-concept. It is important that they acquire media literacy to separate fact from fantasy.

Although this is the end of our exploration of development from infancy through adolescence, we know that change, growth, and development continue beyond adolescence through the period of emerging adulthood, but also throughout life. A solid foundation in childhood and adolescence prepares us for a life full of challenges and rewards.

Chapter Summary

16.1 How does identity develop in adolescence?

In his stage of **identity versus role confusion,** Erikson described the search for identity as the central issue of adolescent development. Adolescents develop a differentiated self that includes their characteristics at various times and in different situations. Marcia proposed two processes necessary to form an identity: exploring the possibilities and making a commitment. The four identity statuses he identified are **identity foreclosure, identity diffusion, identity moratorium,** and **identity achievement.** Adolescents with a strong sense of ethnic identity are better able to resist problem behaviors and more likely to have higher self-esteem. Minority teens benefit when parents use **racial socialization** to instill racial pride and help prepare them to deal with discrimination.

16.2 How do emotions develop in adolescence?

Teens tend to experience more extreme emotions than adults, but self-regulation improves in later adolescence.

Empathy is associated with a secure attachment to parents and underlies development of prosocial behavior. Lack of empathy can contribute to antisocial and delinquent behavior. The incidence of depression increases in adolescence and girls have a higher rate than boys. While girls are more likely to attempt suicide, boys are more likely to die from suicide, which is the third leading cause of death in adolescence.

16.3 How do adolescents' relationships with their parents change?

Although adolescents become more autonomous, parents need to balance autonomy granting with maintaining connectedness to the adolescents. In most cases, parent-adolescent conflict involves everyday, mundane issues like homework and chores. Some conflict with parents is not usually damaging to the relationship and may even improve it in the long run. Divorce generally has negative effects for teens except when conflict between parents subsides as a result.

16.4 What types of peer relationships do adolescents have?

Adolescents spend an increasing amount of time with peers, and relationships become reciprocal and more intimate, especially for girls. Adolescents become more resistant to peer pressure as they get older. Their ideas about the nature of romantic relationships are influenced by family, friends, and the media. The quality of romantic relationships usually is similar to the quality of the adolescents' relationships with parents and friends. Bullying is a threat to the well-being of a number of children and adolescents, and **cyberbullying** makes use of electronic and social media. Schools are safe environments for most adolescents.

16.5 What role do nonparental adults play in adolescents' lives?

Mentors can be naturally occurring relationships or ones that are created as a part of a formal mentoring program. Having a mentor can benefit adolescent development and even act as a protective factor for adolescents who are at risk because these relationships are qualitatively different from other relationships. However, research has failed to find evidence of a strong positive effect of formal mentoring programs. The most effective programs depend on long-term commitment of the mentor.

16.6 What do adolescents do when they are not in school?

In the United States, teens have unstructured time, participate in structured activities such as sports or the arts, and use media. Too much unsupervised time may lead to problem behaviors, but some amount of autonomy is necessary for development of identity. U.S. teens use media for an average of almost 9 hours per day. Social networking can enhance friendships and provide support. Media can constrict **self-complexity** for teens, and minority children may be hurt by stereotypes shown in the media. **Media literacy** can help teens understand how the media are trying to manipulate their thinking in subtle ways.

16.7 What is emerging adulthood and how does it differ from adolescence?

As adult responsibilities are put off to older ages, older adolescents and young adults age 18 to 25 continue to develop their identity prior to making the long-term commitments associated with adult responsibilities. This age has been referred to as **emerging adulthood**.

Key Terms

Cliques   557

Crowds   557

Cyberbullying   561

Delinquency   547

Discrimination   545

Emerging adulthood   575

Ideal self   543

Identity achievement   542

Identity diffusion   542

Identity foreclosure   542

Identity moratorium   542

Identity versus role confusion   541

Media literacy   575

Mentor   567

Natural mentor   566

Negative identity   541

Peer pressure   559

Prejudices   545

Racial socialization   546

Racism   545

Self-complexity   573

Sexting   573

Stereotypes   545

$ SAGE edge™

Sharpen your skills with SAGE edge at edge.sagepub.com/levinechrono

SAGE edge for Students provides a personalized approach to help you accomplish your coursework goals in an easy-to-use learning environment.

Go to edge.sagepub.com/levinechrono for additional exercises and video resources. Select Chapter 16, Social and Emotional Development in Adolescence, for chapter-specific activities. All of the Video Links listed in the margins of this chapter are accessible via this site.

Glossary

Ability grouping   An educational approach that places students of similar ability in learning groups so they can be taught at a level that is most appropriate for their level of understanding.

Abuse   Deliberate and intentional words and actions that cause harm or potential harm to a child; can involve physical, sexual, or psychological abuse.

Accelerated program   A type of program that allows gifted students to move through the standard curriculum more quickly than is typical.

Acceptance/responsiveness   A dimension of parenting that measures the amount of warmth and affection in the parent-child relationship.

Accommodation   Changing mental schemas so they fit new experiences.

Active gene-environment interaction   A situation in which a child's genetic endowment becomes a driving force to seek out experiences that fit her genetic endowments.

Active labor   The second phase in the first stage of labor in which contractions become longer, stronger, and more frequent and the cervix dilates to 4 centimeters.

Adaptive functioning   A person's ability to function independently.

Adolescent growth spurt   The period of rapid increase in height and weight that occurs in early adolescence.

Adrenarche   The increase in adrenal androgen production that occurs early in the pubertal sequence and affects brain development.

Amniocentesis   A test to look for genetic abnormalities prenatally, in which a physician uses a long, thin needle to extract amniotic fluid, which is then tested.

Amnion   The inner fetal membrane that surrounds the fetus and is filled with amniotic fluid.

Anal stage   Freud's second stage, in which toddlers' sexual energy is focused on the anus.

Analytical intelligence   The type of intelligence that is the one closest to *g* or general intelligence and the one prized highly in most schools.

Androgyny   The idea that both sexes can have characteristics that are traditionally considered masculine and traditionally considered feminine.

Animism   Giving human characteristics, such as thought and intention, to inanimate or natural things.

Anorexia nervosa   A condition in which individuals become obsessed with their weight and intentionally restrict food intake to a point that it may become life threatening.

A-not-B error   In a test of object permanence, an infant searches for an object hidden under cloth A, but continues to look under cloth A when it is moved under cloth B.

Antisocial behavior   Actions that hurt other people, physically or emotionally.

Anxiety   A vague fear about events that may or may not occur.

Anxiety disorder   A level of anxiety that is severe, lasts a long time, and interferes with normal functioning.

Anxious ambivalent/resistant attachment   An attachment classification in which the infant is reluctant to move away from his mother to explore and is very distressed when she leaves, but when she returns, he approaches her but also angrily resists her attempt to pick him up.

Anxious avoidant attachment   An attachment classification in which the infant is not distressed when his mother leaves, is as comfortable with the stranger as with his mother, and does not rush to greet his mother when she returns.

Apgar Scale   An assessment of a newborn's overall condition at 1 minute and 5 minutes after birth that is based on the newborn's activity level, pulse, grimace, appearance, and respiration.

Approximate number system (ANS)   An intuitive sense of quantity that appears to be innate.

Archival records   Data collected at an earlier date that are used for research purposes.

Assimilation   Fitting new experiences into existing mental schemas.

Associative play   Sharing toys and interacting with peers, but without a common goal.

Asthma   The most common chronic illness in childhood, in which a child's airways constrict, making it difficult to breathe.

Attachment   An emotional bond to a particular person.

Attachment in the making   The stage from 6 weeks to 6–8 months in which infants develop stranger anxiety, differentiating those they know from those they don't.

Attention deficit/hyperactivity disorder (ADHD)   A persistent pattern of inattention and/or hyperactivity-impulsivity that begins in childhood and interferes with functioning or development.

Authentic assessment   A testing procedure that focuses on the process used in solving complex, real-life problems rather than the product that results from the process.

Authoritarian parents   Parents who combine high levels of control and low levels of warmth, and who expect compliance from the child.

Authoritative parents   Parents who combine high levels of control with a good deal of warmth and encouragement, together with reasonable expectations and explanation of the parents' rules.

Autism spectrum disorder (ASD)   A disorder characterized by pervasive impairment in social communication and interaction and by restricted or repetitive behaviors, interests, or activities. Severity is classified by how much support the individual needs to function effectively.

Autobiographical memory   A coherent set of memories about one's life.

Automaticity   The process by which skills become so well practiced that you can do them without much conscious thought.

Autonomous morality   When children are aware of the rules and realize that they must adhere to them to maintain their interaction with others rather than because an adult has told them what to do.

Average children   Children who receive a number of nominations for "like most" and "like least" that is close to the median in the peer group on a sociometric measure.

Axon   The part of a nerve cell that conducts impulses away from the cell body.

Balanced reading approach   An approach to teaching reading that combines elements of the whole language approach (which emphasizes comprehension and meaning) with elements of the phonics approach (which emphasizes decoding of words).

Behavioral genetics   Research to determine the degree of genetic basis for a behavior, trait, or ability.

Behavioral genomics   The study of the interaction of genes and behavior.

Behaviorism   The theory developed by John B. Watson that focuses on environmental control of observable behavior.

Blastocyst   A hollow ball of cells that consists of the inner cell mass, which becomes the embryo, and an outer ring of cells, which becomes the placenta and chorion.

Body awareness   Conscious knowledge of one's own body parts and movements.

Body image   How a person subjectively sees and feels about his or her physical characteristics.

Body mass index (BMI)   A measure of body fat calculated as a ratio of weight to height.

Broca's area   The part of the brain active in the physical production of speech.

Bulimia   An eating disorder characterized by eating binges, followed by purging (for example, self-induced vomiting or the excessive use of laxatives) to get rid of the food.

Bullying   Repeated exposure to negative actions on the part of one or more other students; includes physical bullying, verbal bullying, and emotional bullying.

Canalization   The degree to which the expression of a gene is influenced by the environment.

Case study   An in-depth study of a single individual or small group of individuals, which uses multiple methods of study.

Centration   Focusing on only one aspect of a situation.

Cephalocaudal   Physical development that proceeds from the head downward through the body.

Cephalocaudal development   A principle whereby development proceeds from the head region down through the body.

Cerebral palsy   A chronic condition that appears early in development and primarily involves problems with body movement and muscle coordination.

Checklist   A prepared list of behaviors, characteristics, or judgments used by observers to assess a child's development.

Child sexual abuse   Any interaction between a child and an adult (or another child) in which the child is used for the sexual stimulation of the perpetrator or an observer.

Child-directed speech   Speech tailored to fit the sensory and cognitive capabilities of infants and children so it holds their attention; includes speaking in a higher pitch with exaggerated intonation and a singsong rhythm and using a simplified vocabulary.

Childhood-onset fluency disorder or stuttering   Difficulty with fluency and time patterning of speech.

Chorion   The outer fetal membrane that surrounds the fetus and gives rise to the placenta.

Chorionic villus sampling (CVS)   A test to look for genetic abnormalities prenatally, in which a small tube is inserted either through the vagina and cervix or through a needle inserted in the abdomen, and a sample of cells from the chorion is retrieved for testing.

Chromosomal disorders   Disorders that result when too many or too few chromosomes are formed or when there is a change in the structure of the chromosome caused by breakage.

Chromosomes   The strands of genes that constitute the human genetic endowment.

Chronosystem   The dimension of time, including one's age and the time in history in which one lives.

Circular reaction   An infant's repetition of a reflexive action that results in a pleasurable experience.

Circumcision   Surgical removal of the foreskin of the penis.

Classical conditioning   The process by which a stimulus (the unconditioned stimulus) that naturally evokes a certain response (the unconditioned response) is paired repeatedly with a neutral stimulus. Eventually the neutral stimulus becomes the conditioned stimulus and evokes the same response, now called the conditioned response.

Classification   The ability to organize objects into hierarchical conceptual categories.

Clear-cut attachment   The stage from 6–8 months to 18 months–2 years, when an infant develops separation anxiety when a person he is attached to leaves him.

Clinical depression   A condition marked by long-lasting and severe feelings of worthlessness and hopelessness, a lack of pleasure, sleep and appetite disturbances, and possibly suicidal thoughts.

Clinical interview   An interview technique in which the interviewer can deviate from a standard set of questions to gather additional information.

Cliques   Small groups of friends who spend time together and develop close relationships.

Coercive family environment   A pattern of family interaction in which parents and children mutually train each other so that the child becomes increasingly aggressive and the parents become less effective in controlling the child's behavior.

Cognitive development   Changes in the way we think, understand, and reason about the world.

Cognitive flexibility   The ability to switch focus as needed to complete a task.

Cognitive processing theory   The theory that learning language is a process of "data crunching," in which the actual process of learning words and their meanings relies on the computational ability of the human brain.

Cohort effect   Differences between groups in a cross-sectional study that are attributable to the fact that the participants have had different life experiences.

Collaborative learning   An educational strategy that allows groups of students who are at different ability levels to work together on a common goal, such as a project or an assignment.

Collectivism   The cultural value that emphasizes obligations to others within your group.

Command strategy   A parenting technique in which the parent does not make any overt threats of punishment, but the child responds to the legitimate authority that the parent has to make a request of the child.

Concordance rate   The degree to which a trait or an ability of one individual is similar to that of another; used to examine similarities between twins and among adopted children and their biological and adoptive parents.

Concrete operations   The third stage in Piaget's theory in which children between 6 and 12 years of age develop logical thinking but still cannot think abstractly.

Concussion   Traumatic brain injuries that change the way your brain functions and may result in headache, memory loss, and confusion.

Conduct disorder   A persistent pattern of behavior marked by violation of the basic rights of others or major age-appropriate social norms or rules.

Connectionist/neural network model   A model of memory in which the process is envisioned as a neural network that consists of concept nodes that are interconnected by links.

Conscience   An autonomous inner guiding system that is based on our understanding of moral rules.

Conservation   The understanding that a basic quantity of something (amount, volume, mass) remains the same regardless of changes in appearance.

Constraints Assumptions that language learners make that limit the alternative meanings that they attribute to new words.

Constructive play   Building or making something for the purposes of play.

Constructivism   The idea that humans actively construct their understanding of the world rather than passively receiving knowledge.

Control group   The group in an experiment that does not get the special treatment and provides a baseline against which the experimental group can be compared.

Controversial children   Children who receive both a large number of nominations for "like most" and a large number of nominations for "like least" from peers on a sociometric measure.

Conventional moral judgment   Moral judgment that moves beyond self-interest to take into account the good of those around you.

Convergent thinking   Finding one correct solution for a problem.

Cooperative play   Play with peers that has a common goal.

Coping   Conscious efforts made to master, tolerate, or reduce stress.

Corpus callosum   The band of fibers that connects the two hemispheres of the brain.

Correlational research design   Research that measures the strength and direction of the relationship between two or more variables that are not created by the experimenter.

Cortisol   A hormone produced as part of the stress response that prepares the body to deal with threat and also shuts down nonessential functions.

Couvade   A sympathetic pregnancy in which a man experiences a variety of symptoms associated with pregnancy or childbirth while his partner is pregnant.

Creative intelligence   The ability to generate ideas and to deal successfully with novelty (sometimes referred to as divergent thinking).

Critical period   A period of time during which development is occurring rapidly and the organism is especially sensitive to damage, which often is severe and irreversible.

Cross-modal transfer of perception   Perception with one sense (for example, seeing an apple) enables recognition of that object with another sense, such as touch.

Cross-sectional design   A research design that uses multiple groups of participants who represent the age span of interest to the researcher.

Cross-sequential design   A research design that uses multiple groups of participants and follows them over a period of time, with the beginning age of each group being the ending age of another group.

Crowds   Large, reputation-based groups that are based on a shared stereotype but whose members do not necessarily spend time together.

Crystallized intelligence   What we already know and can draw on to solve problems.

Cultural neuroscience   The study of the interaction of culture, the mind, and the development of the brain.

Cultural test bias hypothesis   The belief that standardized intelligence tests systematically underestimate the intelligence of minority groups because of bias built into the test.

Culture   The system of behaviors, norms, beliefs, and traditions that form in order to promote the survival of a group that lives in a particular environmental niche.

Cyberbullying   The use of electronic technologies, including e-mails, text messages, digital images, webpages (including social network sites), blogs, or chat rooms, to socially harm others.

Decenter   The ability to think about more than one aspect of a situation at a time.

Delay of gratification   The ability to wait until later to get something desirable.

Delinquency   Youth involvement with criminal activity.

Demandingness/control   A dimension of parenting that measures the amount of restrictiveness and structure that parents place on their children.

Dendrites   The parts of a neuron that receive impulses from other neurons.

Dependent variable   The outcome of interest to the researcher that is measured at the end of an experiment.

Developmental assets Common sense, positive experiences, and qualities that help young people become caring, responsible adults.

Developmental bilingual programs Programs in which English language learners receive instruction in core subjects in their native language until they have the language skills to be instructed in English.

Developmental coordination disorder (DCD) A condition in which delays in reaching motor milestones interfere with daily living and/or academic performance.

Developmental psychopathology An approach that sees mental and behavioral problems as distortions of normal developmental processes rather than as illnesses.

Developmental theory A model of development based on observations that allows us to make predictions.

Deviation IQ A measure of intelligence that is based on the individual's deviation from the norms for a given test.

Diabetes A metabolic disorder in which the body does not produce insulin, or cannot use the insulin produced by the body.

Dialogic reading A technique used to facilitate early literacy, which involves an adult and a child looking at a book together while the adult asks questions and encourages a dialogue, followed by switching roles so the child asks questions of the adult.

Difficult temperament A child's general responsiveness marked by a more negative mood, intense responses, slow adaptation to change, and irregular patterns of eating, sleeping, and elimination.

Discovery learning An approach to teaching that emphasizes allowing children to discover for themselves new information and understanding.

Discrimination Negative behavior directed at people on the basis of their race, ethnicity, religion, or other factors.

Disengaged parents Parents who do not set limits or rules for their children and are not emotionally connected to them.

Disequilibrium A state of confusion in which your schemas do not fit your experiences.

Disinhibited social engagement disorder An attachment disorder in which children approach strangers indiscriminately, not differentiating between attachment figures and other people.

Disorganized/disoriented attachment An attachment classification in which behavior is unpredictable and odd and shows no coherent way of dealing with attachment issues; often linked with parental abuse or neglect.

Disruptive Mood Dysregulation Disorder Severe and frequent temper tantrums that are out of proportion with the situation.

Divergent thinking The ability to find as many possible solutions to a problem as possible rather than the one "correct" solution.

Dizygotic (DZ) twins Twins formed when a woman produces two ova or eggs, which are fertilized by two sperm; genetically DZ twins are as similar as any siblings.

Dominant genes Genes that are usually expressed in the phenotype.

Doula A trained, knowledgeable companion who supports a woman during her labor and delivery.

Drive reduction The idea that human behavior is determined by the motivation to satisfy or reduce the discomfort caused by biological needs or drives.

Dynamic assessment A testing procedure that uses a test-intervene-test procedure to assess the examinee's potential to change.

Dynamic systems theory The theory that all aspects of development interact and affect each other in a dynamic process over time.

Dyslexia An alternative term for a specific learning disorder that is characterized by problems with accurate or fluent word recognition, poor decoding, and poor spelling abilities.

Early labor The first phase in the first stage of labor in which contractions are usually not painful but the cervix begins to thin out and dilate.

Easy temperament A child's general responsiveness marked by positive mood, easy adaptation to change, and regularity and predictability in patterns of eating, sleeping, and elimination.

Ectoderm The outermost layer of the inner cell mass that later becomes the skin, sense organs, brain, and spinal cord.

Effortful control The ability to consciously control one's behavior.

Ego   The part of the personality that contends with the reality of the world and controls the basic drives.

Egocentric speech   A limitation of young children's communication due to their inability to take the perspective of other people into account.

Egocentrism   The inability to see or understand things from someone else's perspective.

Elaboration   A memory strategy that involves creating extra connections, like images or sentences, which can tie information together.

Embryo   The developing organism from conception to the end of the second month of a pregnancy.

Embryonic stage   The prenatal stage that lasts from 2 weeks to 2 months postconception.

Emergent literacy   The set of skills that develop before children begin formal reading instruction, which provide the foundation for later academic skills.

Emerging adulthood   A transition time between adolescence and adulthood, from 18–25 years of age.

Emotion   The body's physiological reaction to a situation, the cognitive interpretation of the situation, communication to another person, and actions.

Emotion schemas   All the associations and interpretations that an individual connects to a certain emotion.

Emotional intelligence   The ability to understand and control one's emotions, to understand the emotions of others, and to use this understanding in human interactions.

Emotion-focused strategies   Coping strategies that are designed to reduce or manage emotional distress.

Empathy   Sharing the feelings of other people.

Encoding processes   The transformation processes through which new information is stored in long-term memory.

Endoderm   The innermost layer of the inner cell mass that later becomes the respiratory system, digestive system, liver, and pancreas.

English as a second language (ESL) pull-out programs   Programs in which students are taught English in a separate classroom.

Enrichment approach   An educational approach for gifted children in which the curriculum is covered but in greater depth, breadth, or complexity than is done in a typical classroom.

Epigenetics   A system by which genes are activated or silenced in response to events or circumstances in the individual's environment.

Equifinality   Different developmental pathways may result in the same outcome.

Equilibration   An attempt to resolve uncertainty to return to a comfortable cognitive state.

Ethnic constancy   The understanding that race or ethnicity remains the same across time and in different settings.

Ethnic identity   A person's attitudes toward the ethnic group to which they feel they belong.

Ethnography   A technique in which a researcher lives with a group of people as a participant observer, taking part in the group's everyday life while observing and interviewing people in the group.

Ethology   The study of the adaptive value of animal and human behavior in the natural environment.

Evocative gene-environment interaction   A situation in which children's genetic endowment causes them to act in a way that draws out or "evokes" certain responses from those around them.

Executive function   The aspect of brain organization that coordinates attention and memory and controls behavioral responses for the purpose of attaining a certain goal.

Exosystem   Settings that the child never enters but that affect the child's development nevertheless, such as the parents' place of work.

Expectancy effects   The effect that the expectations of others can have on one's self-perception and behavior.

Experience-dependent brain development   Development that occurs in response to specific learning experiences.

Experience-expectant brain development   Development that occurs when we encounter experiences that our brain *expects* as a normal event.

Experimental group   The group in an experiment that gets the special treatment that is of interest to the researcher.

Experimental research design   A research design in which an experimental group is administered a treatment and the outcome is compared with a control group that does not receive the treatment.

Expressive language   The written or spoken language we use to convey our thoughts, emotions, or needs.

Externalizing (or other-directed) behaviors   Behaviors, such as aggressive or destructive behavior, in which the child "acts out" on the environment.

Extinction   In operant conditioning, the process by which a behavior stops when it receives no response from the environment.

False belief   The understanding that someone else may believe something that a child knows to be untrue.

False belief paradigm   An experimental task used to assess a child's understanding that others may believe something the child knows to be untrue.

Fast mapping   A process by which children apply constraints and their knowledge of grammar to learn new words very quickly, often after a single exposure.

Fertilization   The process by which a sperm penetrates an egg.

Fetal alcohol spectrum disorders (FASDs)   A range of impairments in a child resulting from consumption of alcohol during a pregnancy; associated with any subset of characteristics of fetal alcohol syndrome at varying levels of severity and other more subtle or functional deficits.

Fetal alcohol syndrome (FAS)   A condition in the child resulting from heavy or binge consumption of alcohol during a pregnancy; associated with abnormal facial features, small stature, and a small head and functional problems such as problems with learning, memory, and attention span.

Fetal stage   The prenatal stage that lasts from the beginning of the third month postconception until birth.

Fetus   The developing organism from the end of the eighth week postconception until birth.

Fine motor skills   Skills that involve small movements, mostly of the hands and fingers, but also of the lips and tongue.

Fluid intelligence   Intelligence that allows us to quickly and effectively solve novel problems for which we have little training.

Food insecurity   A situation in which food is often scarce or unavailable, causing people to overeat when they do have access to food.

Forgotten half   High school students who graduate from high school but do not continue their education by going to college and are not well prepared for the transition to work.

Formal operations   Piaget's fourth stage in which people 12 and older think both logically and abstractly.

Foster care   The temporary placement of children in a family that is not their own because of unhealthy situations within their birth family.

Free association   The process used by psychoanalysis in which one thinks of anything that comes to mind in relation to a dream or another thought to reveal the contents of the unconscious mind.

Friendship   A mutual relationship marked by companionship, closeness, and affection.

Fuzzy trace theory   The theory that there are two memory systems: a systematic, controlled memory for exact details and an automatic, intuitive memory for the gist, or meaning, of events.

Games with rules   Making up rules for a game or playing games with preestablished rules.

Gender constancy   The understanding that despite superficial changes, one's gender remains constant.

Gender identity   Stage when children can identify gender but their concept of gender relies on external appearance.

Gender segregation   A preference for playing with other children of the same gender.

Gender stability   Stage when children understand that their gender will remain stable over time, but aren't sure that gender won't change if they do activities usually performed by the other gender.

Gene   A segment of DNA on a chromosome that creates proteins that are the basis for the body's development and functioning.

Gene therapy   Treatment of genetic disorders through implanting or disabling specific genes.

Generalist genes   Genes that affect many related abilities.

Generalize   To draw inferences from the findings of research on a specific sample about a larger group or population.

Genetic-epistemology   The study of the development of knowledge through biological adaptation and development of the mind.

Genital stage   Freud's fifth and final stage in which people 12 and older develop adult sexuality.

Genome   All of a person's genes, including those that are active and those that are silent.

Genome-wide association   A system that allows scientists to examine the whole human genome at once.

Genotype   All the genes that make up a human being, or the specific genes at a particular location on a chromosome.

Germinal stage   The prenatal stage that lasts from conception to 2 weeks postconception.

Gestational age   The length of time since the conception of a developing organism.

Gifted (or talented) children   Children and youth who exhibit high performance capability in intellectual, creative, and/or artistic areas; possess an unusual leadership capacity; or excel in specific academic fields.

Global self-esteem   The feelings you have about your own general self-worth.

Goal-corrected partnership   The stage of development of attachment from 18 months on, when toddlers create reciprocal relationships with their mothers.

Goodness of fit   How well a child's temperamental characteristics match the demands of the child's environment.

Gross motor skills   Skills that involve the large muscle groups of the body—for example, the legs and arms.

Guilt   Feelings children have when they think about the negative aspects of something they have done, particularly moral failures.

Habituation   The reduction in the response to a stimulus that is repeated.

Hemispheres   The two halves of the brain.

Heritability   A measure of the extent to which genes determine a particular behavior or characteristic.

Heteronomous morality   Moral judgments based on the dictates of authority.

Hostile attribution bias   The tendency to interpret the innocent behaviors of others as hostile rather than benign.

Hygiene hypothesis   The idea that living in a germ-free environment is causing our immune system to become more reactive to allergens.

Hypothesis   A testable prediction about the nature and causes of behavior.

Hypothetico-deductive reasoning   The ability to form hypotheses about how the world works and to reason logically about these hypotheses.

Id   According to psychoanalytic theory, the part of the personality that consists of the basic drives, such as sex and hunger.

Ideal self   The characteristics one aspires to in the future.

Identity achievement   The choice of an identity following exploration of the possibilities.

Identity diffusion   A lack of interest in developing an identity.

Identity foreclosure   Commitment to an identity before exploring possible options.

Identity moratorium   A time of exploration in search of identity, with no commitment made yet.

Identity versus role confusion   Erik Erikson's stage during adolescence when teens are dealing with consolidating their identity.

Imaginary audience   The egocentric belief that one is the center of other people's attention much of the time.

Immanent justice   The belief that unrelated events are automatic punishment for misdeeds.

Immersion programs   Programs in which English language learners are taught academic subjects in English.

Imprinting   In ethology, the automatic process by which animals attach to their mothers.

Incremental theories   Theories in which development is a result of continuous quantitative changes.

Independent variable   The variable in an experiment that the researcher manipulates.

Individualism The cultural value that emphasizes the importance of the individual with emphasis on independence and reliance on one's own abilities.

Inductive discipline   A parenting technique that involves setting clear limits for children and explaining the consequences for negative behavior, why the behavior was wrong, and what the child might do to fix the situation.

Industry versus inferiority   The time in middle childhood during which Erikson says that children begin to learn what it takes to become an adult in their society.

Infant mortality   The rate of infant death within the first year of life.

Infant states Different levels of consciousness used to regulate the amount of stimulation an infant receives; states range from crying to deep sleep.

Infantile amnesia Adults' inability to remember experiences that happened to them before they were about 3 years of age.

Infertility The inability to conceive within 1 year of frequent, unprotected sex.

Inhibition The ability to stop more automatic behaviors in order to stay on task and ignore distractions.

Inhibitory control The ability to stop more automatic cognitive responses to do what is needed to carry out a task correctly.

Inner cell mass A solid clump of cells in the blastocyst, which later develops into the embryo.

Intellectual disability A type of intellectual impairment that includes a low score on a standardized test of intelligence (usually 70 to 75 or lower), deficits in cognitive functioning, and impaired adaptive functioning.

Intelligence Those qualities that help us adapt successfully so that we achieve our goals in life.

Intelligence quotient (IQ) Originally a measure of intelligence calculated based on the ratio of a child's mental age to chronological age, largely replaced now by the deviation IQ.

Interactionism A theory of language development that proposes the child's biological readiness to learn language interacts with the child's experiences with language in the environment to bring about language development.

Internal working model A mental representation of particular attachment relationships a child has experienced that shapes expectations for future relationships.

Internalization The process by which individuals adopt the attitudes, beliefs, and values held by their society.

Internalizing (or self-directed) behaviors Behaviors in which a child's emotions are turned inward and become hurtful to themselves.

Interviews A data collection technique in which an interviewer poses questions to a respondent.

Intuitive thought According to Piaget, the beginning forms of logic developing during the preoperational stage.

Joint attention A process in which an individual looks at the same object that someone else is looking at, but also looks at the person to make sure that they are both involved with the same thing.

Knowledge telling A style of writing (typical of younger children) in which the writer proceeds with little or no evidence of planning or organization of ideas, with the goal of telling as much as he knows about a topic.

Knowledge transforming A style of writing in which the goal is to convey a deeper understanding of a subject by taking information and transforming it into ideas that can be shared with a reader.

Language A system of symbols we use to communicate with others or to think.

Language disorder A disorder in which a child's understanding and use of language is significantly below his nonverbal intelligence.

Latency stage Freud's fourth stage, involving children ages 6 to 12, when the sex drive goes underground.

Lateralization The localization of a function in one hemisphere of the brain or the other.

Leisure repertoire theory The theory that says if children develop a wide repertoire of activities while young, they will be more likely to continue to participate in physical activity as they get older.

Longitudinal design A research design that follows one group of individuals over time and looks at the same or similar measures at each point of testing.

Love withdrawal A parenting technique in which parents withhold their love until a child conforms to the parents' expectations for his behavior.

Low birth weight A full-term infant who weighs less than 5 pounds, 4 ounces.

Macrosystem Cultural norms that guide the nature of the organizations and places that make up one's everyday life.

Malpresentation An abnormal positioning of the fetus in the uterus.

Maltreatment Any act committed by a parent or caregiver that results in harm or potential harm to a child.

Mandatory reporters Individuals who work with children who are required by law to report suspicions of child maltreatment to authorities.

Media literacy The skills to understand the underlying purposes and messages of media.

Menarche   A girl's first menstrual period.

Mental age   The age level at which a child is performing on a test of mental ability.

Mentor   A constructed relationship in which a nonparental adult provides a range of functions to a young person.

Mesoderm   The middle layer of the inner cell mass that later becomes the muscles, bones, blood, heart, kidney, and gonads.

Mesosystem   The interaction among the various microsystems, such as a child's school and home.

Meta-analysis   A statistical procedure that combines data from different studies to determine whether there is a consistent pattern of findings across studies.

Metacognition   The ability to think about and monitor one's own thoughts and cognitive activities.

Metalinguistic ability   The ability to think about and talk about language.

Metamemory   The understanding of memory, how it works, and how to use it effectively.

Microsystem   In ecological theory, the face-to-face interaction of the person in her immediate settings, such as home, school, or friendship groups.

Mindblindness   The inability to understand and theorize about other people's thoughts.

Mirror neurons   Neurons that fire both when an individual acts and when the individual observes the same action performed by another.

Miscarriage   The natural loss of a pregnancy before the fetus reaches a gestational age of 20 weeks.

Molecular genetics   Research focused on the identification of particular genes to describe how these genes work within the cell.

Monozygotic (MZ) twins   Twins formed when a woman produces one egg that is fertilized by one sperm and the resulting ball of cells splits to form two individuals with the same genes.

Moral judgment   The way people reason about moral issues.

Moral knowledge   Understanding of right and wrong.

Morpheme   The smallest unit in a language that has meaning.

Motor schema   Infants' organization of knowledge through action on the world.

Multifactorial inheritance disorders   Disorders that result from the interaction of many genes in interaction with environmental influences.

Multifinality   The same pathways may lead to different developmental outcomes.

Mutations   Changes that occur in the structure of a gene.

Mutual exclusivity constraint   An assumption made by language learners that there is one (and only one) name for an object.

Myelination   The process of laying down a fatty sheath of myelin on the neurons.

Nativism   A theory of language development that human brains are innately wired to learn language and that hearing spoken language triggers the activation of a universal grammar.

Natural mentor   A nonparental adult who provides support and guidance to a young person.

Nature   The influence of genetic inheritance on development.

Negative identity   An identity that is in direct opposition to that which parents or other adults would support.

Negative reinforcement   A response that makes a behavior more likely to happen again because it removes an unpleasant stimulus.

Neglect   Failure to provide for the basic physical, emotional, medical, or educational needs of a child or to protect the child from harm or potential harm.

Neglected children   Children who receive relatively few nominations either as "like most" or as "like least" on a sociometric measure.

Neurons   The cells that make up the nervous system of the body.

Neuropsychology   The study of the interaction of the brain and behavior.

Neurotransmitters   Chemicals that transmit nerve impulses across a synapse from one nerve cell to another.

Niche picking   A process in which people express their genetic tendencies by finding environments that match and enhance those tendencies.

Nocturnal enuresis   An involuntary emptying of the bladder during sleep beyond the age at which children usually gain bladder control.

Non-normative stress Stress that results from a relatively rare occurrence that often overwhelms the individual.

Nonshared environment The different experiences that siblings in the same family have in that environment.

Norm The average or typical performance of an individual of a given age on a test.

Normative stress Stress that is predictable and that most people go through, and which requires a moderate and relatively brief response.

Nuclear family A family consisting of a husband, a wife, and their biological and/or adopted children.

Nucleotides Organic molecules containing a chemical base, a phosphate group, and a sugar molecule.

Nurture The influence of learning and experiences in the environment on development.

Obese Being at or above the 95th percentile of the body mass index (BMI) for children of the same age and sex.

Object permanence The understanding that objects continue to exist when no one is interacting with them.

Observer bias The tendency for an observer to notice and report events that he is expecting to see.

Obsessive-compulsive disorder (OCD) A disorder marked by obsessions or intrusive thoughts and repeated behaviors that people feel compelled to do to control the obsessive thoughts.

Onlooker behavior Watching other children play.

Open adoptions Adoptions in which the children and their biological and adoptive families have access to each other.

Operant conditioning The process by which the likelihood of a response is increased or decreased due to the consequences that follow that response.

Operationalizing a concept Defining a concept in a way that allows it to be measured.

Operations Mental actions that follow systematic, logical rules.

Oppositional defiant disorder A pattern of behavior marked by defiant, disobedient, and hostile behavior toward authority figures.

Oral stage Freud's first stage, in which infants' biological energy is centered on the mouth area.

Organogenesis The process in prenatal development by which all of the major organ systems of the body are laid down.

Other-oriented induction A parenting technique in which the child is asked to think about the consequences of the child's behavior for someone else.

Overregularization A type of grammatical error in which children apply a language rule to words that don't follow it (for example, adding an *s* to make the plural of an irregular noun such as *foot*).

Overweight Being at or above the 85th percentile and lower than the 95th of the body mass index (BMI) compared to children of the same age and sex.

Ovulation The release of a mature egg from an ovary.

Ovum An unfertilized egg.

Parallel play Playing next to a peer with the same type of materials, but not interacting with the other child.

Passive gene-environment interaction A situation in which a child's family shares his own genetically determined abilities and interests.

Peer pressure Influence exerted by peers to get others to comply with their wishes or expectations.

Peer review A process in which professionals critique an article and make suggestions for improvement before a decision is made whether to publish it.

Perception The process of interpreting and attaching meaning to sensory information.

Perceptual bias The tendency to see and understand something based on the way you expected it to be.

Permissive parents Parents who provide a great deal of warmth and acceptance but have few, if any, rules or restrictions.

Personal fable The belief (often held by teenagers) that you are in some way unique and different from all other people.

Phallic stage Freud's third stage, in which children ages 3 to 6 overcome their attraction to the opposite-sex parent and begin to identify with the same-sex parent.

Phenotype A person's bodily traits and characteristics.

Phobia An irrational fear of something specific that is so severe that it interferes with day-to-day functioning.

Phoneme The smallest distinct sound in a particular language.

Phonics (or basic skills) approach   An approach to teaching reading that starts with basic elements like letters and phonemes and teaches children that phonemes can be combined into words before moving on to reading as a whole.

Phonology   The study of the sounds of a language.

Physical development   Biological changes that occur in the body and brain, including changes in size and strength and integration of sensory and motor activities.

Placenta   The organ that supports a pregnancy by bringing oxygen and nutrients to the embryo from the mother through the umbilical cord and carrying away fetal waste products.

Plasticity   The ability of an immature brain to change in form and function.

Play disruption   An inability to play because the child's emotions are preventing the kind of free expression linked with the fun of play.

Play therapy   A way to help children work through difficult feelings with the help of an adult who is trained to understand play as a type of communication.

Pleasure principle   The idea that the id seeks immediate gratification for all of its urges.

Pleiotropic effects   The many different influences any single gene may have.

Polygenic inheritance   Numerous genes may interact to promote any particular trait or behavior.

Popular children   Children who receive a lot of nominations as "like most" and few as "like least" on a sociometric measure.

Popular-antisocial children   Children who are popular with peers by combining prosocial behavior with aggression as a way to manipulate people.

Popular-prosocial children   Children who are popular among peers because they are low on aggression and have a number of desirable characteristics.

Positive youth development   An approach to finding ways to help all young people reach their full potential.

Postconventional moral judgment   Moral judgment that moves beyond society as a defining factor of what is moral or right and is based on universal principles that apply to all.

Postformal operations   The cognitive ability to consider multiple perspectives and bring together seemingly contradictory information.

Postpartum depression   A severe depression that typically begins within the first three months after childbirth that lasts for more than 2 weeks; symptoms are severe enough that they interfere with the woman's ability to function.

Posttraumatic stress disorder (PTSD)   Reexperiencing a traumatic event through intrusive thoughts, distressing dreams, flashbacks, or extreme reactions in situations similar to the original trauma.

Power assertion   A disciplinary technique that emphasizes control of the child's behavior through physical and nonphysical punishment.

Practical intelligence   The ability to solve everyday problems by changing yourself or your behavior to fit the environment better, changing the environment, or moving to a different environment in which you can be more successful.

Practice play   Performing a certain behavior repetitively for the mere pleasure of it.

Pragmatics   The rules guiding the way we use language in social situations.

Preattachment   The stage of development of attachment from birth to 6 weeks, in which infant sensory preferences bring infants into close connection with parents.

Precocious puberty   A condition in which pubertal changes begin at an extraordinarily early age (as young as 6 or 7 years of age).

Preconventional moral judgment   Moral judgment that is marked by self-interest and motivation based on rewards and punishments.

Prejudices   Negative attitudes toward individuals based on their race, ethnicity, religion, or other factors.

Premature birth   A birth that occurs before a gestational age of 37 weeks.

Premoral reasoning   The inability to consider issues on the basis of their morality.

Preoperational stage   Piaget's second stage of development, in which children ages 2 to 7 do not yet have logical thought, and instead think magically and egocentrically.

Prepubescence   The period before puberty when hormonal changes begin.

Primary sex characteristics   The body structures necessary for reproduction—the vagina, ovaries, and uterus of the female, and the testes and penis of the male.

Private speech   Talking to oneself, often out loud, to guide one's own actions.

Problem-focused strategies   Coping strategies that focus on changing or improving a stressful situation.

Processing speed   The efficiency with which one can perform cognitive tasks.

Proprioception   The sense of knowing where the parts of your body are located in space.

Prosocial behavior   Actions that help and support other people.

Proximodistal   Development that proceeds from the central axis of the body toward the extremities.

Pruning   The deterioration and disappearance of synapses that are not used.

Psychoanalytic theory   Freud's theory in which the way we deal with biological urges moves the person through a series of stages that shape our personality.

Psychosexual stages   Freud's idea that at each stage sexual energy is invested in a different part of the body.

Psychosocial stages   Erikson's stages that are based on a central conflict to be resolved involving the social world and the development of identity.

Puberty   The physical changes that make adolescents capable of sexual reproduction.

Punishment   Administering a negative consequence or taking away a positive reinforcement to reduce the likelihood of an undesirable behavior occurring.

Qualitative changes   Changes in the overall nature of what you are examining.

Quantitative changes   Changes in the amount or quantity of what you are measuring.

Questionnaires   A written form of a survey.

Racial socialization   Efforts by minority parents to teach their children about discrimination, prepare them to deal with these experiences, and teach them to take pride in their heritage.

Racism   A pervasive system of advantage and disadvantage based on race.

Random assignment   Assigning participants to the experimental and control groups by chance so that the groups will not systematically differ from each other.

Reactive attachment disorder (RAD)   A disorder marked by an inability to form attachments to caregivers.

Reality principle   The psychoanalytic concept that the ego has the ability to deal with the real world and not just drives and fantasy.

Recast   The act of repeating what children say but in a more advanced grammar to facilitate language learning.

Receptive language   The ability to understand words or sentences.

Recessive genes   Genes that are generally not expressed in the phenotype unless paired with another recessive gene.

Recursive thinking   The ability to think about other people thinking about your thinking.

Reflexes   Patterned, involuntary motor responses that are controlled by the lower brain centers.

Reinforcement   A response to a behavior that causes that behavior to happen more.

Rejected children   Children who receive a lot of nominations as "like least" and few as "like most" on a sociometric measure.

Rejected-aggressive children   Children who are rejected by peers because they are aggressive, annoying, or socially unskilled.

Rejected-withdrawn children   Children who are rejected by peers because they are socially withdrawn and anxious.

Rejection sensitivity   The extent to which a child is affected by peer rejection.

Relationship maintenance   A parenting technique in which the parents try to create a positive relationship with their child so that the parents will have a greater influence on the child's behavior.

Reliability   The ability of a measure to produce consistent results.

Replicate   To find the same results as in a previous research study.

Resilience   The ability to bounce back from adversity or to thrive despite negative life circumstances.

Reversibility   The ability to reverse mental operations.

Rites of passage   Rituals that publicly mark a change in status from child to adult.

Rough-and-tumble play   Play that looks like fighting or wrestling, where the goal is not to hurt or win, but to have fun.

Scaffolding   The idea that more knowledgeable adults and children support a child's learning by providing help to move the child just beyond his current level of capability.

Schedules of reinforcement   Schedules (ratio or interval) on which reinforcement can be delivered based on a fixed or variable number of responses or fixed or variable lengths of time.

Schema   A cognitive framework that places concepts, objects, or experiences into categories or groups of associations.

Schizophrenia   A serious mental disorder in which individuals have difficulty discriminating external reality from their own internal states.

Scientific thinking   The type of thinking scientists use when they set out to test a hypothesis.

Scripts   Memory for the way a common occurrence in one's life, such as grocery shopping, takes place.

Secondary sex characteristics   Physical characteristics that are associated with gender that do not directly affect the sex organs, such as breast development in females or deepening of the voice in males.

Secure attachment   A strong, positive emotional bond with a person who provides comfort and a sense of security.

Secure base for exploration   The use of a parent to provide the security that an infant can rely on as she explores the environment.

Selective attention   The process of tuning in to certain things while tuning out others.

Self-complexity   The number of different ways in which an individual defines herself.

Self-concept   How we think about or describe ourselves.

Self-conscious emotions   Emotions that depend on awareness of oneself, such as pride, guilt, and shame.

Self-efficacy   A belief in our ability to influence our own functioning and our life circumstances.

Self-esteem   How we feel about characteristics we associate with ourselves.

Self-esteem movement   School-based programs designed to boost students' self-esteem, with the goal of eventually improving their academic performance.

Self-fulfilling prophecy   The process by which expectations or beliefs lead to behaviors that help ensure that you fulfill the initial prophecy or expectation.

Self-oriented induction   A parenting technique in which the child is asked to think about the consequences that the child might experience as a result of his behavior.

Semantic bootstrapping   The use of conceptual categories to create grammatical categories.

Semantics   The study of the meanings of words.

Sensations   The information from the environment that is picked up by our sense organs.

Sensorimotor stage   Piaget's first stage in which infants understand the world through the information they take in through their senses and through their actions on their environment.

Separation anxiety   Distress felt when separated from a parent.

Separation anxiety disorder   An anxiety disorder marked by developmentally inappropriate and excessive amount of anxiety when the child is separated from a primary attachment figure.

Seriation   The ability to put objects in order by height, weight, or some other quality.

Sex trafficking   The forcible removal of children from their families for the purposes of prostitution or pornography.

Sexting   Sending nude or seminude pictures of oneself online.

Sexual orientation/preference   Sexual attraction to the same- or opposite-sex partners.

Sexually transmitted disease (STD)   A pathology that can result from a sexually transmitted infection.

Sexually transmitted infection (STI)   An infection caused by a microorganism that is transmitted by direct sexual contact.

Shame   A feeling that occurs as a result of personal failure or when children attribute their bad behavior to an aspect of themselves that they believe they cannot change.

Short-term memory   Brief, temporary storage of information in memory.

Single gene disorders   Genetic disorders caused by a single recessive gene or mutation.

Slow-to-warm temperament   A general responsiveness marked by a slow adaptation to new experiences and moderate irregularity in eating, sleeping, and elimination.

Small for gestational age   Babies who are smaller in size than normal for their gestational age.

Social cognition   The ways we use cognitive processes to understand our social world.

Social cognitive theory   The theory that individuals learn by observing others and imitating their behavior.

Social comparison   Comparing one's own performance or characteristics to those of other people.

Social desirability   The tendency of respondents to answer questions in a way to please the researcher or to make them look good in the researcher's eyes.

Social or pragmatic communication disorder   Difficulty with appropriate use of both verbal and nonverbal communication.

Social policy   Government or private policies for dealing with social issues.

Social promotion   Promoting a child who has not mastered grade-level material to keep the child in a class with same-age peers.

Social referencing   Using the reaction of others to determine how to react in ambiguous situations.

Social status   The level of peer acceptance or peer rejection of an individual in the peer group.

Social-emotional development   Changes in the ways we connect to other individuals and express and understand emotions.

Socialization   The process of instilling the norms, values, attitudes, and beliefs of a culture in its children.

Sociobiology   The application of principles of evolution to the development of social behavior and culture.

Socioeconomic status   A person's social standing based on a combined measure of income, education, and occupation.

Sociometry   A research technique used to assess a child's social status within the peer group.

Solitary independent play   Engaging actively with toys that are different from those being used by other children.

Specific learning disorder   Difficulty with learning and academic performance based on impairment in reading, written expression, and/or mathematics.

Speech-sound disorder   Difficulty producing or using sounds at an age-appropriate level.

Spermarche   The beginning of production of viable sperm.

Stage theories   Theories of development in which each stage in life is seen as qualitatively different from the ones that come before and after.

Standardized test   A test that is administered and scored in a standard or consistent way to all examinees.

Stepfamilies   Families in which there are two adults and at least one child from a previous relationship of one of the adults; there also may be biological children of the couple.

Stereotype threat   The anxiety that results when individuals feel they are behaving in ways that confirm negative stereotyped expectations of a group with which they identify.

Stereotypes   Conclusions made about someone based solely on the group with which he or she is identified.

Strange Situation   Mary Ainsworth's experimental procedure designed to assess security of attachment in infants.

Stranger anxiety   Fearfulness that infants develop at about 6 months of age toward people they do not know.

Substance use disorder (SUD)   Use of drugs that is marked by impaired control, social impairment, risky use, and tolerance build-up and withdrawal symptoms.

Sudden infant death syndrome (SIDS)   The unexpected death of an apparently healthy infant.

Superego   Freud's concept of the conscience or sense of right and wrong.

Surveys   A data collection technique that asks respondents to answer a common set of questions.

Sustained attention   The process of maintaining focus over time.

Symbolic/sociodramatic play   Using symbolic representations and imagination for play.

Synapse   The place where the axon from one neuron meets the dendrite of another neuron.

Synaptogenesis   The development of new synapses.

Syntactic bootstrapping   The use of syntax to learn the meaning of new words (semantics).

Syntax   The grammar of a language.

Taxonomic constraint   An assumption language learners make that two objects that have features in common can have a name in common, but that each object also can have its own individual name.

Telegraphic speech   A stage in language development in which children only use the words necessary to get their point across and omit small words that are not necessary (for example, *Go bye-bye*).

Temperament   The general emotional style an individual displays in responding to experiences in the world.

Teratogens   Agents that can disrupt prenatal development and cause malformations or termination of the pregnancy.

Theory of core knowledge   The theory that basic areas of knowledge are innate and built into the human brain.

Theory of mind   The ability to understand self and others as agents who act on the basis of their mental states.

Theory of multiple intelligences   Gardner's idea that there are a number of different types of intelligence that are all relatively independent of each other.

Thin ideal   The idea promoted by media images that it is best for girls and women to be thin.

Toxic stress   Stress that results in strong, frequent, and prolonged activation of the body's stress response system without any protective buffering from a supportive adult relationship.

Transductive reasoning   Thought that connects one particular observation to another by creating causal links where none exist.

Transition   The third phase in the first stage of labor in which contractions come in rapid succession and last up to 90 seconds each, with little or no pause between them, and which ends when the cervix has dilated 10 centimeters.

Transitional bilingual education programs   Programs in which English language learners receive some instruction in their native language while they also receive concentrated instruction in learning English.

Transitional probability   The likelihood that one particular sound will follow another one to form a word.

Triarchic theory   Sternberg's idea that intelligence represents a balance of analytical, creative, and practical abilities.

Trophoblast   The outer ring of cells in the blastocyst that later develops into the support system for the pregnancy.

Two-way immersion program   Programs in which children who are native speakers of English and children who are not work together in a classroom where both English and the children's other native language are used.

Ultrasound   A prenatal test that uses high-frequency sound waves to create an image of the developing embryo's size, shape, and position in the womb.

Unconscious mind   The part of the mind that contains thoughts and feelings about which we are unaware.

Universal grammar   A hypothesized set of grammatical rules and constraints proposed by Noam Chomsky, thought to underlie all languages and to be hardwired in the human brain.

Unoccupied behavior   Looking around at whatever occurs, but engaging in no activity.

Validity   The ability of a research tool to accurately measure what it purports to measure.

Variable   A characteristic that can be measured and that can have different values.

Violation of expectation   A research methodology based on the finding that babies look longer at unexpected or surprising events.

Visual acuity   The ability to see things in sharp detail.

Visual perspective-taking   The understanding that other people can see an object from a point of view that is different from one's own.

Vocabulary burst   The rapid growth of a child's vocabulary that often occurs in the second year.

Wernicke's area   The part of the brain that helps us understand the meaning in speech.

Whole language instruction   A way to teach reading that emphasizes understanding the meaning of words from the context in which they appear.

Whole object bias   An assumption made by language learners that a word describes an entire object rather than just some portion of it.

Working memory   The amount of information we can actively hold in our conscious mind at one time.

Wraparound program   A comprehensive set of services offered to families to strengthen them or reunite them.

Zone of proximal development   According to Vygotsky, this is what a child cannot do on her own but can do with help from someone more skilled or knowledgeable.

Zygote A fertilized egg.

References

Abdel-Hamid, H. Z. (2011). *Cerebral palsy*. Retrieved from http://www.emedicine.medscape.com/article/1179555-overview

AbdelMalik, P., Husted, J., Chow, E. C., Bassett, A. S. (2003). Childhood head injury and expression of schizophrenia in multiply affected families. *Archives of General Psychiatry, 60*(3), 231–236. doi: 10.1001/archpsyc.60.3.231

Aber, L., Morris, P., & Raver, C. (2012). Children, families and poverty: Definitions, trends, emerging science and implications for policy. *SRCD Social Policy Report, 26*(3), 1–21.

Abma, J. C., Martinez, G. M., & Copen, C. E. (2010). Teenagers in the United States: Sexual activity, contraceptive use, and childbearing, National Survey of Family Growth 2006–2008. *Vital and Health Statistics, 23*(30), 1–47.

Abreu-Villac, Y., Seidler, F. J., Tate, C. A., Cousins, M. M., & Slotkin, T. A. (2004). Prenatal nicotine exposure alters the response to nicotine administration in adolescence: Effects on cholinergic systems during exposure and withdrawal. *Neuropsychopharmacology, 29*, 879–890.

Abrutyn, S., & Mueller, A. S. (2014). Are suicidal behaviors contagious in adolescence? Using longitudinal data to examine suicide prevention. *American Sociologist, 79*(2), 211–227.

Abushaikha, L., & Massah, R. (2012). The roles of the father during childbirth: The lived experiences of Arab Syrian parents. *Health Care For Women International, 33*(2), 168–181. doi: 10.1080/07399332.2011.610534

Academy of Nutrition and Dietetics. (2012). *Promoting positive body image in kids*. Retrieved from http://www.eatright.org/Public/content.aspx?id=6753

Accornero, V., Anthony, J., Morrow, C., Xue, L., Mansoor, E., Johnson, A., . . . Bandstra, E. (2011). Estimated effect of prenatal cocaine exposure on examiner-rated behavior at age 7 years. *Neurotoxicology and Teratology, 33*(3), 370–378. doi: 10.1016/j.ntt.2011.02.014

Achiron, R., Lipitz, S., & Achiron, A. (2001). Sex-related differences in the development of the human fetal corpus callosum: In utero ultrasonographic study. *Prenatal Diagnosis, 21*, 116–120.

Ackerman, P. L. (2005). Ability determinants of individual differences in skilled performance. In R. J. Sternberg & J. E. Pretz (Eds.), *Cognition and intelligence: Identifying the mechanisms of the mind* (pp. 142–159). New York, NY: Cambridge University Press.

Adamczyk-Robinette, S. L., Fletcher, A. C., & Wright, K. (2002). Understanding the authoritative parenting-early adolescent tobacco use link: The mediating role of peer tobacco use. *Journal of Youth and Adolescence, 31*(4), 311–318.

Adams, R., & Laursen, B. (2001). The organization and dynamics of adolescent conflict with parents and friends. *Journal of Marriage and Family, 63*(1), 97–110.

Addy, S., Engelhardt, W., & Skinner, C. (2013). *Basic facts about low-income children: Children under 6 years, 2011*. National Center for Children in Poverty. Retrieved from http://www.nccp.org/publications/pub_1076.html

ADHD Educational Institute. (2014). *Aetiology of ADHD*. Retrieved from http://www.adhd-institute.com/What-is-ADHD/Aetiology.aspx

Adolph, K. E., & Berger, S. E. (2006). Motor development. In W. Damon & R. Lerner (Series Eds.), & D. Kuhn & R. S. Siegler (Vol. Eds.), *Handbook of child psychology: Vol. 2: Cognition, perception and language* (6th ed., pp. 161–213). New York, NY: John Wiley & Sons.

Adoption and Foster Care Analysis and Reporting System. (2013). Preliminary FY 2012 estimates as of November 2013. *The AFCARS Report, No. 20*. Retrieved from http://www.acf.hhs.gov/sites/default/files/cb/afcarsreport20.pdf

Agache, A., Leyendecker, B., Schäfermeier, E., & Schölmerich, A. (2014). Paternal involvement elevates trajectories of life satisfaction during transition to parenthood. *European Journal of Developmental Psychology, 11*(2), 259–277.

Ahn, S., & Miller, S. A. (2012). Theory of mind and self-concept: A comparison of Korean and American children. *Journal of Cross-Cultural Psychology, 43*(5), 671–686. doi: 10.1177/0022022112441247

Ainsworth, M. D. S. (1979). Infant-mother attachment. *American Psychologist, 34*(10), 932–937.

Ainsworth, M. D. S., & Bell, S. M. (1970). Attachment, exploration and separation: Illustrated by the behavior of one-year-olds in a strange situation. *Child Development, 41*(1), 49–67.

Ainsworth, M. D. S., Blehar, M. C., Waters, E., & Wall, S. (1978). *Patterns of attachment*. Hillsdale, NJ: Erlbaum.

Ainsworth, M. D. S., & Bowlby, J. (1989). An ethological approach to personality development. *American Psychologist, 46*(4), 333–341.

Akers, K. G., Martinez-Canabal, A., Restivo, L., Yiu, A. P., De Cristofaro, A., Hsiang, H., . . . Frankland, P. W. (2014). Hippocampal neurogenesis regulates forgetting during adulthood and infancy. *Science, 344*(6184), 598–602. doi: 10.1126/science.1248903

Akhgarnia, G. (2011). Overconnectivity in brain found in autism. San Diego State University NewsCenter. Retrieved from http://newscenter.sdsu.edu/sdsu_newscenter/news.aspx?s=73005

Akhtar, N. (2005). Is joint attention necessary for early language learning? In B. D. Homer & C. S. Tamis-LeMonda (Eds.), *The development of social cognition and communication* (pp. 165–179). Mahwah, NJ: Erlbaum.

Alamargot, D., & Chanquoy, L. (2001). Development of expertise in writing. In G. Rijlaarsdam (Series Ed.), D. Alargot, & L. Chanquoy, *Studies in Writing: Vol 9. Through the Models of Writing* (pp. 185–218). Norwell, MA: Kluwer Academic.

Alberts, A., Elkind, D., & Ginsberg, S. (2007). The personal fable and risk-taking in early adolescence. *Journal of Youth and Adolescence, 36,* 71–76.

Alberts, B., Johnson, A., Lewis, J., Raff, M., Roberts, K., & Walter, P. (2002). *Molecular biology of the cell* (4th ed.). New York, NY: Garland Science.

Alcohol Justice. (2011). *From alcoholic energy drinks to supersized alcopops.* Retrieved from http://www.alcohol-justice.org/images/stories/AEDreportFINAL_1.pdf

Aldwin, C. M. (2012). *Stress, coping, and development: An integrative perspective* (2nd ed.). New York, NY: Guilford Press.

Alexander, G. M., & Hines, M. (1994). Gender labels and play styles: Their relative contribution to children's selection of playmates. *Child Development, 65,* 869–879.

Alexander-Passe, N. (2006). How dyslexic teenagers cope: An investigation of self-esteem, coping and depression. *Dyslexia: An International Journal of Research and Practice, 12*(4), 256–275.

Alfaro, E. C., Umaña-Taylor, A. J., & Bámaca, M. Y. (2006). The influence of academic support on Latino adolescents' academic motivation. *Family Relations, 55,* 279–291.

Alford, S., & Hauser, D. (2009). *Adolescent sexual health in Europe and the U.S.—Why the difference?* (3rd ed.). Washington, DC: Advocates for Youth. (Updated from *Adolescent sexual health in Europe and the U.S.—Why the difference?* by A. Feijoo, 2000 [1st ed.] and 2001 [2nd ed.], Washington, DC: Advocates for Youth)

Ali, M. M., & Dwyer, D. S. (2009). Estimating peer effects in adolescent smoking behavior: A longitudinal analysis. *Journal of Adolescent Health, 45*(4), 402–408.

Alic, M. (2006). Handedness. In *Gale encyclopedia of children's health: Infancy through adolescence.* Retrieved from http://www.encyclopedia.com/doc/1G2-3447200259.html

Alijotas-Reig, J., & Garrido-Gimenez, C. (2013). Current concepts and new trends in the diagnosis and management of recurrent miscarriage. *Obstetrical & Gynecological Survey, 68*(6), 445–466. doi: 10.1097/OGX.0b013e31828aca19

Allen, J. P., Seitz, V., & Apfel, N. H. (2007). The sexually mature teen as a whole person: New directions in prevention and intervention for teen pregnancy and parenthood. In J. L. Aber, S. J. Bishop-Josef, S. M. Jones, K. T. McLearn, & D. A. Phillips (Eds.), *Child development and social policy: Knowledge for action* (pp. 185–200). Washington, DC: American Psychological Association.

Allhusen, V., Belsky, J., Booth-LaForce, C., Bradley, R., Brownell, C. A., Burchinal, M., . . . Weinraub, M. (2005). Duration and developmental timing of poverty and children's cognitive and social development from birth through third grade. *Child Development, 76*(4), 795–810.

Allix, N. M. (2000). The theory of multiple intelligences: A case of missing cognitive matter. *Australian Journal of Education, 44,* 272–288.

Alloway, T. (2010). *Improving working memory: Supporting students' learning.* Thousand Oaks, CA: Sage.

Alloway, T., Gathercole, S., & Pickering, S. J. (2006). Verbal and visuospatial short-term and working memory in children: Are they separable? *Child Development, 77*(6), 1698–1716.

Almendrala, A. (2014, May 19). *The U.S. is the only developed nation with a rising maternal mortality rate.* Retrieved from http://www.huffingtonpost.com/2014/05/19/us-maternal-mortality-rate_n_5340648.html

Almon, J. (2003). The vital role of play in early childhood education. In S. Olfman (Ed.), *All work and no play: How educational reforms are harming our preschoolers* (pp. 17–42). Westport, CT: Praeger.

Alomar, L., & Zwolinski, M. (2002). Quinceañera! A celebration of Latina womanhood. *Voices: The Journal of New York Folklore, 28.* Retrieved from http://www.nyfolklore.org/pubs/voic28-3-4/onair.html

Alvino, J. (1995). *Considerations and strategies for parenting the gifted child* (Publication RM95218). Storrs, CT: The National Research Center on the Gifted and Talented, University of Connecticut.

Amato, P. R. (2005). The impact of family formation change on the cognitive, social, and emotional well-being of the next generation. *Future of Children, 15*(2), 75–96.

Amato, P. R. (2010). Research on divorce: Continuing trends and new developments. *Journal of Marriage and Family, 72,* 650–666.

Amato, P. R. (2012). The well-being of children with gay and lesbian parents. *Social Science Research, 41*(4), 771–774.

Amato, P. R., & Anthony, C. J. (2014). Estimating the effects of parental divorce and death with fixed effects models. *Journal of Marriage and Family, 76*(2), 370–386.

Amato, P. R., & Gilbreth, J. G. (1999). Nonresident fathers and children's well-being: A meta-analysis. *Journal of Marriage and Family, 61,* 557–573.

Ambert, A. (1997). *Parents, children and adolescents.* New York, NY: Haworth Press.

American Academy of Child and Adolescent Psychiatry. (2005). *Foster care*. Retrieved from http://www.aacap.org/cs/root/facts_for_families/foster_care

American Academy of Matrimonial Lawyers. (2009). *Ten tips for divorcing parents*. Retrieved from http://www.aaml.org/go/library/publications/stepping-back-from-anger/ten-tips-for-divorcing-parents/

American Academy of Pediatrics. (2001). Organized sports for children and preadolescents. *Pediatrics, 107*(6), 1459–1462.

American Academy of Pediatrics. (2004). *Caring for your school-age child: Ages 5 to 12* (Rev. ed., E. L. Schor, ed.). New York, NY: Bantam.

American Academy of Pediatrics. (2005). The changing concept of sudden infant death syndrome: Diagnostic coding shifts, controversies regarding the sleeping environment, and new variables to consider in reducing risk. *Pediatrics, 116*, 1245–1255.

American Academy of Pediatrics. (2006). *Choking prevention and first aid for infants and children*. Elk Grove Village, IL: Author.

American Academy of Pediatrics. (2007). Childhood: Growing pains. *Healthy Children, 24–25*.

American Academy of Pediatrics. (2008). *Baby walkers: A dangerous choice*. Retrieved from http://www.healthychildren.org/English/safety-prevention/at-home/Pages/Baby-Walkers-A-Dangerous-Choice.aspx

American Academy of Pediatrics. (2009a). *Caring for your baby and young child: Birth to age 5* (5th ed.). New York, NY: Bantam.

American Academy of Pediatrics. (2009b). Policy statement. *Pediatrics, 123*(1), 188.

American Academy of Pediatrics. (2009c). Recommendations for preventive pediatric health care. *Pediatrics, 96*, 373–374.

American Academy of Pediatrics. (2011a). ADHD: Clinical practice guideline for the diagnosis, evaluation, and treatment of attention-deficit/hyperactivity disorder in children and adolescents. *Pediatrics, 128*(5), 1007–1022. doi: 10.1542/peds.2011-2654.

American Academy of Pediatrics. (2011b). Media use by children younger than 2 years. *Pediatrics, 128*(5), 1040–1045. doi: 10.1542/peds.2011–1753.

American Academy of Pediatrics. (2013). *Common food allergies*. Retrieved from http://www.healthychildren.org/English/healthy-living/nutrition/pages/Common-Food-Allergies.aspx

American Academy of Pediatrics. (n.d.). *Fetal alcohol spectrum disorders program*. Retrieved from http://www.aap.org/en-us/advocacy-and-policy/aap-health-initiatives/fetal-alcohol-spectrum-disorders-toolkit/Pages/Frequently-Asked-Questions.aspx#ques2

American Academy of Pediatrics Committee on Bioethics. (2001). Ethical issues with genetic testing in pediatrics. *Pediatrics, 107*(6),1451–1455. Reaffirmed October 2004.

American Academy of Pediatrics Committee on Drugs. (2001). The transfer of drugs and other chemicals into human milks. *Pediatrics, 108*(3), 776–789.

American Academy of Pediatrics Committee on Psychosocial Aspects of Child and Family Health (1998, 2012). Guidance for effective discipline. *Pediatrics, 101*(4), 723–728.

American Academy of Pediatrics Committee on Public Education. (2001). American Academy of Pediatrics: Children, adolescents and television. *Pediatrics, 107*(2), 423–426.

American Academy of Pediatrics Section on Breastfeeding. (2005). Breastfeeding and the use of human milk. *Pediatrics, 115*, 496–506.

American Association of Diabetes Educators. (2014). Management of children with diabetes in the school setting. *Diabetes Educator, 40*(1), 116–121.

American Association of Intellectual and Developmental Disabilities. (2013). *Definition of intellectual disabilities*. Retrieved from http://www.aaidd.org/content_100.cfm?navID=21

American Association of Retired Persons. (2014). *Grandfacts*. Retrieved from http://www.aarp.org/relationships/friends-family/grandfacts-sheets/

American Association of University Women Educational Foundation. (2004). *Under the microscope—A decade of gender equity projects in the sciences*. Washington, DC: Author.

American Association of University Women. (2009). *Position on single sex education*. Retrieved from http://www.aauw.org/act/issue_advocacy/actionpages/singlesex.cfm

American College of Obstetricians and Gynecologists. (2014). Safe prevention of the primary cesarean delivery. *Obstetrics & Gynecology, 123*, 693–711.

American Congress of Obstetricians and Gynecologists. (2005). *Smoking cessation during pregnancy. ACOG Committee Opinion (No. 316)*.

American Congress of Obstetricians and Gynecologists. (2007). *You and your baby: Prenatal care, labor and delivery, and postpartum care*. Retrieved from http://www.acog.org/publications/patient_education/ab005.cfm

American Congress of Obstetricians and Gynecologists. (2009). ACOG Practice Bulletin No. 107: Induction of labor. *Obstetrics & Gynecology, 114*(2, Part 1), 386–397.

American Congress of Obstetricians and Gynecologists. (2013a). *Frequently asked questions: Ultrasound exams*. Retrieved from http://www.acog.org/~/media/For%20Patients/faq025.pdf?dmc=1&ts=20140613T0856481728

American Congress of Obstetricians and Gynecologists. (2013b). Weight gain during pregnancy. Committee Opinion No 548. *Obstetrics and Gynecology, 121*, 210–212.

American Dental Association. (2005). Tooth eruption: The primary teeth. *Journal of the American Dental Association, 136*, 1619.

American Dental Association. (2014). ADA uses fluoride toothpaste to fight high cavity rate in children. Retrieved from http://www.ada.org/en/press-room/news-releases/2014-archive/february/ada-uses-fluoride-toothpaste

American Foundation for Suicide Prevention and Suicide Prevention Resource Center. (2011). *After suicide: A toolkit for schools.* Newton, MA: Education Development Center.

American Lung Association. (2012). *Trends in asthma morbidity and mortality.* Chicago, IL: American Lung Association.

American Medical Association. (2008). *Prenatal screening questionnaire.* Retrieved from http://www.ama-assn.org/ama1/pub/upload/mm/464/ped_screening.pdf

American Optometric Association. (2013). *Infant vision: Birth to 24 months.* Retrieved from http://www.aoa.org/patients-and-public/good-vision-throughout-life/childrens-vision/infant-vision-birth-to-24-months-of-age

American Pregnancy Association. (2007). *Epidural anesthesia.* Retrieved from http://www.americanpregnancy.org/laborn birth/epidural.html

American Psychiatric Association. (2013). *Diagnostic and statistical manual of mental disorders* (5th ed.). Arlington, VA: American Psychiatric Association.

American Psychological Association. (2004). *Briefing sheet: An overview of the psychological literature on the effects of divorce on children.* Retrieved from http://www.apa.org/about/gr/issues/cyf/divorce.aspx

American Psychological Association. (2005). *Lesbian and gay parenting.* Washington, DC: Author.

American Psychological Association. (2010). *Stress in America: Findings.* Washington, DC: Author. Retrieved from http://www.apa.org/news/press/releases/stress/national-report.pdf

American Psychological Association. (2014a). *Mental health and abortion.* Retrieved from http://www.apa.org/pi/women/programs/abortion/

American Psychological Association. (2014b). *PsycINFO.* Retrieved from http://www.apa.org/pubs/databases/psycinfo/index.aspx

American Psychological Association. (2014c). *Research in brain function and learning.* Retrieved from http://www.apa.org/education/k12/brain-function.aspx?item=1

American Psychological Association Presidential Task Force on Posttraumatic Stress Disorder and Trauma in Children and Adolescents. (2008). *Children and trauma: An update for mental health professionals.* Washington, DC: APA.

American Sexual Health Association. (2014). *STDs/STIs.* Retrieved from http://www.ashastd.org/std-sti.html

American Social Health Association. (1999–2011). *Herpes resource center.* Retrieved from http://www.ashastd.org/herpes/herpes_learn_pregnancy.cfm

American Youth Policy Forum. (2014). *About us.* Retrieved from http://www.aypf.org/about/

America's Future Workforce. (2013). *School to Work Opportunities Act of 1994.* Retrieved from http://americasfutureworkforce.org/2013/10/26/opportunities/

America's Great Outdoors. (2011). *America's great outdoors: A promise to future generations.* Retrieved from http://www.americasgreatoutdoors.gov/

America's Promise Alliance. (2009). *Cities in crisis 2009: Closing the graduation gap.* Retrieved from http://www.americas promise.org/Our-Work/Dropout-Prevention/Cities-in-Crisis.aspx

Anagnostou, K., Islam, S., King, Y., Foley, L., Pasea, L., Bond, S., . . . Clark, A. (2014). Assessing the efficacy of oral immunotherapy for the desensitisation of peanut allergy in children (STOP II): A phase 2 randomised controlled trial. *The Lancet.* Published Online January 30, 2014. Retrieved from http://dx.doi.org/10.1016/

Anderson, C. A., Shibuya, A., Ihori, N., Swing, E. L., Bushman, B. J., Sakamoto, A., . . . Saleem, M. (2010). Violent video game effects on aggression, empathy, and prosocial behavior in Eastern and Western countries: A meta-analytic review. *Psychological Bulletin, 136*(2), 151–173.

Anderson, D. I., Roth, M. B., & Campos, J. J. (2005). Reflexes. In *Encyclopedia of human development.* Thousand Oaks, CA: Sage. Retrieved from http://www.sage-ereference.com/humandevelopment/Article_n517.html

Anderson, D. R., & Hanson, K. G. (2013). What researchers have learned about toddlers and television. *Zero to Three, 33*(4), 4–10.

Anderson, D. R., Levin, S. R., & Lorch, E. P. (1977). The effects of TV program pacing on the behavior of preschool children. *Educational Communication & Technology, 25*(2), 159–166.

Anderson, D. R., & Pempek, T. A. (2005). Television and very young children. *American Behavioral Scientist, 48*(5), 505–522.

Anderson, J. R., Van Ryzin, M. J., & Doherty, W. J. (2010). Developmental trajectories of marital happiness in continuously married individuals: A group-based modeling approach. *Journal of Family Psychology, 24*, 587–596.

Anderson, K. (2005). *US "whittling away at death penalty."* Washington, DC: BBC News website. Retrieved from http://www.news.bbc.co.uk/2/hi/americas/4314207.stm

Andreou, G., & Karapetsas, A. (2004). Verbal abilities in low and highly proficient bilinguals. *Journal of Psycholinguistic Research, 33*(5), 357–364.

Angier, N. (2011, December 26). Now we are six. *The New York Times,* pp. D1.

Annie E. Casey Foundation. (2014). *Helping America's kids have a brighter future.* Retrieved from http://www.aecf.org/

Anobile, G., Stievano, P., & Burr, D. C. (2013). Visual sustained attention and numerosity sensitivity correlate with math achievement in children. *Journal of Experimental Child Psychology, 116*(2), 380–391. doi: 10.1016/j.jecp.2013.06.006

Arbuthnot, K. (2011). *Filling in the blanks: Understanding standardized testing and the Black-White achievement gap.* Charlotte, NC: IAP Information Age.

Arcelus, J., Mitchell, A. J., Wales, J., & Nielson, S. (2011). Mortality rates in patients with anorexia nervosa and other eating disorders. A meta-analysis of 36 studies. *Archives of General Psychiatry, 68*(7), 724–731.

Archibald, A. B., Graber, J. A., & Brooks-Gunn, J. (2003). Pubertal processes and physiological growth in adolescence. In G. R. Adams, M. D. Berzonsky, & M. A. Malden

(Eds.), *Blackwell handbook of adolescence* (pp. 24–47). Malden, MA: Blackwell.

Armbruster, B. B., Lehr, F., & Osborn, J. M. (2001). *Putting reading first: The research building blocks for teaching children to read*. Washington, DC: National Institute for Literacy.

Arnett, J. J. (2000). Emerging adulthood: A theory of development from the late teens through the twenties. *American Psychologist, 55,* 469–480.

Arteaga, S. S., & Lamb, Y. (2008). Expert review of key findings on children exposed to violence and their families from the Safe Start Demonstration Project. *Best Practices in Mental Health: An International Journal, 4*(1), 99–107.

Arthur, A. E., Bigler, R. S., & Ruble, D. N. (2009). An experimental test of the effects of gender constancy on sex typing. *Journal of Experimental Child Psychology, 104*(4), 427–446. doi: 10.1016/j.jecp.2009.08.002

Artman, L., Cahan, S., & Avni-Babad, D. (2006). Age, schooling and conditional reasoning. *Cognitive Development, 21*(2), 131–145. doi: 10.1016/j.cogdev.2006.01.004

Asato, M. R., Sweeney, J. A., Luna, B. (2006). Cognitive processes in the development of TOL performance. *Neuropsychologia, 44*(12), 2259–2269.

Asendorpf, J. B., & Baudonniere, P. (1993). Self-awareness and other-awareness: Mirror self-recognition and synchronic imitation among unfamiliar peers. *Developmental Psychology, 29*(1), 88–95.

Ashiabi, G. S., & O'Neal, K. K. (2008). A framework for understanding the association between food insecurity and children's developmental outcomes. *Child Development Perspectives, 2*(2), 71–77.

Astill, R. G., Van der Heijden, K. B., Van IJzendoorn, M. H., & Van Someren, E. J. (2012). Sleep, cognition, and behavioral problems in school-age children: A century of research meta-analyzed. *Emotional Bulletin, 138*(6), 1109–1138.

Astington, J. W., & Filippova, E. (2005). Language as the route into other minds. In B. F. Malle & S. D. Hodges (Eds.), *Other minds* (pp. 209–222). New York, NY: Guilford Press.

Atwell, J. E., Otterloo, J. V., Zipprich, J., Winter, K., Harriman, K., Salmon, D. A., Halsey, N. A., & Omer, S. B. (2013). Nonmedical vaccine exemptions and pertussis in California, 2010. *Pediatrics, 132,* 624–630.

Aud, S., KewalRamani, A., & Frohlich, L. (2011). *America's youth: Transitions to adulthood* (NCES 2012-026). U.S. Department of Education, National Center for Education Statistics. Washington, DC: U.S. Government Printing Office.

Aunola, K., Stattin, H., & Nurmi, J. (2000). Parenting styles and adolescents' achievement strategies. *Journal of Adolescence, 23*(2), 205–222.

Ayduk, O., Mendoza-Denton, R., Mischel, W., Downey, G., Peake, P. K., & Rodriguez, M. (2000). Regulating the interpersonal self: Strategic self-regulation for coping with rejection sensitivity. *Journal of Personality and Social Psychology, 79*(5), 776–792.

Ayres, M., & Leve, L. D. (2006). Gender identity and play. In D. P. Fromberg & D. Bergen (Eds.), *Play from birth to twelve: Contexts, perspective, and meanings* (pp. 41–46). New York, NY: Routledge.

Bacher, R. (2013). *Taking care of your child's fever.* Retrieved from http://www.webmd.com/children/guide/fever-care-young-children

Bachman, J. G., O'Malley, P. M., Freedman-Doan, P., Trzesniewski, K. H., & Donnellan, M. B. (2011). Adolescent self-esteem: Differences by race/ethnicity, gender and age. *Self-Identity, 10*(4), 445–473, doi: 10.1080/15298861003794538

Baek, H. (2002). A comparative study of moral development of Korean and British children. *Journal of Moral Education, 31*(4), 373–391.

Bafunno, D., & Camodeca, M. (2013). Shame and guilt development in preschoolers: The role of context, audience and individual characteristics. *European Journal of Developmental Psychology, 10*(2), 128–143.

Bagnell, K. (2001). *The little immigrants: The orphans who came to Canada.* Toronto, ON, Canada: Dundurn Press.

Bagwell, C. L., & Schmidt, M. E. (2011). *Friendships in childhood and adolescence.* New York, NY: Guilford.

Baham, M. E., Weimer, A. A., Braver, S. L., & Fabricius, W. V. (2008). Sibling relationships in blended families. In J. Pryor (Ed.), *The International Handbook of Stepfamilies* (pp. 175–207). Hoboken, NJ: Wiley & Sons.

Bailey, A., LeCouteur, A., Gottesman, I., & Bolton, P. (1995). Autism as a strongly genetic disorder: Evidence from a British twin study. *Psychological Medicine, 25*(1), 63–77.

Bailey, J. A., Hill, K. G., Hawkins, J. D., Catalano, R. F., & Abbott, R. D. (2008). Men's and women's patterns of substance use around pregnancy. *Birth: Issues in Perinatal Care, 35*(1), 50–59.

Bailey, R. (2005). Physical development and growth. In N. Salkind (Ed.), *Encyclopedia of human development* (pp. 1001–1008). Thousand Oaks, CA: SAGE.

Baillargeon, R. (1994). How do infants learn about the physical world? *Current Directions in Psychological Science, 3*(5), 133–140.

Baillargeon, R. (2008). Innate ideas revisited: For a principle of persistence in infants' physical reasoning. *Perspectives on Psychological Science, Special Issue: From Philosophical Thinking to Psychological Empiricism, 3*(1), 2–13.

Baillargeon, R., Li, J., Ng, W., & Yuan, S. (2009). An account of infants' physical reasoning. In A. Woodward & A. Needham (Eds.), *Learning and the infant mind* (pp. 66–116). New York, NY: Oxford University Press.

Baillargeon, R., Needham, A., & DeVos, J. (1992). The development of young infants' intuitions about support. *Early Development & Parenting, 1*(2), 69–78.

Baillargeon, R., Spelke, E. S., & Wasserman, S. (1985). Object permanence in five-month-old infants. *Cognition, 20*(3), 191–208.

Baker, A. L., & Ben-Ami, N. (2011). To turn a child against a parent is to turn a child against himself: The direct and indirect effects of exposure to parental alienation strategies on self-esteem and well-being. *Journal of Divorce & Remarriage, 52*(7), 472–489.

Baker, K., & Raney, A. A. (2007). Equally super? Gender-role stereotyping of superheroes in children's animated programs. *Mass Communication and Society, 10*(1), 25–41.

Bakermans-Kranenburg, M. J., van IJzendoorn, M. H., & Juffer, F. (2003). Less is more: Meta-analyses of sensitivity and attachment interventions in early childhood. *Psychological Bulletin, 129*(2), 195–215.

Balaban, M. T., & Reisenauer, C. D. (2005). Sensory development. In *Encyclopedia of human development*. Thousand Oaks, CA: Sage. Retrieved from http://www.sage-ereference.com/humandevelopment/Article_n555.html

Balbernie, R. (2010). Reactive attachment disorder as an evolutionary adaptation. *Attachment & Human Development, 12*(3), 265-281.

Baldry, A. C., & Farrington, D. P. (2000). Bullies and delinquents: Personal characteristics and parental styles. *Journal of Community & Applied Social Psychology, 10*(1), 17–31.

Baldwin, D. A., & Moses, L. J. (2001). Links between social understanding and early word learning: Challenges to current accounts. *Social Development, 10*(3), 309–329.

Bali Travel Guidebook. (2002). *Royal Odalan and tooth filing ceremony (Mepandes)*. Retrieved from http://www.klubkokos.com/guidebook/royal_odalan.htm

Ballard, W., Hall, M. N., & Kaufmann, L. (2010). Do dietary interventions improve ADHD symptoms in children? *Journal of Family Practice, 59*(4), 234–235.

Banaschewski, T., & Brandeis, D. (2007). What electrical brain activity tells us about brain function that other techniques cannot tell us—A child psychiatric perspective. *Journal of Child Psychology and Psychiatry, 4*(5), 415–435.

Bandstra, E., Morrow, C., Accornero, V., Mansoor, E., Xue, L., & Anthony, J. (2011). Estimated effects of in utero cocaine exposure on language development through early adolescence. *Neurotoxicology and Teratology, 33*(1), 25–35. doi: 10.1016/j.ntt.2010.07.001

Bandstra, E. S., Morrow, C. E., Mansoor, E., & Accornero, V. H. (2010). Prenatal drug exposure: Infant and toddler outcomes. *Journal of Addictive Disorders, 29*(2), 245–258.

Bandura, A. (1986). *Social foundations of thought and action*. Englewood Cliffs, NJ: Prentice Hall.

Bandura, A., Caprara, G. V., Barbaranelli, C., Pastorelli, C., & Regalia, C. (2001). Sociocognitive self-regulatory mechanisms governing transgressive behavior. *Journal of Personality and Social Psychology, 80*(1), 125–135.

Bandura, A., Ross, D., & Ross, S. A. (1963). Imitation of film-mediated aggressive models. *Journal of Abnormal and Social Psychology, 66*(1), 3–11.

Banerjee, S. C., & Greene, K. (2007). Antismoking initiatives: Effects of analysis versus production media literacy interventions on smoking-related attitude, norm, and behavioral intentions. *Health Communication, 22,* 37–48.

Barac, R., & Bialystok, E. (2012). Bilingual effects on cognitive and linguistic development: Role of language, cultural background, and education. *Child Development, 83,* 413–422.

Barber, B. K. (1994). Cultural, family, and personal contexts of parent-adolescent conflict. *Journal of Marriage and Family, 56*(2), 375–386.

Barcelona Field Studies Centre. (2010). *Data presentation: Scatter graphs*. Retrieved from http://geographyfieldwork.com/DataPresentationScatterGraphs.htm

Barker, D., Gluckman, P., Godfrey, K., Harding, J., Owens, J., & Robinson, J. (1993). Fetal nutrition and cardiovascular disease in adult life. *Lancet, 341*(8850), 938–941.

Barkin, S., Ip, E., Richardson, I., Klinepeter, S., Finch, S., & Krcmar, M. (2006). Parental media mediation styles for children aged 2 to 11 years. *Archives of Pediatrics & Adolescent Medicine, 160*(4), 395–401.

Barkley, R. A. (2006). Attention-deficit/hyperactivity disorder. In D. A. Wolfe & E. J. Mash (Eds.), *Behavioral and emotional disorders in adolescents* (pp. 91–152). New York, NY: Guilford Press.

Barnett, W. S., Schulman, K., & Shore, R. (2004). Class size: What's the best fit? *NIEER Policy Matters, 9,* 1–11. Retrieved from http://www.nieer.org/resources/policy briefs/9.pdf

Barnhart, R. D., Davenport, M. J., Epps, S. B., & Nordquist, V. M. (2003). Developmental coordination disorder. *Physical Therapy, 83,* 722–731.

Baron-Cohen, S. (1995). *Mindblindness*. Cambridge, MA: MIT Press.

Barr, R., Lauricella, A., Zack, E., & Calvert, S. L. (2010). Infant and early childhood exposure to adult-directed and child-directed television programming: Relations with cognitive skills at age four. *Merrill-Palmer Quarterly, 56*(1), 21–48. doi: 10.1353/mpq.0.0038

Barlett, C., Harris, R., & Bruey, C. (2008). The effect of the amount of blood in a violent video game on aggression, hostility, and arousal. *Journal of Experimental Social Psychology, 44*(3), 539–546.

Bartlett, E. E. (2004). The effect of fatherhood on the health of men: A review of the literature. *Journal of Men's Health and Gender, 1*(2–3), 159–169.

Bassuk, E. L., Murphy, C., Coupe, N. T., Kenney, R. R., & Beach, C. A. (2011). *America's youngest outcasts: 2010.* Needham, MA: National Center on Family Homelessness.

Bates, E. (1990). Language about me and you: Pronominal reference and the emerging concept of self. In D. Cicchetti & M. Beeghly (Eds.), *The self in transition* (pp. 165–182). Chicago, IL: University of Chicago Press.

Bauer, K., Laska, M., Fulkerson, J., & Neumark-Sztainer, D. (2011). Longitudinal and secular trends in parental encouragement for healthy eating, physical activity, and dieting throughout the adolescent years. *Journal of Adolescent Health, 49*(3), 306–311. doi: 10.1016/j.jadohealth.2010.12.023

Bauer, P. J. (2007). Recall in infancy: A neurodevelopmental account. *Current Directions in Psychological Science, 16*(3), 142–146.

Bauer, P. J., & Leventon, J. S. (2013). Memory for one-time experiences in the second year of life: Implications for the status of episodic memory. *Infancy, 18*(5), 755-781. doi: 10.1111/infa.12005

Baumeister, R. F., Campbell, J. D., Krueger, J. I., & Vohs, K. D. (2003). Does high self-esteem cause better performance, interpersonal success, happiness, or healthier lifestyles? *Psychological Science in the Public Interest, 4*(1), 1–44.

Baumgartner, S. E., Valkenburg, P. M., & Peter, J. (2011). The influence of descriptive and injunctive peer norms on adolescents' risky sexual online behavior. *Cyberpsychology, Behavior, and Social Networking, 14*(12), 753–758. doi: 10.1089/cyber.2010.0510

Baumrind, D. (1967). Child care practices anteceding three patterns of preschool behavior. *Genetic Psychology Monographs, 75*(1), 43–88.

Baumrind, D. (1971). Current patterns of parental authority. *Developmental Psychology Monograph, 4*(1), Part 2, 1–103.

Baumrind, D. (1991a). Effective parenting during the early adolescent transition. In P. A. Cowan & E. M. Hetherington (Eds.), *Family transitions* (pp. 111–163). Hillsdale, NJ: Erlbaum.

Baumrind, D. (2012). Differentiating between confrontive and coercive kinds of parental power-assertive disciplinary practices. *Human Development, 55*(2), 35–51. doi: 10.1159/000337962

Baumrind, D. (2013). Authoritative parenting revisited: History and current status. In R. E. Larzelere, A. Morris, & A. W. Harrist (Eds.), *Authoritative parenting: Synthesizing nurturance and discipline for optimal child development.* Washington, DC: American Psychological Association. doi: 10.1037/13948–000

Baumrind, D., Larzelere, R. E., & Owens, E. B. (2010). Effects of preschool parents' power assertive patterns and practices on adolescent development. *Parenting: Science And Practice, 10*(3), 157-201. doi: 10.1080/15295190903290790

Bayley, N. (1969). *Manual for the Bayley Scales of Infant Development.* New York, NY: The Psychological Corporation.

BBC News. (1998). *Evel Knievel's son smashes stunt record.* Retrieved from http://www.news.bbc.co.uk/2/hi/in_depth/60039.stm

Beam, M. R., Chen, C., & Greenberger, E. (2002). The nature of adolescents' relationships with their 'very important' nonparental adults. *American Journal of Community Psychology, 30*(2), 305–325.

Bear, M. F., Connors, B. W., & Paradiso, M. A. (2007). *Neuroscience exploring the brain* (3rd ed.). Baltimore, MD: Lippincott, Williams & Wilkins.

Bearce, K., & Rovee-Collier, C. (2006). Repeated priming increases memory accessibility in infants. *Journal of Experimental Child Psychology, 93*(4), 357-376. doi: 10.1016/j.jecp.2005.10.002

Beasley, N. M. R., Hall, A., Tomkins, A. M., Donnelly, C., Ntimbwa, P., Kivuga, J., . . . Bundy, D. A. P. (2000). The health of enrolled and non enrolled children of school age in Tanga, Tanzania. *Acta Tropica, 76*(3), 223.

Beaudet, A. L. (2013). The utility of chromosocal microarray analysis in developmental and behavioral pediatrics. *Child Development, 84*(1), 121–132.

Becher, J. C. (2006). *Insights into early fetal development.* Royal College of Physicians of Edinburgh and Royal College of Physicians and Surgeons of Glasgow. Retrieved from http://www.behindthemedicalheadlines.com/articles/insights -into-early-fetal-development

Beemsterboer, S. N., Homburg, R., Gorter, N. A., Schats, R., Hompes, P. G. A., & Lambalk, C. B. (2006). The paradox of declining fertility but increasing twinning. *Human Reproduction, 21*(6), 1531–1532.

Beesdo, K., Knappe, S., & Pine, D. S. (2009). Anxiety and anxiety disorders in children and adolescents: Developmental issues and implications for DSM-V. *Psychiatric Clinics of North America, 32*(3), 483–524.

Beighle, A. (2012). *Increasing physical activity through recess.* San Diego, CA: Active Living Research.

Beilock, S. L., Gunderson, E. A., Ramirez, G., & Levine, S. C. (2010). Female teachers' math anxiety affects girls' math achievement. *Proceedings of The National Academy of Sciences of The United States of America, 107*(5), 1860–1863.

Bell, J. (2008). *Yale professor recognized for commitment to children and youth.* Retrieved from http://www.ziglercenter .yale.edu/documents/CTVoicesaward-Gilliam.pdf

Bell, J. F., Wilson, J. S., & Liu, G. C. (2008). Neighborhood greenness and 2-year changes in body mass index of children and youth. *American Journal of Preventive Medicine, 5*(6), 547–553.

Bell, S. M., & Ainsworth, M. D. (1972). Infant crying and maternal responsiveness. *Child Development, 43*(4), 1171–1190.

Bellin, H. F., & Singer, D. G. (2006). My magic story car: Video based play intervention to strengthen emergent literacy of at-risk preschoolers. In D. G. Singer, R. M. Golinkoff, & K. Hirsh-Pasek (Eds.), *Play=learning* (pp. 101–123). New York, NY: Oxford University Press.

Belsky, J. (2005). Attachment theory and research in ecological perspective. In K. E. Grossmann, K. Grossmann, & E. Waters (Eds.), *Attachment from infancy to adulthood: The major longitudinal studies* (pp. 71–97). New York, NY: Guilford Press.

Belsky, J., Burchinal, M., McCartney, K., Vandell, D. L., Clarke-Stewart, K. A., Owen, M. T., & the NICHD Early Child Care Research Network. (2007). Are there long-term effects of early child care? *Child Development, 78*(2), 681–701.

Belsky, J., Houts, R. M., & Fearon, R. (2010). Infant attachment security and the timing of puberty: Testing an evolutionary hypothesis. *Psychological Science, 21*(9), 1195–1201.

Belsky, J., & Kelly, J. (1994). *The transition to parenthood: How a first child changes a marriage.* New York, NY: Delacorte Press.

Bem, S. L. (1989). Genital knowledge and gender constancy in preschool children. *Child Development, 60*(3), 649–662.

Bemiller, M. (2010). Mothering from a distance. *Journal of Divorce and Remarriage, 51*(3), 169–184.

Bengtson, V. L. (2001). Beyond the nuclear family: The increasing importance of multigenerational bonds [The Burgess Award Lecture]. *Journal of Marriage and Family, 63*, 1–16.

Bengtsson, S. L., Nagy, Z., Skare, S., Forsman, L., Forssberg, H., & Ullén, F. (2005). Extensive piano practicing has regionally specific effects on white matter development. *Nature Neuroscience, 8*(9), 1148–1150.

Benner, A. D., & Mistry, R. S. (2007). Congruence of mother and teacher educational expectations and low-income youth's academic competence. *Journal of Educational Psychology, 99*(1), 140–153.

Benson, E. S. (2004). Heritability: It's all relative. *APA Monitor, 35*(4), 44. Retrieved from http://www.apa.org/monitor/apr04/herit.aspx

Berenbaum, S. A., Martin, C. L., Hanish, L. D., Briggs, P. T., & Fabes, R. A. (2008). Sex differences in children's play. In J. B. Becker, K. J. Berkley, N. Gear, E. Hampson, & J. P. Herman (Eds.), *Sex differences in the brain from genes to behavior* (pp. 275–290). New York, NY: Oxford University Press.

Berg, S. J., & Wynne-Edwards, K. E. (2001). Changes in testosterone, cortisol, and estradiol levels in men becoming fathers. *Mayo Clinic Proceedings, 76*, 582–592.

Bergen, A. W., van den Bree, M. M., Yeager, M. M., Welch, R. R., Ganjei, J. K., Haque, K. K., . . . Kaye, W. H. (2003). Candidate genes for anorexia nervosa in the 1p33–36 linkage region: Serotonin 1D and delta opioid receptor loci exhibit significant association to anorexia nervosa. *Molecular Psychiatry, 8*(4), 397–406.

Berger, U., Weitkamp, K., & Strauss, B. (2009). *European Eating Disorders Review, 17*(2), 128–136.

Bergh, S., & Erling, A. (2005). Adolescent identity formation: A Swedish study of identity status using the EOM-EIS-II. *Adolescence, 40*(158), 377–396.

Bergsma, L., & Ingram, M. (2001). *Blowing smoke—Project evaluation final report.* Retrieved from http://www.scenesmoking.org/research/BlowingSmoke.pdf

Berk, L. E., Mann, T. D., & Ogan, A. T. (2006). Make-believe play: Wellspring for development of self-regulation. In D. G. Singer, R. M. Golinkoff, & K. Hirsh-Pasek (Eds.), *Play=learning* (pp. 74–100). New York, NY: Oxford University Press.

Berk, L. E., & Winsler, A. (1995). *Scaffolding children's learning: Vygotsky and early childhood education.* Washington, DC: National Association for the Education of Young Children.

Berlin, M., Vinnerljung, B., & Hjern, A. (2011). School performance in primary school and psychosocial problems in young adulthood among care leavers from long term foster care. *Children and Youth Services Review, 33*(12), 2489–2497.

Berman, M. G., Jonides, J., & Kaplan, S. (2008). The cognitive benefits of interacting with nature. *Psychological Science, 19*(12), 1207–1212.

Bernard, K., Dozier, M., Bick, J., Lewis-Morrarty, E., Lindhiem, O., & Carlson, E. (2012). Enhancing attachment organization among maltreated children: Results of a randomized clinical trial. *Child Development, 83*(2), 623–636.

Bernier, A., Beauchamp, M. H., Bouvette-Turcot, A., Carlson, S. M., & Carrier, J. (2013). Sleep and cognition in preschool years: Specific links to executive functioning. *Child Development, 84*(5), 1542–1553.

Berti, A. E., Garattoni, C., & Venturini, B. (2000). The understanding of sadness, guilt, and shame in 5-, 7-, and 9-year-old children. *Genetic, Social, and General Psychology Monographs, 126*(3), 293–318.

Best, C. C., & McRoberts, G. W. (2003). Infant perception of non-native consonant contrasts that adults assimilate in different ways. *Language and Speech, 46*(2–3), 183–216.

Best, J. R., Miller, P. H., & Jones, L. L. (2009). Executive functions after age 5: Changes and correlates. *Developmental Review, 29*(3), 180–200.

Bhanot, R., & Jovanovic, J. (2005). Do parents' academic gender stereotypes influence whether they intrude on their children's homework? *Sex Roles, 52*(9–10), 597–607.

Bialystok, E. (2001). *Bilingualism in development: Language, literacy, and cognition.* New York, NY: Cambridge University Press.

Bialystok, E. (2007). Acquisition of literacy in bilingual children: A framework for research. *Language Learning, 57*, 45–77.

Bialystok, E. (2011). Reshaping the mind: The benefits of bilingualism. *Canadian Journal of Experimental Psychology, 65*(4), 229–235.

Bialystok, E., & Craik, F. I. M. (2010). Cognitive and linguistic processing in the bilingual mind. *Current Directions in Psychological Science, 19*(1), 19–23.

Bialystok, E., Craik, F. I. M., Green, D. W., & Gollan, T. H. (2009). Bilingual minds. *Psychological Science in the Public Interest, 10*(3), 89–129.

Bialystok, E., & Viswanathan, M. (2009). Components of executive control with advantages for bilingual children in two cultures. *Cognition, 112*(3), 494–500.

Bianchi, S. M., Robinson, J. P., & Milkie, M. A. (2006). *Changing rhythms of American family life.* New York, NY: Russell Sage Foundation.

Biasini, F. J., Grupe, L., Huffman, L., & Bray, N. W. (1999). Mental retardation: A symptom and a syndrome. In S. Netherton, D. Holmes, & C. E. Walker (Eds.), *Comprehensive textbook of child and adolescent disorders* (pp. 6–23). New York, NY: Oxford University Press.

Biblarz, T. J., & Gottainer, G. (2000). Family structure and children's success: A comparison of widowed and divorced single-mother families. *Journal of Marriage and Family, 62*, 533–548.

Biddle, B. J., & Berliner, D. C. (2002). Small class size and its effects. *Educational Leadership, 59*(5), 12–23.

Bieber, L., Dince, P., Drellich, M., Grand, H., Gundlach, R., Kremer, M., . . . Bieber, T. (1962). *Homosexuality: A psychoanalytic study of male homosexuals.* New York, NY: Basic Books.

Biggs, M., Gould, H., & Foster, D. (2013). Understanding why women seek abortions in the US. *BMC Women's Health, 1329.* doi: 10.1186/1472-6874-13-29

Biggs, S. N., Lushington, K., Martin, A. J., van den Heuvel, C., & Kennedy, J. D. (2013). Gender, socioeconomic and ethnic difference in sleep patterns in school-aged children. *Sleep Medicine, 14,* 1304–1309.

Binder, E. B., Bradley, R. G., Liu, W., Epstein, M. P., Deveau, T. C., Mercer, K. B., . . . Ressler, K. J. (2008). Association of *FKBP5* polymorphisms and childhood abuse with risk of posttraumatic stress disorder symptoms in adults. *JAMA, 299*(11), 1291–1305.

Bingham, A., & Pennington, J. L. (2007). As easy as ABC: Facilitating early literacy enrichment experiences. *Young Exceptional Children, 10*(2), 17–29.

Birbeck, D., & Drummond, M. (2005). Interviewing, and listening to the voices of, very young children on body image and perceptions of self. *Early Child Development and Care, 175*(6), 579–596.

Bittner, A., Egger, H. L., Erkanli, A., Costello, E. J., Foley, D. L., & Angold, A. (2007). What do childhood anxiety disorders predict? *Journal of Child Psychology and Psychiatry, 48*(12), 1174–1183.

Black, M. H., Smith, N., Porter, A. H., Jacobsen, S. J., & Koebnick, C. (2012). Higher prevalence of obesity among children with asthma. *Obesity, 20,* 1041–1047.

Black, M. M., Hess, C. R., & Berenson-Howard, J. (2000). Toddlers from low-income families have below normal mental, motor, and behavior scores on the Revised Bayley Scales. *Journal of Applied Developmental Psychology, 26*(6), 655–666.

Blackwell, G. L. (2010). A little help along the way. *Outlook, 104*(1), 16–19.

Blair, C., & Razza, R. (2007). Relating effortful control, executive function, and false belief understanding to emerging math and literacy ability in kindergarten. *Child Development, 78*(2), 647–663. doi: 10.1111/j.1467-8624.2007.01019.x

Blair, C., Zelazo, P. D., & Greenberg, M. T. (2005). The measurement of executive function in early childhood. *Developmental Neuropsychology, 28*(2), 561–571.

Blakemore, S. J., & Choudhury, S. (2006). Development of the adolescent brain: Implications for executive function and social cognition. *Journal of Child Psychology and Psychiatry, 47*(3), 296–312.

Blanchard, R. (2008). Review and theory of handedness, birth order, and homosexuality in men. *Laterality, 13*(1):51–70.

Blasi, C., Bjorklund, D. F., & Soto, P. (2003). Effects of a knowledge base manipulation on children's recall. *Estudios De Psicología, 24*(1), 91–100. doi: 10.1174/021093903321329085

Blasi, C. H., & Bjorklund, D. F. (2003). Evolutionary developmental psychology: A new tool for better understanding human ontogeny. *Human Development, 46,* 259–281.

Blass, E. M., & Hoffmeyer, L. B. (1991). Sucrose as an analgesic in newborn humans. *Pediatrics, 87,* 215–218.

Blondal, K., & Adalbjarnardottir, S. (2014). Parenting in relation to school dropout through student engagement: A longitudinal study. *Journal of Marriage & Family, 76*(4), 778–795.

Blumenthal, H., Leen-Feldner, E. W., Babson, K. A., Gahr, J. L., Trainor, C. D., & Frala, J. L. (2011). Elevated social anxiety among early maturing girls. *Developmental Psychology, 47*(4), 1133–1140.

Boazman, J., & Sayler, M. (2011). Personal well-being of gifted students following participation in an early college-entrance program. *Roeper Review, 33*(2), 76–85.

Bobo, J. K., Klepinger, D. H., & Dong, F. B. (2006). Changes in the prevalence of alcohol use during pregnancy among recent and at-risk drinkers in the NLSY cohort. *Journal of Women's Health, 15*(9), 1061–1070.

Bocarro, J., Kanters, M. A., Casper, J., & Forrester, S. (2008). School physical education, extracurricular sports, and lifelong active living. *Journal of Teaching in Physical Education, 27*(2), 155–166.

Boelema, S. R., Harakeh, Z., Ormel, J., Hartman, C. A., Vollebergh, W. M., & van Zandvoort, M. E. (2013). Executive functioning shows differential maturation from early to late adolescence: Longitudinal findings from a TRAILS study. *Neuropsychology, 28*(2), 177–187. doi: 10.1037/neu0000049

Boergers, J., Gable, C. J., & Owens, J. A. (2014). Later school start time is associated with improved sleep and daytime functioning in adolescents. *Journal of Developmental and Behavioral Pediatrics, 35*(1), 11–17. doi: 10.1097/DBP.0000000000000018

Boets, B., Op de Beeck, H. P., Vandermosten, M., Scott, S. K., Gillebert, C. R., Mantini, D., . . . Ghesquière, P. (2013). Intact but less accessible phonetic representations in adults with dyslexia. *Science, 342*(6163), 1251–1254.

Bogin, B., & Varela-Silva, M. I. (2010). Leg length, body proportion, and health: A review with a note on beauty. *International Journal of Environmental Research and Public Health, 7,* 1047–1075.

Bohannon, J. N., & Bonvillian, J. D. (2005). Theoretical approaches to language acquisition. In J. B. Gleason (Ed.), *The development of language* (6th ed., pp. 230–291). Boston, MA: Pearson.

Boksa, P. (2008). Maternal infection during pregnancy and schizophrenia. *Journal of Psychiatry & Neuroscience, 33*(3), 183–185.

Bonawitz, E., Shafto, P., Gweon, H., Goodman, N. D., Spelke, E., & Schulz, L. (2011). The double-edged sword of pedagogy: Instruction limits spontaneous exploration and discovery. *Cognition, 120*(3), 322-330. doi: 10.1016/j.cognition.2010.10.001

Bonny, J. W., & Lourenco, S. F. (2013). The approximate number system and its relation to early math achievement: Evidence from the preschool years. *Journal of Experimental Child Psychology, 114*(3), 375–388.

Booth, A., & Amato, P. R. (2001). Parental predivorce relations and offspring postdivorce well-being. *Journal of Marriage and Family, 63*(1), 197–212.

Booth-LaForce, C., Oh, W., Kim, A. H., Rubin, K. H., Rose-Krasnor, L., & Burgess, K. (2006). Attachment, self-worth, and peer-group functioning in middle childhood. *Attachment & Human Development, 8*(4), 309–325.

Booth-LaForce, C., & Oxford, M. L. (2008). Trajectories of social withdrawal from grades 1 to 6: Prediction from early parenting, attachment, and temperament. *Developmental Psychology, 44*(5), 1298–1313.

Bornstein, D. (2014). Teaching children to calm themselves. *The New York Times.* Retrieved from http://opinionator. blogs.nytimes.com/2014/03/19/first-learn-how-to-calm-down/?_php=true&_type=blogs&_r=0

Bornstein, M. H., Hahn, C., Bell, C., Haynes, O. M., Slater, A., Golding, J., . . . ALSPAC Study Team. (2006). Stability in cognition across early childhood: A developmental cascade. *Psychological Science, 17*(2), 151–158.

Borntrager, C., Davis, J. L., Bernstein, A., & Gorman, H. (2009). A cross-national perspective on bullying. *Child & Youth Care Forum, 38*(3), 121–134.

Borse, N. N., Gilchrist, J., Dellinger, A. M., Rudd, R. A., Ballesteros, M. F., & Sleet, D. A. (2008). *CDC childhood injury report: Patterns of unintentional injuries among 0–19 year olds in the United States, 2000–2006.* Atlanta, GA: Centers for Disease Control and Prevention, National Center for Injury Prevention and Control.

Bortolus, R., Parazzini, F., Chatenoud, L., Benzi, G., Bianchi, M. M., & Marini, A. (1999). The epidemiology of multiple births. *Human Reproduction Update, 5*(2), 179–187.

Bosma, H., & Gerlsma, C. (2003). From early attachment relations to the adolescent and adult organization of self. In J. Valsiner & K. J. Connolly (Eds.), *Handbook of developmental psychology* (pp. 450–488). Thousand Oaks, CA: Sage.

Boston Women's Health Book Collective. (2005). *Our bodies, ourselves: A new edition for a new era.* New York, NY: Simon & Schuster.

Bouchard, S. (2011). Could virtual reality be effective in treating children with phobias? *Expert Review of Neurotherapeutics, 11*(2), 207–213. doi: 10.1586/ern.10.196

Bouchard, T., Lykken, D. T., McGue, M., & Segal, N. (1990). Sources of human psychological differences: The Minnesota Study of Twins Reared Apart. *Science, 250*(4978), 223–228.

Bouchez, C. (2008). *Childbirth options: What's best?* Retrieved from http://www.webmd.com/baby/features/childbirth-options-whats-best

Bouchez, C. (2010). *Separating pregnancy myths and facts.* Retrieved from http://www.cbsnews.com/news/separating-pregnancy-myths-and-facts/

Boulet, S., Schieve, L., & Boyle, C. (2011). Birth weight and health and developmental outcomes in U.S. children, 1997–2005. *Maternal & Child Health Journal, 15*(7), 836–844. doi: 10.1007/s10995-009-0538-2

Boulos, R., Vikre, E., Oppenheimer, S., Chang, H., & Kanarek, R. B. (2012). ObesiTV: How television is influencing the obesity epidemic. *Physiology & Behavior, 107*(1), 146–153.

Bower, B. (2004). The brain's word act: Reading verbs revs up motor cortex areas. *Science News, 165*(6), 83.

Bower, B. (2005). Investing on a whiff. *Science News, 167*(23), 356–357.

Bowlby, J. (1958). The nature of the child's tie to his mother. *International Journal of Psycho-Analysis, 39,* 350–373.

Bowlby, J. (1969). *Attachment and loss: Vol. 1. Attachment.* New York, NY: Basic Books.

Bowman, L. L., Levine, L. E., Waite, B. M., & Gendron, M. (2010). Can students really multitask? An experimental study of instant messaging while reading. *Computers & Education, 54*(4), 927–931.

Bowman, S. A., Gortmaker, S. L., Ebbeling, C. B., Pereira, M. A., & Ludwig, D. S. (2004). Effects of fast food consumption on energy intake and diet quality among children in a national household survey. *Pediatrics, 113*(1, pt. 1), 112–118.

Boyce, P., Condon, J., Barton, J., & Corkindale, C. (2007). First-time fathers' study: Psychological distress in expectant fathers during pregnancy. *Australian & New Zealand Journal of Psychiatry, 41*(9), 718–725.

Boyd, R. (2008). Do people only use 10 percent of their brains? *Scientific American.* Retrieved from http://www.scientificamer ican.com/article.cfm?id= people-only-use-10-percent-of-brain

Bradley, R. H., & Corwyn, R. F. (2002). Socioeconomic status and child development. *Annual Review of Psychology, 53,* 371–399.

Bradley, R. H., Corwyn, R. F., McAdoo, H. P., & Garcia Coll, C. (2001). The home environments of children in the United States: Part I. Variations by age, ethnicity, and poverty status. *Child Development, 72*(6), 1844–1867.

Brainerd, C. J., & Reyna, V. F. (2004). Fuzzy-trace theory and memory development. *Developmental Review, 24*(4), 396–439.

Braithwaite, D. O., Schrodt, P., & DiVerniero, R. (2009). Stepfamilies. In H. T. Reis & S. Sprecher (Eds.), *Encyclopedia of human relationships* (pp. 1595–1598). Thousand Oaks, CA: Sage.

Branch, D. W., & Scott, J. R. (2003). Early pregnancy loss. In J. S. Scott, R. S. Gibbs, B. Y. Karlan, & A. F. Haney (Eds.), *Danforth's obstetrics and gynecology* (9th ed., pp. 75–87). Philadelphia, PA: Lippincott.

Branum, A. M., & Lukacs, S. L. (2009). Food allergy among children in the United States. *Pediatrics, 124*(6), 1549–1555.

Brasacchio, T., Kuhn, B., & Martin, S. (2001). *How does encouragement of invented spelling influence conventional spelling development?.* [serial online]. Retrieved from ERIC, Ipswich, MA.

Bratton, S. C., Ray, D., & Rhine, T. (2005). The efficacy of play therapy with children: A meta-analytic review of treatment outcomes. *Professional Psychology: Research and Practice, 36*(4), 376–390.

Braungart-Rieker, J., Courtney, S., & Garwood, M. M. (1999). Mother- and father-infant attachment: Families in context. *Journal of Family Psychology, 13*(4), 535–553.

Bregman, J. (2005). Apgar Score. *Encyclopedia of Human Development*. Thousand Oaks, CA: Sage. Retrieved from http://www.sage-ereference.com/humandevelopment/Article_n

Breier, J., Simos, P. G., & Fletcher, J. M. (2002). Abnormal activation of tempoparietal language areas during phonetic analysis in children with dyslexia. *Neuropsychology, 17,* 610–621.

Bremner, J. G., Johnson, S. P., Slater, A., Mason, U., Foster, K., Cheshire, A., & Spring, J. (2005). Conditions for young infants' perception of object trajectories. *Child Development, 76*(5), 1029–1043.

Brennan, A., Marshall-Lucette, S., Ayers, S., & Ahmed, H. (2007). A qualitative exploration of the Couvade syndrome in expectant fathers. *Journal of Reproductive & Infant Psychology, 25*(1), 18–39.

Brisch, K. H., Bechinger, D., Betzler, S., Heinemann, H., Kächele, H., Pohlandt, F., . . . Buchheim, A. (2005). Attachment quality in very low-birthweight premature infants in relation to maternal attachment representations and neurological development. *Parenting: Science and Practice, 5*(4), 311–331.

Britsch, B., Callahan, N., & Peterson, K. (2010). The power of partnerships. *Outlook, 104*(1), 13–15.

Brody, G. H., Chen, Y., Murry, V. M., Ge, X., Simons, R. L., Gibbons, F. X., . . . Cutrona, C. E. (2006). Perceived discrimination and the adjustment of African-American youths: A five year longitudinal analysis with contextual moderation effects. *Child Development, 77*(5), 1170–1189.

Brody, L. E. (2005). The study of exceptional talent. *High Ability Studies, 16*(1), 87–96.

Brody, L. R., & Hall, J. A. (2008). Gender and emotion in context. In M. Lewis & J. Haviland (Eds.), *Handbook of emotions* (3rd ed., pp. 395–408). New York, NY: Guilford.

Broesch, T., Callaghan, T., Henrich, J., Murphy, C., & Rochat, P. (2011). Cultural variations in children's mirror self-recognition. *Journal of Cross-Cultural Psychology, 42*(6), 1018–1029.

Broglio, S. P., Eckner, J. T., Martini, D., Sosnoff, J. J., Kutcher, J. S., & Randolph, C. (2011). Cumulative head impact burden in high school football. *Journal of Neurotrauma, 28*(10), 2069–2078.

Bronfenbrenner, U. (1970). *Two worlds of childhood: U.S. and U.S.S.R.* New York, NY: Russell Sage Foundation.

Bronfenbrenner, U. (1975). Reality and research in the ecology of human development. *Proceedings of the American Philosophical Society, 119*(6), 439–469.

Bronfenbrenner, U. (1977). Toward an experimental ecology of human development. *American Psychologist, 32*(7), 513–531.

Bronfenbrenner, U. (1986). Ecology of the family as a context for human development: Research perspectives. *Developmental Psychology, 22*(6), 723–742.

Brooks, C., Pearce, N., & Douwes, J. (2013). The hygiene hypothesis in allergy and asthma: An update. *Current Opinion in Allergy & Clinical Immunology, 13*(1), 70–77.

Brophy-Herb, H. E., Lee, R. E., Nievar, M. A., & Stollak, G. (2007). Preschoolers' social competence: Relations to family characteristics, teacher behaviors and classroom climate. *Journal of Applied Developmental Psychology, 28*(2), 134–148.

Browder, D. M., Wakeman, S. Y., Spooner, F., Ahlgrim-Delzell, L., & Algozzine, B. (2006). Research on reading instruction for individuals with significant cognitive disabilities. *Exceptional Children, 72*(4), 392–408.

Brown, A. S., & Susser, E. (2008). Prenatal nutritional deficiency and risk of adult schizophrenia. *Schizophrenia Bulletin, 34*(6), 1054–1063.

Brown, B. B. (1993). Peer groups and peer cultures. In S. S. Feldman & G. R. Elliott (Eds.), *At the threshold: The developing adolescent* (pp. 171–196). Cambridge, MA: Harvard University Press.

Brown, B. B. (2004). Adolescents' relationships with peers. In R. M. Lerner & L. Steinberg (Eds.), *Handbook of adolescent psychology* (pp. 363–394). Hoboken, NJ: Wiley.

Brown, B., Bakken, J. P., Ameringer, S. W., & Mahon, S. D. (2008). A comprehensive conceptualization of the peer influence process in adolescence. In M. J. Prinstein & K. A. Dodge (Eds.), *Understanding peer influence in children and adolescents* (pp. 17–44). New York, NY: Guilford Press.

Brown, B. B., & Klute, C. (2006). Friendships, cliques, and crowds. In G. R. Adams & M. D. Berzonsky (Eds.), *Blackwell handbook of adolescence* (pp. 330–348). Malden, MA: Blackwell.

Brown, J. D., & Bobkowski, P. S. (2011). Older and Newer Media: Patterns of Use and Effects on Adolescents' Health and Well-Being. *Journal of Research On Adolescence, 21*(1), 95–113. doi: 10.1111/j.1532-7795.2010.00717.x

Brown, N., Gallagher, R., Fowler, C., & Wales, S. (2010). The role of parents in managing asthma in middle childhood: An important consideration in chronic care. *Collegian, 17*(2), 71–76.

Browne, J. V. (2005). Preterm infants. *Encyclopedia of human development*. Thousand Oaks, CA: Sage. Retrieved from http://www.sage-ereference.com/humandevelopment/Article_n496.html

Brownell, C., & Carriger, M. S. (1990). Changes in cooperation and self-other differentiation during the second year. *Child Development, 61,* 1164–1174.

Bruder, C. E. G., Piotrowski, A., Gijsbers, A. A. C. J., Andersson, R., Erickson, S., Diaz de Stahl, T., . . . Dumanski, J. P. (2008). Phenotypically concordant and discordant monozygotic twins display different DNA copy-number-variation profiles. *The American Journal of Human Genetics, 82*(3), 763–771.

Brunsma, D. L. (2005). Interracial families and the racial identification of mixed-race children: Evidence from the Early Childhood Longitudinal Study. *Social Forces, 84*(2), 1131–1157.

Brunton, P. J., & Russell, J. A. (2008). The expectant brain: Adapting for motherhood. *Nature Reviews Neuroscience, 9*(1), 11–25.

Bruskas, D. (2008). Children in foster care: A vulnerable population at risk. *Journal of Child and Adolescent Psychiatric Nursing, 21*, 70–77.

Brüske, I., Flexeder, C., & Heinrich, J. (2014). Body mass index and the incidence of asthma in children. *Current Opinion in Allergy and Clinical Immunology, 14*(2),155–160.

Bryan, C. L., Sims, S. K., Hester, D. J., & Dunaway, D. L. (2013). Fifteen years after the Surgeon General's Report: Challenges, changes, and future directions in physical education. *Quest, 65*(2), 139–150.

Bryant, B. J., & Bryant, J. P. (2014). Relative weights of the backpacks of elementary school children. *Journal of School Nursing, 30*(1), 19–23.

Bryant, G. A., & Barrett, H. C. (2007). Recognizing intentions in infant-directed speech. *Psychological Science, 18*(8), 746–751.

Buckley, K. W. (1989). *Mechanical man: John Broadus Watson and the beginnings of behaviorism.* New York, NY: Guilford Press.

Buist, K. L., & Vermande, M. (2014). Sibling relationship patterns and their associations with child competence and problem behavior. *Journal of Family Psychology, 28*(4), 529–537. doi: 10.1037/a0036990

Burdi, A. R., Huelke, D. F., Snyder, R. G., & Lowrey, G. H. (1969). Infants and children in the adult world of automobile safety design: Pediatric and anatomical considerations for design of child constraints. *Journal of Biomechanics, 2*, 267–280.

Bureau of Labor Statistics. (2012). *Table 5: Employment status of the population by sex, marital status, and presence and age of own children under 18, 2010–2011 annual averages.* Retrieved from http://www.bls.gov/news.release/famee.t05.htm

Bureau of Labor Statistics. (2014a). *College enrollment and work activity of 2013 high school graduates.* Retrieved from http://www.bls.gov/news.release/hsgec.nr0.htm

Bureau of Labor Statistics. (2014b). *Occupational outlook handbook.* Retrieved from http://www.bls.gov/ooh/

Burghardt, G. M. (2004). Play and the brain in comparative perspective. In R. L. Clements & L. Fiorentino (Eds.), *The child's right to play—A global approach* (pp. 293–308). Westport, CT: Praeger.

Burt Solorzano, C. M., & McCartney, C. R. (2010). Obesity and the pubertal transition in girls and boys. *Reproduction, 140*(3), 399–410.

Bushman, B. J. (2006). Effects of warning and information labels on attraction to television violence in viewers of different ages. *Journal of Applied Social Psychology, 36*(9), 2073–2078. doi: 10.1111/j.0021-9029.2006.00094.x

Bushman, B. J., & Cantor, J. (2003). Media ratings for violence and sex. *American Psychologist, 58*(2), 130–141.

Bussey, K., & Bandura, A. (1999). Social cognitive theory of gender development and differentiation. *Psychological Review, 106*(4), 676–713.

Butte, N. F., Fox, M. K., Briefel, R. R., Siega-Riz, A. M., Dwyer, J. T., Deming, D. M., & Reidy, K. C. (2010). Nutrient intakes of U.S. infants, toddlers, and preschoolers meet or exceed dietary reference intakes. *Journal of the American Dietetic Association, Supplement, 110*, S27–S37.

Butterworth, G. (2003). Pointing is the royal road to language for babies. In S. Kita (Ed.), *Pointing: Where language, culture, and cognition meet* (pp. 9–33). Mahwah, NJ: Erlbaum.

Byers-Heinlein, K., Burns, T. C., & Werker, J. F. (2010). The roots of bilingualism in newborns. *Psychological Science, 21*(3), 343–348.

Byrd, C. M. (2012). The measurement of racial/ethnic identity in children: A critical review. *Journal of Black Psychology, 38*(1), 3–31. doi: 10.1177/0095798410397544

Cacciatore, J. (2009). Appropriate bereavement practice after the death of a Native American child. *Families in Society, 90*(1), 46–50.

Cadoret, R. J., Troughton, E., & O'Gorman, T. W. (1987). Genetic and environmental factors in alcohol abuse and antisocial personality. *Journal of Studies on Alcohol, 48*, 1–8.

Cadoret, R. J., Yates, W. R., Troughton, E., Woodworth, G., & Steward, M. A. (1995). Genetic-environmental interaction in the genesis of aggressivity and conduct disorders. *Archives of General Psychiatry, 52*(11), 916–924.

Cain, K. M. (2005). School years. In N. J. Salkind (Ed.), *Encyclopedia of human development* (pp. 1116–1125). Thousand Oaks, CA: Sage.

Calafat, A., García, F., Juan, M., Becoña, E., & Fernández-Hermida, J. (2014). Which parenting style is more protective against adolescent substance use? Evidence within the European context. *Drug and Alcohol Dependence, 138*, 185–192. doi: 10.1016/j.drugalcdep.2014.02.705

Caldwell, B. M., & Bradley, R. H. (2003). *Home Observation for Measurement of the Environment: Administration Manual.* Tempe: Family & Human Dynamics Research Institute, Arizona State University.

Caldwell, P. H. Y., Nankivell, G., & Sureshkumar, P. (2013). Simple behavioural interventions for nocturnal enuresis in children. *Cochrane Database of Systematic Reviews 7.* Art. No.: CD003637. doi: 10.1002/14651858.CD003637.pub3

Calhoun, F., & Warren, K. (2006). Fetal alcohol syndrome: Historical perspectives. *Neuroscience and Biobehavioral Reviews, 31*, 168–171.

California Department of Developmental Services. (1999). *Changes in the population of persons with autism and pervasive developmental disorders in California's developmental services system: 1987 through 1998.* Sacramento, CA: Author.

California Department of Education. (2013). *Textbook weight in California: Summary of the state board of education action.* Retrieved from http://www.cde.ca.gov/ci/cr/cf/txtbkwght.asp

The California Endowment. (2013, October 15). UC Study: Students prefer new, healthier school meals [Press Release]. Retrieved from http://tcenews.calendow.org/releases/uc-study:-students-prefer-new-healthier-school-meals

Camilli, G., Vargas, S., & Yurecko, M. (2003, May 8). Teaching children to read: The fragile link between science and federal education policy. *Education Policy Analysis Archives, 11*(15). Retrieved from http://epaa.asu.edu/epaa/v11n15/

Camodeca, M., & Goossens, F. A. (2005). Aggression, social cognitions, anger and sadness in bullies and victims. *Journal of Child Psychology and Psychiatry, 46*(2), 186–197. doi: 10.1111/j.1469-7610.2004.00347.x

Camos, V., & Barrouillet, P. (2011). Developmental change in working memory strategies: From passive maintenance to active refreshing. *Developmental Psychology, 47*(3), 898–904. doi: 10.1037/a0023193

Campbell, B. C. (2011). Adrenarche and middle childhood. *Human Nature, 22*, 327–349. doi: 10.1007/s12110-011-9120-x

Campbell, S. B., Spieker, S., Burchinal, M., Poe, M. D., & NICHD Early Child Care Research Network. (2006). Trajectories of aggression from toddlerhood to age 9 predict academic and social functioning through age 12. *Journal of Child Psychology and Psychiatry, 47*(8), 791–800.

Campos, J. J., Bertenthal, B. I., & Kermoian, R. (1992). Early experience and emotional development: The emergence of wariness of heights. *Psychological Science, 3*(1), 61–64.

Campos, J. J., Kermoian, R., & Zumbahlen, M. R. (1992). Socioemotional transformations in the family system following infant crawling onset. In N. Eisenberg & R. A. Fabes (Eds.), *Emotion and its regulation in early development* (pp. 25–40). San Francisco, CA: Jossey-Bass.

Canals, J., Hernández-Martínez, C., Esparó, G., & Fernández-Ballart, J. (2011). Neonatal Behavioral Assessment Scale as a predictor of cognitive development and IQ in full-term infants: A 6-year longitudinal study. *Acta Paediatrica, 100*(10), 1331–1337.

Cannon, J. S., Lipscomb, S., & Public Policy Institute of California. (2011). *Early grade retention and student success: Evidence from Los Angeles.* San Francisco. CA: Public Policy Institute of California.

Cano, F., & Cardelle-Elawar, M. (2004). An integrated analysis of secondary school students' conceptions and beliefs about learning. *European Journal of Psychology of Education, 19*(2), 167–187.

Capizzano, J., & Adams, G. (2003). *Children in low-income families are less likely to be in center-based care.* Washington, DC: Urban Institute.

Carbo, M. (1996). Whole language vs. phonics: The great debate. *Principal, 75*, 36–38.

Carlson, V. J., & Harwood, R. L. (2003). Attachment, culture, and the caregiving system: The cultural patterning of everyday experiences among Anglo and Puerto Rican mother-infant pairs. *Infant Mental Health Journal, 24*(1), 53–73.

Carney, A. B., & Merrell, K. W. (2001). Bullying in schools: Perspectives on understanding and preventing an international problem. *School Psychology International, 22*(3), 364–382.

Carper, R. A., & Courchesne, E. (2005). Localized enlargement of the frontal cortex in early autism. *Biological Psychiatry, 57*(2), 126–133.

Carranza, J., Gonzalez-Salinas, D., & Ato, E. (2013). A longitudinal study of temperament continuity through IBQ, TBAQ and CBQ. *Infant Behavior & Development, 36*(4), 749–761.

Carter, C. S. (2005). The chemistry of child neglect: Do oxytocin and vasopressin mediate the effects of early experience? *Proceedings of the National Academy of Sciences, 102*(51), 18247–18248.

Cartwright, K. B., Galupo, M., Tyree, S. D., & Jennings, J. (2009). Reliability and validity of the Complex Postformal Thought Questionnaire: Assessing adults' cognitive development. *Journal of Adult Development, 16*(3), 183–189. doi: 10.1007/s10804-009-9055-1

Carver, C. S., Scheier, M. F., & Weintraub, J. K. (1989). Assessing coping strategies: A theoretically based approach. *Journal of Personality and Social Psychology, 56*(2), 267–283.

Carver, K., Joyner, K., & Udry, J. R. (2003). National estimates of adolescent romantic relationships. In P. Florsheim (Ed.), *Adolescent romantic relations and sexual behavior: Theory, research, and practical implications* (pp. 23–56). Mahwah, NJ: Erlbaum.

Carver, P. R., Egan, S. K., & Perry, D. G. (2004). Children who question their heterosexuality. *Development Psychology, 40*(1), 43–53.

Carver, P. R., Yunger, J. L., & Perry, D. G. (2003). Gender identity and adjustment in middle childhood. *Sex Roles, 49*(3-4), 95–109.

Casalin, S. Luyten, P., Vliegen, N., & Neurs, P. (2012). The structure and stability of temperament from infancy to toddlerhood: A one-year prospective study. *Infant Behavior & Development, 35*(1), 94–108.

Casey, D. M., Ripke, M. N., & Huston, A. C. (2005). Activity participation and the well-being of children and adolescents in the context of welfare reform. In J. L. Mahoney, R. W. Larson, & J. S. Eccles (Eds.), *Organized activities as contexts of development* (pp. 65–84). Mahwah, NJ: Erlbaum.

Caspi, A., McClay, J., Moffitt, T. E., Mill, J., Martin, J., Craig, I. W., . . . Poulton, R. (2002). Role of genotype in the cycle of violence in maltreated children. *Science, 297*(5582), 851–854.

Caspi, A., Sugden, K., Moffit, T., Taylor, A., Craig, I. W., Harrington, H., . . . Poulton, R. (2003). Influence of life stress on depression: Moderation by a polymorphism in the 5-HTT gene. *Science, 301*, 386–389.

Cattell, R. B. (1963). Theory of fluid and crystallized intelligence: A critical experiment. *Journal of Educational Psychology, 54*, 1–22.

Causey, K., Gardiner, A., & Bjorklund, D. F. (2008). Evolutionary developmental psychology and the role of plasticity in ontogeny and phylogeny. *Psychological Inquiry, 19*(1), 27–30.

Ceci, S. J., Bruck, M., & Loftus, E. F. (1998). On the ethics of memory implantation research. *Applied Cognitive Psychology, 12*(3), 230–240.

Celce-Murcia, M., & Olshtain, E. (2001). *Discourse and context in language teaching: A guide for language teachers.* New York, NY: Cambridge University Press.

Center for Public Education. (2005). *Teacher quality and student achievement: Key lessons learned.* Retrieved from http://www.education.com/reference/article/Ref_Key_lessons_findings

Center of Excellence for Medical Multimedia. (n.d.). *Types of malpresentation.* Retrieved from http://www.pregnancyatoz.org/Labor-and-Delivery/Malpresentation/Types-of-Malpresentation

Center on the Developing Child at Harvard University. (2010). *The foundations of lifelong health are built in early childhood.* Retrieved from http://www.developingchild.harvard.edu

Center on the Developing Child at Harvard University (2011). *Building the brain's "air traffic control" system: How early experiences shape the development of executive function: Working Paper No. 11.* Retrieved from http://www.developingchild.harvard.edu

Centers for Disease Control and Prevention, Division of Nutrition and Physical Activity. (2007). *Does breastfeeding reduce the risk of pediatric overweight? Research to Practice Series No. 4.* Atlanta, GA: Author. Retrieved from http://www.cdc.gov/nccdphp/dnpa/nutrition/pdf/breastfeeding_r2p.pdf

Centers for Disease Control and Prevention. (2005). *Intellectual disability.* Retrieved from http://www.cdc.gov/ncbddd/dd/mr2.htm

Centers for Disease Control and Prevention. (2007a). *Trends in reportable sexually diseases transmitted in the United States, 2007.* Retrieved from http://www.cdc.gov/nchhstp/newsroom/docs/STDTrendsFactSheet.pdf

Centers for Disease Control and Prevention. (2007b). *What do we know about tobacco use and pregnancy?* Retrieved from http://www.cdc.gov/reproductivehealth/TobaccoUsePregnancy/index.htm

Centers for Disease Control and Prevention. (2008a). *Birth defects: Data and statistics.* Retrieved from http://www.cdc.gov/ncbddd/birthdefects/data.html

Centers for Disease Control and Prevention. (2008b). *STDs and pregnancy—CDC fact sheet.* Retrieved from http://www.cdc.gov/std/STDFact-STDs&Pregnancy.htm

Centers for Disease Control and Prevention (2009a). *Birth to 24 months: Girls length-for-age and weight-for-age percentiles.* Retrieved from http://www.cdc.gov/growthcharts/data/who/grchrt_boys_24lw_9210.pdf

Centers for Disease Control and Prevention (2009b). *Birth to 24 months: Boys length-for-age and weight-for-age percentiles.* http://www.cdc.gov/growthcharts/data/who/grchrt_boys_24lw_9210.pdf

Centers for Disease Control and Prevention. (2009c). *Eliminating perinatal HIV transmission.* Retrieved from http://www.cdc.gov/actagainstaids/ottl/pdf/ottl_curriculum.pdf

Centers for Disease Control and Prevention. (2009d). *Toys.* Retrieved from http://www.cdc.gov/nceh/lead/tips/toys.htm

Centers for Disease Control and Prevention. (2010a). *Attention-deficit/hyperactivity disorder (ADHD).* Retrieved from http://www.cdc.gov/ncbddd/adhd/

Centers for Disease Control and Prevention. (2010b). *Families, clinicians and schools: Working together to improve asthma management.* Retrieved from http://www.cdc.gov/Features/ManageAsthma/

Centers for Disease Control and Prevention. (2010c). *Youth violence: Facts at a glance.* Retrieved from http://www.cdc.gov/ViolencePrevention/pdf/YV-DataSheet-a.pdf

Centers for Disease Control and Prevention. (2011a). *About BMI for children and teens.* Retrieved from http://www.cdc.gov/healthyweight/assessing/bmi/childrens_bmi/about_childrens_bmi.html#How%20is%20BMI%20used%20with%20children%20and%20teens

Centers for Disease Control and Prevention. (2011b). *How much physical activity do children need?* Retrieved from http://www.cdc.gov/physicalactivity/everyone/guidelines/children.html

Centers for Disease Control and Prevention. (2011c). *National diabetes fact sheet: National estimates and general information on diabetes and prediabetes in the United States, 2011.* Atlanta, GA: Department of Health and Human Services, Centers for Disease Control and Prevention.

Centers for Disease Control and Prevention. (2011d). Progress toward implementation of human papillomavirus vaccination—the Americas, 2006–2010. *Morbidity & Mortality Weekly Report, 60*, 1382–1384.

Centers for Disease Control and Prevention. (2011e). *Sexually transmitted diseases—interactive data 1996–2011.* Retrieved from http://wonder.cdc.gov/std-std-race-age.html

Centers for Disease Control and Prevention. (2012a). Alcohol use and binge drinking among women of childbearing age—United States, 2006–2010. *MMWR: Morbidity and Mortality Weekly Reports, 61*(28), 534–538.

Centers for Disease Control and Prevention. (2012b). *Concerns about autism.* Retrieved from http://www.cdc.gov/vaccinesafety/Concerns/Autism/Index.html

Centers for Disease Control and Prevention. (2012c). Estimated HIV incidence in the United States, 2007–2010. *HIV Surveillance Supplemental Report 2012, 17*(4).

Centers for Disease Control and Prevention. (2012d). *Fetal alcohol spectrum disorders.* Retrieved from http://www.cdc.gov/ncbddd/fas/fasask.htm#character

Centers for Disease Control and Prevention. (2012e). *Parent's guide to childhood immunizations.* Atlanta, GA: GPO.

Centers for Disease Control and Prevention. (2012f). *Playground injuries: Fact sheet.* Retrieved from http://www.cdc.gov/HomeandRecreationalSafety/Playground-Injuries/playgroundinjuries-factsheet.htm

Centers for Disease Control and Prevention. (2012g). *Suffocation: The reality.* Retrieved from http://www.cdc.gov/safechild/Suffocation/index.html

Centers for Disease Control and Prevention. (2012h). *Vital signs: Child injury.* Retrieved from http://www.cdc.gov/vitalsigns/ChildInjury/

Centers for Disease Control and Prevention (2012i). *Youth risk behavior surveillance—United States, 2011.* MMWR Surveillance Summaries, 61(No. SS4).

Centers for Disease Control and Prevention. (2013a). *Autism spectrum disorders (ASDs): Data and statistics.* Retrieved from http://www.cdc.gov/ncbddd/autism/data.html

Centers for Disease Control and Prevention. (2013b). *Autism spectrum disorders (ASDs): Related topics.* Retrieved from http://www.cdc.gov/ncbddd/autism/topics.html

Centers for Disease Control and Prevention. (2013c). *Cancer prevention and control.* Retrieved from http://www.cdc.gov/cancer/dcpc/data/children.htm

Centers for Disease Control and Prevention. (2013d). *Infertility FAQs.* Retrieved from http://www.cdc.gov/reproductivehealth/Infertility/index.htm#1

Centers for Disease Control and Prevention. (2013e). *Injury prevention and control: Data and statistics.* Retrieved from http://www.cdc.gov/injury/wisqars/LeadingCauses.html

Centers for Disease Control and Prevention. (2013f). *Pertussis (whooping cough).* Retrieved from http://www.cdc.gov/pertussis/about/signs-symptoms.html

Centers for Disease Control and Prevention. (2013g). *Pregnancy-related deaths.* Retrieved from http://www.cdc.gov/reproductivehealth/MaternalInfantHealth/Pregnancy-relatedMortality.htm

Centers for Disease Control and Prevention. (2013h). *Sexually transmitted infections among young Americans.* Retrieved from http://www.cdc.gov/nchhstp/newsroom/2013/SAM-Infographic-2013.html?s_cid=nchhstp-nr-sam-008

Centers for Disease Control and Prevention. (2013i). Three cases of Congenital Rubella Syndrome in the postelimination era—Maryland, Alabama, and Illinois, 2012. *Morbidity and Mortality Weekly Report.* Retrieved from http://www.cdc.gov/mmwr/preview/mmwrhtml/mm6212a3.htm

Centers for Disease Control and Prevention. (2013j). *U.S. breastfeeding rates continue to rise* [Press release]. Retrieved from http://www.cdc.gov/media/releases/2013/p0731-breastfeeding-rates.html

Centers for Disease Control and Prevention (2013k). *Vital signs: Repeat births among teens— United States 2007–2010.* Retrieved from http://www.cdc.gov/mmwr/preview/mmwrhtml/mm6213a4.htm?s_cid=mm6213a4_w

Centers for Disease Control and Prevention. (2013l). *Youth violence: National statistics.* Retrieved from http://www.cdc.gov/violenceprevention/youthviolence/stats_at-a_glance/vca_temp-trends.html

Centers for Disease Control and Prevention. (2014a). *Assistive reproductive technology (ART).* Retrieved from http://www.cdc.gov/ART/index.htm

Centers for Disease Control and Prevention. (2014b). *Attention-deficit/hyperactivity disorder (ADHD).* Retrieved from http://www.cdc.gov/ncbddd/adhd/diagnosis.html

Centers for Disease Control and Prevention. (2014c). *Autism spectrum disorder (ASD) screening and diagnosis.* Retrieved from http://www.cdc.gov/ncbddd/autism/screening.html

Centers for Disease Control and Prevention. (2014d). *Autism spectrum disorder (ASD) data and statistics.* Retrieved from http://www.cdc.gov/ncbddd/autism/data.html

Centers for Disease Control and Prevention. (2014e). *Child maltreatment: Definitions.* Retrieved from http://www.cdc.gov/violenceprevention/childmaltreatment/definitions.html

Centers for Disease Control and Prevention. (2014f). *During pregnancy.* Retrieved from http://www.cdc.gov/pregnancy/during.html

Centers for Disease Control and Prevention. (2014g). *Fetal alcohol spectrum disorders (FASDs).* Retrieved from http://www.cdc.gov/ncbddd/fasd/data.html

Centers for Disease Control and Prevention. (2014h). *HIV among youth.* Retrieved from http://www.cdc.gov/hiv/risk/age/youth/index.html

Centers for Disease Control and Prevention. (2014i). *Suicide prevention: Youth suicide.* Retrieved from http://www.cdc.gov/violenceprevention/pub/youth_suicide.html

Centers for Disease Control and Prevention. (2014j). *Tobacco use and pregnancy.* Retrieved from http://www.cdc.gov/Reproductivehealth/TobaccoUsePregnancy/index.htm

Centers for Disease Control and Prevention. (2014k). *Understanding teen dating violence.* Retrieved from http://www.cdc.gov/violenceprevention/pdf/teen-dating-violence-2014-a.pdf

Centers for Disease Control and Prevention. (2014l). *Youth and tobacco use.* Retrieved from http://www.cdc.gov/tobacco/data_statistics/fact_sheets/youth_data/tobacco_use/index.htm

Centers for Disease Control and Prevention. (2014m). Youth risk behavior surveillance—United States, 2013. Morbidity and mortality weekly report, June 13, 2014. *Surveillance Summaries, 63*(4).

Centers for Disease Control and Prevention. (n.d.). *Know your concussion ABCs.* Retrieved from http://www.cdc.gov/concussion/pdf/TBI_factsheets_PARENTS-508-a.pdf

Central Intelligence Agency. (2014). *World fact book.* Retrieved from https://www.cia.gov/library/publications/the-world-factbook/rankorder/2223rank.html

Cernoch, J. M., & Porter, R. H. (1985). Recognition of maternal axillary odors by infants. *Child Development, 56*(6), 1593–1598.

Chamberlain, D. B. (1999). Babies don't feel pain: A century of denial in medicine. *Journal of Prenatal & Perinatal Psychology & Health, 14*(1-2), 145–168.

Chang, E. S., Greenberger, E., Chen, C., Heckhausen, J., & Farruggia, S. P. (2010). Nonparental adults as social resources in the transition to adulthood. *Journal of Research on Adolescence, 20*(4), 1065–1082. doi: 10.1111/j.1532-7795.2010.00662.x

Chang, M. (2011). Motherhood rooted: Asian and Pacific Islander moms in the U.S. embrace ancient post-birth traditions. *Hyphen*, 23. Retrieved from http://www.hyphenmagazine.com/magazine/issue-23-bittersweet/motherhood-rooted

Chaplin, T. M., & Aldao, A. (2013). Gender differences in emotion expression in children: A meta-analytic review. *Psychological Bulletin, 139*(4), 735–765.

Charles, C., Louv, R., Bodner, L., Guns, B., & Stahl, D. (2009). *Children and nature 2009: A report on the movement to reconnect children to the natural world.* Children & Nature Network. Retrieved from http://www.childrenandnature.org/downloads/CNNMovement2009.pdf

Charlesworth, L., Wood, J., & Viggiani, P. (2011). Middle childhood. In E. D. Hutchison, Ed., *Dimensions of human behavior: The changing life course* (4th ed., pp. 175–226). Thousand Oaks, CA: Sage.

Chawarska, K., Klin, A., Paul, R., & Volkmar, F. (2007). Autism spectrum disorder in the second year: Stability and change in syndrome expression. *Journal of Child Psychology and Psychiatry, 48*(2), 128–138.

Cheadle, J. E., Amato, P. R., & King, V. (2010). Patterns of nonresident father contact. *Demography, 47*(1), 205–225.

Chein, J., Albert, D., O'Brien, L., Uckert, K., & Steinberg, L. (2011). Peers increase adolescent risk taking by enhancing activity in the brain's reward circuitry. *Developmental Science, 14*(2), F1–F10. doi: 10.1111/j.1467-7687.2010.01035.x

Chen, C., Greenberger, E., Farruggia, S., Bush, K., & Dong, Q. (2003). Beyond parents and peers: The role of important non-parental adults (VIPs) in adolescent development in China and the United States. *Psychology in the Schools, 40*(1), 35–50.

Cheng, J., & Monroe, M. C. (2012). Connection to nature: Children's affective attitude toward nature. *Environment and Behavior, 44*(1), 31–49.

Chernella, J. M. (1991). Symbolic inaction in rituals of gender and procreation among the Garifuna (Black Caribs) of Honduras. *Ethos, 19*(1), 52–67.

Chess, S., & Thomas, A. (1999). *Goodness of fit: Clinical applications from infancy through adult life.* Philadelphia, PA: Brunner/Mazel.

Chess, S., Thomas, A., & Birch, H. G. (1965). *Your child is a person: A psychological approach to childhood without guilt.* New York, NY: Viking Press.

Child Care Aware of America. (2013a). *Child/staff ratios.* Retrieved from http://www.naccrra.org/about-child-care/state-child-care-licensing/child/staff-ratios

Child Care Aware of America. (2013b). *We can do better - Child Care Aware of America's ranking of state child care center regulations and oversight, 2013 update.* Arlington, VA: Author.

Child Trends. (2012a). *Births to unmarried women.* Retrieved from http://www.childtrendsdatabank.org/sites/default/files/75_Births_to_Unmarried_Women.pdf

Child Trends. (2012b). *Unintentional injuries.* Retrieved from http://www.childtrends.org/wp-content/uploads/2012/11/122_Unintentional_Injuries.pdf

Child Trends. (2013a). *High school dropout rates.* Retrieved from http://www.childtrends.org/?indicators=high-school-dropout-rates

Child Trends. (2013b). *Physical development and daily health.* Publication # 2013-09. Bethesda, MD: Child Trends.

Child Trends. (2014a). *Late or no prenatal care.* Retrieved from http://www.childtrends.org/wp-content/uploads/2012/11/25_Prenatal_Care.pdf

Child Trends. (2014b). *Unintentional injuries.* Retrieved from http://www.childtrends.org/?indicators=unintentional-injuries

Child Welfare Information Gateway. (2011). *How many children were adopted in 2007 and 2008?* Washington, DC: U.S. Department of Health and Human Services, Children's Bureau.

Child Welfare Information Gateway. (2013). *Parenting a child who has been sexually abused: A guide for foster and adoptive parents.* Washington, DC: U.S. Department of Health and Human Services, Children's Bureau. Retrieved from https://www.childwelfare.gov/pubs/f_abused/f_abused.pdf#page=1&view=Introduction

Child Welfare Information Gateway. (2014). *Mandatory reporters of child abuse and neglect.* Washington, DC: U.S. Department of Health and Human Services, Children's Bureau.

Children's Hospital of Philadelphia. (1996–2014). *Children act fast. . . . So do poisons!* Retrieved from http://www.chop.edu/service/poison-control-center/resources-for-families/preventing-poisonings-from-medicines-household-chemicals-pesticides-and-lead.html

Chin, J. J., & Ludwig, D. (2013). Increasing children's physical activity during school recess periods. *American Journal of Public Health, 103*(7), 1229–1234.

Chin, Y. S. (2014). Trafficked boys overlooked. *Juvenile Justice Information Exchange.* Retrieved from http://jjie.org/trafficked-boys-overlooked-underrepresented/

Chitiyo, M., & Wheeler, J. J. (2006). School phobia: Understanding a complex behavioural response. *Journal of Research in Special Educational Needs, 6*(2), 87–91.

Choe, D., Olson, S. L., & Sameroff, A. J. (2013). The interplay of externalizing problems and physical and inductive discipline during childhood. *Developmental Psychology, 49*(11), 2029–2039. doi: 10.1037/a0032054

Chomsky, N. (1968). *Language and mind.* New York, NY: Harcourt, Brace & World.

Christakis, D. A., Garrison, M. M., Herrenkohl, T., Haggerty, K., Rivara, F. P., Zhou, C., & Liekweg, K. (2013). Modifying media content for preschool children:

A randomized controlled trial. *Pediatrics, 131*(3), 431–438. doi: 10.1542/peds.2012–1493

Christakis, D. A., & Zimmerman, F. J. (2007). Violent television viewing during preschool is associated with antisocial behavior during school age. *Pediatrics, 120*(5), 993–999.

Chumlea, W. C., Schubert, C. M., Roche, A. F., Kulin, H. E., Lee, P. A., Himes, J. H., Sun, S. S. (2003). Age at menarche and racial comparisons in US girls. *Pediatrics, 111*(1), 110–113.

Chye, T. T., Teng, T. K., Hao, T. H., & Seng, J. T. C. (2008). *The new art and science of pregnancy and childbirth: What you want to know from your obstetrician.* Hackensack, NJ: World Scientific.

Cianciolo, A. J., & Sternberg, R. J. (2004). *Intelligence: A brief history.* Malden, MA: Blackwell.

Cicchetti, D., & Toth, S. L. (2009). The past achievements and future promises of developmental psychopathology: The coming of age of a discipline. *Journal of Child Psychology and Psychiatry, 50*(1–2), 16–25.

Cicirelli, V. G. (1994). Sibling relationships in cross-cultural perspective. *Journal of Marriage and Family, 56*(1), 7–20.

Cillessen, A. N., Bukowski, W. M., & Haselager, G. T. (2000). Stability of sociometric categories. *New Directions for Child and Adolescent Development, 88,* 75–93.

Clark, C. (1969). Television and social controls: Some observation of the portrayal of ethnic minorities. *Television Quarterly, 9*(2), 18–22.

Clark, M. A., & Fox, M. K. (2009). Nutritional quality of the diets of US public school children and the role of the school meal programs. *Journal of the American Dietetic Association, 109*(2 Supplement), S44–S56.

Clarke-Stewart, A., & Brentano, C. (2006). *Divorce: Causes and consequences.* New Haven, CT: Yale University Press.

Clarke-Stewart, K., Vandell, D. L., McCartney, K., Owen, M. T., & Booth, C. (2000). Effects of parental separation and divorce on very young children. *Journal of Family Psychology, 14*(2), 304–326.

Clayton, H., Li, R., Perrine, C., & Scanlon, K. (2013). Prevalence and reasons for introducing infants early to solid foods: Variations by milk feeding type. *Pediatrics, 131*(4), e1108–e1114. doi: 10.1542/peds.2012-2265

Clearfield, M. W., & Jedd, K. E. (2013). The effects of socioeconomic status on infant attention. *Infant and Child Development, 22*(1), 53–67. doi: 10.1002/icd.1770

Cleland, V., Crawford, D., Baur, L. A., Hume, C., Timperio, A., & Salmon, J. (2008). A prospective examination of children's time spent outdoors, objectively measured physical activity and overweight. *International Journal of Obesity, 32,* 1685–1693.

Cobbina, J. E., & Oselin, S. S. (2011). It's not only for the money: An analysis of adolescent versus adult entry into street prostitution. *Sociological Inquiry, 81*(3), 310–332. doi: 10.1111/j.1475–682X.2011.00375.x

Coe, C. L., & Lubach, G. R. (2008). Fetal programming: Prenatal origins of health and illness. *Current Directions in Psychological Science, 17*(1), 36–41.

Cohany, S. R., & Sok, E. (2007). Trends in labor force participation of married mothers of infants. *Monthly Labor Review, 130,* 9–16.

Cohen, G. J., & the American Academy of Pediatrics Committee on Psychosocial Aspects of Child and Family Health. (2002). Helping children and families deal with divorce and separation. *Pediatrics, 110,* 1019–1023.

Cohen, L. B., Chaput, H. H., & Cashon, C. H. (2002). A constructivist model of infant cognition. *Cognitive Development, 17*(3–4), 1323–1343.

Coie, J. D., Dodge, K. A., & Coppotelli, H. (1982). Dimensions and types of social status: A cross-age perspective. *Developmental Psychology, 18*(4), 557–570.

Coleman, M., Ganong, L. H., & Warzinik, K. (2007). *Family life in twentieth century America.* Westport, CT: Greenwood Press.

Coll, C., Bearer, E. L., & Lerner, R. M. (2004). Conclusions: Beyond nature versus nurture to more complex, relational, and dynamic developmental systems. In C. Coll, E. L. Bearer, & R. M. Lerner (Eds.), *Nature and nurture: The complex interplay of genetic and environmental influences on human behavior and development* (pp. 225–230). Mahwah, NJ: Erlbaum.

The College Board. (2013). 2013 SAT Report on College & Career readiness. New York, NY: Author.

Collins, R. L., Elliott, M. N., Berry, S. H., Kanouse, D. E., Kunkel, D., Hunter, S. B., & Miu, A. (2004). Watching sex on television predicts adolescent initiation of sexual behavior. *Pediatrics, 114,* e280–e289.

Collins, W. A., & Laursen, B. (2004). Parent-adolescent relationships and influences. In R. M. Lerner & L. Steinberg (Eds.), *Handbook of adolescent psychology* (2nd ed., pp. 331–361). Hoboken, NJ: Wiley.

Colombo, J., & Mitchell, D. W. (2009). Infant visual habituation. *Neurobiology of Learning and Memory, 92*(2), 225–234.

Comalli, P. E., Wapner, S., & Werner, H. (1962). Interference effects of Stroop color-word test in childhood, adulthood, and aging. *Journal of Genetic Psychology, 100,* 47–53.

Compas, B. E., Connor-Smith, J. K., Saltzman, H., Thomsen, A. H., & Wadsworth, M. E. (2001). Coping with stress during childhood and adolescence: Problems, progress, and potential in theory and research. *Psychological Bulletin, 127,* 87–127.

Compas, B. E., Jaser, S. S., Dunn, M. J., & Rodriguez, E. M. (2012). Coping with chronic illness in childhood and adolescence. *Annual Review of Clinical Psychology, 8,* 455–480.

Comstock, G., & Scharrer, E. (2003). Meta-analyzing the controversy over television violence and aggression. In D. A. Gentile (Ed.), *Media violence and children* (pp. 205–226). Westport, CT: Praeger.

Conboy, B. T., & Kuhl, P. K. (2011). Impact of second-language experience in infancy: Brain measures of first- and second-language speech perception. *Developmental Science, 14*(2), 242–248.

Condon, E., Crepinsek, M., & Fox, M. (2009). School meals: Types of foods offered to and consumed by children at lunch and breakfast. *Journal of the American Dietetic Association, 109*(2), S67–S78.

Coontz, S. (2000). Historical perspectives on family diversity. In D. H. Demo, K. R. Allen, & M. A. Fine (Eds.), *Handbook of family diversity* (pp. 15–31). New York, NY: Oxford University Press.

Cooper, S. M., McLoyd, V. C., Wood, D., & Hardaway, C. R. (2008). Racial discrimination and mental health. In S. M. Quintana & C. McKown (Eds.), *Handbook of race, racism, and the developing child* (pp. 278–312). Hoboken, NJ: Wiley.

Copeland, W., Shanahan, L., Miller, S., Costello, E., Angold, A., & Maughan, B. (2010). Outcomes of early pubertal timing in young women: A prospective population-based study. *American Journal of Psychiatry, 167*(10), 1218–1225.

Coplan, R. J., & Arbeau, K. A. (2009). Peer interactions and play in early childhood. In K. H. Rubin & W. M. Bukowski (Eds.), *Handbook of peer interactions, relationships, and groups* (pp. 143–161). New York, NY: Guilford Press.

Coplan, R. J., & Armer, M. (2007). A "multitude" of solitude: A closer look at social withdrawal and nonsocial play in early childhood. *Child Development Perspectives, 1*(1), 26–32.

Corballis, M. C. (2006). *The recursive mind: The origins of human language, thought, and civilization.* Princeton, NJ: Princeton University Press.

Correll, S. J. (2004). Constraints into preferences: Gender, status, and emerging career aspirations. *American Sociological Review, 69*(1), 93–113.

Costello, J., & Angold, A. (2011). Contributions from epidemiology. In J. Garber, P. R. Costanzo, & T. J. Strauman (Eds.), *Depression in adolescent girls: Science and Prevention* (pp. 25–34). New York, NY: Guilford Press.

Côté, S. M., Vaillancourt, T., LeBlanc, J. C., Nagin, D. S., & Tremblay, R. E. (2006). The development of physical aggression from toddlerhood to pre-adolescence: A nation wide longitudinal study of Canadian children. *Journal of Abnormal Child Psychology, 34*(1), 71–85.

Council for Exceptional Children. (2009). *Learning disabilities.* Retrieved from http://www.cec.sped .org/AM/Template.cfm?Section=Learning_Disabilities &Template=/TaggedPage/TaggedPageDisplay.cfm& TPLID=37&ContentID=5629

Courage, M. L., & Howe, M. L. (2004). Advances in early memory development research: Insights about the dark side of the moon. *Developmental Review, 24*(1), 6–32.

Courage, M. L., Reynolds, G. D., & Richards, J. E. (2006). Infants' attention to patterned stimuli: Developmental change from 3 to 12 months of age. *Child Development, 77*(3), 680–695.

Courchesne, E., Chisum, H. J., Townsend, J., Cowles, A., Covington, J., Egaas, B., . . . Press, G. A. (2000). Normal brain development and aging: Quantitative analysis at in vivo MR imaging in healthy volunteers. *Radiology, 216,* 672–682.

Courtney, M. E. (2009). The difficult transition to adulthood for foster youth in the US: Implications for the state as corporate parent. *Society for Research in Child Development Social Policy Report, 23*(1), 3–11, 14–18.

Cox, M., Paley, B., Payne, C. C., & Burchinal, M. (1999). The transition to parenthood: Marital conflict and withdrawal and parent-infant interactions. In M. J. Cox & J. Brooks-Gunn (Eds.), *Conflict and cohesion in families: Causes and consequences* (pp. 87–104). Mahwah, NJ: Erlbaum.

Crain, E. F. (2000). Environmental threats to children's health: A challenge for pediatrics: 2000 Ambulatory Pediatric Association (APA) presidential address. *Pediatrics, 106*(4, Part 2), 871–875.

Crawford, J. (1995). *Bilingual education: History, politics, theory and practice.* Los Angeles, CA: Bilingual Educational Services.

Crawford, M., & Kaufman, M. R. (2008). Sex trafficking in Nepal: Survivor characteristics and long-term outcomes. *Violence Against Women, 14*(8), 905–916.

Crespo, C. J., Smit, E., Troiano, R. P., Bartlett, S. J., Macera, C. A., & Andersen, R. E. (2001). Television watching, energy intake, and obesity in US children: Results from the third National Health and Nutrition Examination Survey, 1988–1994. *Archives of Pediatrics and Adolescent Medicine, 155*(3), 360–365.

Crick, N. R., Grotpeter, J. K., & Bigbee, M. A. (2002). Relationally and physically aggressive children's intent attributions and feelings of distress for relational and instrumental peer provocations. *Child Development, 73*(4), 1134–1142.

Critchley, C. R., & Sanson, A. V. (2006). Is parent disciplinary behavior enduring or situational? A multilevel modeling investigation of individual and contextual influences on power assertive and inductive reasoning behaviors. *Journal of Applied Developmental Psychology, 27*(4), 370–388.

Crocetti, E., Rubini, M., & Meeus, W. (2008). Capturing the dynamics of identity formation in various ethnic groups: Development and validation of a three-dimensional model. *Journal of Adolescence, 31*(2), 207–222.

Crockenberg, S., & Leerkes, E. (2003). Infant negative emotionality, caregiving, and family relationships. In A. C. Crouter & A. Booth (Eds.), *Children's influence on family dynamics* (pp. 57–78). Mahwah, NJ: Erlbaum.

Cromer, L., & Goldsmith, R. (2010). Child sexual abuse myths: Attitudes, beliefs, and individual differences. *Journal of Child Sexual Abuse, 19*(6), 618–647.

Crosnoe, R., Riegle-Crumb, C., Field, S., Frank, K., & Muller, C. (2008). Peer group contexts of girls' and boys' academic experiences. *Child Development, 79*(1), 139–155.

Cross, J., & Fletcher, K. L. (2009). The challenge of adolescent crowd research: Defining the crowd. *Journal of Youth and Adolescence, 38*(6), 747–764.

Crosson-Tower, C. (2003). *The role of educators in preventing and responding to child abuse and neglect.* Washington, DC: U.S. Department of Health and Human Services, Office on Child Abuse and Neglect.

Culp, A. M., Culp, R. E., Blankemeyer, M., & Passmark, L. (1998). Parent Education Home Visitation Program: Adolescent and nonadolescent mother comparison after six months of intervention. *Infant Mental Health Journal, 19*(2), 111–123.

Cummings, C. M., Caporino, N. E., & Kendall, P. C. (2014). Comorbidity of anxiety and depression in children and adolescents: 20 years after. *Psychological Bulletin, 140*(3), 816–845. doi: 10.1037/a0034733

Cunningham, F. G., Bangdiwala, S., Brown, S. S., Dean, T. M., Frederiksen, M., Rowland Hogue, C. J., . . . Zimmet, S. C. (2010). National Institutes of Health Consensus Development Conference Statement: Vaginal birth after cesarean: New insights. March 8–10, 2010. *Obstetrics & Gynecology, 115*(6), 1279–1295.

Cunningham, F. G., Leveno, K. J., Bloom, S. L., Hauth, J. C., Gilstrap, L., III, & Wenstrom, K. D. (2005). *Williams obstetrics* (22nd ed.). New York, NY: McGraw-Hill.

Curry, P., De Amicis, L., & Gilligan, R. (2011). *The effect of cooperative learning on inter-ethnic relations in schools.* Paper presented at the 2011 Society for Research on Educational Effectiveness Conference, Washington, DC.

Curtis, N. M., Ronan, K. R., & Borduin, C. M. (2004). Multisystemic treatment: A meta-analysis of outcome studies. *Journal of Family Psychology, 18*(3), 411–419.

Curtiss, S. (1977). *Genie: A psycholinguistic study of a modern day "wild child."* New York, NY: Academic Press.

Dahl, G. B., & Lochner, L. (2008). *The impact of family income on child achievement: Evidence from the Earned Income Tax Credit* (NBER Working Paper No. 14599). Cambridge, MA: National Bureau of Economic Research.

Damon, W. (2006). Socialization and individuation. In G. Handel (Ed.), *Childhood socialization* (pp. 3–9). New Brunswick, NJ: Aldine Transaction.

Danner, F., & Phillips, B. (2008). Adolescent sleep, school start times, and teen motor vehicle crashes. *Journal of Clinical Sleep Medicine, 4*(6), 533–535.

Dapretto, M., Davies, M. S., Pfeifer, J. H., Scott, A. A., Sigman, M., Bookheimer, S. Y., & Iacoboni, M. (2006). Understanding emotions in others: Mirror neuron dysfunction in children with autism spectrum disorders. *Nature Neuroscience, 9*(1), 28–30.

Darke, K., Clewell, B., & Sevo, R. (2002). Meeting the challenge: The impact of the National Science Foundation's program for women and girls. *Journal of Women and Minorities in Science and Engineering, 8*(3–4), 285–303.

Darley, J. M., & Batson, C. (1973). 'From Jerusalem to Jericho': A study of situational and dispositional variables in helping behavior. *Journal of Personality and Social Psychology, 27*(1), 100–108.

Darling, N., Cumsille, P., & Martínez, M. L. (2008). Individual differences in adolescents' beliefs about the legitimacy of parental authority and their own obligation to obey: A longitudinal investigation. *Child Development, 79*(4), 1103–1118.

Darling, N., Dowdy, B. B., VanHorn, M. L., & Caldwell, L. L. (1999). Mixed-sex settings and the perception of competence. *Journal of Youth and Adolescence, 28*(4), 461–480.

Darling, N., Hamilton, S. F., & Shaver, K. H. (2003). Relationship outside the family: Unrelated adults. In G. R. Adams & M. D. Berzonsky (Eds.), *Blackwell handbook of adolescence* (pp. 349–370). Malden, MA: Blackwell.

D'Augelli, A. R. (2003). Lesbian and bisexual female youth aged 14 to 21: Developmental challenges and victimization experiences. *Journal of Lesbian Studies, 7*(4), 9–29.

Davidov, M., Grusec, J. E., & Wolfe, J. L. (2012). Mothers' knowledge of their children's evaluations of discipline: The role of type of discipline and misdeed, and parenting practices. *Merrill-Palmer Quarterly, 58*(3), 314–340. doi: 10.1353/mpq.2012.0018

Davidson, T. (2003). Developmental coordination disorder. In E. Thackery & M. Harris, Eds., *Gale Encyclopedia of Mental Disorders, Volume 2*, pp. 301–303. Detroit, MI: Thomson.

Davies, P. G., Spencer, S. J., Quinn, D. M., & Gerhardstein, R. (2002). Consuming images: How television commercials that elicit stereotype threat can restrain women academically and professionally. *Personality and Social Psychology Bulletin, 28*(12), 1615–1628.

Davis, B. E., Moon, R. Y., Sachs, H. C., & Ottolini, M. C. (1998). Effects of sleep position on infant motor development. *Pediatrics, 102*(5), 1135–1140.

Davis, D. L., Webster, P., Stainthorpe, H., Chilton, J., Jones, L., & Doi, R. (2007). Declines in sex ratio at birth and fetal deaths in Japan, and in U.S. whites but not African Americans. *Environmental Health Perspectives, 115*(6), 941–946.

Davis, E. P., Glynn, L. M., Waffarn, F., & Sandman, C. A. (2011). Prenatal maternal stress programs infant stress regulation. *Journal of Child Psychology and Psychiatry, 52*(2), 119–129.

Davis, E. P., & Sandman, C. A. (2010). The timing of prenatal exposure to maternal cortisol and psychosocial stress is associated with human infant cognitive development. *Child Development, 81*(1), 131–148.

Davis, L., Mohay, H., & Edwards, H. (2003). Mothers' involvement in caring for their premature infants: An historical overview. *Journal of Advanced Nursing, 42*(6), 578–586.

Davis-Kean, P. E., Jager, J., & Collins, W. A. (2009). The self in action: An emerging link between self-beliefs and behaviors in middle childhood. *Child Development Perspectives, 3*(3), 184–188.

Dawson, G. (2008). Early behavioral intervention, brain plasticity, and the prevention of autism spectrum disorder. *Development and Psychopathology, 20*(3), 775–803. doi: 10.1017/S0954579408000370

Dawson, G., Jones, E. H., Merkle, K., Venema, K., Lowy, R., Faja, S., Kamara, D., . . . Webb, S. J. (2012). Early behavioral intervention is associated with normalized brain activity in young children with autism. *Journal of the American Academy of Child and Adolescent Psychiatry, 51*(11), 1150–1159. doi: 10.1016/j.jaac.2012.08.018

Dawson, P., & Guare, R. (2013). *Executive skills in children and adolescents: A practical guide to assessment and intervention* (2nd ed.). New York, NY: Guilford Press.

Daxinger, L., & Whitelaw, E. (2012). Understanding transgenerational epigenetic inheritance via the gametes in mammals. *Nature Reviews Genetics, 13*(3), 153–162. doi: 10.1038/nrg3188

Day, N. L., Goldschmidt, L., & Thomas, C. A. (2006). Prenatal marijuana exposure contributed to the prediction of marijuana use at age 14. *Addiction, 101*(9), 1313–1322.

de Baulny, H. O., Abadie, V., Feillet, F., & de Parscau, L. (2007). Management of phenylketonuria and hyperphenylalaninemia. *Journal of Nutrition, 137*, 1561S–1563S.

de Bruyn, E. H., & Cillessen, A. N. (2006). Popularity in early adolescence: Prosocial and antisocial subtypes. *Journal of Adolescent Research, 21*(6), 607–627.

de Cos, P. L. (2001). *California's public schools: What experts say about their mission and functions.* Sacramento, CA: California Research Bureau.

De Goede, I. A., Branje, S. T., & Meeus, W. J. (2009). Developmental changes in adolescents' perceptions of relationships with their parents. *Journal of Youth and Adolescence, 38*(1), 75–88.

de Groot, M. J., Hoeksma, M., Blau, N., Reijngoud, D. J., & van Spronsen, F. J. (2010). Pathogenesis of cognitive dysfunction in phenylketonuria: Review of hypotheses. *Molecular Genetics and Metabolism, 99*, S86–S89.

de Haan, M. (2007). *Infant EEG and event-related potentials.* New York, NY: Psychology Press.

de Permentier, P. (2012). An anatomical perspective on growing pains in children. *Journal of The Australian Traditional Medicine Society, 18*(1), 33–34.

Dearing, E., McCartney, K., & Taylor, B. A. (2001). Change in family income-to-needs matters more for children with less. *Child Development, 72*(6), 1779–1793.

Deater-Howe, N., Rinaldi, C. M., Jennings, M., & Petrakos, H. (2002). "No! The lambs can stay out because they got cozies": Constructive and destructive sibling conflict, and pretend play. *Child Development, 73*, 1460–1473.

DeCasper, A. J., & Spence, M. J. (1986). Prenatal maternal speech influences newborns' perception of speech sounds. *Infant Behavior & Development, 19*(2), 133–150.

DeCasper, A., & Fifer, W. P. (1987). Of human bonding: Newborns prefer their mothers' voices. In J. Oates & S. Sheldon (Eds.), *Cognitive development in infancy* (pp. 111–118). Hillsdale, NJ: Erlbaum.

Declercq, E. R., Sakala, C., Corry, M. P., & Applebaum, S. (2006). *Listening to mothers II: Report of the second national U.S. survey of women's childbearing experiences.* New York, NY: Childbirth Connection.

DeLoache, J. S., Chiong, C., Sherman, K., Islan, N., Vanderborght, M., Troseth, G. L., . . . O'Doherty, K. (2010). Do babies learn from baby media? *Psychological Science, 21*(11), 1570–1574.

DeLoache, J. S., & Gottlieb, A. (2000). *A world of babies.* New York, NY: Cambridge University Press.

Demaray, M. K., & Malecki, C. K. (2003). Perceptions of the frequency and importance of social support by students classified as victims, bullies, and bully/victims in an urban middle school. *School Psychology Review, 32*(3), 471–489.

Demetriou, A., Christou, C., Spanoudis, G., & Platsidou, M. (2002). The development of mental processing: Efficiency, working memory, and thinking. *Monographs of the Society for Research in Child Development, 67*(1, Serial No. 268).

Demir, M., & Urberg, K. A. (2004). Friendship and adjustment among adolescents. *Journal of Experimental Child Psychology, 88*(1), 68–82.

Demuth, K. (1990). Subject, topic, and Sesotho passive. *Journal of Child Language, 17*(1), 67–84.

Denham, S. A., Renwick, S. M., & Holt, R. W. (1991). Working and playing together: Predictions of preschool social-emotional competence from mother-child interaction. *Child Development, 62*(2), 242–249.

Dennissen, J. J. A., Asendorpf, J. B., & van Aken, M. A. G. (2008). Childhood personality predicts long-term trajectories of shyness and aggressiveness in the context of demographic transitions in emerging adulthood. *Journal of Personality, 76*(1), 67–99.

Deoni, S. C., Mercure, E., Blasi, A., Gasston, D., Thomson, A., Johnson, M., . . . Murphy, D. G. (2011). Mapping infant brain myelination with magnetic resonance imaging. *Journal of Neuroscience, 31*(2), 2106–2110.

Der, G., Batty, G., & Deary, I. J. (2006). Effect of breast feeding on intelligence in children: Prospective study, sibling pairs analysis, and meta-analysis. *BMJ: British Medical Journal, 333*(7575), 929–930. doi: 10.1136/bmj.38978.699583.55

Desmarais, C., Sylvestre, A., Meyer, F., Bairati, I., & Rouleau, N. (2008). Systematic review of the literature on characteristics of late-talking toddlers. *International Journal of Language & Communication Disorders, 43*(4), 361–389.

Desrochers, J. E., & Houck, G. (2013). *Depression in children and adolescents: Guidelines for school practice.* Silver Spring, MD, & Bethesda, MD: National Association of School Nurses & National Association of School Psychologists.

Detterman, D. K., & Thompson, L. A. (1997). What is so special about special education? *American Psychologist, 52*(10), 1082–1090.

DeVito, D. (Producer), & Niccol, A. (Director). (1997). *Gattaca* [Motion picture]. USA: Columbia Pictures.

Dewey, K. G. (2003). Is breastfeeding protective against child obesity? *Journal of Human Lactation, 19*(1), 9–18.

Diamond, A. (2006). The early development of executive functions. In E. Bialystok & F. I. M. Craik (Eds.), *Lifespan cognition: Mechanisms of change* (pp. 70–95). Oxford, UK: Oxford University Press.

Diamond, A. (2009). The interplay of biology and the environment broadly defined. *Developmental Psychology, 45*(1), 1–8.

Diamond, A., Barnett, W., Thomas, J., & Munro, S. (2007). Preschool program improves cognitive control. *Science, 318*(5855), 1387–1388. doi: 10.1126/science.1151148

Diamond, L. M. (2006). What we got wrong about sexual identity development: Unexpected findings from a longitudinal study of young women. In A. M. Omoto & H. S. Kurtzman (Eds.), *Sexual orientation and mental health: Examining identity and development in lesbian, gay, and bisexual people* (pp. 73–94). Washington, DC: American Psychological Association.

Diamond, L. M., & Savin-Williams, R. C. (2009). Adolescent sexuality. In R. M. Lerner & L. Steinberg (Eds.), *Handbook of adolescent psychology. Vol. I: Individual bases of adolescent development* (3rd ed.). Hoboken, NJ: Wiley.

Dick, D. M., & Rose, R. J. (2004). Behavior genetics: What's new? What's next? In J. Lerner & A. E. Alberts (Eds.), *Current directions in developmental psychology* (pp. 3–10). Upper Saddle River, NJ: Pearson Prentice Hall.

Diego, M. A., Hernandez-Reif, M., Field, T., Friedman, L., & Shaw, K. (2001). HIV adolescents show improved immune function following massage therapy. *International Journal of Neuroscience, 106*, 35–45.

Dieter, J. N. I., Field, T., Hernandez-Reif, M., Emory, E. K., & Redzepi, M. (2003). Stable preterm infants gain more weight and sleep less after five days of massage therapy. *Journal of Pediatric Psychology, 28*(6), 403–411.

DiFiori, J. P., Benjamin, H. J., Brenner, J., Gregory, A., Jayanthi, N., Landry, G. L., & Luke, A. (2014). Overuse injuries and burnout in youth sports: A position statement from the American Medical Society for Sports Medicine. *Clinical Journal of Sports Medicine, 24*(1), 3–20.

DiLauro, E., & Schreiber, L. (2012). Supporting parents and child development through home visiting. *Zero to Three.* Retrieved from http://www.zerotothree.org/public-policy/policy-toolkit/homevisitssing_mar5.pdf

Dilworth-Bart, J. E., Khurshid, A., & Vandell, D. L. (2007). Do maternal stress and home environment mediate the relation between early income-to-need and 54-months attentional abilities? *Infant and Child Development, 16*(5), 525–552.

Diorio, J., & Meaney, M. J. (2007). Maternal programming of defensive responses through sustained effects on gene expression. *Journal of Psychiatry and Neuroscience, 32*(4), 275–284.

DiPietro, J. A., Caulfield, L., Costigan, K. A., Merialdi, M., Nguyen, R. H. N., Zavaleta, N., & Gurewitsch, E. D. (2004). Fetal neurobehavioral development: A tale of two cities. *Developmental Psychology, 40*(3), 445–456.

Dishion, T. J., & Owen, L. D. (2002). A longitudinal analysis of friendships and substance use: Bidirectional influence from adolescence to adulthood. *Developmental Psychology, 38*(4), 480–491.

Dittmar, H., Halliwell, E., & Ive, S. (2006). Does Barbie make girls want to be thin? The effect of experimental exposure to images of dolls on the body image of 5- to 8-year-old girls. *Developmental Psychology, 42*(2), 283–292.

Divorce Statistics. (2012). *Divorce statistics and divorce rate in the USA.* Retrieved from http://www.divorcestatistics.info/divorce-statistics-and-divorce-rate-in-the-usa.html

Dohnt, H. K., & Tiggemann, M. (2006). Body image concerns in young girls: The role of peers and media prior to adolescence. *Journal of Youth and Adolescence, 35*(2), 141–151.

Dolan, A., & Coe, C. (2011). Men, masculine identities and childbirth. *Sociology of Health & Illness, 33*(7), 1019–1034. doi: 10.1111/j.1467–9566.2011.01349.x

Dombrowski, S. C., Noonan, K., & Martin, R. P. (2007). Low birth weight and cognitive outcomes: Evidence for a gradient relationship in an urban, poor, African American birth cohort. *School Psychology Quarterly, 22*(1), 26–43.

Domenech Rodriguez, M., Donovick, M., & Crowley, S. (2009). Parenting styles in a cultural context: Observations of "protective parenting" in first-generation Latinos. *Family Process, 48*(2), 195–210.

Doris, J. M. (2002). *Lack of character: Personality and moral behavior.* New York, NY: Cambridge University Press.

Dowling, E., & Elliott, D. (2012). Promoting positive outcomes for children experiencing change in family relationships. In S. Roffey (Ed.), *Positive relationships: Evidence based practice across the world* (pp. 109–126). New York, NY: Springer Science and Business Media.

Downey, G., Lebolt, A., Rincón, C., & Freitas, A. L. (1998). Rejection sensitivity and children's interpersonal difficulties. *Child Development, 69*(4), 1074–1091.

Dozier, M., Zeanah, C. H., & Bernard, K. (2013). Infants and toddlers in foster care. *Child Development Perspectives, 7*(3), 166–171. doi: 10.1111/cdep.12033

Dr. Seuss Enterprises. (2002–2004). *All about Dr. Seuss.* Retrieved from http://www.catinthehat.org/history.htm

Draucker, C., Martsolf, D. S., Roller, C., Knapik, G., Ross, R., & Stidham, A. (2011). Healing from childhood sexual abuse: A theoretical model. *Journal of Child Sexual Abuse, 20*(4), 435–466. doi: 10.1080/10538712.2011.588188

Drewes, A. A. (2005). Play in selected cultures: Diversity and universality. In E. Gil & A. A. Drewes (Eds.), *Cultural issues in play therapy* (pp. 26–71). New York, NY: Guilford Press.

Drews, F. A., Yazdani, H., Godfrey, C. N., Cooper, J. M., & Strayer, D. L. (2009). Text messaging during simulated driving. *Human Factors, 51*(5), 762–770.

Drouin, M., & Davis, C. (2009). R u txting? Is the use of text speak hurting your literacy? *Journal of Literacy Research, 41*(1), 46–67.

Dube, E. M., & Savin-Williams, R. D. (1999). Sexual identity development among ethnic sexual-minority male youth. *Developmental Psychology, 35*(6), 1389–1398.

Dublin, S., Lydon-Rochelle, M., Kaplan, R. C., Watts, D. H., & Critchlow, C. W. (2000). Maternal and neonatal outcomes after induction of labor without an identified indication. *American Journal of Obstetrics & Gynecology, 183*(4), 986–994.

DuBois, D. L. (2007). *Effectiveness of mentoring program practices.* Alexandria, VA: MENTOR.

DuBois, D. L., Holloway, B. E., Valentine, J. C., & Cooper, H. (2002). Effectiveness of mentoring programs for youth: A meta-analytic review. *American Journal of Community Psychology, 30*(2), 157–197.

DuBois, D. L., & Silverthorn, N. (2005). Characteristics of natural mentoring relationships and adolescent adjustment: Evidence from a national study. *Journal of Primary Prevention, 26*(2), 69–92.

Duckworth, A. L., & Seligman, M. E. P. (2005). Self-discipline outdoes IQ in predicting academic performance of adolescents. *Psychological Science, 16*(12), 939–944.

Duff, F. J., & Clarke, P. J. (2011). Practitioner review: Reading disorders: What are the effective interventions and how should they be implemented and evaluated? *Journal of Child Psychology and Psychiatry, 52*(1), 3–12.

Dumontheil, I., Apperly, I. A., & Blakemore, S. (2010). Online usage of theory of mind continues to develop in late adolescence. *Developmental Science, 13*(2), 331–338. doi: 10.1111/j.1467-7687.2009.00888.x

Duncan, G. J., Huston, A. C., & Weisner, T. S. (2007). *Higher ground: New hope for the working poor and their children.* New York, NY: Russell Sage.

Duncan, R. M., & Cheyne, J. A. (2002). Private speech in young adults: Task difficulty, self-regulation, and psychological predication. *Cognitive Development, 16,* 889–906.

Dunifon, R. (2013). The influence of grandparents on the lives of children and adolescents. *Child Development Perspectives, 7*(1), 55–60.

Dunn, J. (2002). The adjustment of children in stepfamilies: Lessons from community studies. *Child and Adolescent Mental Health, 7*(4), 154–161.

Dunn, J. (2004). *Children's friendships.* Malden, MA: Blackwell.

Dunn, J. (2005). Naturalistic observation of children and their families. In S. Greene & D. Hogan (Eds.), *Researching children's experience: Methods and approaches* (pp. 87–101). Thousand Oaks, CA: Sage.

Dunn, J., Cheng, H., O'Connor, T. G., & Bridges, L. (2004). Children's perspectives on their relationships with their nonresident fathers: Influences, outcomes and implications. *Journal of Child Psychology and Psychiatry, 45*(3), 553–566.

Dunn, J., Fergusson, E., & Maughan, B. (2006). Grandparents, grandchildren, and family change. In A. Clarke-Stewart & J. Dunn (Eds.), *Families count* (pp. 299–318). New York, NY: Cambridge University Press.

Duong, T. H., Jansson, U., & Hellström, A. (2013). Vietnamese mothers' experiences with potty training procedure for children from birth to two years of age. *Journal of Pediatric Urology, 9*(6 Pt A), 808–814.

Dush, C., Taylor, M. G., & Kroeger, R. A. (2008). Marital happiness and psychological well-being across the life course. *Family Relations, 57*(2), 211–226. doi: 10.1111/j.1741-3729.2008.00495.x

Dutra, L. M., & Glantz, S. A. (2014). Electronic cigarettes and conventional cigarette use among U.S. adolescents: A cross-sectional study. *JAMA Pediatrics, 168*(7), 610–617.

Duvander, A., & Andersson, G. (2006). Gender equality and fertility in Sweden: A study on the impact of the father's uptake of parental leave on continued childbearing. *Marriage and Family Review, 39*(1), 121–142.

Dweck, C. S. (1999). Caution—Praise can be dangerous. *American Educator, 23*(1), 1–5.

Dyer, S., & Moneta, G. B. (2006). Frequency of parallel, associate, and cooperative play in British children of different socioeconomic status. *Social Behavior and Personality, 34*(5), 587–592.

Eccles, J. S. (1999). The development of children ages 6 to 14. *Future of Children, 9*(2), 30–44.

Eccles, J. S. (2004). Schools, academic motivation, and stage environment fit. In R. M. Lerner & L. Steinburg (Eds.), *Handbook of adolescent psychology* (2nd ed., pp. 125–153). Hoboken, NJ: Wiley.

Eccles, J. S., & Roeser, R. W. (2009). Schools, academic motivation, and stage-environment Fit. In R. M. Lerner & L. Steinber (Eds.) *Handbook of Adolescent Psychology* (3rd ed.) (pp. 404–434). Hoboken, NJ: John Wiley & Sons.

Eccles, J. S., & Templeton, J. (2002). Extracurricular and other after-school activities for youth. *Review of Educational Research, 26,* 113–180.

Eckerman, C. O., & Didow, S. M. (1996). Nonverbal imitation and toddlers' mastery of verbal means of achieving coordinated action. *Developmental Psychology, 32*(1), 141–152.

Eckstein, D., Aycock, K. J., Sperber, M. A., McDonald, J., Van Wiesner, V., Watts, R. E., & Ginsburg, P. (2010). A review of 200 birth-order studies: Lifestyle characteristics. *Journal of Individual Psychology, 66*(4), 408–434.

Edgren, A. R. (2002). Prematurity. In D. S. Blanchfield & J. L. Longe (Eds.), *Gale encyclopedia of medicine* (Vol. 4, 2nd ed., pp. 2706–2708). Detroit, MI: Gale.

Edin, K., & Kefalas, M. (2005). *Promises I can keep: Why poor women put motherhood before marriage.* Berkeley and Los Angeles: University of California Press.

Education Commission of the States. (2014). *50-state analysis*. Retrieved from http://ecs.force.com/mbdata/mbquestU ?SID=a0i70000004j3cq&rep=Kq02&Q=Q3195

Education Resources Information Center. (n.d.). *About the ERIC collection.* Retrieved from http://www.eric.ed .gov/ERICWebPortal/resources/html/collection/about_ collection.html

Education Week. (2004). *Reading.* Retrieved from http:// www.edweek.org/rc/issues/reading/

Egeghy, P. P., Sheldon, D. M., Stout, E. A., Cohen-Hubal, N. S., Tulve, L. J., Melnyk, M. K., . . . Coan, A. (2007). *Important exposure factors for children: An analysis of laboratory and observational field data characterizing cumulative exposure to pesticides* (EPA Report 600/R-07/013). Washington, DC: Environmental Protection Agency.

Egger, H. (2009). Toddler with temper tantrums: A careful assessment of a dysregulated preschool child. In C. A. Galanter & P. S. Jensen (Eds.), *DSM-IV-TR casebook and treatment guide for child mental health* (pp. 365–384). Arlington, VA: American Psychiatric Publishing.

Ehrenberg, M., Regev, R., Lazinski, M., Behrman, L. J., & Zimmerman, J. (2014). Adjustment to divorce for children. In L. Grossman, & S. Walfish (Eds.), *Translating psychological research into practice* (pp. 1–7). New York, NY: Springer.

Eigsti, I., Zayas, V., Mischel, W., Shoda, Y., Ayduk, O., Dadlani, M. B., . . . Casey, B. J. (2006). Predicting cognitive control from preschool to late adolescence and young adulthood. *Psychological Science, 17*(6), 478–484.

Eisenberg, N., Hofer, C., Spinrad, T. L., Gershoff, E. T., Valiente, C., Losoya, S. H., . . . Maxon, E. (2008). Understanding mother-adolescent conflict discussions: Concurrent and across-time prediction from youths' dispositions and parenting: III. Descriptive analyses and correlations. *Monographs of the Society for Research in Child Development, 73*(2), 54–80.

Eisenberg, N., Hofer, C., & Vaughan, J. (2007). Effortful control and its socioemotional consequences. In J. J. Gross (Ed.), *Handbook of emotion regulation* (pp. 287–306). New York, NY: Guilford Press.

Eisenberg, N., Morris, A. S., McDaniel, B., & Spinrad, T. L. (2009). Moral cognitions and prosocial responding in adolescence. In R. M. Lerner & L. Steinberg (Eds.), *Handbook of adolescent psychology* (3rd ed., Vol. 1, pp. 229–265). Hoboken, NJ: Wiley.

Eisenberg, N., Spinrad, T. L., & Sadovsky, A. (2006). Empathy-related responding in children. In M. Killen & J. Smetana (Eds.), *Handbook of moral development* (pp. 517–549). Mahwah, NJ: Erlbaum.

Elbert, T., Pantev, C., Wienbruch, C., Rockstroh, B., & Taub, E. (1995). Increased cortical representation of the fingers of the left hand in string players. *Science, 270*(5234), 305–307.

Eliot, L. (1999). *What's going on in there? How the brain and mind develop in the first five years of life.* New York, NY: Bantam Books.

Eliot, M., & Cornell, D. G. (2009). Bullying in middle school as a function of insecure attachment and aggressive attitudes. *School Psychology International, 30*(2), 201–214.

Eliot, M., Cornell, D., Gregory, A., & Fan, X. (2010). Supportive school climate and student willingness to seek help for bullying and threats of violence. *Journal of School Psychology, 48*(6), 533–553.

Elkind, D., & Bowen, R. (1979). Imaginary audience behavior in children and adolescents. *Developmental Psychology, 15*(1), 38–44.

Elliott, S., & Umberson, D. (2004). Recent demographic trends in the US and implications for well-being. In J. Scott, J. Treas, & M. Richards (Eds.), *The Blackwell companion to the sociology of families* (pp. 34–53). Malden, MA: Blackwell.

Elliott, W. (2009). Children's college aspirations and expectations: The potential role of children's development accounts (CDAs). *Children and Youth Services Review, 31,* 274–283.

Ellis, B. J., & Essex, M. J. (2007). Family environments, adrenarche, and sexual maturation: A longitudinal test of a life history model. *Child Development, 78*(6), 1799–1817.

Ellsworth, C. P., Muir, D. W., & Hains, S. M. J. (1993). Social competence and person-object differentiation: An analysis of the still-face effect. *Developmental Psychology, 29*(1), 63–73.

Else-Quest, N. M., Hyde, J. S., & Linn, M. C. (2010). Cross-national patterns of gender differences in mathematics: A meta-analysis. *Psychological Bulletin, 136*(1), 103–127.

Ely, R. (2005). Language and literacy in the school years. In J. B. Gleason (Ed.), *The development of language* (6th ed., pp. 396–443). Boston, MA: Pearson.

Engle, M. (2004). Kids and sports. *New York University Child Study Center Letter, 9*(1), 1–7.

Engles, R. C. M. E., Knibbe, R. A., Drop, M. J., & deHaan, Y. T. (1997). Homogeneity of cigarette smoking within peer groups: Influence or selection? *Health Education and Behavior, 24*(6), 801–811.

Entwisle, D. R., Alexander, K. L., & Olson, L. S. (2000). Early work histories of urban youth. *American Sociological Review, 65*(2), 279–297.

Entwisle, D. R., Alexander, K. L., & Olson, L. S. (2005). Urban teenagers: Work and dropout. *Youth & Society, 37*(1), 3–32.

Erickson, L. D., McDonald, S., & Elder, G. R. (2009). Informal mentors and education: Complementary or compensatory resources? *Sociology of Education, 82*(4), 344–367.

Erikson, E. H. (1963). *Childhood and society* (2nd ed.). New York, NY: Norton.

Erikson, E. H. (1968). *Identity, youth and crisis.* New York, NY: W. W. Norton.

Eriksson, J. G., Kajantie, E., Osmond, C., Thornburg, K., & Barker, D. J. (2009). Boys live dangerously in the womb. *American Journal of Human Biology, 22*(3), 300–305.

Erlandsson, K., & Lindgren, H. (2009). From belonging to belonging through a blessed moment of love for a child—The birth of a child from the fathers' perspective. *Journal of Men's Health, 6*(4), 338–344. doi: 10.1016/j.jomh.2009.09.029

Erol, R. Y., & Orth, U. (2011). Self-esteem development from age 14 to 30 Years: A longitudinal study. *Journal of Personality and Social Psychology, 101*(3), 607–619.

Ersoy, B., Balkan, C., Gunay, T., & Egemen, A. (2005). The factors affecting the relation between the menarcheal age of mother and daughter. *Child: Care, Health and Development, 31*(3), 303–308.

Espinosa, L. M. (2002). High-quality preschool: Why we need it and what it looks like. *Preschool Policy Matters, 1*, 1–11.

Espinoza, P., da Luz Fontes, A., & Arms-Chavez, C. J. (2014). Attributional gender bias: Teachers' ability and effort explanations for students' math performance. *Social Psychology of Education, 17*(1), 105–126. doi: 10.1007/s11218-013-9226-6

Esposito, D. H., Holman, R. C., Haberling, D. L., Tate, J. E., Podewils, L. J., Glass, R. I., & Parashar, U. (2011). Baseline estimates of diarrhea-associated mortality among United States children before rotavirus vaccine introduction. *Pediatric Infectious Diseases Journal, 30*(11), 942–947.

Essex, M. J., Boyce, W. T., Hertzman, C., Lam, L. L., Armstrong, J. M., Neumann, S. M. A., & Kobor, M. S. (2013). Epigenetic vestiges of early developmental adversity: Childhood stress exposure and DNA methylation in adolescence. *Child Development, 84*(1), 58–75.

Evans, G. W., Jones-Rounds, M. L., Belojevic, G., & Vermeylen, F. (2012). Family income and childhood obesity in eight European cities: The mediating roles of neighborhood characteristics and physical activity. *Social Science & Medicine, 75*(3), 477–481.

Evins, A. E., Green, A. I., Kane, J. M., & Murray, R. M. (2012). The effect of marijuana use on the risk for schizophrenia. *Journal of Clinical Psychiatry, 73*(11), 1463–1468.

Eyberg, S. M., Nelson, M. M., & Boggs, S. R. (2008). Evidence-based psychosocial treatments for children and adolescents with disruptive behavior. *Journal of Clinical Child and Adolescent Psychology, 37*, 215–237.

Eyer, D. (1992). *Mother-infant bonding: A scientific fiction.* New Haven, CT: Yale University Press.

Faden, V., Ruffin, B., Newes-Adeyi, G., & Chen, C. (2010). The relationship among pubertal stage, age, and drinking in adolescent boys and girls. *Journal of Child & Adolescent Substance Abuse, 19*(1), 1–15.

Fagan, J. F., Holland, C. R., & Wheeler, K. (2007). The prediction, from infancy, of adult IQ and achievement. *Intelligence, 35*(3), 225–231. doi: 10.1016/j.intell.2006.07.007

Fagard, J. (2006). Normal and abnormal early development of handedness. *Developmental Psychobiology, 48*(6), 413–417.

Fagot, B. I. (1997). Attachment, parenting, and peer interactions of toddler children. *Developmental Psychology, 33*(3), 489–499.

Fahlman, S. E. (n.d.). *Smiley lore :-).* Retrieved from http://www.cs.cmu.edu/~sef/sefSmiley.htm

FairTest. (2013). *College-bound seniors SAT scores by family income.* http://www.fairtest.org/college-admissions-tests-show-testdriven-schooling

FairTest.org. (2013). *2013 College bound seniors total group profile report.* Retrieved from http://media.collegeboard.com/digitalServices/pdf/research/2013/TotalGroup-2013.pdf

Falbo, T. (2012). Only children: An updated review. *Journal of Individual Psychology, 68*(1), 38–49.

Fan, J., Gu, X., Guise, K. G., Liu, X., Fossella, J., Wang, H., & Posner, M. I. (2009). Testing the behavioral interaction and integration of attentional networks. *Brain and Cognition, 70*(2), 209–220.

Fancy, S. P., Harrington, E. P., Yuen, T. J., Silbereis, J. C., Zhao, C., Baranzini, S. E., & Rowitch, D. H. (2011). Axin2 as regulatory and therapeutic target in newborn brain injury and remyelination. *Nature Neuroscience, 14*(8), 1009–1016.

Fang, X., Brown, D. S., Florence, C. S., & Mercy, J. A. (2012). The economic burden of child maltreatment in the United States and implications for prevention. *Child Abuse & Neglect, 36*(2), 156–165. doi: 10.1016/j.chiabu.2011.10.006

Fantuzzo, J. W., Bulotsky-Sheare, R., Fusco, R. A., & McWayne, C. (2005). An investigation of preschool classroom behavioral adjustment problems and social-emotional school readiness competencies. *Early Childhood Research Quarterly, 20*(3), 259–275. doi: 10.1016/j.ecresq.2005.07.001

Fantuzzo, J. W., Perlman, S. M., & Dobbins, E. K. (2011). Types and timing of child maltreatment and early school success: A population-based investigation. *Children and Youth Services Review, 33*(8), 1404–1411.

Farrelly, M. C., Davis, K. C., Haviland, M. L., Messeri, P., & Healton, C. G. (2005). Evidence of a dose-response relationship between "truth" antismoking ads and youth smoking prevalence. *American Journal of Public Health, 95*(3), 425–431.

Farrington, D. P., Loeber, R., Stallings, R., & Ttofi, M. M. (2011). Bullying perpetration and victimization as predictors of delinquency and depression in the Pittsburgh Youth Study. *Journal of Aggression, Conflict and Peace Research, 3*(2), 74–81.

Farroni, T., Massaccesi, S., Pividori, D., & Johnson, M. (2004). Gaze following in newborns. *Infancy, 5*(1), 39–60.

Farroni, T., Menon, E., & Johnson, M. H. (2006). Factors influencing newborns' preference for faces with eye contact. *Journal of Experimental Child Psychology, 95*(4), 298–308.

Farruggia, S. P., Bullen, P., & Davidson, J. (2013). Important nonparental adults as an academic resource for youth.

Journal of Early Adolescence, 33(4), 498–522. doi: 10.1177/0272431612450950

Fast, I. (1985). Infantile narcissism and the active infant. *Psychoanalytic Psychology, 2*(2), 153–170.

FDA. (2014). *FDA allows marketing for first-of-its-kind postnatal test to help diagnose developmental delays and intellectual disabilities in children.* Retrieved from http://www.fda.gov/NewsEvents/Newsroom/PressAnnouncements/ucm382179.htm

Federal Interagency Forum on Child and Family Statistics. (2009). *America's children: Key national indicators of well-being.* Washington, DC: U.S. Government Printing Office.

Federal Interagency Forum on Child and Family Statistics. (2013a). *America's children: Key national indicators of well-being, 2013.* Washington, DC: Government Printing Office.

Federal Interagency Forum on Child and Family Statistics. (2013b). *High school academic coursetaking.* Retrieved from http://www.childstats.gov/americaschildren/edu3.asp

Feinberg, M. E., Reiss, D., Neiderhiser, J. M., & Hetherington, E. M. (2005). Differential association of family subsystem negativity on siblings' maladjustment: Using behavior genetic methods to test process theory. *Journal of Family Psychology, 19*(4), 601–610.

Fekkes, M., Pijpers, F. I. M., & Verloove-Vanhorick, S. P. (2005). Bullying: Who does what, when and where? Involvement of children, teachers and parents in bullying behavior. *Health Education Research. 20*(1), 81–91.

Feld, S., & Schieffelin, B. B. (1998). Hard words: A functional basis for Kaluli discourse. In D. Brenneis & R. K. S. Macauley (Eds.), *The matrix of language* (pp. 56–74). Boulder, CO: Westview Press.

Feldman, R., Rosenthal, Z., & Eidelman, A. I. (2014). Maternal-preterm skin-to-skin contact enhances child physiologic organization and cognitive control across the first 10 years of life. *Biological Psychiatry, 75*(1), 56–64. doi: 10.1016/j.biopsych.2013.08.012

Feldman, R., Weller, A., Zagoory-Sharon, O., & Levine, A. (2007). Evidence for a neuroendocrinological foundation of human affiliation: Plasma oxytocin levels across pregnancy and the postpartum period predict mother-infant bonding. *Psychological Science, 18*(11), 965–970. doi: 10.1111/j.1467-9280.2007.02010.x

Felsenthal, R. (2006). As they grow. Pregnancy & birth: Pregnancy myths. *Parents (10836373), 81*(11), 199.

Fender, J. G., Richert, R. A., Robb, M. B., & Wartella, E. (2010). Parent teaching focus and toddlers' learning from an infant DVD. *Infant & Child Development, 19*(6), 613–627. doi: 10.1002/icd.713

Ferguson, B., Graf, E., & Waxman, S. R. (2014). Infants use known verbs to learn novel nouns: Evidence from 15- and 19-month-olds. *Cognition, 131*(1), 139–146. doi: 10.1016/j.cognition.2013.12.014

Ferguson, C. J., Muñoz, M. E., & Medrano, M. R. (2012). Advertising influences on young children's food choices and parental influence. *Journal of Pediatrics, 160*(3), 452–455.

Ferguson, C. J., San Miguel, C., Kilburn, J. C., & Sanchez, P. (2007). The effectiveness of school-based anti-bullying programs: A meta-analytic review. *Criminal Justice Review, 32*(4), 401–414.

Ferguson, R. W., Green, A., & Hansen, L. M. (2013). *Game changers: Stats, stories and what communities are doing to protect young athletes.* Washington, DC: Safe Kids Worldwide.

Ferguson, T. J., Stegge, H., Miller, E. R., & Olsen, M. E. (1999). Guilt, shame, and symptoms in children. *Developmental Psychology, 35*(2), 347–357.

Fergusson, D. M., Boden, J. M., & Horwood, L. J. (2008). Exposure to childhood sexual and physical abuse and adjustment in early adulthood. *Child Abuse & Neglect, 32*(6), 607–619.

Fernald, A. (1985). Four-month-olds prefer to listen to motherese. *Infant Behavior and Development, 8*, 181–195.

Fernald, A., & Morikawa, H. (1993). Common themes and cultural variation in Japanese and American mothers' speech to infants. *Child Development, 64*, 637–656.

Fernald, A., Pinto, J. P., Swingley, D., Weinberg, A., & McRoberts, G. W. (2001). Rapid gains in speed of verbal processing by infants in the 2nd year. In M. Tomasello & E. Bates (Eds.), *Language development: The essential readings* (pp. 49–56). Malden, MA: Blackwell.

Fernyhough, C., & Fradley, E. (2005). Private speech on an executive task: Relations with task difficulty and task performance. *Cognitive Development, 20*(1), 103–120.

Field, T. (2007). *The amazing infant.* Malden, MA: Blackwell.

Field, T., Diego, M., & Hernandez-Reif, M. (2007). Massage therapy research. *Developmental Review, 27*(1), 75–89.

Field, T., Hernandez-Reif, M., Diego, M., Feijo, L., Vera, Y., & Gil, K. (2004). Massage therapy by parents improves early growth and development. *Infant Behavior & Development, 27*(4), 435–442.

Field, T., Morrow, C., Valdeon, C., Larson, S., Kuhn, C., & Schanberg, S. (1992). Massage reduces anxiety in child and adolescent psychiatric patients. *Journal of the American Academy of Child and Adolescent Psychiatry, 31*, 125–131.

Fifer, W. P., Monk, C. E., & Grose-Fifer, J. (2004). Prenatal development and risk. In G. Bremner & A. Fogel (Eds.), *Blackwell handbook of infant development* (pp. 505–542). Malden, MA: Blackwell.

Figueiredo, B., Costa, R., Pacheco, A., & Pais, A. (2009). Mother-to-infant emotional involvement at birth. *Maternal and Child Health Journal, 13*(4), 539–549. doi: 10.1007/s10995-008-0312-x

Filipek, P. A., Accardo, P. J., Baranek, G. T., Cook, E. H., Jr., Dawson, G., Gordon, B., . . . Volkmar, F. R. (1999). The screening and diagnosis of autism spectrum disorders. *Journal of Autism and Developmental Disorders, 29*(2), 439–484.

Filippova, E., & Astington, J. (2010). Children's understanding of social-cognitive and social-communicative aspects of discourse irony. *Child Development, 81*(3), 913–928.

Finer, L. B., & Zolna, M. R. (2012). Unintended pregnancy in the United States: Incidence and disparities, 2006. *Contraception, 84*(5), 478–485.

Finkelhor, D. (2009). The prevention of childhood sexual abuse. *Future of Children, 19*(2), 169–194.

Finkelhor, D., & Hashima, P. Y. (2001). The victimization of children and youth: A comprehensive overview. In S. O. White (Ed.), *Handbook of youth and justice* (pp. 48–78). New York, NY: Kluwer Academic.

Finkelhor, D., Ormrod, R., Turner, H., & Hamby, S. L. (2005). The victimization of children and youth: A comprehensive, national survey. *Child Maltreatment, 10*(1), 5–25.

Finkelhor, D., Turner, H., Ormrod, R., & Hamby, S. L. (2009). Violence, abuse, and crime exposure in a national sample of children and youth. *Pediatrics, 124*(5), 1411–1423.

Finkenauer, C., Engels, R. C. M. E., Meeus, W., & Oosterwegel, A. (2002). Self and identity in early adolescence: The pains and gains of knowing who and what you are. In T. M. Brinthaupt & R. P. Lipka (Eds.), *Understanding early adolescent self and identity: Applications and interventions* (pp. 25–56). Albany: State University New York Press.

Finn, A. S., Sheridan, M. A., Kam, C. L. H., Hinshaw, S., & D'Esposito, M. (2010). Longitudinal evidence for functional specialization of the neural circuit supporting working memory in the human brain. *Journal of Neuroscience, 30*(33), 11062–11067.

Firth, N., Frydenberg, E., & Greaves, D. (2008). Perceived control and adaptive coping: Programs for adolescent students who have learning disabilities. *Learning Disability Quarterly, 31*(3), 151–165.

Flanagan, D., Mascolo, J., & Hardy-Braz, S. (2006–2012). *Standardized testing.* Retrieved from http://www.education.com/reference/article/standardized-testing

Flavell, J. H. (1999). Cognitive development: Children's knowledge about the mind. *Annual Review of Psychology, 50*, 21–45.

Flavell, J. H., Miller, P. H., & Miller, S. A. (2002). *Cognitive development* (4th ed.). Upper Saddle River, NJ: Prentice Hall.

Fleming, A. S., Corter, C., Stallings, J., & Sneider, M. (2002). Testosterone and prolactin are associated with emotional responses to infant cries in new fathers. *Hormones and Behavior, 42*, 399–413.

Fletcher, A. C., & Jefferies, B. C. (1999). Parental mediators of associations between perceived authoritative parenting and early adolescent substance use. *Journal of Early Adolescence, 19*(4), 465–487.

Fletcher, A. C., Walls, J. K., Cook, E. C., Madison, K. J., & Bridges, T. H. (2008). Parenting style as a moderator of associations between maternal disciplinary strategies and child well-being. *Journal of Family Issues, 29*(12), 1724–1744. doi: 10.1177/0192513X08322933

Fletcher, G. E., Zach, T., Pramanik, A. K., & Ford, S. P. (2009). Multiple births. *E-Medicine.* Retrieved from http://www.emedicine.com/ped/TOPIC2599.HTM

Foerde, K., Knowlton, B. J., & Poldrack, R. A. (2006). Modulation of competing memory systems by distraction. *Proceedings of the National Academy of Sciences, 103*(31), 11778–11783.

Fogel, A. (2002). *Infancy* (4th ed.). Belmont, CA: Wadsworth.

Fombonne, E., Zakarian, R., Bennett, A., Meng, L., & McLean-Heywood, D. (2005). Pervasive developmental disorders in Montreal, Quebec, Canada: Prevalence and links with immunizations. *Pediatrics, 118*(1), 139–150.

Fonagy, P., Target, M., & Gergely, G. (2006). Psychoanalytic perspectives on developmental psychology. In D. J. Cohen & D. Cicchetti (Eds.), *Developmental psychopathology: Theory and method* (Vol. 1, pp. 701–749). Hoboken, NJ: Wiley.

Food Research and Action Center. (2010). *School breakfast program.* Retrieved from http://frac.org/federal-foodnutrition-programs/school-breakfast-program/

Foorman, B. R., Francis, D. J., Fletcher, J. M., Schatschneider, C., & Mehta, P. (1998). The role of instruction in learning to read: Preventing reading failure in at-risk children. *Journal of Educational Psychology, 90*(1), 37–55.

Forhan, S. E., Gottlieb, S. L., Sternberg, M. R., Xu, F., Datta, S. D., McQuillan, G. M., Berman, S. M., & Markowitz, L. E. (2009). Prevalence of sexually transmitted infections among female adolescents aged 14 to 19 in the United States. *Pediatrics, 124*(6), 1505–1512.

Forry, N. D., Iruka, I., Kainz, K., Tout, K., Torquati, J., Susman-Stillman, A., . . . Smith, S. (2012). *Identifying profiles of quality in home-based child care, issue brief OPRE 2012-20.* Washington, DC: Office of Planning, Research and Evaluation, Administration for Children and Families, U.S. Department of Health and Human Services.

Fotek, P. (2012). *Natal teeth.* U. S. National Library of Medicine. Retrieved from http://www.nlm.nih.gov/medlineplus/ency/article/003268.htm

Fox, B. (2001). The formative years: How parenthood creates gender. *Canadian Review of Sociology and Anthropology, 28*(4), 373–390.

Fox, G. (2006). Development in family contexts. In L. Combrinck-Graham (Ed.), *Children in family contexts* (pp. 26–50). New York, NY: Guilford Press.

Fraley, R., & Heffernan, M. E. (2013). Attachment and parental divorce: A test of the diffusion and sensitive period hypotheses. *Personality and Social Psychology Bulletin, 39*(9), 1199-1213.

Franceschini, S., Gori, S., Ruffino, M., Pedrolli, K., & Facoetti, A. (2012). A causal link between visual spatial attention and reading acquisition. *Current Biology, 22*, 814–819.

Franco, I., von Gontard, A., & De Gennaro, M. (2013). Evaluation and treatment of nonmonosymptomatic nocturnal enuresis: A standardization document from the International Children's Continence Society. *Journal of Pediatric Urology, 9*(2), 234–243. doi: 10.1016/j.jpurol.2012.10.026

Franic, S., Middeldorp, C. M., Dolan, C. V., Ligthart, L., & Boomsma, D. I. (2010). Childhood and adolescent anxiety and depression: Beyond heritability. *Journal of the*

American Academic of Child and Adolescent Psychiatry, 49, 820–829.

Frank, D. A., Augustyn, M., Knight, W. G., Pell, T., & Zuckerman, B. (2001). Growth, development, and behavior in early childhood following prenatal cocaine exposure: A systematic review. *Journal of the American Medical Association, 285*(12), 1613–1625.

Frank-Briggs, A. (2011). Attention deficit hyperactivity disorder (ADHD). *Journal of Pediatric Neurology, 9*(3), 291–298.

Franklin, B., Jones, A., Love, D., Puckett, S. Macklin, J., & White-Means, S. (2012). Exploring mediators of food insecurity and obesity: A review of the recent literature. *Journal of Community Health, 37*(1), 253–264.

Franklin, J., Rifkin, L., & Pascual, P. (2001). Serving the very young and the restless. In D. G. Singer & J. L. Singer (Eds.), *Handbook of children and the media* (pp. 507–520). Thousand Oaks, CA: Sage.

Frederick, C. B., Snellman, K., & Putnam, R. D. (2014). Increasing socioeconomic disparities in adolescent obesity. *Proceedings of the National Academy of Sciences, 111*(4), 1338–1342.

Freeman, N. K. (2007). Preschoolers' perceptions of gender appropriate toys and their parents' beliefs about genderized behaviors: Miscommunication, mixed messages, or hidden truths? *Early Childhood Education Journal, 34*(5), 357–366.

Freeman, N. K., & Somerindyke, J. (2001). Social play at the computer: Preschoolers scaffold and support peers' computer competence. *Information Technology in Childhood Education Annual, 12*, 203–213.

Freisthler, B., Merritt, D. H., & LaScala, E. A. (2006). Understanding the ecology of child maltreatment: A review of the literature and directions for future research. *Child Maltreatment, 11*(3), 263–280.

French, S., Seidman, E., Allen, L., & Aber, J. (2006). The development of ethnic identity during adolescence. *Developmental Psychology, 42*(1), 1–10.

Freud, A. (1965). *Normality and pathology in childhood.* New York, NY: International Universities Press.

Freud, S. (1950). A note on the unconscious in psycho-analysis (1912). In *Collected papers* (Vol. IV, pp. 22–29). London, UK: Hogarth Press.

Freud, S. (1953). Two encyclopedia articles (1922): (a) Psychoanalysis. In *Collected papers* (Vol. V, pp. 107–130). London, UK: Hogarth Press.

Freud, S. (1959). Character and anal erotism (1908). In *Collected papers* (Vol. II, pp. 45–50). London, UK: Hogarth Press.

Frey, N. (2005). Retention, social promotion, and academic redshirting: What do we know and need to know? *Remedial and Special Education, 26*(6), 332–346.

Fried, L. E., Williams, S., Cabral, H., & Hacker, K. (2013). Developmental differences in risk factors for suicide attempts among 9th and 11th grade youth: A longitudinal perspective. *Journal of School Nursing, 29*(2), 113–122.

Fried, P. A., & Makin, J. E. (1987). Neonatal behavioural correlates of prenatal exposure to marihuana, cigarettes and alcohol in a low risk population. *Neurotoxicology and Teratology, 9*(1), 1–7.

Friedman, H. S., Tucker, J. S., Schwartz, J. E., Martin, L. R., Tomlinson-Keasey, C., Wingard, D. L., & Criqui, M. H. (1995). Childhood conscientiousness and longevity. *Journal of Personality & Social Psychology, 68*, 696–703.

Friedman, M. J. (2006). *Sesame Street educates and entertains internationally.* Retrieved from http://www.america.gov/st/washfile-english/2006/April/20060405165756jmn amdeirf0.4207117.html

Fries, A. B. W., Ziegler, T. E., Kurian, J. R., Jacoris, S., & Pollak, S. D. (2005). Early experience in humans is associated with changes in neuropeptides critical for regulating social behavior. *Proceedings of the National Academy of Sciences, 102*(47), 17237–17240.

Frith, U. (2003). *Autism: Explaining the enigma.* Malden, MA: Blackwell.

Frömel, K., Stelzer, J., Groffik, D., & Ernest, J. (2008). Physical activity of children ages 6-8: The beginning of school attendance. *Journal of Research In Childhood Education, 23*(1), 29-40.

Froschl, M., & Sprung, B. (2008). A positive and pro-active response to young boys in the classroom. *Exchange: The Early Childhood Leaders' Magazine, 182*, 34–36.

Fu, D. (1997). Vygotsky and Marxism. *Education and Culture, 14*(1), 10–17.

Fuhs, M. W., & Day, J. D. (2011). Verbal ability and executive functioning development in preschoolers at head start. *Developmental Psychology, 47*(2), 404–416.

Furco, A. (2013). A research agenda for K–12 school-based service-learning: Academic achievement and school success. *International Journal of Research on Service-Learning and Community Engagement, 1*(1), 11–22.

Furman, W., & Collins, W. A. (2009). Adolescent romantic relationships and experiences. In K. H. Rubin, W. M. Bukowski, & B. Laursen (Eds.), *Handbook of peer interactions, relationships, and groups* (pp. 341–360). New York, NY: Guilford Press.

The Future of Children. (2010). *About the Future of Children.* Retrieved from http://futureofchildren.org/futureofchildren/about/

Gagnon, S., Huelsman, T. J., Reichard, A. E., Kidder-Ashley, P., Griggs, M., Struby, J., & Bollinger, J. (2014). Help me play! Parental behaviors, child temperament, and preschool peer play. *Journal of Child and Family Studies, 23*(5), 872–884. doi: 10.1007/s10826–013–9743–0

Gaillard, V., Barrouillet, P., Jarrold, C., & Camos, V. (2011). Developmental differences in working memory: Where do they come from? *Journal of Experimental Child Psychology, 110*(3), 469–479.

Galan, H. L., & Hobbins. J. C. (2003). Intrauterine growth restriction. In J. S. Scott, R. S. Gibbs, B. Y. Karlan, & A. F. Haney (Eds.), *Danforth's obstetrics and gynecology* (9th ed., pp. 203–217). Philadelphia, PA: Lippincott.

Galler, J. R., Bryce, C. P., Waber, D. P., Hock, R. S., Harrison, R., Eaglesfield, G., & Fitzmaurice, G. (2012a). Infant malnutrition predicts conduct problems in adolescents. *Nutritional Neuroscience, 15*(4), 186–192. doi: 10.1179/1476830512Y.0000000012

Galler, J. R., Bryce, C., Waber, D. P., Zichlin, M. L., Fitzmaurice, G. M., & Eaglesfield, D. (2012b). Socioeconomic outcomes in adults malnourished in the first year of life: A 40-year study. *Pediatrics, 130*(1), e1–e7.

Gallup, G. G., Anderson, J. R., & Shillito, D. J. (2002). The mirror test. In M. Bekoff, C. Allen, & G. M. Burghardt (Eds.), *The cognitive animal: Empirical and theoretical perspectives on animal cognition* (pp. 325–334). Cambridge, MA: MIT Press.

Ganger, J., & Brent, M. R. (2004). Reexamining the vocabulary spurt. *Developmental Psychology, 40*(4), 621–632.

Ganong, L. H., Coleman, M., & Jamison, T. (2011). Patterns of stepchild–stepparent relationship development. *Journal of Marriage and Family, 73*(2), 396–413. doi: 10.1111/j.1741-3737.2010.00814.x

Garan, E. M. (2001). Beyond the smoke and mirrors. *Phi Delta Kappan, 82*(7), 500–506.

Garber, A. K., Park, J., Brindis, C. D., Vaughn, B., Barry, M., Guzman, L., & Berger, A. (2013). *Adolescent health highlights: Physical development and daily health habits.* Child Trend Publication #2013-09. Bethesda, MD: Child Trends.

Garces, E., Thomas, D., & Currie, J. (2002). Longer-term effects of Head Start. *American Economic Review, 9*(4), 999–1012.

García, F., & Gracia, E. (2009). Is always authoritative the optimum parenting style? Evidence from Spanish families. *Adolescence, 44*(173), 101–131.

Gardephe, C. D., & Ettlinger, S. (1993). *Don't pick up the baby or you'll spoil the child and other old wives' tales about pregnancy and parenting.* San Francisco, CA: Chronicle Books.

Gardner, H. (1976). *The shattered mind.* New York, NY: Vintage Books.

Gardner, H. (1993). *Frames of mind: The theory of multiple intelligences.* New York, NY: Basic Books.

Gardner, H. (1999). *Intelligence reframed.* New York, NY: Basic Books.

Gardner, H., & Connell, M. (2000). Response to Nicholas Allix. *Australian Journal of Education, 44*, 288–293.

Gardner, H., & Moran, S. (2006). The science of multiple intelligences theory: A response to Lynn Waterhouse. *Educational Psychologist, 41*(4), 227–232.

Gardner, H., & Traub, J. (2010). A debate on "multiple intelligences." In D. Gordon (Ed.), *Cerebrum 2010: Emerging ideas in brain science* (pp. 34–61). Washington, DC: Dana Press.

Gardner, R. M., Stark, K., Friedman, B. N., & Jackson, N. A. (2000). Predictors of eating disorder scores in children ages 6 through 14: A longitudinal study. *Journal of Psychosomatic Research, 49*(3), 199–205.

Garmy, P., Nyberg, P., & Jakobsson, U. (2012). Sleep and television and computer habits of Swedish school-age children. *Journal of School Nursing, 28*, 469–476.

Garrett, B. (2009). *Brain & behavior: An introduction to biological psychology.* Thousand Oaks, CA: Sage.

Gartner, L. M., Morton, J., Lawrence, R. A., Naylor, A. J., O'Hare, D., Schanler, R. J., & Eidelman, A. I. (2005). Breastfeeding and the use of human milk. *Pediatrics, 115*(2), 496–506.

Garven, S., Wood, J. M., Malpass, R. S., & Shaw, J. S. (1998). More than suggestion: The effect of interviewing techniques from the McMartin Preschool case. *Journal of Applied Psychology, 83*(3), 347–359.

Gaskins, I. W., & Pressley, M. (2007). Teaching metacognitive strategies that address executive function processes within a schoolwide curriculum. In L. Meltzer (Ed.), *Executive function in education: From theory to practice* (pp. 261–286). New York, NY: Guilford Press.

Gass, K., Jenkins, J., & Dunn, J. (2007). Are sibling relationships protective? A longitudinal study. *Journal of Child Psychology and Psychiatry, 48*(2), 167–175.

Gates, G. J. (2011). *How many people are lesbian, gay, bisexual, and transgender?* Los Angeles, CA: The Williams Institute.

Gates, G. J. (2013). *LGBT parenting in the United States.* Los Angeles: The Williams Institute, UCLA School of Law.

Gathercole, S. E., Pickering, S. J., Ambridge, B., & Wearing, H. (2004). The structure of working memory from 4 to 15 years of age. *Developmental Psychology, 40*(2), 177–190.

Gauvain, M., & Parke, R. D. (2010). Socialization. In M. H. Bornstein (Ed.), *Handbook of cultural developmental science* (pp. 239–258). New York, NY: Psychology Press.

Gay, P. (1999). Sigmund Freud. *Time.* Retrieved from http://205.188.238.181/time/time100/scientist/

Gazzaniga, M., Ivry, R. B., & Mangun, G. R. (2013). *Cognitive neuroscience: The biology of the mind* (4th ed.). Cambridge, MA: MIT Press.

Ge, X., Brody, G. H., Conger, R. D., Simons, R. L., & Murry, V. M. (2002). Contextual amplification of pubertal transition effects on deviant peer affiliation and externalizing behavior among African-American children. *Developmental Psychology, 38*(1), 42–54.

Geangu, E., Benga, O., Stahl, D., & Striano, T. (2010). Contagious crying beyond the first days of life. *Infant Behavior & Development, 33*(3), 279–288. doi: 10.1016/j.infbeh.2010.03.004

Gelber, A. M., Isen, A., & National Bureau of Economic Research. (2011). *Children's schooling and parents' investment in children: Evidence from the Head Start Impact Study.* NBER Working Paper No. 17704. Washington, DC: National Bureau of Economic Research.

Gennetian, L., & Miller, C. (2000). *Reforming welfare and rewarding work: Final report on the Minnesota Family Investment Program: Vol. 2. Effects on children.* New York, NY: MDRC. Retrieved from http://www.mdrc.org/publications/206/full.pdf

Gentile, D. A. (2003). Introduction. In D. A. Gentile (Ed.), *Media violence and children* (pp. ix–xi). Westport, CT: Praeger.

Gentile, D. A., & Anderson, C. A. (2003). Violent video games: The newest media violence hazard. In D. A. Gentile (Ed.), *Media violence and children* (pp. 131–152). Westport, CT: Praeger.

Gentile, D. A., Coyne, S., & Walsh, D. A. (2011). Media violence, physical aggression, and relational aggression in school age children: A short-term longitudinal study. *Aggressive Behavior, 37*(2), 193–206.

Gentile, D. A., Linder, J. R., & Walsh, D. A. (2003). *Looking through time: A longitudinal study of children's media violence consumption at home and aggressive behaviors at school.* ERIC Document ED474790.

George, C., Solomon, J., & McIntosh, J. (2011). Divorce in the nursery: On infants and overnight care. *Family Court Review, 49*(3), 521–528.

Gerard, M. (2004). What's a parent to do? Phonics and other stuff. *Childhood Education, 83*(3), 159–160.

Gerhardstein, P., Dickerson, K., Miller, S., & Hipp, D. (2012). Early operant learning is unaffected by socio-economic status and other demographic factors: A meta-analysis. *Infant Behavior and Development, 35,* 472–478.

Gernsbacher, M. A., Dawson, M., & Goldsmith, H. H. (2005). Three reasons not to believe in an autism epidemic. *Current Directions in Psychological Science, 14*(2), 55–58.

Gershoff, E. (2013). Spanking and child development: We know enough now to stop hitting our children. *Child Development Perspectives, 7*(3), 133–137.

Gettler, L. T., McDade, T. W., & Kuzawa, C. W. (2011). Cortisol and testosterone in Filipino young adult men: Evidence for co-regulation of both hormones by fatherhood and relationship status. *American Journal of Human Biology, 23,* 609–620.

Ghetti, S., & Angelini, L. (2008). The development of recollection and familiarity in childhood and adolescence: Evidence from the dual-process signal detection model. *Child Development, 79*(2), 339–358.

Ghoting, S. N., & Martin-Díaz, P. (2006). *Early literacy storytimes @ your library: Partnering with caregivers for success.* Chicago, IL: American Library Association.

Gibbs, J. C. (2014). *Moral development and reality* (3rd ed.). New York, NY: Oxford University Press.

Gibbs, J. C., Basinger, K. S., Grime, R. L., & Snarey, J. R. (2007). Moral judgment development across cultures: Revisiting Kohlberg's universality claims. *Developmental Review, 27*(4), 443–500.

Gibson, E. J., & Walk, R. D. (1960). The 'visual cliff.' *Scientific American, 202*(4), 64–71.

Giedd, J. (2008). The teen brain: Insights from neuroimaging. *Journal of Adolescent Health, 42,* 335–343.

Giedd, J. N. (2004). Structural magnetic resonance imaging of the adolescent brain. *Annals of the New York Academy of Sciences, 1021,* 77–85.

Giedd, J. N., & Rapoport, J. L. (2010). Structural MRI of pediatric brain development: What have we learned and where are we going? *Neuron, 67*(5), 728–734.

Gielen, U. P., & Jeshmaridian, S. S. (1999). Lev S. Vygotsky: The man and the era. *International Journal of Group Tension, 28*(3/4), 273–301.

Gil, E., & Shaw, J. A. (2014). *Working with children with sexual behavior problems.* New York, NY: Gilford Press.

Gilbert, S. F. (2000). *Developmental biology.* Sunderland, MA: Sinauer.

Gilbert, S. F. (2006). *Developmental biology* (8th ed.). Sunderland, MA: Sinauer.

Gilchrist, J., Ballesteros, M. F., & Parker, E. M. (2012). Vital Signs: Unintentional injury deaths among persons aged 0–19 Years—United States, 2000–2009. *Morbidity and Mortality Weekly Report, 61.* Centers for Disease Control and Prevention.

Gilliam, W. S. (2005). *Prekindergarteners left behind: Expulsion rates in state prekindergarten systems.* Retrieved from http://childstudycenter.yale.edu/faculty/pdf/Gilliam05.pdf

Gilliam, W. S., & Shahar, G. (2006). Preschool and child care expulsion and suspension: Rates and predictors in one state. *Infants & Young Children, 19*(3), 228–245. doi: 10.1097/00001163-200607000-00007

Gilligan, C. (1987). *Adolescent development reconsidered.* 10th Annual Konopka Lecture. Retrieved from http://www.konopka.umn.edu/peds/ahm/prod/groups/med/@pub/@med/documents/asset/med_ 21792.pdf

Ginn, J. D. (2008). *At issue: Bilingual education.* Detroit, MI: Thomson-Gale.

Gjerdingen, D. K., & Center, B. A. (2005). First-time parents' postpartum changes in employment, childcare, and housework responsibilities. *Social Science Research, 34,* 103–116.

Glantz, S. A., Mitchell, S., Titus, K., Polansky, J. R., Kaufmann, R. B., & Bauer, U. E. (2011). *Smoking in top-grossing movies—United States, 2010. Centers for Disease Control and Prevention.* Retrieved from http://www.cdc.gov/mmwr/preview/mmwrhtml/mm6027a1.htm?s_cid=mm6027a1_w

Glaser, S. (1993). Intelligence testing. *Congressional Quarterly Researcher, 3,* 649–672.

Glatter, R. (2014). *E-cigarettes: Turning harm reduction into harm addiction?* Retrieved from http://www.forbes.com/sites/robertglatter/2014/07/01/e-cigarettes-turning-harm-reduction-into-harm-addiction/

Gleason, J. B. (2005). The development of language: An overview and a preview. In J. B. Gleason (Ed.), *The development of language* (6th ed., pp. 1–38). Boston, MA: Pearson.

Gleitman, L. (1990). The structural sources of verb meaning. *Language Acquisition, 1,* 3–50.

Godwin, H. A. (2009). *Lead exposure and poisoning in children.* Los Angeles, CA: UCLA.

Gogtay, N., Giedd, J. N., Lusk, L., Hayashi, K. M., Greenstein, D., Vaituzis, A. C., . . . Thompson, P. M. (2004). Dynamic mapping of human cortical development during childhood through early adulthood. *Proceedings of the National Academy of Sciences, 101*(21), 8174–8179.

Goldberg, R. J., Higgins, E. L., Raskind, M. H., & Herman, K. L. (2003). Predictors of success in individuals with learning disabilities: A qualitative analysis. *Learning Disabilities Research and Practice, 18*(4), 222–236.

Goldfield, B. A., & Snow, C. E. (2005). Individual differences—Implications for the study of language acquisition. In J. B. Gleason (Ed.), *The development of language* (6th ed., pp. 292–323). Boston, MA: Pearson.

Goldman, L., & Smith, C. (1998). Imagining identities: Mimetic constructions in Huli child fantasy play. *Journal of the Royal Anthropological Institute, 4*(2), 207–234.

Goldsmith, H. H., Lemery, K. S., Aksan, N., & Buss, K. A. (2000). Temperamental substrates of personality. In V. J. Molfese & D. L. Molfese (Eds.), *Temperament and personality development across the life span* (pp. 1–32). Mahwah, NJ: Erlbaum.

Goldstein, J. R. (2011). A secular trend toward earlier male sexual maturity: Evidence from shifting ages of male young adult mortality. *PLoS ONE, 6*(8), e14826. doi: 10.1371/journal.pone.0014826

Goldstein, S., & Brooks, R. B. (2005). The future of children today. In S. Goldstein & R. B. Brooks (Eds.), *Handbook of resilience in children* (pp. 397–400). New York, NY: Springer.

Goldstein, T. R., & Winner, E. (2012). Enhancing empathy and theory of mind. *Journal of Cognition and Development, 13*(1), 19–37.

Goleman, D. (1995). *Emotional intelligence.* New York, NY: Bantam Books.

Good, C. D., Johnsrude, I., Ashburner, J., Henson, R. N., Friston, K. J., & Frackowiak, R. S. (2001). Cerebral asymmetry and the effects of sex and handedness on brain structure: A voxel-based morphometric analysis of 465 normal adult human brains. *NeuroImage, 14*(3), 685–700.

Good, C., Aronson, J., & Harder, J. (2008). Problems in the pipeline: Stereotype threat and women's achievement in high-level math courses. *Journal of Applied Developmental Psychology, 29*(1), 17–28. doi: 10.1016/j.appdev.2007.10.004

Good, C., Aronson, J., & Inzlicht, M. (2003). Improving adolescents' standardized test performance: An intervention to reduce the effects of stereotype threat. *Journal of Applied Developmental Psychology, 24*(6), 645–662.

Gopnik, A., Meltzoff, A. N., & Kuhl, P. K. (1999). *The scientist in the crib.* New York, NY: William Morrow.

Gormley, W. T., Phillips, D., & Gayer, T. (2008). Preschool programs can boost school readiness. *Science, 320,* 1723–1724.

Gorrese, A., & Ruggieri, R. (2012). Peer attachment: A meta-analytic review of gender and age differences and associations with parent attachment. *Journal of Youth and Adolescence, 41*(5), 650–672.

Gosso, Y., Morais, M. L. S., & Otta, E. (2007). Pretend play of Brazilian children: A window into different cultural worlds. *Journal of Cross-Cultural Psychology, 38*(5), 539–558.

Gottlieb, G. (1991). Experiential canalization of behavioral development: Theory. *Developmental Psychology, 27*(1), 4–13.

Gouin, K., Murphy, K., Shah, P. S., & Knowledge Synthesis Group on Determinants of Low Birth Weight and Preterm Births. (2011). Effects of cocaine use during pregnancy on low birthweight and preterm birth: Systematic review and meta-analyses. *American Journal of Obstetrics and Gynecology, 204*(4), 340, e1–12.

Gould, S. J. (1996). *The mismeasure of man.* New York, NY: W. W. Norton.

Governors' Highway Safety Association. (2014). *Distracted driving laws.* Retrieved from http://www.ghsa.org/html/stateinfo/laws/cellphone_laws.html

Grabe, S., Ward, L. M., & Hyde, J. S. (2008). The role of the media in body image concerns among women: A meta-analysis of experimental and correlational studies. *Psychological Bulletin, 134*(3), 460–476.

Grady, D. (2007). Promising dystrophy drug clears early test. *The New York Times.* Retrieved from http://www.nytimes.com/2007/12/27/health/27drug.html

Graham-Bermann, S. A., Howell, K., Habarth, J., Krishnan, S., Loree, A., & Bermann, E. A. (2008). Toward assessing traumatic events and stress symptoms in preschool children from low-income families. *American Journal of Orthopsychiatry, 78*(2), 220–228. doi: 10.1037/a0013977

Grall, T. (2011). *Custodial mothers and fathers and their child support: 2009.* Washington, DC: U.S. Department of Commerce, Economics and Statistics Administration.

Granic, I., & Patterson, G. R. (2006). Toward a comprehensive model of antisocial development: A dynamic systems approach. *Psychological Review, 113*(1), 101–131.

Grasso, D. J., Ford, J. D., & Briggs-Gowan, M. J. (2013). Early life trauma exposure and stress sensitivity in young children. *Journal of Pediatric Psychology, 38*(1), 94–103. doi: 10.1093/jpepsy/jss101

Gray, L., Watt, L., & Blass, E. M. (2000). Skin-to-skin contact is analgesic in healthy newborns. *Pediatrics, 105*(1), e14.

Gray, M. R., & Steinberg, L. (1999). Unpacking authoritative parenting: Reassessing a multidimensional construct. *Journal of Marriage and Family, 61,* 574–587.

Graziano, P. A., Slavec, J., Hart, K., Garcia, A., & Pelham, W. E. (2014). Improving school readiness in preschoolers with behavior problems: Results from a summer treatment program. *Journal of Psychopathology and Behavioral Assessment.* doi: 10.1007/s10862-014-9418-1

Gredebäck, G., Fikke, L., & Melinder, A. (2010). The development of joint visual attention: A longitudinal study of gaze following during interactions with mothers and strangers. *Developmental Science, 13*(6), 839–848. doi: 10.1111/j.1467-7687.2009.00945.x

Greene, A. (2004). *From first kicks to first steps: Nurturing your baby's development from pregnancy through the first year of life.* New York, NY: McGraw-Hill.

Greene, S. M., Anderson, E. R., Hetherington, E. M., Forgatch, M. S., & DeGarmo, D. S. (2003). Risk and resilience after divorce. In F. Walsh (Ed.), *Normal family processes* (3rd ed., pp. 96–120). New York, NY: Guilford Press.

Greene, S. M., Sullivan, K., & Anderson, E. R. (2008). Divorce and custody. In M. Hersen & A. M. Gross (Eds.), *Handbook of clinical psychology: Vol. 2. Children and adolescents* (pp. 833–855). Hoboken, NJ: Wiley.

Greenfield, P. M., Keller, H., Fuligni, A., & Maynard, A. (2003). Cultural pathways through universal development. *Annual Review of Psychology, 54*, 461–490.

Greenglass, E. R. (2002). Work stress, coping and social support: Implications for women's occupational well-being. In D. L. Nelson & R. J. Burke (Eds.), *Gender work stress and health* (pp. 85–96). Washington, DC: American Psychological Association.

Greenough, W. T., Black, J. E., & Wallace, C. S. (1987). Experience and brain development. *Child Development, 58*(3), 539–559.

Greenwald, A. G., & Nosek, B. A. (2001). Health of the Implicit Association Test at age 3. *Zeitschrift Für Experimentelle Psychologie, 48*(2), 85–93. doi: 10.1026//0949-3946.48.2.85

Greenwald, A. G., Poehlman, A. T., Uhlmann, E. L., & Banaji, M. R. (2009). Understanding and using the Implicit Association Test: III. Meta-analysis of predictive validity. *Journal of Personality and Social Psychology, 97*, 17–41.

Gregory, A., Cornell, D., Fan, X., Sheras, P., Shih, T., & Huang, F. (2010). Authoritative school discipline: High school practices associated with lower bullying and victimization. *Journal of Educational Psychology, 102*(2), 483–496.

Griffin, S. (2004). Building number sense with number worlds: A mathematics program for young children. *Early Childhood Research Quarterly, 19*(1), 173–180. doi: 10.1016/j.ecresq.2004.01.012

Grigorenko, E. L., & Dozier, M. (2013). Introduction to the special section on genomics. *Child Development, 84*(1), 6–16.

Grills-Taquechel, A. E., Norton, P., & Ollendick, T. H. (2010). A longitudinal examination of factors predicting anxiety during the transition to middle school. *Anxiety, Stress & Coping: An International Journal, 23*(5), 493–513.

Grossman, J. B., Chan, C. S., Schwartz, S. O., & Rhodes, J. E. (2012). The test of time in school-based mentoring: The role of relationship duration and re-matching on academic outcomes. *American Journal of Community Psychology, 49*(1–2), 43–54.

Grotevant, H. D., McRoy, R. G., Wrobel, G. M., & Ayers-Lopez, S. (2013). Contact between adoptive and birth families: Perspectives from the Minnesota/Texas Adoption Research Project. *Child Development Perspectives, 7*(3), 193–198. doi: 10.1111/cdep.12039

Grusec, J. E., Goodnow, J. J., & Kuczynski, L. (2000). New directions in analyses of parenting contributions to children's acquisition of values. *Child Development, 71*(1), 205–211.

Guglielmi, R. S. (2008). Native language proficiency, English literacy, academic achievement, and occupational attainment in limited-English-proficient students: A latent growth modeling perspective. *Journal of Educational Psychology, 100*(2), 322–342.

Guilford, J. P. (1950). Creativity. *American Psychologist, 5*, 444–454.

Gunn, B., Simmons, D., & Kameenui, E. (1995). *Emergent literacy: Synthesis of the research (Technical Report No. 19)*. University of Oregon: National Center to Improve the Tools of Educators.

Gunnar, M. R., & Cheatham, C. L. (2003). Brain and behavior interface: Stress and the developing brain. *Infant Mental Health Journal, 24*(3), 195–211.

Gunnar, M. R., & Quevedo, K. (2007). The neurobiology of stress and development. *Annual Review of Psychology, 58*, 145–173.

Gunnoe, M. L., & Hetherington, E. M. (2004). Stepchildren's perceptions of noncustodial mothers and noncustodial fathers: Differences in socioemotional involvement and associations with adolescent adjustment problems. *Journal of Family Psychology, 18*(4), 555–563.

Guo, Y., Connor, C. M., Tompkins, V., & Morrison, F. J. (2011). Classroom quality and student engagement: Contributions to third-grade reading skills. *Frontiers in Psychology, 2,* 1–10.

Gupta, R., Holdford, D., Bilayer, L., Dyer, A., Holl, J. L., & Meltzer, D. (2013). *JAMA Pediatrics, 167*(11), 1026–1031.

Gupta, R. S., Springston, E. E., Warrier, M. R., Smith, B., Kumar, R., Pongracic, J., & Holl, J. L. (2011). The prevalence, severity, and distribution of childhood food allergy in the United States. *Pediatrics 128*(1), e9–17.

Guralnick, M. (2005). Early intervention for children with intellectual disabilities: Current knowledge and future prospects. *Journal of Applied Research in Intellectual Disabilities, 18*, 313–324.

Gurung, R. A. R. (2005). How do students really study (and does it matter)? *Teaching of Psychology, 32*(4), 239–241.

Gustafson, G. E., Wood, R. M., & Green, J. A. (2000). Can we hear the causes of infants' crying? In R. G. Barr, B. Hopkins, & J. A. Green (Eds.), *Crying as a sign, a symptom, & a signal: Clinical emotional and developmental aspects of infant and toddler crying* (pp. 22–28). New York, NY: Cambridge University Press.

Guttmacher Institute. (2012). *Facts on American teens' sexual and reproductive health*. Retrieved from http://www.guttmacher.org/pubs/fb_ATSRH.html

Hackshaw, A., Rodeck, C., & Boniface, S. (2011). Maternal smoking in pregnancy and birth defects: A systematic review based on 173,687 malformed cases and 11.7 million controls. *Human Reproduction Update, 17*(5), 589–604.

Haden, C. A. (2003). Joint encoding and joint reminiscing: Implications for young children's understanding and remembering of personal experiences. In R. Fivush & C. A. Haden (Eds.), *Autobiographical memory and the construction of a narrative self* (pp. 49–69). Mahwah, NJ: Erlbaum.

Hafen, C. A., Laursen, B., Burk, W. J., Kerr, M., & Stattin, H. (2011). Homophily in stable and unstable adolescent friendships: Similarity breeds constancy. *Personality and Individual Differences, 51*(5), 607–612. doi: 10.1016/j.paid.2011.05.027

Haight, W., Black, J., Ostler, T., & Sheridan, K. (2006). Pretend play and emotion learning. In D. G. Singer, R. M. Golinkoff, & K. Hirsh-Pasek (Eds.), *Play=learning* (pp. 209–230). New York, NY: Oxford University Press.

Haight, W., & Miller, P. J. (1992). The development of everyday pretend play: A longitudinal study of mothers' participation. *Merrill-Palmer Quarterly, 38*(3), 331–349.

Haight, W. L., & Black, J. E. (2001). A comparative approach to play: Cross-species and cross-cultural perspectives of play in development. *Human Development, 44*, 228–234.

Haight, W. L., Wang, X., Fung, H., Williams, K., & Mintz, J. (1999). Universal, developmental, and variable aspects of young children's play: A cross-cultural comparison of pretending at home. *Child Development, 70*(6), 1477–1488.

Haith, M. M., Bergman, T., & Moore, M. (1977). Eye contact and face scanning in early infancy. *Science, 198*, 853–855.

Haker, H., Kawohl, W., Herwig, U., & Rössler, W. (2013). Mirror neuron activity during contagious yawning—An fMRI study. *Brain Imaging and Behavior, 7*(1), 28–34. doi: 10.1007/s11682-012-9189-9

Halfon, N., & Newacheck, P. W. (2010). Evolving notions of childhood chronic illness. *Journal of the American Medical Association, 303*, 665–666.

Halim, M. L., & Ruble, D. (2010). Gender identity and stereotyping in early and middle childhood. In J. C. Chrisler, & D. R. McCreary (Eds.), *Handbook of gender research in psychology* (pp. 495–525). New York, NY: Springer.

Hall, G. S. (1904). *Adolescence*. Englewood Cliffs, NJ: Prentice Hall.

Halle, C., Dowd, T., Fowler, C., Rissel, K., Hennessy, K., MacNevin, R., & Nelson, M. A. (2008). Supporting fathers in the transition to parenthood. *Contemporary Nurse, 31*(1), 57–70.

Hallinan, M. T., & Kubitschek, W. (1999). Curriculum differentiation and high school achievement. *Social Psychology of Education, 3*, 41–62.

Halpern, C. T., Spriggs, A. L., Martin, S. L., & Kupper, L. L. (2009). Patterns of intimate partner violence victimization from adolescence to young adulthood in a nationally representative sample. *Journal of Adolescent Health, 45*(5), 508–516.

Hamblen, J., & Barnett, E. (2009). *PTSD in children and adolescents*. U.S. Department of Veterans' Affairs. Retrieved from http://www.ptsd.va.gov/professional/pages/ptsd_in_children_and_adolescents_overview_for_professionals.asp

Hamilton, B. E., & Ventura, S. J. (2012). Birth rates for U.S. teenagers reach historic lows for all age and ethnic groups. *NCHS Data Brief*. Retrieved from http://www.cdc.gov/nchs/data/databriefs/db89.htm

Hamilton, M. A., & Hamilton, S. F. (1997). *Learning well at work: Choices for quality*. Washington, DC: U.S. Department of Education/U.S. Department of Labor.

Hamilton, S. F., & Hamilton, M. A. (1999). *Building strong school-to-work systems: Illustrations of key components*. Washington, DC: U.S. Department of Education/U.S. Department of Labor.

Hamm, J. V., Farmer, T. W., Lambert, K., & Gravelle, M. (2014). Enhancing peer cultures of academic effort and achievement in early adolescence: Promotive effects of the SEALS intervention. *Developmental Psychology, 50*(1), 216–228.

Hamm, J. V., Schmid, L., Farmer, T. W., & Locke, B. (2011). Injunctive and descriptive peer group norms and the academic adjustment of rural early adolescents. *Journal of Early Adolescence, 31*, 41–73. doi: 10.1177/0272431610384486

Hammen, C., & Rudolph, K. D. (2003). Childhood mood disorders. In E. J. Mash & R. A. Barkley (Eds.), *Child psychopathology* (2nd ed., pp. 233–278). New York, NY: Guilford Press.

Hankin, B. L., Abramson, L. Y., Moffitt, T. E., Silva, P. A., McGee, R., & Angell, K. E. (1998). Development of depression from preadolescence to young adulthood: Emerging gender differences in a 10-year longitudinal study. *Journal of Abnormal Psychology, 107*(1), 128–140.

Hanrahan, C. (2006). Sleep. In K. Krapp & J. Wilson (Eds.), *Gale encyclopedia of children's health: Infancy through adolescence* (Vol. 4, pp. 1676–1680). Detroit, MI: Gale.

Hansen, M. B., & Markman, E. M. (2009). Children's use of mutual exclusivity to learn labels for parts of objects. *Developmental Psychology, 45*(2), 592–596.

Hansen, T. (2012). Parenthood and happiness: A review of folk theories versus empirical evidence. *Social Indicators Research, 108*(1), 29–64. doi: 10.1007/s11205–011–9865-y

Hanson, S., Hunter, L., Bormann, J., & Sobo, E. (2009). Paternal fears of childbirth: a literature review. *Journal of Perinatal Education, 18*(4), 12–20. doi: 10.1624/105812409X474672

Hardy, S. A., & Carlo, G. (2011), Moral identity: What is it, how does it develop, and is it linked to moral action? *Child Development Perspectives, 5*, 212–218.

Harlow, H. F. (1958). The nature of love. *American Psychologist, 13*(12), 673–685.

Harris, B. (1979). Whatever happened to Little Albert? *American Psychologist, 34*(2), 151–160.

Harris Interactive. (2013). *Four in five Americans believe parents spanking their children is sometimes appropriate*. Retrieved from http://www.harrisinteractive.com/vault/Harris%20Poll%2067%20-%20Spanking_9.26.13.pdf

Harris, J. R. (1995). Where is the child's environment? A group socialization theory of development. *Psychological Review, 102*(3), 458–489.

Harris, J. R. (1998/2009). *The nurture assumption: Why children turn out the way they do*. New York, NY: Free Press.

Harris, S. (2004). Bullying at school among older adolescents. *Prevention Researcher, 11*(3), 12–14.

Harrison, K. (2000). The body electric: Thin ideal media and eating disorders in adolescents. *Journal of Communication, 50*(3), 119–143.

Harrison, K. (2006). Scope of self: Toward a model of television's effects on self-complexity in adolescence. *Communication Theory, 16*(2), 251–279.

Hart Research Associates. (2011). *A national survey of parents' knowledge, attitudes, and self-reported behaviors concerning sports safety*. Washington, DC: Safe Kids Worldwide.

Hart, B., & Risley, T. R. (1995). *Meaningful differences in the everyday experience of young American children*. Baltimore, MD: Paul H. Brookes.

Harter, S. (1999). *The construction of the self*. New York, NY: Guilford Press.

Harter, S. (2006a). The development of self-esteem. In M. H. Kernis (Ed.), *Self-esteem issues and answers: A sourcebook of current perspectives* (pp. 144–150). New York, NY: Psychology Press.

Harter, S. (2006b). The self. In N. Eisenberg, W. Damon, & R. M. Lerner (Eds.), *Handbook of child psychology: Vol. 3. Social, emotional, and personality development* (6th ed., pp. 505–570). Hoboken, NJ: Wiley.

Harter, S. (2012). *The construction of the self: Developmental and sociocultural foundations* (2nd ed.). New York, NY: Guilford Press.

Hartman, A. (2003). Family policy: Dilemmas, controversies, and opportunities. In F. Walsh (Ed.), *Normal family processes* (3rd ed., pp. 635–662). New York, NY: Guilford Press.

Hartman, L. R., Magalhães, L., & Mandich, A. (2011). What does parental divorce or marital separation mean for adolescents? A scoping review of North American literature. *Journal of Divorce & Remarriage, 52*(7), 490–518. doi: 10.1080/10502556.2011.609432

Hartmann, K., Viswanathan, M., Palmieri, R., Gartlehner, G., Thorp, J. R., & Lohr, K. (2005). Outcomes of routine episiotomy: A systematic review. *JAMA: Journal of The American Medical Association, 293*(17), 2141–2148.

Hartshorne, J. K. (2009, January 8). How birth order affects your personality. *Scientific American*. Retrieved from http://www.scientificamerican.com/article/ruled-by-birth-order/

Harvard Medical School. (2010). Direct-to-consumer genetic testing kits. *Harvard Women's Health Watch, 18*(1), 1-3.

Haselager, G. T., Cillessen, A. N., Van Lieshout, C. M., Riksen-Walraven, J. A., & Hartup, W. W. (2002). Heterogeneity among peer-rejected boys across middle childhood: Developmental pathways of social behavior. *Developmental Psychology, 38*(3), 446–56.

Hasler, B. P., & Clark, D. B. (2013). Circadian misalignment, reward related brain function, and adolescent alcohol involvement. *Alcoholism: Clinical and Experimental Research, 37*(4), 558–565. doi: 10.1111/acer.12003

Hatzenbuehler, M. L. (2011). The social environment and suicide attempts in lesbian, gay, and bisexual youth. *Pediatrics, 127*(5), 896–903.

Haworth, C. M. A., Kovas, Y., Harlaar, N., Hayiou-Thomas, M. E., Petrill, S. A., Dale, P. S., & Plomin, R. (2009). Generalist genes and learning disabilities: A multivariate genetic analysis of low performance in reading, mathematics, language and general cognitive ability in a sample of 8000 12-year-old twins. *Journal of Child Psychology and Psychiatry, 50*(10), 1318–1325.

Hawthorne, P. (2002). Positively *Sesame Street. Time.* Retrieved from http://www.time.com/time/magazine/article/0,9171,901020930-353521,00.html

Hay, C., Meldrum, R., & Mann, K. (2010). Traditional bullying, cyber bullying, and deviance: A general strain theory approach. *Journal of Contemporary Criminal Justice, 26*(2), 130–147. doi: 10.1177/1043986209359557

Hay, D. F. (2006). Yours and mine: Toddlers' talk about possessions with familiar peers. *British Journal of Developmental Psychology, 24*(1), 39–52. doi: 10.1348/026151005X68880

Hay, D. F., Caplan, M., & Nash, A. (2009). The beginnings of peer relations. In K. H. Rubin, W. M. Bukowski, & B. Laursen (Eds.), *Handbook of peer interactions, relationships, and groups* (pp. 121–142). New York, NY: Guilford Press.

Hay, D. F., Hurst, S., Waters, C. S., & Chadwick, A. (2011). Infants' use of force to defend toys: The origins of instrumental aggression. *Infancy, 16*(5), 471–489. doi: 10.1111/j.1532–7078.2011.00069.x

Hay, D. F., & Ross, H. S. (1982). The social nature of early conflict. *Child Development, 53*(1), 105–113.

Hay, J. F., Pelucchi, B., Estes, K., & Saffran, J. R. (2011). Linking sounds to meanings: Infant statistical learning in a natural language. *Cognitive Psychology, 63*(2), 93–106.

Hayne, H. (2004). Infant memory development: Implications for childhood amnesia. *Developmental Review, 24*(1), 33–73.

Hazan, C., & Shaver, P. (1987). Romantic love conceptualized as an attachment process. *Journal of Personality and Social Psychology, 52*(3), 511–524.

Head Start. (2014). *About Early Head Start*. Retrieved from http://eclkc.ohs.acf.hhs.gov/hslc/tta-system/ehsnrc/Early%20Head%20Start/about.html

Head Start Family and Child Experiences Survey (FACES). (2007). Retrieved from http://www.acf.hhs.gov/programs/opre/hs/faces/reports/faces_findings_06/faces06_children.html

Health Resources and Services Administration. (n.d.). *Prenatal services*. Retrieved from http://mchb.hrsa.gov/programs/womeninfants/prenatal.html

Healthy People 2020. (2013). *Physical activity*. Retrieved from http://healthypeople.gov/2020/topicsobjectives2020/objectiveslist.aspx?topicId=33

Heath, P. (2005). *Parent-child relations: History, theory, research, and context.* Upper Saddle River, NJ: Pearson.

Hebert, K. R., Fales, J., Nangle, D. W., Papadakis, A. A., & Grover, R. L. (2013). Linking social anxiety and adolescent romantic relationship functioning: Indirect effects and the importance of peers. *Journal of Youth and Adolescence, 42*(11), 1708–1720. doi: 10.1007/s10964–012–9878–0

Hechtman, P., Kaplan, F., Ayleran, J., Boulay, B., Andermann, E., de Braekeleer, M., . . . Scriber, C. (1990). More than one mutant allele causes infantile Tay-Sachs disease in French-Canadians. *American Journal of Human Genetics, 47*(5), 815–822.

Heckman, J. J. (2011). The economics of inequality. *American Educator, 35*(1), 31–35, 47.

Heckman, J. J., & LaFontaine, P. A. (2010). The American high school graduation rate: Trends and levels. *Review of Economics and Statistics, 92*(2), 244–262.

Heilemann, T., & Santhiveeran, J. (2011). How do female adolescents cope and survive the hardships of prostitution? A content analysis of existing literature. *Journal of Ethnic & Cultural Diversity in Social Work: Innovation in Theory, Research & Practice, 20*(1), 57–76. doi: 10 .1080/15313204.2011.545945

Heisler, E. J. (2012). The *U.S. infant mortality rate: International comparisons, underlying factors, and federal programs.* Washington, DC: Congressional Research Service.

Helt, M. S., Eigsti, I. M., Snyder, P. J., & Fein, D. A. (2010). Contagious yawning in autistic and typical development. *Child Development, 81*(5), 1620–1631.

Hennessey, B. A. (2007). Promoting social competence in school-aged children: The effects of the Open Circle Program. *Journal of School Psychology, 45*(3), 349–360.

Hennighausen, K. H., & Lyons-Ruth, K. (2005). Disorganization of behavioral and attentional strategies toward primary attachment figures: From biologic to dialogic processes. In C. S. Carter, L. Ahnert, K. E. Grossmann, S. B. Hrdy, M. E. Lamb, S. W. Porges, & N. Sachser (Eds.), *Attachment and bonding: A new synthesis* (pp. 269–300). Cambridge, MA: MIT Press.

Hennighausen, K. H., & Lyons-Ruth, K. (2010). Disorganization of attachment strategies in infancy and childhood. In *Encyclopedia on early childhood development.* Centre of Excellence for Early Childhood Development. Retrieved from http://www.enfant-encyclo-pedie.com/pages/PDF/Hennighausen-LyonsRuthANGxp_rev.pdf

Henry, B., Caspi, A., Moffitt, T. E., Harrington, H. L., & Silva, P. A. (1999). Staying in school protects boys with poor self-regulation in childhood from later crime: A longitudinal study. *International Journal of Behavioral Development, 23*(4), 1049–1073.

Hepper, P. G., Wells, D. L., & Lynch, C. (2005). Prenatal thumb sucking is related to postnatal handedness. *Neuropsychologia, 43*(3), 313–315.

Herman-Giddens, M. E. (2006). Recent data on pubertal milestones in United States children: The secular trend toward earlier development. *International Journal of Andrology, 29,* 241–246. doi: 10.1111/j.1365–2605.2005.00575.x

Herman-Giddens, M. E. (2013). The enigmatic pursuit of puberty in girls. *Pediatrics, 132*(6), 1125–1126. doi: 10.1542/peds.2013-3058

Herman-Giddens, M., Steffes, J., Harris, D., Slora, E., Hussey, M., Dowshen, S., . . . Reiter, E. (2012). Secondary sexual characteristics in boys: Data from the Pediatric Research in Office Settings Network. *Pediatrics, 130*(5), e1058–e1068. doi: 10.1542/peds.2011-3291

Herrnstein, R. J., & Murray, C. (1994). *The bell curve: Intelligence and class structure in American life.* New York, NY: Free Press.

Herschensohn, J. (2007). *Language development and age.* New York, NY: Cambridge University Press.

Hersey, J. C., & Jordan, A. (2007). *Reducing children's TV time to reduce the risk of childhood overweight: The children's media use study: Highlights report.* Retrieved from http://www.rocklandsteps.org/files/TV_Time_Highligts[1].pdf

Hetherington, E. M. (2006). The influence of conflict, marital problem solving and parenting on children's adjustment in nondivorced, divorced and remarried families. In A. Clarke-Stewart & J. Dunn (Eds.), *Families count: Effects on child and adolescent development* (pp. 203–237). New York, NY: Cambridge University Press.

Hetherington, E. M., & Kelly, J. (2002). *For better or for worse: Divorce reconsidered.* New York: W.W. Norton & Company.

Hetherington, E. M., Reiss, D., & Plomin, R. (Eds.). (1994). *Separate social words of siblings: The impact of nonshared environment on development.* Hillsdale, NJ: Erlbaum.

Hickman, G. R., Bartholomew, M., Mathwig, J., & Heinrich, R. S. (2008). Differential developmental pathways of high school dropouts and graduates. *Journal of Educational Research, 102*(1), 3–14.

HighScope Educational Research Foundation. (2014). HighScope Perry Preschool Study Lifetime Effects: The HighScope Perry Preschool Study Through Age 40 (2005). Retrieved from http://www.highscope.org/Content. asp?ContentId=219

Hill, C., Corbett, C., & St. Rose, A. (2010). *Why so few? Women in science, technology, engineering and mathematics.* Washington, DC: AAUW. Retrieved from http:// www.aauw.org/learn/research/upload/whysofew.pdf

Hill, J. L., Brooks-Gunn, J., & Waldfogel, J. (2003). Sustained effects of high participation in early intervention for low-birth-weight premature infants. *Developmental Psychology, 39*(4), 730–744.

Hill, N. E., Bromell, L., Tyson, D. F., & Flint, R. (2007). Developmental commentary: Ecological perspectives on parental influences during adolescence. *Journal of Clinical Child and Adolescent Psychiatry, 36*(3), 367–377.

Hinde, E. R., & Perry, N. (2007). Elementary teachers' application of Jean Piaget's theories of cognitive development during social studies curriculum debates in Arizona. *The Elementary School Journal, 108*(1), 63–79.

Hindman, A. H., & Morrison, F. J. (2011). Family involvement and educator outreach in Head Start. *Elementary School Journal, 111*(3), 359–386. doi: 10.1086/657651

Hines, M. (2006). Prenatal testosterone and gender-related behaviour. *European Journal of Endocrinology, 155,* S115–S121.

Hiscock, H. (2006). The crying baby. *Australian Family Physician, 35*(9), 680–684.

Hiscock, H., & Wake, M. (2002). Randomised controlled trial of behavioural infant sleep intervention to improve infant sleep and maternal mood. *BMJ: British Medical Journal, 324,* 1062–1065.

Hiss, W. C., & Franks, C. W. (2014). *Defining promise: Optional standardized testing policies in American college and university admission.* Arlington, VA: National Association for College Admission Counseling.

Hoeve, M., Dubas, J. S., Eichelsheim, V. I., van der Laan, P. H., Smeenk, W., & Gerris, J. R. M. (2009). The relationship between parenting and delinquency: A meta-analysis. *Journal of Abnormal Child Psychology, 37*(6), 749–775.

Hoff, E., & Naigles, L. (2002). How children use input to acquire a lexicon. *Child Development, 73*(2), 418–433.

Hoffman, M. L. (2000). *Empathy and moral development.* New York, NY: Cambridge University Press.

Holbreich, M., Genuneit, J., Weber, J., Braun-Fahrlander, C., & von Mutius, E. (2012). The prevalence of asthma, hay fever and allergic sensitization in Amish children. *Journal of Allergy and Clinical Immunology, 129*(2), Supplement, Page AB130. doi: 10.1016/j.jaci.2011.12.433

Holbreich, M., Genuneit, J., Weber, J., Braun-Fahrlander, C., Waser, M., & von Mutius, E. (2012). Amish children living in northern Indiana have a very low prevalence of allergic sensitization. *Journal of Allergy and Clinical Immunology, 129*(6), 1671–1673.

Holcombe, E., Peterson, K., & Manlove, J. (2009). Ten reasons to still keep the focus on teen childbearing. *Child Trends Research Brief.* Retrieved from http://www.childtrends.org/Files//Child_Trends-2009_04_01_RB_KeepingFocus.pdf

Holfeld, B., & Grabe, M. (2012). Middle school students' perceptions of and responses to cyber bullying. *Journal of Educational Computing Research, 46*(4), 395–413.

Hollich, G., Golinkoff, R. M., & Hirsh-Pasek, K. (2007). Young children associate novel words with complex objects rather than salient parts. *Developmental Psychology, 43*(5), 1051–1061.

Holliday, R. E., Brainerd, C. J., & Reyna, V. F. (2011). Developmental reversals in false memory: Now you see them, now you don't! *Developmental Psychology, 47,* 442–449.

Holmes, B. M. (2007). In search of my "one-and-only": Romance-related media and beliefs in romantic relationship destiny. *Electronic Journal of Communication, 17*(3&4). Retrieved from http://www.cios.org/EJCPUBLIC/017/3/01735.HTML

Holmes, E., Sasaki, T., & Hazen, N. L. (2013). Smooth versus rocky transitions to parenthood: Family systems in developmental context. *Family Relations, 62*(5), 824–837. doi: 10.1111/fare.12041

Holt, K., & Barzel, R. (2013). *Oral health and learning: When children's health suffers, so does their ability to learn.* Washington, DC: National Maternal and Child Oral Health Resource Center.

Honein, M. A., Paulozzi, L. J., & Erickson J. D. (2001). Continued occurrence of Accutane-exposed pregnancies. *Teratology, 64*(3), 142–147.

Hopkins, B., & Johnson, S. P. (2005). *Prenatal development of postnatal functions.* Westport, CT: Praeger.

Hopson, J. L. (1998, September/October). Fetal psychology: Your baby can feel, dream and even listen to Mozart in the womb. *Psychology Today, 31,* 44–48.

Horn, I. B., Brenner, R., Rao, M., & Cheng, T. L. (2006). Beliefs about the appropriate age for initiating toilet training: Are there racial and socioeconomic differences? *Journal of Pediatrics, 149*(2), 165–168.

Hornor, G. (2010). Child sexual abuse: Consequences and implications. *Journal of Pediatric Health Care, 24*(6), 358–364.

Howes, C., & Matheson, C. C. (1992). Sequences in the development of competent play with peers: Social and social pretend play. *Developmental Psychology, 28*(5), 961–974.

Hoyland, A., Dye, L., & Lawton, C. L. (2009). A systematic review of the effect of breakfast on the cognitive performance of children and adolescents. *Nutrition Research Reviews, 22,* 220–243.

Hu, V. W. (2013). From genes to environment: Using integrative genomics to build a "systems-level" understanding of autism spectrum disorders. *Child Development, 84*(1), 89-103.

Huang, B. H. (2014). The effects of age on second language grammar and speech production. *Journal of Psycholinguistic Research, 43*(4), 397–420. doi: 10.1007/s10936–013–9261–7

Huang, C. (2010). Mean-Level change in self-esteem from childhood through adulthood: Meta-analysis of longitudinal studies. *Review of General Psychology, 14*(3), 251–260.

Hubel, D. H., & Wiesel, T. N. (1965). Comparison of the effects of unilateral and bilateral eye closure on cortical unit responses in kittens. *Journal of Neurophysiology, 28,* 1029–1040.

Hudson, J. I., Hiripi, E., Pope, H. G., & Kessler, R. C. (2007). The prevalence and correlates of eating disorders in the national comorbidity survey replication. *Biological Psychiatry, 61*(3), 348–358.

Huelke, D. F. (1998). An overview of anatomical considerations of infants and children in the adult world of automobile safety design. *Annual Proceedings of the Association for the Advancement of Automotive Medicine, 42,* 93–113.

Huitt, W. (2003). *The information processing approach to cognition. Educational Psychology Interactive.* Valdosta,

GA: Valdosta State University. Retrieved from http://www .edpsycinteractive.org/topics/cognition/infoproc.html

Huizink, A. C., & Mulder, E. J. H. (2006). Maternal smoking, drinking or cannabis use during pregnancy and neurobehavioral and cognitive functioning in human offspring. *Neuroscience & Biobehavioral Reviews, 30*(1), 24–41.

Human Genome Project Information. (2003). *CFTR: The gene associated with cystic fibrosis.* Retrieved from http:// www.ornl.gov/sci/techresources/Human_Genome/posters/chromosome/cftr.shtml

Human Genome Project Information. (2008a). *Evaluating gene tests: Some considerations.* Retrieved from http:// www.ornl.gov/sci/techresources/Human_Genome/ resource/testeval.shtml

Human Genome Project Information. (2008b). *U.S. Human Genome Project research goals.* Retrieved from http:// www.ornl.gov/sci/techresources/Human_Genome/hg5yp/ index.shtml

Human Genome Project Information. (2009). *Insights learned from the human DNA sequence.* Retrieved from http://www.ornl.gov/sci/techresources/Human_Genome/ project/journals/insights.shtml

Human Genome Research Institute. (2012). *International HapMap Project.* Retrieved from http://www.genome .gov/10001688

The Human Rights Campaign. (2012). *Growing up LGBT in America: HRC youth survey report key findings.* Washington, DC: Author.

Humphrey, J. H. (2003). *Child development through sport.* New York, NY: Haworth Press.

Humphrey, J. H. (2004). *Childhood stress in contemporary society.* New York, NY: Haworth Press.

Hurd, N. M., Sánchez, B., Zimmerman, M. A., & Caldwell, C. H. (2012). Natural mentors, racial identity, and educational attainment among African American adolescents: Exploring pathways to success. *Child Development, 83*(4), 1196–1212.

Hurd, N. M., & Zimmerman, M. A. (2010). Natural mentoring relationships among adolescent mothers: A study of resilience. *Journal of Research on Adolescence, 20*(3), 789–809.

Hurn, C. J. (2002). IQ. In D. L. Levinson, P. W. Cookson, Jr., & A. R. Sadovnik (Eds.), *Education and sociology: An encyclopedia* (pp. 399–402). New York, NY: Routledge Falmer.

Huston, A. C., Anderson, D. R., Wright, J. C., Linebarger, D. L., & Schmitt, K. L. (2001). *Sesame Street* viewers as adolescents: The recontact study. In S. M. Fisch & R. T. Truglio (Eds.), *"G" is for growing—Thirty years of research on children and* Sesame Street (pp. 131–146). Mahwah, NJ: Erlbaum.

Huttenlocher, P. E. (1999). Synaptogenesis in human cerebral cortex and the concept of critical periods. In N. A. Fox, L. A. Leavitt, & J. G. Warhol (Eds.), *The role of early experience in infant development* (pp. 15–28). New York, NY: Johnson & Johnson.

Hyde, J. (2014). Gender similarities and differences. *Annual Review of Psychology, 65*, 373–398. doi: 10.1146/ annurev-psych-010213-115057

Hyde, M. M., Lamb, Y., Arteaga, S. S., & Chavis, D. (2008). National evaluation of the Safe Start Demonstration Project: Implications for mental health practice. *Best Practices in Mental Health, 4*(1), 108–122.

Iannelli, V. (2006). *New treatment for diarrhea.* Retrieved from http://pediatrics.about.com/cs/pediatricadvice/a/lacto bacillus.htm

Impett, E. A., Sorsoli, L., Schooler, D., Henson, J. M., & Tolman, D. L. (2008). Girls' relationship authenticity and self-esteem across adolescence. *Developmental Psychology, 44*(3), 722–733.

Institute of Education Sciences. (2007). *Intervention: Dialogic reading.* Retrieved from http://ies.ed.gov/ncee/ wwc/reports/early_ed/dial_read/

Institute of Medicine and the National Research Council Institute of Medicine of the National Academies. (2013). *Confronting commercial sexual exploitation and sex trafficking of minors in the United States.* Retrieved from http://www.iom.edu/~/media/Files/Report%20 Files/2013/Sexual-Exploitation-Sex-Trafficking/ sextraffickingminors_rb.pdf

Ip, S., Chung, M., Raman, G., Chew, P., Magula, N., DeVine, D., Trikalinos, T., & Lau, J. (2007). *Breastfeeding and maternal and infant health outcomes in developed countries.* Evidence Report-Technology Assessment No. 153. AHRQ Publication No. 07-E007. Rockville, MD: Agency for Health Care Research and Quality.

Ireson, J., Hallam, S., & Plewis, I. (2001). Ability grouping in secondary schools: Effects on pupils' self-concepts. *British Journal of Educational Psychology, 71*(2), 315–326.

Irish, L., Kobayashi, I., & Delahanty, D. L. (2010). Long-term physical health consequences of childhood sexual abuse: A meta-analytic review. *Journal of Pediatric Psychology, 35*(5), 450–461.

Isaacs, E. B., Fischl, B. R., Quinn, B. T., Chong, W. K., Gadian, D. G., & Lucas, A. (2010). Impact of breast milk on intelligence quotient, brain size, and white matter development. *Pediatric Research, 67*(4), 357–62.

Isay, R. A. (1996). Psychoanalytic therapy with gay men: Developmental considerations. In R. P. Cabaj & T. S. Stein (Eds.), *Textbook of homosexuality and mental health* (pp. 451–469). Washington, DC: American Psychiatric Association.

Ito, T., Ando, H., Suzuki, T., Ogura, T., Hotta, K., Imamura, Y., . . . Handa, H. (2010). Identification of a primary target of thalidomide teratogenicity. *Science, 327*(5971), 1345–1350.

Iverson, J. M., Capirci, O., Volterra, V., & Goldin-Meadow, S. (2008). Learning to talk in a gesture-rich world: Early communication in Italian vs. American children. *First Language, 28*(2), 164–181.

Iverson, J. M., & Goldin-Meadow, S. (2005). Gesture paves the way for language development. *Psychological Science, 16,* 368–371.

Ivkovich, D., Collins, K. L., Eckerman, C. O., Krasnegor, N. A., & Stanton, M. E. (1999). Classical delay eyeblink conditioning in 4- and 5-month-old infants. *Psychological Science, 10,* 4–8.

Izard, C. E. (2007). Basic emotions, natural kinds, emotion schemas and a new paradigm. *Perspectives on Psychological Science, 2*(3), 260–280.

Jaakola, J. K., & Gissler, M. (2007). Are girls more susceptible to the effects of prenatal exposure to tobacco smoke on asthma? *Epidemiology, 18,* 573–576.

Jack, F., MacDonald, S., Reese, E., & Hayne, H. (2009). Maternal reminiscing style during early childhood predicts the age of adolescents' earliest memories. *Child Development, 80*(2), 496–505.

Jack, R. E., Blais, C., Scheepers, C., Schyns, P. G., & Caldara, R. (2009). Cultural confusions show that facial expressions are not universal. *Current Biology, 19*(18), 1543–1548.

Jackson, C., Brown, J. D., & L'Engle, K. L. (2007). R-rated movies, bedroom televisions, and initiation of smoking by white and black adolescents. *Archives of Pediatrics & Adolescent Medicine, 161*(3), 260–268.

Jackson, K. M., & Nazar, A. M. (2006). Breastfeeding, the immune response, and long-term health. *Journal of the American Osteopathic Association, 106*(4), 203–207.

Jacobs, B. A., & Lefgren, L. (2004). Remedial education and student achievement: A regression continuity analysis. *The Review of Economics and Statistics, 86*(1), 226–244.

Jacobs, J. E., Davis-Kean, P., Bleeker, M., Eccles, J. S., & Malanchuk, O. (2005). I can, but I don't want to: The impact of parents, interests, and activities on gender differences in math. In A. Gallagher & J. Kaufman (Ed.), *Gender differences in mathematics* (pp. 246–263). New York, NY: Cambridge University Press.

Jacques, E. (2013). Treating nocturnal enuresis in children and young people. *British Journal of School Nursing, 8*(6), 275–278.

Jaffee, S. R., Bowes, L., Ouellet-Morin, I., Fisher, H. L., Moffitt, T. E., Merrick, M. T., & Arseneault, L. (2013). Safe, stable, nurturing relationships break the intergenerational cycle of abuse: A prospective nationally representative cohort of children in the United Kingdom. *Journal of Adolescent Health, 53*(4, Suppl), S4–S10. doi: 10.1016/j.jadohealth.2013.04.007

Jaffee, S., & Hyde, J. S. (2000). Gender differences in moral orientation: A meta-analysis. *Psychological Bulletin, 126*(5), 703–726.

Jambunathan, S., Burts, D. C., & Pierce, S. (2000). Comparisons of parenting attitudes among five ethnic groups in the United Sates. *Journal of Comparative Family Studies, 31*(4), 395–406.

James, K. H., Engelhardt, L. (2012). The effects of handwriting experience on functional brain development in preliterate children. *Trends in Neuroscience and Education, 1*(1), 32–42. Retrieved from http://dx.doi.org/10.1016/j.tine.2012.08.001

James, W. (1990). *The principles of psychology.* Cambridge, MA: Harvard University Press. (Original work published in 1890)

Janisse, J. J., Bailey, B. A., Ager, J., and Sokol, R. J. (2014). Alcohol, tobacco, cocaine, and marijuana use: Relative contributions to preterm delivery and fetal growth restriction. *Substance Abuse, 35*(1): 60–67. doi: 10.1080/08897077.2013.804483

Jauniaux, E., & Greenough, A. (2007). Short and long term outcomes of smoking during pregnancy. *Early Human Development, 83*(11), 697–698.

Jenkins, L. J., Yang, Y-J., Goh, J., Hong, Y-Y., Park, D. C. (2010). Cultural differences in the lateral occipital complex while viewing incongruent scenes. *Social Cognitive and Affective Neuroscience, 5*(2–3), 236–241.

Jensen, A. C., & Whiteman, S. D. (2014). Parents' differential treatment and adolescents' delinquent behaviors: Direct and indirect effects of difference-score and perception-based measures. *Journal of Family Psychology, 28*(4), 549–559. doi: 10.1037/a0036888

Jensen, A. C., Whiteman, S. D., Fingerman, K. L., & Birditt, K. S. (2013). 'Life still isn't fair': Parental differential treatment of young adult siblings. *Journal of Marriage and Family, 75*(2), 438–452.

Jepsen, J., & Martin, H. (2006). *Born too early: Hidden handicaps of premature children.* London, UK: Karnac Books.

Jimerson, S. R., & Ferguson, P. (2007). A longitudinal study of grade retention: Academic and behavioral outcomes of retained students through adolescence. *School Psychology Quarterly, 22*(3), 314–339.

Jin, M., Jacobvitz, D., Hazen, N., & Jung, S. (2012). Maternal sensitivity and infant attachment security in Korea: Cross-cultural validation of the Strange Situation. *Attachment & Human Development, 14*(1), 33–44.

Johnson, C. P., & Walker, W. O. (2006). Mental retardation: Management and prognosis. *Pediatrics in Review, 27,* 249–256.

Johnson, D., & Sulzby, E. (1999). Addressing the literacy needs of emergent and early readers. *Pathways to School Improvement.* Retrieved from http://www.ncrel.org/sdrs/areas/issues/content/cntareas/reading/li100.htm

Johnson, S. R., Cooper, M. N., Jones, T. W., & Davis, E. A. (2013). Long-term outcome of insulin pump therapy in children with type 1 diabetes assessed in a large population-based case-control study. *Diabetologia, 56*(11), 2392–2400.

Johnson, V. E., & de Villiers, J. G. (2009). Syntactic frames in fast mapping verbs: Effects of age, dialect, and clinical status. *Journal of Speech, Language, and Hearing Research, 52*(3), 610–622.

Johnson, V., Simon, P., & Mun, E. (2014). A peer-led high school transition program increases graduation rates among Latino males. *Journal of Educational Research, 107*(3), 186–196.

Johnston, J. R., Walters, M. G., & Olesen, N. W. (2005). Is it alienating parenting, role reversal or child abuse? A study of children's rejection of a parent in child custody disputes. *Journal of Child Custody, 5*, 191–218.

Johnston, L. D., O'Malley, P. M., Bachman, J. G., & Schulenberg, J. E. (2007). *Monitoring the Future national survey results on drug use, 1975–2006: Volume I, Secondary school students* (NIH Publication No. 07-6205). Bethesda, MD: National Institute on Drug Abuse.

Johnston, L. D., O'Malley, P. M., Miech, R. A., Bachman, J. G., & Schulenberg, J. E. (2014). *Monitoring the Future national results on drug use: 1975–2013: Overview, Key Findings on Adolescent Drug Use.* Ann Arbor: Institute for Social Research, The University of Michigan.

Jones, C. (2014). New law tackles high school football collisions head on. *SF Gate.* Retrieved from http://www.sfgate.com/preps/article/New-California-law-limits-schools-full-contact-5636585.php

Jones, E. G., Renger, R., & Kang, Y. (2007). Self-efficacy for health-related behaviors among deaf adults. *Research in Nursing & Health, 30*(2), 185–192.

Jones, E. M., & Landreth, G. (2002). The efficacy of intensive individual play therapy for chronically ill children. *International Journal of Play Therapy, 11*(1), 117–140.

Jones, M. C. (1924). A laboratory study of fear: The case of Peter. *Pedagogical Seminary, 31*, 308–315.

Jones, P. (1995). Contradictions and unanswered questions in the Genie case: A fresh look at the linguistic evidence. *Language & Communication, 15*(3), 261–280.

Jones, W., & Klin, A. (2013). Attention to eyes is present but in decline in 2-6-month-old infants later diagnosed with autism. *Nature, 504*(7480), 427–431. doi: 10.1038/nature12715

Jorde, L. B., Carey, J. C., Bamshad, M. J., & White, R. L. (2006). *Medical genetics* (3rd ed.). St. Louis, MO: Mosby.

Joseph, J. (2001). Separated twins and the genetics of personality differences: A critique. *American Journal of Psychology, 114*(1), 1–30.

Josselyn, S. A., & Frankland, P. W. (2012). Infantile amnesia: A neurogenic hypothesis. *Learning & Memory, 19*(9), 423–433.

Jurkovic, G. J., Thirkield, A., & Morrell, R. (2001). Parentification of adult child of divorce: A multidimensional analysis. *Journal of Youth and Adolescence, 30*(2), 245–257.

Jusko, T. A., Henderson, C. R., Lanphear, B. P., Dory-Slechta, D. A., Parsons, P. J., & Canfield, R. L. (2008). Blood lead concentrations < 10 µg/dL and child intelligence at 6 years of age. *Environmental Health Perspectives, 116*(2), 243–248.

Jussim, L., & Harber, K. D. (2005). Teacher expectations and self-fulfilling prophecies: Knowns and unknowns, resolved and unresolved controversies. *Personality and Social Psychology Review, 9*(2), 131–155. doi: 10.1207/s15327957pspr0902_3

Juster, F. T., Ono, H., & Stafford, F. (2004). *Changing times of American youth: 1981–2003.* Ann Arbor, MI: Institute for Social Research, University of Michigan. Retrieved from http://www.umich.edu/news/Releases/2004/Nov04/teen_time_report.pdf

Justice, L. M., McGinty, A. S., Piasta, S. B., Kaderavek, J. N., Fan, X. (2010). Print focused read-alouds in preschool classrooms: Intervention effectiveness and moderators of child outcomes. *Speech and Hearing Services in Schools, 41*, 504–520.

Juvonen, J. (2013). Peer rejection among children and adolescents: Antecedents, reactions, and maladaptive pathways. In C. DeWall (Ed.), *The Oxford handbook of social exclusion* (pp. 101–110). New York, NY: Oxford University Press.

Kahan, D. (2008). Recess, extracurricular activities and active classrooms: Means for increasing elementary school students' physical activity. *Journal of Physical Education, Recreation & Dance, 79*(2), 26–31, 39.

Kahn, M. (2002). *Basic Freud: Psychoanalytic thought for the twenty first century.* New York, NY: Basic Books.

Kail, R. (2000). Speed of information processing: Developmental change and links to intelligence. *Journal of School Psychology, 38*, 51–61.

Kail, R. V., & Ferrer, E. (2007). Processing speed in childhood and adolescence: Longitudinal models for examining developmental change. *Child Development, 78*(6), 1760–1770.

Kalb, C. (2004, January 26). Brave new babies. *Newsweek,* pp. 45–53.

Kalb, C. (2005, February 28). When does autism start? *Newsweek,* pp. 45–47, 50–53.

Kalben, B. B. (2002). *Why men die younger: Causes of mortality differences by sex.* SOA Monograph M-LI01-1. Schaumberg, IL: Society of Actuaries.

Kaler, S. R., & Freeman, B. J. (1994). Analysis of environmental deprivation: Cognitive and social development in Romanian orphans. *Journal of Child Psychology and Psychiatry, 35*(4), 769–781.

Kalter, N. (1990). *Growing up with divorce.* London, UK: Collier Macmillan.

Kaltiala-Heino, R., Kosunen, E., & Rimpela, M. (2003). Pubertal timing, sexual behaviour and self-reported depression in middle adolescence. *Journal of Adolescence, 26*, 531–545.

Kamii, C., Rummelsburg, J., & Kari, A. (2005). Teaching arithmetic to low-performing, low-SES first graders. *Journal of Mathematical Behavior, 24*(1), 39–50.

Kandel, D. B., & Lesser, G. S. (1972). *Youth in two worlds.* San Francisco, CA: Jossey-Bass.

Kaneshiro, N. K., & Zieve, D. (2011). *Shaken baby syndrome.* Retrieved from http://www.nlm.nih.gov/medlineplus/ency/article/000004.htm

Kanner, L. (1949). Problems of nosology and psychodynamics of early infantile autism. *American Journal of Orthopsychiatry, 19,* 416–426.

Kanters, M. A., Bocarro, J., & Casper, J. (2008). Supported or pressured? An examination of agreement among parents and children on parent's role in youth sports. *Journal of Sport Behavior, 31*(1), 64–80.

Kapadia, S. (2008). Adolescent-parent relationships in Indian and Indian immigrant families in the US: Intersections and disparities. *Psychology and Developing Societies, 20,* 257–275.

Kaplan, S. (1995). The restorative benefits of nature: Toward an integrative framework. *Journal of Environmental Psychology, 15*(3), 169–182.

Kaplow, J. B., Gipson, P. Y., Horwitz, A. G., Burch, B. N., & King, C. A. (2014). Emotional suppression mediates the relation between adverse life events and adolescent suicide: Implications for prevention. *Prevention Science, 15*(2), 177–185. doi: 10.1007/s11121-013-0367-9

Kaplowitz, P. (2006). Pubertal development in girls: Secular trends. *Current Opinion in Obstetrics and Gynecology, 18*(5), 487–491.

Kaplowitz, P. B. (2008). Link between body fat and the timing of puberty. *Pediatrics, 121*(Supplement No. 3), S208–S217.

Kaplowitz, P. B., Speiser, P. W., Windle, M. L., Levitsky, L. L., Poth, M. P. M., & Kemp, S. (2013). *Precocious puberty.* Retrieved from http://emedicine.medscape.com/article/924002-overview

Kapoun, J. (1998, July/August). Teaching undergrads WEB evaluation: A guide for library instruction. *C&RL News, 522–523.* Retrieved from http://www.ala.org/ala/mgrps/divs/acrl/publications/crlnews/1998/jul/teachingundergrads.cfm

Karmiloff, K., & Karmiloff-Smith, A. (2001). *Pathways to language.* Cambridge, MA: Harvard University Press.

Karney, B. R., Beckett, M. K., Collins, R. L., & Shaw, R. (2007). *Adolescent romantic relationships as precursors of healthy adult marriages: A review of theory, research, and programs.* Santa Monica, CA: RAND Corporation TR-488-ACF. (Technical report prepared by the RAND Labor and Population Program for the U.S. Department of Health and Human Services).

Karoly, L. A., Greenwood, P. W., Everingham, S. S., Hoube, J., Kilburn, M. R., Rydell, C. P., . . . Chiesa, J. (1998). *Investing in our children: What we know and don't know about the costs and benefits of early childhood interventions.* Santa Monica, CA: RAND.

Karpouzis, F., & Bonello, R. (2012). Nutritional complementary and alternative medicine for pediatric attention-deficit/hyperactivity disorder. *Ethical Human Psychology and Psychiatry, 14*(1), 41–60.

Karuza, E. A., Newport, E. L., Aslin, R. N., Starling, S. J., Tivarus, M. E., & Bavelier, D. (2013). The neural correlates of statistical learning in a word segmentation task: An fMRI study. *Brain and Language, 127*(1), 46–54. doi: 10.1016/j.bandl.2012.11.007

Karwelt, N. L. (1999). *Grade retention: Prevalence, timing, and effects* [CRESPAR Report No. 33]. Baltimore, MD: Johns Hopkins University.

Kasbekar, N. (2013). *Baby myths and facts.* Retrieved from http://kidshealthpartners.com/baby-myths-and-facts/

Katz, V. L. (2003). Prenatal care. In J. S. Scott, R. S. Gibbs, B. Y. Karlan, & A. F. Haney (Eds.), *Danforth's obstetrics and gynecology* (9th ed., pp. 1–33). Philadelphia, PA: Lippincott.

Kavšek, M. (2004). Predicting later IQ from infant visual habituation and dishabituation: A meta-analysis. *Journal of Applied Developmental Psychology, 25*(3), 369–393.

Kayyal, M. H., & Russell, J. A. (2013). Americans and Palestinians judge spontaneous facial expressions of emotion. *Emotion, 13*(5), 891–904.

Kazdin, A. E., & Benjet, C. (2003). Spanking children: Evidence and issues. *Current Directions in Psychological Science, 12*(3), 99–103.

Kazdin, A. E., & Marciano, P. L. (1998). Childhood and adolescent depression. In E. J. Mash & R. A. Barkley (Eds.), *Treatment of childhood disorders* (2nd ed., pp. 211–248). New York, NY: Guilford Press.

Keel, P. K., & Forney, K. J. (2013). Psychosocial risk factors for eating disorders. *International Journal of Eating Disorders, 46,* 433–439.

Kelo, M., Martikainen, M., & Eriksson, E. (2011). Self-care of school-age children with diabetes: An integrative review. *Journal of Advanced Nursing, 67*(10), 2096–2108.

Kemp, N., & Bryant, P. (2003). Do beez buzz? Rule-based and frequency-based knowledge in learning to spell plurals. *Child Development, 74*(1), 63–74.

Kempe, C. H., Silverman, F. N., Steele, B. F., Droegemuller, W., Silver, A. K. (1962). The battered child syndrome. *Journal of the American Medical Association, 187,* 17–24.

Kenneady, L. M., & Intercultural Development Research Association. (2004). *Good for nothing in grade retention.* Retrieved from http://www.idra.org/IDRA_Newsletter/June_-_July_2004%3A_Self-Renewing_Schools%E2%80%A6Leadership/Good_for_Nothing_In_grade_Retention

Kennedy, H. (1997). Karl Heinrich Ulrichs: First theorist of homosexuality. In V. A. Rosario (Ed.), *Science and homosexualities* (pp. 26–45). New York, NY: Routledge.

Kennell, J., Klaus, M., McGrath, S., Robertson, S., & Hinkley, C. (1991). Continuous emotional support during labor in a US hospital. A randomized controlled trial. *Journal of the American Medical Association, 265*(17), 2197–2201.

Kennell, J. H., & Klaus, M. H. (1979). Early mother–infant contact: Effects on the mother and the infant. *Bulletin of the Menninger Clinic, 43*(1), 69–78.

Kenney-Benson, G. A., Pomerantz, E. M., Ryan, A. M., & Patrick, H. (2006). Sex differences in math performance: The role of children's approach to schoolwork. *Developmental Psychology, 42*(1), 11–26.

Kessenich, M. (2003). Developmental outcomes of premature, low birth weight, and medically fragile infants. *Newborn & Infant Nursing Reviews, 3*(3), 80–87.

Khurana, A., Romer, D., Betancourt, L. M., Brodsky, N. L., Giannetta, J. M., & Hurt, H. (2013). Working memory ability predicts trajectories of early alcohol use in adolescents: The mediational role of impulsivity. *Addiction, 108*(3), 506–515. doi: 10.1111/add.12001

KidsHealth. (2008). *10 things that might surprise you about being pregnant.* Retrieved from http://kidshealth.org/parent/pregnancy_newborn/pregnancy/pregnancy.html

KidsHealth. (2013). *Backpack safety.* Retrieved from http://kidshealth.org/parent/firstaid_safe/outdoor/backpack.html#a_Problems_Backpacks_Can_Pose

Kiesner, J., Kerr, M., & Stattin, H. (2004). "Very important persons" in adolescence: Going beyond in-school, single friendships in the study of peer homophily. *Journal of Adolescence, 27,* 545–560.

Kim, H. (2011). Consequences of parental divorce for child development. *American Sociological Review, 76*(3), 487–511.

Kim, J. (2009). Type-specific intergenerational transmission of neglectful and physically abusive parenting behaviors among young parents. *Children and Youth Services Review, 31*(7), 761–767.

Kim, K. H. (2005). Can only intelligent people be creative? A meta-analysis. *Journal of Secondary Gifted Education, 16*(2–3), 57–66.

Kim, Y. S., Leventhal, B. L., Koh, Y. J., Fombonne, E., Laska, E., Lim, E. C., . . . Grinker, R. R. (2011). Prevalence of autism spectrum disorders in a total population sample. *American Journal of Psychiatry, 168*(9), 904–912.

Kim-Cohen, J., Caspi, A., Taylor, A., Williams, B., Newcombe, R., Craig, I. W., & Moffitt, T. E. (2006). MAOA, maltreatment, and gene-environment interaction predicting children's mental health: New evidence and a meta-analysis. *Molecular Psychiatry, 11*(10), 903–913.

Kimonis, E. R., Fanti, K., Goldweber, A., Marsee, M. A., Frick, P. J., & Cauffman, E. (2014). Callous-unemotional traits in incarcerated adolescents. *Psychological Assessment, 26*(1), 227–237. doi: 10.1037/a0034585

Kinsbourne, M. (2009). Development of cerebral lateralization in children. In C. R. Reynolds & E. Fletcher-Janzen (Eds.), *Handbook of clinical child neuropsychology* (3rd ed., pp. 47–66). New York, NY: Springer.

Király, I., Csibra, G., & Gergely, G. (2013). Beyond rational imitation: Learning arbitrary means actions from communicative demonstrations. *Journal of Experimental Child Psychology, 116*(2), 471–486. doi: 10.1016/j.jecp.2012.12.003

Kirk, E., Howlett, N., Pine, K. J., & Fletcher, B. (2013). To sign or not to sign? The impact of encouraging infants to gesture on infant language and maternal mind-mindedness. *Child Development, 84*(2), 574–590. doi: 10.1111/j.1467-8624.2012.01874.x

Kirkorian, H. L., Wartella, E. A., & Anderson, D. R. (2008). Children and electronic media. *Future of Children, 18*(1), 39–62.

Kirschner, F., Paas, F., & Kirschner, P. A. (2009). A cognitive load approach to collaborative learning: United brains for complex tasks. *Educational Psychology Review, 21*(1), 31–42.

Kirsh, S. J. (2012). *Children, adolescents, and media violence: A critical look at the research* (2nd ed.). Thousand Oaks, CA: Sage.

Kitayama, S., & Park, J. (2010). Cultural neuroscience of the self: Understanding the social grounding of the brain. *Social Cognitive and Affective Neuroscience, 5,* 111–129.

Kitzman, H., Olds, D., Cole, R., Hanks, C., Anson, E., Arcoleo, K., . . . Holmberg, J. (2010). Enduring effects of prenatal and infancy home visiting by nurses on children: Follow-up of a randomized trial among children at age 12 years. *Archives of Pediatrics & Adolescent Medicine, 164*(5), 412–418. doi: 10.1001/archpediatrics.2010.76

Klaczynski, P. A. (2001). Analytic and heuristic processing influences on adolescent reasoning and decision-making. *Child Development, 72*(3), 844–861. doi: 10.1111/1467-8624.00319

Klahr, A. M., Rueter, M. A., McGue, M., Iacono, W. G., & Burt, S. A. (2011). The relationship between parent-child conflict and adolescent antisocial behavior: Confirming shared environmental mediation. *Journal of Abnormal Child Psychology, 39*(5), 683–694.

Kleibeuker, S. W., Koolschijn, P. P., Jolles, D. D., Schel, M. A., De Dreu, C. W., & Crone, E. A. (2013). Prefrontal cortex involvement in creative problem solving in middle adolescence and adulthood. *Developmental Cognitive Neuroscience, 5,* 197–206. doi: 10.1016/j.dcn.2013.03.003

Klein, P. D. (1997). Multiplying the problems of intelligence by eight: A critique of Gardner's theory. *Canadian Journal of Education, 22*(4), 377–394.

Klemm, W. R. (2013). *What learning cursive does for your brain.* Retrieved from http://www.psychologytoday.com/blog/memory-medic/201303/what-learning-cursive-does-your-brain

Kling, K. C., Hyde, J. S., Showers, C. J., & Buswell, B. N. (1999). Gender differences in self-esteem: A meta-analysis. *Psychological Bulletin, 125,* 470–500.

Kobus, K. (2003). Peers and adolescent smoking. *Addiction, 98,* 37–55.

Kochanska, G., & Aksan, N. (2006). Children's conscience and self-regulation. *Journal of Personality, 74*(6), 1587–1617.

Kochanska, G., Barry, R. A., Aksan, N., & Boldt, L. J. (2008). A developmental model of maternal and child contributions to disruptive conduct: The first six years. *Journal of Child Psychology and Psychiatry*, 49(11), 1220–1227.

Kogan, M. D., Overpeck, M. D., Hoffman, H. J., & Casselbrant, M. L. (2000). Factors associated with tympanostomy tube insertion among preschool-age children in the United States. *American Journal of Public Health*, 90(2), 245–250.

Kohlberg, L. (1966). A cognitive-developmental analysis of children's sex-role concepts and attitudes. In E. E. Maccoby (Ed.), *The development of sex differences* (pp. 82–173). Palo Alto, CA: Stanford University Press.

Kohlberg, L. (1987). The development of moral judgment and moral action. In L. Kohlberg (Ed.), *Child psychology and childhood education* (pp. 259–328). White Plains, NY: Longman.

Kohlberg, L. (2005). Moral stages and moralization: The cognitive-developmental approach. In C. Lewis & J. G. Bremner (Eds.), *Developmental psychology II: Social and language development* (Vol. 5, pp. 201–231). Thousand Oaks, CA: Sage.

Kokko, K., & Pulkkinen, L. (2005). Stability of aggressive behavior from childhood to middle age in women and men. *Aggressive Behavior*, 31(5), 485–497.

Kokko, K., Tremblay, R. E., Lacourse, E., Nagin, D. S., & Vitaro, F. (2006). Trajectories of prosocial behavior and physical aggression in the middle childhood: Links to adolescent school dropout and physical violence. *Journal of Research on Adolescence*, 16(3), 403–428.

Kolkman, M. E., Kroesbergen, E. H., & Leseman, P. M. (2013). Early numerical development and the role of nonsymbolic and symbolic skills. *Learning and Instruction*, 25, 95–103. doi: 10.1016/j.learninstruc.2012.12.001

Konijn, E. A., Bijvank, M. N., & Bushman, B. J. (2007). I wish I were a warrior: The role of wishful identification in the effects of violent video games on aggression in adolescent boys. *Developmental Psychology*, 43(4), 1038–1044.

Koplan, J. P., Liverman, C. T., & Kraak, V. I. (Eds.). (2005). *Preventing childhood obesity: Health in the balance.* Washington, DC: National Academies Press.

Kopp, C. B., & Krakow, J. B. (1982). *Child development: Development in social context.* Upper Saddle River, NJ: Pearson.

Korjenevitch, M., & Dunifon, R. (2010). *Child care center quality and child development.* Ithaca, NY: Cornell University College of Human Ecology.

Kotila, L. E., Schoppe-Sullivan, S. J., & Kamp Dush, C. M. (2013). Time in parenting activities in dual-earner families at the transition to parenthood. *Family Relations, 62,* 795–807.

Kotrla, K. (2010). Domestic minor sex trafficking in the United States. *Social Work,* 55(2), 181–187.

Kovack-Lesh, K. A., Oakes, L. M., & McMurray, B. (2012). Contributions of attentional style and previous experience to 4-month-old infants' categorization. *Infancy, 17*(3), 324–338. doi: 10.1111/j.1532–7078.2011.00073.x

Kovács, Á. M., & Mehler, J. (2009). Cognitive gains in 7-month-old bilingual infants. *Proceedings of the National Academy of Sciences of the United States of America, 106*(16), 6556–6560.

Kovas, Y., & Plomin, R. (2007). Learning abilities and disabilities: Generalist genes, specialist environments. *Current Directions in Psychological Science, 16*(5), 284–288.

Kovas, Y. Y., Haworth, C. A., Harlaar, N. N., Petrill, S. A., Dale, P. S., & Plomin, R. R. (2007). Overlap and specificity of genetic and environmental influences on mathematics and reading disability in 10-year-old twins. *Journal of Child Psychology and Psychiatry,* 48(9), 914–922.

Kowalski, R. M., & Limber, S. P. (2007). Electronic bullying among middle school students. *Journal of Adolescent Health,* 41(6 Supplement), S22–S30.

Kraft, N., & Wheeler, J. (2003). Service learning and resilience in disaffected youth: A research study. In J. Eyler & S. H. Billig (Eds.), *Deconstructing service learning: Research exploring context, participation, and impacts* (pp. 213–238). Greenwich, CT: Information Age.

Krähenbühl, S., & Blades, M. (2006). The effect of interviewing techniques on young children's responses to questions. *Child: Care, Health & Development,* 32(3), 321–331.

Krcmar, M., Grela, B., & Lin, K. (2007). Can toddlers learn vocabulary from television? An experimental approach. *Media Psychology,* 10(1), 41–63.

Krevans, J., & Gibbs, J. C. (1996). Parents' use of inductive discipline: Relations to children's empathy and prosocial behavior. *Child Development,* 67(6), 3263–3277.

Kristensen, P., & Bjerkedal, T. (2007). Explaining the relation between birth order and intelligence. *Science,* 316(5832), 1717.

Kristjansson, B., Petticrew, M., MacDonald, B., Krasevec, J., Janzen, L., Greenhalgh, T., . . . Welch, V. (2007). School feeding for improving the physical and psychosocial health of disadvantaged students. *Cochrane Database of Systematic Reviews,* 1, Art. No.: CD004676.

Kristjánsson, K. (2004). Empathy, sympathy, justice and the child. *Journal of Moral Education,* 33(3), 291–305. doi: 10.1080103057240042000733064

Kroger, J., Martinussen, M., & Marcia, J. E. (2010). Identity status change during adolescence and young adulthood: A meta-analysis. *Journal of Adolescence,* 33(5), 683–698. doi: 10.1016/j.adolescence.2009.11.002

Kronk, C. M. (1994). Private speech in adolescents. *Adolescence,* 29(116), 781–804.

Kuhl, P. K., Conboy, B. T., Padden, D., Nelson, T., & Pruitt, J. (2005). Early speech perception and later language development: Implications for the "critical period." *Language Learning and Development,* 1(3 & 4), 237–264.

Kuhn, D. (2009). Adolescent thinking. In R. M. Lerner & L. Steinberg (Eds.), *Handbook of adolescent psychology.*

Vol. 1: Individual bases of adolescent development (3rd. ed.). Hoboken, NJ: Wiley.

Kuo, F. E., & Taylor, A. (2004). A potential natural treatment for Attention-Deficit/Hyperactivity Disorder: Evidence from a national study. *American Journal of Public Health, 94*(9), 1580–1586.

Kutscher, M. (2008). *ADHD—Living without brakes.* Philadelphia, PA: Jessica Kingsley.

Lablanc, L., Richardson, W., & McIntosh, J. (2005). The use of applied behavioural analysis in teaching children with autism. *International Journal of Special Education, 20*(1), 13–34.

Labouvie-Vief, G. (2006). Emerging structures of adult thought. In J. A. Arnett & J. L. Tanner (Eds.), *Emerging adults in America: Coming of age in the 21st century* (pp. 59–84). Washington, DC: American Psychological Association.

Lacelle, C., Hébert, M., Lavoie, F., Vitaro, F., & Tremblay. R. E. (2012). Sexual health in women reporting a history of child sexual abuse. *Child Abuse & Neglect, 36,* 247–259.

Lachance, J. A., & Mazzocco, M. M. M. (2006). A longitudinal analysis of sex differences in math and spatial skills in primary school age children. *Learning and Individual Differences, 16*(3), 195–216.

Ladd, G. W., Kochenderfer-Ladd, B., Eggum, N. D., Kochel, K. P., & McConnell, E. M. (2011). Characterizing and comparing the friendships of anxious-solitary and unsociable pre-adolescents. *Child Development, 82*(5), 1434–1453.

Lagercrantz, H., & Slotkin, T. A. (1986). The "stress" of being born. *Scientific American, 254,* 100–107.

LaGravenese, R. (Director). (2007). *Freedom writers* [Motion picture]. United States: Paramount.

Laible, D. (2007). Attachment with parents and peers in late adolescence: Links with emotional competence and social behavior. *Personality and Individual Differences, 43*(5), 1185–1197.

Laird, J. A., & Feldman, S. S. (2004). Evaluation of the Summerbridge Intervention Program: Design and preliminary findings. In G. D. Borman & M. Boulay (Eds.), *Summer learning: Research, policies, and programs* (pp. 199–229). Mahwah, NJ: Erlbaum.

Lamb, M. E., Sternberg, K., Orbach, Y., Esplin, P., Stewart, H., & Mitchell, S. (2003). Age differences in children's responses to open ended invitations in the course of forensic interviews. *Journal of Consulting and Clinical Psychology, 71,* 926–934.

Lamborn, S. D., Mounts, N. S., Steinberg, L., & Dornbusch, S. M. (1991). Patterns of competence and adjustment among adolescents from authoritative, authoritarian, indulgent, and neglectful families. *Child Development, 62*(5), 1049–1065.

Lammas, C., & Poland, G. (2014). *Motor skills: The handbook for referrers.* Halton, UK: Bridgewater Community Health Care.

Lampl, M., & Johnson, M. L. (2011). Infant growth in length follows prolonged sleep and increased naps. *Sleep: Journal of Sleep and Sleep Disorders Research, 34*(5), 641–650.

Landgren, K., & Hallström, I. (2011). Parents' experience of living with a baby with infantile colic—A phenomenological hermeneutic study. *Scandinavian Journal of Caring Sciences, 25*(2), 317–324. doi: 10.1111/j.1471–6712.2010.00829.x

Landrum, T. J., & Kauffman, J. M. (2006). Behavioral approaches to classroom management. In C. M. Evertson & C. S. Weinstein (Eds.), *Handbook of classroom management: Research, practice and contemporary issues.* Mahwah, NJ: Erlbaum.

Lane, J. (1994). *History of genetics timeline.* Retrieved from http://www.accessexcellence.org/AE/AEPC/WWC/1994/genetic stln.php

Långström, N., Rahman, Q., Carlström, E., & Lichtenstein, P. (2010). Genetic and environmental effects on same-sex sexual behavior: A population study of twins in Sweden. *Archives of Sexual Behavior, 39*(1), 75–80. doi: 10.1007/s10508-008-9386-1

Lansford, J. E., Chang, L., Dodge, K. A., Malone, P. S., Oburu, P., Palmérus, K., . . . Quinn. N. (2005). Physical discipline and children's adjustment: Cultural normativeness as a moderator. *Child Development, 76*(6), 1234–1246. doi: 10.1111/j.1467–8624.2005.00847.x

Lansford, J. E., & Deater-Deckard, K. (2012). Childrearing discipline and violence in developing countries. *Child Development, 83*(1), 62–75. doi: 10.1111/j.1467-8624.2011.01676.x

Lansford, J. E., Deater-Deckard, K., Dodge, K. A., Bates, J. E., & Pettit, G. S. (2004). Ethnic differences in the link between physical discipline and later adolescent externalizing behaviors. *Journal of Child Psychology and Psychiatry 45*(4), 801–812.

Lansford, J. E., Putallaz, M., Grimes, C. L., Schiro-Osman, K. A., Kupersmidt, J. B., & Coie, J. D. (2006). Perceptions of friendship quality and observed behaviors with friends: How do sociometrically rejected, average, and popular girls differ? *Merrill-Palmer Quarterly, 52*(4), 694–720.

Lany, J., & Saffran, J. R. (2010). From statistics to meaning: Infants' acquisition of lexical categories. *Psychological Science, 21*(2), 284–291.

Lapierre, M. A., Piotrowski, J. T., & Linebarger, D. L. (2012). Background television in the homes of US children. *Pediatrics, 130*(5), 839–846.

Lapsley, D. K. (2006). Moral stage theory. In M. Killen & J. Smetana (Eds.), *Handbook of moral development* (pp. 37–66). Mahwah, NJ: Erlbaum.

Larson, J. P. (2002). Genetic counseling. In D. S. Blachfield & J. L. Longe (Eds.), *Gale encyclopedia of medicine* (Vol. 3, 2nd ed., pp. 1429–1431). Detroit, MI: Gale.

Larson, R. (2004). How U.S. children and adolescents spend time: What it does (and doesn't) tell us about their development. In J. Lerner & A. E. Alberts (Eds.), *Current directions in developmental psychology* (pp. 134–144). Upper Saddle River, NJ: Pearson Prentice Hall.

Larson, R. (2008). Family mealtimes as a developmental context. *Society for Research in Child Development Social Policy Report, 22*(4), 12.

Larson, R. W., & Brown, J. R. (2007). Emotional development in adolescence: What can be learned from a high school theater program? *Child Development, 78*(4), 1083–1099.

Laskey, A., Stump, T., Perkins, S., Zimet, G., Sherman, S., & Downs, S. (2012). Influence of race and socioeconomic status on the diagnosis of child abuse: A randomized study. *Journal of Pediatrics, 160*(6), 1003–1008.

Latzman, R. D., Naifeh, J. A., Watson, D., Vaidya, J. G., Heiden, L. J., Damon, J. D., . . . Young, J. (2011). Racial differences in symptoms of anxiety and depression among three cohorts of students in the Southeastern United States. *Psychiatry: Interpersonal and Biological Processes, 74,* 332–348.

Laursen, B., Coy, K. C., & Collins, W. (1998). Reconsidering changes in parent–child conflict across adolescence: A meta-analysis. *Child Development, 69*(3), 817–832. doi: 10.2307/1132206

Laursen, B., Furman, W., & Mooney, K. A. (2006). Predicting interpersonal competence and self-worth from adolescent relationships and relationship networks: Variable-centered and person-centered perspectives. *Merrill-Palmer Quarterly, 52*(3), 572–600.

Law, K. L., Stroud, L. R., LaGasse, L. L., Niaura, R., Liu, J., & Lester, B. (2003). Smoking during pregnancy and newborn neurobehavior. *Pediatrics, 111*(6), 1318–1323.

Laycock, J., & Meeran, K. (2013). *Integrated endocrinology.* Hoboken, NJ: Wiley-Blackwell.

LD OnLine. (2008a). *Celebrity quiz.* Retrieved from http://www.ldonline.org/article/5938

LD OnLine. (2008b). *LD basics: What is a learning disability?* Retrieved from http://www.ldonline.org/ldbasics/whatisld

Le, H. (2000). Never leave your little one alone—Raising an Ifaluk child. In J. DeLoache & A. Gottlieb (Eds.), *A world of babies* (pp. 199–222). New York, NY: Cambridge University Press.

Lebedeva, G. C., & Kuhl, P. K. (2010). Sing that tune: Infants' perception of melody and lyrics and the facilitation of phonetic recognition in songs. *Infant Behavior and Development, 33*(4), 419–430.

Lecanuet, J., Graniere-Deferre, C., & DeCasper, A. (2005). Are we expecting too much from prenatal sensory experiences? In B. Hopkins & S. P. Johnson (Eds.), *Prenatal development of postnatal functions* (pp. 31–49). Westport, CT: Praeger.

Leconte, P., & Fagard, J. (2006). Lateral preferences in children with intellectual deficiency of idiopathic origin. *Developmental Psychobiology, 48*(6), 492-500.

Lee, H., Andrew, M., Gebremariam, A., Lumeng, J., & Lee, J. (2014). Longitudinal associations between poverty and obesity from birth through adolescence. *American Journal of Public Health, 104*(5), e70–e76.

Lee, H., Harris, K., & Lee, J. (2013). Multiple levels of social disadvantage and links to obesity in adolescence and young adulthood. *Journal of School Health, 83*(3), 139–149.

Lee, J., & Menon, R. (2006). Growth hormone treatment of children with nongrowth-hormone-deficient short stature. *Patient Care For The Nurse Practitioner,* 22–27.

Lee, J. C., & Staff, J. (2007). When work matters: The varying impact of work intensity on high school dropout. *Sociology of Education, 80*(2), 158–178.

Lee, J. M., Appugliese, D., Kaciroti, N., Corwyn, R. F., Bradley, R. H., & Lumeng, J. C. (2007). Weight status in young girls and the onset of puberty. *Pediatrics, 119,* e624–630.

Lee, M. D., MacDermid, S. M., Dohring, P. L., & Kossek, E. E. (2005). Professionals becoming parents: Socialization, adaptation and identity transformation. In E. E. Kossek & S. J. Lambert (Eds.), *Work and life integration: Organization, cultural and individual perspectives* (pp. 287–317). Mahwah, NJ: Erlbaum.

Leffel, K., & Suskind, D. (2013). Parent-directed approaches to enrich the early language environments of children living in poverty. *Seminars In Speech and Language, 34*(4), 267–278. doi: 10.1055/s-0033–1353443

LeHalle, H. (2006). Cognitive development in adolescence: Thinking freed from concrete constraints. In S. Jackson & L. Goossens (Eds.), *Handbook of adolescent development.* New York, NY: Psychology Press.

Lehman, E. B., & Erdwins, C. J. (2004). The social and emotional adjustment of young, intellectually gifted children. In S. M. Moon (Ed.), *Social/emotional issues, underachievement, and counseling of gifted and talented students* (pp. 1–8). Thousand Oaks, CA: Corwin.

Lehman, J. D. (2005). *Understanding marriage, family, and intimate relationships.* Springfield, IL: Charles C Thomas.

Lehmann, C. (2004). Brain studies could affect death penalty case outcome. *Psychiatric News, 39*(24), 10–34.

Lemish, D. (2007). *Children and television: A global perspective.* Oxford, UK: Blackwell.

Lengua, L. J., Honorado, E., & Bush, N. R. (2007). Contextual risk and parenting as predictors of effortful control and social competence in preschool children. *Journal of Applied Developmental Psychology, 28*(1), 40–55. doi: 10.1016/j.appdev.2006.10.001

Lenhart, A., & Madden, M. (2007). *Social networking websites and teens: An overview.* Retrieved from http://www.pewinter net.org/PPF/r/198/report_display.asp

Lenhart, A., Madden, M., Smith, A., Purcell, K., Zickuhr, K., & Rainie, L. (2011). *Teens, kindness and cruelty on social network sites.* Pew Internet & American Life Project. Retrieved from http://pewinternet.org/Reports/2011/Teens-and-social-media/Summary/Majority-of-teens.aspx

Lerner, R. M. (1982). Children and adolescents as producers of their own development. *Developmental Review, 2,* 342–370.

Leslie, M. (2000). The vexing legacy of Lewis Terman. *Stanford Magazine.* Retrieved from http://www.stanfordalumni.org/news/magazine/2000/julaug/articles/terman.html

Leventhal, J. M. (2003). Test of time: "The battered child syndrome" 40 years later. *Clinical Child Psychology and Psychiatry, 8*(4), 543–545.

Levine, L. E. (1983). Mine: Self-definition in 2-year-old boys. *Developmental Psychology, 19*(4), 544–549.

Levine, L. E. (2002). Kohlberg, Lawrence (1927–1987). In N. J. Salkind (Ed.), *Child development* (pp. 225–226). New York, NY: Macmillan Reference USA.

Levine, L. E., & Conway, J. M. (2010). Self–other awareness and peer relationships in toddlers: Gender comparisons. *Infant and Child Development, 19,* 455–464.

Levine, L. E., & Waite, B. M. (2002). Television and the American child. *Clio's Psyche, 9*(1), 24–26.

LeVine, R. A., Dixon, S., LeVine, S., Richman, A., Leiderman, P. H., Keefer, C. H., & Brazelton, T. B. (1994). *Child care and culture: Lessons from Africa.* Cambridge, UK: Cambridge University Press.

Lewin, T. (2013, October 28). New milestone emerges: Baby's first iphone app. *The New York Times,* p. A17.

Lewis, C., & Carpendale, J. (2002). Social cognition. In P. K. Smith & C. H. Hart (Eds.), *Blackwell handbook of childhood social development* (pp. 375–393). Malden, MA: Blackwell.

Lewis, E. E., Dozier, M., Ackerman, J., & Sepulveda-Kozakowski, S. (2007). The effect of placement instability on adopted children's inhibitory control abilities and oppositional behavior. *Developmental Psychology, 43,* 1415–1427.

Lew-Williams, C., Pelucchi, B., & Saffran, J. R. (2011). Isolated words enhance statistical language learning in infancy. *Developmental Science, 14*(6), 1323–1329. doi: 10.1111/j.1467-7687.2011.01079.x

Lew-Williams, C., & Saffran, J. R. (2012). All words are not created equal: Expectations about word length guide infant statistical learning. *Cognition, 122*(2), 241–246. doi: 10.1016/j.cognition.2011.10.007

Li, Q. (2007). Bullying in the new playground: Research into cyberbullying and cyber victimization. *Australasian Journal of Educational Technology, 23,* 435–454.

Li, R., Darling, N., Maurice, E., Barker, L., & Grummer-Strawn, L. M. (2005). Breastfeeding rates in the United States by characteristics of the child, mother, or family: The 2002 National Immunization Survey. *Pediatrics, 115*(1), e31–e37.

Light, K. C., Smith, T. E., Johns, J. M., Brownley, K. A., Hofheimer, J. A., & Amico, J. A. (2000). Oxytocin responsivity in mothers of infants: A preliminary study of relationships with blood pressure during laboratory stress and normal ambulatory activity. *Health Psychology, 19*(6), 560–567.

Lillard, A. S., Lerner, M. D., Hopkins, E. J., Dore, R. A., Smith, E. D., & Palmquist, C. M. (2013). The impact of pretend play on children's development: A review of the evidence. *Psychological Bulletin, 139*(1), 1–34. doi: 10.1037/a0029321

Lim, M. M., Wang, Z., Olazábal, D. E., Ren, X., Terwilliger, E. F., & Young, L. J. (2004). Enhanced partner preference in a promiscuous species by manipulating the expression of a single gene. *Nature, 429,* 754–757.

Lim, M. M., & Young, L. J. (2006). Neuropeptidergic regulation of affiliative behavior and social bonding in animals. *Hormones and Behavior, 50*(4), 506–517.

Limosin, F., Rouillon, F., Payan, C., Cohen, J. M., & Strub, N. (2003). Prenatal exposure to influenza as a risk factor for adult schizophrenia. *Acta Psychiatrica Scandinavica, 107*(5), 331–335.

Lindberg, L. D. (1996). Women's decisions about breastfeeding and maternal employment. *Journal of Marriage and the Family, 58*(1), 239–251.

Lindsey, E. W., & Colwell, M. J. (2003). Preschoolers' emotional competence: Links to pretend and physical play. *Child Study Journal, 33*(1), 39–52.

Lindsey, E. W., & Mize, J. (2000). Parent-child physical and pretense play: Links to children's social competence. *Merrill-Palmer Quarterly, 46*(4), 565–591.

Lips, H. M. (2006). *A new psychology of women* (3rd ed.). New York, NY: McGraw-Hill.

Lisha, N. E., Grana, R., Sun, P., Rohrbach, L., Spruijt-Metz, D., Reifman, A., & Sussman, S. (2014). Evaluation of the psychometric properties of The Revised Inventory of the Dimensions of Emerging Adulthood (IDEA-R) in a sample of continuation high school students. *Evaluation & The Health Professions, 37*(2), 156–177. doi: 10.1177/0163278712452664

Loeber, R., & Hay, D. (1997). Key issues in the development of aggression and violence from childhood to early adulthood. *Annual Review of Psychology, 48,* 371–410.

Logsdon, M. C., Wisner, K., & Shanahan, B. (2007). Evidence on postpartum depression: 10 publications to guide nursing practice. *Issues in Mental Health Nursing, 28,* 445–451.

London, B., Downey, G., Bonica, C., & Paltin, I. (2007). Social causes and consequences of rejection sensitivity. *Journal of Research on Adolescence, 17*(3), 481–506.

Long, J. M., Mareno, N., Shabo, R., & Wilson, A. H. (2012). Overweight and obesity among White, Black, and Mexican American children: Implications for when to intervene. *Journal for Specialists in Pediatric Nursing, 17*(1), 41–50.

Lonigan, C. J., Purpura, D. J., Wilson, S. B., Walker, P. M., & Clancy-Menchetti, J. (2013). Evaluating the components of an emergent literacy intervention for preschool children at risk for reading difficulties. *Journal of Experimental Child Psychology, 114*(1), 111–130. doi: 10.1016/j.jecp.2012.08.010

López, F., Menez, M., & Hernández-Guzmán, L. (2005). Sustained attention during learning activities: An observational study with pre-school children. *Early Child Development and Care, 175*(2), 131–138.

Lord, C., Risi, S., DiLavore, P. S., Shulman, C., Thurm, A., & Pickles, A. (2006). Autism from 2 to 9 years of age. *Archives of General Psychiatry, 63*(6), 694–701.

Lorence, J., & Dworkin, A. G. (2006). Elementary grade retention in Texas and reading achievement among racial groups: 1994–2002. *Review of Policy Research, 23*(5), 999–1033.

Louv, R. (2008). *Last child in the woods: Saving our children from nature-deficit disorder.* Chapel Hill, NC: Algonquin Books.

Lovering, D. (2007). Smiley emoticon 25 years old? :-O. *The Hartford Courant*, p. E2.

Lowell, D., Carter, A., Godoy, L., Paulicin, B., & Briggs-Gowan, M. (2011). A randomized controlled trial of Child FIRST: A comprehensive home-based intervention translating research into early childhood practice. *Child Development, 82*(1), 193–208. doi: 10.1111/j .1467-8624.2010.01550.x

Luby, J. L. (2010). Preschool depression: The importance of identification of depression early in development. *Current Directions in Psychological Science, 19*(2), 91–95.

Lucas, S. R. (1999). *Tracking inequality. Stratification and mobility in American high schools.* New York, NY: Teachers College Press.

Luckey, A. J., & Fabes, R. A. (2005). Understanding nonsocial play in early childhood. *Early Childhood Education Journal, 33*(2), 67–72.

Ludwig, J., & Phillips, D. A. (2008). Long-term effects of Head Start on low-income children. *Annals of the New York Academy of Sciences, 1136*, 257–268.

Luhmann, M., Hofmann, W., Eid, M., & Lucas, R. E. (2012). Subjective well-being and adaptations to life-events: A meta-analysis on differences between cognitive and affective well-being. *Journal of Personality and Social Psychology, 102*, 592–615. doi: 10.1037/a0025948.

Luna, B., Paulsen, D. J., Padmanabhan, A., & Geier, C. (2013). The teenage brain: Cognitive control and motivation. *Current Directions in Psychological Science, 22*(2), 94–100.

Lydon-Rochelle, M. T., Cárdenas, V., Nelson, J. C., Holt, V. L., Gardella, C., & Easterling, T. R. (2007). Induction of labor in the absence of standard medical indications: Incidence and correlates. *Medical Care, 45*(6), 505–512.

Lykken, D. T., McGue, M., Tellegen, A., & Bouchard, T. J. (1992). Emergenesis: Genetic traits that may not run in families. *American Psychologist, 47*(12), 1565–1577.

Lynch, A. D., Lerner, R. M., & Leventhal, T. (2013). Adolescent academic achievement and school engagement: An examination of the role of school-wide peer culture. *Journal of Youth and Adolescence, 42*(1), 6–19.

Lyon, T. D., & Ahern, E. C. (2011). Disclosure of child sexual abuse. In J. E. B. Myers (Ed.), *The APSAC handbook on child maltreatment* (3d. ed., pp. 233–252). Newbury Park, CA: Sage.

Lyons-Ruth, K., & Jacobvitz, D. (2008). Attachment disorganization: Genetic factors, parenting contexts, and developmental transformation from infancy to adulthood. In J. Cassidy, & P. R. Shaver (Eds.), *Handbook of attachment: Theory, research, and clinical applications* (2nd ed., pp. 666–697). New York, NY: Guilford Press.

Ma, H., Unger, J. B., Chou, C., Sun, P., Palmer, P. H., Zhou, Y., . . . Johnson, C. A. (2008). Risk factors for adolescent smoking in urban and rural China: Findings from the China seven cities study. *Addictive Behaviors, 33*(8), 1081–1085.

Maccoby, E. E. (2002). Gender and group process: A developmental perspective. *Current Directions in Psychological Science, 11*(2), 54–58.

MacDorman, M. F. (2013). QuickStats: Infant mortality rates,* by race and Hispanic ethnicity of mother—United States, 2000, 2005, and 2009. *Morbidity and Mortality Weekly Report.* Retrieved from http://www.cdc.gov/ mmwr/preview/mmwrhtml/mm6205a6.htm

MacDorman, M. F., Hoyert, D. L., & Mathews, T. J. (2013). Recent declines in infant mortality in the United States, 2005–2011. *NCHS Data Brief, 120*, 1–7. Retrieved from http://www.cdc.gov/nchs/data/databriefs/db120.htm

MacDorman, M. F., Mathews, T. J., & Declercq E. (2014). Trends in out-of-hospital births in the United States, 1990–2012. NCHS data brief, no. 144. Hyattsville, MD: National Center for Health Statistics. Retrieved from http://www.cdc.gov/nchs/data/databriefs/db144.htm

MacFarlane, A. (1975). Olfaction in the development of social preferences in the human neonate. *Ciba Foundation Symposium, 33*, 103–117.

MacKenzie, M. J., Nicklas, E., Waldfogel, J., & Brooks-Gunn, J. (2013). Spanking and child development across the first decade of Life. *Pediatrics, 132*, e1118–e1125.

MacMillan, R., McMorris, B. J., & Kruttschnitt, C. (2004). Linked lives: Stability and change in maternal circumstances and trajectories of antisocial behavior in children. *Child Development, 75*(1), 205–220.

MacNeil, G. A., & Newell, J. M. (2004). School bullying: Who, why, and what to do. *Prevention Researcher, 11*(3), 15–17.

Madon, S., Guyll, M., Willard, J., & Scherr, K. (2011). Self-fulfilling prophecies: Mechanisms, power, and links to social problems. *Social and Personality Psychology Compass, 5*(8), 578–590.

Madsen, S. D., & Collins, W. (2011). The salience of adolescent romantic experiences for romantic relationship qualities in young adulthood. *Journal of Research on Adolescence, 21*(4), 789–801.

Mahler, M. S., Bergman, A., & Pine, F. (2000). *The psychological birth of the human infant: Symbiosis and individuation.* New York, NY: Basic Books.

Mahler, M. S., Pine, F., & Bergman, A. (1975). *The psychological birth of the human infant.* New York, NY: Basic Books.

Mahoney, J. L., Harris, A. L., & Eccles, J. S. (2006). Organized activity participation, positive youth development, and the over-scheduling hypothesis. *Society for Research in Child Development Social Policy Report, 20*(4), 3–30.

Mahoney, J. L., Stattin, H., & Lord, H. (2004). Unstructured youth recreation centre participation and antisocial behaviour development: Selection influences and the moderating role of antisocial peers. *International Journal of Behavioral Development, 28*(6), 553–560.

Makel, M. C., Plucker, J. A., & Hegarty, B. (2012). Replications in psychology research: How often do they really occur? *Perspectives on Psychological Science, 7*(6), 537–542. doi: 10.1177/1745691612460688

Malanga, C. J., & Kosofsky, B. E. (2003). Does drug abuse beget drug abuse? Behavioral analysis of addiction liability in animal models of prenatal drug exposure. *Developmental Brain Research, 147*(1–2), 47–57.

Malina, R. M., Bouchard, C., & Oded, B. (2004). *Growth maturation and physical activity.* Champaign, IL: Human Kinetics.

Mampe, B., Friederici, A. D., Christophe, A., & Wermke, K. (2009). Newborns' cry melody is shaped by their native language. *Current Biology, 19*(23), 1994–1997.

Management of Acute Malnutrition in Infants (MAMI) Project. (2009). Management of Acute Malnutrition in Infants (MAMI) Project: Summary Report. Retrieved from http://www.actionagainsthunger.org/publication/2009/10/summary-report-management-acute-malnutrition-infants-mami-project

Mancillas, A. (2006). Challenging the stereotypes about only children: A Review of the literature and implications for practice. *Journal of Counseling & Development, 84*(3), 268–275.

Mandara, J., Gaylord-Harden, N. K., Richards, M. H., & Ragsdale, B. L. (2009). The effects of changes in racial identity and self-esteem on changes in African American adolescents' mental health. *Child Development, 80*(6), 1660–1675.

Mandel, S., & Sharlin, S. A. (2006). The non-custodial father: His involvement in his children's lives and the connection between his role and the ex-wife's, child's and father's perception of that role. *Journal of Divorce & Remarriage, 45*(1/2), 79–95.

Mandela, N. (1994). *Long walk to freedom.* Boston, MA: Little, Brown.

Manlove, J., Terry-Humen, E., Papillo, A. R., Franzetta, K., Williams, S., & Ryan, S. (2002). Preventing teenage pregnancy, childbearing, and sexually transmitted diseases: What the research shows. *Child Trends Research Brief, American Teens Series.* Washington, DC: Child Trends and the Knight Foundation.

March of Dimes. (2008). *The cost of prematurity to U.S. employers. Retrieved* from http://marchofdimes.com/peristats/pdfdocs/cts/ThomsonAnalysis2008_SummaryDocument_final121208.pdf

March of Dimes. (2013). *Preterm: United States, 2000–2010.* Retrieved from http://www.marchofdimes.com/peristats/ViewSubtopic.aspx?reg=99&top=3&stop=60&lev=1&slev=1&obj=1&dv=ms

March of Dimes. (2014a). *Genetic counseling.* Retrieved from http://www.marchofdimes.org/pregnancy/genetic-counseling.aspx

March of Dimes. (2014b). *Peristats.* Retrieved from http://www.marchofdimes.org/peristats/ViewSubtopic.aspx?reg=99&top=3&stop=60&lev=1&slev=1&obj=1&dv=ms

March, P. D., & Schub, T. (2013). *Sexual abuse in children and adolescents: Females.* Glendale, CA: Cinahl Information Systems.

Marcia, J. E. (1966). Development and validation of ego-identity status. *Journal of Personality and Social Psychology, 3*(5), 551–558.

Marcus, S., & Heringhausen, J. (2009). Depression in child-bearing women: When depression complicates pregnancy. *Primary Care, 36*(1), 151.

Markman, E. M. (1990). Constraints children place on word meanings. *Cognitive Science, 14*(1), 57–77.

Markovits, H., Benenson, J., & Dolenszky, E. (2001). Evidence that children and adolescents have internal models of peer interactions that are gender differentiated. *Child Development, 72*(3), 879–886.

Markowitz, L. E., Hariri, S., Lin, C., Dunne, E. F., Steinau, M., McQuillan, G., & Unger, E. R. (2013). Reduction in Human Papillomavirus (HPV) prevalence among young women following HPV vaccine introduction in the United States, National Health and Nutrition Examination Surveys, 2003–2010. *Journal of Infectious Diseases, 208,* 385–393.

Marks, A. K., Szalacha, L. A., Lamarre, M., Boyd, M. J., & Coll, C. G. (2007). Emerging ethnic identity and interethnic group social preferences in middle childhood: Findings from the Children of Immigrants Development in Context (CIDC) study. *International Journal of Behavioral Development, 31*(5), 501–513.

Marks, L. (2012). Same-sex parenting and children's outcomes: A closer examination of the American psychological association's brief on lesbian and gay parenting. *Social Science Research, 41*(4), 735–751.

Markstrom, C. A., & Iborra, A. (2003). Adolescent identity formation and rites of passage: The Navajo Kinaalda ceremony for girls. *Journal of Research on Adolescence, 13*(4), 399–425.

Marlier, L., Schaal, B., & Soussignan, R. (1998). Neonatal responsiveness to the odor of amniotic and lacteal fluids: A test of perinatal chemosensory continuity. *Child Development, 69*(3), 611–623.

Marsh, H. W., Seaton, M., Trautwein, R., Ludtke, O., Hau, K. T., O'Mara, A. J., & Craven, R. G. (2008). The big-fish-little-pond-effect stands up to critical scrutiny: Implications for theory, methodology, and future research. *Educational Psychology Review, 20*(3), 319–350.

Martin, C. L., & Fabes, R. A. (2001). The stability and consequences of young children's same-sex peer interactions. *Developmental Psychology, 37*(3), 431–446. doi: 10.1037/0012-1649.37.3.431

Martin, J. A., Hamilton, B. E., & Osterman, M. J. K. (2012). Three Decades of Twin Births in the United States, 1980–2009. *NCHS Data Brief, No. 80.* Retrieved from http://www.cdc.gov/nchs/data/databriefs/db80.pdf

Martin, J. A., Hamilton, B. E., Osterman, M. J. K., Curtin, S. C., & Mathews, T. J. (2013). Births: Final data for 2012. *National vital statistics reports, 62*(9). Hyattsville, MD:

National Center for Health Statistics. Retrieved from http://www.cdc.gov/nchs/data/nvsr/nvsr62/nvsr62_09.pdf

Martin, J., Hiscock, H., Hardy, P., Davey, B., & Wake, M. (2007). Adverse associations of infant and child sleep problems and parent health: An Australian population study. *Pediatrics, 119*(5), 947–955.

Martin, J., & Sokol, B. (2011). Generalized others and imaginary audiences: A neo-Meadian approach to adolescent egocentrism. *New Ideas In Psychology, 29*(3), 364–375.

Martin, M. T., Emery, R. E., & Peris, T. S. (2004). Single-parent families—Risk, resilience and change. In M. Coleman & L. H. Ganong (Eds.), *Handbook of contemporary families* (pp. 282–301). Thousand Oaks, CA: Sage.

Martinez, C. R., & Forgatch, M. S. (2002). Adjusting to change: Linking family structure transitions with parenting and boys' adjustment. *Journal of Family Psychology, 16*, 107–117.

Martinez, I., & Garcia, J. F. (2008). Internalization of values and self-esteem among Brazilian teenagers from authoritative, indulgent, authoritarian, and neglectful homes. *Family Therapy, 35*(1), 43–59.

Martínez, R. S., Aricak, O., Graves, M. N., Peters-Myszak, J., & Nellis, L. (2011). Changes in perceived social support and socioemotional adjustment across the elementary to junior high school transition. *Journal of Youth and Adolescence, 40*(5), 519–530.

Martins, A., & Calheiros, M. M. (2012). Construction of a self-complexity scale for adolescents. *Psychological Assessment, 24*(4), 973–982.

Martins, C., & Gaffan, E. A. (2000). Effects of early maternal depression on patterns of infant-mother attachment: A meta-analytic investigation. *Journal of Child Psychology and Psychiatry, 41*(6), 737–746.

Martins, N., & Harrison, K. (2012). Racial and gender differences in the relationship between children's television use and self-esteem: A longitudinal panel study. *Communication Research, 39*(3), 338–57.

Maslova, E., Bhattacharya, S., Lin, S., & Michels, K. (2010). Caffeine consumption during pregnancy and risk of preterm birth: A meta-analysis. *American Journal of Clinical Nutrition, 92*(5), 1120–1132.

Masoni, M. A., Trimarchi, G., dePunzio, C., & Fioretti, P. (1994). The couvade syndrome. *Journal of Psychosomatic Obstetrics and Gynaecology, 15*(3), 125–131.

Masten, A. S. (2001). Ordinary magic: Resilience process in development. *American Psychologist, 56*(3), 227–238.

Mathematical Association of America. (1998). *Birthday surprises.* Retrieved from http://www.maa.org/mathland/mathtrek_11_23_98.html

Matsumoto, D. (1992). American-Japanese cultural differences in the recognition of universal facial expressions. *Journal of Cross-Cultural Psychology, 23*(1), 72–84.

Matsumoto, D. (2006). Are cultural differences in emotion regulation mediated by personality traits? *Journal of Cross-Cultural Psychology, 37*(4), 421–437.

Matsumoto, D., & Assar, M. (1992). The effects of language on judgments of universal facial expressions of emotion. *Journal of Nonverbal Behavior, 16*(2), 85–99.

Matsumoto, D., Consolacion, T., & Yamada, H. (2002). American-Japanese cultural differences in judgments of emotional expressions of different intensities. *Cognition and Emotion, 16*(6), 721–747.

Matsumoto, D., & Juang, L. (2004). *Culture and psychology* (3rd ed.). Belmont, CA: Wadsworth/Thomson.

Matte-Gagné, C., & Bernier, A. (2011). Prospective relations between maternal autonomy support and child executive functioning: Investigating the mediating role of child language ability. *Journal of Experimental Child Psychology, 110*(4), 611–625. doi: 10.1016/j.jecp.2011.06.006

Maughan, B., Collishaw, S., & Stringaris, A. (2013). Depression in childhood and adolescence. *Journal of the Canadian Academy of Child and Adolescent Psychiatry / Journal De L'académie Canadienne De Psychiatrie De L'enfant Et De L'adolescent, 22*(1), 35–40.

Maurer, D., & Maurer, C. (1988). *The world of the newborn.* New York, NY: Basic Books.

May, P. A., Blankenship, J., Marais, A., Gossage, J., Kalberg, W. O., Joubert, B., . . . Seedat, S. (2013). Maternal alcohol consumption producing fetal alcohol spectrum disorders (FASD): Quantity, frequency, and timing of drinking. *Drug and Alcohol Dependence, 133*(2), 502–512. doi: 10.1016/j.drugalcdep.2013.07.013

Mayo Clinic Staff. (1998–2014). *Concussion.* Retrieved from http://www.mayoclinic.org/diseases-conditions/concussion/basics/definition/con-20019272

Mayo Clinic Staff. (2008). *Children's illness: Top 5 causes of missed school.* Retrieved from http://www.mayoclinic.com/print/childrens-conditions/CC00059/METHOD=print

Mayo Clinic Staff. (2010). *Childhood asthma.* Retrieved from http://www.mayoclinic.com/health/childhood-asthma/DS00849

Mayo Clinic Staff. (2011). *Reye's syndrome.* Retrieved from http://www.mayoclinic.org/diseases-conditions/reyes-syndrome/basics/definition/con-20020083

Mayo Clinic Staff. (2012a). *Antidepressants: Safe during pregnancy?* Retrieved from http://www.mayoclinic.org/healthy-living/pregnancy-week-by-week/in-depth/antidepressants/art-20046420

Mayo Clinic Staff. (2012b). *Strep throat.* Retrieved from http://www.mayoclinic.org/diseases-conditions/strep-throat/basics/definition/con-20022811

Mayo Clinic Staff. (2013). *Chronic stress puts your health at risk.* Retrieved from http://www.mayoclinic.com/health/stress/SR00001

Mayo Clinic Staff. (2014). *Sudden infant death syndrome (SIDS).* Retrieved from http://www.mayoclinic.org/diseases-conditions/sudden-infant-death-syndrome/basics/definition/con-20020269

McCabe, L. A., & Brooks-Gunn, J. (2007). With a little help from my friends? Self-regulation in groups of young children. *Infant Mental Health Journal, 28*(6), 584–605.

McCarthy, F., O'Keeffe, L., Khashan, A., North, R., Poston, L., McCowan, L., . . . Kenny, L. (2013). Association between maternal alcohol consumption in early pregnancy and pregnancy outcomes. *Obstetrics & Gynecology, 122*(4), 830–837. doi: 10.1097/AOG.0b013e3182a6b226

McClain, M., & Pfeiffer, S. (2012). Identification of gifted students in the United States today: A look at state definitions, policies, and practices. *Journal of Applied School Psychology, 28*(1), 59–88.

McCleery, J., Akshoomoff, N., Dobkins, K., & Carver, L. (2009). Atypical face versus object processing and hemispheric asymmetries in 10-month-old infants at risk for autism. *Biological Psychiatry, 66*(10), 950–957. doi: 10.1016/j.biopsych.2009.07.031

McClellan, J., & Stock, S. (2013). Practice parameter for the assessment and treatment of children and adolescents with schizophrenia. *Journal of the American Academy of Child & Adolescent Psychiatry, 52*(9), 976–990.

McClelland, M. M., Acock, A. C., Piccinin, A., Rhea, S. A., & Stallings, M. C. (2013). Relations between preschool attention span-persistence and age 25 educational outcomes. *Early Childhood Research Quarterly, 28*(2), 314–324.

McClun, L. A., & Merrell, K. W. (1998). Relationship of perceived parenting styles, locus of control orientation, and self-concept among junior high age students. *Psychology in the Schools, 35*(4), 381–390.

McClure, M. M., & Fitch, R. H. (2005). Hormones. In N. J. Salkind (Ed.), *Encyclopedia of human development* (pp. 646–649). Thousand Oaks, CA: Sage.

McCoy, K., Cummings, E. M., & Davies, P. T. (2009). Constructive and destructive marital conflict, emotional security and children's prosocial behavior. *Journal of Child Psychology and Psychiatry, 50*(3), 270–279.

McCrink, K., & Wynn, K. (2004). Large-Number Addition and Subtraction by 9-Month-Old Infants. *Psychological Science, 15*(11), 776–781. doi: 10.1111/j.0956-7976.2004.00755.x

McCurdy, L., Winterbottom, K., Mehta, S., & Roberts, J. (2010). Using nature and outdoor activity to improve children's health. *Current Problems in Pediatric and Adolescent Health Care, 40*(5), 102–117.

McDonell, M. G., & McClellan, J. M. (2007). Early-onset schizophrenia. In E. J. Mash & R. A. Barkley (Eds.), *Assessment of childhood disorders* (pp. 526–550). New York, NY: Guilford Press.

McElwain, N. L., Booth-LaForce, C., Lansford, J. E., Wu, X., & Dyer, W. J. (2008). A process model of attachment-friend linkages: Hostile attribution biases, language ability, and mother-child affective mutuality as intervening mechanisms. *Child Development, 79*(6), 1891–1906.

McGivern, R. F., Andersen, J., Byrd, D., Mutter, K.L., & Reilly, J. (2002). Cognitive efficiency on a match to sample task decreases at the onset of puberty in children. *Brain and Cognition, 50*, 73–89.

McGlone, M. S., & Aronson, J. (2006). Sterotype threat, identity salience and spatial reasoning. *Journal of Applied Developmental Psychology, 27*, 486–493.

McGue, M., Elkins, I., Walden, B., & Iacono, W. G. (2005). Perceptions of the parent-adolescent relationship: A longitudinal investigation. *Developmental Psychology, 41*(6), 972–984.

McGuffin, P., Riley, B., & Plomin, R. (2001). Genomics and behavior: Toward behavioral genomics. *Science, 291*(5507), 1232–1249.

McHale, S. M., Kim, J., Whiteman, S., & Crouter, A. C. (2004). Links between sex-typed time use in middle childhood and gender development in early adolescence. *Developmental Psychology, 40*(5), 868–881.

McHale, S. M., Whiteman, S. D., Kim, J., & Crouter, A. C. (2007). Characteristics and correlates of sibling relationships in two-parent African American families. *Journal of Family Psychology 21*(2), 227–235.

McIntosh, J., Smyth, B., Kelaher, M., Wells, Y., & Long, C. (2010). *Post-separation parenting arrangements and developmental outcomes for infants and children.* Canberra, Australia: Attorney General's Department.

McKeachie, W., & Sims, B. (2004). Review of *Educational Psychology: A century of contributions* [A project of Division 15 (Educational Psychology) of the American Psychological Association]. *Educational Psychology Review, 16*(3), 283–298.

McKim, M. K., Cramer, K. M., Stuart, B., & O'Connor, D. L. (1999). Infant care decisions and attachment security: The Canadian Transition to Child Care Study. *Canadian Journal of Behavioural Science, 31*(2), 92–106.

McKown, D., & Weinstein, R. S. (2008). Teacher expectations, classroom context, and the achievement gap. *Journal of School Psychology, 46*(3), 235–261.

McLanahan, S., & Carlson, M. S. (2004). Fathers in fragile families. In M. E. Lamb (Ed.), *The role of the father in child development* (4th ed., pp. 368–396). Hoboken, NJ: Wiley.

McLoyd, V. C. (1998). Socioeconomic disadvantage and child development. *American Psychologist, 53*(2), 185–204.

McLoyd, V. C. (2000). Childhood poverty. In A. E. Kazdin (Ed.), *Encyclopedia of psychology* (pp. 251–257). New York, NY: Oxford University Press.

McLoyd, V. C., Hill, N. E., & Dodge, K. A. (2005). Ecological and cultural diversity in African American family life. In V. C. McLoyd, N. E. Hill, & K. A. Dodge (Eds.), *African American family life* (pp. 3–20). New York, NY: Guilford Press.

McMahon, R. J., & Kotler, J. S. (2006). Conduct problems. In D. A. Wolfe & E. J. Mash (Eds.), *Behavioral and emotional disorders in adolescents* (pp. 153–225). New York, NY: Guilford Press.

McManus, I. C. (2002). *Right hand, left hand: The origins of asymmetry in brains, bodies, atoms and cultures.* London, UK/Cambridge, MA: Weidenfeld & Nicolson/Harvard University Press.

McPherson, F. (2001). *Elaborating the information for better remembering*. Retrieved from http://www.memory-key.com/improving/strategies/study/elaborating

Mead, S. (2006). Evidence suggests otherwise: The truth about boys and girls. *Education Sector*. Retrieved from http://www.educationsector.org/usr_doc/ESO_BoysAndGirls.pdf

Meaney, M. J. (2004). The nature of nurture: Maternal effects and chromatin remodeling. In J. T. Cacioppo & G. G. Bentson (Eds.), *Essays in social neuroscience* (pp. 1–14). Cambridge, MA: MIT Press.

Meaney, M. J. (2010). Epigenetics and the biological definition of gene x environment interactions. *Child Development, 81*, 41–79.

Mecca, A. M., Smelser, N. J., & Vasconcellos, J. (1989). *The social importance of self-esteem*. Berkeley: University of California Press.

Meeus, W. (2011). The study of adolescent identity formation 2000–2010: A review of longitudinal research. *Journal of Research on Adolescents, 21*(1), 75–94.

Meeus, W., van de Schoot, R., Keijsers, L., & Branje, S. (2012). Identity statuses as developmental trajectories: A five-wave longitudinal study in early-to-middle and middle-to-late adolescents. *Journal of Youth & Adolescence, 41*(8), 1008–1021.

Meeus, W., van de Schoot, R., Keijsers, L., Schwartz, S. J., & Branje, S. (2010). On the progression and stability of adolescent identity formation: A five-wave longitudinal study in early-to-middle and middle-to-late adolescence. *Child Development, 81*(5), 1565–1581.

Mehal, J. M., Esposito, D. H., Holman, R. C., Tate, J. E., Callinan, L. S., & Parashar, U. D. (2012). Risk factors for diarrhea-associated infant mortality in the United States, 2005–2007. *Pediatric Infectious Diseases Journal, 31*(7), 717–721.

Meier, A., & Allen, G. (2009). Romantic relationships from adolescence to young adulthood: Evidence from the National Longitudinal Study of Adolescent Health. *Sociological Quarterly, 50*(2), 308–335.

Meltzoff, A. N. (1999). Born to learn: What infants learn from watching us. In N. Fox & J. G. Worhol (Eds.), *The Role of Early Experience in Infant Development*. Skillman, NJ: Pediatric Institute.

Meltzoff, A. N., & Moore, M. K. (1997). Explaining facial imitation: A theoretical model. *Early Development and Parenting, 6*(3–4), 179–192.

Menacker, F., & Hamilton, B. E. (2010). Recent trends in cesarean delivery in the United States. *NCHS Data Brief, 35*. Hyattsville, MD: National Center for Health Statistics.

Mendle, J., Turkheimer, E., & Emery, R. E. (2007). Detrimental psychological outcomes associated with early pubertal timing in adolescent girls. *Developmental Review, 27*(2), 151–171. doi: 10.1016/j.dr.2006.11.001

Mendola, K. (1999). *Natural childbirth options*. Retrieved from http://www.webmd.com/baby/guide/natural-childbirth-options

Menéndez, R. (Director). (1988). *Stand and deliver* [Motion picture]. United States: American Playhouse.

Meng, Y., Babey, S. H., & Wolstein, J. (2012). Asthma-related school absenteeism and school concentration of low-income students in California. *Preventing Chronic Disease, 9*, 110312. doi: http://dx.doi.org/10.5888/pcd9.110312

Menken, K., & Solorza, C. (2014). No child left bilingual: Accountability and the elimination of bilingual education programs in New York City schools. *Educational Policy, 28*(1), 96–125.

Menn, L., & Stoel-Gammon, C. (2005). Phonological development: Learning sounds and sound patterns. In J. B. Gleason (Ed.), *The development of language* (6th ed., pp. 39–61). Boston, MA: Pearson.

Mennella, J. A., Griffin, C. E., & Beauchamp, G. K. (2004). Flavor programming during infancy. *Pediatrics, 113*(4), 840–845.

Mennella, J. A., Pepino, M. Y., & Reed, D. R. (2005). Genetic and environmental determinants of bitter perception and sweet preferences. *Pediatrics, 115*(2), e216–e222.

Mensah, F. K., Bayer, J. K., Wake, M., Carlin, J. B., Allen, N. B., & Patton, G. C. (2013). Early puberty and childhood social and behavioral adjustment. *Journal of Adolescent Health, 53*(1), 118–124.

MENTOR. (2012). *National Mentoring Partnership*. Retrieved from http://www.mentoring.org/

Merck Manual. (2008). *Function and dysfunction of the cerebral lobes*. Retrieved from http://www.merck.com/mmpe/sec16/ch210/ch210a.html#sec16-ch210-ch210a-313

Merck Manual Home Health Handbook. (2013). *Overview of chromosomal disorders*. Retrieved from http://www.merckmanuals.com/home/childrens_health_issues/chromosomal_and_genetic_abnormalities/overview_of_chromosomal_disorders.html

Merrell, K. W., Cohn, B. P., & Tom, K. M. (2011). Development and validation of a teacher report measure for assessing social-emotional strengths of children and adolescents. *School Psychology Review, 40*(2), 226–241.

Merriam-Webster. (2010). *Heteronomous*. Retrieved from http://www.merriam-webster.com/dictionary/heteronomous

Mickalide, A. D., & Hansen, L. M. (2012). *Coaching our kids to fewer injuries: A report on youth sports safety*. Washington, DC: Safe Kids Worldwide. Retrieved from http://www.safekids.org/assets/docs/safety-basics/sports/2012-sports.pdf

Mielke, K. W. (2001). A review of research on the educational and social impact of *Sesame Street*. In S. M. Fisch & R. T. Truglio (Eds.), *"G" is for growing—Thirty years of research on children and* Sesame Street (pp. 83–96). Mahwah, NJ: Erlbaum.

Mikami, A. Y., Lerner, M. D., & Lun, J. (2010). Social context influences on children's rejection by their peers. *Child Development Perspectives, 4*(2), 123–130.

Miller, A. M., & Harwood, R. L. (2002). The cultural organization of parenting: Change and stability of behavior patterns during feeding and social play across the first year of life. *Parenting: Science and Practice, 2*(3), 241–272.

Miller, N. B., Cowan, P. A., Cowan, C. P., Hetherington, E. M., & Clingempeel, W. G. (1993). Externalizing in preschoolers and early adolescents: A cross-study replication of a family model. *Developmental Psychology, 29*(1), 3–18.

Miller, P. H., Slawinski Blessing, J., & Schwartz, S. (2006). Gender differences in high school students' views about science. *International Journal of Science Education, 28*(4), 363–381.

Miller-Perrin, C. L., & Perrin, R. D. (1999). *Child maltreatment: An introduction.* Thousand Oaks, CA: Sage.

Milteer, R. M., & Ginsburg, K. R. (2012). The importance of play in promoting healthy child development and maintaining strong parent-child bond: Focus on children in poverty. *Pediatrics, 129*(1), 204–213.

Mischel, W., & Ayduk, O. (2004). Willpower in a cognitive-affective processing system: The dynamics of delay of gratification. In R. F. Baumeister & K. D. Vohs (Eds.), *Handbook of self-regulation: Research, theory, and applications* (pp. 99–129). New York, NY: Guilford Press.

Mischel, W., Ayduk, O., Berman, M. G., Casey, B. J., Gotlib, I. H., Jonides, J., . . . Shoda, Y. (2011). 'Willpower' over the life span: Decomposing self-regulation. *Social Cognitive and Affective Neuroscience, 6*(2), 252–256. doi: 10.1093/scan/nsq081

Mitchell, J. E., Peterson, C. B., Myers, T., & Wonderlich, S. (2001). Combining pharmacotherapy and psychotherapy in the treatment of patients with eating disorders. *Psychiatric Clinics of North America, 24*(2), 315–323.

Mitchell, M. B., Kuczynski, L., Tubbs, C. Y., & Ross, C. (2010). We care about care: Advice by children in care for children in care, foster parents and child welfare workers about the transition into foster care. *Child and Family Social Work, 15,* 176–185.

Miyake, K., & Yamazaki, K. (1995). Self-conscious emotions, child rearing, and child psychopathology in Japanese culture. In J. P. Tangney & K. W. Fischer (Eds.), *Self-conscious emotions: The psychology of shame, guilt, embarrassment, and pride* (pp. 488–504). New York, NY: Guilford Press.

Moffitt, T. E., & Caspi, A. (2001). Childhood predictors differentiate life-course persistent and adolescence-limited antisocial pathways among males and females. *Development and Psychopathology, 13*(2), 355–375.

Moilanen, K. L., Shaw, D. S., & Maxwell, K. L. (2010). Developmental cascades: Externalizing, internalizing, and academic competence from middle childhood to early adolescence. *Development and Psychopathology, 22*(3), 635–653. doi: 10.1017/S0954579410000337

Moll, H., & Tomasello, M. (2006). Level I perspective-taking at 24 months of age. *British Journal of Developmental Psychology, 24*(3), 603–613.

Monahan, K. C., Lee, J. M., & Steinberg, L. (2011). Revisiting the impact of part-time work on adolescent adjustment: Distinguishing between selection and socialization using propensity score matching. *Child Development, 82*(1), 96–112.

Montgomery, M. J. (2005). Psychosocial intimacy and identity: From early adolescence to emerging adulthood. *Journal of Adolescent Research, 20*(3), 346–374.

Moon, C., Lagercrantz, H., & Kuhl, P. (2013). Language experienced in utero affects vowel perception after birth: A two-country study. *Acta Paediatrica, 102*(2), 156–160.

Moon, W. J., Provenzale, J., Sarikaya, B., Ihn, Y. K., Morlese, J., Chen, S., & DeBellis, M. D. (2011). Diffusion tensor imaging assessment of white matter maturation in childhood and adolescence. *American Journal of Roentgenology, 197*(3), 704–712.

Moore, F. (2102, October 5). *GLAAD's 'Where We Are On TV' report finds LGBT television characters at record high.* Retrieved from http://www.huffingtonpost.com/2012/10/05/glaads-where-we-are-on-tv-report-gay-characters_n_1942313.html

Moore, K. L., & Persaud, T. V. N. (2003). *The developing human: Clinically oriented embryology* (7th ed.). Philadelphia, PA: W. B. Saunders.

Moore, M. J., White, G. L., & Moore, D. L. (2007). Association of relative backpack weight with reported pain, pain sites, medical utilization, and lost school time in children and adolescents. *Journal of School Health, 77,* 232–239.

Moore, M., & Meltzoff, A. N. (2008). Factors affecting infants' manual search for occluded objects and the genesis of object permanence. *Infant Behavior & Development, 31*(2), 168–180.

Moran, E. (2000). Dick and Jane readers. In S. Pendergast & T. Pendergast (Eds.), *St. James encyclopedia of popular culture* (Vol. 1, pp. 700–701). Detroit, MI: St. James Press.

Morgan, S., Koren, G., & Bozzo, P. (2013). Is caffeine consumption safe during pregnancy? *Canadian Family Physician, 59*(4), 361–362.

Morgane, P. J., Austin-LaFrance, R., Brozino, J. D., Tonkiss, J., Diaz-Cintra, S., Cintra, L., . . . Galler, J. R. (1993). Prenatal malnutrition and development of the brain. *Neuroscience and Biobehavioral Reviews, 17*(1), 91–128.

Morris, S. A., Bailis, S. A., & Wiswell, T. E. (2014). Circumcision rates in the United States: Rising or falling? What effect might the New Affirmative Pediatric Policy Statement have? *Mayo Clinic Proceedings, 89*(5), 677–686.

Moss, E., Cyr, C., Bureau, J., Tarabulsy, G. M., & Dubois-Comtois, K. (2005). Stability of attachment during the preschool period. *Developmental Psychology, 41*(5), 773–783.

Moustafa, M. (2001). Contemporary reading instruction. In T. Loveless (Ed.), *The great curriculum debate* (pp. 247–267). Washington, DC: The Brookings Institution Press.

Mueller, F. O., & Cantu, R. C. (2011). *Catastrophic sports injury research*. Retrieved from http://www.unc.edu/depts/nccsi/2011Allsport.pdf

Mundy, P. (2003). The neural basis of social impairments in autism: The role of the dorsal medial-frontal cortex and anterior cingulate system. *Journal of Child Psychology and Psychiatry, 44*(6), 793–809.

Munhall, P. L. (2007). *Nursing research: A qualitative perspective* (4th ed.). Sudbury, MA: Jones & Bartlett.

Munroe, R. L., & Romney, A. K. (2006). Gender and age differences in same-sex aggregation and social behavior: A four-culture study. *Journal of Cross-Cultural Psychology, 37*, 3–19.

Munsch, J., & Blyth, D. A. (1993). An analysis of the functional nature of adolescents' supportive relationships. *Journal of Early Adolescence, 13*(2), 132–153.

Munsch, J., Woodward, J., & Darling, N. (1995). Children's perceptions of their relationships with coresiding and non-custodial fathers. *Journal of Divorce and Remarriage, 23*(1–2), 39–54.

Murch, S. H., Anthony, A., Casson, D. H., Malik, M., Berelowitz, M., Dhillon, A. P., . . . Walker-Smith, J. A. (2004). Retraction of an interpretation. *Lancet, 363*(9411), 750.

Murnen, S. K., Smolak, L., Mills, J., & Good, L. (2003). Thin, sexy women and strong, muscular men: Grade-school children's responses to objectified images of women and men. *Sex Roles, 49*(9–10), 427–437.

Murray, A. (2012). The relationship of parenting style to academic achievement in middle childhood. *The Irish Journal of Psychology, 33*(4), 137–152. doi: 10.1080/03033910.2012.724645

Murray, R., & Ramstetter, C. (2013). The crucial role of recess in school. *Pediatrics, 131*(1), 183–188. doi: 10.1542/peds.2012-2993

Mustanski, B., Birkett, M., Greene, G. J., Rosario, M., Bostwick, W., & Everett, B. G. (2014). The association between sexual orientation, identity and behavior across race/ethnicity, sex, and age in a probability sample of high school students. *American Journal of Public Health, 104*(2), 237–244.

Muzzatti, B., & Agnoli, F. (2007). Gender and mathematics: Attitudes and stereotype threat susceptibility in Italian children. *Developmental Psychology, 43*(3), 747–759.

Myers, B. J. (1984). Mother-infant bonding: Rejoinder to Kennell and Klaus. *Developmental Review, 4*(3), 283–288.

Naigles, L. R., Hoff, E., Vear, D., Tomasello, M., Brandt, S., Waxman, S. R., & Childers, J. B. (2009). Flexibility in early verb use: Evidence from a multiple-N diary study: VII. General discussion. *Monographs of the Society for Research in Child Development, 74*(2), 91–104.

Naimi, T. S., Brewer, R. D., Mokdad, A., Clark, D., Serdula, M. K., & Marks, J. S. (2003). Binge drinking among U.S. adults. *Journal of the American Medical Association, 289*(1), 70–75.

Nakagawa, M., Lamb, M. E., & Miyaki, K. (1992). Antecedents and correlates of the Strange Situation behavior of Japanese infants. *Journal of Cross-Cultural Psychology, 23*(3), 300–310.

Nansel, T. R., Overpeck, M., Pilla, R. S., Ruan, W. J., Simons-Morton, B., & Scheidt, P. (2001). Bullying behaviors among U.S. youth: Prevalence and association with psychosocial adjustment. *Journal of the American Medical Association, 285*(16), 2094–2100, 2141–2142.

Nathanson, A. I. (1999). Identifying and explaining the relationship between parental mediation and children's aggression. *Communication Research, 26*, 124–143.

National Association for Sport and Physical Education. (2009). *Active start: A statement of physical activity guidelines for children birth to five years* (2nd ed.). Reston, VA: Author.

National Cancer Institute. (2010). *Human papillomavirus (HPV) vaccines*. Retrieved from http://www.cancer.gov/cancertopics/factsheet/Prevention/HPV-vaccine

National Cancer Institute Fact Sheet. (2006). *Gene therapy for cancer: Questions and answers*. Retrieved from http://www.cancer.gov/cancertopics/factsheet/Therapy/gene

National Center for Children in Poverty. (2014). *Juvenile justice in the U.S. Facts for Policymakers*. Retrieved from http://www.nccp.org/publications/pub_1038.html

National Center for Education Statistics. (2004a). *Educational attainment of high school dropouts 8 years later*. Retrieved from http://nces.ed.gov/pubs2005/2005026.pdf

National Center for Education Statistics. (2004b). *Trends in educational equity for girls and women: 2004* [NCES 2000–021]. U.S. Department of Education. Washington, DC: U.S. Government Printing Office.

National Center for Education Statistics. (2012). *The nation's report card: Writing 2011*. Retrieved from http://nces.ed.gov/nationsreportcard/pdf/main2011/2012470.pdf

National Center for Education Statistics. (2013a). *Institutional retention and graduation rates for undergraduate students (NCES 2013-037)*. Retrieved from http://nces.ed.gov/programs/coe/indicator_cva.asp

National Center for Education Statistics. (2013b). *The nation's report card: A first look: 2013 mathematics and reading (NCES 2014-451)*. Washington, DC: Institute of Education Sciences, U.S. Department of Education.

National Center for Environmental Health. (2011). *Asthma in the US: Growing every year*. Retrieved from http://www.cdc.gov/VitalSigns/pdf/2011-05-vitalsigns.pdf

National Center for Health Statistics. (2011). *Teenagers in the United States: Sexual activity, contraceptive use, and childbearing, 2006–2010*. National Survey of Family Growth. Series 23, Number 31. Retrieved from http://www.cdc.gov/nchs/data/series/sr_23/sr23_031.pdf

National Center for HIV/AIDS, Viral Hepatitis, STD, and TB Prevention. (2011). *HIV among youth*. Retrieved from http://www.cdc.gov/hiv/youth/pdf/youth.pdf

National Center for HIV/AIDS, Viral Hepatitis, STD & TB Prevention (n.d.). *AIDS trends*. Retrieved from http://www.cdc.gov/hiv/pdf/statistics_surveillance_aidstrends.pdf

National Center for Injury Protection and Control. (2011). *WISQARS online, fatal injury reports*. Retrieved from http://www.cdc/gov/injury/wisqars/fatal.html

National Center for Learning Disabilities. (2010). *LD explained*. Retrieved from http://www.ncld.org/ld-basics/ld-explained

National Child Traumatic Stress Network. (2009). *Sexual development and behavior in children: Information for parents and caregivers*. Retrieved from dhss.alaska.gov/ocs/Documents/Publications/pdf/sexualdevelop-children.pdf

National Child Traumatic Stress Network. (n.d.). *What is child traumatic stress?* Retrieved from http://www.nctsnet.org/sites/default/files/assets/pdfs/what_is_child_traumatic_stress_0.pdf

National Diabetes Education Program. (2006). *Overview of diabetes in children and adolescents*. Retrieved from http://ndep.nih.gov/media/youth_factsheet.pdf

National Endowment for the Arts. (2007). *To read or not to read: A question of national consequence*. Research Report No. 47. Washington, DC: Author.

National Heart, Lung and Blood Institute. (2007). *What is sickle-cell anemia?* Retrieved from http://www.nhlbi.nih.gov/health/dci/Diseases/Sca/SCA_WhatIs.html

National Human Genome Research Institute (2007). *A guide to your genome*. Retrieved from http://www.genome.gov/Pages/Education/AllAbouttheHumanGenomeProject/GuidetoYourGenome07.pdf

National Human Genome Research Institute. (2010). *An overview of the human genome project*. Retrieved from http://www.genome.gov/12011239

National Human Genome Research Institute. (2011a). *Chromosome abnormalities*. Retrieved from http://www.genome.gov/11508982#6

National Human Genome Research Institute. (2011b). *ELSI research priorities and possible research topics*. Retrieved from http://www.genome.gov/27543732

National Human Genome Research Institute. (2011c). *Frequently asked questions about genetic disorders*. Retrieved from http://www.genome.gov/19016930

National Institute of Alcohol Abuse and Alcoholism. (2004). *NIAAA council approves definition of binge drinking*. Retrieved from http://pubs.niaaa.nih.gov/publications/Newsletter/winter2004/Newsletter_Number3.pdf

National Institute of Child Health and Human Development. (2006). *Phenylketonuria (PKU)*. Retrieved from http://www.nichd.nih.gov/health/topics/phenylketonuria.cfm

National Institute of Child Health and Human Development. (2010). *Back to Sleep public education campaign*. Retrieved from http://www.nichd.nih.gov/sids/

National Institute of Child Health and Human Development. (2012). *What causes learning disabilities?* Retrieved from http://www.nichd.nih.gov/health/topics/learning/conditioninfo/pages/causes.aspx

National Institute of Child Health and Human Development Early Child Care Research Network. (1997). The effects of infant child care on infant-mother attachment security: Results of the NICHD study of early child care. *Child Development, 68*(5), 860–879.

National Institute of Child Health and Human Development Early Child Care Research Network. (2001). Child care and common communicable illnesses: Results from the National Institute of Child Health and Human Development Study of Early Child Care. *Archives of Pediatric Adolescent Medicine, 155*(4), 481–488.

National Institute of Child Health and Human Development Early Child Care Research Network. (2005). Duration and developmental timing of poverty and children's cognitive and social development from birth through third grade. *Child Development, 76*(4), 795–810. doi: 10.1111/j.1467-8624.2005.00878.x

National Institute of Justice. (2011). *Prevalence of teen dating violence*. Retrieved from http://www.nij.gov/nij/topics/crime/intimate-partner-violence/teen-dating-violence/prevalence.htm

National Institute of Mental Health. (2009). *The diagnosis of autism spectrum disorders*. Retrieved from http://www.nimh.nih.gov/health/publications/autism/complete-index.shtml#pub3

National Institute of Neurological Disorders and Stroke. (2008). *Autism fact sheet*. Retrieved from http://www.ninds.nih.gov/disorders/autism/detail_autism.htm

National Institute of Neurological Disorders and Stroke. (2011). *Cerebral palsy: Hope through research*. Retrieved from http://www.ninds.nih.gov/disorders/cerebral_palsy/detail_cerebral_palsy.htm#179323104

National Institute on Deafness and Other Communication Disorders. (2013). *Cochlear implants*. Retrieved from http://www.nidcd.nih.gov/health/hearing/pages/coch.aspx

National Institute on Drug Abuse. (2010). *NIDA InfoFacts: Marijuana*. Retrieved from http://www.nida.nih.gov/Infofacts/marijuana.html

National Institute on Drug Abuse. (2014). *Drug facts: High school and youth trends*. Retrieved from http://www.drugabuse.gov/publications/drugfacts/high-school-youth-trends

National Institutes of Health. (2009). *Infant-newborn development*. Retrieved from http://www.nlm.nih.gov/MEDLINEPLUS/ency/article/002004.htm

National Institutes of Health. (2012a). *How is asthma diagnosed?* Retrieved from http://www.nhlbi.nih.gov/health/health-topics/topics/asthma/diagnosis.html

National Institutes of Health. (2012b). *What causes asthma?* Retrieved from http://www.nhlbi.nih.gov/health/health-topics/topics/asthma/causes.html

National Institutes of Health. (2013). *Intellectual disability*. Retrieved from http://www.nlm.nih.gov/medlineplus/ency/article/001523.htm

National Institutes of Health. (2014). *Recommendations for use of antiretroviral drugs in pregnant HIV-1-infected women for maternal health and interventions to reduce perinatal HIV transmission in the United States*. Retrieved from http://aidsinfo.nih.gov/guidelines

National Reading Panel. (2000). Alphabetics Part II: Phonics instruction. In *Report of the National Reading Panel: Teaching children to read: An evidence-based assessment of the scientific research literature on reading and its implications for reading instruction: Reports of the subgroups*. Rockville, MD: NICHD Clearinghouse.

National Research Council. (2011). *Adverse effects of vaccines: Evidence and causality*. Washington, DC: National Academies Press.

National Research Council and Institute of Medicine. (2004). *Community programs to promote youth development*. Retrieved from http://www.nationalacademies.org/bocyf/youth_development_brief.pdf

National Research Council, Commission on Behavioral and Social Sciences and Education. (1997). *Political debate interferes with research on educating children with limited English proficiency*. Retrieved from http://www8.nationalacademies.org/onpinews/newsitem.aspx?recordid=5286

National Science Foundation. (2012). *Science and Engineering Indicators 2012: Student coursetaking in high school mathematics and science*. Retrieved from http://www.nsf.gov/statistics/seind12/c1/c1s2.htm

National Science Foundation. (2013). *Women, minorities and persons with disabilities in Science and Engineering*. Retrieved from http://www.nsf.gov/statistics/wmpd/2013/digest/theme2_1.cfm

National Scientific Council on the Developing Child. (2005/2014). *Excessive stress disrupts the architecture of the developing brain: Working Paper 3*. (Updated ed.). Retrieved from http://www.developingchild.harvard.edu

National Sexual Violence Resource Center. (2013). *An overview of healthy childhood sexual development*. Enola, PA: Author.

National Sleep Foundation. (2013). *Children and sleep*. Retrieved from http://www.sleepfoundation.org/article/sleep-topics/children-and-sleep

National Society of Genetic Counselors. (n.d.). *Understanding and collecting your family history*. Retrieved from http://nsgc.org/p/cm/ld/fid=52

National Writing Project. (2014). *Writing, technology and teens*. Retrieved from http://www.nwp.org/cs/public/print/resource/2432

National Youth Violence Prevention Resource Center. (2008). *School violence fact sheet*. Retrieved from http://www.safeyouth.org/scripts/facts/school.asp

Natsuaki, M. N., Biehl, M. C., & Ge, X. (2009). Trajectories of depressed mood from early adolescence to young adulthood: The effects of pubertal timing and adolescent dating. *Journal of Research on Adolescence, 19*(1), 47–74. doi: 10.1111/j.1532-7795.2009.00581.x

Neber, H., Finsterwald, M., & Urban, N. (2001). Cooperative learning with gifted and high-achieving students: A review and meta-analyses of 12 studies. *High Ability Studies, 12*(2), 199–214.

Neisser, U., Boodoo, G., Bouchard, T. J., Boykin, A. W., Brody, N., Ceci, S. J., . . . Urbina, S. (1996). Intelligence: Knowns and unknowns. *American Psychologist, 51*(2), 77–101.

Nelson, C. (1999). How important are the first 3 years of life? *Applied Developmental Science, 3*(4), 235–238.

Nelson, K. (1993). The psychological and social origins of autobiographical memory. *Psychological Science, 4*(1), 7–14.

Nelson, K. (2014). Events, narratives, memory: What develops. In C. A. Nelson (Ed.), *Memory and affect in development: The Minnesota symposia on child psychology* (Vol. 26, pp. 1–24). New York, NY: Psychology Press.

Nemours Foundation. (1995–2012). *Tips for divorcing parents*. Retrieved from http://kidshealth.org/parent/emotions/feelings/divorce.html#

Neonatology on the Web. (2007, April 29). *Incubators for infants*. Retrieved from http://www.neonatology.org/classics/portroyal.html

Neppl, T. K., Donnellan, M., Scaramella, L. V., Widaman, K. F., Spilman, S. K., Ontai, L. L., & Conger, R. D. (2010). Differential stability of temperament and personality from toddlerhood to middle childhood. *Journal of Research on Personality, 44*(3), 386–396.

Neuman, Å., Hohmann, C., Orsini, N., Pershagen, G., Eller, E., Kjaer, H., . . . Bergström, A. (2012). Maternal smoking in pregnancy and asthma in preschool children: A pooled analysis of eight birth cohorts. *American Journal of Respiratory and Critical Care Medicine, 186*(10), 1037–1043. doi: 10.1164/rccm.201203-0501OC

Neuman, S. B., Kaefer, T., Pinkham, A., & Strouse, G. (2014). Can babies learn to read? A randomized trial of baby media. *Journal of Educational Psychology, 106*(3), 815–830.

Neumark, D., & Rothstein, D. (2005). *Do school-to-work programs help the "Forgotten Half"?* The Institute for the Study of Labor, Discussion Paper No. 1740. Bonn, Germany.

Neumark-Sztainer, D. (2008). Family meals in adolescence: Findings from Project EAT. *Society for Research in Child Development Social Policy Reports, 22*(4), 11.

Neville, H. J., Stevens, C., Pakulak, E., Bell, T. A., Fanning, J., Klein, S., & Isbella, E. (2013). Family-based training program improves brain function, cognition, and behavior in lower socioeconomic status preschoolers. *Proceedings of the National Academy of Sciences of the United States of America, 110*, 12138–12143.

Newcombe, N. S. (2011). Three families of isms. *Child Development Perspectives, 5*(3), 171–172.

Newcombe, N. S., Sluzenski, J., & Huttenlocher, J. (2005). Preexisting knowledge versus on-line learning: What do young infants really know about spatial location? *Psychological Science, 16*(3), 222–227.

Newman, J., Bidjerano, T., Özdogru, A. A., Kao, C., Özköse-Biyik, C., & Johnson, J. J. (2007). What do they usually do after school? A comparative analysis of fourth-grade children in Bulgaria, Taiwan, and the United States. *Journal of Early Adolescence, 27,* 431–456.

Nicholas, J., & Geers, A. E. (2007). Will they catch up? The role of age at cochler implantation in the spoken language development of children with severe to profound hearing loss. *Journal of Speech, Language, and Hearing Research, 50*(4), 1048–1062.

Nield, L. S., Cakan, N., & Kamat, D. (2007). A practical approach to precocious puberty. *Clinical Pediatrics, 46*(4), 299–306.

Nielsen. (2011). *Kids today: How the class of 2011 engages with media.* Retrieved from http://www.nielsen.com/us/en/insights/news/2011/kids-today-how-the-class-of-2011-engages-with-media.html

Nielsen. (2014). *Hugging the curve: Opportunistic on-demand users have spiked overall viewing.* Retrieved from http://www.nielsen.com/us/en/insights/news/2014/hugging-the-curve-opportunistic-on-demand-users-have-spiked-overall-viewing.html

Nijhof, K. S., & Engels, R. C. M. E. (2007). Parenting styles, coping strategies, and the expression of homesickness. *Journal of Adolescence, 30*(5), 709–720.

Nikčević, A. V., & Nicolaides, K. H. (2014). Search for meaning, finding meaning and adjustment in women following miscarriage: A longitudinal study. *Psychology & Health, 29*(1), 50–63. doi: 10.1080/08870446.2013.823497

Nikulina, V., Widom, C. S., & Czaja, S. (2010). The role of childhood neglect and childhood poverty in predicting mental health, academic achievement and crime in adulthood. *American Journal of Community Psychology, 48,* 309–321.

Nisbett, R. E., Aronson, J., Blair, C., Dickens, W., Flynn, J., Halpern, D. F., & Turkheimer, E. (2012). Intelligence: New findings and theoretical developments. *American Psychologist, 67*(2), 130–159.

Nomaguchi, K. M., & Milkie, M. A. (2003). Costs and rewards of children: The effect of becoming a parent on adults' lives. *Journal of Marriage and Family, 65*(2), 356–374.

Nomi, T. (2010). The effects of within-class ability grouping on academic achievement in early elementary years. *Journal of Research on Educational Effectiveness, 3*(1), 56–92.

Nosek, B. A., Smyth, F. L., Sriram, N. N., Lindner, N. M., Devos, T., Ayala, A., . . . Greenwald, A. G. (2009). National differences in gender–science stereotypes predict national sex differences in science and math achievement. *PNAS Proceedings of The National Academy of Sciences of The United States of America, 106*(26), 10593–10597. doi: 10.1073/pnas.0809921106

Nowak, K. L., & Rauh, C. (2008). Choose your "buddy icon" carefully: The influence of avatar androgyny, anthropomorphism and credibility in online interactions. *Computers in Human Behavior, 24,* 1473–1493.

Nsamenang, A. B., & Lo-oh, J. L. (2010). Afrique noir. In M. H. Bornstein (Ed.), *Handbook of cultural developmental science* (pp. 383–407). New York, NY: Psychology Press.

Nucci, L., & Turiel, E. (2009). Capturing the complexity of moral development and education. *Mind, Brain, and Education, 3*(3), 151–159.

O'Donnell, L., Myint, U. A., O'Donnell, C. R., & Stueve, A. (2003). Long-term influence of sexual norms and attitudes on timing of sexual initiation among urban minority youth. *Journal of School Health, 73*(2), 68–75.

O'Keefe, L. (2014). Parents who read to their children nurture more than literary skills. *AAP News.* Retrieved from http://aapnews.aappublications.org/content/early/2014/06/24/aapnews.20140624-2.full.pdf+html

O'Keeffe, G., Clarke-Pearson, K., & Council on Communications and Media. (2011). The impact of social media on children, adolescents, and families. *Pediatrics, 127*(4), 800–804. doi: 10.1542/peds.2011–0054

O'Leary, P., & Barber, J. (2008). Gender differences in silencing following childhood sexual abuse. *Journal of Child Sexual Abuse, 17*(2), 133–143.

O'Mea, M. L. (2013). Implementing applied behavior analysis for effective orientation and mobility instruction of students with multiple disabilities. *Journal of Visual Impairment & Blindness, 107*(1), 65–70.

Oatley, K., Keltner, D., & Jenkins, J. M. (2006). *Understanding emotions* (2nd ed.). Malden, MA: Blackwell.

Office of Juvenile Justice and Delinquency Prevention. (2005). *Drinking in America: Myths, realities, and prevention policy.* Washington, DC: U.S. Department of Justice, Office of Justice Programs, Office of Juvenile Justice and Delinquency Prevention.

Office of National Drug Control Policy. (2014). *Marijuana resource center: State laws related to marijuana.* Retrieved from http://www.whitehouse.gov/ondcp/state-laws-related-to-marijuana

Ogden, C. L., Carroll, M. D., Kit, B. K., & Flegal, K. M. (2014). Prevalence of childhood and adult obesity in the United States, 2011–2012. *Journal of the American Medical Association, 311*(8), 806–814.

Olds, S. B., London, M. L., & Ladewig, P. A. (2002). *Maternal-newborn nursing: A family and community-based approach* (6th ed.). Upper Saddle River, NJ: Prentice Hall.

Olds, T., Maher, C., Blunden, S., & Matricciani, L. (2010). Normative data on the sleep habits of Australian children and adolescents. *Sleep, 33*(10), 1381–1388.

Olson, S. L., Bates, J. E., Sandy, J. M., & Lanthier, R. (2000). Early developmental precursors of externalizing behavior in middle childhood and adolescence. *Journal of Abnormal Child Psychology, 28*(2), 119–133.

Olweus, D. (2001). Peer harassment: A critical analysis and some important issues. In J. Juvonen & S. Graham (Eds.), *Peer harassment in school: The plight of the vulnerable and victimized* (pp. 3–20). Guilford Publications, Inc.

Olweus, D. (2003). A profile of bullying at school. *Educational Leadership, 60*(6), 12–17.

Ongley, S. F., & Malti, T. (2014). The role of moral emotions in the development of children's sharing behavior. *Developmental Psychology, 50*(4), 1148–1159. doi: 10.1037/a0035191

Oppenheimer, L. (1986). Development of recursive thinking: Procedural variations. *International Journal of Behavioral Development, 9*(3), 401–411.

Organisation for Economic Co-operation and Development. (2012). *Infant mortality.* Retrieved from http://www.oecd.org/social/family/CO1.1%20Infant%20mortality%20-%20updated%20081212.pdf

Organisation Economic Co-operation and Development. (2013). *Country Note: Education at a glance 2013: United States.* Retrieved from http://www.oecd.org/edu/United%20States%20_EAG2013%20Country%20Note.pdf

Osgood, D. W., Anderson, A. L., & Shaffer, J. N. (2005). Unstructured leisure in the after-school hours. In J. L. Mahoney, R. W. Larson, & J. S. Eccles (Eds.), *Organized activities as contexts of development* (pp. 45–64). Mahwah, NJ: Erlbaum.

Outdoor Foundation. (2012). *Outdoor Recreation Participation Report 2012.* Retrieved from http://www.outdoorfoundation.org/pdf/ResearchParticipation2012.pdf

Owens, M. E., & Todt, E. H. (1984). Pain in infancy: Neonatal reaction to a heel lance. *Pain, 20*(1), 77–86. doi: 10.1016/0304-3959(84)90813-3

Pachter, L. M., & Garcia Coll, C. (2009). Racism and child health: A review of the literature and future directions. *Journal of Developmental and Behavioral Pediatrics, 30,* 255–263.

Pagan, J. L., Rose, R. J., Viken, R. J., Pulkkinen, L., Kaprio, J., & Dick, D. M. (2006). Genetic and environmental influences on stages of alcohol use across adolescence and into young adulthood. *Behavior Genetics, 36*(4), 483–497.

Pajares, F. (2002). *Overview of social cognitive theory and of self-efficacy.* Retrieved from http://www.emory.edu/EDUCATION/mfp/eff.html

Pajares, F. (2005). Self-efficacy during childhood and adolescence. In F. Pajares, & T. C. Urdan (Eds.), *Self-efficacy beliefs of adolescents* (pp. 339–367). Charlotte, NC: Information Age.

Pajares, F., & Schunk, D. H. (2002). Self and self-belief in psychology and education: An historical perspective. In J. Aronson (Ed.), *Improving academic achievement* (pp. 5–21). New York, NY: Academic Press.

Pakkenberg, B., & Gundersen, H. J. G. (1997). Neocortical neuron number in humans: Effect of sex and age. *Journal of Comparative Neurology, 384,* 312–320.

Palo Alto Medical Foundation. (2014). *Unintentional injuries & violence.* Retrieved from http://www.pamf.org/teen/health/diseases/injury.html

Palusci, V. J., Crum, P., Bliss, R., & Bavolek, S. J. (2008). Changes in parenting attitudes and knowledge among inmates and other at-risk populations after a family nurturing program. *Children and Youth Services Review, 30*(1), 79–89.

Pan, B. A. (2005). Semantic development. In J. B. Gleason (Ed.), *The development of language* (6th ed., pp. 112–147). Boston, MA: Pearson.

Papalia, D. E., Olds, S. W., & Feldman, R. D. (1998). *Human development* (7th ed.). New York, NY: McGraw-Hill.

Parasuraman, R. (1998). The attentive brain: Issues and prospects. In R. Parasuraman (Ed.), *The attentive brain* (pp. 3–15). Cambridge, MA: MIT Press.

Parent, A. S., Teilmann, G., Juul, A., Skakkebaek, N. E., Toppari, J., & Bourguignon, J. P. (2003). The timing of normal puberty and the age limits of sexual precocity: Variations around the world, secular trends, and changes after migration. *Endocrine Reviews, 24*(5), 668–693.

Parent Teacher Association. (2006). *Progress for American Children—2006 National PTA Annual Report.* Retrieved from http://www.pta.org/2006_Annual_Report.pdf

Parker, K., & Wang, W. (2013, March 14). *Modern parenthood: Roles of moms and dads converge as they balance work and family.* Washington, DC: Pew Research, Social & Demographic Trends. Retrieved from http://www.pewsocialtrends.org/2013/03/14/modern-parenthood-roles-of-moms-and-dads-converge-as-they-balance-work-and-family/

Parks, S. E., Annest, J. L., Hill, H. A., & Karch, D. L. (2012). *Pediatric abusive head trauma: Recommended definitions for public health surveillance and research.* Atlanta, GA: Centers for Disease Control and Prevention.

Parmer, S. M., Salisbury-Glennon, J., Shannon, D., & Struempler, B. (2009). School gardens: An experiential learning approach for a nutrition education program to increase fruit and vegetable knowledge, preference, and consumption among second-grade students. *Journal of Nutrition Education and Behavior, 41*(3), 212–217.

Parten, M. (1932). Social participation among pre-school children. *Journal of Abnormal and Social Psychology, 27*(3), 243–269.

Pasley, K., & Moorefield, B. S. (2004). Stepfamilies changes and challenges. In M. Coleman & L. H. Ganong (Eds.), *Handbook of contemporary families* (pp. 317–330). Thousand Oaks, CA: Sage.

Pate, R., Pfeiffer, K., Trost, S., Ziegler, P., & Dowda, M. (2004). Physical activity among children attending preschools. *Pediatrics*, *114*(5 Part 1), 1258–1263.

Patterson, C. J. (2006). Children of lesbian and gay parents. *Current Directions in Psychological Science*, *15*(5), 241–244.

Pauli-Pott, U., Becker, K., Mertesacker, T., & Beckmann, D. (2000). Infants with "colic"—Mothers' perspectives on the crying problem. *Journal of Psychosomatic Research*, *48*(2), 125–132.

Paulson, A., & Teicher, S. A. (2006). Move to single-sex classes fans debate. *Christian Science Monitor*. Retrieved from http://www.csmonitor.com/2006/1026/p02s01-legn.html

Paus, T., Zijdenbos, A., Worsley, K., Collings, D. L., Blumenthal, J., Giedd, J. N., . . . Evans, A. C. (1999). Structural maturation of neural pathways in children and adolescents: In vivo study. *Science*, *283*(5409), 1908–1911.

Pavlov, I. P. (1927). *Conditioned reflexes: An investigation of the physiological activity of the cerebral cortex*. Retrieved from http://www.ivanpavlov.com/lectures/ivan_pavlov-lecture_002.htm

PDR Network. (2010). *Physicians' desk reference* (64th ed.). Retrieved from http://www.pdrhealth.com/drugs/rx/rx-a-z.aspx

Pearson, P. D. (2004). The reading wars. *Educational Policy*, *18*(1), 216–252.

Peck, S. C., Roeser, R. W., Zarrett, N., & Eccles, J. S. (2008). Exploring the roles of extracurricular activity quantity and quality in the educational resilience of vulnerable adolescents: Variable- and pattern-centered approaches. *Journal of Social Issues*, *64*(1), 135–155.

Peets, K., Hodges, E. E., Kikas, E., & Salmivalli, C. (2007). Hostile attributions and behavioral strategies in children: Does relationship type matter? *Developmental Psychology*, *43*(4), 889–900.

Pellegrini, A. D. (2002). Rough-and-tumble play from childhood through adolescence: Development and possible functions. In P. K. Smith & C. Hart (Eds.), *Blackwell handbook of childhood social development* (pp. 438–453). Malden, MA: Blackwell.

Pellegrini, A. D. (2005). *Recess—Its role in education and development*. Mahwah, NJ: Erlbaum.

Pellis, S. M., & Pellis, V. C. (2007). Rough-and-tumble play and the development of the social brain. *Current Directions in Psychological Science*, *16*(2), 95–98.

Pelucchi, B., Hay, J. F., & Saffran, J. R. (2009). Statistical learning in a natural language by 8-month-old infants. *Child Development*, *80*(3), 674–685.

Pempek, T. A., Demers, L. B., Hanson, K. G., Kirkorian, H. L., & Anderson, D. R. (2011). The impact of infant-directed videos on parent-child interaction. *Journal of Applied Developmental Psychology*, *32*(1), 10–19.

Pereda, N., Guilera, G., Forns, M., & Gómez-Benito, J. (2009). The international epidemiology of child sexual abuse: A continuation of Finkelhor (1994). *Child Abuse & Neglect*, *33*(6), 331–342.

Petanjek, Z., Judaš, M., Šimic, G., Rašin, M., Uylings, H. M., Rakic, P., & Kostović, I. (2011). Extraordinary neoteny of synaptic spines in the human prefrontal cortex. *PNAS Proceedings of The National Academy of Sciences of The United States of America*, *108*(32), 13281–13286.

Peter J. Peterson Foundation. (2013). *Americans spend over twice as much per capita on healthcare as the average developed country*. Retrieved from http://pgpf.org/Chart-Archive/0006_health-care-oecd

Peters, E., Riksen-Walraven, J., Cillessen, A. N., & de Weerth, C. (2011). Peer rejection and HPA activity in middle childhood: Friendship makes a difference. *Child Development*, *82*(6), 1906–1920.

Peterson, C. (2002). Children's long-term memory for autobiographical events. *Developmental Review*, *22*(3), 370–402.

Peterson, C. C., Wellman, H. M., & Slaughter, V. (2012). The mind behind the message: Advancing theory-of-mind scales for typically developing children, and those with deafness, autism, or Asperger syndrome. *Child Development*, *83*(2), 469–485. doi: 10.1111/j.1467–8624.2011.01728.x

Petitto, L. A., Katerelos, M., Levy, B. G., Gauna, K., Tétreault, K., & Ferraro, V. (2001). Bilingual signed and spoken language acquisition from birth: Implications for the mechanisms underlying early bilingual language acquisition. *Journal of Child Language*, *28*(2), 453–496.

Pett, M. A., Wampold, B. E., Turner, C. W., & Vaughan-Cole, B. (1999). Paths of influence of divorce on preschool children's psychosocial adjustment. *Journal of Family Psychology*, *13*(2), 145–164.

Petterson, S. M., & Albers, A. B. (2001). Effects of poverty and maternal depression on early childhood development. *Child Development*, *72*(6), 1794–1813.

Pew Internet & American Life Project. (2012). *Teens, smartphones, and texting*. Retrieved from http://www.pewinternet.org/2012/03/19/teens-smartphones-texting/

Pfeiffer, S. I. (2012). Current perspectives on the identification and assessment of gifted students. *Journal of Psychoeducational Assessment*, *30*(1), 3–9.

Phinney, J. S. (1989). Stages of ethnic identity development in minority group adolescents. *Journal of Early Adolescence*, *9*(1–2), 34–49.

Phinney, J. S., Kim-Jo, T., Osorio, S., & Vilhjalmsdottir, P. (2005). Autonomy and relatedness in adolescent-parent disagreements: Ethnic and developmental factors. *Journal of Adolescent Research*, *20*(1), 8–39.

Piaget, J. (1952). *The origins of intelligence in children*. New York, NY: W. W. Norton.

Piaget, J. (1954). *The construction of reality in the child*. New York, NY: Basic Books.

Piaget, J. (1955). *The language and thought of the child*. New York, NY: Meridian Books.

Piaget, J. (1962). *Play, dreams and imitation in childhood*. New York, NY: W. W. Norton.

Piaget, J. (1963). *The origins of intelligence in children.* New York, NY: W. W. Norton.

Piaget, J. (1965). *The moral judgment of the child.* New York, NY: Free Press.

Piaget, J. (1973). *The language and thought of the child.* New York, NY: Meridian World.

Piaget, J. (1999). The stages of intellectual development of the child. In A. Slater & D. Muir (Eds.), *Blackwell reader in developmental psychology* (pp. 35–42). Malden, MA: Blackwell.

Piaget, J., & Inhelder, B. (1956). *The child's conception of space.* London, UK: Routledge.

Pianta, R. C., Barnett, W. S., Burchinal, M., & Thornburg, K. R. (2009). The effects of preschool education: What we know, how public policy is or is not aligned with the evidence base, and what we need to know. *Psychological Science in the Public Interest, 10,* 51–88.

Pietromonaco, P. R., & Barrett, L. F. (2000). The internal working models concept: What do we really know about the self in relation to others? *Review of General Psychology, 4*(2), 155–175.

Pietschnig, J., Voracek, M., & Formann, A. K. (2010). Mozart effect–Shmozart effect: A meta-analysis. *Intelligence, 38*(3), 314–323.

Pinker, S. (1984). *Language learnability and language development.* Cambridge, MA: Harvard University Press.

Pinkleton, B. E., Austin, E., Chen, Y., & Cohen, M. (2012). The role of media literacy in shaping adolescents' understanding of and responses to sexual portrayals in mass media. *Journal of Health Communication, 17*(4), 460–476. doi: 10.1080/10810730.2011.635770

Pinkleton, B. E., Austin, E. W., Cohen, M., Miller, A., & Fitzgerald, E. (2007). A statewide evaluation of the effectiveness of media literacy training to prevent tobacco use among adolescents. *Health Communication, 21,* 23–34.

Pinquart, M., & Teubert, D. (2010). A meta-analytic study of couple interventions during the transition to parenthood. *Family Relations, 59*(3), 221–231. doi: 10.1111/j.1741-3729.2010.00597.x

Pinto, S., & Schub, T. (2013). *Sexual abuse in children and adolescents: Males.* Cinahl. Glendale, CA: Information Systems.

Piper, P. S. (2000). Better read that again: Web hoaxes and misinformation. *Searcher, 8*(8). Retrieved from http://www.highbeam.com/doc/1G1-65575479.html

Plant, T. M. (2006). The role of KiSS-1 in the regulation of puberty in higher primates. *European Journal of Endocrinology, 155,* S11–S16. doi: 10.1530/eje.1.02232

Planty, M., Provasnik, S., & Daniel, B. (2007). *High school course taking: Findings from the condition of education 2007* [NCES 2007–065]. U.S. Department of Education. Washington, DC: National Center for Education Statistics.

Platek, S. M., Critton, S. R., Myers, T. E., & Gallup, G. G., Jr. (2003). Contagious yawning: The role of self-awareness and mental state attribution. *Cognitive Brain Research, 17,* 223–227.

Plomin, R. (2011). Commentary: Why are children in the same family so different? Non-shared environment three decades later. *International Journal of Epidemiology, 40*(3), 582–592. doi: 10.1093/ije/dyq144

Plomin, R. (2013). Child development and molecular genetics: 14 years later. *Child Development, 84*(1), 104–120.

Plomin, R., Asbury, K., & Dunn, J. (2001). Why are children in the same family so different? Non-shared environment a decade later. *Canadian Journal of Psychiatry, 46,* 225–233.

Plomin, R., DeFries, J. C., Craig, I. W., & McGuffin, P. (2003a). Behavioral genetics. In R. Plomin, J. C. DeFries, I. W. Craig, & P. McGuffin (Eds.), *Behavioral genetics in the postgenomic era* (pp. 3–15). Washington, DC: American Psychological Association.

Plomin, R., DeFries, J. C., Craig, I. W., & McGuffin, P. (2003b). Behavioral genomics. In R. Plomin, J. C. DeFries, I. W. Craig, & P. McGuffin (Eds.), *Behavioral genetics in the postgenomic era* (pp. 531–540). Washington, DC: American Psychological Association.

Poehner, M. E. (2007). Beyond the test: L2 dynamic assessment and the transcendence of mediated learning. *Modern Language Journal, 91*(3), 323–340.

Pollet, T. V. (2007). Genetic relatedness and sibling relationship characteristics in a modern society. *Evolution and Human Behavior, 28*(3), 176–185.

Polman, H., de Castro, B. O., & van Aken, M. A. G. (2008). Experimental study of the differential effects of playing versus watching violent video games on children's aggressive behavior. *Aggressive Behavior, 34*(3), 256–264.

Pong, S., Johnston, J., & Chen, V. (2010). Authoritarian parenting and Asian adolescent school performance: Insights from the US and Taiwan. *International Journal of Behavioral Development, 34*(1), 62–72. doi: 10.1177/0165025409345073

Ponitz, C. C., McClelland, M. M., Matthews, J. S., & Morrison, F. J. (2009). A structured observation of behavioral self-regulation and its contribution to kindergarten outcomes. *Developmental Psychology, 45*(3), 605–619.

Pool, M. M., Koolstra, C. M., & van der Voort, T. H. A. (2003). Distraction effects of background soap operas on homework performance: An experimental study enriched with observational data. *Educational Psychology, 23*(4), 361–380.

Porter, N. (2012). *High turnover among early childhood educators in the United States.* Retrieved from http://www.childresearch.net/projects/ecec/2012_04.html

Porter, R. (2013). Milestones in sexual development from puberty in girls. *The Merck Manual: Home Health Handbook, 2004–2011.* http://www.merckmanuals.com/home/womens_health_issues/biology_of_the_female_reproductive_system/puberty_in_girls.html

Posada, G., & Jacobs, A. (2001). Child–mother attachment relationships and culture. *American Psychologist, 56*(10), 821–822. doi: 10.1037/0003-066X.56.10.821

Posner, M. I., Rothbart, M. K., & Sheese, B. E. (2007). Attention genes. *Developmental Science, 10*(1), 24–29.

Posner, R. B. (2006). Early menarche: A review of research on trends in timing racial differences, etiology and psychosocial consequences. *Sex Roles, 54*(5/6), 315–322.

Poti, J. M., Duffey, J. J., & Popkin, B. M. (2014). The association of fast food consumption with poor dietary outcomes and obesity among children: Is it the fast food or the remainder of the diet? *American Journal of Clinical Nutrition, 99*(1), 162–171.

Poulin F., & Dishion, T. (2008). Methodological issues in the use of peer sociometric nominations with middle school youth. *Social Development [serial online], 17*(4), 908–921.

Powell, L., & Nguyen, B. (2013). Fast-food and full-service restaurant consumption among children and adolescents: Effect on energy, beverage, and nutrient intake. *JAMA Pediatrics, 167*(1), 14–20.

Powers, K. (2006–2014). *Authentic assessment.* Retrieved from http://www.education.com/reference/article/authentic-assessment

Prebble, S. C., Addis, D., & Tippett, L. J. (2013). Autobiographical memory and sense of self. *Psychological Bulletin, 139*(4), 815–840. doi: 10.1037/a0030146

Preissler, M. A., & Bloom, P. (2007). Two-year-olds appreciate the dual nature of pictures. *Psychological Science, 18*(1), 1–2.

Preissler, M. A., & Carey, S. (2004). Do both pictures and words function as symbols for 18- and 24-month-old children? *Journal of Cognition and Development, 5*(2), 185–212.

Price, A., Wake, M., Ukoumunne, O., & Hiscock, H. (2012). Five-year follow-up of harms and benefits of behavioral infant sleep intervention: Randomized trial. *Pediatrics, 130*(4), 643–651. doi: 10.1542/peds.2011-3467

Price, M. (2009). The left brain knows what the right hand is doing. *Monitor on Psychology, 40*(1), 60.

Primack, B. A., Gold, M. A., Land, S. R., & Fine, M. J. (2006). Association of cigarette smoking and media literacy about smoking among adolescents. *Journal of Adolescent Medicine, 39,* 465–472.

Provost, M. A., & LaFreniere, P. J. (1991). Social participation and peer competence in preschool children: Evidence for discriminant and convergent validity. *Child Study Journal, 21*(1), 57–72.

Prynn, P. (2012). Nocturnal enuresis in children and adolescents. *Practice Nurse, 42*(6), 20-24.

Public Broadcasting Service. (2001). *Timeline: The bilingual education controversy.* Retrieved from http://www.pbs.org/kcet/publicschool/roots_in_history/bilingual.html

Public Health Agency of Canada. (2003). *Infant attachment: What professionals need to know.* Retrieved from http://www.phac-aspc.gc.ca/mh-sm/mhp-psm/pub/fc-pc/prof_know-eng.php

Pugh, K. R., Frost, S. J., Rothman, D. L., Hoeft, F., DelTufo, S. N., Mason, G. F., . . . Fulbright, R. K. (2014). Glutamate and choline levels predict individual differences in reading ability in emergent readers. *Journal of Neuroscience, 34*(11), 4082–4089.

Puma, M., Bell, S., Cook, R., Heid, C., Broene, P., Jenkins, F., Mashburn, A., & Downer, J. (2012). *Third grade follow-up to the Head Start Impact Study Final Report, Executive Summary.* OPRE Report # 2012-45b. Washington, DC: Office of Planning, Research and Evaluation, Administration for Children and Families, U.S. Department of Health and Human Services.

Punch, S. (2012). Studying transnational children: A multi-sited, longitudinal, ethnographic approach. *Journal of Ethnic & Migration Studies, 38*(6), 1007–1023. doi: 10.1080/1369183X.2012.677181

Putnam, F. W. (2003). Ten-year research update review: Child sexual abuse. *Journal of the American Academy of Child and Adolescent Psychiatry, 42*(3), 269–278.

Quee, P. J., Meijer, J. H., Islam, M., Aleman, A., Alizadeh, B. Z., Meijer, C. J., & van den Heuvel, E. R. (2014). Premorbid adjustment profiles in psychosis and the role of familial factors. *Journal of Abnormal Psychology, 123*(3), 578–587. doi: 10.1037/a0037189

Quenqua, K. (2013). Infants are fed solid food too soon, C.D.C. finds. *New York Times.* Retrieved from http://www.nytimes.com/2013/03/25/health/many-babies-fed-solid-food-too-soon-cdc-finds.html?_r=0

Quiocho, A. M. L., & Daoud, A. M. (2006). Dispelling myths about Latino parent participation in school. *Educational Forum, 70*(3), 255–267.

Radesky, J. S., Silverstein, M., Zuckerman, B., & Christakis, D. A. (2014). Infant self-regulation and early childhood media exposure. *Pediatrics, 133*(5), e1172–e1178. doi: 10.1542/peds.2013–2367

Raeff, C. (2004). Within culture complexities: Multifaceted and interrelated autonomy and connectedness characteristics in late adolescent selves. In M. F. Mascolo & J. Li (Eds.), Culture and developing selves: Beyond dichotomization. *New Directions for Child and Adolescent Development, 104,* 61–78. San Francisco, CA: Jossey-Bass.

Raeff, C., Greenfield, P. M., & Quiroz, B. (2000). Conceptualizing interpersonal relationships in the cultural contexts of individualism and collectivism. In S. Harkness, C. Raeff, & C. M. Super (Eds.), *Variability in the social construction of the child: New Directions for Child and Adolescent Development, 87* (pp. 59–74). San Francisco, CA: Jossey-Bass.

Raley, A. B., & Lucas, J. L. (2006). Stereotype or success? Prime-time television's Portrayals of gay male, lesbian, and bisexual characters. *Journal of Homosexuality, 51*(2), 19–38.

Ram, A., Finzi, R., & Cohen, O. (2002). The non-custodial parent and his infant. *Journal of Divorce & Remarriage, 36*(3–4), 41–55.

Rampage, C., Eovaldi, M., Ma, C., & Weigel-Foy, C. (2003). Adoptive families. In F. Walsh (Ed.), *Normal family processes* (3rd ed., pp. 210–232). New York, NY: Guilford Press.

Rampersaud, G. C., Pereira, M. A., Girard, B. L., Adams, J., & Metzl, J. D. (2005). Breakfast habits, nutritional status, body weight, and academic performance in children and adolescents. *Journal of the American Dietetic Association, 105*(5), 743–760.

Ramsey-Rennels, J. L., & Langlois, J. H. (2007). How infants perceive and process faces. In A. Slater & M. Lewis (Eds.), *Introduction to infant development* (pp. 191–215). New York, NY: Oxford University Press.

Randler, C., & Frech, D. (2009). Young people's time-of-day preferences affect their school performance. *Journal of Youth Studies, 12*(6), 653–667.

Raphel, S. (2008). Kinship care and the situation for grandparents. *Journal of Child and Adolescent Psychiatric Nursing, 21*, 118–120.

Ratjen, F., & Döring, G. (2003). Cystic fibrosis. *Lancet, 361*(9358), 681–689.

Raver, C., Blair, C., & Willoughby, M. (2013). Poverty as a predictor of 4-year-olds' executive function: New perspectives on models of differential susceptibility. *Developmental Psychology, 49*(2), 292-304. doi: 10.1037/a0028343

Redshaw, M., & Martin, C. (2011). Motherhood: A natural progression and a major transition. *Journal of Reproductive and Infant Psychology, 29*(4), 305–307. doi: 10.1080/02646838.2011.639510

Reed, R. K. (2005). *Birthing fathers: The transformation of men in American rites of birth.* New Brunswick, NJ: Rutgers University Press.

Reef, S., & Redd, S. (2008). Congenital rubella syndrome. In Centers for Disease Control and Prevention (Ed.), *Manual for the surveillance of vaccine-preventable diseases* (4th ed.). Retrieved from http://www.cdc.gov/vaccines/pubs/surv- manual/chpt15-crs.htm

Reeves, J. (2006). Recklessness, rescue and responsibility: Young men tell their stories of the transition to fatherhood. *Practice, 18*(2), 79–90.

Regnerus, M. (2012). How different are the adult children of parents who have same-sex relationships? Findings from the New Family Structures Study. *Social Science Research, 41*(4), 752–770.

Reichow, B. (2012). Overview of meta-analyses on early intensive behavioral intervention for young children with autism spectrum disorders. *Journal of Autism and Developmental Disorders, 42*(4), 512–520.

Reid, J. A., & Piquero, A. R. (2014). Age-graded risks for commercial sexual exploitation of male and female youth. *Journal of Interpersonal Violence, 29*(9), 1747–1777. doi: 10.1177/0886260513511535

Reif, A., Rosler, M., Freitag, C. M., Schneider, M., Eujen, A., Kissling, C., . . . Retz, W. (2007). Nature and nurture predispose to violent behavior: Serotonergic genes and adverse childhood environment. *Neuropsychoparmacology, 32*(11), 2375–2383.

Reis, S. M. (2004). Series introduction. In R. J. Sternberg (Ed.), *Definitions and conceptions of giftedness* (pp. ix-xxi). Thousand Oaks, CA: Corwin.

Reis, S. M., & Renzulli, J. S. (2010). Is there still a need for gifted education? An examination of current research. *Learning & Individual Differences, 20*(4), 308–317.

Ren, W., Lui, S., Deng, W., Li, F., Li, M., Huang, X., . . . Gong, Q. (2013). Anatomical and functional brain abnormalities in drug-naive first-episode schizophrenia. *American Journal of Psychiatry, 170*(11), 1308–1316. doi: 10.1176/appi.ajp.2013.12091148

Repacholi, B. M., & Gopnik, A. (1997). Early reasoning about desires: Evidence from 14- and 18-month-olds. *Developmental Psychology, 33*(1), 12–21.

RESOLVE: The National Fertility Association. (2014). *Fast facts about infertility.* Retrieved from http://www.resolve.org/about/fast-facts-about-fertility.html

Rew, L., Carver, T., & Li, C. (2011). Early and risky sexual behavior in a sample of rural adolescents. *Issues in Comprehensive Pediatric Nursing, 34*(4), 189–204. doi: 10.3109/01460862.2011.619861

Reynolds, A. J., Temple, J. A., Robertson, D. L., & Mann, E. A. (2001). Long-term effects of an early childhood intervention on educational achievement and juvenile arrest: A 15-year follow-up of low-income children in public schools. *JAMA, 285*(18), 2339–2346.

Reynolds, B. M., & Juvonen, J. (2011). The role of early maturation, perceived popularity, and rumors in the emergence of internalizing symptoms among adolescent girls. *Journal of Youth and Adolescence, 40*(11), 1407–1422. doi: 10.1007/s10964–010–9619–1

Reynolds, C. R. (2000). Why is psychometric research on bias in mental testing so often ignored? *Psychology, Public Policy, and Law, 6*(1), 144–150.

Rhodes, J. E., & DuBois, D. L. (2006). Understanding and facilitating the youth mentoring movement. *Social Policy Report, 20*(3), 1–19.

Rhodes, J. E., Ebert, L., & Fischer, K. (1992). Natural mentors: An overlooked resource in the social networks of young, African American mothers. *American Journal of Community Psychology, 20*(4), 445–461.

Ricard, M., Girouard, P. C., & Gouin Décairie, T. (1999). Personal pronouns and perspective taking in toddlers. *Journal of Child Language, 26*(3), 681–697.

Rich, S. S., DiMarco, N. M., Huettig, C., Essery, E. V., Andersson, E., & Sanborn, C. F. (2005). Perceptions of health status and play activities in parents of overweight Hispanic toddlers and preschoolers. *Family and Community Health, 28*(2), 130–141.

Richmond, M. K., Stocker, C. M., & Rienks, S. L. (2005). Longitudinal associations between sibling relationship quality, parental differential treatment, and children's adjustment. *Journal of Family Psychology, 19*(4), 550–559.

Rideout, V. (2013). *Zero to eight: Children's media use in America 2013.* Common Sense Media. Retrieved from http://www.commonsensemedia.org/research/zero-to-eight-childrens-media-use-in-america-2013

Rideout, V., Foehr, U. G., & Roberts, D. F. (2010). *Generation M²: Media in the lives of 8- to 18-year-olds.*

A Kaiser Family Foundation Study. Retrieved from http://www.kff.org/ent media/upload/8010.pdf

Rideout, V. J., & Hamel, E. (2006). *The media family: Electronic media in the lives of infants, toddlers, preschoolers and their parents.* Retrieved from http://www.kff.org/entmedia/upload/7500.pdf

Ridgers, N. D., Saint-Maurice, P. F., Welk, G. J., Siahpush, M., & Huberty, J. (2011). Differences in physical activity during school recess. *Journal of School Health, 81*(9), 545–551.

Ringelhann, B., Hathorn, M. K., Jilly, P., Grant, F., & Parniczky, G. (1976). A new look at the protection of hemoglobin AS and AC genotypes against plasmodium falciparum infection: A census tract approach. *American Journal of Human Genetics, 28*(3), 270–279.

Rishel, C. W., Cottrell, L., Cottrell, S., Stanton, B., Gibson, C., & Bougher, K. (2007). Exploring adolescents' relationships with non-parental adults using the Non-Parental Adult Inventory (N.P.A.I.). *Child & Adolescent Social Work Journal, 24*(5), 495–508.

Ritchey, K. D., & Speece, D. L. (2006). From letter names to word reading: The nascent role of sublexical fluency. *Contemporary Educational Psychology, 31*(3), 301–327.

Rittle-Johnson, B., & Siegler, R. S. (1999). Learning to spell: Variability, choice, and change in children's strategy use. *Child Development, 70*(2), 332–348.

Rivadeneyra, R., Ward, L. M., & Gordon, M. (2007). Distorted reflections: Media exposure and Latino adolescents' conceptions of self. *Media Psychology, 9*(2), 261–290.

Robb, M. B., Richert, R. A., & Wartella, E. A. (2009). Just a talking book? Word learning from watching baby videos. *British Journal of Developmental Psychology, 27*(1), 27–45. doi: 10.1348/026151008X320156

Robers, S., Zhang, J., & Truman, J. (2012). *Indicators of school crime and safety: 2011* (NCES 2012-002/NCJ 236021). National Center for Education Statistics, Washington, DC: U.S. Department of Education, and Bureau of Justice Statistics, Office of Justice Programs, U.S. Department of Justice. Washington, DC.

Roberts, D. (2002). *Shattered bonds: The color of child welfare.* New York, NY: Basic Civitas Books.

Robinson, J. L., Zahn-Waxler, C., & Emde, R. N. (1994). Patterns of development in early empathic behavior: Environmental and child constitutional influences. *Social Development, 3*(2), 125–145.

Robinson-Riegler, G., & Robinson-Riegler, B. (2008). *Cognitive psychology: Applying the science of the mind.* Boston, MA: Pearson/Allyn & Bacon.

Robnett, R. D., & Leaper, C. (2013). Friendship groups, personal motivation, and gender in relation to high school students' STEM career interest. *Journal of Research on Adolescence, 23*(4), 652–664. doi: 10.1111/jora.12013

Rochat, P. (2001). Origins of self-concept. In G. Bremner & A. Fogel (Eds.), *Blackwell handbook of infant development* (pp. 191–212). Malden, MA: Blackwell.

Rochat, P. (2011). Possession and morality in early development. *New Directions for Child and Adolescent Development, 132,* 23–38.

Roche, K. M., & Ghazarian, S. R. (2012). The value of family routines for the academic success of vulnerable adolescents. *Journal of Family Issues, 33*(7), 874–897.

Rochlin, M. (2008). *Heterosexual questionnaire—Handout: A lesson plan from* Creating Safe Space for GLBTQ Youth: A Toolkit. Adapted for use by Advocates for Youth. Retrieved from http://www.advocatesforyouth.org/index.php?option=com_content&task=view&id=223&Itemid=129 (Original work published in 1977).

Rodkey, E., & Pillai Riddell, P. (2013). The infancy of infant pain research: The experimental origins of infant pain denial. *Journal of Pain, 14*(4), 338–350. doi: 10.1016/j.jpain.2012.12.017

Rodkin, P. C., Farmer, T. W., Pearl, R., & Van Acker, R. (2000). Heterogeneity of popular boys: Antisocial and prosocial configurations. *Developmental Psychology, 36*(1), 14–24.

Rodriguez, E. T., & Tamis-LeMonda, C. S. (2011). Trajectories of the home learning environment across the first 5 years: Associations with children's vocabulary and literacy skills at prekindergarten. *Child Development, 82*(4), 1058–1075.

Rodriguez, E. T., Tamis-LeMonda, C. S., Spellmann, M. E., Pan, B. A., Raikes, H., Lugo-Gil, J., & Luze, G. (2009). The formative role of home literacy experiences across the first three years of life in children from low-income families. *Journal of Applied Developmental Psychology, 30*(6), 677–694.

Roeser, R. W., & Peck, S. C. (2003). Patterns and pathways of educational achievement across adolescence: A holistic-developmental perspective. In W. Damon, S. C. Peck, & R. W. Roeser (Eds.), *New directions for child and adolescent development: Vol. 101. Person-centered approaches to studying human development in context* (pp. 39–62). San Francisco, CA: Jossey-Bass.

Rogers, J. M. (2009). Tobacco and pregnancy. *Reproductive Toxicology, 28*(2), 152–160.

Rogers, L., Zosuls, K. M., Halim, M., Ruble, D., Hughes, D., & Fuligni, A. (2012). Meaning making in middle childhood: An exploration of the meaning of ethnic identity. *Cultural Diversity and Ethnic Minority Psychology, 18*(2), 99–108.

Rogol, A., Roemmich, J., & Clark, P. (2002). Growth at puberty. *Journal of Adolescent Health, 31*(6), 192–200.

Rose, A. J., Schwartz-Mette, R. A., Smith, R. L., Asher, S. R., Swenson, L. P., Carlson, W., & Waller, E. M. (2012). How girls and boys expect disclosure about problems will make them feel: Implications for friendships. *Child Development, 83*(3), 844–863.

Rose, A., & Rudolph, K. D. (2006). A review of sex differences in peer relationship processes: Potential trade-offs for the emotional and behavioral development of girls and boys. *Psychological Bulletin, 132,* 98–131.

Rose, S. A., Feldman, J. F., Jankowski, J. J., & Van Rossem, R. (2012). Information processing from infancy to 11 years: Continuities and prediction of IQ. *Intelligence, 40*(5), 445–457. doi: 10.1016/j.intell.2012.05.007

Rose, S. A., Feldman, J. F., & Wallace, I. F. (1992). Infant information processing in relation to six-year cognitive outcomes. *Child Development, 63*(5),1126–1141.

Rosenstein, D., & Oster, H. (2005). Differential facial responses to four basic tastes in newborns. In P. Ekman & E. L. Rosenberg (Eds.), *What the face reveals: Basic and applied studies of spontaneous expression using the facial action coding system (FACS)* (2nd ed., pp. 302–327). New York, NY: Oxford University Press.

Rosenthal, R., & Jacobson, L. (1968). *Pygmalion in the classroom: Teacher expectation and pupils' intellectual development.* New York, NY: Rinehart & Winston.

Rosenzweig, M. R., Breedlove, S. M., & Watson, N. V. (2005). *Biological psychology* (4th ed.). Sunderland, MA: Sinauer.

Ross, M., & Wang, Q. (2010). Why we remember and what we remember: Culture and autobiographical memory. *Perspectives on Psychological Science, 5*(4), 401–409. doi: 10.1177/1745691610375555

Rostad, K., Yott, J., & Poulin-Dubois, D. (2012). Development of categorization in infancy: Advancing forward to the animate/inanimate level. *Infant Behavior & Development, 35*(3), 584–595. doi: 10.1016/j.infbeh.2012.05.005

Rothbart, M. K. (2007). Temperament, development, and personality. *Current Directions in Psychological Science, 16*(4), 207–212.

Rothbart, M. K., Ahadi, S. A., Hershey, K. L., & Fisher, P. (2001). Investigations of temperament at three to seven years: The Child's Behavior Questionnaire. *Child Development, 72*(5), 1394–1408.

Rothbart, M. K., Derryberry, D., & Hershey, K. (2000). Stability of temperament in childhood: Laboratory infant assessment to parent report at seven years. In V. J. Molfese & D. L. Molfese (Eds.), *Temperament and personality development across the life span* (pp. 85–119). Mahwah, NJ: Erlbaum.

Rothbaum, R., Kakinuma, M., Nagaoka, R., & Azuma, H. (2007). Attachment and AMAE: Parent-child closeness in the United States and Japan. *Journal of Cross-Cultural Psychology, 38*(4), 465–486. doi: 10.1177/0022022107302315

Rovee-Collier, C. (1999). The development of infant memory. *Current Directions in Psychological Science, 8*(3), 80–85.

Rowe, D. C. (2003). Assessing genotype-environment interactions and correlations in the postgenomic era. In R. Plomin, J. C. DeFries, I. W. Craig, & P. McGuffin (Eds.), *Behavioral genetics in the postgenomic era* (pp. 71–86). Washington, DC: American Psychological Association.

Rowe, M. L. (2008). Child-directed speech: Relation to socioeconomic status, knowledge of child development and child vocabulary skill. *Journal of Child Language, 35*(1), 185–205.

Rowe, M. L., & Goldin-Meadow, S. (2009). Differences in early gesture explain SES disparities in child vocabulary size at school entry. *Science, 323*(5916), 951–953.

Roze, E., Meijer, L., Van Braeckel, K. N., Ruiter, S. A., Bruggink, J. L., & Bos, A. F. (2010). Developmental trajectories from birth to school age in healthy term-born children. *Pediatrics, 126*(5), e1134–e1142.

Rubin, K. H., Lynch, D., Coplan, R., Rose-Krasnor, L., & Booth, C. L. (1994). "Birds of a feather . . .": Behavioral concordances and preferential personal attraction in children. *Child Development, 65*(6), 1778–1785.

Ruble, D. N., Taylor, L. J., Cyphers, L., Greulich, F. K., Lurye, L. E., & Shrout, P. E. (2007). The role of gender constancy in early gender development. *Child Development, 78*(4), 1121–1136.

Rudy, D., & Grusec, J. E. (2006). Authoritarian parenting in individualist and collectivist groups: Associations with maternal emotion and cognition and children's self-esteem. *Journal of Family Psychology, 20*(1), 68–78.

Rueda, M., Posner, M. I., & Rothbart, M. K. (2005). The development of executive attention: Contributions to the emergence of self-regulation. *Developmental Neuropsychology, 28*(2), 573–594. doi: 10.1207/s15326942dn2802_2

Ruffman, T., Perner, J., & Parkin, L. (1999). How parenting style affects false belief understanding. *Social Development, 8*(3), 395–411.

Rumberger, R. W. (2013). *Poverty and high school dropouts.* Retrieved from http://www.apa.org/pi/ses/resources/indicator/2013/05/poverty-dropouts.aspx

Russell, A., Hart, C. H., Robinson, C. C., & Olsen, S. F. (2003). Children's sociable and aggressive behavior with peers: A comparison of the US and Australia, and contributions of temperament and parenting styles. *International Journal of Behavioral Development, 27*(1), 74–86.

Russell, J. A. (1994). Is there universal recognition of emotion from facial expressions? A review of the cross-cultural studies. *Psychological Bulletin, 115*(1), 102–141.

Ryan, A. M., Shim, S., & Makara, K. A. (2013). Changes in academic adjustment and relational self-worth across the transition to middle school. *Journal of Youth and Adolescence, 42*(9), 1372–1384. doi: 10.1007/s10964-013-9984-7

Ryan, R. M., Fauth, R. C., & Brooks-Gunn, J. (2006). Childhood poverty: Implications for school readiness and early childhood education. In B. Spodek & O. Saracho (Eds.), *Handbook of research on the education of young children* (2nd ed., pp. 323–346). Mahwah, NJ: Erlbaum.

Ryder, J. F., Tunmer, W. E., & Greaney, K. T. (2008). Explicit instruction in phonemic awareness and phonemically based decoding skills as an intervention strategy for struggling readers in whole language classrooms. *Reading & Writing, 21*(4), 349–369.

Rymer, R. (1993). *Genie: An abused child's flight from silence.* New York, NY: Harper.

Sachs, J. (2005). Communication development in infancy. In J. B. Gleason (Ed.), *The development of language* (6th ed., pp. 39–61). Boston, MA: Pearson.

Sadker, D., & Zittleman, K. R. (2009). *Still failing at fairness: How gender bias cheats boys and girls in school and what we can do about it.* New York, NY: Scribner.

Sadker, M., & Sadker, D. (1995). *Failing at fairness: How our schools cheat girls.* New York, NY: Touchstone.

SafeKids. (2007). No. 1 cause of injury in elementary school: Playground accidents. *Safe Kids E-Newsletter, 19*(19). Retrieved from http://www.nlcsafekids.org/0907E-Newsletter.pdf

SafeKids USA. (2011). *Sport and recreation safety fact sheet.* Retrieved from http://www.safekids.org/our-work/research/fact-sheets/sport-and-recreation-safety-fact-sheet.html

Saffran, J. R., Johnson, E. K., Aslin, R. N., & Newport, E. L. (1999). Statistical learning of tone sequences by human infants and adults. *Cognition, 70*(1), 27–52.

Sahin, N. H., & Gungor, I. (2010). Prevention of congenital anomalies and the roles of healthcare professionals. In E. Pereira & J. Soria (Eds.), *Handbook of prenatal diagnosis: Methods, issues, and health impacts* (p. 1–39). Hauppauge, NY: Nova Science Publishers.

Sakai, T., Demura, S., & Fujii, K. (2012). Relationship between body composition and BMI in preschool children. *Sport Sciences for Health, 7*(1), 5–12.

Saleh, M., Lazonder, A. W., & De Jong, T. (2005). Effects of within-class ability grouping on social interaction, achievement, and motivation. *Instructional Science, 33*(2), 105–119. doi: 10.1007/s11251–004–6405-z

Sales, J. M., & Fivush, R. (2005). Social and emotional functions of mother-child reminiscing about stressful events. *Social Cognition, 23*(1), 70–90.

Salkind, N. J. (2004). *Introduction to theories of human development.* Thousand Oaks, CA: Sage.

Salkind, N. J. (2005). Puberty. In *Encyclopedia of human development.* Thousand Oaks, CA: Sage. Retrieved from http://www.sage-ereference.com/humandevelopment/Article_n507.html

Salmela-Aro, K. (2012). Transition to parenthood and positive parenting: Longitudinal and intervention approaches. *European Journal of Developmental Psychology, 9*(1), 21–32. doi: 10.1080/17405629.2011.607584

Salmons, B. (2010). One step closer to unraveling the genetics of autism spectrum disorder. *British Journal of Developmental Disabilities, 56*(111, Pt. 2), 167–169.

Sameroff, A. (2010). A unified theory of development: A dialectic integration of nature and nurture. *Child Development, 81*(1), 6–22.

Sameroff, A. J., & Haith, M. M. (1996). Interpreting developmental transitions. In A. J. Sameroff & M. M. Haith (Eds.), *The five to seven year shift: The age of reason and responsibility* (pp. 3–16). Chicago, IL: University of Chicago Press.

SAMHSA. (2009). *Depression takes its toll.* Retrieved from http://www.samhsa.gov/samhsanewsletter/Volume_17_Number_3/YouthAdultDepression.aspx

SAMHSA (2012). *2012 national strategy for suicide prevention: How you can play a role in preventing suicide.* Retrieved from http://surgeongeneral.gov/library/reports/national-strategy-suicide-prevention/factsheet.pdf

Sammons, W. A. H., & Lewis, J. M. (1985). *Premature babies: A different beginning.* St. Louis, MO: Mosby.

Sandnabba, N. K., & Ahlberg, C. (1999). Parents' attitudes and expectations about children's cross-gender behavior. *Sex Roles, 40*(3–4), 249–263.

Sandstrom, M. J., & Zakriski, A. L. (2004). Understanding the experience of peer rejection. In J. B. Kupersmidt & K. A. Dodge (Eds.), *Children's peer relations: From development to intervention* (pp. 101–118). Washington, DC: American Psychological Association.

Sann, C., & Streri, A. (2007). Perception of object shape and texture in human newborns: Evidence from cross-modal transfer tasks. *Developmental Science, 10*(3), 399–410.

Sassu, K. A., Elinoff, M. J., Bray, M. A., & Kehle, T. J. (2004). *Bullies and victims: Information for parents.* Retrieved from http://www.nasponline.org/resources/handouts/revisedPDFs/bulliesvictims.pdf

Sato, Y., Sogabe, Y., & Mazuka, R. (2010). Discrimination of phonemic vowel length by Japanese infants. *Developmental Psychology, 46*(1), 106–119.

Savin-Williams, R. C., & Diamond, L. M. (1999). Sexual orientation. In W. K. Silverman (Ed.), *Development issues in the clinical treatment of children* (pp. 241–258). Needham Heights, MA: Allyn & Bacon.

Savin-Williams, R. C., & Ream, G. L. (2003). Sex variations in the disclosure to parents of same-sex attractions. *Journal of Family Psychology, 17*(3), 429–438.

Saxbe, D. E., & Repetti, R. L. (2009). Brief report: Fathers' and mothers' marital relationship predicts daughters' pubertal development two years later. *Journal of Adolescence, 32*(2), 415–423.

Saygin, Z. M., Norton, E. S., Osher, D. E., Beach, S. D., Cyr, A. B., Ozernov-Palchik, O., Yendiki, A., Fischl, B., Gaab, N., & Gabrieli, J. D. E. (2013). Tracking the roots of reading ability: White matter volume and integrity correlate with phonological awareness in prereading and early-reading kindergarten children. *Journal of Neuroscience, 33*(33), 13251–13258.

Sayler, M. F., & Brookshire, W. K. (2004). Social, emotional and behavior adjustment of accelerated students, students in gifted classes, and regular students in eighth grade. In S. M. Moon (Ed.), *Social/emotional issues, underachievement, and counseling of gifted and talented students* (pp. 9–19). Thousand Oaks, CA: Corwin.

Saylor, M. M., Ganea, P. A., & Vazquez, M. D. (2011). What's mine is mine: Twelve-month olds use possession pronouns to identify referents. *Developmental Science, 14*(4), 859–864.

Scarlett, W. G., Naudeau, S., Salonius-Pasternak, D., & Ponte, I. (2005). *Children's play.* Thousand Oaks, CA: Sage.

Scarr, S. (1992). Developmental theories for the 1990s: Development and individual differences. *Child Development, 63*, 1–19.

Scarr, S., & McCartney, K. (1983). How people make their own environments: A theory of genotype environment effects. *Child Development, 54*(2), 424–435.

Schalet, A. (2007). Adolescent sexuality viewed through two different cultural lenses. In M. S. Tepper & A. F. Owens (Eds.), *Sexual health: Moral and cultural foundations* (Vol. 3, pp. 365–387). Westport, CT: Praeger.

Schiffer, M. (Writer), & Avildsen, J. G. (Director). (1989). *Lean on me* [Motion picture]. United States: Warner Bros.

Schlam, T. R., Wilson, N. L., Shoda, Y., Mischel, W., & Ayduk, O. (2013). Preschoolers' delay of gratification predicts their body mass 30 years later. *Journal of Pediatrics, 162*(1), 90–93. doi: 10.1016/j.jpeds.2012.06.049

Schmader, T. (2010). Stereotype threat deconstructed. *Current Directions in Psychological Science, 19*(1), 14–18.

Schmidt, J., Shumow, L., & Kackar, H. (2007). Adolescents' participation in service activities and its impact on academic, behavioral, and civic outcomes. *Journal of Youth and Adolescence, 36*(2), 127–140.

Schmidt, L. A., & Tasker, S. L. (2000). Childhood shyness: Determinants, development and "depathology." In W. R. Crozier (Ed.), *Shyness: Development, consolidation and change* (pp. 30–46). New York, NY: Routledge.

Schmidt, M. E., & Anderson, D. R. (2007). The impact of television on cognitive development and educational achievement. In N. Pecora, J. P. Murray, & E. A. Wartella (Eds.), *Children and television: Fifty years of research* (pp. 65–84). Mahwah, NJ: Erlbaum.

Schmidt, M. E., Pempek, T. A., Kirkorian, H. L., Lund, A. F., & Anderson, D. R. (2008). The effects of background television on the toy play behavior of very young children. *Child Development, 79*(4), 1137–1151.

Schmit, S., & Matthews, H. (2013, August). *Better for babies: A study in state infant and toddler child care policies. CLASP.* Retrieved from http://www.clasp.org/resources-and-publications/files/BetterforBabies2.pdf

Schneider Rosen, K., & Burke, P. B. (1999). Multiple attachment relationships within families: Mothers and fathers with two young children. *Developmental Psychology, 35*(2), 436–441.

Schneider, W. (2002). Memory development in childhood. In U. Goswami (Ed.), *Blackwell handbook of childhood cognitive development* (pp. 236–256). Malden, MA: Blackwell.

Schneider, W., Bjorklund, D. F., & Maier-Bruckner, W. (1996). The effects of expertise and IQ on children's memory: When knowledge is, and when it is not enough. *International Journal of Behavioral Development, 19*(4), 773–796. doi: 10.1080/016502596385578

Schneider, W., Kron, V., Hünnerkopf, M., & Krajewski, K. (2004). The development of young children's memory strategies: First findings from the Würzburg Longitudinal Memory Study. *Journal of Experimental Child Psychology, 88*(2), 193–209. doi: 10.1016/j.jecp.2004.02.004

Scholte, R. H. J., Engels, R. C. M. E., de Kemp, R. A. T., Harakeh, Z., & Overbeek, G. (2007). Differential parental treatment, sibling relationships and delinquency in adolescence. *Journal of Youth and Adolescence, 36*(5), 661–671.

Schoppe-Sullivan, S. J., Diener, M. L., Mangelsdorf, S. C., Brown, G. L., McHale, J. L., & Frosch, C. A. (2006). Attachment and sensitivity in family context: The roles of parent and infant gender. *Infant and Child Development, 15*(4), 367–385.

Schulman, C. (2001). *Losing baby teeth.* Retrieved from http://www.parents.com/kids/hygiene/tooth-care/losing-baby-teeth/

Schuntermann, P. (2007). The sibling experience: Growing up with a child who has pervasive developmental disorder or mental retardation. *Harvard Review of Psychiatry, 15*(3), 93–108.

Schwarz, S. W., & Peterson, J. (2010). *Adolescent obesity in the United States: Facts for policymakers.* New York. NY: National Center for Children in Poverty.

Schweinhart, L. J. (2013). Long-term follow-up of a preschool experiment. *Journal of Experimental Criminology, 9*(4), 389–409. doi: 10.1007/s11292-013-9190-3

Scott, L. K. (2013). Presence of Type 2 diabetes risk factors in children. *Pediatric Nursing, 39*(4), 190–196.

Scott, R. M., & Baillargeon, R. (2009). Which penguin is this? Attributing false beliefs about object identity at 18 months. *Child Development, 80*(4), 1172–1196.

Scriver, C. R. (2007). The PAH gene, phenylketonuria, and a paradigm shift. *Human Mutation, 28*(9), 831–845.

Search Institute. (2012). *What kids need: Developmental assets.* Retrieved from http://www.search-institute.org/developmental-assets

Seaton, E. K., Scottham, K., & Sellers, R. M. (2006). The status model of racial identity development in African American adolescents: Evidence of structure, trajectories, and well-being. *Child Development, 77*(5), 1416–1426. doi: 10.1111/j.1467-8624.2006.00944.x

Sebastian, R. S., Wilkinson Enns, C., & Goldman, J. D. (2009). US adolescents and MyPyramid: Associations between fast-food consumption and lower likelihood of meeting recommendations. *Journal of the American Dietetic Association, 109*(2), 226–235.

Sedgh, G., Singh, S., Shah, I. H., Åhman, E., Henshaw, S. K., & Bankole, A. (2012). Induced abortion: Incidence and trends worldwide from 1995 to 2008. *The Lancet, 379*(9816), 625–632. doi: 10.1016/S0140-6736(11)61786-8

Sedlak, A. J., Mettenburg, J., Basena, M., Petta, I., McPherson, K., Greene, A., & Li, S. (2010). *Fourth National Incidence Study of Child Abuse and Neglect (NIS–4): Report to Congress.* Washington, DC: U.S. Department of Health and Human Services, Administration for Children and Families.

Segal, M. (2004). The roots and fruits of pretending. In E. F. Zigler, D. G. Singer, & S. J. Bishop-Josef (Eds.), *Children's play—The roots of reading* (pp. 33–48). Washington, DC: Zero to Three Press.

Segovia, C., Hutchinson, I., Laing, D. G., & Jinks, A. L. (2002). A quantitative study of fungiform papillae and taste pore density in adults and children. *Developmental Brain Research, 138*(2), 135–146. doi: 10.1016/S0165-3806(02)00463-7

Sellers, R. M., Copeland-Linder, N., Martin, P. P., & Lewis, L. (2006). Racial identity matters: The relationship between racial discrimination and psychological functioning in African-American adolescents. *Journal of Research on Adolescence, 16*(2), 187–216.

Semrud-Clikeman, M. (2014). *Research in brain function and learning. American Psychological Association.* Retrieved from http://www.apa.org/education/k12/brain-function.aspx?item=1

Sénéchal, M., Ouellette, G., Pagan, S., & Lever, R. (2012). The role of invented spelling on learning to read in low-phoneme awareness kindergartners: A randomized-control-trial study. *Reading & Writing, 25*(4), 917–934.

Seo, Y., Abbott, R. D., & Hawkins, J. D. (2008). Outcome status of students with learning disabilities at ages 21 and 14. *Journal of Learning Disabilities, 41*(4), 300–314.

Serbin, L. A., Stack, D. M., & Kingdon, D. (2013). Academic success across the transition from primary to secondary schooling among lower-income adolescents: Understanding the effects of family resources and gender. *Journal of Youth and Adolescence, 42*(9), 1331–1347. doi: 10.1007/s10964-013-9987-4

Serrano, E., & Powell, A. (2013). *Healthy eating for children 2 to 5 years old: A guide for parents and caregivers* (Publication 384-150). Blacksburg: Virginia Cooperative Extension.

Sesame Street Workshop. (2014). *Sweeping the clouds away for 43 years—and counting.* Retrieved from http://www.sesameworkshop.org/what-we-do/our-initiatives/sesame-street/

Sesma, A., Mannes, M., & Scales, P. C. (2005). Positive adaptation, resilience, and the developmental asset framework. In S. Goldstein & R. B. Brooks (Eds.), *Handbook of resilience in children* (pp. 281–296). New York, NY: Springer.

Setliff, A. E., & Courage, M. L. (2011). Background television and infants' allocation of their attention during toy play. *Infancy, 16*(6), 611–639. doi: 10.1111/j.1532-7078.2011.00070.x

Shahaeian, A., Peterson, C. C., Slaughter, V., & Wellman, H. M. (2011). Culture and the sequence of steps in theory of mind development. *Developmental Psychology, 47*(5), 1239–1247. doi: 10.1037/a0023899

Shakoor, S., Jaffee, S. R., Bowes, L., Ouellet-Morin, I., Andreou, P., Happé, F., Moffitt, T. E., & Arseneault, L. (2012). A prospective longitudinal study of children's theory of mind and adolescent involvement in bullying. *Journal of Child Psychology & Psychiatry, 53*(3), 254–261. doi: 10.1111/j.1469-7610.2011.02488.x

Shamir-Essakow, G., Ungerer, J. A., & Rapee, R. M. (2005). Attachment, behavioral inhibition, and anxiety in preschool children. *Journal of Abnormal Child Psychology, 33*(2), 131–143.

Shanahan, T. (2004). Critiques of the National Reading Panel report. In P. McCardle & V. Chhabra (Eds.), *The voice of evidence in reading research* (pp. 235–265). Baltimore, MD: Brooks.

Shapiro, L. R., Hurry, J., Masterson, J., Wydell, T. N., & Doctor, E. (2009). Classroom implications of recent research into literacy development: From predictors to assessment. *Dyslexia, 15*(1), 1–22.

Shaver, P. R., & Mikulincer, M. (2014). Attachment bonds in romantic relationships. In M. Mikulincer & P. R. Shaver (Eds.), *Mechanisms of social connection: From brain to group* (pp. 273–290). Washington, DC: American Psychological Association.

Shaw, D. S., Owens, E. B., & Giovannelli, J. (2001). Infant and toddler pathways leading to early externalizing disorders. *Journal of the American Academy of Child and Adolescent Psychiatry, 40*(1), 36–43.

Shayer, M., & Ginsburg, D. (2009). Thirty years on—a large anti-Flynn effect? (II): 13- and 14-year-olds. Piagetian tests of formal operations norms 1976-2006/7. *British Journal of Educational Psychology, 79*(3), 409–418.

Shea, A. K., & Steiner, M. (2008). Cigarette smoking during pregnancy. *Nicotine and Tobacco Research, 10*(2), 267–278.

Shearer, C. L., Crouter, A. C., & McHale, S. (2005). Parents' perceptions of changes in mother-child and father-child relationships during adolescence. *Journal of Adolescent Research, 20*(6), 662–684.

Sheldon, A., & Strange, W. (1982). The acquisition of /r/ and /l/ by Japanese learners of English: Evidence that speech production can precede speech perception. *Applied Psycholinguistics, 3*(3), 243–261.

Shelov, S. P., & Altmann, T. R. (2009). *Caring for your baby and young child* (5th ed.). Elk Grove, IL: American Academy of Pediatrics.

Shepard, S., & Metzler, D. (1988). Mental rotation: Effects of dimensionality of objects and type of task. *Journal of Experimental Psychology: Human Perception and Performance, 14*(1), 3–11.

Shield, J., & Mullen, M. C. (2012). *Healthy eating, healthy weight for kids and teens.* Washington, DC: Eat Right Press, Academy of Nutrition and Dietetics.

Shih, J. H., Eberhard, N. K., Hammen, C., & Brennan, P. A. (2006). Differential exposure and reactivity to interpersonal stress predict sex differences in adolescent depression. *Journal of Clinical Child and Adolescent Psychology, 35,* 103–115.

Shih, P., Keehn, B., Oram, J. K., Leyden, K. M., Keown, C. L., & Müller, R. (2011). Functional differentiation of posterior superior temporal sulcus in autism: A functional connectivity magnetic resonance imaging study. *Biological Psychiatry, 70*(3), 270–277. doi: 10.1016/j.biopsych.2011.03.040

Shoda, Y., Mischel, W., & Peake, P. K. (1990). Predicting adolescent cognitive and self-regulatory competencies from preschool delay of gratification: Identifying diagnostic conditions. *Developmental Psychology, 26*(6), 978–986.

Shonkoff, J. P., Garner, A. S., & Committee on Psychosocial Aspects of Child and Family Health, Committee on Early Childhood, Adoption and Department Care, and Section on Development and Behavioral Pediatrics. (2012). The lifelong effects of early childhood adversity and toxic stress. *Pediatrics, 129*(1), e232–e246.

Shonkoff, J. P., & Phillips, D. A. (2000). *From neurons to neighborhoods: The science of early childhood development.* Washington, DC: National Academy Press.

Short, M. A., Gradisar, M., Lack, L. C., & Wright, H. R. (2013). The impact of sleep on adolescent depressed mood, alertness and academic performance. *Journal of Adolescence, 36*(6), 1025–1033. doi: 10.1016/j.adolescence.2013.08.007

Sibley, C. G., & Overall, N. C. (2008). Modeling the hierarchical structure of attachment representations: A test of domain differentiation. *Personality and Individual Differences, 44,* 238–249.

Sicherer, S. H., Mahr, T., & The American Academy of Pediatrics Section on Allergy and Immunology. (2010). Management of food allergy in the school setting. *Pediatrics, 126*(6), 1232–1239.

Siega-Riz, A. M., Deming, D. M., Reidy, K. C., Fox, M. K., Condon, E., & Briefel, R. R. (2010). Food consumption patterns of infants and toddlers: Where are we now? *Journal of the American Dietetic Association,* supplement, 110, S38–S51.

Siegel, D. H. (2012). Growing up in open adoption: Young adult's perspectives. *Families in Society, 93*(2), 133–140.

Siegel, D. H. (2013). Open adoption: Adoptive parents' reactions two decades later. *Social Work, 58*(1), 43–52. doi: 10.1093/sw/sws053

Siegler, R., & Crowley, K. (1991). The microgenetic method: A direct means for studying cognitive development. *American Psychologist, 46*(6), 606–620.

Siennick, S. E. (2013). Still the favorite? Parents' differential treatment of siblings entering young adulthood. *Journal of Marriage and Family, 75*(4), 981–994.

Silberglitt, B., Jimerson, S. R., Burns, M. K., & Appleton, J. J. (2006). Does the timing of grade retention make a difference? Examining the effects of early versus later retention. *School Psychology Review, 35*(1), 134–141.

Silvers, J. A., McRae, K., Gabrieli, J. E., Gross, J. J., Remy, K. A., & Ochsner, K. N. (2012). Age-related differences in emotional reactivity, regulation, and rejection sensitivity in adolescence. *Emotion, 12*(6), 1235–1247. doi: 10.1037/a0028297

Sim, L., Lebow, J., & Billings, M. (2013). Eating disorders in adolescents with a history of obesity. *Pediatrics, 132*(4), e1026–e1030. doi: 10.1542/peds.2012-3940

Simcock, G., & Hayne, H. (2002). Breaking the barrier? Children fail to translate their preverbal memories into language. *Psychological Science, 13*(3), 225–231.

Simola, P. P., Liukkonen, K. K., Pitkäranta, A. A., Pirinen, T. T., & Aronen, E. T. (2012). Psychosocial and somatic outcomes of sleep problems in children: A 4-year follow-up study. *Child: Care, Health and Development, 40*(1), 60–67. doi: 10.1111/j.1365–2214.2012.01412.x

Simpson, J. L. (2007). Causes of fetal wastage. *Clinical Obstetrics and Gynecology, 50*(1), 10–30.

Simpson, R., de Boer-Ott, S., Griswold, D., Myles, B. S., Byrd, S., Ganz, J., et al. (2005). *Autism spectrum disorders: Interventions and treatments for children and youth.* Thousand Oaks, CA: Corwin.

Singer, D. G., & Revenson, T. A. (1996). *A Piaget primer* (Rev. ed.). New York, NY: Penguin Books.

Singh, A. S., Mulder, C., Twisk, J. W., van Mechelen, W., & Chinapaw, M. J. (2008). Tracking of childhood overweight into adulthood: A systematic review of the literature. *Obesity Review, 9*(5), 474–88.

Sirois, S., & Jackson, I. R. (2012). Pupil dilation and object permanence in infants. *Infancy, 17,* 61–78. doi: 10.1111/j.1532-7078.2011.00096.x

Skafida, V. (2012). Juggling work and motherhood: The impact of employment and maternity leave on breastfeeding duration: A survival analysis on growing up in Scotland. *Maternal and Child Health Journal, 16*(2), 519–527.

Skinner, B. F. (1953). *Science and human behavior.* New York, NY: Macmillan.

Skinner, B. F. (1991). *Verbal behavior.* Acton, MA: Copley. (Original work published in 1957)

Skinner, M. K., Haque, C. M., Nilsson, E., Bhandari, R., & McCarrey, J. R. (2013). Environmentally induced transgenerational epigenetic reprogramming of primordial germ cells and the subsequent germ line. *PLoS ONE, 8*(7), 1–15. doi: 10.1371/journal.pone.0066318

Skogerbø, A., Kesmodel, U., Denny, C., Kjaersgaard, M., Wimberley, T., Landrø, N., & Mortensen, E. (2013). The effects of low to moderate alcohol consumption and binge drinking in early pregnancy on behaviour in 5-year-old children. *BJOG: An International Journal of Obstetrics & Gynaecology, 120*(9), 1042–1050. doi: 10.1111/1471–0528.12208.

Skuse, D., Bruce, H., Dowdney, L., & Mrazek, D. (2011). *Child psychology and psychiatry: Frameworks for practice*. Hoboken, NJ: Wiley.

Slater, A., Field, T., & Hernandez-Reif, M. (2007). The development of the senses. In A. Slater & M. Lewis (Eds.), *Introduction to infant development*. New York, NY: Oxford University Press.

Sleet, D. A., Ballesteros, M. F., & Borse, N. N. (2010). A review of unintentional injuries in adolescents. *Annual Review of Public Health, 31*, 195–212.

Slotkin, T. A. (2008). If nicotine is a developmental neurotoxicant in animal studies, dare we recommend nicotine replacement therapy in pregnant women and adolescents? *Neurotoxicology and Teratology, 30*(1), 1–19.

Smetana, J. G. (2011). *Adolescents, families, and social development: How teens construct their worlds*. Malden, MA: Wiley-Blackwell.

Smetana, J. G., Metzger, A., & Campione-Barr, N. (2004). African American late adolescents' relationships with parents: Developmental transitions and longitudinal patterns. *Child Development, 75*(3), 932–947.

Smilansky, S. (1968). *The effects of sociodramatic play on disadvantaged preschool children*. New York, NY: Wiley.

Smith, A. (2013). *Head Start Trauma Smart: Creating trauma-informed Head Start communities*. Region Seven Head Start Association. Retrieved from http://www.saintlukeshealthsystem.org/sites/default/files/files/Head%20Start%20Trauma%20Smart%20Article-Summer%202013%20Magazine(1).pdf

Smith-Spangler, C., Brandeau, M., Hunter, G., Bavinger, J., Pearson, M., Eschbach, P., . . . Bravata, D. (2012). Are organic foods safer or healthier than conventional alternatives?: A systematic review. *Annals of Internal Medicine, 157*(5), 348–366.

Smolak, L. (2004). Body image in children and adolescents: Where do we go from here? *Body Image, 1*(1), 15–28.

Smotherman, W. P., & Robinson, S. R. (1996). The development of behavior before birth. *Developmental Psychology, 32*(3), 425–434.

Smyke, A., Zeanah, C., Gleason, M., Drury, S., Fox, N., Nelson, C., & Guthrie, D. (2012). A randomized controlled trial comparing foster care and institutional care for children with signs of reactive attachment disorder. *American Journal of Psychiatry, 169*(5), 508–514.

Snow, K. (n.d.). *Research news you can use: Debunking the play vs. learning dichotomy*. National Association for the Education of Young Children. Retrieved from http://www.naeyc.org/content/research-news-you-can-use-play-vs-learning

Snow, R. E. (1995). Pygmalion and intelligence? *Current Directions in Psychological Sciences, 4*(6), 169–171.

Snow, R. F. (1981, June/July). Martin Couney. *American Heritage Magazine, 32*(4). Retrieved from http://www.americanheritage.com/articles/magazine/ah/1981/4/1981_4_90.shtml

Snowling, M. J., & Hulme, C. (2011). Evidence-based interventions for reading and language difficulties: Creating a virtuous circle. *British Journal of Educational Psychology, 81*, 1–23.

Society for Neuroscience. (2007). The adolescent brain. *Brain Briefings*. Retrieved from http://www.sfn.org/index.aspx?pagename=brainBriefings_Adolescent_brain

Society for Research in Child Development. (2007). *Ethical standards for research with children*. Retrieved from http://www.srcd.org/index.php?option=com_content&task=view&id=68&Itemid=499

Solomon, S., & Knafo, A. (2007). Value similarity in adolescent friendships. In T. C. Rhodes (Ed.), *Focus on adolescent behavior research* (pp 133–155). Hauppauge, NY: Nova Science.

Sorace, A. (2006). The more, the merrier: Facts and beliefs about the bilingual mind. In S. Della Sala (Ed.), *Tall tales about the mind and brain: Separating fact from fiction* (pp. 193–203). Oxford, UK: Oxford University Press.

Sorhagen, N. S. (2013). Early teacher expectations disproportionately affect poor children's high school performance. *Journal of Educational Psychology, 105*(2), 465–477.

Southam-Gerow, M. A., & Chorpita, B. F. (2007). Anxiety in children and adolescents. In E. J. Mash & R. A. Barkley (Eds.), *Assessment of childhood disorders* (pp. 347–397). New York, NY: Guilford Press.

Southern Regional Education Board. (2001). *Finding alternatives to failure: Can states end social promotion and reduce retention rates?* Atlanta, GA: Author.

Southgate, V., Senju, A., & Csibra, G. (2007). Action anticipation through attribution of false belief by 2-year-olds. *Psychological Science, 18*(7), 587–592.

SPARK. (2009–2014). *The impact of budget cuts on physical education*. Retrieved from http://visual.ly/effect-budget-cuts-physical-education

Sparks, B. F., Friedman, S. D., Shaw, D. W., Aylward, E. H., Echelard, D., Artru, A. A., . . . Dager, S. R. (2002). Brain structural abnormalities in young children with autism spectrum disorder. *Neurology, 29*(2), 184–192. doi: 10.1212/WNL.59.2.184

Spelke, E. S. (2000). Core knowledge. *American Psychologist, 55*(11), 1233–1243.

Spelke, E. S., & Kinzler, K. D. (2007). Core knowledge. *Developmental Science 10*(1), 89–96.

Spencer, J. P., Clearfield, M., Corbetta, D., Ulrich, B., Buchanan, P., & Schöner, G. (2006). Moving toward a grand theory of development: In memory of Esther Thelen. *Child Development, 77*(6), 1521–1538.

Spencer, J. P., Perone, S., & Buss, A. (2011). Twenty years and going strong: A dynamic systems revolution in motor and cognitive development. *Child Development Perspectives, 5*, 260–266.

Spera, C. (2005). A review of the relationship among parenting practices, parenting styles, and adolescent school achievement. *Educational Psychology Review, 17*(2), 125–146.

Spielberg, S. (Director). (1982). *E.T.: The extra-terrestrial* [Motion picture]. United States: Universal.

Spitzer, R. L. (1981). The diagnostic status of homosexuality in DSM-III: A reformulation of the issues. *American Journal of Psychiatry, 138*, 210–215.

Sprengelmeyer, R., Perrett, D. I., Fagan, E. C., Cornwell, R. E., Lobmaier, J. S., Sprengelmeyer, A., . . . Young, A. W. (2009). The cutest little baby face: A hormonal link to sensitivity to cuteness in infant faces. *Psychological Science, 20*(2), 149–154.

Squeglia, L. M., Jacobus, J., & Tapert, S. F. (2009). The influence of substance use on adolescent brain development. *Journal of Clinical EEG & Neuroscience, 40*(1), 31–38.

Squeglia, L. M., Pulido, C., Wetherill, R. R., Jacobus, J., Brown, G. G., & Tapert, S. F. (2012). Brain response to working memory over three years of adolescence: Influence of initiating heavy drinking. *Journal of Studies on Alcohol and Drugs, 73*(5), 749–760.

Sroufe, L. A. (2005). Attachment and development: A prospective, longitudinal study from birth to adulthood. *Attachment and Human Development, 7*(4), 349–367.

Sroufe, L. A. (2009). The concept of development in developmental psychopathology. *Child Development Perspectives, 3*, 178–183.

Sroufe, L. A., Carlson, E., & Shulman, S. (1993). Individuals in relationships: Development from infancy through adolescence. In D. C. Funder, R. D. Parke, C. Tomlinson-Keasey, & K. Widaman (Eds.), *Studying lives through time* (pp. 315–342). Washington, DC: American Psychological Association.

Sroufe, L. A., Egeland, B., Carlson, E., & Collins, W. A. (2005). Placing early attachment experiences in developmental context. In K. E. Grossmann, K. Grossmann, & E. Waters (Eds.), *Attachment from infancy to adulthood* (pp. 48–70). New York, NY: Guilford Press.

St. James-Roberts, I. (2007). Helping parents to manage infant crying and sleeping: A review of the evidence and its implications for services. *Child Abuse Review, 16*(1), 47–69.

St. Rose, A. (2010). Why so few? Women in science, technology, engineering, and mathematics. *Outlook, 104*(1), 8–11.

Stebbins, L. F. (2001). *Work and family in America: A reference handbook*. Santa Barbara, CA: ABC-CLIO.

Steffens, M. C., Jelenec, P., & Noack, P. (2010). On the leaky math pipeline: Comparing implicit math-gender stereotypes and math withdrawal in female and male children and adolescents. *Journal of Educational Psychology, 102*(4), 947–963. doi:10.1037/a0019920

Steinberg, L., Mounts, N. S., Lamborn, S. D., & Dornbusch, S. M. (1991). Authoritative parenting and adolescent adjustment across varied ecological niches. *Journal of Research on Adolescence, 1*(1), 19–36.

Steinberg, L., & Silk, J. S. (2002). Parenting adolescents. In M. H. Bornstein (Ed.), *Handbook of parenting* (2nd ed., pp. 103–133). Mahwah, NJ: Erlbaum.

Steiner, G., & Smith, J. A. (1999). *Learning: Nineteen scenarios from everyday life*. Cambridge, UK: Cambridge University Press.

Steinhausen, H. C. (2009). The heterogeneity of causes and courses of attention-deficit/hyperactivity disorder. *Acta Psychiatrica Scandinavica, 120*(5), 392–399.

Sterling, E. W., & Best-Boss, A. (2013). *Your child's teeth: A complete guide for parents*. Baltimore, MD: Johns Hopkins University Press.

Stern, M., Karraker, K., McIntosh, B., Moritzen, S., & Olexa, M. (2006). Prematurity stereotyping and mothers' interaction with their premature and full-term infants during the first year. *Journal of Pediatric Psychology, 31*(6), 597–607.

Sternberg, R. J. (2002a). Beyond g: The theory of successful intelligence. In R. J. Sternberg & E. L. Grigorenko (Eds.), *The general factor of intelligence: How general is it?* (pp. 447–479). Mahwah, NJ: Erlbaum.

Sternberg, R. J. (2002b). Raising the achievement of all students: Teaching for successful intelligence. *Educational Psychology Review, 14*(4), 383–393.

Sternberg, R. J. (2003a). Creative thinking in the classroom. *Scandinavian Journal of Educational Research, 47*(3), 325–338.

Sternberg, R. J. (2003b). Our research program validating the triarchic theory of successful intelligence: Reply to Gottfredson. *Intelligence, 31*(4), 399–413.

Sternberg, R. J., Castejón, J. L., Prieto, M. D., Hautamäki, J., & Grigorenko, E. L. (2001). Confirmatory factor analysis of the Sternberg Triarchic Abilities Test in three international samples: An empirical test of the triarchic theory of intelligence. *European Journal of Psychological Assessment, 17*(1), 1–16.

Sternberg, R. J., & Detterman, D. K. (Eds.). (1986). *What is intelligence? Contemporary viewpoints on its nature and definition*. Norwood, NJ: Ablex.

Sternstein, A. (2007). Childhood obesity: An ounce of prevention is worth a pound. *Family Practice Recertification, 29*(3), 19–29.

Stice, E., & Shaw, H. (2004). Eating disorder prevention programs: A meta-analytic review. *Psychological Bulletin, 130*(2), 206–227.

Stiefel Laboratories. (2008). *Contraception counseling referral program*. Retrieved from http://www.soriatane.com/media/ContraceptCounseling.pdf

Stiles, J. (2009). On genes, brains and behavior: Why should developmental psychologists care about brain development? *Child Development Perspectives, 3*, 196–202.

Stipek, D. J. (2002). School entry age. In R. E. Tremblay, M. Boivin, & R. DeV. Peters (Eds.), *Encyclopedia on early childhood development* [online]. Montreal, Quebec, Canada: Centre of Excellence for Early Childhood. Retrieved from http://www.child-encyclopedia.com/Pages/PDF/StipekANGxp.pdf

Stipek, D. J., Gralinski, H., & Kopp, C. B. (1990). Self-concept development in the toddler years. *Developmental Psychology, 26*(6), 972–977.

Storey, A. E., Walsh, C. J., Quinton, R. L., & Wynne-Edwards, K. E. (2000). Hormonal correlates of paternal responsiveness in new and expectant fathers. *Evolution and Human Behavior, 21*(2), 79–95.

Stormshak, E. A., Comeau, C. A., & Shepard, S. A. (2004). The relative contribution of sibling deviance and peer deviance in the prediction of substance use across middle childhood. *Journal of Abnormal Child Psychology, 32*(6), 635–649. doi: 10.1023/B:JACP.0000047212.49463.c7

Story, M., Kaphingst, K. M., & French, S. (2006). The role of schools in obesity prevention. *Future of Children, 16*(1), 109–142.

Stowe, L. A., & Sabourin, L. (2005). Imaging the processing of a second language: Effects of maturation and proficiency on the neural processes involved. *IRAL: International Review of Applied Linguistics in Language Teaching, 43*(4), 329–353.

Strayer, D. L., Drews, F. A., & Crouch, D. J. (2006). Fatal distraction? A comparison of the cell phone driver and the drunk driver. *Human Factors, 48*(2), 381–391.

Strelau, J. (1998). *Temperament: A psychological perspective.* New York, NY: Plenum.

Strohschein, L. (2005). Parental divorce and child mental health trajectories. *Journal of Marriage and Family, 67*(5), 1286–1300.

Sturm, L. (2004). Temperament in early childhood: A primer for the perplexed. In *Zero to Three.* Retrieved from http://www.zero tothree.org/site/DocServer/v0124–4a.pdf?docID=1761&AddInterest=1158

Subrahmanyam, K., & Greenfield, P. (2008). Online communication and adolescent relationships. *Future of Children, 18*(1), 119–146.

Substance Abuse and Mental Health Services Administration, Office of Applied Studies. (2007). *The NSDUH Report: Youth activities, substance use, and family income.* Rockville, MD: Author.

Substance Abuse and Mental Health Services Administration. (2009). *National report finds low levels of substance use among pregnant women, but higher levels in new mothers.* Retrieved from http://www.samhsa.gov/newsroom/advisories/0905202210.aspx

Sullivan, R. M., & Toubas, P. (1998). Clinical usefulness of maternal odor in newborns: Soothing and feeding preparatory responses. *Biology of the Neonate, 74*(6), 402–408.

Sumter, S. R., Bokhorst, C. L., Steinberg, L., & Westenberg, P. (2009). The developmental pattern of resistance to peer influence in adolescence: Will the teenager ever be able to resist? *Journal of Adolescence, 32*(4), 1009–1021. doi: 10.1016/j.adolescence.2008.08.010

Suomen Akatemia (Academy of Finland). (2013, October 22). New evidence for role of specific virus causing type 1 diabetes. *ScienceDaily.* Retrieved November 21, 2014, from www.sciencedaily.com/releases/2013/10/131022091721.htm

Super, C. M. (1976). Environmental effects on motor development: The case of African infant precocity. *Developmental Medicine & Child Neurology, 18*(5), 561–567.

Surkan, P. J., Zhang, A., Trachtenberg, F., Daniel, D. B., McKinlay, S., & Bellinger, D. C. (2007). Neuropsychological function in children with blood lead levels <10 µg/dL. *NeuroToxicology, 28*(6), 1170–1177.

Susman-Stillman, A., Kalkose, M., Egeland, B., & Waldman, I. (1996). Infant temperament and maternal sensitivity as predictors of attachment security. *Infant Behavior & Development, 19*(1), 33–47.

Suzuki, L. K., & Beale, I. I. (2006). Personal Web home pages of adolescents with cancer: Self-presentation, information dissemination, and interpersonal connection. *Journal of Pediatric Oncology Nursing, 23*(3), 152–161.

Suzuki, L. K., & Calzo, J. P. (2004). The search for peer advice in cyberspace: An examination of online teen bulletin boards about health and sexuality. *Journal of Applied Developmental Psychology, 25*(6), 685–698.

Svanberg, P. O. G. (1998). Attachment, resilience and prevention. *Journal of Mental Health, 7*(6), 543–578.

Svensson, R., & Oberwittler, D. (2010). It's not the time they spend, it's what they do: The interaction between delinquent friends and unstructured routine activity on delinquency: Findings from two countries. *Journal of Criminal Justice, 38*(5), 1006–1014.

Swanson, H. (2006–2014). *Dynamic assessment.* Retrieved from http://www.education.com/reference/article/dynamic-assessment

Symonds, W. C., Schwartz, R. B., & Ferguson, R. (2011). *Pathways to prosperity: Meeting the Challenge of Preparing Young Americans for the 21st Century.* Report issued by the Pathways to Prosperity Project, Harvard Graduate School of Education.

Szyf, M., & Bick, J. (2013). DNA methylation: A mechanism for embedding early life experiences in the genome. *Child Development, 84*(1), 49–57.

Taddio, A. (2001). Pain management for neonatal circumcision. *Paediatric Drugs, 3*(2), 101–111.

Tamis-LeMonda, C. S., Bornstein, M. H., & Baumwell, L. (2001). Maternal responsiveness and children's achievement of language milestones. *Child Development, 72*(3), 748–767.

Tamis-LeMonda, C. S., Cristofaro, T. N., Rodriguez, E. T., & Bornstein, M. H. (2006). Early language development: Social influences in the first years of life. In L. Balter & C. S. Tamis-LeMonda (Eds.), *Child psychology: A handbook of contemporary issues* (2nd ed., pp. 79–108). New York, NY: Psychology Press.

Tandon, R., Gaebel, W., Barch, D. M., Bustillo, J., Gur, R. E., Heckers, S., . . . Carpenter, W. (2013). Definition and description of schizophrenia in the *DSM-5. Schizophrenia Research, 150*(1), 3–10. doi: 10.1016/j.schres.2013.05.028

Tanimura, M., Okuma, K., & Kyoshima, K. (2007). Television viewing, reduced parental utterance, and delayed speech development in infants and young children. *Archives of Pediatrics & Adolescent Medicine, 161,* 618–619.

Tardif, T., & Wellman, H. M. (2000). Acquisition of mental state language in Mandarin- and Cantonese-speaking children. *Developmental Psychology, 36*(1), 25–43.

Task Force on Sudden Infant Death Syndrome. (2011). SIDS and other sleep-related infant deaths: Expansion of recommendations for a safe infant sleeping environment. *Pediatrics, 128,* 1030–1039.

Taylor, A., & Kuo, F. E. (2009). Children with attention deficits concentrate better after walk in the park. *Journal of Attention Disorders, 12*(5), 402–409.

Taylor, A., Kuo, F. E., & Sullivan, W. C. (2002). Views of nature and self-discipline: Evidence from inner-city children. *Journal of Environmental Psychology, 22,* 49–63.

Taylor, B. (2006). Vaccines and the changing epidemiology of autism. *Child Care, Health and Development, 32*(5), 511–519.

Tenenbaum, H. R., & Ruck, M. D. (2007). Are teachers' expectations different for racial minority than for European American Students?: A meta-analysis. *Journal of Educational Psychology, 99*(2), 253–273.

Terlecki, M. S., Newcombe, N. S., & Little, M. (2008). Durable and generalized effects of spatial experience on mental rotation: Gender differences in growth patterns. *Applied Cognitive Psychology, 22*(7), 996–1013.

Texas Education Agency. (2004). *Foundations of reading: Effective phonological awareness instruction and progress monitoring.* Retrieved from http://www.meadowscenter.org/vgc/downloads/primary/guides/PA_Guide.pdf

Thelen, E. (1989). Self-organization in developmental processes: Can systems approaches work? In M. R. Gunnar & E. Thelen (Eds.), *Systems and development: The Minnesota symposia on child psychology* (pp. 77–117). Hillsdale, NJ: Erlbaum.

Thelen, E., Corbetta, D., Kamm, K., Spencer, J. P., Schneider, K., & Zernicke, R. F. (1993). The transition to reaching: Mapping intention and intrinsic dynamics. *Child Development, 64*(4), 1058–1098.

Thelen, E., Fisher, D. M., & Ridley-Johnson, R. (2002). The relationship between physical growth and a newborn reflex. *Infant Behavior & Development, 25*(1), 72–85.

Thomas, A., & Chess, S. (1977). *Temperament and development.* New York, NY: Brunner/Mazel.

Thompson, L. A., Fagan, J. F., & Fulker, D. W. (1991). Longitudinal prediction of specific cognitive abilities from infant novelty preference. *Child Development, 62,* 530–538.

Thompson, M. P., Kingree, J. B., & Desai, S. (2004). Gender differences in long-term health consequences of physical abuse of children: Data from a nationally representative survey. *American Journal of Public Health, 94*(4), 599–604.

Thorne, B. (1994). *Gender play—Girls and boys in school.* New Brunswick, NJ: Rutgers University Press.

Tiedemann, J. (2000). Parents' gender stereotypes and teachers' beliefs as predictors of children's concept of their mathematical ability in elementary school. *Journal of Educational Psychology, 92*(1), 144–151.

Tiggemann, M. (2001). Children's body image: It starts sooner than you think. *Virtually Healthy, 19,* 3.

Tillman, K. H. (2007). Family structure pathways and academic disadvantage among adolescents in stepfamilies. *Sociological Inquiry, 77,* 383–424.

Tinbergen, N. (1963). On aims and methods of ethology. *Zeitschrift für Tierpsychologie, 20,* 410–433.

Tison, J., Chaudhary, N., & Cosgrove, L. (2011, December). *National phone survey on distracted driving attitudes and behaviors.* (Report No. DOT HS 811 555). Washington, DC: National Highway Traffic Safety Administration. Retrieved from http://www.distraction.gov/download/research-pdf/8396_DistractedDrivingSurvey-120611-v3.pdf

Tither, J. M., & Ellis, B. J. (2008). Impact of fathers on daughters' age at menarche: A genetically and environmentally controlled sibling study. *Developmental Psychology, 44*(5), 1409–1420.

Tokolahi, E. (2014). Developmental coordination disorder: The domain of child and adolescent mental health occupational therapists? *New Zealand Journal of Occupational Therapy, 61*(1), 21–25.

Torff, B. (1996). How are you smart? Multiple intelligences and classroom practices. *The NAMTA Journal, 21*(2), 31–43.

Torff, B., & Gardner, H. (1999). The vertical mind—The case for multiple intelligences. In M. Anderson (Ed.), *The development of intelligence* (pp. 139–159). Hove, East Sussex, UK: Psychology Press.

Tornello, S. L., Emery, R., Rowen, J., Potter, D., Ocker, B., & Xu, Y. (2013). Overnight custody arrangements, attachment, and adjustment among very young children. *Journal of Marriage and Family, 75*(4), 871–885.

Tracy, J. L., & Robins, R. W. (2006). Appraisal antecedents of shame and guilt: Support for a theoretical model. *Personality and Social Psychology Bulletin, 32,* 1339–1351.

Tracy, J. L., & Robins, R. W. (2008). The nonverbal expression of pride: Evidence for cross-cultural recognition. *Journal of Personality and Social Psychology, 94*(3), 516–530.

Tracy, J. L., Robins, R. W., & Lagattuta, K. H. (2005). Can children recognize pride? *Emotion, 5*(3), 251–257.

Trautwein, U., Ludtke, O., Marsh, H. W., Koller, O., & Baumert, J. (2006). Tracking, grading, and student motivation: Using group composition and status to predict self-concept and interest in ninth-grade mathematics. *Journal of Educational Psychology, 98*(4), 788–806.

Trevarthen, C. (1991). Reviewed work(s): *Developmental Psychology in the Soviet Union by Jaan Valsiner. Soviet Studies, 43*(1), 183–187.

Trzaskowski, M., Shakeshaft, N. G., & Plomin, R. (2013). Intelligence indexes generalist genes for cognitive abilities. *Intelligence, 41*(5), 560–565. doi: 10.1016/j.intell.2013.07.011

Ttofi, M. M., & Farrington, D. P. (2011). Effectiveness of school-based programs to reduce bullying: A systematic and meta-analytic review. *Journal of Experimental Criminology, 7*(1), 27–56.

Tu, M. T., Lupien, S. J., & Walker, C. (2005). Measuring stress responses in postpartum mothers: Perspectives from studies in human and animal populations. *Stress: The International Journal on the Biology of Stress, 8*(1), 19–34.

Tucker, P. (2008). The physical activity levels of preschool-aged children: A systematic review. *Early Childhood Research Quarterly, 23*(4), 547–558.

Tulsky, D. S., Carlozzi, N. E., Chevalier, N., Espy, K. A., Beaumont, J. L., & Mungas, D. (2013). National Institutes of Health Toolbox Cognition Battery (NIH Toolbox CB): Validation for children between 3 and 15 years: V. NIH Toolbox Cognition Battery (CB): Measuring working memory. *Monographs of The Society For Research in Child Development, 78*(4), 70–87. doi: 10.1111/mono.12035

Turkheimer, E., Haley, A., Waldron, M., D'Onofrio, B., & Gottesman, I. I. (2003). Socioeconomic status modifies heritability of IQ in young children. *Psychological Science, 14*(6), 623–628.

Turkheimer, E., & Waldron, M. (2000). Nonshared environment: A theoretical, methodological, and quantitative review. *Psychological Bulletin, 126*(1), 78–108.

Turkington, C. A. (2002). Infertility therapies. In J. L. Longe & D. S. Blanchfield (Eds.), *Gale encyclopedia of medicine* (Vol. 2, 2nd ed., pp. 1831–1833). Detroit, MI: Gale.

Twenge, J. M. (2006). *Generation me: Why today's young Americans are more confident, assertive, entitled—and more miserable than ever before.* New York, NY: Free Press.

Twenge, J. M., & Campbell, W. (2001). Age and birth cohort differences in self-esteem: A cross-temporal meta-analysis. *Personality and Social Psychology Review, 5*(4), 321–344. doi: 10.1207/S15327957PSPR0504_3

Twenge, J. M., Campbell, W., & Foster, C. A. (2003). Parenthood and marital satisfaction: A meta-analytic review. *Journal of Marriage and Family, 65*(3), 574–583. doi: 10.1111/j.1741-3737.2003.00574.x

Twenge, J. M., & Nolen-Hoeksema, S. (2002). Age, gender, race, socioeconomic status, and birth cohort differences on the Children's Depression Inventory: A meta-analysis. *Journal of Abnormal Psychology, 111,* 578–588.

Tyree, T. (2011). African American stereotypes in reality television. *Howard Journal of Communications, 22*(4), 394–413. doi: 10.1080/10646175.2011.617217

Tyrka, A. R., Graber, J. A., & Brooks-Gunn, J. (2000). The development of disordered eating: Correlates and predictors of eating problems in the context of adolescence. In A. J. Sameroff, M. Lewis, & S. Miller (Eds.), *Handbook of developmental psychopathology* (2nd ed., pp. 607–624). New York, NY: Plenum Press.

Tyrrell, M. (2005). School phobia. *Journal of School Nursing, 21*(3), 147–151.

Tyson, J. E., Nehal, A. P., Langer, J., Green, C., & Higgins, R. D. (2008). Intensive care for extreme prematurity—Moving beyond gestational age. *New England Journal of Medicine, 358,* 1672–1681.

Tzuriel, E., & Egozi, G. (2010). Gender differences in spatial ability of young children: The effects of training and processing strategies. *Child Development, 81,* 1417–1430.

UC Davis Health System. (2013). *Experimental gene therapy treatment for duchenne muscular dystrophy offers hope for youngster. News from UC Davis Health System.* Retrieved from http://www.ucdmc.ucdavis.edu/publish/news/newsroom/7450

Ullman, S. E., & Filipas, H. H. (2005). Gender differences in social reactions to abuse disclosures, post-abuse coping, and PTSD of child sexual abuse survivors. *Child Abuse and Neglect, 29,* 767–782.

Umaña-Taylor, A. J., Gonzales-Backen, M. A., & Guimond, A. B. (2009). Latino adolescents' ethnic identity: Is there a developmental progression and does growth in ethnic identity predict growth in self-esteem? *Child Development, 80*(2), 391–405.

United Cerebral Palsy. (2007). *Vocabulary tips: Cerebral palsy—Facts & figures.* Retrieved from http://www.ucp.org/ucp_ generaldoc.cfm/1/9/37/37–37/447

United Nations Committee on the Rights of the Child. (2013). *General comment No. 17 (2013) on the right of the child to rest, leisure, play, recreational activities, cultural life and the arts (art. 31).* Retrieved from http://www2.ohchr.org/english/bodies/crc/docs/GC/CRC-C-GC-17_en.doc+&cd=6&hl=en&ct=clnk&gl=us

Urdan, T., Solek, M., & Schoenfelder, E. (2007). Students' perceptions of family influences on their academic motivation: A qualitative analysis. *European Journal of Psychology of Education, 22*(1), 7–21. doi: 10.1007/BF03173686

Uro, G., & Barrio, A. (2013). *English Language Learners in America's Great City Schools: Demographics, achievement, and staffing.* Washington, DC: Council of the Great City Schools.

U.S. Census Bureau. (2008a). *Current population survey (CPS)—Definitions and explanations.* Retrieved from http://www.census.gov/population/www/cps/cpsdef.html

U.S. Census Bureau. (2011a). *Back to school: 2011–2012.* Document CB11-FF.15. Retrieved from http://www.census.gov/newsroom/releases/pdf/cb11ff-15_school.pdf

U.S. Census Bureau. (2011b). *Half of young children in the U.S. are read to at least once a day, Census Bureau Reports.* Retrieved from http://www.census.gov/newsroom/releases/archives/children/cb11-138.html

U.S. Census Bureau. (2012a). *Family Households by Number of Own Children Under 18 Years of Age: 2000 to 2010.* Retrieved from http://www.census.gov/compendia/statab/2012/tables/12s0064.pdf

U.S. Census Bureau. (2012b). *Historical poverty tables: Families.* Retrieved from http://www.census.gov/hhes/www/poverty/data/historical/families.html

U.S. Consumer Product Safety Commission (2010). *Public playground safety handbook.* Retrieved from http://www.cpsc.gov//PageFiles/122149/325.pdf

U.S. Department of Agriculture. (2010). *Dietary guidelines for Americans: Report of the Dietary Guidelines Advisory Committee on the Dietary Guidelines for Americans, 2010.* Retrieved from http://www.cnpp.usda.gov/DGAs2010-DGACReport.htm

U.S. Department of Agriculture. (2012). *Dietary guidelines consumer brochure.* Retrieved from http://www.choosemyplate.gov/print-materials-ordering/dietary-guidelines.html

U.S. Department of Education. (2006). *Secretary Spellings announces more choices in single sex education.* Retrieved from http://www.ed.gov/news/pressreleases/2006/10/10242006.html

U.S. Department of Education. (2013). *The biennial report to Congress on the implementation of the title III state formula grant program.* School years 2008–10. Retrieved from http://www.ncela.us/files/uploads/3/biennial_report_0810.pdf

U.S. Department of Education. (n.d.-a). *Building the legacy: IDEA 2004.* Retrieved from http://idea.ed.gov/explore/view/p/,root,regs,300,A,300%252E8,

U.S. Department of Education. (n.d.-b). *Early learning: American's middle class promise begins early.* Retrieved from https://www.ed.gov/early-learning#fn1

U.S. Department of Energy Genome Programs. (2008). *Genomics and its impact on science and society: The human genome project and beyond (2008).* Retrieved from http://www.ornl.gov/sci/techresources/Human_Genome/publicat/primer2001/primer11.pdf

U.S. Department of Energy Genome Programs. (2012). *Human Genome Project information.* Retrieved from http://www.ornl.gov/sci/techresources/Human_Genome/home.shtml

U.S. Department of Health and Human Services. (2005a). *Code of federal regulations.* Retrieved from http://www.hhs.gov/ohrp/humansubjects/guidance/45cfr46.htm

U.S. Department of Health and Human Services. (2005b). *U.S. Surgeon General releases advisory on alcohol use in pregnancy.* Health and Human Services Press Release. Retrieved from http://www.surgeongeneral.gov/pressreleases/sg02222005.html

U.S. Department of Health and Human Services. (2006). *Fact sheet: Preventing infant mortality.* Retrieved from http://www.hhs.gov/news/factsheet/infant.html

U.S. Department of Health and Human Services. (2007, November 5). *Fact sheet: Positive youth development.* Retrieved from http://www.acf.hhs.gov/programs/fysb/content/positive youth/factsheet.htm

U.S. Department of Health and Human Services. (2011). *Child maltreatment 2010.* Washington, DC: Government Printing office.

U.S. Department of Health and Human Services. (2012a). *Bulimia nervosa fact sheet.* Retrieved from http://www.womenshealth.gov/publications/our-publications/factsheet/bulimia-nervosa.html#c

U.S. Department of Health and Human Services. (2012b). *Pregnancy and childbirth.* Retrieved from http://www.aids.gov/hiv-aids-basics/prevention/reduce-your-risk/pregnancy-and-childbirth/

U.S. Department of Health and Human Services. (2012c). *Preventing tobacco use among youth and young adults: A report of the Surgeon General.* Atlanta, GA: U.S. Department of Health and Human Services, Centers for Disease Control and Prevention, National Center for Chronic Disease Prevention and Health Promotion, Office on Smoking and Health.

U.S. Department of Health and Human Services. (2013). *Child maltreatment 2012.* Retrieved from http://www.acf.hhs.gov/programs/cb/research-data-technology/statistics-research/child-maltreatment

U.S. Department of Justice, Bureau of Justice Statistics, *National Crime Victimization Survey (NCVS), 1992–2010.* Retrieved from http://nces.ed.gov/pubs2012/2012002.pdf

U.S. Department of Labor. (2010). *Fact Sheet #28: The Family and Medical Leave Act of 1993.* Retrieved from http://www.dol.gov/whd/regs/compliance/whdfs28.htm

U.S. Environmental Protection Agency. (2013). *Cancer incidence and mortality for children ages 0–19 years, 1992–2009.* Retrieved from http://www.epa.gov/ace/health/childhood_cancer.html

U.S. Environmental Protection Agency. (2012). *Children's health protection.* Retrieved from http://www.yosemite.epa.gov/ochp/ochpweb.nsf/content/homepage.htm

U.S. Food and Drug Administration. (2013). *Public health advisory: FDA recommends that over-the-counter (OTC) cough and cold products not be used for infants and children under 2 years of age.* Retrieved from http://www.fda.gov/drugs/drugsafety/postmarketdrugsafetyinformation forpatientsandproviders/drugsafetyinformationforhealth careprofessionals/publichealthadvisories/ucm051137.htm

U.S. National Library of Medicine. (2010a). *X chromosome.* Retrieved from http://ghr.nlm.nih.gov/chromosome=X

U.S. National Library of Medicine. (2010b). *Y chromosome.* Retrieved from http://ghr.nlm.nih.gov/chromosome/Y

U.S. National Library of Medicine. (2011). *DNA structure.* Retrieved from http://ghr.nlm.nih.gov/handbook/basics/dna

U.S. National Library of Medicine. (2013). *Ear infections.* Retrieved from http://www.nlm.nih.gov/medlineplus/earinfections.html

U.S. Preventive Services Task Force. (2010). *Screening for obesity in children and adolescents.* Recommendation Statement. Retrieved from http://www.uspreventiveservicestaskforce.org/uspstf10/childobes/chobesrs.htm

Vaglio, S. (2009). Chemical communication and mother-infant recognition. *Communicative and Integrative Biology, 2*(3), 279–281.

Valkenburg, P. M., & Peter, J. (2007). Online communication and adolescent well-being: Testing the stimulation versus the displacement hypothesis. *Journal of Computer-Mediated Communication, 12*(4), 1169–1182.

van der Veer, R. (2007). *Lev Vygotsky.* New York, NY: Continuum.

Van Doorn, M. D., Branje, S. T., & Meeus, W. J. (2011). Developmental Changes in Conflict Resolution Styles in Parent-Adolescent Relationships: A Four-Wave Longitudinal Study. *Journal of Youth and Adolescence, 40*(1), 97–107.

van IJzendoorn, M. H., & Sagi-Schwartz, A. (2008). Cross-cultural patterns of attachment: Universal and contextual dimensions. In J. Cassidy & P. R. Shaver (Eds.), *Handbook of attachment: Theory, research, and clinical applications* (2nd ed., pp. 880–905). New York, NY: Guilford Press.

van Jaarsveld, C. H. M., Fidler, J. A., Simon, A. E., & Wardle, J. (2007). Persistent impact of pubertal timing on trends in smoking, food choice, activity, and stress in adolescence. *Psychosomatic Medicine, 69*(8), 798–806.

Van, P. (2012). Conversations, coping, & connectedness: A qualitative study of women who have experienced involuntary pregnancy loss. *Omega: Journal of Death and Dying, 65*(1), 71–85.

Van Ryzen, M. J., Carlson, E. A., & Sroufe, L. A. (2012). Attachment discontinuity in a high-risk sample. *Attachment & Human Development, 13*(4), 381–401.

Vance, E. (2007). Cuteness: We know it when we see it. *Observer, 20*(6), 8.

VanCleave, J., Gortmaker, S. L., & Perrin, J. M. (2010). Dynamics of obesity and chronic health conditions among children and youth. *Journal of the American Medical Association, 303*(7), 623–630.

Vandell, D. (2000). Parents, peer groups, and other socializing influences. *Developmental Psychology, 36*(6), 699–710.

Vandenbosch, L., & Eggermont, S. (2011). Temptation Island, The Bachelor, Joe Millionaire: A prospective cohort study on the role of romantically themed reality television in adolescents' sexual development. *Journal of Broadcasting & Electronic Media, 55*(4), 563–580. doi: 10.1080/08838151.2011.620663

VanderBerg, K. A. (2007). Individualized developmental care for high risk newborns in the NICU: A practice guideline. *Early Human Development, 83*(7), 433–442.

Vandewater, E. A., Rideout, V. J., Wartella, E. A., Huang, X., Lee, J. H., & Shim, M. (2007). Digital childhood: Electronic media and technology use among infants, toddlers, and preschoolers. *Pediatrics, 119,* e1006–e1015.

Vandivere, S., Malm, K., & Radel, L. (2009). *Adoption USA: A chartbook based on the 2007 National Survey of Adoptive Parents.* Washington, DC: U.S. Department of Health and Human Services, Office of the Assistant Secretary for Planning and Evaluation. Retrieved from http://aspe.hhs.gov/hsp/09/NSAP/chartbook/index.pdf

VanTassel-Baska, J. (2014). Performance-based assessment: The road to authentic learning for the gifted. *Gifted Child Today, 37*(1), 41–47.

Vaquero, E., & Kao, G. (2008). Do you like me as much as I like you? Friendship reciprocity and its effects on school outcomes among adolescents. *Social Science Research, 37*(1), 55–72.

Vargas, J. S. (2005). *A brief biography of B. F. Skinner.* Retrieved from http://www.bfskinner.org/BFSkinner/AboutSkinner.html

Varnhagen, C. K., McFall, G., Pugh, N., Routledge, L., Sumida-MacDonald, H., & Kwong, T. E. (2010). Lol: New language and spelling in instant messaging. *Reading and Writing, 23*(6), 719–733.

Vasilyeva, M., Huttenlocher, J., & Waterfall, H. (2006). Effects of language intervention on syntactic skill levels in preschoolers. *Developmental Psychology, 42*(1), 164–174.

Vasilyeva, M., Waterfall, H., & Huttenlocher, J. (2008). Emergence of syntax: Commonalities and differences across children. *Developmental Science, 11*(1), 84–97.

Vaughan, B. S., March, J. S., & Kratochvil, C. J. (2012). The evidence-based pharmacological treatment of paediatric ADHD. *International Journal of Neuropsychopharmacology, 15*(1), 27–39.

Veenstra, R., Lindenberg, S., Munniksma, A., & Dijkstra, J. (2010). The complex relation between bullying, victimization, acceptance, and rejection: Giving special attention to status, affection, and sex differences. *Child Development, 81*(2), 480–486.

Venezia, A., & Jaeger, L. (2013). Transitions from high school to college. *Future of Children, 23*(1), 117–136.

Venkatesh, S. (2008). *Gang leader for a day: A rogue sociologist takes to the streets.* New York, NY: Penguin Press.

Vernon-Feagans, L., Garrett-Peters, P., Willoughby, M., & Mills-Koonce, R. (2012). Chaos, poverty, and parenting: Predictors of early language development. *Early Childhood Research Quarterly, 27*(3), 339–351.

Véronneau, M., & Dishion, T. J. (2011). Middle school friendships and academic achievement in early adolescence: A longitudinal analysis. *Journal of Early Adolescence, 31*(1), 99–124. doi: 10.1177/0272431610384485

Vespa, J., Lewis, J. M., & Krelder, R. M. (2013). *American's Families and Living Arrangements: 2012. Current Population Reports, P20–570.* Washington, DC: U.S. Census Bureau.

Vialle, W., Ashton, T., Carlon, G., & Rankin, F. (2001). Acceleration: A coat of many colours. *Roeper Review, 24*(1), 14–19.

Vickers, B. (2005). Cognitive model of the maintenance and treatment of post-traumatic stress. *Clinical Child Psychology and Psychiatry, 10*(2), 217–234.

Vidal, J. (2014). Dutch arrest 44 Greenpeace activists blocking Russian Arctic oil tanker. *The Guardian.* Retrieved from http://www.theguardian.com/environment/2014/may/01/greenpeace-russian-arctic-oil-tanker

Visu-Petra, L., Cheie, L., & Benga, O. (2008). Short-term memory performance and metamemory judgments in preschool and early school-age children: A quantitative and qualitative analysis. *Cognitie, Creier, Comportament/Cognition, Brain, Behavior, 12*(1), 71–101.

Viswanathan, M., Visco, A. G., Hartmann, K., Wechter, M. E., Gartlehner, G., Wu, J. M.,. . . Lohr, K. N. (2006). *Cesarean delivery on maternal request.* Rockville, MD: Agency for Healthcare Research and Quality. Evidence Report/Technology Assessment, 133.

Vogt Yuan, A. (2007). Gender Differences in the Relationship of Puberty with Adolescents' Depressive Symptoms: Do Body Perceptions Matter? *Sex Roles, 57*(1/2), 69–80. doi: 10.1007/s11199-007-9212-6

Volkarsky, K. B. (2010). *Diet quality of American school-age children.* New York, NY: Nova Science.

Volkmar, F. R., & Tsatsanis, K. (2002). Psychosis and psychotic conditions in childhood and adolescence. In D. T. Marsh & M. A. Fristad (Eds.), *Handbook of serious emotional disturbance in children and adolescents* (pp. 266–283). Hoboken, NJ: Wiley.

Volpe, J. J. (2009). Cerebellum of the premature infant: Rapidly developing, vulnerable, clinically important. *Journal of Child Neurology, 24*(9), 1085–1104.

Volterra, V., Caselli, M. C., Capirci, O., & Pizzuto, E. (2005). Gesture and the emergence and development of language. In M. Tomasello & D. I. Slobin (Eds.), *Beyond nature-nurture* (pp. 3–40). Mahwah, NJ: Erlbaum.

von Kries, R., Koletzko, B., Sauerwald, T., von Mutius, E., Barnert, D., Grunert, V., & von Voss, H. (1999). Breast feeding and obesity: Cross-sectional study. *British Medical Journal, 319*, 147–150.

Vora, S. (n.d.). Pregnancy myth busters. *Parents.* Retrieved from http://www.parents.com/pregnancy/my-body/is-it-safe/pregnancy-myth-busters/

Voyer, D., Voyer, S., & Bryden, M. P. (1995). Magnitude of sex differences in spatial abilities: A meta-analysis and consideration of critical variables. *Psychological Bulletin, 117*(2), 250–270.

Vrugt, A., & Oort, F. J. (2008). Metacognition, achievement goals, study strategies and academic achievement: Pathways to achievement. *Metacognition and Learning, 30*, 123–146.

Vygotsky, L. S. (1962). *Thought and language.* Cambridge, MA: MIT Press. (Original work published in 1934)

Vygotsky, L. S. (1978a). Interaction between learning and development. In M. Cole, V. John-Steiner, & E. Souberman (Eds.), *Mind in society: The development of higher psychological processes* (pp. 79–91). Cambridge, MA: Harvard University Press.

Vygotsky, L. S. (1978b). *Mind in society: The development of higher psychological processes.* Cambridge, MA: Harvard University Press.

Vygotsky, L. S. (1986). *Thought and language.* Cambridge, MA: MIT Press.

Waddington, C. H. (1942). Canalization of development and the inheritance of acquired characters. *Nature, 150*, 563–564.

Wadhwa, P. D. (2005). Psychoneuroendocrine processes in human pregnancy influence fetal development and health. *Psychoneuroendocrinology, 30*(8), 724–743.

Wahlstrom, D., White, T., & Luciana, M. (2010). Neurobehavioral evidence for changes in dopamine system activity during adolescence. *Neuroscience and Biobehavioral Reviews, 34*(5), 631–648. doi: 10.1016/j.neubiorev.2009.12.007

Wakefield, A. J., Murch, S. H., Anthony, A., Linnell, J., Casson, D. M., Malik, M.,. . . Walker-Smith, J. A. (1998). Ileal-lymphoid-nodular hyperplasia, non-specific colitis, and pervasive developmental disorder in children. *Lancet, 351*(9103), 637–641.

Walcott, D. D., Pratt, H. D., & Patel, D. R. (2003). Adolescents and eating disorders: Gender, racial ethnic, sociocultural and socioeconomic issues. *Journal of Adolescent Research, 18*(3), 223–243.

Walker, L. J. (2006). *Gender and morality.* In M. Killen & J. G. Smetana (Eds.), *Handbook of moral development* (pp. 93–115). Erlbaum: Mahwah.

Walker, L. J., & Frimer, J. A. (2009). 'The song remains the same': Rebuttal to Sherblom's re-envisioning of the legacy of the care challenge. *Journal of Moral Education, 38*(1), 53–68.

Walker, S. K. (2005). Use of parenting newsletter series and other child-rearing information sources by mothers of infants. *Family and Consumer Sciences Research Journal, 34*(2), 153–172.

Wallach, M. A., & Kogan, N. (1965). *Modes of thinking in young children: A study of the creativity-intelligence distinction.* New York, NY: Holt, Rinehart & Winston.

Walum, H., Westberg, L., Henningsson, S., Neiderhiser, J. M., Reiss, D., Igl, W., . . . Lichtenstein, P. (2008). Genetic variation in the vasopressin receptor 1a gene (AVPR1A) associates with pair-bonding behavior in humans. *Proceedings of the National Academy of Sciences, 105*(37), 14153–14156.

Wang, Q. (2008). Being American, being Asian: The bicultural self and autobiographical memory in Asian Americans. *Cognition, 107*, 743–751.

Wang, A., Peterson, G. W., & Morphey, L. (2007). Who is more important for early adolescents' developmental choices? Peers or parents? *Marriage & Family Review, 42*(2), 95–122.

Wang, J., Iannotti, R. J., & Nansel, T. R. (2009). School bullying among adolescents in the United States: Physical, verbal, relational, and cyber. *Journal of Adolescent Health, 45*(4), 368–375.

Wang, M., & Sheikh-Khalil, S. (2014). Does parental involvement matter for student achievement and mental health in high school? *Child Development, 85*(2), 610–625. doi: 10.1111/cdev.12153

Wang, Q. (2006). Culture and the development of self-knowledge. *Current Directions in Psychological Science, 15*(4), 182–187.

Wappner, R., Cho, S., Kronmal, R. A., Schuett, V., & Seashore, M. R. (1999). Management of phenylketonuria for optimal outcome: A review of guidelines for phenylketonuria management and a report of surveys of parents, patients, and clinic directors. *Pediatrics, 104*(6), e68.

Ward, L. M. (2004). Wading through the stereotypes: Positive and negative associations between media use and black adolescents' conception of self. *Developmental Psychology, 40*(2), 284–294.

Ward, L. M., & Friedman, K. (2006). Using TV as a guide: Associations between television viewing and adolescents' sexual attitudes and behavior. *Journal of Research on Adolescence, 16*(1), 133–156.

Warnick, M. (2010). Mom. Pregnancy myths busted. *American Baby, 72*(2), 24.

Wasser, H., Bentley, M., Borja, J., Goldman, B., Thompson, A., Slining, M., & Adair, L. (2011). Infants perceived as "fussy" are more likely to receive complementary foods before 4 months. *Pediatrics, 127*(2), 229-237.

Wasserman, J. D. (2012). A history of intelligence assessment: The unfinished tapestry. In D. P. Flanagan & P. L. Flanagan (Eds.), *Contemporary intellectual assessment* (pp. 3–55). New York, NY: Guilford.

Waterhouse, L. (2006). Multiple intelligences, the Mozart effect, and emotional intelligence: A critical review. *Educational Psychologist, 41*(4), 207–225.

Watkins, B. (2011). Eating Disorders: An Overview. In B. Lask & I. Frampton (Eds.), *Eating disorders and the brain*. Hoboken, NJ: Wiley.

Watson, J. B., & Rayner, R. (1920). Conditioned emotional reactions. *Journal of Experimental Psychology, 3*(1), 1–14.

Watson, J. D. (2003). *DNA: The secret of life*. New York, NY: Knopf.

Watson, M. W., & Fischer, K. W. (1977). A developmental sequence of agent use in late infancy. *Child Development, 48*, 828–836.

Watson, M. W., & Fischer, K. W. (1980). Development of social roles in elicited and spontaneous behavior during the preschool years. *Developmental Psychology, 16*(5), 483–494.

Waxman, S., Fu, X., Arunachalam, S., Leddon, E., Geraghty, K., & Song, H. (2013). Are nouns learned before verbs? Infants provide insight into a long-standing debate. *Child Development Perspectives, 7*(3), 155–159. doi: 10.1111/cdep.12032

Weatherspoon, L. J., Venkatesh, S., Horodynski, M. A., Stommel, M., & Brophy-Herb, H. E. (2013). Food patterns and mealtime behaviors in low-income mothers and toddlers. *Journal of Community Health Nursing, 30*(1), 1–15.

WebMD. (2013). *Autism symptoms, causes, treatment, and more*. Retrieved from http://www.webmd.com/brain/autism/mental-health-autism

Wechsler, D. (2003). *Wechsler intelligence scale for children* (4th ed.). San Antonio, TX: Pearson.

Weech, A. A. (1954). Signposts on the highway of growth. *American Journal of Diseases of Children, 88*(4), 452–457.

Weems, C. F. (2008). Developmental trajectories of childhood anxiety: Identifying continuity and change in anxious emotion. *Developmental Review, 28*(4), 488–502.

Weersing, V. R., & Brent, D. A. (2010). Treating depression in adolescents using individual cognitive-behavioral therapy. In J. R. Weisz & A. Kazdin (Eds.), *Evidence-based psychotherapies for children and adolescents* (2nd ed., pp. 126–139). New York, NY: Guilford Press.

Weichold, K., Silbereisen, R. K., & Schmitt-Rodermund, E. (2003). Short-term and long-term consequences of early versus late physical maturation in adolescents. In C. Hayward (Ed.), *Gender differences at puberty* (pp. 241–276). Cambridge, UK: Cambridge University Press.

Weigard, A., Chein, J., Albert, D., Smith, A., & Steinberg, L. (2014). Effects of anonymous peer observation on adolescents' preference for immediate rewards. *Developmental Science, 17*(1), 71–78. doi: 10.1111/desc.12099

Weil, L. G., Fleming, S. M., Dumontheil, I., Kilford, E. J., Weil, R. S., Rees, G., . . . Blakemore, S. (2013). The development of metacognitive ability in adolescence. *Consciousness and Cognition: An International Journal, 22*(1), 264–271. doi: 10.1016/j.concog.2013.01.004

Weimer, J. (2001). *The economic benefits of breastfeeding: A review and analysis* [Food Assistance and Nutrition Research Report No. 13]. Washington, DC: U.S. Department of Agriculture Economic Research Service.

Weinfield, N. S., Whaley, G. J. L., & Egeland, B. (2004). Continuity, discontinuity, and coherence in attachment from infancy to late adolescence: Sequelae of organization and disorganization. *Attachment and Human Development, 6*(1), 73–97.

Weintraub, S., Bauer, P. J., Zelazo, P., Wallner-Allen, K., Dikmen, S. S., Heaton, R. K., . . . Gershon, R. C. (2013). National Institutes of Health Toolbox Cognition Battery (NIH Toolbox CB): Validation for children between 3 and 15 years: I. NIH Toolbox Cognition Battery (CB): Introduction and pediatric data. *Monographs of The Society for Research in Child Development, 78*(4), 1–15. doi: 10.1111/mono.12031

Weisleder, A., & Fernald, A. (2013). Talking to children matters: Early language experience strengthens processing and builds vocabulary. *Psychological Science, 24*(11), 2143–2152. doi: 10.1177/0956797613488145

Weisman, O., Zagoory-Sharon, O., & Feldman, R. (2014). Oxytocin administration, salivary testosterone, and father–infant social behavior. *Progress in Neuro-Psychopharmacology & Biological Psychiatry, 49*, 47–52. doi: 10.1016/j.pnpbp.2013.11.006

Weitz, T., Moore, K., Gordon, R., & Adler, N. (2008). You say "regret" and I say "relief": A need to break the polemic about abortion. *Contraception, 78*(2), 87–89. doi: 10.1016/j.contraception.2008.04.116

Wells, N. M., & Evans, G. W. (2003). Nearby nature: A buffer of life stress among rural children. *Environment and Behavior, 35*(3), 311–330.

Wenger, A., & Fowers, B. J. (2008). Positive illusion in parenting: Every child is above average. *Journal of Applied Social Psychology, 38*(3), 611–634.

Wenig, M. (2014). *Yoga for kids.* Retrieved from http://www.yogajournal.com/lifestyle/210

Werner, E. E. (1992). The children of Kauai: Resiliency and recovery in adolescence and adulthood. *Journal of Adolescent Health, 13*(4), 262–268.

Werner, E. E. (2005). What can we learn about resilience from large-scale longitudinal studies? In S. Goldstein & R. B. Brooks (Eds.), *Handbook of resilience in children* (pp. 91–106). New York, NY: Springer.

Werner, E. E., & Smith, R. S. (1985). *Vulnerable but invincible: A study of resilient children.* New York, NY: McGraw-Hill.

Wertsch, J. V. (1985). *Vygotsky and the social formation of mind.* Cambridge, MA: Harvard University Press.

Westerveld, M., Sass, K. J., Chelune, G. J., Hermann, B. P., Barr, W. B., Loring, D. W., . . . Spencer, D. D. (2000). Temporal lobectomy in children: Cognitive outcome. *Journal of Neurosurgery, 92*(1), 24–30.

Westling, E., Andrews, J. A., Hampson, S. E., & Peterson, M. (2008). Pubertal timing and substance use: The effects of gender, parental monitoring and deviant peers. *Journal of Adolescent Health, 42,* 555–563.

Wheeler, L., Buckley, R., Gerald, L. B., Merkle, S., & Morrison, T. A. (2009). Working with schools to improve pediatric asthma management. *Pediatric Asthma, Allergy & Immunology, 22*(4), 197–207.

Whitehurst, G. J. (1992). *Dialogic reading: An effective way to read to preschoolers.* Retrieved from http://www.readingrockets.org/article/400

Whitehurst, G. J., & Chingos, M. M. (2011). *Class size: What research says and what it means for state policy.* Washington, DC: The Brookings Institute.

Wier, L., Miller, A., & Steiner, C. (2009). *Sports injuries in children requiring hospital emergency care, 2006.* HCUP Statistical Brief #75. Rockville, MD: Agency for Healthcare Research and Quality. Retrieved from http://www.hcup-us.ahrq.gov/reports/statbriefs/sb75.jsp

Williams, K., & Umberson, D. (1999). Medical technology and childbirth: Experiences of expectant mothers and fathers. *Sex Roles, 21*(3–4), 147–168.

Williams, S., Mastergeorge, A. M., & Ontai, L. L. (2010). Caregiver involvement in infant peer interactions: Scaffolding in a social context. *Early Childhood Research Quarterly, 25*(2), 251–266.

Williams, S., Ontai, L. L., & Mastergeorge, A. M. (2010). The development of peer interaction in infancy: Exploring the dyadic processes. *Social Development, 19*(2), 348–368.

Williamson, D. M., Abe, K., Bean, C., Ferré, C., Henderson, Z., & Lackritz, E. (2008). Current research in preterm birth. *Journal of Women's Health, 17*(10), 1545–1549.

Williams-Rautiolla, S. (2008). *Cooney, Joan Ganz.* The Museum of Broadcast Communications. Retrieved from http://www.museum.tv/archives/etv/C/htmlC/cooneyjoan/cooneyjoan.htm

Wills, T. A., Sargent, J. D., Stoolmiller, M., Gibbons, F. X., & Gerrard, M. (2008). Movie smoking exposure and smoking onset: A longitudinal study of mediation processes in a representative sample of U.S. adolescents. *Psychology of Addictive Behaviors, 22*(2), 269–277.

Wilson, E. O. (1975). *Sociobiology: The new synthesis.* Cambridge, MA: Harvard University Press.

Wilson, L. (2014). Environmental exposure: Educating the childbirth educator. *International Journal of Childbirth Education, 29*(1), 32–40.

Wilson, V. (2013). Type 2 diabetes: An epidemic in children. *Nursing Child and Young People, 25*(2), 14–17.

Windsor, J., Benigno, J. P., Wing, C. A., Carroll, P. J., Koga, S. F., Nelson, C. A., . . . Zeanah, C. H. (2011). Effect of foster care on young children's language learning. *Child Development, 82*(4), 1040–1046.

Winerman, L. (2005). The mind's mirror. *Monitor on Psychology, 36*(9), 48.

Winickoff, J., Friebely, J., Tanski, S., Sherrod, C., Matt, G., Hovell, M., & McMillen, R. (2009). Beliefs about the health effects of "thirdhand" smoke and home smoking bans. *Pediatrics, 123*(1), e74–e79. doi: 10.1542/peds.2008-2184

Winn, W. (2004). Cognitive perspectives in psychology. In D. H. Jonassen (Ed.), *Handbook of research for educational communications and technology* (2nd ed., pp. 79–112). New York, NY: Simon & Schuster.

Winsler, A., Feder, M., Way, E. L., & Manfra, L. (2006). Maternal beliefs concerning young children's private speech. *Infant and Child Development, 15*(4), 403–420. doi: 10.1002/icd.467

Winsler, A., Madigan, A. L., & Aquilino, S. A. (2005). Correspondence between maternal and paternal parenting styles in early childhood. *Early Childhood Research Quarterly, 20*(1), 1–12.

Winsler, A., & Naglieri, J. (2003). Overt and covert verbal problem-solving strategies: Developmental trends in use, awareness, and relations with task performance in children aged 5 to 17. *Child Development, 74*(3), 659–678.

Witvliet, M., Brendgen, M., Van Lier, P. C., Koot, H. M., & Vitaro, F. (2010). Early adolescent depressive symptoms: Prediction from clique isolation, loneliness, and perceived social acceptance. *Journal of Abnormal Child Psychology, 38*(8), 1045–1056.

Wolak, J., Finkelhor, D., Mitchell, K. J., & Ybarra, M. L. (2008). Online "predators" and their victims: Myths, realities and implications for prevention treatment. *American Psychologist, 63*(2), 111–128.

Wolfe, D. A., & Mash, E. J. (Eds.). (2006). *Behavioral and emotional disorders in adolescents: Nature, assessment, and treatment.* New York, NY: Guilford Press.

Wolters Kluwer Health. (2009). *Professional guide to diseases* (9th ed.). Philadelphia, PA: Lippincott, Williams & Wilkins.

Wonderlich, A. L., Ackard, D. M., & Henderson, J. B. (2005). Childhood beauty pageant contestants: Associations with adult disordered eating and mental health. *Eating Disorders: The Journal of Treatment & Prevention, 13*(3), 291–301.

Wong, C. A., Eccles, J. S., & Sameroff, A. (2003). The influence of ethnic discrimination and ethnic identification on African American adolescents' school and socioemotional adjustment. *Journal of Personality, 71*(6), 1197–1232.

Wong, C. A., & Taylor, E. D. (1996). The effects of peer influences and negative peer orientation on African American and European American students' values and achievement. Poster presented at the biennial meeting of the SRA, Boston.

Wong, C., Berkowitz, Z., Dorell, C., Anhang Price, R., Lee, J., & Saraiya, M. (2011). Human papillomavirus vaccine uptake among 9- to 17-year-old girls: National Health Interview Survey, 2008. *Cancer, 117*(24), 5612–5620.

Woodward, A. L. (2009). Infants' grasp of others' intentions. *Current Directions in Psychological Science, 18*(1), 53–57.

World Health Organization. (2011). *Making pregnancy safer: Skilled birth attendants.* Retrieved from http://www.who.int/making_pregnancy_safer/topics/skilled_birth/en/index.html

World Health Organization. (2012). *Children: Reducing mortality.* Retrieved from http://www.who.int/mediacentre/factsheets/fs178/en/

Wray, N., & Visscher, P. (2008). Estimating trait heritability. *Nature Education, 1*(1), 29.

Wright, J. C., Huston, A. C., Scantlin, R., & Kotler, J. (2001). The Early Window Project: *Sesame Street* prepares children for school. In S. M. Fisch & R. T. Truglio (Eds.), *"G" is for growing—Thirty years of research on children and Sesame Street* (pp. 97–114). Mahwah, NJ: Erlbaum.

Wynn, K. (1992). Addition and subtraction by human infants. *Nature, 358*(6389), 749–750.

Xu, H., Wen, L., Rissel, C., & Baur, L. (2013). Smoking status and factors associated with smoking of first-time mothers during pregnancy and postpartum: Findings from the Healthy Beginnings Trial. *Maternal & Child Health Journal, 17*(6), 1151–1157.

Yatvin, J. (2002). Babes in the woods: The wanderings of the National Reading Panel. *Phi Delta Kappan, 83*(5), 364–369.

Yi, C. (2013). *The psychological well-being of East Asian youth.* New York, NY: Springer.

Yoshikawa, H., Aber, J., & Beardslee, W. R. (2012). The effects of poverty on the mental, emotional, and behavioral health of children and youth: Implications for prevention. *American Psychologist, 67*(4), 272–284.

Yu, T., Pettit, G. S., Lansford, J. E., Dodge, K. A., & Bates, J. E. (2010). The interactive effects of marital conflict and divorce on parent-adult children's relationships. *Journal of Marriage and Family, 72*(2), 282–292.

Yurgelun-Todd, D. (2007). Emotional and cognitive changes during adolescence. *Current Opinion in Neurobiology, 17*(2), 251–257.

Zadok-Levitan, O., & Bronz, R. (2004). Adults with learning disabilities who are successful at work. *Man and Work, 13*(1–2), 44–60, 69–70.

Zakriski, A. L., & Coie, J. D. (1996). A comparison of aggressive-rejected and nonaggressive: Rejected children's interpretations of self-directed and other-directed rejection. *Child Development, 67*(3), 1048–1070. doi: 10.1111/j.1467-8624.1996.tb01782.x

Zarbatany, L., McDougall, P., & Hymel, S. (2000). Gender-differentiated experience in the peer culture: Links to intimacy in preadolescence. *Social Development, 9*(1), 62–79.

Zeanah, C. H., Smyke, A. T., Koga, S. F., Carlson, E., & Bucharest Early Intervention Project Core Group. (2005). Attachment in institutionalized and community children in Romania. *Child Development, 76*(5), 1015–1028.

Zelazo, N. A., Zelazo, P. R., Cohen, K. M., & Zelazo, P. D. (1993). Specificity of practice effects on elementary neuromotor patterns. *Developmental Psychology, 29*(4), 686–691.

Zelazo, P. D. (2004–2014). *Executive Function Part Two: The development of executive function in infancy and early childhood.* Aboutkidshealth. Retrieved from http://www.aboutkidshealth.ca/en/news/series/executivefunction/pages/executive-function-part-two-the-development-of-executive-function-in-infancy-and-early-childhood.aspx

Zelazo, P. D. (2006). The Dimensional Change Card Sort (DCCS): A method of assessing executive function in children. *Nature Protocols, 1*, 297–301.

Zelazo, P. D., Anderson, J. E., Richler, J., Wallner-Allen, K., Beaumont, J. L., & Weintraub, S. (2013). National Institutes of Health Toolbox Cognition Battery (NIH Toolbox CB): Validation for children between 3 and 15 years: II. NIH Toolbox Cognition Battery (CB): Measuring executive function and attention. *Monographs of The Society for Research in Child Development, 78*(4), 16–33. doi: 10.1111/mono.12032

Zero to Three. (2012). *Sleep myths.* Retrieved from http://www.zerotothree.org/child-development/sleep/sleep-myth.html

Zettergren, P. (2005). Childhood peer status as predictor of midadolescence peer situation and social adjustment. *Psychology in the Schools, 42*(7), 745–757.

Zevenbergen, A. A., & Whitehurst, G. J. (2008). In A. van Kleeck, S. A. Stahl, & E. B. Bauer (Eds.), *On reading books to children: Parents and teachers* (pp. 170–194). Mahwah, NJ: Erlbaum Taylor & Francis e-Library.

Zhang, N., Baker, H. W., Tufts, M., Raymond, R. E., Salihu, H., & Elliott, M. R. (2013). Early childhood lead exposure and academic achievement: Evidence from Detroit public schools, 2008–2010. *American Journal of Public Health, 103*(3), e72–e77.

Zhang, T., & Meaney, M. J. (2010). Epigenetics and the environmental regulation of the genome and its function. *Annual Review of Psychology, 61*, 439–466.

Zhang, Y., Haraksingh, R., Grubert, F., Abyzov, A., Gerstein, M., Weissman, S., & Urban, A. E. (2013). Child development and structural variation in the human genome. *Child Development, 84*(1), 34–48.

Zhou, Q., Hofer, C., Eisenberg, N., Reiser, M., Spinrad, T. L., & Fabes, R. A. (2007). The developmental trajectories of attention focusing, attentional and behavioral persistence, and externalizing problems during school-age years. *Developmental Psychology, 43*(2), 369–385.

Zigler, E., & Bishop-Josef, S. J. (2006). The cognitive child versus the whole child: Lessons from 40 years of Head Start. In D. G. Singer, R. M. Golinkoff, & K. Hirsh-Pasek (Eds.), *Play=learning* (pp. 15–35). New York, NY: Oxford University Press.

Zimmer-Gembeck, M. J., & Skinner, E. A. (2008). Adolescents coping with stress: Development and diversity. *Prevention Researchers, 15*(4), 3–7.

Zimmerman, F. J., Christakis, D. A., & Meltzoff, A. N. (2007). Associations between media viewing and language development in children under age two years. *Journal of Pediatrics, 151*, 364–368.

Zimmerman, M. A., Bingenheimer, J. B., & Notaro, P. C. (2002). Natural mentors and adolescent resiliency: A study with urban youth. *American Journal of Community Psychology, 30*(2), 221–243.

Ziol-Guest, K. M., & McKenna, C. C. (2014). Early childhood housing instability and school readiness. *Child Development, 85*(1), 103–113.

Zook, R. (2010). *Why Computer Engineer Barbie is good for women in tech.* Retrieved from http://www.mashable.com/2010/03/09/computer-engineer-barbie/

Zosuls, K. M., Ruble, D. N., Tamis-LeMonda, C. S., Shrout, P. E., Bornstein, M. H., & Greulich, F. K. (2009). The acquisition of gender labels in infancy: Implications for gender-typed play. *Developmental Psychology, 45*(3), 688–701. doi: 10.1037/a0014053

Author Index

Subject Index

SAGE researchmethods

The essential online tool for researchers from the world's leading methods publisher

Find exactly what you are looking for, from basic explanations to advanced discussion

More content and new features added this year!

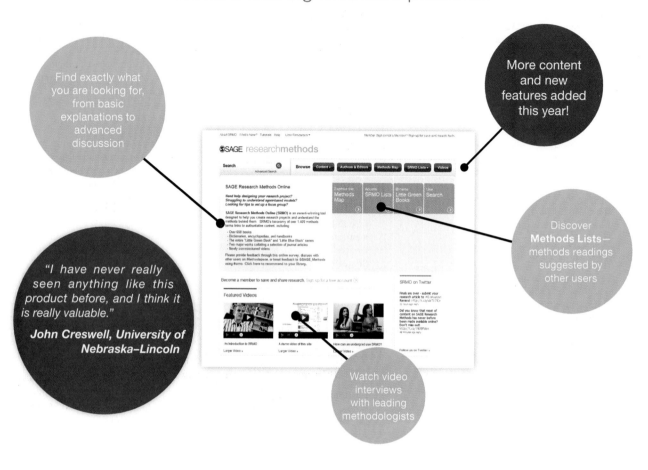

"I have never really seen anything like this product before, and I think it is really valuable."

John Creswell, University of Nebraska–Lincoln

Discover **Methods Lists**—methods readings suggested by other users

Watch video interviews with leading methodologists

Explore the **Methods Map** to discover links between methods

Search a custom-designed taxonomy with more than 1,400 qualitative, quantitative, and mixed methods terms

Uncover more than 120,000 pages of book, journal, and reference content to support your learning

Find out more at
www.sageresearchmethods.com